W9-AYG-435

Contents

Cover Story

Some time late during the first century of the new millenium, acoustic guitar manufacturers genetically followed up and improved their original "SmartWood" instruments originating from the late 20th century. After over 40 years of organic laboratory testing, a complex hybrid wood embryo was developed, enabling acoustic guitars to literally be grown in some midwestern areas of the U.S. and other countries. This process involved using a specially formulated embryo shaped like a large, disfigured potato developed after elaborate scientific wood grafting experimentation. Once the specific graft mix was tested (rosewood/walnut/mahogany/maple were the most popular hybrids) under lab conditions, this man-made seed was planted into a natural soil base, which had very critical growing characteristics. This sprouted a new breed of "guitar farmers", who now could see their planted woodies grow up and enlarge before their very eyes.

Initially, many guitar mutants grew up as a result of inconsistent moisture, fertilization experimentation, and especially those instruments which broke the soil with their necks facing south. During the early years, entire guitar harvests had warped necks and other unsightly wooden aberrations. While most of the bad guitar crops were thrown away, the ones which could be salvaged were embedded with an untamperable electronic chip, that when scanned, read "Second".

As more knowledge was acquired during this exciting new organic process, the results became more predictable. Even sophisticated archtops could be grown with a high degree of quality assurance. Once an instrument was fully-grown, guitar farmers could simply go out to the field and harvest them with only slight digging needed around the underground lower bouts. These new acoustic guitar "bodies" were then shipped per a monthly quota allotment to a guitar manufacturer (some larger companies even owned their own "Woodie Wonderlands"), where they underwent final wood finishing, followed by the installation of metal hardware. Since each body was uniquely different, every finished instrument had a tonal quality of its own. Eventually, the diminishing base of musicians and collectors sought out only those instruments with the best tone. Figured wood was no longer an issue, since both killer flame and quilt patterns could now be easily organically duplicated.

As the earth's forests continued to shrink during the beginning of the new millenium's 3rd century, natural wood was reserved only for special projects, and the world's remaining supply was now tightly controlled by an ultra-powerful organization called IWPA (International Wood Preservation Agency). As guitar manufacturers lost their ability to use natural wood products, these new self-grown hybrid instruments became the only guitars available to musicians, and huge premiums for older, collectible guitars (pre-2198) became a reality. Eventually, even this new generation of guitar growing was outlawed, due to governments reclaiming the acreage in an effort to stop a worldwide food shortage. Towards the end of this organic growing period, some instruments were engineered to grow into special monster reproductions of popular, late 20th century instruments. Over 35 meters in length, these giants were highly prized by the new generation of NBA "Skyplayers", perfect for their new genetically enhanced 10-meter arms. It is one of these last organic, monster vintage crops that is pictured on this edition's front cover, shown finished per an ad agency advertisement.

Centuries later, as both vintage and organic guitars succumbed to the wear and tear of guitar playing, older wood instruments became both rare and unobtainable, since composite materials had long before replaced natural wood. By the year 2500, guitar playing had virtually come to an end, since most music was now easily electronically synthesized, and could be reprogrammed into any conceivable musical style, shape or form - all without having to pay any guitar players for studio time. At this point, older acoustic instruments had become an oddity, with a few wealthy collectors and museums owning the few remaining specimins.

> **Back Cover Photo**
> 1990 Martin D-45 Custom Deluxe, SN# 493546
> Courtesy of Buddy Summer
> (Previously owned by Chris Martin IV, president & CEO of Martin Guitar Co.)

BLUE BOOK of ACOUSTIC GUITARS

EDITION

by Steven Cherne
Edited by S.P. Fjestad

$24.95
Publisher's Softcover
Suggested List Price

Publisher's Limited
Edition Hardcover
Suggested List Price - $44.95

VALUES • INFORMATION • IDENTIFICATION • GRADING

FIFTH EDITION BLUE BOOK OF ACOUSTIC GUITARS

Publisher's Note: This book is the result of nonstop and continual guitar research obtained by attending guitar shows, communicating with guitar dealers and collectors throughout the country each year, and staying on top of trends as they occur. This book represents an analysis of prices for which both recently manufactured and collectible guitars have actually been selling for during that period at an average retail level.

Although every reasonable effort has been made to compile an accurate and reliable guide, guitar prices may vary significantly depending on such factors as the locality of the sale, the number of sales we were able to consider, famous musician endorsement of certain models, regional economic conditions, and other critical factors.

Accordingly, no representation can be made that the guitars listed may be bought or sold at prices indicated, nor shall the editor or publisher be responsible for any error made in compiling and recording such prices.

Copyright © 1998 Blue Book Publications, Inc.
All Rights Reserved.

Blue Book Publications, Inc.
8009 34th Avenue South, Suite 175
Minneapolis, MN 55425 U.S.A.
Phone: 800-877-4867 (U.S.A. and Canada orders only)
Phone: 612-854-5229
Fax: 612-853-1486
Email: guitars@bluebookinc.com
Web site: http://www.bluebookinc.com

Published and printed in the United States of America
ISBN No. 1-886768-16-1
Library of Congress Catalog Card Number 98-88663

Distributed in part by Music Sales Corporation and Omnibus Press
Order # BP 10038
257 Park Avenue South, New York, NY 10010 USA
Phone: 212-254-2100 Fax: 212-254-2013 Email: 71360.3514@compuserve.com

No part of this publication may be reproduced in any form whatsoever, by photograph, mimeograph, FAX transmission, or any other mechanical or electronic means. Nor can it be broadcast or transmitted, by translation into any language, nor by recording electronically or otherwise, without the express written permission from the publisher - except by a reviewer, who may quote brief passages for critical articles and/or reviews.

The percentage breakdown of a guitar's condition factor with respective values per condition as utilized in the Photo Percentage Grading System™ is a trademark of Blue Book Publications, Inc. Any unauthorized usage of this grading system for the evaluation of a guitar's values and photo percentage breakdown is expressly forbidden by the publisher.

Production Manager - **Tom Heller**

Cover Layout & Design, Compositing, and Lettering, PPGS color layout - **Walter Horishnyk**

Text Formatting & Layout - **Tom Heller**

Art Director - **Walter Horishnyk**

Cover Source Photography - **Paul Goodwin**

PPGS Color Photography - **S. P. Fjestad**

Alphabetical/Special Sections Photo Placement and Programming - **Tom Lundin**

Printer - **Jeff Kuhnz & crew at Action Printing**, located in Fond du Lac, WI

This publication was published and printed in the United States of America.

Foreword

Let's face it - one of the main reasons you bought this book is that sometime real soon, you are going to get asked "Know anything about this old flat top?", and the proverbial follow up "What do you think it's worth?" For those two perennial all-pro questions, you can rest assured you now have the right stuff between your fingers.

Many older *Blue Book of Guitars* readers will have already noticed that last year's award-winning "Fat Boy" (908 page 4th Edition) has been replaced by 2 obese relatives - namely, the 5th Editions of the *Blue Book of Acoustic Guitars* and the *Blue Book of Electric Guitars*. This all new, 5th Edition acoustic publication is now focused on acoustics and acoustic electrics only. If you want the definitive book on electric instruments, the 5th Edition *Blue Book of Electric Guitars* is a similar one-stop shopping center for electric guitar information and up-to-date pricing.

You will note a pricing structure change throughout the A-Z sections. Rather than listing 7 or 8 values for individual models, this new 5th Edition now lists between 2 and 4 prices. If a guitar is currently manufactured, it will have the current manufacturer's suggested retail, 100% (new) price, in addition to values for both Excellent and Average condition factors (if the model has been produced long enough to warrant used prices). For out of production and older vintage instruments, only, Excellent and Average prices are typically listed. We felt this was less confusing and more helpful to most of you that don't want to be bothered in trying to split finer grading factors.

We are proud to offer you the best editorial content we've ever published. Michael Longworth, former Martin historian, has penned a new article, "What Kind of Guitar Do You Want?" - a must read for anyone interested in acoustic instruments. It covers all the bases, and you will be a smarter buyer/seller once you've read it. Additionally, Walter Carter, Gibson's historian, has written the definitive article on Gibson LP Reissues. Even though this is an electric guitar article, we have published it here so you can get a feel for the contents of the *Blue Book of Electric Guitars*.

In this 5th Edition, the color Photo Percentage Grading System has been has been expanded to include more acoustic instruments. Percentage grading is still listed to give you more visual information on condition factors other than Excellent and Average.

Perhaps more important than anything else are the additional information and updates in this new publication. The content has become staggering - good news for the reader, bad news for the ever bulging page count. Both the Gibson and Martin sections have been completely revised and price updated, while the National listings are now fully fleshed out. When you consider the expanded Trademark Index, Serialization, Anatomy of an Acoustic Guitar, Glossary, thorough Index, and other valuable sections, it becomes apparent that most of the information in this 5th Edition *Blue Book of Acoustic Guitars* is simply not available anywhere else, at any price!

Once again, I would like to thank you for helping, supporting and believing in this project, it's come along way since 1993! Not to be overlooked are the manufacturers, luthiers, and related industry shakers who have taken their valuable time to work with us - we really appreciate it, and couldn't have done it without you As in the past, keep your comments and suggestions coming in. It is the single best way of helping us to take the pulse of this marketplace.

Sincerely,

S.P. Fjestad
Editor & Publisher
Blue Book of Acoustic Guitars™

Acknowledgements & Dedication

CONTRIBUTING WRITERS

The Fifth Edition of the *Blue Book of Acoustic Guitars* can finally be acknowledged as the book used by the professionals and collectors because it is written by the professionals and collectors! The number of Contributing Editors who took their time to help in the individual sections of the book should be commended for their contributions to research and for "setting the story straight". Wherever possible, the *Blue Book of Acoustic Guitars* has specifically pointed out the text where certain ideas or concepts originated. Readers are encouraged to buy the original text and get the full story!

Jim Fisch & L. B. Fred
Authors, *Epiphone: The House of Stathopoulo*

Robert Hartman
Author, *The Larsons' Creations, Guitars and Mandolins*

Jay Pilzer
Contributing Author,
20th Century Guitar Magazine
New Hope Guitar Traders

Jim Speros
Stromberg Research

INDEPENDENT WRITERS AND RESEARCHERS

In addition to the comments and revisions by the professional writers, a number of independent writers and researchers took it upon themselves to add supplementary text and descriptions. All of these gentlemen should be commended for their contributions to research. Furthermore, for taking the time and sharing personal observations, *Blue Book of Acoustic Guitars* would like to thank them for their consideration in answering correspondence, questions, and out-of-the-blue phone calls.

William C. Kaman, II
(Travis Bean research)
Kaman Music Corporation

Dave Hull
(Gibson, Martin, and National research)

Fred Oster
(Gibson, Martin, and National research)

Walter Murray
Frankenstein Fretworks

Vincent Motel
(GRD Archivist)

Dave Pavlick
(Richelieu and Castelfidardo research)

Keith Smart

Mitch Walters
(C & R Guitars research)

Sam J. Maggio

Brian Gidyk
(Gittler Correspondent)

Hal Hammer, Jr.

R. Steven Graves

Dr. Neil J. Gunther

John Carl Hansen

Bud Herber

Chuck Richards

Dale Smith

AUTHOR ACKNOWLEDGEMENTS

While the number of books written on guitars and guitar builders may occupy one shelf in a bookcase, the wealth of information between the covers is growing in leaps and bounds. In addition to the in-house research staff at **Blue Book Publications**, certain books are still key cornerstones for this project. Textual ideas are fully credited to the authors, and we strongly urge anyone to purchase (if he/she hasn't already) these books for personal reference. **The following authors are in no way involved with the publication of this book, nor associated with Blue Book Publcations, Inc.** However, to properly give credit where credit is due.

I wish to acknowledge the work that these gentlemen have done in documenting histories of guitar companies:

Paul Day - *The Burns Book, The Guru's Guitar Guide*
Jim Fisch - *L.B. Fred, Epiphone: The House of Stathopoulo*
Michael Wright - *Guitar Stories Volume I*
Willie G. Moseley - *Stellas and Stratocasters, Guitar People*
Yasuhiko Iwanade - *The Beauty of the Burst, The Galaxy of Strats*

George Gruhn and Walter Carter - *Gruhn's Guide to Vintage Guitars, Acoustic Guitars, Electric Guitars and Basses*
Walter Carter - *Gibson: 100 Years of an American Icon, The Martin Book, The History of The Ovation Guitar*
Tom Wheeler - *American Guitars*
Tony Bacon - *The Ultimate Guitar Book*

Paul Bechtoldt - *G&L: Leo's Legacy, Guitars from Neptune* (with Doug Tulloch)
Hans Moust - *The Guild Book*
Richard Smith - *Fender: The Sound Heard 'Round the World, The Rickenbacker Book*
Adrian Ingram - *The ES-175 Book*
A.R. Duchossoir, *Guitar Identification*

CONTRIBUTING EDITORS

Dave Rogers and Eddy Thurston
Dave's Guitar Shop

Scott Freilich
Top Shelf Music

Bill Stapelton
American Music

Craig Brody
Guitar Broker

Art Wiggs
Wings Guitar Products

Brian Goff
Bizarre Guitars

John and Rhonda Kinnemire
JK Lutherie

Bob Ohman
Fine and Not so Fine European Guitars

Kevin Macy
Guitars, Effects, Effect Schematics

Chad Speck
Encore Music

Stan Werbin
Frog Elderly Instruments

Fred Matt & Tracy Pace
CD Ltd.

Leroy Braxton

David Belzer

Jerry Grote
Guitar Center (Vintage)

Anthony Huvard
Luthiers Around the World

Garrie Johnson
Southwest Vintage

Lee Walker -
Sound Pad Music

Jimmy Gravity
J.Gravity Strings

Scott Hoyt,
Hershberger Music

Jay Wolfe
Wolfe Guitars

Stan Jay
Mandolin Bros.

Jim Dombrowski
Jim's Music

Rick Powell
Tim Kummer
MARS Music

Haidin Demaj - Maton

Howie's Guitar Haven
Florida

Charles "Duke" and Fritzie Kramer
D & F Products

Ed Roman - World Class Guitars

Frank Finocchio

Tony Davanzo -
Guitar Makers Connection

Frank Ford
Richard Johnson
Gryphon String Instruments

Marc Silber
K & S Guitars

PHOTOGRAPHY ADVISORY BOARD

S. P. Fjestad
Paul Goodwin
Dave's Guitar Shop - LaCrosse, Wisconsin
Willie's American Guitars - St. Paul, Minnesota
LaVonne Wagener Music Savage, Minnesota
Hal Hammer, Jr.

A number of collectors, dealers, and private individuals allowed the *Blue Book of Acoustic Guitars* access to their collections, and assisted it's effort in collecting those images. The *Blue Book of Acoustic Guitars* would like to express its gratitude to:

Darryl Alger - Pastime Music
Buddy Summer - Nancy's Music Box
Scott Chinery - The Chinery Collection
Nate Westgor (and Skip) - Willie's American Guitars
Elliot Rubinson - Thoroughbred Music
Mike Coulson - Fine Vintage Guitars
Ryland Fitchet - Rockohaulix
Robert Saunders - Music Go Round
John J. Beeson - The Music Shoppe
Gerald Culbertson, Jr.
Bob Dobyne
Mike Routhier - Northeast TV

Pressly Lee
Ronn David - Vintage World
Rick King - Guitar Maniacs
Howie's Guitar Haven
Phil Willhoite - Phil's Guitar Works
Steve Burgess
Jim Furniss
Cassi International
John Miller

ADVISORY BOARD

Advisory Board members have access to specialty information or act in capacities "behind the scenes". Informal meetings may start serious, but fun's gonna break out pretty quick!

Lawrence Acunto
James Acunto
20th Century Guitar

Robert and Cindy Benedetto
Benedetto Archtop Guitars

Jurgen Engler - Die Krupps

Fred Austin - Far Away Guitars

Thomas Bauer -
Uncle Tom's Music

J. W. Black
Fred Stuart
John Page
and other hard working members of the Fender Custom Shop

David Maddux -
Fender U.S. Production

David Baas -
Roadworthy Guitars and Amps

Larry Briggs - Strings West

Dr. Thomas Van Hoose

Carl R. (Bob) Vail

Jim Rosenberg - Epiphone

Eric Futterer - Renaissance Records

John Brinkmann -
Waco Vintage Instruments

Mark Chatfield -
Cowtown Guitars

Chip Brauer - The Guitar Man

Dale B. Hanson -
Vintage Strings

Gregg Hopkins -
Vintage Amp Restoration

Steve Helgeson -
Moonstone Guitars

Larry Jenssen -
Slow Hand Guitars

Hap Kuffner -
Kuffner International Inc.

Tim Lanham and Doug Will -
L & W Corporation

Gordy and Marcia Lupo -
Gordy's Music

Tom Murphy -
Guitar Preservation

Joe Naylor - Reverend Guitars

Mike and Margaret Overly -
The Guitar Encyclomedia

Seymour Duncan

Dave Prescott - Arista Records

Jim Shine

Mark Pollock -
Charley's Guitar Shop
Greater Southwest Guitar Show

Lisa Sharken - Guitar Shop

Chuck McMillen
L & W Corporation

Billy Ray and Claudia Bush -
Frankfurt, Germany

Eugene Sharpey -
Sharp Recording and Entertainment

Dil Shaw

Mayner Greene

Kent Armstrong

Bill Acton - Guild

Ronald Rothman -
Rothman's Guitars

Rick Nielsen - Cheap Trick

Greg Schrecengost - Hofner

Russ Spaeth -
Music Exchange

Larry and Wendy Davis
WD Music Products, Inc.

Tim Swartz -
TubeTone Amplifiers

Dana Sutcliffe -
St. Louis Music

Gerald Weber -
Kendrick Amplifiers

Andy MacKenzie

Michael Holmes

Jimmy Wallace -
Sound Southwest

Jonas Aronson - Amanda's Texas Underground

Steve Ridinger
Michael Campion
Gary Patrick - Danelectro

Doug Zeno - Economical Audio

Jay Hostetler - Stewart-MacDonlad Guitar Shop Supply

Guy Bruno -
Wow! Nice Guitars

Dick Butler -
The String Collector

Skip Calvin -
Fort Wayne Guitar Exchange

Mario A. Campa and John E. DeSilva - Toys From the Attic

Jim Colclasure -
The Guitarcheologist

Gary S. Dick -
Gary's Classic Guitars

Aad Overeem

Roy Gentry

Don Pennington

Richard Friedman -
Sam Ash Music Stores

Michael Gardner -
Blue Heart Music Store

Larry Henrikson - Ax in Hand

Rock and Roll Hall of Fame and Museum

Paul Huber and Terry Breese -
Huber and Breese

Dave Hinson -
Hazard Ware Inc.

Greg Kurczewski - Rockhaus

John Evans - Green Bay, WI

Ward Meeker
Dave Kyle
Eric Shoaf -
Vintage Guitar Magazine

Alex Pepiak
Guitar Digest

Barry Moorhouse
The Bass Book

John Sprung
American Guitar Center

Paul Ruta

Evert Jepma

Roland Lozier -
Lozier Piano & Music

Ed Benson
Just Jazz Magazine

Charles H. Chapman

Joe Mass

Mr. Geoff Leach
Impress Corporation

Chizuru Shimano
Rittor Music, Inc.

Ron Middlebrook
Centerstream Publishing

Michael Mair
Vintage Paper

Simon Blundell - Rose-Morris

Brian Weinberg

Gunter Janssen
Vintage Guitar News

Steven A. Wilson
Dave McCumiskey -
Music Sales Corporation

EXTRA SPECIAL "ROCK ALBUM"-STYLE THANK YOU CREDITS!

Big "Thank You" go out to Chad Speck (Minneapolis' home away from home - that's a comfy couch!), Steve Speck, Paul Day, Persian Kitty on the 'net, www.baldtaco.com ("spankware" internet support), Daryl Jamison (SWR), Tommy Williams (Horizon Music Inc.), Scott Post (Furman Sound), Jon Edwards (Coffin Case Company), and Zebulon Cash-Lane (Aka ZEB!).

Long Suffering Family and Friends: My wife, Michelle, Al and Linda Cherne (parents), Curt and Amy Cherne, Craig Cherne, Mona Liska, Keith and Jan Cherne, Dorothy Cherne, Steve Blankenship, Dean Bolinger, Karyn Hill, Target and Fluffy.

Blue Book Germany: A bier-soaked "Danke" to Billy Ray and Claudia Bush, Thomas Bauer, Jens Ritter (Ritter Basses), and Nik Huber (Nik Huber Guitars).

Author/Musician Steve Cherne uses Reverend Guitars, Frye Acoustic-Electrics, Ritter basses, Soldano guitar amps, SWR bass amps, Peavey P.A. gear, Alesis synths, Guiness Stout, and Summit ales.

Steven Cherne, — **Blue Book Publications, Inc**

How to Use This Book

This new, **Fifth Edition** *Blue Book of Acoustic Guitars™* continues to use a similar size format which was established in the Third Edition. While there are still hundreds of pages of specific guitar models and pricing, the Fifth Edition continues to be more of an all out informational source than strictly a "hold-your-hand" pricing guide. In theory, you should be able to read the trademark name off the headstock of the guitar (where applicable), and be able to find out the country of origin, date(s) produced, and other company/model-related facts for that guitar. Many smaller, out-of-production trademarks and/or companies which are only infrequently encountered in the secondary marketplace are intentionally not priced in this text, as it is pretty hard to pin a tail on a donkey that is nowhere to be seen. Unfortunately, the less information known about a trademark is typically another way of asking the seller, "Would you take any less? After all, nobody seems to know anything about it." In other words, don't confuse rarity with desirability when it comes to these informational "blackholes." As in the past, if you own a current edition of the *Blue Book of Acoustic Guitars™* and still have questions, we will try to assist you in identifying/pricing your guitar(s). Please refer to page 42 for this service.

The prices listed in the Fifth Edition *Blue Book of Acoustic Guitars™* **are based on average national retail prices for both vintage and modern guitars. This is NOT a wholesale pricing guide; prices reflect the numbers you typically see on a guitar's price tag. More importantly, do not expect to walk into a music store, guitar or pawn shop and think that the proprietor should pay you the retail price listed within this text for your instrument(s). Dealer offers on most models could be 20%-50% less than values listed, depending upon locality, desirability, and profitability.**

In other words, if you want to receive 100% of the price (retail value), then you have to do 100% of the work (become the retailer which also includes assuming 100% of the risk). Business is business, and making a profit is what helps keep the UPS man delivering on a daily basis and the specially priced Big Macs™ brought in for lunch to the overworked employees.

Currently manufactured guitars are typically listed with the manufacturer's suggested retail, a 100% price (may reflect market place discounting), and in most cases include prices for both excellent and average condition factors. Please consult our 16-page color Photo Percentage Grading System™ (pages 49-64) to learn more about the condition of your guitar(s). This is the first time, to our knowledge, that color plates have been utilized to accurately illustrate each guitar's unique condition factor. Since condition is the overriding factor in price evaluation, study these photos carefully to learn more about the condition of your specimen(s).

For your convenience, an explanation of factors that can affect condition and pricing, guitar grading systems, how to convert them, and description of individual condition factors appear on pages 47-48 to assist you in learning more about guitar grading systems and individual condition factors. Please read these pages carefully, as the values in this publication are based on the grading/condition factors listed. This will be especially helpful when evaluating older vintage instruments. Remember, the price is wrong if the condition factor isn't right.

All values within this text assume original condition. From the vintage marketplace or (especially) a collector's point of view, any repairs, alterations, modifications, "enhancements", "improvements", "professionally modified to a more desirable configuration", or any other non-factory changes usually detract from an instrument's value. Please refer to **page 47** regarding an explanation to finishes, repairs, alterations/modifications, and other elements which have to be factored in before determining the correct condition. Depending on the seriousness of the modification/alteration, you may have to go down a condition factor or two when re-computing price for these alterations. Determining values for damaged and/or previously repaired instruments will usually depend on the parts and labor costs necessary to return them to playable and/or original specifications. **The grading lines within the Fifth Edition have been changed to reflect this edition's change to only listing the Excellent and Average condition factors.**

You may note that this new Fifth Edition contains quite a few more black-and-white photos (almost 400) of individual models/variations to assist you with more visual identification.

The **Fifth Edition** *Blue Book of Acoustic Guitars*™ provides many company histories, notes on influential luthiers and designers, and other bits of knowledge as a supplement to the straight pricing text. Hopefully, this information will be shared to alleviate those "gray areas" of the unknown, and shed light on the efforts of those luthiers/companies who build the guitars that we play and cherish.

We have designed an easy-to-use (and consistent) text format throughout this publication to assist you in finding specific information within the shortest amount of time, and there is a lot of information!

1. Trademark manufacturer, brand name, or importer are listed in bold face type with a thin, screened, "perforated" line running through the center and will appear alphabetically as follows:

MARTIN

GIBSON

COLLINGS

2. Manufacturer/trademark information and production dates (if possible) are listed directly beneath the trademark heading:

Instruments produced in Fullerton, California since 1978.

3. A company overview, model information recap, and/or other relatively useful pieces of information may follow within a smaller block of text:

This brand name belonged to Marcelo Barbero (1904-1955), considered one of the great flamenco guitar makers.

4. When a proper model-by-model listing is not available (due to space considerations), a small paragraph may follow with the company history and related production data. These paragraphs may also include current retail prices. The following example is from Luthier Tim Scheerhorn:

The Mahogany/Spruce Regal Body model ($2,450) has a book-matched quartersawn Sitka Spruce top, solid mahogany back and sides, and a two-piece mahogany neck. The Mahogany/Spruce Large Body model has similar specifications, but with a larger body size for additional volume and projection (list $2,650).

5. The next major classification under a heading name may include a category name which appears in upper-case, is flush left, and inside an approximately 3 1/2 inch shaded box. A category name refers mostly to a guitar's primary configuration:

ACOUSTIC

ACOUSTIC ELECTRIC

6. A sub-classification of the category name (upper and lower-case description slightly indented inside a longer and lighter shaded box) usually indicates a grouping or series which has to be further defined under the category name:

SIGNATURE SERIES

ELITE ACOUSTIC SERIES

7. Model names appear flush left, are bolded in upper case, and appear in alpha-numerical (normally) sequence which are grouped under the various subheadings:

DS-2H 12-Fret (Collings)

8. Variations within a model appear as sub-models, are indented, and appear in both upper and lower case type:

70 F Flamenco

Model sub-variations appear in the text under the description/pricing of the main model(s).

9. Model/sub-model descriptions appear directly under model/sub-model names and appear as follows:

— dreadnought style, solid cedar top, round soundhole, maple bound body, wood rosette, mahogany back/sides/neck, 14/20 Fret, rosewood fingerboard with double dot inlay at 12th Fret, rosewood bridge with white pins, 3 per side vintage chrome tuners. Available in natural satin finish. Mfg. beginning 1996.

10. Pricing. Directly underneath the model description is the pricing line for that model. You will notice that this new **Fifth Edition** *Blue Book of Acoustic Guitars*™ features only one price line

throughout. Typically, it includes the Mfr.'s Sug. Retail on currently manufactured instruments, a 100% price (this may reflect industry discounting, if any), and, if applicable, a single price for both Excellent and Average condition factors. When the following price line is encountered,

Grading	100%	EXCELLENT	AVERAGE
Mfr.'s Sug. Retail $1,149	$875	$550	$395

it automatically indicates the guitar is currently manufactured and the manufacturer's suggested retail price is shown left of the 100% column. **The 100% price on a new instrument is what you can typically expect to pay for that instrument, and may reflect a discount off the Manufacturer's Suggested Retail price. The values for the remaining Excellent and Average condition factors represent actual selling prices for used instruments in these two conditions.**

An "N/A" instead of a price means that a firm market price is **Not Available** within a certain condition factor. Also, $TBA has been inserted instead of prices for those models **To Be Announced** at a future date.

Musical instruments, like other consumer goods (for example: automobiles, appliances, or electronics) may be discounted to promote consumer spending. Discounting is generally used as a sales tool within the music industry and includes many music/guitar establishments, chain stores, mail-order companies, and other retailers to help sell merchandise. Discounted prices depend on each region's unique local market place economics (some markets may not discount at all, but offer quality service and support/advice after your purchase).

The 100% condition factor, when encountered in a currently manufactured guitar, assumes the guitar has not been previously sold at retail and includes a factory warranty. A currently manufactured new instrument must include EVERYTHING the factory originally provided with the instrument - including the case (if originally included), warranty card, instruction manual (if any), hang tags (if any), etc. Simply refer to the correct condition column of the instrument in question and refer to the price listed directly underneath.

A price line with 2 values listed (as the example below demonstrates) indicates a discontinued, out of production model with values shown for Excellent and Average condition factors only. 100% prices have intentionally not been listed, since the longer an instrument has been discontinued, the less likely you will find it in 100% condition. On recently discontinued models (within the past several years), 100% values (new condition) will typically be approximately 25% - 100% higher than the Excellent price, depending on the desireability factor of that specific out-of-production make and model (including any extra-cost options). 100% discontinued pricing on major trademark models will normally be priced towards the upper end of this percentage spread, while lesser known out-of-production models will fall within the bottom end.

Grading	100%	EXCELLENT	AVERAGE
		$665	$400

Obviously, "Mfr.'s Sug. Retail" will not appear in the left margin, but a model note may appear below the price line indicating the last Manufacturer's Suggested Retail price. Also, an N/A (Not Available) may appear in place of values for instruments that are not commonly encountered in lower condition factor(s). Some instruments that are only 10 years old and have never been taken out-of-the-case (unplayed), may not be 100% (new), as the finish may have slightly cracked, tarnished, faded, or deteriorated. **100% is new -- no excuses, period**.

The following price line indicates that this model has been in production for a short time only, and used guitars simply do not exist yet. Also, the 100% price is not listed, as this type of guitar is typically of limited production and/or special order, and dealer/consumer discounts usually do not apply.

Mfr.'s Sug. Retail $1,299

11. While the current Manufacturer's Suggested Retail price is included on current models whenever possible, the Last Suggested Retail price for discontinued models may appear in smaller typeface flush right directly underneath the price line:

Last Sug. Mfr.'s Retail was $649.

12. Manufacturer's notes, model information, and available options appear in smaller type and are significant as they contain both important model changes and other up-to-date information:

Early models may have mahogany back and sides.

13. Extra cost features/special orders and other value added/subtracted items (add-ons for currently manufactured guitars reflect a retail price), are placed directly under individual price lines, and appear bolder than other descriptive typeface:

Add $200 for 'Floating Pickup' system.
Add $250 for the 18 in. body width.

14. A grading line will appear at the top of each page where applicable. This new grading line shown below has been designed specifically for the new **Fifth Edition** *Blue Book of Acoustic Guitars,*TM and reflects the 100% value (this price represents industry discounting, if any, in

Grading	100%	EXCELLENT	AVERAGE

addition to the value of a discontinued instrument in 100% or new condition). Next to 100%, left to right, are the Fifth Edition standard Excellent and Average condition factors. These two new condition factors will hopefully eliminate some of the "grading graffiti" on these types of instruments, where a single percentage or abbreviation doesn't do them justice.

To find a particular acoustic guitar in this book, first identify the name of the manufacturer, trademark, importer, brand name, or in some cases - headstock logo. Refer to this listing within the correct alphabetical section. Next, locate the correct category name (**Acoustic, Acoustic Electric**). Models will be listed first alpha-numerically (Model J-180, J-200, etc.) then by model name (Savannah, Vicksburg, etc.). Once you find the correct model or sub-model under its respective heading or subheading, determine the acoustic guitar's original condition factor (see the **Photo Percentage Grading System**TM on pages 49-64), and simply find the corresponding condition column (Excellent or Average) to ascertain the correct price. Special/limited editions usually appear last under a manufacturer's heading. **In order to save time when looking up a particular model(s), you may want to look first at our expanded Index on pages 467-471. Also, the Trademark Index located on pages 452-466 is the only up-to-date and comprehensive listing of current acoustic manufacturers and luthiers in print - use both of them, they can be very helpful!**

Additional sections in this publication that will be of special interest are the Serialization Charts, Anatomy/Glossary of An Acoustic Guitar, and Strings/Pickups. When using the Serialization Charts, make sure your model is listed and find the serial number within the yearly range listings. However, **do not date your instrument on serial number information alone!** Double check parts/finish variations in the text accompanying the model, or reference the coding on your instrument's potentiometers (tone and volume knobs), if applicable on an acoustic electric model. More research and data regarding serialization is still being compiled, and updates will continue to be published in future editions of the ***Blue Book of Acoustic Guitars***TM.

COLLECTIBLE TODAY, COMMODITY TOMORROW?

A Publisher's Overview of the Acoustic Guitar Marketplace

Fully understanding today's acoustic guitar industry is to realize that the marketplace components are significantly different than those for electric guitars. The talented, new crop of luthiers which has blossomed nicely over the past 10-15 years, is now making a major difference in those areas previously dominated by major models and trademarks. Since tonal quality has now become Polar North for players who know the difference, many buyers are now purchasing a new Taylor, Collings, Larrivee, Martin, Heritage, Guild, Gibson, etc., rather than buy a more expensive vintage instrument that doesn't sound as good. While still competitive, this part of the acoustic guitar biz is now flourishing, and the real winner is today's consumer.

Remember - just because a guitar is currently manufactured in limited quantities does not necessarily guarantee collectibility. In this situation, a guitar, like anything else in current production, becomes a commodity which responds to only two things - supply & demand. You could make it more complicated, but supply and demand are the only two factors determining an instrument's price that is currently in production. While it sounds easy, understanding the individual components of these supply and demand curves gets more complicated when applying them to real world situations.

A good example is limited edition instruments currently manufactured - many of them reissues of older classic models. Many older vintage instruments with a fixed supply now depend solely on demand to determine today's price tags. Since only so many "1st generation" acoustic guitars were originally built, only a small percentage of these will remain in excellent original condition 20-30 years later.

What's important here is to remember these original models were meant to play, not collect, resulting in only a small number remaining in excellent original condition. With pre-war Martin D-28s pushing $20,000 these days, there can be a lot of pressure for a manufacturer to put out resissues in an attempt to tap into some of this "surplus" vintage money.

Because of this, today's reissues have a different focus. This new crop may be more of a marketing gimmick and advertising campaign to try and take advantage of the high vintage prices being paid for their "1st generation relatives", even though the Japanese "drunken sailor" buying frenzy for vintage instruments is now a shadow of what it used to be. These recent 2nd (in some cases, even 3rd!) generation descendants of the original classics are, in many cases, priced $1,000's less than the originals. It remains to be seen if these new generations of guitar "trading cards" will turn out to be more desirable in the future.

After all, since most new reissues/limited editions are not played, their condition factor ends up on one square - namely NIC (New In Case). With supply and condition now being fixed, the only way to get an increase in price is to get an increase in demand.

While many players, collectors, and investors hope the vintage marketplace (i.e. fixed, out of production supply with fixed or increasing demand) will raise pricing, guitar manufacturers scrutinize vintage guitar economics as an opportunity to reissue or further eulogize by a commemorative/special edition. When vintage prices increase drastically, new reissues/special editions/commemoratives have become the easiest way manufacturers can use the current marketplace to help them bolster the bottom line.

On a final note, it is obvious to anyone who has attended recent NAMM shows and reads the guitar mags regularly that this is one of the better times for comparing quality and overall value against price. With Asian markets shaky and desperate to sell their products into America, while domestic manufacturers try to match them in both quality & price point, this is perhaps the most opportune time ever for a new guitar buyer. So do your homework, keep pluckin' those G-strings, and above all else, have fun while you're doing it.

Token Tidbits From Turbulent Toyland

"Honest to God, this older Martin was originally owned by Gene Autry!"

"Are you sure about that?"

"Yeah. One of our local musicians got to meet Autry back in the 50's at the Grand Ol Opry. This guy had a new Gibson that Autry liked, and they swapped guitars that night."

"What do you mean $1,750? I saw an ad for the same model on the 'net the other day priced at $3,250. I may be stupid, but I'm not dumb!"

"Honestly, if I took any less, I'd be losing money."

"Whadda ya mean that $1,000 guitar I bought from your store 2 weeks ago for $700 that's been played twice is only worth $425 cash right now? Shouldn't you give me some KY Jelly for that type of rectal penetration? How late are you open?"

"Don't try to figure it out, just have a new box of price tags ready."

"Really can't say over the phone - I'd have to see the instrument first. Could be anywhere from a-hundred and twenty-five bucks to over $700, depending on condition. We could waste another twenty minutes talking about this, or you could hold it closer to the microphone so I could see it better."

"Make me your best offer, and I'll let you know how much too low you are."

"No I don't, but what would you possibly use a mandolin neck without frets and a rounded headstock for anyway?" - Washington D.C. Guitar Show comeback to a question from a disguised Monica Lewinsky.

"Outside of a replaced fingerboard, new frets, non-original tuners & pickups, and the new sparkle lime green paint job, this guitar is all original."

"Don't miss Guitar Center's Blowout this Labor Day weekend! Prices have been slashed over 50%! Save hundreds! For a limited time only, Washburn acoustics are as low as $200, and Samick's new lineup now starts at less than $100!"

"I don't care what it says in the *Blue Book of Acoustic Guitars*. Around here, an instrument like that doesn't bring over $350 - period!"

"Yes Jesse, I know you're the new governor of Minnesota, but you can't expect me to take your H&K MP-5 machine gun in trade for this new limited edition Martin D-45."

"This is all the cash I got on me, and I gotta have gas for the way home. Take it or leave it."

"Look pal, older D'Angelico New Yorkers are selling for at least thirty grand these days. My guitar actually sounds better, and it's priced at only $650!"

"But I can buy it through a catalog for only $350, get a free case, and don't have to pay sales tax. Why can't you match that price?"

raveling the firearms collectors shows in the mid 1960's I was introduced to a longtime collector, Harvey (Knox) Baldwin, a longtime resident of Nashville, Tennessee. Knox and I became fast friends often attending national gun shows together where we shared lodging. Those long weekends afforded discussions covering a volume of subjects. My music interest sparked Knox's informing me he owned a guitar that had once been the property of Hank Williams Sr. Initially I figured Knox was teasing me with this story.

After listening for years to this tale, it was clear Knox was telling me a factual story. It did, of course, help when Knox finally showed me the album cover that pictured the guitar with Hank Jr. at a very young age and Connie Francis. The guitar was easily recognizable, as the wood grain top is like a fingerprint - a one of a kind.

Fate placed the Baldwin and Williams families living near one another, as well as having children near the same age. Hank Jr. frequented the Baldwin home often as part of teenagers coming and going on a regular basis. Hank Jr. was fascinated with firearms at an early age, often spending time around the Baldwin home learning about firearms through Knox's collection. When Hank Jr. became of age he began acquiring firearms for his personal collection from Mr. Baldwin. During an early acquisition, Hank Jr. traded his father's handmade guitar to Knox as part payment in a deal. Knox had foresight Hank Sr.'s life and times would cause the guitar to become quite valuable as part of country music history. Well, he was correct, as I'm the proof!!!!

For years I would sneak the Hank Williams Sr. guitar into my conversations with Knox. Without exception, I would ask him to quote me a price on the darn thing.

He would respond in some fashion putting me off so that he might price it to me at a later date. Well years passed and no price was ever quoted. Eight years ago, during one of those late night conversations, I pleaded with him to price the guitar this one time so I might say YES or never press him again for a figure. After a long thoughtful pause he quoted a price so high he was sure I would not step up to make the buy. Well he was wrong!! It has been mine since that night along with the album cover picturing Hank Jr., Connie Francis, and the famous guitar.

Two years ago, I acquired a Colt .45 automatic taken from Hank Sr. by a Tennessee highway patrolman, as Hank Sr. partied too close to the Governor's mansion, as well Hank Sr.'s hat - but those are stories for another time.

Jack A. Puglisi
Sportsman & Singer

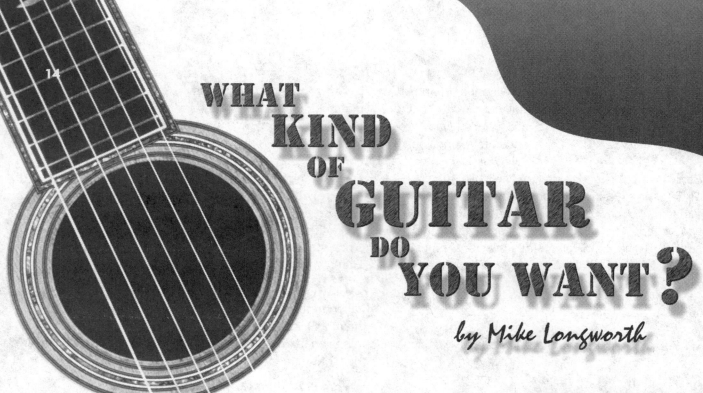

WHAT KIND OF GUITAR DO YOU WANT?

by Mike Longworth

SIZE

One of the first things people ask me is, "What is your favorite guitar?" This is a question that I answer with a question - "What am I going to do with it?" For backing up a bluegrass band, I would use a Dreadnought or other large guitar. If I were recording, as I did in the early 60's, I would use a 000 size. If I were going to lie down on the sofa with the guitar on my belly to pick and sing to myself, a 0 or 00 would be best. Occasionally, a very small instrument like a size 5 is nice, or other ¾ size guitar.

Please note that most of my comments relate to Martin sizes and shapes. It's only natural - I have worked with Martins for over 40 years, and was an employee of the Martin Company for 27 years. Most of my comments can be applied to other brands, though their measurements can vary.

Guitar player/collector James Furniss and his Martin Acoustic.
(Photo courtesy Hal Hammer, Jr.)

FOR INVESTMENT OR FOR PLAYING?

Whether you are buying a new or used guitar, investment value may be a factor. If you are buying new, and are concerned about resale value, you should investigate the track records of the used instruments. *The Blue Book of Acoustic Guitars* is a good source of information for checking on both price and ages. A used newer model may be worth more or less than half of the new price. Do not expect the value to rise over the retail for a few years. A newer used guitar might give you more bang for the buck.

Newer manufacturers and small makers may not have such track records. You will be on your own in deciding which makers or guitars might be in demand in the future. With electric guitars (out of my field), it appears to me that there is considerable influence in "which rock superstar is playing

ABOUT THE AUTHOR

Mike Longworth is a native of Chattanooga, TN, and is an acoustic musician, former collector, pearl inlay artist, and author with over 40 years of experience. He plays five-string banjo, acoustic guitar, and bass. He served with the United States Air Force in several capacities during the 1950's. Mike joined C.F. Martin & Co. in 1968 as a pearl inlay artist to reissue the famous D-45 guitar, and went on to be their Consumer Relations Manager and Historian. His book, *Martin Guitars: A History*, first published in 1975, has seen four editions. Mr. Richard Johnston and Dick Boak are preparing a fifth edition.

Photo by Don Fisher

Mike suggested several guitar designs, including the D-41, the D-40BLE, the OM-40 Limited Edition (double top pearl model), the 1935 reissue, and worked as a member of the Guitar-of-the-Month team through 1994.

He retired to Tennessee after 27 years with Martin. He is now disabled, and resides in Bell Buckle with his wife, Sue, and where he occasionally makes an ornate ukulele when he feels like it, and is so inclined. He has never sold one of his ukuleles. Mike says he is guitared-out, and now prefers to work with ukuleles and banjos.

which model?" It is also apparent that this type of influence will change over the years, so it may be a short-term effect.

If you are primarily concerned with the playability of an instrument, your job is easier. There are a number of small makers that produce good sounding and good quality guitars. Many of them are friends of mine, so I will not point out particular brands. That is subjective and mostly personal opinion.

The downside of the small or independent makers is partly what the future of their operation might be. The fact that someone makes a fine guitar does not mean they will not be making clocks instead of guitars next year. A

warranty is only effective for the period the maker is in business, unless they are bought out by someone with an interest in carrying on the guarantees. I solve this problem by NOT offering any warranty!

Which small makers will be in demand in future years? No one knows, but it is a relatively long shot. I personally recommend seeking out makers or small factories with some years in the business, preferably a second or third generation family heritage. A corporate entity is also more assurance that one person will not sink the ship. On the other hand, there are times when you are excited about a small maker or their product, and want to promote them without compensation

because you believe in their product. I have done that, and might do it again. Unless you are a dyed-in-the-wool fan of some artist, I do not recommend buying solely on the fact that their name is attached to it. Make sure it fits YOUR needs, not theirs. Also, I have heard of cases where an artist would use a particular brand on a recording for the tone, then grab another for their endorsement on the album cover.

STEEL OR NYLON?

Most people reading this article will have their own answer for this. It is opinion, preference, and musical style that play a part in your decision. For classic guitar styles, you will want nylon strings, and European-made guitars are often preferred. For country, blues, jazz or bluegrass, steel is most common. (Yes, I know Willie uses nylon.) Within the realm of what is commonly known as folk music, most play whatever they like, and are less bound by size, brand, and other considerations. This is not to say that some players do not have certain preferences, but that it varies from one artist to another.

PRICING

One problem with which I have difficulty is the art of purchasing a guitar from an individual. At one time, prices were less dramatic, and people put low prices on old merchandise. This idea is almost obsolete. While at Martin, I noticed a trend of the sellers, some even without musical interest, doing more research before pricing. They would call a few dealers, read the *Blue Book of Acoustic Guitars*, or consult the Internet. When they called you, they already knew what they THOUGHT their guitar was worth. We didn't usually buy, sell, or appraise instruments, but we got the calls anyway.

In case you are selling instead of buying, this next bit of information will be useful. First of all, *Blue Book of Acoustic Guitars* prices are approximate, and the actual sale prices can vary from one part of the country to the next, or by condition. Something may sell high in New York, but for less in Tennessee or the Midwest. Secondly, the appraisal prices are the prices a dealer might charge when they sell you a guitar, not what they would give you for yours.

Most owners I have encountered say, "Dealer X appraised it at $2,000 - I won't take a penny less!" These poor folks are at a disadvantage. If you can find the ultimate retail customer, I wish you well. In most cases, the dealer knows or thinks they know where it might sell, and at what price. They will buy for perhaps 50% of retail. This will vary with the dealer and with the desirability and the value of the item involved.

Consignment is better if you are not in a hurry. Most dealers I know charge 15%-25% commis-

sion, depending on the item, price, and desirability. If you do not know the next owner, having a dealer do it for you is a good idea. They DO earn their commission. They have to clean it up, sometimes adjust and repair, (usually at your expense), and advertise it. They have the responsibility to take care of the item, keep good strings on it, and eventually ship it out, etc. Personally, if I don't have anyone in mind for an instrument, I will trust it to a reputable dealer.

WOODS

Many woods are used for guitars. Spruce is usually used for the top. The most common primary woods for sides and backs are mahogany, rosewood, and maple. There are, of course, many others. I can only give my personal opinion and a generalization on these woods. Any particular guitar may have the traits of another wood.

Mahogany is an excellent wood for a guitar, and has a bright treble sound that tends to separate the individual notes. Some flat-pickers prefer this type of tone for single note picking. Rosewood has a deeper sound, and may be best for bass rhythm backup. Maple is

somewhere in the middle. The final judgement is in your own ear. Also, note that you can get much the same effect by reducing the size of your guitar. A 000 size will usually be brighter than a Dreadnought, as will a thinner body design on a jumbo.

Ebony and rosewood are the two primary woods for fingerboards and bridges. Ebony is harder, slicker, basically black, and sometimes has light streaks. Rosewood is softer, and somewhat more subject to wear. I like both. Choose for yourself. I will say that most manufacturers use the ebony for their more expensive guitars.

Master Luthier Augustine Lo Prinzi inspecting a book-matched back. (Photo courtesy of Hal Hammer Jr.)

FRETS

Some players prefer narrow, medium, or wide frets. I prefer medium. For mandolins and banjos, many seem to like narrow frets. This is largely a personal preference. Worn frets would not cause me to turn down a guitar. I never felt fret replacement to be a major modification affecting much of the value if well done. Originality buffs may disagree. It is a factor you must consider if you have to add to the cost of a fret job.

FINISH

Finishes are of several types: lacquer, polyurethane, and French polish. French polish is rarely seen these days. It is a hand-applied, hand-rubbed finish, very time consuming and fairly soft. Lacquer is used for most brands. It is medium hard, which varies according to brand and application. Polyurethane finish is very hard, looks good, but is hard to repair. Most guitars made in the Far East seem to be finished in this manner. Presently, I am experimenting with a Minwax™ Handrubbed Polyurethane finish on my latest ukulele, but have not developed a final opinion on its quality for the purpose.

Another finish consideration is gloss or semi-gloss, and even flat finish. I always preferred semi-gloss or flat. They do not glare under stage and TV lighting. You can see the wood and trim-

Bridges being glued to the top of guitars. (Photo courtesy of Martin Guitar Co., Nazareth, PA)

mings, not the glare of the finish. These have one disadvantage - they will become shiny where they are subjected to constant rubbing, such areas as where your arm crosses the top, the back of the neck, etc. Polished finishes are more popular. Then there is the "what happened to the finish on your guitar?" factor, a rude question, often asked by the unknowing public.

NECKS

The neck is all important, but largely a matter of personal taste. Personally, I like a neck with a teeny bit more width than standard. Obviously, the standard width will be more popu-

lar. Then you have flat and curved fingerboards. Most steel string guitar fingerboards are curved, though an old one is sometimes flat. Classic boards are almost always flat, as are most banjos, mandolins, and ukuleles. Consider solid vs. slotted heads - In my opinion, slotted heads are prettier, but they are not practical for the stage. If you break a string on a slotted head guitar, you are out of business until you find another guitar, or sit down and replace it. With solid heads, I know of at least one top professional who will tell you a joke, and upon finishing it, has replaced the string, and is ready to go again. This is not possible with a slotted head.

CRACKS

Cracks do indeed alter the value of a guitar. My experience and opinion are that cracks in the sides and backs, if repairable without patching, are far less of a problem than cracked tops. Perhaps this is because the tops show when you're playing, and they are also subject to more stress. Cracks in necks can also affect the value.

ACTION

Again, this is mostly a personal opinion. What you play, how hard you play, the gauge of your strings, and your playing style are all factors. If your action is too low, a new bridge saddle and/or a new nut will often correct it. If the action is too high, you should judge whether an action judgement at the bridge saddle and/or the nut would solve the problem. If it will not do the job, you might encounter a neck set, cutting down of the bridge, leveling of uneven frets, straightening necks, etc. The validity of each available option is a matter of opinion. The expertise of the person doing the work should be a consideration. Major work should always be entrusted to a competent repairperson.

TUNERS

I am frequently asked about tuners. Most often you do not have a choice if you are buying a used guitar, so condition is important. On many old-style tuners, repair is not practical, and replacements are expensive, or just not available. Of modern tuners, my favorites are Schallers, and for new old-style tuners, the Stewart MacDonald Waverly machines or similar machines by Martin would be my choices.

BRIDGES

If the bridge has a small crack, it can probably be repaired, especially since the advent of cyanoacrylate glues used with ebony or rosewood dust. This type of work should be done by a professional repairperson. This glue can damage the finish of the top.

If the crack is very open, a bridge must usually be ordered, or specially made for the job. I do not recommend the use of a bridge that does not approximate the original for that specific vintage guitar. I have seen bridges that I like, but are not standard. Some have a curved layout for the bridge pinholes. This is probably superior, because there are fewer holes along a single grain line in the wood. Note that such a thing would adversely affect the value of a used collector's item.

Gluing together the two pieces of rosewood to form a "back".
(Photo courtesy of Martin Guitar Co., Nazareth, PA)

BINDINGS

Most bindings are some form of plastic. Some makers pride themselves on their wood bindings. Pearl is a factor on some higher priced models and collectors items. This is more often abalone top and body trim as used by Martin from the 1830's through the early 1940's, reintroduced in 1968, and now used by almost every manufacturer. Abalone and white oyster pearl are used mostly on fingerboards. Pearl will add beauty and value to your instrument, but does not usually affect the tone quality. If tone, and not fanciness is your goal, you can eliminate pearl models, and seek the same specs on a guitar without the pearl trimming. Personally, I am addicted to pearl...

BRACING

When considering the bracing, I can speak only of flat-top guitars. Most often used is the Martin style "X" bracing or some variation thereof. Another is transverse bracing that is straight across the guitar. I consider the "X" to be the superior of the two. Some makers have their own design for bracing.

PRICING AGAIN

Now we will revisit pricing, which is what the *Blue Book of Acoustic Guitars* is all about. The seller wants as much as they can get,

Gluing kerfing to the body. (Photo courtesy of Martin Guitar Co., Nazareth, PA)

and the buyer wants it as cheaply as possible. This presents a haggling situation, and since I am not good at it, I avoid saying much about it. Personally, I am more of a take-it-or-leave-it man. I guess you have to know what or with whom you are dealing in such cases. When working with a dealer, you must remember that they have overhead and employees they have to feed. They cannot exist without a profit. One of my favorite sayings is, "You cannot buy at retail, sell at retail, and live on the profit!" Asking prices and "gettin'" prices are not necessarily the same. Often there is at least a little movement necessary to come to terms.

I hope that I have given you some guidance in determining what kind of guitar you wish to buy. The opinions are my own, and do not necessarily represent the opinions of the publisher, other dealers, or knowledgeable people. No responsibility is accepted by the author or publishers for the use of the information contained herein . A friend once told me, "If two persons agree on everything, one of them is unnecessary." Keep that in mind, and listen to other opinions as well as mine. ■

Mike Longwoth

C.F. Martin & Co. historian (retired)

"YOU CANNOT BUY AT RETAIL, SELL AT RETAIL, AND LIVE ON THE PROFIT!"

JERRY'S SCRAP BOOK

Marty Balin of Jefferson Starship, 6/1/96

Roger Hodgson, formerly of Supertramp, 4/14/98

Garth Brooks & Jerry Adler, 8/16/93

Garth Brooks, 8/16/93

Jimmy Buffett, 10/18/97

For this all-new *Blue Book of Acoustic Guitars*, a wide range of photos from the world of rock & roll, as well as country music has been selected.

One of the nicest people in the music industry has to be Garth Brooks. We've met twice, and he's just the friendliest guy you'll ever meet. After 10 minutes with Garth, you feel like old friends. Included is a photo of Garth & myself taken the first time we met over 5 years ago.

Besides being a really great person, Garth is also one of the finest and hardest working performers you'll ever see. No one leaves a Garth concert disappointed!

George Strait, 10/22/91

Pete Townshend of The Who, 10/26/96

Daryl Hall of Hall & Oates, 5/28/98

Kenny Loggins, 10/21/91

Paul Stanley, 6/24/95

Alan Jackson, 8/2/97

All photos courtesy Jerry Scott Adler ©

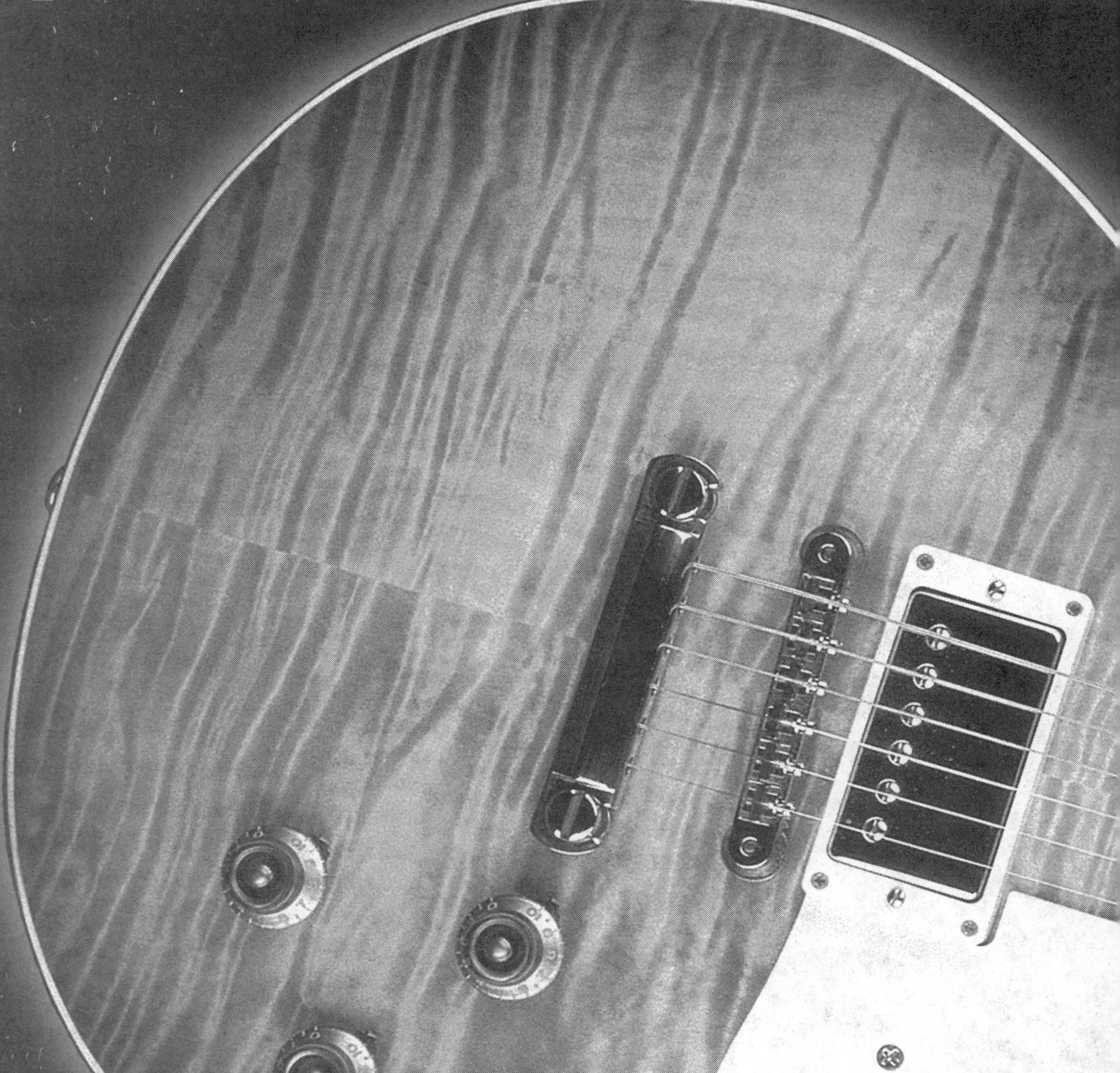

Keeping the Flame Alive!

BY WALTER CARTER

With original sunburst Les Paul Standards going anywhere from $25,000 to $60,000 or higher, it's not surprising to see a healthy demand for Gibson's dead-on accurate '59 Les Paul Flametop Reissue, which currently lists for $11,250. But there's more than just a healthy demand for new Reissues. Reissues have a 20-year history of their own now, and there's a growing aura of mystery and mystique around the model—the kind of buzz that may indicate a "sleeper" is about to awaken in the vintage and collectible market.

ABOUT THE AUTHOR

Walter Carter has been involved in the Nashville music world as an author, journalist, songwriter and musician since 1971. From 1993-98 he was the historian of the Gibson guitar company, where he wrote the book *Gibson Guitars: 100 Years of an American Icon*. His three books co-authored with vintage guitar dealer George Gruhn have become primary source books for vintage guitar photos and identification. He has also written books on Martin, Gibson and Epiphone.

He is the co-writer of the 1988 hit country song "Life as We Knew It" by Kathy Mattea, and he currently plays mandola in the Nashville Mandolin Ensemble.

Granted, buyers have always looked at the '59 Reissue as an investment, thanks in no small part to Gibson marketing of the model as such, but their interest goes beyond the typical questions of "What's it worth?" and "Will it hold its value?" They want to know "What's the startup point for the Historic Collection?" or "When did the Replica era begin" or "Was my guitar made by Tom Murphy?"

These questions may seem esoteric, anal or irrelevant now, particularly since by most traditional definitions of "collectible," the Les Paul Reissue is not a collectible. After all, it's still in production (though somewhat limited). You can buy now or wait until next year. The only thing different will be the price, and the price difference will probably reflect either inflation or Gibson's policy of raising prices every year rather than an increase in demand.

On the other hand, these esoteric issues are just the type that delineated pre-CBS from post-CBS in Fender history, Loar-period from post-Loar in Gibson history-delineations that mean hundreds or even thousands of dollars of difference in values between otherwise similar instruments. Furthermore, no other reissues attract this kind of interest and scrutiny. Not Gibson's korina reissues of the Flying V and Explorer, which cost more than the Les Paul and are produced in much smaller numbers. Not even the goldtop Les Paul reissues and the Black Beauty (Les Paul Custom) reissues.

So what is it about the reissue of the sunburst Standard that makes it special? More pertinent to today's guitar buyers, what specific characteristics are going to be valued the highest in tomorrow's vintage market? Is it the flame in the top, the finish color or overall accuracy of the reproduction that's most important? In other words, which Reissue is the best buy?

**But first,
which Reissue is which?**

PRE-REISSUES

History usually holds some clues, but when it came to bringing back the Les Paul Standard, Gibson appears to have been clueless. As everyone knows, Gibson changed the finish on the Les Paul Standard from gold to sunburst in 1958 and then killed off the model at the tail end of 1960 in favor of the SG body style (although it was still called Les Paul Standard for three more years). The first surge of demand for the old Standards came in the late '60s, and it came from players. Gibson reissued the Les Paul in 1968 with goldtop finish and, for reasons no one has ever explained, single-coil P-90 pickups rather than humbuckers. Maybe someone in marketing had a friend or a family member who thought the goldtop P-90 Les Paul version was the coolest ever. Who knows?

A year later, in another misguided move, Gibson replaced the goldtop with a cherry sunburst Les Paul Deluxe, which was the right color, but with mini-humbucking pickups, which were wrong. The minis were an identification mark of the Epiphone line, but because Epi production was about to be moved to Japan, it's likely that someone in engineering feathered his cap with a plan to use up existing stock. Hey, a humbucker's a humbucker, right? Doesn't matter how big it is.

Until 1976 Gibson didn't offer a Les Paul Standard in the catalog, but the company made them anyway. All a dealer had to do was order a Deluxe with full-size humbuckers and he got a Standard, complete with "Standard" on the truss rod cover. Judging from the numerous sightings today of standards with six-digit serial numbers (1970-75), a lot of guitar buyers wanted a Standard like the old Standard. But what they were getting was a far cry from the original, thanks to Gibsons numerous "improvements" in the model, such as polyurethane-coated pickup wire, a wider peghead, a three-piece neck (instead of the original one-piece), a four-layer "pancake" body (instead of the original two

layers) and a three-piece top (instead of two bookmatched pieces). These changes may have made sense at the time to engineers and accountants and maybe even to marketing people, but not to guitar players.

Keep in mind that by the mid 1970s, intracompany communications at Gibson were probably at an all-time low. Marketing and other corporate offices of Norlin Industries (Gibson's parent company,) were located in Lincolnwood, Illinois. Kalamazoo, the original home of Gibson, was technically just a manufacturing facility. Although the Kalamazoo plant was still the heart and soul of Gibson as far as the guitar world was concerned, Les Pauls were no longer being made there; Les Paul production had been moved to the Nashville plant that had opened in 1974. Surely there

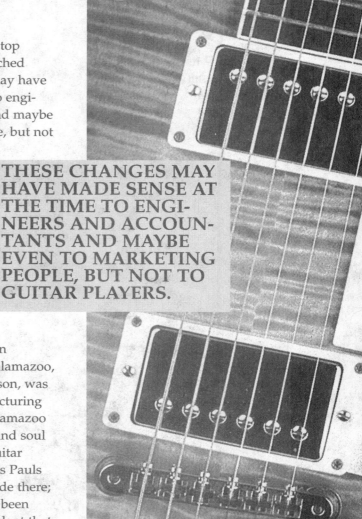

THESE CHANGES MAY HAVE MADE SENSE AT THE TIME TO ENGINEERS AND ACCOUNTANTS AND MAYBE EVEN TO MARKETING PEOPLE, BUT NOT TO GUITAR PLAYERS.

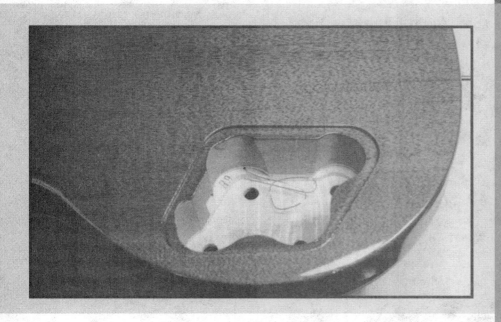

R9 stamp in the cavity. Reissue model numbers are R8, R9 and R0, for 1958, 1959 and 1960, respectively. The lip on the edge of the cavity is there because the floor of the cavity is routed parallel to the top of the guitar. On regular production models, the floor is flat and parallel to the back of the guitar.

were some people in the Gibson organization who knew what was happening in the guitar market, but if they tried to pass the word along, it got lost in the corporate structure.

By 1974 or '75 the demand for original-style sunburst Les Pauls was strong enough that a dealer took matters into his own hands. Chris Lovell, one of the owners of Strings and Things in Memphis, called Kalamazoo and asked if the original Les Paul Standard specs were still around. They were, and Lovell placed a custom order. He asked for a narrower headstock than the current style, narrow binding in the cutaway, a deeper carve in the top, full-size humbuckers and a two-piece flamed maple top. Lovell also told Gibson not even to bother with finishing the top. The bright yellow center of Gibson's 1970s cherry sunburst finish was so garish and ugly compared to the deep amber of the originals that Lovell had Gibson put a clear coat on the top, which he then sent out to be stripped and refinished to the original look.

That was the first reissue. All the key elements of today's Reissue were important (if not fully implemented) from the beginning: the original styling (headstock size, binding width, top carving), the original sound (humbuckers), the original finish and a curly maple top.

Hold it right there. When did the curly top become important? Many of the originals had curly tops—some of them with dramatic "flame"—but not all of them by any means. The reason was probably pragmatic: Gibson used curly maple when it was available. Curly maple obviously was appreciated by Gibson, as illustrated by the curly pieces that were chosen for the bookmatched backs of F-5 mandolins as far back as the early 1920s. But Gibson never promoted curly maple in connection with Les Paul tops, for fear of running out. Which apparently they did from time to time. Nevertheless, sometime between 1961 and 1974, Les Paul players had clearly fallen for the flame. The flame top had become as much a part of the classic look as the thin binding or the small headstock.

The Strings and Things reissues marked the beginning of the reissue era, but they weren't much of a reissue. Some were so bad they had to be returned, and Strings and Things only ended up with a total of 28 guitars from 1975-78.

From Gibson's point of view, the Strings and Things Les

Pauls were probably a fly in the ointment of smooth production. Twenty-eight guitars in four years? Hardly a demand worth cultivating. Gibson's only response was to begin officially listing the Les Paul Standard, which the company had been making anyway for the past five years, in 1976.

The movement may have been barely perceptible, but Strings and Things had gotten the ball rolling on the Les Paul reissues. The next push came in 1978, and again it came from a dealer. Jimmy Wallace, who was working at the time for Arnold & Morgan in Dallas, saw the Strings and Things reissues and made a trip to Kalamazoo to personally pick out some maple tops for his own order of reissues. Gibson made some reissues for Wallace, who sold most of them to Japanese customers and then ordered more.

> Flame to the edge. In the years of Plus and Premium Plus tops, the distinction between Reissue and Premium Plus was that the flame on the Reissue top extended all the way to the edge while the flame on the PP top, even though it may have been equally as dramatic, stopped short of the edge.

BY THIS TIME, ONE OF THE MOST GLARING DEFICIENCIES OF NEW LES PAULS (COMPARED TO THE ORIGINALS) WAS THE HUMBUCKING PICKUP.

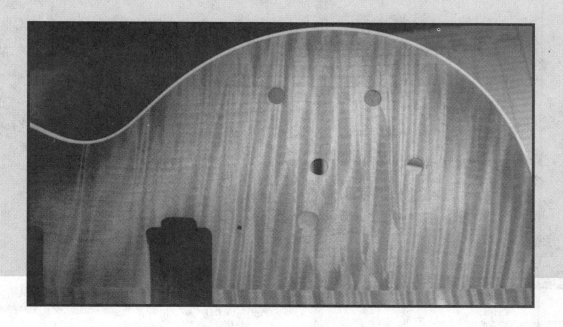

Like the Strings and Things reissues, Wallace's had a nice top but that was about it. The rest of the guitar was standard Gibson issue for the period.

Someone in Kalamazoo took notice, but what could anyone in Kalamazoo do? Les Pauls were made in Nashville. Possibly fired up by a rivalry between the Kalamazoo and Nashville plants, the Les Paul Kalamazoo appeared in 1979. It was basically a Les Paul Standard with no pickup covers, the klunky rectangular tune-o-matic bridge and "KM" on the truss rod cover. It would have had nothing to do with the evolution of reissues except that it had a two-piece flamed maple top. Because Les Pauls weren't in the Kalamazoo plant's domain, the Les Paul KM was offered in a "limited" run of 1500. Coincidentally-or maybe not-1500 was about the total number of original sunburst Les Pauls produced from 1958-60.

Whether it was rivalry between plants or increased market awareness, the Nashville plant jumped into the reissue action in 1980. By this time, one of the most glaring deficiencies of new Les Pauls (compared to the originals) was the humbucking pickup. In preparation for its first attempt at a reissue, Gibson assigned engineer Tim Shaw the job of designing a reissue of the original Patent-Applied-For humbucking pickup—within certain restrictions. "This was 1980 and Norlin was already feeling the pinch," Shaw said, referring to Gibson's long decline through the 1970s and early '80s. "We weren't allowed to do much retooling. We redid the bobbin because it was worn out. We got some old bobbins and put the square hole back in. We did it without the T-hole, which stood for Treble."

To replicate the magnets, Shaw gathered up magnets from original PAFs and sent them to a lab to be analyzed. "Most were Alnico 2's," he said, "but some were 5's. In the process of making an Alnico 5, they stick a magnet in a huge coil for orientation, but an unoriented 5 sounds a lot like a 2. They started with Alinco 2 and then switched to Alnico 5."

Shaw discovered that the original magnets were a little thicker than 1980 production magnets. "Magnetic strength is largely a function of the area of the polarized face; increasing the face size gives you more power," he explained. So he specified the thicker magnet for the new PAF.

Wiring on the originals was #42 gauge, which Gibson still used. However, the original wire had an enamel coating and the current wire had a polyurethane coat, which also was of a different thickness or "buildup" than that of the original, which affected capacitance. Norlin refused to go the extra mile-or extra buck, as it

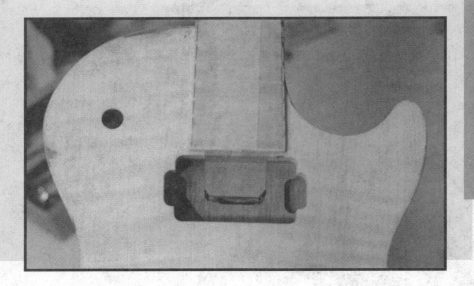

Neck tenon and shoulder shape. The longer neck tenon of the Reissue effects a "smile" in the pickup cavity. The shoulder on the bass side meets the body at a slight slope, which to the eye of a Les Paul aficionado is easily distinguishable from the 90-degree angle on the production model.

were. Enamel-coated wire cost a dollar more per pound than poly-coated. Shaw could change the spec on the buildup without additional expense, so the thickness of the coating was the same as on the original wire, but he was forced to use the poly coat. The difference is easy to see: purple wire on the originals, orange on the reissues.

Shaw later found a spec for the number of turns on a spec sheet for a 1957 ES-175. "It specified 5,000 turns because a P-90 had 10,000 turns and they cut it in half," Shaw said. In reality, however, originals had anywhere from 5,000 to 6,000 turns, depending on how tight the coil was wound. Shaw later met Seth Lover, who designed and patented Gibson's humbucker, at a NAMM show. Lover laughed when asked about a spec for windings, and he told Shaw, "We wound them until they were full."

The spec for resistance was even less exact, Shaw said. The old ohmeter was graduated in incre-ments of .5 (500 ohms). Anywhere between 3.5 and 4 on the meter (3,500 to 4,000 ohms) met the spec. Consequently, Shaw pointed out, there is no such thing as an exact reissue or replica of the 1959 PAF pickup. There can only be a replica of one original PAF, or an average PAF. As Gibson would find out in the early 1990s, the same could be said about the entire guitar.

Shaw's PAF reissue debuted on Gibson's new Nashville-made Les Paul Heritage 80 in 1980. Compared to anything Gibson had previously made (which is to say, compared to nothing), it was an excellent reissue of a sunburst Les Paul Standard. It had a nice top, thin binding in the cutaway, nickel-plated parts, more accurate sunburst finish and smaller headstock, but the body shape, body size and three-piece neck, among other details, were just regular production. It appears that Gibson still didn't understand the demand for an accurate reissue, because Gibson accompanied the Heritage 80 with fancier versions: the

Heritage 80 Elite, with an ebony fingerboard that had no relevance to the reissue market (although it did have a one-piece neck) and the Heritage 80 Award, with gold plated hardware that also had no relevance to the reissue market.

The Heritage 80 was still not good enough for those who wanted a Standard like the original Standard, and the push for a more accurate reissue came once again from dealers and from the Kalamazoo plant. In 1982, Jimmy Wallace opened his own store in the Dallas area and continued ordering what were becoming known as "Jimmy Wallace Reissues." At the same time, Leo's Music in Oakland, California, and Guitar Trader in Redbank, New Jersey, began ordering reissues. These dealers requested more accurate specs for body size, body carving and neck shape, although they usually didn't get them. Also in 1982, the Kalamazoo plant added fuel to the fire with the Les Paul Standard '82, which was distinguished from the Heritage 80 primarily by its one-piece neck and the fact that it was made in Kalmazoo.

REISSUE

Finally, in 1983, Gibson reclaimed the reissue market from the dealers by introducing the Les Paul Reissue. Not a '59 Reissue, not a '60 Reissue, just a cherry sunburst Reissue. By 1984 it was also offered with goldtop finish. By 1985 it had the smaller headstock of the originals, but it was still only a close approximation.

The Reissue had an appeal to collectors or tradition-minded buyers from the beginning. Obviously, such features as nickel-plating, finish color and binding depth had nothing to do with playability. Yet it was still priced within a player's reach. In 1984 it listed for $1,599; the production Les Paul Standard was $999 and the Custom was $1,099. Anything over $1,000 in the mid-1980s may seem beyond the average player's reach, but the Reissue was only in the middle range of Gibson's line, the same price as the B.B. King model. Gibson's high-end archtops, such as the Super 400CES or Johnny Smith, listed for $2,599.

As the reissue market was growing, Gibson was going down the tubes. The Kalamazoo plant was closed in 1984, and in 1986 Gibson was sold to Henry Juszkiewicz and two partners. Where the previous management had squandered Gibson's brand-name value on such forgettable models as the Sonex (with parti-

cle-board body) and the Q-series (with crude Strat-like body shape and various pickup combinations), the new owners recognized the potential of Gibson's tradition as they rebuilt the company. The first price list under their regime marked the debut of the Historic Collection. However, the Les Paul Reissue (previously a Custom Shop offering) was assigned to the Les Paul Collection; the Historic Collection was reserved for electric archtops such as the Byrdland and Super 400CES. Juszkiewicz did bump the price of the Reissue up more than he did the other models, and for the next two years, it listed for about double the price of the Standard.

Through the 1980s and into the 1990s, the Les Paul Reissue remained virtually unchanged. However, two historic-related developments from 1990, though not directly related to the Les Paul Reissue, would soon push the Reissue onward to "replica" status.

The first major step forward (or back to the past) was a new PAF reissue pickup, designed by Gibson R&D head J.T. Riboloff. Among other improvements, Riboloff had original PAF magnets analyzed and matched for performance as well as composition, and he brought the coil wire back to the original enamel-coated style, easily distinguishable from the urethane-wrapped wire by its blue hue. The new '57 Classic pickup debuted in 1990 on several models

> ## AS THE REISSUE MARKET WAS GROWING, GIBSON WAS GOING DOWN THE TUBES.

1958 Figured top
Les Paul Model

with historic appeal, including the Les Paul Reissue.

At the same time, Riboloff designed a new Les Paul model using the 1960 sunburst Standard as a starting point. The new model had the thin binding in the cutaway, the small headstock, various shades of sunburst finish and the inked-on serial number of the Reissue. But it had a slim, 1960-style neck profile, hot ceramic-magnet pickups with no pickup covers and "1960" stamped on the pickguard. It is clearly not a reissue. of the classic Les Paul Standard, although it was named, ironically, the Les Paul Classic.

In 1991 Juszkiewicz distanced the Reissue from the Classic, Standard and other regular production models by listing it in the Historic Collection. The collectible status of Historic models was underscored by the Les Paul Reissue's list price of $4,199, almost three times that of the Standard ($1,499) and more than double that of the Classic ($1,699).

The problem was that the differences between the Reissue and the Classic were on paper. In reality, the Classic was actually closer to the original sunburst Les Paul than the Reissue was. The Classic headstock was correct (the Reissue was smaller than that of the Standard, but not small enough). The Classic had push-in tuner bushings (again, the correct

vintage style) where the Reissue had standard screw-in bushings. And the Classic had aged (yellowed) fingerboard inlays, which looked like those of an original Standard.

To further blur the line between the Classic and the Reissue, Gibson introduced the Classic Plus in the spring of 1991. It had a curlier top than the Classic but not as curly as the Reissue. Late in 1991, Gibson offered the Reissue with the thin 1960-style neck of the Classic, naming it the '60 Flametop Reissue. At that point the thick-neck version then became the '59 Flametop Reissue.

For dealers, and ultimately for buyers, the Reissue was separated from the Standard and Classic at the January 1992 NAMM trade show when Juszkiewicz inaugurated a new Historic program for dealers. In an audacious stroke of creative financing, he convinced dealers to help him with his startup costs by ponying up $10,000 (which Gibson would return in one year, with interest). The headliners of the new program were korina reissues of the Flying V and Explorer, priced at $10,000. A dealer had to be a Historic dealer to be able to sell a Les Paul Reissue.

There was still the problem of accuracy, however. With increasingly curlier tops on Classics (the Classic Premium Plus was soon to come), it was still a more attractive reissue-style guitar than the Reissue. Some Classic tops were flamed enough that "enterprising" dealers changed

out the pickguard and truss rod cover and added a pair of pickup covers. Voila! A Reissue. A $2,000 upgrade (in list price). So in early 1992, the Reissue was changed to incorporate the more accurate features of the Classic.

THE R9

The upgraded Reissue of 1992 was still essentially a Classic with different pickups and a better top. By delineating tops into various grades (Classic, Plus and Reissue), Gibson had established a value on a curly top. In late 1991 the difference between a Classic and a Classic Plus was $400, and in early 1992, a price reduction on the Plus narrowed the difference to only $200. The difference in price between the Classic Plus and the Flametop Reissue was $2,200. Obviously it would take more than a nicer top on a Reissue to justify the huge price differential. It would take nothing short of a replica of an original sunburst Les Paul, and Gibson put together a team to take the Reissue "all the way" back to 1959.

Today, Gibson's Custom Shop is a stand alone division (officially either the Custom, Art, Historic division or the Custom Manufacturing division) with its own building, its own staff, responsible for the models in the Historic Collection as well as "Custom" production models, such as the ES-336 or the Leland Sklar Bass. In the early 1990s, however, the Custom Shop "staff" didn't really exist. It was an undefined group within the regular production facility at Gibson's

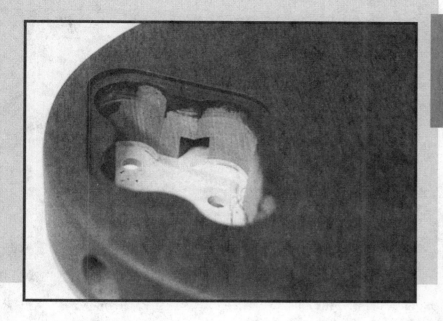

Small channel. The square channel leading from the control cavity to the pickup cavity is 1/2-inch wide on the Reissue, 3/4-inch wide on production models.

Nashville division, aka "Gibson USA" or simply "the plant." Members of this Custom Shop group were called upon as needed to fulfill custom orders for dealers.

Tom Murphy, who had been with Gibson since 1989 and was working on improving Les Pauls, was tapped to head the group that would develop the "replica." Murphy describes his role variously as "crusader" and "babysitter." "I'd talk about the Reissue and people would walk off," he recalled. "But I'd take it home and sleep on it."

Gibson owned no original 1959 Les Pauls, so the company borrowed one from Nashville dealer Crawford White. Engineer Matthew Klein created a digital "map" so that every nuance of the body shape could be matched and maintained. Two more '59s were extensively measured in the shop, and Murphy estimates he inspected and measured another 25 at guitar shows. Just as Tim Shaw

had found in his research into original PAFs, the Reissue team found great variance in the original guitar measurements, and the final product would be a best average of the various examples.

The team went the extra mile in replicating the originals, even in areas most guitar players would never know. The originals had a longer neck tenon (the part that fits into the body) which may make a slight difference in the stability of the neck. The originals had a control cavity floor that was routed parallel to the curved top of the guitar (rather than parallel to the flat back of the guitar), so that it was deeper at one end, which made no difference in sound or performance. The origi-

> **THE TEAM WENT THE EXTRA MILE IN REPLICATING THE ORIGINALS, EVEN IN AREAS MOST GUITAR PLAYERS WOULD NEVER KNOW.**

nals had a 1/2-inch square channel routed between the control cavity and the pickup cavity (production models have a 3/4-inch square channel). The originals had rounded fingerboard edges and more rounded body edges. Everything was faithfully replicated.

Keith Medley, who left Gibson in 1993 to make guitars on his own and who has since returned to Gibson's R&D department, hand-made protoypes #1 and #2 with Murphy. The Replica, as the guitar world called it, or the R9 as the Custom Shop people called it, debuted at the January 1993 NAMM show in Anaheim. And a new era began.

Or did it? It appears that for once in Gibson history, there is a clear-cut line of delineation. Reissue through 1992; R9 beginning in 1993. But that would be too easy. The introduction indeed marks the beginning of a new period for the Reissue, but it's a period of mystery and mystique.

When the R9 debuted in 1993, it was still coming off the

regular production line. Tom Murphy painted the finish on the first 25 sunbursts and the first 15 goldtops (considerable research

one at a time on an older carver that Custom used (and still uses) for carving archtop guitars, such as the L-5 and Super 400.

THE FUTURE OF THE LES PAUL REISSUE MARKET IS DEPENDENT ON SEVERAL FACTORS, NONE OF WHICH IS ABSOLUTE.

1959 Flametop
Les Paul Standard

had gone into replicating the original goldtop finish also). Then he monitored production but did no more finish work through the end of 1993.

In late 1993 Gibson separated the Custom Shop from the plant and gave it divisional status, complete with its own facility three doors down from the plant. Murphy made the move into the new division, and from the beginning of 1994 until Nov. 2 of that year (his last day at Gibson), he put the finish, the silkscreen logo and the serial number on every sunburst and goldtop Reissue.

The "deep dish" top, which according to Murphy is more accurately described as "the flat-bellied dimpled top," was problematic. The multi-station top carvers that Gibson uses for production guitars have a master wheel that follows a template or form for the top. The wheel was too large to conform to the Reissue curve. "The wheel wouldn't fall down into the dimple," Murphy said. Consequently, all the Reissue tops had to be carved

Late in 1994 the Reissues changed slightly, and the "babysitter" noticed. The tops were coming back from the plant, after sanding and binding, a little flatter than they were supposed to be. Murphy discovered that the carving form was laying at an odd angle. The day before he left, he hand-scraped the form, and the tops made from that form, from late 1994 and early 1995, are to him "the coolest carving," different from any other period.

THE FUTURE

The R9—the ultimate replica-did not settle the Les Paul Reissue issue, at least not for those who want to know whether a Reissue will increase in value. Again, the appeal is based on the accuracy of the replication and the curl in the top. Unfortunately for those who would like to bet on a sure thing, neither of these characteristics is settled.

One would think that a curly top will always be appreciated and valued. After all, curly maple has been loved by instru-

ment makers for centuries (note that any photos of fine violins always show the back as well as the front). It's the flame that gives each instrument not only its beauty but also a unique identity. Vic Da Pra's book, *Sunburst Alley* illustrates the effect that flamey pieces of wood can have on a guitar lover. They inspired an entire new lexicon to describe flamed maple, including such terms as ribbon curl (regular, irregular, medium and heavy), 3D curl, pinstripes, variegated curl, light blister, heavy medullary grain and deep striations. Exceptional examples inspired such descriptions as "chevrons of maple figure ascending heavenward" or "fractionating, shattering and radiating" as well as such terms as lovely, luscious, dramatic, incomparable, bewitching, sinuous, striking, spectacular and drop-dead killer.

In addition to curly maple's visual appeal, it's a well-known fact that it's rare, occurring randomly in something like 10 percent of maple trees. But that doesn't mean it's scarce. As the Reissue gained in popularity, Gibson foresaw a shortage and set about securing a supply for the future. "One of the problems in 1994, when I first came to work here, was that they had maybe 75 curly maple tops a month, and they lost about half in the kiln," said Gene Nix, head of a woodbuying team that Gibson put together in 1994. "And what they were buying was actually defective before they turned it into a guitar. The material they wanted was hard maple, and that's not near as intense with the figure as the soft maple is. The other problem was the sourcing. They were looking in all the wrong places. We put together a wood team here at the plant and defined what we wanted and then went out and developed some suppliers."

Soft maple rather than hard maple? Nix looked at the tops of originals and discovered that some were soft maple and some were hard maple, so his quest for soft maple did not represent a deviation from original Les Paul specs.

The next step was to develop and educate suppliers. The wood was out there, but it was not economical to produce. Because soft maple has more defects than hard maple, a log of soft maple produces less wood. And it has to be quarter-sawn to get the most flame. Furthermore, the difficulty in matching various pieces of curly maple makes it less than desirable for the furniture market, so sawmills didn't want to fool with it. But with Gibson as a willing buyer, suppliers began going to the log yards and picking out potentially flamed maple logs before they were run through the regular milling process.

The result of Gibson's wood team efforts is a ready supply of flamed tops. The $400-500 "value" that Gibson had assigned to

flamed tops in the early 1990s became a moot point in 1998 when Gibson abolished Premium Plus and Plus tops in the regular Les Paul line and even abolished the sunburst finish on the Classic. Now there was no way to get a flamed top on a Standard unless it was a Reissue (or some other Custom Shop creation). Despite the appearance of scarcity, however, highly flamed tops abound in the Les Paul line, on the popular new Double-Cutaway Standard and on the Joe Perry signature Les Paul Standard.

Also, a funny thing happened on the way to the Flametop Appreciation Society. Some people decided that flame didn't matter at all, at least not at the premium price Gibson was asking. They ordered a Reissue, but hold the flame, please. By the end of 1994, Gibson was offering a '58 Plaintop Reissue at around half the price of the Flametop version. (The year 1958 was not known for yielding more plain tops than curly tops; it was just the only year still available from the sunburst era.)

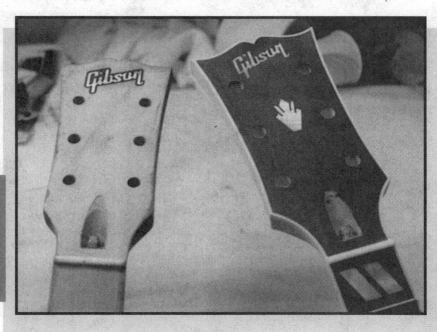

Holly peghead veneer. Before finishing, it's easy to see the difference between a white holly peghead veneer on a Reissue and the black fiberboard veneer of production models.

The question of accuracy of replication was settled with the R9 in 1993-almost. The top carving may be questionable from time to time, but there's still the matter of the finish. Initially, the R9 (as well as previous Reissues) was finished to look the same as an original

A finished R9 on a rack, a rare sight. Demand exceeds production for the '59 Flametop Reissues, so most are packed and shipped as soon as the finish is dry.

1959 Les Paul Standard looks today—like a 40-year-old guitar, with the cherry finish faded somewhat, with the binding and fingerboard inlay yellowing with age. Buyers did not want a new-looking guitar. Gibson's Heritage Cherry Sunburst finish provided that slightly faded vintage look, and it was the preferred finish over the optional Dark Cherry Sunburst finish, which had a brighter cherry look that made the guitar look brand new.

So what is the correct finish? One fraction of the market believes that the best finish

INITIALLY, THE R9 (AS WELL AS PREVIOUS REISSUES) WAS FINISHED TO LOOK THE SAME AS AN ORIGINAL 1959 LES PAUL STANDARD LOOKS TODAY-LIKE A 40-YEAR-OLD GUITAR...

Gibson ever put on an R9 was done by Tom Murphy. People call Gibson asking if a certain Reissue were made in the Tom Murphy era. It's gotten to the point where people are buying new Reissues and then sending them to Murphy, who is the proprietor of Guitar Preservation in Marion, Illinois, to strip and apply the "correct" finish.

But the "correct" finish for a Les Paul Reissue is a changing notion, Murphy says. For some now, it is the "Brockburst," a ref-

erence to the guitar, formerly owned by Brian Brock, that graces the cover of Tom Wheeler's *American Guitars.* That's a darker cherry than the standard Reissue finish. "I saw a change in taste starting about late '95," Murphy said. "People are seeing guitars with bold enough tops that they could handle a darker cherry sunburst. Now they're ready to take that darker sunburst on some of those killer tops. I've had several requests for that style of color on the top. Maybe the Reissue is so established that we could look at them like they'd look brand new. It couldn't happen before because the guitar was so inaccurate. I thought that was pretty good testimony for the guitars."

But once again the '58 Plaintop Reissue (R8) skews the sample. In 1998 Gibson started offering it with a curly top—though not nearly as curly as the R9—for an upcharge of $525. To avoid getting caught up in the curly top confusion of the Plus and Premium Plus, Gibson offered the R8 only in Butterscotch and Vintage Red finishes. And people bought it.

Then there's the issue of rarity—an important issue in the collectible/investment market. The R9 is not rare. Production has been averaging around 500 per year, although it may be cut back from time to time so that Gibson's Custom Shop doesn't end up with all its fortunes riding on one model. But there are already more R9s than there were original sunburst Les Paul Standards.

The future of the Les Paul Reissue market is dependent on several factors, none of which is absolute. Degree of accuracy makes a difference—the R9 is likely to be more desirable than the previous versions. An accurate finish is important to most, but not all buyers, and even then, "accurate" is a matter of disagreement. Degree or quality of the figuration of the top makes a difference. That's obvious from the descriptions of instruments for sale; they almost always include an assessment of the top. But again, not to all buyers. And rarity is yet to be established; production is ongoing and subject to Gibson's whim.

The Les Paul Reissue does have a future as a collectible and/or investment, due to the fact that people like a cherry sunburst Les Paul Standard. No, people **love** a cherry sunburst Les Paul Standard, and they're always going to. Younger recording artists like them, too, so there's not likely to be a market-killing generational change of preference. People love a sunburst Les Paul more if it's in its classic form, which is to say 1958-60 specs. And most people love it more if it has a flamed top.

With this much information, the future of the Les Paul Reissue market would be easy to predict, except for the fact that it's still in production and still subject to interpretation. A whim in the marketplace, or a nod from an influential guitarist toward a certain version of the model, could change everything. Just as the appeal of the Les Paul Standard is a personal, subjective thing, perhaps the best advice to a prospective buyer is to check prices and then to make it a personal, subjective decision. The love of an instrument may turn out to be the best hedge against an unpredictable market. ∎

Edwin Wilson, right, and Matt Klein, the keepers of the flame in Gibson's Custom division today.

Anatomy of an Acoustic Guitar

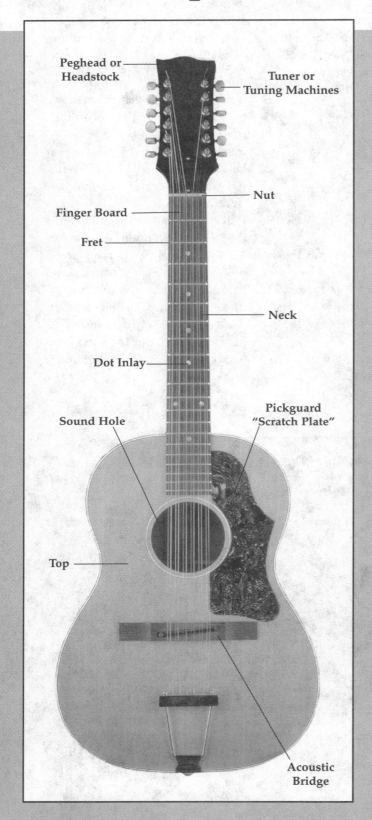

Peghead or Headstock

Tuner or Tuning Machines

Nut

Finger Board

Fret

Neck

Dot Inlay

Sound Hole

Pickguard "Scratch Plate"

Top

Acoustic Bridge

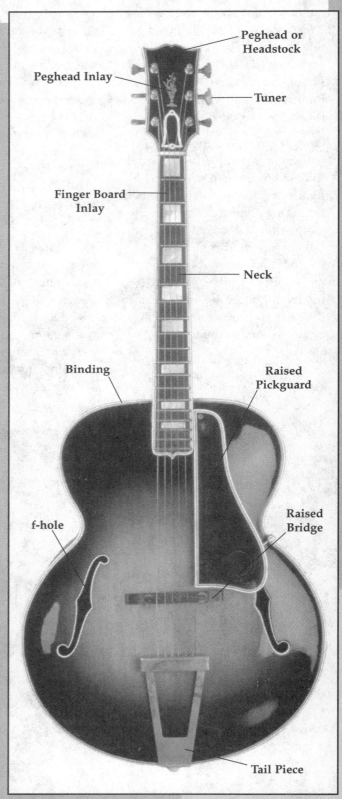

Peghead or Headstock

Peghead Inlay

Tuner

Finger Board Inlay

Neck

Binding

Raised Pickguard

f-hole

Raised Bridge

Tail Piece

This glossary is divided into 4 sections: **General Glossary; Hardware: Bridges, Pegs, Tailpieces, and Tuners; Pickups;** and **Book Terminology.** If you are looking for something and can't find it in one section, please check the others. If you can't find it after you've been through the whole glossary, give us a call. We value your input for future editions.

GENERAL GLOSSARY

ABALONE - Shellfish material used in instrument ornamentation.

ACOUSTIC - Generic term used for hollow bodied instruments that rely on the body to produce the amplified sound of the instrument, rather than electronic amplification.

ACOUSTIC ELECTRIC - A thin hollow bodied instrument that relies on a pickup to further amplify its sound.

ACTION - Everybody wants a piece of it. It is also the height the strings are off of the fingerboard, stretched between the nut and bridge.

ARCH/ARCHED TOP - The top of an instrument that has been carved or pressed to have a "rounded" top.

AVOIDIRE - blonde mahogany.

BINDING (bound) - Trim that goes along the outer edge of the body, neck or peghead. It is made out of many different materials, natural and synthetic.

BODY - The main bulk of the instrument, usually. It is where the bridge, tailpiece and pickguard are located. On acoustics, the soundhole, or holes, are located on the body top, usually, and the sound is amplified inside it. On electrics it is where the pickups are routed into and the electronics housing is stored. It is what the player cradles.

BOLT ON/BOLT ON NECK - Construction technique that involves attaching the neck to the body by means of bolts or screws. Bolt-on necks are generally built and finished separately from the guitar body, and parts are assembled together later.

BOUND See BINDING.

BOUT/BOUTS - The rounded, generally, side/sides on the top and bottom of an instrument's body.

BRIDGE - Component that touches the top of the instrument and transfers vibrations from string to body. It is usually attached by glue or screws but is also found to be held in place by string tension, the same as a violin.

CARVED TOP See ARCH TOP.

CELLO TAIL ADJUSTER - The Cello tail adjuster is a 1/8" diameter black nylon-type material which attaches to the tailpiece and loops around an endpin jack (or ebony endpin). Nylon, of course, replaced the real (if unstable) gut material several years ago. This tail adjuster is used on virtually every cello tailpiece in the world, and figures prominently in a number of archtop guitar designs.

CUTAWAY - An area that has been cut away on the treble bout, or both bouts, to allow access to the higher frets. See FLORENTINE and VENETIAN.

DING - small mark or dent on a guitar. Also the noise you swear you hear when your guitar hits another object, thus causing the mark.

DREADNOUGHT - A generic term used to describe steel string guitar configuration consisting of a boxy body and solid headstock.

EBONIZED - A process by which the wood has been stained dark to appear to be ebony; alternatively, also referring to something black in color (such as bridge adjuster wheels) made to blend in with ebony fittings on an archtop guitar.

EBONOL - A synthetic material that is used as replacement for wood (generally as a fingerboard).

ELECTRIC - A generic term referencing the fact that the instrument relies on pickups to amplify its sound.

F-HOLE - Stylized "f" shaped soundhole that is carved into the top of various instruments, most commonly acoustic. It usually comes in pairs.

FINGERBOARD - An area on top of the neck that the string is pressed against to create the desired note (frequency).

FINISH - The outer coat of an instrument. The sealant of the wood. The protector of the instrument. How many ways do you say it? It's all of the above, it's the finish.

FLAT TOP - Term used to describe an acoustic steel stringed instrument whose top is flat.

FLORENTINE - sharp point on the treble forward horn of a body cutaway. See also VENETIAN.

FRET - A strip of metal that is embedded at specific intervals into the fingerboard.

FRETBOARD - Another way of saying fingerboard and specifying that it has frets embedded into it.

GOLPEADOR - protective (generally clear) plate added to top of flamenco guitars for *tapping*.

GRAPHITE - Used in various forms of instrument construction because of its rigidity and weight, this type of carbon is used in the body, neck and nut.

HARDWARE - Generic term for the bridge, tailpiece, tuners or vibrato system.

HEADLESS - This means the instrument has no peghead.

HEADSTOCK See PEGHEAD.

HEEL - On the backside of an instrument, the heel is located at the base of the neck where the neck meets the body.

INLAY - Decoration or identifying marks on an instrument that are inlaid into one of the surface areas. They are made of a number of materials, though abalone, pearl and wood are the most common.

LOCKING TUNERS - These tuners are manufactured with a locking mechanism built right into them, thus preventing string slippage.

LOGO - An identifying feature on an instrument: it could be a symbol or a name; and it could appear as a decal, an inlay, or painted on (and it could be missing).

MOTHER OF PEARL - A shellfish (oyster/clam) material used for inlay.

NATO - A lower grade or quality of mahogany, sometimes referred to as "lumberyard" mahogany.

NECK - The area that the strings of the instrument are stretched along, the peghead sits at the top, the body lies at the bottom.

OCTAVE - In Western Notation, every 12 frets on a stringed instrument is an octave in the musical scale of things.

PEARL - Short for Mother of Pearl, the inside shell from a shellfish. See MOTHER OF PEARL.

PEARLOID - A synthetic material made of plastic and pearl dust.

PEGHEAD - The area at the top of an instrument where the tuning machines, or pegs, are located.

PHENOLIC - A synthetic material that is used as fingerboard wood replacement.

PICKGUARD - A piece of material used to protect the instrument's top or finish from gouges that are caused by the pick or your fingers.

PICKUP - An electronic device that translates string vibrations into the electronic signal needed for amplification of the sound. See PICKUP Section.

PURFLING - Decorative trim that is found running along the inside of the binding.

RELIEF - The upward slope of the fingerboard that keeps the strings off the frets.

RESONATOR - A metal device located in some instruments that is the means of their amplification.

REVERSE HEADSTOCK (Reverse Peghead) - On this instrument the peghead has been flipped over from the normal configuration and the tuners are all on the highest note side of the instrument (tuners are all located on one side).

ROSETTE - A decorative design that is placed around the soundhole.

SADDLE - The area that a string passes over to create the length needed for an exact note (frequency).

SCALE LENGTH - The area between the nut and bridge over which the strings of the instrument are stretched.

SCALLOPED - This is what the area on the fingerboard between the frets is called when it has been scooped out, creating a dip between the frets.

SCRATCH PLATE - Slang for Pickguard. See PICKGUARD.

SEMI-ACOUSTIC - term used to describe a shallow bodied instrument that is constructed with a solid piece of wood running the length of the center of the body.

SLOTTED PEGHEAD - A peghead usually associated with classic style instruments. The peghead has slots running lengthwise that allows access to the tuners.

SOUNDHOLE - A hole found in the top of acoustic instruments (mostly), that allows the sound to be projected from the body.

STRINGS - They are the substance that is stretched between the tuners/pegs and the bridge/tailpiece. The weight of the string is what determines the range of frequencies it will cover.

SUNBURST (Sunburst Finish) - A finish that is dark at the edge of the instrument's top and gets progressively lighter towards the middle.

THINLINE - Original Gibson terminology referring to a hollow bodied instrument that has a shallow depth of body.

THROUGH BODY (Thru Body; Neck Through) - Type of construction that consists of the neck wood extending through the entire length of the instrument and the pieces of wood that make up the body being attached to the sides of the neck wood (called *wings*).

TREMOLO - A regular increase and decrease in the volume of a continuous sound. Many tremolo effects units have controls for Speed (number of volume changes per time period) and Depth (amount of volume change that occurs).

TRUSS ROD - A rod, or rods, placed in necks made of wood to create stability and a means of adjustment.

VENETIAN - rounded point on the treble forward horn of a body cutaway. See also FLORENTINE.

VIBRATO - The act of physically lengthening or shortening the medium (in this case, it will be strings) to produce a fluctuation in frequency. The pitch altering mechanism on your guitar is a vibrato, not a tremolo!

VOLUTE (Also Neck Volute) - Additional protruding wood used as a strengthening support where an angled-back headstock is spliced to the end of the neck. This carved (or shaped) piece of the neck is also refered to as a "handstop".

WINGS - The body pieces attached to the sides of a through body neck blank, thus forming a complete body.

ZERO FRET - The zero fret is a length of fret wire fitted into a fret slot which is cut at the exact location as that of a conventional nut. The fingerboard is generally cut off 1/8" longer than usual, at which point the nut is fitted. When used in conjunction with the zero fret, the nut serves as a string guide. The fret wire used on the zero fret is usually slightly larger than that used on the fingerboard itself - the slightly higher zero fret establishes the open string's height above the fingerboard.

HARDWARE: BRIDGES, PEGS, TAILPIECES AND TUNERS

ACOUSTIC BRIDGE - The bridge on an acoustic instrument is usually glued to the top and though pins are usually used there are still numerous ways of holding the strings taut.

BANJO TUNERS - tuners that are perpendicular to the peghead and pass through it, as opposed to being mounted on the side of the peghead, (like classic style peghead tuners).

BIGSBY VIBRATO - A vibrato system that involves a roller bar with little pegs that run in a perpendicular line, around which you hook the string balls. One end of the bar has an arm coming off of it, a spring is located under the arm, and the entire apparatus is connected to a trapeze tailpiece. The bridge is separate from the vibrato system. This vibrato was designed by Paul Bigsby.

BRIDGE - Component that touches the top of the instrument and transfers vibrations from string to body. It is usually attached by glue or screws but is also found to be held in place by string tension, the same as a violin.

BRIDGE PIN - A peg that passes through the bridge anchoring one end of the string for tuning.

DOUBLE LOCKING VIBRATO - A vibrato system that locks the strings into place by tightening down screws on each string, thus stopping the string's ability to slip. There is also a clamp at the top of the fingerboard that holds the strings from the tuners. These more modern designs were formulated separately by Floyd Rose and the Kahler company. As guitarist Billy Gibbons (ZZ Top) is fond of saying, the locking vibratos give you the ability to "turn Steel into Rubber, and have 'er bounce back on a dime". See VIBRATO SYSTEM.

FIXED BRIDGE - One piece, usually metal, usually on electric instruments, unit that contains the saddles, bridge and tailpiece all in one and is held onto the body by screws.

FRICTION PEGS - Wooden dowels that rely on the friction created between itself and the wood of the hole it is put in to keep the tension of the strings constant.

HEADLESS - Term meaning that the instrument's headstock is missing. The top of the neck is capped with a piece of hardware that acts like a regular tailpiece on the instrument body.

LOCKING TUNERS - These tuners are manufactured with a locking mechanism built into them, thus preventing string slippage.

NUT - Device located at the top of the fingerboard (opposite from the bridge) that determines the action and spacing of the strings.

PEGS -See FRICTION PEGS.

PINS - Pegs that are used to anchor the strings in place on the bridge.

ROLLER BRIDGE - This is a Gretsch trademark feature. It is an adjustable metal bridge that sits on a wooden base, the saddles of this unit sit on a threaded bar and are easily moved back and forth to allow personal string spacing.

SADDLE/SADDLES - A part of the bridge that holds the string/strings in place, helps transfer vibrations to the instrument body and helps in setting the action.

SET-IN - Guitar construction that involves attaching the neck to the body by gluing a joint (such as a dovetail). Set necks cannot be adjusted by shims as their angle of attachment to the body is pre-set in the design.

SINGLE LOCKING VIBRATO - A vibrato system that locks the strings on the unit to keep them from going out of tune during heavy arm use. This style of vibrato does not employ a clamping system at the top of the fingerboard.

STANDARD VIBRATO - Usually associated with the Fender Stratocaster, this unit has the saddles on top and an arm off to one side. The arm allows you to bend the strings, making the frequencies (notes) rise or drop. All of this sits on a metal plate that rocks back and forth. Strings may have an area to attach to on top or they may pass through the body and have holding cups on the back side. A block of metal, usually called the Inertia Block, is generally located under the saddles to allow for increased sustain. The block travels through the instrument's body and has springs attached to it to create the tension necessary to keep the strings in tune. See VIBRATO SYSTEM.

STEINBERGER BRIDGE - A bridge designed by Ned Steinberger, it combines the instrument bridge and tuners all in one unit. It is used with headless instruments.

STOP TAILPIECE - This piece of hardware is attached to the top of an instrument by screws and has slots in it to hold the string balls. Generally used with a tunomatic bridge.

STRINGS THROUGH ANCHORING - A tailpiece that involves the strings passing through an instrument's body and the string balls are held in place by cups.

STUD TAILPIECE - See STOP TAILPIECE.

TAILPIECE - The device that holds the strings at the body end of the scale. It may be all in one unit that contains the saddle/saddles also, or stands alone.

TIED BRIDGE - Style of bridge usually associated with "classical" style instruments that have the strings secured by tying them around the bridge.

TRAPEZE TAILPIECE - A type of tailpiece that is hinged, has one end attached to the bottom bout of the instrument and the other end has grooves in it to hold the string balls.

TREM/TREMOLO/TREMOLO ARM - Terms inaccurately used to mean Vibrato System. See VIBRATO SYSTEM.

TUNER/TUNERS - Mechanical device that is used to stretch the string/strings. These are located on the peghead.

TUNABLE STOP TAILPIECE - A tailpiece that rests on a pair of posts and has small fine tuning machines mounted on top of it.

TUNOMATIC BRIDGE - A bridge that is attached to the instrument's top by two metal posts and has adjustable saddles on the topside.

VIBRATO - Generic term used to describe Vibrato System.

VIBRATO SYSTEM - A device that stretches or slackens the strings by the means of a lever, the arm or bar, and a fulcrum, the pivot pins or blades.

WANG BAR - Slang term used for Vibrato System.

WHAMMY (WHAMMY BAR) - Slang terms used for Vibrato System.

WRAPOVER BRIDGE - A self contained bridge/tailpiece bar device that is attached to the body, with the strings wrapping over the bar.

WRAPUNDER BRIDGE - The same as above except the strings wrap under the bar.

PICKUPS

ACTIVE ELECTRONICS - A form of electronic circuitry that involves some power source, usually a 9 volt battery. Most of the time the circuit is an amplification circuit, though it may also be onboard effects circuitry.

AMPLIFY/AMPLIFICATION - To increase, in this case to increase the volume of the instrument.

'FLOATING' PICKUP - A magnetic pickup that is suspended over (versus being built into) the top of the guitar, just below the fingerboard. This enables the guitar to be used acoustically or electrically. Examples include the Benedetto pickup, the DeArmond #1100G, or the Gibson Johnny Smith pickup.

"JAZZ" PICKUP - A pickup, suspended ('floating') or built-in on an archtop guitar that gives the instrument a traditional, mainstream jazz sound.

PARAMETRIC EQUALIZER - An equalizer that allows you to specifically choose which range of frequencies you wish to affect.

PASSIVE ELECTRONICS - Electronic circuitry that has no power supply. Usually it consists of filter circuitry.

PIEZO (PIEZOELECTRIC) - A crystalline substance that induces an electrical current caused by pressure or vibrations.

PREAMP - An electronic circuit that amplifies the signal from the pickup/s and preps it for the amplifier.

SOUNDHOLE - An opening in the instrument's top (usually), that allows the amplified sound out of the body cavity.

TRANSDUCER/TRANSDUCER PICKUP
- A device that converts energy from one form to another, in this instance it is the vibrations caused by the strings, moving along the wood and being converted into electrical energy for amplification.

BOOK TERMS

This glossary section should help you understand the jargon used in the model descriptions of the instruments in this text.

3 PER SIDE - Three tuners on each side of the peghead on a six string instrument.

3/2 PER SIDE - This is in reference to a 5 string instrument with three tuners on one side of the peghead and two tuners on the other.

335 STYLE - refers to an instrument that has a semi-hollowbody cutaway body style similar to that of the Gibson 335.

4 ON A SIDE - Four tuners on one side of the peghead on a 4-string instrument.

4 PER SIDE - Four tuners on each side of the peghead an eight string instrument.

4/1 PER SIDE - On an instrument with five strings this would mean four tuners are on one side of the peghead, and one is on the other.

4/2 PER SIDE - Four tuners on one side and two on the other side of a peghead.

4/3 PER SIDE - This instrument has seven strings with four of the tuners located on one side of the peghead and three on the other side.

5 ON A SIDE - All the tuners on one side of the peghead on a 5-string instrument.

6 ON A SIDE - All six tuners on one side of the peghead on a 6-string instrument.

6 PER SIDE - Six tuners on each side of the peghead on an twelve string instrument.

6/1 PER SIDE - A seven string instrument with six tuners on one side and one on the other.

7 ON ONE SIDE - A term referring to a seven string instrument with all the tuners on the peghead are on one side.

12/14 FRET - Term in which the first number describes the fret at which the neck joins the body, and the second number is the total number of frets on the fingerboard.

CLASSICAL STYLE - This term refers to a gut or nylon string instruments fashioned after the original guitar design. Used predominately in classical music, this design features a 12/19 fretboard, round soundhole, slotted (or 'open') headstock, and a tied-end bridge.

DREADNOUGHT STYLE - This term refers to steel string instruments that are fashioned after the traditional build of a Martin instrument, a boxy type instrument with squared top and bottom bouts, approximately 14 inches across the top bouts, 16 inches across the bottom bouts, there is not much of a waist and the depth of instrument is about 4-5 inches.

DUAL CUTAWAY - Guitar design with two forward horns, both extending forward an equal amount (See OFFSET DOUBLE CUTAWAY, SINGLE CUTAWAY).

FLAMENCO STYLE - The Flamenco style guitar is similar to the Classical style, save for the addition of the (generally clear) 'tap plate'. by the bridge.

JAZZ STYLE - A body shape similar to the traditional jazz arch-top or semi-hollowbody design; or affiliated parts of such models.

OFFSET DOUBLE CUTAWAY - Guitar design with two forward horns, the top (bass side) horn more prominent of the two (See DUAL CUTAWAY, SINGLE CUTAWAY).

N/A (Also $ N/A) - "Not Available". Finding a "Not Available" code while reviewing this text indicates that a model in a particular given grade cannot be found in the secondary marketplace.

POINT FINGERBOARD - A fingerboard that has a "V-ed" section on it at the body end of the fingerboard.

POINT(Y) HEADSTOCK - Tip of the headstock narrows (i.e. Charvel/Jackson or Kramer models).

SINGLE CUTAWAY - Guitar design with a single curve into the body, allowing the player access to the upper frets of the fretboard (See DUAL CUTAWAY, OFFSET DOUBLE CUTAWAY).

SLEEK - A more modern body style, perhaps having longer forward horns, more contoured body, or a certain aerodynamic flair (!).

TBA (Also $ TBA) - "To Be Announced"; specific stated item or amount is currently unavailable from the manufacturer. TBA is generally used when a new model is unveiled, but a suggested list price has not yet been announced.

TELE STYLE - A single cutaway 'plank' body similar to the original Fender Telecaster; also refers to the style of fixed bridge.

THROUGH BODY (Neck-Through Construction) - Type of construction that consists of the neck wood extending through the entire length of the instrument and the pieces of wood that make up the body being attached to the sides of the neck wood.

TUNOMATIC STOP TAILPIECE - This unit is a combination bridge/tailpiece that has adjustable (tunomatic) saddles mounted on a wrap around tailpiece.

VOLUME/TONE CONTROL - The instrument has a volume and a tone control. If a two (2) precedes the term then there are two volume and two tone controls.

KNOW YOUR WOODS!

Throughout the text of the **Blue Book of Acoustic Guitars**, readers may notice different woods used in the construction of guitars and basses. The following table is presented to help understand the different names that describe the woods used in guitar building.

WOOD NOMENCLATURE

COMMON NAME	LATIN NAME	FAMILY	OTHER NAMES
AMERICAN WOODS			
Maple	Acer Macrophyllum	Aceraceae	-
Rock Maple	Acer Saccharum	Aceraceae	Hard Maple, White Maple
Walnut	Juglans Hindsii	Juglancaceae	California Walnut, Claro Walnut
Madrone	Arbutus Menziessi	Ericaceae	-
Sycamore	Acer Pseudoplatanus	Aceraceae	-
SOUTH AND CENTRAL AMERICAN WOODS			
Bocate	Cordia spp.	-	Mexican Rosewood
Cocobola	Dalbergia Retusa	Leguminosae	Granadillo
Mahogany	Swietinia Macrophylla	Meliaceae	-
Purpleheart	Peltogne spp.	Leguminosae	Amaranth, Violetwood, Morado Saka, Koroboreli, Tananeo, Pau Roxo
Tulipwood	Dalbergia Fructescens	Leguminosae	Jacaranda Rosa, Pinkwood, Pau Rosa
AFRICAN WOODS			
Bubinga	Guibouria Demusi	Leguminosae	African Rosewood
Ebony	Diospryus Crassiflora	Ebenaceae	Gabon Ebony
Wenge	Millettia Laurentii	Leguminosae	Panga Panga
Cocobola	Microberlinia Brazzavillensis	Leguminosae	Zebrano, Zingana, Allene, Ele, Amouk
INDIAN WOODS			
Ebony	Diospryus Ebenaceae	Ebenaceae	-
Macassar Ebony	Diospryus Celebica	Ebenaceae	Striped Ebony
Rosewood	Dalbergia Latifoloa	Leguminosae	Bombay Rosewood, Sissoo, Biti, Ervadi, Kalaruk
Vermillion	Pterocarpu Dalbergoides	Leguminosae	Paduak, Andaman Rosewood
PACIFIC RIM WOODS			
Lacewood	Carwellia Sublimis	Protaceae	Australian Silky Oak
Koa	Acacia Koa	-	-

(Wood information courtesy Mica Wickersham, Alembic)

COMMON GUITAR ABBREVIATIONS

These abbreviations may be found as prefixes and suffixes with a company's model names, and may indicate a special quality about that particular designation. This list should be viewed as being a guide, as there is no agreed upon standard in the industry; a lot of companies will have their own letters or numbers which are that instrument's company code.

A	Ash	F	Fretless or Florentine	N	Natural
B	Bass, Brazilian Rosewood, or Blue (finish)	H	Herringbone	OM	Orchestra Model
BK	Black (finish)	J	Jumbo	R	Reverse (headstock) or Red (finish)
C	Cutaway	K	Koa	S	Spanish, Solid Body, Special or Super
D	Dreadnought or Double	L	Left Handed	SG	Solid Guitar
DC	Double Cutaway	LE	Limited Edition	T	Tremolo or Thinline
E	Electric	LQBA	Leo Quan Bad Ass	V	V shaped Neck, Venetian, Vibrato or Vintage Series
ES	Electric (Electro) Spanish	M	Mahogany or Maple		

A Unique Concept The *Blue Book of Acoustic Guitars*™ is the only book that:

- Provides reference text as well as pricing information on over 1,000 trademarks!
- Supplies 32 full color and almost 400 b/w photos for easier guitar identification!
- Utilizes several guitar grading systems, including the **Photo Percentage Grading System**™ for condition factors, in addition to converting this system to other existing grading systems.
- Is updated annually and provides the freshest information available on both the vintage market, as well as currently manufactured models!
- Is based on actual selling prices. These are real world prices you can actually expect to pay - as opposed to artificial prices that are not based on each guitar's unique condition factor.
- Offers you personal consultation by mail on special questions you may have! (No book can cover everything.)
- Gives detailed serial number information on 28 major guitar manufacturers! Much of this serialization is simply not available anywhere else, at any price!

Individual appraisals and /or additional research can be performed for $20.00 per guitar

(see the "Correspondence Inquiries" section below for more information on this service).

Buying, Selling, or Trading?

Interested in buying or selling a particular guitar(s)? Or maybe hesitating because you are unsure of what a fair market price should be? Depending on what you are interested in, a referral will be made that will enable you to be sure that you are getting what you paid for (or getting paid a fair price). This referral service is designed to help all those people who are worried or scared about purchasing a potentially "bad guitar" or getting "ripped off" when selling. There is no charge for this referral service - we are simply connecting you with the best person(s) possible within your field of collecting to ensure that you get a fair deal. This sort of matchmaking can make a world of difference on potentially buying or selling a guitar. Please phone or write the *Blue Book of Acoustic Guitars*™ for both availability and dealer referrals that can be relied upon for both buying and selling. All replies are treated strictly confidential. Replies should be directed to address at right.

Blue Book Publications, Inc.
Attn: Guitar B/S/T
8009 34th Avenue South Ste. 175
Minneapolis, MN 55425 USA
FAX: 612-853-1486
Email: guitars@bluebookinc.com
Web: http://www.bluebookinc.com

Correspondence Inquiries

As with any ongoing publication, certain models and variations will not be included within the scope of the text. As expanded research uncovers model variations and new companies, the book's body of text will always have some gray areas. Not believing in ivory towers and one-way traffic, this publisher offers a mechanism for the consumer to get further information about models not listed in these pages. No book can ever be totally complete in a collectible field as broad as this. For that reason, we are offering correspondence inquiries to help you obtain additional information on items not listed, or even questions on the data and prices provided.

Answering your correspondence (including letters, FAXes, and Email) under normal circumstances takes us between 10-14 working days, one of the fastest turn-around times in the industry. To make sure we can assist you with any correspondence, please include good quality photos of the specimen in question, any information available about that particular specimen, including manufacturer, model, body style, color/finish, unusual or other discernible features (if any) that will assist us with identifying your guitar(s). The charge for this comprehensive research program is $20.00 per instrument. In addition to payment, be sure to include both your address and phone number, giving us an option of how to contact you for best service. To keep up with this constant onslaught of correspondence, we have a large network of both dealers and collectors who can assist us (if necessary) to answer most of your questions within this time frame.

Remember, the charge for this research service is $20.00 per guitar and payment must accompany your correspondence, and will be answered in a FIFO system (first in first out). Thank you for your patience - it's a big job.

All correspondence regarding information and appraisals (not potential contributions or buying/selling guitars) should be directed to:

Blue Book Publications, Inc.
Attn: Guitar Correspondence
8009 34th Avenue South Ste. 175
Minneapolis, MN 55425 USA
FAX: 612-853-1486
Email: guitars@bluebookinc.com
Web: http://www.bluebookinc.com

SORRY - No order or request for research paid by credit card will be processed without a credit card expiration date.

Interested In Contributing ?

We always said that once you publish a book, you will always find out what you don't know. This publication is no different. However, an annual publication should always get better. Accumulating new research is an ongoing process with the results being published in each new edition.

The *Blue Book of Acoustic Guitars*™ has been the result of non-stop and continual guitar research obtained by working with both manufacturers and luthiers (including visiting their production facilities whenever we get the opportunity). Lutherie organizations, individual workshops, music stores, guitar shops, pawn shops, second-hand stores, and going to a lot of guitar/trade shows also hone our chops. Also of major importance is speaking directly with acknowledged experts (published and unpublished), reading books/catalogues/company promo materials, gathering critical and up-to-date manufacturer/luthier information obtained from NAMM Shows and the makers themselves, and observing and analyzing market trends by following major vintage dealer and collector pricing and trends.

If you feel that you can contribute in any way to the materials published herein, I would encourage you to submit hard copy regarding your potential additions, revisions, corrections, or any other pertinent information that you feel would enhance the benefits this book provides to its readers. Unfortunately, I am unable to take your information over the phone (this protects both of us)! Join the top notch crowd of Contributing Editors, and see that your information can make a difference!

All materials sent in for possible inclusion into the upcoming 6th Edition of the *Blue Book of Acoustic Guitars*™ should be either mailed, FAXed, or Emailed to us by June 1st, 1999 at the address listed below:

Blue Book Publications, Inc.
Attn: Guitar Contributions
8009 34th Avenue South Ste. 175
Minneapolis, MN 55425 USA
FAX: 612-853-1486
Email: guitars@bluebookinc.com
Web: http://www.bluebookinc.com

Once you have sent in your contributions, I will contact you at a later date to discuss possible inclusion in upcoming editions. I do appreciate your time and consideration in this matter, and will try to respond quickly to any correspondence sent my way.

Steven Cherne, Author

Blue Book of Acoustic Guitars

Authors & References

ACHARD, KEN,
The Fender Guitar, The Bold Strummer, Ltd., Westport CT, 1990

ACHARD, KEN,
The History and Development of the American Guitar, The Bold Strummer, Ltd., Westport CT, 1990

BACON, TONY,
The Ultimate Guitar Book, Alfred A. Knopf, Inc., New York NY, 1991

BACON, TONY AND DAY, PAUL,
The Fender Book, GPI/Miller Freeman Inc., San Francisco CA, 1992

BACON, TONY AND DAY, PAUL,
The Gibson Les Paul Book, GPI/Miller Freeman Inc., San Francisco CA, 1993

BACON, TONY AND DAY, PAUL,
The Gretsch Book, GPI/Miller Freeman Inc., San Francisco CA, 1996

BACON, TONY AND DAY, PAUL,
The Guru's Guitar Guide, Track Record Publishing, London England, 1990

BACON, TONY AND DAY, PAUL,
The Rickenbacker Book, GPI/Miller Freeman Inc., San Francisco CA, 1994

BACON, TONY AND MOORHOUSE, BARRY,
The Bass Book, GPI/Miller Freeman Inc., San Francisco CA, 1995

BECHTOLDT, PAUL,
G&L: LEO'S LEGACY,
Woof Associates, 1994

BECHTOLDT, PAUL AND TULLOCH, DOUG,
Guitars from Neptune - A Definitive Journey Into Danelectro Mania, JK Lutherie, Harrison OH, 1996

BENEDETTO, ROBERT,
Making an Archtop Guitar - The Definitive Work on the Design and Construction of an Acoustic Archtop Guitar, Centerstream Publishing, Anaheim Hills CA, 1996

BISHOP, IAN C.,
The Gibson Guitar, The Bold Strummer, Ltd., Westport CT, 1990

BISHOP, IAN C.,
The Gibson Guitar From 1950 Vol. 2, The Bold Strummer, Ltd., Westport NY 1990

BLASQUIZ, KLAUS,
The Fender Bass, Hal Leonard Publishing Corp., Milwaukee WI, 1990

BRIGGS, BRINKMAN AND CROCKER,
Guitars, Guitars, Guitars, All American Music Publishers, Neosho MO, 1988

BROZEMAN, BOB,
The History & Artistry of National Resonator Instruments, Centerstream Publishing, Anaheim Hills CA, 1993

CARTER, WALTER,
Epiphone, The Complete History, Hal Leonard Corporation, Milwaukee WI, 1995

CARTER, WALTER,
Gibson Guitars, 100 Years of an American Icon, General Publishing, Inc., New York NY, 1994

CARTER, WALTER,
The History of the Ovation Guitar, Hal Leonard Corporation, Milwaukee WI, 1996

CARTER, WALTER,
The Martin Book, GPI/Miller Freeman Inc., San Francisco CA, 1995

DAY, PAUL,
The Burns Book, The Bold Strummer, Ltd., Westport Connecticut, 1990

DENYER, RALPH,
The Guitar Handbook, Alfred A. Knopf Inc., New York NY, 1982

DUCHOSSOIR, A.R.,
Gibson Electrics, Hal Leonard Publishing Corp., Milwaukee WI, 1981

DUCHOSSOIR, A.R.,
Gibson Electrics - The Classic Years, Hal Leonard Publishing Corp., Milwaukee WI, 1994

DUCHOSSOIR, A.R.,
Guitar Identification, Hal Leonard Publishing Corp., Milwaukee WI, 1983

DUCHOSSOIR, A.R.,
The Fender Stratocaster, Hal Leonard Publishing Corp., Milwaukee WI, 1989

DUCHOSSOIR, A.R.,
The Fender Telecaster, Hal Leonard Publishing Corp., Milwaukee WI, 1991

ERLEWINE, VINOLPAL AND WHITFORD,
Gibson's Fabulous Flat-Top Guitars, Miller Freeman Books, San Francisco CA, 1994

EVANS, TOM AND MARY ANNE,
Guitars from the Renaissance to Rock, Facts on File, New York NY, 1977

FISCH, JIM, & FRED, L.B.
Epiphone: The House of Stathopoulo, Amsco Publications (Music Sales Corporation), New York NY, 1996

FULLERTON, GEORGE,
Guitar Legends, Centerstream Publishing, Fullerton CA, 1993

GIEL, KATE, ET AL,
Ferrington Guitars, HarperCollins, New York NY, 1992

GILTRAP, GORDON & MARTEN, NEVILLE,
The Hofner Guitar - A History, International Music Publications Limited, Essex England, 1993

GRUHN AND CARTER,
Acoustic Guitars and Other Fretted Instruments, Miller Freeman Inc., San Francisco CA, 1993

GRUHN AND CARTER,
Electric Guitars and Basses, GPI/Miller Freeman Inc., San Francisco CA, 1994

GRUHN AND CARTER,
Gruhn's Guide to Vintage Guitars, GPI/Miller Freeman Inc., San Francisco CA, 1991

HARTMAN, ROBERT CARL,
The Larsons' Creations, Guitars and Mandolins, Centerstream Publishing, Fullerton CA, 1995

HOWE, STEVE,
The Steve Howe Guitar Collection, GPI/Miller Freeman, Inc., San Francisco CA, 1993

IWANADE, YASUHIKO,
The Beauty of the 'Burst, Rittor Music, Tokyo Japan, 1997

IWANADE, YASUHIKO,
The Galaxy of Strats, Rittor Music, Tokyo Japan, 1998

JUAN, CARLOS,
Collectables & Vintage, American Guitar Center, Stuttgart Germany, 1995

LONGWORTH, MIKE,
Martin Guitars, a History, 4 Maples Press Inc., Minisink Hills PA, 1987

MOSELEY, WILLIE G.,
Classic Guitars U.S.A., Centerstream Publishing, Fullerton CA, 1992

MOSELEY, WILLIE G.,
Stellas & Stratocasters, Vintage Guitar Books, Bismarck ND, 1994

MOSELEY, WILLIE G.,
Guitar People, Vintage Guitar Books, Bismarck ND, 1997

MOUST, HANS,
The Guild Guitar Book, The Company and the Instruments, 1952-1977, Guitar Archives Publications, The Netherlands, 1995

RICH, BILL AND NIELSEN, RICK,
Guitars of the Stars, Volume 1: Rick Nielsen, Gots Publishing Ltd., A Division of Rich Specialties, Inc., Rockford IL, 1993
Rittor Music, Bizarre Guitars, Vol. 2, Japan, 1993

RITTOR MUSIC,
Guitar Graphic, Vol. 1, Tokyo Japan, 1994

RITTOR MUSIC,
Guitar Graphic, Vol. 2, Tokyo Japan, 1995

RITTOR MUSIC,
Guitar Graphic, Vol. 3, Tokyo Japan, 1995

RITTOR MUSIC,
Guitar Graphic, Vol. 4, Tokyo Japan, 1996

RITTOR MUSIC,
Guitar Graphic, Vol. 5, Tokyo Japan, 1996

RITTOR MUSIC,
Guitar Graphic, Vol. 6, Tokyo Japan, 1997

RITTOR MUSIC,
Guitar Graphic, Vol. 7, Tokyo Japan, 1997

RITTOR MUSIC,
Guitar Graphic, Vol. 8, Tokyo Japan, 1998

SCHMIDT, PAUL WILLIAM,
Acquired of the Angels: The lives and works of master guitar makers John D'Angelico and James L. D'Aquisto, The Scarecrow Press, Inc., Metuchen, NJ, 1991

SCOTT, JAY,
'50s Cool: Kay Guitars, Seventh String Press, Hauppauge NY, 1992

SCOTT, JAY,
The Guitars of the Fred Gretsch Company, Centerstream Publishing, Fullerton CA, 1992

SCOTT, JAY & DA PRA, VIC,
'Burst 1958-'60 Sunburst Les Paul, Seventh String Press, Hauppauge NY, 1994

SMITH, RICHARD R.,
Fender - The Sound Heard 'Round the World, Garfish Publishing Company, Fullerton CA, 1995

SMITH, RICHARD R.,
Fender Custom Shop Guitar Gallery, Hal Leonard COrporation, Milwaukee WI, 1996

SMITH, RICHARD R.,
The History of Rickenbacker Guitars, Centerstream Publishing, Fullerton CA, 1989

TEAGLE, JOHN,
Washburn Over One Hundred Years of Find Stringed Instruments, Music Sales Corp, New York NY, 1996

VAN HOOSE, THOMAS A.,
The Gibson Super 400, Miller Freeman, Inc., San Francisco, 1991

WHEELER, TOM,
American Guitars, HarperCollins Publishers, New York NY, 1990

WHEELER, TOM,
The Guitar Book, A Handbook for Electric & Acoustic Guitarists, Harper & Row, New York NY, 1974

WHITE, FORREST, FENDER
The Inside Story, GPI/Miller Freeman Books, San Francisco CA, 1994

WRIGHT, MICHAEL,
Guitar Stories, Volume One, Vintage Guitar Books, Bismarck ND, 1995

Y ou've bought this book so you're obviously interested in stringed instruments. Being knowledgeable about any subject is a good idea and having the up-to-the-minute-news is the best form of knowledge. We recommend the following publications for instrument information, collecting news, updates and show announcements, luthier and artist insights and loads of other information that might interest you.

Periodicals Listings

20TH CENTURY GUITAR
Seventh String Press, Inc., 135 Oser Avenue, Hauppauge, New York 11788
Phone number: 516-273-1674, (FAX) 516-435-9057
Published monthly. 12 month subscription is $15.00 in the USA.

ACOUSTIC GUITAR
String Letter Publishing, Inc., P.O. Box 767, San Anselmo, Californa 94979-0767; 255 West End Avenue, San Rafael, California 94901
Phone number: 415-485-6946, (FAX) 415-485-0831
Email: slp@stringletter.com
Published monthly. 12 month subscription is $29.95 in the USA.

BASS PLAYER
Miller Freeman, Inc., 411 Borel Avenue #100, San Mateo, California 94402
Phone number: 800-234-1831
(415-358-9500), (FAX) 415-358-9966
Email: bassplayer@mfi.com
Published monthly. 12 month subscription is $29.95 in the USA.

BASSICS
924 Sea Cliff Dr., Carlsbad, California 92009.
Phone number: 760-931-9433 (FAX)760-931-0159
Email: bassicRG@aol.com, or lynngarant@aol.com
http://www.bassics.com
Published quarterly. 4 issue/year subscription is $12.00, 2 years for $22.00 in the USA.

DOWNBEAT
102 N. Haven Road, Elmhurst, Illinois 60126-3379.
Gitarre & Bass (Germany)
MM-Musik-Media-Verlag GmbH, An Der Wachsfabrik 8, Koln 50996 Germany
Phone number: 011-39-2236-96217
(FAX) 011-39-2236-96217-5
Published monthly.

GITARRE & BASS (GERMANY)
MM-Musik-Media-Verlag GmbH, An Der Wachsfabrik 8, Koln, 50996 Germany
Phone number: 011-39-2236-96217
(FAX) 011-39-2236-96217-5
Published monthly.

GUITAR DIGEST
P.O. Box 66, The Plains, Ohio 45780
Phone number: 740-797-3351,
(FAX) 740-592-4614
Email: alexmac@frognet.net
Published 6 times a year. A six issue subscription is $10.00 in the USA.

**GUITAR FOR
THE PRACTICING MUSICIAN**
Cherry Lane Magazines, Inc., Six East 32nd St., New York, NY 10016
Phone number: 212-561-3000
Published monthly. 12 month subscription is $22.95 in the USA, and a two year subscription is $37.95 in the USA.

GUITAR ONE
Cherry Lane Magazines, Inc., Six East 32nd St., New York, NY 10016
Phone number: 212-561-3000 Published monthly. Available on the newstands for $4.95 per issue in the USA.

THE GUITAR MAGAZINE (UK)
Link House Magazines Ltd., Link House, Dingwall Avenue, Croyden CR9 2TA, England.
Phone number: 011-44-181-686-2599
(FAX) 011-44-181-781-1158
Email: 101574.223@compuserve.com
Published monthly.

GUITAR PLAYER
Miller Freeman, Inc., 411 Borel Avenue #100, San Mateo, California 94402
Phone number: 800-289-9939
(415-358-9500), (FAX) 415-358-9966
Email: guitplyr@mfi.com.
Published monthly. 12 month subscription is $29.95 in the USA.

GUITAR SHOP
Cherry Lane Magazines, Inc., Six East 32nd St., New York, NY 10016
Phone number: 212-561-3000
Published bimonthly. 12 month subscription is $17.75 in the USA.

GUITAR WORLD
Harris Publications, Inc., 1115 Broadway, New York, New York 10010
Phone number: 800-866-2886
Email: sounding.board@guitarworld.com
World Wide Web: http://www.guitarworld.com
Published monthly. 12 month subscription is $19.95 in the USA.

GUITAR WORLD ACOUSTIC

Harris Publications, Inc., 1115 Broadway,
New York, New York 10010
Phone number: 212-807-7100,
(FAX) 212-627-4678
Email: sounding.board@guitarworld.com
World Wide Web: http://www.guitarworld.com
 Published monthly. 12 month subscription is
$19.94 in the USA.

GUITARIST (UK)

Alexander House, Forehill, Ely,
Cambs CB7 4AF, England
Phone number: 011-44-1353-665577
(FAX) 011-44-1353-662489
Email: guitarist@musicians-net.co.uk
 Published monthly.

GUITARIST (FRANCE)

10, Rue De la Paix, Boulogne, France 92100

JAZZTIMES

8737 Colesville RD., 5th Floor, Silver
Spring, MD 02910-3921
Phone: 888-458-4637
 Published 10 times/year. A one year subscrip-
tion is $23.95 in the USA.

JUST JAZZ GUITAR

P.O. Box 76053, Atlanta, Georgia 30358-1053
Phone number: 404-250-9298,
(FAX) 404-250-9298
Email: jazzgtr@onramp.net
 Published 4 times a year. A one year subscrip-
tion scription is $36 in the USA.

MUSICIAN

33 Commercial Street,
Gloucester, Massachusetts 01930
Phone number: 800-347-6969
(212-536-5208)
 Published monthly, yearly subscription is
$19.97 in the USA.

MUSICO PRO

Music Maker Pubilcations, Inc., 5412
Idylwild Trail, Suite 100, Boulder,
Colorado 80301
Phone number: 303-516-9118
(FAX) 303-516-9119
A music/gear magazine is published in
Spanish (available in U.S., Argentine, Chile,
Mexico, and Spain).
 Published 9 times a year. Subscription is
$14.95 in the USA.

THE NATIONAL INSTRUMENT EXCHANGE

John B. Kinnemeyer, 11115 Sand Run,
Harrison, Ohio 45030
Phone number: 800-827-0682
(513-353-3320), (FAX) 513-353-3320
Email: guitar@jklutherie.com
World Wide Web:
http://www.jklutherie.com/nie
 Published monthly. Guitar Buy and Sell
Newsletter. 12 issue subscription is $15.00 in
the USA.

STACCATO

Manfred Hecker and Carsten Durer, editors.
Akazienweg 57, Cologne, 50827 Germany
Phone number: 011-39-221-5301560
(FAX) 011-39-221-5302286
Email: staccato@vva.com

VINTAGE GUITAR MAGAZINE

Alan J. Greenwood, P.O. Box 7301,
Bismarck, North Dakota 58507
Phone number: 701-255-1197
(FAX) 701-255-0250
 Published monthly. 12 month subscription is
$27.95 in the USA.

VINTAGE GUITAR NEWS (GERMANY)

Verlag Gunter Janssen, Eggensteinerstr. 46,
Stutensee, D-76297 Germany
Phone number: +49-7244-740063,
(FAX) +49-7244-740064
Email: 101574.223@compuserve.com
 Published six times yearly.

In addition to the regular publications
put out by these publishers, most offer
Special Edition (i.e., yearly buyers'
guides, new product reviews, market
overviews, etc.) magazines that are
released annually, or bi-annually.

BLUE BOOK of GUITARS™
a blast from the past!

Past issues of the *Blue Book of Guitars*™ are
available in **limited quantities**. This is the
easiest way to bone up on past pricing trends!

Call **1-800-877-4867** for availability.

All prices include 4th class S/H.

1st Edition - published in 1993
Original retail price $19.95
Out of print - **$20.00**

2nd Edition - published in 1994
Original retail price $24.95
Out of print - **$20.00**

3rd Edition - published in 1996
Original retail price $29.95
Out of print - **$15.00**

4th Edition - published in 1997
Original retail price $29.95
Out of print - **$20.00**

UNDERSTANDING FACTORS
THAT CAN AFFECT CONDITION & PRICING

Rating the condition factor of a guitar is, at best, still subjective, while at worst, totally misrepresentative. We've attempted to give a few examples of things that may affect the pricing and desirability of vintage acoustic guitars, but it's really impossible to accurately ascertain the correct condition factor without the instrument in your grubby little hand. Even then, three different "experts" will probably come up with slightly different grades, not to mention different values based on different reasons. We tend to think that common sense plays a big part in the vintage marketplace. Listed below are major factors to consider when determining both the condition and value of any used acoustic instrument. Also, please study the PPGS color photographs carefully on pages 49-64 to learn more about the factors described below.

FINISH-- An original finish in good shape is, of course, the most desirable. A light professional overspray will negatively affect the value of a guitar somewhat. A refinish will put it into the "below average" catagory in almost every case. A professional, well done refinish is better than an amateur job. However, in either case expect the value of the instrument to be lower than the average prices listed in this book. An exception might be a case where there's only one or two examples of a highly desirable item, and condition obviously takes a back seat to rarity.

MAJOR REPAIRS--Many older guitars have had repairs, of course. A well-done neck reset won't affect the overall value that much. Replaced bridges will have an affect but the better the work, the less it will hurt. A replaced neck, fingerboard, part of a side, top or back will cause the price to drop noticably. Again, if it's an especially rare item, the rarity might supercede most of that. If it's the only one you can find, well, you just might have to pay the price.

MODIFICATIONS--Any non-factory modification on an original guitar is going to hurt the value. To decide to put a shaded top finish on a 1940 D-28, for example, will cost you the price of refinishing, plus at least $10,000 in loss of value! Less visable but still important would be modifi-cations on braces, shaving necks, and even installing a pickup jack. Think really really hard before you do any of these things to your vintage guitar. You won't get a second chance to make it original.

**REPLACEMENT TUNERS
AND OTHER NON-ORIGINAL PARTS**--Many older guitars have been fitted with new tuners somewhere along the way. These days there are good replacement tuners available that fit the original holes, etc. There are also sleeves that will make an oversized hole into the correct size for original style tuners. Even a good, appropriate replacement set will have a negative affect on value, even though it constitutes a playing improvement over what was available twenty years ago.

CRACKS--Acoustic guitars are made of wood and cracks do happen. Unfortunately, unattended cracks tend to get bigger and usually do not go back together perfectly. Any crack will affect value, but a small, professionally well repaired crack will take much less of a bite out of the price than a large gaping crack that wouldn't go together properly.

FRETS--A good analogy for frets would be found in the vintage car market: you rarely find a vintage car with original tires. Guitars were made to be played and frets do wear out. A good professional fret job using factory spec parts should not affect the value of your instrument. Again, this question won't come up with a mint, unplayed guitar.

COSMETICS--The cleaner an instrument, the more it's worth. Don't ever underestimate the value of eye appeal. A mint, unplayed, original condition guitar with tags will always bring more than the prices for "excellent" condition. On the other hand, an instrument with most of the finish worn off from years of use might bring less than the average shown here.

Guitars, even vintage ones, are meant to be played. Enjoy yours, take proper care of it, play it once in awhile, and don't let temperature, humidity factors get to extremes. ∎

Understanding & Converting Guitar Grading Systems

Since the new *5th Edition Blue Book of Acoustic Guitars*™ now uses the descriptive grading system of Average & Excellent factors to describe condition, please study the color acoustic guitar condition photos on the following pages carefully to help understand and identify each acoustic guitar's unique condition factor. These photos, with condition factors, serve as a guideline, not an absolute. Remember, if the condition factor isn't right, the price is wrong!

The conversion chart listed below has been provided to help you convert to the Photo Percentage Grading System™ and several others. All percentage descriptions and/or possible conversions made thereof, are based on original condition - alterations, repairs, refinishing work, and any other non-original alterations that have changed the condition of an instrument must be listed additionally and typically subtracted from the values based on condition throughout this text (please refer to page 47 for an explanation of these critical factors affecting both condition and price).

ACOUSTIC GUITAR CONDITION FACTORS WITH EXPLANATIONS

ADDITIONAL PPGS/DESCRIPTIVE/NUMERICAL CONDITION FACTORS

100% - New - New with all factory materials, including warranty card, owner's manual, case, and other items that were originally included by the manufacturer. On currently manufactured instruments, the 100% price refers to an instrument not previously sold at retail. On out-of-production instruments (including dealer "new, old stock," or NOS), the longer a guitar has been discontinued, the less likely you will find it in 100% condition. Some instruments that are less than 20 years old and have never been taken out-of-the-case (unplayed) may not be 100% (new), as the finish may have slightly cracked, tarnished, faded, or deteriorated. Remember, there are no excuses in 100% condition.

Both Excellent & Average condition factors can be subdivided slightly, depending on wear factors, within the range of conditions. Obviously, an Average acoustic with a lot of body wear is less desirable than an Average acoustic with little body wear - and should be prices accordingly.

Excellent - The Excellent condition factor comprises the range of conditions from 98% Mint to 90% Excellent (a '9'). Though this range is none too broad, the intent is to capture a description that indicates a very clean, (barely) used guitar. The sort of guitar that looks "brand new", but does not have the manufacturer's warranty. See photos 1, 2, 7, 8, 21, 22, 31 & 32

Average - The Average guitar condition factor indicates an acoustic guitar that has been in a player's hands and has suffered a bit because of the usage. A good condition indicator for an Average guitar is the dents, chips, and dings on the body, or scratches on the top and back. The Average condition range includes conditions between 85% (Very Good+) down to 60% (Good) wherein the amount of noticeable wear on the body is the factor that indicates an Average condition.

For Above Average conditions, refer to photos 11, 12, 25, & 26

For Average condition, please observe photos 3, 4, 5, 6, 9, 10, 13, 14, 17, 18, 23, 24, 29 & 30

Below Average is represented by photos 15, 16, 19, 20, 27 & 28

95% - 98%- Excellent Plus - 9+ - Only very slightly used and/or played very little, may have minor "case" wear or light dings on exterior finish only, without finish checking, very close to new condition, also refers to a currently manufactured instrument that has previously sold at retail, even though it may not have been played. May have a slight scratch - otherwise as new. See photos 1 & 2 (95% condition).

90% - Excellent - 9 - Light exterior finish wear with a few minor dings, no paint chips down to the wood, normal nicks and scratches, light observable neck wear in most cases, 9 quesadillas with homemade guacamole and salsa. See photos 7, 8, 31, & 32.

80% - Very Good+ (VG+) Above Average - 8 - More exterior finish wear (20% of the original finish is gone) that may include minor chips that extend down to the wood, body wear, but nothing real serious, nice shape overall, with mostly honest player wear. See photos 3, 4, 9, 10, 11, 12, 25 & 26.

70% - Very Good (VG) - Average - 7 - More serious exterior finish wear that could include some major gauges and nicks, player arm wear, and/or fret deterioration. See photos 5, 6, 13, 14, 17, 18, 23, & 24.

60% - Good (G) - Subaverage - 6 - Noticeable wear on most areas - normally this consists of some major belt buckle wear and finish deterioration, may include cracking, possible repairs or alterations. When this condition factor is encountered, normally an instrument should have all logos intact, original pickups, minor headstock damage, and perhaps a few non-serious alterations, with or without original case. See photos 15, 16, 27, 28, 29 & 30.

40% - Fair (F) - Below Average - 4 - Major features are still discernible, major parts missing, probably either refinished or repaired, structurally sound, though many times encountered with non-factory alterations. See photos 19 & 20.

20% - Poor (P) - 2 - Ending a life sentence of hard labor, must still be playable, most of the licks have left, family members should be notified immediately, normally not worthy unless the ad also mentions pre-war D-45, "If you paid more for another one like this, this could be your last chance to be a Chump again," a couple of reheated Lil' Smokies and the rest of a two-week old tin of unrefrigerated Kipper snacks.

1960 Gibson Hummingbird - Ser. #unknown, Cherry Sunburst finish, Excellent overall condition. There's nothing like kicking off the Photo Percentage Grading System by giving your fans the bird - in this case a clean Hummingbird from the first year of production. A great model with great appointments - just soak in the multiple-ply body binding, parallelogram fingerboard inlays, Gibson logo and crown headstock inlay, and bound fingerboard. Of course, the hummingbird and flowers on the pickguard complete the package.

1964 Gibson J-200 - Ser. #62460, Natural Blonde finish, approx. 80% (VG+) overall condition. This condition factor qualifies as the bottom end of Excellent condition for instruments of this vintage. Observe wear underneath "mustache" bridge and nicks on back of neck. Observe 3-piece neck, spectacular book-matched flame maple on back, and extra holes on back of headstock (which are usually indicative of replacement tuners). Also, examine neck inlays and definitive pickguard graphics on this model. The J-200 series has many variations.

1952 Gibson SJ-200 - Ser. # unknown, Blonde finish, Approx. 70% (VG) overall - Average condition for its age. The Southerner Jumbo (SJ) model featured a 16 inch body width. In 1942, the first factory order batch had rosewood back and sides; but all batches after that featured mahogany. The loops up by the headstock are cleverly coiled string ends. By the early 1950s the crown inlay had replaced the "Only a Gibson is Good Enough" banner inlay on the headstock. Also, compare the SJ "mustache" bridge with the bridge on the J-200 in Photos 3 & 4.

1967 Gibson B-25 - Ser. # unknown, Translucent Red custom color finish, Excellent condition. Traditionally, these models are encountered in a Cherry Sunburst or Natural (top) finish. After Norlin acquired Gibson in the late 1960s, they spent some of that corporate money "jazzing up" various models to compete with Fender - hence the custom colors. Note a small amount of dings on the top, but still in very nice condition overall.

A Gibson-era Epiphone Texan (FT 79 N) - Ser. #424923, Natural finish, Average (70%-80% or VG - VG+) overall condition. No major wear in any one area, just normal scratches, dings, and handling marks. Two-piece mahogany back with normal horizontal finish weather checking. Astute Epiphone acoustic aficionados will recognize the replaced tuners. Note 'E' logo on bell and wear on upper neck.

Guild D3 JN-T - Ser. #180154, Natural finish, 80% (VG+) overall condition. Notice considerable wear on left side of pickguard below soundhole - the only major area of deterioration on this instrument outside of normal nicks and scratches. This dreadnought features a 2-piece bookmatched spruce top, mahogany back and neck, rosewood fingerboard with dot inlays, and enclosed tuners.

1957 Martin D-18 - Ser. #168235, Natural finish, approx. 70% (VG) overall condition. Close inspection reveals a top surface crack running from the bridge to the bottom of the body. Unprofessional attempts when repairing Martins (and other flattop guitars) will lower values more significantly than an original instrument with natural cracking. Readers without bifocals will still note small operation ID numbers between tuning machines.

1945 Martin D-18 - Ser. #92775, Natural finish, approx. 60% (G) overall condition (back side lowers the average). This condition factor qualifies as the lower end of the Average condition. Examine wear along the sides of the neck above soundhole. Also note the splitting of the top as well as the scratch marks on the 2-piece bookmatched mahogany back and relative lack of wear on neck.

1934 Martin R-18 - Ser. # unknown, Dark Mahogany finish, 70% (VG) overall condition. For this vintage, this instrument is in Average condition. Small arch top body style with round soundhole and trapeze tailpiece. Note finish deterioration around left side of soundhole and neck, and continuing to top of body. Nice back with minimal scratching. Normal neck wear (although upper back has a few scratches and some finish loss). This Martin is all original - not a bad pre-war Martin. Originality is Polar North for Martin collectors.

1924 Gibson L-4 - Ser. #92109, Regular finish, approx. 50% (G-) overall condition. Definitely, a Below Average specimen. Note the nasty cracks on right front side of body in addition to more than normal scratches and dings on back side of body caused by excessive jean rivet damage - also note missing pickguard. Observe early Gibson script logo on headstock. Remember - this guitar may have been originally transported by horse and buggy, steam train, or a "brand new" Ford Model T truck!

1946 Epiphone Emperor - Ser. #55580, Natural finish, 95% (EXC+) overall condition. In wide bodies, Boeing has the 747, and Epiphone had the 18-inch Emperor. Spectacular bookmatched flame maple multi-bound backside with 7-piece laminate neck. Double inlay blocks on fretboard, tortoise shell multi-layered pickguard, and split trapeze tailpiece are all hallmarks of this model.

21 22

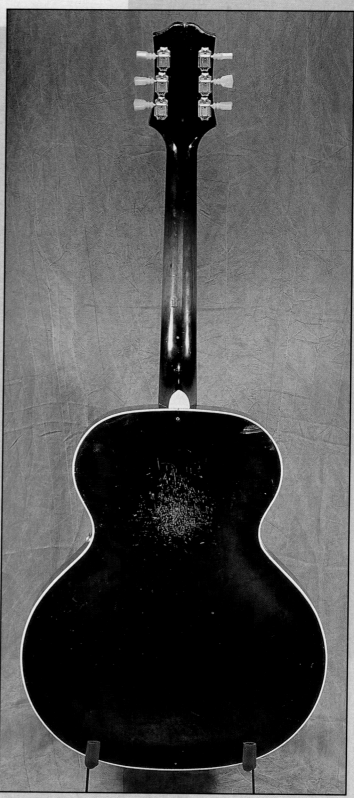

1950 Epiphone Zenith - Ser. # unknown, Regular finish, 70% (VG) overall condition. Back side of this instrument is living proof of what a belt buckle can do to the finish over a period of time (and lower the condition factor 10%). Sunburst finish on back of neck reveals 3-piece laminate construction. Trapeze tailpiece (note dulling due to oxidation on this guitar), dot inlays, and adjustable rosewood bridge are all standard features on this model.

23

24

1942 Gibson Super 400 - Ser. #97668, Regular finish, 80% (VG+) overall condition. Examine finish scratches on upper top of front and sides of back. Gibson's top-of-the-line carved top acoustic featured an 18-inch body width. Note the bookmatched flame maple back, as well as the front and back headstock inlays. A marbled celluloid pickguard and Super 400 logo on heel complete the package.

25   26

 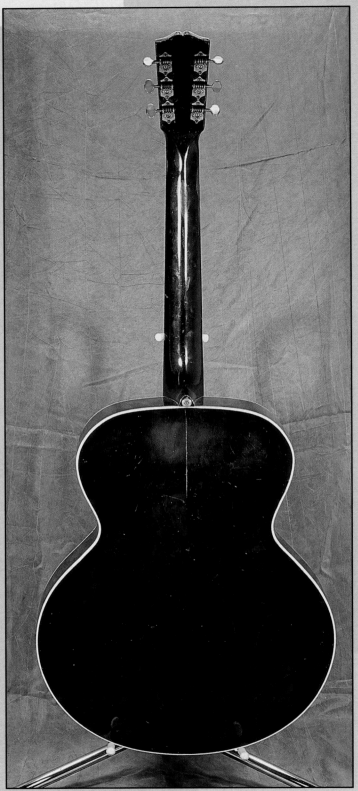

1935 Gibson L7 - Ser. #90980, Regular finish, approx. 60% (G) condition. The amount of wear qualifies this guitar as being on the down side of the Average condition for instruments of this vintage. While this instrument does not exhibit extreme wear in any one area, multiple scratches and nicks on front, in addition to back of neck wear, reduce this specimen's overall condition to 60%. Observe unusual fretboard inlays, small headstock, and dark finished maple back. All original with no major problems.

1938 Gibson L-7 - Ser. #unknown, Blonde finish, 60%-70% (G) overall or around Average condition for this vintage. Note cracks from left F-hole to lower/upper bouts and inside the tailpiece. Eagle eye readers will quickly call a foul on the floating pickup appearing in an Acoustic Guitar book, but this model is built primarily like an acoustic (just think of it like an extra olive in your martini). Slightly tarnished tailpiece could be buffed back up - and then it's time to hit the jazz clubs uptown.

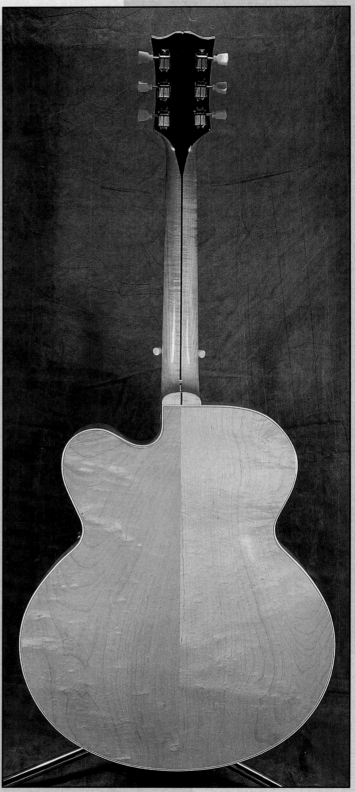

1953 Gibson L-7C - Ser. #A-13922, Natural finish, approx. 90% overall condition (Excellent), dings and gouges on lower body bout hurt this guitar's overall condition from 95% to 90%. Professional repairs could bring the price tag back to the 95% value. Examine exceptionally clean bookmatched back and very little wear on back of 2-piece neck. Trapeze tailpiece shows normal dulling due to oxidation. Parallelogram inlays, rosewood bridge, and layered black pickguard are standard features on this model.

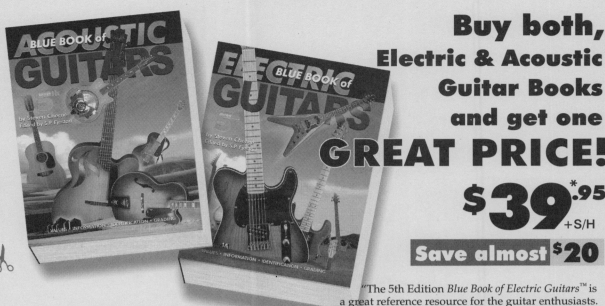

Buy both, Electric & Acoustic Guitar Books and get one GREAT PRICE!

$39.95* +S/H

Save almost $20

"The 5th Edition *Blue Book of Electric Guitars*™ is a great reference resource for the guitar enthusiasts. I can only guess at the work involved in gathering so much information."
Paul Reed Smith — *PRS Guitars*

"This 5th Edition *Blue Book of Acoustic Guitars*™ will provide dealers, collectors, and serious guitar enthusiasts with an invaluable resource, incredibly thorough and packed with detail."
C.F. Martin IV — *Chairman & CEO, C. F. Martin & Co.*

Call 1-800-877-4867 to order

Call Toll-Free to order the (Domestic Orders) 1-800-877-4867
BLUE BOOK OF ELECTRIC/ACOUSTIC GUITARS™

☐ 5th Edition Blue Book of Electric Guitars .... **$33.95** | $29.95+$4 4th class S/H
Price above includes 4th class S/H, please add $2 more for 1st class (UPS)

☐ 5th Edition Blue Book of Acoustic Guitars .... **$28.95** | $24.95+$4 4th class S/H
Price above includes 4th class S/H, please add $2 more for 1st class (UPS)

Best Deal! Save almost $20

☐ Both Electric & Acoustic Guitar Books........ **$45.95** | $39.95+$6* UPS S/H
Price above includes UPS S/H

Please allow 2-4 weeks for delivery (4th class), 3-7 business days(UPS).
Prices vary outside of the U.S., call for more information.

Call 1-800-877-4867 or return this order card with information & payment. Sorry no COD's.

International 612-854-5229, FAX 612-853-1486
Please send payment to: Blue Book Publications, Inc.
8009 34th Ave. S. Suite 175, Dept. G5oc
Minneapolis, MN 55425   U.S.A

Name_____
Company_____
Address_____ Sorry, no P.O. Box addresses on UPS deliveries. _____
City_____ State_____ Zip_____
Credit Card No._____Exp._____
Daytime Phone No._____
Signature_____

Form of Payment:
☐ Personal Check
☐ Money Order
☐ Cashier's Check
☐ Visa
☐ Master Card
☐ Discover
☐ American Express

Order on the Web at:
www.bluebookinc.com

Call (Domestic Orders) to order 1-800-877-4867

☐ 5th Edition Blue Book of Electric Guitars .... **$33.95** $29.95+$4 4th class S/H
Price above includes 4th class S/H, please add $2 more for 1st class (UPS)

☐ 5th Edition Blue Book of Acoustic Guitars .... **$28.95** $24.95+$4 4th class S/H
Price above includes 4th class S/H, please add $2 more for 1st class (UPS)

Best Deal! Save almost $20

☐ Both Electric & Acoustic Guitar Books........ **$45.95** $39.95+$6* UPS S/H
Price above includes UPS S/H

Please allow 2-4 weeks for delivery (4th class), 3-7 business days(UPS).
Prices vary outside of the U.S., call for more information.

Call 1-800-877-4867 or return this order card
with information & payment. Sorry no COD's.

International 612-854-5229, FAX 612-853-1486
Please send payment to: Blue Book Publications, Inc.
8009 34th Ave. S. Suite 175, Dept. G5oc
Minneapolis, MN 55425   U.S.A

Name_____
Company_____
Address_____ Sorry, no P.O. Box addresses on UPS deliveries.
City_____State_____Zip_____
Credit Card No._____Exp._____
Daytime Phone No._____
Signature_____

Form of Payment:
☐ **Personal Check**
☐ **Money Order**
☐ **Cashier's Check**
☐ **Visa**
☐ **Master Card**
☐ **Discover**
☐ **American Express**

Order on the Web at:
www.bluebookinc.com

Call (Domestic Orders) **to order**
1-800-877-4867

Call Toll-Free to order the **1-800-877-4867**™
BLUE BOOK OF ELECTRIC/ACOUSTIC GUITARS™

Buy both,
Electric & Acoustic Guitar Books and get one
GREAT PRICE!
$39.*95
+S/H
Save almost $20

"This 5th Edition *Blue Book of Acoustic Guitars*™ will provide dealers, collectors, and serious guitar enthusiasts with an invaluable resource, incredibly thorough and packed with detail."

C.F. Martin IV — *Chairman & CEO, C. F. Martin & Co.*

"The 5th Edition *Blue Book of Electric Guitars*™ is a great reference resource for the guitar enthusiasts. I can only guess at the work involved in gathering so much information."

Paul Reed Smith — *PRS Guitars*

Call **to order**
1-800-877-4867

A

A

See chapter on House Brands.

This trademark has been identified as a House Brand of the Alden department store chain. One of the models shares similarities with the Harmony-built **Stratotone** of the 1960s, while a previously identified model dates back to the 1950s.

(Source: Willie G. Moseley, Stellas & Stratocasters)

ABILENE

Instruments produced in Asia by Samick. Distributed in the U.S. by Advantage Worldwide.

The Abilene trademark is distributed in the U.S. by Advantage Worldwide. The Abilene trademark is offered on a range of acoustic, acoustic/electric, and solid body electric guitars and practice amplifers. The guitars are built by Samick of Korean, and the electric guitar models feature designs based on popular American models.

ACOUSTIC

There are a full range of acoustic models, ranging from the two classical guitars (**AC 15G** and **AC 25 G**), to the dreadnoughts **AW 15** (Black, Sunburst, and White) and **AW 20** and **AW 25G**. All have laminated nato bodies, and 'natural' tops. The AW 25G has a Blond spruce top. The top of the line **AW 270 HS** is a herringbone-bound dreadnought with a cedar top. Both the **AW 15 EM** and **AW 115 DE** dreadnoughts are acoustic/electric models with volume and tone controls.

ACADEMY

Instruments built in Korea. Distributed by Lark in the Morning of Mendocino, California.

Academy offers nice quality steel string guitars, 4-, 5-, and 6-string banjos, and chord harps.

A.C.E.

Instruments currently built in Somersworth, New Hampshire. Distributed by A.C.E. Guitars of Somersworth, New Hampshire.

A.C.E. Guitars currently offers 4 different acoustic/electric guitar models. One model is a thinline Classical with "Total Tonal Control" electronics. Prices currently $TBA. For further information regarding specifications and pricing, contact A.C.E. Guitars via the Index of Current Manufacturers located in the rear of this edition.

AIRCRAFT

Instruments built in Japan.

Guitars carrying the Aircraft logo are actually manufactured by the Morris company, who also build instruments for such brandnames as their own Morris trademark, as well as the Hurricane logo.

ALEX

See DOMINO.

Instruments manufactured in Japan circa mid to late 1960s. Distributed by Maurice Lipsky Music Company, Inc. of New York, New York.

Alex acoustic guitar models featured laminated mahogany tops, backs, and sides, as well as internal fan bracing. The Alex acoustic was offered with standard size (retail list $29.95), concert size (retail list $34.50), grand concert (retail list $37.50), or in a 12-string configuration (retail list $80.00).

(Domino catalog courtesy John Kinnemeyer, JK Lutherie)

ALHAMBRA

Instruments currently built in Spain. Distributed by Manufacturas Alhambra, S. L., of Alicante, Spain.

Alhambra classical guitars are medium to very high quality Spanish instruments. Models are constructed with either solid cedar (and Red cedar) or solid spruce tops, cypress or Brazilian rosewood (model **Lut. Rio Professional**) (or laminated rosewood or laminated sycamore) sides. In addition to their traditional classical models, Alhambra also offers a single cutaway classical model (**5 P CTW**), a folk model (**J 3**), a dreadnought model (**W 3**), as well as two 10-string instruments (a bandurria and a laud). Retail list prices range from $425 up to $8,000 depending on design, inlays, and woods used in construction.

RANDY ALLEN

Instruments built in Colfax, California since 1982.

Luthier Randy Allen began repairing guitars and other stringed instruments in 1980. Two years later, Allen built his first custom guitar. Luthier Allen has been handcrafting quality acoustic guitars, acoustic resonator guitars, and mandolins for over fifteen years. All Allen guitars are built on a custom order basis.

All acoustic guitar models have options ranging from a cutaway body configuration, abalone edging, different fingerboard inlays, and wood bindings (call for price confirmation).

Standard features on the acoustic guitar models include East Indian Rosewood or Honduran Mahogany back and sides, a Sitka spruce top; bound Ebony fingerboards, bridge, and peghead overlay; and a bound headstock and mother of pearl position dots. Basic models include the **Dreadnaught** ($2,595), **Small Jumbo** ($2,795), the **Parlor** ($2,795), and the **OM** ($2,795). Allen recently introduced a new design for the **S J**

Cutaway that features a redesigned bridge and softer cutaway; the model has a Sitka spruce top, Indian rosewood back and sides, ebony fittings, and gold hardware.

In 1996, Allen debuted a new series of Resophonic guitars. The **Allen Resonator** guitar models are equipped with high quality hardware, and a spun resonator cone. The chrome plated cover plate is held in position with machine screws (as opposed to wood screws, which may strip out over time). The top, back, and sides are maple (a spruce top is available on request). This model is configured either as a square neck or round neck, and is available on a custom order basis starting at $2,595 (retail list) with a custom fitted hardshell case. Allen's mandolins start at $2,395, and feature maple back and sides, a bone nut and saddle, maple or mahogany neck, and choice of an f-hole or round soundhole in addition to the standard features found on the guitar models. For further information, contact luthier Randy Allen throught the Index of Current Manufacturers located in the back of this book.

RICHARD C. ALLEN

Instruments currently built in Almonte, California.

Luthier R.C. Allen has been playing guitar since his high school days in the late 1940s. Allen has been playing, collecting, repairing, and building guitars for a great number of years. After working sixteen years as a warehouseman for a paper company, Allen began doing repair work for west coast guitar wholesaler/distributors like C. Bruno and Pacific Music. In 1972, Allen began building guitars full time.

Allen's designs focus on hollowbody and semi-hollowbody guitars. While he has built some electrics, the design was semi-hollow (similar to the Rickenbacker idea) with a flat top/back and f-holes. Currently, Allen focuses on *jazz*-style archtops.

ALMANSA

GUITARRAS ALMANSA.

Instruments currently built in Almansa, Spain. Distributed by Guitarras Almansa of Almansa (Albacete), Spain.

Almansa has been producing fine quality classical guitars for nearly a decade. Under the directorship of Pedro-Angel Lopez, Almansa continues their focus of providing a wide range of models.

ACOUSTIC

All the nylon-stringed Almansa guitars are built to a 650 mm (25.6") scale length, and feature a multicolored wood rosette, wood body binding, and 19 fret fingerboard.

The basic **Studio** models (400 series models) feature a solid cedar or solid spruce top, laminated mahogany back and sides, and Indian rosewood fingerboard. Higher level models (420s and 430s) feature back and sides of bubinga or laminated Indian rosewood. The **Conservatory** models (450 and 460 series) have solid Indian rosewood back and sides, and models with installed pickup systems also have a rounded cutaway. The fully handmade **Concert** models like the **Professional Jacaranda** have first quality Indian or Brazilian rosewood back and sides and German Spruce tops, while the **Gran Concierto** model has an ornate headstock and is built of selected woods that have been naturally dried for years.

Almansa also offers several **Flamenco** models, with sycamore or cypress wood construction. Models are available in Studio, Conservatory, or Concert level construction.

Current retail prices were not available for this edition.

ALMCRANTZ

Instruments built in America in the late 1800s.

An Almcrantz acoustic guitar bearing a label reading "July 1895" was featured in the first edition of Tom Wheeler's reference book "American Guitars" (HarperCollins Publishers, New York). Research is continuing on the company history, and further information will be updated in future editions of the **Blue Book of Guitars**.

ALOHA

Instruments built in San Antonio, Texas and Chicago, Illinois. Distributed by the Aloha Publishing and Musical Instrument Company of Chicago, Illinois.

The Aloha company was founded in 1935 by J. M. Raleigh. True to the nature of a "House Brand" distributor, Raleigh's company distributed both Aloha instruments and amplifiers and Raleigh brand instruments through his Chicago office. Acoustic guitars were supplied by Harmony, and initial amplifiers and guitars were supplied by the Alamo company of San Antonio, Texas. By the mid 1950s, Aloha was producing their own amps, but continued using Alamo products.

(Source: Michael Wright, Vintage Guitar Magazine)

ALOSA

See SANDNER.

ALVAREZ

Alvarez instruments are currently manufactured in either Japan and Korea. Distributed by St. Louis Music of St. Louis, Missouri.

The St. Louis Music Supply Company was originally founded in 1922 by Bernard Kornblum as a violin shop. In 1957, Gene Kornblum (Bernard's son) joined the family business.

The Alvarez trademark was established in 1965, and the company was the earliest of Asian producers to feature laminate-body guitars with solid wood tops. Initially, Alvarez guitars were built in Japan during the late 1960s, and distributed through St. Louis Music.

St. Louis Music also distributed the Electra and Westone brands of solid body electrics. St. Louis Music currently manufactures Crate and Ampeg amplifiers in the U.S., while Alvarez instruments are designed in St. Louis and produced overseas.

ACOUSTIC

All Alvarez acoustic steel string guitars (except models 5212, 5214 and 5216) have a stylized *double A* shell logo inlay and rosewood veneer on their pegheads. **Regent** series models are the entry level to the Alvarez line, and generally feature laminated tops, backs, and sides. **Artist** series

5004 Rosewood
courtesy Alvarez

models feature more exotic woods, and have shell and pearl inlay work. **Professional** series models have solid tops. The acoustic/electric **Fusion** series models currently feature the Alvarez System 500 bridge pickup/on-board EQ.

Artist Series

5002 MAHOGANY CLASSIC — classical style, laminated spruce top, round soundhole, bound body, wooden inlay rosette, mahogany back/sides, nato neck, 12/19 fret rosewood fingerboard, rosewood bridge, rosewood veneer on peghead, 3 per side gold tuners. Available in Natural finish. Disc. 1998.

$225 $125
Last Mfr.'s Sug. Retail was $410.

5004 ARTIST ROSEWOOD (Formerly ROSEWOOD CLASSIC) — similar to 5002, except has rosewood back/sides. Available in Natural finish. Current mfr.

Mfr.'s Sug. Retail	$579	$435	$285	$195

5014 ARTIST FOLK (Formerly MOUNTAIN FOLK) — folk style, laminated spruce top, round soundhole, multi-layer black/white body binding, black/white ring inlay rosette, tortoise pickguard, mahogany back/sides/neck, 14/20 fret rosewood fingerboard with pearl dot inlay, stylized bird wings inlay at 12th fret, rosewood bridge with white black dot pins, blackface peghead with pearl logo inlay, 3 per side chrome die cast tuners. Available in Sunburst finish. Mfr. 1995 to date.

Mfr.'s Sug. Retail	$479	$350	$235	$155

5019 MIDNIGHT SPECIAL — dreadnought style, laminated spruce top, round soundhole, multi-layer black/white body binding, abalone shell rosette, black pickguard, mahogany back/sides, nato neck, 14/20 fret rosewood fingerboard with pearl dot inlay, stylized bird wings inlay at 12th fret, rosewood bridge with white pearl dot pins, 3 per side chrome tuners. Available in Black finish. Current mfr.

Mfr.'s Sug. Retail	$629	$475	$300	$200

5020 MOUNTAIN DELUXE (Formerly MOUNTAIN) — dreadnought style, laminated spruce top, round soundhole, multi-layer black/white body binding, synthetic shell rosette, black pickguard, mahogany back/sides/neck, 14/20 fret rosewood fingerboard with pearl dot inlay/stylized bird wings inlay at 12th fret, rosewood bridge with black pearl dot pins, rosewood veneer on peghead, 3 per side chrome tuners. Available in Natural and Sunburst finishes. Mfr. 1991 to 1995, 1997 to date.

Mfr.'s Sug. Retail	$499	$375	$245	$160

5020 M — similar to 5020 Mountain, except has laminated mahogany top. Disc. 1995.

$215 $125
Last Mfr.'s Sug. Retail was $400.

5020 SB Mountain Deluxe Sunburst — similar to 5020 Mountain. Available in Sunburst finish. Current mfr.

Mfr.'s Sug. Retail	$499	$375	$245	$160

5021 — similar to 5020, except has a 12-string configuration, 6 per side tuners. Disc. 1993.

$215 $140
Last Mfr.'s Sug. Retail was $425.

5040 KOA — dreadnought style, laminated koa top, round soundhole, 3 stripe bound body and rosette, brown pickguard, koa back/sides, nato neck, 14/20 fret rosewood fingerboard with pearl dot inlay, stylized bird wings inlay at 12th fret, rosewood bridge with black pearl dot pins, koa veneer on peghead, 3 per side chrome tuners. Available in Natural finish. Disc. 1998.

$215 $140
Last Mfr.'s Sug. Retail was $500.

5043 BURGUNDY (Also BURGUNDY ARTIST) — dreadnought style, laminated oak top, round soundhole, multi bound body, abalone rosette, oak back/sides, mahogany neck, 20 fret rosewood fingerboard with pearl cross inlay, rosewood bridge with black white dot pins, oak peghead veneer with pearl logo inlay, 3 per side diecast tuners. Available in Burgundy Stain finish. Mfr. 1994 to date.

Mfr.'s Sug. Retail	$629	$475	$300	$215

5055 BLUESMAN — jumbo style, laminated spruce top, 2 f-holes, multi-bound body, mahogany back/sides/neck, 14/20 fret bound rosewood fingerboard with pearl dot inlay, stylized bird wings inlay at 12th fret, rosewood bridge with white black dot pins, blackface peghead with pearl logo inlay, 3 per side chrome die cast tuners. Available in Sunburst finish. Mfr. 1995 to date.

Mfr.'s Sug. Retail	$599	$450	$285	$175

5072 JUMBO (Also ARTIST JUMBO) — jumbo style, laminated spruce top, round soundhole, tortoise pickguard, abalone bound body/rosette, mahogany back/sides, 14/20 fret rosewood fingerboard with pearl dot inlay, stylized bird wings inlay at 12th fret, rosewood bridge with white black dot pins, rosewood peghead veneer with pearl logo inlay, 3 per side diecast tuners. Available in Natural finish. Mfr. 1994 to date.

Mfr.'s Sug. Retail	$619	$465	$300	$200

5220 C — single cutaway dreadnought style, spruce top, round soundhole, 3 stripe bound body and rosette, black pickguard, mahogany back/sides, nato neck, 20 fret rosewood fingerboard with pearl dot inlay, rosewood bridge with black pearl dot pins, 3 per side chrome tuners. Available in Natural finish. Disc. 1995.

$175 $115
Last Mfr.'s Sug. Retail was $350.

5224 — dreadnought style, solid spruce top, round soundhole, 5 stripe bound body/rosette, mahogany back/sides, nato neck, 14/20 fret rosewood fingerboard with dot inlay, rosewood bridge with white pearl dot pins, 3 per side chrome tuners. Available in Natural finish. Disc. 1988.

$240 $125
Last Mfr.'s Sug. Retail was $450.

5002 Mahogany
courtesy Alvarez

5055 Bluesman
courtesy Alvarez

Grading	100%	EXCELLENT	AVERAGE

5225 Rosewood — similar to the 5224, except features rosewood back/sides. Available in Natural finish. Mfr. 1981 to 1992.

	$250	$125

Last Mfr.'s Sug. Retail was $459.

5227 Rosewood Special — similar to the 5225, except has laminated spruce top. Disc. 1985.

	$175	$115

Last Mfr.'s Sug. Retail was $349.

5237 CURLY MAPLE — dreadnought style, laminated spruce top, round soundhole, 5 stripe bound body/rosette, curly maple back/sides, nato neck, 14/20 fret rosewood fingerboard with pearl dot inlay/stylized bird wings inlay at 12th fret, rosewood bridge with white pearl dot pins, 3 per side chrome tuners. Available in Sunburst finish. Disc. 1995.

	$250	$155

Last Mfr.'s Sug. Retail was $475.

AD 60 K ARTIST KOA — dreadnought style, koa top, round soundhole, black pickguard, ivory body, white pearl rosette, koa back/sides, mahogany neck, 14/20 fret bound rosewood fingerboard with stylized Alvarez *slash* inlay at 12th fret, rosewood bridge with white pearl dot pins, 3 per side chrome tuners. Available in Natural gloss finish. Mfr. 1998 to date.

Mfr.'s Sug. Retail	$579	$435	$285	$195

AJ 60-12 ARTIST MAPLE JUMBO 12-STRING — dreadnought style, koa top, round soundhole, black pickguard, ivory body, white pearl rosette, koa back/sides, mahogany neck, 14/20 fret bound rosewood fingerboard with stylized Alvarez *slash* inlay at 12th fret, rosewood bridge with white pearl dot pins, 3 per side chrome tuners. Available in Natural gloss finish. Mfr. 1998 to date.

Mfr.'s Sug. Retail	$599	$450	$300	$195

Professional Series

5009 PROFESSIONAL ROSEWOOD CLASSIC — classical style, solid spruce top, round soundhole, bound body, wooden inlay rosette, rosewood back/sides, nato neck, 19 fret rosewood fingerboard, rosewood bridge, rosewood veneer on peghead, 3 per side gold tuners. Available in Natural finish. Current mfr.

Mfr.'s Sug. Retail	$679	$500	$340	$225

5022 HERRINGBONE PROFESSIONAL (Formerly GLENBROOKE) — dreadnought style, solid spruce top, round soundhole, tortoise pickguard, herringbone bound body/rosette, rosewood back/sides, mahogany neck, 14/20 fret rosewood fingerboard with pearl dot inlay, stylized bird wings inlay at 12th fret, rosewood bridge with white pearl dot pins, rosewood peghead veneer with pearl logo inlay, 3 per side chrome tuners. Available in Natural finish. Current mfr.

Mfr.'s Sug. Retail	$649	$485	$325	$215

5028 MAHOGANY PRO — dreadnought style, solid spruce top, round soundhole, tortoise pickguard, black/white multi-layer bound body, black/white inlay rosette, mahogany back/sides/neck, 14/20 fret rosewood fingerboard with pearl dot inlay/stylized *bird wings* inlay at 12th fret, rosewood bridge with white pearl dot pins, 3 per side chrome tuners. Available in Natural satin finish. Current mfr.

Mfr.'s Sug. Retail	$499	$375	$245	$165

5030 TIMBERLINE SATIN — dreadnought style, solid spruce top, round soundhole, tortoise pickguard, black/white multi-layer bound body, abalone shell inlay rosette, mahogany back/sides/neck, 14/20 fret rosewood fingerboard with stylized *diamond* inlay at 12th fret, rosewood bridge with white pearl dot pins, 3 per side chrome tuners. Available in Natural satin finish. Current mfr.

Mfr.'s Sug. Retail	$619	$465	$300	$200

5031 Timberline — similar to the 5030 Timberline Satin. Available in Natural gloss finish. Current mfr.

Mfr.'s Sug. Retail	$649	$485	$325	$215

5032 TIMBER RIDGE — dreadnought style, solid spruce top, round soundhole, tortoise pickguard, wood body binding, wood inlay rosette, mahogany back/sides/neck, 14/20 fret rosewood fingerboard with pearl dot inlay, stylized bird wings inlay at 12th fret, rosewood bridge with white pearl dot pins, rosewood peghead veneer with pearl logo inlay, 3 per side chrome tuners. Available in Natural finish. Mfd. 1994 to 1998.

	$375	$215

Last Mfr.'s Sug. Retail was $640.

5037 WILDWOOD 12-STRING — dreadnought style, solid cedar top, round soundhole, 5 stripe bound body/rosette, mahogany back/sides, nato neck, 14/20 fret rosewood fingerboard with pearl dot inlay, 12th fret has stylized bird wings inlay, rosewood bridge with white black dot pins, rosewood veneer on peghead, 6 per side gold tuners with amber buttons. Available in Natural finish. Current mfr.

Mfr.'s Sug. Retail	$819	$625	$395	$265

In 1995, solid spruce top replaces original item.

5045 MOUNTAIN — dreadnought style, solid spruce top, round soundhole, wood body binding, wood inlay rosette, mahogany back/sides/neck, 14/20 fret rosewood fingerboard with pearl dot inlay, stylized bird wings inlay at 12th fret, rosewood bridge with white pearl dot pins, peghead logo decal, 3 per side chrome tuners. Available in Vintage satin finish. Disc. 1995.

	$265	$160

Last Mfr.'s Sug. Retail was $500.

5045 G Graphite Pro (Formerly 5045 G Mountain) — similar to 5045, except has wood herringbone body binding, graphite bridge. Mfr. 1996 to date.

Mfr.'s Sug. Retail	$599	$450	$295	$200

5022 Glenbrooke
courtesy Alvarez

Grading	100%	EXCELLENT	AVERAGE

5054 (GOLDEN CHORUS) — dreadnought style, solid spruce top, round soundhole, herringbone bound body and rosette, tortoise pickguard, rosewood back/sides, nato neck, 14/20 fret rosewood fingerboard with pearl dot inlay, 12th fret has stylized bird wings inlay, rosewood bridge with white pearl dot pins, rosewood veneer on peghead, 6 per side chrome tuners. Available in Natural finish. Disc. 1994.

		$300	$185

Last Mfr.'s Sug. Retail was $600.

5062 WILDWOOD (Also WILDWOOD NATURAL) — dreadnought style, solid spruce top, round soundhole, 5 stripe bound body/rosette, mahogany back/sides, nato neck, 14/20 fret rosewood fingerboard with pearl dot inlay, 12th fret has stylized bird wings inlay, rosewood bridge with white black dot pins, 3 per side chrome tuners. Available in Natural finish. Current mfr.

Mfr.'s Sug. Retail	$649	$495	$325	$215

5063 Wildwood Special — similar to 5062, except has gold tuners with amber buttons. Available in Natural finish. Disc. 1993.

		$215	$115

Last Mfr.'s Sug. Retail was $430.

5202 MAHOGANY — classical style, solid spruce top, round soundhole, bound body, wooden inlay rosette, African mahogany back/sides, nato neck, 19 fret rosewood fingerboard, rosewood bridge, rosewood veneer on peghead, 3 per side gold tuners. Available in Natural finish. Disc. 1997.

		$275	$165

Last Mfr.'s Sug. Retail was $525.

5224 MAHOGANY — dreadnought style, solid spruce top, round soundhole, 3 stripe bound body/rosette, black pickguard, mahogany back/sides, nato neck, 14/20 fret rosewood fingerboard with pearl dot inlay, rosewood bridge with black dot pins, rosewood veneer on peghead, 3 per side chrome tuners. Available in Natural finish. Disc. 1995.

		$240	$140

Last Mfr.'s Sug. Retail was $450.

5225 — similar to 5224, except has tiger rosewood back/sides, bound fingerboard, bound peghead. Disc. 1994.

		$250	$150

Last Mfr.'s Sug. Retail was $460.

6010 ELEGANCE SIGNATURE — dreadnought style, solid spruce top, round soundhole, multi-layer bound body, abalone rosette, mahogany back/sides/neck, 14/20 fret bound rosewood fingerboard with pearl *double A* inlay at 12th fret, rosewood bridge with white pearl dot pins, bound peghead with rosewood veneer/pearl logo inlay, 3 per side gold die cast tuners. Available in Natural finish. Mfd. 1995 to 1997.

		$425	$260

Last Mfr.'s Sug. Retail was $775.

6015 Elegance Rose — similar to the 6010, except features a solid mahogany back, multi-layer maple/rosewood body binding, tortoise pickguard, 14/20 fret rosewood fingerboard with pearl rose inlay at 12th fret, rosewood bridge with black pearl dot pins. Available in Natural semi-gloss finish. Mfr. 1995 to date.

Mfr.'s Sug. Retail	$999	$715	$270	$180

6020 C Elegance Cutaway — similar to the 6010, except features florentine cutaway body, Honduras mahogany back/sides, abalone shell body binding, 14/20 fret bound rosewood fingerboard with pearl inlay at 12th fret, rosewood bridge with black pearl dot pins, ornate pearl headstock inlay. Available in Natural gloss finish. Current mfr.

Mfr.'s Sug. Retail	$1,399	$715	$270	$180

PD 100 PROFESSIONAL DREADNOUGHT — dreadnought style, solid spruce top, round soundhole, abalone/ivory body binding, abalone rosette, black pickguard, rosewood back/sides, mahogany neck, 14/20 fret bound rosewood fingerboard with fancy pearl leaves/vine inlay, bound peghead, rosewood bridge with black abalone dot pins, 3 per side gold tuners. Available in Natural gloss finish.

Mfr.'s Sug. Retail	$899	$675	$450	$295

Regent Standard Series

5201 REGENT CLASSIC (Also 5201 CLASSIC) — classical style, laminated spruce top, round soundhole, black body binding, wood mosaic rosette, mahogany back/sides/neck, 12/19 fret rosewood fingerboard, rosewood bridge, 3 per side tuners with plastic buttons. Available in Vintage Stain finish. Mfr. 1994 to 1995, 1997 to date.

Mfr.'s Sug. Retail	$199	$150	$95	$65

Add $100 for **Model 5201 VP** (retail list $299).

5208 N — dreadnought style, laminated spruce top, round soundhole, bound body, 3 stripe rosette, black pickguard, mahogany back/sides/neck, 14/20 fret rosewood fingerboard with pearl dot inlay, rosewood bridge with black pins, 3 per side chrome tuners. Available in Natural finish. Mfd. 1995 to 1997.

		$135	$85

Last Mfr.'s Sug. Retail was $250.

5208 M — similar to 5208 N, except has laminated mahogany top. Mfd. 1995 to 1997.

		$120	$70

Last Mfr.'s Sug. Retail was $225.

5209 REGENT — dreadnought style, laminated spruce top, round soundhole, single layer black body binding, black/white ring rosette, tortoise pickguard, mahogany back/sides/neck, 14/20 fret rosewood fingerboard with dot inlay, rosewood bridge with black pins, 3 per side chrome tuners. Available in Natural gloss finish. Current mfr.

Mfr.'s Sug. Retail	$219	$165	$100	$75

Add $90 for **Model 5209 VP** (retail list $309).

5208 N
courtesy Alvarez

Grading	100%	EXCELLENT	AVERAGE

5210 SATIN — dreadnought style, laminated spruce top, round soundhole, bound body, 3 stripe rosette, tortoise pickguard, mahogany back/sides/neck, 14/20 fret rosewood fingerboard with pearl dot inlay, rosewood bridge with white pins, 3 per side chrome tuners. Available in Natural satin finish. Mfd. 1994 to 1997.

		$175	$100

Last Mfr.'s Sug. Retail was $335.

RD 20 REGENT STANDARD (Formerly 5212 REGENT SPECIAL) — dreadnought style, laminated spruce top, round soundhole, multi-layer black/white body binding, 3 stripe rosette, tortoise pickguard, mahogany back/sides/neck, 14/20 fret rosewood fingerboard with dot inlay, rosewood bridge with white pins, 3 per side chrome tuners. Available in Natural gloss and Sunburst finishes. Current mfr.

Mfr.'s Sug. Retail	$279	$200	$140	$95

In 1996, Sunburst finish was discontinued.
Add $90 for **Model RD 20 VP** (retail list $369).

RD 20 S Regent Standard Solid Top — similar to the RD 20, except has solid spruce top. Available in Natural gloss finish. Mfr. 1998 to date.

Mfr.'s Sug. Retail	$339	$255	$165	$115

RD 20-12 Regent Standard 12-String — similar to the RD 20, except has 12-string configuration, 6 per side tuners. Available in Natural gloss finish. Mfr. 1998 to date.

Mfr.'s Sug. Retail	$289	$215	$145	$100

5212 BK — similar to the 5212 Regent Special, except has black pickguard. Available in Black finish. Disc. 1997.

		$200	$120

Last Mfr.'s Sug. Retail was $380.

5216 FOLK — similar to 5212, except has parlor style (folk) body configuration. Disc. 1997.

		$140	$85

Last Mfr.'s Sug. Retail was $265.

Regent Deluxe Series

5003 ARTIST MAHOGANY — classical style, laminated spruce top, round soundhole, multi-layer black body, wood mosaic rosette, mahogany back/sides/neck, 12/19 fret rosewood fingerboard, rosewood bridge, slotted headstock, 3 per side tuners with plastic buttons. Available in Antique Natural gloss finish. Current mfr.

Mfr.'s Sug. Retail	$379	$285	$185	$125

5214 REGENT DELUXE — dreadnought style, spruce top, round soundhole, multi-layer black/white body binding, black/white ring rosette, black pickguard, mahogany back/sides/neck, 14/20 fret rosewood fingerboard with dot inlay, rosewood bridge with black pins, 3 per side chrome tuners. Available in Natural gloss finish. Current mfr.

Mfr.'s Sug. Retail	$399	$300	$195	$130

5214 12 Regent Deluxe 12-String — similar to 5214, except has 12-string configuration, 6 per side tuners. Current mfr.

Mfr.'s Sug. Retail	$579	$435	$285	$195

RD 30 BK REGENT DELUXE (BLACK), RD 30 SB REGENT DELUXE (SUNBURST) — dreadnought style, spruce top, round soundhole, multi-layer black/white body binding, black/white ring rosette, black pickguard, mahogany back/sides/neck, 14/20 fret rosewood fingerboard with dot inlay, rosewood bridge with black pins, 3 per side chrome tuners. Available in Gloss Black (**RD 30 BK**) and Sunburst (**RD 30 SB**) finish. Mfr. 1998 to date.

Mfr.'s Sug. Retail	$389	$295	$185	$125

RD 30 L Regent Deluxe Left Handed — similar to the RD 30 BK, except in left-handed configuration. Available in Natural gloss finish. Mfr. 1998 to date.

Mfr.'s Sug. Retail	$399	$300	$195	$130

RD 50 Regent Deluxe Rosewood — similar to the RD 30 BK, except has rosewood back/sides. Available in Natural gloss finish. Mfr. 1998 to date.

Mfr.'s Sug. Retail	$449	$325	$225	$150

RF 30 REGENT DELUXE FOLK — similar to RD 30 BK, except in folk body configuration. Available in Natural gloss finish. Mfr. 1998 to date.

Mfr.'s Sug. Retail	$379	$285	$185	$125

Silver Anniversary Series

2551 ROSEWOOD — dreadnought style, solid spruce top, round soundhole, 5 stripe bound body, abalone rosette, rosewood back/sides, mahogany neck, 14/20 fret rosewood fingerboard with pearl diamond inlay, rosewood bridge with white black dot pins, rosewood veneer on bound peghead with Silver Anniversary inlay, 3 per side chrome tuners. Available in Natural finish. Disc. 1997.

		$375	$225

Last Mfr.'s Sug. Retail was $650.

2551/12 12-String — similar to 2551 Rosewood, except has 12-string configuration, 6 on a side tuners. Disc. 1995.

		$425	$250

Last Mfr.'s Sug. Retail was $800.

2552 — dreadnought style, spruce top, round soundhole, 5 stripe bound body, abalone rosette, mahogany back/sides/neck, 14/20 fret rosewood fingerboard with pearl dot inlay, rosewood bridge with black white dot pins, rosewood veneer on peghead, 3 per side chrome tuners. Available in Natural finish. Disc. 1993.

		$225	$125

Last Mfr.'s Sug. Retail was $400.

5212 Regent Special
courtesy Alvarez

Grading		100%	EXCELLENT	AVERAGE

2555 JUMBO — jumbo style, florentine cutaway, laminated spruce top, round soundhole, 5 stripe bound body, abalone flake rosette, mahogany back/sides/neck, 21 fret rosewood fingerboard with abalone offset bar inlay, rosewood bridge with black white pins, rosewood veneer on bound peghead with Silver Anniversary inlay, 3 per side chrome tuners. Available in Natural and Sunburst finishes. Disc. 1995.

$550 $325
Last Mfr.'s Sug. Retail was $1,050.

This model was available with an Alvarez Bi-Phonic pickup system.

In 1995, Natural finish was discontinued.

2555 BK (Folk) — similar to the 2555, except has folk body configuration, single florentine cutaway, abalone body binding, abalone rosette. Available in Gloss Black finish. Mfd. 1994 only.

$450 $300
Last Mfr.'s Sug. Retail was $900.

ACOUSTIC ELECTRIC

Artist Series Acoustic Electric

5019 AV — dreadnought style, laminated spruce top, round soundhole, 5 stripe bound body, abalone inlay rosette, black pickguard, mahogany back/sides, nato neck, 14/20 fret rosewood fingerboard with pearl dot inlay/stylized bird wings inlay at 12th fret, rosewood bridge with white pearl dot pins, 3 per side chrome tuners, bridge pickup system, 3 band EQ. Available in Black finish. Mfd. 1994 only.

$425 $265
Last Mfr.'s Sug. Retail was $825.

This model is similar to Model 5019, with electronics.

5072 C BK
courtesy Alvarez

5020 C MOUNTAIN DELUXE CUTAWAY, 5020 C S MOUNTAIN DELUXE CUTAWAY — dreadnought style, single rounded cutaway body, spruce top, round soundhole, multi-layer black/white body binding, synthetic shell rosette, tortoise pickguard, mahogany back/sides/neck, 14/20 fret rosewood fingerboard with stylized *diamond* inlay at 12th fret, rosewood bridge with black pearl dot pins, 3 per side chrome tuners, bridge pickup system, volume/tone controls, System 500 electronics. Available in Natural (**Model 5020 C**) and Brown (**Model 5020 C S**) gloss finishes.

Mfr.'s Sug. Retail	$879	$675	$435	$295

5072 C BK (FUSION JUMBO) — single round cutaway jumbo style, laminated spruce top, round soundhole, multi bound body, abalone rosette, black pickguard, mahogany back/sides/neck, 20 fret rosewood fingerboard with pearl dot inlay/stylized bird wings inlay at 12th fret, rosewood bridge with white pearl dot pins, bound blackface peghead with abalone logo, 3 per side chrome die cast tuners, piezo bridge pickups, 3 band EQ, System 500 electronics. Available in Black finish. Mfr. 1995 to date.

Mfr.'s Sug. Retail	$979	$740	$495	$325

This model is similar to Model 5072 Jumbo, with electronics.

5088 C (FUSION DELUXE) — dreadnought style, single rounded cutaway, laminated spruce top, round soundhole, tortoise pickguard, 3 stripe bound body/rosette, mahogany back/sides/neck, 20 fret rosewood fingerboard with pearl dot inlay, pearl curlicue inlay at 12th fret, rosewood bridge with black white dot pins, pearl logo peghead inlay, 3 per side diecast tuners, piezo bridge pickups, 3 band EQ, System 500 electronics. Available in Natural finish. Mfr. 1994 to date.

Mfr.'s Sug. Retail	$929	$695	$450	$300

5088 C BK (Fusion Deluxe) — similar to 5088C, except has black pickguard, abalone flake rosette, white black dot bridge pins. Available in Black finish. Mfr. 1994 to date.

Mfr.'s Sug. Retail	$999	$755	$500	$335

This model was also available in a White finish with no pickguard (Model 5088 C WH). The White finish was discontinued in 1996.

5088/12 12-String — similar to 5088 C, except has 12-string configuration, 6 per side tuners. Mfd. 1994 only.

$435 $275
Last Mfr.'s Sug. Retail was $850.

AC 40 C ARTIST CUTAWAY CLASSIC — classical style, rounded cutaway body, spruce top, round soundhole, multi-layer black body binding, wood mosaic rosette, rosewood back/sides, mahogany neck, 12/19 fret rosewood fingerboard, rosewood bridge, 3 per side gold tuners with plastic buttons, piezo bridge pickups, 3 band EQ, System 500 electronics. Available in Natural gloss finish. Mfr. 1998 to date.

Mfr.'s Sug. Retail	$849	$650	$415	$285

Fusion Series Acoustic Electric

5008 C CLASSIC — classical style, single rounded cutaway, laminated spruce top, round soundhole, bound body, wooden inlay rosette, mahogany back/sides/neck, 19 fret rosewood fingerboard, rosewood wraparound bridge, rosewood peghead veneer with pearl logo inlay, 3 per side gold tuners with plastic buttons, piezo bridge pickups, 3 band EQ. Available in Natural finish. Mfd. 1994 only.

$485 $295
Last Mfr.'s Sug. Retail was $900.

5080 N FUSION DELUXE THINLINE (NATURAL) — dreadnought style, thinline rounded cutaway body, spruce top, round soundhole, multi-layer black/white body binding, abalone shell rosette, mahogany back/sides/neck, 20 fret rosewood fingerboard with pearl dot inlay/stylized bird wings inlay at 12th fret, rosewood bridge with black pearl dot pins, abalone logo peghead inlay, 3 per side chrome tuners, piezo bridge pickups, volume/tone controls, System 500 electronics. Available in Natural gloss finish. Current mfr.

Mfr.'s Sug. Retail	$779	$585	$375	$265

5088 C
courtesy Alvarez

5083 N
courtesy Alvarez

5220 CEQVS
courtesy Alvarez

Grading	100%	EXCELLENT	AVERAGE

5081 N Fusion Deluxe Thinline (Blue) — similar to 5080 N, except has flamed maple top, maple back/sides. Available in Transparent Blue gloss finish. Current mfr.

Mfr.'s Sug. Retail	$819	$600	$395	$265

5082 N — similar to 5080 N, except has laminated curly maple top, curly maple back and sides. Available in Transparent Violin finish. Disc. 1995.

	$400	$250

Last Mfr.'s Sug. Retail was $800.

5083 N Fusion Deluxe Thinline (Sunburst) — similar to 5080 N, except has flame maple top, maple back/sides. Available in Transparent Red gloss finish. Current mfr.

Mfr.'s Sug. Retail	$819	$600	$395	$265

In 1996, Sunburst finish replaced Transparent Red finish.

5084 N — similar to 5080 N. Available in Black gloss finish. Mfd. 1994 to 1996.

	$375	$235

Last Mfr.'s Sug. Retail was $750.

5220 C EQ FUSION STANDARD (Also 5220 C EQ CH, 5220 C EQ VS) — dreadnought style, single rounded cutaway body, spruce top, round soundhole, 3 stripe bound body and rosette, black pickguard, mahogany back/sides, nato neck, 20 fret rosewood fingerboard with pearl dot inlay, rosewood bridge with black pearl dot pins, 3 per side chrome tuners, bridge pickup system, 3 band EQ. Available in Natural finish. Current mfr.

Mfr.'s Sug. Retail	$699	$525	$340	$225

Add $50 for Cherry **(Model 5220 C EQ CH FUSION STANDARD)** or Sunburst **(Model 5220 C EQ VS FUSION STANDARD)** finishes.

This model was similar to the Model 5220 C, with electronics.

Professional Series Acoustic Electric

5086 WILDWOOD — single cutaway dreadnought style, solid spruce top, round soundhole, 5 stripe bound body/rosette, mahogany back/sides, nato neck, 14/20 fret rosewood fingerboard with pearl dot inlay, 12th fret has stylized bird wings inlay, rosewood bridge with white black dot pins, 3 per side gold tuners with amber buttons, and bi-phonic pickup system and controls. Available in Natural finish. Disc. 1995.

	$500	$275

Last Mfr.'s Sug. Retail was $950.

This model was similar to the model 5062, with electronics.

PC 50 C PROFESSIONAL CLASSIC — classical style, rounded cutaway body, solid spruce top, round soundhole, multi-layer black body binding, wood mosiac rosette, rosewood back/sides, mahogany neck, 12/19 fret rosewood fingerboard, rosewood bridge, slotted headstock, 3 per side gold tuners with plastic buttons, piezo bridge pickup, volume/tone controls, System 500 electronics. Available in Natural gloss finish. Mfr. 1998 to date.

Mfr.'s Sug. Retail	$999	$715	$270	$180

PF 90 C PROFESSIONAL FOLK CUTAWAY — folk style, single rounded cutaway body, solid spruce top, round soundhole, ivory/herringbone body binding, abalone rosette, rosewood back/sides, mahogany neck, 14/20 fret bound rosewood fingerboard with pearl *slash* inlay at 12th fret, rosewood bridge with white black dot pins, bound peghead, 3 per side chrome die cast tuners. Available in Natural gloss finish.

Mfr.'s Sug. Retail	$799	$600	$395	$265

Regent Standard Series Acoustic Electric

RD 20 C REGENT STANDARD CUTAWAY — dreadnought style, laminated spruce top, round soundhole, multi-layer black/white body binding, 3 stripe rosette, tortoise pickguard, mahogany back/sides/neck, 14/20 fret rosewood fingerboard with dot inlay, rosewood bridge with white pins, 3 per side chrome tuners, piezo bridge pickup, volume/tone controls, 3 band EQ. Available in Natural gloss finish. Current mfr.

Mfr.'s Sug. Retail	$389	$295	$195	$130

This model is similar to the Model RD 20, with electronics.

Regent Deluxe Series Acoustic Electric

RD 30 C REGENT DELUXE CUTAWAY — dreadnought style, single rounded cutaway body, spruce top, round soundhole, multi-layer black/white body binding, black/white ring rosette, black pickguard, mahogany back/sides/neck, 14/20 fret rosewood fingerboard with dot inlay, rosewood bridge with black pins, 3 per side chrome tuners, piezo bridge pickup, volume/tone controls, System 500 electronics. Available in Natural gloss finish. Mfr. 1998 to date.

Mfr.'s Sug. Retail	$549	$425	$265	$175

Willow Ridge Series Acoustic Electric

2531 — single round cutaway classical style, spruce top, round soundhole, wooden inlay rosette, bound body, mahogany back/sides/neck, 19 fret rosewood fingerboard, rosewood wraparound bridge, 3 per side chrome tuners with plastic buttons, piezo bridge pickups, 3 band EQ. Available in Natural finish. Mfd. 1994 only.

	$525	$325

Last Mfr.'s Sug. Retail was $1,050.

2532 — single round cutaway dreadnought style, spruce top, black pickguard, 3 stripe bound body/rosette, maple back/sides, mahogany neck, 22 fret rosewood fingerboard with pearl dot inlay, rosewood bridge with white black dot pins, 3 per side diecast tuners, piezo bridge pickups, 3 band EQ. Available in Natural finish. Disc. 1995.

	$550	$325

Last Mfr.'s Sug. Retail was $1,050.

2533 — similar to 2532, except has mahogany back/sides. Available in Natural finish. Disc. 1995.

	$525	$325

Last Mfr.'s Sug. Retail was $1,050.

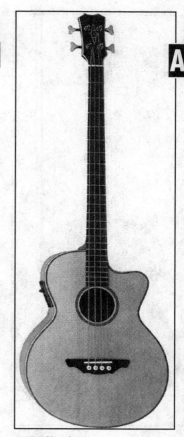

4070 Wildwood Bass
courtesy Alvarez

ACOUSTIC ELECTRIC BASS

Traditional Series

4070 ACOUSTIC BASS — single round jumbo style, laminated spruce top, round soundhole, 3 stripe bound body/rosette, mahogany back/sides/neck, 23 fret rosewood fingerboard, rosewood bridge with white black dot pins, bound rosewood peghead with pearl logo inlay, 2 per side diecast tuners, piezo bridge pickups, 3 band EQ. Available in Natural gloss finish. Mfr. 1994 to date.

Mfr.'s Sug. Retail	$1,149	$875	$575	$385

Add $50 for Black finish (**Model 4070 BK**).

In 1996, Black finish was discontinued.

ALVAREZ YAIRI

Instruments built in Japan from 1966 to date. Current production is based in Kani, Japan. Distributed by in the U.S. by St. Louis Music of St. Louis, Missouri.

These handcrafted guitars are built by craftsmen under the direction of luthier/designer Kazuo Yairi. Yairi, who learned to construct violins and guitars from his father, started his own company to produce handmade guitars in larger quantities.

Alvarez Yairi acoustics were imported to the U.S. starting in 1966, and were exclusively distributed by St. Louis Music. Alvarez Yairi instruments are now a division of Alvarez and St. Louis Music. These quality acoustic guitars are designed by both luthier Yairi in Japan and the designers at St. Louis Music. Instruments are both adjusted at the Alvarez Yairi factory in Japan, and re-inspected after shipping at St. Louis Music before delivery to dealers.

ACOUSTIC

All Alvarez Yairi acoustic steel string guitars have abalone or pearl peghead logo inlay.

All Alvarez Yairi models may be purchased with Alvarez Natural Response or System 500 pickups.
Add $110 for installed BP Natural Response pickup (without volume/tone control).
Add $135 for installed BT Natural Response pickup (with volume/tone control).
Add $300 for installed System 500 pickup.

FY 40 CAROLINA FOLK — dreadnought *clinched waist* style, solid Canadian spruce top, round soundhole, ivoroid/wood bound top and back, 3 stripe rosette, mahogany back/sides/neck, 14/20 fret rosewood fingerboard with snowflake inlay, rosewood bridge, rosewood headstock veneer, 3 per side chrome tuners. Available in Natural finish. Mfd. circa mid 1970s.

$450 $300

JY 10 NASHVILLE JUMBO — jumbo style, solid spruce top, round soundhole, tortoise pickguard, ivoroid bound body, abalone purfling/rosette, maple back/sides, mahogany neck, 14/20 fret rosewood fingerboard with pearl dot inlay, 12th fret pearl curlicue inlay, ebony bridge with white black dot pins, ebony veneered bound peghead, 3 per side gold tuners. Available in Sunburst finish. Mfd. 1994 to 1998.

$775 $450
Last Mfr.'s Sug. Retail was $1,400.

Classic Series

All classical guitars have rosewood veneer on their pegheads.

CY 110 MAHOGANY CLASSIC — classical style, solid cedar top, round soundhole, black multi-ply body binding, wooden mosaic rosette, Honduran mahogany back/sides, mahogany neck, 12/19 fret rosewood fingerboard, rosewood bridge, slotted headstock, 3 per side gold tuners with pearloid buttons. Available in Natural semi-satin finish. Current mfr.

Mfr.'s Sug. Retail	$899	$675	$465	$300

CY 116 BURLED (Formerly CY116 LA GRANJA) — classical style, solid cedar top, round soundhole, maple body binding, wooden mosaic rosette, burled mahogany back/sides, mahogany neck, 12/19 fret ebony fingerboard, rosewood bridge, rosewood veneer headstock, slotted headstock, 3 per side gold tuners with pearloid buttons. Available in Antique gloss finish. Mfr. 1975 to date.

Mfr.'s Sug. Retail	$1,199	$925	$640	$415

CY 118 Jacaranda — similar to CY 116, except has jacaranda back/sides, wood multi-layer body binding. Current mfr.

Mfr.'s Sug. Retail	$1,299	$975	$675	$450

CY 125 EL LORCA — classical style, solid cedar top, round soundhole, wooden inlay rosette and stripe on headstock, three stripe bound body, rosewood sides, rosewood bookmatched back, mahogany neck, 12/19 fret ebony fingerboard, rosewood bridge and headstock veneer, 3 per side gold tuners with pearloid buttons. Available in Natural finish. Mfd. circa mid 1970s.

$450 $300

CY 130 CONQUISTADOR — classical style, cedar top, round soundhole, wooden inlay rosette, 3 stripe bound body, rosewood sides, 2 piece rosewood back, mahogany neck/headstock, 12/19 fret ebony fingerboard, carved headstock design, rosewood bridge, 3 per side gold tuners with pearloid buttons. Available in Natural finish. Mfd. circa mid 1970s.

$500 $375

CY 132 C Conquistador Cutaway — similar to the CY 130 Conquistador, except has single *stepped down* cutaway. Mfd. circa mid 1970s.

$450 $325

CY 118 Jacaranda
courtesy Alvarez Yairi

Grading	100%	EXCELLENT	AVERAGE

CY 135 CONCERT MASTER — classical style, Canadian cedar top, round soundhole, wooden inlay bound body and rosette, jacaranda sides, jacaranda bookmatched back, mahogany neck/headstock, 12/19 fret ebony fingerboard, ebony bridge, 3 per side gold tuners with pearloid buttons. Available in Natural finish. Mfd. circa mid 1970s.

		$550	$400

CY 140 CONCERT MASTER (Formerly CY 140 GRAND CONCERT MASTER) — classical style, solid cedar top, round soundhole, multi-layer wood body binding, wood mosaic rosette, jacaranda back/sides, mahogany neck, 12/19 fret ebony fingerboard, rosewood bridge, slotted headstock, 3 per side gold tuners with pearl buttons. Available in Antique Natural gloss finish. Mfd. circa mid 1970s to date.

Mfr.'s Sug. Retail	$1,549	$1,150	$825	$550

Dreadnought Series

DY 50 N — dreadnought style, cedar top, round soundhole, 3 stripe bound body, abalone rosette, tortoise pickguard, jacaranda back/sides, mahogany neck, 14/20 fret bound rosewood fingerboard with abalone diamond inlay, rosewood bridge with white pearl dot pins, rosewood veneer on bound peghead, 3 per side gold tuners. Available in Natural finish. Mfd. 1991 to 1995.

		$650	$395

Last Mfr.'s Sug. Retail was $1,275.

DY 51 BLUE RIDGE — dreadnought style, solid cedar top, round soundhole, ivoroid bound body, herringbone rosette, burled mahogany back/sides, nato mahogany neck, 14/20 fret ebony fingerboard with snowflake inlay, ebony bridge, burled mahogany headstock veneer, mother-of-pearl headstock inlay, 3 per side chrome tuners. Available in Natural finish. Mfd. circa mid 1970s.

		$445	$300

DY 52 SILVER LARK — dreadnought style, solid Canadian spruce top, round soundhole, white maple bound body, herringbone rosette, walnut pickguard, walnut back/sides, mahogany neck, 14/20 fret ebony fingerboard with snowflake inlay, ebony bridge, mother-of-pearl headstock inlay, walnut veneer on peghead, 3 per side chrome tuners. Available in Natural finish. Mfd. circa mid 1970s.

		$490	$350

This model had a solid oboncol wood pickguard (adhesive backed for optional installation) available.

DY 53 SILVER HARP — dreadnought style, solid Canadian spruce top, round soundhole, white maple bound body, herringbone rosette, burled mahogany back/sides, nato mahogany neck, 14/20 fret ebony fingerboard with snowflake inlay, ebony bridge, mother-of-pearl headstock inlay, 3 per side chrome tuners. Available in Natural satin finish. Mfd. circa mid 1970s.

		$495	$300

This model had a solid oboncol wood pickguard (adhesive backed for optional installation) available.

DY 53 N — jumbo style, spruce top, round soundhole, 5 stripe bound body and rosette, tortoise pickguard, rosewood back/sides, mahogany neck, 14/20 fret bound rosewood fingerboard with pearl block inlay, rosewood bridge with white pearl dot pins, rosewood veneer on bound peghead, 3 per side chrome tuners. Available in Natural finish. Mfd. 1991 to 1995.

		$575	$350

Last Mfr.'s Sug. Retail was $1,100.

In 1994, coral rosewood back/sides replaced original item.

DY 54 SILVER FAWN — dreadnought style, solid Canadian spruce top, round soundhole, maple bound body, turquoise/wood rosette, oboncol back/sides, nato mahogany neck, 14/20 fret black ebony fingerboard with snowflake inlay, ebony bridge, rosewood inlay on lower body bout, mother-of-pearl headstock inlay, 3 per side chrome tuners. Available in Natural finish. Mfd. circa mid 1970s.

		$475	$325

This model had a solid oboncol wood pickguard (adhesive backed for optional installation) available.

DY 57 WINCHESTER DREADNOUGHT — dreadnought style, solid Canadian spruce top, round soundhole, ivoroid/wood marquetry bound body, herringbone rosette, mahogany back/sides, nato mahogany neck, 14/20 fret ebony fingerboard with dot inlay, ebony bridge, 3 per side chrome tuners. Available in Natural finish. Mfd. circa mid 1970s.

		$425	$250

DY 58 DREADNOUGHT NINE — dreadnought style, solid Canadian spruce top, round soundhole, ivoroid bound body, wood inlay rosette, mahogany back/sides/neck, 14/20 fret ebony fingerboard with pearl dot inlay, ebony bridge, mahogany headstock veneer, tortoiseshell pickguard, 3 + 6 per side chrome tuners. Available in Natural finish. Mfd. circa mid 1970s.

		$485	$325

This nine-stringed guitar combines three single bass-side strings with three pairs of treble strings. This model will also function as a six string acoustic.

DY 68 RAMBLING TWELVE — dreadnought style, solid Canadian spruce top, round soundhole, wood inlay bound body, wood inlay rosette, mahogany back/sides/neck, 14/20 fret ebony fingerboard with pearl dot inlay, ebony bridge, mahogany headstock veneer, abalone logo inlay on headstock, tortoiseshell pickguard, 6 per side chrome tuners, abalone inlays on bridge pins. Available in Natural finish. Mfd. circa mid 1970s.

		$485	$300

DY 75 — dreadnought style, spruce top, round soundhole, wooden inlay bound body/rosette, tortoise pickguard, rosewood back/sides, mahogany neck, 14/20 fret rosewood fingerboard with pearl dot inlay, Direct Coupled rosewood bridge, rosewood veneer on bound peghead, 3 per side chrome tuners. Available in Natural finish. Mfd. 1991 to 1995.

		$700	$425

Last Mfr.'s Sug. Retail was $1,300.

The original design circa mid 1970s featured a bound ebony fingerboard with abalone dot inlays and ebony bridge (DY75 LEXINGTON DREADNOUGHT).

Grading	100%	EXCELLENT	AVERAGE

A

DY 76 HERRINGBONE TWELVE — dreadnought style, solid Canadian spruce top, round soundhole, ivoroid bound body, 3 stripe wood rosette, rosewood back/sides/neck, 14/20 fret ebony fingerboard with snowflake inlay, ebony bridge, rosewood headstock veneer, abalone logo inlay on headstock, tortoiseshell pickguard, 6 per side chrome tuners, abalone inlays on bridge pins. Available in Natural finish. Mfd. circa mid 1970s.

$465 $315

DY 77 N — dreadnought style, solid spruce top, round soundhole, herringbone bound body/rosette, tortoise pickguard, rosewood back/sides, mahogany neck, 14/20 fret ebony fingerboard with abalone diamond inlay, rosewood Direct Coupled bridge, rosewood veneer on bound peghead, 3 per side chrome tuners. Available in Natural finish. Mfd. 1991 to 1995.

$625 $375

Last Mfr.'s Sug. Retail was $1,200.

DY 78 HERRINGBONE TRI-BACK — dreadnought style, Canadian spruce top, round soundhole, herringbone bound body, herringbone rosette, burled thuya pickguard, rosewood sides, three piece rosewood/mahogany/rosewood back, mahogany neck, 14/20 fret ebony fingerboard with pearl snowflake inlay, ebony bridge, burled thuya veneer on peghead, 3 per side chrome tuners. Available in Natural finish. Mfd. circa mid 1970s.

$525 $325

DY 85 STANDARD ABALONE — dreadnought style, Canadian spruce top, round soundhole, abalone and celluloid bound body and soundhole, black pickguard, burled mahogany sides, three piece burled mahogany/rosewood/burled mahogany back, nato mahogany neck, 14/20 fret ebony fingerboard with abalone inlay, ebony bridge, internal lacquering, 3 per side gold Grover tuners. Available in Natural finish. Mfd. circa mid 1970s.

$625 $350

DY 87 JUMBO DOUBLE NECK — dreadnought style, solid Canadian spruce top, shared oval soundhole, celluloid bound body, wood inlay rosette, mahogany back/sides, mahogany necks, 14/20 fret ebony fingerboard with snowflake inlay, double ebony bridge, black headstocks, 3 per side headstock (6 string), 6 per side headstock (12 string), chrome tuners. Available in Natural finish. Mfd. circa mid 1970s.

$625 $400

DY 90 — dreadnought style, solid spruce top, round soundhole, abalone bound body and rosette, black pickguard with Alvarez Yairi logo in abalone, rosewood back/sides, mahogany neck, 14/20 fret bound ebony fingerboard with abalone diamond inlay, abalone bound ebony bridge with black pearl dot pins, rosewood peghead veneer with abalone logo inlay, 3 per side gold tuners. Available in Natural finish. Mfd. circa mid 1970s to 1995.

$790 $475

Last Mfr.'s Sug. Retail was $1,475.

The original design featured a jacaranda three piece back, jacaranda sides, Canadian spruce top, and internal lacquering as well as the abalone appointments (DY90 SUPER ABALONE).

DY 92 LUTE BACK — dreadnought style, spruce top, round soundhole, herringbone bound body and rosette, 33 piece mahogany/rosewood/maple lute style rounded back, 14/20 fret bound ebony fingerboard with pearl dot inlay, ebony bridge with black pearl dot pins, 3 per side gold tuners. Available in Natural finish. Mfr. circa 1975 to 1993.

$1,475 $900

Last Mfr.'s Sug. Retail was $2,775.

The DY 92 was produced in limited quanities.

DY 96 ABALONE SUPREME — dreadnought style, Canadian spruce top, round soundhole, abalone bound body and rosette, bookmatched jacaranda back with inlaid middle strip of marquetry, jacaranda sides, abalone bound jacaranda pickguard, 14/20 fret abalone bound ebony fingerboard with abalone diamond shaped inlays, ebony bridge with abalone inlay, 3 per side gold tuners, abalone bound headstock. Available in Natural finish. Mfr. circa mid 1970s.

$750 $475

Innovative Series

DY 52 CANYON CREEK — dreadnought style, solid spruce top, round soundhole, 3 stripe body binding, shell rosette, tortoise pickguard, rosewood back/sides, mahogany neck, 14/20 fret rosewood fingerboard with pearl dot inlay/12th fret pearl snowflake inlay, Direct Coupled ebony bridge with black pearl dot pins, rosewood veneer on peghead, 3 per side chrome tuners. Available in Natural gloss finish. Mfr. 1991 to date.

Mfr.'s Sug. Retail	$1,249	$950	$650	$425

In 1994, coral rosewood back/sides replaced original item.

DY 80 Canyon Creek 12-String — similar to the DY 52, except has 12-string configuration, 6 per side chrome tuners. Available in Natural gloss finish. Mfr. 1991 to date.

Mfr.'s Sug. Retail	$1,299	$975	$650	$435

DY 70 MAPLE GRAPHITE — dreadnought style, solid spruce top, round soundhole, tortoise shell bound body/rosette, flamed maple back/sides, mahogany neck, 14/20 fret rosewood fingerboard with pearl dot inlay/12th fret pearl curlicue inlay, graphite bridge with black abalone dot pins, graphite peghead veneer with pearl logo inlay, 3 per side chrome tuners. Available in Natural gloss finish. Mfr. 1994 to date.

Mfr.'s Sug. Retail	$1,099	$825	$570	$385

DY 71 Koa Graphite — similar to DY 70, except has tortoise pickguard, tortoise shell/ivory body binding, koa back/sides, graphite bridge/bridge plate. Current mfr.

Mfr.'s Sug. Retail	$1,149	$875	$575	$390

Signature Series

All Signature models have Kazuo Yairi's signature on them.

DY52 Canyon Creek
courtesy Alvarez Yairi

A

Grading	100%	EXCELLENT	AVERAGE

AY 20 SIGNATURE — concert style, solid cedar top, round soundhole, wood bound body, abalone rosette, walnut back/sides, mahogany neck, 14/20 fret rosewood fingerboard, 12th fret abalone diamond/slash inlay, rosewood bridge with black abalone dot pins, walnut peghead veneer with abalone logo inlay, 3 per side gold tuners. Available in Natural finish. Mfd. 1994 to 1998.

		$700	$450

Last Mfr.'s Sug. Retail was $1,250.

DY 61 SIGNATURE — dreadnought style, solid cedar top, round soundhole, maple/wood body binding, abalone shell rosette, burled mahogany back/sides, mahogany neck, 14/20 fret ebony fingerboard/12th fret pearl diamond/abalone slash inlay, rosewood bridge with black abalone dot pins, burl mahogany veneer on peghead with abalone/wooden strip inlays, abalone logo peghead inlay, 3 per side gold tuners with amber buttons. Available in Natural semi-satin finish. Mfr. 1991 to date.

Mfr.'s Sug. Retail	$1,499	$1,124	$750	$500

In 1994, burled mahogany back/sides replaced original item.

DY 69 — similar to DY 61, except has spruce top, tortoise pickguard, wooden inlay rosette, burled mahogany back/sides, upper belly bridge with white abalone dot pins. Mfd. 1994 only.

		$725	$450

Last Mfr.'s Sug. Retail was $1,350.

DY 72 12-String — similar to DY 61, except has 12 strings and rosewood veneer on peghead. Disc. 1997.

		$665	$400

Last Mfr.'s Sug. Retail was $1,275.

YM 1 YAIRI MASTER MAHOGANY — dreadnought style, solid cedar top, multi-layer wood body binding, abalone shell rosette, solid mahogany back/sides, mahogany neck, 14/20 fret rosewood fingerboard, 12th fret abalone stripe/pearl cross inlay, rosewood bridge with black pearl dot pins, ebony veneered peghead with pearl logo inlay, 3 per side gold die cast tuners. Available in Natural semi-satin finish. Mfr. 1995 to date.

Mfr.'s Sug. Retail	$1,399	$1,100	$725	$475

YM 2 Yairi Master Ovangkol — similar to the YM 1, except features solid spruce top, solid ovangkol back/sides. Current mfr.

Mfr.'s Sug. Retail	$1,499	$1,150	$750	$500

Traditional Series

DY 38 WOOD RIDGE — dreadnought style, solid spruce top, round soundhole, 3 stripe body binding, 5 stripe rosette, black pickguard, mahogany back/sides/neck, 14/20 fret rosewood fingerboard with pearl dot inlay/12th fret has pearl snowflake inlay, rosewood bridge with black white dot pins, 3 per side chrome tuners. Available in Natural gloss finish. Mfr. 1991 to date.

Mfr.'s Sug. Retail	$899	$675	$465	$300

In 1996, flamed maple back/sides replaced mahogany back/sides.

DY 45 WOOD RIDGE SUNBURST (Formerly DY WOOD RIDGE VINTAGE, DY 45 VINTAGE DREADNOUGHT) — dreadnought style, solid spruce top, round soundhole, 3 stripe body binding, 5 stripe rosette, black pickguard, mahogany back/sides/neck, 14/20 fret rosewood fingerboard with pearl dot inlay/12th fret has pearl snowflake inlay at 12th fret, ebony bridge with black white dot pins, 3 per side chrome tuners. Available in Dark Satin Antique finish. Mfr. 1975 to date.

Mfr.'s Sug. Retail	$899	$675	$465	$300

In 1996, Sunburst mahogany finish replaced Dark Satin Antique finish.

DY 46 Gloss Vintage Dreadnought — similar to the DY45 Vintage Dreadnought, except had gloss finish. Mfd. circa mid 1970s.

		$400	$250

DY 74 WELLINGTON — dreadnought style, solid spruce top, round soundhole, 5 stripe bound body and rosette, tortoise pickguard, rosewood back/sides, mahogany neck, 14/20 fret ebony fingerboard with varying pearl inlay, ebony bridge with white pearl dot pins, rosewood veneer on peghead, 3 per side chrome tuners. Available in Natural gloss finish. Mfr. circa 1975 to date.

Mfr.'s Sug. Retail	$1,219	$975	$615	$425

The original design circa mid 1970s featured an ebony fingerboard and bridge, and jacaranda veneer peghead (DY74 WELLINGTON ROSEWOOD).

DY 74 C (Formerly DY74 C Wellington Cutaway) — similar to DY74, except has single rounded cutaway. Mfr. circa 1975 to date.

Mfr.'s Sug. Retail	$1,319	$1,000	$650	$435

DY 74 S Wellington Sunburst — similar to DY74 Wellington Rosewood, except has brown sunburst finish. Mfr. circa mid 1970s.

		$550	$325

DC 1 Virtuoso
courtesy Alvarez Yairi

Grading	100%	EXCELLENT	AVERAGE

DY 91 ADVANCED KOA (Also DELUXE KOA) — dreadnought style, solid spruce top, round soundhole, abalone bound body and rosette, flamed koa back/sides, black pickguard with Alvarez Yairi logo in abalone, mahogany neck, 14/20 fret bound ebony fingerboard with abalone diamond inlay, abalone bound ebony bridge with black pearl dot pins, koa peghead veneer with abalone logo inlay, 3 per side gold tuners. Available in Natural gloss finish. Mfr. 1994 to date.

Mfr.'s Sug. Retail	$1,749	$1,300	$850	$585

Virtuoso Series

DC 1 VIRTUOSO 12-STRING — rounded shoulder dreadnought style, solid spruce top, round soundhole, ivoroid bound body, herringbone purfling/rosette, Indian rosewood back/sides, mahogany neck, 12/19 fret ebony fingerboard with pearl cross/elispe inlay, ebony bridge with white pearl dot pins, tortoise pickguard, ebony veneered peghead with pearl logo inlay, 6 per side chrome die cast tuners. Available in Natural gloss finish. Mfr. 1995 to date.

Mfr.'s Sug. Retail	$1,599	$1,200	$825	$550

GY 2 (VIRTUOSO DELUXE) — single round cutaway jumbo style, solid spruce top, round soundhole, tortoise pickguard, ivoroid bound body, abalone purfling/rosette, lacewood back/sides, mahogany neck, 20 fret bound ebony fingerboard with pearl dot inlay, 12th fret pearl curlicue inlay, abalone bound ebony bridge, rosewood veneered peghead with pearl logo inlay, 3 per side gold die cast tuners. Available in Natural finish. Mfd. 1995 to 1997.

		$1,000	$625

Last Mfr.'s Sug. Retail was $2,000.

This instrument was co-designed with Jerry Garcia.

ACOUSTIC ELECTRIC

Classic Series Acoustic Electric

CY 127 CE CUTAWAY CLASSIC — shallow depth classical style body, rounded cutaway, solid cedar top, round soundhole, multi-layer wood body binding, wood mosaic rosette, rosewood back/sides, mahogany neck, 12/19 fret ebony fingerboard, rosewood bridge, slotted headstock, 3 per side gold tuners with pearloid buttons, Alvarez Natural Response pickup system and volume/tone control. Available in Natural gloss finish. Mfr. 1991 to date.

Mfr.'s Sug. Retail	$1,399	$1,050	$675	$450

GY 2 Virtuoso
courtesy Alvarez Yairi

Custom Series Acoustic Electric

YC 1 CUSTOM CUTAWAY (NYLON STRING) — sloped rounded cutaway body, solid spruce top, round soundhole, multi-layer tortoise body binding, turquoise rosette, rosewood back/sides, mahogany neck, 12/20 fret ebony fingerboard with turquoise inlay, rosewood bridge, slotted headstock, 3 per side gold tuners with pearloid buttons, piezo bridge pickup, volume/tone controls, System 500 electronics. Available in Natural gloss finish. Current mfr.

Mfr.'s Sug. Retail	$1,899	$1,425	$900	$625

YC 2 Custom Cutaway (Steel String) — similar to the YC 1, except features graphite bridge, solid headstock, 3 per side gold tuners. Available in Natural gloss finish. Current mfr.

Mfr.'s Sug. Retail	$1,899	$1,425	$900	$625

Dreadnought Series Acoustic Electric

DY 45 AV — dreadnought style, solid spruce top, round soundhole, 3 stripe bound body, 5 stripe rosette, black pickguard, mahogany back/sides/neck, 14/20 fret rosewood fingerboard with pearl dot inlay, 12th fret has pearl snowflake inlay at 12th fret, ebony bridge with black white dot pins, 3 per side chrome tuners, piezo bridge pickup, 3 band EQ. Available in Dark Satin Antique finish. Mfd. 1994 only.

		$575	$350

Last Mfr.'s Sug. Retail was $1,075.

This model is similar to DY45, with electronics.

DY 50 NEQ — dreadnought style, cedar top, round soundhole, 3 stripe bound body, abalone rosette, tortoise pickguard, jacaranda back/sides, mahogany neck, 14/20 fret bound rosewood fingerboard with abalone diamond inlay, rosewood bridge with white pearl dot pins, rosewood veneer on bound peghead, 3 per side gold tuners, piezo bridge pickup, 3 band EQ. Available in Natural finish. Mfd. 1994 only.

		$825	$500

Last Mfr.'s Sug. Retail was $1,575.

This model is similar to DY50 N, with electronics.

DY 77 NEQ — dreadnought style, solid spruce top, round soundhole, herringbone bound body/rosette, tortoise pickguard, rosewood back/sides, mahogany neck, 14/20 fret ebony fingerboard with abalone diamond inlay, rosewood Direct Coupled bridge, rosewood veneer on bound peghead, 3 per side chrome tuners, piezo bridge pickup, 3 band EQ. Available in Natural finish. Mfd. 1994 only.

		$795	$465

Last Mfr.'s Sug. Retail was $1,500.

This model is similar to DY77 N, with electronics.

Express Series Acoustic Electric

DY 87 — dreadnought style, rounded cutaway body, curly maple top, round soundhole, 5 stripe bound body and rosette, maple back/sides, mahogany neck, 21 fret ebony fingerboard with pearl dot inlay, 12th fret has pearl snowflake inlay, ebony bridge with white abalone dot pins, 3 per side chrome tuners, bridge pickup, 3 band EQ. Available in Transparent Black finish. Mfd. 1991 to 1995.

		$775	$500

Last Mfr.'s Sug. Retail was $1,450.

Grading	100%	EXCELLENT	AVERAGE

DY 87/12 — similar to DY87, except has 12 strings, 6 per side tuners. Available in Violin Sunburst finish. Mfd. 1991 to 1995.

	$850	**$500**

Last Mfr.'s Sug. Retail was $1,575.

Fusion Series Acoustic Electric

The DY 88 Express Pro was renamed the Fusion Series in 1998.

DY 88 BK ADVANCED ACOUSTIC ELECTRIC (Formerly DY 88 EXPRESS PRO) — dreadnought style, rounded cutaway *Closed Chamber* body, spruce top, abalone/ivory body binding, mahogany back/sides/neck, 23 fret ebony fingerboard with pearl dot inlay/pearl snowflake inlay on 12th fret, ebony bridge with white abalone dot pins, 3 per side gold tuners, Hexaphonic piezo bridge pickup, System 500 electronics. Available in Gloss Black finish. Mfr. 1991 to 1997, 1998 to date.

Mfr.'s Sug. Retail	$1,799	$1,350	$850	$595

In 1998, a spruce top and mahogany back and sides replaced the original curly maple top and maple back and sides.

DY 88 BK 12 Advanced Acoustic Electric (Formerly DY 88/12 Express Pro) — similar to DY 88 BK, except has 12-string configuration, 6 per side gold tuners. Available in Gloss Black finish. Mfr. 1991 to date.

Mfr.'s Sug. Retail	$1,949	$1,450	$950	$650

DY 88 PW Advanced Acoustic Electric — similar to DY 88 BK. Available in Gloss White finish. Mfr. 1998 to date.

Mfr.'s Sug. Retail	$1,799	$1,350	$850	$595

SY 88 BK Advanced Acoustic Electric — similar to DY 88 BK, except features a thinline body, small *Closed Chamber* body, ivory body binding. Available in Gloss Black finish. Mfr. 1998 to date.

Mfr.'s Sug. Retail	$1,449	$1,100	$725	$495

Innovative Series Acoustic Electric

YB 1 BARITONE — jumbo style, solid spruce top, round soundhole, 5 stripe body binding, shell rosette, rosewood back/sides, mahogany neck, 14/20 fret ebony fingerboard, ebony bridge with white abalone dot pins, 3 per side gold tuners, piezo bridge pickup, volume/tone controls, System 500 electronics. Available in Natural gloss finish. Current mfr.

Mfr.'s Sug. Retail	$1,899	$1,425	$900	$625

Signature Series Acoustic Electric

All Signature models have Kazuo Yairi's signature on them.

AYL 1 LUTHIER CUTAWAY — dreadnought style, rounded cutaway body, solid spruce top, round soundhole, synthetic tortoise body binding, abalone shell rosette, mahogany back/sides/neck, 14/20 fret rosewood fingerboard/12th fret pearl diamond/abalone slash inlay, rosewood bridge with black abalone dot pins, 3 per side gold tuners, piezo bridge pickup, volume/tone controls, System 500 electronics. Available in Natural semi-gloss finish. Current mfr.

Mfr.'s Sug. Retail	$1,549	$1,150	$750	$525

DY 62 SIGNATURE CUTAWAY — dreadnought style, rounded cutaway body, solid cedar top, round soundhole, maple body binding, abalone shell rosette, burled mahogany back/sides, mahogany neck, 14/20 fret rosewood fingerboard/12th fret pearl diamond/abalone slash inlay, rosewood bridge with black abalone dot pins, burl mahogany veneer on peghead with abalone/wooden strip inlays, abalone logo peghead inlay, 3 per side gold tuners with amber buttons, piezo bridge pickup, volume/tone controls, System 500 electronics. Available in Natural semi-satin finish. Mfd. 1991 to date.

Mfr.'s Sug. Retail	$1,649	$1,225	$825	$550

This model is similar to DY61, with electronics.

Traditional Series Acoustic Electric

DY 38 C CUTAWAY — dreadnought style, sloped rounded cutaway body, solid spruce top, round soundhole, 3 stripe body binding, 5 stripe rosette, black pickguard, flamed maple back/sides, mahogany neck, 14/20 fret rosewood fingerboard with pearl dot inlay/12th fret has pearl snowflake inlay, rosewood bridge with black white dot pins, 3 per side chrome tuners. Available in Natural gloss finish. Mfr. 1991 to date.

Mfr.'s Sug. Retail	$1,249	$950	$625	$425

This model is similar to the DY 38, with electronics.

DY 74 CEQ (Also DY 74 CEQ1) — dreadnought style, rounded cutaway body, solid spruce top, round soundhole, 5 stripe body binding/rosette, tortoise pickguard, rosewood back/sides, mahogany neck, 14/20 fret ebony fingerboard with varying pearl inlay, ebony bridge with white pearl dot pins, rosewood veneer on peghead, 3 per side chrome tuners, piezo bridge pickups, 3 band EQ/System 500 electronics. Available in Natural gloss finish. Mfr. 1995 to date.

Mfr.'s Sug. Retail	$1,449	$1,100	$725	$495

This model is similar to DY74, with electronics.

Virtuoso Series Acoustic Electric

GY 1 — dreadnought style, rounded cutaway body, solid spruce top, round soundhole, 5 stripe bound body and rosette, tortoise pickguard, rosewood back/sides, mahogany neck, 20 fret bound ebony fingerboard with varied abalone inlay, rosewood bridge with white abalone dot pins, rosewood veneer on bound peghead with pearl tulip inlay, 3 per side gold tuners, bridge pickup, 3 band EQ. Available in Natural finish. Mfd. 1991 to 1996.

	$850	**$525**

Last Mfr.'s Sug. Retail was $1,700.

This model was co-designed with Jerry Garcia.

Grading	100%	EXCELLENT	AVERAGE

WY 1 VIRTUOSO WEIR — jumbo style, rounded cutaway body, solid cedar top, round soundhole, multi-layer wood body binding, abalone shell rosette, rosewood back/sides, mahogany neck, 14/20 fret ebony fingerboard/12th fret has pearl diamond/abalone slash inlay, Direct Coupled ebony bridge with black abalone dot pins, rosewood veneer on peghead with abalone and wooden strip inlays, 3 per side gold tuners, piezo bridge pickup, 3 band EQ/System 500 electronics. Available in Natural semi-satin finish. Mfr. 1991 to date.

Mfr.'s Sug. Retail	$1,699	$1,275	$825	$550

In 1994, folk style body replaced original item.

This model was co-designed with Bob Weir.

WY 1 BK Virtuoso Weir (Black) — similar to WY1 Virtuoso (folk style body), except features solid spruce top, abalone shell body binding. Available in Gloss Black finish. Mfr. 1995 to date.

Mfr.'s Sug. Retail	$1,699	$1,275	$825	$550

WY 1 12 Virtuoso Weir 12-String — similar to WY1 Virtuoso (folk style body), except has 12-string configuration, 6 per side tuners. Available in Natural Semi-satin finish. Mfr. 1996 to date.

Mfr.'s Sug. Retail	$1,849	$1,395	$900	$625

WY 1 K Koa — similar to WY1 Virtuoso (folk style body), except features koa top/back/sides, abalone rosette, abalone body binding, fingerboard dot inlay, snowflake bridge inlay. Available in Natural Gloss finish. Mfr. 1998 to date.

Mfr.'s Sug. Retail	$1,789	$1,350	$875	$595

WY 1 SB Sunburst — similar to WY1 Virtuoso (folk style body), except features maple back/sides, abalone rosette, abalone body binding, fingerboard dot inlay. Available in Sunburst finish. Mfr. 1998 to date.

Mfr.'s Sug. Retail	$1,789	$1,350	$875	$595

AMADA

Instruments currently produced in Luby, Czech Republic. Distributed by Geneva International Corporation of Wheeling, Illinois.

Amada classical guitars and mandolins (as well as Lidl orchestra instruments) are made by Strunal Manufacture of Luby. These guitars are available in five fractional sizes for the younger entry level student. Amada believes that fitting the right size guitar to the physical size of the student aids in the learning curve, as opposed to younger students struggling with a full sized guitar.

The fractional scale runs from 1/4, 1/2, 3/4, 7/8, up to full size. The scale lengths range from 17" (1/4 size), to 20 1/4" (1/2 size), 24" (3/4 size), 24 1/2" (7/8 size), up to 25 1/2" (Full size). Corresponding metric measurements run from 440 mm to 650 mm.

Models are offered in oak or mahogany back and sides, and are available in a high gloss or matte Natural finish.

WY 1 Virtuoso
courtesy Alvarez Yairi

ACOUSTIC

Classical Nylon String Series

All the models in Amada's Classical Nylon string series have a spruce top, round soundhole, classical style slotted headstock, 3 per side tuners, and tied bridge.

MODEL 4635 (4/4 Size) — spruce top, 25 1/2" scale, oak back/sides, rosewood fingerboard, rosewood bridge. Available in Natural high gloss finish. Current mfr.
Mfr.'s Sug. Retail $240

Model 4635 PM (4/4 Size) — similar to the Model 4635. Available in Natural matte finish. Current mfr.
Mfr.'s Sug. Retail $232

MODEL 4655 (4/4 Size) — spruce top, 25 1/2" scale, mahogany back/sides, rosewood fingerboard, rosewood bridge. Available in Natural high gloss finish. Current mfr.
Mfr.'s Sug. Retail $240

Model 4655 PM (4/4 Size) — similar to the Model 4655. Available in Natural matte finish. Current mfr.
Mfr.'s Sug. Retail $232

MODEL 5432 (7/8 Size) — spruce top, 24 1/2" scale, oak back/sides, rosewood fingerboard, rosewood bridge. Available in Natural high gloss finish. Current mfr.
Mfr.'s Sug. Retail $198

Model 5432 PM (7/8 Size) — similar to the Model 5432. Available in Natural matte finish. Current mfr.
Mfr.'s Sug. Retail $190

MODEL 5452 (7/8 Size) — spruce top, 24 1/2" scale, mahogany back/sides, rosewood fingerboard, rosewood bridge. Available in Natural high gloss finish. Current mfr.
Mfr.'s Sug. Retail $198

Model 5452 PM (7/8 Size) — similar to the Model 5452. Available in Natural matte finish. Current mfr.
Mfr.'s Sug. Retail $190

MODEL 5437 (3/4 Size) — spruce top, 22 1/2" scale, oak back/sides, rosewood fingerboard, rosewood bridge. Available in Natural high gloss finish. Current mfr.
Mfr.'s Sug. Retail $192

Model 5437 PM (3/4 Size) — similar to the Model 5437. Available in Natural matte finish. Current mfr.
Mfr.'s Sug. Retail $184

A

MODEL 5457 PM (3/4 Size) — spruce top, 22 1/2" scale, mahogany back/sides, rosewood fingerboard, rosewood bridge. Available in Natural matte finish. Current mfr.
Mfr.'s Sug. Retail $184

MODEL 5433 (1/2 Size) — spruce top, 21" scale, oak back/sides, rosewood fingerboard, rosewood bridge. Available in Natural high gloss finish. Current mfr.
Mfr.'s Sug. Retail $190

Model 5433 PM (1/2 Size) — similar to the Model 5433. Available in Natural matte finish. Current mfr.
Mfr.'s Sug. Retail $182

MODEL 5453 (1/2 Size) — spruce top, 21" scale, mahogany back/sides, rosewood fingerboard, rosewood bridge. Available in Natural high gloss finish. Current mfr.
Mfr.'s Sug. Retail $190

Model 5453 PM (1/2 Size) — similar to the Model 5453. Available in Natural matte finish. Current mfr.
Mfr.'s Sug. Retail $182

MODEL 5434 (1/4 Size) — spruce top, 17" scale, oak back/sides, rosewood fingerboard, rosewood bridge. Available in Natural high gloss finish. Current mfr.
Mfr.'s Sug. Retail $184

MODEL 4735 (4/4 Size) — solid cedar top, 25 1/2" scale, oak back/sides, rosewood fingerboard, rosewood bridge. Available in Natural high gloss finish. Current mfr.
Mfr.'s Sug. Retail $342

Model 4735 PM (4/4 Size) — similar to the Model 4735. Available in Natural matte finish. Current mfr.
Mfr.'s Sug. Retail $332

MODEL 4755 (4/4 Size) — solid cedar top, 25 1/2" scale, mahogany back/sides, rosewood fingerboard, rosewood bridge. Available in Natural high gloss finish. Current mfr.
Mfr.'s Sug. Retail $342

Model 4755 PM (4/4 Size) — similar to the Model 4755. Available in Natural matte finish. Current mfr.
Mfr.'s Sug. Retail $332

MODEL 5732 (7/8 Size) — solid cedar top, 24 1/2" scale, oak back/sides, rosewood fingerboard, rosewood bridge. Available in Natural high gloss finish. Current mfr.
Mfr.'s Sug. Retail $342

MODEL 5752 (7/8 Size) — solid cedar top, 24 1/2" scale, mahogany back/sides, rosewood fingerboard, rosewood bridge. Available in Natural high gloss finish. Current mfr.
Mfr.'s Sug. Retail $342

MODEL 5737 (3/4 Size) — solid cedar top, 22 1/2" scale, oak back/sides, rosewood fingerboard, rosewood bridge. Available in Natural high gloss finish. Current mfr.
Mfr.'s Sug. Retail $342

MODEL 5757 (3/4 Size) — solid cedar top, 22 1/2" scale, mahogany back/sides, rosewood fingerboard, rosewood bridge. Available in Natural high gloss finish. Current mfr.
Mfr.'s Sug. Retail $342

MODEL 8010 (4/4 Size) — solid spruce top, 25 1/2" scale, beechwood back/sides. Available in Natural high gloss finish. Current mfr.
Mfr.'s Sug. Retail $179

MODEL 8011 (3/4 Size) — solid spruce top, 24" scale, beechwood back/sides. Available in Natural high gloss finish. Current mfr.
Mfr.'s Sug. Retail $159

MODEL 8012 (1/2 Size) — solid spruce top, 20 1/4" scale, beechwood back/sides. Available in Natural high gloss finish. Current mfr.
Mfr.'s Sug. Retail $139

6-String Archtop
courtesy Dale Unger

AMALIO BURGUET

Instruments currently produced in Spain. Distributed by Saga Musical Instruments of San Francisco, California.

Amalio Burguet acoustics are offered in the classical and flamenco configurations. Handmade in Spain, these guitars feature a solid cedar or solid spruce top, mahogany neck, rosewood or ebony fingerboard, rosewood bridge, an inlaid marquetry rosette, clear high gloss finish, gold-plated tuners, and a slotted 3 per side headstock. Models feature rosewood, walnut, mahogany, cypress, or sycamore back and sides.

AMERICAN ACOUSTECH

Instruments currently produced in Rochester, New York.

American Acoustech is currently producing guitar models. For further information, please contact American Acoustech via the Index of Current Manufacturers located in the back of this edition.

AMERICAN ARCHTOP

Instruments built in Stroudsburg, Pennsylvania since 1996.

Dale Unger is currently handcrafting archtop guitars designed by Robert Benedetto. Unger, a former apprentice to Benedetto for four years, grew up in the Nazareth, Pennsylvania area, and recalls building *Martin-style flat top acoustics during the 1970s!* His twenty-plus years building guitars part-time was a great backround for the four years working and studying with Benedetto.

Grading	100%	EXCELLENT	AVERAGE

7-String Archtop
courtesy Dale Unger

ACOUSTIC

All of Unger's archtops are available in a 16" or 17" wide body, and a depth of 2 5/8" or 3". Bodies have a single cutaway, and feature solid maple sides and matching maple neck. The 21 fret fingerboard, bridge, fingerrest, and tailpiece are all made of solid ebony. Scale length is 25". Models feature black Schaller tuning machines, Natural or Blonde finishes, and are available with or without binding. Unger also offers the option of floating or built-in Benedetto pickups.

Add $50 for tone control on a suspended pickup.

Add $50 for ebony tuning buttons.

Add $150 for built-in humbucker pickup with volume and tone controls.

Add $250 for name inlayed on tailpiece.

Add $300 for Violin finish.

The **American Dream** model with laminated maple top and back is available in 6- or 7-string configurations, with the retail price of $2,950. This model is also offered with a laminated German spruce top and European flamed maple back for $3,950.

The **American Legend** features voiced top and back plates of solid German spruce (top) and flamed European maple (back). Suggested list price is $5,950. The new **American Collector Series** model lists at $8,000 (contact Unger for specifications).

Unger's top of the line **The American** (suggested list price is $12,500) has special design inlays and hand-voiced top and back plates of select aged woods.

AMIGO

Instruments currently manufactured in Europe. Distributed by Midco International of Effingham, Illinois.

Amigo acoustic guitars are designed and priced with students and entry level players in mind.

ACOUSTIC

The Amigo line of classical guitars features two 1/2 scale guitars. The **AM 10** steel string ($79.95) and the **AM 15** nylon string ($79.95) models both feature spruce tops and maple backs and sides. The **AM 10** has a sunburst finish; the **AM 15** features a solid spruce top.

Amigo offers two 3/4 scale guitars. The **AM 20** steel string ($109) and **AM 30** nylon string ($109) models again both feature spruce tops and maple backs and sides. The **AM 20** has a sunburst finish; the **AM 30** has a natural solid spruce top.

There are two full sized acoustics in the Amigo line: the **AM 40** classical ($149) has a natural-amber laminate top, and beech back and sides. The **AM 50** classical ($169) has a solid spruce top and maple back and sides.

ANDERSEN STRINGED INSTRUMENTS

Instruments built in Seattle, Washington since 1978. Instruments are available through luthier Steven Andersen, and Pioneer Music (Portland, Oregon).

Luthier Steven Andersen built his first guitar in 1973, and has earned his living solely as a guitar maker since 1978. Andersen specializes in custom building to meet the player's needs. Working alone, Andersen builds two or three instruments at a time, generally completing sixteen to eighteen a year. Andersen guitars have been sold across the U.S., as well as in a dozen countries around the world. Although Steven Andersen doesn't actively pursue the endorsements of famous musicians, he has been fortunate in having a number of well known players purchase his instruments (Steve Miller, Bill Frisell, and mandolinist Sam Bush).

Andersen currently features six different archtop guitar models, and one flattop acoustic model. The Concert model flattop guitar ($3,500) is offered with numerous top/sides/back tone wood options. In addition to his guitar models, Andersen also builds A-Style mandolins ($3,000), A-Style mandolas ($3,300), and mandocellos ($4,000).

ACOUSTIC ARCHTOP

Andersen archtop guitars all share certain specifications. The body depth is three inches, and the scale lengths available are either 24.9" or 25.4". The soundboard is crafted of either Engelman or Sitka spruce. The back, sides and neck are highly figured maple; and the pickguard, bridge, fretboard and peghead face are ebony. The instrument's tailpiece is a graphite composite with an ebony veneer. The archtops are finished in Amber Blonde or Clear Blonde. Andersen does offer several options on various models, as well as suggestions for floating pickups. The base price also includes a standard hardshell case.

While work backlog is around twenty months, a delivery date will be confirmed when an order is placed. For those who prefer to purchase a guitar without the wait, Andersen occasionally has completed guitars available for sale (call for information).

Add $200 for left-handed configuration.

Add $300 for Sunburst finish.

Add $500 for Adirondack Spruce soundboard.

Add $600 for 7-string configuration.

Add $1,000 to $4,000 for Brazilian rosewood.

The **Emerald City** ($8,500) and **Metropolitan** ($7,500) are the most ornate members of the Andersen family of archtop guitars. The designs are reminiscent of the Art Deco style popular in the 1930s and 1940s. Construction details include hand engraved mother-of-pearl inlays, ivoroid binding around the body, f-holes, neck and and peghead; and the most highly figured maple for the back, sides, and neck. The Emerald City is available in either a 17" or 18" body width, and the Metropolitan is only available in a 17" body width. The Metropolitan was designed in collaboration with vintage guitar enthusiasts John G. Stewart and K. C. Wait.

The **Emerald City Reserve** ($11,000) is a limited edition model built with rare woods reserved especially for this model. Wood combinations include a European spruce top and European maple back, or an Adirondack spruce top with a 90-year-old one piece American maple back. Further model specifications will be supplied by Andersen.

The **Model 17** ($6,000) and the **Model 18** ($6,200) are elegant in their simplicity. The Model 17 has a 17" body width, and the Model 18 has an 18" body width. By using a minimal amount of inlay and decoration, Andersen is able to build a guitar whose design and materials are first class, yet at a price somewhat less than the more ornate instruments. Body, f-holes, neck and peghead are bound in ivoroid.

The **Oval Hole Archtop** model ($5,200) is designed as an archtop with a warmer sound than a traditional model. Andersen feels that the oval soundhole allows the guitar to sustain more than an f-hole top. The overall design of this model is intended to make the guitar as lightweight and resonant as possible.

Andersen's newest model is the **Model 14** Archtop guitar ($5,500). The Model 14 is designed as an option for guitarist who travel on airplanes. Due to space consideration, and the tightening of regulations regarding "carry-on" luggage, Andersen devised an archtop guitar that is full sized where it needs to be, and reduced where the designs allows. Thus, the scale length (25.4"), neck size and shape, and bridge/soundboard design retain their usual size. The body and peghead size then are reduced: the body width is 14", and the depth is 2" (or 2.5"). Pickup choices range from Armstrong, Bartolini, or EMG. Andersen collaborated with guitarist Bill Frisell on this new electrified archtop model.

ANGELICA

Instruments built in Japan from circa 1967 to 1975.

The Angelica trademark is a brandname used by UK importers Boosey & Hawkes on these entry level guitars and basses based on classic American designs. Some of the original designs produced for Angelica are actually better in quality.

(Source: Tony Bacon and Paul Day, The Guru's Guitar Guide)

Angelica instruments were not distributed to the U.S. market. Some models may be encountered on the Eastern Seaboard, but the average price for these guitars ranges around $100 to $150.

ANGELO

Instruments produced in Thailand. Distributed by T. Angelo Industrial Co., Ltd., of Bangkok, Thailand.

Don't let the Thailand address fool you - the T. Angelo Industrial company is building credible acoustic and electric guitar models based on classic American designs. The prices are in the entry to intermediate players range, with acoustic retailing between $185 to $260, acoustic/electrics ranging from $499 to $595. The **A'50** and **A'60 Vintage** Strat-ish models fall between $450 to $545. Hot-rodded modern designs with locking tremolo systems run a bit higher ($540 to $675).

ANGUS

Instruments built in Laguna Beach, California since the mid 1970s.

Luthier Mark Angus built his first guitar over two decades ago, and combines his many years as a player and craftsman to deliver an exceptionally versatile instrument. Angus currently works full time as head of the repair department at the Guitar Shoppe in Laguna Beach, California, and builds between six to eight guitars a year. The Guitar Shoppe, which is owned by Kirk Sand (see SAND GUITARS) and Jim Matthews, produces some of the finest custom instruments built today as well as being one of the premier repair facilities on the West Coast.

ACOUSTIC

Angus guitars are handcrafted instruments consisting of Honduran mahogany necks, Engleman, Sitka or European spruce bodies, Indian Rosewood back and sides, and an ebony fretboard. These custom guitars come in many shapes and sizes, including one model with a seven piece back of maple and rosewood. Prices run between $2,000 and $3,000 per instrument on the average. For further information, contact luthier Angus via the Index of Current Manufacturers listed in the back of this book.

ANTARES

Instruments manufactured in Korea. Distributed in the U.S. market by Vega Musical Instruments (VMI) Industries of Brea, California.

Antares guitars are designed for entry level musicians and guitar students. Designs range from a six string classical model, to six string steel string models of various finishes and even a twelve string model. Advertised prices start at $100 and up. VMI also supplies student level 10 and 20 watt guitar amplifiers under the "Animal" trademark.

ANTONIO ESTEBAN

Instruments currently produced in Spain.

Antonio Esteban classical guitars are currently available in the European market. **Models 10** and **30** are constructed with mahogany (bubinga on **Model 20**) bodies, Canadian cedar tops, and palisander fingerboards and bridges. The top of the line **Model 40** has a palisander body, and ebony fingerboard. Antonio Esteban also offers a Flamenco model (**Model 40 F**) with tap plates and a palisander fingerboard.

ANTONIO LORCA

Instruments currently built in Spain. Distributed in the U.S. market by David Perry Guitar Imports.

Antonio Lorca Guitars feature solid cedar tops on flamenco style acoustics. Student models begin at $369, recital models begin at $529, and concert level guitars begin at $599 (prices quoted are 1996 retail, current retail prices may differ). For additional information, please contact David Perry Guitar Imports through the index of Current Manfacturers located in the back of this edition.

APOLLONIO GUITARS

Instruments currently built in Rockport, Maine.

Luthier Nick Appollonio, a musician interested in Celtic music, estimates that he has built about 600 stringed instruments such as lutes, louds, mandolins, mandocellos, and guitars. Prices vary on the commissioned works.

APPLAUSE

Instruments manufactured in Korea from 1980 to date. Distributed by the Kaman Music Corporation of Bloomfield, Connecticut.

Applause guitars were originally produced in New Hartford, Connecticut from 1975 to 1979.

The Applause instruments were originally designed to be the entry level version of the Ovation guitars. In 1975, the new line of guitars was first offered to Ovation dealers as the "Ovation Medallion". A year later, models under the Applause trademark were offered to Kaman distributors. The Medallion name ran into some trademark claim problems, and was changed to

AA 35
courtesy Applause

Matrix. Matrix "Applauses" carried a list price of $249. In 1983, The Ovation Celebrity (also Korean, with U.S. produced synthetic backs) was introduced, again serving as an entry point to Ovation guitars.

Applause instruments feature the same guitar design and synthetic "bowl back" that the American built Ovations possess. While engineered and manufactured with the same attention to quality, production of these models overseas is Kaman's key to offering good quality guitars for players on a budget.

Applause guitars are offered in acoustic and acoustic/electric models. The acoustic/electrics offer similar under-the-saddle piezoelectric systems with volume and tone controls as the Ovation guitars. Models encoded with an "AA" are Applause Acoustics, while an "AE" denotes an Applause Electric. The "AN" code indicates an Applause Nylon string model.

ACOUSTIC

All Applause instruments feature a solid Walnut bridge, Sitka spruce top (some models may be laminated tops), Ping tuning machines, a steel reinforced truss rod, and solid mahogany neck, mother-of-pearl inlay dots.

Grading	100%	EXCELLENT	AVERAGE

All models are available in a Natural finish; some models may also be Black, White, Brownburst, "Barnboard" (enhanced grain), and Purpleburst.

AA 12 — 1/2 size single round cutaway, 3 stripe bound body/rosette, mini bowl, 20 fret bound fingerboard with pearl dot inlay, 3 per side tuners. Available in Natural finish. Current mfr.

Mfr.'s Sug. Retail	$260	$200	$115	$80

AA 13 — similar to AA 12, except has 3/4 size body. Current mfr.

Mfr.'s Sug. Retail	$280	$225	$125	$90

AA 31 — dreadnought style, black pickguard, 5 stripe bound body/rosette, deep bowl, 14/20 fret fingerboard with pearl dot inlay, body matching peghead, 3 per side tuners. Available in Barnboard, Brownburst and Natural finishes. Current mfr.

Mfr.'s Sug. Retail	$310	$250	$145	$100

AA 33 — classic style, bound body, decal rosette, deep bowl, 12/19 fret fingerboard, wraparound walnut bridge, 3 per side gold tuners. Available in Natural finish. Current mfr.

Mfr.'s Sug. Retail	$310	$250	$145	$100

AA 35 — dreadnought style, black pickguard, 5 stripe bound body/rosette, deep bowl, 14/20 fret fingerboard with pearl dot inlay, 6 per side tuners. Available in Black and Natural finishes. Current mfr.

Mfr.'s Sug. Retail	$390	$315	$175	$125

ACOUSTIC ELECTRIC

AE 32 — dreadnought style, black pickguard, 5 stripe bound body/rosette, deep bowl, 14/20 fret bound fingerboard with pearl diamond inlay, 3 per side tuners. Available in Natural finish. Current mfr.

Mfr.'s Sug. Retail	$390	$315	$175	$125

AE 34 — single round cutaway classic style, bound body, decal rosette, shallow bowl, 12/19 fret fingerboard, wraparound walnut bridge, 3 per side gold tuners. Available in Natural finish. Current mfr.

Mfr.'s Sug. Retail	$430	$350	$195	$140

AE 35 — dreadnought style, black pickguard, 5 stripe bound body/rosette, deep bowl, 14/20 fret fingerboard with pearl dot inlay, 6 per side tuners. Available in Black and Natural finishes. Current mfr.

Mfr.'s Sug. Retail	$470	$375	$190	$155

AE 36 — dreadnought style, black pickguard, 5 stripe bound body/rosette, deep bowl, 14/20 fret bound fingerboard with pearl diamond inlay, 3 per side tuners. Available in Barnboard, Brownburst, Natural and White finishes. Current mfr.

Mfr.'s Sug. Retail	$410	$325	$165	$135

AE 38 — dreadnought style, black pickguard, 5 stripe bound body/rosette, shallow bowl, 14/20 fret bound fingerboard with pearl diamond inlay, 3 per side tuners. Available in Barnboard, Black, Brownburst, Natural, Purpleburst and White finishes. Current mfr.

Mfr.'s Sug. Retail	$450	$360	$195	$145

ACOUSTIC ELECTRIC BASS

AE 40 — single round cutaway dreadnought style, Sitka spruce top, round soundhole, 5 stripe bound body/rosette, deep bowl, mahogany neck, 19 fret walnut fingerboard with pearl dot inlay, strings thru walnut bridge, logo decal on peghead, 2 per side chrome tuners. Available in Black and Natural finishes. Current mfr.

Mfr.'s Sug. Retail	$490	$395	$205	$160

AE 40F — similar to AE 40, except features a fretless neck. Current mfr.

Mfr.'s Sug. Retail	$515	$415	$215	$160

ARBITER

Instruments built in Japan during the mid 1960s to late 1970s.

The ARBITER trademark is the brand of a UK importer. Original models are of entry level quality, later models are good quality copy designs and some original designs.

(Source: Tony Bacon and Paul Day, The Guru's Guitar Guide)

ARBOR

Instruments currently manufactured in Asia. Distributed in the U.S. by Midco International of Effingham, Illinois.

AE 32
courtesy Applause

AE 36
courtesy Applause

Grading	100%	EXCELLENT	AVERAGE

Arbor guitars are aimed at the entry level student to the intermediate player. The Midco International company has been importing and distributing both acoustic and solid body guitars to the U.S. market for a good number of years, and now offers a five-year warranty on their acoustic guitar line.

Model coding carries an A for an acoustic model. The double digits after the prefix (such as A30) indicates a regular acoustic, and triple digits following the prefix (like A700) for acoustic/electric models.

ACOUSTIC

Unless specified otherwise, Acoustic models feature a dreadnought body size, mahogany neck, sides and back, rosewood fingerboard with dot position markers, rosewood bridge, 3+3 headstock, and chromed tuning machines.

A 12 — spruce top, 12-string configuration, black pickguard. Available in natural finish. Current mfr.

Mfr.'s Sug. Retail	$300	$225	$135	$95

A 19 — spruce top, black multiple binding on top and back. Available in natural finish. Mfr. 1997 to date.

Mfr.'s Sug. Retail	$230	$175	$110	$80

A 20 — spruce top, mahogany back and sides, black pickguard. Available in natural finish. Current mfr.

Mfr.'s Sug. Retail	$260	$195	$120	$85

This model is also available in a left-handed configuration (A 20L) for the same retail price.

A 29 — spruce top, mahogany back and sides, bound fingerboard, white multiple binding on top and back, center marquetry stripe on back. Available in natural finish. Mfr. 1997 to date.

Mfr.'s Sug. Retail	$260	$195	$120	$85

A 30 — spruce top, mahogany back and sides, black pickguard. Available in gloss black finish. Current mfr.

Mfr.'s Sug. Retail	$270	$225	$130	$90

This model is also available in a white finish as model A 45.

A 39 C — concert size classical body, spruce top, mahogany back and sides, multiple binding on top and back, center marquetry stripe on back, chrome butterfly button tuning machines. Available in natural finish. Mfr. 1997 to date.

Mfr.'s Sug. Retail	$230	$175	$110	$80

A 40 — spruce top, mahogany back and sides, black pickguard. Available in tobacco burst finish. Current mfr.

Mfr.'s Sug. Retail	$270	$225	$130	$90

A 60 — jumbo body, spruce top, ovancol back and sides, black pickguard. Available in natural finish. Current mfr.

Mfr.'s Sug. Retail	$460	$350	$225	$150

Arbor by Washburn Series

AW 1 N — concert size body, spruce top, mahogany back and sides, rosewood fingerboard and bridge. Available in natural finish. Current mfr.

Mfr.'s Sug. Retail	$270	$225	$130	$90

AW 2 N — dreadnought body, select spruce top, mahogany back and sides, rosewood fingerboard and bridge. Available in natural finish. Current mfr.

Mfr.'s Sug. Retail	$300	$225	$135	$95

AW 3 — dreadnought body, select spruce top, mahogany back and sides, rosewood fingerboard and bridge, die cast tuning machines. Available in natural finish. Current mfr.

Mfr.'s Sug. Retail	$350	$275	$175	$125

AW 5 S — dreadnought body, solid spruce top, scalloped spruce bracing, mahogany back and sides, rosewood fingerboard and bridge, Grover tuning machines. Available in natural finish. Current mfr.

Mfr.'s Sug. Retail	$480	$350	$225	$150

AW 6 S — dreadnought body, solid spruce top, scalloped spruce bracing, ovankol back and sides, rosewood fingerboard and bridge, Grover tuning machines. Available in natural finish. Current mfr.

Mfr.'s Sug. Retail	$520	$395	$250	$175

ACOUSTIC ELECTRIC

All acoustic/electric models have a single rounded cutaway, chromed tuning machines, rosewood fingerboards and bridges, and piezo pickups.

A 20 E — dreadnought non-cutaway body, spruce top, mahogany back and sides, black pickguard, 1 volume/1 tone controls. Available in natural finish. Current mfr.

Mfr.'s Sug. Retail	$300	$225	$135	$100

A 600 — spruce top, nato back and sides, hardwood fingerboard with white dot position markers, hardwood bridge, piezo pickup, black pickguard, 1 volume/1 tone controls. Available in natural finish. Current mfr.

Mfr.'s Sug. Retail	$340	$250	$150	$100

Add $10 for Tobaccoburst (A 600TB) or Wine Red (A 600WR).

A 800 CS — slim dreadnought body, curly maple top, mahogany back and sides, rosewood fingerboard with white dot and diamond position markers, rosewood bridge, gold hardware, piezo pickup, 4 band EQ preamp, volume slider. Available in cherry burst finish. Current mfr.

Mfr.'s Sug. Retail	$520	$395	$250	$175

This model is also available in a Transparent Black finish (A 800TBK).

Grading	100%	EXCELLENT	AVERAGE

Arbor by Washburn Acoustic/Electric Series

AW 2 CE — dreadnought body with single cutaway, select spruce top, mahogany back and sides, rosewood fingerboard and bridge, active electronic pickup system. Available in natural finish. Current mfr.

Mfr.'s Sug. Retail	$430	$325	$200	$150

 This model is also available in a Gloss Black finish (Model AW 2 CEB).

AW 3 CE — dreadnought body with single cutaway, select spruce top, mahogany back and sides, rosewood fingerboard and bridge, die cast tuning machines, active electronic pickup system. Available in natural finish. Current mfr.

Mfr.'s Sug. Retail	$500	$375	$225	$150

ACOUSTIC ELECTRIC BASS

A 100 — spruce top, mahogany back and sides, multiple binding, piezo pickup, 2 per side headstock, 1 volume/1 tone controls. Available in natural finish. Current mfr.

Mfr.'s Sug. Retail	$500	$375	$225	$150

ARCH CRAFT

Instruments built by the Kay Musical Instrument Company of Chicago, Illinois during the early 1930s.

These entry level acoustic flat-top and archtop guitars were built by Kay (one of the three U.S. *jobber* guitar companies), and distributed through various outlets.

(Source: Michael Wright, Vintage Guitar Magazine)

ARIA

ARIA PRO II

Instruments produced in Japan since 1957. Current models are produced in the U.S., Japan, Korea, China, Indonesia, and Spain. Distributed in the U.S. market by Aria USA/NHF of Pennsauken, New Jersey.

ARIA is the trademark of the Arai Company of Japan, which began producing guitars in 1957. Prior to 1975, the trademark was either **ARIA**, or **ARIA DIAMOND**. Original designs in the 1960s gave way to a greater emphasis on replicas of American designs in the late 1970s. Ironically, the recognition of these well-produced replicas led to success in later years as the company returned to producing original designs. The Aria trademark has always reflected high production quality, and currently there has been more emphasis on stylish designs (such as the Fullerton guitar series, or in bass designs such as the AVB-SB).

The Arai company has produced instruments under their Aria/Aria Diamond/Aria Pro II trademark for a number of years. They have also built instruments distributed under the Univox and Cameo labels as well. Aria also offers the Ariana line of acoustic steel-string and nylon-string models.

ACOUSTIC

1 AF 075 D (Also Designated AW-75 F) — grand concert folk style, spruce top, round soundhole, black pickguard, bound body, 5 stripe rosette, mahogany back/sides/neck, 14/20 fret rosewood fingerboard with pearl dot inlay, rosewood bridge with black pins, 3 per side nickel tuners. Available in Natural finish. Current mfr.

Mfr.'s Sug. Retail	$369	$275	$185	$125

1 AF 530 — grand concert folk style, solid spruce top, round soundhole, black pickguard, bound body, 5 stripe rosette, maple back/sides, mahogany neck, 14/20 fret rosewood fingerboard with pearl dot inlay, rosewood bridge with black pins, 3 per side deluxe tuners. Available in Natural finish. Mfr. 1998 to date.

Mfr.'s Sug. Retail	$599	$450	$295	$200

AK Series

 AK Series guitars are currently produced in Korea.

AK 70 — classic style, mahogany top, round soundhole, bound body, wooden inlay rosette, mahogany back/sides/neck, 12/19 fret rosewood fingerboard/bridge, 3 per side nickel tuners. Available in Natural finish. Mfd. 1991 to 1993.

		$100	$65

 Last Mfr.'s Sug. Retail was $200.

1 AK 75 — classic style, spruce top, round soundhole, bound body, wooden inlay rosette, mahogany back/sides/neck, 12/19 fret rosewood fingerboard/bridge, 3 per side nickel tuners. Available in Natural finish. Mfr. 1991 to date.

Mfr.'s Sug. Retail	$379	$285	$190	$125

AK 100 — similar to AK 75, except has different rosette and rosewood veneer on peghead. Disc. 1993.

		$120	$80

 Last Mfr.'s Sug. Retail was $240.

AK 200 3/4 — similar to AK 75, except is three-quarter body size. Disc. 1993.

		$120	$80

 Last Mfr.'s Sug. Retail was $240.

AK 200 — similar to AK 75, except has different rosette and rosewood veneer on peghead. Disc. 1993.

		$120	$80

 Last Mfr.'s Sug. Retail was $240.

1 AK 210 — classic style, select cedar top, round soundhole, bound body, wooden inlay rosette, mahogany back/sides/neck, 12/19 fret rosewood fingerboard/bridge, 3 per side chrome tuners. Available in Natural finish. Mfr. 1994 to date.

Mfr.'s Sug. Retail	$399	$300	$195	$130

Grading		100%	EXCELLENT	AVERAGE

AK 310 — similar to AK 210, except has gold tuners. Mfr. 1994 to 1996.

$219 $125

$105

Mfr.'s Sug. Retail was $439.

1 AK 320 — classic style, solid cedar top, round soundhole, multiple bound body, wooden inlay rosette, mahogany back/sides/neck, 12/19 fret rosewood fingerboard/bridge, 3 per side chrome tuners. Available in Natural finish. Mfr. 1997 to date.

Mfr.'s Sug. Retail $549 $415 $270 $180

AK 600 — classic style, solid spruce top, round soundhole, 5 stripe bound body, wooden inlay rosette, rosewood back/sides, mahogany neck, 12/19 fret rosewood fingerboard/bridge, rosewood veneer on peghead, 3 per side gold tuners. Available in Natural finish. Mfd. 1991 to 1996.

$190 $120

Last Mfr.'s Sug. Retail was $400.

AK 900 — similar to AK 600, except has solid cedar top. Mfd. 1991 to 1996.

$225 $150

Last Mfr.'s Sug. Retail was $559.

1 AK 920 — classic style, solid cedar top, round soundhole, bound body, wooden inlay rosette, rosewood back/sides, mahogany neck, 12/19 fret rosewood fingerboard/bridge, rosewood veneer on peghead, 3 per side gold tuners. Available in Natural finish. Mfr. 1997 to date.

Mfr.'s Sug. Retail $659 $495 $325 $215

AK 1000 — classic style, spruce top, round soundhole, bound body, wooden inlay rosette, mahogany back/sides/neck, 12/19 fret rosewood fingerboard/bridge, rosewood peghead veneer, 3 per side nickel tuners. Available in Natural finish. Mfd. 1991 to 1993.

$350 $230

Last Mfr.'s Sug. Retail was $700.

AW Series

1 AW 73 N — dreadnought style, spruce top, round soundhole, black pickguard, bound body, 5 stripe rosette, mahogany back/sides/neck, 14/20 fret rosewood fingerboard with white dot inlay, rosewood bridge, 3 per side nickel tuners. Available in Natural gloss finish. Mfr. 1996 to date.

Mfr.'s Sug. Retail $299 $200 $100 $85

1 AW 73 C — similar to the 1 AW 73 N, except has single cutaway. Available in Black, Blue sunburst, Natural, and Red sunburst. Mfr. 1996 to date.

Mfr.'s Sug. Retail $369 $270 $170 $135

AW 70 — dreadnought style, mahogany top, round soundhole, black pickguard, bound body, 5 stripe rosette, mahogany back/sides/neck, 14/20 fret rosewood fingerboard with pearl dot inlay, rosewood bridge with black pins, 3 per side nickel tuners. Available in Walnut finish. Mfd. 1991 to 1993.

$100 $65

Last Mfr.'s Sug. Retail was $200.

1 AW 75 D — dreadnought style, spruce top, round soundhole, black pickguard, bound body, 5 stripe rosette, mahogany back/sides/neck, 14/20 fret rosewood fingerboard with pearl dot inlay, rosewood bridge with black pins, 3 per side nickel tuners. Available in Black, Black Sunburst, Blue Sunburst, Brown Sunburst, Natural, Red Sunburst, and White finishes. Current mfr.

Mfr.'s Sug. Retail $369 $270 $170 $135

Add $20 for Black, Black Sunburst, Blue Sunburst, Brown Sunburst, Red Sunburst, and White finishes (retail list $389).

1 AW 75 LDN — similar to the 1 AW 75 D, except in left-handed configuration. Available in Natural gloss finish only. Mfr. 1995 to date.

Mfr.'s Sug. Retail $399 $280 $180 $135

AW 100 — dreadnought style, spruce top, round soundhole, black pickguard, bound body, 3 stripe rosette, black pickguard, mahogany back/sides/neck, 14/20 fret rosewood fingerboard with pearl dot inlay, rosewood bridge with black white dot pins, 3 per side chrome tuners. Available in Natural finish. Disc. 1991.

$140 $90

Last Mfr.'s Sug. Retail was $275.

AW 100 C — similar to AW-100, except has single round cutaway. Disc. 1991.

$150 $100

Last Mfr.'s Sug. Retail was $300.

1 AW 110 N — dreadnought style, cedar top, round soundhole, black pickguard, bound body, 3 stripe rosette, black pickguard, mahogany back/sides/neck, 14/20 fret rosewood fingerboard with pearl dot inlay, rosewood bridge with black white dot pins, 3 per side chrome tuners. Available in Natural semi-gloss finish. Mfr. 1991 to date.

Mfr.'s Sug. Retail $399 $280 $180 $135

1 AW 110 C — similar to 1 AW 110 N, except has single rounded cutaway. Mfr. 1991 to date.

Mfr.'s Sug. Retail $469 $350 $230 $160

AW 110 CT — similar to 1 AW 110 C, except in a 12-string configuration. Disc 1991.

$175 $115

Last Mfr.'s Sug. Retail was $350.

1 AW 110 LN — similar to 1 AW 110 N, except in left-handed configuration. Mfr. 1996 to date.

Mfr.'s Sug. Retail $449 $340 $220 $150

Grading	100%	EXCELLENT	AVERAGE

1 AW 110 T — similar to 1 AW 110 N, except in a 12-string configuration. Mfr. 1996 to date.

Mfr.'s Sug. Retail	$479	$360	$240	$160

1 AW 130 X — dreadnought style, solid spruce top, round soundhole, mahogany back/sides/neck, 14/20 fret rosewood fingerboard with white dot inlay, rosewood bridge, 3 per side chrome diecast tuners. Available in Natural semi-gloss finish. Mfr. 1997 to date.

Mfr.'s Sug. Retail	$369	$275	$185	$125

1 AW 200 — dreadnought style, spruce top, round soundhole, bound body, 3 stripe rosette, black pickguard, ovankol back/sides/neck, 14/20 fret rosewood fingerboard with pearl dot inlay, rosewood bridge with white black dot pins, 3 per side chrome diecast tuners. Available in Antique Violin, Brown Sunburst, Black, and Natural finishes. Mfr. 1991 to date.

Mfr.'s Sug. Retail	$479	$365	$235	$160

In 1993, Brown Sunburst finish was discontinued.

In 1996, Antique Violin finish was discontinued.

1 AW 200 C — similar to 1 AW 200, except has single round cutaway. Available in Black and Natural finishes. Mfr. 1991 to date.

Mfr.'s Sug. Retail	$499	$375	$240	$160

AW 200 F — similar to 1 AW 200, except has folk style body. Disc. 1993.

			$130	$90

Last Mfr.'s Sug. Retail was $379.

1 AW 200 L — similar to 1 AW 200, except in left-handed configuration. Available in Natural gloss finish only. Mfr. 1997 to date.

Mfr.'s Sug. Retail	$529	$395	$265	$175

1 AW 200 T — similar to AW-200, except has 12 strings, 6 per side tuners. Mfr. 1991 to date.

Mfr.'s Sug. Retail	$579	$435	$285	$190

AW 250 — dreadnought style, figured maple top, round soundhole, black pickguard, 3 stripe bound body/rosette, flamed maple back/sides, mahogany neck, 14/20 fret rosewood fingerboard with pearl dot inlay, rosewood bridge with white black dot pins, 3 per side chrome diecast tuners. Available in Black Sunburst and Vintage Sunburst finishes. Mfd. 1994 to 1996.

			$225	$150

Last Mfr.'s Sug. Retail was $450.

1 AW 300 N — dreadnought style, spruce top, round soundhole, black pickguard, 3 stripe bound body/rosette, rosewood back/sides, mahogany neck, 14/20 fret rosewood fingerboard with pearl dot inlay, rosewood bridge with white black dot pins, 3 per side gold tuners. Available in Black Sunburst and Natural finishes. Mfr. 1997 to date.

Mfr.'s Sug. Retail	$659	$495	$320	$220

In 1998, the Black Sunburst finish was discontinued.

1 AW 310 N — dreadnought style, cedar top, round soundhole, herringbone bound body/rosette, tortoiseshell pickguard, ovankol back/sides, mahogany neck, 14/20 fret rosewood fingerboard with pearl dot inlay, rosewood bridge with white black dot pins, 3 per side gold tuners. Available in Natural semi-gloss finish. Mfr. 1991 to 1992, 1996 to date.

Mfr.'s Sug. Retail	$659	$495	$320	$220

In 1997, rosewood back and sides replaced original item.

AW 310 C — similar to 1 AW 310, except has single round cutaway and ovankol back and sides. Mfd. 1991 to 1992.

			$200	$130

Last Mfr.'s Sug. Retail was $400.

AW 310 T — similar to AW 310, except has 12 strings. Mfd. 1991 to 1996.

			$185	$115

Last Mfr.'s Sug. Retail was $400.

AW 320 T — similar to AW 310, except has 12 strings, gold hardware. Mfd. 1991 to 1996.

			$225	$150

Last Mfr.'s Sug. Retail was $450.

AW 410 — jumbo style, cedar top, round soundhole, herringbone bound body/rosette, black pickguard, ovankol back/sides, mahogany neck, 14/20 fret rosewood fingerboard with pearl dot inlay, rosewood bridge with white black dot pins, 3 per side chrome diecast tuners. Available in Natural finish. Mfd. 1991 to 1992.

			$180	$120

Last Mfr.'s Sug. Retail was $360.

1 AW 420 N — dreadnought style, solid cedar top, round soundhole, black pickguard, 3 stripe bound body, mahogany back/sides, mahogany neck, 14/20 fret bound rosewood fingerboard with pearl dot inlay, rosewood bridge with black pins, 3 per side chrome diecast tuners. Available in Natural gloss finish. Mfr. 1997 to date.

Mfr.'s Sug. Retail	$669	$500	$325	$225

AW 600 — dreadnought style, spruce top, round soundhole, black pickguard, 3 stripe bound body/rosette, rosewood back/sides, mahogany neck, 14/20 fret bound rosewood fingerboard with pearl dot inlay, rosewood bridge with white black dot pins, rosewood veneer on bound peghead, 3 per side chrome diecast tuners. Available in Natural finish. Disc. 1996.

			$205	$120

Last Mfr.'s Sug. Retail was $479.

In 1994, gold tuners replaced original item.

This model was also available with mahogany back/sides.

A

AW 620 — dreadnought style, solid cedar top, round soundhole, tortoiseshell pickguard, 3 stripe bound body, rosewood back/sides, mahogany neck, 14/20 fret bound rosewood fingerboard with pearl dot inlay, rosewood bridge with white black dot pins, 3 per side gold tuners. Available in Natural satin finish. Disc. 1994.

		$205	$120

Last Mfr.'s Sug. Retail was $500.

1 AW 630 — dreadnought style, solid spruce top, round soundhole, tortoiseshell pickguard, 3 stripe bound body, ovankol back/sides, mahogany neck, 14/20 fret bound rosewood fingerboard with pearl dot inlay, rosewood bridge with white black dot pins, 3 per side gold tuners. Available in Black and Natural gloss finishes. Mfr. 1996 to date.

Mfr.'s Sug. Retail	$779	$580	$370	$260

AW 650 — similar to AW 600, except had solid spruce top, mahogany back/sides, gold tuners. Mfd. 1994 to 1996.

		$225	$150

Last Mfr.'s Sug. Retail was $450.

AW-700 — dreadnought style, solid spruce top, round soundhole, black pickguard, 3 stripe bound body/rosette, rosewood back/sides, mahogany neck, 14/20 fret rosewood fingerboard with pearl diamond inlay, rosewood bridge with white black dot pins, rosewood veneer peghead, 3 per side gold diecast tuners. Available in Natural finish. Mfd. 1991 only.

		$195	$125

Last Mfr.'s Sug. Retail was $390.

AW 800 — dreadnought style, solid spruce top, round soundhole, tortoise shell pickguard, herringbone bound body/rosette, rosewood back/sides, mahogany neck, 14/20 fret rosewood fingerboard with pearl diamond inlay, rosewood bridge with white black dot pins, rosewood veneer on peghead, 3 per side gold diecast tuners. Available in Natural finish. Disc. 1996.

		$240	$155

Last Mfr.'s Sug. Retail was $559.

AW 800 T — similar to AW 800, except has 12 strings, 6 per side tuners. Disc. 1996.

		$275	$180

Last Mfr.'s Sug. Retail was $599.

1 AW 830 N — dreadnought style, solid spruce top, round soundhole, tortoise shell pickguard, herringbone bound body/rosette, rosewood back/sides, mahogany neck, 14/20 fret rosewood fingerboard with pearl diamond inlay, rosewood bridge with white black dot pins, 3 per side gold diecast tuners. Available in Natural gloss finish. Mfr. 1996 to date.

Mfr.'s Sug. Retail	$699	$525	$350	$235

1 AW 830 T — similar to 1 AW 830, except has 12 strings, 6 per side tuners. Mfr. 1996 to date.

Mfr.'s Sug. Retail	$749	$560	$370	$250

1 AW 920 N — dreadnought style, solid cedar top, round soundhole, tortoiseshell pickguard, abalone bound body/rosette, rosewood back/sides, mahogany neck, 14/20 fret rosewood fingerboard with pearl diamond inlay, rosewood bridge with white black dot pins, 3 per side gold tuners. Available in Natural finish. Mfr. 1996 to date.

Mfr.'s Sug. Retail	$1,159	$870	$565	$380

1 AW 930 N — dreadnought style, solid spruce top, round soundhole, tortoiseshell pickguard, abalone bound body/rosette, rosewood back/sides, mahogany neck, 14/20 fret rosewood fingerboard with pearl diamond inlay, rosewood bridge with white black dot pins, 3 per side gold tuners. Available in Natural finish. Mfr. 1996 to date.

Mfr.'s Sug. Retail	$1,199	$900	$590	$395

1 AW 930 T — similar to 1 AW 930, except has 12 strings, 6 per side tuners. Mfr. 1996 to date.

Mfr.'s Sug. Retail	$1,299	$975	$640	$430

LW Series

LJ 8 — jumbo style, cedar top, round soundhole, 3 stripe bound body/rosette, black pickguard, bubinga back/sides, mahogany neck, 14/20 fret rosewood fingerboard with pearl dot inlay, ebonized maple bridge with white black dot pins, 3 per side chrome diecast tuners. Available in Natural finish. Mfd. 1994 to 1996.

		$265	$175

Last Mfr.'s Sug. Retail was $530.

LW 8 — similar to LJ 8, except has dreadnought style, spruce top, ovankol back/sides. Available in Natural finish. Mfd. 1994 to 1996.

		$265	$175

Mfr.'s Sug. Retail was $530.

LW 10 — dreadnought style, spruce top, round soundhole, 3 stripe bound body/rosette, black pickguard, mahogany back/sides/neck, 14/20 fret rosewood fingerboard with pearl dot inlay, ebonized maple bridge with white black dot pins, 3 per side chrome diecast tuners. Available in Black, Natural, Tobacco Brown and Wine Red finishes. Mfd. 1991 to 1992.

		$280	$190

Last Mfr.'s Sug. Retail was $560.

LW 10 T — similar to the LW 10, except in a 12-string configuration. Mfd. 1991 to 1992.

		$295	$195

Last Mfr.'s Sug. Retail was $575.

LW-12 — dreadnought style, cedar top, round soundhole, herringbone bound body/rosette, tortoise pickguard, walnut back/sides, mahogany neck, 14/20 fret rosewood fingerboard with pearl dot inlay, ebonized maple bridge with white black dot pins, rosewood veneer on peghead, 3 per side chrome diecast tuners. Available in Black and Natural finishes. Disc. 1992.

		$270	$180

Last Mfr.'s Sug. Retail was $540.

LW 12 T — similar to the LW 12, except in a 12-string configuration. Mfd. 1991 to 1992.

		$305	$200

Last Mfr.'s Sug. Retail was $575.

Grading	100%	EXCELLENT	AVERAGE

LW 14 — dreadnought style, sycamore top, round soundhole, herringbone bound body/rosette, black pickguard, walnut back/sides, mahogany neck, 14/20 fret rosewood fingerboard with pearl dot inlay, ebonized maple bridge with white black dot pins, sycamore veneer on peghead, 3 per side chrome diecast tuners. Available in Tobacco Sunburst finish. Disc. 1993.

	$285	$190	
		Last Mfr.'s Sug. Retail was $575.	

LW 18 — dreadnought style, spruce top, round soundhole, 5 stripe bound body/rosette, rosewood back/sides, mahogany neck, 14/20 fret rosewood fingerboard with pearl dot inlay, ebonized maple bridge with white black dot pins, rosewood veneer on peghead, 3 per side chrome diecast tuners. Available in Natural finish. Disc. 1993.

	$300	$195	
		Last Mfr.'s Sug. Retail was $600.	

LW 18 T — similar to LW-18, except has 12 strings, 6 per side tuners. Disc. 1993.

	$320	$210	
		Last Mfr.'s Sug. Retail was $640.	

SW Series

SW 8 — dreadnought style, solid cedar top, round soundhole, tortoise shell bound body/rosette/pickguard, mahogany back/sides/neck, 14/20 fret rosewood fingerboard with pearl dot inlay, ebonized maple bridge with white black dot pins, rosewood veneer on peghead, 3 per side chrome diecast tuners. Available in Natural finish. Disc. 1993.

	$320	$210	
		Last Mfr.'s Sug. Retail was $640.	

SW 8 C — similar to SW 8, except has single round cutaway. Disc. 1993.

	$360	$240	
		Last Mfr.'s Sug. Retail was $715.	

SW 8 CT — similar to SW 8, except has single round cutaway, 12 strings, 6 per side tuners. Disc. 1993.

	$375	$245	
		Last Mfr.'s Sug. Retail was $750.	

SW 8 T — similar to SW 8, except has 12 strings, 6 per side tuners. Disc. 1993.

	$335	$220	
		Last Mfr.'s Sug. Retail was $670.	

Concert Classic Series

Instruments made in Spain. All instruments in this series have classical style body, round soundhole, wood inlay rosette, mahogany neck, 12/19 fret fingerboard, tied rosewood bridge, rosewood veneered slotted peghead, 3 per side tuners with pearloid buttons. Available in Natural finish.

1 AC 25 — solid cedar top, African sapelli back/sides, rosewood fingerboard, nickel hardware. Mfr. 1995 to date.

Mfr.'s Sug. Retail	$395	$285	$140	$115

1 AC 35 — solid cedar top, African sapelli back/sides, rosewood fingerboard, gold hardware. Mfr. 1995 to date.

Mfr.'s Sug. Retail	$495	$355	$170	$135

AC 35 A — similar to AC 35, except has **alto (530mm scale)** style, solid spruce top, single flat cutaway. Disc. 1997.

	$200	$135	
		Last Mfr.'s Sug. Retail was $495.	

1 AC 50 — solid cedar top, rosewood back/sides/fingerboard, gold hardware. Mfr. 1995 to date.

Mfr.'s Sug. Retail	$695	$540	$270	$225

This model was also available with a spruce top (Model AC 50 S). Model AC 50 S was discontinued in 1997.

AC 50 A — similar to AC 50, except has **alto (530mm scale)** style, single flat cutaway. Disc. 1997.

	$395	$225	
		Last Mfr.'s Sug. Retail was $695.	

This model was optionally available with a solid spruce top.

AC 75 CB — **contra bass (750mm scale)** style, solid cedar top, African sapelli back/sides, rosewood fingerboard, gold hardware. Disc. 1997.

	$495	$350	
		Last Mfr.'s Sug. Retail was $1,095.	

AC 75 B — similar to AC 75 CB, except has **bass (700mm scale)** style. Disc. 1997.

	$495	$350	
		Last Mfr.'s Sug. Retail was $1,095.	

1 AC 80 — solid spruce top, rosewood back/sides, ebony fingerboard, gold hardware. Mfr. 1995 to date.

Mfr.'s Sug. Retail	$995	$750	$500	$355

AC 85 A — single flat cutaway **alto (530mm scale)** style, solid spruce top, rosewood back/sides, ebony fingerboard, gold hardware. Disc. 1997.

	$535	$355	
		Last Mfr.'s Sug. Retail was $1,075.	

AC 90 CB — **contra bass (750mm scale)** style, solid spruce top, rosewood back/sides, ebony fingerboard, gold hardware.

	$630	$415	
		Last Mfr.'s Sug. Retail was $1,255.	

Grading	100%	EXCELLENT	AVERAGE

AC 90 B — similar to AC 90 CB, except has **bass (700mm scale)** style.

$630 $415
Last Mfr.'s Sug. Retail was $1,255.

Pepe Series

The Pepe Series models are made in Spain. All instruments in this series have classical style body, solid cedar top, round soundhole, wood inlay rosette, African sapelli back/sides, mahogany neck, 12/19 fret rosewood fingerboard, tied rosewood bridge, rosewood veneered slotted peghead, 3 per side gold tuners with pearloid buttons. Available in Natural finish. Mfr. 1995 to date.

PS 48 — 480mm scale.
| Mfr.'s Sug. Retail | $375 | $280 | $195 | $140 |

PS 53 — 530mm scale.
| Mfr.'s Sug. Retail | $375 | $280 | $195 | $140 |

PS 58 — 580mm scale.
| Mfr.'s Sug. Retail | $375 | $280 | $195 | $140 |

ACOUSTIC ELECTRIC

3 AW 73 CE — dreadnought style, single cutaway, spruce top, round soundhole, black pickguard, bound body, 5 stripe rosette, mahogany back/sides/neck, 14/20 fret rosewood fingerboard with white dot inlay, rosewood bridge, 3 per side nickel tuners, piezo pickups, volume/tone controls. Available in Black and Natural finishes. Mfr. 1996 to date.
| Mfr.'s Sug. Retail | $449 | $340 | $225 | $150 |

3 AW 200 E — dreadnought style, spruce top, round soundhole, bound body, 3 stripe rosette, black pickguard, ovankol back/sides/neck, 14/20 fret rosewood fingerboard with pearl dot inlay, rosewood bridge with white black dot pins, 3 per side chrome diecast tuners, piezo pickup, and 3 band EQ. Available in Black and Natural finishes. Mfr. 1991 to date.
| Mfr.'s Sug. Retail | $579 | $435 | $285 | $190 |

3 AW 200 CE — similar to 3 AW 200 E, except has single round cutaway, piezo pickup, 3 band EQ. Mfr. 1991 to date.
| Mfr.'s Sug. Retail | $649 | $490 | $320 | $215 |

3 AW 200 CTE — similar to AW-200 CE, except has 12 strings, 6 per side tuners, piezo pickup, 3 band EQ. Available in Natural finish only. Current mfr.
| Mfr.'s Sug. Retail | $699 | $525 | $340 | $230 |

AW 310 CE — dreadnought style, single round cutaway, cedar top, round soundhole, herringbone bound body/rosette, ovankol back/sides, mahogany neck, 14/20 fret rosewood fingerboard with pearl dot inlay, rosewood bridge with white black dot pins, 3 per side chrome diecast tuners, piezo pickup, 3 band EQ. Available in Natural finish. Mfd. 1991 to 1992.

$235 $155
Last Mfr.'s Sug. Retail was $470.

CES 50 — single round cutaway classic style, spruce top, bound body, wooden inlay rosette, mahogany body/neck, 22 fret extended rosewood fingerboard, rosewood bridge, 3 per side gold tuners, piezo pickups, volume/tone control. Available in Black, Natural and White finishes. Mfd. 1992 to 1994.

$300 $195
Last Mfr.'s Sug. Retail was $600.

This model is a solid body with a routed out soundhole and installed plastic dish for resonance.

CE-42
courtesy Aria Pro II

3 CE 40 N — deep nylon string single round cutaway classical style, spruce top, round soundhole, mahogany neck, bound body, rosewood back/sides/neck, 19 fret rosewood fingerboard/bridge, 3 per side gold tuners, Fishman Matrix pickup with 4 band EQ. Available in Natural finish. Mfr. 1996 to date.
| Mfr.'s Sug. Retail | $749 | $560 | $370 | $250 |

The 3 CE 40 N has a body depth of 100 mm (3.9 inches).

3 CE 42 N — similar to the 3 CE 40 N, except has a shallow body depth. Mfr. 1996 to date.
| Mfr.'s Sug. Retail | $749 | $560 | $370 | $250 |

The 3 CE 42 N has a body depth of 75 mm (2.9 inches).

CE 60 — single round cutaway classic style, spruce top, round soundhole, bound body, wooden inlay rosette, mahogany back/sides/neck, 19 fret rosewood fingerboard/bridge, rosewood veneer on peghead, 3 per side gold tuners, piezo pickups with 3 band EQ. Available in Natural finish. Mfd. 1991 to 1994.

$350 $230
Last Mfr.'s Sug. Retail was $700.

CE 60 S — similar to CE 60, except has 22 fret extended fingerboard with pearl dot inlay, steel strings with white black dot bridge pins. Disc. 1994.

$350 $230
Last Mfr.'s Sug. Retail was $700.

CE 60/14 — similar to CE 60, except has 22 fret extended fingerboard. Disc. 1994.

$350 $230
Last Mfr.'s Sug. Retail was $700.

FEA 10 — single round cutaway dreadnought style, cedar top, round soundhole, bound body, wooden inlay rosette, mahogany back/sides/neck, 22 fret rosewood fingerboard with pearl dot inlay, rosewood bridge with black pearl dot pins, 3 per side diecast tuners, piezo pickup, 3 band EQ. Available in Natural and Walnut finishes. Mfd. 1992 to 1995.

$440 $275
Last Mfr.'s Sug. Retail was $900.

Grading	100%	EXCELLENT	AVERAGE

FEA 15 — similar to FEA 10, except has spruce top. Available in Brown Sunburst, Natural and Transparent Black finishes. Disc. 1993.

$475 $315
Last Mfr.'s Sug. Retail was $950.

FEA 16 N — single round cutaway dreadnought style, figured sycamore top, round soundhole, bound body, wooden inlay rosette, mahogany back/sides/neck, 22 fret rosewood fingerboard with pearl dot inlay, rosewood bridge with black pearl dot pins, 3 per side diecast tuners, piezo pickup, 3 band EQ. Available in Natural finish. Mfd. 1994 only.

$525 $345
Last Mfr.'s Sug. Retail was $1,050.

FEA 20 — single round cutaway dreadnought style, sycamore top, round soundhole, bound body, abalone designed rosette, sycamore back/sides, mahogany neck, 22 fret bound rosewood fingerboard with pearl dot inlay, rosewood bridge with black pearl dot pins, 3 per side gold diecast tuners, piezo pickup, 3 band EQ. Available in See through Black and See through Blue finishes. Mfd. 1991 to 1996.

$605 $380
Last Mfr.'s Sug. Retail was $1,300.

Concert Classic Series Acoustic Electric

Instruments made in Spain. All instruments in this series have classical style body with a single rounded cutaway, round soundhole, wood inlay rosette, mahogany neck, 12/19 fret fingerboard, tied rosewood bridge, rosewood veneered slotted peghead, 3 per side tuners with pearloid buttons. Available in Natural finish.

The acoustic electric Concert Classic models are all equipped with Fishman Matrix electronics.

3 AC 25 CE — solid cedar top, African sapelli back/sides, rosewood fingerboard, nickel hardware. Mfr. 1998 to date.

Mfr.'s Sug. Retail	$650	$495	$325	$215

3 AC 35 CE — solid cedar top, African sapelli back/sides, rosewood fingerboard, gold hardware. Mfr. 1998 to date.

Mfr.'s Sug. Retail	$750	$575	$365	$250

3 AC 50 CE — solid cedar top, rosewood back/sides/fingerboard, gold hardware. Mfr. 1998 to date.

Mfr.'s Sug. Retail	$950	$725	$465	$300

3 AC 80 CE — solid spruce top, rosewood back/sides, ebony fingerboard, gold hardware. Mfr. 1998 to date.

Mfr.'s Sug. Retail	$1,250	$945	$635	$445

Elecord Series

Elecord series guitars feature Fishman Matrix pickups and electronics, and a single rounded cutaway.

3 FET 01 — single rounded cutaway large body, spruce top, oval soundhole, bound body, soundhole rosette, daowood back/sides, mahogany neck, 22 fret bound rosewood fingerboard with pearl snowflake inlay, rosewood bridge with white black dot pins, bound peghead, 3 per side gold tuners, Fishman Matrix pickup, 4 band EQ. Available in Blue Shade, Black and Natural finishes. Mfr. 1996 to date.

Mfr.'s Sug. Retail	$789	$590	$390	$265

In 1997, Blue Shade finish was discontinued.

3 FET 02 — single rounded cutaway small body, spruce top, oval soundhole, bound body, soundhole rosette, daowood back/sides, mahogany neck, 22 fret bound rosewood fingerboard with pearl snowflake inlay, rosewood bridge with white black dot pins, bound peghead, 3 per side gold tuners, Fishman Matrix pickup, 4 band EQ. Available in Blue Shade, Black, Natural, and Vintage sunburst finishes. Mfr. 1996 to date.

Mfr.'s Sug. Retail	$789	$590	$390	$265

In 1997, Blue Shade and Vintage sunburst finishes were discontinued; See through Blue and Violin sunburst finishes were introduced.

3 FET 03 — similar to the 3 FET 02, except has a Silky Oak top/back/sides. Available in Amber, See through Black, and Blue Shade finishes. Mfr. 1996 to date.

Mfr.'s Sug. Retail	$859	$645	$425	$285

In 1997, See Through Black and Blue Shade finishes were discontinued.

FET 85 — single sharp cutaway jumbo style, arched spruce top, oval soundhole, 5 stripe bound body/rosette, chestnut back/sides, mahogany neck, 21 fret bound rosewood fingerboard with pearl diamond inlay, rosewood bridge with black pearl dot pins and pearl diamond inlay, bound peghead with chestnut veneer, 3 per side gold diecast tuners, piezo pickup, 3 band EQ. Available in Amber Natural and Antique Sunburst finishes. Mfd. 1991 to 1992.

$700 $460
Last Mfr.'s Sug. Retail was $1,400.

This model had rosewood back/sides optionally available.

FET 100 — cutaway jumbo style, arched chestnut/spruce laminated top, oval soundhole, 3 stripe bound body and rosette, chestnut arched back/sides, maple neck, 21 fret bound ebony fingerboard with abalone/pearl split block inlay, rosewood bridge with white pearl dot pins and pearl diamond inlay, bound peghead, 3 per side gold diecast tuners, piezo pickup, 3 band EQ. Available in Amber Natural, Blue Shade and Red Shade finishes. Mfd. 1991 to 1992.

$750 $495
Last Mfr.'s Sug. Retail was $1,500.

FET 500 (formerly the FET SPL) — round cutaway jumbo style, spruce top, oval soundhole, 5 stripe bound body and rosette, mahogany arched back/sides/neck, 21 fret rosewood bound fingerboard with pearl dot inlay, rosewood bridge with white pearl dot pins, bound peghead, 3 per side diecast tuners, piezo pickup, volume/tone control. Available in Antique Sunburst, Black Sunburst and Transparent Red finishes. Mfd. 1991 to 1992.

$285 $190
Last Mfr.'s Sug. Retail was $575.

FET-01
courtesy Aria Pro II

Grading	100%	EXCELLENT	AVERAGE

FET-02
courtesy Aria Pro II

FET 600 (formerly the FET DLX) — cutaway jumbo style, arched sycamore top, oval soundhole, 5 stripe bound body and rosette, sycamore arched back/sides, mahogany neck, 21 fret bound rosewood fingerboard with pearl diamond inlay, rosewood bridge with white pearl dot pins, bound peghead, 3 per side diecast tuners, piezo pickup, 3 band EQ. Available in Amber Natural and Antique Sunburst finishes. Mfd. 1991 to 1992.

	$380	$250

Last Mfr.'s Sug. Retail was $765.

FET 600/12 — similar to the FET 600, except in a 12-string configuration. Mfd. 1991 to 1992.

	$380	$250

Last Mfr.'s Sug. Retail was $765.

Sandpiper Series

The Sandpiper Series was introduced in 1998. Models feature solid spruce tops, arched backs, fine ornamentation, and Fishman electronics.

3 SP-1 SANDPIPER — folk style, single rounded cutaway body, solid spruce top, round soundhole, pearl/ivory body binding, pearl rosette, rosewood back/sides, mahogany neck, 21 fret ebony fingerboard with pearl inlay, rosewood bridge with black pins, 3 per side gold tuners, Fishman Matrix Pro pickup, volume/brilliance/3 band EQ, phase switch. Available in Natural finish. Mfr. 1998 to date.
Mfr.'s Sug. Retail $2,499

3 SP-2 Sandpiper — similar to the 3 SP-1, except features inset soundhole mosaic, rosewood fingerboard, PZP-6 piezo pickup, volume/mid contour/3 band EQ, PR-500 electronics. Available in Natural finish. Mfr. 1998 to date.
Mfr.'s Sug. Retail $1,999

3 SP-3 Sandpiper — similar to the 3 SP-1, except features rosewood fingerboard, Fishman pickup, volume/mid contour/3 band EQ. Available in Natural finish. Mfr. 1998 to date.
Mfr.'s Sug. Retail $1,779

3 SP-4 Sandpiper — similar to the 3 SP-1, except features Pau Ferro back/sides, rosewood fingerboard, Fishman pickup, volume/mid contour/3 band EQ. Available in Blue Sunburst, Natural, and Sunburst finishes. Mfr. 1998 to date.
Mfr.'s Sug. Retail $1,779

ACOUSTIC ELECTRIC BASS

4 FEB 02 — single rounded cutaway body, spruce top, oval soundhole, bound body, daowood back/sides, maple neck, 24 fret bound rosewood fingerboard with pearl dot inlay, string through rosewood bridge, bound peghead, 2 per side gold tuners, Fishman Matrix pickup, 4 band EQ. Available in Black and Natural finishes. Mfr. 1996 to date.

Mfr.'s Sug. Retail	$839	$625	$415	$280

In 1997, Black finish was discontinued; Violin sunburst finish was introduced.

4 FEB DLX — single round cutaway dreadnought style, arched flame maple top, f holes, multi bound body, figured maple back/sides/neck, 21 fret rosewood fingerboard with pearl snowflake inlay, string thru rosewood bridge, flame maple peghead veneer with pearl flower/logo inlay, 2 per side gold tuners, piezo bridge pickup, 4 band EQ. Available in Brown Sunburst, Natural and Violin Sunburst finishes. Mfd. 1994 to 1997.

	$500	$330

Last Mfr.'s Sug. Retail was $1,040.

4 FEB STD — similar to FEB DLX, except has spruce top, mahogany back/sides, chrome tuners. Mfd. 1994 to 1996.

	$425	$280

Last Mfr.'s Sug. Retail was $900.

Sandpiper Bass Series

4 SPB 04 SANDPIPER BASS 4-STRING — single rounded cutaway body, solid spruce top, round soundhole, ivory body binding, ivory rosette, rosewood back/sides, maple neck, 24 fret ebony fingerboard with pearl inlay, rosewood bridge with black pins, 2 per side gold tuners, Fishman pickup, volume/3 band EQ. Available in Natural finish. Mfr. 1998 to date.
Mfr.'s Sug. Retail $2,199

4 SPB 05 Sandpiper Bass 5-String — similar to the 4 SPB 04, except has 5-string configuration, 3/2 per side tuners. Available in Natural finish. Mfr. 1998 to date.
Mfr.'s Sug. Retail $2,499

4 SPB 05 FL Sandpiper Bass 5-String Fretless — similar to the 4 SPB 05 5-String, except has fretless fingerboard. Available in Natural finish. Mfr. 1998 to date.
Mfr.'s Sug. Retail $2,499

4 SPB 06 Sandpiper Bass 6-String — similar to the 4 SPB 04, except has 6-string configuration, 3 per side tuners. Available in Natural finish. Mfr. 1998 to date.
Mfr.'s Sug. Retail $2,499

ARIANA

Instruments currently built in Asia. Distributed in the U.S. market by Aria USA/NHF of Pennsauken, New Jersey.

Ariana is one of the trademarks of the Arai Company of Japan, which began producing guitars in 1957. Aria offers the Ariana line of acoustic steel-string and nylon-string models for beginner to intermediate guitar students as a quality instrument at affordable prices.

ARIRANG

Instruments built in Korea during the early 1980s.

This trademark consists of entry level copies of American designs, and some original designs.

(Source: Tony Bacon and Paul Day, The Guru's Guitar Guide)

ARISTONE

See FRAMUS.

See also BESSON.

Instruments made in West Germany during the late 1950s through the early 1960s.

While ARISTONE was the brandname for a UK importer, these guitars were made by and identical to certain FRAMUS models. Research also indicates that the trademark BESSON was utilized as well.

(Source: Tony Bacon and Paul Day, The Guru's Guitar Guide)

ARITA

Instruments manufactured in Japan.

Arita instruments were distributed in the U.S. market by the Newark Musical Merchandise Company of Newark, New Jersey.

(Source: Michael Wright, Guitar Stories Volume One)

ARMY & NAVY SPECIAL

See chapter on House Brands.

This trademark has been identified as a Gibson built budget line available only at military post exchanges (PXs) towards the end of World War I (1918). They will have a label different from the standard Gibson label of the time, yet still be credited to the *Gibson Mandolin - Guitar Co.* of 'Kalamazoo, Mich., USA'. As a Gibson-built budget line instrument, these guitars do not possess an adjustable truss rod in the neck.

(Source: Walter Carter, Gibson: 100 Years of an American Icon)

ART & LUTHERIE

Instruments currently produced in La Patrie, Canada. Distibuted by La Si Do, Inc. of St. Laurent (Quebec), Canada.

Art & Lutherie models are an affordable line of acoustic guitars by La Si Do that complements their higher end models from Godin and Simon & Patrick. Lead by *Guitare Luthier* Daniel Gervais, Art & Lutherie produces guitars built with Canadian tonewoods such as wild cherry, maple, and walnut (gives those trees from the Rain Forest a little breathing room!).

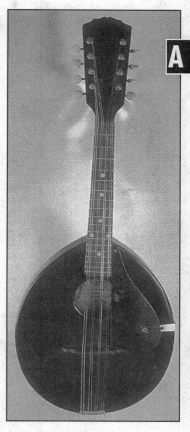

Army & Navy Mandolin
courtesy Darrell Spatafore

ACOUSTIC

ART & LUTHERIE (Model 8568) — 3 ply wild cherry laminated top, wild cherry back/sides, round soundhole, big leaf maple neck, walnut fingerboard with a white dot inlay, solid headstock, 3 per side chrome tuners, black pickguard, and walnut bridge with white bridgepins. Available in Almond Brown **(Model 8568)**, Antique Burst **(Model 8582)**, Black **(Model 8605)**, Chestnut Brown **(Model 8629)**, Transparent Blue **(Model 9190)**, and Transparent Red **(Model 9176)** satin lacquer finish. Current mfr.

    Mfr.'s Sug. Retail   **$299**

        Add $137 for EPM EQ electronic pickup (retail list is $436).

Art & Lutherie Cutaway (Model 9213) — similar to the Art & Lutherie model, except features a single sloped shoulder cutaway body. Available in Almond Brown CW **(Model 9213)**, Antique Burst CW **(Model 9237)**, Black CW **(Model 9251)**, Chestnut Brown CW **(Model 9275)**, Transparent Blue CW **(Model 9312)**, and Transparent Red CW **(Model 9299)** satin lacquer finish. Current mfr.

    Mfr.'s Sug. Retail   **$359**

        Add $137 for EPM EQ electronic pickup (retail list is $496).

Art & Lutherie Cedar Top (Model 0180) — similar to the Art & Lutherie model, except features a solid cedar top. Available in Natural semi-gloss lacquer finish. Current mfr.

    Mfr.'s Sug. Retail   **$339**

        Add $137 for EPM EQ electronic pickup **(Model 0197)**.

Ami Series

Drawing inspiration from those turn-of-the-century parlor guitars, Art & Lutherie also offers the **Ami** model. This model has full scale fingerboard yet scaled down body size designed with children in mind.

AMI NYLON STRING (Model 8704) — 3 ply laminated wild cherry top, wild cherry back/sides, round soundhole, maple neck, walnut fingerboard, classical style tied walnut bridge, slotted headstock, 3 per side tuners. Available in Almond Brown lacquer finish. Mfr. 1998 to date.

    Mfr.'s Sug. Retail   **$269**

        Add $137 for EPM EQ electronic pickup **(Model 11230)**.

Ami Nylon String Cedar Top (Model 11155) — similar to the Ami Nylon String model, except features a solid cedar top. Available in Natural lacquer finish. Mfr. 1998 to date.

    Mfr.'s Sug. Retail   **$295**

        Add $137 for EPM EQ electronic pickup **(Model 11162)**.

Ami Steel String (Model 8643) — similar to the Ami Nylon String, except features a solid headstock, walnut bridge with white bridgepins, chrome tuners. Available in Almond Brown **(Model 8643)**, Antique Burst **(Model 8667)**, Black **(Model 9404)**, Chestnut Brown **(Model 8681)**, Transparent Blue **(Model 9152)**, and Transparent Red **(Model 9138)** lacquer finishes. Mfr. 1998 to date.

    Mfr.'s Sug. Retail   **$269**

        Add $137 for EPM EQ electronic pickup (retail list is $406).

A

Augustino LoPrinzi
in his workshop

ARTESANO

Distributed by Juan Orozco Corporation of Maunabo, Puerto Rico.

Artesano acoustics are currently available in the U.S. market. For further information regarding models and pricing, please contact the Juan Orozco Corporation through the Index of Current Manufacturers located in the back of this edition.

ARTISAN

Instruments produced in Japan.

Artisan instruments were distributed in the U.S. market by the Barth-Feinberg company of New York.

(Source: Michael Wright, Guitar Stories Volume One)

ARTISTA

Instruments built in Spain. Distributed by Musicorp, a division of MBT of Charleston, South Carolina.

These reasonably priced handmade guitars are designed for the beginning classical guitar student. The Artista line features three models: the **Granada** ($275) has an Oregon Pine top, Sapelle (mahogany) body, and a jacaranda fingerboard; the **Morena** ($350) has the same Oregon Pine top combined with a Mongoy (Brazilian jacaranda) body, and mahogany neck; and the **Segovia** ($525) features a solid cedar top, rosewood back and sides, and a rosewood fingerboard.

ASAMA

Instruments built in Japan during the early 1980s.

Guitars with this trademark are generally medium to good quality copies of American design as well as some original designs.

(Source: Tony Bacon and Paul Day, The Guru's Guitar Guide)

ASHLAND

These instruments are manufactured in Asia. Distributed by V M I Industries of Brea, California.

Ashland instruments are manufactured for the entry level or beginning guitarist. Ashland offers three dreadnought style guitars with a spruce top and mahogany back and sides. Prices start at $249 (AD 26), to $269 (AD 36), up to $299 (AD 39). A fourth model, the AE 16 ($279) is an acoustic/electric that features a fingerboard-mounted pickup with adjustable polepieces.

ASPEN

Instruments produced in Korea between 1987 to 1991. Distributed by International Music Corporation (IMC) of Fort Worth, Texas.

Aspen was a trademark used by the International Music Corporation on a number of imported acoustic guitars and banjos. The A series featured laminated tops/bodies, and had a retail price range between $200 up to $570. Aspen's high end **Aspen Luthier** (or **AL**) series had solid wood tops, and a retail new price range between $790 to $1,500.

Aspen A-Series guitars carry a used price around $100, depending on condition; the AL-Series rates a bit higher around $300 to $400.

ASPRI CREATIVE ACOUSTICS

Distributed by Aspri Creative Acoustics of Montreal, Canada.

Further information is still being researched for future editions of the **Blue Book of Guitars**. For information regarding model specifications and pricing, please contact Aspri Creative Acoustics via the Index of Current Manufacturers located in the rear of this edition.

ASTURIAS

Instruments built on the island of Kyushu, Japan. Distribution in the U.S. market by J.T.G. of Nashville, located in Nashville, Tennessee.

The Asturias Workshops in southern Japan employ seventeen people who have worked at Asturias most of their lives or have a family connection. Guided by chief luthier Wataru Tsuji, these luthiers take great care with their production methods to ensure a quality guitar.

ATLAS

See chapter on House Brands.

This trademark has been identified as a "House Brand" of the RCA Victor Records Stores.

(Source: Willie G. Moseley, Stellas & Stratocasters)

AUDITION

See chapter on House Brands.

This trademark has been identified by researcher Willie G. Moseley as a "House Brand" of the F. W. Woolworth (Woolco) department stores.

Further information from authors Tony Bacon and Paul Day indicate that guitars with this trademark originated in Japan (later Korea) during the 1960s and 1970s.

(Source: Tony Bacon and Paul Day, The Guru's Guitar Guide)

AUGUSTINO LOPRINZI

Instruments currently built in Florida.

Luthier Augustino LoPrinzi originally was trained by his father to be a barber. A self-taught guitar builder, LoPrinzi's original Flemmington, New Jersey barbershop also had a guitar workshop in the back. After ten years dividing his interests, LoPrinzi (and his brother Thomas) founded LoPrinzi guitars in New Jersey in 1972. The business grew from a two- and three-man operation into a staff of 18 employees. Modern production techniques enabled the LoPrinzi brothers to pare the number of employees back to 7 while still producing 60 to 80 guitars a month in 1975. LoPrinzi, tired of overseeing production, sold the business to Maark Corporation (a subsidiary of AMF). Refusing to sign a "Non-compete" clause, LoPrinzi opened "Augustino Guitars" two weeks later - and literally right next door to his original plant! He continued to produce guitars there until 1978, and then moved to Florida. The AMF-owned LoPrinzi company continued producing guitars for a number of years, and finally closed the doors in 1980. Years later, Augustino called AMF to request his old trademark back. Working with vice president Dick Hargraves, Augustino officially had the trademark transferred back, and has combined it to form the current "Augustino LoPrinzi" line of classical guitars. LoPrinzi still builds classical guitars full time (about 8 guitars a month), and is assisted by his daughter, Donna Chavis, and woodworker Bill Kreutzer.

(Source: Hal Hammer)

Through the years, Augustino LoPrinzi has consulted or designed instruments for many companies including Guild, Martin, Kramer, Fender, and others. His high quality limited production classical guitars feature quality tonewoods, and range in price from $2,300 to $3,100. LoPrinzi also builds several flamenco models, and a smaller number of steel string acoustics. For further information regarding models, availability, and pricing, please contact luthier LoPrinzi via the Index of Current Manufacturers located in the rear of this book.

Augustino Loprinzi

AUSTIN

Instruments currently built in Korea and China. Distributed by St. Louis Music of St. Louis, Missouri.

Asian-produced Austin instruments are good quality entry or student level acoustic and electric guitars.

ACOUSTIC

The **AU 339 N 39 Guitar** (list $120) is a classical model with a spruce top, agathis back and sides, Nato/mahogany neck, and hardwood fingerboard; the full sized **AU 560 Concert Classic** (list $229) has a laminated spruce top, mahogany back/sides/neck, rosewood bridge and fingerboard, and inlaid marquetry soundhole rosette.

There are four dreadnought models, one of which is an acoustic/electric model. The **AU 341 S Dreadnought** (list $150) has a spruce top, mahogany back and sides, and rosewood fingerboard. The **AU 506 Ozark** has similar construction, and also features a rosewood bridge, chrome tuners, and a gloss finish (list $219). The **AU 506** is optionally available in a Gloss Black finish for $239. The 12-string **AU 518 Osage** dreadnought has a laminated spruce top, mahogany back and sides, hardwood bridge and fingerboard, chrome tuners, 5-ply body binding, and a pearl inlaid logo (list $299).

For folk style guitars, Austin offers two models. The **AU 339 S** model (list $120) has a spruce top, agathis back and sides, and a Nato/mahogany neck with hardwood fingerboard. The **AU 502 Meramac Folk** (list $229) has a spruce top and mahogany back and sides, along with a maple neck and rosewood fingerboard and bridge.

ACOUSTIC ELECTRIC

The **AU 520 Table Rock** (list $359) has a cutaway dreadnought body with laminated spruce top, mahogany back/sides/neck, diecast tuners, pearl inlaid logo, bridge pickup with volume and 3 band EQ controls, and a Natural Gloss finish. The **AU 520** is optionally available in a Gloss Black finish for $379.

AVON

Instruments built in Japan during the early to late 1970s.

The AVON trademark is the brandname of a UK importer. Avons are generally low to medium quality copies of American designs.

(Source: Tony Bacon and Paul Day, The Guru's Guitar Guide)

AXELSON

Instruments currently built in Duluth, Minnesota.

Luthier Randy Axelson has been providing top-notch guitar repair, restoration, and custom guitar building on a regular basis. For information, pricing, and availability contact luthier Axelson through the Index of Current Manufacturers located in the back of this book.

AXEMAN

Instruments built in Japan during the late 1970s.

The AXEMAN trademark is the brandname of a UK importer. The guitars are generally medium quality copies of American designs.

(Source: Tony Bacon and Paul Day, The Guru's Guitar Guide)

AXTECH

Instruments currently built in Korea.

Axtech instruments are generally entry level to medium quality solid body and acoustic guitars based on Classic American designs.

A

B

B & J

See chapter on House Brands.

This trademark has been identified as a House Brand of the B & J company.

(Source: Willie G. Moseley, Stellas & Stratocasters)

BACON & DAY

See VEGA.

BALDWIN

Instruments produced initally in England by Burns; later models were shipped by components and assembled in Booneville, Arkansas. Baldwin guitars and basses were produced between 1965 to 1970. Distribution of instruments handled by the Baldwin Piano Company of Cinncinnati, Ohio.

In 1962, as Leo Fender's health was faltering, he discussed the idea of selling Fender Electric Instruments company to Don Randall (head of Fender Sales). While Randall toyed with the idea even as late as the summer of 1963, they eventually concluded to sell to a third party who had money. Negotiations began with the Baldwin Piano Company in April of 1964, who offered $5 million (minus Fender's liabilities). When talks bogged down over acoustic guitar and electric piano operations, Randall met with representatives of the Columbia Broadcasting System (CBS). An agreement with CBS was signed in October, 1964, for $13 million that took effect in January of 1965.

Baldwin, outbid by CBS but still looking to diversify its product lines, then bought the Burns manufacturing facilities from Jim Burns (regarded as "the British Leo Fender") in September, 1965. U.S. distributed models bore the Baldwin trademark. During Baldwin's first year of ownership, only the logos were changed on the imported guitars. In 1966, the Burns-style scroll headstock was redesigned; and in 1967 the *700* series was debuted. The Baldwin company then began assembling the imported Burns parts in Booneville, Arkansas.

Baldwin acquired the Gretsch trademark when Fred Gretsch, Jr. sold the company in 1967. As part of a business consolidation, the New York Gretsch operation was moved to the Arkansas facility in 1970. Baldwin then concentrated their corporate interests in the Gretsch product line, discontinuing further Baldwin/Burns models. However, it is interesting to note that many Burns-style features (like the bridge vibrato) began to turn up on Gretsch models after 1967. For further Baldwin/Gretsch history, see GRETSCH.

(Source: Paul Day, The Burns Book; and Michael Wright, Vintage Guitar Magazine)

BARBERO

Instruments were built in Spain.

This brandname belonged to Marcelo Barbero (1904-1955), considered one of the great flamenco guitar makers.

(Source: Tony Bacon, The Ultimate Guitar Book)

CARL BARNEY

Instruments built in Southbury, Connecticut since 1968.

Luthier Carl Barney started building classical guitars in 1968, and built his first archtop guitar in 1972. Two years later, Barney built a guitar for jazz legend Sal Salvador - and began a long friendship and collaboration with Salvador (Barney later created the **Sal Salvador Artist** model for Salvador in 1980).

All guitars are handcrafted by Barney in his workshop. Since the mid 1970s, Barney has been searching and stockpiling fine instrument woods. In 1976, Barney purchased a good-sized quanity of Gaboon ebony, as well as Brazilian and Indian rosewood. Barney currently uses figured woods for all models, and has a supply of figured maple for special commisions. Barney began using Adirondack (American Red) spruce for guitar tops since 1993, which is whiter in appearance than Sitka spruce (which is also available).

Since mid 1996, Barney has built over eighty archtop guitars. Although archtops have been Barney's focus since 1974, he has also built over 100 classical, flat-top acoustics, and solid body electrics since the mid 1970s. Prices quoted are for base models; for further information please contact luthier Barney through the Index of Current Manufacturers located in the rear of this book.

ACOUSTIC

Add $100 for 18" body width.

Barney offers three versions of his **Jazzmaker Series** archtop guitars. The **Jazzmaker I** features a hand-carved top and back, figured maple back and sides, *4-line* top binding, *1-line* back/fingerboard/headstock binding, small fingerboard markers, unbound f-holes, ebony tailpiece and pickguard, and is available in 16" and 17" body widths. The retail price in a Sunburst finish is $3,300; Natural finish is $3,500.

The **Jazzmaker II** is the standard custom model. This model has a hand-carved top and back, highly figured maple back and sides, *7-line* top binding, *4-line* back/fingerboard/headstock binding, block fingerboard markers, bound f-holes, ebony bridge and tailpiece and pickguard, and is available in 16" and 17" body widths. The retail price in a Sunburst finish is $3,800; Natural finish is $4,000.

The **Jazzmaker Deluxe** is similar to the Jazzmaker II, except has exceptionally figured maple back and sides; *7-line* binding on top, back, and headstock; split block fingerboard inlay; *4-line* binding on fingerboard and f-holes; inlaid ebony heel cap, inlaid ebony veneer on the back of headstock. The retail price in a Sunburst finish is $4,200; Natural finish is $4,400.

Jazzmaker II
courtesy Carl Barney

Sal Salvador model
courtesy Carl Barney

The **OV Jazz Model** is an oval soundhole guitar similar to the 1960s Howard Robert Epiphone model. Retail prices start at $2,600 for the basic model, and increase up to $3,400 to the deluxe version based on the amount of detail and inlay work.

The current **Sal Salvador Artist** model is based on the third model Barney built for Salvador, and is the second Artist model design (the first design was created in 1981). The model has an Adirondack spruce top, flamed maple back and sides, abalone/pearl split block fingerboard inlay/headstock/heel cap. The ebony tailpiece and pickguard also have decorative inlays. This model is available with a built-in pickup, or with a floating pickup. The body width is 16", and the body depth 2 3/4" depth. The Salvadore Artist model is available with a Natural top/tinted back and sides, Natural, and 4 color Sunburst finishes. Retail list price is $4,500, and includes a hard shell case.

In addition to the Archtop models, Barney also offers flatop top steel strings models (list $1,400), classicals ($1,800), and even solid body electric designs ($1,000).

BARON (U.S. MFR.)

See chapter on House Brands.

This trademark has been identified as a *House Brand* of the RCA Victor Records Store; furthermore, KAY exported guitars bearing this trademark to the Thibouville-Lamy company of France.

(Source: Willie G. Moseley, Stellas & Stratocasters)

BARRINGTON

Instruments produced in Japan during the late 1980s. Distribution in the U.S. market was handled by Barrington Guitars of Barrington, Illinois.

Barrington Guitars offered both solid body electric guitars and basses during the late 1980s, as well as acoustic and acoustic/electric models. The guitar models were produced in Japan by Terada. The company now specializes in brass instruments as the L.A. Sax Company of Barrington, Illinois.

ACOUSTIC

Barrington offered both acoustic and acoustic/electric Barrington Gruhn signature series models as well. The acoustics were similar to a design prototype produced in collaboration between George Gruhn and Collings guitars in 1988; and the Barrington models carried a new retail list price between $1,225 and $1,325 (a Fishman transducer pickup was optional equipment on the four models). The **AT-1** and **AT-2** f-hole archtops listed new at $1,650.

BILL BARTOLINI

Instruments built in 1960s.

Bartolini now produces a line of high quality guitar pickups in Livermore, California.

Luthier Bill Bartolini used to build classical guitars in California during the 1960s. Bartolini estimates that perhaps only a dozen guitars were built. Research on resonances produced during this time formed the basis for his pickup designs, and his clear, high quality pickups are standard features on numerous luthiers' creations.

(Information courtesy Bill Bartolini)

BAUER

See S.S. STEWART.

George Bauer, a noted guitar builder in Philadelphia during the late 1800s, entered into a partnership with banjo producer S.S. Stewart. The two produced guitars under the Stewart & Bauer trademark. After Stewart passed away, Bauer continued to release instruments under the Stewart & Bauer label, and also under the Monogram trademark.

(Source: Tom Wheeler, American Guitars)

BAY STATE

Instruments manufactured in Boston, Massachusetts from 1865 to the early 1900s.

The Oliver Ditson Company, Inc. was formed in 1835 by music publisher Oliver Ditson (1811-1888). Ditson was a primary force in music merchandising, distribution, and retail sales on the East Coast. He also helped establish two musical instrument manufacturers: The John Church Company of Cincinnati, Ohio, and Lyon & Healy (Washburn) in Chicago, Illinois.

In 1865 Ditson established a manufacturing branch of his company under the supervision of John Haynes, called the John C. Haynes Company. This branch built guitars for a number of trademarks, such as **Bay State**, **Tilton**, and **Haynes Excelsior**.

(Source: Tom Wheeler, American Guitars)

B.C. RICH

Instruments currently built in Hesperia, California (American Handmade series) and Asia (NJ, Platinum and Bronze series). Distributed by B.C. Rich Guitars International, Inc. of San Bernadino, California and B.C. Rich Guitars USA.

Import models (NJ, Platinum, and Bronze Series) distributed by Davitt & Hanser Music of Cincinnati, Ohio.

Luthier Bernardo Chavez Rico used to build classical and flamenco guitars at Bernardo's Valencian Guitar Shop, the family's business in Los Angeles. During the mid 1960s folk music boom (and boom in guitar sales), a distributor suggested a name change - and B.C. Rich guitars were born. Between 1966 and 1968, Rico continued to build acoustic guitars, then changed to solid body electrics. The company began producing custom guitars based on Fender and Gibson designs, but Rico wanted to produce designs that represented his tastes and ideals. The Seagull solid body (first produced in 1971) was sleek, curvy, and *made for rock & roll*. Possessing a fast neck, hot-rodded circuitry and pickups, and a unique body profile was (and still is) an eye-catching design.

In 1974, Neal Mosher joined the company. Mosher also had a hand in some of the guitars designed, and further explored other designs with models like the Mockingbird, Eagle, Ironbird, and the provocatively-named Bich. The first 6-tuners-on-a-side headstocks began to appear in 1981. In the mid 1980s, B.C. Rich moved from Los Angeles to El Monte, California.

The company began to import models in the **U.S. Production Series**, Korean-produced kits that were assembled in the U.S. between 1984 to 1986. In 1984, the Japanese-built **N.J. Series** line of B.C. Rich designs were introduced, and were built by the Terada company for two years. Production of the N.J. series was moved to Korea in 1986 (models were built in the Cort factory).

In 1988, Rico licensed the Korean-built lower priced **Platinum** and entry level **Rave Series** to the Class Axe company, and later licensed the B.C. Rich name and designs in 1989. Class Axe moved production of the U.S.-built guitars to a facility in Warren, New Jersey, and stepped up importation of the N.J. (named after Nagoya, Japan - not New Jersey), Platinum, and Rave Series models.

Unfortunately, the lower priced series soon began to show a marked drop in quality. In 1994, Rico came back out of semi-retirement, retook control over his trademark, and began to rebuild the company. Rico became partners with Bill Shapiro, and the two divided up areas of responsibility. Rico once more began building acoustic and high end electrics at his Hesperia facilities; and Shapiro began maintaining quality control over the imported N.J., Platinum, and U.S. series in San Bernadino. In 1998, Davitt & Hanser Music of Cincinnati, Ohio began distributing the import models (NJ, Platinum, and Bronze Series).

(Additional model commentary courtesy Bernie Rich, President/Founder of B.C. Rich International, May 1997)

Grading	100%	EXCELLENT	AVERAGE

ACOUSTIC

Signature Series

The Signature Series acoustics are hand crafted in the U.S.
Add $100 for 6 on a side headstock (acoustic models).
Add $150 for an installed Fishman Matrix 4 band EQ.

B20-D — dreadnought style, solid spruce top, round soundhole, white body binding, solid mahogany back/sides, mahogany neck, 21 fret rosewood fingerboard with white dot inlay, rosewood bridge, white pearl dot bridge pins, 3 per side chrome tuners. Available in Stained High Gloss finish. Current mfr.

Mfr.'s Sug. Retail	$1,299	$910	$600	$420

This model is also available with a solid black finish with white body binding or solid white finish with black body binding.

B20-C Cutaway — similar to B20-D, except has single rounded cutaway. Available in Natural High Gloss finish. Current mfr.

Mfr.'s Sug. Retail	$1,399	$980	$645	$445

This model is also available with a solid black finish with white body binding or solid white finish with black body binding.

B20-C DS Cutaway — similar to the B20-D, except has a solid red cedar top, single rounded cutaway, diamond shaped soundhole with abalone and rosewood inlays. Current mfr.

Mfr.'s Sug. Retail	$1,499	$1,050	$690	$480

This model is also available with a solid black finish with white body binding or solid white finish with black body binding.

B30-D — dreadnought sized flat top body, select spruce top, round soundhole, rosewood bound body, abalone rosette, solid quilted maple back/sides, mahogany neck, 21 fret rosewood fingerboard with abalone diamond inlay, rosewood bridge, white pearl dot bridge pins, 3 per side chrome tuners. Available in Natural, Transparent Blue, Transparent Emerald Green, Transparent Pagan Gold, and Transparent Red finishes. Current mfr.

Mfr.'s Sug. Retail	$1,499	$1,050	$690	$480

B30-C — similar to B30-D, except has a single rounded cutaway. Current mfr.

Mfr.'s Sug. Retail	$1,499	$1,050	$690	$480

B35-D — dreadnought style, select spruce top, round soundhole, white body binding, solid rosewood back/sides, mahogany neck, 14/21 fret bound ebony fingerboard with abalone cloud inlay, ebony bridge with pearl cloud inlay, white pearl dot bridge pins, peghead with abalone logo inlay, 3 per side chrome tuners. Available in Natural finish. Mfr. 1995 to date.

Mfr.'s Sug. Retail	$1,699	$1,190	$785	$545

B35-C — similar to B35-D, except has a single rounded cutaway. Current mfr.

Mfr.'s Sug. Retail	$1,699	$1,190	$785	$545

B41-C DIAMOND — single round cutaway flat top body, select spruce top, diamond shaped soundhole, abalone purfling/rosette, rosewood back/sides, mahogany neck, 21 fret bound ebony fingerboard with abalone cloud inlay, ebony bridge with pearl cloud inlay, white pearl dot bridge pins, bound rosewood veneered peghead with abalone logo inlay, 3 per side Grover Imperial gold tuners. Available in Natural finish. Mfr. 1995 to date.

Mfr.'s Sug. Retail	$2,699	$2,025	$1,325	$890

B41-D — similar to B41-C, except has noncutaway dreadnought style body, 14/21 fret rosewood fingerboard. Available in Natural finish. Mfr. 1995 to 1996.

			$1,325	$800

Last Mfr.'s Sug. Retail was $2,495.

Elite Acoustic Series

Elite Series acoustic guitars are imported to the U.S. market.

BR40D — dreadnought style, solid spruce top, round soundhole, mahogany back/sides, mahogany neck, 21 fret rosewood fingerboard with white dot inlay, rosewood bridge, white pearl dot bridge pins, 3 per side chrome tuners. Available in Natural and Sunburst high gloss finishes. Current mfr.

Mfr.'s Sug. Retail	$479	$335	$225	$155

Grading	100%	EXCELLENT	AVERAGE

BR60D — dreadnought style, solid cedar top, round soundhole, mahogany back/sides, abalone body binding, mahogany neck, 21 fret rosewood fingerboard with pearl eagle inlay, rosewood bridge, white pearl dot bridge pins, 3 per side gold plated die cast tuners. Available in Natural satin finish. Current mfr.

Mfr.'s Sug. Retail	$689	$480	$320	$220

Add $200 for factory installed Fishman Matrix 4 band EQ system/bridge transducer.

BR65DE — dreadnought style, solid spruce top, round soundhole, mahogany back/sides, white body binding, mahogany neck, 21 fret bound rosewood fingerboard with white dot inlay, rosewood bridge, white pearl dot bridge pins, 3 per side chrome tuners, Fishman Matrix EQ system. Available in Gloss Black finish. Current mfr.

Mfr.'s Sug. Retail	$899	$630	$415	$290

BR65DCE — similar to the BR65DE, except has single rounded cutaway. Current mfr.

Mfr.'s Sug. Retail	$899	$630	$415	$290

BR70D — dreadnought style, solid spruce top, round soundhole, rosewood back/sides, abalone/white body binding, abalone rosette, mahogany neck, 21 fret bound rosewood fingerboard with cats eye position markers, rosewood bridge, white pearl dot bridge pins, bound headstock, 3 per side tuners. Available in Natural Gloss finish. Current mfr.

Mfr.'s Sug. Retail	$649	$455	$300	$210

Add $200 for factory installed Fishman Matrix 4 band EQ system/bridge transducer.

B D DEY

Instruments currently built in the Czech Republic. Distributed by B D Dey Musical Instruments of the Czech Republic.

The Czech Republic is beginning to be the place for companies looking for an alternative to Asian guitar production. Various areas in the Czech Republic have a reputation for excellent instrument craftsmanship, evolving from the earlier days of violin and viola production. Of course, now that capitalism is back, making some money on well-built instruments isn't bad either. B D Dey Musical Instruments is one such modern company that is making a bid for European (and perhaps) American market success. B D Dey is currently offering 5 different electric guitar models, and a 6- and 12-string jumbo acoustic guitar model.

ACOUSTIC

The **Rieger-Kloss** jumbo guitar model features a solid spruce top, mahogany veneer back and sides, maple neck, 1 4/20 ebony fingerboard with pearl dot inlays, ebony bridge, 3 (or 6, depending on the configuration) per side chrome tune rs, plastic pickguard. The acoustics are available in Natural and Sunburst finishes; both configurations are also available with a piezo pickup an d onboard equalizer.

BEAR CREEK GUITARS

Instruments currently built in Monterey, California. Distributed by Bear Creek Guitars of Monterey, California.

Bear Creek Guitars builds fine handmade Hawaiian steel guitars in the "Weissenborn" tradition. The instruments are styled after the classic steel guitars of the 1920s but with beautiful craftsmanship and more attention to details than the originals. The price range for the four styles available runs from $1,800 to $3,500. Bear Creek instruments are played and recommended by noted musician/author Bob Brozman.

BELTONA

Instruments currently built in Leeds, England.

Beltona produces custom-made resonator instruments, all out of metal construction. Beltona manufactures all of their own parts. All guitars are made to customer specifications, as well as the custom engraving.

The Beltona Shop produces a limited number of instruments per year. Current models include a triple resonator guitar, a single resonator guitar (either 12 or 14 fret), and an electro resonator model, as well as mandolin and ukulele models. For further information regarding prices and specifications, please contact Beltona through the Index of Current Manufacturers located in the back of this book.

ROBERT BENEDETTO

Instruments currently built in East Stroudsburg, Pennsylvania.

Robert Benedetto
courtesy Robert and Cindy Benedetto

Master Luthier Robert Benedetto has been handcrafting fine archtop guitars since 1968. Benedetto was born in New York in 1946. Both his father and grandfather were master cabinetmakers, and Benedetto's uncles were musicians. While growing up in New Jersey, Benedetto began playing the guitar professionally at age thirteen. Being near the New York/New Jersey jazz music scene, Benedetto had numerous opportunities to perform repair and restoration work on other classic archtops. Benedetto built his first archtop in 1968, and his pre-eminence in the field is evidenced by his having made archtop guitars longer than any living builders and has a growing list of endorsers. Current endorsers range from Jimmy Bruno and Kenny Burrell to Earl Klugh and Andy Summers.

Benedetto moved to Homosassa, Florida in 1976. Three years later, he relocated to Clearwater, Florida. A veteran innovator, Benedetto began concentrating on the acoustic properties of the guitar designs, and started a movement to strip away unnecessary adornment (inlays, bindings) in 1982. While continuing his regular work on archtop building, Benedetto also built violins between 1983-1987. Violinist extraordinaire Stephane Grappelli purchased one of his violins in 1993. Benedetto even built a small number of electric solid body guitars and basses (which debuted at the 1987 NAMM show) in addition to his regular archtop production schedule.

Benedetto moved to his current location in East Stroudsberg, Pennsylvania in 1990, and continues to produce instruments from that location. His endorsers span three generations of jazz guitarists. Not since John D'Angelico has anyone made as many archtop guitars nor had as many well known players endorsing and recording with his guitars. Closer scrutiny reveals nuances found only from a maker of his stature. His minimalist delicate inlay motif has become a trademark as have his novel use of black, rather than gold, tuning machines, black bridge height adjustment wheels, and an ebony nut (versus bone), all of which harmonize with the ebony fittings throughout the guitar. He is the originator of the solid ebony tailpiece, uniquely fastened to the guitar with cello tail adjustor. Likewise, he was the first to use exotic and natural wood veneers on the headstock and pioneered the use of violin-pigments to shade his guitars. His *honey blonde* finish is now widely used within the guitar industry. Benedetto is also well known for refining the 7-string archtop and is that unique model's most prolific maker.

Benedetto is the Archtop Guitar Construction Editor and "Guitar Maintenance" columnist for **Just Jazz Guitar** magazine, and is the author of **Making an Archtop Guitar** (Centerstream Publishing, 1994). He released his 9 1/2 hour instructional video, **Archtop Guitar Design & Construction**, in November 1996. He is currently at work on a second book tenatively entitled "Anecdotes, Insights, and Facts about Archtop Guitar Construction". His forthcoming biography is being written by eminent jazz guitar historian Adrian Ingram. Benedetto serves on the board of Association of Stringed Instrument Artisans and endorses E&O Mari "La Bella" strings. He also markets the **Benedetto** *floating* pickup, a standard size humbucking pickup, and solid ebony tailpiece for his (and other) archtop acoustic guitars.

(Biographical information courtesy Cindy Benedetto)

As of August 1997, luthier Bob Benedetto has built over 675 instruments. While the majority are archtop guitars, he has also produced 157 electric solid body guitars, 52 electric basses, 48 violins, 5 violas, 2 mandolins, and one cello. Benedetto currently schedules his production to a limited 12 to 15 archtop guitars a year, as well as a few violins.

ACOUSTIC ARCHTOP

Limelite
courtesy John Bender

All Benedetto guitars share some similar design and construction features. All tops and backs are hand graduated and tuned, and all models feature a single cutaway (except the Americana model). They have a 25" scale, and the necks feature 21 frets. Bodies may be 16", 17", or 18" across the lower bout, and have a depth of 3" (the 18" body has an additional $1,200 charge). Hardware includes a suspended *Benedetto* jazz mini-humbucker with volume control mounted on pickguard/fingerrest, black ebonized bridge height adjusters, an adjustable truss rod, and Schaller M6 tuning machines with solid ebony or gold buttons. The fingerboard, bridge, pickguard, fingerrest, truss rod cover, and harp-style tailpiece are all handcrafted of solid ebony, and the guitars are finished in high gloss nitrocellulose lacquer. Color choices include a Traditional Sunburst, Cremona Sunburst, Honey Blonde, Blonde, or Natural. The suggested retail price includes a deluxe hardshell case.

MANHATTAN— carved select aged spruce top, carved select flamed maple back with matching sides, black/white binding, 3-piece flamed maple neck, Neo-classical (no inlays) fingerboard, narrow **Chuck Wayne**-style fingerrest, black or gold Schaller tuners with solid ebony buttons. Current mfr.
List Price $17,500

FRATELLO— carved select aged spruce top, carved select flamed maple back with matching sides, black/white binding, 3-piece flamed maple neck, traditional-style bound pickguard, large mother-of-pearl fingerboard inlays, gold Schaller M6 tuners with gold buttons. Current mfr.
List Price $17,500

THE 7-STRING— 7-string configuration, carved select aged spruce tops, carved flamed maple back with matching sides, black/white binding, 3-piece flamed maple neck, Neo-classical fingerboard, narrow **Chuck Wayne**-style fingerrest, gold Schaller tuners with solid ebony buttons. Current mfr.
List Price $17,500

LA VENEZIA — carved European spruce top, flamed European maple back/sides, 3-piece flamed maple neck, Neo-classical fingerboard, no body binding, large flared headstock, ebony nut, chamfered f-holes, no fingerrest, solid ebony endpin, black Schaller tuners with solid ebony buttons. Available in Cremona lacq Sunburst finish. Current mfr.
List Price $20,000

The La Venezia was inspired by a unique guitar built for Chuck Wayne in 1982, and features an intermingling of design ideas from violin and archtop building.

AMERICANA— 18" body width, carved select aged spruce tops, non-cutaway body, carved select flamed maple back with matching sides, black/white binding, 3-piece flamed maple neck, large flared headstock, Neo-classical (no inlays) fingerboard, narrow **Chuck Wayne**-style fingerrest, gold Schaller tuners with solid Ebony buttons. Current mfr.
List Price $27,500

Both the Americana and Limelite models offer a tribute to the early days of archtop building and big bands.

LIMELITE— carved select aged spruce tops, carved flamed maple back with matching sides, 3-piece flamed maple neck, large flared headstock, split fingerboard inlay, traditionally-shaped bound pickguard, intricate inlay work on the pickguard/tailpiece, gold Schaller tuners with solid ebony buttons. Current mfr.
List Price $35,000

CREMONA — hand carved/graduated/tuned European cello wood top and back, matching sides, fine line binding, flamed maple neck, large flared burl-veneered headstock with elegant mother-of-pearl/abalone inlay, gold Schaller tuners with gold (or solid ebony or mother of pearl) buttons. Current mfr.
List Price $50,000

The Cremona was Benedetto's first standard model. Current options include headstock-matching inlay on tailpiece and pickguard, and split block mother of pearl fingerboard inlay.

Renaissance Series

Renaissance Series instruments are very custom, one-of-a-kind archtop guitars. While the features may vary, the most distinct similarity between them are the clustered sound openings (unique to Benedetto) which range in design and location from one instrument to another. To date, only two instruments have been constructed - the *Il Fiorentino*, and the *Il Palissandro* (a third is in the works). List price on these models is $35,000. All Renaissance series instruments will have their own name.

The *Il Palissandro* model has a 16" width, non-cutaway body, and features a European spruce top, Indian rosewood back and sides, one-piece Honduran mahogany neck, ebony fingerboard/bridge/tailpiece/endpin, rosewood binding/natural wood purfling, a classical-style tapered neck heel, serpentine-style headstock with flamed curly maple and rosewood border/flamed curly maple truss rod cover, no fingerrest and no pickup.

Benedetto La Cremona Azzurra
courtesy Scott Chinery

BENTLY

Instruments are manufactured in Asia. Distributed by the St. Louis Music company of St. Louis, Missouri.

B

Bently instruments are entry level to medium quality solid body guitars and basses that feature designs based on classic American favorites.

BESSON

See FRAMUS.

See also ARISTONE.

Instruments made in West Germany during the late 1950s through the early 1960s.

While BESSON was the brandname for a UK importer, these guitars were made by and identical to certain FRAMUS models. Research also indicates that the trademark ARISTONE was utilized as well.

(Source: Tony Bacon and Paul Day, The Guru's Guitar Guide)

BEVERLY

See chapter on House Brands.

This trademark has been identified as a "House Brand" of SELMER UK in England.

(Source: Willie G. Moseley, Stellas & Stratocasters)

BI LEVEL GUITARS

See LA JOLLA LUTHIERS.

BIG HEART

Instruments built in the U.S. since 1998. Distributed by the Big Heart Slide Company of Placentia, California.

In 1998, the Big Heart Slide Company debuted their own guitar model, the **Big Heart BrassTop**. The Big Heart Slide Company is well known for their various aluminum, porcelain, and glass slides; the guitar model is an electric hollow body guitar set up for the slide technique, and features a full brass top. Retail prices range from $750 to $1,200. For further information and specifications, contact the Big Heart Slide Company via the Index of Current Manufacturers located in the back of this edition.

BLACK HILLS

See chapter on House Brands.

This trademark has been identified as a *House Brand* of the Wall Drug stores.

(Source: Willie G. Moseley, Stellas & Stratocasters)

TOM BLACKSHEAR

Instruments currently built in San Antonio, Texas.

Luthier Tom Blackshear builds high quality Classical guitar models. For further information, please contact luthier Blackshear via the index of Current Manufacturers located in the back of this book.

BLAIR GUITARS LTD.

Instruments currently built in Ellington, Connecticut.

Designer Douglas Blair has over twenty years experience in the music field, and has been building his own guitars since his teens. Blair has recorded 3 independent EP/LPs, and toured with acts like *Run 21* and "W.A.S.P.". Throughout his professional playing career, Blair found himself constantly switching between his electric guitar and an Ovation acoustic on a stand for live performances. In 1990, Blair conceived of the **Mutant Twin** guitar model as a way to solve the problem, which combined a solid body half with an "acoustic" half (with hollow tuned sound chamber and Fishman preamp). Prototypes were developed with the aid of Ovation R & D designer Don Johnson in 1990, and the guitar debuted in Boston in 1991. Blair Guitars Ltd. debuted at the 1994 NAMM winter show.

In 1997, Blair's design was licensed to Guild (FMIC) as the new Slash signature **Crossroads** custom design doubleneck guitar. This model is available in Black or Crimson Transparent finishes (Guild retail list $4,000).

ACOUSTIC

Blair recently introduced the **ASIA Acoustic 12**, a "Dual Format 12-string model with 6 pairs of unison strings and nylon strings. This guitar has a cedar top, mahogany neck, mahogany/koa back and sides, Steinberger tuners, Fishman piezo bridge pickup, active volume/tone/controls, discrete outputs, and a 3-way format selector (list price $1,999).

BLUE LION

Instruments built in Santa Margarita, California since 1975.

The Blue Lion company of Robert and Janita Baker is more known for the dulcimers they produce, but they did build an estimated 6 to 8 acoustic guitars a year. The model is dubbed the **B 1 Standard**, and many custom options were featured.

The last list price recorded for the B 1 Standard was $1,650 (with case).

BLUERIDGE

Instruments currently produced in Asia. Distributed by Saga Musical Instruments of San Francisco, California.

Blueridge acoustics are dreadnought style guitars designed in part for the entry level to intermediate guitar player. These guitars feature a solid spruce top, mahogany neck, bound rosewood fingerboard with mother of pearl position dots, rosewood bridge, a concentric circle rosette, black pickguard, natural satin or clear high gloss finish, chrome sealed tuners, and a solid 3 per side headstock. Models feature rosewood or mahogany back and sides.

BLUESOUTH

Instruments currently built in Muscle Shoals, Alabama.

Ronnie Knight began Bluesouth Guitars in 1991 with the idea of building stringed musical instruments which celebrate the musical heritage of the American South. Blues, jazz, country, rock, and spiritual music were all created in the southern American states. This small area from Texas to the Carolinas, from Kentucky to Florida, has been the hotbed of the world's musical culture in the twentieth century. Several small towns within the southeast have had a huge impact on today's popular music: Muscle Shoals, Alabama, Macon, Georgia, and Clarksdale, Mississippi.

The results of this project have been unique, light-bodied guitars with large, comfortable necks. Bluesouth contends that "fierce individualism" is the key ingredient in their guitar making operation. Starting in a small shop over a record store in early 1992, Bluesouth moved to a much larger industrial facility in the spring of 1995. To date, the company offers 7 models, including 2 electric basses. Bluesouth also builds its own cases and pickups in house.

(Company history courtesy Ronnie Knight, April 17, 1996)

ACOUSTIC

Bluesouth guitars offers two acoustic models, an archtop model and a flattop model. The arch top **Storyville** model has a single cutaway body with hand carved European spruce top, European maple back and sides, 5-ply black/ivoroid body bin ding, hard maple neck, and ivoroid bound ebony fingerboard. The list price of $5,300 includes a case. The **Tutweiler** (list $2,195, case included) has a solid spruce top, mahogany back and sides, ivoroid body binding, mahogany neck, and rosewood fingerboard.

BOAZ ELKAYAM GUITARS

Instruments currently built in North Hollywood, California.

Boaz Elkayam hand builds commissioned guitars, customized prototypes, classical and flamenco style guitars, mandolins, and his new 'Travel Guitar'. Elkayam, the son of a violin builder, was taught building techniques of stringed instruments, and has performed restoration work on museum pieces.

ACOUSTIC

Luthier Elkayam handcrafts his guitars using traditional lutherie techniques, and eschews the use of power tools. Elkayam prefers to build with top-of-the-line woods such as Brazilian and Indian rosewood, Macassar and Gaboon ebony, Hond uran mahogany, German and Canadian spruce, and Alaskan red cedar. Pieces are limited to a small yearly output.

JOSEPH BOHMANN

Instruments built in Chicago, Illinois from 1878 to the late 1920s.

Luthier Joseph H. Bohmann was born in Neumarkt (Bohemia), Czechoslovakia in 1848. He later emigrated to America, and then founded Bohmann's American Musical Industry in 1878. Bohmann's Perfect Artist violins won a number of international honors, and his American mandolin model was the top of the line in both the Montgomery Ward and Sears catalogues in 1894. By 1900, Bohmann was offering thirteen grades of guitars.

(Source: Michael Wright, Vintage Guitar Magazine)

BOOM BASSES

See KEN DONNELL.

BOUCHET

Instruments built in Paris, France from 1946 to possibly the late 1970s.

Luthier and painter Robert Bouchet (1898-1986) began building guitars in Paris in the mid 1940s. A keen guitarist, he produced very high quality guitars in small numbers.

(Source: Tony Bacon, The Ultimate Guitar Book)

DANA BOURGEOIS GUITARS

Instruments currently produced in Lewiston, Maine. Distributed by Akai Musical Instrument Corporation of Fort Worth, Texas.

Luthier Dana Bourgeois has spent almost twenty-five years honing his craft as a custom builder and restorer of vintage guitars. Before starting his own company, Bourgeois was a co-founder of Schoenberg guitars. Bourgeois designed the acclaimed Schoenberg Soloist, and personally voiced each Schoenberg guitar during its construction by the C.F. Martin company. He later served as design consultant to Gibson during the start up of their acoustic guitar plant in Montana. While working as a product designer for Paul Reed Smith, he learned CAD drawing from Bob Taylor (Taylor Guitars).

Bourgeois currently builds guitars with his own company, and applies his knowledge of traditional and modern techniques to current designs. One such technique is the "voicing" of each piece of wood by tapping and listening. During construction, further tap-tuning and adjusting the thickness of the guitar's top tunes the wood resonance. This process allows the top to respond to a greater range of frequencies, which results in a more "articulate" and balanced acoustic guitar.

(Company history courtesy Dana Bourgeois Guitars)

ACOUSTIC ARCHTOP

A-500 (17")— 17" body width, spruce top, curly maple back/sides, 2 f-holes, 3-piece curly maple neck, ivoroid body/neck/peghead binding, black/white/black purfling, 20 fret ebony fingerboard with Deco block fingerboard inlay, ebony peghead veneer, ebony adjustable bridge/metal tailpiece, raised bound black pickguard, 3 per side gold Schaller tuners with ebony buttons, floating Kent Armstrong custom pickup. Current mfr.

Mfr.'s Sug. Retail $8,580

Bozo custom Archtop courtesy Bozo
Podunavac

ACOUSTIC

All Bourgeois guitars feature an ebony fretboard and bridge, single piece mahogany neck, Adirondack spruce bracing, mother of pearl headstock inlay, ebony end and bridge pins with mother of pearl dots, and a gloss lacquer finish on body and neck. Retail price includes hardshell case.

Add $240 for TMC acoustic pickup.

Dreadnought Series

RICKY SKAGGS SIGNATURE — dreadnought style, master grade spruce top, Indian rosewood back/sides, round soundhole, abalone rosette, ivoroid body/neck/peghead binding, black/white/black top and back purfling, herringbone backstripe, squared headstock with rosewood veneer, 14/20 fret ebony fingerboard with pearl square and diamond inlay, ebony belly bridge, tortoiseshell pickguard, 3 per side nickel Waverly tuners. Current mfr.

Mfr.'s Sug. Retail $4,000

Ricky Skaggs Country Boy — similar to the Ricky Skaggs Signature, except features mahogany back/sides, wood rosette, tortoiseshell-style body binding, black/white top purfling, black line backstripe, black bound fingerboard with mother of pearl dot position markers, 3 per side vintage-style Gotoh tuners. Mfr. 1998 to date.

Mfr.'s Sug. Retail $2,960

Jumbo Orchestra Model Series

JOMC-DLX — Jumbo OM style body with single rounded cutaway, spruce top, Indian rosewood back/sides, round soundhole, abalone rosette, ivoroid body/neck/peghead binding, abalone top purfling and black/white/black back and side purfling, fancy herringbone backstripe, flared rounded headstock with ebony veneer, 14/20 fret ebony fingerboard with pearl floral inlay, ebony belly bridge, tortoiseshell pickguard, 3 per side gold Schaller tuners with ebony buttons. Current mfr.

Mfr.'s Sug. Retail $4,850

Orchestra Model Series

OM — OM style body, spruce top, mahogany back/sides, round soundhole, wood rosette, tortoiseshell-style body binding, black/white top purfling, black line backstripe, squared headstock with Indian rosewood veneer, 14/20 fret black bound ebony fingerboard with mother of pearl dot position markers, ebony belly bridge, tortoiseshell pickguard, 3 per side gold Gotoh tuners. Current mfr.

Mfr.'s Sug. Retail $2,850

OMC (Orchestra Model Cutaway) — similar to the OM, except features single rounded cutaway body, Indian rosewood back/sides, abalone rosette, black/white/black top purfling, multi-color herringbone backstripe, pearl square and diamond fingerboard inlay. Current mfr.

Mfr.'s Sug. Retail $3,650

Slope D Cutaway Series (12 Fret)

MARTIN SIMPSON SIGNATURE MODEL — dreadnought style body with sloped cutaway, spruce top, Indian rosewood back/sides, round soundhole, abalone rosette, ivoroid body/neck/peghead binding, black/white/black top purfling, multi-color herringbone backstripe, flared rounded headstock with ebony veneer, 12/19 fret ebony fingerboard with leaf inlay, ebony belly bridge, 3 per side chrome Schaller tuners, special signature label. Current mfr.

Mfr.'s Sug. Retail $4,100

Martin Simpson European — similar to the Martin Simpson Signature Model, except features cedar top, mahogany back/sides, wood rosette, mother of pearl position markers, 3 per side vintage-style Gotoh tuners. Mfr. 1998 to date.

Mfr.'s Sug. Retail $3,450

RALPH S. BOWN

Instruments currently built in York, England.

This independent luthier is currently building high quality guitars. For further information, please contact Ralph Bown via the Index of Current Manufacturers located in the back of this edition.

BŎ ZO

Instruments currently built in Englewood, Florida.

Master Luthier Bozidar Podunavac has been creating guitars for forty years. Bozo (pronounced Bo-Zho) was originally apprenticed to luthier Milutin Mladenuvic in his native Yugoslavia. In 1959, Bozo and his wife Mirjana emigrated to the U.S., and were located in Chicago, Illinois. Bozo initially did repair work for various music stores, and later opened his own shop in 1965. His original guitars were designed after the dreadnought body style, but changed to his own original 'Bell Western' design in 1968.

The Podunavacs moved to Escondido (near San Diego), California in 1972, and to San Diego three years later. In 1978, Bozo opened a school of lutherie, which he ran for a number of years. The family later relocated to Florida, where the current guitar building is based today. Although Podunavac is currently retired, he was enticed back into making the guitars he loves by a prominent musical instrument dealer. Bozo was one of the luthiers contacted by esteemed collector Scott Chinery for a model in the *Blue Guitars Collection*. Bozo still constructs guitars on a limited basis.

In the late 1970s, some guitars based on Bozo's designs were constructed in Japan. Research still continues on the nature and designation of these models.

ACOUSTIC

Known for both his flattop and arch top guitar designs, Bozo is currently building arch top models only. Instruments feature very ornate detailing and inlay work, as well as a large distinct headstock. The guitars feature hand-selected European woods, carved tops, elaborate abalone and herringbone inlays, and wood binding (no plastic or celluloid is used on his guitars). Contact luthier Podunavac for price quotes and commission dates.

Master Luthier Bozidar Podunavac courtesy
Bozo Podunavac

BRADFORD

See chapter on House Brands.

This trademark has been identified as a *House Brand* of the W. T. Grant company, one of the old style *Five and Dime* retail stores. W. T. Grant offered the Bradford trademarked guitars during the mid 1960s. Many of the instruments have been identified as produced by Guyatone in Japan. Bradford models ranged from flattop acoustics to thinline hollowbody and solidbody electric guitars and basses.

(Source: Michael Wright, Vintage Guitar Magazine)

BRADLEY

Instruments produced in Japan.

The American distributor for this trademark was Veneman Music of Bethesda, Maryland.

(Source: Michael Wright, Guitar Stories Vol. 1)

BREEDLOVE

Instruments built in Tumalo, Oregon since 1990. Distributed by the Breedlove Guitar Company of Tumalo, Oregon.

Larry Breedlove and Steve Henderson spent time refining their lutherie skills with Bob Taylor (Taylor Guitars). The two partners then moved up into the Pacific Northwest and founded the Breedlove Guitar Company in 1990. Henderson and Breedlove experimented with other tonewoods, and offer instruments built with high quality aged woods like walnut, myrtlewood, and red cedar as well as the traditional maple, spruce, rosewood, and mahogany.

Breedlove is also focusing on mandolin models. Breedlove mandolins feature solid flamed maple backs and sides, carved solid Sitka spruce tops, ebony bridge/fingerboard/peghead veneers, and Schaller tuners. All models are available in a classic Sunburst finish. The **Cascade** (retail list $2,395) is modeled after the CM guitar body design. The **Columbia** (list $2,395) is similar to the Cascade, except features an oval soundhole and x-shaped top bracing. The **Oregon** (list $1,995) is a tear drop shaped mandolin with parallel bracing, and the **Olympic** (list $1,995) is a similar tear drop shape with an oval soundhole and x-braced top.

In 1997, Breedlove developed a new system that designates model description. This system consists of three parts: a letter (or letters) indicates the body shape:

C	Concert
CM	Concert Asymmetrical
RD	Dreadnought
MJ	Jumbo
EG	Gerhard Jumbo
SC	S Series Concert
SD	S Series Dreadnought
SJ	S Series Jumbo

The first number indicates body depth:

1	Shallow (4 1/16" at tail)
2	Deep (4 9/16" at tail)

The second number indicates body cutaway style:

0	non-cutaway
2	sharp (pointed horn) cutaway
5	soft (rounded horn) cutaway

An optional 'X' following the model designation indicates traditional 'X-bracing'.

ACOUSTIC

Breedlove guitars feature an asymmetrical peghead, 25 1/2" scale, and an ebony *pinless* bridge. Breedlove offers several different abalone and mother of pearl fingerboard inlay patterns. Wood options for the back and sides include Walnut, Maple, Myrtlewood (add $100), Rosewood (add $200), Koa (add $525), Striped Ebony ($Call), and Brazilian Rosewood ($Call). Different solid wood options for guitar's top Englemann Spruce (add $150), Adirondack Spruce (add $350), Redwood (add $175), and Bear Claw Sitka Spruce (add $175). Various other options such as different appointments, abalone rosettes, fingerboard inlay patterns, and electronic packages are also available at additional costs (Contact Breedlove for price quotations).

Add $200 for Fishman Matrix Natural pickup system.

Add $230 for L.R. Baggs Ribbon RTS pickup system.

Add $400 for L.R. Baggs Dual Source pickup system.

Add $350 for twelve-string configuration.

Add $350 for left-handed configuration.

Premier Line Standard Models

All Breedlove Premier Line instruments have ivoroid or black plastic binding, top and back purflings, and abalone rosettes. Bridges, fingerboards, and peghead veneers are made of ebony. The following suggested retail list prices are for guitars with Sitka spruce tops and Mahogany back and sides (price includes a case).

Add $495 for Classic Appointments (choice of Bloodwood, Koa, Maple, Walnut, or Rosewood body/fingerboard/and headstock binding, top/side/back purfling, and a V-shaped tailstrip.

C 1 0 — concert style shallow body, extensive purfling on body/neck/fingerboard, 14/20 fret bound ebony fingerboard with pearl dot inlay, ebony *pinless* bridge, bound peghead, ebony peghead veneer, 3 per side gold Schaller tuners. Available in satin finish. Current mfr.

C 1 0 body dimensions: Body Length - 19 7/8 inches, Body Width - 15 3/8 inches, Body Depth - 4 1/16 inches.

Mfr.'s Sug. Retail   **$2,195**

Bozo headstock inlay detail courtesy Bozo Podunavac

"Large and Small" custom Archtops courtesy Bozo Podunavac

Breedlove C 2 0
courtesy Breedlove Guitar Company

C 1 2 — concert style shallow body with sharp cutaway. Similar construction details as the C 1 0. Current mfr.
Mfr.'s Sug. Retail $2,495

C 1 5 — concert style shallow body with soft cutaway. Similar construction details as the C 1 0. Current mfr.
Mfr.'s Sug. Retail $2,595

C 2 0 — concert style deep body, extensive purfling on body/neck/fingerboard, 14/20 fret bound ebony fingerboard with pearl dot inlay, ebony *pinless* bridge, bound peghead, ebony peghead veneer, 3 per side gold Schaller tuners. Available in satin finish. Current mfr.

C 2 0 body dimensions: Body Length - 19 7/8 inches, Body Width - 15 3/8 inches, Body Depth - 4 9/16 inches.
Mfr.'s Sug. Retail $2,195

C 2 2 — concert style deep body with sharp cutaway. Similar construction details as the C 2 0. Current mfr.
Mfr.'s Sug. Retail $2,495

C 2 5 (Formerly C 5) — concert style deep body with soft cutaway. Similar construction details as the C 2 0. Current mfr.
Mfr.'s Sug. Retail $2,595

CM — concert style asymetrical (similar to the C 2 0, except longer and wider) body, extensive purfling on body/neck/fingerboard, 14/20 fret bound ebony fingerboard with pearl dot inlay, ebony *pinless* bridge, bound peghead, ebony peghead veneer, 3 per side gold Schaller tuners. Available in satin finish. Current mfr.

CM body dimensions: Body Length - 21 1/8 inches, Body Width - 16 1/8 inches, Body Depth - 4 5/16 inches.
Mfr.'s Sug. Retail $3,295

EG 1 5 (ED GERHARD CUSTOM) — jumbo style shallow body with soft cutaway, choice of tone wood on top/back/sides, extensive purfling on body/neck/fingerboard, 14/20 fret bound ebony fingerboard with pearl dot inlay, ebony *pinless* bridge, bound peghead, ebony peghead veneer, 3 per side gold Schaller tuners. Available in satin finish. Current mfr.
Mfr.'s Sug. Retail $3,295

MJ 2 0 — jumbo style deep body, extensive purfling on body/neck/fingerboard, 14/20 fret bound ebony fingerboard with pearl dot inlay, ebony *pinless* bridge, bound peghead, ebony peghead veneer, 3 per side gold Schaller tuners. Available in satin finish. Current mfr.

MJ 2 0 body dimensions: Body Length - 21 inches, Body Width - 17 inches, Body Depth - 4 9/16 inches.
Mfr.'s Sug. Retail $2,295

MJ 2 2 — jumbo style deep body with sharp cutaway. Similar construction details as the MJ 2 0. Current mfr.
Mfr.'s Sug. Retail $2,595

RD 2 0 X — dreadnought style deep body, extensive purfling on body/neck/fingerboard, 14/20 fret bound ebony fingerboard with pearl dot inlay, ebony *pinless* bridge, bound peghead, ebony peghead veneer, 3 per side gold Schaller tuners. Available in Natural satin finish. Current mfr.

RD 2 0 X body dimensions: Body Length - 20 1/8 inches, Body Width - 16 1/8 inches, Body Depth - 4 9/16 inches.
Mfr.'s Sug. Retail $2,195

RD 2 2 X — jumbo style deep body with sharp cutaway. Similar construction details as the RD 2 0 X. Current mfr.
Mfr.'s Sug. Retail $2,495

Special Edition Models

DESCHUTES (Formerly C2 DESCHUTES) — concert style deep body with sharp cutaway, figured mahogany back/sides, herringbone purfling, striped ebony rosette/peghead veneer, 14/20 fret bound ebony fingerboard with mother of pearl trout and trout fly inlays, ivoroid neck binding, ebony *pinless* bridge, bound peghead, 3 per side gold Schaller tuners. Available in satin finish. Current mfr.
Mfr.'s Sug. Retail $3,195

This model is dedicated to the Deschutes River and the sport of Fly Fishing.

ED GERHARD SIGNATURE — jumbo style shallow body with soft cutaway, Sitka spruce top, rosewood back/sides, koa binding, wood rosette, 14/20 fret bound ebony fingerboard with pearl dot inlay, ebony *pinless* bridge, bound peghead, ebony peghead veneer, 3 per side gold mini tuners with oversized buttons. Available in satin finish. Current mfr.
Mfr.'s Sug. Retail $2,995

NORTHWEST (Formerly C5 NORTHWEST) — concert style deep body with soft cutaway, myrtlewood back/sides, maple neck, walnut binding, 14/20 fret bound ebony fingerboard with hand-engraved abalone and mother of pearl reproductions of North West Indian totems (whale and fish motifs), ebony *pinless* bridge, bound peghead, ebony peghead veneer, 3 per side gold Schaller tuners. Available in satin finish. Current mfr.
Mfr.'s Sug. Retail $3,395

S Series Models

The **S Series** guitars may not be as ornate as the regular line but are built with the same materials at the Breedlove facility with the same attention to detail. The primary difference is in the appointments, less purflings, a simpler bridge, abalone rosette, and a rosewood peghead veneer. The following suggested retail list prices are for guitars with Sitka spruce tops and Walnut back and sides (price includes a case).
Add $100 for Western Red Cedar top.
Add $100 for Myrtlewood back and sides.
Add $200 for Rosewood back and sides.

SC 2 0 — concert style deep body, Sitka spruce top, walnut back/sides, round soundhole, top purfling, one piece wood rosette, ebony fingerboard/pinless bridge, rosewood peghead veneer, 3 per side asymmetrical headstock with gold Grover tuners. Available in satin finish. Current mfr.

SC 2 0 body dimensions: Body Length - 19 7/8 inches, Body Width - 15 3/8 inches, Body Depth - 4 9/16 inches.
Mfr.'s Sug. Retail $1,695

SC 2 5 — concert style deep body with soft cutaway. Similar construction details as the SC 2 0. Current mfr.
Mfr.'s Sug. Retail $1,995

SD 2 0 X — dreadnought style deep body, round soundhole, walnut back/sides, top purfling, one piece wood rosette, ebony fingerboard/pinless bridge, rosewood peghead veneer, 3 per side asymmetrical headstock with gold Grover tuners, Available in satin finish. Current mfr.

> SD body dimensions: Body Length - 20 1/8 inches, Body Width - 16 1/8 inches, Body Depth - 4 9/16 inches.

Mfr.'s Sug. Retail $1,695

SJ 1 0 — jumbo style shallow body, round soundhole, walnut back/sides, top purfling, one piece wood rosette, ebony fingerboard/pinless bridge, rosewood peghead veneer, 3 per side asymmetrical headstock with gold Grover tuners, Available in satin finish. Current mfr.

Mfr.'s Sug. Retail $1,795

SJ 1 5 — jumbo style shallow body with soft cutaway. Similar construction details as the SJ 1 0. Current mfr.

Mfr.'s Sug. Retail $2,095

SJ 2 0 — jumbo style deep body. Similar construction details as the SJ 1 0. Current mfr.

Mfr.'s Sug. Retail $1,795

> The SJ 2 0 model was offered in a Twelve String configuration as a separate model up to 1998. Retail list price for Walnut back/sides was $1,995; Rosewood back/sides were $2,145. Models featured similar construction details as the SJ 2 0, with 6 per side tuners.

SJ 2 5 — jumbo style deep body with soft cutaway. Similar construction details as the SJ 1 0. Current mfr.

Mfr.'s Sug. Retail $2,095

BRIDWELL WORKSHOP

Instruments produced in Palatine, Illinois.

The Bridwell Workshop is currently building high quality guitars. For further information, please contact the Bridwell Workshop via the Index of Current Manufacturers located in the back of this edition.

CLINT BRILEY

Instruments currently built in Florida.

This company was founded by Clint Briley in 1989, motivated by his experience of making new parts for his vintage National Duolian Resonator guitar. Briley, a machinist, has a background in die making. With assistance from local luthier/repairman (and friend) Charlie Jirousek, Briley hand built necks and steel bodies as he established his new company.

(Source: Hal Hammer)

> Briley currently offers two models that feature his own spun resonator cones and parts. The Cutaway Steel Body ($1,500) has a mahogany neck and rosewood fingerboard, and meets the metal body at the twelfth fret. The Econo-Steel ($800) has no cutaway on its steel body.

Cutaway Steel Body model
courtesy Clint Briley

BRONSON

See chapter on House Brands.

While this trademark has been identified as a *House Brand*, the distributor is still unknown.

(Source: Willie G. Moseley, Stellas & Stratocasters)

BRUKO

Instruments currently built in Germany. Distributed by Lark in the Morning of Mendocino, California.

Bruko Instruments consists of solid wood ukuleles and half-size miniature guitars.

C. BRUNO & SON

See chapter on House Brands.

C. Bruno & Son was originally formed in Macon, Georgia in 1834. The company has been in the music distribution business since then. C. Bruno & Son guitars were built by another manufacturer, and distributed by the company. C. Bruno & Son distributors is currently part of Kaman Music Corporation.

> In 1838, Charles Bruno and C.F. Martin entered into a partnership to produce and distribute acoustic guitars. These specific guitars are labeled with both names, and were produced in New York. In 1839, Martin moved the company to Nazareth, Pennsylvania and dissolved the partnership. C.F. Martin did not provide the guitars that bear the "Bruno" or "C. Bruno & Sons" logos on the peghead.

(Source: Mike Longworth, Martin Guitars)

CYNDY BURTON

Instruments currently built in Portland, Oregon.

Luthier Cyndy Burton builds high quality acoustic guitars. For further information concerning specifications and pricing, please contact Burton through the Index of Current Manufacturers located in the back of this edition.

JOHN BUSCARINO

Instruments currently built in Largo, Florida. Distributed by the Buscarino Guitar Company of Largo, Florida.

Luthier John Buscarino apprenticed with Master acoustic guitar builder Augustino LoPrinzi for over a year in 1978, and with Bob Benedetto of archtop lutherie fame from 1979 to 1981. Later that year, Buscarino formed **Nova U.S.A.**, which built high quality solid body electrics, and acoustic/electric instruments. In 1990, Buscarino changed the company name to **Buscarino Guitars** to reflect the change to building acoustic instruments. Buscarino continues to produce limited production custom guitars, and is currently focusing on archtop guitar building.

Buscarino Virtuoso
courtesy Scott Chinery

ACOUSTIC ARCHTOP

Buscarino archtop guitars are offered with a variety of options such as custom finishes, Tree of Life inlay, neck or tailpiece inlays. There is no charge for a suspended pickup. Contact luthier Buscarino for pricing information.

Add $100 for a built-in humbucker pickup.

Add $100 for bound fingerboard.

Add $650 for AAA highly figured wood.

Add $800 for a 7-string configuration.

Add $800 for an 18" body width.

Add $800 for wood binding.

Add $800 for left-handed configuration.

Add $1,200 for European cello woods.

Add $1,500 for the Poly-Drive MIDI system.

ARTISAN (16" or 17")— carved single-A aged spruce top, carved single-A flamed maple back with matching sides, Venetian cutaway, black/white body binding, 3-piece flamed maple neck, 25" scale, 22 fret ebony fingerboard, ebony pickguard/tailpiece/truss rod cover, 3 per side gold M6 Schaller tuners with solid ebony buttons. Available in Natural high gloss lacquer finish. Current mfr.

Mfr.'s Sug. Retail   **$4,200**

Add $300 for Honey Blonde, Vintage Natural finishes.

Add $300 for solid white binding on f-holes.

Add $500 for a Sunburst finish.

Price includes a 3-ply case.

MONARCH (16" or 17")— carved double-A aged spruce top, carved double-A flamed maple back with matching sides, Venetian cutaway, bound f-holes, black/white body binding, 3-piece flamed maple neck, 25" scale, 22 fret ebony fingerboard, ebony pickguard/tailpiece/truss rod cover, 3 per side gold M6 Schaller tuners with solid ebony buttons. Available in Honey Blonde, Natural, Traditional Sunburst, and Vintage Natural high gloss lacquer finishes. Current mfr.

Mfr.'s Sug. Retail   **$6,000**

Add $300 for a Sunburst finish.

Price includes a double arched 5-ply case.

Buscarino's Monarch archtop is produced through associative efforts with Master Luthier Bob Benedetto.

VIRTUOSO (16" or 17")— carved master grade aged spruce top, carved master grade flamed maple back with matching sides, Venetian cutaway, bound f-holes, fine line black/white body binding, 3-piece flamed maple neck, 25" scale, 22 fret ebony fingerboard with block inlay, ebony pickguard/tailpiece/truss rod cover, bound pickguard, 3 per side gold M6 Schaller tuners with solid ebony buttons. Available in Honey Blonde, Natural, Traditional Sunburst, and Vintage Natural high gloss lacquer finishes. Current mfr.

Mfr.'s Sug. Retail   **$10,000**

Add $300 for a Sunburst finish.

Price includes a double arched 5-ply case.

ACOUSTIC

The Cabaret model is optionally available with lattice bracing or flying braces, Gilbert tuners, or internal (or external) electronics (call for price quote).

Add $350 for wood binding.

Add $350 for RMC Diffu pickup system.

Add $500 for RMC Poly-Drive II Outside MIDI electronics.

Add $800 for the 7-string configuration.

Add $1,000 for RMC Poly-Drive IV built-in electronics.

CABARET— Engleman spruce (or Sitka spruce or Western cedar) top, flame maple (or mahogany or Indian rosewood or Bolivian rosewood) carved back with matching sides, rounded cutaway, round soundhole, black plastic binding with multiple purflings, Honduran mahogany neck, 25 1/2" scale, ebony fingerboard, ebony bridge with abalone inlay, slotted headstock, 3 per side Schaller Deluxe tuners with ebony buttons. Available in Natural high gloss lacquer finish. Current mfr.

Body Width 13 7/8", Body Depth 3 1/2".

Mfr.'s Sug. Retail   **$3,000**

Price includes a custom double arched 5-ply case with crushed velvet lining.

Grand Cabaret — similar construction as Cabaret. Offered in a larger body style.

Body Width 14 3/8", Body Depth 3 3/4".

Mfr.'s Sug. Retail   **$3,300**

Price includes a custom double arched 5-ply case with crushed velvet lining.

C

CADENZA

Instruments currently produced in Korea. Distributed by the Kimex Company of Seoul, Korea.

Cadenza features a wide range of steel-string, classical, and bass acoustic guitars.

CALVIN CRAMER

Instruments built in Markneukirchen, Germany since 1996. Distributed in the U.S. by Musima North America of Tampa, Florida.

Calvin Cramer concert guitars debuted in the United States, Canada, and South American markets in 1996. The guitars are built by Musima, Germany's largest acoustic guitar manufacturer. The company headquarters in Markneukirchen, Germany are near the Czech border.

In 1991, Musima was purchased by industry veteran Helmet Stumpf following the German re-unification. The Musima facilities currently employ 130 workers, and continue to produce Musima stringed instruments as well as the Calvin Cramer concert guitars.

CAMPELLONE

M. CAMPELLONE GUITARS.

Instruments currently built in Providence, Rhode Island.

Luthier Mark Campellone originally began building solid body guitars in the late 1970s, and turned his attention to archtops around 1987. All of his models are constructed of solid wood, and feature carved tops and backs.

Campellone's 17" width guitars are offered in two versions. The Full-sized 17" has a 21" body length, while the Short 17" has a body length of 20 1/2" and a more 'compact' feel to the instrument.

Campellone Special
courtesy Mark Campellone

ACOUSTIC

Campellone currently offers three models of solid wood carved acoustics: each model is available in a 16", 17", or 18" Venetian cutaway body, body depth of 2 7/8" to 3 3/8"; with fingerboard scales of 24.5", 25", or 25.5", nut width of 1 11/16" or 1 3/4", with an optional 'floating' pickup system. All three models have genuine shell inlays, and gold plated hardware. Finishes include Natural, Tinted Blonde, and a variety of Transparent Sunbursts.
Add $200 for floating pickup system.
Add $250 for the 18" body.

SPECIAL SERIES — hand graduated select spruce top, hand graduated back of choicest figured maple with matching rims, multi-bound top, back, fingerboard, peghead, f-holes, and tortoiseshell style pickguard, figured maple neck, ebony fingerboard with five-piece 'keystone' position markers of mother-of-pearl and abalone, ebony bridge, Special Series peghead inlay, rear peghead inlay, bridge bass inlay, shell truss rod cover, Special series tailpiece, and custom case.
Mfr.'s Sug. Retail $6,500

DELUXE SERIES — hand graduated select spruce top, hand graduated back of highly figured maple with matching rims, multi-bound top, back, fingerboard, peghead, and tortoiseshell style pickguard, bound f-holes, figured maple neck, ebony fingerboard with three-piece 'keystone' position markers, ebony bridge, Deluxe Series peghead inlay, and Deluxe series tailpiece.
Mfr.'s Sug. Retail $4,750

STANDARD SERIES — hand graduated spruce top, hand graduated figured maple back with matching rims, multi-bound top, single-bound back, fingerboard, peghead, and tortoiseshell style pickguard, maple neck, rosewood fingerboard, bridge, and tailpiece applique.
Mfr.'s Sug. Retail $3,500

CAPITAL

See chapter on House Brands.

This Gibson built budget line of guitars has been identified as a *House Branzd* of the J. W. Jenkins Company of Kansas City. While built to the same standards as other Gibson guitars, they lack the one 'true' Gibson touch: an adjustable truss rod. House Brand Gibsons were available to musical instrument distributors in the late 1930s and early 1940s.

(Source: Walter Carter, Gibson Guitars: 100 Years of an American Icon)

CARELLI

Instruments built in Chicago, Illinois circa mid 1930s. Distributor unidentified.

Carelli archtop guitars were produced in the 1930s by the Harmony Guitar company. Harmony, well known for producing an estimated 57 "different" brands throughout its history, was the largest *jobber* production house in the history of guitar production. The Carelli trademark, or distributing company is yet unidentified.

ACOUSTIC ARCHTOP

The Carelli *Artist E* that was documented at the 19th Annual Dallas Vintage Guitar show has a number of features similar to Harmony's **Cremona** models. Harmony began producing the Cremona series circa 1934, and these models featured carved solid tops and laminated curly maple backs. The Carelli *Artist E* bears the same distinct features as the Cremona model #7. It is estimated that the model shown in the picture is a mid (1935 or 1936) 1930s vintage.

Carelli Artist E
courtesy Gary Sullivan

Grading	100%	EXCELLENT	AVERAGE

(Source: Jim Fisch, author (with L.B. Fred) of Epiphone: The House of Stathopoulo; and Gary Sullivan, owner)

CARSON ROBISON

See chapter on House Brands.

Carson J. Robison was a popular country singer and songwriter in the 1930s who endorsed a RECORDING KING flattop model. RECORDING KING was the "House Brand" for Montgomery Ward, and GIBSON built the high end models for the line (cheaper models were built by someone else). Early models had only a white paint stencil of "Carson J. Robison" on the peghead (hence this listing) but later models had the Recording King Logo as well.

(Source: Walter Carter, Gibson Guitars: 100 Years of an American Icon)

CARVIN

Instruments produced in Escondido, California since 1969. Previous production was located in Covina, California from 1949 to 1969. Carvin instruments are sold through direct catalog sales, as well as through their three factory stores in California: San Diego, Santa Ana, and Hollywood.

In 1946, Lowell Kiesel founded Kiesel Electronics in Los Angeles, California. Three years later, the Kiesel family settled in Covina, California and began the original catalog business of manufacturing and distributing lap steel guitars, small tube amps and pickups. The Carvin trademark was derived from Kiesel's two oldest sons, **Car**son and Ga**vin**. Guitars were originally offered in kit form, or by parts since 1949; Carvin began building complete guitars in 1964. By 1978, the glued set-neck design replaced the bolt-on necks. The majority of the current guitar and bass models currently feature a neck-through design.

Carvin has always been a mail-order only company, and offers the players a wide range of options on the individual models. Even though they can't be tried out before they're bought, Carvin offers a 10 day money back guarantee. Because Carvin sells factory direct, they are not stocked in music stores; by requesting a catalog the careful shopper will also find a difference between the new list price and the actual sales price.

Carvin offers a full range of guitar and bass replacement parts in their full line catalog. The Carvin company also offers mixing boards, power amplifiers, powered mixers, P.A. speakers, monitor speakers, guitar combo amps/heads/cabinets, and bass amps/cabinets as well.

For current information regarding the Carvin line of electric guitars and basses, please refer to the **5th Edition Blue Book of Electric Guitars**.

ACOUSTIC ELECTRIC

AC175 — single cutaway hollowed-out mahogany body, spruce top, round soundhole, thru body mahogany neck, 24 fret ebony fingerboard with pearl dot inlay, ebony bridge with black pins, blackface peghead with screened logo, 3 per side gold tuners, transducer bridge Fishman pickup, volume/treble/bass controls, active electronics. Available in Classic White, Ferrari Red, Jet Black, Natural, Pearl Blue, Pearl Red and Pearl White finishes. Mfr. 1994 to date.

Mfr.'s Sug. Retail	$1,599	$699	$525	$450

AC275 JUMBO — similar to the AC175, except the mahogany body in 1 1/2" wider, and features a F60 acoustic transducer with volume/treble/bass controls and active electronics. Mfr. 1996 to date.

Mfr.'s Sug. Retail	$1,699	$749	$575	$475

AC275-12 — similar to the AC275, except in 12-string configuration and 6 per side headstock. Mfr. 1997 to date.

Mfr.'s Sug. Retail	$1,799	$799	$625	$500

ACOUSTIC ELECTRIC BASS

All acoustic bass models have a 34" scale, and are available in these standard colors: Classic White, Ferrari Red, Jet Black, Pearl Blue, Pearl Red, Pearl White, and a Tung Oil finish. Translucent finishes are optionally available.

Add $100 for flamed maple (FT) top.

Add $150 for quilted maple (QT) top.

Add $150 for flamed koa (FKT) top.

AC40 — offset double cutaway semi-hollow mahogany body, AAA Englemann spruce top, through body mahogany neck, 24 fret ebony fingerboard with pearl dot inlay, fixed acoustic-style bridge, 4 on a side tuners, Carvin F40 acoustic bridge transducer, master volume control, bass/treble tone controls. Current mfr.

Mfr.'s Sug. Retail	$1,499	$699	$525	$425

This model has fretless fingerboard (AC40F) optionally available.

AC50 — similar to the AC40, except in a 5 string configuration, 3/2 per side tuners. Current mfr.

Mfr.'s Sug. Retail	$1,669	$769	$595	$475

This model has fretless fingerboard (AC50F) optionally available.

CATALINA

See chapter on House Brands.

This trademark has been identified as a "House Brand" of the Abercrombie & Fitch company.

(Source: Willie G. Moseley, Stellas & Stratocasters)

Campellone Deluxe
courtesy Mark Campellone

AC 275 Jumbo
courtesy Carvin

CATALUNA

Instruments currently built in Taiwan, Republic of China. Distributed by Reliance International Corporation of Taiwan, Republic of China.

Reliance International's Cataluna instruments are entry level to medium quality acoustic guitars. The **Apex** series features 4 traditional style dreadnought style acoustics, and two classical acoustics. **Apex** series instruments feature spruce tops, Nato backs/sides/necks, and rosewood fingerboards. For further information regarding prices and specifications, contact Reliance International Corporation via the Index of Current Manufacturers located in the back of this edition.

C B ALYN

Instruments currently built in Pacific Palisades, California.

The **Rosebud** models are high quality, solid top (no soundholes) acoustic guitars with a piezo pickup system. Retail list ranges from $1,499 (basic) to $1,599 (**RB70 Artist**).

CELEBRITY

Instruments are built in Korea, and distributed by the Kaman Music Corporation of Bloomfield, Connecticut since the late 1980s.

The Celebrity line of bowl back guitars was introduced in 1983 as a Korean-built entry level *introduction* to the American-built Ovation line. Celebrity models offer similar design features, and a variety of options as their overseas production saves money on their retail price. The Celebrity trademark was also applied to a number of solid body electrics based on popular American designs.

CFOX

Also CHARLES FOX GUITARS.

Instruments built in Healdsburg, California from 1997 to date.

Charles Fox Guitars debuted at the 1998 NAMM industry show in January, and introduced the newest line of high quality hand crafted acoustic guitar models. While the company is new, the luthier and designer is not - Charles Fox has a worldwide reputation as a luthier, educator, and consultant in the field of guitar building. The CFox guitar line is the product of Fox's 30 years experience as an artist, craftsman, and teacher.

Charles Fox (b. 1943) did his undergraduate work at the Art Institute of Chicago and completed his postgraduate work at Northwestern University in 1966. Fox began building his own guitars in 1968, and since then has worked both as a custom guitar builder and as the head of his own guitar production shop. In the late 1970s and early 1980s, Fox's GRD Guitars (see GRD) were among the first instruments to define the market for high end electric guitars.

In 1973, Fox founded the first school for guitar builders in North America, the Guitar Research and Design Center. In recent years Fox has founded and directed the American School of Lutherie in Healdsburg, California; and has been a founder and educational co-ordinator of the Healdsburg Guitar Festival.

ACOUSTIC

All 4 of the CFox models are available in 3 different quality series. Left-handed configurations are available at no extra charge. For custom inlay work or Brazilian rosewood back/sides, please contact Charles Fox Guitars via the Index of Current Manufacturers located in the back of this edition.
Add $150 for Engelmann spruce soundboard.
Add $150 for Western red cedar soundboard.
Add $175 for extended fretboard.
Add $250 for German spruce soundboard.
Add $350 for cocobola back and sides.
Add $400 for figured maple back and sides.
Add $400 for wood binding.
Add $500 for wood binding, cutaway configuration.
Add $500 for koa back and sides.
Add $500 for standard cutaway.
Add $700 for abalone trim.
Add $750 for compounded cutaway.

C CONCERT (NAPA SERIES) — solid AAA Sitka spruce top, carbon-graphite reinforced Honduran mahogany neck, 25 1/2" scale, Honduran mahogany back/sides, black top binding, round soundhole with rosette, 14/21 fret ebony fingerboard, ebony peghead overlay with mother of pearl logo, ebony bridge with ebony bridgepins, ebony end pin, 3 per side nickel Grover tuners. Available in Natural finish. Mfr. 1998 to date.

Total Length 39 3/4", Body Width 14 13/16" (lower bout), Body Thickness 3 1/4" (heel) to 4" (end).
Mfr.'s Sug. Retail   **$2,800**

C Concert (Sonoma Series) — similar to the C Concert (Napa Series), except features Indian rosewood back/sides, grained ivoroid top binding, grained ivoroid neck/headstock binding, abalone rosette, ebony bridgepins with abalone dots, 3 per side chrome Schaller tuners. Available in Natural finish. Mfr. 1998 to date.
Mfr.'s Sug. Retail   **$3,200**

C Concert (Frisco Series) — similar to the C Concert (Napa Series), except features master grade Sitka spruce top, Indian rosewood back/sides, ebony end graft, grained ivoroid body binding, grained ivoroid neck/headstock binding, abalone rosette, ebony bridgepins with abalone dots, 3 per side gold Schaller tuners with ebony buttons. Available in Natural finish. Mfr. 1998 to date.
Mfr.'s Sug. Retail   **$3,700**

AC 50 Bass
courtesy Carvin

AE 185
courtesy Carvin

D DREADNOUGHT (NAPA SERIES) — solid AAA Sitka spruce top, carbon-graphite reinforced Honduran mahogany neck, 25 1/2" scale, Honduran mahogany back/sides, black top binding, round soundhole with rosette, 14/21 fret ebony fingerboard, ebony peghead overlay with mother of pearl logo, ebony bridge with ebony bridgepins, ebony end pin, 3 per side nickel Grover tuners. Available in Natural finish. Mfr. 1998 to date.

> Total Length 40 7/8", Body Width 15 5/8" (lower bout), Body Thickness 3 7/8" (heel) to 4 7/8" (end).
> Mfr.'s Sug. Retail $2,800

D Dreadnought (Sonoma Series) — similar to the D Dreadnought (Napa Series), except features Indian rosewood back/sides, grained ivoroid top binding, grained ivoroid neck/headstock binding, abalone rosette, ebony bridgepins with abalone dots, 3 per side chrome Schaller tuners. Available in Natural finish. Mfr. 1998 to date.
> Mfr.'s Sug. Retail $3,200

D Dreadnought (Frisco Series) — similar to the D Dreadnought (Napa Series), except features master grade Sitka spruce top, Indian rosewood back/sides, ebony end graft, grained ivoroid body binding, grained ivoroid neck/headstock binding, abalone rosette, ebony bridgepins with abalone dots, 3 per side gold Schaller tuners with ebony buttons. Available in Natural finish. Mfr. 1998 to date.
> Mfr.'s Sug. Retail $3,700

H HYBRID (NAPA SERIES) — solid AAA Sitka spruce top, carbon-graphite reinforced Honduran mahogany neck, 25 1/2" scale, Honduran mahogany back/sides, black top binding, round soundhole with rosette, 14/21 fret ebony fingerboard, ebony peghead overlay with mother of pearl logo, ebony bridge with ebony bridgepins, ebony end pin, 3 per side nickel Grover tuners. Available in Natural finish. Mfr. 1998 to date.

> Total Length 40 5/8", Body Width 14 7/8" (lower bout), Body Thickness 3 1/4" (heel) to 4" (end).
> Mfr.'s Sug. Retail $2,800

H Hybrid (Sonoma Series) — similar to the H Hybrid (Napa Series), except features Indian rosewood back/sides, grained ivoroid top binding, grained ivoroid neck/headstock binding, abalone rosette, ebony bridgepins with abalone dots, 3 per side chrome Schaller tuners. Available in Natural finish. Mfr. 1998 to date.
> Mfr.'s Sug. Retail $3,200

H Hybrid (Frisco Series) — similar to the H Hybrid (Napa Series), except features master grade Sitka spruce top, Indian rosewood back/sides, ebony end graft, grained ivoroid body binding, grained ivoroid neck/headstock binding, abalone rosette, ebony bridgepins with abalone dots, 3 per side gold Schaller tuners with ebony buttons. Available in Natural finish. Mfr. 1998 to date.
> Mfr.'s Sug. Retail $3,700

H-12 HYBRID (NAPA SERIES) — solid AAA Sitka spruce top, carbon-graphite reinforced Honduran mahogany neck, 25 1/2" scale, Honduran mahogany back/sides, black top binding, round soundhole with rosette, 12/19 fret ebony fingerboard, ebony peghead overlay with mother of pearl logo, ebony bridge with ebony bridgepins, ebony end pin, 3 per side nickel Grover tuners. Available in Natural finish. Mfr. 1998 to date.

> Total Length 39 1/8", Body Width 14 7/8" (lower bout), Body Thickness 3 1/4" (heel) to 4" (end).
> Mfr.'s Sug. Retail $2,800

H-12 Hybrid (Sonoma Series) — similar to the H-12 Hybrid (Napa Series), except features Indian rosewood back/sides, grained ivoroid top binding, grained ivoroid neck/headstock binding, abalone rosette, ebony bridgepins with abalone dots, 3 per side chrome Schaller tuners. Available in Natural finish. Mfr. 1998 to date.
> Mfr.'s Sug. Retail $3,200

H-12 Hybrid (Frisco Series) — similar to the H-12 Hybrid (Napa Series), except features master grade Sitka spruce top, Indian rosewood back/sides, ebony end graft, grained ivoroid body binding, grained ivoroid neck/headstock binding, abalone rosette, ebony bridgepins with abalone dots, 3 per side gold Schaller tuners with ebony buttons. Available in Natural finish. Mfr. 1998 to date.
> Mfr.'s Sug. Retail $3,700

SJ SMALL JUMBO (NAPA SERIES) — solid AAA Sitka spruce top, carbon-graphite reinforced Honduran mahogany neck, 25 1/2" scale, Honduran mahogany back/sides, black top binding, round soundhole with rosette, 14/21 fret ebony fingerboard, ebony peghead overlay with mother of pearl logo, ebony bridge with ebony bridgepins, ebony end pin, 3 per side nickel Grover tuners. Available in Natural finish. Mfr. 1998 to date.

> Total Length 41 7/8", Body Width 16 1/4" (lower bout), Body Thickness 3 1/2" (heel) to 4 1/4" (end).
> Mfr.'s Sug. Retail $2,800

SJ Small Jumbo (Sonoma Series) — similar to the SJ Small Jumbo (Napa Series), except features Indian rosewood back/sides, grained ivoroid top binding, grained ivoroid neck/headstock binding, abalone rosette, ebony bridgepins with abalone dots, 3 per side chrome Schaller tuners. Available in Natural finish. Mfr. 1998 to date.
> Mfr.'s Sug. Retail $3,200

SJ Small Jumbo (Frisco Series) — similar to the SJ Small Jumbo (Napa Series), except features master grade Sitka spruce top, Indian rosewood back/sides, ebony end graft, grained ivoroid body binding, grained ivoroid neck/headstock binding, abalone rosette, ebony bridgepins with abalone dots, 3 per side gold Schaller tuners with ebony buttons. Available in Natural finish. Mfr. 1998 to date.
> Mfr.'s Sug. Retail $3,700

CHAPIN

Instruments currently built in San Jose, California.

Handcrafted Chapin guitars feature carefully thought out designs that provide ergonomic comfort and a wide palette of tones. All Chapin guitars are handcrafted by luthiers Bill Chapin and Fred Campbell; all guitars feature the Campbell/Chapin locking dovetail set-in neck joint.

The Chapin Insight guitar inspection camera features a small-bodied camera on a flexible mount that allows the luthier/repairman an inside view of the acoustic guitar to help solve internal problems. This low-light camera features 3.6 mm lens for ultra close crack inspection, and has an RCA output that feeds directly into a VCR or camcorder for video documentation. The Insight (list $349) operates on a 9 volt battery - so it is mobile as well. The

Grading	100%	EXCELLENT	AVERAGE

importance to collectors? Now there is a tool for proper guitar authentication: the internal signatures and dates of an acoustic (or semi-hollow body) guitar can be read in seconds - and right at the guitar show, if necessary!

For current information on Chapin's electric models, please refer to the **5th Edition Blue Book of Electric Guitars**.

ACOUSTIC ELECTRIC

All of Chapin's models are available with additional options such as choice of wood(s), pickups, or hardware (call for price quote). Retail prices listed below reflect the base price.

Chapin's acoustic electric **Eagle** (list $1,850) is available in nylon or steel string configuration. It features semi-solid body design with tuned acoustic chambers, spruce (or maple) top, rosewood acoustic-style bridge or electric-style bridge with piezo pickups (steel string model only), and Gilbert or Sperzel tuners. The **Eagle Custom** model has a figured redwood or mater-grade spruce top, interchangeable ebony soundports, figured wood binding, violin-style purfling, acoustic transducer, and Gilbert tuners with abalone inlay (retail list is $3,475).

CHARVEL

Instruments currently produced in Korea. Distributed by Jackson/Charvel Guitar Company (Akai Musical Instruments) of Fort Worth, Texas.

Instruments originally produced in the U.S between 1978 to 1985; later (post-1985) production was based in the U.S., Japan, and Korea.

Trademark established in 1978 by the Charvel Manufacturing Company.

125 S
courtesy Charvel

In the late 1970s, Wayne Charvel's Guitar Repair shop in Azusa, California acquired a reputation for making custom high quality bodies and necks. Grover Jackson began working at the shop in 1977, and a year later bought out Charvel and moved the company to San Dimas. Jackson debuted the Charvel custom guitars at the 1979 NAMM show, and the first catalog depicting the bolt-neck beauties and custom options arrived in 1981.

The standard models from *Charvel Manufacturing* carried a list price between $880 to $955, and the amount of custom options was staggering. In 1983, the Charvel company began offering neck-through models under the **Jackson** trademark.

Grover Jackson licensed the Charvel trademark to the International Music Corporation (IMC) in 1985; the company was sold to them a year later. In late 1986 production facilities were moved to Ontario, California. Distribution eventually switched from Charvel/Jackson to the Jackson/Charvel Guitar company, currently a branch of the Akai Musical Instruments company. As the years went by and the Charvel line expanded, its upper end models were phased out and moved into the Jackson line (which had been the Charvel/Jackson Company's line of custom made instruments) and were gaining more popularity. For example, the **Charvel Avenger** (mfd. 1991 to 1992), became the **Jackson Rhoads EX Pro** (mfd. 1992 to date). For further details, see the **Jackson** guitars section in this edition.

In 1988, Charvel sent a crew of luthiers to Japan for a year or so to crosstrain the Japanese builders on building methods for custom built guitars. The resulting custom instruments had a retail list price between $1,000 to $1,300. U.S. custom built guitars have a four digit serial number, the Japanese custom built models have a six digit serial number. Numbers may be prefaced with a "C", which may stand for "Custom" made (this point has not been completely verified).

By the early 1990s, the only Charvel models left were entry level 'Strat'-style electrics and dreadnought and jumbo-style (full bodied and cutaways) acoustic guitars. In the late 1990s, even the electrics were phased out in favor of the acoustic and acoustic/electric models.

(Early Charvel history courtesy Baker Rorick, Guitar Shop magazine; additional information courtesy Roland Lozier, Lozier Piano & Music)

ACOUSTIC

125S — dreadnought style, solid spruce top, round soundhole, 7 stripe bound body/rosette, mahogany back/sides/neck, 14/20 fret bound rosewood fingerboard with abalone dot inlay, rosewood bridge with white black pins, rosewood veneered peghead with pearl logo inlay, 3 per side chrome tuners. Available in Natural and Tobacco Sunburst finishes. Mfd. 1994 to 1996.

$300 $175
Last Mfr.'s Sug. Retail was $595.

125SE — similar to 125S, except has transducer bridge pickup, 3 band EQ. Available in Natural and Tobacco Sunburst finishes. Mfd. 1994 to 1996.

$350 $210
Last Mfr.'s Sug. Retail was $695.

150SC — single round cutaway dreadnought style, solid spruce top, round soundhole, 7 stripe bound body/rosette, rosewood back/sides, mahogany neck, 14/20 fret bound rosewood fingerboard with abalone dot inlay, rosewood bridge with white black pins, rosewood veneered peghead with pearl logo inlay, 3 per side chrome tuners. Available in Natural and Tobacco Sunburst finishes. Mfd. 1994 to 1996.

$300 $175
Last Mfr.'s Sug. Retail was $595.

150SEC — similar to 150SC, except has transducer bridge pickup, 3 band EQ. Available in Natural and Tobacco Sunburst finishes. Mfd. 1994 to 1996.

$350 $200
Last Mfr.'s Sug. Retail was $695.

525 — single round cutaway dreadnought style, spruce top, round soundhole, 5 stripe bound body and rosette, mahogany arched back/sides/neck, 22 fret bound rosewood fingerboard with pearl dot inlay, rosewood bridge with white black dot pins, bound peghead with abalone Charvel logo inlay, 3 per side chrome tuners. Available in Cherry Sunburst, Metallic Black, Natural and Tobacco Sunburst. Disc. 1994.

$200 $125
Last Mfr.'s Sug. Retail was $400.

550
courtesy Charvel

625 C
courtesy Charvel

Grading		100%	EXCELLENT	AVERAGE

525D — similar to 525, except has transducer bridge pickup with 3 band EQ. Available in Metallic Black, Natural and Tobacco Sunburst finishes. Disc. 1994.

			$200	$125

Last Mfr.'s Sug. Retail was $500.

550 — dreadnought style, spruce top, round soundhole, black pickguard, 3 stripe bound body/rosette, mahogany back/sides/neck, 25.6" scale, 14/20 fret rosewood fingerboard with abalone dot inlay, rosewood bridge with black white dot pins, rosewood veneered peghead with pearl logo inlay, 3 per side chrome tuners. Available in Mahogany and Natural finishes. Mfr. 1994 to date.

Mfr.'s Sug. Retail	$275	$200	$125	$90

Add $20 for single round cutaway **(Model 550C)**, available in Natural finish only.

550E — similar to 550, except has transducer bridge pickup, 3 band EQ. Available in Natural finish. Mfr. 1994 to date.

Mfr.'s Sug. Retail	$350	$250	$150	$100

Add $25 for single round cutaway **(Model 550CE)**, available in Natural finish only.

625 — single round cutaway jumbo style, spruce top, round soundhole, 5 stripe bound body and rosette, nato back/sides, mahogany neck, 25.6" scale, 20 fret rosewood fingerboard with abalone dot inlay, rosewood bridge with white black dot pins, rosewood veneer on peghead with abalone Charvel logo inlay, 3 per side gold tuners. Available in Cherry Sunburst, Metallic Black, Natural, and Tobacco Sunburst finishes. Mfr. 1992 to date.

Mfr.'s Sug. Retail	$365	$275	$150	$100

In 1997, abalone inlay was changed to faux abalone.

625C — similar to 625, except has abalone bound body/rosette, rosewood back/sides, 24 fret bound extended fingerboard, abalone dot pins, bound peghead, transducer bridge pickup, 3 band EQ, active electronics. Mfr. 1992 to date.

Mfr.'s Sug. Retail	$645	$475	$300	$200

625C-12 — similar to 625, except has 12-string configuration, abalone bound body/rosette, rosewood back/sides, 24 fret bound extended fingerboard, abalone dot pins, bound peghead, 6 per side tuners, transducer bridge pickup, 3 band EQ, active electronics. Available in Metallic Black, Natural, and Tobacco Sunburst finishes. Mfr. 1994 to date.

Mfr.'s Sug. Retail	$695	$560	$280	$230

625D — similar to 625, except has transducer bridge pickup, 3 band EQ, active electronics.

Mfr.'s Sug. Retail	$475	$350	$175	$125

625F — similar to 625, except has figured maple top. Available in Tobacco Sunburst, Transparent Black and Transparent Red. Mfd. 1994 to 1995.

			$325	$200

Last Mfr.'s Sug. Retail was $650.

725 E
courtesy Charvel

725 — jumbo style, solid spruce top, round soundhole, 7 stripe bound body/rosette, mahogany back/sides/neck, 14/20 fret rosewood fingerboard with pearl offset dot inlay, rosewood bridge with white black pins, rosewood veneered peghead with pearl logo inlay, 3 per side chrome tuners. Available in Natural finish. Mfd. 1994 to 1996.

			$200	$125

Last Mfr.'s Sug. Retail was $495.

725E — similar to 725, except has transducer bridge pickup, 3 band EQ. Available in Natural finish. Mfd. 1994 to 1996.

			$300	$175

Last Mfr.'s Sug. Retail was $595.

750E — jumbo style, solid spruce top, round soundhole, 7 stripe bound body/rosette, figured maple back/sides, mahogany neck, 14/20 fret rosewood fingerboard with pearl offset dot inlay, rosewood bridge with white black pins, figured maple veneered peghead with pearl logo inlay, 3 per side gold tuners. Available in Natural finish. Mfd. 1994 to 1996.

			$350	$200

Last Mfr.'s Sug. Retail was $695.

CM-100 — dreadnought style, cedar top, round soundhole, multibound body, 3 stripe rosette, figured mahogany back/sides, mahogany neck, 14/20 fret bound rosewood fingerboard with pearl dot inlay, ebony bridge with white black dot pins, bound rosewood veneered peghead with pearl logo inlay, 3 per side chrome tuners. Available in Natural finish. Mfd. 1994 only.

			$400	$275

Last Mfr.'s Sug. Retail was $895.

CM-400 LIMITED EDITION — jumbo style, solid spruce top, round soundhole, maple bound/abalone purfling body, abalone rosette, jacaranda back/sides, mahogany neck, 14/20 fret ebony fingerboard with pearl cloud inlay, ebony bridge with black abalone dot pins, abalone bound rosewood veneered peghead with abalone logo inlay, 3 per side gold tuners. Available in Natural finish. Mfd. 1994 only.

			$1,950	$1,250

Last Mfr.'s Sug. Retail was $3,995.

ACOUSTIC ELECTRIC

325SL — double offset cutaway asymmetrical style, spruce top, offset wedge soundhole, bound body and soundhole, nato back/sides/neck, 22 fret rosewood fingerboard with offset abalone dot inlay, rosewood bridge with white pearl dot pins, rosewood veneer with abalone Charvel logo, 3 per side chrome tuners, transducer bridge pickup, 3 band EQ, active electronics. Available in Black, Bright Red and Turquoise finishes. Mfd. 1992 to 1994.

			$250	$150

Last Mfr.'s Sug. Retail was $500.

Grading	100%	EXCELLENT	AVERAGE

325SLX — similar to 325SL, except has figured maple top, rosewood back/sides, bound fingerboard with shark fin inlay, bound peghead, active electronics with built-in chorus. Available in Cherry Sunburst, Tobacco Sunburst and Transparent Red finishes.

$300 $195
Last Mfr.'s Sug. Retail was $600.

ATX — single cutaway hollow mahogany body, bound maple top, maple neck, 24 fret rosewood fingerboard with offset pearl dot inlay, strings through rosewood bridge, six on side one chrome tuners, Fishman transducer bridge pickup, volume/3 band EQ controls. Available in Black, Deep Metallic Blue, Dark Metallic Red and Deep Metallic Violet finishes. Mfd. 1993 to 1996.

$450 $295
Last Mfr.'s Sug. Retail was $895.

ATX (Trans) — similar to ATX, except has figured maple top. Available in Tobacco Sunburst, Transparent Black and Transparent Violet finishes. Disc. 1996.

$500 $325
Last Mfr.'s Sug. Retail was $995.

ACOUSTIC ELECTRIC BASS

425 SL — offset double rounded cutaway asymmetrical style, spruce top, offset wedge soundhole, bound body and soundhole, nato back/sides/neck, 22 fret rosewood fingerboard with offset abalone inlay, rosewood bridge with abalone dot inlay, abalone Charvel logo peghead inlay, 2 per side chrome tuners, transducer bridge pickup, 3 band EQ, active electronics. Available in Bright Red, Metallic Black and Turquoise finishes. Mfd. 1992 to 1994.

$275 $175
Last Mfr.'s Sug. Retail was $550.

425SLX — similar to 425SL, except has figured maple top, rosewood back/sides, bound fingerboard/peghead, active electronics with built-in chorus. Available in Cherry Sunburst, Tobacco Sunburst and Transparent Red finishes. Mfd. 1992 to 1994.

$325 $200
Last Mfr.'s Sug. Retail was $650.

ATX BASS — single cutaway hollow mahogany body, bound maple top, maple neck, 22 fret rosewood fingerboard with offset pearl dot inlay, strings through rosewood bridge, 4 on one side chrome tuners, volume/3 band EQ controls. Available in Black, Deep Metallic Blue, and Deep Metallic Violet finishes. Mfd. 1993 to 1996.

$500 $300
Last Mfr.'s Sug. Retail was $995.

ATX Bass (Trans) — similar to ATX Bass, except has figured maple top. Available in Tobacco Sunburst, Transparent Black, and Transparent Violet finishes.

$550 $350
Last Mfr.'s Sug. Retail was $1,095.

625 C 12
courtesy Charvel

CHARVETTE

Instruments produced in Korea from 1989 to 1994. Charvette, an entry level line to Charvel, was distributed by the International Music Corporation of Ft. Worth, Texas.

The Charvette trademark was distributed by the Charvel/Jackson company as a good quality entry level guitar based on their original Jackson USA "superstrat" designs. Where the Charvel and Jackson models may sport 'Jackson' pickups, Charvettes invariably had 'Charvel' pickups to support a company/product unity.

ACOUSTIC ELECTRIC

500 — single round cutaway flat top style, maple top, plectrum shape soundhole, one stripe bound body/rosette, bolt-on maple neck, 22 fret rosewood fingerboard with pearl dot inlay, rosewood bridge with black pins, 6 on one side tuners, black hardware, 6 piezo bridge pickups, volume/treble/bass controls, active electronics. Available in Ferrari Red, Midnite Black and Snow White finish. Mfd. 1991 to 1992.

$225 $125
Last Mfr.'s Sug. Retail was $495.

CHATWORTH

Instruments currently built in England.

Luthier Andy Smith is currently building high quality guitars. For further information, please contact luthier Smith via the Index of Current Manufacturers located in the rear of this book.

CHRIS

See chapter on House Brands.

This trademark has been identified as a separate budget line of guitars from the Jackson-Guldan company of Columbus, Ohio.

(Source: Willie G. Moseley, Stellas & Stratocasters)

CHRIS LARKIN

CHRIS LARKIN CUSTOM GUITARS.

Instruments built in Ireland since 1977.

Since 1977, Chris Larkin Custom Guitars have been based at Castlegregory, County Kerry, on the west coast of Ireland. Chris Larkin works alone hand building a range of original designs to custom order to a very high level of quality from the finest

625 D
courtesy Charvel

available materials. The range is wide ("it stops me from becoming bored!") including acoustic, electric, archtop, and semi-acoustic guitars; acoustic, electric, semi-acoustic, and upright 'stick' basses; and archtop mandolins. 'One-off' designs are also built and Chris admits to having made some very high spec copies when offered enough money!

(Company information courtesy Chris Larkin, Chris Larkin Custom Guitars)

As each instrument is hand made to order, the customer has a wide choice of woods, colours, fret type, fingerboard radius, neck profile, and dimensions within the design to enable the finished instrument to better suit the player. All Larkin instruments from 1980 on have a shamrock as the headstock inlay. Sales are worldwide through distributors in some areas, or direct from the maker.

Serialization

Since 1982, a simple six digit system has been used. The first two digits indicate the year, the next two the month, and the final two the sequence in that month. For example, 970103 was the third instrument in January 1997. Before 1982 the numbers are a bit chaotic! Chris Larkin has full documentation for almost every instrument that he has ever built, so he can supply a history from the serial number in most cases.

ACOUSTIC

ASAP acoustic flat top models are lightly built for performances with an emphasis on balanced tone. This model is available in various configurations such as a nylon string, a 12-string, an acoustic bass model, and a jumbo. Prices run from $2,400 up to $2,890. All models feature a Highlander pickup and preamp system, and gold tuners.

ASAS archtop guitars are available in two acoustic models and one semi-acoustic (both acoustic models feature fingerboard mounted custom made humbuckers). All models are built from European spruce and highly figured maple, and have multiple binding on body, neck, headstock, and scratchplate. The archtops are available with a Florentine cutaway ($3,785) and Venetian cutaway ($4,000). The ASA Semi-hollow (list $3,440) has a cedar sustain block running from neck to tail, 2 Schaller G50 humbuckers, and a stop tailpiece.

CIMARRON GUITARS

Instruments built in Ridgeway, Colorado since 1978.

In addition to the hand crafted acoustic models, luthier John Walsh produces electric semi-acoustic guitars as well.

Early in his career, it was estimated that Walsh produced 24 acoustic guitars a year. The acoustic guitar models featured Sitka spruce tops, maple or mahogany necks, and ebony fingerboards on standard models to custom configurations. The thinline Model One has bent wood sides, Rio Grande pickups, Sperzel tuners, and numerous custom options (contact Walsh for retail prices).

CITATION

Instruments produced in Japan.

The U.S. distributor of Citation guitars was the Grossman company of Cleveland, Ohio.

(Source: Michael Wright, Guitar Stories Volume One)

HARVEY CITRON

Instruments built in Woodstock, New York since 1983.

Luthier Harvey Citron has been building high quality, innovative, solid body guitars since the early 1970s. Citron, a noted guitarist and singer, co-founded the Veillette-Citron company in 1975. During the partnership's eight years, they were well known for the quality of their handcrafted electric guitars, basses, and baritone guitars. Citron also designed the **X-92 Breakaway** model for Guild and was a regular contributing writer for several guitar magazines.

Citron instruments are available direct from Harvey Citron, or through a limited number of dealers. Citron maintains a current price list and descriptions of his models at his web site. His **Basic Guitar Set-Up and Repair** instructional video is available from Homespun Tapes; Citron's cleverly designed **Guitar Stand** has a list price of $499.

ACOUSTIC ELECTRIC

All Acoustic Electric models are available with or without a headstock at no additional charge.
Add $450 for MIDI capability (Acoustic Electric models).

AEG — offset double cutaway body, 25 1/2" scale, six on a side headstock, magnetic pickup/piezo bridge transducers, active electronics, volume/blend/tone controls. Current mfr.
Mfr.'s Sug. Retail $3,799

ACOUSTIC ELECTRIC BASS

All Acoustic Electric models are available with or without a headstock at no additional charge.

Fingerboards available in fretless configuration at no additional cost.

A 5 — offset double cutaway body, 35" scale, 5-string configuration, five on a side headstock, magnetic pickup/piezo bridge transducers, on-board electronics, volume/blend/tone controls. Mfr. 1998 to date.
Mfr.'s Sug. Retail $2,799

AE4 — offset double cutaway body, 34" scale, bolt-on neck, four on a side headstock, magnetic pickup/piezo bridge transducers, active electronics, volume/blend/tone controls located on upper bass horn. Current mfr.
Mfr.'s Sug. Retail $3,799

AE5 — similar to the AE4, except has 35" scale and 5-string configuration. Current mfr.
Mfr.'s Sug. Retail $3,999

COLLINGS

Instruments built in Austin, Texas since 1986. Distributed by Collings Guitars, Inc. of Austin, Texas.

Luthier Bill Collings was born in Michigan, and raised in Ohio. In 1973, Collings moved from Ohio to Houston, Texas, and originally did guitar repair work. Colling's first flattop guitars date from this period. In 1980, Collings relocated his workshop

Grading	100%	EXCELLENT	AVERAGE

to Austin, Texas. In addition to his flattop guitars, he also began building archtop guitars. Collings Guitars was founded in 1986. Today, the company maintains tight quality control over their production, and consumer demand remains high.

(Company information courtesy Collings Guitars)

A small number of Collings guitars have turned up on the secondary market; the majority of these instruments are in very good to excellent condition and are in as much demand as the new instruments from Collings dealers. Be aware of retail list prices and the demand wherein when shopping in the secondary markets.

LABEL IDENTIFICATION

1975-1979: Models do not have a label; instead, there is a signature in ink on the inside back strip.

1979-1984: Light brown oval label with brown ink marked *Bill Collings, Luthier* and illustrated with logs floating in a river.

1984-1989: Darker brown oval label with brown ink marked *Bill Collings, Luthier* and illustrated with logs and guitars floating in a river.

1989 to date: Light brown oval label with black ink marked *Collings, Austin, Texas.*

Flattop Serialization

1975-1987: Guitars do not posses a serial number. Most are marked with a handwritten date on the underside of the top. Some guitars from 1987 may have a serial number.

1988 to date: Guitars began a consecutive numbering series that began with number 175. The serial number is stamped on the neck block.

Archtop Serialization

Before 1991: Archtops before 1991 had their own separate serialization.

1991 to date: Archtops are now numbered with a two part serial number. The first number indicates the archtop as part of the general company serialization, and the second number indicates the ranking in the archtop series list.

ACOUSTIC ARCHTOP

In addition to their well known flattop acoustic models, the Collings handcrafted **Archtop** model is offered in a 17" wide body ($13,500) and an 18" wide body ($14,500).

Prior to 1997, a 16" wide body was offered (original retail list was $10,000), but has since been discontinued.

Collings 18" Special
courtesy Scott Chinery

ACOUSTIC

Collings guitars are offered with a number of options, such as abalone top border inlays, custom inlays, tuning machines, wood binding, and body wood, including Brazilian rosewood (please call for prices and availability). All models are available with these following options:

Add $150 for Engelmann spruce top.
Add $225 for abalone rosette.
Add $250 for koa top.
Add $300 for left-handed configuration.
Add $150 for German spruce top.
Add $350 for sunburst top.
Add $350 for maple body and neck.
Add $500 for rounded single cutaway.
Add $500 for koa back and sides.

BABY — 3/4 size dreadnought style, spruce top, ivoroid binding, herringbone purfling, round soundhole, ivoroid/wood stripe rosette, tortoise style pickguard, East Indian rosewood back/sides, mahogany neck, 24 1/8" scale, 14/20 fret bound ebony fingerboard with pearl diamond/square inlay, ebony bridge with white black dot pins, rosewood veneer on bound peghead with mother of pearl logo inlay, 3 per side nickel Waverly tuners. Available in Natural finish. Mfr. 1997 to date.

Total Length 36 1/2", Body Length 17 1/8", Body Width 12 1/2", Body Thickness 3 15/16".

Mfr.'s Sug. Retail	$2,700	$2,195	$N/A	$N/A

C Series

C-10 — folk style, spruce top, round soundhole, tortoise style pickguard, ivoroid bound body/rosette, mahogany back/sides/neck, 25 1/2" scale, 14/20 fret bound ebony fingerboard, ebony bridge with white black dot pins, rosewood veneer on bound peghead with mother of pearl logo, 3 per side gold Kluson tuners. Available in Natural finish. Current mfr.

Total Length 39 1/2", Body Length 19 1/4", Body Width 14 3/4", Body Thickness 4 1/4".

Mfr.'s Sug. Retail	$2,550	$2,175	$N/A	$N/A

In 1992, this model was also available in Blonde, Blue, Midnight Black, and Red finishes with a pearloid pickguard and pearloid headstock veneer.

In 1995, nickel Schaller mini-tuners replaced original item.

C-10 Deluxe — similar to C-10, except has East Indian rosewood back/sides, pearl dot fingerboard inlay, ebony peghead veneer with pearl logo inlay, gold Schaller mini tuners. Available in Natural finish. Current mfr.

Mfr.'s Sug. Retail	$2,950	$2,500	$N/A	$N/A

In 1995, nickel Schaller mini-tuners replaced original item.

C-100 — similar to C-10, except has larger body dimensions. Disc. 1995.

Body Length 20 1/8", Body Width 16", Body Thickness 4 1/2".

	$1,275	$N/A

Last Mfr.'s Sug. Retail was $2,225.

Grading	100%	EXCELLENT	AVERAGE

C-100 Deluxe — similar to C-10 Deluxe, except has larger body dimensions. Disc. 1995.

Body Length 20 1/8", Body Width 16", Body Thickness 4 1/2".

		$1,500	$N/A

Last Mfr.'s Retail was $2,725.

CJ COLLINGS JUMBO — folk style, spruce top, round soundhole, tortoise style pickguard, double black/white strip purfling, black/white strip rosette, East Indian back/sides, mahogany neck, 25 1/2" scale, 14/20 fret ivoroid bound ebony fingerboard with pearl dot markers, ebony bridge with white black dot pins, ebony veneer on ivoroid bound peghead with mother of pearl logo, 3 per side nickel Waverly tuners. Available in Natural finish. Mfr. 1995 to date.

Total Length 40 1/4", Body Length 20 1/8", Body Width 16", Body Thickness 4 7/8".

Mfr.'s Sug. Retail	$3,050	$2,600	$N/A	$N/A

D Series

D-1 — dreadnought style, spruce top, round soundhole, tortoise pickguard, 3 stripe bound body/rosette, mahogany back/sides/neck, 25 1/2" scale, 14/20 fret bound ebony fingerboard, ebony bridge with white black dot pins, rosewood veneer on bound peghead with pearl logo inlay, 3 per side chrome Gotoh tuners. Available in Natural finish. Current mfr.

Total Length 40 1/4", Body Length 20", Body Width 15 5/8", Body Thickness 4 7/8".

Mfr.'s Sug. Retail	$2,550	$2,175	$N/A	$N/A

In 1995, nickel Waverly tuners replaced original item.

D-2 — similar to D-1, except has Indian rosewood back/sides, pearl diamond/square peghead inlay. Disc. 1995.

		$1,275	$N/A

Last Mfr.'s Sug. Retail was $2,300.

D-2H — dreadnought style, spruce top, ivoroid binding, herringbone purfling, round soundhole, ivoroid/wood stripe rosette, tortoise style pickguard, East Indian rosewood back/sides, mahogany neck, 14/20 fret bound ebony fingerboard with pearl diamond/square inlay, ebony bridge with white black dot pins, rosewood veneer on bound peghead with mother of pearl logo inlay, 3 per side nickel Waverly tuners. Available in Natural finish. Current mfr.

Mfr.'s Sug. Retail	$2,700	$2,295	$N/A	$N/A

D-3 — similar to D-2H, except has abalone purfling/rosette, no fingerboard inlays, and gold Waverly tuners. Current mfr.

Mfr.'s Sug. Retail	$3,275	$2,775	$N/A	$N/A

DS-2H 12-FRET — dreadnought style, spruce top, ivoroid binding, herringbone purfling, round soundhole, ivoroid/wood stripe rosette, tortoise style pickguard, East Indian rosewood back/sides, mahogany neck, 25 1/2" scale, 12/20 fret bound ebony fingerboard with pearl diamond/square inlay, ebony bridge with white black dot pins, rosewood veneer on bound slotted peghead with mother of pearl logo inlay, 3 per side nickel Waverly tuners. Available in Natural finish. Mfr. 1995 to date.

Total Length 40 1/8", Body Length 20 7/8", Body Width 15 5/8", Body Thickness 4 1/8".

Mfr.'s Sug. Retail	$3,100	$2,700	$N/A	$N/A

OM Series

OM-1 — grand concert style, spruce top, round soundhole, tortoise pickguard, 3 stripe bound body/rosette, mahogany back/sides/neck, 25 1/2" scale, 14/20 fret bound ebony fingerboard with pearl dot markers, ebony bridge with white black dot pins, rosewood veneer on bound peghead with mother of pearl logo inlay, 3 per side chrome Gotoh tuners. Available in Natural finish. Current mfr.

Total Length 39 1/2", Body Length 19 1/4", Body Width 15", Body Thickness 4 1/8".

Mfr.'s Sug. Retail	$2,550	$2,175	$N/A	$N/A

In 1995, nickel Waverly tuners replaced original item.

OM-2 — similar to OM-1, except has Indian rosewood back/sides, pearl diamond/square peghead inlay. Disc. 1995.

		$1,295	$N/A

Last Mfr.'s Sug. Retail was $2,300.

OM-2H — grand concert style, spruce top, ivoroid binding, herringbone purfling, round soundhole, ivoroid/wood stripe rosette, tortoise style pickguard, East Indian rosewood back/sides, mahogany neck, 14/20 fret bound ebony fingerboard with pearl diamond/square inlay, ebony bridge with white black dot pins, rosewood veneer on bound peghead with mother of pearl logo inlay, 3 per side nickel Waverly tuners. Available in Natural finish. Current mfr.

Mfr.'s Sug. Retail	$2,700	$2,295	$N/A	$N/A

OM-3 — similar to OM-2H, except has abalone purfling/rosette, no fingerboard inlays, and gold Waverly tuners. Current mfr.

Mfr.'s Sug. Retail	$3,275	$2,775	$N/A	$N/A

000-2H 12-FRET — orchestra style, spruce top, ivoroid binding, herringbone purfling, round soundhole, ivoroid/wood stripe rosette, tortoise style pickguard, East Indian rosewood back/sides, mahogany neck, 25 1/2" scale, 12/20 fret bound ebony fingerboard with pearl diamond/square inlay, ebony pyramid bridge with white black dot pins, rosewood veneer on bound slotted peghead with mother of pearl logo inlay, 3 per side nickel Waverly slot-head tuners. Available in Natural finish. Mfr. 1994 to date.

Total Length 39 1/2", Body Length 20 1/4", Body Width 15", Body Thickness 4 1/8".

Mfr.'s Sug. Retail	$3,100	$2,650	$N/A	$N/A

Grading	100%	EXCELLENT	AVERAGE

SJ Small Jumbo Series

SJ SMALL JUMBO — small jumbo style, spruce top, round soundhole, tortoise pickguard, double black/ivoroid strip purfling, black/white wood and nitrate strip rosette, maple back/sides/neck, 25 1/2" scale, 14/20 fret bound ebony fingerboard with modern pearl diamond inlay, ebony bridge with white black dot pins, ebony veneer on bound peghead with pearl diamond and logo inlay, 3 per side gold Schaller mini tuners. Available in Natural finish. Current mfr.

Total Length 40 1/4", Body Length 20 1/8", Body Width 16", Body Thickness 4 1/2".

Mfr.'s Sug. Retail	$3,250	$2,750	$N/A	$N/A

COLLOPY

Instruments currently built in San Francisco, California.

Luthier Rich Collopy has been building and performing repairs on guitars for the past 25 years. In the last year, Collopy opened a retail musical instrument shop in addition to his repairs and building. For further information concerning specifications and pricing, please contact luthier Collopy via the Index of Current Manufacturers located in the rear of this edition.

BILL COMINS

Instruments built in Willow Grove, Pennsylvania since 1991.

Bill Comins has been a guitar player since the age of six. While attending Temple University, Comins majored in Jazz Guitar Performance as well as performing professionally and teaching.

Following his backround in building and repairing stringed instruments, Comins maintained his own repair/custom shop in addition to working in a violin repair shop for 4 years after college. In 1991, Comins met with Master Luthier Bob Benedetto. Benedetto's shared knowledge inspired Comins to develop his own archtop guitar design. Comin's archtop guitar design is based in part on his professional guitar playing backround, and has devised a guitar that is comfortable to play. Comins currently offers 4 different archtop models.

Realizing that other players may have tastes that vary from his, Comins offers a number of following options to his standard models like the choice of tone woods, cutaway or non-cutaway design, 16", 17", or 18" lower bout, choice of an oval soundhole or f-holes, parallel or X-bracing, and a 7-string configuration.

ACOUSTIC ARCHTOP

The following is standard on all Comins Archtop guitars: Handcarved solid Sitka or Engelmann spruce tops, handcarved solid maple back and matching sides, a 16" or 17" lower bout, 3 1/8" body depth, violin style floating ebony tail piece, adjustable ebony bridge, choice of f-holes or an oval sound hole, 25" scale; and a 22 fret ebony fingerboard. List prices include a 3-ply hardshell case.

There is no charge for other scale lengths (24 3/4", 25 1/2", etc.), an oval sound hole, non-cutaway body, or other body depths. Wood binding may run between $300 to $600; other options are available on request. Contact luther Comins via the Index of Current Manuacturers located in the back of this edition.

Add $250 for fancy split block pearl fingerboard inlay.

Add $300 for 18" lower bout.

Add $700 for 7-string configuration.

The **Chester Avenue** model (list $5,450) features a select Sitka or Englemann spruce top that is hand carved from solid woods, and nicely figured maple back and sides. The bound ebony fingerboard has 22 frets; ebony is also featured in the adjustable bridge and violin style floating tail piece. The **Chester Avenue** is available in Sunburst or Honey blonde finishes, and features multi-laminated bindings and purfling around the top, bottom, peghead, f-holes, and raised pickguard. The gold Schaller mini tuning machines have ebony buttons, and the model comes equipped with a Benedetto Suspended pickup with volume control.

In 1996, Comins introduced the **Classic** model archtop. Its design is similar to the Chester Avenue, but features a 3-piece laminated figured neck, bound f-holes/unbound ebony pickguard, and has slightly less ornate appointments. The **Classic** carries a suggested retail of $4,950.

The **Concert** model ($3,950) is another archtop with a hand carved top and back and three-piece maple neck. The body, neck, and headstock are bound, while the chamfered f-holes and Chuck Wayne-style raised pickguard are not. The Concert model is available only in a Sunburst finish.

The violin-style finish and straight forward appointments of the **Parlor** archtop are reminiscent of a violin. This model also features the 3-piece laminated neck, no raised pickguard, and mini tuning machines in a black finish with ebony buttons. The Parlor (list $3,500) is available with an oval soundhole or classically-styled f-holes. The Parlor is also optionally available with violin-style purfling around the top and back (add $250).

Comins Chester Avenue
courtesy Scott Chinery

CONCERTONE

See chapter on House Brands.

This trademark has been identified as a "House Brand" of Montgomery Wards. Instruments were built by either KAY or HARMONY.

(Source: Michael Wright, Guitar Stories Volume One)

CONDE HERMANOS

Instruments produced in Madrid, Spain. Distributed by Luthier Music Corporation of New York City, New York.

Conde Hermanos offers a wide range of Classical, Concert-grade Classical, Flamenco, and Concert-grade Flamenco acoustic guitars built in Madrid, Spain. These models are constructed with the medium level to professional classical guitarist in mind.

ACOUSTIC

AC/EC Classical Series

AC Series Concert Classical guitars feature German Spruce or Canadian red cedar tops, Indian rosewood back and sides, cedar neck, and an ebony fingerboard. Prices (in U.S.) range from $3,100 (**Model AC 22**), to $4,310 (**Model AC 23**); the **Model AC 23 R** has Brazilian rosewood

Grading	100%	EXCELLENT	AVERAGE

(Jacaranda) back and sides (retail U.S. $5,361). The 8-string **Model AC 23 R.8** also features Brazilian rosewood (Jacaranda) back and sides (retail U.S. $CALL) and is available in a 10-string configuration. The top of the line **Felipe V** has a retail price of $9,271.

The **EC** Studio classical guitars, like the Concert classicals, have German Spruce or Canadian red cedar tops, Indian rosewood back and sides, cedar neck, and an ebony fingerboard. U.S. retail prices range from $1,226 (**Model EC 1**), to $1,607 (**Model EC 2**), to $2,271 (**Model EC 3**).

AF/EF Flamenco Series

Conde Hermano's **AF Series** Concert Flamenco guitars have German Spruce tops, Indian rosewood back and sides, cedar neck, and an ebony fingerboard. These flamenco models are equipped with a transparent tapping plate ("Golpeador transparente") and choice of machine head or wooden peg tuners. Prices (in U.S.) range from $3,097 (**Model AF 24**), to $4,310 (**Model AF 25**); the **Model AF 25 R** has Brazilian rosewood (Jacaranda) back and sides (retail U.S. $5,362). The top of the line **Felipe V Flamenco** has a retail price of $9,271. Other models include the **Model A 26** ($4,310), **Model A 27** ($2,555), and **Model A 28** ($1,987).

The **EF** Studio Flamenco guitars feature Spanish cypress back and sides, German Spruce or Canadian red cedar tops, cedar neck, and an ebony fingerboard. Flamenco models are equipped with a transparent tapping plate and choice of machine head or wooden peg tuners. U.S. retail prices range from $1,226 (**Model EF 4**), to $1,394 (**Model EF 5**). The **Model EF 5 N** features Indian rosewood back and sides (retail U.S. $1,607).

CONN

Instruments built in Japan circa 1968 to 1978.

The U.S. distributor for Conn brandname instruments was Conn/Continental Music Company of Chicago, Illinois. The Conn trademark is perhaps more recognizable on their brass band instruments. Conn offered both classical models and 6- and 12-string acoustic steel-string models, built by Aria and Company in Japan. Many models of student level to intermediate quality, and some feature a bolt-on neck instead of the usual standard.

(Source: Michael Wright, Guitar Stories Volume One)

CONQUEROR

Instruments produced in Japan circa 1970s (estimated).

The Conqueror label is found on classical-style acoustic guitars.

These models have a spruce top, round soundhole, geometric rosette (black, red, green, yellow pattern), nato back and sides, one piece nato neck ("steel reinforced"), 12/19 fret laminated fingerboard (perhaps bubinga), nato bridge. The slotted headstock has three per side ivory-colored plastic tuners. The soundboard is stained redwood color, the back/sides/neck stained mahogany. They have a distinctive coat of arms and armor plastic ornament on the headstock, with the work "Conqueror" in Old English typeface. A similar crest can be found on the interior paper label inside the body, and a *Made in Japan* label on the back of the headstock.

Conqueror acoustics in average condition are valued around $60.

(Source: Walter Murray, Frankenstein Fretworks)

CONRAD

Instruments produced in Japan circa 1972 to 1978.

The Conrad trademark was a brandname used by U.S. importers David Wexler and Company of Chicago, Illinois. The Conrad product line consisted of 6- and 12-string acoustic guitars, thinline hollowbody electrics, solid body electric guitars and basses, mandolins, and banjos. Conrad instruments were produced by Kasuga International (Kasuga and Tokai USA, Inc.), and featured good quality designs specifically based on popular American designs.

(Source: Michael Wright, Guitar Stories Volume One)

CONTESSA

Instruments built in Italy between 1966 to early 1970s. Distributed in the U.S. by M. Hohner, Inc. of Hicksville, New York.

The Contessa trademark covered a wide range of medium quality guitars and solid state amplifiers. The **HG** series (for Hohner Guitars?) featured acoustic ("Folk, Classical, and Country & Western") and original design solid body electrics.

(Source: Tony Bacon and Paul Day, The Guru's Guitar Guide)

ACOUSTIC

HG 01 — dreadnought style, spruce top, round soundhole, mahogany back/sides, 18 fret rosewood fingerboard with white dot inlay, rosewood bridge with white pins, black pickguard, 3 per side Contessa tuners with plastic buttons. Available in Natural finish. Mfd. circa early 1970s.

Length 38 1/2", Body Width 14 1/2".

$75 $35
Last Mfr.'s Sug. Retail was $79.95.

HG 06 J — dreadnought style, spruce top, round soundhole, mahogany back/sides, 20 fret rosewood fingerboard with white dot inlay, rosewood bridge with white black-dot pins, black pickguard (half covers soundhole rosette), 3 per side Contessa tuners. Available in Natural finish. Mfd. circa early 1970s.

Length 40 1/4", Body Width 14 1/2".

$90 $50
Last Mfr.'s Sug. Retail was $99.95.

HG 12 J — dreadnought style, spruce top, round soundhole, mahogany back/sides, 21 fret rosewood fingerboard, rosewood bridge, black pickguard, 3 per side Contessa tuners. Available in Natural finish. Mfd. circa early 1970s.

Length 42 1/2", Body Width 14 1/4".

$95 $50
Last Mfr.'s Sug. Retail was $139.95.

CONTINENTAL

See also CONN.

Instruments produced in Japan.

As well as distributing the Conn guitars, the Continental Music Company of Chicago, Illinois also distributed their own brandname guitars under the Continental logo in the U.S.

(Source: Michael Wright, Guitar Stories Volume One)

COOG INSTRUMENTS

Instruments currently built in Santa Cruz, California.

Luthier Ronald Cook runs Coog Instruments as a hobby/semi-business. Cook's primary focus is on handcrafted folk instruments such as guitars and dulcimers, but has also constructed various electric guitars, hurdy-gurdies, and harpsichords through the years. Cook also performs repair work on antique or vintage stringed instruments.

Cook's building and repairs are conducted in his spare time; thus, the lead time on a custom guitar or dulcimer order is a bit longer than running down to your local "guitar club mega-gigantic store" and buying one off the wall. If patience and a custom built folk instrument is what you're into, then please call luthier Cook via the Index of Current Manufacturers located in the back of this edition.

CORDOBA

Instruments produced in Spain. Distributed exclusively in the U.S. by Guitar Salon International of Santa Monica, California.

The Cordoba line of classical guitars is designed for the characteristics of a handmade guitar, but priced for the serious student. Prices range from $579 up to $2,739.

ACOUSTIC

30 R — classical style, solid cedar top, round soundhole, laminated mahogany back/sides, mahogany neck, 650 mm scale, 12/19 fret rosewood fingerboard, rosewood tied bridge, slotted headstock, 3 per side nickel plated tuners. Available in Natural finish. Current mfr.
   Mfr.'s Sug. Retail $579

40 R — similar to the 30 R, except features laminated rosewood back/sides, maple purfling, gold plated tuners. Available in Natural finish. Current mfr.
   Mfr.'s Sug. Retail $759

50 R — similar to the 30 R, except features laminated rosewood back/sides, ebony-reinforced Honduran cedar neck, ebony fingerboard, gold plated tuners. Available in Natural finish. Current mfr.
   Mfr.'s Sug. Retail $939

50 EC — similar to the 50 R, except features a single rounded cutaway body, slightly narower fingerboard, Fishman transducer. Available in Natural finish. Current mfr.
   Mfr.'s Sug. Retail $1,679

60 R — similar to the 50 R, except features rosewood back/sides, maple purfling. Available in Natural finish. Current mfr.
   Mfr.'s Sug. Retail $1,239

70 R — similar to the 60 R, except features German spruce top, ebony-reinforced Spanish cedar neck, detailed headstock/purfling/rosette. Available in Natural finish. Current mfr.
   Mfr.'s Sug. Retail $1,239

70 F Flamenco — similar to the 70 R, except features solid cypress back/sides, translucent tap plate. Available in Natural finish. Current mfr.
   Mfr.'s Sug. Retail $1,459

90 — similar to the 70 R, except features quartersawn German spruce (or cedar) top, solid Indian rosewood back/sides. Available in Natural high gloss lacquer finish. Current mfr.
   Mfr.'s Sug. Retail $2,099

110 — similar to the 70 R, except features quartersawn German spruce (or cedar) top, solid Indian rosewood back/sides, detailed headstock/purfling/rosette. Available in Natural high gloss lacquer finish. Current mfr.
   Mfr.'s Sug. Retail $2,739

CORT

Instruments currently produced in Inchon and Taejon, Korea; and Surabuya, Indonesia. Distributed in the U.S. by Cort Musical Instrument Company, Ltd. of Northbrook, Illinois.

Since 1960, Cort has been providing students, beginners and mid-level guitar players quality acoustic, semi-hollow body, and solid body guitars and basses. All Cort instruments are produced in Asia in Cort company facilities, which were established in 1973. Cort is one of the few U.S. companies that owns their overseas production facilities. Cort also produces most of their own electronics (pickups, circuit boards, and other guitar parts); additional parts and custom pieces are available under the **MightyMite** trademark.

The Cort engineering and design center is located in Northbrook, Illinois. Wood is bought from the U.S. and Canada, and shipped to their production facilities in Korea. Cort instruments are then produced and assembled in the main Cort factories in Korea. After shipping the finished instruments back to the U.S., all instruments are checked in the Illinois facilities as part of quality control prior to shipping to the dealer.

In addition to their traditional designs, Cort also offers a large number of their own designs, as well as featured designs by other luthiers. Beginning in 1996, Cort began commissioning designs from noted luthier Jerry Auerswald; this lead to other

Grading	100%	EXCELLENT	AVERAGE

designs from such noted U.S. luthiers as Jim Triggs, Bill Conklin, and Greg Curbow. Cort has also worked with guitarists Larry Coryell and Matt "Guitar" Murphy on their respective signature series models (the **LCS-1** and the **MGM-1**).

Cort's left-handed models are generally a special order, and produced in limited quanities. There is an additional $30 charge for left-handed configuration models in the current production line-up.

ACOUSTIC

Cort Custom Shop Models

Cort briefly offered specialty versions of their acoustic models: **SJ-DLX** (retail list $1,295); The **SF-CLASSIC** (retail list $995), and the **NAT-28 DLX** (retail list $795) between 1996 to 1998.

Natural Series

NATURAL — dreadnought style, solid cedar top, round soundhole, maple bound body, wood design rosette, mahogany back/sides/neck, 14/20 fret rosewood fingerboard with double dot inlay at 12th fret, rosewood bridge with white pins, 3 per side vintage chrome tuners. Available in Natural Satin finish. Mfr. 1996 to date.

Mfr.'s Sug. Retail	$479	$335	$225	$175

Natural DLX — similar to the Natural, except has solid rosewood back, rosewood sides, stylized inlay at 12th fret, vintage gold tuners. Mfd. 1996 to 1998.

			$425	$250

Last Mfr.'s Sug. Retail was $795.

Resonator Series

ADR6 — dreadnought style resonator guitar, spruce top, mahogany back/sides, mahogany rounded neck, multiple ivory body binding, a 14/20 fret rosewood fingerboard with white dot inlays, resonator cone/soundwell, two mesh soundholes, spider bridge, 3 on a side chrome diecast tuners. Available in Natural Glossy and Tobacco Sunburst finishes. Mfd. 1996 to 1998.

			$375	$225

Last Mfr.'s Sug. Retail was $699.

ADS6 — similar to the ADR6, except has square neck and chrome open tuning machines. Mfd. 1996 to 1998.

			$395	$225

Last Mfr.'s Sug. Retail was $750.

Solid Top Series

EARTH 100 — dreadnought style, solid spruce top, round soundhole, tortoise pickguard, black body binding, 4 ring rosette, maple back/sides/neck, 14/20 fret rosewood fingerboard with dot inlay, rosewood bridge with white pins, 3 per side chrome diecast tuners. Available in 'Tone Finish' finish. Mfr. 1998 to date.

Mfr.'s Sug. Retail	$299	$225	$135	$100

EARTH 200 — dreadnought style, solid spruce top, round soundhole, tortoise pickguard, herringbone bound body/rosette, mahogany back/sides/neck, 14/20 fret rosewood fingerboard with dot inlay, stylized inlay at 12th fret, rosewood bridge with white pins, 3 per side chrome Grover tuners. Available in Natural Satin finish. Current mfr.

Mfr.'s Sug. Retail	$389	$275	$150	$100

Earth 200 LH — similar to the Earth 200, except in left-handed configuration. Current mfr.

Mfr.'s Sug. Retail	$419	$295	$175	$125

Earth 200-12 — similar to the Earth 200, except in 12-string configuration, 6 per side tuners. Mfr. 1998 to date.

Mfr.'s Sug. Retail	$479	$335	$225	$150

Earth 200 GC — similar to the Earth 200, except in a Grand Concert style body, and featuring a solid cedar top, no pickguard. Mfr. 1996 to date.

Mfr.'s Sug. Retail	$389	$325	$150	$100

Earth 500 — similar to the Earth 200, except has gold Grover tuners. Available in Natural Glossy finish. Current mfr.

Mfr.'s Sug. Retail	$469	$325	$225	$150

Earth 900 — similar to the Earth 200, except has solid cedar top, bound fingerboard with abalone inlays, and gold classic tuners. Mfr. 1998 to date.

Mfr.'s Sug. Retail	$595	$425	$275	$195

Earth 1000 — similar to the Earth 200, except has rosewood sides and back, abalone finderboard/soundhole inlays, and gold Grover tuners. Available in Natural Glossy finish. Current mfr.

Mfr.'s Sug. Retail	$595	$425	$275	$195

Western Series (Formerly AJ Series)

AJ 850 — dreadnought style, spruce top, round soundhole, tortoise pickguard, black body/rosette binding, mahogany back/sides/neck, 14/20 fret rosewood fingerboard with dot inlay, rosewood bridge with white pins, 3 per side chrome diecast tuners. Available in 'Tone Finish' finish. Current mfr.

Mfr.'s Sug. Retail	$279	$195	$125	$90

AJ 860 — dreadnought style, spruce top, round soundhole, black pickguard, multiple black body/rosette binding, mahogany back/sides/neck, 14/20 fret rosewood fingerboard with dot inlay, rosewood bridge with white pins, 3 per side chrome diecast tuners. Available in Natural Satin finish. Current mfr.

Mfr.'s Sug. Retail	$299	$200	$125	$90

AJ 870 — similar to the AJ 860, except available in Natural Glossy or Tobacco Sunburst finishes. Current mfr.

Mfr.'s Sug. Retail	$349	$250	$175	$125

Grading	100%	EXCELLENT	AVERAGE

AJ 870 BK — similar to the AJ 870, except in Black finish. Disc. 1998.

		$200	$125

Last Mfr.'s Sug. Retail was $399.

AJ 870 C — similar to the AJ 870, except has a transducer pickup mounted in the bridge. Disc. 1998.

Mfr.'s Sug. Retail	$399	$280	$180	$130

AJ 870 12 — similar to the AJ 870, except in a 12-string configuration, 6 per side tuners. Available in Natural Glossy finish only. Current mfr.

Mfr.'s Sug. Retail	$389	$275	$175	$125

ACOUSTIC ELECTRIC

MR Series

All the MR Series acoustic electric models feature a Fishman transducer pickup and EQ.

MR710 F — dreadnought style, single cutaway body, spruce top, round soundhole, black body binding, 4 ring rosette, maple back/sides/neck, 14/20 fret rosewood fingerboard with offset dot inlay, rosewood bridge with white pins, 3 per side chrome diecast tuners, Fishman acoustic pickup, Fishman Deluxe EQ with 3 band sliders and mid frequency sweep/volume controls. Available in Natural 'Tone Finish' finish. Mfr. 1998 to date.

Mfr.'s Sug. Retail	$495	$350	$225	$150

MR720 F — single cutaway dreadnought style, spruce top, round soundhole, tortoiseshell pickguard, multiple ivory body binding/rosette, mahogany back/sides/neck, 14/20 fret rosewood fingerboard with offset dot inlay, rosewood bridge with white pins, 3 per side chrome Grover tuners, Fishman acoustic pickup, Fishman Deluxe EQ with 3 band sliders and mid frequency sweep/volume controls. Available in Natural Glossy, Natural Satin, and See Through Black finishes. Current mfr.

Mfr.'s Sug. Retail	$550	$395	$250	$175

MR730 FX (Previously MR730 F) — similar to the MR720 F, except has a solid spruce top, Fishman Prefix EQ system. Available in Natural Satin finish only. Current mfr.

Mfr.'s Sug. Retail	$650	$450	$300	$225

MR750 F (Also MR750 FX) — similar to the MR720 F, except has a bound flamed maple top, bound neck/headstock, Fishman Prefix EQ system, tortoise pickguard, gold Grover tuners. Available in Amber Satin, See Through Black, See Through Blue, See Through Red, and Tobacco Sunburst finishes. Current mfr.

Mfr.'s Sug. Retail	$695	$495	$325	$225

MR770 F — similar to MR750 F, except has a rounded profile back. Current mfr.

Mfr.'s Sug. Retail	$695	$495	$325	$225

MR780 FX — similar to MR750 F, except has quilted maple top, maple back/sides, maple neck, white body binding, gold diecast tuners. Available in Blue Burst and Red Burst finishes. Mfr. 1998 to date.

Mfr.'s Sug. Retail	$750	$525	$350	$250

SF/SJ Series

The SF and SJ Series acoustic/electrics feature a single cutaway and narrower waist design than the dreadnought style Solid Top models.

SF1 — single cutaway body, spruce top, round soundhole, bound body, rosette, maple back/sides/neck, 14/20 fret rosewood fingerboard with offset dot inlay, rosewood bridge with white pins, 3 per side chrome diecast tuners, SlimJim pickup, Cort EQ with 3 band/volume sliders. Available in Natural Satin finish. Current mfr.

Mfr.'s Sug. Retail	$550	$395	$250	$175

Early models may have mahogany back/sides, and mahogany neck.

SF5 X (Previously SF5) — similar to SF1, except has solid cedar top, mahogany back/sides/neck, gold Grover tuners, Fishman acoustic pickup, Fishman Prefix EQ with 3 band/contour/volume sliders. Available in Natural Satin finish. Mfr. 1996 to 1997 (as SF5), 1998 to date.

Mfr.'s Sug. Retail	$659	$475	$300	$225

SJ5 (Also SJ5 X) — similar to the SF1, except has a deeper body, solid spruce top, mahogany back/sides/neck, gold Grover tuners, Fishman acoustic pickup, Fishman Prefix EQ with 3 band/contour/volume sliders. Available in Natural Satin finish. Current mfr.

Mfr.'s Sug. Retail	$659	$475	$300	$225

SJ10 (Also SJ10 X) — similar to the SJ5, except has rosewood back and sides, abalone binding on body/soundhole, abalone position inlays. Available in Natural Glossy finish. Mfr. 1996 to date.

Mfr.'s Sug. Retail	$895	$625	$425	$295

ACOUSTIC ELECTRIC BASS

MR720 BF — single cutaway dreadnought style, spruce top, round soundhole, multiple ivory body binding/rosette, maple back/sides, mahogany neck, 15/20 fret rosewood fingerboard with offset dot inlay, rosewood bridge with white pins, 2 per side chrome diecast tuners, Fishman acoustic pickup, Fishman Deluxe EQ with 3 band sliders and mid frequency sweep/volume controls. Available in Natural Glossy and See Through Black finishes. Current mfr.

Mfr.'s Sug. Retail	$795	$575	$375	$250

Price includes gig bag.

CORTEZ

Instruments built in Japan circa 1969 to 1988. Distributed in the U.S. market by Westheimer Musical Industries of Chicago, Illinois.

Cortez acoustics were produced in Japan, and imported to the U.S. market as an affordable alternative in the acoustic guitar market. Westheimer's Cortez company and trademark could be viewed as a stepping stone towards his current **Cort** company (See CORT).

COSI

Instruments built in Les Plages, France. Distributed by Applications de technologies Nouvelles (ATN) International of Les Plages, France.

Designer J. C. Lagarde's CoSI (**Co**mposite **S**tring **I**nstruments) brand of upright basses feature wood soundboards and graphite back and sides. The wood top maintains the proper response, while the graphite body maintains a stable equilibrium regardless of room temperature. CoSI instruments are recognized worldwide for their acoustic qualities, and are priced such that students and professionals can easily afford to have proper sound. For further information regarding CoSI instruments, please contact Applications de technologies Nouvelles International via the Index of Current Manufacturers located in the back of this edition.

CRAFTER

Instruments are currently built in Korea. Distributed in the U.S. by HSS (a Division of Hohner, Inc.), located in Richmond, Virginia.

The Crafter guitar line consists of acoustic guitars with wood tops and either fiberglass or traditional wood backs. The acoustic/electric models are equipped with Shadow pickup systems with built-in four band EQs. Retail list prices range from $369 up to $679.

In 1998, Crafter introduced a new acoustic/electric Mandolin with similar construction techniques like the guitars. The M70E 8-string mandolin is available in Classic Natural (with spruce top) and Marine Sunburst or Red Sunburst (with tiger maple top).

ACOUSTIC

The all acoustic Crafter model is the **MD 60** (list $369) with tiger maple top, ash back and sides, mahogany neck, and rosewood fingerboard and bridge.

ACOUSTIC ELECTRIC

Crafter's acoustic/electric models are equipped with Shadow pickup systems with built-in four band EQs.

Dreadnought Series

The **ED 100 EQ** (list $549) has a spruce top, koa back and sides, mahogany neck, rosewood fingerboard and bridge, and a Natural Satin finish.

Fiberglass Back Series

All 4 models feature fiberglass backs and wood tops. The **FA 820 EQ** (list $489) has an ash top, mahogany neck, rosewood fingerboard and bridge, and an Antique Sunburst finish. The **FSD 400 EQ** is similar in construction design, except features a tiger maple top with f-holes, and Cherry Sunburst finish (list $579). The **FSG 250** (list $429) has a spruce top, mahogany neck, rosewood fingerboard and bridge, and Cherry Sunburst or optional Transparent Black finish (**Model FSD 320 EQ**). The optional Transparent Black finish is an additional $100 (retail list $529). The **FSG 280 EQ** is similar, except features a tiger maple top (list $569).

Mini Series

The Crafter Mini Series debuted in 1997. The travel-style **Mini RF 30** has a fiberglass back, full scale mahogany neck and rosewood fingerboard, and a spruce top. The RF 30 is available in Natural, Blue Stain, and Black Stain finishes (retail list $299). The acoustic/electric **RF 40 E** has a similar construction, and includes a piezo bridge pickup with volume and tone controls. The RF 40 E (list $339) is available in Green Stain, Purple Stain, and Tobacco Sunburst finishes.

Super Jumbo Series

The **SJC 330 EQ** Super Jumbo has a spruce top, and is available in a Tobacco Sunburst finish (list $589); the **SJC 390 EQ** (list $679) has a similar construction design. The **SJ 270** Super Jumbo has a tiger maple top, mahogany back/sides/neck, rosewood fingerboard, and Tobacco Sunburst finish (list $499).

CRAFTERS OF TENNESSEE, LLC

Instruments currently built in Old Hickory, Tennessee.

President Mark Taylor's company is currently offering a range of high quality, ornate **Rich & Taylor** Living Legend Signature Model banjos, as well as the **Tut Taylor** series of Resophonic guitars. Tut Taylor began his musical career in the 1930s, playing the mandolin. He quickly moved to the resophonic guitar, and developed his style playing with a flat pick. Tut Taylor has recorded several albums and toured extensively with John Hartford and Norman Blake, among other well-known entertainers.

ACOUSTIC

All **Tut Taylor Signature Model** resphonic guitars feature a solid peghead with an ebony overlay, bound ebony fingerboard with intricate abalone inlay, an *old style* sound well with parallelogram openings, an aluminum cast and machined spider, and improved design brass cover plate.

The **Tennessean** model (retail list $1,495) has a 12-fret square Honduran mahogany neck, bound top and back Honduran mahogany body, nickel hardware, and a Brown Sunburst finish. The **Virginian**'s 12-fret square neck and body are constructed of flamed maple, and has a multi-bound top and back in a Vintage Brown Sunburst finish. Available with nickel hardware (retail $1,695) or 24 karat gold plated hardware (retail $1,995). The top of the line **Californian** resonator guitar has a solid walnut 12-fret squared neck, and a walnut body with mulit-bound top and back. Finished in natural walnut, the Californian is offered with nickel hardware (retail $1,795) or hand-engraved 24 karat gold plated hardware (retail $2,095).

CRAFTSMAN

Instruments produced in Japan during the late 1970s through the mid 1980s.

Craftsman built entry level to medium quality copies of American designs.

(Source: Tony Bacon and Paul Day, The Guru's Guitar Guide)

TOM CRANDALL

Instruments currently built in Phoenix, Arizona.

Instruments previously built in Iowa City, Iowa (beginning in 1990).

Luthier Tom Crandall has been building guitars and doing repairs for the past 6 to 7 years. Now located in Phoenix, Crandall continues to build a limited number of flat-top and archtop acoustic guitars. For further information, please contact luthier Tom Crandall via the Index of Current Manufacturers located in the back of this edition.

CRESTLINE

Instruments built in Japan circa mid to late 1970s. Distributed by the Grossman Music Corporation of Cleveland, Ohio.

These entry level to intermediate solid body guitars featured designs based on classic American favorites. Crestline offered a wide range of stringed instruments, including classical, folk, dreadnought, and 12-string acoustics; solid body electric guitars and basses; amplifiers; banjos, mandolins, and ukeleles. Considering the amount of instruments available, the Crestline trademark was probably used on guitars built by one of the bigger Japanese guitar producers and 'rebranded' for the U.S. market. One model reviewed at a vintage guitar show was based on Gibson's Les Paul design, and had Grover tuners, 2 Japanese covered humbuckers, and decent wood.

CROMWELL

See chapter on House Brands.

While the distribution of this trademark was handled by midwestern mail order companies, Gibson built this line of budget guitars sometime in the mid 1930s to the early 1940s. While the guitars were built to roughly similar Gibson standards, they lack the adjustable truss rod in the neck that differentiates them from a true Gibson of the same period.

(Source: Walter Carter, Gibson Guitars: 100 Years of an American Icon)

CUMBUS

Distributed by Lark in the Morning of Mendocino, California.

These instruments are traditional stringed instruments of Turkey, and include the *Cumbus* 12-string fretless banjo, 12-string banjo guitar, *Cumbus* saz, *Cumbus* banjo mandolin, and others.

WILLIAM R. CUMPIANO

Instruments currently built in Northampton, Massachusetts.

Luthier William Cumpiano trained under Michael Gurian in the early 1970s at the Michael Gurian Workshop, as well as working with Michael Millard in the mid 1970s. After training with Millard, Cumpiano opened his own lutherie shop.

For the past 25 years, William R. Cumpiano has been making guitars in the North American, European, and Latin American traditions, primarily on a commission basis. Over the years, he has achieved wide recognition in the field for his innovative designs and fine craftsmanship, as well as for having authored the principle textbook ("Guitarmaking: Tradition and Technology") and for his numerous feature articles in guitar magazines, such as **Acoustic Guitar** and **Guitarmaker**. Cumpiano has supplied custom-made instruments to some of the finest and most prominent guitarists in the United States.

(Biographical material courtesy of William R. Cumpiano, September 1997)

CURBOW

Instruments currently built in Morgantown, Georgia.

Luthier Greg Curbow offers a line of high quality stringed instruments that feature **Rockwood** necks. The *Rockwood* material is a composite of birch and phenolic based resins formed under pressure and heat, which produces a neck unaffected by changes in temperature and humidity. Curbow basses and guitars are hand-crafted directly at the Curbow workshop in the North Georgia mountains.

For current information on Curbow electric guitars and basses, please refer to the **5th Edition Blue Book of Electric Guitars**.

ACOUSTIC ELECTRIC BASS

ACOUSTIC ELECTRIC 4 — mahogany back and sides, quilted maple top, Rockwood neck, fretless Rockwood fingerboard, 2 per side headstock, chrome hardware, fixed bridge, custom Bartolini piezo and magnetic pickup system, Current mfr.

Mfr.'s Sug. Retail $9,995

Price includes a hardshell case.

This model is available in a 30" or 34" scale, and in 5-, 6-, and 7-string configurations.

CUSTOM KRAFT

See chapter on House Brands.

This trademark has been identified as a *House Brand* of St. Louis Music. The St. Louis Music Supply Company was founded in 1922 by Bernard Kornblum, originally as an importer of German violins. The St. Louis, Missouri-based company has been a distributor, importer, and manufacturer of musical instruments over the past seventy-five years.

In the mid 1950s, St. Louis Music distributed amplifiers and guitars from other producers such as Alamo, Harmony, Kay, Magnatone, Rickenbacker, and Supro. By 1960, the focus was on Harmony, Kay, and Supro: all built "upstream" in Chicago, Illinois. 1960 was also the year that St. Louis Music began carrying Kay's **Thinline** single cutaway electric guitar.

Custom Kraft was launched in 1961 as St. Louis Music's own house brand. The first series of semi-hollowbody Custom Kraft **Color Dynamic** Electric guitars were built by **Kay**, and appear to be Thinline models in Black, Red, and White. In 1963, a line of solid body double cutaway electrics built by **Valco** were added to the catalog under the Custom Kraft moniker, as well as Kay-built archtop and flat-top acoustic.

In 1967, Valco purchased Kay, a deal that managed to sink both companies by 1968. St. Louis Music continued advertising both companies models through 1970, perhaps NOS supplies from their warehouse. St. Louis Music continued to offer Custom Kraft guitars into the early 1970s, but as their sources had dried up so did the trademark name. St. Louis Music's next trademark guitar line was **Electra** (then followed by **Westone**, and **Alvarez**).

> Custom Kraft models are generally priced according to the weirdness/coolness factor, so don't be surprised to see the range of prices from $125 up to $400! The uncertainty indicates a buyer-directed market, so if you find one that you like, don't be afraid to haggle over the price. The earlier KAY and VALCO built guitars date from the 1960s, while later models were probably built in Japan.

(Source: Michael Wright, Vintage Guitar magazine)

CYCLONE

Instruments produced in Japan.

Cyclone guitars were distributed in the U.S. market by Leban Imports of Baltimore, Maryland.

(Source: Michael Wright, Guitar Stories Volume One)

DAVID DAILY

Instruments currently built in the U.S. Distributed by Kirkpatrick Guitar Studio of Baltimore, Maryland.

Luthier David Daily has been building high quality classical model guitars for the past few years. For further information regarding model specifications and pricing, please contact the Kirkpatrick Guitar Studio via the Index of Current Manufacturers located in the back of this edition.

DAIMARU

Instruments produced in Japan.

Daimaru guitars were distributed in the U.S. by the Daimaru New York Corporation of New York, New York.

(Source: Michael Wright, Guitar Stories Volume One)

DAION

Some guitars may also carry the trademark of JOODEE or YAMAKI.

Instruments were built in Japan circa late 1970s through the mid 1980s. Distributed by MCI, Inc. of Waco, Texas.

Originally, these Japanese-produced high quality guitars were based on popular U.S. designs in the 1970s, but turned to original designs in the 1980s. The Daion logo was applied to a range of acoustic, semi-hollow body, and solid body guitars and basses. Some Daion headstocks also feature a stylized tuning fork logo.

Grading	100%	EXCELLENT	AVERAGE

ACOUSTIC

Heritage Series

The Heritage series was Daion's top of the line for acoustic models. The following models were produced circa late 1970s to the early 1980s.

To date, reliable market prices for this model series are not available.

78 DAION HERITAGE — dreadnought style, solid cedar top with hand-stained mahogany finish, hardwood neck, round soundhole, maple binding, mahogany sides/2 piece back, 14/20 fret rosewood fingerboard with brass dot inlay, rosewood bridge with brass saddle, brass nut, rosewood string pins, 3 per side gold plated sealed tuning machines. Available in Natural finish.

78/12 Daion Heritage — similar to the 78 Daion Heritage, except in a 12-string configuration, slotted headstock, 6 per side tuners.

79 DAION HERITAGE — similar to the 78 Daion Heritage, except has spruce or solid cedar top and brass binding. Available in gloss Black finish.

80 DAION HERITAGE — dreadnought style, solid spruce top with hand-stained ovancol facing, nato neck, oval soundhole, maple binding, ovancol back/sides, 14/20 fret maple bound rosewood fingerboard with brass dot inlay, tortoise pickguard, rosewood bridge with brass saddle, brass nut, maple bound headstock with carved Daion design inlay, rosewood string pins, 3 per side gold plated sealed tuning machines. Available in Natural finish.

Maplewood Series

The Maplewood Series debuted in 1980. The dreadnought-styled **MS-100** had a spruce top, maple back/sides/neck/fingerboard, brown dot inlays, sealed tuners, 3 on a side headstock, and a Natural Blonde finish. The **MS-101** was similar, but featured a hand-rubbed Tan finish. A 12-string configuration with slotted headstock and 6 on a side plate tuners was called the **MS-100/12**.

Reliable market prices for these models are not available.

Mark Series

The Mark Series was offered circa late 1970s to the early 1980s. Truss rod access was at the body end of the neck, through the soundhole.

MARK I — dreadnought style, solid cedar top, hardwood neck, round soundhole, black binding, mahogany sides/back, 14/20 fret rosewood fingerboard with white dot inlay, rosewood bridge, rosewood pickguard, 3 per side chrome sealed tuning machines. Available in Natural finish.

$120 $70
Last Mfr.'s Sug. Retail was $255.

Mark I/12 — similar to the Mark I, except has a 12-string configuration, slotted headstock, 6 on a side tuners.

$140 $90
Last Mfr.'s Sug. Retail was $289.50.

MARK II — dreadnought style, solid cedar top, hardwood neck, round soundhole, white binding, redwood sides/2 piece back, 14/20 fret rosewood fingerboard with white dot inlay, rosewood bridge, rosewood pickguard, 3 per side chrome sealed tuning machines. Available in Natural finish.

$145 $95
Last Mfr.'s Sug. Retail was $299.50.

Mark II/12 — similar to the Mark II, except has a 12-string configuration, slotted headstock, 6 on a side tuners.

$155 $100

Last Mfr.'s Sug. Retail was $315.

MARK III — dreadnought style, spruce top, maple neck, round soundhole, white binding, maple sides/2 piece back, 14/20 fret maple fingerboard with brown dot inlay, maple bridge, rosewood pickguard, 3 per side chrome sealed tuning machines. Available in Natural finish.

$165 $105

Last Mfr.'s Sug. Retail was $340.

Mark III/12 — similar to the Mark III, except has a 12-string configuration, slotted headstock, 6 on a side tuners.

$180 $110

Last Mfr.'s Sug. Retail was $380.

MARK IV — dreadnought style, solid cedar top, hardwood neck, round soundhole, black binding, 5-layer maple/rosewood soundhole purfling, rosewood sides/2 piece back, 14/20 fret rosewood fingerboard with offset slash inlay, bone nut, rosewood bridge with bone saddle, rosewood pickguard, 3 per side chrome rotomatic tuners. Available in Natural finish.

$190 $125

Last Mfr.'s Sug. Retail was $395.

Mark IV/12 — similar to the Mark IV, except has a 12-string configuration, slotted headstock, 6 on a side tuners.

$205 $130

Last Mfr.'s Sug. Retail was $425.

MARK V — dreadnought style, solid cedar top, hardwood neck, round soundhole, herringbone binding/soundhole purfling, rosewood sides/2 piece back, 14/20 fret rosewood fingerboard with offset white dot inlay, bone nut, rosewood *smile*-shaped bridge with bone saddle, rosewood pickguard, 3 per side chrome sealed tuners. Available in Natural finish.

$235 $150

Last Mfr.'s Sug. Retail was $479.

Mark V/12 — similar to the Mark V, except has a 12-string configuration, slotted headstock, 6 on a side tuners.

$240 $155

Last Mfr.'s Sug. Retail was $495.

DAKOTA

Instruments currently built in Asia. Distributed by Sound Trek Distributors of Tampa, Florida.

Dakota Guitars' acoustic models are constructed with traditional 'old world' craftsmanship augmented by high tech computer designs. Dakota models are named after America's rare wild life, and are quite recognizable by their abalone bound headstock which features a white pearl "Snow-covered mountain top" inlay.

While Dakota Guitars has announced that the current models are being built in "Limited Quantities", they have not yet disclosed how limited those quantities are.

ACOUSTIC

Dakota Guitars' models are built with solid bone nuts and saddles, Sperzel U.S.A. tuners, abalone and white pearl inlays, and solid Engelmann spruce or tiger maple tops. Retail list prices include a case.

BH1 BIG HORN — grand concert style, solid Englemann spruce top, round soundhole, abalone binding, Indian rosewood back/sides, 14/20 fret fingerboard with inlay, bone nut, bridge with bone saddle, 3 per side tuners. Available in Natural finish. Current mfr.

Mfr.'s Sug. Retail $899

B1 BUCK — dreadnought style, solid Englemann spruce top, round soundhole, abalone binding, Indian rosewood back/sides, 14/20 fret fingerboard with inlay, bone nut, bridge with bone saddle, 3 per side tuners. Available in Natural finish. Current mfr.

Mfr.'s Sug. Retail $915

W1 WOLF — dreadnought style, tiger maple top, round soundhole, tiger maple back/sides, 14/20 fret fingerboard with inlay, bone nut, bridge with bone saddle, 3 per side tuners. Available in Gloss See-Thru Black finish with matching headstock. Current mfr.

Mfr.'s Sug. Retail $749

ACOUSTIC ELECTRIC

Dakota Guitars' acoustic/electric models feature a Max-Q 1 preamp system built in.

C1 COUGAR — dreadnought style, single rounded cutaway, solid Englemann spruce top, round soundhole, abalone and wood rosette, Indian rosewood back/sides, 14/20 fret fingerboard with inlay, bone nut, bridge with bone saddle, 3 per side tuners, Max-Q 1 Deluxe pickup. Available in Natural finish. Current mfr.

Mfr.'s Sug. Retail $949

E1 EAGLE — grand concert style, single rounded cutaway, solid Englemann spruce top, round soundhole, abalone binding, Indian rosewood back/sides, 14/20 fret fingerboard with inlay, bone nut, bridge with bone saddle, 3 per side tuners, Max-Q 1 Deluxe pickup. Available in Natural finish. Current mfr.

Mfr.'s Sug. Retail $1,049

G1 GRIZZLY — dreadnought style, single rounded cutaway, solid Englemann spruce top, round soundhole, abalone binding, Indian rosewood back/sides, 14/20 fret fingerboard with inlay, bone nut, bridge with bone saddle, 3 per side tuners, Max-Q 1 Deluxe pickup. Available in Natural finish. Current mfr.

Mfr.'s Sug. Retail $1,065

TED DALACK

Instruments currently built in Gainesville, Georgia.

Luthier Ted Dalack has been handcrafting custom flat-top steel string acoustic guitars for a number of years. Prices on Dalack's custom-built instuments range from $3,000 to $5,000.

Dalack also offers repairs, restorations, and custom services on all fretted instruments. Dalack's shop is an authorized factory service repair shop for Martin, Fender, and Guild. For further information regarding custom-built instruments or repairs, contact Ted Dalack via the Index of Current Manufacturers located in the back of this edition.

DALLAS

Instruments were made in England, West Germany, and Japan during the early to mid 1960s.

Some guitars may also carry the trademark of TUXEDO.

The DALLAS and TUXEDO trademarks are the brandnames used by a UK importer/distributor. Early solid body guitars were supplied by either FENTON-WEILL or VOX in Britain, with entry level German and Japanese original design guitars imported in.

(Source: Tony Bacon and Paul Day, The Guru's Guitar Guide)

D'AGOSTINO

Instruments produced in Italy by the EKO company between 1978 and 1982. After 1982, instruments were produced in Japan (then later Korea).

Instrument production was contracted to the EKO custom shop in Milwaukee, Wisconsin. Distributed by PMS Music of New York, New York.

Pat D'Agostino (ex-Gibson/Maestro effects) began his own instrument importing company in 1975. The D'Agostino Corporation of New Jersey began importing acoustic dreadnoughts, then introduced the Italian-built **Benchmark Series** of guitars in 1977. These models featured laminated neck thru designs, 2 humbuckers and a 3 per side headstock. Production then moved to Korea in the early 1980s, although some better models were built in Japan during the 1990s. Pat, assisted by Steven D'Agostino and Mike Confortti, has always maintained a high quality control level and limited quantities.

(Source: Michael Wright, Vintage Guitar Magazine)

D'Angelico 17" Special
courtesy John Miller

D'ANGELICO

Instruments built in New York City, New York between 1932 and 1964.

Master Luthier John D'Angelico (1905-1964) was born and raised in New York City, New York. In 1914, he apprenticed to his Granduncle, and learned the luthier trade of building stringed instruments and repair. After 18 years of working on stringed instruments, he opened his own shop on Kenmare Street (D'Angelico was 27). D'Angelico guitars were entirely handcrafted by D'Angelico with assistance by shop employees such as Vincent DiSerio (assistant/apprentice from 1932 to 1959). In the early 1950s, D'Angelico's workshop had a bench and counter for guitar work, and a showcase with new United or Favilla guitars, used "trade-ins" and a few amplifiers from Nat Daniel's Danelectro or Everett Hull's Ampeg company. A very young James D'Aquisto became the second assistant to the shop in 1953.

In 1959, the building where D'Angelico worked and lived was condemned by the city due to an unsafe foundation. While scouting out new locations, D'Angelico and DiSerio had a serious argument over finances. DiSerio left and accepted work at the Favilla guitar plant. After a number of months went by, D'Angelico and D'Aquisto finally reopened the guitar shop at its new location. Unfortunately, D'Angelico's health began to take a turn for the worse. John D'Angelico passed away in his sleep in September of 1964.

Both models Excel and New Yorker were in demand as they were being built, and are still in demand today from jazz guitar players and collectors. John D'Angelico created 1,164 serialized guitars, as well as unnumbered mandolins, and novelty instruments.

(Source: Paul William Schmidt, Acquired of the Angels)

ACOUSTIC

Luthier John D'Angelico built archtop guitars with either 16", 17", or 18" across the lower bout. All his guitars share similarities in the basic structure, but there are numerous variations in the craftsmanship of the bracing, depth, neck shaping, and cosmetic features based on customer's preference. D'Angelico built models with either a cutaway or non-cutaway body, and some with either a round or an oval sound hole.

Because each guitar was normally custom built per individual specifications, there is very little standardized pricing structure within the variations. The price range of a D'Angelico guitar can get as low as $10,000-$15,000 for a repaired, player's grade instrument; while the high range can be in excess of $100,000 - specifically depending on the condition, rarity, and even previous owner premium in some cases. It is highly recommended that several professional appraisals be secured before buying/selling/trading any D'Angelico guitar.

With the rise of the "archtop renissance" in the 1990s, a number of current luthiers are offering very high quality archtops in the same price range as the player's grade D'Angelicos (various models that have had professional repair). As a result, the player's grade D'Angelico market is fairly soft these days while challenged by the instruments of such builders as Triggs, Mortoro, De Cava, and a number of others (most 'used' Benedetto models are not found in the $10,000 range).

'60 D'Angelico New Yorker
courtesy Dr. Tom Van Hoose

D'ANGELICO BY VESTAX

Instruments currently built in Japan. These models are not distributed in the U.S. market.

Vestax is currently offering a number of high quality D'Angelico archtop guitar models in other parts of the world's musical instrument market (i.e. not the U.S. market). These models remain true to the D'Angelico designs from which they are derived, and do have high quality workmanship.

Retail list pricing from specification sheets were in Japanese Yen - but as they do not apply to the U.S. market, they will not be quoted below. Various body widths and specifications are unknown to date.

ACOUSTIC

There are 5 different D'Angelico models offered by Vestax; four are full acoustics which are augmented by floating pickups, and the fifth is a semi-hollow body model with 2 humbuckers. The **D'Angelico New Yorker (Model Big Body NYI-1)** has a single rounded cutaway bound body, set-in neck, 22 fret bound fingerboard with pearl block inlays, bound headstock, bound pickguard, adustable rosewood bridge/'stairstep' rosewood solid tailpiece, gold hardware, pearl logo/'New Yorker' logo inlay, and 3 per side 'butterbean' tuners. This model is offered in a smaller body width as the **New Yorker (Model Small Body NYS-1)** with similar construction details.

The **New Yorker (Model Big Body NYL-2)** is also similar to the NYL-1, but features an adjustable rosewood bridge/gold-plated metal 'stairstep' bridge, re-issue Grover Imperial tuners. This model is offered in a smaller body width as the **New Yorker (Model Small Body NYS-2)**. Both of the "-2" have retail list prices that are roughly 1/3 the list price of the "-1" series, leading to the question of laminated bodies versus hand carved bodies. This question has not yet been resolved.

The Semi-Acoustic (or semi-hollow body) **New Yorker Semi Acoustic Type (Model NY22-3)** has a single cutaway bound body, 2 bound f-holes, bound neck/headstock/raised pickguard, 2 humbuckers, tune-o-matic bridge/stop tailpiece, gold hardware, 2 volume/2 tone controls, 3 way selector switch. The headstock detail is similar to the 4 full acoustic models.

D'ANGELICO II

Instruments built in the U.S. Distributed by Archtop Enterprises, Inc. of Merrick, New York.

The D'Angelico II company is currently producing high quality reproductions of John D'Angelico's New Yorker and Excel models. Models share similar construction features such as Spruce tops, figured Maple back and sides, Ebony fingerboard with mother-of-pearl inlays, and gold-plated Grover tuners and tailpiece. All guitars are individually handcrafted and hand engraved.

The 18" New Yorker is offered in cutaway ($12,000) and non-cutaway ($11,750) versions, and in a Sunburst or Antique Natural finish. The Excel cutaway model ($11,500), Style B non-cutaway ($9,500), and Jazz Classic ($7,250) share a 17" body (measured across the lower bout). A smaller single pickup electric model called the Jazz Artist ($4,650) has a 16" body. Finally, a semi-hollowbody electric archtop called the Fusion ($3,750) is offered in Antique Natural, New Yorker Sunburst, or Flaming Red nitro cellulose lacquer finish.

D'ANGELICO REPLICA

Instruments built in Grass Valley, California since 1994. Distributed by The Working Musician of Arcadia, California.

Frank W. Green, author of the book **D'Angelico, What's in a Name**, is currently offering a replica of the D'Angelico Excel **(Deluxe LB-175)**. The D'Angelico replicas are officially sanctioned by the current nameowner.

Green's book, now offered by Centerstream Publishing, details the D'Angelico guitars from the point of view of the players and owners. The book contains a number of personal stories that bring to life the D'Angelico mystique.

(Centerstream Publishing, P.O. Box 17878, Anaheim Hills CA 92807, phone or fax 714.779.9390)

ACOUSTIC ARCHTOP

Green is offering the **Excel Deluxe LB-175**, an instrument with a 17 1/2" lower bout, handcarved Engelmann spruce top, western curly maple back and sides, a curly maple neck, bound ebony fingerboard with 'split block' inlays, Grover tuners, and gold plated *stairstep* tailpiece. Retail list prices range between $10,000 to $18,000. An 18 1/2" **New Yorker** has a retail price between $12,000 to $20,000. The top of the line instruments allow for personalizing and custom features as long as they fall within the parameters of what the master would do.

D'AQUISTO

Instruments built in Huntington, New York, as well as Greenport, New York, between 1965 to 1995.

Master Luthier James L. D'Aquisto (1935-1995) met John D'Angelico around 1953. At the early age of 17, D'Aquisto became D'Angelico's apprentice, and by 1959 was handling the decorative procedures and other lutherie jobs. When D'Angelico had a falling out with another member of the shop during the move of the business, D'Aquisto began doing actual building and shaping work. This lutherie work continued until the time of D'Angelico's death in 1964. The loss of D'Angelico in 1964 not only affected D'Aquisto personally, but professionally. Although he took over the business and shop with the encouragement of D'Angelico's brother, business under his own trademark started slowly. D'Aquisto continued to work in D'Angelico's shop repairing instruments at the last address - 37 Kenmare Street, New York City, New York. Finally, one year after D'Angelico's death, D'Aquisto summoned the nerve to build a guitar with the **D'Aquisto** inlay on the headpiece.

In 1965, D'Aquisto moved his shop to Huntington, New York, and sold his first instrument, styled after a D'Angelico New Yorker. Most of D'Aquisto's traditional design instruments are styled after John D'Angelico's Excel and New Yorker, with D'Aquisto adding refinements and improvements. D'Aquisto set up a deal with the Swedish-based Hagstrom company to produce guitars based on his designs in 1968, and the Ampeg company was one of the U.S. distributors. In 1973, D'Aquisto relocated his business once again, this time setting up shop in Farmingdale, New York. He produced his first flat top guitar in 1975, and his first solid body electric one year later. The Fender Musical Instrument Corporation produced a number of D'Aquisto-designed guitars beginning in the 1980s, and two models in the Designer series (D'Aquisto Ultra and Deluxe) are still in production today at the Fender USA Custom shop.

In the late 1980s, D'Aquisto again moved his shop to Greenport, New York, and continued to produce instruments from that location. In 1987, D'Aquisto broke away from archtop design tradition when he debuted the **Avant Garde**. The Excel and New Yorker style models were discontinued in 1991, as D'Aquisto concentrated on creating more forward-looking and advanced archtops. In 1994, models such as the **Solo** with four soundholes (only nine built), and **Centura** models were introduced. James L. D'Aquisto passed away in April, 1995.

D'Aquisto Centura
courtesy Scott Chinery

(Source: Paul William Schmidt, Acquired of the Angels)

James D'Aquisto built several hundred instruments, from archtops to flat tops to solid body electrics. Prices for his work may start at $10,000, with the model configuration and special order embellishments adding considerably to the base price. Like D'Angelico, most of D'Aquisto's instruments were made to order and varied in dimensions and details. When buying/selling/appraising a D'Aquisto, it is the recommendation of the Blue Book of Guitars that two or three professional appraisals be obtained.

DAVE MAIZE

Instruments currently built in Talent, Oregon.

Luthier Dave Maze hand-builds acoustic bass guitars with environmentally-friendly woods (either from a sustained yield source, a non-endangered species or reclaimed material).

Dave Maize instruments typically have redwood or cedar soundboards and bodies of figured black walnut, maple, black locust or other select woods. Standard features include solid wood construction throughout, 34" scale, 24 fret neck, Sperzel tuners, adjustable truss rod and a beautiful peghead inlay. Maize offers several custom options (prices vary). The 4-string acoustic bass model has a retail price of $2,100 and the 5-string model lists at $2,350.

J. THOMAS DAVIS

Instruments currently built in Columbus, Ohio.

Luthier Tom Davis estimates that while he builds a handful of custom guitars each year, his primary focus is on repair work. Davis has over twenty years experience in guitar building and repair. For futher information about repair work or custom guitar pricing, please contact luthier Tom Davis via the Index of Current Manufacturers located in the back of this book.

K.D. DAVIS GUITARS

Instruments currently built in Sonoma, California.

Luthier Kevin D. Davis is currently building hand crafted custom guitars. For futher information concerning model specification and pricing, please contact luthier Kevin Davis via the Index of Current Manufacturers located in the rear of this edition.

WILLIAM DAVIS

Instruments currently built in Boxford, Maine.

William Davis' handbuilt guitars are available through his Boxford, Maine lutherie. For up-to-date information concerning models and pricing, please contact luthier William Davis via the Index of Current Manufacturers located in the rear of this edition.

Dave Maize acoustic bass courtesy Dave Maize

DE CAVA

Instruments currently built in Stratford, Connecticut.

Born and raised in Stratford, Connecticut, luthier James R. De Cava began playing guitar and banjo as a teenager. De Cava began performing repairs on his guitars simply because there were few repair people around at the time. While spending time meeting others with similar interests, De Cava came into contact with Paul Morrisey and Bob Flesher at **Liberty Banjo Co.** De Cava worked for them between 1975 to the early 1980s cutting and inlaying mother of pearl with intricate designs. Through the years De Cava has built many different stringed instruments (banjos, mandolins, flat top and solid body guitars). De Cava now focuses on archtop guitar building.

De Cava briefly offered the Classic model ($5,490), which featured a flame or quilted maple top, fancy scroll position markers on the fingerboard, a pearl nut, an engraved pearl truss rod cover, and hand-engraved inlay pieces on the peghead (front and back)/pickguard/tailpiece/heel. An 18" body width was available at no extra charge.

ACOUSTIC

All De Cava archtop guitars share similar features such as a solid hand-carved Sitka or Adirondack spruce top, carved maple back with matching sides, ebony fingerboard, hinged ebony tailpiece, an adjustable bridge, ebony pickguard, ebony peghead overlays, and bound f-holes. De Cava offers his models in either a 16" or 17" body width, with parallel or X-bracing. Prices include a hard shell case.

Add $125 (and up) for special fingerboard inlays.

Add $200 for Blonde finish.

Add $200 (and up) for floating or built-in pick-up.

Archtop Series

De Cava's **Stratford** (list $3,950) is his traditional style guitar model, and features three layer body binding/single layer bound peghead and fingerboard, gold plated trim and tuners, pearl peghead logo, ebony truss rod cover, and gold and ebony tailpiece. Available in a traditional Sunburst finish.

The **Stylist** model ($7,450) is the deluxe model, with the highly figured maple back and sides, multi-layer bindings on the body/neck/peghead, 5-piece laminated figured maple neck, hand cut and engraved pearl pattern throughout the guitar, hand engraved pearl truss rod cover, and gold plated Schaller tuners with ebony buttons. The **Stylist** is available in either 16", 17", or 18" body widths; and Antique, Natural, or Sunburst finishes. A 7-string configuration is available at no extra charge.

Signature Series

De Cava has two new models, the **Signature Jazz** and the **Signature Blues**. The **Signature Blues** model was designed in conjunction with blues guitarist Debbie Davis. The Signature models are lightweight, contemporary hand-carved hollow body archtops with all the sleek contours of a solid body. Signature Series models have a 15 1/4" body width, 2 1/4" body depth, either a single neck pickup (Jazz model) or double pickups (Blues model), tune-o-matic style bridge/ebony tailpiece, and Neo Classic fingerboard. The retail price of $3,450 includes a durable gig bag. The Signature models are optionally available with the customer's signature inlaid in pearl, and fingerboard inlays.

De Cava Classic courtesy James R. De Cava

DEAN

Instruments currently produced in Plant City, Florida (Custom Shop and all the USA series) and Korea (all of the American Spirit series). Distributed by Armadillo Enterprises of Clearwater, Florida.

Previously, Dean guitars with the set-neck design were built in Evanston, Illinois from 1977 to 1986. In 1985, Dean began production of some models in Japan and Korea. Dean production from 1986 to 1993 was based in Asia.

The original Evanston, Illinois-based company was founded by Dean Zelinsky in 1977, after graduating from high school in 1976. Zelinsky, fond of classic Gibson designs, began building high quality electric solid body instruments and eventually started developing his own designs. Originally, there were three models: The **V** (similar to the Flying V), The **Z** (**Explorer body shape**), **and the ML** (sort of a cross between the V and an Explorer - and named after the initials of Matt Lynn, Zelinsky's best friend growing up). As the company's guitars gained popularity, production facilities were moved to Chicago in 1980.

Zelinsky originally got into the guitar building business to fill a void he felt the larger companies had: a high quality, set neck, eye-catching stage guitar. Though new designs continued to be developed, manufacturing of these instruments was shifted more and more to overseas builders. In 1986, Dean closed the USA Shop, leaving all construction to be completed overseas. The U.S. market had shifted towards the then-popular bolt neck *super-strat* design, and Zelinsky's personal taste leaned in the opposite direction.

Zelinsky sold Dean Guitars in 1990 to Oscar Medros, founder and owner of Tropical Music (based in Miami, Florida). The Dean Guitars facility in Plant City, Florida is currently run by Tracy Hoeft and Jon Hill, and new guitars are distributed to markets in the U.S., Japan, Korea, and Europe.

Zelinsky has estimated that between 6,000 and 7,000 (possibly 8,000) guitars were built in the U.S. between 1977 and 1986.

It has been estimated by various Dean collectors that the Japanese Dean models were built by the ESP Guitar company in Japan (circa 1986 to 1989).

In 1998, the Dean Guitar company introduced the Dean Stack in the Box (retail new $44.95), a stereo headphone amp that can be hooked up to home stereos; and the Dean Mean 16 (list $109.95), a 16 watt solid state amp with overdrive.

Grading	100%	EXCELLENT	AVERAGE

ACOUSTIC

Dean Artist CS
courtesy Armadillo Enterprises

D-1 — dreadnought style, laminated spruce top, round soundhole, maple neck, rosewood fingerboard with dot inlays, mahogany back/sides, enclosed chrome tuning machines. Available in Natural finish. Mfd. 1991 to 1992.

	$125	$85

Last Mfr.'s Sug. Retail was $199.

ARTIST CS (Model DGA-ACS) — jumbo style, single rounded cutaway medium thin body, solid spruce top, round soundhole, body binding, mahogany back/sides, 14/20 fret fingerboard with white dot inlay, triangular Dean rosewood bridge, 3 per side Grover tuners, chrome hardware. Available in Classic Black and Gloss Natural finishes. Mfr. 1998 to date.
Mfr.'s Sug. Retail $399

CONCERT C (Model DGA-CC) — classical style, single rounded cutaway body, select cedar top, round soundhole, multi-ply body binding, mahogany back/sides, 12/19 fret fingerboard, slotted headstock, tied bridge, 3 per side tuning machines. Available in Gloss Natural finish. Mfr. 1998 to date.
Mfr.'s Sug. Retail $249

Masters Series

Masters Series acoustics are produced in Czechoslovakia.

MASTERS SD (Model DGA-MSD) — dreadnought style, solid cedar top, round soundhole, wood body binding, mahogany back/sides, 14/20 fret fingerboard with white dot inlay, triangular Dean rosewood bridge, 3 per side Schaller tuners, chrome hardware. Available in Satin Natural finish. Mfr. 1998 to date.
Mfr.'s Sug. Retail $449

Masters SS (Model DGA-MSS) — similar to the Masters SD, except features a solid spruce top, mahogany neck. Available in Gloss Natural finish. Mfr. 1998 to date.
Mfr.'s Sug. Retail $499

Masters SR (Model DGA-MSR) — similar to the Masters SD, except features a solid spruce top, rosewood back/sides, mahogany neck. Available in Gloss Natural finish. Mfr. 1998 to date.
Mfr.'s Sug. Retail $569

Resonator Series

RESONATOR C (Model DGA-RC) — single rounded cutaway body, metal resonator plate, multi-ply body binding, mahogany back/sides, 'biscuit' bridge, chrome hardware, 3 per side tuning machines. Available in Black Satin and Natural Mahogany finishes. Mfr. 1998 to date.
Mfr.'s Sug. Retail $399

RESONATOR SP (Model DGA-RSP) — dreadnought style, metal resonator plate, multi-ply body binding, mahogany back/sides, mahogany neck, 'spider' bridge, chrome hardware, 3 per side tuning machines. Available in Cherry Sunburst and Natural Mahogany finishes. Mfr. 1998 to date.
Mfr.'s Sug. Retail $449

Dean Master SD
courtesy Armadillo Enterprises

Tradition Series

The **AcousticPack (Model DGP-AP)** is an all-in-one starter system that includes a Tradition One acoustic guitar in Gloss Natural, a guitar strap, Dean picks, and a guitar tuner. This complete package retails for $269.

D

Grading	100%	EXCELLENT	AVERAGE

TRADITION ONE (Model DGA-T1) — dreadnought style, select spruce top, round soundhole, body binding, mahogany back/sides, 14/20 fret fingerboard with white dot inlay, triangular Dean rosewood bridge, 3 per side die cast tuners. Available in Gloss Natural finish. Mfr. 1998 to date.

  Mfr.'s Sug. Retail $229

    Add $20 for left-handed configuration **(Model DGA-T-L)**. Available in Gloss Natural finish only.

  Tradition S — similar to the Tradition One, except features a solid spruce top, 3 per side Grover tuners. Available in Gloss Natural finish. Mfr. 1998 to date.

  Mfr.'s Sug. Retail $299

ACOUSTIC ELECTRIC

ARTIST CSE (Model DGA-ACSE) — jumbo style, single rounded cutaway medium thin body, solid spruce top, round soundhole, abalone binding, Dean "Wing" design rosette, solid rosewood sides, rosewood back, 14/24 fret extended fingerboard with block inlays, triangular Dean rosewood bridge, 3 per side Grover tuners, gold hardware, piezo bridge pickup, Shadow 5 band EQ. Available in Classic Black, Gloss Amber, and Gloss Natural finishes. Mfr. 1998 to date.

  Mfr.'s Sug. Retail $699

MASTERS SE (Model DGA-MSE) — dreadnought style, solid spruce top, round soundhole, wood body binding, mahogany back/sides, mahogany neck, 14/20 fret fingerboard with white dot inlay, triangular Dean rosewood bridge, 3 per side Schaller tuners, chrome hardware, piezo bridge pickup, Shadow 5 band EQ. Available in Gloss Natural finish. Mfr. 1998 to date.

  Mfr.'s Sug. Retail $599

Performer Series

PERFORMER E — jumbo style, single rounded cutaway body, select spruce top, round soundhole, body binding, mahogany back/sides, 14/20 fret fingerboard with white dot inlay, triangular Dean rosewood bridge, 3 per side die cast tuners, chrome hardware, piezo bridge pickup, volume/tone controls. Available in Classic Black and Gloss Natural finishes. Mfr. 1998 to date.

  Mfr.'s Sug. Retail $299

  Performer SE (Model DGA-PSE) — similar to the Performer E, except features a solid spruce top, abalone binding, extended fingerboard, 3 per side Grover tuners, Shadow 5 band EQ. Available in Classic Black and Gloss Natural finishes. Mfr. 1998 to date.

  Mfr.'s Sug. Retail $499

    Add $20 for left-handed configuration **(Model DGA-PSE-L)**. Available in Gloss Natural finish only.

  Performer DSE (Model DGA-PDSE) — similar to the Performer E, except features a solid spruce top, solid rosewood sides, rosewood back, abalone binding, 14/24 fret extended fingerboard with block inlays, Dean "Wing" design rosette, 3 per side Grover tuners, gold hardware, Shadow 5 band EQ. Available in Classic Black and Gloss Natural finishes. Mfr. 1998 to date.

  Mfr.'s Sug. Retail $599

Resonator Series

RESONATOR CE (Model DGA-RCE) — single rounded Dean cutaway body, metal resonator plate, multi-ply body binding, mahogany back/sides, 'biscuit' bridge, chrome hardware, 3 per side tuning machines, chrome lipstick pickup, volume/tone controls. Available in Natural Mahogany finish. Mfr. 1998 to date.

  Mfr.'s Sug. Retail $499

RESONATOR GCE (Model DGA-RGCE) — single rounded Dean cutaway body, metal resonator plate, multi-ply body binding, mahogany back/sides, 'biscuit' bridge, gold hardware, 3 per side tuning machines, humbucker pickup, volume/tone controls. Available in Black Satin finish. Mfr. 1998 to date.

  Mfr.'s Sug. Retail $599

Stage Series

STAGE ACOUSTIC (Model DGK-SA) — offset double cutaway hollow basswood body, round soundhole, body binding, set-in neck, 22 fret rosewood fingerboard with dot inlay, rosewood bridge, chrome hardware, small offset V-shaped headstock, 3 per side tuners. Available in Classic Black, Cherry Sunburst, Transparent Blue, and Transparent Purple finishes. Mfr. 1998 to date.

  Mfr.'s Sug. Retail $499 $350 $225 $150

  Stage Acoustic Deluxe (Model DGK-SD) — similar to the Stage Acoustic, except features a flame maple top, gold hardware, Shadow piezo bridge, volume/tone controls. Available in Flame Black, Flame Cherry Sunburst, Flame Gloss Natural, and Flame Red finishes. Mfr. 1998 to date.

  Mfr.'s Sug. Retail $599 $425 $275 $195

    Add $20 for left-handed configuration **(Model DGK-SD-L)**. Available in Flame Gloss Natural finish only.

Tradition Series

TRADITION SE (Model DGA-TSE) — dreadnought style, solid spruce top, round soundhole, body binding, mahogany back/sides, 14/20 fret fingerboard with white dot inlay, triangular Dean rosewood bridge, 3 per side Grover tuners, piezo bridge pickup, Shadow 5 band EQ. Available in Gloss Natural finish. Mfr. 1998 to date.

  Mfr.'s Sug. Retail $399

Dean Artist CSE
courtesy Armadillo Enterprises

Dean Resonator CE
courtesy Armadillo Enterprises

ACOUSTIC ELECTRIC BASS

PERFORMER BASS CE (Model DGA-PBCE) — jumbo style, single rounded cutaway body, spruce top, round soundhole, multi-ply body binding, mahogany back/sides, 20 fret fingerboard with white dot inlay, triangular Dean rosewood bridge, 2 per side Grover tuners, chrome hardware, piezo bridge pickup, 4 band EQ. Available in Satin Natural finish. Mfr. 1998 to date.

Mfr.'s Sug. Retail $399

DEAR

Instruments currently produced in Asia. Distributed by L.A. Guitar Works of Reseda, California.

Dear guitars are medium quality acoustic guitars that feature a wood top mated to a shallow fiberglass back. The Dear design is similar to the design pioneered by Ovation, except instead of a rounded 'bowl' back the Dear design is squared. At the given list price point, it is estimated that the Dear guitar tops are laminated, not solid.

ACOUSTIC ELECTRIC

The three Dear acoustic/electric models have a cutaway body, onboard preamp and bridge-mounted pickup system. The **DAC-480E** has a round soundhole, spruce top, and a retail price of $299. The **DAC-485E** features similar construction, with a highly flamed maple top (list $319). Instead of a round soundhole, the **DAC-500E** has a pair of f-holes.

In addition to the acoustic/electrics, Dear also offers two classical style/synthetic back models. The EL 1500 (list $439) has a cedar top and matte finish; the EL 2000 has a spruce top (list $459).

DECCA

Instruments produced in Japan.

The Decca trademark is a brandname used by U.S. importers Decca Records.

(Source: Michael Wright, Guitar Stories Volume One)

DEERING

Guitars were built in Lemon Grove, California from 1989-1991. Deering has produced high quality banjos in Lemon Grove since 1975.

In 1975, Greg and Janet Deering began producing the quality banjos that the company is known for. While continuing to offer innovative banjo designs, the Deerings also offer several models from entry level to professional play.

Deering offers a banjo model that is tuned and played like a guitar. The MB-6 is designed for the guitar player who doesn't have to *learn banjo to play banjo*. The MB-6 is also available in a 12-string configuration.

In the late 1980s, Deering offered 4 different solid body guitar models in 2 variations that carried a retail price between $1,498-$2,850. The guitar models were also offered with some custom options, but were only produced for little over one year.

DEY

See **B D DEY.**

DIASONIC

Instruments produced in Japan, circa unknown.

It is estimated that Diasonic instruments were constructed in the 1970s, as their headstock design skirts infringing on Gibson's standard design.

The Diasonic folk style acoustic has a spruce top, geometric pattern rosette, nato back and sides, 14/20 fret rosewood fingerboard with rectangular pearloid inlay, 3 per side chrome tuners, adjustable saddle, white bridge pins, and tortoise pickguard.

Diasonic instruments in average condition command about $100.

(Source: Walter Murray, Frankenstein Fretworks)

DILLON

Instruments currently built in Bloomsburg, Pennsylvania.

Dillon Guitars offers quality custom built instruments. For further information, contact Dillon Guitars via the Index of Current Manufacturers located in the back of this book.

DITSON

Instruments manufactured in Boston, Massachusetts from 1865 to the early 1900s.

The Oliver Ditson Company, Inc. was formed in 1835 by music publisher Oliver Ditson (1811-1888). Ditson was a primary force in music merchandising, distribution, and retail sales on the East Coast. He also helped establish two musical instrument manufacturers: The **John Church Company** of Cincinnati, Ohio, and **Lyon & Healy** (Washburn) in Chicago, Illinois.

In 1865 Ditson established a manufacturing branch of his company under the supervision of John Haynes, called the **John C. Haynes** Company. This branch built guitars for a number of trademarks, such as **Bay State**, **Tilton**, and **Haynes Excelsior**.

(Source: Tom Wheeler, American Guitars)

D. J. ARGUS

Instruments built in New York, New York circa early 1990s. Distributed through Rudy's Music Shop of New York City, New York.

D. J. Argus archtops featured traditional D'Angelico stylings, solid spruce tops, laminated curly maple back and sides, engraved tailpieces, and Grover Imperial tuners. Research continues on the D. J. Argus archtop models for future editions of the **Blue Book of Guitars.**

Dean Performer DSE
courtesy Armadillo Enterprises

Dean Tradition One
courtesy Armadillo Enterprises

DOBRO

Instruments previously manufactured by Original Musical Instruments Company, located in Huntington Beach, California. In 1997, production was moved to Nashville, Tennessee. Distributed by the Gibson Guitar Corporation of Nashville, Tennessee.

The original Dobro company was formed in 1928 in Los Angeles, California.

The Dopyera family emigrated from the Austro-Hungary area to Southern Califonia in 1908. In the early 1920s, John and Rudy Dopyera began producing banjos in Southern California. They were approached by guitarist George Beauchamp to help solve his 'volume' (or lack thereof) problem with other instruments in the vaudeville orchestra. In the course of their conversation, the idea of placing aluminum resonators in a guitar body for amplification purposes was developed. John Dopyera and his four brothers (plus some associates, like George Beauchamp) formed National in 1925. The initial partnership between Dopyera and Beauchamp lasted for about two years, and then John Dopyera left National to form the Dobro company. The Dobro name was chosen as a contraction of the <u>Do</u>pyera <u>Bro</u>thers (and it also means *good* in Slavic languages).

The Dobro and National companies were later remerged by Louis Dopyera in 1931 or 1932. The company moved to Chicago, Illinois in 1936, and a year later granted Regal the rights to manufacture Dobros. The *revised* company changed its name to **VALCO** in 1943, and worked on war materials during World War II. In 1959, VALCO transferred the Dobro name and tools to Emil Dopyera. Between 1966 and 1967, the Dobro trademark was sold to Semie Moseley, of Mosrite fame. Moseley constructed the first Dobros out of parts from Emil's California plant, and later built his own necks and bodies. Moseley also built *Mobros*, a Mosrite-inspired Dobro design. After Mosrite collapsed, the name was still held by Moseley; so in the late 1960s, Emil's company produced resonator guitars under the tradename of **Hound Dog** and **Dopera** (note the missing 'y') **Originals**. When the Dobro name finally became available again, Emil and new associates founded the Original Musical Instruments Company, Inc. (OMI) in 1970. OMI has been producing Dobros ever since.

In 1985, Chester and Mary Lizak purchased OMI from Gabriela and Ron Lazar; and eight years later in 1993, OMI was purchased by the Gibson Guitar Corporation, and production continued to be centered in California. The production of Dobro instruments was moved to Nashville, Tennessee in the Spring of 1997.

(Early company history courtesy Bob Brozman, The History and Artistry of National Resonator Instruments)

ACOUSTIC

33 Series

33 Series instruments have 2 f-holes (instead of mesh-covered soundholes) 'biscuit' bridge, and a 10 1/2" inverted resonator cone.

CHROME PLATED 33 (Model DM33) — hollow style, chrome plated bell brass body, 2 f-holes, single cone resonator, maple neck, 14/19 fret rosewood fingerboard with white dot inlay, biscuit bridge/trapeze tailpiece, chrome hardware, 3 per side tuners. Available in Hawaiian (palm trees), Lattice D, Plain, or Sailboat sand-blasted designs on back. Mfr. 1996 to date.

Mfr.'s Sug. Retail	$1,799	$1,440	$770	$560

33 Deluxe California Girl (Model DM33 DLX C) — simlar to the Chrome Plated 33, except has sand-blasted 'California Girl' design on back. Mfr. 1996 to date.

Mfr.'s Sug. Retail	$2,299	$1,840	$1,190	$780

33 Deluxe Mesa (Model DM33 DLX M) — similar to the Chrome Plated 33, except has mesa style sand-blasted design on back. Mfr. 1996 to date.

Mfr.'s Sug. Retail	$2,099	$1,680	$1,090	$715

Steel 33 (Model DS33) — similar to the Chrome Plated 33, except has steel body. Available in Amberburst and Darkburst finishes. Mfr. 1996 to date.

Mfr.'s Sug. Retail	$1,499	$1,200	$780	$500

Wood 33 (Model DW33) — similar to the Chrome Plated 33, except has 3-ply laminated maple body. Available in Natural finish. Mfr. 1996 to date.

Mfr.'s Sug. Retail	$1,299	$1,040	$670	$440

DOBRO D (Model DM33 D) — similar to the Chrome Plated 33, except has sand-blasted flower design on back. Disc. 1996.

		$855	$495

Last Mfr.'s Sug. Retail was $1,499.

The models DM33 D. H. and S have all been incorporated into variations of the current Chrome Plated 33 model (see above).

Hawaiian (Model DM33 H) — similar to the Chrome Plated 33, except has sand-blasted palm tree/beach design on back. Disc. 1996.

		$855	$495

Last Mfr.'s Sug. Retail was $1,499.

Sailboat (Model DM33 S) — similar to the Chrome Plated 33, except has sand-blasted sailing ship design on back. Disc. 1996.

		$855	$495

Last Mfr.'s Sug. Retail was $1,499.

60 Roundneck Series

The 60 Roundneck Series, like their Squareneck counterparts, have a 12/19 fingerboard, 3-ply laminated wood bodies, 10 1/2" resonator, and a original-style spider bridge. The Roundneck series has a rounded ('Spanish') neck.

Model 33 H
courtesy Gibson Guitar Company

Grading	100%	EXCELLENT	AVERAGE

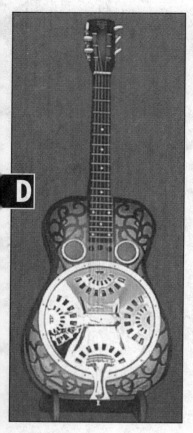

Model 66 S
courtesy Gibson Guitar Company

60 CLASSIC (Model DW60) — hollow style, 3-ply laminated maple top/back/sides, 2 screened/3 smaller uncovered sound-holes, single cone resonator, maple neck, 12/19 fret rosewood fingerboard with white dot inlay, spider bridge/trapeze tailpiece, solid peghead with logo decal, chrome hardware, 3 per side tuners. Available in Amber, Natural, and Sunburst finishes. Current mfr.

Mfr.'s Sug. Retail	$1,399	$1,120	$730	$475

60 Classic Darkburst (Model DW60 DB) — similar to 60 Classic. Available in Darkburst finish. Current mfr.

Mfr.'s Sug. Retail	$1,299	$1,040	$670	$440

Classic 60 Amber — similar to 60 Classic, except has bound body. Available in Amber finish. Disc. 1996.

		$610	$370

Last Mfr.'s Sug. Retail was $1,149.

This model was also available with a square neck (Model DW60 A S).

Classic 60 Mahogany (Formerly Mahogany Classic) (Model DW60 MN) — similar to 60 Classic, except has mahogany body, 2 screened/3 clear soundholes, bound body/fingerboard/peghead, pearl diamond/dot fingerboard inlay. Available in Natural finish. Disc. 1996.

		$660	$400

Last Mfr.'s Sug. Retail was $1,249.

This model was also available with a square neck (Model DW60 MN S).

Classic 60 Natural (Formerly Natural Classic) (Model DW60 N) — similar to 60 Classic, except has bound body. Available in Natural finish. Disc. 1996.

		$610	$370

Last Mfr.'s Sug. Retail was $1,149.

This model was also available with a square neck (Model DW60 N S).

Classic 60 Sunburst (Model DW60 S) — similar to 60 Classic, except has bound body. Available in 3 Tone Sunburst finish. Disc. 1996.

		$640	$385

Last Mfr.'s Sug. Retail was $1,199.

This model was also available with a square neck (Model DW60 S S).

Classic 60 Walnut (Formerly Walnut Classic) (Model DW60 WN) — hollow style, walnut top, 2 screened/3 clear soundholes, single cone resonator, walnut back/sides, maple neck, 14/19 fret bound ebony fingerboard with pearl vine inlay, spider bridge/trapeze tailpiece, chrome hardware, slotted peghead with logo decal, 3 per side tuners with plastic buttons. Available in Natural finish. Disc. 1996.

		$690	$415

Last Mfr.'s Sug. Retail was $1,299.

This model was also available with a square neck (Model DW60 WN S).

ZEPHYR SUNBURST (Model DW60 ZSC) — single sharp cutaway hollow style, maple top, multiple soundholes, single cone resonator, bound body, maple back/sides/neck, 19 fret ebony fingerboard with abalone seagull inlay, spider bridge/trapeze tailpiece, chrome hardware, slotted peghead, 3 per side tuners with plastic buttons. Available in Sunburst finish. Disc. 1995.

		$740	$445

Last Mfr.'s Sug. Retail was $1,399.

F60 CLASSIC (Formerly F HOLE CLASSIC) (Model DWF60) — hollow style, laminated maple top, 2 f-holes, single cone resonator, maple back/sides/neck, 12/19 fret rosewood fingerboard with pearl dot inlay, spider bridge/trapeze tailpiece, slotted peghead with logo decal, chrome hardware, 3 per side tuners with plastic buttons. Available in Blackburst, TobaccoBurst, and VintageBurst finishes. Current mfr.

Mfr.'s Sug. Retail	$1,099	$880	$575	$375

60 Squareneck Series

The 60 Squareneck Series is constructed similar to the Roundneck models, except have a squared ('Hawaiian') neck for lap steel-style playing, high nut, and 2 mesh-covered soundholes.

27 DELUXE (Model DW27 DLX) — hollow style, laminated figured maple top/back/sides, 2 smaller screened soundholes, single cone resonator with parallelogram sound holes, maple neck, 12/19 fret rosewood fingerboard with elaborate pearl inlay, spider bridge/trapeze tailpiece, solid peghead with logo decal, chrome hardware, 3 per side tuners. Mfr. 1996 to date.

Mfr.'s Sug. Retail	$1,799	$1,440	$770	$560

60 SQUARENECK (Model DW60) — hollow style, laminated maple top/back/sides, 2 screened/3 smaller uncovered sound-holes, single cone resonator with squared sound holes, maple neck, 12/19 fret rosewood fingerboard with pearl dot inlay, spider bridge/trapeze tailpiece, solid peghead with logo decal, chrome hardware, 3 per side tuners. Available in Amberburst, Natural, and Sunburst finishes. Current mfr.

Mfr.'s Sug. Retail	$1,399	$1,120	$730	$475

60 Squareneck Darkburst (Model DW60 DBS) — similar to 60 Squareneck. Available in Darkburst finish. Current mfr.

Mfr.'s Sug. Retail	$1,299	$1,040	$670	$440

F60 Classic Squareneck (Model DWF60 S) — hollow style, laminated maple top, 2 f-holes, single cone resonator, maple back/sides/neck, 12/19 fret rosewood fingerboard with pearl dot inlay, spider bridge/trapeze tailpiece, slotted peghead with logo decal, chrome hardware, 3 per side tuners with plastic buttons. Available in Blackburst, TobaccoBurst, and VintageBurst finishes. Current mfr.

Mfr.'s Sug. Retail	$1,099	$880	$575	$375

Grading	100%	EXCELLENT	AVERAGE

MODEL 63 (Formerly DOBRO 8-String) (Model DW63) — similar to the F60 Squareneck, except has 8-string configuration, 2 screened/3 smaller uncovered soundholes, 4 per side slotted headstock, redesigned bridge. Available in Natural and Sunburst finishes. Mfr. 1996 to date.

Mfr.'s Sug. Retail	$1,399	$1,120	$730	$475

Acoustic Series

MAHOGANY TROUBADOUR (Model DWTRUMH) — Available in Natural finish. Mfr. 1996 to date.

Mfr.'s Sug. Retail	$1,499	$1,200	$780	$510

Spruce Top Troubadour (Model DWTRUSP) — similar to the Mahogany Troubador, except has a spruce top. Mfr. 1996 to date.

Mfr.'s Sug. Retail	$1,699	$1,360	$885	$580

Artist Signature Series

The Artist Signature models are limited edition models that are signed up on the headstock by the Artist involved with the specialty design (Dobro also offers the same design in an unsigned/un-numbered edition as well).

JERRY DOUGLAS LTD (Model DWJDS LTD) — hollow style with internal soundposts and tone bars, bound mahogany top/back/sides, 2 screened/3 smaller uncovered soundholes, single cone resonator with squared sound holes, 25" scale, mahogany neck, 12/19 fret bound rosewood fingerboard with pearl dot inlay (dots begin at 5th fret), spider bridge/trapeze tailpiece, solid peghead with logo decal/signature, chrome hardware, 3 per side tuners. Available in Natural finish. Mfr. 1996 to date.

Mfr.'s Sug. Retail	$2,399	$1,920	$1,250	$815

Jerry Douglas (Model DWJDS) — similar to the Jerry Douglas Ltd, except has no signature on peghead. Mfr. 1996 to date.

Mfr.'s Sug. Retail	$1,899	$1,520	$990	$650

JOSH GRAVES LTD (Model DWJOSH LTD) — hollow style, bound wood body, 2 screened soundholes, single cone resonator, 25" scale, 12/19 fret rosewood fingerboard with pearl dot inlay, spider bridge/trapeze tailpiece, solid peghead with logo decal/signature, chrome hardware, 3 per side tuners. Available in Sunburst finish. Mfr. 1996 to date.

Mfr.'s Sug. Retail	$2,399	$1,920	$1,250	$815

This model is based on Graves' own 1928 Model 37.

Josh Graves (Model DWJOSH) — similar to the Josh Graves Ltd, except has no signature on peghead. Mfr. 1996 to date.

Mfr.'s Sug. Retail	$1,899	$1,520	$990	$650

PETE BROTHER OSWALD KIRBY LTD (Model DWOS LTD) — hollow style, bound wood body, 2 screened soundholes, single cone resonator with parallelogram soundwell holes, 12/19 fret rosewood fingerboard with pearl dot inlay (position markers begin at 5th fret), 'V'-shaped roundneck, metal high-nut adaptor, spider bridge/trapeze tailpiece, slotted peghead with logo decal/signature, chrome hardware, 3 per side tuners. Available in Sunburst finish. Mfr. 1996 to date.

Mfr.'s Sug. Retail	$2,399	$1,920	$1,250	$815

This model is based on Kirby's own 1928 Model 27.

Pete Brother Oswald Kirby (Model DWOS) — similar to the Pete Brother Oswald Kirby Ltd, except has no signature on peghead. Mfr. 1996 to date.

Mfr.'s Sug. Retail	$1,899	$1,520	$990	$650

AL PERKINS LTD (Model DWPERKINSLTD) — hollow style, bound figured maple top/back/sides, 2 f-holes, single cone resonator with engraved pointsettia palmplate, 12/19 fret bound rosewood fingerboard with pearl dot inlay (dots begin at 5th fret), spider bridge/trapeze tailpiece, solid peghead with logo decal/signature, gold hardware, 3 per side tuners. Available in Translucent Black finish. Mfr. 1996 to date.

Mfr.'s Sug. Retail	$2,399	$1,920	$1,250	$815

Al Perkins (Model DWPERKINS) — similar to the Al Perkins Ltd, except has no signature on peghead. Mfr. 1996 to date.

Mfr.'s Sug. Retail	$1,899	$1,520	$990	$650

TOM SWATZELL LTD (Model DWTS LTD) — hollow style, bound wood body, 2 screened/3 smaller uncovered soundholes, single cone resonator with engraved diamond palmplate/coverplate, 12/19 fret bound ebony fingerboard with abalone diamond inlay (position markers begin at 5th fret), spider bridge/trapeze tailpiece, slotted peghead with logo decal/signature, chrome hardware, 3 per side tuners. Available in Sunburst finish. Mfr. 1996 to date.

Mfr.'s Sug. Retail	$2,399	$1,920	$1,250	$815

Tom Swatzell (Model DWTS) — similar to the Tom Swatzell Ltd, except has no signature on peghead. Mfr. 1996 to date.

Mfr.'s Sug. Retail	$1,899	$1,520	$990	$650

Bottleneck Series

Bottleneck Series instruments are specifically designed for 'bottleneck'-style guitar playing, and feature a flat 14/19 fret fingerboard, 'biscuit' bridge, and a single 9 1/2" resonator cone.

CHROME-PLATED 90 (Model DM90) — hollow style, chrome plated bell brass body, 2 f-holes, single cone resonator, maple neck, 14/19 fret rosewood fingerboard with white dot inlay, biscuit bridge/trapeze tailpiece, chrome hardware, solid peghead, 3 per side tuners. Available in Chrome finish. Current mfr.

Mfr.'s Sug. Retail	$1,799	$1,440	$770	$560

90 Deluxe (Model DM90 DLX) — similar to the Chrome-Plated 90, except features a bound ebony fingerboard with pearl diamond inlays, sand-blasted Palm Tree scene on front and back. Mfr. 1996 to date.

Mfr.'s Sug. Retail	$2,099	$1,680	$1,090	$715

Wood Body 90
courtesy Gibson Guitar Company

Grading	100%	EXCELLENT	AVERAGE

STEEL BODY 90 (Model DS90) — similar to the Chrome-Plated 90, except has a steel body. Available in Amberburst and Darkburst finishes. Mfr. 1996 to date.

Mfr.'s Sug. Retail	$1,499	$1,200	$780	$510

WOOD BODY 90 (Model DW90) — similar to the Chrome-Plated 90, except features a wood body. Available in Sunburst finish. Current mfr.

Mfr.'s Sug. Retail	$1,299	$1,040	$670	$440

Wood Body 90 Deluxe (Model DW90 DLX) — similar to the Wood Body 90, except features a bound peghead, bound ebony fingerboard with pearl diamond inlay. Mfr. 1996 to date.

Mfr.'s Sug. Retail	$1,799	$1,440	$770	$560

Wood Body 90 Soft Cutaway (Model DW90 SFT) — similar to the Wood Body 90, except has single rounded cutaway, slotted headstock, multiple soundholes in 2 diamond-shaped groups. Available in Natural and Darkburst finishes. Current mfr.

Mfr.'s Sug. Retail	$1,599	$1,280	$830	$545

HULA BLUES (Model DWHB) — hollow style, maple top, 2 f-holes, single cone resonator, maple back/sides/neck, 12/19 fret rosewood fingerboard with pearl dot inlay, spider bridge/trapeze tailpiece, chrome hardware, slotted peghead, 3 per side tuners. Available in Brown/Cream or Green/Cream screened Hawaiian scenes (front and back) finishes. Current mfr.

Mfr.'s Sug. Retail	$1,099	$880	$575	$375

Engraved Art Series

The Engraved Art Series models have triple chrome-plated bell brass bodies, 'biscuit' bridge, and single 10 1/2" resonator cone. The hand-engraved designs are inspired by the models of the late 1920s.

CHRYSANTHEMUM (Model DM3000) — hollow style, chrome plated bell brass body, 2 f-holes, single cone resonator, hard rock maple neck, 14/19 fret bound ebony fingerboard with mother of pearl diamond inlay, spider bridge/trapeze tailpiece, pearl logo peghead inlay, chrome hardware, 3 per side tuners. Available in engraved Swirl of Flowers finish on front/back/sides/coverplate/palmplate. Mfr. 1996 to date.

Mfr.'s Sug. Retail	$4,999	$4,000	$2,060	$1,700

Deco (Model DM20) — similar to the Chrysanthemum, except features unbound peghead, unbound rosewood fingerboard with pearl dot inlays. Available in engraved Art Deco (stylized geometric line designs) front and back finish. Mfr. 1995 to date.

Mfr.'s Sug. Retail	$2,499	$2,000	$1,300	$850

Dobro Shield (Model DM1000) — similar to the Chrysanthemum, except features mother of pearl cloud and D-O-B-R-O inlays. Available in engraved Flower pattern on front, Dobro Shield on back finish. Current mfr.

Mfr.'s Sug. Retail	$3,599	$2,880	$1,870	$1,225

This model has been nicknamed the Dobro Special.

Lily of the Valley (Model DM75) — similar to the Chrysanthemum in construction. Available in engraved Lily of the Valley (blossoms and leaves) design finish on front/back/sides/coverplate/palmplate. Current mfr.

Mfr.'s Sug. Retail	$2,799	$2,240	$1,460	$950

Rose (Model DM36) — similar to the Chrysanthemum, except features unbound peghead, unbound rosewood fingerboard with pearl dot inlays. Available in engraved Wild Rose (rose and vine) design finish on front/back/palmplate. Current mfr.

Mfr.'s Sug. Retail	$2,299	$1,840	$1,190	$780

Special Edition Series

Special Edition models were offered with round (Spanish) or square (Hawaiian) necks (square neck models were designated with an *S* after the model code).

CURLY MAPLE SPECIAL (Model DWS60 C) — hollow style, curly maple back/sides, single cone resonator, maple neck, 12/19 fret rosewood fingerboard with white dot inlay, spider bridge/trapeze tailpiece, solid peghead with logo decal, chrome hardware, 3 per side tuners. Available in Natural finish. Disc. 1995.

		$955	$575

Last Mfr.'s Sug. Retail was $1,799.

Koa Special (Model DWS60 K) — similar to the Curly Maple Special, except has koa back and sides. Disc. 1995.

		$1,480	$895

Last Mfr.'s Sug. Retail was $2,799.

Mahogany Special (Model DWS60 M) — similar to the Curly Maple Special, except has mahogany back and sides. Disc. 1995.

		$850	$530

Last Mfr.'s Sug. Retail was $1,599.

Rosewood Special (Model DWS60 R) — similar to the Curly Maple Special, except has rosewood back and sides. Disc. 1995.

		$1,060	$640

Last Mfr.'s Sug. Retail was $1,999.

ACOUSTIC BASS

Resonator-equipped Acoustic bass models debuted in 1995. Both models listed are available with an optional fretless fingerboard.

MODEL D DELUXE (Model DBASS) — hollow style, bound laminated maple top/back/sides, 2 screened/3 smaller uncovered soundholes, single cone resonator, maple neck, 18/24 fret rosewood fingerboard with white dot inlay, spider bridge/trapeze tailpiece, solid peghead with logo decal, chrome hardware, 2 per side tuners. Available in Darkburst finish. Mfr. 1995 to date.

Mfr.'s Sug. Retail	$1,899	$1,520	$990	$650

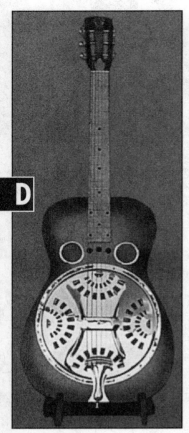

Hound Dog 101
courtesy Gibson Guitar Company

Grading	100%	EXCELLENT	AVERAGE

Model D Deluxe Natural (Model DBASS N). — similar to the Model D Deluxe in construction. Available in Natural finish. Mfr. 1995 to date.

Mfr.'s Sug. Retail	$1,999	$1,600	$1,040	$680

MODEL F (Model FBASS) — similar to the Model D, except has 2 f-holes. Available in BlackBurst, TobaccoBurst, and VintageBurst finishes. Mfr. 1996 to date.

Mfr.'s Sug. Retail	$1,499	$1,200	$780	$510

The Model F bass is not available in a fretless configuration. The Model F Deluxe versions are, however.

Model F Deluxe (Model FBASS DLX) — similar to the Model F in construction. Available in DarkBurst finish. Mfr. 1996 to date.

Mfr.'s Sug. Retail	$1,899	$1,520	$990	$650

Model F Deluxe Natural (Model FBASS DLX N) — similar to the Model F in construction. Available in Natural finish. Mfr. 1996 to date.

Mfr.'s Sug. Retail	$1,999	$1,600	$1,040	$680

MODEL F DELUXE 5 STRING (Model DBASS DLX 5) — similar to the Model F, except has a 5-string configuration. Available in DarkBurst finish. Mfr. 1996 to date.

Mfr.'s Sug. Retail	$2,099	$1,680	$1,090	$715

Model F Deluxe 5 String Natural (Model DBASS DLX N 5) — similar to the Model F Deluxe 5 String in construction. Available in Natural finish. Mfr. 1996 to date.

Mfr.'s Sug. Retail	$2,199	$1,760	$1,145	$745

DOLCE

See chapter on House Brands.

This trademark has been identified as the House Brand used by such stores as Marshall Fields, Macy's, and Gimbles.

(Source: Willie G. Moseley, Stellas & Stratocasters)

DOMINO

Instruments manufactured in Japan circa mid to late 1960s. Distributed by Maurice Lipsky Music Company, Inc., of New York, New York.

These Japanese-produced guitars and basses were imported to the U.S. market by the Maurice Lipsky company of New York, New York (Domino was a division of The Orpheum Manufacturing Company). Domino offered a wide range of Vox- and Fender-derived solid body models, and Gibson-esque 335 semi-hollow (or perhaps completely hollow) models. In 1967, the Domino design focus spotlighted copies of Fender's Jazzmaster/Jaguar and Mustang models renamed the **Spartan** and the **Olympic**. You just know that these guitars are the product of the 1960s, as the Domino catalog claimed that their guitars had "Lightning Fast Action - Psychedelic Sounds - Elegant Mod Styling". As they say on late night commercials, "Now how much will you pay?" But Wait!

The entire Domino product line featured Japanese hardware and pickups. Domino's **Thunder-Matic** line of drums featured 6 ply shells, and internal adjustable mufflers.

(Source: Michael Wright, Guitar Stories Volume One; Domino catalog courtesy John Kinnemeyer, JK Lutherie)

Sometimes you just can't stop. Here's some more "Features built into Every Domino:"

1) Mallory 'Full Range' adjustable pickups.

2) Mark Steel "Lightning Fast" Speed Scale Jazz Neck - the shorter distances between frets permits easier fingering and, naturally faster handling.

3) Mark Steel 3 ounce tremolo/micrometric roller bridge, 6 coats of gloss lacquer.

4) extra value(!) $400 worth of dramatic sound, features, superb styling, handling - yet Domino prices start as low as $22.50 - Compare and You'll Agree!

> Domino guitars may look cool from a distance, but up close they're a tough tone nut to crack. Prices in the vintage market range from $75 to $175 (in excellent condition) as many players bypass the wacky 1960s models to look for a newer model entry level guitar.

For further information regarding Domino electric guitars, please refer to the **5th Edition Blue Book of Electric Guitars**.

ACOUSTIC

The **MARK V NYLON** model was a classical-style acoustic with laminated top/back/sides, round soundhole, a slotted headstock, tied bridge, and featured 3 per side tuners (retail list was $90).

KEN DONNELL

Instruments built in Chico, California during the late 1980s to the early 1990s. Distributed by Donnell Enterprises of Chico, California.

Luthier Ken Donnell offered an acoustic bass that was optionally augmented with a magnetic pickup in the soundhole or an internal Donnell Mini-Flex microphone system. Currently, Boom basses are not in production while Donnell focuses on the development of the **Donnell Mini-Flex** microphone system.

This internal mini-microphone installs inside the acoustic guitar with no modifications to the guitar itself. The mic and gooseneck clip to an interior brace near the soundhole, and the cable runs along the bass side of the fingerboard to the output jack. Other models are installed through the endblock of the guitar in place of the strap button. The Mini-Clip series is offered in a number of different models (featuring different low impedence microphones). For further product information, contact Donnell Enterprises.

Boom basses have a cedar soundboard, mahogany back, sides, and neck, and rosewood fingerboards and bridges. The tuning machines are chrome Schallers. The basses have a 32" scale (45 1/2" overall), and a six inch depth. The neck joined the non-cutaway body at the 14th fret, and had 19 frets overall. The original suggested list price (direct from the company) was $1,600.

DORADO

Instruments produced in Japan circa early 1970s. Distributed in the U.S. by the Baldwin Piano and Organ Company of Cincinnati, Ohio.

The Dorado trademark was briefly used by Baldwin (during its Gretsch ownership) on a product line of Japanese-built acoustics and electric guitars and basses.

> Dorado instruments are of decent quality, but are often found at slightly inflated asking prices due to the attachment of the Gretsch name. Remember, these are 1970s Japanese guitars imported in by Gretsch during their phase of Baldwin ownership! Dorados are sometimes rightly priced between $125 to $175; but many times they are tagged at prices double that. Of course, what a guitar is tagged at and what it sells at (cash talks, baby!) are always two different animals.

(Source: Walter Murray, Frankenstein Fretworks; and Michael Wright, Vintage Guitar Magazine)

MICHAEL DUNN

Instruments currently built in Vancouver (British Columbia), Canada.

Michael Dunn apprenticed for three years under maestros Jose Orti and Jose Ferrer at George Bowden's workshop in Palma De Mallorca, Spain in 1966. As a guitarist, Dunn was fascinated by Django Reinhardt's acoustic style of jazz. Dunn's interest in the Maccaferri guitar design, along with his backround of the Spanish guitar-building tradition, is the basis for his modern interpretation of Maccaferri-styled models. Dunn also offers two classical style models, a flamenco style acoustic, and a Weissenborn-style acoustic Hawaiian guitar.

Dunn uses spruce or cedar for the tuned soundboard, and an ebony fingerboard on top of a Honduran Mahogany neck. Models have a brass tailpiece, and are finished with a French polish process. A slotted peghead is optional. The **Mystery Pacific** model (list price $3,000) was developed from the original design patented by Mario Maccaferri in 1930. The Mystery Pacific is fitted with an internal soundbox and reflector, and posseses the D-shaped soundhole, cedar soundboard, and rosewood back and sides. The **Stardust** (list $2,500) has an oval soundhole, and features Paduak or a similar medium density tropical hardwood for the back and sides. The scale length of the **Belleville** is 670 mm, as compared to the Stardust's 640 mm scale. Construction of the longer-scaled Belleville (list $2,500) is similar to the Stardust model.

In addition to the three Maccaferri-derived models, Dunn also builds a 660 mm scale Classical guitar (list $3,000); a 1939 Hauser-type Classical (650 mm scale length) guitar for $3,000; a Flamenco model (list $ 2,500); and a Weissenborn-style acoustic Hawaiian guitar model (list $2,500).

GUITARES MAURICE DUPONT

Instruments currently built in France. Distributed by Paul Hostetter of Santa Cruz, California.

After spending a number of years repairing and restoring Selmer/Maccaferri guitars, luthier Maurice Dupont began building Selmer replicas that differ in the fact the Dupont features a one-piece neck with adjustable trussrod inside (Selmers had a three piece neck), and better construction materials. Dupont also hand builds his own classical, flamenco, steel-string, and archtop guitars. Both the **Excellence** and **Privilege** archtops are offered in 16" or 17" bodies, and with a Florentine or Venetian cutaway. For further information on either the Selmer-type guitars, or his other Dupont models, please contact Paul Hostetter in Santa Cruz, California.

(Dupont history courtesy Paul Hostetter)

DURANGO

Instruments currently produced in Asia. Distributed by Saga Musical Instruments of San Francisco, California.

Durango full-sized classical acoustics are designed in part for the entry level guitar student, and features laminated spruce tops, birch back and sides, black body binding, a matte finish, chrome hardware, and 3 per side slotted headstocks. For further information regarding models and pricing, contact Saga Musical Instruments through the Index of Current Manufacturers located in the rear of this edition.

DURANGO

Instrument production and dates of production unknown. Distributed by Sayre Woods Music & Band Instrument Company of Madison Township, New Jersey.

Guitarist/**Blue Book** reader Kenneth Heller offers this yet unspecified Durango trademark for your inspection. The inside label reads "Distributed by Sayre Woods Music & Band Instrument Company of Madison Township, New Jersey"; model "# SAY 622"; serial "#-283" (or perhaps G000315). Other readers with information concerning the Durango trademark are invited to write to the **Blue Book of Guitars** for future inclusions.

(Information courtesy Kenneth Heller)

W.J. DYER & BRO.

See LARSON BROTHERS (1900-1944).

From the 1880s to the 1930s, the Dyer store in St. Paul was *the* place for musical merchandise for the midwest in the areas northwest of Chicago. They sold about anything music related on the market at that time. The Larson brothers of Maurer & Co., Chicago were commissioned to build a line of **Symphony** harp-guitars and **Symphony** harp-mandolin orchestra pieces along with the J.F. Stetson brand of guitars. They started building these great instruments circa 1910.

The original design of these harp-style instruments came from that of Chris Knutsen who had been building that style since 1898. The early Larsons showed a resemblance to the Knutsen ideas but evolved to a final design by 1912. The harp-guitars are labeled **Style #4** through **#8** whereas the higher the number, the better the grade of material and intricacy of the trim. The Style #4 is very plain with dot inlays in the fingerboard and no binding on the back. The Style #8 has a pearl trimmed top, fancy peghead inlay and the beautiful tree-of-life fingerboard. This tree-of-life pattern is also used on the fanciest Maurers and Prairie States having the 12 fret-to-the-body necks.

Dyer Symphony Harp Guitar Style #7
courtesy Robert Carl Hartman

The harp-mandolin series includes a harp-mandola and harp-mando-cello also in different degrees of ornamentation. Some of the Stetson guitars are Larson-made, but others were possibly made by Harmony, Lyon & Healy, or others. If the Stetson trademark is burned into the inside back strip, it is probably a Larson.

For more information regarding other Larson-made brands, see **Maurer**, **Prairie State**, **Euphonon**, **Wm. C. Stahl**, and **The Larson Brothers**.

For more detailed information regarding all Larson brands, see The Larsons' Creations, G Carl Hartman, Centerstream Publishing, P.O. Box 17878, Anaheim Hills CA 92807, phone/fax (714) 779-9390.

D

ECCLESHALL

Instruments built in England since the early 1970s.

Luthier Christopher J. Eccleshall is known for the high quality guitars that he produces. Eccelshall also builds violins, mandolins, and banjos. Some of his original designs carry such model designations like **Excalibur**, **EQ**, and **Craftsman**. Luthier Eccleshall was also the first UK maker to have Japanese-built solid body guitars.

(Source: Tony Bacon and Paul Day, The Guru's Guitar Guide)

ROB EHLERS

Instruments built in Oregon since 1985.

Luthier Rob Ehlers has been building high quality acoustic steel string guitars in his workshop over the last ten years. For information regarding availability, pricing, and model nomenclature, please contact luthier Ehlers through the Index of Current Manufacturers located in the rear of this book.

EHLERS & BURNS

See EHLERS.

Instruments custom built in Oregon from 1974 to 1984.

The E & B (EHLERS & BURNS) trademark was used by luthiers Rob Ehlers and Bruce Burns during a ten year period. Most instuments produced then were custom ordered. After 1984, Bruce Burns was no longer involved in the construction of the instruments.

EICHELBAUM CUSTOM GUITARS

Instruments currently built in Santa Barbara, California.

Eichelbaum Custom Guitars is offering three different models of hand crafted acoustic guitars. These models are also available with a number of custom options, thus personalizing the guitar to the owner.

Models are constructed with Master-grade woods: Sitka spruce tops, Indian rosewood back and sides, honduran Mahogany necks, and ebony fingerboards/bridges/binding (with maple or Koa)/endpins. The **Sierra Orchestra Model** retails at $1,650, the **Sierra Jumbo Model** is priced at $1,950, and the **Sierra Cutaway Model** is $2,050. All prices include a deluxe hardshell case. For further information regarding the specifications, custom options, and pricing please contact Eichelbaum Custom Guitars through the Index of Current Manufacturers located in the back of this edition.

F-100 Acoustic
courtesy Donn Eisele

EISELE

Instruments currently built in Kailua, Hawaii.

Donn H. Eisele began playing guitar about thirty years ago, and started collecting in the past ten years. In 1989, Eisele began building guitars as a hobby; he decided to pursue it full time in early 1995.

Eisele offers a range of both flat top and archtop acoustic guitars. All models have a wide range of custom features available, and both prices include a hardshell case.

Eisele's flattop guitars include such standard features as mahogany back and sides, one piece or laminated mahogany neck, Sitka spruce or Western red cedar top, ebony or rosewood fingerboard with dot inlays, ebony or rosewood bridge, single body binding (white, ivoroid, or tortoises), chrome Schaller tuners, and a nitrocellulose lacquer finish. The Standard list price begins at $2,500. The **F-00** has a 15" body similar to a Gibson L-00, while the **F-OM**'s 15" body resembles a Martin OM. The **F-100** is the 16" version of the F-00, and the **F-J** model is a 16" jumbo shaped like a Gibson J-185. The 17" **F-SJ** jumbo resembles a Gibson J-200.

Eisele's Archtop guitar is featured in a 16" or 17" body, and the Standard has a list price begining at $4,750. The Archtop includes such standard features as hand carved back of big leaf maple with matching sides, 1 piece or laminated figured maple neck, hand carved Englemann or Sitka spruce top, ebony fingerboard/finger rest/bridge/tailpiece, black/white/black body purfling, ivoroid fingerboard binding, gold Schaller tuners, and a nitrocellulose lacquer finish.

EKO

Instruments currently built in Asia. Distributed by EKO Musical Instruments of Montelupone, Italy.

Instruments were formerly built in Italy from the early 1960s through 1987. Distribution in the U.S. market by the LoDuca Bros. of Milwaukee, Wisconsin.

The LoDuca Bros. musical distribution company was formed in 1941 by brothers Tom and Guy LoDuca. Capitalizing on money made through their accordian-based vaudevillian act, lessons, and accordian repair, the LoDucas began importing and selling Italian accordians. Throughout the 1940s and 1950s, the LoDucas built up a musical distributorship with accordians and sheet music. By the late 1950s, they were handling Magnatone amplifiers and guitars.

In 1961, the LoDucas teamed up with Italy-based Oliviero Pigini & Company to import guitars. Pigini, one of the LoDuca's accordian manufacturers, had formed the EKO company in anticipation of the boom in the guitar market. The LoDucas acted as technical designers and gave input on EKO designs (as well as being the exclusive U.S. dealers), and EKO built guitars for their dealers. Some of the sparkle finishes were no doubt inspired by the accordians produced in the past. In fact, the various on/off switches and tone settings are down right reminiscent of accordian voice settings! The plastic covered-guitars lasted through to the mid 1960s, when more conventional finishes were offered. EKO also built a number of guitars for Vox, Goya, and Thomas companies.

By 1967 EKO had established dealers in 57 countries around the world. During the late 1960s and early 1970s the guitar market began to get soft, and many guitar builders began to go out of business. EKO continued on, but cut back the number

17" Archtop
courtesy Donn Eisele

Ranger 12 Acoustic 1967 EKO Catalog

of models offered. In the late 1970s, EKO introduced a *custom shop* branch that built neck-through designed guitars for other trademarks. Once such company was **D'Agostino**, and EKO produced the **Bench Mark** models from 1978 to 1982.

The EKO company kept producing models until 1985. By the mid-1980s, the LoDuca Bros. company had begun concentrating on guitar case production, and stopped importing the final *Alembic-styled* set-neck guitars that were being produced. The original EKO company's holdings were liquidated in 1987.

Currently, the EKO trademark has again been revived in Italy, and appears on entry level solid body guitars built in Asia. The revived company is offering a wide range of acoustic, classical, and solid body electric guitars and amplifiers - all with contemporary market designs.

(Eko history source: Michael Wright, Guitar Stories Volume One)

The Loduca Bros., Inc. company is still in Milwaukee, and can be reached at the Lo Duca Building, 400 N. Broadway, Milwaukee, Wisconsin 53202 (414.347.1400, FAX 414.347.1402).

ACOUSTIC

The current Eko (Asian-produced) product line has a wide range of classical (**Conservatorio** and **Studio** series), classical models with EQ and piezo bridges (**Classic EQ**), jumbo-style acoustic/electrics (**Electro-Acoustic** series), and dreadnought models (**Acoustic** series). The current acoustic models all have different, re-styled headstocks from the earlier Eko Italian-production models.

EL CID

Instruments produced in Asia. Distributed by the L.A. Guitar Works of Reseda, California.

El Cid classical guitars are offered in **King** and **Queen** designated models that have slotted headstocks, solid spruce or cedar tops, and rosewood or lacewood back/sides. List price for either model is $799 (with hardshell case).

EL DEGAS

Instruments produced in Japan.

The El Degas trademark was a brandname used by U.S. importers Buegeleisen & Jacobson of New York, New York.

(Source: Michael Wright, Guitar Stories Volume One)

ELGER

Instruments originally produced in Ardmore, Pennsylvania from 1959 to 1965. Elger began importing instruments produced in Japan during the early 1960s.

Elger instruments were distributed in the U.S. by the Elger Company of Ardmore, Pennsylvania. The roots of the Elger company were founded in 1954 by Harry Rosenbloom when he opened Medley Music in Bryn Mawr, Pennsylvania. In 1959, Rosenbloom decided to produce his own acoustic guitars as the Elger Company (named after his children, Ellen and Gerson). Rosenbloom soon turned from U.S. production to Japanese when the Elger company became partners with Hoshino Gakki Gen, and introduced the **Ibanez** trademark to the U.S. market. Elger did maintain the Pennsylvania facilities to check incoming shipments and correct any flaws prior to shipping merchandise out to their dealers. For further company history, see **Ibanez**.

(Source: Michael Wright, Guitar Stories Volume One)

JEFFREY R. ELLIOT

Instruments built in Portland, Oregon.

Luthier Jeffrey R. Elliot began professionally building guitars in 1966. Elliot builds between six to eight classical or steel string guitars on a yearly basis. A variety of woods are available for the top and body; inlay work and designs are custom ordered. Prices begin around $4,000.

Elliot's last given address was 2812 SE 37th Avenue, Portland, Oregon (97202).

EMPERADOR

Instruments built in Japan by the Kasuga company circa 1966 to 1992. Distributed by Westheimer Musical Instruments of Chicago, Illinois.

The Emperador trademark was a brandname used in the U.S. market by the Westheimer Musical Instruments of Chicago, Illinois. The Emperador trademark was the Westheimer company's entry level line to their Cort products line through the years. Emperador models are usually shorter-scaled entry level instruments, and the trademark can be found on both jazz-style thinline acoustic/electric archtops and solid body electric guitars and basses.

ENCORE

Instruments are currently produced in Asia. Distributed by John Hornby Skewes & Co., Ltd. of Garforth (Leeds), England.

The **Encore** trademark is the brandname of UK importer John Hornby Skewes & Co., Ltd. The company was founded in 1965 by the namesake, Mr. John Hornby Skewes. The Encore line consists of solidly built guitars and basses that feature designs based on popular American favorites. Encore instruments are of medium to good quality, and their model E83 bass was named *Most Popular U.K. Bass Guitar* in 1992, 1993, 1994, and 1995.

In addition to the Encore line, the John Hornby Skewes company distributes the Vintage instruments line (see VINTAGE).

ACOUSTIC

The current Encore line of acoustic guitars is well represented by over 22 models. In addition to the steel string acoustics, there are currently 6 classical models (three full size, two 3/4 scale, and one 1/2 scale), and construction ranges from a beech laminate top to solid spruce, with either a maple laminate or beech laminate back and sides.

CE 500 (CUTAWAY) — dreadnought style, single rounded cutaway, round soundhole, laminated spruce top, Nato back/side/neck, 14/20 fret rosewood fingerboard with white dot inlay, rosewood bridge, chrome hardware, 3 per side headstock, black pickguard. Available in Natural finish. Current mfr.
   Mfr.'s Sug. Retail $TBA

E Series

E 400 N DREADNOUGHT (Also E 400 S) — dreadnought style, round soundhole, laminated spruce top, Nato back/side/neck, 14/20 fret rosewood fingerboard with white dot inlay, rosewood bridge, chrome hardware, 3 per side headstock, black pickguard. Available in Natural (E 400 N) and Natural Satin (E 400 S) finishes. Current mfr.
   Mfr.'s Sug. Retail $TBA

   E 600 N — similar to the E 400, except has herringbone binding/rosette, custom inlay at 12th fret.
   Mfr.'s Sug. Retail $TBA

   W 250 (Also W 250 TS) — similar to the E 400, except has ebonised hardwood fingerboard, spruce bridge. Available in Natural (W 250) and Tobacco Sunburst (W 250 TS) finishes. Current mfr.
   Mfr.'s Sug. Retail $139

   W 260 — similar to the W 250, except features spruce top, mahogany back and sides, rosewood fingerboard, rosewood bridge. Available in Natural finish. Current mfr.
   Mfr.'s Sug. Retail $219

      This model is available in a left-handed configuration (Model W 260 LH).

ACOUSTIC ELECTRIC

CE Series

CE 500 EA — dreadnought style, single rounded cutaway, round soundhole, laminated spruce top, Nato back/side/neck, 14/20 fret rosewood fingerboard with white oval inlay, rosewood bridge, 3 per side headstock, black pickguard, chrome hardware, piezo pickup, volume/tone controls. Available in Natural finish. Current mfr.
   Mfr.'s Sug. Retail $TBA

      This model is available in a left-handed configuration (Model LH 500 EA).

   CE 500 EAJ — similar to the CE 500 EA, except has a 3 band EQ, white dot inlays. Current mfr.
   Mfr.'s Sug. Retail $TBA

EM 132 — jumbo style, single rounded cutaway, round soundhole, flame maple top, ash back/sides, nato neck, 14/20 fret rosewood fingerboard with white diamond inlay, rosewood bridge, 3 per side headstock, chrome hardware, piezo pickup, 3 band EQ controls. Available in Gold Flame finish. Current mfr.
   Mfr.'s Sug. Retail $TBA

EA Series

EA 400 N — dreadnought style, round soundhole, laminated spruce top, Nato back/side/neck, 14/20 fret rosewood fingerboard with white dot inlay, rosewood bridge, chrome hardware, 3 per side headstock, black pickguard, piezo pickup, volume/tone controls. Available in Natural finish. Current mfr.
   Mfr.'s Sug. Retail $TBA

   EA 250 — similar to the EA 400 N, except features ebonized hardwood fingerboard, spruce bridge. Current mfr.
   Mfr.'s Sug. Retail $179

EY 50 ELECTRO — dreadnought style, single rounded cutaway, round soundhole, birdseye maple top, ash back/sides, Nato neck, 14/20 fret rosewood fingerboard with white dot inlay, rosewood bridge, 3 per side headstock, chrome hardware, piezo pickup, 4 band EQ. Available in Wine Red finish. Current mfr.
   Mfr.'s Sug. Retail $TBA

ENSENADA

Instruments produced in Japan, circa 1970s. Distributed by Strum & Drum of Chicago, Illinois.

The Ensenada trademark was a brandname of U.S. importers Strum & Drum of Chicago, Illinois. Strum and Drum were later owners of the National trademark, acquired when Valco's holdings were auctioned off. Ensenada instruments were distributed between roughly 1973 to 1974.

   (Source: Michael Wright, Guitar Stories Volume One)

EPI

Instruments produced in China or Indonesia. Distributed by Epiphone (Gibson Musical Instruments) of Nashville, Tennessee.

Epi stringed instruments are the entry level line to the current Epiphone range of guitars and basses.

Grading		100%	EXCELLENT	AVERAGE

ACOUSTIC

ED-100 (Model ED10) — Available in Natural Matte finish. Current mfr.

Mfr.'s Sug. Retail	$209	$145	$100	$70

EC-100 (Model EC10) — Available in Natural Matte finish. Current mfr.

Mfr.'s Sug. Retail	$189	$145	$100	$70

EPIPHONE

Instruments produced in Korea since 1983. Epiphone is a division of Gibson Musical Instruments of Nashville, Tennessee.

The original Epiphone company was based in New York, New York from 1930 to 1953; and later in Philadelphia, Pennsylvania from 1954 to 1957.

When Epiphone was purchased by Gibson, production moved to Kalamazoo, Michigan from 1958 to 1969; then to Japan from 1970 to 1983. Some specialty models were built in Nashville, Tennesee in 1982 to 1983, also from 1989 to 1994.

E

Emperor 1939 Reissue
courtesy The Epiphone Company

According to family history, Anastasios Stathopoulo (b. 1863) began constructing musical instruments in his home town of Sparta, Greece in 1873. He moved to the U.S. with his family is 1903, settling in New York City, where he produced a full range of stringed instruments bearing his own name up until the time of his death in 1915. The company, which soon became known as "The House of Statopoulo", continued under the direction and ownership of his wife, Marianthe (b. 1875) and eldest son, Epaminondas (Epi [b. 1893]).

Following Marianthe's death in 1923, The House of Statopoulo was incorporated with Epi as president and majority shareholder, his sister Alkminie (Minnie [1897-1984]) as treasurer, and brother Orpheus (Orphie [1899-1973]) as secretary. They immediately announced "The new policy of business" would be "the production of banjos, tenor banjos, banjo mandolins, banjo guitars, and banjo ukuleles under the registered trademark of **Epiphone**". The name "Epiphone" was a combination of Epi's nickname with the Greek word for sound, "phone". Their elegant "Recording" line of tenor banjos was considered to be amongst the finest ever made. These were joined in the late 1920s by a full line of Recording model guitars. In 1928, the company's name was changed to "The Epiphone Banjo Co."

The **Masterbilt** series of guitars was introduced in 1931 and marked Epiphone's entrance into the production of modern, carved, "f"-hole archtop guitars, based on violin construction principles. Indeed, at the time of their introduction, the Materbilt guitar line was the most complete selection of "f"-hole guitars available from any instrument maker in the world. Complementary Spanish and Hawaiian flattop models and carved-top mandolins were likewise included under the Masterbilt aigis. Soon, Epiphone advertisements would claim that it was "The World's Largest Producer of First Grade Fretted Instruments". Whether this was an accurate boast or not, it set the stage for a two decade rivalry between Epiphone and its largest competitor, Gibson.

By 1935, the company was now known simply as "Epiphone, Inc.", and was producing its "Electar" brand of electric Hawaiian and Spanish guitars, as well as amplifiers which were designed by electronics pioneer and Danelectro founder, Nat Daniels (1912-1994). That same year marked the introduction of the flagship 18 3/8" **Emperor** model archtop guitar and signaled the re-design and enlargement of the company's entire Masterbilt archtop line.

Notable Epiphone innovations in this era included the first patented electronic pickup with individual pole pieces and the distinctive "Frequensator" tailpiece. Both were designed by salesman and acknowledged jack-of-all-trades, Herb Sunshine (1906-1988), and in production by 1937. In 1940, the company also introduced a full line of well respected bass violins produced under the watchful eye of the youngest of the Stathopoulo brothers, Frixo (b. 1905) who had joined the firm in the early 1930s.

During this period, Epiphone's growing product line was considered second to none, and could boast such endorsers as George Van Eps (with the Ray Noble Orchestra), Carmen Mastren (with Tommy Dorsey), Allan Reuss (with Benny Goodman's band), and many, many more.

Epi Stathopoulo died from leukemia in 1943 at the age of 49, and this, combined with the many hardships incurred during World War II, set the company on a downward spiral. Orphie Stathopoulo, who took over as president, was unable to recapture the momentum of the prewar years, and constant friction between he and his brother Frixo (now vice-president) began to pull the company apart at the seams.

In 1951, simmering labor problems resulted in a strike which shut down the New York plant for several months. During this time, Orphie sold a stake in the business to the large distribution company, Continental Music. Continental moved production to Philadelphia, and most instruments manufactured from 1952 to 1957 were made there. It is doubtful, however, if much was produced in the final two years, as Epiphone was rapidly being overtaken by new entrants into the guitar market, notably Fender and Guild, the later of which had ironically been started by many former Epiphone employees under the leadership of Alfred Dronge and former Epiphone executive, George Mann.

It had become increasingly apparent that Epiphone was no longer capable of developing the new products necessary to capture the imagination of the guitar-buying public and its financial viability had come to an end. Following Frixo's sudden death in 1957, Orphie, by now the company's sole owner, approached Gibson president Ted McCarty, who had previously expressed interest in buying Epiphone's bass violin production. A deal was signed and trucks were dispatched from Kalamazoo to New York and Philadelphia to make the move. Records during this time period indicate that the out-of-work ex-Epiphone workers in New Berlin, New York "celebrated" by hosting a bonfire behind the plant with any available lumber (both finished and unfinished!). When the vans returned to the Gibson warehouse in Michigan, McCarty realized (much to his surprise) that not only had he received the bass making operation, but all the jigs, fixtures, and machinery necessary for making guitars, plus much of the work in progress. For the sum of $20,000, Gibson had acquired it's once mighty rival (including what would become the most profitable trademark) lock, stock, and barrel.

It was decided that Epiphone would be re-established as a first rate guitar manufacturer, so that Gibson's parent company CMI (Chicago Musical Instruments) could offer a product comparable in every way to Gibson. This was done primarily as a way of offering music stores which, due to existing contractual obligations in a particular sales area, were not allowed to carry the exclusive Gibson line. The Epiphone brand could now be offered to competing retailers who were also carrying

Grading	100%	EXCELLENT	AVERAGE

many of the other well-known brands which were distributed by the giant CMI. Though Epiphone was set up as an autonomous company, in a separate part of the Gibson complex, parallel product lines were soon established, and Gibson was (in effect) competing with itself.

After Epiphone was moved to Kalamazoo, instruments were built in the U.S through 1969. In 1970, production was moved overseas. Instruments were originally built in Japan (1970-1983), but during the early 1980s, Japanese production costs became pricey due to the changing ratio of the dollar/yen.

Since 1984, the majority of guitars have been produced in Korea. However, there have been a number of models like the Spirit, Special, USA Pro, and USA Coronet that were produced in Nashville, Tennessee. These models are the exception to the rule. Epiphone currently offers a very wide range of acoustic, semi-hollow, and solid body electric guitars.

In 1998, Epiphone offered the new **EZ-Bender**, a detachable "B" string bender that can be installed on any guitar equipped with a stop bar tailpiece. The EZ-Bender can be installed with no modifications whatsoever to the guitar.

(Source: N.Y. Epiphone information by L.B. Fred and Jim Fisch, Epiphone: The House of Stathopoulo)

(Additional Epiphone history courtesy Walter Carter, Epiphone: The Complete History)

PRODUCTION LOCATION:

Epiphone guitars have been produced in a wide range of places. The following list gives a rough approximation to production facilities by year.

Epiphone-owned production:

Guitars produced from the late 1920s up to the time of Gibson's purchase of the company are known by collectors as "New York Epiphones".

New York, NY	**Late 1920s to 1952**
Philadelphia, PA	**1952 to 1957**

Gibson-owned production:

Kalamazoo, MI	**1958 to 1969**	
Japan	**1970 to 1983**	
Taiwan	**1979 to 1981**	
Nashville, TN	**1982 to 1983**	**(Spirit, Special, U.S. Map)**
Korea	**1983 to date**	
Japan	**1988 to 1989**	**(Spotlights, Thinlines)**
Nashville, TN	**1989 to 1994**	**(USA Pro)**
Nashville, TN	**1991 to 1994**	**(USA Coronet)**
China	**1997 to date**	
Indonesia	**1997 to date**	

For information regarding archtop models with built-in pickups, please refer to the Epiphone Electric Archtop section in the **5th Edition Blue Book of Electric Guitars**.

RECORDING MODELS

Recording Model Series

Recording Model archtop guitars feature an asymetrical body with angled cutaway on treble bout. Some models had flat tops, others an arched top (see descriptions below). Recording Model guitars are relatively rare in the vintage guitar market. These models were introduced during the 1920s, and discontinued around 1931.

RECORDING MODEL A — graduated spruce top, maple or mahogany back/sides, single black body binding, 25" scale, rosewood fingerboard with dot inlay, 3 per side tuners, pin bridge or trapeze tailpiece. Available in Natural or Natural with shaded top finishes.

	$1,800	$800

Recording Model B — similar to Recording Model A, except features bound rosewood fingerboard with paired diamond inlay.

	$2,200	$1,100

Recording Model C — similar to Recording Model A, except features carved spruce top, bound ebony fingerboard with paired diamond inlay, single white body binding. Available in Shaded top finish.

	$3,000	$1,800

Some models may have rosewood fingerboards with block inlay; some models may have a black pickguard.

Recording Model D — similar to Recording Model A, except features carved spruce top, bound ebony fingerboard with pearloid block inlay, single white body binding, black pickguard. Available in Shaded top finish.

	$3,500	$2,000

Recording Model E — similar to Recording Model A, except features carved spruce top, laminated curly maple body, 3-ply white body binding, bound ebony fingerboard with celluloid blocks with floral engraving, black pickguard, gold plated tuners. Available in Shaded top finish.

	$4,000	$2,300

ACOUSTIC ARCHTOP

All high-end professional model Epiphone tenor guitars should be considered rarities, and bring a price comparable to their 6-string counterparts.

BEVERLY — flat spruce top, 2 segmented f-holes, raised black pickguard, mahogany arched back, mahogany sides/neck, 14/20 fret rosewood fingerboard with pearl dot inlay, adjustable rosewood bridge/trapeze tailpiece, blackface peghead, 3 per side tuners. Available in Brown finish. Mfd. 1931 to 1937.

13" body width.

Grading	100%	EXCELLENT	AVERAGE
		$500	$325

(For historical interest, this instrument originally sold for $35.)

BLACKSTONE — carved spruce top, f-holes, raised black pickguard, bound body, maple back/sides, 14/20 fret bound rosewood fingerboard with pearl dot inlay, adjustable rosewood bridge/trapeze tailpiece, bound blackface peghead with pearl logo inlay, 3 per side plate mounted tuners. Available in Ebony and Sunburst finish. Mfd. 1931 to 1951.

14 3/4" Body width.

1931-1932		$850	$550
1933-1935		$600	$350
1936-1951		$750	$500

The Ebony finish was briefly available from 1931 to 1932.

In 1931, engraved pearloid peghead overlay with pearl Masterbilt banner peghead inlay was added.

In 1934, 15 1/2" body width, mahogany back/sides, redesigned unbound peghead with redesigned inlay replaced original items.

In 1936, parallelogram fingerboard inlay replaced original item, auditorium style body, maple back/sides, diamond/script logo peghead inlay replaced respective items.

In 1939, center dip style peghead replaced respective item.

In 1941, Blonde finish became optionally available.

Blackstone Tenor — similar to the Blackstone, except features a 4-string tenor configuration. Mfd. 1931 to 1949.

1931-1932		$850	$550
1933-1935		$600	$350
1936-1951		$750	$500

BROADWAY — carved spruce top, f-holes, raised black pickguard, multibound body, walnut back/sides, mahogany neck, 14/20 fret bound ebony fingerboard with pearl diamond inlay, adjustable ebony bridge/trapeze tailpiece, blackface peghead with pearl Masterbilt banner/logo inlay, 3 per side nickel tuners. Available in Sunburst finish. Mfd. 1931 to 1957.

16 3/8" body width.

1931-1934		$1,800	$850
1935-1957		$2,200	$1,450

In 1934, bound pickguard, block fingerboard inlay, vine/block logo peghead inlay, gold hardware replaced original items; carved back added to design.

In 1937, 17 3/8" body width, redesigned pickguard/tailpiece/logo replaced respective items, bound peghead replaced original item.

In 1939, maple back/sides, Frequensator tailpiece, redesigned peghead replaced respective items.

In 1941, Blonde finish was optionally available.

In 1944, pearl flower peghead inlay replaced respective item.

In 1949, Broadway Regent (cutaway body) was introduced.

(For historical interest, this instrument originally sold for $175.)

Bretton Tenor — tenor version of the Broadway model. Mfd. 1931 to 1936.

15 1/2" body width.

		$900	$575

This tenor model was originally called the Bretton from its introduction in 1931 to 1936. The name was changed to Broadway Tenor in 1937.

Broadway Tenor — similar to the Blackstone, except features a 4-string tenor configuration. Mfd. 1937 to 1949.

1937-1949		$2,200	$1,450

Broadway Regent — similar to the Blackstone, except features a single rounded cutaway body. Mfd. 1949 to 1957.

1949-1957		$3,000	$2,000

BYRON — carved spruce top, mahogany back/sides, single body binding, mahogany neck, 20 fret rosewood fingerboard with dot inlay, f-holes, 3 per side tuners with plastic buttons, nickel hardware, tortoiseshell pickguard, trapeze tailpiece. Available in Sunburst Top finish. Mfd. 1949 to 1955.

15 3/8" body width.

		$650	$375

DE LUXE — carved spruce top, 2 f-holes, multibound body, black/white diagonal purfling on top, figured maple back/sides, 5 piece carved figured maple neck, 14/20 fret bound rosewood fingerboard with pearl slotted diamond inlay, adjustable rosewood bridge/trapeze tailpiece, bound blackface peghead with pearl Masterbilt banner inlay, 3 per side gold die cast tuners. Available in Sunburst finish. Mfd. 1931 to 1957 (New York).

16 3/8" body width.

1931-1935		$3,500	$1,500
1936-1937		$3,500	$1,500
1937-1957		$4,000	$2,000

In 1959, 70 instruments were produced in Gibson's Kalamazoo plant.

1959		$1,900	$900

In 1934, floral fingerboard inlay, vine/logo peghead inlay replaced original items, raised white pickguard was added.

Grading	100%	EXCELLENT	AVERAGE

In late 1935, (grand auditorium style) 17 3/8" body width, redesigned black pickguard, bound f-holes, resigned tailpiece replaced original items, cloud fingerboard inlay, script peghead logo replaced respective items.

In 1937, Frequensator tailpiece replaced respective item.

In 1939, Natural finish was optionally available.

In 1949, De Luxe Regent (cutaway body) was introduced.

Under Gibson ownership, this model was re-introduced in 1958/1959. By 1965, the model was available by special order; and discontinued in 1970.

Empire (De Luxe Tenor) — tenor version of the De Luxe model. Mfd. 1931 to 1935.

15 1/2" body width.

1931-1935		$3,500	$1,500

De Luxe Regent — similar to the De Luxe, except has a single round cutaway body. Mfd. 1949 to 1958.

		$5,000	$3,250

Some models may feature the flower peghead inlay.

DEVON — carved spruce top, mahogany back/sides, single bound body, mahogany neck, 20 fret rosewood fingerboard with oval inlay, f-holes, 3 per side tuners, nickel hardware, bound tortoiseshell logo with 'E' logo, Frequensator tailpiece. Available in Sunburst top and Natural finishes. Mfd. 1949 to 1957.

17 3/8" body width.

		$1,000	$600

EMPEROR (Mfr. 1935 to 1957) — carved spruce top, multibound f-holes, raised bound tortoise pickguard, multibound body, maple back/sides/neck, carved back, 14/20 fret bound ebony fingerboard with pearl split block inlay, adjustable ebony bridge/logo engraved trapeze tailpiece, bound peghead with pearl vine/logo inlay, 3 per side gold tuners. Available in Cremona Brown Sunburst finish. Mfd. 1935 to 1957.

18 1/2" body width.

1935-1936		$5,000	$3,000
1937-1957		$4,800	$2,800

In 1937, Frequensator tailpiece replaced original items.

In 1939, pearl block/abalone triangle fingerboard, redesigned peghead replaced original items; Natural finish optionally available.

By the mid 1940s, rosewood fingerboard replaced original item.

In 1948, Emperor Regent (cutaway body) was introduced. A limited number of cutaway Emperors bearing the label Soloist Emperor were produced in 1948 as well.

(For historical interest, this instrument originally sold for $400.)

Emperor (Mfr. 1958 to 1970) — reintroduced by Gibson in 1958. Available by special order only in 1963, discontinued 1970.

		$2,400	$1,625

Emperor Cutaway (New York Mfr.) — similar to Emperor, except has single round cutaway. Mfd. 1948 to 1955.

		$7,000	$4,500

OLYMPIC — carved spruce or poplar top, mahogany back/sides, single body binding, mahogany neck, segmented f-holes, 20 fret rosewood fingerboard with dot inlay, small black pickguard, 3 per side tuners with plastic buttons. Available in Golden Brown and Brown with Sunburst top. Mfd. 1931 to 1949.

13" body width.

		$550	$300

In 1939, large tortoiseshell pickguard replaced original item.

Olympic Tenor — tenor version of the Olympic model. Mfd. 1937 to 1949.

		$550	$300

RITZ — carved spruce top, maple back/sides, tortoiseshell body binding, cello style f-holes, cherrywood neck, 20 fret rosewood fingerboard with dot inlay, trapeze tailpiece. Available in Natural opaque finish only. Mfd. 1941 to 1949.

15 1/4" body width.

		$600	$375

Ritz Tenor — tenor version of the Ritz model. Mfd. 1941 to 1949.

		$600	$375

ROYAL — carved spruce top, mahogany back and sides, single body binding, segmented f-holes, 2-piece mahogany neck, 20 fret rosewood fingerboard with dot inlay, black pickguard, trapeze tailpiece. Available in Brown with Sunburst top finish. Mfd. 1931 to 1935.

15 1/2" body width.

		$650	$325

In 1933, American walnut back/sides replaced original item.

SPARTAN — carved spruce top, round soundhole, raised black pickguard, one stripe rosette, bound body, maple back/sides, mahogany neck, 14/20 fret bound rosewood fingerboard with pearl dot inlay, adjustable rosewood bridge/nickel trapeze tailpiece, bound peghead with pearl wedge/logo inlay, 3 per side nickel tuners. Available in Sunburst finish. Mfd. 1934 to 1949.

16 3/8" body width.

Epiphone Ritz
courtesy Clay Leighton

Grading	100%	EXCELLENT	AVERAGE
1934-1935		$900	$600
1936-1949		$750	$450

In 1936, carved back added to design; f-holes, walnut back/sides, block fingerboard inlay, column/logo peghead inlay replaced original items.

In 1939, center dip peghead replaced original item.

In 1941, white mahogany back/sides replaced respective item. Blonde finish optionally available.

(For historical interest, this instrument originally sold for $100.)

Regent Tenor — bound body, mahogany back/sides, trapeze tailpiece. Mfd. 1934 to 1936.

15 1/2" body width.

	EXCELLENT	AVERAGE
	$575	$425

This model originally was the companion tenor model to the Spartan guitar. Discontinued in favor of the Spartan Tenor, introduced in 1937.

Spartan Tenor — similar to the Regent Tenor. Mfd. 1937 to 1949.

15 1/2" body width.

	EXCELLENT	AVERAGE
	$750	$525

The Regent tenor guitar was the original companion to the Spartan guitar. The Regent was discontinued in 1936 in favor of the Spartan Tenor.

TUDOR — carved spruce top, curly maple back/sides, carved back, 3-ply body binding, 5-ply maple/mahogany neck, segmented f-holes, bound black pickguard, gold hardware, trapeze tailpiece. Available in Brown with Sunburst top. Mfd. 1932 to 1936.

16 3/8" body width.

	EXCELLENT	AVERAGE
	$2,500	$1,200

TRIUMPH (Mfr. 1931 to 1957) — 15 1/2" body width, carved spruce top, f-holes, raised black pickguard, bound body, walnut back/sides, mahogany neck, 14/20 fret bound rosewood fingerboard with pearl diamond inlay, adjustable rosewood bridge/trapeze tailpiece, bound peghead with pearl *Masterbilt* banner/logo inlay, 3 per side nickel tuners. Available in Sunburst finish. Mfd. 1931 to 1957.

	EXCELLENT	AVERAGE
1931-1932	$750	$450
1933-1935	$950	$650
1936-1957	$1,500	$900

In 1933, the body was redesigned to 16 3/8" across the lower bout.

In 1934, maple back/sides, unbound peghead with pearl fleur-de-lis/logo inlay replaced original items; carved back added to design.

In 1935, redesigned script peghead logo replaced respective item.

In 1936, the body was redesigned to 17 3/8" across the lower bout.

In 1937, bound pickguard, Frequensator tailpiece replaced original items, bound peghead replaced respective item.

In 1939, Frequensator tailpiece replaced respective item.

In 1941, redesigned peghead replaced respective item, Blonde finish optionally available.

In 1949, redesigned pickguard with stylized E, column peghead inlay replaced respective items.

In 1949, the Triumph Regent (cutaway body) was introduced.

(For historical interest, this instrument originally sold for $125.)

Triumph (Mfr. 1958 to 1970) — reintroduced by Gibson in 1958. Available by special order only in 1963, discontinued 1970.

	EXCELLENT	AVERAGE
	$900	$650

Triumph Regent — similar to Triumph, except has single round cutaway. Mfd. 1949 to 1958.

	EXCELLENT	AVERAGE
	$2,500	$1,200

Hollywood Tenor — tenor version of the Triumph. Mfd. 1931 to 1936.

	EXCELLENT	AVERAGE
	$1,700	$1,100

This model was originally called the Hollywood from its introduction in 1934 to 1936. The name was changed to Triumph Tenor in 1937.

Triumph Tenor — similar to the Hollywood Tenor. Mfd. 1937 to 1957.

	EXCELLENT	AVERAGE
	$1,800	$950

ZENITH — carved spruce top, f-holes, raised black pickguard, bound body, maple back/sides, mahogany neck, 14/20 fret rosewood fingerboard with pearl dot inlay, adjustable rosewood bridge/trapeze tailpiece, blackface peghead, 3 per side single unit nickel tuners with plastic buttons. Available in Sunburst finish. Mfd. 1931 to 1957.

13 5/8" body width.

	EXCELLENT	AVERAGE
	$850	$450

In 1934, (grand concert style) 14 3/8" body width, walnut back/sides replaced original items, pearl wedge/logo peghead inlay added.

In 1936, 16 3/8" body width introduced.

In 1937, diamond/script logo peghead inlay replaced respective item. Tenor and Plectrum version of the Zenith were available.

1942 Epiphone Zenith
courtesy Robert Aponte

E

In 1942, redesigned peghead replaced original item.

In 1954, pearl oval peghead inlay replaced respective item. Blonde finish optionally available.

(For historical interest, this instrument originally sold for $50.)

Melody Tenor — tenor version of the Zenith, walnut back/side. Mfd. 1931 to 1936.

13 1/4" body width.

$850 $450

This model was originally called the Melody from its introduction in 1931 to 1936. The name was changed to Zenith Tenor in 1937.

Zenith Tenor — similar to the Melody tenor. Mfd. 1937 to 1957.

13 1/4" body width.

$850 $450

ACOUSTIC

In 1998, Epiphone began offering guitar and accessory packages for that "one stop shopping" experience for entry level guitars. Actually, the notion of a guitar package plus strings, a tuner, a gigbag, and a 'How-To' video makes perfect sense for the first time guitar student.

The **C-10 Gig Rig** package (list $299) includes a C-10 nylon string acoustic guitar, Qwik-Tune quartz tuner, black gigbag, strap, picks, and a 30 minute Guitar Essentials Hal Leonard video tape. The **PR-100 Gig Rig** (list $329) is similar, but substitutes a PR-100 steel string guitar.

AJ (Advanced Jumbo) Series

AJ-15 (Model EAA1) — sloped shoulder jumbo style, select spruce top, round soundhole, black pickguard, bound body, stripe rosette, mahogany back/sides/neck, 14/20 fret fingerboard with pearl dot inlay, rosewood bridge with black bridgepins, 3 per side chrome tuners. Available in Ebony, Natural and Vintage Sunburst finishes. Mfr. 1998 to date.
Mfr.'s Sug. Retail $299

AJ-15L (Model EAA2) — similar to AJ-15, except in a left-handed configuration. Available in Natural finish. Mfr. 1998 to date.
Mfr.'s Sug. Retail $324

AJ-1512 (Model EAA3) — similar to AJ-15, except in a 12-string configuration, 6 per side tuners. Available in Natural finish. Mfr. 1998 to date.
Mfr.'s Sug. Retail $349

AJ-18S (Model EAA4) — similar to AJ-15, except has a solid spruce top, single rounded cutaway body, no pickguard, diamond fingerboard inlay/block inlay at 12th fret, gold hardware. Available in Ebony, Natural, and Vintage Sunburst finishes. Mfr. 1998 to date.
Mfr.'s Sug. Retail $389

AJ-18SL (Model EAA5) — similar to AJ-18S, except in a left-handed configuration. Available in Natural finish. Mfr. 1998 to date.
Mfr.'s Sug. Retail $414

AJ-1812S (Model EAA6) — similar to AJ-18S, except in a 12-string configuration, 6 per side tuners. Available in Natural finish. Mfr. 1998 to date.
Mfr.'s Sug. Retail $429

AJ-1812SL (Model EAA7) — similar to AJ-18S, except in a left-handed 12-string configuration, 6 per side tuners. Available in Natural finish. Mfr. 1998 to date.
Mfr.'s Sug. Retail $454

AJ-28S (Model EAT1) — similar to AJ-15, except has a solid spruce top, bound body/fingerboard/headstock, diamond fingerboard inlay/block inlay at 12th fret, rosewood headstock veneer. Available in Ebony, Natural, and Vintage Sunburst finishes. Mfr. 1998 to date.
Mfr.'s Sug. Retail $599

AJ-35S (Model EAT2) — similar to AJ-15, except has a solid spruce top, triple-ply body binding, abalone rosette, dot fingerboard inlay/block inlay at 12th fret, rosewood headstock veneer, gold hardware. Available in Ebony, Natural, and Vintage Sunburst finishes. Mfr. 1998 to date.
Mfr.'s Sug. Retail $679

AJ-45S (Model EAA8) — similar to AJ-15, except has a solid spruce top, 24.75" scale, bound body, blackface headstock with screened logo, tortoiseshell pickguard, 3 per side vintage-style tuners. Available in Vintage Sunburst finish. Mfr. 1998 to date.
Mfr.'s Sug. Retail $649

The AJ-45S is based on Gibson's J-45 model.

ALHAMBRA (CLASSICAL) — spruce top, curly maple back/sides, round soundhole, mahogany neck, 12/20 fret rosewood fingerboard, rosewood bridge, slotted headstock. Mfd. 1938 to 1941.

14 3/8" body width.

$1,000 $625

BARCELONE (CLASSICAL) — maple back/sides, 25 1/2" scale, black body binding, gold hardware, pearloid tuner buttons. Mfd. 1963 to 1969.

14 1/4" body width.

$525 $375

Grading	100%	EXCELLENT	AVERAGE

BARD — 12-string configuration, spruce top, mahogany back/sides, multiple-bound body, 24 3/4" scale, oval peghead inlay. Mfd. 1962 to 1970.

		$700	$500

Bluegrass Series

BISCUIT RESOPHONIC (Model EFB1) — resonator model with round neck, chrome hardware, 2 f-holes. Available in Black, Brown, Heritage Cherry Sunburst, Red Brown Mahogany, and Translucent Blue finishes. Current mfr.

Mfr.'s Sug. Retail	$569	$400	$275	$195

Spider Resophonic (Model EFSP) — similar to Biscuit Resophonic, except has square neck, 2 mesh-covered soundholes, slotted headstock. Current mfr.

Mfr.'s Sug. Retail	$569	$400	$275	$195

C (Classical) Series

C-10 (Model EC15) — Available in Natural Satin finish. Mfr. 1997 to date.

Mfr.'s Sug. Retail	$229	$175	$100	$70

Add $10 for Natural gloss finish.

C-25 (Model EC25) — classical style. Available in Natural Satin finish. Current mfr.

Mfr.'s Sug. Retail	$269	$200	$135	$95

C-40 (Model EC40) — classical style. Available in Natural gloss finish. Current mfr.

Mfr.'s Sug. Retail	$299	$210	$150	$100

CLASSIC — spruce top, mahogany back/sides, tortoise body binding. Mfd. 1963 to 1970.

		$275	$175

CONCERT (CLASSICAL) — maple back/sides, mutiple-body bindings, bound rosewood fingerboard (extends over soundhole), rosewood bridge, slotted peghead, gold hardware. Available in Natural finish. Mfd. 1938 to 1941.

16 1/2" body width.

		$1,400	$925

DON EVERLY SQ-180 (Model EAQ1) — star fingerboard inlay, soundhole-surrounding pickguard. Available in Ebony finish. Current mfr.

Mfr.'s Sug. Retail	$519	$375	$250	$175

DOVE (Model EADV) — double parallelogram fingerboard inlay, dove artwork on tortoiseshell pickguard, moustache-style bridge with wing inlay, bound fingerboard. Available in Cherry and Natural finish. Mfr. 1998 to date.

Mfr.'s Sug. Retail	$549			

This model is based on Gibson's Dove acoustic guitar.

EJ-200 (Model EAJ2) — jumbo style, spruce top, round soundhole, tortoise pickguard with engraved flowers/pearl dot inlay, 3 stripe bound body/rosette, maple back/sides/neck, 14/20 fret bound pointed fingerboard with pearl crown inlay, rosewood mustache bridge with pearl block inlay, white black dot bridge pins, bound blackface peghead with pearl crown/logo inlay, 3 per side gold tuners. Available in Ebony, Natural and Vintage Sunburst finishes. Current mfr.

Mfr.'s Sug. Retail	$799	$600	$400	$275

EJ-212 — similar to the EJ-200, except has 12-string configuration, 6 per side tuners. Available in Black, Natural, and Vintage Sunburst finishes. Current mfr.

Mfr.'s Sug. Retail	$819	$625	$425	$275

ELVIS PRESLEY EJ-200 (Model EAEP) — similar to the EJ-200, except has special fingerboard inlay, yellow "Elvis" graphic on lower bout, special graphic pickguard. Available in Black finish. Current mfr.

Mfr.'s Sug. Retail	$799	$575	$375	$275

Elvis Presley EJ-200 CE (Model EEEP) — similar to the Elvis Presley EJ-200, except features single rounded cutaway, piezo bridge pickup, volume/tone controls. Available in Black finish. Current mfr.

Mfr.'s Sug. Retail	$999	$695	$450	$325

EL DORADO — squared shoulder dreadnought, spruce top, mahogany back and sides, multiple body binding, bound fingerboard with single parallelogram inlay, oval headstock inlay. Available in Natural finish. Mfd. 1963 to 1970.

		$1,000	$750

EO-1 — rounded cutaway, spruce top, round soundhole, 3 stripe bound body/rosette, mahogany back/sides/neck, 21 fret bound rosewood fingerboard with pearl dot inlay, rosewood bridge with white black dot pins, rosewood veneer on bound peghead with star/crescent inlay, 3 per side chrome tuners. Available in Natural finish. Mfd. 1992 to date.

		$325	$200

Last Mfr.'s Sug. Retail was $630.

ESPANA (CLASSICAL) — maple back/sides, black bound body. Available in Walnut finish. Mfd. 1962 to 1969.

		$350	$250

EXCELLENTE — squared shoulder dreadnought style, spruce top, rosewood back/sides, multiple body binding, round soundhole, bound ebony fingerboard with cloud inlay, pearl and abalone peghead inlay, eagle inlay on pickguard, tunomatic bridge, gold hardware. Available in Natural finish. Mfd. 1963 to 1970.

		$5,300	$3,500

Excellente (Model EAEX) — Contemporary re-issue. Available in Natural and Vintage Sunburst finishes. Current mfr.

Mfr.'s Sug. Retail	$1,499	$1,050	$695	$475

Grading	100%	EXCELLENT	AVERAGE

FOLKSTER — 14 1/4" body width, spruce top, mahogany back/sides, rosewood fingerboard with dot inlay, 2 white pickguards. Mfd. 1966 to 1970.

$375 $225

FT Series

Between 1980 to 1982, Epiphone offered a number of additional FT Series models. The **FT-120** (retail list $170) was offered in a Natural finish, while the **FT-130** (list $190) was featured in Brown Sunburst. All other models were available in a Natural finish. The **FT-140** had a retail list price of $200; the **FT-145**, list $220; **FT-150**, list $270; **FT-160**, list $250; **FT-165**, list $300. The **FT-165** was produced between 1980 to 1981.

Most secondary prices on these early 1980s FT Series models range between $95 to $125.

FT DE LUXE — spruce top, maple back/sides, round soundhole, multiple body binding, maple neck, bound rosewood fingerboard with cloud inlay, tortoise pickguard, trapeze tailpiece, vine peghead inlay, gold hardware. Available in Natural and Sunburst finishes. Mfd. 1939 to 1942.

16 1/2" body width.

$3,000 $1,650

This model is similar to the De Luxe Archtop, except in a flat-top configuration.

De Luxe Cutaway — similar to the FT De Luxe, except features a single rounded cutaway body, flower peghead inlay. Mfd. 1954 to 1957.

17 3/8" body width.

$3,500 $1,800

FT 27 — spruce top, mahogany back/sides, bound top, 14/20 fret rosewood fingerboard with dot inlay, Masterbilt peghead decal, rosewood bridge. Available in Sunburst finish. Mfd. 1935 to 1941.

14 1/2" body width.

$550 $375

FT 30 (CABALLERO) — OO style, mahogany top, round soundhole, tortoise pickguard, mahogany back/sides/neck, 14/20 fret rosewood fingerboard with pearl dot inlay, rosewood bridge with white pins, 3 per side tuners with plastic buttons. Available in Natural finish. Mfd. 1941 to 1949.

14 1/2" body width.

1941-1949 $700 $400

The FT 30 was renamed the Caballero by Gibson in 1958. Mfd. 1958 to 1970.

1958-1970 $375 $295

In 1958, tortoise pickguard with logo was introduced.

In 1961, non logo pickguard replaced original item.

In 1963, adjustable saddle replaced original item.

FT 37 — spruce top, quartered walnut back/sides, cherry neck, 20 fret rosewood fingerboard with dot inlay, tortoiseshell pickguard, rosewood bridge, 3 per side tuners with plastic buttons. Available in Yellow Sunburst top and Natural finishes. Mfd. 1935 to 1941.

15 1/2" body width.

$800 $525

FT 45 (CORTEZ) — OO style, spruce top, round soundhole, tortoise pickguard, white body binding, walnut back/sides, cherry neck, 20 fret rosewood fingerboard with pearl dot inlay, rosewood bridge with white pins, metal logo plate mounted on peghead, 3 per side tuners. Available in Natural and Sunburst finishes. Mfd. 1941 to 1949.

14 1/2" body width.

1941-1949 $800 $500

The FT 45 was renamed the Cortez by Gibson in 1958. Mfd. 1958 to 1970.

1956-1970 $550 $400

In 1962, Natural finish with adjustable bridge became optionally available.

FT 50 — OO style, spruce top, round soundhole, mahogany back/sides, tortoiseshell body binding, cherry neck, tortoise pickguard, 14/20 fret bound rosewood fingerboard with dot inlay, rosewood bridge, 3 per side tuners with plastic buttons. Available in Natural finish. Mfd. 1941 to 1949.

14 1/2" body width.

$900 $550

FT 75 — spruce top, curly maple back/sides, multiple body binding, mahogany neck, 20 fret bound rosewood fingerboard with parallelogram inlay, rosewood bridge, 3 per side open back tuners. Available in Cherry Burst, Natural, and Sunburst finishes. Mfd. 1935 to 1942.

16 1/2" body width.

$1,400 $825

FT 79 (TEXAN) — dreadnought style, spruce top, walnut back/sides, cherry neck, 20 fret bound rosewood fingerboard with parallelogram inlay, rosewood bridge, 3 per side open back tuners. Available in Natural and Sunburst finish. Mfd. 1941 to 1957.

16 1/2" body width.

$1,200 $695

In 1949, a new jumbo body style was introduced.

In 1954, curly maple back/sides replaced original item.

Epiphone FT-130
courtesy Bob Dobyne

E

Grading	100%	EXCELLENT	AVERAGE

The FT 79 was renamed the Texan by Gibson in 1958. Mfd. 1958 to 1970.

| | | $800 | $500 |

Texan (Model EATX) — contemporary model. Available in Natural and Vintage Sunburst finishes. Current mfr.
Mfr.'s Sug. Retail $899 $625 $425 $295

FT 110 (FRONTIER) — dreadnought style, spruce top, curly maple back/sides, 5-piece cherry neck, 20 fret bound rosewood fingerboard with slotted block inlay, rosewood bridge, 3 per side open back tuners. Available in Natural and Sunburst finish. Mfd. 1941 to 1957.

16 1/2" body width.

| | | $1,800 | $950 |

In 1949, a new jumbo body style was introduced.

The FT 110 was renamed the Frontier by Gibson in 1958. Mfd. 1958 to 1970.

| | | $1,000 | $675 |

Frontier (Model EAFT) — contemporary re-issue. Available in Natural and Vintage Sunburst finishes.
Mfr.'s Sug. Retail $999 $695 $450 $325

Frontier Left-Handed (Model EAFTL) — similar to Frontier, except in left-handed configuration. Available in Natural and Vintage Sunburst finishes. Mfr. 1997 to 1998.

| | | $675 | $400 |

Last Mfr.'s Sug. Retail was $1,269.

FT 140 (Korea Mfr.) — spruce top, mahogany back/sides, bolt-on neck, zero fret, 20 fret rosewood fingerboard with pearl dot inlay, black pickguard, rosewood bridge with black buttons, 3 per side chrome tuners. Available in Natural finish. Mfd. 1973 to 1976.

| | | $175 | $100 |

Last Mfr.'s Sug. Retail was $145.

HUMMINGBIRD (Model EAHB) — dreadnought style, bound body, double parallelogram block inlays, flowers/hummingbird artwork on tortoiseshell pickguard, 3 per side chrome vintage-style tuners. Available in Heritage Cherry Sunburst finishes. Current mfr.
Mfr.'s Sug. Retail $599 $425 $275 $175

This model is based on Gibson's Hummingbird acoustic guitar.

MADRID (Mfr. 1931 to 1941) — spruce top, curly maple back/sides, tortoise body binding, 12/19 fret fingerboard. Available in Natural finish. Mfd. 1931 to 1941.
1931-1935

| | | $2,200 | $1,250 |

This model was originally introduced as an f-hole guitar, Hawaiian (or Spanish) style.

In 1936, the Madrid was re-designated as a Jumbo size, 16 1/2" body width, round soundhole, Hawaiian style only.
1936-1941

| | | $2,000 | $950 |

Madrid (Mfr. 1962 to 1970) — classical style, mahogany back/sides, tortoise body binding. Available in Natural finish. Mfd. 1962 to 1970.

| | | $350 | $225 |

NAVARRE — Hawaiian style, spruce top, mahogany back/sides/neck, round soundhole, 20 fret bound rosewood fingerboard with dot inlay, tortoiseshell pickguard, rosewood bridge, 3 per side tuners with plastic buttons. Available in Brown finish. Mfd. 1931 to 1941.

16 1/2" body width.

| | | $1,500 | $950 |

PR Series

PR-100 (Model EA10) — dreadnought style, spruce top, round soundhole, black pickguard, stripe rosette, mahogany back/sides/neck, 14/20 fret rosewood fingerboard with dot inlay, rosewood bridge with black pins, 3 per side chrome tuners. Available in Ebony, Natural Gloss, and Vintage Sunburst finishes. Mfr. 1997 to date.
Mfr.'s Sug. Retail $249 $175 $115 $80

PR-200 (Model EA20) — dreadnought style, spruce top, round soundhole, black pickguard, stripe rosette, bound body, mahogany back/sides/neck, 14/20 fret rosewood fingerboard with pearl dot inlay, rosewood bridge with white pins, 3 per side chrome tuners. Available in Natural Satin finish. Mfr. 1992 to date.
Mfr.'s Sug. Retail $309 $225 $150 $100

In 1998, Ebony, Natural Gloss, and Vintage Sunburst finishes were introduced (previously a $15 option).

PR-350 (Model EA35) — dreadnought style, spruce top, round soundhole, tortoise pickguard with stylized *E*, 3 stripe bound body/rosette, mahogany back/sides/neck, 14/20 fret rosewood fingerboard with pearl snowflake inlay, pearl crown/logo inlay, 3 per side chrome tuners. Available in Natural finish. Mfr. 1992 to date.
Mfr.'s Sug. Retail $369 $275 $175 $125

In 1998, Ebony and Vintage Sunburst finishes were introduced (previously a $10 option).

PR-350 C (Model EA3C) — similar to the PR-350, except features a single rounded cutaway body. Available in Natural finish. Current mfr.
Mfr.'s Sug. Retail $409 $300 $200 $150

In 1998, Ebony and Vintage Sunburst finishes were introduced (previously a $10 option).

PR-350 M (Model EM35) — similar to PR-350, except has mahogany top. Mfd. 1993 to 1998.

| | | $200 | $125 |

Last Mfr.'s Sug. Retail was $379.

PR-200
courtesy The Epiphone Company

Grading	100%	EXCELLENT	AVERAGE

PR-350 S (Model EAOS) — similar to PR-350, except has spruce top. Mfr. 1992 to date

Mfr.'s Sug. Retail	$409	$300	$200	$150

In 1998, Ebony and Vintage Sunburst finishes were introduced (previously a $10 option).

PR-350 S Left-Handed (Model EAOL) — similar to the PR-350 S, except in left-handed configuration. Available in Natural finish. Current mfr.

Mfr.'s Sug. Retail	$434	$325	$225	$150

PR-350-12 (Model EA3T) — similar to the PR-350 S, except has 12-string configuration. Available in Natural finish. Current mfr.

Mfr.'s Sug. Retail	$399	$300	$200	$135

PR-400 (Model EA40) — Available in Natural finish. Mfr. 1997 to date.

Mfr.'s Sug. Retail	$459	$325	$225	$150

PR-720 S — dreadnought style, solid spruce top, round soundhole, tortoiseshell pickguard, 3 stripe rosette, bound body, African ovankol back/sides, mahogany neck, 14/20 fret rosewood fingerboard with pearl diamond inlay, rosewood bridge with white pins, 3 per side chrome tuners. Available in Natural finish. Mfd. 1992 only.

		$225	$135

PR-775 S — dreadnought style, solid spruce top, round soundhole, tortoiseshell pickguard, abalone bound body/rosette, rosewood back/sides, mahogany neck, 14/20 fret bound rosewood fingerboard with abalone pearl block/triangle inlay, rosewood bridge with white black dot pins, rosewood veneer on bound peghead with crescent/star/logo inlay, 3 per side chrome tuners. Available in Natural finish. Disc. 1996.

		$250	$175

Last Mfr.'s Sug. Retail was $500.

PR-775-12 — similar to the PR-775 S, except in 12-string configuration.

		$250	$175

Last Mfr.'s Sug. Retail was $500.

PR-800 S (Model EA80) — Available in Natural finish. Disc. 1998.

		$325	$200

Last Mfr.'s Sug. Retail was $619.

SERENADER — 12-string configuration, 14 1/4" body width, mahogany back/sides, 25 1/2" scale, adjustable saddle, dot fingerboard inlay. Available in Walnut finish. Mfd. 1963 to 1970.

		$700	$400

SEVILLE (Mfr. 1938 to 1941) — classical style, spruce top, round soundhole, mahogany back/sides, mahogany neck, 12/20 fret rosewood extended fingerboard, rosewood bridge, slotted headstock. Available in Natural finish. Mfd. 1938 to 1941.

14 3/8" body width.

		$500	$325

Seville (Mfr. 1961 to 1970) — classical style, mahogany back/sides, 25 1/2" scale, tortoise body binding. Available in Natural finish. Mfd. 1961 to 1970.

14 1/4" body width.

		$350	$250

The Seville model was offered with a ceramic pickup between 1961 to 1964 as the Seville Electric.

SONGWRITER (Model EABM) (Formerly BLUESMASTER) — slope shouldered folk style, bound body. Available in Ebony, Natural, and Vintage Sunburst finishes. Current mfr.

Mfr.'s Sug. Retail	$679	$475	$300	$225

TROUBADOUR — squared shoulder dreadnought style, spruce top, maple back/sides, multiple body binding, 12/19 fret rosewood fingerboard with slotted block inlay, 2 white pickguards, solid peghead, gold hardware. Available in Walnut finish. Mfd. 1963 to 1970.

		$400	$275

ACOUSTIC ELECTRIC

AJ (Advanced Jumbo) Acoustic Electric Series

AJ-15 E (Model EEA1) — sloped shoulder jumbo style, solid Sitka spruce top, round soundhole, black pickguard, bound body, stripe rosette, mahogany back/sides/neck, 14/20 fret fingerboard with pearl dot inlay, rosewood bridge with black bridgepins, 3 per side chrome tuners, piezo pickup, Electar preamp system. Available in Ebony, Natural and Vintage Sunburst finishes. Mfr. 1998 to date.

Mfr.'s Sug. Retail	$329

AJ-18S CE (Model EEA2) — similar to AJ-15 E, except has single rounded cutaway body, no pickguard, diamond fingerboard inlay/block inlay at 12th fret, gold hardware, piezo pickup, Electar Epiphone 6 preamp system. Available in Ebony, Natural, and Vintage Sunburst finishes. Mfr. 1998 to date.

Mfr.'s Sug. Retail	$549

AJ-30 CE (Model EEA3) — similar to AJ-15 E, except has single rounded cutaway body, dot fingerboard inlay/block inlay at 12th fret, piezo pickup, Electar Epiphone 6 preamp system. Available in Ebony, Natural, and Vintage Sunburst finishes. Mfr. 1998 to date.

Mfr.'s Sug. Retail	$679

E

Grading	100%	EXCELLENT	AVERAGE

C-70 CE
courtesy The Epiphone Company

AJ-40 TLC (Model EE4C) — similar to AJ-15 E, except has single rounded cutaway body, no pickguard, bound body, dot fingerboard inlay/block inlay at 12th fret, gold hardware, piezo pickup, Electar Epiphonic 2000 preamp system. Available in Ebony, Natural, and Vintage Sunburst finishes. Mfr. 1998 to date.

Mfr.'s Sug. Retail	$699		

AJ-45S E (Model EEA8) — similar to AJ-15 E, except has 24.75" scale, bound body, blackface headstock with screened logo, tortoiseshell pickguard, 3 per side vintage-style tuners, piezo pickup, Electar Epiphone 6 preamp system. Available in Vintage Sunburst finish. Mfr. 1998 to date.

Mfr.'s Sug. Retail	$779		

The AJ-45S is based on Gibson's J-45 model.

C-70 CE (Model EOC7) — classic style, single rounded cutaway body, spruce top, round soundhole, bound body, wooden inlay rosette, rosewood back/sides, mahogany neck, 19 fret rosewood fingerboard, rosewood tied bridge, rosewood peghead veneer with circles/star design, 3 per side chrome tuners with pearl buttons, piezo pickup, volume/3 band EQ. Available in Natural finish. Current mfr.

Mfr.'s Sug. Retail	$649	$475	$325	$225

Selena C-70 CE (Model EESE) — similar to the C-70 CE, except features Selena signature graphic on body. Available in Black finish. Mfr. 1997 only.

		$475	$295

Last Mfr.'s Sug. Retail was $899.

CABALLERO (Model EECB) — contemporary re-issue. Available in Natural finish. Mfr. 1997 to date.

Mfr.'s Sug. Retail	$1,299	$900	$600	$425

Epiphone Chet Atkins Series

CHET ATKINS SST STANDARD (Model ECSS) — semi-solid thinline acoustic. Available in Ebony, Heritage Cherry Sunburst, and Natural finishes. Current mfr.

Mfr.'s Sug. Retail	$599	$425	$250	$175

Chet Atkins CEC (Model ECCE) — Available in Antique Natural finish. Mfr. 1995 to date.

Mfr.'s Sug. Retail	$599	$425	$250	$175

Chet Atkins Custom (Model ECSF) — Available in Heritage Cherry Sunburst and Natural Finishes. Current mfr.

		$375	$225

Last Mfr.'s Sug. Retail was $699.

Chet Atkins Deluxe (Model ECBE) — Available in Heritage Cherry Sunburst and Natural finishes. Current mfr.

		$400	$250

Last Mfr.'s Sug. Retail was $749.

DOVE A/E (Model EEDV) — double parallelogram fingerboard inlay, dove artwork on tortoiseshell pickguard, moustache-style bridge with wing inlay, bound fingerboard, piezo pickup, Electar preamp system. Available in Cherry and Natural finish. Mfr. 1998 to date.

Mfr.'s Sug. Retail	$679		

This model is based on Gibson's Dove acoustic guitar.

JOHN LENNON EJ-160 E (Model EEEJ) — dreadnought style, bound body/fingerboard, trapezoid fingerboard inlay, built-in pickup, volume/tone controls (on top), tortoiseshell pickguard, screened 'John Lennon' signature on body. Available in Natural and Vintage Cherry Sunburst finishes. Mfr. 1997 to date.

Mfr.'s Sug. Retail	$1,149	$800	$525	$375

In 1998, Natural finish was discontinued.

EJ-200 CE (Model EEJ2) — similar to the EJ-200 (Model EAJ2), except features piezo bridge pickup, volume/tone controls. Available in Black, Natural, and Vintage Sunburst finishes. Current mfr.

Mfr.'s Sug. Retail	$909	$625	$450	$325

EO-2 (Model EO2E) — rounded cutaway folk style, arched walnut top, oval soundhole, 3 stripe bound body/rosette, walnut back/sides, mahogany neck, 21 fret bound rosewood fingerboard with pearl dot inlay, rosewood bridge with white black dot pins, rosewood veneer on bound peghead with star/crescent inlay, 3 per side chrome tuners, piezo pickup, volume/tone controls. Available in Natural finish. Mfd. 1992 to date.

		$425	$250

Last Mfr.'s Sug. Retail was $799.

This model has a wooden butterfly inlay between the soundhole and bridge.

JEFF "SKUNK" BAXTER (Model EAJB) — Available in Ebony, Red Brown Mahogany, Natural, and Vintage Sunburst. Current mfr.

Mfr.'s Sug. Retail	$819	$575	$375	$275

PR-5 E (Model EEP5) — single sharp cutaway folk style, figured maple top, round soundhole, multi-bound body/rosette, mahogany back/sides/neck, 20 fret bound rosewood fingerboard with pearl diamond slot inlay, rosewood bridge with white black dot pins, blackface peghead with pearl crown/logo inlay, 3 per side gold tuners, piezo bridge pickup, 4 band EQ. Available in Black, Natural, and Vintage Sunburst finishes. Mfd. 1992 to date.

Mfr.'s Sug. Retail	$699	$495	$325	$225

PR-5 E Artist (Model EEA5) — Available in Heritage Cherry Sunburst, Vintage Sunburst, and White finishes. Current mfr.

Mfr.'s Sug. Retail	$799	$575	$375	$250

PR-5 E Left-Handed (Model EEP5L) — similar to the PR-5 E, except in a left-handed configuration. Available in Natural finish. Current mfr.

Mfr.'s Sug. Retail	$724	$500	$325	$225

Grading		100%	EXCELLENT	AVERAGE

PR-6 E (Model EEP6) — Available in Heritage Cherry Sunburst, Translucent Amber, Translucent Red, and Tobacco Sunburst finish. Disc. 1998.

			$400	$250

Last Mfr.'s Sug. Retail was $769.

PR-7 E (Model EEP7) — Available in Heritage Cherry Sunburst, Natural, Orange Sunburst, Translucent Black, and Vintage Cherry Sunburst. Current mfr.

Mfr.'s Sug. Retail	$749	$525	$350	$250

PR-200 E (Model EE20) — dreadnought style, spruce top, round soundhole, tortoise pickguard with stylized *E*, 3 stripe bound body/rosette, mahogany back/sides/neck, 14/20 fret rosewood fingerboard with pearl snowflake inlay, pearl crown/logo inlay, 3 per side chrome tuners. Available in Natural finish. Mfd. 1992 to date.

Mfr.'s Sug. Retail	$379	$275	$175	$125

PR-350 E (Model EE35) — Available in Natural finish. Disc. 1998.

			$250	$165

Last Mfr.'s Sug. Retail was $459.

Add $10 for Ebony and Vintage Sunburst finishes.

PR-350 12 String E (Model EE3T) — similar to PR-350 E, except features 12-string configuration. Available in Natural finish. Disc. 1998.

			$275	$195

Last Mfr.'s Sug. Retail was $529.

PR-350 C E (Model EE3C) — similar to PR-350 E, except features a single rounded cutaway body. Available in Natural finish. Current mfr.

Mfr.'s Sug. Retail	$499	$350	$250	$175

In 1998, Ebony and Vintage Sunburst finishes were introduced (previously a $10 option).

PR-350 M E (Model EME5) — similar to PR-350 E, except has mahogany top, piezo bridge pickup. Mfd. 1993 to 1998.

			$275	$165

Last Mfr.'s Sug. Retail was $499.

PR-775 SC E (Model EO77) — single rounded cutaway body, gold hardware, Electar preamp system. Available in Antique Natural finish. Mfr. 1997 to date.

Mfr.'s Sug. Retail	$799	$575	$375	$250

PR-800 S E (Model EE80) — dreadnought style, gold hardware, Electar preamp system. Available in Natural finish. Current mfr.

Mfr.'s Sug. Retail	$719	$525	$350	$250

ACOUSTIC ELECTRIC BASS

EL CAPITAN (Model EBEC) — jumbo style, maple body, set-in maple neck, 34" scale, rosewood fingerboard with dot inlay, piezo bridge pickup, Para-EQ preamp system. Available in Ebony, Natural, and Vintage Sunburst finishes. Current mfr.

Mfr.'s Sug. Retail	$949	$675	$450	$325

El Capitan Cutaway (Model EBC4) — similar to El Capitan, except features a single rounded cutaway body. Available in Ebony, Natural, and Vintage Sunburst finishes. Current mfr.

Mfr.'s Sug. Retail	$1,029	$750	$500	$350

El Capitan Cutaway Fretless (Model EBC4F) — similar to El Capitan, except features a single rounded cutaway body, fretless fingerboard. Available in Ebony, Natural, and Vintage Sunburst finishes. Disc. 1998.

			$575	$350

Last Mfr.'s Sug. Retail was $1,099.

El Capitan 5 String Cutaway (Model EBC5) — similar to El Capitan, except features a single rounded cutaway body, 5-string configuration, 3/2 per side tuners. Available in Ebony, Natural, and Vintage Sunburst finishes. Current mfr.

Mfr.'s Sug. Retail	$1,049	$800	$550	$375

El Capitan 5 String Cutaway Fretless (Model EBC5F) — similar to the El Capitan 5 String Cutaway, except features a fretless fingerboard. Available in Ebony, Natural, and Vintage Sunburst finishes. Current mfr.

Mfr.'s Sug. Retail	$1,049	$800	$550	$375

ERNIE BALL'S EARTHWOOD

Instruments produced in San Luis Obispo, California in the early to mid 1970s.

After finding great success with prepackaged string sets and custom gauges, Ernie Ball founded the Earthwood company to produce a four string acoustic bass guitar. George Fullerton built the prototype, as well as helping with other work before moving to Leo Fender's CLF Research company in 1974. Earthwood offered both the acoustic bass guitar and a lacquer finished *solid body* guitar with large sound chambers in 1972, but production was short lived (through February 1973). In April of 1975, bass guitar operations resumed on a limited basis for a number of years.

EROS

Instruments were produced in Japan between the early 1970s through the early 1980s.

The EROS trademark is the brandname of a UK importer. These guitars were generally entry level copies of American designs.

(Source: Tony Bacon and Paul Day, The Guru's Guitar Guide)

ESPANA

Instruments produced in Asia. Distributed in the U.S. by Espana Guitars (Buegeleisen & Jacobson) of New York, New York.

Espana trademark acoustic guitars were distributed by Buegeleisen & Jacobson of New York, New York under the "Espana Guitars" company name during the early 1970s. The New York distributors Buegeleisen & Jacobson also imported in **Kent** and **Val Dez** guitars during the same time period. That's why all three "companies" shared the same address: 5 Union Square, New York (New York, 10003)!

ACOUSTIC

These Espana acoustic models have been described as having "inlay" on the fingerboards and rosettes. This inlay may vary from model to model. All guitar models are equipped with a "stress channel" style truss rod.

Classical Models

2000 — nylon string configuration, 25" scale, spruce top, round soundhole, mahogany back/sides, 18 fret rosewood fingerboard, 7-piece mahogany neck, rosewood bridge, 3 per side tuners. Available in Natural finish. Mfd. circa early 1970s.

$75 $40
Last Mfr.'s Sug. Retail was $100.

2001 (3/4 Size) — similar to the 2000, except features a 22" scale, rosewood bridge with inlay. Available in Natural finish. Mfd. circa early 1970s.

Length 35", Body Width 16 1/4", Body Thickness 3 3/4".

$75 $40
Last Mfr.'s Sug. Retail was $110.

2002 — nylon string configuration, 25" scale, spruce top, round soundhole, mahogany back/sides, marquetry on back, 18 fret rosewood fingerboard, 7-piece mahogany neck, rosewood bridge with inlay, 3 per side tuners. Available in Natural finish. Mfd. circa early 1970s.

Body Width 18 1/4", Body Thickness 4 1/4".

$80 $45
Last Mfr.'s Sug. Retail was $125.

2004 — nylon string configuration, 25 1/2" scale, spruce top, round soundhole, rosewood back/sides, 18 fret rosewood fingerboard, 7-piece mahogany neck, rosewood bridge, 3 per side tuners. Available in Natural finish. Mfd. circa early 1970s.

Body Width 18 7/8", Body Thickness 4 3/8".

$100 $70
Last Mfr.'s Sug. Retail was $165.

2006 — similar to the 2004, except has additional inlay, rosewood bridge with inlay, 3 per side gold-plated tuners. Available in Natural hand-rubbed finish. Mfd. circa early 1970s.

$125 $80
Last Mfr.'s Sug. Retail was $250.

Dreadnought Models

2100 — dreadnought style, 25" scale, spruce top, round soundhole, mahogany back/sides, 21 fret rosewood fingerboard, 7-piece mahogany neck, adjustable rosewood bridge, 3 per side tuners. Available in Natural finish. Mfd. circa early 1970s.

Length 18", Body Thickness 3 7/8".

$75 $40
Last Mfr.'s Sug. Retail was $100.

2102 — similar to the 2100. Available in Natural finish. Mfd. circa early 1970s.

Length 18 1/4", Body Thickness 4 1/4".

$75 $45
Last Mfr.'s Sug. Retail was $125.

2104 — similar to the 2100, except features round soundhole with inlay, rosewood back/sides, adjustable bridge. Available in Natural finish. Mfd. circa early 1970s.

Length 18 7/8", Body Thickness 4 3/8".

$95 $55
Last Mfr.'s Sug. Retail was $165.

2106 — dreadnought style, 25" scale, spruce top, round soundhole with inlay, rosewood back/sides, 21 fret rosewood fingerboard, 7-piece mahogany neck, adjustable rosewood bridge, 3 per side tuners. Available in Natural finish. Mfd. circa early 1970s.

Length 20", Body Thickness 4 3/8".

$100 $60
Last Mfr.'s Sug. Retail was $175.

2108 12-STRING — similar to the 2106, except has 12-string configuration, 6 per side tuners, 18 fret rosewood fingerboard, additional inlay. Available in Natural finish. Mfd. circa early 1970s.

Length 20", Body Thickness 4 3/8".

$110 $65
Last Mfr.'s Sug. Retail was $195.

Grading	100%	EXCELLENT	AVERAGE

2114 TENOR — dreadnought style, 23" scale, spruce top, round soundhole, mahogany back/sides, 20 fret rosewood fingerboard, 7-piece mahogany neck, adjustable rosewood bridge, 3 per side tuners. Available in Natural finish. Mfd. circa early 1970s.
Length 18 1/4", Body Thickness 4 1/4".

$80 $45
Last Mfr.'s Sug. Retail was $125.

ESPANOLA

Instruments are produced in Korea. Distributed by V.J. Rendano Music Company, Inc. of Youngstown, Ohio.

The wide range of Espanola acoustic guitars are designed and priced with the entry level or student guitarist in mind. Suggested new retail prices range from $200 up to $450 on the Korean-produced acoustic guitar models; $450 on the resonator-style models; $125 to $300 on four Paracho, Mexico classicals; and $350 to $550 on 4-string acoustic bass guitars.

La ESPANOLA
(GUITARRAS ESPANOLA)

Instruments currently built in Paracho (Michoacan), Mexico.

Guitarras Espanola has been hand crafting classical guitars through three generations. The guitars are built of exotic Mexican woods in the artisan tradition workshop, and feature cedar tops, mahogany or walnut sides, as well as Siricote or Palo Escrito woods.

ESTESO

Guitars were built in Spain.

The Esteso label indicated instruments built by Domingo Esteso (1882 - 1937). Originally trained at the Madrid workshop of Manuel Ramirez, Esteso later set up shop in the same town, and his instruments were widely praised.
   (Source: Tony Bacon, The Ultimate Guitar Book)

ESTEVE

Instruments currently built in Alboraya (Valencia), Spain. Distributed by Fernandez Music of Irvine, California.

Esteve guitars are built in an artisan workshop in Spain, and have solid tops as well as traditional Spanish integrated neck/body construction. There is a wide range of classical and flamenco guitars available, as well as requintos and special models (bass, contrabass, and an octave guitar).

ACOUSTIC

The workshop classical models range in price from $450 to $850, and feature Dark mahogany bodies and rosewood fingerboards up to walnut or rosewood bodies. The models that are **Hand Assembled by individual artisans** have solid rosewood bodies and ebony fingerboards; these models are priced at $1,350 to $1,550. **Deluxe Artisan models** have more exotic woods like South American rosewood and special bracings; these special models range in price from $2,550 to $5,300.

Flamenco models (with a clear tap plate) feature sycamore back and sides and double rosewood purfling (retail list $825). The **Deluxe Artisan Flamenco models** range from $1,350 (solid Mukali with ebony fingerboard) up to to $2,600 (Indian rosewood body). Wooden tuning pegs (instead of metal) are an additional $100.

EUPHANON COMPANY

See WALTER LIPTON.

EUPHONON

See LARSON BROTHERS (1900-1944).

The Euphonon brand of guitars and mandolins was made by the Larson brothers of Maurer & Co. in Chicago from the early-1930s till the demise of the company in 1944. This brand was added to the other Larson brands to accommodate the larger size guitars and mandolins the industry started producing at that time to meet the players' demand for more volume. A new style of purfling was used for this brand consisting of alternating strips of black and white woods instead of the marquetry used in the past. The top-of-the-line instruments have abalone trimmed tops.

The Larsons made Euphonon guitars in two main types: the traditional round-hole and the dreadnought. The round-hole guitar sizes range from 15" student grade to 16", 17", 19" and a very rare 21" in the better and best grades. Many of the better and all of the best grades have laminated top braces and laminated necks. Euphonons have backs and sides made of oak, maple, mahogany, or rosewood.

Some of the fret markers used on the Euphonons and the larger Prairie State guitars are the same as the ones used on the earlier Maurers and Prairie States of the smaller body sizes. The fancier trimmed instruments often have engraved pearl fret markers along with a similar inlay on each end of the bridge. The Euphonon guitars are quite rare, of very high quality, and are sought by players and collectors.

For more information regarding other Larson-made brands, see **MAURER, PRAIRIE STATE, WM. C. STAHL, W.J. DYER,** and **THE LARSON BROTHERS.**

   For more detailed information regarding all Larson brands, see The Larsons' Creations, Guitars and Mandolins, by Robert Carl Hartman, Centerstream Publishing, P.O. Box 17878, Anaheim Hills CA 92807, phone/fax (714) 779-9390.

15" Euphonon acoustic w/Stahl label
courtesy Robert Carl Hartman

KENT EVERETT

Instruments currently built in Atlanta, Georgia.

Luthier Kent Everett has been crafting guitars since 1977. Everett had 18 years experience in performing guitar repairs during his early days custom building acoustics, and now focuses directly on guitar building only.

Everett has a number of custom headstock/fingerboard inlay packages available (call for pricing and availability). All models are also offered with the following options:
Add $25 for Black or Gold Grover mini tuners.
Add $75 for purfled peghead with fine black/white line.
Add $85 for Black plastic of Tortoiseshell bound soundhole.
Add $90 for left-handed configuration.
Add $120 for aged Sitka spruce top (1960s) or Figured Sitka.
Add $250 for Venetian cutaway.

ACOUSTIC

Emerald Series

All models feature an AAA Sitka spruce top, mahogany neck, ebony peghead overlay/fingerboard/bridge, lacewood fingerboard binding and appointments, ivoroid or tortoise shell body binding, bone saddle, abalone inlays/rosette, tortoise shell (or black or clear or no) pickguard, small emerald at 12th fret, and a natural high gloss nitrocellulose finish. The following four models are offered in two different wood packages: **Mahogany** back and sides, or **Rosewood** back and sides. Prices include an arched top hardshell case.

A.C. — extra large body, tight waist. Current mfr.

Mahogany
Mfr.'s Sug. Retail	$2,247

Rosewood
Mfr.'s Sug. Retail	$2,328

L — small body, Grand Concert shape. Current mfr.

Mahogany
Mfr.'s Sug. Retail	$2,247

Rosewood
Mfr.'s Sug. Retail	$2,328

This model has either a 24 3/4" scale or 25 2/5" scale lengths available.

N — dreadnought size, larger soundhole. Current mfr.

Mahogany
Mfr.'s Sug. Retail	$2,247

Rosewood
Mfr.'s Sug. Retail	$2,328

P — medium body, slightly smaller than a dreadnought. Current mfr.

Mahogany
Mfr.'s Sug. Retail	$2,247

Rosewood
Mfr.'s Sug. Retail	$2,328

Elite Series

In 1996, Everett began offering three new high end guitar *packages*. These premium **Elan Instruments** feature wood bindings, select shell inlays, ebony bound soundholes, and AAA-plus quality woods.

ELITE — figured sitka top, ebony or ziricote with multiple black/white body binding, lacewood bound fingerboard extension, mother of pearl logo, 14kt gold line peghead trim, gold plated Waverly or Schaller (with ebony) tuners, special decorative inlay options, copper/white side position markers, paua shell rosette. Mfr. 1996 to date.

Rosewood
Mfr.'s Sug. Retail	$3,400

Sierra Series

SIERRA — figured sitka top, vermillion with black/white body binding, lacewood bound fingerboard extension, mother of pearl logo, black or gold Grover mini-tuners with ebony buttons, silver/white side position markers, lacewood or koa rosette. Mfr. 1996 to date.

Mahogany
Mfr.'s Sug. Retail	$2,800

Rosewood
Mfr.'s Sug. Retail	$2,870

Everett Model L
courtesy Kent Everett

Silver Series

SILVER — figured sitka top, vermillion with black/white body binding, lacewood or ziricote bound square fingerboard end, mother of pearl logo, sterling silver line peghead trim, nickel plated Waverly tuners, abalone fingerboard inlay, silver/white side position markers, paua shell rosette. Mfr. 1996 to date.

Mahogany	
Mfr.'s Sug. Retail	$2,975
Rosewood	
Mfr.'s Sug. Retail	$3,045

EVERGREEN

Instruments currently built in Cove, Oregon.

Jerry Nolte's Evergreen Mountain Instruments was started in 1972. Nolte produces about twelve guitars a year. His acoustics feature cedar or spruce tops; 3-piece mahogany necks; rosewood fingerboard and bridge; back and sides of American black walnut, maple, koa, and cherry; and hand-rubbed violin varnish. Prices start at under $1,000.

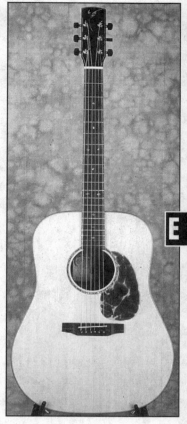

Everett Model N
courtesy Kent Everett

E

E

FAIR LADY

Instruments currently produced in China. Distributed by Kwo Hsiao Company, Ltd., of Taipei, Taiwan.

The Kwo Hsiao Company, Ltd. is currently offering a wide range of student level to intermediate grade acoustic guitar models. Models range from classical-style nylon strings, to dreadnought and jumbo style models (some with single rounded cutaways), and include models with built-in piezo bridge pickups and preamp systems. Models feature a spruce top, nato wood back and sides, rosewood fingerboard and bridge, and a solid headstock with 3 per side chrome tuners. Most intriguing is the **Model FAW-688**, with its double cutaway body design. For further information regarding the Fair Lady line of guitars, please contact the Kwo Hsiao Company, Ltd. through the Index of Current Manufacturers located in the back of this edition.

FASCINATOR

See chapter on House Brands.

This Gibson built budget line of guitars has been identified as a *House Brand* of the Tonk Bros. company of Chicago, Illinois. While built to the same standards as other Gibson guitars, they lack the one true 'Gibson' touch: an adjustable truss rod. House Brand Gibsons were available to musical instrument distributors in the late 1930s and early 1940s.

(Source: Walter Carter, Gibson Guitars: 100 Years of an American Icon)

FAVILLA

Instruments built in New York City, New York between 1890 to 1973.

In 1888, brothers John and Joseph Favilla left their home country of Italy and moved to Manhattan in New York City. Two years later, they founded **Favilla Brothers**, which later became **Favilla Guitars, Inc**. The workshop moved to Brooklyn in 1929, and later back to Manhattan.

Frank Favilla (John's elder son) began running the facility in the late 1940s. The company moved to larger facilities in Brooklyn in 1959, and in 1965 moved to a 20,000 square-foot plant out in Long Island. The larger facilities employed between fifteen and twenty workers, and the staff produced about 3,000 acoustic guitars a year. Higher production costs were one of the factors that led to the plant closing in 1973.

In 1970, Tom Favilla (third generation) began importing guitars from Japan. Japanese Favillas had the company name in script; American-built Favillas will have the family crest on the headstock.

(Source: Tom Wheeler, American Guitars)

FENDER

Instruments currently produced in Corona, California (U.S.), Mexico, Japan, Tianjin (China), and Korea. Distributed by the Fender Musical Instruments Corporation of Scottsdale, Arizona.

Trademark established circa 1948 in Fullerton, California.

Clarence Leonidas Fender was born in 1909, and raised in Fullerton, California. As a teenager he developed an interest in electronics, and soon was building and repairing radios for fellow classmates. After high school, Leo Fender held a bookkeeping position while he still did radio repair at home. After holding a series of jobs, Fender opened up a full scale radio repair shop in 1939. In addition to service work, the Fender Radio Service store soon became a general electronics retail outlet. However, the forerunner to the Fender Electric Instruments company was a smaller two-man operation that was originally started as the K & F company in 1945. Leo Fender began modestly building small amplifiers and electric lap steels with his partner, Clayton Orr *Doc* Kaufman. After K & F dissolved, Fender then formed the Fender Electric Instrument company in 1946, located on South Pomona Avenue in Fullerton, California. The company sales, though slow at first, began to expand as his amplifiers and lap steel began meeting acceptance among West Coast musicians. In 1950, Fender successfully developed the first production solid body electric guitar. Originally the Broadcaster, the name was quickly changed to the Telecaster after the Gretsch company objected to the infringement of their *Broadkaster* drum sets.

Soon Fender's inventive genius began designing new models through the early 1950s and early 1960s. The Fender *Precision* Bass guitar was unveiled in 1951. While there is some kind of an existing background for the development of an electric solid body guitar, the notion of a 34" scale instrument with a fretted neck that could replace an upright acoustic doublebass was completely new to the music industry. The Precision bass (so named because players could fret the note 'precisely') coupled with a Fender Bassman amplifier gave the bass player more sonic projection. Fender then followed with another design in 1954, the Stratocaster. The simplicity in design, added to the popular sounds and playability, makes this design the most copied world wide. Other popular models of guitars, basses, and amplifiers soon followed.

By 1964, Fender's line of products included electric guitars, basses, steel guitars, effects units, acoustic guitars, electric pianos, and a variety of accessories. Leo's faltering health was a factor in putting the company up for sale, and first offered it to Don Randall (the head of Fender Sales) for a million and a half dollars. Randall opened negotiations with the Baldwin Piano & Organ company, but when those negotiations fell through, offered it to the conglomerate CBS (who was looking to diversify the company holdings). Fender (FEIC) was purchased by CBS on January 5, 1965 (actually in December of 1964) for thirteen million dollars. Leo Fender was kept on as a *special consultant* for five years, and then left when then contract was up in 1970. Due to a ten year *no compete* clause, the next Leo Fender-designed guitars did not show up in the music industry until 1976 (Music Man).

While Fender was just another division of CBS, a number of key figures left the company. Forrest White, the production manager, left in 1967 after a dispute in producing solid state amplifiers. Don Randall left in 1969, disenchanted with corporate life. George Fullerton, one of the people involved with the Stratocaster design, left in 1970. Obviously, the quality in Fender products did not drop the day Leo Fender sold the company. Dale Hyatt, another veteran of the early Fender days, figured

Grading	100%	EXCELLENT	AVERAGE

that the quality on the products stayed relatively stable until around 1968 (Hyatt left in 1972). But a number of cost-cutting strategies, and attempts to produce more products had a deteriorating effect. This reputation leads right to the classic phrase heard at vintage guitar shows, "Pre-CBS?".

In the early 1980s, the Fender guitar empire began to crumble. Many cost-cutting factors and management problems forced CBS to try various last ditch efforts to salvage the instrument line. In March of 1982, Fender (with CBS' blessing) negotiated with Kanda Shokai and Yamano Music to establish **Fender Japan**. After discussions with Tokai (who built a great Fender Strat replica, among other nice guitars), Kawai, and others, Fender finally chose Fuji Gen Gakki (based in Matsumoto, about 130 miles northwest of Tokyo). In 1983 the **Squier** series was built in Japan, earmarked for European distribution. The Squier trademark came from a string-making company in Michigan (V.C. Squier) that CBS had acquired in 1965.

In 1984 CBS decided to sell Fender. Offers came in from IMC (Hondo, Charvel/Jackson), and the Kaman Music Corporation (Ovation). Finally, CBS sold Fender to an investment group led by William Schultz in March for twelve and a half million dollars. This investment group formally became the Fender Musical Instruments Corporation (FMIC). As the sale did not include production facilities, USA guitar production ceased for most of 1985. It has been estimated that 80% of the guitars sold between late 1984 and mid-1986 were made in Japan. Soon after, a new factory was built in Corona, California, and USA production was restored in 1986 and continues to this day.

In 1990, the Fender (FMIC) company built an assembly facility in Mexico to offset rising costs of oriental production due to the weakening of the American dollar in the international market. Fender also experimented with production based in India from 1989 to 1990. The Fender (FMIC) company currently manufactures instruments in China, Japan, Korea, Mexico, and the U.S.

As reported in the March 1998 edition of **MMR**, Fender CEO Schultz sent out a letter to Fender dealers (dated January 9, 1998) which discussed the company establishing a "limited number" of Fender mail-order catalog dealers. Fender has announced specific guidelines as to what is allowed in mail-order catalog sales. Most importantly, Fender "announced a minimum advertised price (MAP) policy applicable to mail-order catalogs only", stated Schultz, "The MAP for mail-order catalogs is set at a maximum 30 percent off the Fender suggested retail price, and will be enforced unilaterally by Fender".

What this does to the Fender retail price overall is basically lower the bar for dealers - but the impact on regular guitar stores has not been fully realized. While it's one thing to buy because of a discounted price through a catalog, it's a different situation to walk into a dealer's shop and be able to "test drive" a guitar before it is purchased. Retail music stores have to be aware that there is now an outside source (not under their control) that may dictates minimum sales prices - the national catalogs. Of course, retail shops still control the maximum sale price applied to an instrument. Readers familiar to the **Blue Book of Guitars** will note both the Manufacturer's suggest retail price and the appropriate discounted price (100% listing) under currently produced models.

(Source for earlier Fender history: Richard R. Smith, Fender: The Sound Heard 'Round the World)

PRODUCTION MODEL CODES

Current Fender instruments are identified by a *part number* that consists of a three digit location/facility code and a four digit model code (the two codes are separated by a hyphen). An example of this would be:

010 - 9200

(The 010-9200 part number is the California-built Stevie Ray Vaughn model.)

As Fender guitars are built in a number of locations worldwide, the three digit code will indicate where production took place (this does not indicate where the parts originated, however; just assembly of components). The first digit differentiates between Fender bridges and Floyd Rose tremolos:

0	**Fender Product, non-Floyd Rose**
1	**Floyd Rose Bridge**
3	**Guild Product**

The second/third digit combination designates the production location:

10	**U.S., Guitar (Corona)**
13	**Mexico, Guitar and Bass (Ensenada)**
19	**U.S., Bass (Corona)**
25	**Japan, Guitar and Bass**
27	**Japan, Guitar and Bass**
33	**Korea, Guitar and Bass**
33	**China, Guitar and Bass**
33	**Indonesia, Guitar and Bass**
50	**Guild Product, Acoustic and Electric (Rhode Island)**
94	**Spain, Acoustic Guitar (Classical)**

The four digits on the other side of the hyphen continue defining the model. The fourth/fifth digit combination is the product designation. The sixth digit defines left-handedness, or key parts inherent to that product. The final seventh digit indicates which type of wood fingerboard. Any digits that follow the second hyphen (eighth/ninth/tenth) are color descriptions (01 = Blond, 02 = Lake Placid Blue, etc.) Happy Hunting!

For further information on Fender electric models, please refer to the **5th Edition Blue Book of Electric Guitars**.

ACOUSTIC

AG Series

AG Series acoustics were discontinued in 1994, in favor of the DG Series. AG Series models were produced in Asia.

AG-10 — dreadnought style, spruce top, round soundhole, black pickguard, 5 stripe bound body/rosette, mahogany back/sides/neck, 14/20 fret rosewood fingerboard with pearl dot inlay, rosewood bridge with black white dot pins, 6 on one side chrome tuners. Available in Natural finish. Disc. 1994.

$100 $70

Last Mfr.'s Sug. Retail was $230.

Fender D'Aquisto Ultra
courtesy Scott Chinery

Grading	100%	EXCELLENT	AVERAGE

AG-15 — similar to AG-10, except has high gloss finish. Disc. 1994.

$100 $65
Last Mfr.'s Sug. Retail was $250.

AG-20 — similar to AG-10, except has rosewood back/sides. Disc. 1994.

$110 $75
Last Mfr.'s Sug. Retail was $280.

California Series

The California series was discontinued in 1994. California Series models were produced in Asia.

AVALON — folk style, spruce top, round soundhole, black pickguard, 3 stripe bound body/rosette, mahogany back/sides/neck, 14/20 fret bubinga fingerboard with pearl dot inlay, bubinga strings thru bridge, 6 on one side die-cast tuners. Available in Natural finish. Mfd. 1987 to 1994.

$120 $75
Last Mfr.'s Sug. Retail was $300.

CATALINA — dreadnought style, spruce top, round soundhole, black pickguard, 3 stripe bound body/rosette, mahogany back/sides/neck, 14/20 fret rosewood fingerboard with pearl dot inlay, rosewood bridge with white black dot pins, 6 on one side die-cast tuners. Available in Black finish. Mfd. 1987 to 1994.

$150 $95
Last Mfr.'s Sug. Retail was $370.

Concord — similar to Catalina, except has bubinga fingerboard/bridge. Available in Natural finish. Mfd. 1987 to 1994.

$135 $90
Last Mfr.'s Sug. Retail was $300.

LA BREA — single round cutaway dreadnought style, spruce top, round soundhole, black pickguard, 3 stripe bound body/rosette, mahogany back/sides/neck, 21 fret rosewood fingerboard with pearl dot inlay, rosewood bridge with white black dot pins, 6 on one side chrome tuners, acoustic pickup, volume/tone control. Available in Natural finish. Mfd. 1987 to 1994.

$195 $125
Last Mfr.'s Sug. Retail was $480.

Add $10 for Black finish.
Add $20 for Sunburst finish.
Add $30 for figured maple top/back/sides.

MALIBU — dreadnought style, sycamore top, round soundhole, black pickguard, sycamore back/sides, mahogany neck, 14/20 fret rosewood fingerboard with pearl dot inlay, rosewood bridge with white black dot inlay, 6 on one side die-cast tuners. Available in Dark Violin Sunburst finish. Mfd. 1987 to 1994.

$150 $95
Last Mfr.'s Sug. Retail was $385.

MONTARA — single round cutaway dreadnought style, spruce top, oval soundhole, bound body, multi-ring rosette, mahogany back/sides/neck, convex back, 21 fret rosewood fingerboard with pearl dot inlay, rosewood bridge with white pins, 6 on one side die-cast tuners with pearl buttons, acoustic pickup, volume/treble/mid/bass controls. Available in Natural finish. Mfd. 1990 to 1994.

$250 $175
Last Mfr.'s Sug. Retail was $650.

Add $10 for Black finish.
Add $20 for Sunburst finish.
Add $80 for flame maple top/back/sides/neck.

NEWPORTER — dreadnought style, mahogany top, round soundhole, black pickguard, 3 stripe bound body/rosette, mahogany back/sides/neck, 14/20 fret rosewood fingerboard with pearl dot inlay, rosewood bridge with white black dot pins, 6 on one side die-cast tuners. Available in Natural finish. Disc. 1994.

$125 $80
Last Mfr.'s Sug. Retail was $325.

Redondo — similar to the Newporter, except has spruce top. Available in Natural finish. Disc. 1994.

$150 $110
Last Mfr.'s Sug. Retail was $335.

Santa Maria — similar to the Newporter, except has spruce top, tortoise pickguard. Available in Natural finish. Mfd. 1989 to 1994.

$150 $90
Last Mfr.'s Sug. Retail was $360.

SAN LUIS REY — dreadnought style, solid spruce top, round soundhole, black pickguard, rosewood back/sides, mahogany neck, 14/20 fret rosewood fingerboard with pearl snowflake inlay, 6 on one side chrome tuners. Available in Natural finish. Mfd. 1990 to 1994.

$175 $110
Last Mfr.'s Sug. Retail was $445.

San Marino — similar to the San Luis Rey, except has 3 stripe bound body/rosette, mahogany back/sides/neck, 14/20 fret rosewood fingerboard with pearl dot inlay. Available in Natural finish. Mfd. 1989 to 1994.

$150 $95
Last Mfr.'s Sug. Retail was $370.

Grading	100%	EXCELLENT	AVERAGE

SAN MIGUEL — single round cutaway dreadnought style, spruce top, round soundhole, black pickguard, 3 stripe bound body/rosette, mahogany back/sides/neck, 14/20 fret rosewood fingerboard with pearl dot inlay, rosewood bridge with white black dot pins, 6 on one side tuners. Available in Natural finish. Disc. 1994.

	$145	$90	

Last Mfr.'s Sug. Retail was $360.

This model was optionally available in a left-handed configuration.

CG Series

The CG Series is Fender's classical guitars (with nylon strings). CG Series models were produced in Asia.

CG-5 (Model 094-0500-021) — classical style, nato top/back/sides, round soundhole, nato neck, 12/18 fret rosewood fingerboard, slotted headstock, 3 per side chrome tuners. Available in Satin finish. Mfr. 1995 to 1998.

	$75	$45	

Last Mfr.'s Sug. Retail was $155.

CG-7 (Model 094-0700-021) — similar to the CG-5, except features spruce top, meranti back/sides, 12/19 fret fingerboard. Available in Gloss finish. Mfr. 1995 to date.

Mfr.'s Sug. Retail	$179	$125	$85	$60

DG Series

The DG Series acoustics are steel-string dreadnought designs. The DG series was introduced in 1995, filling the same niche as the AG and Spring Hill series. DG Series models are produced in Asia.

Fender's **DG-3 ValuePak** (Model 095-0300-021) features a DG-3 acoustic, polish, polishing cloth, picks, strings, gig bag, and chord book. The **DG-3 ValuePak** has a retail list price of $319.

DG-3 VALUEPAK (Model 095-0300-021) — dreadnought style, spruce top, round soundhole, black pickguard, nato back/sides, 14/20 fret rosewood fingerboard with white dot inlay, 6 on one side die-cast tuners. Available in Natural finish. Mfr. 1995 to date.

Mfr.'s Sug. Retail	$319	$225	$125	$85

DG-5 (Model 095-0500-021) — dreadnought style, nato top/back/sides, round soundhole, 14/20 fret rosewood fingerboard, rosewood bridge, black plastic pickguard, 3 per side chrome tuners. Available in Satin finish. Mfr. 1995 to 1998.

	$85	$55	

Last Mfr.'s Sug. Retail was $175.

DG-7 (Model 095-0700-021) — dreadnought style, spruce top, round soundhole, meranti back/sides, 14/20 fret rosewood fingerboard, rosewood bridge, pickguard, 3 per side chrome tuners. Available in High Gloss Natural finish. Mfr. 1995 to date.

Mfr.'s Sug. Retail	$219	$150	$90	$70

DG-9 (Model 095-0900-021) — dreadnought style, select spruce top, round soundhole, mahogany back/sides, 14/20 fret rosewood fingerboard, rosewood bridge, black pickguard, 3 per side chrome tuners. Available in Satin finish. Mfr. 1997 to date.

Mfr.'s Sug. Retail	$259	$175	$100	$70

DG-10 (Model 095-1000-021) — dreadnought style, select spruce top, round soundhole, mahogany back/sides, 14/20 fret rosewood fingerboard, rosewood bridge, black pickguard, 3 per side chrome tuners. Available in Satin finish. Mfd. 1995 to 1996.

	$95	$65	

Last Mfr.'s Sug. Retail was $269.

DG-10 LH (Model 095-1020-021) — similar to the DG-10, except in a left-handed configuration. Mfr. 1995 to date.

Mfr.'s Sug. Retail	$339	$250	$140	$100

DG-10-12 (Model 095-1012-021) — similar to the DG-10, except in a 12-string configuration. Mfr. 1995 to date.

Mfr.'s Sug. Retail	$359	$250	$150	$115

DG-11 (Model 095-1100-021) — dreadnought style, spruce top, round soundhole, nato back/sides, 14/20 fret rosewood fingerboard with dot inlay, rosewood bridge, black pickguard, 3 per side chrome tuners. Available in Black (-006), Sunburst (-032), and Natural (-021) gloss finishes. Mfr. 1998 to date.

Mfr.'s Sug. Retail	$299	$210	$135	$95

DG-15 (Model 095-1500-021) — similar to the DG-10 model. Available in Jet Black (-006), Gloss Sunburst (-032), and Natural (-021) finishes. Mfd. 1995 to 1998.

	$150	$100	

Last Mfr.'s Sug. Retail was $359.

DG-16 (Model 095-1600-021) — dreadnought style, spruce top, round soundhole, mahogany back/sides, 14/20 fret rosewood fingerboard with snowflake inlay, rosewood bridge, black pickguard, 3 per side die-cast tuners. Available in Black (-006), Sunburst (-032), and Natural (-021) gloss finishes. Mfr. 1998 to date.

Mfr.'s Sug. Retail	$369	$260	$175	$125

DG-20 S (Model 095-2000-021) — dreadnought style, solid spruce top, round soundhole, mahogany back/sides, 14/20 fret rosewood fingerboard, rosewood bridge, tortoiseshell pickguard, 3 per side chrome tuners. Available in Natural Gloss finish. Mfr. 1995 to date.

Mfr.'s Sug. Retail	$449	$325	$200	$150

DG-21 S (Model 095-2100-021) — dreadnought style, solid spruce top, round soundhole, rosewood back/sides, 14/20 fret rosewood fingerboard, rosewood bridge, tortoiseshell pickguard, 3 per side gold die-cast tuners. Available in Natural Gloss finish. Mfr. 1995 to date.

Mfr.'s Sug. Retail	$499	$350	$225	$150

Grading	100%	EXCELLENT	AVERAGE

DG-22 S (Model 095-2200-021) — dreadnought style, solid spruce top, round soundhole, figured maple back/sides, 14/20 fret rosewood fingerboard, rosewood bridge, tortoiseshell pickguard, 3 per side gold die-cast tuners. Available in Cherry (-030), Natural (-021), and Sunburst (-032) Gloss finishes. Mfr. 1995 to date.

Mfr.'s Sug. Retail	$529	$375	$250	$175

DG-24 (Model 095-2400-021) — dreadnought style, wood bound mahogany top/back/sides, round soundhole, wood inlay rosette, 14/20 fret rosewood fingerboard, rosewood bridge, 3 per side chrome die-cast tuners with pearloid buttons. Available in Satin finish. Mfr. 1997 to date.

Mfr.'s Sug. Retail	$499	$350	$225	$150

DG-25 S (Model 095-2500-021) — similar to the DG-24, except has solid cedar top. Available in Satin finish. Mfr. 1997 to date.

Mfr.'s Sug. Retail	$549	$385	$250	$175

DG-31 S (Model 095-3100-021) — dreadnought style, solid Englemann spruce top, round soundhole, mahogany back/sides, 14/20 fret rosewood fingerboard, rosewood bridge, 3 per side chrome die-cast tuners. Available in Gloss finish. Mfr. 1995 to date.

Mfr.'s Sug. Retail	$549	$385	$250	$175

DG-31 S LH (Model 095-3120-021). — similar to the DG-31, except in a left-handed configuration. Available in Gloss finish. Mfr. 1995 to date.

Mfr.'s Sug. Retail	$559	$395	$250	$195

DG-31-12 (Model 095-3112-021) — similar to the DG-31, except in a 12-string configuration, spruce top, 6 per side tuners. Available in Gloss finish. Mfr. 1995 to date.

Mfr.'s Sug. Retail	$529	$375	$250	$195

DG-41 S (Model 095-4100-021) — dreadnought style, solid Englemann spruce top, round soundhole, rosewood back/sides, 14/20 fret rosewood fingerboard, rosewood bridge, tortoiseshell pickguard, 3 per side gold die-cast tuners. Available in Gloss finish. Mfd. 1995 to date.

Mfr.'s Sug. Retail	$599	$425	$275	$195

DG-41-12 (Model 095-4112-021) — similar to the DG-41, except in 12-string configuration. Available in Gloss finish. Mfr. 1995 to date.

Mfr.'s Sug. Retail	$689	$495	$325	$225

F Series

F Series instruments were produced circa late 1970s through the early 1980s, and featured a flat top/dreadnought design. Models ranged from the F-3 (retail price $149) up to the F-115 (retail price $895); the **F-200 series** ranged in price from the F-200 (retail price $300) up to the F-360S-12 12-string (retail price $535). Used market prices depend on condition and demand; regular F series models range from $50 to $150 - F-200 series models range from $125 to $200.

FC Series

FC Series instruments were produced circa late 1970s through the early 1980s, and featured a classical design, slotted headstock. Suggested list prices ranged from $165 (FC-10) up to $395 (FC-130S). Used market prices may range from $75 to $150, depending on demand and condition.

FG Series

Fender also offered a **FG-210S**, a solid spruce top dreadnought with mahogany neck/back/sides with a rosewood fingerboard/bridge from 1990 to 1994. Suggested retail price was $360.

Fender (U.S.A. Mfr.) Acoustic Models

Fender Concert Acoustic
courtesy C. W. Green

CONCERT (Mfr. 1963-1970) — dreadnought style, 15 3/8" body width, spruce top, round soundhole, maple back/sides, bound top/back, bolt-on maple neck with neckplate, 25 1/2" scale, 20 fret rosewood fingerboard with pearl dot inlays, 6 on a side chrome tuners, rosewood bridge with white bridgepins, single ply pickguard, aluminum support rod (through body). Available in Natural finish. Mfd. 1963 to 1970.

		$650	$500

In 1966, mahogany, rosewood, vermillion, or zebrawood back and sides were optionally available.

In 1968, Sunburst finish was optionally available.

KING — dreadnought style, 15 5/8" body width, spruce top, round soundhole, mahogany back/sides, multiple bound top/back, bolt-on maple neck with neckplate, 25 1/2" scale, 21 fret bound rosewood fingerboard with pearl dot inlays, 6 on a side chrome tuners, aluminum support rod (through body). Available in Natural finish. Mfd. 1963 to 1966.

		$875	$600

This model was optionally available with back and sides of Brazilian rosewood, Indian rosewood, vermillion, or zebrawood.

KINGMAN (Previously KING) — similar to the King model. Available in Natural or Sunburst finishes. Mfd. 1966 to 1971.

		$795	$550

In 1968, maple, rosewood, or vermillion back and sides were optionally available; Black, Custom Colors, and Antigua finishes were optionally available.

Shenandoah — similar to the Kingman, except features 12-string configuration, 6 per side tuners. Mfd. 1965 to 1971.

		$795	$550

In 1967, Antigua (silver to black sunburst) finish was optionally available.

In 1968, Black and Sunburst finishes were optionally available.

Wildwood Acoustic — similar to the Kingman, except features beechwood back/sides, 3-ply pickguard, block fingerboard inlay. Available in injected-dye colors (primary color of green, blue, and gold). Mfd. 1966 to 1971.

$680 $540

The Wildwood finish was the result of a seven year process in Germany where dye was injected into growing beech trees. Veneers for laminating were available after the beech trees were harvested.

MALIBU (Mfr. 1965-1971) — dreadnought style, 14 7/8" body width, spruce top, round soundhole, mahogany back/sides, mahogany neck, one-ply bound top, 25 1/2" scale, 14/20 fret rosewood fingerboard with dot inlay, rosewood bridge. Available in Black, Mahogany, and Sunburst finishes. Mfd. 1965 to 1971.

$500 $325

Villager — similar to the Malibu, except features 12-string configuration, 6 per side tuners. Mfd. 1965 to 1971.

$550 $350

In 1969, Sunburst finish was optionally available.

NEWPORTER (Mfr. 1965-1971) — dreadnought style, 14 3/8" body width, spruce top, round soundhole, mahogany back/sides, mahogany neck, one-ply bound top, 25 1/2" scale, 14/20 fret rosewood fingerboard with dot inlay, rosewood bridge. Available in Mahogany finish. Mfd. 1965 to 1971.

$500 $325

In 1968, Mahogany top, 3-ply pickguard, and Black finish was optionally available.

Redondo (Mfr. 1969-1971) — similar to the Newporter, except features a spruce top. Mfd. 1969 to 1971.

$500 $325

PALOMINO — dreadnought style, 15 3/8" body width, spruce top, round soundhole, mahogany back/sides, mahogany neck, 3-ply bound top and back, 25 1/2" scale, 14/20 fret rosewood fingerboard with dot inlay, rosewood bridge, tuners with plastic buttons. Available in Black Vermillion, Mahogany, and Sunburst finishes. Mfd. 1968 to 1971.

$500 $325

Gemini Series

The Gemini I and II were offered between 1983 to 1994 (later models only during the 1990s) and had spruce tops and Nato or mahogany back/sides. Retail list prices ranged from $265 up to $315. Used market prices range around $125 to $150.

GC Series

GC-23 S (Model 095-2300-021) — grand concert style, solid spruce top, round soundhole, mahogany back/sides, 14/20 fret rosewood fingerboard, rosewood bridge, 3 per side chrome die-cast tuners. Available in Gloss finish. Mfr. 1997 to date.

Mfr.'s Sug. Retail $429 $300 $200 $150

Springhill Series

Springhill Series models were produced in Asia.

LS-10 — dreadnought style, solid spruce top, round soundhole, tortoise pickguard, mahogany back/sides/neck, 14/20 fret bound rosewood fingerboard with pearl dot inlay, rosewood bridge with black pearl dot pins, ebony veneered peghead with pearl logo inlay, 3 per side chrome tuners. Available in Natural finish. Mfd. 1994 to 1995.

$675 $500

Last Mfr.'s Sug. Retail was $1,700.

LS-20 (Model 095-4000) — similar to LS-10, except has rosewood back/sides, ebony fingerboard/bridge, gold tuners. Mfd. 1994 to 1995.

$900 $625

Last Mfr.'s Sug. Retail was $2,075.

Add $200 for Fishman electronics and left-handed configuration**LS-20LH** (Model 095-4020-320)

This model was available in a left-handed configuration as LH-20LH (Model 095-4020-220).

LS-30 — similar to LS-10, except has figured maple back/sides, ebony fingerboard/bridge, bound peghead, gold tuners. Mfd. 1994 to 1995.

$895 $595

Last Mfr.'s Sug. Retail was $2,000.

LS-40C — single sharp cutaway dreadnought style, solid spruce top, round soundhole, tortoise pickguard, mahogany back/sides/neck, 14/20 fret bound rosewood fingerboard with pearl dot inlay, rosewood bridge with black pearl dot pins, ebony veneered peghead with pearl logo inlay, 3 per side chrome tuners. Available in Natural finish. Disc. 1994.

$850 $575

Last Mfr.'s Sug. Retail was $1,900.

LS-50C — similar to LS-40C, except has rosewood back/sides, ebony fingerboard/bridge, gold tuners. Disc. 1994.

$875 $625

Last Mfr.'s Sug. Retail was $2,100.

LS-60C — similar to LS-40C, except has figured maple back/sides, ebony fingerboard/bridge, bound peghead, gold tuners. Disc. 1994.

$875 $650

Last Mfr.'s Sug. Retail was $2,200.

Grading	100%	EXCELLENT	AVERAGE

SB Series

SB Series models were produced in Asia.

SB-15 (Model 095-4515) — jumbo style, solid spruce top, round soundhole, tortoise pickguard, mahogany back/sides/neck, 14/20 fret bound rosewood fingerboard with pearl dot inlay, rosewood bridge with black pearl dot pins, ebony veneered peghead with pearl logo inlay, 3 per side chrome tuners. Available in Natural finish. Mfd. 1994 to 1995.

	$800	$575

Last Mfr.'s Sug. Retail was $1,925.

SB-25 (Model 095-4525) — similar to SB-15, except has rosewood back/sides, ebony fingerboard/bridge, gold tuners. Mfd. 1994 to 1995.

	$850	$650

Last Mfr.'s Sug. Retail was $2,125.

SB-35 — similar to SB-15, except has figured maple back/sides, ebony fingerboard/bridge, bound peghead, gold tuners. Mfd. 1994 to 1995.

	$875	$625

Last Mfr.'s Sug. Retail was $2,100.

SB-45C — single sharp cutaway jumbo style, solid spruce top, round soundhole, tortoise pickguard, mahogany back/sides/neck, 14/20 fret bound rosewood fingerboard with pearl dot inlay, rosewood bridge with black pearl dot pins, ebony veneered peghead with pearl logo inlay, 3 per side chrome tuners. Available in Natural finish. Mfd. 1994 to 1995.

	$800	$525

Last Mfr.'s Sug. Retail was $2,000.

SB-55C — similar to SB-45C, except has rosewood back/sides, ebony fingerboard/bridge, gold tuners. Mfd. 1994 to 1995.

	$875	$650

Last Mfr.'s Sug. Retail was $2,200.

SB-65C — similar to SB-45C, except has figured maple back/sides, ebony fingerboard/bridge, bound peghead, gold tuners. Mfd. 1994 to 1995.

	$900	$695

Last Mfr.'s Sug. Retail was $2,300.

SX Series

600 SX — dreadnought style, spruce top, round soundhole, tortoise pickguard, 5 stripe bound body/rosette, nato back/sides/neck, 14/20 fret rosewood fingerboard with pearl dot inlay, rosewood bridge with white black dot pins, rosewood veneered peghead with pearl logo inlay, 3 per side chrome tuners. Available in Natural finish. Mfd. 1994 to 1995.

	$150	$90

Last Mfr.'s Sug. Retail was $405.

800 SX — similar to 600 SX, except has rosewood back/sides, gold hardware. Mfd. 1994 to 1995.

	$175	$100

Last Mfr.'s Sug. Retail was $460.

1000 SX — dreadnought style, solid spruce top, round soundhole, 3 stripe bound body/rosette, mahogany back/sides/neck, 14/20 fret rosewood fingerboard with pearl dot inlay, strings thru rosewood bridge, bound rosewood veneered peghead with pearl logo inlay, 3 per side chrome tuners. Available in Natural finish. Mfd. 1993 to 1995.

	$250	$185

Last Mfr.'s Sug. Retail was $645.

1100 SX — similar to 1000 SX, except has rosewood back/sides, ebony fingerboard/bridge, gold tuners. Mfd. 1993 to 1995.

	$275	$200

Last Mfr.'s Sug. Retail was $780.

1200 SX — dreadnought style, solid spruce top, round soundhole, 3 stripe bound body/rosette, mahogany back/sides/neck, 14/20 fret rosewood fingerboard with pearl dot inlay, strings through rosewood bridge, bound rosewood veneered peghead with pearl logo inlay, 3 per side chrome tuners. Available in Natural finish. Mfd. 1993 to 1995.

	$375	$295

Last Mfr.'s Sug. Retail was $965.

1300 SX — similar to 1200 SX, except has rosewood back/sides, ebony fingerboard with pearl snowflake inlay, ebony bridge, gold tuners. Mfd. 1993 to 1995.

	$475	$350

Last Mfr.'s Sug. Retail was $1,175.

1500 SX — jumbo style, solid spruce top, round soundhole, black pickguard, rosewood back/sides, mahogany neck, 14/20 fret rosewood fingerboard with pearl block inlay, strings through rosewood bridge, bound rosewood veneered peghead with pearl logo inlay, 3 per side gold tuners. Available in Natural finish. Mfd. 1993 to 1995.

	$375	$295

Last Mfr.'s Sug. Retail was $965.

1505 SX — similar to 1500 SX, except has sycamore back/sides. Available in Sunburst top finish. Mfd. 1993 to 1995.

	$375	$300

Last Mfr.'s Sug. Retail was $1,015.

2100 SX — single round cutaway classic style, solid cedar top, round soundhole, 5 stripe bound body, wood inlay rosette, ovankol back/sides, nato neck, 19 fret rosewood fingerboard, rosewood bridge, rosewood veneered peghead, 3 per side gold tuners with pearloid buttons. Available in Natural finish. Mfd. 1994 to 1995.

	$225	$165

Last Mfr.'s Sug. Retail was $640.

Grading	100%	EXCELLENT	AVERAGE

ACOUSTIC ELECTRIC

AG-25 — single round cutaway dreadnought style, spruce top, round soundhole, black pickguard, mahogany back/sides/neck, 20 fret rosewood fingerboard with pearl dot inlay, rosewood bridge with black white dot pins, 6 on one side chrome tuners, piezo bridge pickup, volume/tone slide control. Available in Natural finish. Disc. 1994.

	$135	$90

Last Mfr.'s Sug. Retail was $335.

CG-25 SCE (Model 094-2505-021) — classical style with cutaway design, solid cedar top, round soundhole, ovankol back/sides, nato neck, 12/19 fret rosewood fingerboard, slotted headstock, 3 per side gold tuners, piezo transducer, active EQ. Available in Gloss finish. Mfr. 1995 to date.

Mfr.'s Sug. Retail	$699	$495	$325	$225

DG Cutaway Series

DG-10 CE (Model 095-1005-021) — dreadnought style with cutaway design, spruce top, round soundhole, mahogany back/sides, 14/20 fret rosewood fingerboard, rosewood bridge, black pickguard, 3 per side chrome tuners, bridge transducer, volume/tone controls. Available in Satin finish. Mfr. 1995 to date.

Mfr.'s Sug. Retail	$429	$300	$200	$140

DG-10 CE LH (Model 095-1025-021) — similar to the DG-10 CE, except features a left-handed configuration. Mfr. 1998 to date.

Mfr.'s Sug. Retail	$439	$300	$200	$140

DG-20 CE (Model 095-2005-021) — dreadnought style with cutaway design, solid spruce top, round soundhole, mahogany back/sides, 14/20 fret rosewood fingerboard, rosewood bridge, tortoiseshell pickguard, 3 per side chrome die-cast tuners, piezo pickup, on-board preamp, volume/3 band EQ/mid-sweep controls. Available in Natural Gloss finish. Mfr. 1995 to date.

Mfr.'s Sug. Retail	$559	$395	$250	$175

DG-22 CE (Model 095-2205) — dreadnought style with cutaway design, figured maple top/back/sides, round soundhole, 14/20 fret rosewood fingerboard, rosewood bridge, tortoiseshell pickguard, 3 per side gold die-cast tuners, Fishman Matrix pickup, on-board preamp, volume/3 band EQ/mid-sweep controls. Available in Cherry (-030), Natural (-021), and Sunburst (-032) Gloss finishes. Mfd. 1995 to date.

Mfr.'s Sug. Retail	$729	$525	$325	$225

DG-31 SCE (Model 095-3105) — dreadnought style with cutaway design, solid Englemann spruce top, round soundhole, mahogany back/sides, 14/20 fret rosewood fingerboard, rosewood bridge, tortoiseshell pickguard, 3 per side chrome die-cast tuners, Fishman Acoustic Matrix pickup, on-board preamp, volume/3 band EQ/mid-sweep controls. Available in Black (-006), Cherry Sunburst (-031), and Natural (-021) Gloss finishes. Mfd. 1995 to date.

Mfr.'s Sug. Retail	$799	$560	$375	$250

DG-41 SCE (Model 095-4105-021) — dreadnought style with cutaway design, solid Englemann spruce top, round soundhole, rosewood back/sides, 14/20 fret rosewood fingerboard, rosewood bridge, tortoiseshell pickguard, 3 per side gold die-cast tuners, Fishman Acoustic Matrix Professional pickup, on-board preamp, volume/4 band EQ/phase reversal controls. Available in Gloss finish. Mfd. 1995 to date.

Mfr.'s Sug. Retail	$999	$699	$450	$325

JG Series

JG-12 CE-12 (Model 095-1217-021) — mini-jumbo style with cutaway design, spruce top, round soundhole, mahogany back/sides, 14/20 fret rosewood fingerboard, rosewood bridge, 6 per side chrome die-cast tuners, Fender piezo pickup, on-board preamp, volume/3 band EQ/mid-sweep controls. Available in Satin finish. Mfr. 1998 to date.

Mfr.'s Sug. Retail	$589	$415	$275	$195

JG-26 SCE (Model 095-2605-021) — mini-jumbo style with cutaway design, solid cedar top, round soundhole, mahogany back/sides, 14/20 fret rosewood fingerboard, rosewood bridge, 3 per side chrome die-cast tuners with pearloid buttons, Fishman Acoustic Matrix pickup, on-board preamp, volume/3 band EQ/mid-sweep controls. Available in Satin finish. Mfr. 1997 to date.

Mfr.'s Sug. Retail	$699	$490	$325	$225

SX Series

1105 SXE — dreadnought style, solid spruce top, round soundhole, 3 stripe bound body/rosette, mahogany neck, rosewood back/sides, 14/20 fret ebony fingerboard with pearl dot inlay, strings through ebony bridge, bound rosewood veneered peghead with pearl logo inlay, 3 per side gold tuners, piezo pickup, volume/treble/bass/mix controls. Available in Natural finish. Mfd. 1993 to 1995.

	$275	$200

Last Mfr.'s Sug. Retail was $880.

Grading	100%	EXCELLENT	AVERAGE

1600 SXE — jumbo style, solid spruce top, round soundhole, black pickguard, rosewood back/sides, mahogany neck, 14/20 fret rosewood fingerboard with pearl block inlay, strings through rosewood bridge, bound rosewood veneered peghead with pearl logo inlay, 3 per side gold tuners, piezo pickup, volume/treble/bass/mix controls. Available in Natural finish. Mfd. 1993 to 1995.

	$475	$325

Last Mfr.'s Sug. Retail was $1,065.

Telecoustic Series

TELECOUSTIC STANDARD — single round cutaway style, spruce top, oval soundhole, basswood back/sides, maple neck, 22 fret rosewood fingerboard, rosewood bridge with white pins, 6 on one side chrome tuners with plastic buttons, piezo bridge pickup, volume/treble/bass slide controls. Available in Antique Burst, Black, and Natural finishes. Mfd. 1993 to 1995.

	$525	$350

Last Mfr.'s Sug. Retail was $960.

Telecoustic Custom — similar to Telecoustic Standard, except has bound solid spruce top, mahogany back/sides/neck, pau ferro fingerboard, pau ferro/ebony laminate bridge, Schaller tuners with pearl buttons, active electronics. Available in Antique Burst and Natural finishes. Mfd. 1993 to 1995.

$550

	$1,150	$725

Last Mfr.'s Sug. Retail was $2,150.

Telecoustic Deluxe — similar to Telecoustic Standard, except has mahogany back/sides/neck, rosewood/ebony laminate bridge, pearl tuner buttons. Mfd. 1993 to 1995.

$295

	$625	$425

Last Mfr.'s Sug. Retail was $1,160.

ACOUSTIC ELECTRIC BASS

BG-29 BLACK (Model 095-2900-306) — slimline dreadnought style with cutaway design, maple top, round soundhole, maple back/sides, 14/20 fret rosewood fingerboard, rosewood bridge, 2 per side chrome die-cast tuners, Fishman Acoustic Matrix pickup, on-board preamp, volume/3 band EQ/mid-sweep controls. Available in Black Gloss finish. Mfd. 1995 to date.

Mfr.'s Sug. Retail	$869	$610	$400	$275

List price includes gig bag.

BG-29 Natural (Model 095-2900-321) — similar to the BG-29 Black, except has spruce top, mahogany back/sides. Available in Natural Satin finish. Mfr. 1997 to date.

Mfr.'s Sug. Retail	$809	$570	$375	$250

FERNANDES

Instruments produced in Tokyo, Japan since 1969. Distributed in the U.S. by Fernandes Guitars U.S.A. Inc., of Van Nuys, California.

In 1969, Fernandes Company Ltd. (based in Tokyo, Japan) was established to produce quality classical guitars at an affordable price. Over the next twenty years, Fernandes expanded the line and became one of the largest selling guitar manufacturers in the world. Fernandes is the number one selling guitar in Japan, and at times has held as much as 40% of the Japanese market.

In late 1992, Fernandes Company Ltd. began distributing their entire line of guitars to the U.S. market as Fernandes Guitars U.S.A., Inc. Fernandes Company Ltd. uses only the top facilities located in Japan, Taiwan, China, and Korea to produce their guitars. Once the factory is done manufacturing the guitars, they are shipped to the United States where they are inspected and set up again.

In 1998, Fernandes renamed their instruments. For example, the eye-catching **H-80** art-deco-style guitar model became the **Vertigo Deluxe**. In addition to their **RetroRocket** and **Retrospect** series, Fernandes is concentrating on the newer additions to their line like the **P-Project**, **Native**, **Dragonfly**, and **Lexington** series. Fernandes also offers five different models of practice amps (15 to 20 watts) for guitars and basses.

(Company history courtesy Bryan Wresinski, Fernandes Guitars U.S.A.)

ACOUSTIC ELECTRIC

FAA-400 ACOUSTIC/ELECTRIC — single rounded cutaway body, spruce top, molded back, set-in nato neck, 25 1/4" scale, multi-layer binding, 22 fret rosewood fingerboard, rosewood bridge, chrome hardware, 3 per side tuners, bridge mounted piezo pickup, active pre-amp/3 band EQ. Available in Natural finish. Disc. 1998.

	$295	$175

Last Mfr.'s Sug. Retail was $519.

Reyna (Formerly FAA-500) — similar to the FAA-400, except features a bound flame maple top, bound neck, active preamp with volume/bass/mid/treble slider controls. Available in 3-Tone Sunburst, Black Burst, Cherry Sunburst, and Natural finishes. Current mfr.

Mfr.'s Sug. Retail	$549	$425	$275	$175

Early versions of the FAA-500 were also available in Antique Sunburst and Greyburst finishes.

DANNY FERRINGTON

Instruments built in Santa Monica, California since 1980.

Flanders Archtop
courtesy Martin Flanders

Luthier Danny Ferrington was born and raised in Louisiana. Ferrington's father, Lloyd, was a cabinet maker who had previously played guitar and bass in a local country western combo. Ferrington's first experiences with woodworking were in his father's shop in Monroe, Louisiana.

Ferrington accepted an apprenticeship in 1975 at the Old Time Pickin' Parlour in Nashville, Tennessee. He spent the next five years working with noted acoustic guitar builder Randy Woods. Ferrington's first acoustic was built in 1977, and he continued to hone his craft.

In 1980, Ferrington moved to Los Angeles, California. Ferrington spent a number of years experimenting with different designs, and tones from instruments, and continued building custom guitars. Many of the features on the custom guitars are developed through discussions with the musician commissioning the piece. It is estimated that by 1992, Ferrington had constructed over one hundred custom instruments.

(Source: Kate Geil, et al, the Ferrington Guitars book)

In the late 1980s, the Kramer guitar company was offering several models designed by Ferrington. After Kramer went under, the Ferrington Guitar Company of Long Branch, New Jersey (phone number was previously listed at 908.870.3800) offered essentially the same models (KFS-1, KFT-1, and KFB-1) with Ferrington on the headstock. These models featured a maple neck, rosewood fingerboard, acoustic body, 3-band EQ, and a thinline bridge transducer.

FITZPATRICK JAZZ GUITARS

Instruments currently built in Wickford, Rhode Island.

Luthier Charles Fitzpatrick builds acoustic, acoustic-electric, and semi-hollow body electric archtop guitars in 15", 16", 17", and 18" body widths. The **Jazz Box Select** features single cutaway body consisting of fancy quilted or flamed maple with matching rim and neck, solid carved top of North American spruce, fine line black and white body binding, mother of pearl block fingerboard inlays, gold tuneomatic tailpiece, bound tortoiseshell fingerrest, and a suspended jazz pickup. List prices range from $3,270 (16"), $3,800 (17"), to $4,500 (18"). The list price includes a hardshell case, and Fitzpatrick offers a range of options and custom inlays.

FIVE STAR

See chapter on House Brands.

While this trademark has been identified as a House Brand, the retailer or distributor has not yet been identified. These smaller bodied acoustics have the logo and star position markers painted on, as opposed to the inlay work of a more expensive guitar.

(Source: Willie G. Moseley, Stellas & Stratocasters)

FLANDERS

Instruments built in New England since 1979. Distributed by Fretboard Corner of Lake Ronkonkoma, New York.

Building his first guitar in 1979, Martin Flanders has managed to walk the fine line between old world craftsmanship and modern vision. Flanders gained experience and respect for quality by restoring antique furniture in his father's shop. Living in New England (where select tone woods exist) has afforded Flanders the thrill of harvesting his own stock. Luthier Flanders' business strategy consists of marketing his custom built guitars at a price customers would expect to pay for a 'production' instrument.

ACOUSTIC

Flanders currently offers five guitar models like the **Model 200** (a hybrid carved guitar with tone bars), **Model 300 Executive** single cutaway acoustic archtop, to the stunning archtop like the **Soloist**. The base models are all available with many customization options to choose from.

FLEISHMAN

Instruments currently built in Boulder, Colorado.

Luthier Harry Fleishman has been designing and building high quality guitars and basses since 1975. In addition to the electric solid body models that Fleishman is known for, he also builds a small number of acoustic guitars on a yearly basis. Fleishman is also a current columnist for the Guild of American Luthiers newsletter.

Fleishman designed the Flash model for Hondo during the 1980s, a minimalist body reverse-tuned bass with a number of innovative design features.

ACOUSTIC

Luthier Fleishman is offering two acoustic guitar models, the custom built steel string (or classical style) model (list $3,750 and up), and the **Asymmetric Acoustic** (list $3,950) with multiple sound holes. Fleishman also offers a custom-built Acoustic Bass model (list $3,750 and up).

FLETA

Instruments built in Barcelona, Spain from 1927 to 1977.

Luthier Ignacio Fleta (1897-1977) built classical guitars in Spain that reflected the influence of Antonio de Torres, but featured some of Fleta's design ideas as well. Fleta would varnish the **inside** of the guitar as well, with the intent of brightening the sound. Fleta also added an extra strut under the treble side of the top as a means of increasing volume.

(Source: Tony Bacon, The Ultimate Guitar Book)

RUBEN FLORES

Instruments currently built in Seal Beach, California.

Luthier Ruben Flores is currently hand crafting custom built guitars. For further information regarding pricing and model specifications, please contact luthier Flores via the Index of Current Manudacturers located in the rear of this edition.

E. A. FOLEY

Instruments built in Andover, New Jersey since 1988. Distributed by Foley Guitars, Inc. of Andover, New Jersey.

Luthier Ed Foley has been hand crafting high quality acoustic guitars since the late 1980s. Many of his guitars can be found with a large number of Nashville artists, as well as other recording professionals. Foley headstocks are quite distinct, for they feature the graphic of a cow's skull!

Foley only builds about 15 guitars a year. In addition to his custom bracing, Foley also used graphite to reinforce his contoured necks, and Groove Tubes "Flat Heads" embedded in the headstock for improved sustain.

ACOUSTIC

Ordering a Foley acoustic is exactly like ordering a custom built guitar. True to form, the 1998 Price List runs three pages; the customer starts at the top of page one and makes the necessary choices as the list is run down. At the end of the choices for the model, the customer totals up all additional charges, and that's the retail price. All Foley guitars come with a hardshell case and John Pearse strings.

The base list price for a Foley acoustic is $1,950 (and that begins with the body size). A left-handed configuration is no extra charge; but a body cutaway adds $225 and the 12-string configuration is an additional $200. The basic model consists of a scalloped brace Sitka spruce top, mahogany sides, 2 piece mahogany back, ivoroid or tortoise body binding, black and white rings rosette, dot fingerboard inlay, 24.9" or 25.4" scale, rosewood fingerboard and bridge, 3 per side chrome Schaller tuners, and choice of black, tortoise, or no fingerboard.

Any other custom choice carries an additional cost, such as a choice of Engelmann spruce (or flame koa or Alpine or German spruce) top for $175 (each), Brazilian rosewood back and sides (add $1,450) or flame koa (or flame maple or birdseye maple or quilted maple) for $325 (each). The list of options is actually staggering; but the end result is a custom built guitar the way the customer wanted it. For additional information and pricing, please contact luthier Foley via the Index of Current Manufacturers located in the back of this edition.

FOSTER

Instruments currently built in Covington, Louisiana.

Luthier Jimmy Foster offers repair and restoration work in addition to his current guitar designs, and has been working in the New Orleans area for over twenty five years. In addition to his standard models (listed below), Foster also offers custom orders available with choice of woods, inlays, and trim. For further information, contact luthier Foster through the Index of Current Manufacturers located in the back of this edition.

ACOUSTIC

Flat-Top FT Series

The **FT1** flat-top acoustic has a 17" body width, spruce top, body binding, mahogany back/sides/neck, 25.5" scale, ebony fingerboard/bridge/headstock overlay (retail list $2,450). A piezo bridge pickup is optionally available for an additional $175.

FRAMUS

Instruments currently produced in Markneukirchen, Germany. Distributed by Warwick GmbH & Co. Music Equipment Kg of Markneukirchen, Germany.

Instruments were previously produced in Germany from the late 1940s through the mid 1970s.

In 1996, the trademark was re-introduced in Europe (no U.S. distributors listed to date).

When Frederick Wilfer returned to his home town of Walthersgrun at the end of World War II, he realized that the American-controlled Sudentenland area was soon to fall under control of the Russian forces. With the help of the Americans, Wilfer succeeded in resettling a number of violin makers from Schonbach to Franconia (later in the district of Erlangen). Between 1945 to 1947, Wilfer continued to find homes and employment for the Schonbach violin makers.

In 1946, Wilfer founded the Framus production company, the company name an acronym for **Fra**nconian **Mus**ical instruments. As the company established itself in 1946, Wilfer drew on the knowledge of his violin builder from Schonbach to produce a range of musical instruments including violins and cellos. The new Framus company expanded out of its first couple of production buildings, eventually building a new factory in Bubenreuth in 1955.

The first Framus electric guitars appeared in the 1950s. Due to the presence of American servicemen stationed there, the influence of rock'n roll surfaced earlier in Germany than other European countries. As a result, German guitar builders had a headstart on answering the demand caused by the proliferation of pop groups during the 1960s. Furthermore, as the German production increased, they began exporting their guitars to other countries (including the U.S.). The Framus company stayed active in producing acoustic and electric guitars, and electric basses until the mid 1970s.

In the 1970s, increased competition and serious price undercutting from firms in the Asian market had a serious effect on established companies. Unfortunately, one aspect was to force a number of firms into bankruptcy - and Framus was one of those companies in 1975. However, Wilfer did have the opportunity to watch his son, Hans-Peter Wilfer, establish his own company in 1982 (see WARWICK). Warwick's success allowed Hans-Peter to re-introduce the Framus trademark to the European musical market in 1996. In honor of his father Frederick, Hans-Peter chose to use the world famous Framus trademark when he began offering guitar models in 1996.

(Source: Hans Peter Wilfer, Warwick GmbH & Co. Music Equipment Kg; and Tony Bacon and Paul Day, The Guru's Guitar Guide)

Current Framus instruments (including the electric guitars, Classic and Folk acoustics, and handwired tube guitar amps) are produced at the Warwick facility. Currently, Framus instruments are available in England, Germany, Sweden, and Switzerland; worldwide distribution is in the planning stages.

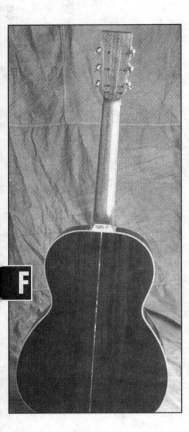

Back Details
courtesy Froggy Bottom

Framus Serialization

In order to properly date the year of issue, most Framus guitars had a separate pair of digits after the main serial number. If the separate pair is present, the two numbers will indicate the year.

FRANCISCAN

Instruments currently produced in Indonesia. Distributed in the U.S. by Kaman Musical Instruments of Bloomfield, Connecticut.

The Franciscan line offers a full line of beginner, student, and intermediate quality guitars, as well as mandolins. Most of the instruments in the line retail between $75 up to $175. Current models feature a blackface peghead with the Franciscan logo in gold script.

(Source: Walter Murray, Frankenstein Fretworks)

ACOUSTIC

The current model line includes models like the **CS-3**, which has a 3/4 size acoustic with a classical-style slotted headstock, 12/18 fret fingerboard, black pickguard, trapeze-style tailpiece, pearloid tuner buttons, and a 2-tone Sunburst finish (retail list $75). The **CS-19** (list $100) is a full sized acoustic folk guitar, with spruce top, round soundhole, black rosette, black body binding, nato back and sides, 14/20 fret laminated fretboard with pearl dot inlay, 3 per side chrome tuners, and hardwood bridge with black bridge pins. The **CS-20 E** is similar in construction to the **CS-19**, except also has a transducer pickup (list $150).

FRANCONIA

Instruments were built in Japan between 1980 and 1985.

The FRANCONIA trademark was a brandname used by a UK importer. The guitars were generally entry level to mid quality copies of American designs.

(Source: Tony Bacon and Paul Day, The Guru's Guitar Guide)

FRANKLIN GUITAR COMPANY

Instruments built in Seattle, Washington from 1976 to date.

Luthier Nick Kukick began the Franklin Guitar Company in 1976. It is estimated that he has been building 36 guitars a year, offered in OM and Jumbo body styles. Kukich's acoustic guitars feature Engelman spruce tops, Indian (or Brazilian) rosewood and koa back/sides, mahogany necks, ebony fingerboards and bridges, and herringbone purfling. Options such as a left-hand configuration, cutaway body design, or inlay/ornamentation was available by customer's specifications.

The last given address for the Franklin Guitar Company was 604 Alaskan Way, Seattle, Washington 98104.

FRESHMAN

Instruments were built in Japan in the mid 1960s.

As an inexpensive, entry level guitar, the Freshman trademark is quite apt: a Senior, it isn't. In fact, it's not even close to a Sophomore.

(Source: Tony Bacon and Paul Day, The Guru's Guitar Guide)

FROGGY BOTTOM

Instruments built in Newfane, Vermont since 1970. Instruments are available through Froggy Bottom Guitars as well as selected dealers.

Luthier Michael Millard initially began Froggy Bottom Guitars as a custom shop back in 1970, as a means to providing guitars crafted for the customers who commission them. Millard, a one-time guitar student of Reverend Gary Davis, responds to the customer's request for certain tone or feel. Although there is a *standard* for each of Millard's models, it is the customer who defines certain parameters that are incorporated in the player's special guitar.

Luthier Millard, who is assisted by his partner Andrew Mueller, also builds "production models" in their two-man shop. These guitars also share more in common with the specially commissioned models than the average production line acoustics. These luthiers are joined by Petria Mitchell, who creates the scrimshaw work on many of the Froggy Bottom heelcaps; and canine "neck carver" Bubba Le Bump.

The name "Froggy Bottom" is derived from the nickname given to land along the Mississippi Delta that is prone to flooding each year. The term was used by the sharecroppers who worked the land, and Millard seeks to capture the spirit of the place and its people in his custom guitar construction.

Grading Identification

Froggy Bottom guitars are offered in four style options on the standard models. Each style adds features to the preceding listing, which defines the different levels of refinement.

Basic: The **Basic** style offers maple trim, a single herringbone rosette ring, 8 ply top purfling, mother-of-pearl peghead logo, a Brazilian rosewood bridge, and chrome Schaller tuners.

Standard: The **Standard** options go one step up with an ebony bridge, abalone position markers, an abalone logo, 2 ring rosette, Maple end inlay and heel cap, and back and side purfling.

Deluxe: Further options in the **Deluxe** category include an abalone rosette, Curly Maple neck heel trim, Gold Schaller tuners, a bound headstock, and a distinctive fretboard inlay.

Limited: The **Limited** style option offers an abalone back seam inlay and abalone top trim inlay to the preceding steps.

Construction Details

All guitar models are offered in four standard back and sides materials such as Mahogany, Indian Rosewood, Curly Maple, and Curly Hawaiian Koa. Each series listed below will have a series of numbers described at the list price: the format follows the Basic/Standard/Deluxe/Limited model.

Soundhole Closeup
courtesy Froggy Bottom

For further information regarding specifications, pricing, and clarity, please contact Michael Millard and Andy Mueller at Froggy Bottom Guitars through the Index of Current Manufacturers located in the back of this book.

ACOUSTIC

Froggy Bottom Guitars has numerous custom options available to the customer. There is no extra charge for nut width variations; all other options do have a price. For price quotes on wood options (like Brazilian rosewood back and sides) or abalone inlays (rosette, backstrip, or trim), please call Froggy Bottom Guitars.

Add $100 for Gold Schaller tuners.

Add $150 for nickel finish Waverly G-98 tuners.

Add $200 for Gold finish Waverly G-98 tuners.

Add $150 for oversized soundhole.

Add $160 for bound headstock (6-string models).

Add $200 for left-handed configuration.

Add $225 for engraved Mammoth Ivory heel cap.

Add $500 (and up) for Florentine or Venetian cutaway body.

Small Body Guitar Models

MODEL A (Also MODEL A-12) — Concert (00) style, 25" scale, Adirondack spruce top, round soundhole, rosette, mahogany neck, 12/20 fret (Model A-12) or 14/20 fret (Model A) fingerboard, solid peghead, 3 per side tuners, tortoise pickguard. Available in Natural finish. Current mfr.

Body length 19 3/4", Body Width 14 1/2", Body Depth 4 1/4".

Mahogany back and sides.
Mfr.'s Sug. Retail (Basic) $2,665
Mfr.'s Sug. Retail (Standard) $2,815
Mfr.'s Sug. Retail (Deluxe) $3,460
Mfr.'s Sug. Retail (Limited) $4,605

Maple back and sides.
Mfr.'s Sug. Retail (Standard) $3,110
Mfr.'s Sug. Retail (Deluxe) $3,810
Mfr.'s Sug. Retail (Limited) $4,970

Koa back and sides.
Mfr.'s Sug. Retail (Standard) $3,435
Mfr.'s Sug. Retail (Deluxe) $4,205
Mfr.'s Sug. Retail (Limited) $5,435

Rosewood back and sides.
Mfr.'s Sug. Retail (Standard) $3,175
Mfr.'s Sug. Retail (Deluxe) $3,875
Mfr.'s Sug. Retail (Limited) $5,045

PARLOR GUITAR — 24 3/4" scale, Adirondack spruce top, round soundhole, rosette, mahogany neck, 12/20 fret fingerboard, slotted peghead, bar-style bridge, 3 per side Waverly tuners, tortoise pickguard. Available in Natural finish. Current mfr.

Body length 20", Body Width 13 3/8", Body Depth 4 1/4".

Mahogany back and sides.
Mfr.'s Sug. Retail (Basic) $3,195
Mfr.'s Sug. Retail (Standard) $3,345
Mfr.'s Sug. Retail (Deluxe) $3,990
Mfr.'s Sug. Retail (Limited) $5,135

Maple back and sides.
Mfr.'s Sug. Retail (Standard) $3,640
Mfr.'s Sug. Retail (Deluxe) $4,340
Mfr.'s Sug. Retail (Limited) $5,500

Koa back and sides.
Mfr.'s Sug. Retail (Standard) $3,965
Mfr.'s Sug. Retail (Deluxe) $4,735
Mfr.'s Sug. Retail (Limited) $5,965

Rosewood back and sides.
Mfr.'s Sug. Retail (Standard) $3,870
Mfr.'s Sug. Retail (Deluxe) $4,610
Mfr.'s Sug. Retail (Limited) $5,845

Grand Concert Guitar Models

MODEL H (Also MODEL H-12) — Grand Concert style, 25 1/4" scale, Engelmann spruce top, round soundhole, rosette, mahogany neck, 12/20 fret (Model H-12) or 14/20 fret (Model H) fingerboard, solid peghead, 3 per side tuners, tortoise pickguard. Available in Natural finish. Current mfr.

Model H: Body length 19 1/8", Body Width 15", Body Depth 4 1/4".

Model H-12: Body length 20 3/8", Body Width 15", Body Depth 4 1/4".

Mahogany back and sides.

Fylde Portuguese Mandola
courtesy Fylde Guitars

Mfr.'s Sug. Retail (Basic) $2,615
Mfr.'s Sug. Retail (Standard) $2,765
Mfr.'s Sug. Retail (Deluxe) $3,120
Mfr.'s Sug. Retail (Limited) $4,555

Maple back and sides.
Mfr.'s Sug. Retail (Standard) $3,060
Mfr.'s Sug. Retail (Deluxe) $3,760
Mfr.'s Sug. Retail (Limited) $4,920

Koa back and sides.
Mfr.'s Sug. Retail (Standard) $3,380
Mfr.'s Sug. Retail (Deluxe) $4,150
Mfr.'s Sug. Retail (Limited) $5,380

Rosewood back and sides.
Mfr.'s Sug. Retail (Standard) $3,120
Mfr.'s Sug. Retail (Deluxe) $3,820
Mfr.'s Sug. Retail (Limited) $4,995

The H-12 model has a 25" scale, and lighter bracing pattern.

Full Size Guitar Models

The **Model D** is based on the ever popular dreadnought body developed by the Martin company. While the traditional dreadnought guitar is both powerful and bass heavy, the Froggy Bottom adds clarity, especially up the neck. The **Model F** evolved out of conversions of Martin arch tops in the New York shop of Matt Umanov. Those early conversions demonstrated the virtues of reducing the body volume of larger instruments and clearly altered the course of contemporary flat top guitar design. Models D, F and F-12, and K share the same basic retail pricing system; only one pricing table is supplied for brevity.

MODEL D — dreadnought style, 25 1/4" scale, Sitka spruce top, round soundhole, rosette, mahogany neck, 14/20 fret fingerboard, solid peghead, 3 per side tuners, pickguard. Available in Natural finish. Current mfr.

Body length 20", Body Width 16", Body Depth 4 1/2".

See Pricing Table on Model K.

MODEL F (Also MODEL F-12) — dreadnought style, 25 1/4" scale, Sitka spruce top, round soundhole, rosette, mahogany neck, 12/20 fret (Model F-12) or 14/20 fret (Model F) fingerboard, solid peghead, 3 per side tuners, tortoise pickguard. Available in Natural finish. Current mfr.

Model F: Body length 20 1/4", Body Width 16", Body Depth 4 1/8".

Model F-12: Body length 21", Body Width 16", Body Depth 4 1/8".

See Pricing Table on Model K.

MODEL K — tight waist/rounded profile body, 25 1/4" scale, Sitka spruce top, round soundhole, rosette, mahogany neck, 14/20 fret fingerboard, solid peghead, 3 per side tuners, pickguard. Available in Natural finish. Current mfr.

Body length 20", Body Width 16", Body Depth 4 1/4".

Mahogany back and sides.
Mfr.'s Sug. Retail (Basic) $2,460
Mfr.'s Sug. Retail (Standard) $2,655
Mfr.'s Sug. Retail (Deluxe) $3,350
Mfr.'s Sug. Retail (Limited) $4,560

Maple back and sides.
Mfr.'s Sug. Retail (Standard) $2,995
Mfr.'s Sug. Retail (Deluxe) $3,700
Mfr.'s Sug. Retail (Limited) $4,930

Koa back and sides.
Mfr.'s Sug. Retail (Standard) $3,330
Mfr.'s Sug. Retail (Deluxe) $4,110
Mfr.'s Sug. Retail (Limited) $5,410

Rosewood back and sides.
Mfr.'s Sug. Retail (Standard) $3,060
Mfr.'s Sug. Retail (Deluxe) $3,770
Mfr.'s Sug. Retail (Limited) $5,000

Jumbo Series

With the revival of interest in older 12 fret guitars (i.e. where the neck joins the body) such as the Martin original D, the **Model B** is designed as a 12 string with a long (26") scale for blues master Paul Geremia (this is THE guitar for those who love the old Stellas of Willie McTell and Leadbelly). The **Model G** is based on the beautiful Gibson L-5 profile. The **Model J** is the original "Froggy Bottom Special", Millard's earliest jumbo model (first built in 1972). Models B-12, G, and J share the same basic retail pricing system; only one pricing table is supplied for brevity.

MODEL B (Also MODEL B-12) — jumbo style, 26" scale, Sitka spruce top, round soundhole, rosette, mahogany neck, 12-string configuration, 12/20 fret fingerboard, solid peghead, 6 per side tuners, pickguard. Available in Natural finish. Current mfr.

Body length 21", Body Width 16 1/2", Body Depth 4 1/2".

See Pricing Table on Model J.

MODEL G — jumbo style, 25 1/4" scale, Sitka spruce top, round soundhole, rosette, mahogany neck, 14/20 fret fingerboard, solid peghead, 3 per side tuners, pickguard. Available in Natural finish. Current mfr.

Body length 20 7/8", Body Width 17", Body Depth 4 3/8".

Fylde Goodfellow
courtesy Fylde Guitars

Fylde Ariel
courtesy Fylde Guitars

See Pricing Table on Model J.

This model is optionally available as a 4-string bass guitar (34" scale).

MODEL J — tight waist jumbo style, 25 1/4" scale, Sitka spruce top, round soundhole, rosette, mahogany neck, 14/20 fret fingerboard, solid peghead, 3 per side tuners, pickguard. Available in Natural finish. Current mfr.

Body length 20 5/8", Body Width 17", Body Depth 4 1/8".

Mahogany back and sides.
Mfr.'s Sug. Retail (Basic) $2,755
Mfr.'s Sug. Retail (Standard) $2,965
Mfr.'s Sug. Retail (Deluxe) $3,585
Mfr.'s Sug. Retail (Limited) $4,870

Maple back and sides.
Mfr.'s Sug. Retail (Standard) $3,310
Mfr.'s Sug. Retail (Deluxe) $3,935
Mfr.'s Sug. Retail (Limited) $5,240

Koa back and side.
Mfr.'s Sug. Retail (Standard) $3,670
Mfr.'s Sug. Retail (Deluxe) $4,360
Mfr.'s Sug. Retail (Limited) $5,745

Rosewood back and sides.
Mfr.'s Sug. Retail (Standard) $3,365
Mfr.'s Sug. Retail (Deluxe) $3,995
Mfr.'s Sug. Retail (Limited) $5,310

Fylde Oberon
courtesy Fylde Guitars

FRONTIER

Instruments were produced in Japan during the early 1980s.

Frontier guitars are decent to good quality original designs as well as copies of American designs. The puzzling one is the signature model of Norris Fant. Guitar collectors or Fan club members who wish to enlighten us on Mr. Fant are invited to write to the **Blue Book of Guitars.**

(Source: Tony Bacon and Paul Day, The Guru's Guitar Guide)

FYLDE

Instruments currently built in Penrith (Cumbria), England.

Luthier Roger Bucknall began building guitars at age nine (back in the late 1950s), and continued occasionally building until he was twenty-one. While he was running a folk club, Bucknall soon had a large number of orders for his designs. A friend offered to finance Bucknall's new endeavor, and Bucknall moved to the Fylde coast of Lancashire in 1973 to begin producing guitars. Rather than set up a one-man shop, Bucknall was determined to enter into full production.

Buckanll continued to expand the business through the 1970s, and by the end of the decade had a staff of around twelve people building twenty guitars a week. Bucjnall estimates that half of the production was being sold to hte U.S. market, the rest in Europe.

In the later half of 1979 to 1980, Bucknall suffered through personal family problems, coupled with a fading market and struggling finances. In 1980, the company went broke, and Fylde Instruments Ltd. was closed down.

Bucknall, with the help of another close friend, continued making about 100 guitars a year under the Fylde Guitars name. He also launched a business making snooker cues at this time.

Bucknall sold the snooker business in 1992 and re-invested in Fylde Guitars. Fylde currently produces around 400 instruments a year. With traditional wood supplies becoming scarce, Bucknall is now seeking a source of renewable new materials for his guitars, and is now committed to not purchasing any more rosewood or ebony unless the wood is coming from a substantial source.

In addition to the numerous guitar models, Fylde Guitars also offers a number of models from the Mandolin family, such as the Mandola, Cittern, Portuguese Mandola, "Octavious" Bouzouki, and the Mandolin. Interested players are invited to call or write to Fylde Guitars for their current catalog and price list.

Fylde Egyptian
courtesy Fylde Guitars

ACOUSTIC

The clever folks at Fylde have named many of the current guitar models after characters in Shakespeare plays (which, in the long run, is more entertaining than a simple model number). The **Ariel** model (list $1,533) has a slotted headstock, and a body design somewhere between a nylon and steel-string guitar design. The Ariel features a cedar top, mahogany back and sides, and a 12/19 fret ebony neck with a 629 mm scale length. The **Goodfellow** (list $1,393) is slightly larger than the Ariel, and has a 14/20 fret rosewood fingerboard.

If you combine a single cutaway with a *Hot Club*-era Selmer acoustic, the results may be a **Caliban** (list $2,191). The D-shaped soundhole and deep cutaway mark this model, constructed with a cedar top, Indian rosewood back and sides, and ebony fingerboard and bridge. The **Egyptian** (list $2,191) features a spruce top, an oval soundhole, and bridge/metal tailpiece with its deep cutaway and Indian rosewood back and sides. Both models feature a 24 fret fingerboard.

The **Falstaff** and **Oberon** models share similar construction such as spruce tops, Indian rosewood back and sides, and an ebony fingerboard and bridge (and a similar list price of $2,093 each). The Falstaff has a dreadnought body appearance and a 68 mm scale, while the Oberon leans toward a grand concert style and 629 mm scale.

Fylde's **Orsino** (list $1,393) acoustic is a dreadnought style guitar with a cedar top and mahogany back and sides. The **Othello** (list $1,393) is very similar to the Orsino, except has a narrower fingerboard and wider frets. Both models feature rosewood fingerboards and bridges.

Sir Toby Bass

The deep-bodied jumbo-style **Magician** (list $1,813) features a cedar top, walnut back and sides, a 5-piece laminated neck, and an ebony fingerboard and bridge.

ACOUSTIC ELECTRIC

The **Model 42** is available with either mahogany (-M) or Indian rosewood (-R) back and sides, with a spruce top, and L.R. Baggs Duet amplification system. The 'M' version has rosewood fingerboard and bridge, while the 'R' version has a shaded spruce top and ebony fingerboard and bridge. The scale length is 648 mm. Retail prices range between $2,093 up to $2,513.

ACOUSTIC BASS

Fylde has two models of acoustic bass, the **King John** (860 mm scale) and the **Sir Toby** (762 mm scale). Both basses feature mahogany back and sides, a voiced cedar top, and rosewood fingerboard and bridge. The **King John** and **Sir Toby** models both retail at $1,393 (each).

G

GAGLIANO

Instruments produced in Korea, circa recent. Distributed by Avnet, Inc.

Gagliano acoustic guitars have the Gagliano trademark name in gold script on the headstock, while their internal label states "Meisel Music, a subsidiary of Avnet, Inc.". Research continues on the Gagliano trademark.

One model observed, a Model 2060 may or may not be indicative of the entire product line: The different components are of various levels of quality and state of technology. For example, the neck is a decent quality nato, with an adjustable truss rod. This neck is about as good a quality as you could expect on this genre of instrument; on the other hand, the bridge is made of plastic and the soundboard is plywood, with a paper-like laminate to make it look like spruce. The internal bracing is also a mish-mash of technological styles.

(Source: Walter Murray, Frankenstein Fretworks)

J.W. GALLAGHER & SONS

Instruments built in Wartrace, Tennessee. Distributed by J.W. Gallagher & Sons of Wartrace, Tennessee.

The Gallagher family settled in Wartrace (about 60 miles southeast of Nashville) back in the late 1820s. John William Gallagher was born in 1915, and in 1939 established a furniture making business. Don Gallagher was born in 1947, and grew up among the tools and wood in the family's woodworking shop. The furniture business converted to guitar production later in the 1960s. Gallagher and his son Don produced 24 guitars in their first year.

In 1976, Don Gallagher took over management of the business, three years before the luthier community lost J.W. Gallagher in 1979. Don Gallagher continues to build acoustic guitars in the family tradition.

(Source: Tom Wheeler, American Guitars)

Gallagher guitars have been built in very limited numbers. From the opening year of 1965 to 1990, only 2,064 guitars were made. According to the Gallagher catalog, early instruments had paper labels. The serial number on these labels indicate the year and month the guitar was made. Starting in 1970, the serialization began to reflect the number of guitars that had been built. This number, along with the model number, is stamped on the neck block inside every Gallagher guitar.

ACOUSTIC

All Gallagher guitars are meticulously handcrafted, using the finest woods available at the workshop. Hardshell cases are an extra charge, but well worth the investment in protecting your Gallagher guitar.

Add $170 for 12-string configuration.

Add $220 for Sunburst finish.

Add $230 for Fishman Acoustic Matrix system.

Add $400 for single cutaway body design.

Add $400 for a slotted headstock.

G Series

The first Gallagher guitar model was built back in 1965, and was designated the G-50 in honor of J.W. Gallagher's age at the time. The **G-50** features mahogany back and sides, a spruce top, and a soundhole edged in black and white wood strips. The rosewood fingerboard has pearl dot inlays, and the guitar has a bound peghead and body that is finished in highly polished lacquer. Retail list price is $2,000. The **G-45** is similar to the G-50, except it does not have the bound headstock and the body binding is in black. List price is also $2,000.

The **G-70** ($2,340) has a two-piece top and a body of rosewood. The bound ebony fingerboard is inlayed with mother-of-pearl diamonds and squares, and the top and the soundhole are bound in herringbone. The **G-65** ($2,180) features a bookmatched rosewood back, and rosewood sides. Black and white wood inlays surround the top and the soundhole, while the nut and saddle are constructed of bone.

In 1968 both Doc and Merle Watson began playing guitars crafted by J.W. and Don. Six years later, Doc Watson requested certain particular features in a guitar that was built for him. This model was the basis for the **Doc Watson Model**. In 1975, Merle received the first cutaway version of this model. The Doc Watson model has a spruce top, mahogany back and sides, and a bridge and fingerboard of ebony. The nut and saddles are constructed of bone, and the top and soundhole have herringbone inlays. List price is $2,165.

Modified G Series

The **G-70M** is a modified version of the G-70 model, and features a bound fingerboard, herringbone trim around the top and soundhole, a longer body design, and the neck joins at the twelfth fret. The **G-45M** is the same size as the G-70M, but features mahogany back and sides, black/white trim around the top and soundhole, and the neck joins at the twelfth fret as well. List price on the G-70M is $2,400, while the G-45M is $2,060.

Grand Concert

Model **GC-70** is similar in appointments to the G-70, except in the grand concert body size. The first GC-70 was built in 1968 for country artist Grandpa Jones. Rosewood back and sides, spruce top, bound ebony fingerboard, ebony bridge, and herringbone trim comprise this model ($2,400).

Special Series

The **71 Special** was introduced in 1970, and features a rosewood back and sides, spruce top, herringbone purfling and soundhole rosette, bound ebony fingerboard, ebony bridge, abalone snowflake inlays. List price is $2,600.

The very first **72 Special** was built by Don Gallagher in late 1977. The body is rosewood, with a spruce top and mahogany neck. Both the bridge and fingerboard are ebony, and the nut and saddle are crafted of bone. The 72 Special carries a list price of $3,100.

71 Special
courtesy Don Gallagher

72 Special
courtesy Don Gallagher

Auditorium Series

A more defined *waist* is featured on the **Ragtime Special**, which is an 'auditorium' size guitar. The model has mahogany back and sides, spruce top, black-bound body and peghead, ebony fingerboard and bridge. Retail list is $2,200. The **A-70** ($2,400) is similar to the GC-70 model, but has a 14 fret neck.

12 String Series

Although any model has an option to be built as a twelve string, Gallagher specifically offers 2 models designated so. The **G-70 12** ($2,510) and the **G-45 12** ($2,170) are similar in construction to their associated models, except both pegheads are equipped with *mini* tuning machines.

KEVIN GALLAGHER

See OMEGA INSTRUMENTS.

BRYAN GALLOUP

Instruments built in Big Rapids, Michigan from 1992 to date.

Luthier Bryan Galloup has been a guitar repairman on vintage guitars for the past 20 years. Galloup began building his own guitars in 1992, and went full time in guitar building in 1995.

Galloup's techniques of neck resets, fretting, bridge and bridge plate replacement were featured in the Guild of American Luthier's *American Luthier* publication; Galloup is also the repair and modification columnist for The Association of Stringed Instrument Artisans' quarterly magazine.

In addition to his acoustic guitar models, Galloup also runs the Bryan Galloup's School of Guitar Building and Repair, a fully equipped wood working shop that is designed to handle the most advanced repairs, restorations, and custom ordered acoustic and electric guitars. Students during the 8 week class are outfitted with their own workbench, hand tools, and supplies and receive a hands-on education in the luthiery arts.

ACOUSTIC

Galloup's acoustic guitar models include the **G-1 American Classic** (list $2,650), the **GD-1 Classic Deluxe** (list $3,800), **GS-2 Hutchinson** (list $2,975), and the **GE-3 Hired Hand** (list $2,495). For further information regarding model specifications and pricing, please contact luthier Bryan Galloup via the Index of Current Manufacturers located in the rear of this book.

MARK GASSER

Instruments currently built in Cottonwood, Arizona. Distributed by GuitArts of Cottonwood, Arizona.

Luthier Mark Gasser has been hand crafting guitars for over eleven years. Gasser studied techniques originated by Bozo Podunavac. Finding that each wood creates its own unique tone, Gasser likes to experiment with non-traditional woods in crafting his guitars.

Gasser's guitars are made from exotic hardwoods, such as African paduak, Alaskan spruce and cedar, and Honduran mahogany. His fretboards are rosewood and ebony. Retail list prices start at $1,695.

GAY

Instruments built in Edmonton (Alberta), Canada between circa early-to-mid 1950s to the mid 1970s.

Luthier Frank Gay maintained his guitar building and repair services for more than two decades in Edmonton. A formidable jazz and classical guitarist, his flattop acoustics were the most recognizable instrument - and oddly enough, his biggest endorsers were country western artists (one notable player was Webb Pierce). Gay guitars are recognized by the exaggerated checkerboard rosette inlays, six on a side headstocks, and the occasional heart-shaped soundhole.

(Source: Teisco Del Rey, Guitar Player magazine)

GENEVA

Instruments produced in the Czech Republic from 1981 to date. Distributed by the Geneva International Corporation of Wheeling, Illinois.

Geneva acoustic guitars have been produced in the Czech Republic since 1981, and carry the same European traditions of quality workmanship. Geneva guitars feature a different bridge design that changes the pitch of the string crossing the bridge's saddle, adding to the transfer of vibrations from the strings to the top via the bridge.

ACOUSTIC

Pro Dreadnought Style Series

D 1 P — dreadnought style, solid cedar top, round soundhole, laminated mahogany back/sides, mahogany neck, rosewood fingerboard with white dot inlay, rosewood bridge, 3 per side Schaller tuners. Available in Natural matte finish. Current mfr.
Mfr.'s Sug. Retail $739

D 5 P — dreadnought style, solid spruce top, round soundhole, solid rosewood back/sides, mahogany neck, ebony fingerboard with abalone inlay, ebony bridge, 3 per side gold tuners. Available in Natural high gloss finish. Current mfr.
Mfr.'s Sug. Retail $1,439

D 61 — dreadnought style, solid cedar top, round soundhole, laminated mahogany back/sides, mahogany neck, rosewood fingerboard with white dot inlay, rosewood bridge, 3 per side Schaller tuners. Available in Natural matte finish. Current mfr.
Mfr.'s Sug. Retail $659

D 62 — dreadnought style, solid spruce top, round soundhole, solid rosewood back/sides, mahogany neck, rosewood fingerboard with white dot inlay, rosewood bridge, 3 per side Schaller tuners. Available in Natural high gloss finish. Current mfr.
    Mfr.'s Sug. Retail $TBA

D 63 — dreadnought style, solid spruce top, round soundhole, solid rosewood back/sides, mahogany neck, ebony fingerboard with abalone inlay, ebony bridge, 3 per side gold tuners. Available in Natural high gloss finish. Current mfr.
    Mfr.'s Sug. Retail $1,499

JV 61 — jumbo style, single rounded cutaway, solid cedar top, round soundhole, laminated mahogany back/sides, mahogany neck, rosewood fingerboard with white dot inlay, rosewood bridge, 3 per side Schaller tuners. Available in Natural matte finish. Current mfr.
    Mfr.'s Sug. Retail $695

Pro Roundback Style Series

Z 122 12-STRING — roundback body design, 12-string configuration, solid spruce top, round soundhole, ebony fingerboard with abalone inlay, ebony bridge, 6 per side tuners. Available in Natural high gloss finish. Current mfr.
    Mfr.'s Sug. Retail $999

Z V 62 6-STRING — roundback body design, solid spruce top, round soundhole, ebony fingerboard with abalone inlay, ebony bridge, 3 per side tuners. Available in Natural high gloss finish. Current mfr.
    Mfr.'s Sug. Retail $869

Select Series

The **GS-10** features a spruce top, round soundhole, rosewood back/sides, bound body, rosewood fingerboard with white diamond-shaped inlays, rosewood bridge, black teardrop-shaped pickguard, 3 per side tuners, and is available in a high gloss finish. The **GS-20** is similar to the GS-10, except features a rounded cutaway body; the **GS-21** is similar to the GS-20 and has an on-board preamp (9 volt) with EQ controls. All prices $TBA.

GIANNINI

Instruments currently built in Brazil. Distributed by Music Industries Corporation of Floral Park, New York.

Giannini acoustics are offered in a wide range of entry level to professional quality instruments.

In the early 1970s, Giannini was distributed in the U.S. by Giannini Guitars at 75 Frost Street, Westbury (New York 11590). If that address seems somewhat familiar, it was shared by Westbury Guitars, the Merson company, and currently Korg USA (Marshall, Parker, Korg).

ACOUSTIC

CRA-65 — dreadnought style, yellow spruce top, round soundhole, Brazilian rosewood back/sides, 19 fret rosewood fingerboard, rosewood bridge, 3 per side tuners. Available in Natural finish. Mfd. circa early 1970s.

Length 40", Body Width 15 1/4", Body Thickness 4".

Model has not traded sufficiently to quote prices.

                                        Last Mfr.'s Sug. Retail was $160.

CRA-125 — dreadnought style, spruce top, round soundhole, Brazilian rosewood back/sides, 20 fret rosewood fingerboard, rosewood bridge, 3 per side tuners. Available in Natural finish. Mfd. circa early 1970s.

Length 43", Body Width 15 1/4", Body Thickness 4".

Model has not traded sufficiently to quote prices.

                                        Last Mfr.'s Sug. Retail was $175.

CRA 6N CRAVIOLA — nylon strings, spruce top, round soundhole, Brazilian rosewood back/sides, 19 fret rosewood fingerboard, rosewood bridge, 3 per side tuners. Available in Natural finish. Mfd. circa early 1970s.

Length 40", Body Width 15 1/4", Body Thickness 4".

Model has not traded sufficiently to quote prices.

                                        Last Mfr.'s Sug. Retail was $150.

This model was also available in a 12-string configuration.

The Craviola is the "kidney bean-shaped" body Giannini model that turns up occasionally in the secondary market. This model may also have a Merson company label.

GIBSON

Instruments produced in Nashville, Tennessee from 1974 to date. Distributed by the Gibson Guitar Corporation of Nashville, Tennessee.

Instruments previously produced in Kalamazoo, Michigan from 1896 to 1901; The Gibson Mandolin-Guitar Manufacturing Company, Limited (which evolved into the Gibson Guitar Corporation) produced instruments in Kalamazoo, Michigan from 1902 to 1984.

Luthier Orville H. Gibson was born in Chateaugay, New York. In 1856 he *moved West* to Kalamazoo, Michigan. City records from 1896-1897 indicate a business address of 114 South Burdick for *O.H. Gibson, Manufacturer, Musical Instruments*. By 1899-1902, the city directories indicate a change to the Second Floor of 104 East Main.

The Gibson Mandolin-Guitar Manufacturing Company, Limited was established at 2:55 p.m. on October 11, 1902. The agreement was formed by John W. Adams (pres.), Samuel H. Van Horn (treasurer), Sylvo Reams (sec. and also production mngr.), Lewis Williams (later secretary and Gen. Mngr.), and Leroy Hornbeck. Orville Gibson was not one of the founding partners, but had a separate contract to be a consultant and trainer. Gibson was also the first to purchase 500 shares of the new company's stock. In 1915, Gibson and the company negotiated a new agreement in which Orville was to be paid a monthly salary for the rest of his life. Orville, who had some troubles with his health back in 1911, was treated in 1916 at

G

the pyschiatric center of St. Lawrence State hospital in Ogdensburg, New York. Orville Gibson died of endocarditis on August 21, 1918.

In 1906 the company moved to 116 East Exchange Place, and the name was changed to Gibson Mandolin Guitar Company. In 1917, production facilities were opened at Parsons Street (the first of a total of five buildings at that location). Chicago Musical Instruments (CMI) acquired controlling interest in Gibson, Inc. in 1944. Maurice H. Berlin (president of CMI) became general secretary and treasurer of Gibson. From this date, the Gibson Sales Department became located in Chicago while the Kalamazoo plant concentrated on production.

In 1935, Gibson began investigating into a prototype electric pickup. Musician Alvino Rey started research with engineers at the Lyon & Healy company (See WASHBURN) in Chicago, and a year later the research was moved in-house to Kalamazoo. In late 1935, Gibson debuted the hexagonal pickup on a lap steel model; this same pickup was applied to an archtop guitar and offered as the ES (Electric Spanish) 150 in 1936. The ES-150 was used by jazz guitarist Charlie Christian, and this model is still known as the "Charlie Christian" model.

After the release of Leo Fender's **Broadcaster** (later **Telecaster**) model, Gibson and guitarist Les Paul collaborated in the release of the solid body Gibson **Les Paul** in 1952. This model was refined with the introduction of the tune-o-matic bridge/stop tailpiece combination, and P.A.F. humbuckers through the 1950s. Under the direction of then Gibson president Ted McCarty, the Gibson company attempted to throw off the tag of being "stodgy" and old fashioned when they introduced the **Flying V** and **Explorer** models in the late 1950s. In this case, they pre-judged the public's tastes by about 10 years! As guitar players' tastes changed in the late 1950s, Gibson discontinued the single cutaway Les Paul model in favor of the double cutaway **SG** in 1960. As the popularity of the electric blues (as championed by Eric Clapton and Michael Bloomfield) grew during the 1960s, Gibson reissued the Les Paul in 1968.

Gibson acquired Epiphone in 1957, and production of Gibson-made Epiphones began in 1959, and lasted until 1969. In 1970, production moved to Japan (or, the Epiphone name was then applied to imported instruments).

In December of 1969, E.C.L. Industries, Inc. took control of CMI. Gibson, Inc. stayed under control of CMI until 1974, when it became a subsidiary of NORLIN Industries (Norlin is named after H. **Nor**ton Stevens, President of E.C.L. and Maurice H. **Ber**lin, President of CMI). A new factory was opened in Nashville, Tennessee the same year.

In 1980, Norlin decided to sell Gibson. Norlin also relocated some of the sales, marketing, administration, and finance personnel from Chicago to the Nashville plant. Main Gibson production was then handled in Nashville, and Kalamazoo became a specialist factory for custom orders. In 1983, then-Gibson president Marty Locke informed plant manager Jim Deurloo that the Kalamazoo plant would close. Final production was June 1984, and the plant closed three months later. [On a side note: Rather than give up on the 65 year old facilities, Jim Deurloo, Marv Lamb, and J.P. Moats started the Heritage Guitar Company in April of 1985. The company is located in the original 1917 building.]

In January of 1986, Henry Juszkiewicz (pres), David Berryman (VP of finance and accounting), and Gary Zebrowski (electronics business) bought Gibson for five million dollars. Since the purchase in 1986, the revived **Gibson USA** company has been at work to return to the level of quality the company had reached earlier. Expansion of the acoustic guitar production began at the Bozeman, Montana facilities. Many hard rock bands and guitarists began playing (and posing) with Gibson guitars, again fueling desire among the players.

Gibson's **Historic Collection** models were introduced in 1991, and custom pieces built at Gibson's Custom Shop began sporting their own **Gibson Custom * Art * Historic** logo on the headstock in 1996. This new division is responsible for producing Historic Collection models, commemorative guitars, custom-ordered and special edition guitars, as well as restoration and repair of vintage models.

In the tail end of 1996, both the Dobro production facilities in California and the Montana mandolin guitar facilities were closed down. New production facilities for both named **Original Musical Instruments** (O.M.I.) is expected to be opened in Nashville, Tennessee in late 1998.

In 1998, Gibson opened up a new dealer level for specialty guitars. The Gibson Historic Collection **Award** models are only available through the (estimated) 50 Award Level dealers, and feature specific year/model designated instruments at an upscale price. As noted elsewhere, the antique and vintage firearm market has authentic reproductions of especially prized models. Whether or not Gibson is building "reproductions" with these designated models, the bottom line is that they are damn fine instruments that any Gibson fan would be honored to own (and play).

(Source: Walter Carter, Gibson Guitars: 100 Years of an American Icon; and Tom Wheeler, American Guitars)

IDENTIFYING FEATURES ON

GIBSON MUSICAL INSTRUMENTS

Gibson Headstock Logo

The most consistent and easily found feature that goes across all models of Gibson production is the **logo**, or lack of one, found on the peghead. The very earliest instruments made are generally found with a star inside a crescent design, or a blank peghead, and labels inside the body. This lasted until approximately 1902.

From 1902 to the late 1920s, *The Gibson*, inlaid in pearl and placed at a slant, is found on the peghead. In the late 1920s, this style of logo was changed to having *The Gibson* read straight across the peghead as opposed to being slanted. Flat top acoustics production began at approximately this time and these instruments generally do not have *The* on the inlay, it just has *Gibson* in script writing. By 1933, this was the established peghead logo for Gibson. Just before WWII, Gibson began making the lettering on the logo thicker and this became standard on most prewar instruments. Right after WWII, the styling of the logo remained but it became slanted once again.

In 1947, the logo that is still in use today made its debut. This logo has a block styling with the *G* having a tail, the *i* dot is touching the *G*, the *b* and *o* are open and the *n* is connected at the bottom. The logo is still slanted. By 1951, the dot on the *i* was no longer connected to the *G*. In 1967, the logo styling became even more squared (pentographed) with the *b* and *o* becoming closed and the *i* dot being removed.

In 1970, Gibson replaced the black tinted piece of wood that had been used on the peghead face with a black fiber that the logo and other peghead inlay were placed into. With the change in peghead facing came a slightly smaller logo lettering. In 1972, the *i* dot reappeared on the peghead logo. In 1981, the *n* is connected at the top of the *o*. There are a few models through the years that do not follow this timeline, ie: reissues and limited editions, but most of the production instruments can be found with the above feature changes.

Gibson Tuners

The configuration of the Kluson tuners used on Gibson instruments can be used to date an instrument. Before 1959, all Kluson tuners with plastic buttons had a single ring around the stem end of the button. In 1960, this was changed to a double ring configuration.

Gibson Peghead Volute

Another dating feature of Gibsons is the use of a peghead volute found on instruments between 1970 and 1973. Also, in 1965 Gibson switched from 17 degrees to 14 degrees on the tilt of the peghead. Before 1950, peghead thickness varied, getting narrower towards the top of the peghead. After 1950, pegheads all became one uniform thickness, from bottom to top.

Common Gibson Abbreviations

C - Cutaway

D - Dreadnought or Double

E - Electric

ES - Electric (Electro) Spanish

GS - Gut String

J - Jumbo

LE - Limited Edition

S - Spanish, Solid Body, Special or Super

SG - Solid Guitar

T - Tremolo or Thinline

V - Venetian or Vibrato

Production Model Codes

For ease in identifying current Gibson production guitar models in the Gibson section, the Gibson four digit **Family Code** (in parenthesis) follows the model's name. Some of the Historic Collection family codes are 8 digits long.

For further information regarding Gibson electric models, please refer to the **5th Edition Blue Book of Electric Guitars**. Gibson Archtop models that feature "floating" pickups or built-in pickups will be featured in the Gibson Electric section of the Electric edition.

Grading	100%	Excellent	Average

ACOUSTIC

While the thought of a Sunburst finished Les Paul model brings many players (and collectors) a case of the warm fuzzies, Gibson acoustic guitar collectors are more partial to a Natural finished acoustic over a similar model finished in Sunburst. As a result, there is a premium for Natural finished Gibson acoustics.

Add 20% to 30% for Natural finish.

BLUE RIDGE — slope shouldered body style, solid spruce top, round soundhole, black pickguard, 3 stripe bound body/rosette, laminated rosewood back/sides, mahogany neck, 14/20 fret rosewood fingerboard with pearl dot inlay, reverse belly rosewood bridge with black white dot pins, blackface peghead with screened logo, 3 per side chrome tuners. Available in Natural finish. Mfd. 1968 to 1979.

	$600	$300

In 1969, standard bridge replaced original item.

In 1973, low impedance pickup became optionally available.

Blue Ridge 12 — similar to Blue Ridge, except has 12 strings, 6 per side tuners. Mfd. 1970 to 1978.

	$500	$275

B Series

B-15 — spruce top, round soundhole, tortoise pickguard, 1 stripe rosette, bound top, mahogany back/sides/neck, 14/20 fret rosewood fingerboard with pearl dot inlay, rosewood bridge with white pins, 3 per side tuners with plastic buttons. Available in Natural finish. Mfd. 1967 to 1971.

	$300	$175

B-25 — spruce top, round soundhole, tortoise pickguard, 3 stripe bound body/rosette, mahogany back, laminated mahogany sides, mahogany neck, 14/20 fret rosewood fingerboard with pearl dot inlay, upper belly on laminated rosewood bridge with adjustable saddle and white pins, blackface peghead with decal logo, 3 per side tuners with plastic buttons. Available in Cherry Sunburst and Natural finishes. Mfd. 1962 to 1977.

1962-1969	$600	$350
1970-1977	$450	$275

In 1965, a plastic Special bridge replaced the laminated rosewood bridge.

In 1968, wood bridge replaced respective item.

B-25 ³⁄₄ — similar to B-25, except is ³⁄₄ size body. Mfd. 1962 to 1968.

	$800	$400

In 1966, Natural finish was discontinued.

1964 B-25
courtesy Sam J. Maggio

Grading	100%	Excellent	Average

Gibson B-25-12-N
courtesy Jason Crisp

B-25-12 — spruce top, round soundhole, tortoise pickguard, bound body/rosette, mahogany back/sides/neck, 14/20 fret rosewood fingerboard with pearl dot inlay, reverse belly rosewood bridge with white pins, blackface peghead with decal logo, 6 per side tuners with plastic buttons. Available in Cherry Sunburst and Natural finishes. Mfd. 1962 to 1977.

1962-1969		$500	$300
1970-1977		$400	$250

In 1963, strings through bridge replaced original item, no bridge pins.

In 1965, redesigned reverse bridge replaced respective item, trapeze tailpiece added.

In 1970, standard bridge with white pins replaced respective item, no trapeze tailpiece, Cherry Sunburst finish was discontinued.

B-45-12 — slope shouldered body, spruce top, round soundhole, tortoise pickguard, 2 stripe bound body/rosette, mahogany back/sides/neck, 14/20 fret rosewood fingerboard with pearl dot inlay, rosewood bridge with adjustable saddle, trapeze tailpiece, blackface peghead with pearl split diamond inlay/logo decal, 6 per side nickel tuners with plastic buttons. Available in Cherry Sunburst finish. Mfd. 1961 to 1979.

1961-1969		$900	$450
1970-1979		$600	$350

In 1962, reverse belly bridge with pins, adjustable saddle replaced original items.

In 1964, string through reverse belly bridge replaced respective item, Natural finish (Model B-45-12 N) optionally available.

In 1965, rectangular bridge/trapeze tailpiece replaced respective item.

In 1970, redesigned pickguard, 12/20 fret fingerboard, standard bridge with pins, Tobacco Sunburst finish replaced original items.

Blues King Series

BLUES KING L-00 — parlor style, spruce top, round soundhole, tortoise pickguard, 3 stripe bound body/rosette, mahogany back/sides/neck, 14/20 fret rosewood fingerboard with pearl dot inlay, straight rosewood bridge with white pins, blackface peghead with pearl logo inlay, 3 per side nickel tuners. Available in Antique Ebony, Natural top/Antique Walnut back/sides and Vintage Sunburst finishes. Mfr. 1994 to 1996.

		$1,100	$550

Last Mfr.'s Sug. Retail was $1,400.

Blues King Special — similar to Blues King L-00, except has Indian rosewood back/sides, bound ebony fingerboard with pearl block inlay, ebony belly bridge with white pins, bound blackface peghead with pearl vase/logo inlay, transducer pickup/preamp system. Available in Antique Natural and Vintage Sunburst finishes. Mfr. 1994 to 1996.

		$1,625	$900

Last Mfr.'s Sug. Retail was $2,500.

C Models

C-0 — spruce top, round soundhole, bound body, rosette decal, mahogany back/sides/neck, 12/19 fret rosewood fingerboard, rosewood wraparound bridge, 3 per side chrome tuners with plastic buttons. Available in Natural finish. Mfd. 1962 to 1971.

		$450	$300

C-1 — spruce top, round soundhole, bound body, 2 stripe rosette, mahogany back/sides/neck, 12/19 fret rosewood fingerboard, rosewood wraparound bridge, 3 per side nickel tuners with plastic buttons. Available in Natural finish. Mfd. 1957 to 1971.

		$500	$350

In 1966, wooden inlay rosette, chrome tuners replaced original items.

C-1 E — similar to C-1, except has ceramic bridge pickup. Mfd. 1960 to 1968.

		$400	$200

C-1 S — similar to C-1, except has student size body. Mfd. 1961 to 1967.

		$250	$150

C-1 D — similar to C-1, except has rounded peghead. Mfd. 1963 to 1971.

		$350	$200

C-2 — spruce top, round soundhole, bound body, 2 stripe rosette, maple back/side, mahogany neck, 12/19 fret rosewood fingerboard, rosewood wraparound bridge with pearl block inlay, 3 per side nickel tuners with plastic buttons. Available in Natural Top/Mahogany Back/Side finish. Mfd. 1960 to 1971.

		$500	$250

In 1966, redesigned rosette, peghead replaced original item.

C-4 — similar to C-2, except has gold tuners. Available in Natural Top/Rosewood Back/Sides finish. Mfd. 1962 to 1968.

		$500	$250

C-6 RICHARD PICK CUSTOM — classic style, spruce top, round soundhole, tortoise bound body, wooden inlay rosette, Brazilian rosewood back/sides, mahogany neck, 12/19 fret ebony fingerboard, wraparound rosewood bridge, rosewood veneered peghead, 3 per side gold tuners. Available in Natural finish. Mfd. 1958 to 1971.

		$850	$500

In 1966, pearl block bridge inlay was added.

Grading	100%	Excellent	Average

C-8 — similar to C-6, except has different rosette pattern, narrow peghead. Mfd. 1962 to 1969.

$650 $300

CF-100 — single sharp cutaway body, spruce top, round soundhole, tortoise pickguard, bound body, 1 stripe rosette, mahogany back/sides/neck, 20 fret bound rosewood fingerboard with pearl trapezoid inlay, rosewood reverse bridge with pearl dot inlay, white bridge pins, blackface peghead with logo decal, 3 per side nickel tuners. Available in Golden Sunburst finish. Mfd. 1950 to 1959.

$2,000 $1,400

In 1952, pearl crown/logo inlay replaced original item.

In 1957, redesigned pickguard replaced original item.

CF-100 E — similar to CF-100, except has one single coil pickup, volume/tone control. Mfd. 1951 to 1959.

$2,500 $1,500

CHICAGO 35 — bell shape dreadnought style, spruce top, round soundhole, tortoise pickguard, 3 stripe bound body/rosette, mahogany back/sides/neck, 14/19 fret rosewood fingerboard with pearl cross inlay, rosewood straight bridge with white pins, blackface peghead with screened logo, 3 per side nickel tuners, transducer pickup/preamp system. Available in Antique Natural and Special Vintage Sunburst finishes. Mfr. 1994 to 1996.

$1,300 $750

Last Mfr.'s Sug. Retail was $2,000.

CITATION — single round cutaway multi-bound body, carved spruce top, bound f-holes, raised multi-bound flamed maple pickguard, figured maple back/sides/neck, 20 fret multi-bound pointed fingerboard with pearl cloud inlay, adjustable ebony bridge with pearl fleur-de-lis inlay on wings, gold trapeze tailpiece with engraved model name, multi-bound ebony veneered peghead with abalone fleur-de-lis/logo inlay, abalone fleur-de-lis inlay on back of peghead, 3 per side gold engraved tuners. Available in Faded Cherry Sunburst, Honeyburst and Natural finishes.

In 1972, Gibson produced only 15 Citation guitars. Ten years later, Gibson produced 3 more (by customer request). These 18 guitars have not traded sufficiently to quote pricing.

Current production instruments are part of the Historic Collection Series, found at the end of this section.

CL (Custom Acoustic Line) Dreadnought Series

The Custom Acoustic Line Series debuted in early 1997. Models feature the Gibson Advanced Bracing pattern and a factory-installed transducer.

CL-20 STANDARD PLUS (CL20) — solid spruce top, round soundhole, black body binding, solid mahogany back/sides, 14/20 fret rosewood fingerboard with abalone snowflake inlay, 'moustache'-style rosewood bridge with white bridgepins, 3 per side gold tuners, 'batwing'-shaped tortoise pickguard. Available in Antique Natural finish. Mfr. 1997 to date.
Mfr.'s Sug. Retail $1,499

This model does not feature the installed transducer.

CL-30 DELUXE (CL30) — solid spruce top, round soundhole, multiple-ply body binding, solid African bubinga back/sides, 14/20 fret rosewood fingerboard with abalone floret inlay, rosewood headstock veneer, mother of pearl headstock logo/abalone floret inlay, 'moustache'-style rosewood bridge with white bridgepins, 3 per side gold tuners, 'batwing'-shaped tortoise pickguard. Available in Antique Natural gloss lacquer finish. Mfr. 1997 to date.
Mfr.'s Sug. Retail $1,849

CL-35 Deluxe Cutaway (CL35) — similar to the CL-30, except features a single Venetian cutaway body. Available in Antique Natural gloss lacquer finish. Mfr. 1997 to date.
Mfr.'s Sug. Retail $1,949

CL-40 ARTIST (CL40) — Sitka spruce top, round soundhole, abalone rosette, multiple-ply body binding, solid rosewood back/sides, 14/20 fret ebony fingerboard with abalone 'angel wing' inlay, mother of pearl headstock logo/abalone 'angel wing' inlay, 'moustache'-style ebony bridge with abalone dot bridgepins, 3 per side gold tuners, 'batwing'-shaped tortoise pickguard. Available in Antique Natural gloss lacquer finish. Mfr. 1997 to date.
Mfr.'s Sug. Retail $2,649

CL-45 Artist Cutaway (CL45) — similar to the CL-40, except features a single Venetian cutaway body. Available in Antique Natural gloss lacquer finish. Mfr. 1997 to date.
Mfr.'s Sug. Retail $2,749

CL-50 SUPREME (CL50) — solid Sitka spruce top, round soundhole, abalone rosette, abalone body binding, solid rosewood back/sides, 14/20 fret ebony fingerboard with abalone 'autumn leaf' inlay, bound headstock, mother of pearl headstock logo/abalone 'autumn leaf' inlay, 'moustache'-style ebony bridge with abalone dot bridgepins, 3 per side gold tuners, 'batwing'-shaped tortoise pickguard. Available in Antique Natural gloss lacquer finish. Mfr. 1997 to date.
Mfr.'s Sug. Retail $4,999

This model is optionally available with a "Tree of Life" fingerboard inlay (with cost upcharge).

Dove (Current Mfr.)
courtesy Gibson USA

DOVE — slope shouldered body, spruce top, round soundhole, tortoise pickguard with dove inlay, 3 stripe bound body/rosette, figured maple back/sides, 14/20 fret bound rosewood fingerboard with pearl parallelogram inlay, enlarged rosewood bridge with black pearl dot pins, pearl dove inlay on bridge wings, blackface peghead with pearl plant/logo inlay, 3 per side gold tuners with pearl buttons. Available in Antique Cherry finish. Mfd. 1962 to 1996.

1962-1968	$2,800	$1,750
1969-1989	$1,200	$750
1990-1996	$1,595	$800

Last Mfr.'s Sug. Retail was $2,450.

In 1969, adjustable bridge replaced original item.

In 1970, non-adjustable bridge replaced respective item.

In 1975, ebony fingerboard replaced original item.

In 1996, the '60s Dove model superceded the original Dove model (see listing below).

Grading	100%	Excellent	Average

'60s DOVE (HLDO) (Previously ACDO) — slope shouldered body, solid Sitka spruce top, round soundhole, 3-ply bound body/rosette, flamed maple back/sides, maple neck, 14/20 fret bound rosewood fingerboard with pearl parallelogram inlay, rosewood dove-wing bridge with mother of pearl inlay, black white dot bridgepins, bound blackface peghead with abalone crown/logo inlay, 3 per side gold tuners, tortoise pickguard with engraved dove inlay. Available in Antique Cherry (Natural top and Cherry finish back and sides) lacquer finish. Current mfr.

Mfr.'s Sug. Retail	$3,999	$2,800	$2,400	$1,600

EVERLY BROTHERS — spruce top, round soundhole, 2 tortoise pickguards, 2 stripe bound body/rosette, maple back/sides, 1 piece mahogany neck, 14/20 fret rosewood fingerboard with pearl star inlay, reverse belly adjustable bridge with pearl dot inlay, blackface peghead with pearl star/logo inlay, 3 per side gold tuners. Available in Black, Cherry Sunburst, Natural Top/Red Back/Sides and Natural Top/Walnut Back/Sides finishes. Mfd. 1962 to 1973.

1962-1968		$7,000	$5,000
1969-1973		$2,500	$2,000

This model also known as Model J-180.

In 1968, black pickguards, Natural Top/Walnut Back/Sides finish replaced original items.

The Everly J-180 (AC18) — jumbo style, spruce top, round soundhole, 2 black pickguards, multistripe bound body/rosette, figured maple back/sides/neck, 14/20 fret bound rosewood fingerboard with pearl star inlay, rosewood mustache bridge with pearl star inlay/white pins, multibound blackface peghead with pearl star/logo inlay, 3 per side nickel tuners. Available in Antique Ebony and Heritage Cherry Sunburst finishes. Mfr. 1994 to 1997.

	$1,300	$700
		Last Mfr.'s Sug. Retail was $2,000.

Everly Cutaway — similar to The Everly, except has single sharp cutaway, tortoise pickguards, gold tuners, transducer pickups/preamp system. Available in Antique Ebony and Heritage Cherry Sunburst finishes. Mfr. 1994 to 1997.

	$1,495	$850
		Last Mfr.'s Sug. Retail was $2,300.

F-25 (FOLKSINGER) — spruce top, round soundhole, 2 white pickguards, 2 stripe bound body/rosette, mahogany back/sides/neck, 12/18 fret rosewood fingerboard with pearl dot inlay, rosewood reverse belly bridge with white pins/2 pearl dot inlay, blackface peghead with screened logo, 3 per side nickel tuners with plastic buttons. Available in Natural finish. Mfd. 1963 to 1970.

	$600	$400

In 1969, redesigned body/peghead, standard bridge replaced original items, white pickguards were discontinued.

FJ-N (FOLKSINGER JUMBO) — spruce top, round soundhole, 2 white pickguards, 3 stripe bound body/rosette, mahogany back/sides/neck, 12/18 fret bound rosewood fingerboard with pearl trapezoid inlay, rosewood reverse bridge with white pins/2 pearl dot inlay, blackface peghead with pearl crown/logo inlay, 3 per side nickel tuners with plastic buttons. Available in Natural finish. Mfd. 1963 to 1968.

	$1,000	$700

FLAMENCO 2 — classic style, spruce top, round soundhole, 2 white pickguards, tortoise bound body, wooden inlay rosette, cypress back/side, mahogany neck, 12/19 fret rosewood fingerboard, rosewood wraparound bridge with pearl block inlay, rosewood veneered peghead with logo decal, 3 per side nickel tuners with plastic buttons. Available in Natural Top/Mahogany Back/Side finish. Mfd. 1963 to 1968.

	$475	$275

Gospel Series

GOSPEL — slope shouldered body, spruce top, round soundhole, tortoise pickguard, 3 stripe bound body/rosette, laminated maple back/sides, maple neck, 14/20 fret ebony fingerboard with pearl dot inlay, ebony bridge with black pearl dot pins, blackface peghead with dove/logo decals, 3 per side chrome tuners. Available in Natural finish. Mfd. 1972 to 1980.

	$800	$500

GOSPEL — dreadnought style, spruce top, round soundhole, tortoise pickguard, multistripe bound body/rosette, mahogany back/sides/neck, 14/20 fret rosewood fingerboard with pearl dot inlay, rosewood bridge with white pins, blackface peghead with screened vase/logo, 3 per side nickel tuners with pearloid buttons. Available in Antique Natural and Natural top/Antique Walnut back/sides finishes. Mfd. 1994 to 1996.

	$695	$450
		Last Mfr.'s Sug. Retail was $1,050.

Gospel AV — similar to Gospel, except has transducer pickup/preamp system. Available in Antique Natural, Natural top/Antique Walnut back/sides and Vintage Sunburst finishes. Mfd. 1994 to 1996.

	$875	$500
		Last Mfr.'s Sug. Retail was $1,350.

GS Series

GS Series classical guitars are not heavily traded in the vintage market. The following prices are estimated market projections.

GS-1 — classic style, round soundhole, bound body, 3 stripe rosette, bound body, 2 stripe rosette, mahogany back/sides/neck, 12/19 fret rosewood fingerboard, rosewood tied bridge with pearl cross inlay, blackface peghead with screened logo, 3 per side tuners with plastic buttons. Available in Natural finish. Mfd. 1950 to 1957.

	$550	$375

GS-2 — similar to GS-1, except has maple back/sides. Mfd. 1954 to 1960.

	$600	$375

Grading	100%	Excellent	Average

GS-5 (Formerly Custom Classic) — similar to GS-1, except has rosewood back/sides. Mfd. 1954 to 1960.

	$750	$400

> This model was originally designated the Custom Classic in 1954. In 1957, it was renamed the GS-5.

GS-35 — classical style, spruce top, round soundhole, bound body, 2 stripe rosette, mahogany back/sides/neck, 12/19 fret ebony fingerboard, rosewood tied bridge, solid blackface peghead with screened logo, 3 per side tuners with plastic buttons. Available in Natural finish. Mfd. 1939 to 1943.

	$650	$300

GS-85 — similar to GS-35, except has rosewood back/sides, pearl bridge inlay. Mfd. 1939 to 1943.

	$850	$400

Hall of Fame Models

> Hall of Fame models celebrate a famous artist's association with a specific acoustic guitar. All Hall of Fame models are numbered, limited editions.

BUDDY HOLLY MODEL (ACBH) — J-45 style, solid Sitka spruce top, round soundhole, bound body, mahogany back/sides, 14/20 fret bound rosewood fingerboard with pearl dot inlay, rosewood bridge, black bridgepins, blackface peghead with abalone banner/logo inlay, 3 per side nickel tuners, teardrop-shaped black pickguard. Available in Vintage Sunburst lacquer finish. Mfr. 1997 to date.

Mfr.'s Sug. Retail $4,999

> This model has a certificate of authenticity signed by Maria Elena Holly (Buddy Holly's widow).

ELVIS KING OF ROCK MODEL (ACEP) — J-200 style, solid Sitka spruce top, round soundhole, bound body, maple back/sides, 14/20 fret bound ebony fingerboard with mother of pearl crown inlay, custom ebony bridge, white bridgepins, bound blackface peghead with mother of pearl crown/logo inlay, 3 per side gold tuners, bound black pickguard with mother of pearl crown inlay. Available in Ebony lacquer finish. Mfr. 1997 to date.

Mfr.'s Sug. Retail $4,999

> This limited edition model is scheduled for 250 instruments. All models certified and endorsed by Graceland.

Elvis Presley Signature Model (ACEP) — similar to the Elvis 'King of Rock' model, except features a premium Sitka spruce top, flamed maple back/sides, 'Elvis Presley' fingerboard inlay with two stars, custom engraved 'Elvis' pickguard, bound blackface peghead with mother of pearl flowerpot/logo inlay, ebony 'moustache' bridge with pearl inlay. Available in Antique Natural lacquer finish. Mfr. 1997 to date.

Mfr.'s Sug. Retail $7,999

> The Elvis Presley Signature model is based on the custom J-200 used by Elvis during his 1969 concert at the International Hotel in Las Vegas.

> Built in cooperation with Graceland, this limited edition model is scheduled for 250 instruments. Models have a signed certificate of authenticity.

SJ HANK WILLIAMS JR. MODEL (ACJS) — Super Jumbo (SJ) style, solid Sitka spruce top, round soundhole, multiple-ply bound body/rosette, mahogany back/sides, 14/20 bound rosewood fingerboard with pearl parallelogram inlay, rosewood bridge, black bridgepins, blackface peghead with pearl logo inlay, 3 per side nickel Kluson-style tuners, teardrop-shaped black pickguard. Available in Vintage Sunburst lacquer finish. Mfr. 1997 to date.

Mfr.'s Sug. Retail $4,999

Heritage Series

HERITAGE — slope shouldered body, round soundhole, tortoise pickguard, 2 stripe bound body/rosette, laminated rosewood back/sides, mahogany neck, 14/20 fret ebony fingerboard with pearl dot inlay, reverse ebony bridge with white pins, adjustable saddle, blackface peghead with logo decal, 3 per side nickel tuners. Available in Natural finish. Mfd. 1965 to 1982.

1965-1969	$1,100	$700
1970-1982	$600	$450

> In 1968, standard bridge replaced original item.

> In 1969, black pickguard, pearl diamond/curlicue/logo peghead inlay replaced original items.

> In 1971, pearl block fingerboard inlay replaced original item, redesigned bridge with pearl curlicue inlay replaced respective item.

> In 1973, bound fingerboard replaced original item.

Heritage 12 — similar to Heritage, except has 12 strings, 6 per side tuners. Mfd. 1968 to 1970.

	$750	$500

Hummingbird Series

HUMMINGBIRD — dreadnought style, spruce top, round soundhole, tortoise pickguard with engraved floral/hummingbird pattern, 3 stripe bound body/rosette, mahogany back/sides/neck, 14/20 fret bound rosewood fingerboard with pearl parallelogram inlay, rosewood bridge with black pearl dot pins, blackface peghead with pearl plant/logo inlay, 3 per side nickel tuners with pearl buttons. Available in Vintage Cherry Sunburst finish. Mfd. 1960 to 1996.

1960-1969	$3,000	$1,500
1970-1989	$1,100	$600
1990-1996	$1,250	$695

Last Mfr.'s Sug. Retail was $2,299.

> Between 1962-1963, some models were produced with maple back/sides.

> In 1969, adjustable saddle replaced original item.

> In 1970, non-adjustable saddle replaced respective item.

Hummingbird (Current Mfr.)
courtesy Gibson USA

Grading	100%	Excellent	Average

In 1973, block fingerboard inlay replaced original item.

In 1984, parallelogram fingerboard inlay replaced respective item.

In 1996, the Early '60s Hummingbird model superceded the original Hummingbird model (see listing below).

EARLY '60s HUMMINGBIRD (HLHB)(Previous ACHB) — dreadnought style, solid Sitka spruce top, round soundhole, bound body, mahogany back/sides, 24 3/4" scale, 14/20 fret bound rosewood fingerboard with mother of pearl parallelogram inlay, rosewood bridge, black bridgepins, blackface peghead with abalone crown/logo inlay, 3 per side nickel tuners, tortoiseshell pickguard with floral/hummingbird design. Available in Heritage Cherry Sunburst lacquer finish. Current mfr.

Mfr.'s Sug. Retail	$2,449	$1,750	$1,475	$975

Jubilee Series

JUBILEE — ¾ size square shouldered body, spruce top, round soundhole, black pickguard, bound body/rosette, mahogany back/sides/neck, 14/20 fret rosewood fingerboard with pearl dot inlay, adjustable rosewood bridge, 3 per side tuners. Available in Natural finish. Mfd. 1970 to 1971.

		$700	$400

Jubilee 12 String — similar to Jubilee, except has 12 strings, 6 per side tuners.

		$500	$300

Jubilee Deluxe — similar to Jubilee, except has multi-wooden binding/purfling, rosewood back/sides.

		$800	$600

J Series

JUMBO — round soundhole, stripe bound body/rosette, mahogany back/sides/neck, 14/19 fret rosewood fingerboard with pearl dot inlay, rectangular rosewood bridge with white pins, blackface peghead with pearl logo inlay, 3 per side nickel tuners, tortoise pickguard. Available in Sunburst finish. Mfd. 1934 to 1936.

		$20,000	$6,000

In 1935, fingerboard binding was added.

Advanced Jumbo — similar to Jumbo, except has rosewood back/sides, pearl diamond/arrow fingerboard inlay, white black dot bridge pins, pearl diamond/arrow peghead inlay. Available in Sunburst finish. Mfd. 1936 to 1940.

		$35,000	$15,000

1936 ADVANCED JUMBO (HLAJ) (Previously ACAJ) — slope shouldered body, solid Sitka spruce top, round soundhole, bound body, Indian rosewood back/sides, 14/20 fret bound rosewood fingerboard with mother of pearl arrow inlay, rosewood bridge, white bridgepins, blackface peghead with abalone crown/logo inlay, 3 per side nickel tuners, "flame" colored pickguard. Available in Vintage Sunburst lacquer finish. Current mfr.

Mfr.'s Sug. Retail	$2,999	$2,100	$1,800	$1,200

J-25 — slope shouldered body, laminated spruce top, round soundhole, tortoise pickguard, bound body/rosette, synthetic back/sides bowl, mahogany neck, 14/20 fret rosewood fingerboard with pearl dot inlay, rosewood bridge with white pins, blackface peghead with screened logo, 3 per side nickel tuners with pearloid buttons. Available in Natural finish. Mfd. 1984 to 1987.

		$550	$350

J-30 — dreadnought body, spruce top, round soundhole, tortoise pickguard, 3 stripe bound body/rosette, mahogany back/sides/neck, 14/20 fret rosewood fingerboard with pearl dot inlay, blackface peghead with pearl banner/logo inlay, rosewood bridge with black pins, 3 per side nickel tuners with pearloid buttons. Available in Antique Walnut and Vintage Sunburst finishes. Mfd. 1985 to date.

Mfr.'s Sug. Retail	$1,400	$1,050	$850	$450

In 1994, reverse bridge with rosewood pins replaced original item.

J-30 Cutaway — similar to J-30, except has single round cutaway, reverse belly bridge with rosewood pins, transducer pickup/preamp system. Available in Antique Walnut and Vintage Sunburst finishes. Mfr. 1994 to date.

Mfr.'s Sug. Retail	$1,750	$1,325	$1,150	$600

Jumbo 35 (Also J-35) — spruce top, round soundhole, bound body, 1-ply stripe rosette, mahogany back/sides/neck, 14/19 fret rosewood fingerboard with pearl dot inlay, rosewood straight bridge with pearl dot inlay, white bridge pins, blackface peghead with screened logo, 3 per side tuners with plastic buttons, "tiger stripe" pickguard. Available in Sunburst finish. Mfd. 1936 to 1942.

		$5,500	$3,000

In 1939, Natural finish was also available.

In 1941, both Natural and Sunburst finishes were available.

J-35 (1985 to 1987 Mfr.) — spruce top, round soundhole, tortoise pickguard, 3 stripe bound body/rosette, maple back/sides/neck, 14/20 fret rosewood fingerboard with pearl dot inlay, rosewood reverse bridge with white black dot pins, blackface peghead with screened logo, 3 per side tuners with plastic buttons. Available in Cherry Sunburst finish. Mfd. 1985 to 1987.

		$800	$450

J-40 — spruce top, round soundhole, black pickguard, bound body, 3 stripe rosette, laminated mahogany back/sides, mahogany neck, 14/20 fret rosewood fingerboard with pearl dot inlay, rosewood strings through bridge, screened peghead logo, 3 per side chrome tuners. Available in Natural finish. Mfd. 1971 to 1982.

		$600	$350

In 1973, 3-piece maple neck replaced original item.

This model was optionally available in Cherry Sunburst finish.

J-30 (Current Mfr.)
courtesy Gibson USA

J-45 — slope shouldered body, spruce top, round soundhole, tortoise shell pickguard, 3 stripe bound body/rosette, mahogany back/sides/neck, 14/20 fret rosewood fingerboard with pearl dot inlay, rosewood bridge with black pins, 3 per side nickel tuners with pearl buttons. Available in Sunburst finish. Mfd. 1942 to 1985.

1942-1945	$3,000	$2,000

This model was originally offered with a single stripe body binding. The banner peghead inlay was offered from 1942 to 1945.

1946	$2,200	$1,800
1947-1954	$2,000	$1,500
1955-1960	$1,800	$1,200
1960-1968	$1,200	$800
1969-1985	$700	$450

Some models were made with maple back and sides, and a small amount in rosewood back and sides. These models command a premium price.

In 1942, multi-ply body binding was offered; In 1943, one stripe body binding replaced multi-ply body binding.

In 1950, upper belly on bridge, 3 stripe body binding replaced original items.

In 1955, redesigned pickguard replaced original item.

In 1956, adjustable bridge became optionally available.

In 1962, Cherry Sunburst finish was offered.

In 1968, belly under bridge replaced respective item.

In 1969, redesigned body/pickguard replaced respective items.

In 1971, non-adjustable saddle became standard.

In 1975, redesigned pickguard, 4 stripe top purfling, tortoise body binding replaced respective items.

In 1981, 3 stripe top purfling replaced respective item.

J-45 Celebrity — similar to J-45, except has rosewood back/sides, abalone *The Gibson* and fern design peghead inlay, 5-ply bound headstock, ebony fingerboard and bridge, 7-ply front and back binding, gold hardware. Mfd. 1985 only.

	$1,800	$1,200

Approximately 100 of these instruments were produced.

EARLY J-45 (HL45)(Previously AC45) — slope shouldered dreadnought style, solid Sitka spruce top, round soundhole, white body binding, mahogany back/sides, 14/20 fret rosewood fingerboard with mother of pearl dot inlay, vintage-style rosewood reverse belly bridge, white bridgepins, blackface peghead with logo inlay, 3 per side vintage-style nickel tuners, teardrop-shaped black pickguard. Available in Vintage Sunburst lacquer finish. Mfr. 1984 to date.

Mfr.'s Sug. Retail $1,799	$1,350	$1,100	$775

Beginning in 1984, the J-45 Reissue was available in Ebony, Natural and Sunburst finishes. When the model was re-designated the Early J-45, the finish was changed to a Vintage Sunburst finish.

J-50 — similar to J-45, except has Natural finish. Mfd. 1947 to 1985.

1946-1959	$2,000	$1,100
1960-1969	$1,200	$700
1970-1985	$700	$450

JUMBO 55 (J-55) (1939 to 1942 Mfr.) — spruce top, round soundhole, tortoise pickguard, bound body, 1 stripe rosette, mahogany back/sides/neck, 14/20 fret bound coffeewood fingerboard with pearl dot inlay, coffeewood mustache bridge with pearl dot inlay, white bridge pins, blackface stairstep peghead with pearl logo inlay, 3 per side tuners with amber buttons. Available in Sunburst finish. Mfd. 1939 to 1942.

	$7,500	$6,000

In 1940, standard peghead replaced original item.

	$6,000	$4,000

In 1941, rosewood fingerboard, wings shaped rosewood bridge with pearl dot inlay replaced original items.

J-55 *(1973 to 1982 Mfr.)* — slope shouldered body, spruce top, round soundhole, tortoise pickguard, bound body, 3 stripe rosette, laminated mahogany back/sides, maple neck, 14/20 fret rosewood fingerboard with pearl dot inlay, rosewood bridge with black white dot pins, blackface peghead with pearl logo inlay, 3 per side chrome tuners. Available in Natural finish. Mfd. 1973 to 1982.

	$650	$300

J-60 — dreadnought body, spruce top, round soundhole, tortoise pickguard, 3 stripe bound body/rosette, rosewood back/sides, mahogany neck, 14/20 fret rosewood fingerboard with pearl dot inlay, rosewood bridge with black pins, 3 per side nickel tuners with pearl buttons. Available in Antique Natural and Vintage Sunburst finishes. Disc. 1998.

	$1,100	$650

Last Mfr.'s Sug. Retail was $1,999.

J-60 TRADITIONAL (CL60) — square shoulder dreadnought, solid Sitka spruce top, round soundhole, abalone body binding, solid rosewood back/sides, 14/20 fret ebony fingerboard with pearl dot inlay, bound headstock with mother of pearl script logo, ebony belly bridge with white bridgepins, 3 per side gold tuners, teardrop-shaped tortoise pickguard. Available in Antique Natural gloss lacquer finish. Mfr. 1997 to date.

Mfr.'s Sug. Retail $2,099

Grading	100%	Excellent	Average

J-100 — spruce top, round soundhole, black pickguard, 2 stripe bound body/rosette, maple back/sides/neck, 14/20 fret rosewood fingerboard with pearl dot inlay, rosewood bridge with black pins, 3 per side nickel tuners with pearl buttons. Available in Natural finish. Mfd. 1985 to 1991.

	$900	**$600**

This model was optionally available with a cedar top.

J-100 XTRA — spruce top, round soundhole, black pickguard, 2 stripe bound body/rosette, mahogany back/sides/neck, 14/20 fret rosewood fingerboard with pearl dot inlay, rosewood bridge with black pins, blackface peghead with pearl crown/logo inlay, 3 per side nickel tuners with pearloid buttons. Available in Antique Walnut and Vintage Sunburst finishes. Disc. 1998.

	$975	**$550**

Last Mfr.'s Sug. Retail was $1,500.

In 1994, tortoise pickguard, mustache bridge with rosewood pins replaced original items.

J-100 Xtra Cutaway — similar to J-100 Xtra, except has single round cutaway, tortoise pickguard, mustache bridge with rosewood pins, transducer pickup/preamp system. Available in Antique Walnut and Vintage Sunburst finishes. Mfd. 1994 to 1998.

	$1,200	**$650**

Last Mfr.'s Sug. Retail was $1,850.

J-180 — spruce top, round soundhole, 2 tortoise pickguards, 3 stripe bound body/rosette, maple back/sides, 1 piece mahogany neck, 14/20 fret rosewood fingerboard with pearl star inlay, reverse belly bridge with black white dot pins, blackface peghead with pearl star/logo inlay, 3 per side nickel tuners with pearloid buttons. Available in Black finish. Mfd. 1986 to 1991.

	$1,000	**$585**

J-180 (HL18) — solid Sitka spruce top, round soundhole, white body binding, maple back/sides, 14/20 fret bound rosewood fingerboard with mother of pearl star inlay, rosewood bridge, white bridgepins, blackface peghead with abalone star/logo inlay, 3 per side nickel tuners, "dual side" black pickguard. Available in Ebony lacquer finish. Current mfr.

Mfr.'s Sug. Retail	**$2,199**	**$1,550**	**$1,325**	**$875**

J-185 — spruce top, round soundhole, tortoise pickguard, 2 stripe bound body/rosette, figured maple back/sides, mahogany neck, 14/20 fret rosewood fingerboard with pearl parallelogram inlay, upper belly rosewood bridge with white pins, pearl cross bridge wings inlay, blackface peghead with pearl crown/logo inlay, 3 per side nickel tuners. Available in Cremona Brown Burst and Natural finishes. Mfd. 1951 to 1958.

	$6,500	**$4,500**

Models in a Natural finish command a premium.

J-200 (Also SJ-200) — spruce top, round soundhole, black pickguard with engraved floral pattern, figured maple back/sides/neck, 14/20 fret bound rosewood fingerboard with pearl crown inlay, rosewood mustache bridge with pearl block inlay, black pearl dot pins, bound peghead with pearl plant/logo inlay, 3 per side gold tuners with pearl buttons. Available in Antique Walnut, Natural and Vintage Sunburst finishes. Mfd. 1946 to 1996.

Rosewood back and sides.

1937-1942	**$25,000 (and Up)**	

Figured maple back and sides.

1946-1959	**$6,000**	**$2,800**
1960-1969	**$3,500**	**$1,800**
1970-1989	**$1,500**	**$800**
1990-1996	**$1,750**	**$1,100**

Last Mfr.'s Sug. Retail was $2,700.

When this model was introduced in 1937, it was known as the Super Jumbo (SJ-200). In 1947, it was renamed in the company catalogs to the J-200. However, many instruments continued to by labeled SJ-200 well into the early 1950s. Some pre-war models with rosewood construction have sold for above $25,000. Pre-War instruments should be determined on a piece-by-piece basis as opposed to the usual market, as this model and many of Gibson's high end instruments were not manufactured during the war - thus, there simply aren't that many guitars available (or as we like to say Up North, it's hard to go fishing when there's not many fish in the pond).

When this model was originally released, it featured a single peghead binding.

In 1948, Natural finish became optionally available.

In 1960, adjustable saddle bridge became an option.

In 1961, tune-o-matic bridge with pearl block inlay replaced original items.

In 1969, adjustable saddle became standard.

In 1971, ebony fingerboard replaced original item, non-adjustable bridge replaced respective item.

In 1979, rosewood fingerboard replaced respective item.

In 1985, mustache bridge with pearl block inlay replaced respective item, multi-bound peghead replaced original item.

In 1994, Antique Ebony finish was introduced, pearl crown fingerboard inlay, gold hardware replaced respective items.

In 1996, the '50s Super Jumbo 200 model superceded the J-200 model (see listing below).

J-200 12-String — similar to J-200, except has 12 strings, 6 per side tuners. Disc. 1998.

	$2,100	**$1,250**

Last Mfr.'s Sug. Retail was $3,200.

1953 Gibson J-200
19th Annual Dallas Show

G

Grading	100%	Excellent	Average

J-200 Celebrity — similar to J-200, except has ornate scroll type fingerboard inlay, fern peghead inlay. Mfd. 1985 only.

	$2,000	$1,500

J-200 Deluxe — spruce top, round soundhole, black pickguard with engraved floral pattern/abalone dot inlay, abalone bound body/rosette, figured maple back/sides/neck, 14/20 fret bound ebony fingerboard with abalone crown inlay, ebony mustache bridge with abalone block inlay/white abalone dot pins, bound blackface peghead with abalone crown/logo inlay, 3 per side gold Grover Imperial tuners. Available in Antique Natural and Vintage Sunburst finishes. Mfd. 1994 to 1996.

	$3,375	$2,075
		Last Mfr.'s Sug. Retail was $5,200.

This model has rosewood back/sides/neck optionally available.

J-200 Jr. — similar to J-200, except has smaller body, nickel tuners. Disc. 1994.

	$1,250	$725
		Last Mfr.'s Sug. Retail was $1,800.

This model was also offered in a 12-string configuration (Model J-200 Jr. 12-String).

'50s SUPER JUMBO 200 (HL20) (Previously AC20) — Sitka spruce top, round soundhole, abalone bound body/rosette, flamed maple back/sides, maple neck, 14/20 fret bound rosewood fingerboard with abalone crown inlay, rosewood mustache bridge with abalone block inlay/white abalone dot pins, bound blackface peghead with abalone crown/logo inlay, 3 per side gold tuners, black pickguard with engraved floral pattern/abalone dot inlay. Available in Antique Natural and Vintage Sunburst lacquer finishes. Current mfr.

Mfr.'s Sug. Retail	$3,999	$2,800	$2,400	$1,600

J-250 R — spruce top, round soundhole, black pickguard with engraved floral pattern, rosewood back/sides, mahogany neck, 14/20 fret bound rosewood fingerboard with pearl crown inlay, rosewood mustache bridge with pearl block inlay, black pearl dot pins, bound peghead with pearl crown/logo inlay, 3 per side gold tuners with pearl buttons. Available in Natural finish. Mfd. 1972 to 1978.

	$850	$375

J-300 — similar to J-250 R, except has 12 strings, 6 per side tuners. Mfd. 1973 only.

	$725	$300

J-1000 — rounded single cutaway body, spruce top, round soundhole, 3 stripe bound body/rosette, rosewood back/sides, mahogany neck, 20 bound rosewood pointed fingerboard with pearl diamond inlay, rosewood mustache bridge with black pearl dot pins, bound blackface peghead with pearl diamond/logo inlay, 3 per side gold tuners. Available in Natural finish. Mfd. 1992 only.

	$1,400	$850
		Last Mfr.'s Sug. Retail was $1,999.

J-1500 — rounded single cutaway body, spruce top, round soundhole, 3 stripe bound body, abalone rosette, rosewood back/sides, mahogany neck, 20 fret bound ebony pointed fingerboard with abalone varied diamond inlay, ebony mustache bridge with white black dot pins, bound blackface peghead with abalone fleur-de-lis/logo inlay, 3 per side gold tuners. Available in Natural finish. Mfd. 1992 only.

	$1,700	$1,100
		Last Mfr.'s Sug. Retail was $2,750.

J-2000/CUSTOM — single rounded cutaway body, spruce top, round soundhole, abalone bound body/rosette, rosewood back/sides, mahogany neck, 20 fret bound ebony point fingerboard with abalone leaf inlay, ebony bridge with white abalone dot pins, abalone leaf bridge wings inlay, bound peghead with leaf/logo inlay, 3 per side gold tuners with pearl buttons, piezo bridge pickup, endpin pickup jack. Available in Antique Natural and Vintage Sunburst finishes. Disc. 1994.

	$2,500	$1,600
		Last Mfr.'s Sug. Retail was $4,010.

JG-0 — spruce top, round soundhole, bound body, 1 stripe rosette, mahogany back/sides/neck, 14/20 fret rosewood fingerboard with pearl dot inlay, rosewood bridge with white pins, logo peghead decal, 3 per side tuners. Available in Natural finish. Mfd. 1970 to 1972.

	$500	$250

JG-12 — similar to JG-0, except has 12 strings, 6 per side tuners. Mfd. 1970 only.

	$450	$200

SJ (SOUTHERNER JUMBO) — spruce top, round soundhole, black pickguard, 2 stripe bound body/rosette, mahogany back/sides/neck, 14/20 fret bound rosewood fingerboard with pearl parallelogram inlays, rosewood bridge with white pins, blackface peghead with pearl banner logo inlay, 3 per side nickel tuners. Available in Sunburst finish. Mfd. 1942 to 1978.

Banner peghead inlay (1942-1945)

1942-1945	$4,500	$3,000

Banner peghead inlay discontinued 1946.

1946-1959	$2,100	$1,100
1960-1969	$1,300	$800
1970-1978	$700	$450

A few early models are found with rosewood back/sides.

In 1946, the banner inlay on the peghead was discontinued.

In 1949, upper belly bridge replaced original item.

In 1954, Natural finish became optionally available.

In 1955, redesigned pickguard replaced original item.

J-2000
courtesy Gibson USA

In 1956, the SJ in Natural finish was renamed the Country-Western Jumbo. In 1960, this new designation was again renamed the SJN (See SJN listing below).

In mid to late 1962, adjustable saddle replaced original item; redesigned body/pickguard replaced respective items.

In 1969, standard style bridge replaced respective item.

In 1970, non-adjustable saddle replaced respective item.

In 1974, 4 stripe body/2 stripe neck binding replaced original items.

SJN (Also SJN Country Western)(Formerly Country-Western Jumbo) — similar to SJ (Southern Jumbo), except has tortoise pickguard. Available in Natural finish. Mfd. 1956 to 1978.

1956-1969		$1,700	$1,100
1970-1978		$700	$450

In 1956, the SJ in Natural finish was renamed the Country-Western Jumbo. In 1960, this new designation was again renamed the SJN.

In 1962, the SJN was again called the Country-Western.

SJ-45 DELUXE — spruce top, round soundhole, tortoise pickguard, abalone bound body, 3 stripe rosette, rosewood back/sides, mahogany neck, 14/20 fret bound rosewood fingerboard with pearl flower inlay, rosewood bridge with white pins, bound blackface peghead with pearl banner/logo inlay, 3 per side gold tuners. Available in Antique Natural and Special Vintage Sunburst finishes. Mfd. 1994 to date.

Mfr.'s Sug. Retail	$3,000	$2,250	$1,950	$1,000

L Series

STYLE L — arched spruce top, round soundhole, bound body, wood inlay rosette, maple back/sides/neck, 13/19 fret ebony fingerboard with pearl dot inlay, ebony bridge/trapeze tailpiece, blackface peghead, 3 per side tuners. Available in Orange Top finish. Mfd. approx. 1903.

	$1,200	$900

L-0 (1926 to 1933 Mfr.) — spruce top, round soundhole, bound body, 2 stripe rosette, maple back/sides, mahogany neck, 12/19 fret ebonized fingerboard with pearl dot inlay, ebony pyramid bridge with black pins, blackface peghead with screened logo, 3 per side tuners with plastic buttons. Available in Amber Brown finish. Mfd. 1926 to 1933.

	$1,000	$700

A few of these instruments are found with black tuner buttons.

In 1928, mahogany top/back/sides, bound soundhole, rosewood fingerboard, rosewood standard bridge with extra white pin replaced original items.

In 1929, straight bridge with no extra pin replaced respective item.

In 1932, 14/19 fret fingerboard replaced original item.

L-0 (1937 to 1942 Mfr.) — similar to L-0, except has spruce top, tortoise or white pickguard. Available in Ebony finish. Mfd. 1937 to 1942.

	$1,200	$850

L-00 — spruce top, round soundhole, tortoise or white pickguard, bound body, 2 stripe rosette, mahogany back/sides/neck, 14/19 fret rosewood fingerboard with pearl dot inlay, rosewood straight bridge with black white dot pins, blackface peghead with screened logo, 3 per side tuners with plastic buttons. Available in Ebony, Natural and Sunburst finishes. Mfd. approx. 1930 to 1945.

	$1,600	$1,000

Models with maple back/sides command a premium (up to 50% for flamed maple).

Early versions of this model have 12/19 fret fingerboards.

In 1934, Sunburst finish became available.

In 1937, ¾ size body became optionally available.

In 1941, Natural finish became optionally available, Ebony finish was discontinued.

In 1942, banner peghead logo found on a few instruments.

L-00 (1936 REISSUE) — spruce top, round soundhole, 2 stripe bound body/rosette, mahogany back/sides/neck, 14/19 fret bound rosewood fingerboard with pearl dot inlay, rosewood bridge with white pins, 3 per side nickel tuners with plastic buttons. Available in Antique Walnut and Vintage Sunburst finishes. Mfd. 1992 to 1996.

	$850	$500

Last Mfr.'s Sug. Retail was $1,300.

L-1 ARCHTOP — carved spruce top, bound round soundhole, raised tortoise pickguard, bound body, 2 rope pattern rosette, birch back/sides, maple neck, 13/19 fret ebony fingerboard with pearl dot inlay, ebony bridge/trapeze tailpiece, slotted peghead, 3 per side tuners with plastic buttons. Available in Orange Top/Mahogany finish. Mfd. 1903 to 1925.

	$600	$350

This model was also produced with maple back/sides.

In 1918, Brown finish replaced original item.

In 1920, 5 ring rosette replaced original item.

Grading	100%	Excellent	Average

L-1 Flat Top — spruce top, round soundhole, bound body, 3 ring rosette, mahogany back/sides, maple neck, 12/19 fret ebony fingerboard with pearl dot inlay, ebony pyramid bridge with black pins, painted peghead logo, 3 per side tuners with plastic buttons. Available in Brown finish. Mfd. 1926 to 1937.

| | **$1,800** | **$1,000** | |

By 1928, bound rosewood fingerboard, 3 stripe bound body/rosette, rosewood belly bridge with white pins, Brown Sunburst finish replaced original items, extra bridge pin was added.

In 1929, straight bridge replaced respective item, extra bridge pin was discontinued.

In 1931, the body and bridge were redesigned, unbound fingerboard replaced respective item.

In 1932, single bound body, 14/19 fret fingerboard replaced respective items.

In 1933, a tortoise pickguard and peghead logo were added.

L-1 (Reissue) — spruce top, round soundhole, 2 stripe bound body/rosette, mahogany back/sides/neck, 14/19 fret bound rosewood fingerboard with pearl dot inlay, rosewood bridge with white pins, 3 per side nickel tuners with plastic buttons. Available in Vintage Cherry Sunburst finish. Current mfr.

| **Mfr.'s Sug. Retail** | **$1,400** | **$1,050** | **$900** | **$500** |

L-2 ARCHTOP (1902 to 1908 Mfr.) — carved spruce top, round soundhole, raised tortoise pickguard, bound body, 3 rope pattern rosette, birch back/sides, maple neck, 13/19 fret ebony fingerboard with pearl dot inlay, adjustable ebony bridge/trapeze tailpiece, snakehead peghead with pearl logo inlay, 3 per side tuners with plastic buttons. Available in Orange Top finish. Mfd. 1902 to 1908.

| | **$1,200** | **$600** | |

L-2 Archtop (1924 to 1926 Mfr.) — carved spruce top, round soundhole, raised tortoise pickguard, bound body, 2 ring rosette, maple back/sides, mahogany neck, 13/19 fret bound ebony fingerboard with pearl dot inlay, adjustable ebony bridge/trapeze tailpiece, snakehead peghead with pearl logo inlay, 3 per side tuners with plastic buttons. Available in Amber finish. Mfd. 1924 to 1926.

| | **$1,300** | **$700** | |

L-2 Flat Top — spruce top, round soundhole, 3 stripe body/rosette, bound body, rosewood back/sides, mahogany neck, 13/19 fret bound ebony fingerboard with pearl dot inlay, ebony pyramid bridge, blackface peghead with pearl logo inlay, 3 per side tuners with plastic buttons. Available in Natural and Sunburst finish. Mfd. 1929 to 1934.

| | **$2,000** | **$1,500** | |

This model was also available with adjustable ebony bridge/trapeze tailpiece.

In 1931, mahogany back/sides, 12/19 fret fingerboard replaced original items, gold sparkle inlay rosette/body, pearl flame peghead inlay were added.

In 1932, rosewood back/sides, 13/19 fret fingerboard adjustable ebony bridge/trapeze tailpiece replaced respective items, raised pickguard was added, gold sparkle inlay no longer available.

In 1933, top glued pickguard, ebony bridge with black pins replaced respective items.

In 1934, 14/19 fret fingerboard replaced respective item.

L-3 — carved spruce top, bound round soundhole, raised tortoise pickguard, bound body, 3 ring wooden inlay rosette, birch back/sides, maple neck, 13/19 fret bound ebony fingerboard with pearl dot inlay, ebony bridge/trapeze tailpiece, blackface peghead with pearl logo inlay, 3 per side tuners with plastic buttons. Available in Orange Top/Mahogany finish. Mfd. 1902 to 1933.

| | **$1,600** | **$1,000** | |

L-4 — arched carved spruce top, oval soundhole, wooden inlay rosette, raised tortoise pickguard, bound soundhole/body, maple back/sides, mahogany neck, 12/20 fret bound ebony pointed fingerboard with pearl dot inlay, ebony bridge/trapeze tailpiece with black pins, bound blackface peghead with pearl logo inlay, 3 per side tuners with buttons. Available in Black finish. Mfd. 1912 to 1956.

1912-1923	**$1,800**	**$1,300**
1924-1935	**$1,750**	**$1,300**
1936-1945	**$1,800**	**$1,200**
1946-1956	**$1,600**	**$1,000**

L-4 models with the truss rod command a higher premium.

In 1914, 3 ring rosette, Mahogany finish replaced original items, Black and Orange finishes optionally available.

In 1918, Mahogany Sunburst finish replaced respective item.

By 1920, rosette and peghead logo inlay were redesigned.

In 1923, tailpiece pins were removed.

In 1927, rosette was redesigned.

In 1928, round soundhole 14/20 fret unbound fingerboard, unbound peghead replaced original items, 2 ring rosette, redesigned peghead logo replaced respective items.

By 1933, bound fingerboard replaced respective item, pearl diamond peghead inlay was added.

In 1935, f-holes, bound pickguard, redesigned fingerboard inlay, redesigned trapeze tailpiece, bound peghead with lily inlay replaced respective items.

In 1937, unbound pickguard replaced respective item, round soundhole was optionally available.

In 1940, Natural finish optionally available.

In 1941, unbound peghead replaced respective item.

In 1946, bound pickguard, multi bound body replaced respective items.

In 1947, laminated pickguard, parallelogram fingerboard inlay replaced respective items.

L-4 C — single pointed cutaway body, arched spruce top, f-holes, raised laminated pickguard, bound body, carved maple back/sides, mahogany neck, 19 fret bound rosewood fingerboard with pearl parallelogram inlay, adjustable rosewood bridge/trapeze tailpiece, blackface peghead with pearl flowerpot/logo inlay, 3 per side tuners with plastic buttons. Available in Natural and Sunburst finishes. Mfd. 1949 to 1971.

1949-1962	$2,200	$1,600
1962-1971	$2,000	$1,400

Add 20% for Natural (Blonde) finish.

L-5 — carved spruce top, f-holes, raised multi-bound pickguard, multi-bound body, carved figured maple back/sides, figured maple/ebony neck, 14/20 fret bound ebony pointed fingerboard with pearl dot inlay, adjustable ebony bridge/trapeze tailpiece, multi-bound blackface snakehead peghead with pearl flowerpot/logo inlay, 3 per side silver plate tuners with pearl buttons, Master Model/Loyd Loar signature labels. Available in Cremona Brown Sunburst finish. Mfd. 1922 to 1958.

Models signed by Lloyd Loar (1922 to 1924).

1922-1924	$30,000 (and Up)	

Loar signature label discontinued in 1924.

1925-1934	$6,000	$3,800

Advanced Body offered in 1935 (17" body width).

1935-1948	$5,000	$3,800
1949-1958	$5,000	$3,500

Some early versions of this instrument have birch back/sides.

In 1924, Loar signature label discontinued.

In 1925, gold tuners replaced original item.

In 1927, Master Model label was discontinued.

In 1929, flat fingerboard with block inlay replaced original items, individual tuners replaced respective item.

In 1935, The Advanced L-5's larger body (17 inches across lower bout), binding, tailpiece, peghead replaced original items, redesigned fingerboard replaced respective item.

In 1936, bound f-holes replaced original item.

In 1937, gold tailpiece with silver insert, Grover Imperial tuners replaced respective items.

In 1939, redesigned tailpiece replaced respective item, pearloid pickguard, Natural finish optionally available.

In 1948, 1 or 2 pickguard mounted pickups became optionally available.

Current production instruments (1934 L-5) are part of the Historic Collection Series, found at the end of this section.

L-5 P (Premiere) (Also L-5 C) — single rounded cutaway body, arched spruce top, bound f-holes, raised multi bound pearloid pickguard, multi-bound body, carved figured maple back/sides, figured maple neck, 14/20 fret multi-bound ebony pointed fingerboard with pearl block inlay, adjustable ebony bridge/gold trapeze tailpiece with silver insert, multi-bound blackface peghead with pearl flowerpot/logo inlay, 3 per side gold tuners. Available in Natural and Sunburst finishes. Mfd. 1939 to 1989.

1939-1941	$12,000	$9,000
1942-1949	$9,000	$6,000
1950-1969	$8,500	$5,500
1970-1989	$6,000	$4,000

In 1948, renamed L-5 C, 1 or 2 pickguard mounted pickups became optionally available.

L-5 CT — similar to L-5 C, except has thin body, shorter scale length. Available in Red finish. Mfd. 1959 to 1961.

	$18,500	$10,000

Also referred to as the George Gobel model. 2 humbucker pickups, 2 volume/tone controls, and a 3 position switch were optionally available.

L-7 — arched spruce top, f-holes, raised bound black pickguard, bound body, carved maple back/sides, mahogany neck, 14/19 fret bound rosewood fingerboard with pearl multi design inlay, adjustable rosewood bridge/trapeze tailpiece, bound blackface peghead with pearl fleur-de-lis/logo inlay, 3 per side tuners with plastic buttons. Available in Sunburst finish. Mfd. 1933 to 1956.

1933-1934	$2,500	$1,800

Advanced Body (17" body width) offered.

1935-1948	$2,100	$1,600
1949-1956	$2,000	$1,500

In 1934, Advanced body, fingerboard/peghead inlay, trapeze tailpiece replaced original items.

In 1937, redesigned trapeze tailpiece replaced respective item.

In 1939, Natural finish became available.

In 1942, multi bound body, parellogram fingerboard inlay, crown peghead inlay replaced respective items.

In 1944, redesigned trapeze tailpiece replaced respective item.

In 1948, laminated pickguard replaced respective item, 1 or 2 pickguard mounted pickups became optionally available.

1935 Gibson L-5
courtesy Garrie Johnson

1937 Gibson L-7
courtesy Southworth Guitars

Grading	100%	Excellent	Average

L-7 C — single rounded cutaway body, arched spruce top, f-holes, raised black laminated pickguard, bound body, carved maple back/sides, mahogany neck, 14/19 fret bound rosewood fingerboard with pearl parallelogram inlay, adjustable rosewood bridge/trapeze tailpiece, bound blackface peghead with pearl crown/logo inlay, 3 per side tuners with plastic buttons. Available in Natural and Sunburst finishes. Mfd. 1948 to 1972.

1948-1968		$4,000	$2,500
1969-1972		$2,300	$1,800

Natural (Blond) finish commands a higher premium.

This model had 1 or 2 pickguard mounted pickups optionally available.

In 1957, redesigned trapeze tailpiece replaced original item.

L-10 — arched spruce top, f-holes, raised black pickguard, bound body, carved maple back/sides, mahogany neck, 14/19 fret bound ebony fingerboard with pearl dot inlay, adjustable ebony bridge/wrapover trapeze tailpiece, blackface peghead with pearl logo inlay, 3 per side nickel tuners. Available in Black finish. Mfd. 1931 to 1939.

1931-1934		$2,500	$1,800

Advanced Body (17" body width) offered.

1935-1939		$2,500	$1,800

In 1934, Advanced Body, bound pickguard, checkered top binding, double triangle fingerboard inlay, redesigned trapeze tailpiece, bound peghead with pearl vase inlay, Red Mahogany finish replaced original items.

In 1935, redesigned tailpiece, redesigned peghead inlay replaced respective items.

L-12 — arched spruce top, f-holes, raised bound black pickguard, bound body, carved maple back/sides, mahogany neck, 14/19 fret bound ebony fingerboard with pearl flowers inlay, adjustable ebony bridge/trapeze tailpiece, bound blackface peghead with pearl vase/logo inlay, 3 per side gold tuners. Available in Red Mahogany Sunburst finish. Mfd. 1932 to 1955.

1932-1934		$2,500	$1,800

Advanced Body (17" body width) offered.

1935-1955		$2,500	$1,800

In 1934, multi-bound pickguard/top/peghead, parallelogram fingerboard inlay, diamond/star peghead inlay replaced original items.

In 1937, redesigned tailpiece replaced original item.

In 1941, bound pickguard/peghead, crown peghead inlay replaced respective items.

L-12 P (Premiere) — similar to L-12, except has single round cutaway. Mfd. 1947 to 1950.

		$3,500	$2,600

L-20 SPECIAL — spruce top, round soundhole, 2 stripe bound body/rosette, rosewood back/sides/neck, 14/19 fret bound rosewood fingerboard with pearl dot inlay, rosewood bridge with white pins, 3 per side gold tuners with plastic buttons, piezo bridge pickup, endpin pickup jack. Available in Antique Natural and Vintage Sunburst finishes. Current mfr.

Mfr.'s Sug. Retail $2,000	$1,500	$1,300	$800

L-30 — arched spruce top, f-holes, raised black pickguard, bound body, maple back/sides, mahogany neck, 14/19 fret ebony fingerboard with pearl dot inlay, adjustable ebony bridge/trapeze tailpiece, blackface peghead with screened logo, 3 per side tuners with plastic buttons. Available in Black finish. Mfd. 1935 to 1943.

		$1,000	$600

In 1936, Dark Mahogany Sunburst finish replaced original item.

In 1938, rosewood bridge replaced original item.

L-37 — similar to L-30, except has Red Mahogany Sunburst finish. Mfd. 1935 to 1941.

		$1,000	$600

In 1936, Brown Sunburst finish replaced original item.

L-47 — arched spruce top, f-holes, raised bound pickguard, tortoise bound body, maple back/sides, mahogany neck, 14/19 fret ebony fingerboard with pearl dot inlay, adjustable ebony bridge/trapeze tailpiece, blackface peghead with screened logo, 3 per side tuners with plastic buttons. Available in Natural and Sunburst finishes. Mfd. 1940 to 1943.

		$650	$400

L-48 — arched mahogany top, f-holes, raised black pickguard, bound body, mahogany back/sides/neck, 14/19 fret rosewood fingerboard with pearl dot inlay, adjustable rosewood bridge/trapeze tailpiece, blackface peghead with screened logo, 3 per side tuners. Available in Cremona Brown Sunburst finish. Mfd. 1946 to 1971.

		$500	$400

A few early instruments have spruce tops, trapezoid fingerboard inlay.

In 1952, spruce top, maple back, mahogany sides replaced original items.

In 1957, mahogany top replaced respective item, some instruments found with mahogany back also.

L-50 — arched spruce top, round soundhole, black pickguard, bound body, maple back/sides, mahogany neck, 14/19 fret ebony fingerboard with pearl dot inlay, adjustable ebony bridge/trapeze tailpiece, blackface peghead with screened logo, 3 per side tuners with plastic buttons. Available in Dark Mahogany Sunburst finish. Mfd. 1932 to 1971.

1932-1942		$1,000	$700
1943-1971		$750	$550

In 1934, redesigned body (16" body width, arched back), raised pickguard, redesigned tailpiece replaced original items.

In 1935, orchestra style body replaced respective item, arched back replaced original item.

In 1936, redesigned tailpiece replaced respective item.

1936 L-30
courtesy Sam J. Maggio

In 1943, redesigned tailpiece replaced original item, 3 per side plate mounted tuners replaced original item.

In 1946, bound pickguard/fingerboard with pearl trapezoid inlay replaced original items, redesigned tailpiece, 3 per side tuners with plastic buttons replaced respective items.

In 1949, laminated pickguard replaced respective item.

L-75 — arched spruce top, f-holes, bound body, mahogany back/sides, mahogany neck, 14/19 fret pearloid fingerboard with pearl multi-design inlay in blocks of rosewood, adjustable rosewood bridge/trapeze tailpiece, pearloid veneered peghead, rosewood diamond peghead inlay with pearl logo, 3 per side tuners with plastic buttons. Available in Natural finish. Mfd. 1932 to 1939.

$800 $550

In 1934, redesigned body/tailpiece, bound rosewood fingerboard with pearl dot inlay, blackface peghead with pearl vase logo inlay replaced original items.

In 1935, carved back replaced original item, orchestra style body, redesigned peghead inlay replaced respective items, raised pickguard added.

L-C (Century of Progress) — spruce top, round soundhole, tortoise pickguard, bound body, 1 stripe rosette, curly maple back/sides, mahogany neck, 14/19 fret bound pearloid fingerboard, rosewood block with pearl diamonds fingerboard inlay, rosewood straight bridge with white pins, bound peghead with pearloid veneer, rosewood wedge with pearl slotted diamond/logo inlay, 3 per side tuners with plastic buttons. Available in Sunburst finish. Mfd. 1933 to 1940.

$3,000 $2,300

In 1938, 2 types of rosewood peghead veneer replaced original item; one featured pearl diamond inlay, the other was bound with pearl slotted diamond/logo inlay.

L-Jr. — carved spruce top, round bound soundhole, birch back/sides, maple neck, 13/19 fret ebony fingerboard with pearl dot inlay, ebony bridge/trapeze tailpiece, tortoise plate with black pins on trapeze tailpiece, slotted peghead, 3 per side tuners with plastic buttons. Available in Brown finish. Mfd. 1919 to 1926.

Body Width 13 1/2".

$500 $350

L-Jr. models with truss rod or factory black finish command a higher premium.

The L-Jr. model is a "budget" version of the L-1 archtop.

LG Series

LG-0 — mahogany top, round soundhole, black pickguard, bound body, 1 stripe rosette, mahogany back/sides/neck, 14/20 fret rosewood fingerboard with pearl dot inlay, rosewood straight bridge, white bridge pins, blackface peghead with screened logo, 3 per side nickel tuners with plastic buttons. Available in Natural finish. Mfd. 1958 to 1974.

$400 $250

In 1962, plastic screw-on bridge replaced original item.

In 1963, redesigned tortoise pickguard replaced original item.

In 1966, rosewood reverse bridge replaced respective item.

In 1969, spruce top, standard bridge replaced respective items.

In 1970, veneerless peghead replaced original item, black pickguard replaced respective item.

LG-1 — spruce top, round soundhole, tortoise pickguard, bound body, 1 stripe rosette, mahogany back/sides/neck, 14/19 fret rosewood fingerboard with pearl dot inlay, rosewood straight bridge with pearl dot inlay, black bridge pins, blackface peghead with screened logo, 3 per side nickel tuners with plastic buttons. Available in Sunburst finish. Mfd. 1947 to 1968.

$800 $600

In 1955, redesigned pickguard, 14/20 fret fingerboard replaced original items.

In 1962, plastic screw-on bridge replaced original item.

LG-2 — red spruce top, round soundhole, tortoise shell pickguard, bound body, 1 stripe rosette, mahogany back/sides/neck, 14/19 fret rosewood fingerboard with pearl dot inlay, rosewood straight bridge with pearl dot inlay, black bridge pins, blackface peghead with screened logo, 3 per side nickel tuners with plastic buttons. Available in Cherry Sunburst and Golden Sunburst finishes. Mfd. 1942 to 1962.

$1,200 $700

Early models are found with banner/logo peghead decals.

$1,600 $1,000

During WWII, Gibson used whatever materials were available to construct instruments. Consequently, there are LG-2's found with mahogany tops, maple back/sides/neck, no truss rods and other little differences from other production models found before and after the war.

In 1955, redesigned pickguard, 14/20 fret fingerboard replaced original items.

In 1961, Cherry Sunburst finish replaced original item.

LG-2 ¾ — similar to LG-2, except has ¾ size body. Mfd. 1949 to 1968.

$850 $600

LG-3 — spruce top, round soundhole, tortoise shell pickguard, 3 stripe bound body/rosette, mahogany back/sides/neck, 14/19 fret rosewood fingerboard with pearl dot inlay, rosewood straight bridge with pearl dot inlay, white bridge pins, blackface peghead with banner/logo decal, 3 per side nickel tuners with plastic buttons. Available in Natural finish. Mfd. 1945 to 1963.

$1,800 $1,200

In 1947, banner peghead decal was removed.

1967 LG-0
courtesy Sam J. Maggio

G

Grading	100%	Excellent	Average
		$1,400	$900

In 1955, redesigned pickguard, 14/20 fret fingerboard replaced original items.

In 1961, adjustable bridge replaced original item.

In early 1962, reverse rosewood bridge with adjustable saddle replaced respective item.

In late 1962, plastic screw-on bridge replaced respective item.

The LG-3 has a "X-braced" top.

NICK LUCAS (GIBSON SPECIAL) — slightly arched spruce top, mahogany back/sides/neck, bound body, bound rosewood fingerboard with dot inlay, rosewood bridge, *The Gibson* headstock logo, special round Nick Lucas label. Available in Sunburst finish. Mfd. 1928 to 1938.

Body Width 13 1/2".

	Excellent	Average
	$3,000	$2,800

Maple- and rosewood-bodied models should bring a higher premium.

The Nick Lucas model underwent redesign at least twice in its short production span. Models can be found with 12, 13, and 14 fret-to-the-body fingerboards in mahogany, rosewood, and maple.

Nick Lucas L-00 body shape variant.

	Excellent	Average
	$5,000	$3,000

Mark Series

All of the following instruments have these features: sloped shouldered body, spruce top, round soundhole, removable pickguard, bound body, mahogany neck, 14/20 fret fingerboard, fan bridge, 3 different replaceable saddles, blackface snakehead peghead, 3 per side tuners. Available in Natural and Sunburst finishes (unless otherwise noted). The Mark series were produced between 1975 to 1979.

MK-35 — spruce top, 2 stripe rosewood soundhole cap, mahogany back/sides, rosewood fingerboard with pearl dot inlay, nickel tuners.

	Excellent	Average
	$550	$300

MK-35-12 — similar to MK-35, except has 12 strings, 6 per side tuners. Mfd. 1977 only.

	Excellent	Average
	$600	$300

Only 12 of these instruments were produced.

MK-53 — spruce top, multi-bound body, 2 stripe rosewood soundhole cap, maple back/sides, rosewood fingerboard with pearl dot inlay, nickel tuners.

	Excellent	Average
	$650	$400

MK-72 — spruce top, 3 stripe rosette, rosewood back/sides, 3 piece ebony/rosewood/ebony fingerboard with pearl dot inlay, nickel tuners.

	Excellent	Average
	$850	$550

MK-81 — spruce top, 3 stripe rosewood rosette cap, multi-bound body, rosewood back/sides, ebony fingerboard with block abalone inlays, gold tuners.

	Excellent	Average
	$900	$625

MK-99 — spruce top, round soundhole with 2 stripe rosewood soundhole cap, red stripe bound body, purple stained rosewood back/sides, purple stained maple neck, 14/20 fret red stripe bound ebony fingerboard with abalone bowtie inlay, ebony fan bridge with silver red dot pins, blackface red bound peghead, 3 per side gold tuners. Available in Natural finish. Mfd. 1975 to 1979.

	Excellent	Average
	$2,500	$1,500

This model was handcrafted and signed by Richard Schneider while he was Gibson's Master Luthier. Only 12 instruments are known to have been made.

Roy Smeck Series

RADIO GRANDE — spruce top, round soundhole, tortoise pickguard, bound body, 1 stripe rosette, rosewood back/sides, mahogany neck, 12/19 fret bound rosewood fingerboard with pearl varying diamond inlay, rosewood straight bridge with black pearl dot pins, blackface peghead with screened model name/logo, 3 per side tuners with plastic buttons. Available in Natural finish. Mfd. 1934 to 1939.

	Excellent	Average
	$2,250	$1,275

Stage Deluxe — similar to Radio Grande, except has mahogany back/sides, pearl dot fingerboard inlay, white pearl dot bridge pins. Available in Sunburst finish. Mfd. 1934 to 1942.

	Excellent	Average
	$1,950	$1,250

Two styles of this model were available: Standard and Hawaiian. The Standard model had the logo only screened on the peghead. The Hawaiian model featured inlaid ivoroid pieces instead of frets. The ivoroid pieces were usually replaced by frets, making the original ivoroid inlay configuration more desired by collectors.

In 1935, bound fingerboard with varying pearl diamond inlay replaced original item.

MODEL O — arched spruce top, oval soundhole, bound body, wood inlay rosette, walnut back/sides, mahogany neck, 12/20 fret bound pointed rosewood fingerboard with pearl dot inlay, rosewood bridge/trapeze tailpiece with black pearl dot pins, bound blackface peghead with pearl logo inlay, friction tuners. Available in Black Top finish. Mfd. 1902 to 1907.

	Excellent	Average
	$5,500	$4,200

The Model O had features from both archtop and flat top construction. Some models have an 18" body width.

This model was also available in a Presentation version, which is extremely rare (the last recorded sale of a Presentation model was for $15,000).

In 1906, a slotted peghead was introduced.

Grading	100%	Excellent	Average

Gibson Harp Guitar
courtesy Tam Milano

STYLE O ARTIST — single sharp cutaway body, carved spruce top, scrolled upper bass bout, oval soundhole, raised tortoise pickguard, bound body, wood inlay rosette, maple back/sides, mahogany neck, 15/22 fret bound extended ebony fingerboard with pearl dot inlay, ebony bridge/trapeze tailpiece with black pearl dot pins, bound blackface peghead with pearl fleur-de-lis/logo inlay, 3 per side diecast tuners. Available in Amber, Black, Mahogany Stain and Mahogany Sunburst finishes. Mfd. 1908 to 1923.

$3,000 $2,500

In 1914, Amber and Mahogany finishes replaced original finishes.

In 1918, redesigned pickguard/peghead inlay replaced original items. Mahogany Sunburst finish replaced respective finish.

STYLE U HARP GUITAR — 6-string/12 bass string configuration, round soundhole, scroll on upper bass bout, maple back and sides, bound soundhole, mahogany bridge, ebony fingerboard with dot inlay, veneer peghead. Available in Black Top/Dark Mahogany back/sides finish. Mfd. 1902 to 1939.

Body width 21".

$5,000 $3,000

Although this model stayed listed in Gibson catalogs until 1939, it's unlikely that models were manufactured after 1924.

Special Custom Models

Special Custom models were designed by Gibson Master Luthier Ren Ferguson. Special Custom models are numbered and have a certificate of authenticity.

DOVE IN FLIGHT (ACDFACGH1) — Dove dreadnought style, hand select solid spruce top, round soundhole, bound body, flamed maple back/sides, 3-piece maple neck, 14/20 fret bound ebony fingerboard with pearl parallelogram inlay, ebony dove-tail bridge with dove inlay, white bridgepins, blackface peghead with mother of pearl "3 Doves in Flight"/logo inlay, Custom Shop seal on back of headstock, 3 per side gold tuners, tortoise pickguard with engraved dove inlay. Available in Antique Cherry (Natural top and Cherry back and sides) lacquer finish. Mfr. 1997 to date.

Mfr.'s Sug. Retail $5,499

MONTANA GOLD J-200 (ACMGANGH1) — J-200 style, hand select solid spruce top, round soundhole, bound body, flamed maple back/sides, flamed maple neck, 14/20 fret bound ebony fingerboard with pearl block inlay, ebony moutache bridge with pearl inlay, white bridgepins, blackface peghead with mother of pearl "Harvested Wheat"/logo inlay, Custom Shop seal on back of headstock, 3 per side gold Imperial tuners, tortoise pickguard with engraved 'Montana Gold'/Wheat inlay. Available in Antique Natural lacquer finish. Mfr. 1997 to date.

Mfr.'s Sug. Retail $4,399

This model's serial number is inside the guitar on the headblock.

RON WOOD SIGNATURE J-200 (ACRW) — J-200 style, hand select solid Sitka spruce top, round soundhole, bound body, flamed maple back/sides, flamed maple neck, 14/20 fret bound ebony fingerboard with abalone flame inlay, ebony moutache bridge with gold lip pearl inlay, white bridgepins, blackface peghead with mother of pearl "Ron Wood" signature/logo inlay, Custom Shop seal on back of headstock, 3 per side gold tuners, dual hand-engraved pickguards with a flame design. Available in Antique Natural lacquer finish. Mfr. 1997 to date.

Mfr.'s Sug. Retail $7,999

This model was designed in conjunction with guitarist Ron Wood (Rolling Stones). Wood personally signed the first 100 labels for this limited edition model.

Super 300 Series

SUPER 300 — arched spruce top, f-holes, raised multi-ply black pickguard, figured maple back/sides, multiple bound body, 3 piece figured maple/mahogany neck, 14/20 fret bound Brazilian rosewood fingerboard with pearl parallelogram inlay, adjustable rosewood bridge/nickel trapeze tailpiece, multi-bound blackface peghead with pearl crown/logo inlay, 3 per side nickel tuners. Available in Golden Sunburst finish. Mfd. 1948 to 1955.

$3,600 $3,200

Super 300 C — similar to Super 300, except has a single rounded cutaway. Mfd. 1957 to 1958.

$6,700 $6,200

Super 400 Series

SUPER 400 — carved spruce top, bound f-holes, raised multi-bound tortoiseshell pickguard, carved maple back/sides, multiple bound body, 3 piece figured maple neck, model name engraved into heel cap, 20 fret bound ebony fingerboard with point on bottom, pearl split block fingerboard inlay, adjustable rosewood bridge with pearl triangle wings inlay, gold trapeze tailpiece with engraved model name, multi-bound blackface peghead with pearl 5 piece split diamond/logo inlay, pearl 3 piece split diamond inlay on back of peghead, 3 per side engraved gold tuners. Available in Brown Sunburst and Natural finishes. Mfd. 1934 to 1955.

Body Width 18".

1934-1939	$10,000	$8,000
1945-1955	$8,000	$6,000

Natural finish instruments command a higher premium.

From 1934 to 1938, Varitone tailpiece replaced respective item.

In 1936, upper bouts were widened.

In 1937, Grover Imperial tuners became optionally available.

In 1938, Kluson Sealfast tuners replaced original item.

In 1939, Natural finish became optionally available.

In 1941, engraved heel cap and rosewood bridge with pearl inlay were discontinued.

Grading	100%	Excellent	Average

Current production instruments (1939 Super 400 in Natural or Cremona Brown) are part of the Historic Collection Series, found at the end of this section.

Super 400 Premier (Super 400 C) — similar to Super 400, except has a single rounded cutaway, multi-bound pearloid pickguard, unhinged Varitone tailpiece. Available in Brown Sunburst and Natural finishes. Mfd. 1937 to 1983.

Pre-War models.

1937-1942	$18,000	$13,500

Post-War models.

1944-1969	$15,000	$8,500
1970-1983	$10,000	$7,500

Natural finish instruments command a higher premium.

Some early models were produced with solid metal tuners.

In 1942, no model name was indicated on heel cap.

This model, like many of Gibson's high end instruments, were not manufactured during World War II.

In 1949, rosewood fingerboard replaced original item.

In 1953, ebony fingerboard replaced respective item.

By 1957, metal tuners replaced original item.

Current production instruments (1939 Super 400 Premier in Natural or Cremona Brown) are part of the Historic Collection Series, found at the end of this section.

CHET ATKINS SUPER 4000 — single rounded cutaway hollow body, bound carved Sitka spruce top, bound f-holes, raised multi-bound tortoiseshell pickguard, carved bookmatched maple back/sides, multiple bound body, 5-piece curly maple neck, 20 fret bound ebony fingerboard, pearl split block fingerboard inlay, adjustable ebony bridge base/gold tune-o-matic bridge, gold trapeze tailpiece with ebony insertsa and abalone fleur-de-lis inlay, multi-bound blackface peghead with pearl 5 piece split diamond/logo inlay, 3 per side gold Kluson tuners with mother of pearl buttons, 'floating' pickup and linear sliding volume control with ebony knob (under raised pickguard). Available in Sunburst and Natural finishes. Mfd. 1997 only.

Mfr.'s Sug. Retail $40,000

It is estimated that only 25 Super 4000 models were built. Only 20 models were available to the public.

Gibson Super 400
courtesy Dr. Tom Van Hoose

Working Musician Models

Working Musician models are available in limited quantities.

BLUESBENDER (WM00) — small body, Sitka spruce top, round soundhole, mahogany back/sides, 3 per side nickel tuners. Available in Antique Walnut satin finish. Mfr. 1998 to date.

Mfr.'s Sug. Retail $1,099

SONGWRITER DREADNOUGHT (WM10) — dreadnought style, Sitka spruce top, round soundhole, mahogany back/sides, 3 per side nickel tuners. Available in Antique Walnut satin finish. Mfr. 1998 to date.

Mfr.'s Sug. Retail $1,099

WORKING MAN 45 (WM45) — soft-shouldered dreadnought style, Sitka spruce top, round soundhole, mahogany back/sides, 3 per side nickel tuners. Available in Antique Walnut satin finish. Mfr. 1998 to date.

Mfr.'s Sug. Retail $1,099

GIBSON HISTORICAL COLLECTION

ACOUSTIC MODELS

The instruments in these series are reproductions of Gibson classics. The instruments are manufactured to the exact specifications of their original release and in several cases, use the same tooling when available. The Gibson Historic Collection first debuted in 1991, and is now part of the Custom and Art Division.

Historic Collection instruments are produced in limited quanities. The few models that do show up in the vintage/used market are always in 95% to 98% condition (as a rule), and will still bring a premium price. Knowledge of the current market value is helpful in determining a price for these instruments.

Historic Collection Carved Top Series

CITATION (HSCTNAGH) — single rounded cutaway multi-bound body, carved spruce top, bound f-holes, raised multi-bound flamed maple pickguard, figured maple back/sides/neck, 20 fret multi-bound pointed fingerboard with pearl cloud inlay, adjustable ebony bridge with pearl fleur-de-lis inlay on wings, gold trapeze tailpiece with engraved model name, multi-bound ebony veneered peghead with abalone fleur-de-lis/logo inlay, abalone fleur-de-lis inlay on back of peghead, 3 per side gold engraved tuners. Available in Natural finish. Current mfr.

Mfr.'s Sug. Retail $32,000

Citation (HSCT[ ]GH) — with Faded Cherry Sunburst (FS) and Honeyburst (HB) finishes.

Mfr.'s Sug. Retail $26,350

1934 L-5 NON-CUTAWAY (HSL5BRGH) — multi-bound body, carved spruce top, layered tortoise pickguard, bound f-holes, maple back/sides/neck, 20 fret bound pointed ebony fingerboard with pearl block inlay, ebony bridge with pearl inlay on wings, model name engraved trapeze tailpiece with chrome insert, multi-bound blackface peghead with pearl flame/logo inlay, 3 per side gold tuners. Available in Cremona Brown Sunburst finish. Current mfr.

Mfr.'s Sug. Retail $6,250

1997 Gibson Super 4000
courtesy Buddy Summer

Grading	100%	EXCELLENT	AVERAGE

L-5 CT (HSLCTNAGH) — single rounded cutaway bound hollow body, carved spruce top, bound f-holes, solid maple back/sides, 5-piece laminated maple neck, 20 fret bound pointed ebony fingerboard with pearl block inlay, ebony bridge/model name engraved trapeze tailpiece with chrome insert, multi-ply bound blackface peghead with pearl flowerpot/logo inlay, 3 per side Schaller M-6 tuners, gold hardware, layered tortoise pickguard. Available in Natural (NA) finish. Mfr. 1998 to date.

    Body Width 17".
    Mfr.'s Sug. Retail   **$13,725**

L-5 CT (HSLCTVSGH) — with Vintage Sunburst finish.
    Mfr.'s Sug. Retail   **$10,975**

L-5 CT (HSLCTFCGH) — with Faded Cherry (FC) finish.
    Mfr.'s Sug. Retail   **$8,225**

1939 SUPER 400 (HSS4NAGH) — arched spruce top, bound f-holes, raised multi-bound mottled plastic pickguard, figured maple back/sides, multiple bound body, 3 piece figured maple/mahogany neck, model name engraved into heel cap, 14/20 fret bound ebony fingerboard with point on bottom, pearl split block fingerboard inlay, adjustable rosewood bridge with pearl triangle wings inlay, gold trapeze tailpiece with engraved model name, multi-bound blackface peghead with pearl 5 piece split diamond/logo inlay, pearl 3 piece split diamond inlay on back of peghead, 3 per side gold Grover Imperial tuners. Available in Natural finish. Disc. 1998.

            $11,750   **$N/A**
                      Last Mfr.'s Sug. Retail was $14,719.

1939 Super 400 (HSS4BRGH) — with Cremona Brown Burst finish.

            $11,000   **$N/A**
                      Last Mfr.'s Sug. Retail was $13,739.

1939 SUPER 400 PREMIER (HS4PNAGH) — single round cutaway body, arched spruce top, bound f-holes, raised multi-bound pearloid pickguard, figured maple back/sides, multiple bound body, 3 piece figured maple/mahogany neck, model name engraved into heel cap, 14/20 fret bound ebony fingerboard with point on bottom, pearl split block fingerboard inlay, adjustable rosewood bridge with pearl triangle wings inlay, gold unhinged *PAF* trapeze tailpiece with engraved model name, multi-bound blackface peghead with pearl 5 piece split diamond/logo inlay, pearl 3 piece split diamond inlay on back of peghead, 3 per side gold Grover Imperial tuners. Available in Natural finish. Disc. 1998.

            $11,750   **$N/A**
                      Last Mfr.'s Sug. Retail was $14,719.

1939 Super 400 Premier (HS4PBRGH) — with Cremona Brown Burst finish.
            $11,000   **$N/A**
                      Last Mfr.'s Sug. Retail was $13,739.

ACOUSTIC ELECTRIC

BOSSA NOVA — nylon string configuration, single round cutaway body, spruce top, round soundhole, 2 stripe bound body/rosette, rosewood back/sides, mahogany neck, 20 fret rosewood fingerboard, rosewood tied bridge, classical style slotted peghead, 3 per side nickel tuners with plastic buttons, ceramic bridge pickup. Available in Natural finish. Mfd. 1971 to 1973.

            $750   **$495**

Chet Atkins Series

CHET ATKINS CE (ARCE) — single rounded cutaway mahogany body with hollow sound chambers, solid spruce top, round soundhole with plastic bowl insert, 2 stripe bound body, wood inlay rosette, mahogany neck, 19 fret rosewood fingerboard, tied rosewood bridge, rosewood veneer on slotted peghead, 3 per side gold tuners with pearl buttons, Gibson piezo bridge pickups, volume/tone control, active electronics. Available in Alpine White (AW), Cedar (CD), Ebony (EB), and Wine Red (WR) finishes. Current mfr.

Mfr.'s Sug. Retail	$1,629	$1,150	$750	$525

    In 1994, Alpine White and Ebony finishes were discontinued.

Chet Atkins CE-AN (ARCE-AN) — similar to the Chet Atkins CE, except available in Antique Natural finish with gold hardware. Current mfr.

Mfr.'s Sug. Retail	$2,978	$2,100	$1,375	$950

CHET ATKINS CEC (ARCC) — similar to Chet Atkins CE, except has solid cedar top. Available in Cedar (CD) and Wine Red (WR) finishes. Current mfr.

Mfr.'s Sug. Retail	$1,733	$1,225	$800	$550

Chet Atkins CEC-AN (ARCC-AN) — similar to the Chet Atkins CEC, except available in Antique Natural finish with gold hardware. Current mfr.

Mfr.'s Sug. Retail	$3,089	$2,150	$1,425	$995

CHET ATKINS STUDIO CE (ARSE) — single rounded cutaway hollow mahogany body, bound body, solid spruce top, 3-piece mahogany neck, 24 fret ebony fingerboard with no inlay, 3 per side tuners with plastic buttons, slotted headstock, gold hardware, bridge-mounted piezo pickup, volume/bass/treble controls. Available in Antique Natural finish with gold hardware. Mfr. 1993 to date.

Mfr.'s Sug. Retail	$3,667	$2,550	$1,695	$1,200

Chet Atkins Studio CEC (ARST) — similar to the Chet Atkins Studio CE, except has a solid cedar top. Available in Antique Natural finish with gold hardware. Current mfr.

Mfr.'s Sug. Retail	$3,802	$2,650	$1,750	$1,250

Grading	100%	EXCELLENT	AVERAGE

CHET ATKINS SST (ARSS) — single round cutaway mahogany body with hollow sound chamber, 5 stripe bound solid spruce top with Chet Atkins' signature, mahogany neck, 21 fret ebony fingerboard with pearl star inlay, ebony bridge with black pearl dot pins, pearl star bridge wings inlay, blackface peghead with pearl star/logo inlay, 3 per side gold tuners, transducer bridge pickup, volume/treble/bass controls, active electronics. Available in Alpine White (AW), Ebony (EB), Heritage Cherry Sunburst (HS), and Wine Red (WR) finishes. Mfd. 1987 to date.

Mfr.'s Sug. Retail	$1,975	$1,400	$895	$550

In 1994, Alpine White and Wine Red finishes were discontinued.

Chet Atkins SST-AN (ARSS-AN) — similar to Chet Atkins SST, except has Antique Natural finish and gold hardware. Current mfr.

Mfr.'s Sug. Retail	$2,691	$1,900	$1,250	$925

In 1994, Translucent Red finish was discontinued.

Chet Atkins SST Flame Top — similar to Chet Atkins SST, except has figured maple top. Available in Antique Natural, Heritage Cherry Sunburst and Translucent Red finishes. Disc. 1995.

		$925	$575

Last Mfr.'s Sug. Retail was $2,179.

In 1994, Translucent Amber finish was introduced, Translucent Red finish was discontinued.

Chet Atkins SST 12 — similar to Chet Atkins SST, except has 12 string configuration, 6 per side tuners. Available in Ebony and Wine Red finishes. Disc. 1994.

		$625	$425

Last Mfr.'s Sug. Retail was $1,250.

Add $250 for Antique Natural finish.

Chet Atkins SST 12 Flame Top — similar to Chet Atkins SST, except has 12 string configuration, flame maple top, 6 per side tuners. Available in Antique Natural, Heritage Cherry Sunburst and Translucent Red finishes. Disc. 1994.

		$800	$525

Last Mfr.'s Sug. Retail was $1,600.

EAS Series

EAS STANDARD — single round cutaway body, solid spruce top, round soundhole, tortoise pickguard, bound body, 2 multi-stripe rings rosette, maple back/sides/neck, 20 fret rosewood fingerboard with pearl dot inlay, rosewood reverse bridge with white pins, blackface peghead with screened logo, 3 per side chrome tuners, bridge pickup, 3 band EQ. Available in Antique Natural, Cherry and Vintage Sunburst finishes. Mfd. 1992 to 1994.

		$650	$425

Last Mfr.'s Sug. Retail was $1,300.

EAS Deluxe — similar to EAS Standard, except has figured maple top, white pickguard, bound fingerboard with trapezoid inlay, pearl crown/logo peghead inlay, nickel tuners with plastic buttons. Available in Vintage Cherry Sunburst finish. Mfd. 1992 to 1994.

		$750	$495

Last Mfr.'s Sug. Retail was $1,500.

EC (Custom Acoustic Line) Dreadnought Series

The Custom Acoustic Line Series debuted in early 1997. Models feature the Gibson Advanced Bracing pattern and a factory-installed transducer with on-board controls.

EC-10 STANDARD (EC10) — single rounded cutaway jumbo style, solid spruce top, round soundhole, body binding, arched maple back, solid maple sides, 24 3/4" scale, 14/20 fret rosewood fingerboard with pearl dot inlay, 'moustache'-style rosewood bridge with white bridgepins, 3 per side nickel tuners, 'batwing'-shaped tortoise pickguard, bridge transducer, volume/brillance/3 band EQ controls, phase switch. Available in Cherry, Blue, and Ebony lacquer finishes. Mfr. 1997 to date.

Mfr.'s Sug. Retail	$1,699

Add $100 for Emerald Forest finish with gold hardware (**Model EC-10 Emerald Forest**).

EC-20 Starburst (EC20) — similar to the EC-10 Standard, except features multiple-ply body binding, mother of pearl starburst-design fingerboard inlay, 3 per side gold tuners, volume/brillance/treble contour/bass frequency/notch controls, phase switch. Available in Antique Natural, Cherry, and Blue finishes. Mfr. 1997 to date.

Mfr.'s Sug. Retail	$2,149

This model is optionally available with abalone floret position markers.

EC-30 BLUES KING ELECTRO (EC30) — single round cutaway jumbo style, solid spruce top, round soundhole, tortoise pickguard, multistripe bound body/rosette, flame maple back/sides, mahogany neck, 14/20 fret bound ebony fingerboard with pearl parallelogram inlay, ebony bridge with white pins, bound blackface peghead with pearl vase/logo inlay, 3 per side gold tuners, transducer bridge pickup, volume/brillance/treble contour/bass frequency/notch controls, phase switch. Available in Antique Natural lacquer finish. Mfr. 1994 to date.

Mfr.'s Sug. Retail	$2,999	$2,100	$1,800	$1,200

Early EC-30 models may have rosewood fingerboards and bridges, nickel tuners. Available in Heritage Cherry Sunburst, Natural top/Antique Chocolate back/sides and Vintage Sunburst finishes.

J-160 E — slope shouldered body, spruce top, round soundhole, tortoise pickguard, 2 stripe bound body/rosette, mahogany back/sides/neck, 15/19 fret bound rosewood fingerboard with pearl block/trapezoid inlay, rosewood bridge with white pins, adjustable saddle, blackface peghead with pearl crown/logo inlay, 3 per side nickel tuners, single coil pickup, volume/tone control. Available in Sunburst finish. Mfd. 1954 to 1979.

1954-1959		$2,000	$1,275
1960-1964		$1,450	$1,100
1965-1968		$1,300	$900
1969-1979		$1,200	$950

EAS Deluxe
courtesy Gibson USA

Grading		100%	EXCELLENT	AVERAGE

J-160 E (Current Mfr.)
courtesy Gibson USA

J-160 E (Reissue) — similar to J-160 E, except has regular saddle. Available in Vintage Sunburst finish. Mfd. 1991 to 1996.

$900 $595

Last Mfr.'s Sug. Retail was $1,900.

LES PAUL JUMBO — slope shouldered body, single rounded cutaway, spruce top, round soundhole, tortoise pickguard, 2 stripe bound body/rosette, rosewood back/sides, mahogany neck, 19 fret rosewood fingerboard with pearl dot inlay, rosewood bridge with black white dot pins, 3 per side chrome tuners, single coil pickup, volume/treble/mid/bass controls, 2 position switch. Available in Natural finish. Mfd. 1970 only.

$850 $575

JOHN AND BILL GILBERT

Instruments are built outside San Francisco, California.

Luthier John Gilbert built his first classical guitar in 1965 as a hobby. By 1974, after performing repair work in addition to his guitar building, Gilbert began concentrating on building full time. In 1991, Gilbert was joined by his son Bill. Gilbert's classical guitars have been favored by a large number of professional players. The design features a responsive projection of volume and tone coloration that depends on the guitarist' playing.

Between 1974 to 1991, John Gilbert built an estimated 140 guitars. Both Gilberts build between 6 to 10 guitars annually.

STEPHEN GILCHRIST

Instruments currently built in Australia. Distributed by the Carmel Music Company of Carmel, California.

Australian luthier Stephen Gilchrist is known for his high qualilty mandolins, mandolas and mandocellos. Gilchrist began building instruments in 1976, and spent 1980 in the U.S. working in Nashville, Tennessee at Gruhn Guitars. After 1980, Gilchrist returned to Australia and continues to produce guitars and mandolins. For further information regarding current model specifications and pricing, contact the Carmel Music Company through the Index of Current Manufacturers located in the back of this edition.

Gilchrist has built a number of acoustic and electric guitars; most of the electric guitars were built between 1987 to 1988. To make identification of these guitars a bit difficult, some models do not have the Gilchrist name anywhere on the instrument - and none of them have a serial number. This edition of the Blue Book of Guitars does not have any information regarding current models on file in the Blue Book Archives.

ROBERT GIRDIS

Instruments currently produced in Seattle, Washington.

1n 1978, luthier Robert Girdis began his studies in guitar construction at the Northwest School of Instrument Design in Seattle. After his first year of intensive studies apprenticeship, Girdis stayed on for a second year as a teaching assistant. In 1981 Girdis established his own workshop of Guemes Island (Washington), sharing a large workshop with a boatbuilder.

After a short time at work in an Anacortes boatyard, Girdis formed a collaboration with a local wildlife artist to make 50 realistic carved cedar duck decoys. Girdis also served as assistant to Guemes Island's artist/sculptor Phillip McCracken, working on several sculptures in progress in wood, stone, and bronze. Returning to his own shop, Girdis began fashioning commissioned guitars and dulcimers as well as performing instrument repair work. Dulcimer construction offered Girdis the chance to experiment with several different designs, and different exotic woods. Girdis then began to focus on building acoustic guitars, and accepting more comissions for steel string models.

Girdis has been featured in Frets Magazine, focusing on the artistic side of the craft. Girdis' guitars are noted for their big acoustic sound and attention to detail in the construction.

ACOUSTIC

The list price for Girdis' acoustic guitars start from $2,400. For further information regar ding specifications and pricings, contact Robert Girdis via the Index of Current Manufacturers located in the back of this edition.

ROBERT L. GIVENS

Instruments built circa 1960-1993.

Luthier Robert L. Givens (1944-1993) began building guitars in 1960, and continued until his untimely death in March of 1993. He built around 1,500 mandolins (about 700 of those for Tut Taylor's GTR company), around 200 guitars, and nearly 750 custom 5 string tenor banjo necks. According to Greg Boyd of the Stringed Instrument Division (Missoula, Montana), Givens built one mandolin a week except during his yearly two week vacation. Givens eschewed modern conveniences like telephones, and business was generally done face to face. Luthier Givens sometimes had one or two part time workers assisting him.

GLOBE

See also GOODMAN.

See chapter on House Brands.

This trademark has been identified as a *House Brand* of the Goodman Community Discount Center, circa 1958-1960.

(Source: Willie G. Moseley, Stellas & Stratocasters)

GODIN

Since 1987, all instruments built in La Patrie and Princeville, Quebec, in Canada; and Berlin, New Hampshire. Distributed by La Si Do, Inc. of St. Laurent, Canada.

Although the trademark and instruments bearing his name are relatively new, Robert Godin has been a mainstay in the guitar building industry since 1972. Godin got his first guitar at age seven and never looked back. By the time he was 15, he was working at La Tosca Musique in Montreal selling guitars and learning about minor repairs and set up work. Before long, Robert's passion for guitar playing was eclipsed by his fascination with the construction of the instruments themselves. In 1968 Godin set up a custom guitar shop in Montreal called Harmonilab. Harmonilab quickly became known for its excellent work and musicians were coming from as far away as Quebec City to have their guitars adjusted. Harmonilab was the first guitar shop in Quebec to use professional strobe tuners for intonating guitars.

Although Harmonilab's business was flourishing, Robert was full of ideas for the design and construction of acoustic guitars. So in 1972, the **Norman Guitar Company** was born. From the beginning the Norman guitars showed signs of the innovations that Godin would eventually bring to the guitar market. Perhaps the most significant item about the Norman history is that it represented the beginning of guitar building in the village of La Patrie, Quebec. La Patrie has since become an entire town of guitar builders - more on that later.

By 1978, Norman guitars had become quite successful in Canada and France, while at the same time the people in La Patrie were crafting replacement necks and bodies for the electric guitar market. Before long there was a lineup at the door of American guitar companies that wanted Godin's crew to supply all their necks and bodies.

In 1980 Godin introduced the Seagull guitar. With many innovations like a bolt-on neck (for consistent neck pitch), pointed headstock (straight string pull) and a handmade solid top, the Seagull was designed for an ease of play for the entry level to intermediate guitar player. Most striking was the satin lacquer finish. Godin borrowed the finishing idea that was used on fine violins, and applied it to the acoustic guitar. When the final version of the Seagull guitar went into production, Godin went about the business of finding a sales force to help introduce the Seagull into the U.S. market. Several independent U.S. sales agents jumped at the chance to get involved with this new guitar, and armed with samples off they went into the market. A couple of months passed, and not one guitar was sold. Rather than retreat back to Harmonilab, Godin decided that he would have to get out there himself and explain the Seagull guitar concept. So he bought himself an old Ford Econoline van and stuffed it full of about 85 guitars, and started driving through New England visiting guitar shops and introducing the Seagull guitar. Acceptance of this new guitar spread, and by 1985 La Si Do was incorporated and the factory in La Patrie expanded to meet the growing demand. Godin introduced the La Patrie brand of classical acoustic guitars in 1982. The La Patrie trademark was used to honor the town's tradition of luthiery that had developed during the first ten years since the inception of the Norman guitars trademark. In 1985, Godin also introduced the Simon & Patrick line (named after his two sons) for people interested in a more traditional instrument. Simon & Patrick guitars still maintained a number of Seagull innovations.

Since Godin's factory had been producing necks and bodies for various American guitar companies since 1978, he combined that knowledge with his background in acoustic guitar design for an entirely new product. The 'Acousticaster' was debuted in 1987, and represented the first design under the Godin name. The Acousticaster was designed to produce an acoustic sound from an instrument that was as easy to play as the player's favorite electric guitar. This was achieved through the help of a patented mechanical harp system inside the guitar. Over the past few years, the Godin name has become known for very high quality and innovative designs. Robert Godin is showing no signs of slowing down, having recently introduced the innovative models Multiac, LGX, and LGX-SA.

Today, La Si Do Inc. employs close to 500 people in four factories located in La Patrie and Princeville, Quebec (Canada), and Berlin, New Hampshire. Models of the La Si Do guitar family are in demand all over the world, and Godin is still on the road teaching people about guitars. In a final related note, the Ford Econoline van "died" with about 300,000 miles on it about 14 years ago.

(Company History courtesy Robert Godin and Katherine Calder [Artist Relations], La Si Do, Inc., June 5, 1996)

Production Model Codes

Godin is currently using a system similar to the original Gretsch system, in that the company is assigning both a model name and a four digit number that indicates the color finish specific to that guitar model. Thus, the four digit code will indicate which model and color from just one number. References in this text will list the four digit variances for color finish within the model designations.

ACOUSTIC ELECTRIC

A 6 6-STRING ACOUSTIC/ELECTRIC (Model 7523) — single rounded cutaway semi-hollow chambered light maple body, solid cedar top, mahogany neck, 25 1/2" scale, 22 fret rosewood fingerboard with offset dot inlay, solid peghead with Godin logo, 3 per side black tuners, rosewood bridge with white bridgepins, L.R. Baggs ribbon transducer, volume/3 band EQ slider controls, on-board preamp. Available in Blue **(Model 7486)**, CognacBurst **(Model 7479)**, and Natural **(Model 7523)** semi-gloss finishes. Current mfr.

Mfr.'s Sug. Retail	$795	$650	$425	$275

Add $100 for Black high gloss finish **(Model 9435)**.

A 12 12-String Acoustic/Electric (Model 9602) — similar to the A 6, except features a maple neck, 12-string configuration, 6 per side headstock. Available in Blue **(Model 10653)**, CognacBurst **(Model 10646)**, and Natural **(Model 9602)** semi-gloss finishes. Mfr. 1997 to date.

Mfr.'s Sug. Retail	$845	$675	$450	$300

Add $100 for Black high gloss finish **(Model 9619)**.

Godin A12
courtesy Godin

Grading	100%	EXCELLENT	AVERAGE

ACS NYLON WITH SYNTH ACCESS (Model 7745) — ((nylon string configuration) single rounded cutaway semi-hollow chambered light maple body, maple top, mahogany neck, 22 fret ebony fingerboard with offset dot inlay, multiple (5) small soundholes on upper bass bout, slotted peghead with "R. Godin" signature logo, 3 per side gold tuners with pearloid buttons, rosewood tied bridge, 6 individual microtransducer bridge saddles, RMC hexaphonic multisensors, volume/3 band EQ/synth volume slider controls, 2 synth (program up/down) push buttons, on-board preamp, 13 pin connector for Roland GR series guitar synths. Available in CognacBurst **(Model 9381)** and Natural **(Model 7745)** semi-gloss finishes. Current mfr.

Mfr.'s Sug. Retail	$995	$795	$525	$350

Add $100 for Blue high gloss finish **(Model 9428)**.

Acousticaster Series

Early Acousticaster models have a black or creme colored controls plate in the bass horn bout.

Godin Acousticaster
courtesy Bill Stevens

ACOUSTICASTER 6 (Model 3518) — single cutaway semi-hollow maple body, solid spruce top, fan bracing with mechanical harp (18 tuned metal tines), rock maple neck, 25 1/2" scale, 22 fret maple or rosewood fingerboard with offset dot inlay, 6 on one side gold tuners, rosewood bridge with white bridgepins, L.R. Baggs bridge transducer, volume/active 3 band EQ. Available in Black high gloss finish (maple fingerboard, **Model 3471**; rosewood fingerboard, **Model 3518**). Current mfr.

Mfr.'s Sug. Retail	$899	$725	$450	$295

This model was initally available in Aqua and White finishes.

Acousticaster 6 Left (Model 3532) — similar to Acousticaster 6, except features a left-handed configuration, rosewood fingerboard (only). Available in Black high gloss finish. Current mfr.

Mfr.'s Sug. Retail	$1,039	$850	$550	$350

This model was initally available in Cherryburst, Cognacburst, and Natural finishes.

Acousticaster Deluxe (Model 3594) — similar to Acousticaster 6, except has semi-hollow mahogany body. Available in Natural high gloss finish (maple fingerboard, **Model 3563**; rosewood fingerboard, **Model 3594**). Current mfr.

Mfr.'s Sug. Retail	$969	$775	$500	$325

This model was initally available in Cherryburst, Cognacburst, and Natural finishes.

Acousticaster 12 — similar to Acousticaster, except has 12 strings, 6 per side tuners. Available Black and White finishes. Disc. 1996.

	$475	$275

Last Mfr.'s Sug. Retail was $960.

Acousticaster Deluxe 12 — similar to Acousticaster, except has semi-hollow mahogany body, 12 strings, 6 per side tuners. Available in Cognacburst and Natural finishes. Disc. 1996.

	$500	$300

Last Mfr.'s Sug. Retail was $1,020.

MultiAc Series

All MultiAc semi-acoutic models feature a dual-chambered mahogany body, solid spruce top, and mahogany neck. **Synth Access** models have an RMC hexaphonic multisensor, while the **Duet** models feature the L.R. Baggs Duet system.

MULTIAC NYLON STRING WITH SYNTH ACCESS (Model 4713) — ((nylon string configuration) single cutaway two-chambered mahogany body, bound spruce top, mahogany neck, 25 1/2" scale, 22 fret ebony fingerboard with offset dot inlay, multiple (5) small soundholes on upper bass bout, slotted peghead with "R. Godin" signature logo, 3 per side gold tuners with pearloid buttons, rosewood tied bridge, 6 individual microtransducer bridge saddles, RMC hexaphonic multisensors, volume/3 band EQ/synth volume slider controls, 2 synth (program up/down) push buttons, on-board preamp, 13 pin connector for Roland GR series guitar synths. Available in Natural semi-gloss finish. Current mfr.

Mfr.'s Sug. Retail	$1,375	$1,100	$725	$475

Add $100 for Natural high gloss finish **(Model 4690)**.

MultiAc Nylon Duet (Model 7615) — similar to MultiAc Nylon String With Synth Access, except has rosewood fingerboard, L.R. Baggs Duet system (ribbon transducer and internal microphone). Available in Natural semi-gloss finish. Current mfr.

Mfr.'s Sug. Retail	$1,075	$875	$550	$375

Add $100 for Natural high gloss finish **(Model 7608)**.

MultiAc Nylon Duet Custom Shop (Model 4836) — similar to MultiAc Nylon Duet, except has ebony fingerboard, abalone bound body/neck/headstock, abalone bridge inlay. Available in Black **(Model 4836)** and Natural **(Model 4843)** high-gloss finish. Mfr. 1998 to date.

Mfr.'s Sug. Retail	$2,745

List price includes a hardshell case.

MULTIAC STEEL STRING WITH SYNTH ACCESS (Model 4812) — (steel string configuration) single cutaway two-chambered mahogany body, bound spruce top, mahogany neck, 25 1/2" scale, 22 fret ebony fingerboard with offset dot inlay, multiple (5) small soundholes on upper bass bout, slotted peghead with "R. Godin" signature logo, 3 per side gold tuners with pearloid buttons, rosewood tied bridge, 6 individual microtransducer bridge saddles, RMC hexaphonic multisensors, volume/3 band EQ/synth volume slider controls, 2 synth (program up/down) push buttons, on-board preamp, 13 pin connector for Roland GR series guitar synths. Available in Natural semi-gloss finish. Current mfr.

Mfr.'s Sug. Retail	$1,425	$1,150	$750	$525

Add $100 for Blue **(Model 7905)**, CognacBurst **(Model 7912)**, and Natural **(Model 4775)** high gloss finishes.

MultiAc Steel Duet (Model 7646) — similar to MultiAc Steel String With Synth Access, except has rosewood fingerboard, L.R. Baggs Duet system (ribbon transducer and internal microphone). Available in Natural semi-gloss finish. Current mfr.

Mfr.'s Sug. Retail	$1,175	$950	$525	$400

Add $100 for Blue **(Model 7899)**, CognacBurst **(Model 7622)**, and Natural **(Model 4639)** high gloss finishes.

Grading	100%	EXCELLENT	AVERAGE

MultiAc Steel Duet Custom Shop (Model 4881) — similar to MultiAc Steel Duet, except has ebony fingerboard, abalone bound body/neck/headstock, abalone bridge inlay. Available in Black (**Model 4881**) and Natural (**Model 4898**) high-gloss finish. Mfr. 1998 to date.

Mfr.'s Sug. Retail $2,845

List price includes a hardshell case.

ACOUSTIC ELECTRIC BASS

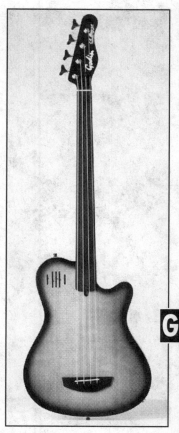

A 4 SEMI-ACOUSTIC BASS (Model 10134) — single rounded cutaway semi-hollow chambered maple body, solid cedar top, maple neck, 34" scale, 22 fret rosewood fingerboard with offset dot inlay, blackface peghead with Godin logo, 4 on a side gold tuners, strings-through rosewood bridge, L.R. Baggs ribbon transducer, volume/3 band EQ slider controls, on-board preamp. Available in CognacBurst (**Model 10141**) and Natural (**Model 10134**) semi-gloss finishes. Current mfr.

Mfr.'s Sug. Retail	$895	$725	$475	$300

Add $100 for Black high gloss finish (**Model 10585**).

A 4 Semi-Acoustic Fretless Bass (Model 10158) — similar to the A 4 Semi-Acoustic Bass, except features a fretless ebony fingerboard. Available in CognacBurst (**Model 10165**) and Natural (**Model 10158**) semi-gloss finishes. Current mfr.

Mfr.'s Sug. Retail	$995	$795	$525	$350

Add $100 for Black high gloss finish (**Model 10578**).

ACOUSTIBASS — single cutaway routed out maple body, bound spruce top, thumb rest, bolt-on maple neck, fretless ebony fingerboard, strings-through ebony bridge, 4 on one side gold tuners, piezo bridge pickup, 4 band EQ. Available in Aqua, Black and White finishes. Disc. 1996.

           $525 $325

Last Mfr.'s Sug. Retail was $1,060.

Acoustibass Deluxe (Model 3754) — similar to Acoustibass, except has routed out mahogany body. Available in Cherryburst, Cognacburst and Natural finishes. Disc. 1998.

           $675 $395

Last Mfr.'s Sug. Retail was $1,159.

Godin A4 AcoustiBass
courtesy Godin

GOLDENTONE

Instruments were produced in Japan during the 1960s.

The Goldentone trademark was used by U.S. importers Elger and its partner Hoshino Gakki Ten as one of the brandnames used in their joint guitar producing venture. Hoshino in Japan was shipping Fuji Gen Gakki-built guitars marketed in the U.S. as Goldentone, Elger, and eventually Ibanez. These solid body guitars featured original body designs in the early to mid 1960s.

(Source: Michael Wright, Guitar Stories Volume One)

GOLDEN WOOD

Instruments currently built in Gualala, California.

The Golden Wood company is currently offering hand crafted guitars. For further information regarding specifications and pricing, please contact the Golden Wood company through the Index of Current Manufacturers located in the back of this edition.

GOODALL

Instruments currently built in Kailua-Kona, Hawaii. Distributed by James Goodall Guitars of Kailua-Kona, Hawaii.

Luthier James Goodall grew up in Lemon Grove, California. Apparently, there must be something in the water, for a number of high profile luthiers (such as Greg Deering, Geoff Stelling, and Larry and Kim Breedlove) have sprung from the same area. Prior to building his first acoustic guitar, Goodall's woodworking experience was limited to his surfboard building during high school (of course, having a father with wood carving knowledge certainly helps). After his intial success, Goodall began building guitars for friends - which lead to a backlog of orders by the mid 1970s. Goodall moved to full time guitar building in 1978.

In 1981, Goodall relocated his shop to Mendocino, California. From 1981 to 1989, he averaged around 40 guitars a year. In 1992, Goodall moved off the mainland to Kailua-Kona, Hawaii. His shop now has five employees, and ships 5 instruments a week. For further information regarding pricing and specifications, please contact Goodall Guitars through the Index of Current Manufacturers located in the back of this edition.

ACOUSTIC

Goodall offers a wide range of custom options, including wood choices, fingerboard inlay, a nd body binding. For models constructed with birdseye maple, Macassar ebony, quilted mahogany, or Brazilian rosewood back and sides (al l with Master Grade tops), please call James Goodall for a price request.

Add $50 for ebony buttons (for Schaller tuners).

Add $70 for gold Schaller tuners.

Add $80 for cedar or redwood top.

Add $130 for Engelmann spruce top.

Add $175 for L.R. Baggs Ribbon transducer pickup.

Add $200 for left-handed configuration.

Add $480 for 12-string configuration.

Add $520 for cutaway body configuration.

Goldklang acoustic
courtesy Hal Hammer

Grand Concert Series

GRAND CONCERT — grand concert (smaller body) style, Alaskan Sitka spruce top, round soundhole, abalone rosette, ebony binding, 14/20 fret ebony fingerboard with abalone dot inlays, ebony bridge with black white dot pins, 3 per side chrome Schaller tuners. Available in Natural finish (with satin finish neck). Current mfr.

Mahogany back/sides, rosewood or maple binding.
Mfr.'s Sug. Retail $2,560

Rosewood back/sides, curly koa binding.
Mfr.'s Sug. Retail $2,750

Curly Koa back/sides, rosewood or maple binding.
Mfr.'s Sug. Retail $2,910

Curly maple back/sides, rosewood binding.
Mfr.'s Sug. Retail $2,990

Curly walnut back/sides, maple binding.
Mfr.'s Sug. Retail $2,990

Jumbo Series

JUMBO — jumbo style, Alaskan Sitka spruce top, round soundhole, abalone rosette, ebony binding, 14/20 fret ebony fingerboard with abalone dot inlays, ebony bridge with black white dot pins, 3 per side chrome Schaller tuners. Available in Natural finish (with satin finish neck). Current mfr.

Mahogany back/sides, rosewood or maple binding.
Mfr.'s Sug. Retail $2,775

Rosewood back/sides, curly koa binding.
Mfr.'s Sug. Retail $2,990

Curly Koa back/sides, rosewood or maple binding.
Mfr.'s Sug. Retail $3,150

Curly maple back/sides, rosewood binding.
Mfr.'s Sug. Retail $3,215

Curly walnut back/sides, maple binding.
Mfr.'s Sug. Retail $3,215

Standard Series

STANDARD — dreadnought style, Alaskan Sitka spruce top, round soundhole, abalone rosette, ebony binding, 14/20 fret ebony fingerboard with abalone dot inlays, ebony bridge with black white dot pins, 3 per side chrome Schaller tuners. Available in Natural finish (with satin finish neck). Current mfr.

Mahogany back/sides, rosewood or maple binding.
Mfr.'s Sug. Retail $2,560

Rosewood back/sides, curly koa binding.
Mfr.'s Sug. Retail $2,750

Curly Koa back/sides, rosewood or maple binding.
Mfr.'s Sug. Retail $2,910

Curly maple back/sides, rosewood binding.
Mfr.'s Sug. Retail $2,990

Curly walnut back/sides, maple binding.
Mfr.'s Sug. Retail $2,990

GOODMAN

See chapter on House Brands.

This trademark has been identified as a *House Brand* of the Goodman Community Discount Center, circa 1961-1964. Previously, the company used the trademark of GLOBE.

(Source: Willie G. Moseley, Stellas & Stratocasters)

GOODMAN GUITARS

Instruments currently built in Brewster, New York.

Luthier Brad Goodman took to woodworking in his early childhood, and by the end of high school has completed several guitars and mandolins. Over the past twenty years, Goodman has continued to refine his guitar building skills by building lutes, mandolins, acoustic flat top and archtop guitars. Goodman is currently focusing on a series of archtop models.

Goodman archtops have similar construction features like AAA figured maple back and sides, S itka spruce tops, 3-piece curly maple necks, ebony fingerboard/tailpiece/bridge/pickguard/ and peghead veneers. Instruments also featur e multiple-layer binding, abalone side dots, gold Schaller tuners, and clear lacquer finishes. Prices range from $2,800 on his **Jazz Classical** (a classical guitar with an arched back) to his Archtop models ($4,000). For further information, please contact luthier Goodman through the Index of Curr ent manufacturers located in the back of this book.

GOYA

Instruments were originally produced in Sweden circa 1900s to mid 1960s. Distributed by Hershman Musical Instrument Company of New York.

Later Goya instruments were built in Korea from the early 1970s to 1996, and were distributed by The Martin Guitar Company, located in Nazareth, Pennsylvania.

The **Goya** trademark was originally used by the Hershman Musical Instrument Company of New York City, New York in the 1950s on models built by Sweden's Levin company (similar models were sold in Europe under the company's Levin trademark). Levin built high quality acoustic flattop, classical, and archtop guitars as well as mandolins. A large number of rebranded *Goya* instruments were imported to the U.S. market.

In the late 1950s, solidbody electric guitars and basses built by Hagstrom (also a Swedish company) were rebranded *Goya* and distributed in the U.S. as well. In 1963 the company changed its name to the Goya Musical Instrument Corporation.

Goya was purchased by Avnet (see **Guild**) in 1966, and continued to import instruments such as the Rangemaster in 1967. By the late 1960s, electric solidbody guitars and basses were then being built in Italy by the EKO company. Avnet then sold the Goya trademark to Kustom Electronics. It has been estimated that the later Goya instruments of the 1970s were built in Japan.

The C. F. Martin company later acquired the Levin company, and bought the rights to the Goya trademark from a company named Dude, Inc. in 1976. Martin imported a number of guitar, mandolin, and banjo string instruments from the 1970s through to 1996. While this trademark is currently discontinued, the rights to the name are still held by the Martin Guitar company.

The Goya company featured a number of innovations that most people are not aware of. Goya was the first classic guitar line to put the trademark name on the headstock, and also created the ball end classic guitar string.

Levin-Era Goya models feature interior paper label with the Goya trademark in a cursive style, and designated "Made by A.B. Herman Carlson Levin - Gothenburg, Sweden". Model and serial number appear on the label, as well as on the neck block.

ACOUSTIC

Grading	100%	EXCELLENT	AVERAGE

G Series

G-1 — classic style, spruce ply top, round soundhole, bound body, rosette decal, mahogany stain ply back/sides, nato neck, 12/19 fret ebonized fingerboard, ebonized tied bridge, 3 per side chrome tuners with white buttons. Available in Natural finish. Disc. 1996.

$60 $35
Last Mfr.'s Sug. Retail was $115.

G-2 — similar to the G-1, except has rosewood stain ply back/sides, 3 per side chrome tuners with pearloid buttons. Available in Natural finish. Disc. 1996.

$75 $50
Last Mfr.'s Sug. Retail was $155.

G-3 — dreadnought style, spruce ply top, round soundhole, black pickguard, bound body, rosette decal, mahogany stain ply back/sides, nato neck, 14/20 fret ebonized fingerboard with pearl dot inlay, ebonized bridge with white pins, screened peghead logo, 3 per side chrome diecast tuners. Available in Natural finish. Disc. 1996.

$70 $45
Last Mfr.'s Sug. Retail was $135.

G-4 — similar to the G-3, except has rosewood stain ply back/sides, rosewood bridge with white pins. Available in Natural finish. Disc. 1996.

$80 $55
Last Mfr.'s Sug. Retail was $170.

G-120 — classic style, spruce top, round soundhole, bound body, wood inlay rosette, mahogany back/sides/neck, 12/18 fret rosewood fingerboard, rosewood tied bridge, 3 per side chrome tuners. Available in Natural finish. Disc. 1996.

$130 $80
Last Mfr.'s Sug. Retail was $260.

G-125 — similar to the G-120, except has a 12/19 fret rosewood fingerboard. Available in Natural finish. Disc. 1996.

$145 $95
Last Mfr.'s Sug. Retail was $290.

G-145 — classic style, cedar top, round soundhole, bound body, wood inlay rosette, rosewood back/sides, mahogany neck, 12/19 fret rosewood fingerboard, rosewood tied bridge, 3 per side gold tuners. Available in Natural finish. Disc. 1996.

$175 $115
Last Mfr.'s Sug. Retail was $350.

G-145 S — similar to G-145, except has solid cedar top. Disc. 1996.

$250 $165
Last Mfr.'s Sug. Retail was $510.

G-215 — grand concert style, spruce top, round soundhole, black pickguard, 3 stripe bound body/rosette, mahogany back/sides/neck, 14/20 fret rosewood fingerboard with pearl dot inlay, rosewood bridge with white black dot pins, rosewood veneered peghead with screened logo, 3 per side chrome tuners. Available in Natural finish. Disc. 1996.

$165 $110
Last Mfr.'s Sug. Retail was $330.

G-215 L — similar to the G-215, except in left-handed configuration. Disc. 1996.

$175 $120
Last Mfr.'s Sug. Retail was $350.

G-230 S — similar to G-215, except has solid spruce top, tortoise pickguard, gold tuners. Disc. 1996.

$200 $130
Last Mfr.'s Sug. Retail was $405.

G-215
courtesy C.F. Martin Company

G-145 S
courtesy C.F. Martin Company

Grading	100%	EXCELLENT	AVERAGE

G-120
courtesy C.F. Martin Company

G-300 — dreadnought style, spruce top, round soundhole, black pickguard, bound body, 3 stripe rosette, mahogany back/sides/neck, 14/20 fret rosewood fingerboard with pearl dot inlay, rosewood bridge with black white dot pins, screened peghead logo, 3 per side diecast tuners. Available in Natural finish. Disc. 1996.

$150 $100
Last Mfr.'s Sug. Retail was $300.

Add $30 for Sunburst finish **(G-300 SB)**.

G-300 L — similar to the G-300, except in left-handed configuration. Disc. 1996.

$160 $110
Last Mfr.'s Sug. Retail was $320.

G-312 — similar to the G-300, except has 3 stripe bound body/rosette, 3 per side chrome tuners. Available in Natural finish. Disc. 1996.

$180 $120
Last Mfr.'s Sug. Retail was $360.

Add $20 for Sunburst finish **(G-312 SB)**.

G-316 H — dreadnought style, spruce top, round soundhole, tortoise pickguard, herringbone bound body/rosette, rosewood back/sides, mahogany neck, 14/20 fret rosewood fingerboard with pearl dot inlay, rosewood bridge with white black dot pins, screened peghead logo, 3 per side chrome tuners. Available in Natural finish. Disc. 1996.

$240 $155
Last Mfr.'s Sug. Retail was $480.

G-318 C — single round cutaway dreadnought style, spruce top, round soundhole, black pickguard, 3 stripe bound body/rosette, mahogany back/sides/neck, 14/20 fret rosewood fingerboard with pearl dot inlay, rosewood bridge with black white dot pins, screened peghead logo, 3 per side chrome tuners. Available in Natural finish. Disc. 1996.

$185 $120
Last Mfr.'s Sug. Retail was $375.

G-330 S — dreadnought style, solid spruce top, round soundhole, tortoise pickguard, multibound body/rosette, rosewood back/sides/neck, 14/20 fret bound ebonized rosewood fingerboard with pearl dot inlay, rosewood bridge with white black dot pins, bound peghead with pearl torch inlay, 3 per side gold tuners. Available in Natural finish. Disc. 1996.

$280 $185
Last Mfr.'s Sug. Retail was $555.

G-335 S — similar to the G-330 S, except has herringbone bound body/rosette, rosewood back/sides, mahogany neck, 14/20 fret bound rosewood fingerboard with pearl snowflake/tree of life inlay. Available in Natural finish. Disc. 1996.

$290 $190
Last Mfr.'s Sug. Retail was $580.

G-415 — dreadnought style, spruce top, round soundhole, black pickguard, multibound body/rosette, mahogany back/sides/neck, 14/20 fret rosewood fingerboard with pearl dot inlay, rosewood bridge with black white dot pins, screened peghead logo, 6 per side chrome tuners. Available in Natural finish. Disc. 1996.

$195 $125
Last Mfr.'s Sug. Retail was $390.

ACOUSTIC ELECTRIC

G-312 E — dreadnought style, spruce top, round soundhole, black pickguard, bound body, 3 stripe rosette, mahogany back/sides/neck, 14/20 fret rosewood fingerboard with pearl dot inlay, rosewood bridge with black white dot pins, screened peghead logo, 3 per side diecast tuners, piezo bridge pickup, volume/tone controls. Available in Natural finish. Disc. 1996.

$235 $155
Last Mfr.'s Sug. Retail was $475.

G-318 CE — single round cutaway dreadnought style, spruce top, round soundhole, black pickguard, 3 stripe bound body/rosette, mahogany back/sides/neck, 14/20 fret rosewood fingerboard with pearl dot inlay, rosewood bridge with black white dot pins, screened peghead logo, 3 per side chrome tuners, piezo bridge pickup, volume/tone control. Available in Natural finish. Disc. 1996.

$260 $170
Last Mfr.'s Sug. Retail was $515.

G-500 — single round cutaway hollow style, round soundhole, multibound body/rosette, mahogany back/sides/neck, 20 fret bound rosewood fingerboard with pearl dot inlay, rosewood bridge with white black dot pins, bound peghead with screened logo, 3 per side chrome tuners, piezo bridge pickup, 3 band EQ. Available in Black, Blueburst and Natural finishes. Disc. 1996.

$300 $195
Last Mfr.'s Sug. Retail was $600.

G-600 — single sharp cutaway dreadnought body, spruce top, round soundhole, black pickguard, multibound body/rosette, mahogany back/sides/neck, 14/20 fret rosewood fingerboard with pearl dot inlay, rosewood bridge with black white dot pins, bound peghead with screened logo, 3 per side chrome tuners, piezo bridge pickup, 3 band EQ. Available in Black and Natural finishes. Disc. 1996.

$290 $190
Last Mfr.'s Sug. Retail was $580.

OSKAR GRAF

Instruments built in Clarendon, Ontario (Canada) since 1970.

G-300
courtesy C.F. Martin Company

Luthier Oskar Graf has been handcrafting classical and steel-string acoustic guitars for over 26 years. In addition, Graf now offers acoustic bass guitars, as well as custom designs and restorations.

Graf has built flamenco style guitars and lutes through the years, and estimates that he has produced maybe 250 guitars (mostly as commissioned pieces). Instruments feature cedar and spruce tops, and rosewood and koa backs and sides.

GRAMMER

Instruments were built in Nashville, Tennessee circa early 1960s until 1971.

The Grammer Guitar Company was founded in the early 1960s in Nashville, Tennessee. Grand Ol' Opry performer Billy Grammer's investment helped start the company after Grammer succeeded R.G.& G. Musical Instrument Company. The company was very active in the Nashville area, and many local performers used these acoustic guitars during the 1960s.

The Grammer Guitar company was later sold to Ampeg (circa unknown, late 1960s), and the later models have an Ampeg "A" logo on the front of the headstock below the Grammer name. Grammer went out of business in 1971; the company's assets (but not the trademark name) was sold at a bankruptcy auction the same year.

(Source: George Gruhn, Vintage Guitar Magazine; and Tom Wheeler, American Guitars)

GRANDE

Instruments built in Japan during the mid to late 1970s. Imported by Jerry O'Hagan of St. Louis Park, Minnesota.

Between 1975 and 1979, Jerry O'Hagan imported the Japanese-built Grande acoustic guitars to the U.S. market. O'Hagan later went on to produce the American-built solid body electric O'Hagan guitars (1979 to 1983).

(Source: Michael Wright, Guitar Stories Volume One)

GRANT

Instruments produced in Japan from the 1970s through the 1980s.

The GRANT trademark was the brandname of a UK importer, and the guitars were medium quality copies of American designs.

(Source: Tony Bacon and Paul Day, The Guru's Guitar Guide)

GRANTSON

Instruments produced in Japan during the mid 1970s.

These entry level guitars featured designs based on popular American models.

(Source: Tony Bacon and Paul Day, The Guru's Guitar Guide)

G R D

GUITAR RESEARCH AND DESIGN.

Instruments built in South Strafford, Vermont between 1978 to 1982. Distributed initially by United Marketing International of Grapevine, Texas; distribution was later retained by Guitar Reseach and Design.

GRD (Guitar Reseach and Design) was founded in 1978 by luthier/designer Charles Fox. The Guitar Reseach and Design company grew out of the School of Guitar Research and Design Center, which was founded by Fox in South Strafford, Vermont in 1973. The GRD Center was the first guitar building school in North America. The GRD company workforce consisted of graduates from the school.

GRD first advertised in **Guitar Player** magazine in the October 1978 issue, and were distributed by United Marketing International of Grapevine, Texas. This same issue also featured pictures of their Chicago NAMM booth on page 23, while page 24 showed a picture of then-GP columnist and vintage guitar expert George Gruhn holding one of their double cutaway models. The ads in the November and December 1978 issues of **Guitar Player** announced that they were available direct to the musician and to select professional sound shops around the country. A letter to customers during this time period who had requested the company's brochures announced that GRD had broken ties with their distributor.

George Gruhn's January 1979 **Guitar Player** column featured GRD instruments. Gruhn called them "one of the most interesting guitars I saw at the entire (NAMM) show...and are capable of producing almost any type of sound. The instruments are beautifully crafted, and while modernistic in design, they were tasteful, reserved, and elegant...it is a significant instrument that demonstrates the future potential in both electrical and physical design." The last mention of GRD was in the January 1981 issue of **Guitar Player** magazine, in which Jim Nollman stated that Charles Fox was designing him a 3/4-size guitar to use in playing slide guitar in Jim's attempt to communicate with whales. And you thought that slide guitar playing only perked up the ears of dogs in the neighborhood!

GRD closed its doors in 1982, and Fox moved to San Francisco to puruse other interests. Fox became a biofeedback therapist, yoga instructor, and professional gambler as he stayed out of the guitar business. However, the lure of teaching and the world of lutherie beckoned, and Fox started the American School of Lutheriy in Healdsburg, California. In 1998, Fox also returned to guitar manufacturing as he founded the CFOX guitar company (see CFOX) which is currently building high quality acoustic guitars.

(Source: Vincent Motel, G R D Historian)

GRD Design Features

Guitar Reseach and Design was an innovative company during the late 1970s. Some of the company's ideas include the thin body acoustic guitar, brass nuts, hexaphonic pickups, and active electronics that featured on-board compression, distortion, and wireless broadcasters.

GRD electric guitars utilized fade/mix controls (instead of the usual toggle switches) to blend the pickups' outputs; and featured coil tap (coil split) and phase switches. GRD electric guitars were also available with built-in 6 band graphic equalizers that offered 18 dB of cut or boost, and parametric equalizers with selectable frequency centers and cut or boost controls (these features are usually associated with P.A. mixing boards).

GRD hardware was manufactured in-house, and the pickups used on the electric models were specially wound and potted by DiMarzio.

What appears to be binding on the solid body models is actually two laminated layers of maple sandwiching a layer of ebonized maple in the center. GRD instruments all feature the highly noticable "Omega" headstock cutaway.

G-500
courtesy C.F. Martin Company

G

Grammer G-10
courtesy John Miller

ACOUSTIC

The 1978 GRD brochure featured 6 acoustic models; but also mentioned 6- and 10-string classic guitars, baroque, flamenco, and smaller sized steel stringed instruments which were available on a custom basis. All braces are fully scalloped, tapered, and floated free of the linings. The phenolic fretboard is relieved over the soundboard. Upper linings are individual tentalones, back linings are solid bent rosewood. The nut and saddle are solid brass (interchangeable saddles of bone, phenolic, and epoxy graphite were available in special order. The body/neck connection was a Spanish-style foot and shelf neck/body joint.

GRD acoustics feature a solid rosewood back and sides, peghead overlay, back linings, center web, bindings, and trim. The standard soundboard was spruce; cedar was optionally available. GRD necks are Honduran mahogany with the head and arm spliced instead of being band sawn from one piece. Headstocks featured 3 per side gold plated Schaller tuners.

On-board electronics featured a transducer pickup and tone control system that required no preamp - one pickup was mounted beneath the bridge, and the second was mounted beneath the fretboard. The on-board electronics featured volume, tone, and balance controls. The output jacks were flush mounted, and the guitars had Strap Lock fittings.

The model **F** and **F 1** were full sized acoustics with a jumbo-esque (tight waist) body style, 660 mm scale, 21 fret fingerboard. The **F 1** model has a single Florentine-style cutaway.

The **T** and **T 1** acoustics were full sized models with a dreadnought-style body, 630 mm scale, 21 fret fingerboard. The **T 1** model has a single Florentine-style cutaway.

The shallow body **S 1** and **S 2** models have a 645 mm scale, and a 21 fret fingerboard. The **S 1** has a single Florentine-style cutaway; the **S 2** is a double (dual) cutaway body.

GRECO

Instruments produced in Japan during the 1960s.

Greco instruments were imported to the U.S. through Goya Guitars/Avnet. Avnet was the same major company that also acquired Guild in 1966.

(Source: Michael Wright, Guitar Stories Volume One)

GREEN MOUNTAIN GUITARS

Instruments built in Tumalo, Oregon by the Breedlove Guitar Company. Distribution is handled by the Breedlove company in Tumalo, Oregon.

Green Mountain Guitars (by Breedlove) offers an acoustic guitar model with an interchangeable neck system for beginning (and growing) guitar students. As the student physically matures, the graduated necks can be changed to match the student's growth. For further information, contact Breedlove Guitar Company via the Index of Current Manufacturers located in the back of this book.

GREMLIN

Instruments built in Asia. Distributed in the U.S. market by Midco International of Effingham, Illinois.

Gremlin guitars are designed for the entry level or student guitarist.

GRETSCH

Instruments currently produced in the U.S. (three current models) since 1995. Other models produced in Japan from 1989 to date. Distributed by the Fred Gretsch Company of Savannah, Georgia.

Instruments originally produced in New York City, New York from the early 1900s to 1970. Production was moved to Booneville, Arkansas from 1970 to 1979. Gretsch (as owned by D. H. Baldwin Piano Company) ceased production (of guitars) in 1981.

Friedrich Gretsch was born in 1856, and emigrated to America when he was 16. In 1883 he founded a musical instrument shop in Brooklyn which prospered. The Fred Gretsch Company began manufacturing instruments in 1883 (while Friedrich maintained his proper name, he "americanized" it for the company). Gretsch passed away unexpectedly (at age 39) during a trip to Germany in April 1895, and his son Fred (often referred to as Fred Gretsch, Sr. in company histories) took over the family business (at 15!). Gretsch Sr. expanded the business considerably by 1916. Beginning with percussion, ukeleles, and banjos, Gretsch introduced guitars in the early 1930s, developing a well respected line of archtop orchestra models. In 1926 the company acquired the rights to K. Zildjian Cymbals, and debuted the Gretsch tenor guitar. During the Christmas season of 1929, the production capacity was reported to be 100,000 instruments (stringed instruments and drums); and a new midwestern branch was opened in Chicago, Illinois. In March of 1940 Gretsch acquired the B & D trademark from the Bacon Banjo Corporation. Fred Gretsch, Sr. retired in 1942.

William Walter Gretsch assumed the presidency of the company until 1948, and then Fred Gretsch, Jr. took over the position. Gretsch, Jr. was the primary president during the great Gretsch heyday, and was ably assisted by such notables as Jimmy Webster and Charles "Duke" Kramer (Kramer was involved with the Gretsch company from 1935 to his retirement in 1980, and was even involved after his retirement!). During the 1950s, the majority of Gretsch's guitar line was focused on electric six string Spanish instruments. With the endorsement of Chet Atkins and George Harrison, Gretsch electrics became very popular with both country and rock-n-roll musicians through the 1960s.

Outbid in their attempt to buy Fender in 1965, the D. H. Baldwin company bought Gretsch in 1967, and Gretsch, Jr. was made a director of Baldwin. Baldwin had previously acquired the manufacturing facilities of England's James Ormstron Burns (Burns Guitars) in September 1965, and Baldwin was assembling the imported Burns parts in Booneville, Arkansas. In a business consolidation, The New York Gretsch operation was moved down to the Arkansas facility in 1970. Production focused on Gretsch, and Burns guitars were basically discontinued.

In January of 1973 the Booneville plant suffered a serious fire. Baldwin made the decision to discontinue guitar building operations. Three months later, long-time manager Bill Hagner formed the Hagner Musical Instruments company and formed an agreement with Baldwin to build and sell Gretsch guitars to Baldwin from the Booneville facility. Baldwin would still retain the rights to the trademark. Another fire broke out in December of the same year, but the operation recovered. Baldwin stepped in and regained control of the operation in December of 1978, the same year that they bought the Kustom Amplifier company in Chanute, Kansas. Gretsch production was briefly moved to the Kansas facility, and by 1982 they moved again to

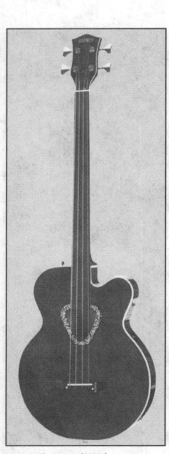

Acoustic Electric Bass (G6176)
courtesy Fred Gretsch Enterprises

Gallatin, Tennessee. 1981 was probably the last date of guitar production, but Gretsch drum products were continued at Tennessee. In 1983 the production had again returned to Arkansas.

Baldwin had experimented briefly with guitar production at their Mexican organ facilities, producing perhaps 100 *Southern Belle* guitars (basically renamed Country Gentlemans) between 1978 and 1979. When Gretsch production returned to Arkansas in 1983, the Baldwin company asked Charles Kramer to come out of retirement and help bring the business back (which he did). In 1984, Baldwin also sold off their rights to Kustom amps. In 1985 Kramer brokered a deal between Baldwin and Fred Gretsch III that returned the trademark back to the family.

Kramer and Gretsch III developed the specifications for the reissue models that are currently being built by the Terada company in Japan. The majority of Japanese-produced Gretsch models are brokered in the U.S. market; however, there has been some "grey market" Japan-only models that have been brought into the U.S. One such model, the **White Penguin Reissue**, was briefly offered through Gretsch to the U.S. market - it is estimated that perhaps a dozen or so were sold through dealers.

In 1995, three models were introduced that are currently built in the U.S: **Country Club 1955** (model G6196-1955), **Nashville 1955** (model G6120-1955), and the **White Falcon I - 1955** (model G6136-1955).

(Later company history courtesy Michael Wright, Guitar Stories Volume One)

Charles Duke Kramer first joined the Gretsch company at their Chicago office in 1935. When Kramer first retired in 1980, he formed D & F Products. In late 1981, when Baldwin lost a lease on one of their small production plants, Kramer went out and bought any existing guitar parts (about three 42-foot semi-trailers worth!). While some were sold back to the revitalized Gretsch company in 1985, Kramer still makes the parts available through his D & F Products company. D & F Products can be reached at: 6735 Hidden Hills Drive, Cincinnati, Ohio 45230 (513.232.4972).

Initial Production Model Codes

The Gretsch company assigned a name and a four digit number to each guitar model. However, they would also assign a different, yet associated number to the same model in a different color or component assembly. This system helped *expedite the ordering system*, says Charles *Duke* Kramer, *you could look at an invoice and know exactly which model and color from one number.* References in this text, while still incomplete, will list variances in the model designations.

Current Production Model Codes

Current Gretsch models may have a *G* preface to the four digit code, and also letters at the end that designate different bridge configuration (like a Bigsby tremolo), or a cutaway body style. Many of the reissue models also have a hyphen and four digit year following the primary model number designation that indicate a certain vintage-style year.

For further information regarding Gretsch electric models, please refer to the **5th Edition Blue Book of Electric Guitars**. Gretsch archtop models with built-in pickups can be found in the Gretsch Electric section of the Electric edition.

Charles "Duke" Kramer

ACOUSTIC ARCHTOP

MODEL 35

Grading	100%	EXCELLENT	AVERAGE

— carved spruce top, f-holes, raised bound black pickguard, bound body, maple back/sides, 3 piece maple/rosewood neck, 14/20 fret ebony fingerboard with pearloid dot inlay, ebony bridge/trapeze tailpiece, rosewood peghead veneer with pearl logo inlay, 3 per side diecast tuners. Available in Dark Red Sunburst finish. Mfd. 1933 to 1949.

Body Width 16".

| | **$295** | **$190** |

In 1936, adjustable maple bridge and black plastic peghead veneer replaced original items.

By 1939, 3 stripe body binding, rosewood fingerboard, tortoise shell tuner buttons, nickel plated hardware, and Brown Sunburst finish became standard.

MODEL 50 — carved spruce top, f-holes, raised black pickguard, bound body, avoidire back, figured maple sides/neck, 14/20 fret bound ebony pointed end fingerboard with pearloid diamond inlay, adjustable maple bridge/trapeze tailpiece, black face peghead with pearl scroll inlay, 3 per side nickel tuners with tortoise buttons. Available in Brown Sunburst finish. Mfd. 1936 to 1949.

Body Width 16".

| | **$300** | **$200** |

This model also available with round soundhole (Model 50R), which was discontinued by 1940.

By 1940, rosewood fingerboard with dot inlay replaced ebony fingerboard with diamond inlay.

MODEL 75 — arched spruce top, raised bound tortoise pickguard, f-holes, bound body, figured maple back/sides, 3 piece maple neck, 14/20 fret bound rosewood pointed end fingerboard with pearloid block inlay, adjustable rosewood stairstep bridge/nickel trapeze tailpiece, black face peghead with large floral/logo inlay, 3 per side nickel tuners. Available in Brown Sunburst finish. Mfd. 1939 to 1949.

Body Width 16".

| | **$395** | **$250** |

Early models had bound pegheads.

By 1940, 3 stripe bound pickguard/body replaced original items, pickguard was also enlarged.

MODEL 100 — arched spruce top, raised bound tortoise pickguard, f-holes, 2 stripe bound body, curly maple back/sides, 3 piece curly maple/rosewood neck, 14/20 fret bound rosewood fingerboard with pearl block inlay, adjustable rosewood stairstep bridge/step tailpiece, bound blackface peghead with pearl floral/logo inlay, 3 per side gold tuners. Available in Natural and Sunburst finishes. Mfd. 1939 to 1955.

Body Width 16".

| | **$400** | **$225** |

Grading	100%	EXCELLENT	AVERAGE

MODEL 150 — carved spruce top, raised bound tortoise pickguard, f-holes, multibound body, curly maple back/sides, curly maple neck, 14/20 fret bound ebony fingerboard with pearl block inlay, adjustable ebony stairstep bridge/stop tailpiece, bound blackface peghead with pearl "Artist"/logo inlay, 3 per side gold tuners. Available in Natural and Sunburst finishes. Mfd. 1935 to 1939.

Body Width 16".

		$525	$300

MODEL 250 — arched spruce top, raised bound tortoise pickguard, bound catseye soundholes, 3 stripe bound body, arched maple back/sides, 14/20 fret bound ebony fingerboard with pearl block inlay, adjustable stylized ebony bridge/trapeze tailpiece, bound blackface peghead with 2 pearl quarter notes/logo inlay, 3 per side gold tuners with pearloid buttons. Available in Sunburst finish. Mfd. 1936 to 1939.

Body Width 16".

		$600	$325

CONSTELLATION (Model 6030) — single round cutaway body, arched spruce top, 2 stripe bound f-holes, raised bound tortoise pickguard, 2 stripe bound body, laminated maple back/sides, 3 piece maple/rosewood neck, 19 fret bound rosewood fingerboard with pearloid block inlay, adjustable rosewood stairstep bridge/gold trapeze tailpiece, bound black face peghead with pearl logo inlay, 3 per side gold tuners. Available in Natural (**Model 6031**) and Sunburst (**Model 6030**) finishes. Mfd. 1951 to 1960.

		$1,250	$825

Originally released as the Synchromatic, it was later known as the Constellation.

By 1955, hump top block fingerboard inlay and ebony bridge/G logo trapeze tailpiece replaced original items.

ELDORADO (Formerly SYNCHROMATIC 400)(Model 6040) — single round cutaway body, arched spruce top, 2 f-holes, 3 stripe bound body, maple back/sides/neck, 21 fret bound ebony fingerboard with pearloid humptop block inlay, adjustable ebony stairstep bridge/gold G logo trapeze tailpiece, bound black face peghead with logo inlay, raised pickguard, 3 per side gold tuners. Available in Natural (**Model 6041**) and Sunburst (**Model 6040**) finishes. Mfd. 1955 to 1970.

Body Width 18".

		$1,500	$875

This model was introduced in 1955 as a custom order only.

By 1968, Natural finish was discontinued.

ELDORADO 18" CARVED TOP (Model G410) — similar to the Eldorado (Model 6040). Available in Sunburst (**Model G410**) and Natural (**Model G410 M**) finishes. Mfr. 1991 to date.

Body Width 18".

Mfr.'s Sug. Retail	$5,700	$4,200	$1,950	$1,395

Add $300 for model in Natural finish (**Model G410 M**).

FLEETWOOD (Model 6038) — similar to Eldorado, except has smaller body, Synchromatic/logo on peghead. Available in Natural (**Model 6039**) and Sunburst (**Model 6038**) finishes. Mfd. 1955 to 1968.

Body Width 17".

		$1,395	$925

In 1959, the thumbnail fingerboard inlays replaced block inlays.

Synchromatic Series

Early Synchromatic models have bulb shaped pegheads. Fingerboard inlay listed as the standard, though models are also found with 'split block', 'thumb print' and other inlay styles.

MODEL 160 (Model 6028) — carved spruce top, raised bound tortoise pickguard, bound catseye soundholes, tortoise bound body, carved curly maple back, curly maple sides, 5 piece maple neck, 14/20 fret bound rosewood fingerboard with pearl block inlay, adjustable stylized rosewood bridge/trapeze tailpiece, bound blackface peghead with pearl model name/logo inlay, 3 per side chrome Grover tuners. Available in Sunburst (**Model 6028**) finish. Mfd. 1939 to 1951.

Body Width 17".

		$1,000	$400

In 1942, Natural finish (Model 6029) became available.

MODEL 200 — carved spruce top, raised bound tortoise pickguard, bound catseye soundholes, 2 stripe bound body, carved flame maple back, curly maple sides, 5 piece maple neck, 14/20 fret bound rosewood fingerboard with pearl humpblock inlay, adjustable stylized rosewood bridge/trapeze tailpiece, bound blackface peghead with pearl model name/logo inlay, 3 per side gold Grover tuners. Available in Natural and Sunburst finishes. Mfd. 1939 to 1949.

Body Width 17".

		$1,000	$675

MODEL 300 (Model 6036) — carved spruce top, raised bound tortoise pickguard, bound catseye soundholes, single bound body, carved flame maple back, curly maple sides, 5 piece maple/rosewood neck, 14/20 fret bound ebony fingerboard with pearl humpblock inlay, adjustable stylized Brazilian rosewood bridge/trapeze tailpiece, bound blackface peghead with pearl model name/logo inlay, 3 per side gold Grover tuners. Available in Natural (**Model 6037**) and Sunburst (**Model 6036**) finishes. Mfd. 1939 to 1959.

Body Width 17".

		$2,000	$1,025

Eldorado G-410 M
courtesy Fred Gretsch Enterprises

G

Grading	100%	EXCELLENT	AVERAGE

G

MODEL 400 (Model 6040) — carved spruce top, raised bound tortoise pickguard, multibound catseye soundholes, multibound body with gold inner stripe, carved flame maple back, curly flame sides, 3 piece curly maple neck, 14/20 fret multibound ebony fingerboard with pearl humpblock with gold stripe inlay, adjustable stylized ebony bridge/trapeze tailpiece, multibound blackface peghead with pearl catseye-stairstep/logo inlay, 3 per side gold Grover Imperial tuners. Available in Natural **(Model 6041)** and Sunburst **(Model 6040)** finishes. Mfd. 1939 to 1955.

    Body Width 18".

		$4,200	$2,500

SYNCHROMATIC (Model G400) — arched spruce top, raised bound tortoise pickguard, bound catseye soundholes, 3 stripe bound body, arched maple back, maple sides/neck, 14/20 fret bound rosewood fingerboard with pearl split humpblock inlay, adjustable stylized ebony bridge/step trapeze tailpiece, bound blackface peghead with pearl model name/logo inlay, 3 per side gold tuners. Available in Sunburst finish. Mfr. 1991 to date.

Mfr.'s Sug. Retail	$1,500	$1,200	$600	$495

Synchromatic C (Model G400 C) — similar to Synchromatic, except has single round cutaway. Available in Sunburst finish. Mfr. 1991 to date.

Mfr.'s Sug. Retail	$1,750	$1,400	$700	$575

Blonde Maple Synchromatic C (Model G400 MC) — similar to Synchromatic C, except has Blonde Maple finish. Available in Natural finish. Mfr. 1991 to 1996.

			$975	$675

        Last Mfr.'s Sug. Retail was $1,850.

Synchromatic C with Pickup (Model G400 CV) — similar to Synchromatic C, except has Filtertron pickup and Bigsby tremolo bridge. Available in Sunburst finish. Mfr. 1994 to date.

Mfr.'s Sug. Retail	$2,400	$1,800	$900	$775

Blonde Maple Synchromatic C with Pickup (Model G400 MCV) — similar to Blonde Maple Synchromatic C, except has Filtertron pickup and Bigsby tremolo. Available in Natural finish. Mfr. 1991 to date.

Mfr.'s Sug. Retail	$2,500	$1,900	$950	$800

17" SYNCHROMATIC LIMITED EDITION (Model G450) — similar to the Synchromatic, except features handcarved spruce top, 'floating' Jazz pickup. Available in Walnut Stain finish. Mfr. 1997 to date.

    Body Width 17".

Mfr.'s Sug. Retail	$5,700	$4,500	$N/A	$N/A

    This Limited Edition model comes with a Certificate of Authenticity signed by Fred Gretsch.

17" Maple Synchromatic Limited Edition (Model G450 M) — similar to the 17" Synchromatic Limited Edition, except features a carved maple top. Mfr. 1997 to date.

    Body Width 17".

Mfr.'s Sug. Retail	$5,700	$4,500	$N/A	$N/A

ORANGE SYNCHROMATIC (Model G460) — similar to the Synchromatic, except features a laminated spruce top. Available in Orange finish. Mfr. 1997 to date.

Mfr.'s Sug. Retail	$1,295	$1,050	$700	$525

Maple Synchromatic (Model G460 M) — similar to the Orange Synchromatic, except features a laminated maple top. Mfr. 1997 to date.

Mfr.'s Sug. Retail	$1,295	$1,050	$700	$525

SYNCHROMATIC JUMBO 125F (Model 6021) — arched spruce top, triangle soundhole, tortoise shell pickguard, 2 stripe bound body/rosette, figured maple back/sides/neck, 14/21 fret bound rosewood fingerboard with pearloid block inlay, adjustable rosewood bridge/stop tailpiece mounted on triangular rosewood base, black face peghead with pearl logo inlay, 3 per side diecast tuners. Available in Natural top, Sunburst back/side finish. Mfd. 1947 to 1954.

			$895	$595

    Some models had tortoise binding all around, other models came with single body binding.

ACOUSTIC

BURL IVES — spruce top, round soundhole, tortoise pickguard, 2 stripe bound body/rosette, mahogany back/sides/neck, 14/19 fret rosewood fingerboard with pearloid dot inlay, rosewood bridge with black pins, black peghead face with Burl Ives/logo, 3 per side tuners with plastic buttons. Available in Natural finish. Mfd. 1952 to 1955.

			$375	$250

FOLK (Model 6003) — spruce top, round soundhole, tortoise pickguard, 3-stripe bound body/rosette, mahogany back/sides/neck, 14/19 fret rosewood fingerboard with pearloid dot inlay, rosewood bridge with black pins, black peghead face with logo, 3 per side tuners with plastic buttons. Available in Natural finish. Mfd. 1951 to 1975.

			$275	$175

    In 1955, this model was named the Grand Concert (Model 6003) and had a slanted peghead logo.

    In 1959, renamed the Jimmy Rogers Model (endorsed by 1950s/1960s pop star Jimmie Rodgers).

    In 1963, renamed Folk Singing Model.

    In 1965, renamed Folk Model.

    In 1967, straight across peghead logo was added, zero fret added.

    In 1969, Mahogany Top (Model 6004) and Sunburst finish (Model 6002) became optional.

*Gretsch Synchromatic
courtesy Thoroughbred Music*

*Synchromatic G-400
courtesy Fred Gretsch Enterprises*

Grading	100%	EXCELLENT	AVERAGE

Rancher (G6022)
courtesy Fred Gretsch Enterprises

RANCHER — spruce top with stylized G brand, triangle soundhole, tortoise pickguard with engraved longhorn steer head, 3 stripe bound body/rosette, maple arched back/sides/neck, 14/21 fret bound rosewood fingerboard with pearloid block inlay, adjustable rosewood bridge/stop tailpiece mounted on triangular rosewood base, black face bound peghead with pearl steer head/logo inlay, 3 per side gold tuners. Available in Golden Red finish. Mfd. 1954 to 1973.

1954-1959		$3,000	$1,975
1960-1964		$2,250	$1,050
1965-1969		$1,500	$875
1970-1973		$1,000	$700

G brand was on bass side of top, fingerboard inlay was inscribed with cows and cactus.

By 1957, gold pickguard and hump top fingerboard inlay with no engraving replaced original items.

In 1959, tan pickguard, thumbnail fingerboard inlay replaced respective items.

In 1961, no G brand on top, and horseshoe peghead inlay replaced original items.

Rancher (1st Reissue) — similar to Rancher, except has block fingerboard inlay with engraved cows and cactus, rosewood bridge with white pins, horseshoe peghead inlay. Mfd. 1975 to 1980.

		$675	$450

In 1978, tri-saddle bridge with white pins replaced respective item.

RANCHER (2nd REISSUE) (Model G6022) — spruce top with G brand, bound triangle soundhole, tortoise pickguard with engraved steerhead, 3 stripe bound body, maple back/sides/neck, 14/21 fret bound rosewood fingerboard with western motif engraved pearl block inlays, rosewood bridge with black white dot pins, bound peghead with pearl steerhead/logo inlay, 3 per side gold tuners. Available in Transparent Orange finish. Mfr. 1991 to date.

Mfr.'s Sug. Retail	$1,550	$1,250	$850	$625

Rancher Double Neck (Model G6022-6/12) — similar to the Rancher-2nd Reissue, except has 6-string and 12-string neck configurations. Mfr. 1997 to date.

Mfr.'s Sug. Retail	$3,200	$2,550	$1,700	$1,275

Rancher C (Model G6022 C) — similar to Rancher-2nd Reissue, except has single round cutaway, single coil pickup, volume/tone control. Current mfr.

Mfr.'s Sug. Retail	$1,600	$1,275	$875	$650

Rancher CV (Model G6022 CV) — similar to Rancher-2nd Reissue, except has single round cutaway, no pickguard, adjustamatic metal bridge with rosewood base/Bigsby vibrato, single coil pickup, volume/tone control. Current mfr.

Mfr.'s Sug. Retail	$1,750	$1,400	$700	$575

1954 Rancher Reissue (Model G6022-1954) — similar to Rancher-2nd Reissue, except features 1954 model specifications. Mfr. 1997 to date.

Mfr.'s Sug. Retail	$1,650	$1,325	$900	$650

Rancher 12 (Model G6022/12) — similar to Rancher-2nd Reissue, except has 12-string configuration, 6 per side tuners. Current mfr.

Mfr.'s Sug. Retail	$1,550	$1,250	$850	$625

Rancher C 12 (Model G6022 C/12) — similar to Rancher-2nd Reissue, except has 12 strings, single round cutaway, 6 per side tuners, single coil pickup, volume/tone control. Current mfr.

Mfr.'s Sug. Retail	$1,600	$1,275	$650	$525

SUN VALLEY (Model 6010) — spruce top, round soundhole, tortoise pickguard, 3 stripe bound body/rosette, mahogany back/sides/neck, 14/20 fret bound rosewood fingerboard with dot inlay, rosewood bridge with black pins, bound peghead, 3 per side chrome tuners. Available in Natural and Sunburst finishes. Mfd. 1959 to 1977.

1959-1964		$525	$350
1965-1969		$450	$300
1970-1977		$395	$250

By 1973, Sunburst finish was optional.

Sun Valley Dreadnought Acoustic (Model G6010) — dreadnought style, solid spruce top, triangle soundhole, 3 stripe bound body, floral pattern rosette, rosewood back/sides, mahogany neck, 14/20 fret bound rosewood fingerboard with pearl diamond inlay, pearl scroll inlay at 12th fret, rosewood bridge with black pearl dot pins, pearl floral bridge wing inlay, bound blackface peghead with pearl floral/logo inlay, 3 per side gold tuners. Available in Natural finish. Mfr. 1991 to date.

Mfr.'s Sug. Retail	$1,250	$1,000	$500	$425

SYNCHROMATIC 300F — spruce top, triangle soundhole, raised pickguard, 3 stripe body/rosette, maple arched back/sides/neck, 14/21 fret bound rosewood fingerboard with pearloid slashed humptop block inlay, adjustable rosewood stairstep bridge/gold trapeze tailpiece, bound cloud peghead with silkscreened Synchromatic/logo, 3 per side gold tuners. Available in Natural top, Dark back/side finish. Mfd. 1947 to 1955.

		$1,250	$825

Synchromatic 400F — similar to Synchromatic 300F, except has larger body. Available in Sunburst back/side finish.

		$2,325	$1,525

WAYFARER JUMBO — dreadnought style, spruce top, round soundhole, lucite pickguard with engraved sailboat/logos, 3 stripe bound body/rosette, red maple back/sides/neck, 14/21 fret bound rosewood fingerboard with pearl split block inlay, rosewood bridge with white pins, black face peghead with logo inlay, 3 per side Grover chrome tuners. Available in Natural finish. Mfd. 1969 to 1972.

		$375	$250

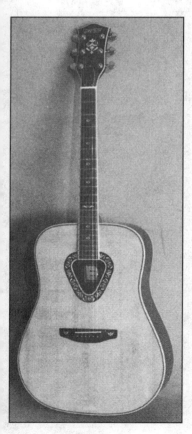

Sun Valley (G6010)
courtesy Fred Gretsch Enterprises

Grading	100%	EXCELLENT	AVERAGE

WHITE FALCON RANCHER (Model G6022 CWF) — single round cutaway jumbo style, solid spruce top with "G" brand, tortoise pickguard, bound triangle soundhole, gold sparkle bound body, maple back/sides/neck, 21 fret gold sparkle bound rosewood fingerboard with western motif engraved pearl block inlays, rosewood bridge with black white dot pins, gold sparkle bound peghead with gold sparkle inlay, 3 per side gold tuners, internal acoustic pickup, volume/3 band EQ controls. Available in White finish. Mfr. 1994 to date.

| Mfr.'s Sug. Retail | $2,500 | $2,000 | $1,000 | $825 |

White Falcon Rancher with Fishman Pickup (Model G6022 CWFF) — similar to the White Falcon Rancher, except features a Fishman transducer pickup. Mfr. 1997 to date.

| Mfr.'s Sug. Retail | $2,800 | $2,250 | $1,475 | $1,075 |

ACOUSTIC ELECTRIC

CRIMSON FLYER (Model G6020) — single round cutaway body, solid spruce top, triangle soundhole, multi bound body, floral pattern rosette, chestnut back/sides, 2 piece mahogany neck, 22 fret rosewood fingerboard with pearl dot inlay, pearl scroll inlay at 12th fret, rosewood bridge with black pearl pins, pearl floral bridge wing inlay, bound body matching peghead with pearl logo inlay, 3 per side gold tuners, active ceramic pickup, volume/tone control. Available in Cherry Sunburst finish. Mfd. 1991 to 1996.

		$675	$450

Last Mfr.'s Sug. Retail was $1,350.

Crimson Flyer V (Model G6020 V) — similar to Crimson Flyer, except has rosewood/metal tuneomatic bridge/Bigsby vibrato. Current mfr.

| Mfr.'s Sug. Retail | $1,650 | $1,325 | $650 | $550 |

NIGHTBIRD (Model G6030) — single round cutaway body, solid spruce top, triangle soundhole, 3 stripe bound body, floral pattern rosette, maple back/sides, 2 piece mahogany neck, 21 fret bound rosewood fingerboard with pearl dot inlay, pearl scroll inlay at 12th fret, rosewood bridge with black pearl dot pins, pearl floral pattern bridge wing inlay, bound blackface peghead with pearl logo inlay, 3 per side gold tuners, active ceramic pickup, volume/tone control. Available in Ebony finish. Current mfr.

| Mfr.'s Sug. Retail | $1,200 | $960 | $480 | $395 |

Nightbird V (Model 6030 V) — similar to Nightbird, except has rosewood/metal tuneomatic bridge/Bigsby vibrato tailpiece. Current mfr.

| Mfr.'s Sug. Retail | $1,500 | $1,200 | $600 | $495 |

Crimson Flyer (G6020)
courtesy Fred Gretsch Enterprises

ACOUSTIC ELECTRIC BASS

ACOUSTIC FRETTED BASS (Model G6175) — single round cutaway body, spruce top, triangle soundhole, 3 stripe bound body, floral pattern rosette, maple back/sides/neck, 23 fret bound rosewood fingerboard with pearl dot inlay, pearl scroll inlay at 12th fret, rosewood strings thru bridge, bound blackface peghead with pearl logo inlay, 2 per side gold tuners, active ceramic pickup, volume/tone control. Available in Transparent Orange finish. Current mfr.

| Mfr.'s Sug. Retail | $1,500 | $1,200 | $800 | $550 |

Acoustic Fretless Bass (Model G6176) — similar to the Acoustic Fretted Bass, except has fretless fingerboard.

| Mfr.'s Sug. Retail | $1,500 | $1,200 | $800 | $550 |

JOHN GREVEN

Instruments currently built in Bloomington, Indiana.

Luthier John Greven has been building guitars for the past thirty years. While he has always been building good sounding acoustics, Greven is perhaps better known for the outstanding quality of his inlay work. Rather than waste words attempting to describe the quality of his guitars, simply contact John Greven through the Index of Current Manufacturers located in the back of this book for specification and pricing information.

Three years ago, Greven devised a faux tortoise shell material that can be used as pickguards or body binding without the problems encountered by the real material. This faux 'shell is available through the Luthier's Mercantile International at P.O. Box 774, Healdsburg CA 95448-0774; or phone 800.477.4437, (FAX) 707.433.8802 (email: LMI@LMII.com, or Web: http://www.lmii.com/~LMI).

STEVEN GRIMES

Instruments currently built in Kula, Hawaii.

Luthier Steven Grimes originally apprenticed with a violin maker and set up his own mandolin shop in Port Townsend, Washington in 1972. During that time period, Grimes also began handcrafting archtop guitars. In Grimes moved to Hawaii, and continues to produce guitars on a custom basis.

Grimes estimates that he produces about 20 guitars a year (half of them are archtops). Customers have choices on size, woods used, color of finish, inlay work, electronic packages, and the neck profile.

ACOUSTIC

Grimes' models include the **Beamer**, a double soundhole flat-top acoustic that is constructed with highly figured wood (list $3,400); the **Jazz Nouveau**, an archtop model with curly maple top/koa body and ebony fingerboard/bridge/pickguard/tailpiece (list $5,600); and the **Montreux**, an archtop model with European spruce top and figured German maple back and sides (list $8,800). Both archtop models are optionally available in a 7-string configuration, with custom inlay, or with a 'floating' pickup. The **Beamer** acoustic is optionally available with custom electronics, a cutaway body, or custom inlays. For further information regarding specifications and pricing, please contact Steven Grimes through the Index of Current Manufacturers located in the back of this book.

Grimes Jazz Laureate
courtesy Scott Chinery

Grimes Archtop
courtesy Stephen Grimes

Prestige Excellence
courtesy Guild Guitars

GRIMSHAW

Instruments produced in England from the 1950s through the late 1970s.

While this company is best known for its high quality archtop guitars, they also produced a notable semi-hollowbody design in the mid 1950s called the Short-Scale. In the early 1960s, Emil Grimshaw introduced the Meteor solid body guitar. The company then focused on both original and copies of American designs from the late 1960s on.

(Source: Tony Bacon and Paul Day, The Guru's Guitar Guide)

GROSSMAN

See chapter on House Brands.

Before World War II, the majority of guitars were sold through mail-order distributors. The Grossman company distributed a number of guitars built for them with their trademark on the headstock.

(Source: Tom Wheeler, American Guitars)

GROVES CUSTOM GUITARS

Instruments currently built in Tucson, Arizona.

Luthier Gordon S. Groves is currently offering hand crafted guitar models. For further information regarding specifications and pricing, please contact luthier Groves via the Index of Current Manufacturers located in the back of this edition.

GUDELSKY MUSICAL INSTRUMENTS

Instruments were built in Vista, California from 1985 to 1996.

Luthier Harris Paul Gudelsky (1964-1996) had apprenticed to James D'Aquisto before starting Gudelsky Musical Instruments. Gudelsky's personal goal was to try to build a more modern version of the archtop guitar. Gudelsky offered a small line of instruments exclusively on a customer order basis that included hollow body archtops (acoustic and electric/acoustic) ranged between $4,290 and $5,500; semi hollow bodies ranged from $4,235 to $4,400; and set-neck solid bodies ranged from $2,450 to $3,500. Paul Gudelsky was found fatally shot at his Vista, California home in May, 1996.

GUGINO

Instruments built in Buffalo, New York between the 1930s and 1940s.

Luthier Carmino Gugino built instruments that featured high quality conventional building (the frets, finish, carving, etc.) combined with very unconventional design ideas. As detailed by Jay Scott, certain models feature necks that screw on to the body, or have asymetrical bodies, or an archtop that has a detachable neck/body joint/bridge piece that is removable from the body.

(Source: Teisco Del Rey, Guitar Player magazine)

GUILD

Instruments produced in Westerly, Rhode Island from 1969 to date. Distributed by the Fender Musical Instrument Corporation (FMIC) of Scottsdale, Arizona. In 1997, Guild (Fender FMIC) opened up a new Guild Custom Shop in Nashville, Tennessee.

Guild was originally located in New York City between 1952 to 1956; production was moved to Hoboken, New Jersey, from late 1956 to 1968.

Contrary to the notions about a "guild of old world-style craftsmen" gathering to build these exceptional guitars, Guild was founded in 1952 by Alfred Dronge (who did hire great guitar builders). Dronge, a Jewish emigrant from Europe, grew up in New York City and took jobs working for various music stores on Park Row. Dronge became an accomplished musician who played both banjo and guitar, and loved jazz music. His experience in teaching music and performing in small orchestras led to the formation of the Sagman and Dronge music store.

After World War II, Dronge gave up the music store in favor of importing and distributing Italian accordions. The Sonola Accordion Company was successful enough to make Dronge a small fortune. It is with this reputation and finances that Dronge formed Guild Guitars, Inc. with ex-Ephiphone sales manager George Mann. Incidentally, the *Guild* name came from a third party who was involved with a guitar amplifier company that was going out of business. As the plant was closing down Dronge and Gene Detgen decided to keep the name. The Guild company was registered in 1952.

As the original New York-based Epiphone company was having problems with the local unions, they decided to move production down to Philadelphia. Dronge took advantage of this decision and attracted several of their ex-luthiers to his company. Some of the workers were of Italian ancestry, and felt more comfortable remaining in the *Little Italy* neighborhood rather than moving to Pennsylvania.

The company was originally located in a New York loft from 1952 through 1956. They expanded into a larger workshop in Hoboken, New Jersey, in late 1956. Finally, upon completion of new facilities, Guild moved to its current home in Westerly, Rhode Island, in 1969.

As pop music in the 1960s spurred on a demand for guitars, musical instrument companies expanded to meet the business growth. At the same time, large corporations began to diversify their holdings. Most people are aware of the CBS decision to buy Fender in 1965, or Baldwin Piano's purchase of the Burns trademark and manufacturing equipment in 1967. In 1966 electronic parts producer Avnet Inc. bought Guild Musical Instruments, and Alfred Dronge stayed on as president. Dronge also hired Jim Deurloo (of Gibson and later Heritage fame) as plant manager in December 1969. Deurloo's commitment to quality control resulted in better consistency of Guild products.

Tragedy occurred in 1972 as Alfred Dronge was killed in an aircraft crash. The relationships he built with the members of the company dissipated, and the driving force of twenty years since the inception was gone. However, Leon Tell (Guild's vice president from 1963 to 1973) became the company president in 1973 and maintained that position until 1983.

In mid August of 1986, Avnet sold Guild to a management/investment group from New England and Tennessee. Officers of the newly formed Guild Music Corporation included company President Jerre R. Haskew (previously Chief Executive Officer and President of the Commerce Union Bank of Chattanooga Tennessee), Executive Vice President of Plant and Operations George A. Hammerstrom, and Executive Vice President of Product Development and Artist Relations George Gruhn (Gruhn later left the company in early 1988).

Unfortunately, the remaining members of the investment group defaulted on bank obligations in November of 1988, leading to a court supervised financial restructuring. The Faas Corporation of New Berlin, Wisconsin (now U.S. Musical Corporation) bought Guild 1n January 1989. Solid body guitar production was discontinued in favor of acoustic and acoustic-electric production (a company strength) although some electric models were reissued in the mid 1990s.

Most recently, the Guild company was purchased by Fender Musical Instrument Corporation in 1995. A recent 1996 catalog shows an arrangement of acoustic and acoustic-electric models, as well as some semi-hollowbody guitars and one solid body electric. Guild has introduced more solid body electrics lately; all current models are based on memorable Guild models from earlier years (such as the Starfire models). In 1997, Guild opened a new Custom Shop in Nashville, Tennessee.

(Reference source for early Guild history: Hans Moust, The Guild Guitar Book; contemporary history courtesy Jay Pilzer; Guild model information courtesy Bill Acton, Guild Guitars)

IDENTIFYING FEATURES ON

GUILD INSTRUMENTS

According to noted authority and Guild enthusiast Jay Pilzer, there are identifying features on Guild instruments that can assist in determining their year of production:

Knobs on Electrics:

1953-58 transparent barrel knobs; 1959-63 transparent yellowish top hat knobs with Guild logo in either chrome or gold; 1964-72 black top hat knobs, Guild logo, tone or vol; circa 1990-present black top hat with Guild logo, no numbers or tone/vol.

Electric Pickguards:

Except for the Johnny Smith/Artist Award (which used the stairstep pickguard), Guild pickguards were rounded, following the shape of the guitar until 1963 when the stairstep became standard on archtop electrics.

Acoustic Pickguards:

Most models have a distinct Guild shape in either tortoise or black with rounded edges that follow the line of guitar, except the F-20, M-20, and new *A* series which have teardrop pickguards.

Headstock Inlays:

The earliest were simple Guild inverted *V* with triangular insert, with *G* logo below, later the triangular insert disappears, Chesterfield introduced on some models by 1957. In general the more elaborate the headstock, the higher price the instrument.

For information regarding archtop models with "floating" or built-in pickups, please refer to the Guild Electric section in the **5th Edition Blue Book of Electric Guitars**.

ACOUSTIC ARCHTOPS

Archtop Models

A-50 GRANADA — hollow non-cutaway style bound body, laminated arched spruce top, f-holes, raised black pickguard, mahogany back/sides/neck, 14/20 fret rosewood fingerboard with pearl dot inlay, adjustable rosewood bridge/trapeze tailpiece, blackface peghead with screened logo, 3 per side nickel tuners. Available in Sunburst finish. Mfd. 1952 to 1968.

Body Width 16 1/4".

	100%	EXCELLENT	AVERAGE
		$375	$200

A-150 — hollow single round cutaway style bound body, carved solid spruce top, f-holes, raised black pickguard, laminated maple back and sides, 20 fret rosewood fingerboard with block inlay, 24 3/4" inch scale, adjustable rosewood bridge/trapeze tailpiece, blackface peghead with screened logo, 3 per side nickel tuners. Available in Sunburst finish. Mfd. 1953 to 1973.

Body Width 17".

	100%	EXCELLENT	AVERAGE
		$1,200	$1,000

A-350 STRATFORD — single round cutaway hollow style, arched spruce top, raised black laminated pickguard, 2 bound f-holes, multibound body, maple back/sides/neck, 20 fret bound rosewood fingerboard with pearl block inlay, adjustable rosewood bridge/harp tailpiece, multibound blackface peghead with pearl shield/logo inlay, 3 per side gold tuners. Available in Sunburst finish. Mfd. 1952 to 1972.

	100%	EXCELLENT	AVERAGE
		$2,200	$1,700

A-500 STUART — single round cutaway hollow style, bound arched solid spruce top, 2 bound f-holes, bound tortoise pickguard, maple back/sides/neck, 20 fret bound ebony fingerboard with pearl block/abalone wedge inlay, adjustable ebony bridge, stylized trapeze tailpiece, bound peghead with pearl shield/logo inlay, 3 per side gold Imperial tuners. Available in Natural and Sunburst finishes. Mfd. 1952 to 1966.

	100%	EXCELLENT	AVERAGE
		$3,200	$2,500

Grading	100%		EXCELLENT	AVERAGE

ARTIST AWARD (Model 350-8300) — single rounded cutaway hollow body, bound hand-carved solid spruce top, 2 bound f-holes, bound tortoise pickguard, solid German figured maple back/sides, 5 piece maple neck, 20 fret bound ebony fingerboard with pearl block/abalone wedge inlay, adjustable ebony bridge, stylized trapeze tailpiece, bound peghead with pearl/abalone inscribed block/logo inlay, 3 per side Imperial tuners, gold hardware, 'floating' Guild single coil pickup. Available in Antique Burst (837) and Blonde (801) finishes. Mfd. 1954 to date.

1954-1959			$2,750	$1,800
1960-1969			$2,200	$1,500
1970-1979			$2,000	$1,250
1980-1989			$1,850	$1,100
1990-1996			$2,000	$1,300
Mfr.'s Sug. Retail	$6,299	$5,100	$3,275	$2,200

This model was originally the Johnny Smith Model, but shortly after its debut Mr. Smith discontinued his association with Guild.

List Price includes deluxe "Alligator" hardshell case.

CA-100 CAPRI — single sharp cutaway hollow style, arched bound spruce top, raised bound black pickguard, 2 f-holes, maple back/sides/neck, 20 fret bound rosewood fingerboard with pearl block inlay, adjustable rosewood bridge/trapeze tailpiece, blackface peghead with pearl shield/logo inlay, 3 per side chrome tuners. Available in Sunburst finish. Mfd. 1956 to 1972.

	$1,000	$750

In 1954, harp tailpiece replaced original item.

ACOUSTIC

A Series

A-25HR — concert size body, spruce top, mahogany back and sides, rosewood fingerboard with dot inlays, rosewood bridge, 3 per side tuners, tortoise shell pickguard. Available in Natural satin finish. Disc. 1998.

	$425	$250

Last Mfr.'s Sug. Retail was $999.

A-25HG — similar to the A-25HR, except has a high gloss finish. Disc. 1995.

	$600	$450

Last Mfr.'s Sug. Retail was $1,099.

A-50 — similar to the A-25HR, except has rosewood back and sides, abalone rosette, ebony fingerboard and bridge. Disc. 1998.

	$850	$575

Last Mfr.'s Sug. Retail was $1,499.

The A-50 steel string model is not to be confused with the earlier A-50 Archtop model.

Dreadnought Series

All models in this series have dreadnought style bodies.

D-4 (Model 350-0100) — solid spruce top, round soundhole, tortoise pickguard, 3 stripe bound body/rosette, arched mahogany back, solid mahogany sides/neck, 14/20 fret rosewood fingerboard with pearl dot inlay, rosewood bridge with white black dot pins, 3 per side chrome tuners. Available in Natural (021) handrubbed satin finish. Current mfr.

Mfr.'s Sug. Retail	$699	$525	$350	$250

Add $150 for D-4 model with Fishman Transducer **(Model 350-0105)**.
Add $300 for D-4 model with Fishman Transducer and preamp **(Model 350-0106)**.
Add $130 for left-handed configuration model D-4 LH **(Model 350-0120)**.
Add $280 for D-4 LH model with Fishman Transducer **(Model 350-0125)**.
Add $430 for D-4 LH model with Fishman Transducer and preamp **(Model 350-0126)**.

D-4 G (Model 350-0140) (Formerly D-4 HG) — similar to D-4. Available in Natural (021) high gloss finish. Mfr. 1990 to 1994, 1998 to date.

Mfr.'s Sug. Retail	$799	$595	$395	$275

Add $150 for D-4 G model with Fishman Transducer **(Model 350-0145)**.
Add $300 for D-4 G model with Fishman Transducer and preamp **(Model 350-0146)**.
Add $130 for left-handed configuration model D-4 G LH **(Model 350-0160)**.
Add $280 for D-4 G LH model with Fishman Transducer **(Model 350-0165)**.
Add $430 for D-4 G LH model with Fishman Transducer and preamp **(Model 350-0166)**.

D-4 12 12-String (Model 350-0900) — similar to D-4, except has 12-string configuration, 6 per side tuners. Available in Natural (721) handrubbed satin finish. Current mfr.

Mfr.'s Sug. Retail	$1,049	$795	$525	$350

Add $150 for D-4 12 model with Fishman Transducer **(Model 350-0905)**.
Add $300 for D-4 12 model with Fishman Transducer and preamp **(Model 350-0906)**.
Add $130 for left-handed configuration model D-4 12 LH **(Model 350-0920)**.
Add $280 for D-4 12 LH model with Fishman Transducer **(Model 350-0925)**.
Add $430 for D-4 12 LH model with Fishman Transducer and preamp **(Model 350-0926)**.

List Price includes hardshell case.

D-15
courtesy Guild Guitars

D-6 — similar to D-4, except has gold hardware. Available in Natural finish. Disc. 1995.

	$425	$250

Last Mfr.'s Sug. Retail was $950.

G

Grading	100%	EXCELLENT	AVERAGE

D-6 HG — similar to D-4, except has gold hardware. Available in Natural high gloss finish. Disc. 1996.

$525 $300

Last Mfr.'s Sug. Retail was $1,100.

D-15 — mahogany top/back/sides/neck, round soundhole, tortoise pickguard, 3 stripe rosette, 14/20 fret rosewood fingerboard with pearl dot inlay, rosewood bridge with white black dot pins, 3 per side chrome tuners. Available in Black, Natural and Woodgrain Red finishes. Mfd. 1987 to 1994.

$425 $275

Last Mfr.'s Sug. Retail was $850.

D-25 (Model 350-0200) — solid spruce top, round soundhole, tortoise pickguard, black bound body, 3 stripe rosette, arched mahogany back, solid mahogany sides/neck, 14/20 fret rosewood fingerboard with pearl dot inlay, rosewood bridge with white black dot pins, 3 per side chrome tuners. Available in Black (706), Natural (721), and Antique (Sun)Burst (737) high gloss finishes. Mfr. 1979 to date.

1979-1989		$425	$275
1990-1998		$550	$300
Mfr.'s Sug. Retail	$1,099 $825	$550	$375

Add $150 for D-25 model with Fishman Transducer (**Model 350-0205**).

Add $300 for D-25 model with Fishman Transducer and preamp (**Model 350-0206**).

Add $130 for left-handed configuration model D-25 LH (**Model 350-0220**).

Add $280 for D-25 LH model with Fishman Transducer (**Model 350-0225**).

Add $430 for D-25 LH model with Fishman Transducer and preamp (**Model 350-0226**).

List price includes hardshell case.

D-25 12 12-String (Model 350-1000) — similar to D-25 except has 12 string configuration, 6 per side tuners. Available in Black (706), Natural (721), and Antique (Sun)Burst (737) high gloss finishes. Current mfr.

Mfr.'s Sug. Retail	$1,249 $950	$625	$425

Add $150 for D-25 12 model with Fishman Transducer (**Model 350-1005**).

Add $300 for D-25 12 model with Fishman Transducer and preamp (**Model 350-1006**).

Add $130 for left-handed configuration model D-25 12 LH (**Model 350-1020**).

Add $280 for D-25 12 LH model with Fishman Transducer (**Model 350-1025**).

Add $430 for D-25 12 LH model with Fishman Transducer and preamp (**Model 350-1026**).

List price includes hardshell case.

1980 D-25
courtesy Sam J. Maggio

D-25 M — similar to D-25, except has mahogany top. Disc. 1995.

$450 $325

D-30 (Model 350-1200) — solid spruce top, round soundhole, arched maple back, solid maple sides, mahogany neck, 14/20 rosewood fingerboard with pearl dot inlay, tortoise pickguard, 3 per side chrome tuners. Available in Black (706), Blonde (701), and Antique (Sun)Burst (737) high gloss finishes. Current mfr.

Mfr.'s Sug. Retail	$1,399 $1,050	$695	$475

Add $150 for D-30 model with Fishman Transducer (**Model 350-1205**).

Add $300 for D-30 model with Fishman Transducer and preamp (**Model 350-1206**).

Add $130 for left-handed configuration model D-30 LH (**Model 350-1220**).

Add $280 for D-30 LH model with Fishman Transducer (**Model 350-1225**).

Add $430 for D-30 LH model with Fishman Transducer and preamp (**Model 350-1226**).

List price includes hardshell case.

D-35 — solid spruce top, round soundhole, tortoise pickguard, bound body, 1 stripe rosette, mahogany back/sides/neck, 14/20 fret rosewood fingerboard with pearl dot inlay, rosewood bridge with white black dot pins, screened peghead logo, 3 per side chrome tuners. Available in Natural finish.

$700 $500

D-40 — solid spruce top, round soundhole, tortoise pickguard, bound body, 3 stripe rosette, mahogany back/sides/neck, 14/20 fret rosewood fingerboard with pearl dot inlay, rosewood bridge with white black dot pins, pearl Chesterfield/logo peghead inlay, 3 per side chrome tuners. Available in Natural finish. Disc. 1991.

$800 $500

Last Mfr.'s Sug. Retail was $1,295.

This model had single sharp cutaway optionally available (Model D-40C).

D-44 — solid spruce top, round soundhole, tortoise pickguard, 5 stripe bound body/rosette, pearwood back/sides, mahogany neck, 14/20 fret ebony fingerboard with pearl dot inlay, ebony bridge with white black dot pins, pearl Chesterfield/logo peghead inlay, 3 per side chrome tuners. Available in Natural and Sunburst finishes. Mfd. 1964 to 1979.

$750 $500

In 1974, maple back/sides replaced original item (Model D-44M).

D-46 — similar to the D-44, except has ash back and sides. Available in Natural and Sunburst finishes. Mfd. 1964 to 1979.

$800 $625

D-50 — solid spruce top, round soundhole, tortoise pickguard, 5 stripe bound body/rosette, rosewood back/sides, mahogany neck, 14/20 fret ebony fingerboard with pearl dot inlay, ebony bridge with white black dot pins, pearl Chesterfield/logo peghead inlay, 3 per side chrome tuners. Available in Natural and Sunburst finishes. Disc. 1994.

$850 $500

Last Mfr.'s Sug. Retail was $1,395.

Guild D-25 M
courtesy Mark Humphrey

G

Grading	100%	EXCELLENT	AVERAGE

1979 D-35 NT
courtesy Sam J. Maggio

D-55 (Model 350-0300) — solid spruce top, round soundhole, tortoise pickguard, 3 stripe bound body, abalone rosette, bookmatched rosewood back, solid rosewood sides, 3 piece mahogany neck, 14/20 fret bound ebony fingerboard with pearl block/abalone wedge inlay, ebony bridge with white abalone dot pins, maple endpin wedge, bound peghead with pearl shield/logo inlay, 3 per side gold tuners. Available in Natural (821) and Antique (Sun)Burst (837) high gloss lacquer finishes. Current mfr.

Mfr.'s Sug. Retail $2,199	$1,650	$1,100	$275

    Add $150 for D-55 model with Fishman Transducer (**Model 350-0305**).

    Add $300 for D-55 model with Fishman Transducer and preamp (**Model 350-0306**).

    Add $130 for left-handed configuration model D-55 LH (**Model 350-0320**).

    Add $280 for D-55 LH model with Fishman Transducer (**Model 350-0325**).

    Add $430 for D-55 LH model with Fishman Transducer and preamp (**Model 350-0326**).

    List price includes deluxe hardshell case.

DK-70 PEACOCK (LIMITED EDITION) — dreadnought style, koa body, ebony fingerboard with abalone cloud inlays, abalone Guild logo inlay on headstock, abalone peacock inlay on pickguard. Available in Natural finish. Mfd. 1995 to 1996.

                   $1,800 $1,100

                             Last Mfr.'s Sug. Retail was $4,999.

    The projected production run of this model was 50 pieces. It is estimated that only half were actually completed.

G-37 — solid spruce top, round soundhole, tortoise pickguard, bound body, 3 stripe rosette, maple back/sides/neck, 14/20 fret rosewood fingerboard with pearl dot inlay, rosewood bridge with white black dot pins, pearl Chesterfield/logo peghead inlay, 3 per side chrome tuners. Available in Black, Natural and Sunburst finishes. Introduced circa 1972.

                   $650 $425

    The G-37 is nearly the same guitar as the D-30, but features chrome tuners (which some D-30s have as well).

G-41 — oversized dreadnought style, solid spruce top, mahogany back and sides, rosewood fingerboard with dot inlay, 26¼ inch scale. Introduced circa 1974.

    Body Width 17".

                   $750 $525

G-75 — (¾ size) dreadnought style, solid spruce top, rosewood back and sides, 25 1/2" scale, ebony fingerboard. Introduced circa 1975.

    Body Width 15".

                   $650 $475

G-212 NT — dreadnought style, 12-string configuration, solid spruce top, round soundhole, tortoise pickguard, w/b/w bound body, 3 stripe rosette, mahogany back/sides/neck, double truss rods, 25 1/2" scale, 14/20 fret rosewood fingerboard, rosewood bridge with white black dot pins, pearl Chesterfield/logo peghead inlay, 6 per side chrome Guild tuners. Available in Natural finish. Mfd. 1974 to 1989.

                   $600 $350

                             Last Mfr.'s Sug. Retail was $895.

    The G-212 was advertised that it was "Built on a D-40 body", according to company literature of the time.

G-312 NT — similar to the G-212 NT, except featured black pickguard, 7-ply white ivoroid binding, rosewood back/sides, 3-piece mahogany neck, ebony fingerboard, Schaller tuners.

                   $550 $400

                           Last Mfr.'s Sug. Retail was $1,130.

    The G-312 advertising announced that "Guild's D-50 body is available in a 12-stringed instrument".

GV-52 — bell shaped flat-top body, solid spruce top, round soundhole, tortoise pickguard, bound body, herringbone rosette, rosewood back/sides, mahogany neck, 14/20 fret ebony fingerboard with pearl dot inlay, ebony bridge with white black dot pins, blackface peghead with pearl Chesterfield/logo inlay, 3 per side gold tuners. Available in Natural finish. Mfd. 1994 to 1995.

                   $575 $375

                           Last Mfr.'s Sug. Retail was $1,150.

Vintage Dreadnought Series

    DV models feature shaved or hand scalloped top bracing.

DV-6 (Model 350-0500) — solid spruce top, round soundhole, solid mahogany back/sides, shaved bracing, vintage herringbone rosette, 14/20 fret rosewood fingerboard with dot inlay, 3 per side gold tuners. Available in Natural (721) handrubbed satin finish. Current mfr.

Mfr.'s Sug. Retail $1,099	$825	$550	$375

    Add $150 for DV-6 model with Fishman Transducer (**Model 350-0505**).

    Add $300 for DV-6 model with Fishman Transducer and preamp (**Model 350-0506**).

    Add $130 for left-handed configuration model DV-6 LH (**Model 350-0520**).

    Add $280 for DV-6 LH model with Fishman Transducer (**Model 350-0525**).

    Add $430 for DV-6 LH model with Fishman Transducer and preamp (**Model 350-0526**).

    List price includes hardshell case.

DV-6 HG (Model 350-0600) — similar to the DV-6. Available in Antique Burst (737) and Natural (721) high gloss lacquer finishes. Mfr. 1998 to date.

Mfr.'s Sug. Retail $1,299	$995	$650	$425

    Add $150 for DV-6 HG model with Fishman Transducer (**Model 350-0605**).

    Add $300 for DV-6 HG model with Fishman Transducer and preamp (**Model 350-0606**).

    Add $130 for left-handed configuration model DV-6 HG LH (**Model 350-0620**).

D-55
courtesy Guild Guitars

Grading	100%	EXCELLENT	AVERAGE

Add $280 for DV-6 HG LH model with Fishman Transducer (**Model 350-0625**).

Add $430 for DV-6 HG LH model with Fishman Transducer and preamp (**Model 350-0626**).

List price includes hardshell case.

DV-52 (Model 350-0700) — solid spruce top, round soundhole, hand-scalloped bracing, tortoise pickguard, 3 stripe bound body, abalone rosette, solid rosewood back/sides, mahogany neck, 14/20 fret ebony fingerboard with pearl dot inlay, ebony bridge with white black dot pins, pearl Chesterfield/logo peghead inlay, 3 per side gold tuners. Available in Natural (721) satin lacquer finishes. Current mfr.

Mfr.'s Sug. Retail	$1,399	$1,050	$695	$475

Add $150 for DV-52 model with Fishman Transducer (**Model 350-0705**).

Add $300 for DV-52 model with Fishman Transducer and preamp (**Model 350-0706**).

Add $130 for left-handed configuration model DV-52 LH (**Model 350-0720**).

Add $280 for DV-52 LH model with Fishman Transducer (**Model 350-0725**).

Add $430 for DV-52 LH model with Fishman Transducer and preamp (**Model 350-0726**).

List price includes hardshell case.

DV-52 HG (Model 350-0800) — similar to DV 52, except features shaved bracing. Available in Antique Burst (737) and Natural (721) high gloss lacquer finishes. Mfr. 1990 to 1994, 1998 to date.

Mfr.'s Sug. Retail	$1,499	$1,125	$750	$500

Add $150 for DV-52 HG model with Fishman Transducer (**Model 350-0805**).

Add $300 for DV-52 HG model with Fishman Transducer and preamp (**Model 350-0806**).

Add $130 for left-handed configuration model DV-52 HG LH (**Model 350-0820**).

Add $280 for DV-52 HG LH model with Fishman Transducer (**Model 350-0825**).

Add $430 for DV-52 HG LH model with Fishman Transducer and preamp (**Model 350-0826**).

List price includes hardshell case.

DV-62 — solid spruce top, round soundhole, tortoise pickguard, herringbone bound body/rosette, rosewood back/sides, mahogany neck, 14/20 fret ebony fingerboard with pearl dot inlay, ebony bridge with white black dot pins, pearl shield/logo peghead inlay, 3 per side gold tuners. Available in Natural and Sunburst finishes. Mfd. 1994 to 1995.

			$750	$495

Last Mfr.'s Sug. Retail was $1,500.

DV-74 PUEBLO (LIMITED EDITION) — dreadnought style, solid spruce top, herringbone top binding, rosewood back and sides, ebony fingerboard with South Sea coral/onyx/turquoise/nickel silver Southwestern motif, South Sea coral/onyx/turquoise/nickel silver design on rosette, chrome silver hardware, Grover Imperial tuners. Mfd. 1996 only.

			$1,400	$1,000

Last Mfr.'s Sug. Retail was $2,499.

In 1996, Guild announced that only 50 of these guitars would be constructed. It is not known if the full production run was completed.

F Series

Guild's F Series flat-top models feature tight waisted bodies and 24 3/4" scale lengths.

F-20 TROUBADOR — solid spruce top, round soundhole, tortoise pickguard, bound body, single rosette, maple back/sides, mahogany neck, 14/20 fret rosewood fingerboard with pearl dot inlay, rosewood bridge with white pins, blackface peghead with screened logo, 3 per side chrome tuners. Available in Natural top/Mahogany Stain back/sides finish. Mfd. 1952 to 1973.

Body Length 18", Body Width 13 1/3", Body Depth 4 1/4".

1952-1956			$650	$450
1957-1973			$600	$400

In 1957, mahogany back/sides replaced original items.

M-20 — similar to F-20, except has mahogany top. Mfd. 1964 to 1973.

			$400	$300

F-30 ARAGON — solid spruce top, round soundhole, black pickguard, bound body, single rosette, maple back/sides, mahogany neck, 14/20 fret rosewood fingerboard with pearl dot inlay, rosewood bridge with white pins, blackface peghead with screened logo, 3 per side chrome tuners. Available in Natural top/Mahogany Stain back/sides finish. Mfd. 1952 to 1985.

Body Length 19 1/4", Body Width 15 1/2", Body Depth 4 1/4".

1952-1956			$800	$550
1957-1985			$750	$500

F-30 R (Limited Edition) — similar to the F-30, except featured rosewood back and sides.

			$1,250	$1,050

Before being put into full production in 1998 (See Model 350-5500), the F-30 R was only available as a Limited Edition model.

M-30 — similar to F-30 Aragon, except has mahogany top, black pickguard. Mfd. 1952 to 1985.

			$650	$350

F-30 HR (Model 350-5300) — solid spruce top, round soundhole, solid mahogany back/sides, 24 3/4" scale, 14/20 fret rosewood fingerboard with dot inlay, 3 per side chrome tuners, black pickguard. Available in Natural (721) handrubbed satin finish. Mfr. 1998 to date.

Mfr.'s Sug. Retail	$1,100

This model, like other current Guild models, will be available with a Fishman Transducer (Model 350-5305) and Fishman Transducer and preamp (Model 350-5306).

F-45 CE
courtesy Guild Guitars

G

Grading	100%	EXCELLENT	AVERAGE

The left-handed configuration model F-30 HR LH (Model 350-5320) is also slated for a Fishman Transducer (Model 350-5325) as well as a Fishman Transducer and preamp (Model 350-5326). All prices are currently $TBA.

List price will include hardshell case.

F-30 HG (Model 350-5400) — similar to the F-30 HR. Available in Antique Burst (737), Black (706), and Natural (721) high gloss finishes. Mfr. 1998 to date.

    Mfr.'s Sug. Retail   **$1,300**

This model, like other current Guild models, will be available with a Fishman Transducer (Model 350-5405) and Fishman Transducer and preamp (Model 350-5406).

The left-handed configuration model F-30 HR LH (Model 350-5420) is also slated for a Fishman Transducer (Model 350-5425) as well as a Fishman Transducer and preamp (Model 350-5426). All prices are currently $TBA.

List price will include hardshell case.

F-30 R (Model 350-5500) — similar to the F-30 HR, except features rosewood back/sides, 3 per side gold tuners. Available in Antique Burst (737) and Natural (721) high gloss finishes. Mfr. 1998 to date.

    Mfr.'s Sug. Retail   **$1,500**

This model, like other current Guild models, will be available with a Fishman Transducer (Model 350-5505) and Fishman Transducer and preamp (Model 350-5506).

The left-handed configuration model F-30 HR LH (Model 350-5520) is also slated for a Fishman Transducer (Model 350-5525) as well as a Fishman Transducer and preamp (Model 350-5526). All prices are currently $TBA.

List price will include hardshell case.

F-40 VALENCIA — solid spruce top, round soundhole, black pickguard, multibound body, 2 stripe rosette, maple back/sides, mahogany neck, 14/20 fret bound rosewood fingerboard with pearl block inlay, rosewood bridge with white pins, blackface peghead with pearl shield/logo inlay, 3 per side chrome tuners. Available in Natural and Sunburst finishes. Mfd. 1952 to 1964.

    Body Length 19 1/4", Body Width 16", Body Depth 4 1/4".

                                    $850   **$700**

M-40 Reissue — similar to F-40, except has pearl Chesterfield/logo peghead inlay. Mfd. 1973 to circa 1985.

        $750   **$500**

F-42 — folk style, spruce top, mahogany back and sides, rosewood fingerboard with dot inlays. Mfd. circa late 1980s.

    Body Width 16".

        $775   **$575**

F-44 — similar to the F-42, except has maple back and sides, multiple bindings, bound fingerboard. Mfd. 1984 to 1988.

        $1,100   **$800**

F-48 — solid spruce top, round soundhole, black pickguard, multibound body, 3 stripe rosette, mahogany back/sides, mahogany neck, 14/20 fret bound rosewood fingerboard with pearl block inlay, rosewood bridge with white black dot pins, bound blackface peghead with pearl shield/logo inlay, 3 per side gold tuners. Available in Natural and Sunburst finishes. Mfd. 1973 to 1975.

    Body Length 21", Body Width 17", Body Depth 5".

        $725   **$525**

F-50 — solid spruce top, round soundhole, black pickguard, multibound body, 3 stripe rosette, figured maple back/sides, mahogany neck, 14/20 fret bound ebony fingerboard with pearl block/abalone wedge inlay, ebony bridge with white black dot pins, bound blackface peghead with pearl shield/logo inlay, 3 per side gold tuners. Available in Natural and Sunburst finishes. Mfd. 1953 to circa 1990.

    Body Length 21", Body Width 17", Body Depth 5".

	100%	AVERAGE
1953-1960	$1,550	$1,200
1961-1974	$1,350	$1,000
1975-1990	$1,300	$950

F-50 R — similar to F-50, except has rosewood back/sides. Mfd. 1964 to circa 1990.

        $1,525   **$975**

F-47 — similar to the F-50 model, except has mahogany construction, rosewood fingerboard with block inlays, and chrome tuners.

        $800   **$625**

F-64 — similar to the F-42, but has rosewood back and sides, bound ebony fingerboard, and bound headstock. Mfd. circa late 1980s.

        $1,100   **$800**

GF-30 — folk style, solid spruce top, arched maple back, and maple sides, rosewood fingerboard with dot inlays, 3 per side headstock, chrome hardware. Mfd. circa late 1980s.

    Body Width 16".

        $700   **$475**

GF-50 — similar to the F-64, except featured dot inlays on the ebony fingerboard, and ebony bridge. Mfd. circa late 1980s.

        $900   **$600**

GF-60 — similar to the F-64 (the original model was renamed). Mfd. circa late 1980s.

        $1,100   **$800**

1973 F-40 SB
courtesy Sam J. Maggio

Grading	100%	EXCELLENT	AVERAGE

GF-60 C — similar to the Gf-60, except has single cutaway body.

		$1,200	$900

STUDIO 24 — double cutaway body, spruce top, maple back and sides, redesigned neck joint that allows access to upper frets. Mfd. circa late 1980s.

		$2,350	$2,000

Designed in conjunction with noted vintage guitar expert George Gruhn.

12 String Series

F-112 — flat-top body, solid spruce top, round soundhole, tortoise pickguard, tortoise bound body, single rosette, mahogany back/sides/neck, 14/20 fret rosewood fingerboard with pearl dot inlay, rosewood bridge with white pins, blackface peghead with screened logo, 6 per side chrome tuners. Available in Natural finish. Mfd. 1968 to 1982.

Body Length - 19 1/4", Body Width 15 1/4", Body Depth 4 1/2".

		$650	$525

F-212 — flat-top body, solid spruce top, round soundhole, tortoise pickguard, multibound body, single rosette, mahogany back/sides/neck, 14/20 fret rosewood fingerboard with pearl dot inlay, rosewood bridge with white pins, blackface peghead with screened logo, 6 per side chrome tuners. Available in Natural finish. Mfd. 1963 to 1985.

Body Length 20", Body Width 15 7/8", Body Depth 5".

		$825	$700

F-212 XL — similar to F-212, except has larger body. Mfd. 1970 to 1985.

Body Length 21", Body Width 17", Body Depth 5".

		$875	$750

F-312 — similar to F-212, except has multibound body, rosewood back/sides, ebony fingerboard. Mfd. 1964 to 1974.

Body Length 21", Body Width 17", Body Depth 5".

		$825	$700

F-412 — flat-top body, solid spruce top, round soundhole, black pickguard, multibound body, 3 stripe rosette, maple back/sides, mahogany neck, 14/20 fret bound ebony fingerboard with pearl block inlay, ebony bridge with white pins, bound blackface peghead with pearl shield/logo inlay, 6 per side gold tuners. Available in Natural finish. Mfd. 1970 to circa 1990.

Body Length 21", Body Width 17", Body Depth 5".

		$1,200	$975

F-512 — flat-top body, solid spruce top, round soundhole, black pickguard, wood bound body, multistripe purfling/rosette, rosewood back/sides, mahogany neck, 14/20 fret bound/purfled ebony fingerboard with pearl block/abalone wedge inlay, ebony bridge with white black dot pins, bound blackface peghead with pearl shield/logo inlay, 6 per side gold tuners. Available in Natural finish. Mfd. 1970 to circa 1990.

Body Length 21", Body Width 17", Body Depth 5".

		$1,450	$1,125

GF-50
courtesy Guild Guitars

Jumbo Series

All models in this series have jumbo style bodies, round soundholes and tortoise pickguards.

JF-4 — solid spruce top, bound body, 3 stripe rosette, mahogany back/sides/neck, 14/20 fret rosewood fingerboard with pearl dot inlay, rosewood bridge with white black dot pins, 3 per side chrome tuners. Available in Natural finish. Disc. 1995.

		$425	$250
			Last Mfr.'s Sug. Retail was $880.

Add $200 for high gloss finish **(Model JF4-HG)**.

JF-4 12 S — similar to JF-4, except has 12-string configuration, 6 per side tuners. Disc. 1994.

		$500	$325
			Last Mfr.'s Sug. Retail was $995.

JF-30 (Model 350-2000) — solid spruce top, arched maple back, solid curly maple sides, bound body, 3 stripe rosette, maple neck, 14/20 fret rosewood fingerboard with pearl dot inlay, rosewood bridge with white black dot pins, pearl Chesterfield/logo peghead inlay, 3 per side gold tuners. Available in Blonde (701), Black (706), and Antique (Sun)Burst (737) high gloss finishes. Current mfr.

Mfr.'s Sug. Retail	$1,499	$1,125	$725	$495

Add $150 for JF-30 model with Fishman Transducer **(Model 350-2005)**.
Add $300 for JF-30 model with Fishman Transducer and preamp **(Model 350-2006)**.
Add $130 for left-handed configuration model JF-30 LH **(Model 350-2020)**.
Add $280 for JF-30 LH model with Fishman Transducer **(Model 350-2025)**.
Add $430 for JF-30 LH model with Fishman Transducer and preamp **(Model 350-2026)**.

List price includes hardshell case.

JF-30 12 12-String (Model 350-2500) — similar to JF-30, except has 12-string configuration, 6 per side tuners. Available in Blonde (701), Black (706), and Antique (Sun)Burst (737) high gloss finishes. Current mfr.

Mfr.'s Sug. Retail	$1,599	$1,200	$795	$500

Add $150 for JF-30 12 model with Fishman Transducer **(Model 350-2505)**.
Add $300 for JF-30 12 model with Fishman Transducer and preamp **(Model 350-2506)**.
Add $130 for left-handed configuration model JF-30 12 LH **(Model 350-2520)**.
Add $280 for JF-30 12 LH model with Fishman Transducer **(Model 350-2525)**.
Add $430 for JF-30 12 LH model with Fishman Transducer and preamp **(Model 350-2526)**.

List price includes hardshell case.

Grading	100%	EXCELLENT	AVERAGE

JF-55 (Model 350-2100) — solid spruce top, scalloped bracing, 3 stripe bound body, abalone rosette, solid rosewood back/sides, mahogany neck, 14/20 fret bound ebony fingerboard with pearl block/abalone wedge inlay, ebony bridge with white abalone dot pins, maple endpin wedge, bound peghead with pearl shield/logo inlay, 3 per side gold tuners. Available in Antique Burst (837) and Natural (821) high gloss finishes. Current mfr.

Mfr.'s Sug. Retail $2,199	$1,650	$1,100	$725

    Add $150 for JF-55 model with Fishman Transducer **(Model 350-2105)**.

    Add $300 for JF-55 model with Fishman Transducer and preamp **(Model 350-2106)**.

    Add $130 for left-handed configuration model JF-55 LH **(Model 350-2120)**.

    Add $280 for JF-55 LH model with Fishman Transducer **(Model 350-2125)**.

    Add $430 for JF-55 LH model with Fishman Transducer and preamp **(Model 350-2126)**.

List price includes deluxe hardshell case.

JF-55 12 12-String (Model 350-2600) — similar to the JF-55, except has 12-string configuration, 6 per side tuners. Available in Natural (821) and Antique (Sun)Burst (837) high gloss finishes.

Mfr.'s Sug. Retail $2,299	$1,725	$1,125	$750

    Add $150 for JF-55 12 model with Fishman Transducer **(Model 350-2605)**.

    Add $300 for JF-55 12 model with Fishman Transducer and preamp **(Model 350-2606)**.

    Add $130 for left-handed configuration model JF-55 12 LH **(Model 350-2620)**.

    Add $280 for JF-55 12 LH model with Fishman Transducer **(Model 350-2625)**.

    Add $430 for JF-55 12 LH model with Fishman Transducer and preamp **(Model 350-2626)**.

List price includes deluxe hardshell case.

JF-65 (Model 350-2900) — solid spruce top, 3 stripe bound body, abalone rosette, arched maple back, solid curly maple sides, maple neck, 14/20 fret bound ebony fingerboard with pearl block/abalone wedge inlay, ebony bridge with white abalone dot pins, maple endpin wedge, bound peghead with pearl shield/logo inlay, 3 per side gold tuners. Available in Blonde (801) and Antique (Sun)Burst (837) finishes. Current mfr.

Mfr.'s Sug. Retail $2,099	$1,575	$1,000	$695

    Add $150 for JF-65 model with Fishman Transducer **(Model 350-2905)**.

    Add $300 for JF-65 model with Fishman Transducer and preamp **(Model 350-2906)**.

    Add $130 for left-handed configuration model JF-65 LH **(Model 350-2920)**.

    Add $280 for JF-65 LH model with Fishman Transducer **(Model 350-2925)**.

    Add $430 for JF-65 LH model with Fishman Transducer and preamp **(Model 350-2926)**.

List price includes deluxe hardshell case.

JF-65 12 12-String (Model 350-2700) — similar to the JF-65, except has 12-string configuration, 6 per side tuners. Available in Blonde (801) and Antique (Sun)Burst (837) high gloss finishes.

Mfr.'s Sug. Retail $2,199	$1,650	$1,100	$725

    Add $150 for JF-65 12 model with Fishman Transducer **(Model 350-2705)**.

    Add $300 for JF-65 12 model with Fishman Transducer and preamp **(Model 350-2706)**.

    Add $130 for left-handed configuration model JF-65 12 LH **(Model 350-2720)**.

    Add $280 for JF-65 12 LH model with Fishman Transducer **(Model 350-2725)**.

    Add $430 for JF-65 12 LH model with Fishman Transducer and preamp **(Model 350-2726)**.

List price includes deluxe hardshell case.

JV-52 — jumbo style, solid spruce top, round soundhole, tortoise pickguard, bound body, herringbone rosette, rosewood back/sides, mahogany neck, 14/20 fret ebony fingerboard with pearl dot inlay, ebony bridge with white black dot pins, blackface peghead with pearl Chesterfield/logo inlay, 3 per side gold tuners. Available in Natural finish. Mfd. 1994 to 1995.

		$800	$425

    Last Mfr.'s Sug. Retail was $1,250.

Mark Series

Instruments in this series are classically styled.

MARK I — mahogany top, round soundhole, simple marquetry rosette, mahogany back/sides/neck, 12/19 fret rosewood fingerboard, tied rosewood bridge, 3 per side nickel tuners. Available in Natural finish. Mfd. 1960 to 1973.

		$375	$255

Mark II — similar to Mark I, except has spruce top, bound body. Mfd. 1960 to 1988.

		$400	$325

Mark III — similar to Mark I, except has spruce top, multibound body, floral rosette marquetry. Mfd. 1960 to 1988.

		$525	$425

Mark IV — spruce top, round soundhole, multi-bound body, marquetry rosette, figured pearwood back/sides, mahogany neck, 12/19 fret ebony fingerboard, tied ebony bridge, 3 per side chrome tuners with pearloid buttons. Available in Natural finish. Mfd. 1960 to 1985.

		$600	$500

This model had figured maple back/sides optionally available.

Mark V — similar to Mark IV, except has ebony bound body, elaborate marquetry rosette, figured maple back/sides, gold tuners with engraved buttons. Mfd. 1960 to 1988.

		$700	$600

This model had rosewood back/sides optionally available.

JF-30
courtesy Guild Guitars

JF-65 12-String
courtesy Guild Guitars

Grading	100%	EXCELLENT	AVERAGE

Mark VI — similar to Mark IV, except has ebony bound body, elaborate marquetry rosette, Brazilian rosewood back/sides, gold tuners with engraved buttons. Mfd. 1966 to 1968.

| | $850 | $500 | |

Guild Custom Shop Series

In 1997, Guild opened a Custom Shop in Nashville, Tennessee. Guild Custom Shop models are bui lt in limited quantities.

45th ANNIVERSARY — solid spruce top, round soundhole, solid maple back/sides, multiple body binding, abalone purfling/rosette, 14/20 fret bound ebony fingerboard with abalone/pearl inlay, ebony bridge, bound peghead with abalone shield/logo inlay, 3 per side gold tuners. Available in Natural finish. Mfr. 1997 only.

| | SN/A | SN/A | |

Last Mfr.'s Sug. Retail was $4,500.

Only 45 instruments will be built. This 45th Anniversary model commemorates Guild's beginning in 1952.

D-100 — solid spruce top, scalloped bracing, round soundhole, black pickguard, maple bound body, abalone purfling/rosette, solid rosewood back/sides, 3 piece mahogany/maple neck, 14/20 fret maple bound ebony fingerboard with abalone crown inlay, ebony bridge with white abalone dot pins, maple endpin wedge, maple bound peghead with abalone shield/logo inlay, 3 per side gold tuners. Available in Natural and Sunburst finishes. Current mfr.

| | $2,200 | SN/A | |

Last Mfr.'s Sug. Retail was $3,600.

D-100 C Dreadnought (Model 350-0400) — similar to D-100, except has handcarved heel. Available in Antique Burst (837) and Natural (821) high gloss lacquer finishes. Current mfr.

| Mfr.'s Sug. Retail | $3,999 | $3,120 | SN/A | SN/A |

Add $150 for D-100 C model with Fishman Transducer (**Model 350-0405**).

Add $300 for D-100 C model with Fishman Transducer and preamp (**Model 350-0406**).

Add $130 for left-handed configuration model D-100 C LH (**Model 350-0420**).

Add $280 for D-100 C LH model with Fishman Transducer (**Model 350-0425**).

Add $430 for D-100 C LH model with Fishman Transducer and preamp (**Model 350-0426**).

List price includes deluxe hardshell case.

JF-100 JUMBO — solid spruce top, scalloped bracing, maple bound body, abalone purfling, abalone rosette, solid rosewood back/sides, 3 piece mahogany neck with maple center strip, 14/20 fret maple bound ebony fingerboard with abalone crown inlay, ebony bridge with white abalone pins, maple endpin wedge, ebony endpin, maple bound peghead with abalone shield/logo inlay, 3 per side tuners. Available in Natural finish. Disc. 1995.

| | $1,950 | SN/A | |

Last Mfr.'s Sug. Retail was $3,700.

JF-100 12 Jumbo 12-String — similar to JF-100, except has 12 strings, 6 per side tuners. Disc. 1995.

| | $2,000 | SN/A | |

Last Mfr.'s Sug. Retail was $4,000.

JF-100 C JUMBO (Model 350-2200) — similar to JF-100, except has hand carved heel. Available in Antique Burst (837) and Natural (821) high gloss lacquer finish. Mfr. 1994 to date.

| Mfr.'s Sug. Retail | $4,299 | $3,450 | SN/A | SN/A |

Add $150 for JF-100 C model with Fishman Transducer (**Model 350-2205**).

Add $300 for JF-100 C model with Fishman Transducer and preamp (**Model 350-2206**).

Add $130 for left-handed configuration model JF-100 C LH (**Model 350-2220**).

Add $280 for JF-100 C LH model with Fishman Transducer (**Model 350-2225**).

Add $430 for JF-100 C LH model with Fishman Transducer and preamp (**Model 350-2226**).

List price includes deluxe hardshell case.

JF-100 C 12 Jumbo 12-String (Model 350-2800) — similar to JF-100 C, except has 12 string configuration, 6 per side tuners. Available in Antique Burst (837) and Natural (821) high gloss lacquer finish. Mfr. 1994 to date.

| Mfr.'s Sug. Retail | $4,499 | $3,600 | SN/A | SN/A |

Add $150 for JF-100 C 12 model with Fishman Transducer (**Model 350-2805**).

Add $300 for JF-100 C 12 model with Fishman Transducer and preamp (**Model 350-2806**).

Add $130 for left-handed configuration model JF-100 C 12 LH (**Model 350-2820**).

Add $280 for JF-100 C 12 LH model with Fishman Transducer (**Model 350-2825**).

Add $430 for JF-100 C 12 LH model with Fishman Transducer and preamp (**Model 350-2826**).

List price includes deluxe hardshell case.

DECO DREADNOUGHT (Model 395-0850) — solid AAA spruce top, scalloped bracings, round soundhole, abalone rosette, bookmatched rosewood back, solid rosewood sides, abalone top binding, 3-piece mahogany neck, abalone-bound black pickguard, 14/20 fret bound ebony fingerboard with abalone Deco inlay, ebony bridge, bound peghead with abalone shield/logo inlay, 3 per side gold tuners. Available in Natural (821) high gloss lacquer finish. Mfr. 1997 to date.

| Mfr.'s Sug. Retail | $3,499 | $2,800 | SN/A | SN/A |

List price includes deluxe hardshell case.

Finesse Dreadnought (Model 395-0805) — similar to the Deco, except has herringbone rosette, unbound peghead, unbound fingerboard with abalone dot inlay, tortoiseshell pickguard, tortoiseshell bound top, Fishman Matrix Natural II pickup. Available in Natural (821)high gloss lacquer finish. Mfr. 1997 to date.

| Mfr.'s Sug. Retail | $2,699 | $2,200 | SN/A | SN/A |

List price includes deluxe hardshell case.

D-100
courtesy Guild Guitars

G

Grading	100%	EXCELLENT	AVERAGE

VALENCIA CONCERT (Model 395-3550) — solid AAA spruce top, shaved bracings, round soundhole, abalone rosette, solid highly figured maple back/sides, abalone top binding, solid figured maple neck, black pickguard, 14/20 fret bound ebony fingerboard with abalone Deco inlay, ebony bridge, bound peghead with abalone shield/logo inlay, 3 per side gold tuners. Available in Antique Burst (837) and Blonde (801) high gloss lacquer finish. Mfr. 1998 to date.

    Mfr.'s Sug. Retail $3,999

        List price includes deluxe hardshell case.

ACOUSTIC BASS

B-30 — grand concert style, spruce top, round soundhole, tortoise pickguard, 3 stripe bound body/rosette, mahogany back/sides/neck, 14/20 fret rosewood fingerboard with pearl dot inlay, rosewood bridge with white pins, pearl Chesterfield/logo peghead inlay, 2 per side chrome tuners. Available in Natural and Sunburst finishes. Mfd. 1987 to 1995.

                $900 $650

                Last Mfr.'s Sug. Retail was $1,400.

B-500 C — similar to B-30, except has single round cutaway, maple back/sides, transducer bridge pickup, volume/concentric treble/bass control, preamp. Available in Natural and Sunburst finishes. Disc. 1994.

                $850 $550

                Last Mfr.'s Sug. Retail was $1,695.

ACOUSTIC ELECTRIC

CCE-100 — single round cutaway classic style, oval soundhole, bound body, wood inlay rosette, mahogany back/sides/neck, 24 fret rosewood fingerboard, rosewood bridge, 3 per side chrome tuners, transducer pickup, 4 band EQ with preamp. Available in Natural finish. Mfd. 1994 to 1995.

                $600 $395

                Last Mfr.'s Sug. Retail was $1,200.

CCE-100 HG — similar to CCE-100, except has gold hardware. Available in Natural high gloss finish. Disc. 1995.

                $700 $450

                Last Mfr.'s Sug. Retail was $1,400.

DCE-1 (Model 350-1306) — single cutaway body, solid spruce top, round soundhole, black pickguard, bound body, 3 stripe rosette, mahogany back/sides/neck, 20 fret rosewood fingerboard with dot inlay, rosewood bridge with white black dot pins, 3 per side gold tuners, transducer pickup, Fishman Acoustic Matrix system. Available in Natural (021) handrubbed satin finish. Mfr. 1994 to date.

    Mfr.'s Sug. Retail $1,099 $825 $550 $395

        Add $200 for left-handed configuration model DCE-1 LH **(Model 350-1326)**.

DCE-1 HG (Model 350-1406) — similar to the DCE-1. Available in Antique Burst (037), Black (006), and Cherry (038) high gloss finishes. Mfr. 1996 to date.

    Mfr.'s Sug. Retail $1,299 $1,000 $650 $425

        Add $200 for left-handed configuration model DCE-1 HG LH **(Model 350-1426)**.

DCE-5 — similar to DCE-1, except has rosewood back/sides, ebony fingerboard, Fishman Prefix On Board Blender system. Available in Natural (721) and Antique (Sun)Burst (737) high gloss finishes. Mfr. 1994 to 1995.

    Mfr.'s Sug. Retail $1,599 $1,200 $795 $575

        Add $130 for left-handed configuration model D-55 LH **(Model 350-0320)**.

        List price includes hardshell case.

Acoustic Electric Traditional (F) Series

    All models in this series have single rounded cutaway folk style body, oval soundhole, tortoise pickguard, 3 stripe bound body/rosette, transducer pickup, volume/4 band EQ preamp system with built in phase reversal, unless otherwise listed.

F-4 CE
courtesy Guild Guitars

F-4 CE (Model 350-3006) — solid spruce top, mahogany back/sides/neck, 14/20 fret rosewood fingerboard with pearl dot inlay, rosewood bridge with white black dot pins, 3 per side chrome tuners, Fishman Acoustic Matrix system. Available in Natural (721) handrubbed satin finish. Current mfr.

    Mfr.'s Sug. Retail $1,199 $900 $595 $395

        Add $200 for left-handed configuration model F-4 CE LH **(Model 350-3026)**.

        Black and Vintage White high gloss finishes were available between 1994 to 1997.

        List price includes hardshell case.

F-4 CE HG (Model 350-3106) — similar to F-4 CE. Available in Antique Burst (737), Black (706), Crimson Red Transparent (738), and Teal Green Transparent (748) high gloss finishes. Mfr. 1998 to date.

    Mfr.'s Sug. Retail $1,399

        Add $200 for left-handed configuration model F-4 CE HG LH **(Model 350-3126)**.

        List price includes hardshell case.

F-4 CE MH — similar to F-4 CE, except has mahogany top. Available in Amber finish. Disc. 1995.

                    $500 $325

                Last Mfr.'s Sug. Retail was $1,050.

F-5 CE (Model 350-3206) — solid spruce top, rosewood back/sides, mahogany neck, 14/20 fret rosewood fingerboard with pearl dot inlay, rosewood bridge with white black dot pins, 3 per side chrome Grover tuners, Fishman Acoustic Matrix system. Available in Black (706), Natural (721), and Antique (Sun)Burst (737) high gloss lacquer finishes. Current mfr.

    Mfr.'s Sug. Retail $1,499 $1,125 $725 $495

        Add $100 for deep body **Model FF-5 CE** (this option was discontinued in 1998).

        Add $200 for left-handed configuration model F-5 CE LH **(Model 350-3226)**.

        List price includes hardshell case.

G

F-25 CE — solid spruce top, mahogany back/sides/neck, 24 fret rosewood fingerboard with pearl dot inlay, rosewood bridge with white black dot pins, 3 per side chrome Grover tuners, volume control, concentric treble/bass control, active preamp. Available in Black, Natural and Sunburst finishes. Disc. 1992.

$600 $395
Last Mfr.'s Sug. Retail was $1,195.

F-30 CE — solid spruce top, flame maple back/sides, mahogany neck, 24 fret rosewood fingerboard with pearl dot inlay, rosewood bridge with white black dot pins, pearl Chesterfield/logo peghead inlay, 3 per side gold Grover tuners. Available in Black, Blonde, Natural and Sunburst finishes. Disc. 1995.

$850 $500
Last Mfr.'s Sug. Retail was $1,495.

F-45 CE — similar to the F-30 CE, except features mahogany back/sides.

$850 $500

F-65 CE (Model 350-3306) — solid spruce top, abalone rosette, curly maple back/sides, mahogany neck, 14/20 fret bound ebony fingerboard with pearl block/abalone wedge inlay, ebony bridge with white abalone dot pins, bound peghead with pearl shield/logo inlay, 3 per side gold Grover tuners, Fishman Prefix On Board Blender system. Available in Antique Burst (837), Black (806), Blonde (801), Crimson Red Transparent (838), Sapphire Blue Transparent (827), and Teal Green Transparent (848) high gloss finishes. Current mfr.

Mfr.'s Sug. Retail $1,999 $1,520 $760 $625
Add $200 for left-handed configuration model F-65 CE LH **(Model 350-3326)**.
Add $200 for left-handed configuration model F-5 CE LH **(Model 350-3226)**.

Early versions of this model had figured maple top with Amber and Sunburst finishes optionally available.

In 1994, transducer pickup, and preamp were introduced.

List price includes deluxe hardshell case.

FS-48 DECEIVER — single cutaway body style, maple fingerboard, pointed headstock design, with piezo pickup and humbucker hidden between the soundhole and bridge. Mfd. circa 1984.

Model has not traded sufficiently to quote pricing.

S-4 Specialist (Formerly Songbird) Series

The S-4 CE Specialist models were previously called the **Songbird** models. The S-4 CE has a body the size of a **Bluesbird**, and has a routed-out acoustic chamber in the mahogany body that is capped with an X-braced solid spruce top.

S-4 CE HR (Model 350-6000) — Bluesbird-style solid mahogany body with (routed out) acoustic chamber, solid spruce top, round soundhole, tortoise pickguard, 3 stripe bound body/rosette, mahogany neck, 22 fret rosewood fingerboard with pearl dot inlay, rosewood bridge with white black dot pins, 3 per side chrome tuners, transducer bridge pickup, volume/concentric treble/bass control, Fishman Acoustic Matrix preamp. Available in Natural (821) handrubbed satin finish. Current mfr.

Mfr.'s Sug. Retail $1,199 $899 $595 $395

List price includes deluxe hardshell case.

S-4 CE HG (Model 350-6100) (Formerly Songbird) — similar S-4 CE HR, except has pearl Chesterfield/logo peghead inlay, gold tuners. Available in Black (806) and Natural (821) high gloss finishes. Current mfr.

Mfr.'s Sug. Retail $1,399 $1,050 $550 $450

List price includes deluxe hardshell case.

Early Songbird models were also available in a White finish.

S-4 CE BG BARRY GIBB SIGNATURE (Model 350-6100) — similar S-4 CE HG. Available in Crimson Red Transparent (838) and Sapphire Blue Transparent (827) custom high gloss finishes. Mfr. 1998 to date.

Mfr.'s Sug. Retail $1,499

This model was designed in conjunction with Barry Gibb (BeeGees).

List price includes deluxe hardshell case.

ACOUSTIC ELECTRIC BASS

B-4 E (Model 350-4006) — single rounded cutaway folk style, solid spruce top, oval soundhole, tortoise pickguard, 3 stripe bound body/rosette, arched mahogany back, mahogany sides/neck, 14/20 fret rosewood fingerboard with pearl dot inlay, rosewood bridge with white black dot pins, 2 per side chrome tuners, transducer pickup, volume/4 band EQ control, Fishman Acoustic Matrix preamp. Available in Natural (721) handrubbed satin finish. Current mfr.

Mfr.'s Sug. Retail $1,299 $995 $650 $425
Add $200 for left-handed configuration model B-4 E LH **(Model 350-4026)**. The left-handed B-4 E LH model is available with a fretless fingerboard **(Model 350-4126)**.

The B-4 E model is available with a fretless fingerboard (Model 350-4106).

List price includes hardshell case.

B-4 E HG (Model 350-4206) — similar to B-4 E, except has multiple-ply body binding. Available in Antique Burst (737), Black (706), Crimson Red Transparent (738), and Teal Green Transparent (748) high gloss finishes. Mfr. 1994 to 1995, 1998 to date.

Mfr.'s Sug. Retail $1,449 $1,100 $725 $495
Add $200 for left-handed configuration model B-4 E HG LH **(Model 350-4026)**. The left-handed B-4 E HG LH model is available with a fretless fingerboard **(Model 350-4326)**.

The B-4 E HG model is available with a fretless fingerboard (Model 350-4306).

List price includes hardshell case.

F-30 CE
courtesy Guild Guitars

Songbird
courtesy Guild Guitars

Grading	100%	EXCELLENT	AVERAGE

B-30 Acoustic Bass
courtesy Guild Guitars

B-4 E MH — similar to B-4E, except has mahogany top. Mfd. 1994 to 1995.

		$575	$375

Last Mfr.'s Sug. Retail was $1,150.

B-30 E (Model 350-4406) — jumbo style, solid spruce top, round soundhole, tortoise pickguard, 3 stripe bound body/rosette, arched mahogany back, mahogany sides/neck, 14/20 fret rosewood fingerboard with pearl dot inlay, rosewood bridge with white pins, pearl Chesterfield/logo peghead inlay, 2 per side chrome tuners, transducer bridge pickup, volume/concentric treble/bass control, Fishman Acoustic Matrix system. Available in Natural (821) and Antique (Sun)Burst (837) high gloss lacquer finishes. Current mfr.

Mfr.'s Sug. Retail	$1,899	$1,425	$950	$625

Add $130 for left-handed configuration model B-30 E LH **(Model 350-4426)**. The left-handed B-30 E LH model is available with a fretless fingerboard **(Model 350-4526)**.

The B-30 E model is available with a fretless fingerboard (Model 350-4506).

List price includes hardshell case.

B-30 E T — similar to B-30E, except has thinline body style. Disc. 1992.

		$795	$525

Last Mfr.'s Sug. Retail was $1,595.

GUITAR FARM

Instruments currently built in Sperryville, Virginia.

The Guitar Farm is currently offering hand crafted guitar models. For further information regarding specifications and pricing, contact The Guitar Farm through the Index of Current Manufacturers located in the rear of this edition.

MICHAEL GURIAN

Instruments built on "Earth, Third Planet from the Sun" (New York, New York) between 1965 and 1982.

Luthier Michael Gurian built quality classical and steel string acoustic guitars, as well as being a major American wood supplier. He debuted his classical designs in 1965 and offered steel string designs four years later. In 1971, at the encouragement of vintage retailer Matt Umanov, Gurian designed a cutaway model that later became a regular part of the product line.

In the early 1970s, Gurian moved his production facilities to Hinsdale, New Hampshire. Gurian's four story mill building housed a large band saw (for slabbing logs), two resaws (cutting slabs to dimension), and various planers. During this time period, Gurian imported ebony, rosewood, mansonia, and spruce; his U.S. sources supplied walnut, maple, and other woods.

Disaster struck in 1979, as a fire consumed their current stock of guitars as well as tooling and machinery. However, Gurian rebuilt by later that year and continued producing guitars until 1982.

Michael Gurian may have stopped offering guitars in 1982, but he still continues to be a major presence in the guitar building industry. Gurian serves as a consultant in guitar design, and his company offers guitar fittings (such as bridge pins) and supplies, custom built marquetry, and guitar-building tools based on his designs.

(Source: The Alembic Report (Guitar Player magazine); and Tom Wheeler, American Guitars)

ACOUSTIC

Michael Gurian was perhaps one of the first smaller guitar producers to combine production techniques with hand crafted sensibilities. Guitars produced at the New Hampshire site were built in 3 distinct phases. In Phase One, the basic guitar parts (tops, backs, necks, fingerboards, etc.) were produced in large lots and inventoried. Gurian's factory did use carving lathes to "rough out" the neck blanks, and heated hydraulic presses to bend the guitar sides. During Phase Two, the company's luthiers would choose "kits" from the part supplies and construct the guitar individually. This allowed the luthiers control over individual guitar's construction and tuning. Finally, in Phase Three, the finished guitars were sent to the finishing technicians to spray the finish. This method would guanantee a similarity in the finishes from one guitar to the next.

The market is wide open on Gurian prices. The majority of guitars are probably in the hands of players and collectors, and as a result do not trade too often. It is estimated that the guitars are more plentiful on the east coast than the rest of the nation, given the location of the production facilities. Finally, as Gurian guitars have not been well notated previously, various dealers perhaps shyed away from dealing an "unknown quanity" when the opportunity arose. The **Blue Book of Guitars** recommends playing a Gurian when they are encountered; let your fingers and ears do the preliminary investigation.

G

WM. HALL & SON

Location and date of production currently unknown.

The **Blue Book of Guitars** was contacted by Lester Groves in regards to an older acoustic guitar he currently owns. The label inside reads *Wm. Hall & Son - 239 Broadway NY*, and carries a serial number of 5138. This acoustic has a spruce top and rosewood sides. The **Blue Book of Guitars** is still trying to figure out if the company is the distributor or the manufacturer! If any knowledgable readers have any information, please contact the **Blue Book** staff for an update in the next edition.

HANNAH

Instruments currently built in Saint John (New Brunswick), Canada.

Luthier Rod Hannah hand builds both dreadnought and 000 12-Fret acoustic guitars in "short lot" sizes (approximately 4 instruments at a time). Hannah guitars are built with recording and performing musicians in mind. Retail list prices start at $4,500 (and up).

HARMONY

Instruments produced in the Chicago, Illinois area between the 1890s to 1975.

Harmony, along with Kay, were the two major producers for instrument wholesalers for a number of years (see chapter on House Brands). When the U.S. manufacturing facilities were closed, the Harmony trademark was sold and later applied to Korean-built instruments from the mid 1970s to the late 1980s.

The Harmony Company of Chicago, Illinois was one of the largest American musical instrument manufacturers. Harmony has the historical distinction of being the largest "jobber" house in the nation, producing stringed instruments for a number of different wholesalers. Individual dealers or distributors could get stringed instruments with their own brandname on it (as long as they ordered a minimum of 100 pieces). At one time the amount of instruments being produced by Harmony made up the largest percentage of stringed instruments being manufactured in the U.S. market (archtops, flat-tops, electric Spanish, Hawaiian bodies, ukeleles, banjos, mandolins, violins and more).

Harmony was founded by Wilhelm J.F. Schultz in 1892. Schultz, a German immigrant and former foreman of Lyon & Healy's drum division, started his new company with four employees. By 1884, the number of employees had grown to forty, and Shultz continued to expand into larger and larger factories through 1904. Shultz built Harmony up to a 125 employee workforce (and a quarter of a million dollars in annual sales) by 1915.

Harmony H6659 Dreadnought
1973 Harmony Catalog

In 1916, the Sears, Roebuck Company purchased Harmony, and seven years later the company had annual sales of 250,000 units. Max Adler, a Sears executive, appointed Jay Kraus as vice-president of Harmony in 1925. The following year Jay succeeded founder Wilhelm Schultz as president, and continued expanding production. In 1930, annual sales were reported to be 500,000 units, with 35 to 40 percent being sold to Sears (catalog sales). Harmony had no branch offices, territorial restrictions, or dealer *reps* - wholesalers purchased the musical instruments and aggressively sold to music stores.

Harmony bought several trademarks from the bankrupt Oscar Schmidt Company in 1939, and their Sovereign and Stella lines were Harmony's more popular guitars. In 1940, Krause bought Harmony by acquiring the controlling stock, and continued to expand the company's production to meet the market boom during the 1950s and 1960s. Mr. Kraus remained president until 1968, when he died of a heart attack. Charles Rubovits (who had been with Harmony since 1935) took over as president, and remained in that position for two years. Kraus' trust still maintained control over Harmony, and trust members attempted to form a conglomerate by purchasing Chicago-based distributor Targ & Dinner and a few other companies. Company (or more properly the conglomerate's) indebtedness led to a liquidation auction to satisfy creditors - although Harmony continued to turn in impressive annual sales figures right up until the company was dissolved in 1974 (or early 1975). The loss of Harmony in the mid 1970s, combined with the decline of Kay/Valco, Inc. in 1969 (or 1970) definitely left the door wide open for Asian products to gain a larger percentage of the entry or student level guitar market (for example, W.M.I. began using the Kay trademark on Teisco-built guitars as early as 1973; these guitars were sold through department store chains through the 1970s).

(Harmony company history courtesy Tom Wheeler, American Guitars)

(Harmony model information courtesy John Kenimire of JK Lutherie, Ryland Fitchett of Rockohaulix, Ronald Rothman of Rothman's Guitars)

Identifying Re-Branded Harmony Trademarks

Harmony reportedly made 57 "different" brands throughout their productive years. Early models featured the Harmony trademark, or remained unlabeled for the numerous wholesalers. In 1928 Harmony introduced the **Roy Smeck Vita** series, and two years later the **Grand Concert** and **Hawaiian** models debuted. The **Vagabond** line was introduced in 1931, the **Cremona** series in 1934, and **Patrician** guitars later in 1938.

As Harmony was purchased by Sears, Roebuck in 1916, Harmony built a number of **Silvertone** models. Harmony continued to sell to Sears even after Kraus bought the company. Harmony bought a number of trademarks from the bankrupt Oscar Schmidt Company in 1939 (such as **La Scala, Stella, Sovereign**), as well as expanding their own brandnames with **Valencia, Monterey, Harmony Deluxe, Johnny Marvin, Vogue**, and many (like **Carelli** from the mid 1930s) that are being researched today! Although the Kay company built most of the **Airline** guitars for the Montgomery Ward stores, Harmony would sometimes be subcontracted to build Airlines to meet the seasonal shopping rush. National (Valco) supplied resonator cones for some Harmony resonator models, and probably bought guitar parts from Harmony in return.

Harmony Production, 1961 to 1975

The Harmony company of 4600 South Kolin Avenue in Chicago, Illinois built a great deal of guitars. Harmony catalogs in the early 1960s proudly proclaimed "We've produced Millions of Instruments but We make them One at a Time". Harmony guitars can be found practically anywhere: the guitar shop, the antique shop, the flea market, the Sunday garage sale right around the corner. Due to the vast numbers of Harmony guitars, and because the majority of them were entry level models, the vintage guitar market's response is a collective shrug of the shoulders as it moves on to the higher dollar American built Fenders and Gibsons, etc.

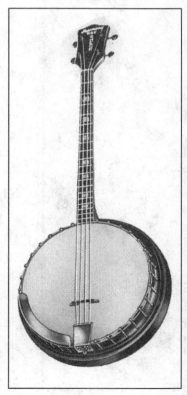

Harmony Roy Smeck Banjo 8125
1964 Harmony Catalog

Harmony "Singing Cowboys" 1057
1964 Harmony Catalog

As a result, the secondary Harmony guitar market is rather hard to pin down. Outside of a few hardy souls like Willie Moseley, Ronald Rothman, Paul Day, and Tony Bacon, very little has been written about Harmony guitar <u>models</u> as a means to identify them. As a result, rather than use the exact model designations, most dealers tend to offer a "Harmony Acoustic", or a "'60s Harmony Archtop" through their ads or at guitar shows. It becomes difficult to track the asking prices of various models if the information regarding that model is not available.

The majority of Harmony guitars encountered today are generally part of the millions produced during the 1960s through the company's closing in 1975. As most of them were entry level models, condition (especially physical condition) becomes a bit more critical in pricing. A dead mint Harmony Rocket is worth the money because it's clean - a beat up, player's grade Rocket might not be worth a second look to the interested party. However, the market interest is the deciding factor in pricing - the intrinsic value of (for example) a laminated body Harmony archtop will be the deciding factor in the asking price to the public.

The **Blue Book of Guitars** continues to seek out additional input on Harmony models, specifications, dates of production, and any serialization information. This year's section is the starting point for defining Harmony products. Additional information gathered on Harmony will be updated in future editions of the **Blue Book of Guitars**.

Harmony Pricing Overview

While Harmony did produce a wide range of acoustic archtop and archtop models with pickups, the majority of models were the entry level or student grade instruments. The average Harmony encountered at a guitar show or secondhand store is probably going to be one of the 1960s production models, and for a player's value, most of these will fall in the under $200 range.

For most models, the secondary market (defined used sales prices) is still undefined. **Prices are listed in models where specific data was available.**

Given the interest in other brand name American-produced guitars, there is the faint beginnings of collector desirability on certain Harmony models. Certainly the Pre-war arched (or carved) top acoustics, Rocket series (especially the **H-59 Rocket III** model), or any of the laminated arch tops in mint condition will begin to bring a higher premium. In this case, condition will be everything - the majority of Harmony guitars encountered <u>have been played</u> and are not in mint condition.

For example, the Harmony/Silvertone guitar models (offered by Sears) may range in price between $225 to $395, depending on configuration and condition. The Silvertone model with the black finish and single cutaway hollow body with the huge aluminum binding (pickguard and 2 humbuckers) may bring $400 if in clean condition.

Harmony Series Designations

In addition to the Harmony trademark, Harmony models also carry the model (series) designation on the headstock, i.e. **Broadway**, **Monterey**, **Patrician**, **Sovereign**, etc. Some of the Sovereign models may further be designated as **"Jet Set"** variations as well. Keep in mind that there are model distinctions within the series.

For further information regarding Harmony electric guitars, please refer to the **5th Edition Blue Book of Electric Guitars**. Archtop guitars with "floating" or built-in pickups can be found in the Harmony Electric section of the Electric edition.

ACOUSTIC

Arched (Top) Series

The 1200 Series Arched Guitars were originally designated the Auditorium models; in 1969, they were renamed to Archtone models.

H 1213 ARCHTONE (Also H 1214 BLONDE, H 1215 BROWN MAHOGANY) — hollow body with white striped edges, arched birch top/birch back/sides, 2 f-holes, 20 fret hard maple fingerboard with white dot inlay, 3 per side tuners, chrome hardware, adjustable bridge/raised tailpiece, raised celluloid pickguard with stencilled Harmony logo. Available in Shaded Brown Sunburst **(Model H 1213)**, Blonde Ivory Enamel with Grained effect **(Model H 1214)**, and Gloss Brown Mahogany with Grained effect **(Model H 1215)** finishes. Disc. circa 1972.

Last Mfr.'s Sug. Retail was $49.95.

The hard maple fingerboard was "grained to resemble rosewood", according to the 1961 Harmony catalog.

HTG 1215 Archtone Tenor — similar to the H 1215 Archtone, except in Tenor (4-string) configuration. Available in Gloss Brown Mahogany finish with Grained effect. Disc. circa 1972.

Last Mfr.'s Sug. Retail was $49.95.

H 1310 CUTAWAY — bound single cutaway body, arched spruce top/maple back, 2 segmented f-holes, 20 fret rosewood fingerboard with pearlette block inlay, pearlette inlaid logo on rosewood peghead veneer, 3 per side tuners, chrome hardware, adjustable bridge/raised tailpiece, raised black pickguard. Available in Shaded Brown finish. Disc. circa 1972.

Length 41", Body Width 16 1/2".

Last Mfr.'s Sug. Retail was $149.50.

H 1311 Cutaway Blonde — similar to the H 1310. Available in Blonde finish. Disc. circa 1965.

Last Mfr.'s Sug. Retail was $105.

Broadway Arched (Top) Series

H 954 BROADWAY (AUDITORIUM SIZE) — bound hollow body, arched select hardwood top/hardwood back/sides, 2 f-holes, 20 fret ebonised maple fingerboard with white dot inlay, 3 per side tuners, chrome hardware, adjustable bridge/raised tailpiece, raised celluloid pickguard with stencilled design. Available in Mahogany Sunburst finish. Disc. circa 1972.

Length 40 3/4", Body Width 15 3/4".

Last Mfr.'s Sug. Retail was $74.50.

Master Arched (Top) Series

H 945 MASTER (AUDITORIUM SIZE) — celluloid bound hollow body, arched hardwood top/back, 2 f-holes, 20 fret ebonised maple fingerboard with white block inlay, 3 per side tuners, chrome hardware, adjustable ebonised bridge/raised tailpiece, raised shell pickguard with stencilled Master logo. Available in Sunburst lacquer finish. Disc. circa 1972.

Length 40", Body Width 15 3/4".

Last Mfr.'s Sug. Retail was $59.95.

Harmony Auditorium Arch Top 1215
1964 Harmony Catalog

Monterey Arched (Top) Series

H 950 MONTEREY LEADER — celluloid bound hollow body, arched hardwood top/back, 2 f-holes, 20 fret ebonised maple fingerboard with white dot inlay, 3 per side tuners, chrome hardware, adjustable ebonised bridge/raised tailpiece, raised black pickguard with stencilled M logo. Available in Figured Red Sunburst finish. Disc. circa 1972.

> Length 40", Body Width 15 3/4".

> Last Mfr.'s Sug. Retail was $69.95.

HTG 950 Monterey Tenor (Also TG 950) — similar to the H 950, except in Tenor (4-string) configuration. Available in Figured Red Sunburst finish. Disc. circa 1972.

> Last Mfr.'s Sug. Retail was $69.50.

H 1325 MONTEREY (GRAND AUDITORIUM) — celluloid bound hollow body, arched spruce top/hardwood back/sides, 2 f-holes, 20 fret bound fingerboard with white dot inlay, 3 per side tuners, chrome hardware, adjustable bridge/raised tailpiece, raised shell pickguard with stencilled M logo. Available in Shaded Brown finish. Disc. circa 1972.

> Length 41", Body Width 16 1/4".

> Last Mfr.'s Sug. Retail was $79.50.

H 1456 MONTEREY (GRAND AUDITORIUM PROFESSIONAL) — celluloid bound hollow body, arched select spruce top/maple back, 2 segmented f-holes, 20 fret celluloid bound rosewood fingerboard with pearlette block inlay, 3 per side tuners, chrome hardware, adjustable bridge/raised tailpiece, raised brown pickguard with stencilled M logo. Available in Sunburst finish. Disc. circa 1968.

> Length 40 1/2", Body Width 16 1/2".

> Last Mfr.'s Sug. Retail was $85.

H 1457 Monterey Blonde — similar to the H 1456, except features raised white pickguard with stencilled M logo. Available in Blonde finish. Disc. circa 1965.

> Last Mfr.'s Sug. Retail was $78.00.

Montclair Arched (Top) Series

H 956 W MONTCLAIR (GRAND AUDITORIUM PROFESSIONAL) — bound hollow body, arched hardwood top/hardwood back/sides, 2 f-holes, 20 fret bound fingerboard with white dot inlay, 3 per side tuners, chrome hardware, adjustable bridge/raised tailpiece, raised white pickguard. Available in Black finish. Disc. circa 1965.

> Length 40 1/2", Body Width 16 1/2".

> Last Mfr.'s Sug. Retail was $65.

H 956 Montclair — similar to the H 956 W, except features white block fingerboard inlay. Available in Black finish. Mfd. 1966 to 1967.

> Length 40 1/2", Body Width 16 1/2".

> Last Mfr.'s Sug. Retail was $75.

Patrician Arched (Top) Series

H 1407 PATRICIAN (AUDITORIUM SIZE) — shell celluloid bound hollow body, arched spruce top/mahogany back/sides, mahogany neck, 2 f-holes, 20 fret rosewood fingerboard with white dot inlay, 3 per side tuners, chrome hardware, adjustable bridge/raised tailpiece, raised shell celluloid pickguard with stencilled P logo. Available in Natural finish. Disc. circa 1972.

> Length 40 3/4", Body Width 15 3/4".

> Last Mfr.'s Sug. Retail was $79.50.

12-STRING SERIES

Many of Harmony's catalogs recommended that "You do not tune a 12-string guitar as high as regular 6-string guitar pitch". As a result, The **Blue Book of Guitars** offers a caution that current owners of these same models may want to tune down to avoid any structural problems (bridges separating or pulling off, top warpage, etc.).

H 1230 GRAND CONCERT 12-STRING — 25 1/4" scale, select spruce top, round soundhole, mahogany back/sides, bound body, mahogany neck, 12/18 fret tapered rosewood fingerboard with white dot position markers, solid headstock, dual-saddle rosewood bridge/chrome metal tailpiece, 6 per side Waverly tuners, black 'batwing' pickguard with silkscreened design. Available in Pumpkin Top/Dark stain body finish. Mfd. circa 1969 to circa 1971.

> Length 40 3/4", Body Width 15 1/8".

> Last Mfr.'s Sug. Retail was $129.50.

H 1270 JUMBO 12-STRING — 25 1/4" scale, select spruce top, round soundhole, mahogany back/sides, bound body, 12/18 fret rosewood fingerboard with white dot position markers, slotted headstock, dual-saddle rosewood bridge/chrome metal tailpiece, 6 per side Waverly tuners, teardrop-shaped black pickguard. Available in Natural finish. Mfd. 1963 to circa 1972.

> Length 40 1/2", Body Width 16", Body Thickness 4 5/16".

> Last Mfr.'s Sug. Retail was $164.50.

Classic Series

Classic Series models are classical guitars with Harmony's "Fan-Rib" construction (a Spanish-style fan-braced top).

H 171 CLASSIC (OR FOLK) — nylon string, 25 1/4" scale, spruce top, round soundhole, hardwood back/sides/neck, 12/19 fret ebonized maple fingerboard, slotted headstock, pinless bridge, 3 per side Waverly tuners. Available in Pumpkin finish. Mfd. 1969 to circa 1971.

> Length 36", Body Width 13 1/8".

> Last Mfr.'s Sug. Retail was $49.95.

The H 171 does not have the fan-rib bracing.

Harmony Master Arch Top 945
1964 Harmony Catalog

H

Harmony Monterey Blond 1457
1964 Harmony Catalog

Harmony H6272 Traditional Classic
1973 Harmony Catalog

H 172 — nylon string, 25 1/4" scale, bound spruce top, fan ribbed, round soundhole with marquetry inlay, hardwood back/sides/neck, 12/19 fret ebonized maple fingerboard, rosewood pinless bridge, 3 per side Waverly tuners. Available in Pumpkin finish. Mfd. 1971 to circa 1973.

Length 38 1/2", Body Width 14 5/8".

Last Mfr.'s Sug. Retail was $79.95.

H 173 — nylon string, bound select spruce top, bound round soundhole, hardwood back/sides/neck, 12/19 fret ebonized maple fingerboard, ebonised maple tie bridge, 3 per side tuners, squared slotted headstock. Available in Natural finish. Disc. 1971.

Length 38 1/2", Body Width 14 5/8".

Last Mfr.'s Sug. Retail was $79.50.

H 174 — nylon string, bound seasoned spruce top, round soundhole with inlay, mahogany back/sides/neck, 12/19 fret fingerboard, rosewood tie bridge, 3 per side tuners, rounded slotted headstock. Available in Natural finish. Disc. circa 1968.

Length 38 1/2", Body Width 14 5/8".

Last Mfr.'s Sug. Retail was $95.

H 175 — nylon string, 25 1/4" scale, black bound select spruce top, fan ribbed, round soundhole with wood marquetry inlay, mahogany neck, hard maple back/sides, 12/19 fret ebonized maple fingerboard, slotted headstock with wood marquetry inlay, pinless bridge with wood marquetry inlay, 3 per side Waverly tuners. Available in Natural gloss finish. Mfd. 1967 to circa 1973.

Length 38 1/2", Body Width 14 5/8".

Last Mfr.'s Sug. Retail was $135.

H 177 — nylon string, 25 1/4" scale, bound seasoned spruce top, bound back, fan ribbed, round soundhole with marquetry inlay, mahogany back/sides/neck, 12/19 fret ebonized hard maple fingerboard, pinless rosewood bridge, slotted headstock, 3 per side Waverly tuners. Available in Pumpkin finish. Mfd. 1969 to circa 1973.

Length 38 1/2", Body Width 14 5/8".

Last Mfr.'s Sug. Retail was $99.50.

H 937 STUDENT GUITAR (NYLON STRING) — nylon string, 24 1/4" scale, hardwood top, round soundhole, hardwood back/sides, 18 fret ebonized maple fingerboard, slotted headstock, pinless bridge, 3 per side Waverly tuners. Available in Natural finish. Mfd. 1969 to circa 1971.

Length 36", Body Width 13 1/8".

Last Mfr.'s Sug. Retail was $41.50.

Flat Top Series

H 150 STUDIO SPECIAL (3/4 SIZE) — dreadnought style, celluloid bound hardwood top, round soundhole, hardwood back/sides, 12/18 fret ebonised maple fingerboard, pinless bridge, white celluloid pickguard, 3 per side tuners. Available in Natural finish. Disc. 1971.

Length 34 1/4", Body Width 13 1/8".

Last Mfr.'s Sug. Retail was $41.50.

H 151 BEST BEGINNERS (3/4 SIZE) — dreadnought style, bound hardwood top, celluloid edge binding, round soundhole, hardwood back/sides, 12/18 fret maple fingerboard, bolted-on pinless bridge, black celluloid 'batwing' pickguard with vine design, solid blackface headstock, 3 per side Waverly tuners. Available in Shaded Brown finish. Disc. 1971.

Length 34 1/4", Body Width 13 1/8", Body Thickness 3 1/4".

Last Mfr.'s Sug. Retail was $41.50.

Harmony designated the H 151 the "Best Beginners or 'Loaner' Guitar".

H 159 JUMBO — dreadnought style, 25 1/4" scale, hardwood top, white striped edge/black pin line, white celluloid bindings, round soundhole with simulated marquetry inlay, hardwood back/sides, 20 fret ebonized maple fingerboard with white dot inlay, ebonized maple pin bridge with white bridgepins, black pickguard with small logo design, 3 per side Waverly tuners. Available in Natural Top/Dark Brown Rosewood body stain finish. Mfd. circa 1969 to 1970.

Length 40 3/4", Body Width 16", Body Thickness 4 1/4".

Last Mfr.'s Sug. Retail was $59.95.

H 162 GRAND CONCERT — dreadnought style, 24 1/4" scale, spruce top, round soundhole, mahogany back/sides, hardwood neck, 14/19 fret rosewood fingerboard with white dot inlay, adjustable truss rod, rosewood pin bridge, shell celluloid pickguard, 3 per side tuners. Available in Natural lacquer finish. Disc. 1970.

Length 39", Body Width 15 1/8".

Last Mfr.'s Sug. Retail was $64.50.

H 162 3/4 — similar to the H 162, except in smaller (3/4) size configuration. Disc. 1970.

Length 32", Body Width 11 1/4".

Last Mfr.'s Sug. Retail was $64.50.

H 165 Grand Concert Mahogany — similar to the H 162, except features a mahogany top, Brazilian rosewood (!!?) fingerboard, pinless bridge. Disc. 1970.

The secondary market is still undefined.

Last Mfr.'s Sug. Retail was $64.50.

H 162/1 FOLK (GRAND CONCERT SIZE) — dreadnought style, 24 1/4" scale, spruce top, round soundhole, mahogany back/sides, 19 fret rosewood fingerboard, adjustable truss rod, pinned bridge, black pickguard, 3 per side Waverly tuners. Available in Natural finish. Mfd. 1971 to 1972.

Length 39", Body Width 15 1/8".

Last Mfr.'s Sug. Retail was $64.50.

H 162 3/4 — similar to the H 162/1. Available in Natural finish. Mfd. 1971 to 1972.

Length 39", Body Width 15 1/8".

Harmony H1233 12-String
1973 Harmony Catalog

Last Mfr.'s Sug. Retail was $64.50.

H 165/1 Folk Mahogany (Grand Concert Size) — similar to the H 162/1, except features a mahogany top and pinless bridge. Mfd. 1971 to 1972.

Length 39", Body Width 15 1/8".

Last Mfr.'s Sug. Retail was $64.50.

H 166 FOLK — dreadnought style, 24 1/4" scale, spruce top, white body binding, round soundhole, hardwood back/sides/neck, 19 fret bound rosewood fingerboard with white dot inlay, pin bridge, 3 per side Waverly tuners, black 'batwing' pickguard with small 'H' logo, white truss rod cover. Available in Pumpkin Top/Dark Rosewood stain gloss finish. Disc. 1971.

Length 40", Body Width 15 1/8".

Last Mfr.'s Sug. Retail was $74.50.

H 167 FOLK — dreadnought style, spruce top, round soundhole, hardwood back/sides, 19 fret bound rosewood fingerboard with white dot inlay, rosewood pin bridge with white bridgepins, 6 on a side tuners, white truss rod cover, black 'batwing' pickguard with small 'H' logo. Available in Natural finish. Mfd. circa 1969 to 1970.

Length 39", Body Width 15 1/8".

Last Mfr.'s Sug. Retail was $74.50.

H 168 Folk — similar to the H 167 Folk. Available in Pumpkin Top/Dark Rosewood Body Color finish. Mfd. circa 1969 to 1970.

Length 39", Body Width 15 1/8".

Last Mfr.'s Sug. Retail was $74.50.

H 180 GRAND CONCERT — dreadnought style, bound selected spruce top, round soundhole, mahogany back/sides, 19 fret bound rosewood fingerboard with white dot inlay, adjustable saddle rosewood pin bridge with white bridgepins, black pickguard with design pattern, 6 on a side Waverly tuners. Available in Antique Mahogany (Antique limed grain over Dark Rosewood stain) finish. Mfd. circa 1969 to 1970.

Length 39", Body Width 15 1/8".

Last Mfr.'s Sug. Retail was $104.50.

H 181 Grand Concert — similar to the H 180, except features inlaid rings rosette. Available in Pumpkin Top/Dark Rosewood stain finish. Mfd. circa 1969 to 1970.

Length 39", Body Width 15 1/8".

Last Mfr.'s Sug. Retail was $104.50.

H 182 GRAND CONCERT — dreadnought style, 24 1/4" scale, bound selected spruce top, round soundhole, mahogany back/sides/neck, 19 fret bound rosewood fingerboard with white dot inlay, bound blackface headstock with decorative design, adjustable pin bridge, teardrop-shaped black pickguard, 3 per side Waverly tuners with white buttons, white truss rod cover. Available in Pumpkin Top/Dark Rosewood body finish. Disc. 1971.

Length 40", Body Width 15 1/8".

Harmony Sovereign Western Special 1203
1964 Harmony Catalog

Last Mfr.'s Sug. Retail was $104.50.

Sovereign Flat Top Series

HTG 1201 TENOR GUITAR — Tenor (4-string) configuration, spruce top/mahogany back/sides, round soundhole, mahogany neck, celluloid edge binding, 14/20 fret fingerboard with white dot inlay, ebonised pin bridge, shell celluloid pickguard, 2 per side tuners. Available in Natural finish. Disc. circa 1972.

Length 34", Body Width 13 1/8".

Last Mfr.'s Sug. Retail was $82.50.

H 1203 GRAND CONCERT SPECIAL (Formerly WESTERN SPECIAL) — dreadnought style, 24 1/4" scale, select spruce top/mahogany back/sides, round soundhole, mahogany neck, 19 fret rosewood fingerboard with white dot inlay, adjustable truss rod, pinless rosewood bridge, 3 per side Waverly tuners. Available in Natural finish. Disc. circa 1972.

Length 40", Body Width 15 1/8".

Last Mfr.'s Sug. Retail was $98.50.

The H 1203 model was originally designated the Western Special. In 1966, it was re-designated the Grand Concert Special.

H 1260 JUMBO — jumbo style, 25 1/4" scale, spruce top/mahogany back/sides, round soundhole, mahogany neck, shell edge binding, 19 fret rosewood fingerboard with white dot inlay, pinless bridge, teardrop-shaped pickguard, 3 per side Waverly tuners. Available in Natural finish. Disc. circa 1972.

Length 40 1/4", Body Width 16", Body Thickness 4 5/16".

Last Mfr.'s Sug. Retail was $119.50.

H 1266 SOVEREIGN DELUXE JUMBO — dreadnought style, 25 1/4" scale, bound spruce top, round soundhole, mahogany back/sides, 14/19 fret rosewood fingerboard with white block inlays, adjustable *mustache*-style bridge with white pins, 2 black *batwing* pickguards (1 per side of soundhole), 3 per side Waverly tuners. Available in Sunburst finish. Mfd. 1969 to circa 1972.

Length 41 1/2", Body Width 16", Body Thickness 4 5/64".

Last Mfr.'s Sug. Retail was $169.50.

H 1265 Sovereign Deluxe Jumbo — similar to the H 1266, except features 2-piece black "State of Alaska"-shaped pickguard. Available in Sunburst finish. Mfd. 1967 to 1968.

Length 41 1/2", Body Width 16", Body Thickness 4 5/64".

Last Mfr.'s Sug. Retail was $159.50.

The H 1265 was the forerunner to the H 1266 model (the H 1266 has a "more sensible" pickguard scheme).

Harmony Sovereign Jumbo 1260
1964 Harmony Catalog

(Harmony) Sovereign H6364 Jet Black Folk
1973 Harmony Catalog

Sovereign "Jet Set" Flat Top Series

H 164 "JET SET" SOVEREIGN FOLK GUITAR — dreadnought style, 24 1/4" scale, select spruce top, bound body, round soundhole with inlaid rings, hardwood back/sides/neck, 14/19 fret rosewood fingerboard with white dot inlay, rosewood pin bridge, white edged tear-drop shaped black pickguard with small 'H' design, 3 per side Waverly tuners. Available in Jet Black gloss finish. Mfd. circa 1971.

Length 39", Body Width 15 1/8".

Last Mfr.'s Sug. Retail was $74.50.

H 1204 "JET SET" SOVEREIGN GRAND CONCERT — dreadnought style, 24 1/4" scale, rosewood top, round soundhole, hardwood back/sides, 19 fret rosewood fingerboard, adjustable truss rod, adjustable pin bridge, 3 per side Waverly tuners. Available in Natural finish. Mfd. circa 1971.

Length 40", Body Width 15 1/8".

Last Mfr.'s Sug. Retail was $99.50.

H 1264 "JET SET" SOVEREIGN JUMBO — dreadnought style, 25 1/4" scale, bound spruce top, round soundhole with wood marquetry inlay, hardwood back/sides, 14/19 fret rosewood fingerboard with white block inlays, adjustable *mustache*-style bridge with white pins, 2 black *batwing* pickguards (1 per side of soundhole), 3 per side Waverly tuners. Available in Jet Black gloss finish. Mfd. 1971 to circa 1972.

Length 41 1/2", Body Width 16", Body Thickness 4 5/64".

Last Mfr.'s Sug. Retail was $159.50.

ACOUSTIC ELECTRIC

H 55 SOVEREIGN DUAL PURPOSE — dreadnought style, 24 1/4" scale, spruce top, round soundhole, mahogany back/sides, 20 fret rosewood fingerboard with white dot inlay, pinless bridge, black teardrop-shaped pickguard, 3 per side Waverly tuners, pickup (concealed under fingerboard), volume/tone controls. Available in Natural finish. Disc. 1971 (as H 55), 1972 to 1975 (as H 655).

Length 40", Body Width 15 1/8", Body Thickness 3 3/4".

Last Mfr.'s Sug. Retail was $137.50.

This model is designated Harmony and Sovereign on the black peghead.

In circa 1973, the H 55 model was redesignated the H 655.

HARPTONE

HARPTONE MANUFACTURING CORPORATION

Instruments built in Newark, New Jersey 1966 to mid-1970s.

The Harptone company was a commercial successor to the Felsberg Company (circa 1893). During the 1930s, Harptone was more known for musical instrument accessories, although a few guitars were built between 1924 and 1942.

The Harptone Manufacturing Corporation was located at 127 South 15th Street in Newark, New Jersey (07107) during the early to mid 1960s. Harptone's main guitar designer was Stan Koontz (who also designed Standel and his own signature guitars). Harptone's guitar product line consisted of mainly acoustic guitar models, including acoustic archtop models.

When Micro-Frets closed operations in Maryland in either 1974 or 1975, the company assets were purchased by David Sturgill. Sturgill, who served as the company president of Grammer Guitars for three years, let his sons John and Danny gain access to leftover Micro-Frets parts. In addition to those parts, they had also purchased the remains of New Jersey's Harptone guitar company. The two assembled a number of solid body guitars which were then sold under the 'Diamond-S' trademark. Unfortunately, that business venture did not catch on, and dissolved sometime in 1976.

(Company history courtesy Tom Wheeler, American Guitars)

Harptone instruments were built between 1966 to the mid-1970s. Research continues on the production dates per model, and as such none of the following models below will have an indicated date(s) of manufacture. Instruments can be dated by examining the components (pickups, hardware, tuners) and especially the potentiometers (where applicable). The Blue Book of Guitars will continue to update further discoveries in future editions.

The secondary market (defined used sales prices) for Harptone guitar models are still undefined. Model pricing can be potentially determined by weighing the value of the components and and craftmanship versus desirability in the vintage guitar market.

For further information regarding Harpton electric models, please refer to the **5th Edition Blue Book of Electric Guitars**.

ACOUSTIC ARCHTOP

520 — 24 5/8" scale, maple top/back/sides, 21 fret rosewood fingerboard, adjustable metal bridge, 3 per side Grover tuners, 2 D'Armond pickups, volume/tone controls, pickup selector switch.

Body Width 16", Body Thickness 1 3/4".

Last Mfr.'s Sug. Retail was $525.

550 S — 24 5/8" scale, spruce top, maple back/sides, 21 fret ebony fingerboard, 3 per side Grover tuners, adjustable metal bridge, 3 per side Grover tuners, 2 D'Armond pickups, volume/tone controls, pickup selector switch.

Body Width 16", Body Thickness 3".

Last Mfr.'s Sug. Retail was $625.

811 — 24 5/8" scale, maple top/back/sides, 21 fret ebony fingerboard, adjustable metal bridge, 3 per side Grover tuners, 2 D'Armond pickups, volume/tone controls, pickup selector switch.

Body Width 17", Body Thickness 3 1/4".

Last Mfr.'s Sug. Retail was $675.

910 — 24 5/8" scale, spruce top, maple back/sides, 21 fret ebony fingerboard, adjustable metal bridge, 3 per side Grover tuners, gold-plated hardware, 2 D'Armond pickups, pickup selector switch.

Body Width 17", Body Thickness 3 1/4".

Harmony Sovereign H-55 Dual Purpose
1964 Harmony Catalog

Last Mfr.'s Sug. Retail was $850.

1000 — 24 5/8" scale, spruce top, maple back/sides, 21 fret ebony fingerboard, adjustable wood bridge, 3 per side Grover tuners, gold-plated hardware, 1 D'Armond pickups, volume/tone controls.

Body Width 18", Body Thickness 3 1/4" .

Last Mfr.'s Sug. Retail was $1,295.

ACOUSTIC

E 6N (EAGLE) — dreadnought style, 24 5/8" scale, sitka spruce top, round soundhole, qrtd. mahogany back, mahogany sides, 20 fret rosewood fingerboard, double truss rod, pin bridge, 3 per side Grover tuners. Available in Natural finish.

Body Width 15 5/8", Body Thickness 4 7/8".

Last Mfr.'s Sug. Retail was $225.

E 12N 12-String (Eagle) — similar to the E 6N, except features mahogany back/sides, 12-string configuration, 6 per side Grover tuners. Available in Natural finish.

Body Width 15 5/8", Body Thickness 4 7/8".

Last Mfr.'s Sug. Retail was $249.95.

F 6NC (FOLK MASTER) — dreadnought style with single rounded cutaway, 24 5/8" scale, sitka spruce top, round soundhole, flamed maple back/sides, 20 fret rosewood fingerboard, double truss rod, adjustable pin bridge, 3 per side Grover tuners. Available in Natural finish.

Body Width 17", Body Thickness 4 7/8".

Last Mfr.'s Sug. Retail was $329.95.

F 12NC 12-String (Folk Master) — similar to the F 6NC, except features maple back/sides, pin bridge, 12-string configuration, 6 per side Grover tuners. Available in Natural finish.

Body Width 17", Body Thickness 4 7/8".

Last Mfr.'s Sug. Retail was $329.95.

L 6N (LARK) — dreadnought style, 24 5/8" scale, sitka spruce top, round soundhole, mahogany back/sides, 20 fret rosewood fingerboard, double truss rod, pin bridge, 3 per side Grover tuners. Available in Natural finish.

Body Width 17", Body Thickness 4 7/8".

Last Mfr.'s Sug. Retail was $269.95.

P 6N (PIONEER) — dreadnought style, 24 5/8" scale, sitka spruce top, round soundhole, mahogany back/sides, 20 fret rosewood fingerboard, double truss rod, pin bridge, 3 per side Grover tuners. Available in Natural finish.

Body Width 16", Body Thickness 4 7/8".

Last Mfr.'s Sug. Retail was $225.

S 6NC (SULTAN) — dreadnought style with single rounded cutaway, 24 5/8" scale, sitka spruce top, round soundhole, flamed maple back/sides, 14/20 fret rosewood fingerboard with white dot inlay, double truss rod, teardrop-shaped black pickguard, adjustable bridge with white pins, unbound *pincher* headstock, 3 per side Grover tuners. Available in Natural finish.

Body Width 16", Body Thickness 4 7/8".

Last Mfr.'s Sug. Retail was $269.

S 12NC 12-String (Sultan) — similar to the S 6NC, except features maple back/sides, pin bridge, 12-string configuration, 6 per side Grover tuners. Available in Natural finish.

Body Width 16", Body Thickness 4 7/8".

Last Mfr.'s Sug. Retail was $295.

Z 6N (ZODIAC) — dreadnought style, 24 5/8" scale, sitka spruce top, round soundhole, rosewood back/sides, 20 fret bound rosewood fingerboard, double truss rod, adjustable pin bridge, 3 per side Grover tuners. Available in Natural finish.

Body Width 15 5/8", Body Thickness 4 7/8".

Last Mfr.'s Sug. Retail was $350.

Z 12N 12-String (Zodiac) — similar to the Z 6N, except features a pin bridge, 12-string configuration, 6 per side Grover tuners. Available in Natural finish.

Body Width 15 5/8", Body Thickness 4 7/8".

Last Mfr.'s Sug. Retail was $375.

Renzi Series

RENZI 100 — nylon string, 25 5/8" scale, Alpine spruce top, round soundhole, mahogany back/sides, 19 fret rosewood fingerboard, hand-engraved headstock, rosewood bridge, 3 per side German tuners. Available in Natural finish.

Last Mfr.'s Sug. Retail was $250.

Renzi 200 — similar to the Renzi 100, except features maple back/sides. Available in Natural finish.

Last Mfr.'s Sug. Retail was $350.

RICHARD HARRIS

Instruments currently built in Indianapolis, Indiana.

Luthier Richard Harris builds custom acoustic "Tele"-style guitars - the models are all acoustic, but are shaped with the single cutaway body like a Tele. For further information regarding his custom guitars, contact Richard Harris through the Index of Current Manufacturers located in the back of this edition.

HERMAN HAUSER

Instruments currently built in Reisbach, Germany.

Instruments built in Munich, Germany since the early 1900s.

Harmony H8025 Baroque Mandolin
1973 Harmony Catalog

Harmony H4095 Baritone Ukulele
1973 Harmony Catalog

Luthier Hermann Hauser (1882-1952) built a variety of stringed instruments throughout his career. While earlier models did not share the same designs as the "Spanish school", Hauser soon adopted designs introduced by Antonio de Torres. In the late 1930s Maestro Andres Segovia moved from a Ramirez guitar to a Hauser built classical, which he played until 1970.

Hermann Hauser was succeeded by his son, Herman Hauser II, and a grandson, Herman Hauser III, who continues the family tradition of building fine acoustic guitars. In the same tradition of his father and grandfather, Hauser III builds perhaps 12 guitars a year utilizing fine aged German spruce and rosewood.

(Source: Tony Bacon, The Ultimate Guitar Book)

HAWK

See FRAMUS and KLIRA.

Instruments were built in West Germany during the early 1960s.

The Hawk trademark was a brandname used by a UK importer. Instruments imported into England were built by either Framus or Klira in Germany, and are identical to their respective builder's models.

(Source: Tony Bacon and Paul Day, The Guru's Guitar Guide)

HAYNES

Instruments manufactured in Boston, Massachusetts from 1865 to the early 1900s.

The Oliver Ditson Company, Inc. was formed in 1835 by music publisher Oliver Ditson (1811-1888). Ditson was a primary force in music merchandising, distribution, and retail sales on the East Coast. He also helped establish two musical instrument manufacturers: The John Church Company of Cincinnati, Ohio, and Lyon & Healy (Washburn) in Chicago, Illinois.

In 1865, Ditson established a manufacturing branch of his company under the supervision of John Haynes, called the John C. Haynes Company. This branch built guitars for a number of trademarks, such as **Bay State**, **Tilton**, and **Haynes Excelsior**.

(Source: Tom Wheeler, American Guitars)

LES HAYNIE

Instruments currently built in Eureka Springs, Arkansas.

Les Haynie hand crafts custom guitars in his shop in Eureka Springs. For further information concerning models and pricing, please contact luthier Haynie through the Index of Current Manufacturers located in the rear of this book.

MICHAEL HEIDEN

Instruments currently built in Chilliwac (British Columbia), Canada. Distributed by Heiden Stringed Instruments of Chilliwac (British Columbia), Canada.

Luthier Micheal Heiden is currently hand crafting some very high quality acoustic guitar models and mandolins. For further information regarding model specifications, custom orders, and pricing, please contact luthier Heiden via the Index of Current Manufacturers located in the back of this edition.

WILLIAM HENDERSON

Instruments built in the U.S. Distributed by Kirkpatrick Guitar Studios of Baltimore, Maryland.

Luthier William Henderson, a rapidly developing talent, is currently building high quality classical guitars.

HENRY GUITAR COMPANY

Instruments built in Asheville, North Carolina since 1994; in 1997 the company moved to Atlanta, Georgia.

Luthier Jeff Henry has been building acoustic guitars for over 2 years in North Carolina. Henry studied under Nick Apollonio of Rockport, Maine before forming his own company. Henry currently offers five different hand crafted acoustic guitar models, as well as custom options. Henry guitars carry a stylized **H** on the headstock, as well as a full label inside the soundhole.

Model Designations

Jeff Henry offers five different acoustic guitar models: the **ML**, his smallest instrument with lively response; **LJ**, a *Little Jumbo* that combines the balance of a ML with the power of a full body; the **Jumbo**, a full sized acoustic; the **D**, a dreadnought sized acoustic; and the **SD**, which is similar to the **D** except has sloped shoulders.

ACOUSTIC

Henry guitars are offered with other custom options such as installed pickups, and additional wood choices on the soundboard, or back and sides.

Add $25 for an exotic wood pickguard.

Add $75 for an exotic wood rosette.

Add $200 for a cutaway body configuration.

Add $200 for a 12 string configuration.

All five models are available in either the Standard or Deluxe package, and the prices include a hardshell case. The **Standard** package (retail $1,500) has a Sikta Spruce or Western Red Cedar soundboard, Mahogany back and sides, a Rosewood fingerboard and bridge, Pearl dots inlay, Ivoroid or Tortoise shell body binding, a herringbone rosette, a tortoiseshell pickguard, and Grover tuners. More upscale is the **Deluxe** package (retail $2,100). The Deluxe offers the same Sikta Spruce or Western Red Cedar soundboard, a Mahogany back with a hardwood backstrip, Mahogany sides, a bound Ebony fingerboard, Ebony bridge, Abalone diamond inlays, Abalone bridge inlay, Rosewood or Maple mitered body binding, an Abalone rosette, a tortoiseshell pickguard, and Schaller tuners.

HERITAGE

Instruments built in Kalamazoo, Michigan since 1985. The Lasar Music Corporation is the exclusive sales and marketing company for Heritage Guitars, Inc.

H-5 Mandolin
courtesy Heritage Guitar Company

H

The Gibson guitar company was founded in Kalamazoo in 1902. The young company continued to expand, and built production facilities at 225 Parsons Street (the first of a total of five buildings at that location) in 1917. In 1974, Gibson was acquired by the Norlin corporation, which also opened facilities the same year in Nashville, Tennessee. However, financial troubles led Norlin to consider shutting down either the Kalamazoo or Nashville facilities in the early 1980s. Even though the Kalamazoo plant was Gibson's home since 1917, the decision was made in July of 1983 by Norlin to close the plant. The doors at 225 Parsons Street closed in the fall of 1984.

Heritage Guitar, Inc. opened in 1985 in the original Gibson building. Rather than uproot and move to Tennessee, Jim Deurloo, Marvin Lamb, and J. P. Moats elected to leave the Gibson company, and stay in Kalamazoo to start a new guitar company. Members of the original trio were later joined by Bill Paige and Mike Korpak (other long time Gibson workers). Korpack left the Heritage company in 1985.

Jim Deurloo began working at Gibson in 1958, and through his career was promoted from neck sander to pattern maker up to general foreman of the pattern shop, machine shop, and maintenance. Deurloo was the plant manager at Guild between 1969 to 1974, and had been involved with the opening and tooling up of the newer Nashville facility in 1974. During this time period, Deurloo was also the head of engineering, and was later promoted to assitant plant manager. In 1978 Deurloo was named plant manager at the Kalamazoo facility.

Marv Lamb was hired by Gibson in 1956 to do hand sanding and other jobs in the wood shop (Lamb was one of the workers on the '58 Korina Flying Vs and Explorers). He was promoted through a series of positions to general foreman of finishing and final assembly, and finally to plant superintendent in 1974 (a position he held until Gibson closed the plant in 1984).

J.P. Moats was hired by Gibson in 1957 for sanding and final cleaning. Through promotions, Moats became head of quality control as well as the supervisor of inspectors, and later the wood inspector. While inspecting wood for Gibson, Moats was also in charge of repairs and custom orders.

Bill Paige, a graduate of the business school at Western Michigan University joined Gibson in 1975 as a cost accountant and other capacities in the accounting department. Paige is currently the Heritage controller, and handles all non-guitar manufacturing functions.

All current owners of Heritage continue to design models, and produce various instruments in the production facilities. Heritage continues to develop new models along with their wide range of acoustic, hollow body, semi-hollow, and electric guitar models. Heritage is also one of the few *new* guitar companies with models that are stocked in vintage and collectible guitar stores worldwide.

Heritage also builds mandolins and a banjo model on a "Limited Availablility" basis. The H-5 Mandolin (retail list $3,725) has a solid spruce top, scrolled body design, curly maple back/rim/one piece neck, ebony fingerboard, bound peghead with mother of pearl/abalone inlays, and gold hardware. Featuring a more traditional body style, the H-50 Mandolin (retail list $1,350) also has a solid spruce top, curly maple back/rim/one piece neck, rosewood fingerboard, 4 on a plate tuners, and chrome hardware. The H-40 Mandolin (retail list $1,200) is similar to the H-50, except has a plain maple back/rim/neck. All three models are available in an Antique Sunburst finish.

The Kalamazoo Standard Banjo (retail list $2,700) has a bound curly maple resonator/neck, maple rim, bound ebony fingerboard with mother of pearl inlays, and chrome hardware. Available in Honey Stain finish.

Heritage offers a wide range of custom features. Unless specified, a hardshell case is optional with the guitar. Cases for the acoustics, jazz guitars, and basses run $160 while the cases for electric guitars are $150; cases for the Super Eagle model are $180.

ACOUSTIC

Heritage's acoustic instruments are available on a limited basis.

H-450 — dreadnought style, solid spruce top, round soundhole, 25 1/2" scale, white bound body, wooden inlay rosette, black pickguard, mahogany back/sides, maple neck, 14/20 fret rosewood fingerboard with mother of pearl dot inlay, rosewood bridge with white pins, 3 per side chrome tuners. Available in Antique Sunburst or Natural finishes on top; Walnut finish on back/sides/neck. Disc. 1990.

	$450	$275

Last Mfr.'s Sug. Retail was $850.

H-480 — narrow waist rounded single cutaway style, solid spruce top, oval soundhole, 25 1/2" scale, white bound body/rosette, carved mahogany back, solid mahogany sides, mahogany neck, 14/21 fret rosewood fingerboard with mother of pearl dot inlay, rosewood bridge with white pins, 3 per side chrome tuners. Available in Antique Sunburst or Natural finishes on top; Walnut finish on back/sides/neck. Disc. 1990.

	$450	$275

Last Mfr.'s Sug. Retail was $850.

HFT-445 (formerly H-445) — dreadnought style, solid spruce top, round soundhole, white bound body and wooden inlay rosette, black pickguard, mahogany back/sides, maple neck, 14/20 fret rosewood fingerboard with pearl dot inlay, rosewood bridge with white pins, 3 per side chrome tuners. Available in Antique Sunburst finish. Mfr. 1987 to date.

Mfr.'s Sug. Retail	$1,300	$1,050	$675	$450

Add $50 for Natural finish.

HFT-475 — single sharp cutaway jumbo style, solid spruce top, round soundhole, 5 stripe bound body and rosette, black pickguard, mahogany back/sides/neck, 20 fret bound rosewood fingerboard with pearl block inlay, rosewood bridge with white pins, bound peghead, 3 per side chrome tuners. Available in Antique Sunburst finish. Current mfr.

Mfr.'s Sug. Retail	$2,050	$1,650	$1,100	$700

Add $50 for Natural finish.
Add $150 for DeArmond pickup.

H-445
courtesy Heritage Guitar Company

Grading	100%	EXCELLENT	AVERAGE

HFT-485 — jumbo style, solid spruce top, round soundhole, 3 stripe bound body/rosette, rosewood pickguard, rosewood back/sides, mahogany neck, 14/21 fret bound rosewood fingerboard with pearl block inlay, rosewood bridge with white pins, bound peghead, 3 per side chrome tuners. Available in Antique Sunburst finish. Current mfr.

Mfr.'s Sug. Retail $2,300	$1,850	$1,200	$775

Add $50 for Natural finish.
Add $150 for DeArmond pickup.

HFT-475
courtesy Heritage Guitar Company

HERNANDEZ y AGUADO

Instruments were built in Madrid, Spain during the 1960s.

Luthiers Manuel Hernandez and Victoriano Aguado combined guitar making skills to build world class classical guitars.

(Source: Tony Bacon, The Ultimate Guitar Book)

H.G. LEACH

Instruments currently built in Cedar Ridge, California.

Harvey G. Leach has been building acoustic guitars for over 25 years. Leach, a former furniture maker from Vermont, began building banjos and mandolins early on in his musical instrument career. In 1979, he built his first guitar, and then gave it to his wife as a wedding present. All H.G. Leach guitars are individually handcrafted, and built to the owner's specifications. He estimates that 20 to 25 guitars are built each year; a basic model may take a week's worth of work (spread out over a three week time), and a fancier model with mother-of-pearl inlays may take five times more time.

Leach is also committed to enviromental concerns, and produces his guitars with domestic or foreign sustainable yield mahogany and Brazilian (or Bolivian) rosewood. Leach also uses a water-based lacquer finish (a nitrocellulose finish is available on request).

ACOUSTIC

Luthier Leach offers a wide range of inlay, abalone trim, wood appointments, and other options to all of his creations (the list is two columns long!). As a result, the custom-ordered guitar is a custom-built guitar, right to the customer's specifications. All list prices include a hardshell case.

Archtop Series

Leach offers an archtop design in two appointment styles, and three body sizes (16", 17", and 18") - as well as a 19" body archtop bass.

EXCELSIOR — choice of maple, mahogany, sycamore, claro walnut, spruce, western red cedar, incense cedar, and redwood; single rounded cutaway body, black (or white or cream or ivoroid) celluloid binding, graphite-reinforced neck, 25.375" scale, 20 fret rosewood or ebony fingerboard with 'zero' fret and abalone or pearl dot inlay, rosewood or ebony bridge, 2 f-holes, 3 per side goldplated Grover tuners, raised pickguard. Current mfr.

Mfr.'s Sug. Retail (16")	$3,295
Mfr.'s Sug. Retail (17")	$3,495
Mfr.'s Sug. Retail (18")	$3,695

ELITE — highly figured back and side woods, single rounded cutaway body, multi-ply binding, graphite-reinforced neck, 25.375" scale, 20 fret rosewood or ebony fingerboard with 'zero' fret and split-block fretboard inlays, brass and pearl peghead inlay, brass or ebony tailpiece, 2 f-holes, 3 per side goldplated Grover Imperial tuners, raised pickguard. Current mfr.

Mfr.'s Sug. Retail (16")	$4,795
Mfr.'s Sug. Retail (17")	$4,995
Mfr.'s Sug. Retail (18")	$5,195

Flattop Series

The standard appointment for the Flattop models is as follows: choice of maple, mahogany, sycamore, claro walnut, spruce, western red cedar, incense cedar, and redwood; dreadnought style body, black (or white or cream or ivoroid) celluloid binding, graphite-reinforced neck, 25.375" scale, 14/20 fret rosewood or ebony fingerboard with 'zero' fret and abalone or pearl dot inlay, rosewood or ebony bridge, Southwest or herringbone rosette, 3 per side goldplated Grover tuners, raised pickguard. Numerous options are available.

FRANCONIA — standard Dreadnought size. Current mfr.

Mfr.'s Sug. Retail	$1,995

Jumbo Series

NYLON — slotted open headstock, designed for nylon string use.

Mfr.'s Sug. Retail	$2,495

CREMONA — the body size is smaller than the Saratoga model, but the same shape (has more balance than the Saratoga as well). Current mfr.

Mfr.'s Sug. Retail	$2,150

SARATOGA — built in the *Grand* size, and has a bassy and loud voicing that is geared towards fingerpicking. Curent mfr.

Mfr.'s Sug. Retail	$2,195

Mini Series

KIRBY — smaller body, neck joins at the twelveth fret. Current mfr.

Mfr.'s Sug. Retail	$2,050

RACHEL — dreadnought body shape, but 20% smaller body; 15 fret neck, standard scale. Current mfr.

Mfr.'s Sug. Retail	$1,950

Special and Limited Edition Series

Leach offers the *Motherlode* option on any guitar model. The Motherlode option has special gold-in-quartz block inlays for the fingerboard (call for pricing and availability).

25th ANNIVERSARY MODEL — single 'Willoughby' cutaway Cremona-style body, abalone trim on top of body/soundhole/fretboard/peghead/truss rod cover, mother of pearl label with Leach family crest and serial number, abalone (or toroise or wood veneer) tuner buttons. Current mfr.

    Mfr.'s Sug. Retail $2,500

        Production is limited to 25 guitars.

ROY ROGERS *BLUESMAN* — dreadnought style body, special Roy Rogers fretboard inlays, Roy Rogers Signature label, abalone trim on top of body/soundhole/fretboard/peghead/truss rod cover, choice of abalone (or tortoise or wood veneer) tuner buttons. Current mfr.

    Mfr.'s Sug. Retail $3,250

THOM BRESH LEGACY — dreadnought style body, spruce top, herringbone trim, round soundhole, birdseye maple neck, rosewood back/sides, 14/20 rosewood fretboard with Merle Travis inlays, 6 on a side Merle Travis design scroll peghead, Merle Travis design pickguard, special pearl label (caricature of Thom drawn by Travis), vintage style tuning machines. Current mfr.

    Mfr.'s Sug. Retail $2,995

        Thom Bresh is the son of legendary guitarist Merle Travis.

    Thom Bresh Spirit — similar to the Thom Bresh Legacy model, with the addition of abalone trim on top of body/soundhole/fretboard/peghead/truss rod cover, and choice of abalone or tortoise or wood veneer tuner buttons. Current mfr.

    Mfr.'s Sug. Retail $3,995

ACOUSTIC ELECTRIC

Leach currently is offering an Electric/Acoustic model called the **Cremona/Willoughby/RMC** that is based on the Cremona. This model incorporates a smaller bodied acoustic with a slim, fast neck, a body cutaway that offers access to all 24 frets, and on-board electronics.

ACOUSTIC BASS

ACOUSTIC BASS — Saratoga body shape and fretless neck. Current mfr.

    Mfr.'s Sug. Retail $2,295

        A fretted neck is an option on this model.

EXCELSIOR BASS — 19" wide body, patterned after the Excelsior archtop model. Current mfr.

    Mfr.'s Sug. Retail $3,795

ELITE BASS — 19" wide body, patterned after the Elite archtop model. Current mfr.

    Mfr.'s Sug. Retail $5,295

1996 Andaluz
courtesy Dennis Hill

DENNIS HILL

Instruments currently built in Panama City, Florida. Distributed by Leitz Music, Inc. of Panama City, Florida.

Dennis Hill has a tradition of music in his life that reaches back to his father, who was a dance band musician. After a five year career in the U.S. Navy (Hill received his Honorable Discharge in 1969), Hill became the student to classical guitar teacher Ernesto Dijk. As Hill's interest in guitars grew, he met Augustino LoPrinzi in 1987. Hill finally became a sales representative for LoPrinzi's guitars, and studied his guitarmaking at LoPrinzi'z shop. Their agreement was that Hill could observe anytime, on any day, but not to disturb LoPrinzi during construction. Questions and answers were reserved for breakfast and lunch; and Hill had to build in his apartments after hours. In 1992, Hill moved to Panama City and established his own shop.

Hill currently builds both classical and flamenco acoustic guitars in the traditional Spanish style, and constructs them with Englemann or European Spruce tops, Cedar necks, Cypress or Maple back and sides, Ebony fingerboards, and Rosewood bridge and bindings. The Flamenco guitar model has a list price from $2,500; the AndaluzD guitar model has a list price from $3,500; and the Primero Classic guitar model has a list price from $5,000. For further information contact Leitz Music, Inc. through the Index of Current Manufacturers located in the back of this book.

(Source: Hal Hammer)

KENNY HILL

HILL GUITAR COMPANY.

See Also NEW WORLD GUITAR COMPANY.

Instruments currently built in Santa Cruz, California. Distributed by the Hill Guitar Company of Ben Lomond, California.

Kenny Hill has been a professional classical guitarist for 25 years, and has performed extensively throughout the United States and Mexico. His ability and experience as a performer result in a special gift for making an instrument that is very playable and appealing to the player, as well as the audience.

He has been awarded two major grants from the California Arts Council. One of those grants was to establish a guitar building program inside Soledad State Prison. He continues to act as a guitar building consultant, there and in other prisons. He is also the founder and director of the **New World Guitar Co.**, listed elsewhere in this directory. Mr. Hill is a regular contributor to several national magazines, including *Guitar, Soundboard*, and *American Lutherie*.

(Biography courtesy Kenny Hill, September 1997)

Kenny Hill has built quality concert classical and flamenco guitars since 1975. He builds about 25 guitars per year in his shop in the mountains outside of Santa Cruz, California. His Kenneth Hill Signature Series instruments are handmade from the finest traditional materials, and sell for $3,600 to $5,000 (special terms are available to dealers).

1996 Flamenco
courtesy Bill Giles

Hill guitars are characterized as having a clear and warm sound, with excellent balance and separation. The neck and action are among the most playable available anywhere.

ACOUSTIC

Old Master Series

The (Classical) guitar models in the Old Master Series seek to emulate the instruments of important historical guitar builders. This project offers the guitarist a chance to own an instrument with the musicial and design characteristics that might otherwise be unavailable due to the scarity or cost of an original.

BARCELONA MODEL — (Built in the style of Ignacio Fleta guitars) Western red cedar top, Indian rosewood back/sides, 650 mm scale, ebony fingerboard, slotted headstock with 3 per side Spanish tuners. Current mfr.
Mfr.'s Sug. Retail $2,800

LA TRIANA FLAMENCO — (Built in the style of Santos Hernandez guitars) Canadian spruce top, cypress back/sides, 650 mm scale, ebony fingerboard, slotted headstock with 3 per side Schaller (or peg) tuners. Current mfr.
Mfr.'s Sug. Retail $1,750

LONDON MODEL (19th CENTURY) — (Built in the style of Louis Panormo guitars) Canadian spruce top, rosewood back/sides, 635 mm scale, ebony fingerboard, slotted headstock with 3 per side Gotoh tuners. Current mfr.
Mfr.'s Sug. Retail $1,950

This style of guitar is nicknamed "Cacahaute" (Peanut) because of its size and distinctive shape.

MADRID MODEL — (Built in the style of Jose Ramirez guitars) Western red cedar top, Indian rosewood back/sides, 650 mm scale, ebony fingerboard, slotted headstock with 3 per side Gotoh tuners. Current mfr.
Mfr.'s Sug. Retail $1,950

MUNICH MODEL — (Built in the style of Herman Hauser I guitars) Canadian spruce top, Indian rosewood back/sides, 640 or 650 mm scale, ebony fingerboard, slotted headstock with 3 per side Schaller tuners. Current mfr.
Mfr.'s Sug. Retail $1,950

PRODIGY (STUDENT MODEL) — spruce or cedar top, Mexican rosewood back/sides, 650 mm scale, granadillo fingerboard, slotted headstock with 3 per side Gotoh tuners. Current mfr.
Mfr.'s Sug. Retail $975

HIRADE

See TAKAMINE (Hirade Series).

HOFFMAN GUITARS

Instruments built in Minneapolis, Minnesota since 1971.

Luthier Charlie Hoffman and Hoffman Guitars offers both high quality handcrafted guitars and high quality instrument repair services. Hoffman Guitars is the factory authorized warranty service for Martin, Gibson, Guild, Fender, Taylor, and other manufacturers.

To date, Charlie Hoffman has built over 360 hand crafted guitars, which are played by such guitarists as Leo Kottke, Dakota Dave Hull, Ann Reed, and many others. Hoffman's website offers a vast plethora of guitar and lutherie information as well.

ACOUSTIC

Given the nature of hand building custom guitars, the following information is more of a guide than an exact specification for the commissioned guitar.

The **Concert Model** was designed with a fingerpicking player in mind, and also works well with vocal accompaniment. This Concert Model is available with a cutaway body, or a 12 fret (body joins the neck at the 12th fret) configuration.

Body Length 18.75", Depth 4.5", Lower Bout 15.25".

Hoffman's **Dreadnought** model is built along the lines of the classic Martin Dreadnought shape, with a somewhat "stiff" top (to accentuate the treble) and a slightly deeper body. This model is also available with a cutaway body, or a 12 fret (body joins the neck at the 12th fret) configuration.

Body Length 20", Depth 5", Lower Bout 15.6".

The **Parlor** guitar is patterned after the numerous 'parlor guitars' of the 1900s to the 1930s, and is standard with a 12 fret neck. It is optional in a slotted or solid headstock.

Body Length 19", Depth 4.125", Lower Bout 13.75".

Hoffman's three primary body shapes are all priced the same - by the nature of the body woods that determine the construction. African Mahogany body woods retail at $2,000; East Indian body woods at $2,200; Koa or Flame Maple body woods are $2,400 each. Given the nature of Brazilian Rosewood or Highly Flamed Koa, the customer must call for an estimate. Other custom features on Hoffman guitars include a custom neck width or contour (no charge), a cutaway body ($400), herringbone purfling ($50), Abalone rosette ($100) or Abalone top edging ($300), or a 12-string configuration ($300). For proper information regarding prices and specifications, contact Charlie Hoffman at Hoffman Guitars through the Index of Current Manufacturers located in the back of this edition.

HOFNER

Instruments are produced in Bubenreuth and Hagenau, Germany. Hofner instruments are distributed in the U.S. by Boosey & Hawkes Musical Instruments, Inc. of Libertyville, Illinois.

The Hofner instrument making company was originally founded by Karl Hofner in 1887. Originally located in Schonbach (in the area now called Czechoslovakia), Hofner produced fine stringed instruments such as violins, cellos, and doublebasses. Karl's two sons, Josef and Walter, joined the company in 1919 and 1921 (respectively), and expanded Hofner's market to North American and the Far East. Production of guitars began in 1925, in the area that was to become East Germany during the "Cold War" era. Following World War II, the Hofner family moved to West Germany and established a new factory in Bubenreuth in 1948. By 1950, new production facilities in Bubenreuth and Hanenau were staffed by over 300 Hofner employees.

The first Hofner electric archtop debuted in the 1950s. While various guitar models were available in Germany since 1949 (and earlier, if you take in the over 100 years of company history), Hofners were not officially exported to England until Selmer of London took over distributorship in 1958. Furthermore, Selmer's British models were specified for the U.K. only - and differ from those available in the German market.

The concept of a violin-shaped bass was developed by Walter Hofner (Karl's son) in 1956. Walter's idea to electrically amplify a bass was new for the company, but the hollow body model itself was based on family design traditions. The **500/1.** model made its debut at the Frankfurt Music Fair the same year. While most people may recognize that model as the *Beatle Bass* popularized by Paul McCartney, the Hofner company also produced a wide range of solid, semi-hollow, and archtop designs that were good quality instruments.

Until 1997, Hofner products were distributed by EMMC (Entertainment Music Marketing Corporation), which focused on distributing the 500/1 Reissue violin electric bass. In 1998, distribution for Hofner products in the U.S. market was changed to Boosey & Hawkes Musical Instruments, Inc. of Libertyville, Illinois. Boosey & Hawkes wasted no time in introducing three jazz-style semi-hollow guitar models, which includes a **New President** (Model HP-55) model guitar. Boosey & Hawkes is also distributing Thomastik guitar and bass strings along with the Hofner accessories.

(Hofner history source: Gordon Giltrap and Neville Marten, The Hofner Guitar - A History; and Tony Bacon, The Ultimate Guitar Book)

(Current Hofner product information courtesy Greg Schrecengost, Boosey & Hawkes Musical Instruments, Inc.)

Model Dating Information

Hofner began installing adjustable truss-rods in their guitar necks beginning in 1960. Any model prior to that year will not have a truss-rod cover.

Hofner Models (1950s to 1970s)

Between the late 1950s and early 1970s, Hofner produced a number of semi-hollow or hollowbody electric guitars and basses that were in demand in England. English distribution was handled by **Selmer** of London, and specified models that were imported. In some cases, English models are certainly different from the 'domestic' models offered in Germany.

There will always be interest in Hofners; either Paul McCartney's earlier association with the **Beatle Bass** or the thrill of a **Committee** or **Golden Hofner**.

Hofner Models (1960s to 1980s)

From the late 1960s to the early 1980s, the company produced a number of guitar models based on popular American designs. In addition, Hofner also built a number of better quality original models such as **Alpha**, **Compact**, and **Razorwood** from the late 1970s to the mid 1980s. However, you have to *know 'em before you tag 'em*. The **Blue Book of Guitars** recommends discussions with your favorite vintage dealers (it's easier to figure them out when they're in front of you). Other inquiries can be addressed either to Boosey & Hawkes or members of the **Blue Book** staff as to models nomenclature and market value.

Used clean big-body hollowbody guitars had been advertised nationally for $750 to $950, with the more ornate models carrying an asking price of $1,500 to $2,200.

Hofner Models (Non-U.S.)

Hofner (and Boosey & Hawkes) is currently offering a wider range of models outside of the U.S. market. In fact, Hofner has 4 different series of acoustic guitars that are not represented below: the child-sized **Jugend-/Schulergitarren** (HS Series), classical-style **Konzertgitarren** (HF Series), enviroment-friendly **Green Line** (HGL Series), and the upscale **Meistergitarrren** (HM Series). Electric models include the **Jazzica Standard** and **Jazzica Special**, **Vice President**, and **New President**, as well as the **Nightingale Standard** and the **Nightingale Special**. Electric bass models are the same. As radio announcer Paul Harvey says, "Now you know the rest of the story"!

HMW 400
courtesy Hohner

HOHNER

Instruments currently produced in Korea, although earlier models from the 1970s were built in Japan. Currently distributed in the U.S. by HSS (a Division of Hohner, Inc.), located in Richmond, Virginia.

The Hohner company was founded in 1857, and is currently the world's largest manufacturer and distributor of harmonicas. Hohner offers a wide range of solidly constructed musical instruments. The company has stayed contemporary with the current market by licensing designs and parts from Ned Steinberger, Claim Guitars (Germany), and Wilkinson hardware.

In addition to their guitar models, Hohner also distributes Sonor drums, Sabian cymbals, and Hohner educational percussion instruments.

Grading		100%	EXCELLENT	AVERAGE

ACOUSTIC

HAG294 — small body, spruce top, round soundhole, bound body, 5 stripe rosette, black pickguard, mahogany back/sides/neck, 12/18 fret ebonized fingerboard with white dot inlay, ebonized bridge, 3 per side diecast tuners. Available in Natural finish. Mfd. 1991 to 1996.

			$60	$40

Last Mfr.'s Sug. Retail was $110.

HAG294C — similar to HAG294, except has classical body styling. Disc. 1996.

			$60	$40

Last Mfr.'s Sug. Retail was $110.

Acoustic Series

HF70 — folk size, spruce top, round soundhole, bound body, black pickguard, mahogany back/sides/neck, 14/20 fret rosewood fingerboard with white dot inlay, rosewood bridge with white pins, 3 per side covered tuners. Available in Natural finish. Current mfr.

Mfr.'s Sug. Retail	$269	$200	$130	$90

HW03 STUDENT MODEL — 3/4 size, spruce top, round soundhole, bound body, black pickguard, mahogany back/sides/neck, 14/20 fret fingerboard, nylon string tied bridge, 3 per side open tuners. Available in Natural finish. Current mfr.

Mfr.'s Sug. Retail	$109	$85	$55	$40

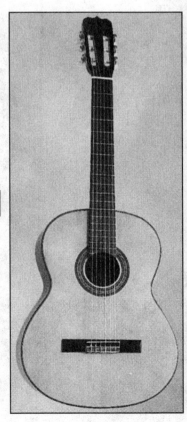

HMC 30
courtesy Hohner

Grading	100%	EXCELLENT	AVERAGE

HMW 600
courtesy Hohner

HW300 (Also HW-300CM) — dreadnought style, mahogany top, round soundhole, single body binding, 5 stripe rosette, black pickguard, mahogany back/sides/neck, 14/20 fret rosewood fingerboard with white dot inlay, rosewood bridge with white pins, 3 per side open tuners. Available in Natural Satin finish. Mfr. 1994 to date.

Mfr.'s Sug. Retail	$189	$150	$95	$65

Add $10 for Natural Gloss finish **(Model HW300G)**.
Add $20 for Gloss Sunburst finish **(Model HW300G-SB)**.

HW400 (Also HMW400) — dreadnought body, spruce top, round soundhole, bound body, 5 stripe rosette, black pickguard, mahogany back/sides/neck, 14/20 fret rosewood fingerboard with white dot inlay, rosewood bridge with white pins, 3 per side covered tuners. Available in Natural and Sunburst finishes. Mfr. 1990 to date.

Mfr.'s Sug. Retail	$269	$200	$130	$90

Add $20 for left-handed configuration **(Model HW400 LH)**.
Add $60 for Black finish.

HW12 — similar to the HW400, except features ashwood back/sides, multiple body binding, bound neck/headstock, 12-string configuration, 6 per side covered tuners. Available in Natural finish. Current mfr.

Mfr.'s Sug. Retail	$339	$250	$175	$125

HMW600 — similar to HMW400, except has herringbone binding and rosette, enclosed chrome tuners. Available in Black and Natural finishes. Disc. 1996.

	$125	$85

Last Mfr.'s Sug. Retail was $290.

HMW1200 — similar to HMW400, except has 12-string configuration, 6 per side tuner. Disc. 1996.

	$150	$100

Last Mfr.'s Sug. Retail was $325.

Solid Top Acoustic Series

HW700S — dreadnought body, solid spruce top, round soundhole, bound body, black pickguard, mahogany back/sides/neck, 14/20 fret rosewood fingerboard with white dot inlay, rosewood bridge with white pins, 3 per side deluxe tuners. Available in Natural finish. Current mfr.

Mfr.'s Sug. Retail	$389	$295	$195	$150

HW720S — similar to HW700S, except features rosewood back and sides. Available in Natural finish. Current mfr.

Mfr.'s Sug. Retail	$469	$350	$225	$150

HW750S — similar to HW700S, except features solid cedar top, ashwood back and sides. Available in Natural finish. Current mfr.

Mfr.'s Sug. Retail	$499	$375	$250	$175

Classical Series

All models in this series have a round soundhole, bound body, wooden inlay rosette, 14/19 fret ebonized fingerboard, nylon strings, tied bridge, 3 per side diecast tuners (unless otherwise noted).

HC03 STUDENT MODEL — 3/4 size body. Available in Natural finish. Current mfr.

Mfr.'s Sug. Retail	$109	$80	$50	$35

HC06 — spruce top, mahogany back/sides. Available in Natural finish. Current mfr.

Mfr.'s Sug. Retail	$139	$100	$70	$50

HC15 — mahogany back/sidestop/neck. Available in Natural Mahogany finish. Current mfr.

Mfr.'s Sug. Retail	$189	$140	$95	$65

HC20 — spruce top, Philipine mahogany back/sides. Available in Natural finish. Current mfr.

Mfr.'s Sug. Retail	$269	$200	$135	$90

HC35S — solid spruce top, rosewood back/sides. Available in Natural finish. Current mfr.

Mfr.'s Sug. Retail	$399	$299	$200	$135

HMC10 — spruce top, mahogany back/sides/neck. Available in Natural finish. Mfd. 1991 to 1996.

	$125	$70

Last Mfr.'s Sug. Retail was $220.

HMC30 — similar to HMC10, except has rosewood back/sides.

	$150	$100

Last Mfr.'s Sug. Retail was $300.

ACOUSTIC ELECTRIC

HAG21 — single round cutaway classic style, solid maple body, spruce top, round soundhole, bound body, wooden inlay rosette, mahogany neck, 20 fret rosewood fingerboard with white dot inlay, rosewood bridge with white pins, 3 per side chrome tuners, piezo bridge pickup, volume/tone control. Available in Natural finish. Mfd. 1990 to 1992.

	$250	$150

Last Mfr.'s Sug. Retail was $500.

HAG22 — similar to HAG21, except has dreadnought style body. Available in Sunburst finish. Disc. 1992.

	$250	$150

Last Mfr.'s Sug. Retail was $500.

HC 35 S
courtesy Hohner

H

Grading	100%	EXCELLENT	AVERAGE

TWP600 — single cutaway dreadnought style, spruce top, trianglular soundhole, bound body, 3 stripe rosette, mahogany back/sides/neck, 20 fret rosewood fingerboard with white dot inlay, rosewood bridge with white pins, 3 per side chrome tuners, piezo bridge pickup, 3 band EQ system. Available in Black, Blue Sunburst, Natural and Pumpkin Burst finishes. Mfd. 1992 to 1996.

	$250	$175	
		Last Mfr.'s Sug. Retail was $550.	

Electro Acoustic Series

EA55CEQ — single cutaway body, spruce top, oval soundhole, bound body, striped rosette, ashwood back/sides, mahogany neck, 22 fret rosewood fingerboard with white dot inlay, rosewood bridge, 2 per side chrome tuners, piezo bridge pickup, volume/4 band EQ controls. Available in Natural and Transparent Red finishes. Current mfr.

Mfr.'s Sug. Retail	$499	$375	$250	$150

EA60CEQ — similar to EA55CEQ, except features maple top. Available in Transparent Blue and Transparent Black finishes. Current mfr.

Mfr.'s Sug. Retail	$525	$395	$250	$175

EA12 — similar to EA55CEQ, except features a 12-string configuration, 6 per side tuners. Available in Transparent Black finish. Current mfr.

Mfr.'s Sug. Retail	$569	$425	$275	$195

EA100CEQ — similar to EA55CEQ, except features a flamed maple top. Available in Natural finish. Current mfr.

Mfr.'s Sug. Retail	$599	$450	$295	$200

EA120CEQ — similar to EA55CEQ, except features a solid cedar top. Available in Natural finish. Current mfr.

Mfr.'s Sug. Retail	$629	$475	$300	$200

EC280CEQ — single cutaway classical style, spruce top, round soundhole, bound body, striped rosette, mahogany back/sides/neck, 19 fret rosewood fingerboard, rosewood bridge, slotted headstock, 3 per side gold tuners, piezo bridge pickup, volume/4 band EQ controls. Available in Natural finish. Current mfr.

Mfr.'s Sug. Retail	$499	$375	$250	$150

ACOUSTIC ELECTRIC BASS

EAB40 — single cutaway body, spruce top, oval soundhole, bound body, striped rosette, ashwood back/sides, mahogany neck, 22 fret rosewood fingerboard with white dot inlay, rosewood bridge, 2 per side chrome tuners, piezo bridge pickup, volume/4 band EQ controls. Available in Natural finish. Current mfr.

Mfr.'s Sug. Retail	$625	$475	$300	$200

Add $70 for maple top with Sunburst finish **(Model EAB50)**.

TWP600B — single cutaway dreadnought style, spruce top, triangle soundhole, bound body, 3 stripe rosette, mahogany back/sides/neck, 20 fret rosewood fingerboard with white dot inlay, strings through rosewood bridge, 2 per side chrome tuners, piezo electric bridge pickup, 3 band EQ system. Available in Black, Blue Sunburst, Natural, Pumpkin Burst and Transparent Red finishes. Mfd. 1992 to 1996.

	$300	$195	
		Last Mfr.'s Sug. Retail was $650.	

EA 60 CEQ
courtesy Hohner

HOLIDAY

See chapter on House Brands.

This trademark has been identified as a "House Brand" distributed by Montgomery Wards and Alden's department stores. Author/researcher Willie G. Moseley also reports seeing a catalog reprint showing Holiday instruments made by Harmony, Kay, **and** Danelectro. Additional information in regards to instruments with this trademark will be welcome, **especially** any Danelectro with a 'HOLIDAY' logo on the headstock. Future updates will be included in upcoming editions of the **Blue Book of Guitars**.

(Source: Willie G. Moseley, Stellas & Stratocasters)

BILL HOLLENBECK

Instruments currently built in Lincoln, Illinois.

Luthier Bill Hollenbeck took a serious interest in guitars as a youth, and used to modify his own instruments in his attempt to improve them. Hollenbeck has a Master's Degree in Industrial Arts, and taught electronics to high school students for twenty-five years. During his teaching years, Hollenbeck met well-known midwestern luthier Bill Barker in 1970, and served as Barker's apprentice as he learned the art of guitar construction. In 1990, Hollenbeck left education to devote himself full-time to guitar building, restoration, and repair. Hollenbeck was featured at the Smithsonian Institute in 1996, and currently offers 4 different archtop guitar models. Prices range from $3,800 to $6,800.

(Source: Hal Hammer)

ACOUSTIC

Hollenbeck currently handcrafts archtop guitars with aged Sitka spruce tops, and back and sides from Birdseye, Flame, or Quilted maple. The truss rod, fingerboard, pickguard, bridge, saddle, and tailpiece are matching ebony or rosewood. Metal parts are polished brass and 24kt gold plated, and inlays are constructed with mother of pearl or abalone. Colors include blonde or lacquer shading. Scale lengths include 24 27/32" or 25 11/32". Models have 2 f-holes, and 3 per side headstocks.

REMINISCE — 16" body.

Mfr.'s Sug. Retail	$6,200

SIMPLICITY — 17" body.

Mfr.'s Sug. Retail	$3,800

17" Archtop
courtesy Bill Hollenbeck

JAZZ REFLECTIONS — 17" body.
Mfr.'s Sug. Retail $6,400

TIME TRAVELER — 18" body.
Mfr.'s Sug. Retail $6,800

Prices include a hardshell case, and a "floating" pickup. An optional Fishman transducer can be mounted in the saddle if requested by the customer.

HOLLISTER GUITARS

Instruments currently built in Dedham, Massachusetts.

Luthier Kent Hollister is currently offering high quality, custom built guitars such as the **Archtop** ($3,000), **Semi-hollow** ($1,900), **Carved Top Solid Body** ($1,500), and **The Plank** ($1,200). The Plank is an electric solid body with neck-through design. Hollister has also created the **Archtop Bass** ($2,800), which features a central soundhole (as opposed to f-holes). Just the thing to swing with the archtop guitarists! For further information contact luthier Kent Hollister through the Index of Current Manufacturers located in the back of this book.

STEPHEN HOLST

Instruments built in Eugene, Oregon since 1984.

Luthier Stephen Holst began building guitars in 1984, and through inspiration and refinement developed the models currently offered. Holst draws on his familiarity of Pacific Northwest tonewoods in developing tonal qualities in his handcrafted instruments. Holst specifically works with the customer commissioning the instrument, tailoring the requests to the specific guitar. In addition, Holst has experimented in other designs such as nylon string, 7- and 12-string, and baritone archtops.

ACOUSTIC

Luthier Holst chooses aged spruce and maple for the tops and backs, and figured eastern hard rock maple for the neck. Fingerboards, bridges, fingerrests, and tailpieces are constructed from ebony. The archtop guitars are finished in Natural Blonde or Sunburst, and feature gold Schaller M6 tuning machines. Both models in the archtop series are offered in a 16", 17", or 18" body width, and have a number of options available, many at no additional charge.

Traditional Series

The **Holst K 100** is designed as a tribute to past glories in archtop construction. The K 100 models are appointed with multiple layers of fine-lined binding throughout the neck, body, f-holes, headstock, and fingerrest. The K 100 has an additional option of engraved mother of pearl inlays on the fretboard, headstock, and tailpiece. The base list price is set at $4,000.

Contemporary Series

Holst's **K 200** series is a contemporary look at the evolution of the archtop design. The K 200 has a more modern feel in its simplicity in design, yet the same attention to building quality as the K 100. The K 200's understated elegance is captured in the all wood binding on the body, neck, and peghead. The f-holes are more contoured, the fingerboard and tailpiece are unadorned, and the fingerrest is narrower in design. Base asking price begins at $3,500.

HONDO

Instruments currently produced in Korea. Distributed by MBT International of Charleston, South Carolina.

Between 1974 to early 1980s some models were produced in Japan.

The Hondo guitar company was originally formed in 1969 when Jerry Freed and Tommy Moore of the International Music Corporation (IMC) of Fort Worth, Texas, combined with the recently formed Samick company. IMC's intent was to introduce modern manufacturing techniques and American quality standards to the Korean guitar manufacturing industry.

The Hondo concept was to offer an organized product line and solid entry level market instruments at a fair market price. The original Korean products were classical and steel-string acoustic guitars. In 1972, the first crudely built Hondo electrics were built. However, two years later the product line took a big leap forward in quality under the new **Hondo II** logo. Hondo also began limited production of guitars in Japan in 1974.

By 1975, Hondo had distributors in 70 countries worldwide, and had expanded to producing stringed instruments at the time. In 1976, over 22,000 of the Bi-Centennial banjos were sold. The company also made improvements to the finish quality on their products, introduced scalloped bracing on acoustics, and began using a higher quality brand of tuning machines.

Hondo was one of the first overseas guitar builders to feature American-built DiMarzio pickups on the import instruments beginning in 1978. By this year, a number of Hondo II models featured designs based on classic American favorites. In 1979, over 790,000 Hondo instruments were sold worldwide. All guitar production returned to Korea in 1983. At that point, the product line consisted of 485 different models!

In 1985, IMC acquired major interest in the Charvel/Jackson company, and began dedicating more time and interest in the higher end guitar market. The Hondo trademark went into mothballs around 1987. However, Jerry Freed started the *Jerry Freed International* company in 1989, and acquired the rights to the Hondo trademark in 1991 (the "Est. 1969" tagline was added to the Hondo logo at this time). Freed began distribution of a new line of Hondo guitars. In 1993, the revamped company was relocated to Stuart, Florida; additional models added to the line were produced in China and Taiwan.

The Hondo Guitar Company was purchased by the MBT International in 1995. MBT also owns and distributes J.B. Player instruments. The Hondo product line was revamped for improved quality while maintaining student-friendly prices. Hondo celebrated their 25th year of manufacturing electric guitars in 1997.

(Source: Tom Malm, MBT International; and Michael Wright, Guitar Stories Volume One)

Hondo guitars generally carried a new retail price range between $179 and $349 (up to $449). While their more unusual-designed model may command a slghtly higher price, the average used price may range between $119 (good condition) up to $199 (clean condition, with case, DiMarzio pickups).

Hollenbeck 18" Time Traveller
courtesy Bill Hollenbeck

Hollister Custom
courtesy Kent Hollister

ACOUSTIC

Hondo currently offers a wide range of dreadnought and classical style guitars. The five models in the **H18** (list $289) series feature select spruce tops, mahogany back/sides, 2-ply binding, chrome tuners, and a gloss finish; models like the **H124** (list $299) and **H125** (list $285) have nato back/sides, and single-ply binding. The Classical guitar models feature a variety of select spruce, nato, and agathis tops, backs, and sides.

Older models, like the 12-string **H-180** with a trapeze tailpiece, may be worth between $100 to $125 on the secondary market.

Deluxe Series

The Deluxe Series was first offered in 1982, and featured 11 classical and 22 steel string acoustic models. The electric line featured 9 variations on the Les Paul theme, including the **H-752** double cutaway LP. A 'strat' of sorts carried the designation **H-760**, a B.C. Rich inspired model with humbuckers and three mini-switches was the **H-930**, and a 335 repro was designated the **H-935**. Many carried a new list price between $229 and $299.

Professional Series

The Professional Series was introduced in 1982, and had a number of classical and steel string models. More importantly, there was a number of electric Strat-style guitars that were presumably built by Tokai in Japan. Tokai was one of the *reproduction* companies of the mid-to-late 1970s that built pretty good *Strats* - much to Fender's displeasure.

Standard Series

Standard Series guitars were also introduced in the early 1980s, and were Hondo's single or double pickup entry level guitars. The acoustic models were beginner's guitars as well. The Standard line did offer 11 banjo models of different add-ons, and 4 distinct mandolins.

HOOTENANNY

See chapter on House Brands.

This trademark has been identified as a "sub-brand" from the budget line of CHRIS guitars by the Jackson-Guldan company. However, another source suggests that the trademark was marketed by the Monroe Catalog House. A rose is a rose is a rose...

(Source: Willie G. Moseley, Stellas & Stratocasters)

HOPF

Instruments made in Germany from the late 1950s through the mid 1980s.

The Hopf name was established back in 1669, and lasted through the mid 1980s. The company produced a wide range of good quality solid body, semi-hollow, and archtop guitars from the late 1950s on. While some of the designs do bear an American design influence, the liberal use of local woods (such as beech, sycamore, or European pine) and certain departures from conventional styling give them an individual identity.

(Source: Tony Bacon, The Ultimate Guitar Book)

DIETER HOPF

Distributed by Luthier Music Corporation.

Dieter Hopf guitars are currently available through the Luthier Music Corporation. Research continues on Dieter Hopf for future editions of the **Blue Book of Guitars**. For current information on pricing and specifications, contact the Luthier Music Corporation via the Index of Current Manufacturers located in the back of this edition.

HOWARD (U.S. MFR.)

Instruments built in New York, New York circa 1930s.

The construction technique and overall appearance indicate the possibility that Epaminondas "Epi" Stathopoulos' Epiphone company built instruments under the Howard trademark for a dealer or distributor. Models that have appeared in the vintage guitar market have the **Howard** brandname and fleur-de-lis inlaid on the headstock. The dealer or distributor involved in the *Howard* trademark has yet to be identified.

(Source: Paul Bechtoldt, Vintage Guitar Magazine, February 1996)

HOYER

Current production instruments are distributed internationally by Mario Pellarin Musikwaren of Cologne, Germany.

Instruments built in West Germany from the late 1950s through the late 1980s.

The Hoyer company produced a wide range of good to high quality solid body, semi-hollow body, and archtop guitars, with some emphasis on the later during the 1960s. During the early 1970s, there was some production of solid bodied guitars with an emphasis on classic American designs.

The Hoyer trademark was re-introduced in the 1990s with the cheerful "A Legend is Back!" motto. Hoyer is currently offering a wide range of acoustic and electric guitars in Europe; a U.S. distributor has not yet been named. Further information on Hoyer instruments is available through the company; contact them through the Index of Current Manufacturers located in the rear of this edition.

(Source: Tony Bacon and Paul Day, The Guru's Guitar Guide)

ACOUSTIC

Hoyer has almost twenty different acoustic models (primarily dreadnought designs) and two resonator guitar models. Models fall under the **Select Top Series** (laminated bodies), **Solid Top Series** (solid wood top and laminated back and sides), and the **Electric Acoustic Series** (which has Fishman Matrix and Prefix systems)

The five Hoyer classical and flamenco acoustic models are currently built in Spain, and are offered in the **Solid Top Series** (laminated wood back and sides) or the **Solid Body Series** (Solid Body Series models still have a solid wood top).

Both the classical style **HC-150E** and **HC-200E** models have an L.R. Baggs RT preamp and ribbon pickup. Both have a solid cedar top, rosewood back and sides, and ebony fingerboards.

Hollenbeck Ebony and Blue
courtesy Scott Chinery

H

Howard acoustic
courtesy of C. W. Green

1950s Hoyer
courtesy Thomas Bauer

BENITO HUIPE

Instruments built in Paracho, Mexico. Distributed by Casa Talamantes of Albuquerque, New Mexico.

Benito Huipe started making guitars in his hometown of Paracho (Michoacan) Mexico, but as a youth, he moved to Los Angeles, California, where he perfected his craft during his 22 years there. While he makes all types of guitars, he is particularly known for the high quality of his flameco guitars. In 1994, he returned to live permanently in Paracho, and continues to produce guitars.

Huipe's basic flamenco guitar of cypress and either spruce or cedar sells for $1,200. Models are available through Casa Talamantes in New Mexico.

THOMAS HUMPHREY

Instruments currently produced in Gardiner, New York. Previous production was located in New York City, New York.

Luthier Thomas Humphrey has been building classical guitars for the past 27 years. In 1985, Humphrey startled the lutherie world when he introduced the **Millennium** models, which featured an innovative, tapered body design and elevated fingerboard. This innovation to the classical guitar represented some of the very few alterations to the fundamental design of the traditional Antonio Torres model. Though initially questioned, the new design has since been universally accepted by both players and other guitar makers.

Luthier Humphrey is known for producing primarily spruce top guitars and (almost exclusively) Brazilian rosewood back and sides. Humphrey produced guitars for the first 27 years in New York City; his workshop now is located in the countryside near the village of Gardiner, New York. Presently, his guitars are used in both recording and concert situations by many of the world's leading guitarists. Humphrey presently produces an estimated twenty-one guitars a year.

Though always changing and modifing the design as well as seeking new innovations, the current embodiment has become somewhat standardized due to a collaboration with the **C.F. Martin Guitar company**. The C.F. Martin company currently is producing three different models.

(Biography courtesy Thomas Humphrey, October, 1997)

According to the Martin Guitar company's Sounding Board newsletter, "a recent survey of 100 of the world's top classical guitarists revealed that approximately 20% play a Humphrey Millenium".

ACOUSTIC

Humphrey's classical design features primarily spruce tops and (almost exclusively) Brazilian rosewood back and sides. The classical model design has a tapered body and elevated fingerboard. For further specifications and questions about pricing, contact luthier Humphrey via the Index of Current Manufacturers located in the back of this edition.

In 1996, Humphrey contracted a standardized design of his design to the C.F. Martin Guitar company of Nazareth, Pennsylvania. The Martin-built versions of Humphrey's design, **Model C-TSH** (Standard Series) and **Model C-1R** (1 Series), were available in late 1996 (nearer to early 1997). The Martin version of the Humphrey design utilizes both spruce and cedar soundboards as well as rosewood and other back and side material in order to reach a wide range of price points. These guitars also have met with tremendous response from many different styles of guitarists.

In late 1997, the C.F. Martin company introduced the Sting Signature version of the Humphrey design **(Model C-MSH** Limited Edition).

HUTTL

Instruments were built in Germany from the 1950s to the 1970s.

The Huttl trademark may not be as well known as other German guitar builders such as Framus, Hopf, or Klira. While their designs may be as original as the others, the quality of workmanship is still fairly rough in comparison. Research continues into the Huttl trademark.

ANTHONY J. HUVARD

Instruments currently built in Sandston, Virginia.

Luthier Anthony J. Huvard builds a limited number of high quality guitars. Huvard also offers a very comprehensive website called **Luthiers Around The World**, which offers information regarding indepentent luthiers and lutherie products. For additional information, please contact Anthony J. Huvard through the Index of Current Manufacturers located in the back of this edition.

HYUNDAI

Instruments currently built in Korea. Distributed in the U.S. through Hyundai Guitars of West Nyack, New York.

Hyndai offers a range of medium quality guitars designed for beginning students that have designs based on popular American classics.

IBANEZ

Instruments produced in Japan since the early 1960s, and some models produced in Korea since the 1980s. Ibanez guitars are distributed in the U.S. by Ibanez USA (Hoshino) in Bensalem, Pennsylvania. Other distribution offices include Quebec (for Canada), Sydney (for Australia), and Auckland (for New Zealand).

The Ibanez trademark originated from the Fuji plant in Matsumoto, Japan. In 1932, the Hoshino Gakki Ten, Inc. factory began producing instruments under the Ibanez trademark. The factory and offices were burned down during World War II, and were revived in 1950. By the mid 1960s, Hoshino was producing instruments under various trademarks such as Ibanez, Star, King's Stone, Jamboree, and Goldentone.

In the mid-1950s, Harry Rosenbloom opened the Medley Music store outside Philadelphia. As the Folk Music boom began in 1959, Rosenbloom decided to begin producing acoustic guitars and formed the Elger company (named after Rosenbloom's children, Ellen and Gerson). Elger acoustics were produced in Ardmore, Pennsylvania between 1959 and 1965.

In the 1960s, Rosenbloom travelled to Japan and found a number of companies that he contracted to produce the Elger acoustics. Later, he was contacted by Hoshino to form a closer business relationship. The first entry level solid body guitars featuring original designs first surfaced in the mid 1960s, some bearing the Elger trademark, and some bearing the Ibanez logo. One of the major keys to the perceived early Ibanez quality is due to Hoshino shipping the guitars to the Elger factory in Ardmore. The arriving guitars would be re-checked, and set up prior to shipping to the retailer. Many distributors at the time would just simply ship *product* to the retailer, and let surprises occur at the unboxing. By reviewing the guitars in a separate facility, Hoshino/Ibanez could catch any problems before the retailer - so the number of perceived flawed guitars was reduced at the retail/sales end. In England, Ibanez was imported by the Summerfield Brothers, and sometimes had either the **CSL** trademark or no trademark at all on the headstock. Other U.K. distributors used the **Antoria** brandname, and in Australia they were rebranded with a **Jason** logo.

In the early 1970s, the level of quality rose as well as the level of indebtedness to classic American designs. It has been argued that Ibanez' reproductions of Stratocasters and Les Pauls may be equal to or better than the quality of Norlin era Gibsons or CBS era Fenders. While the **Blue Book of Guitars** would rather stay neutral on this debate (we just list them, not rate them), it has been suggested by outside sources that next time *close your eyes and let your hands and ears be the judge*. In any event, the unauthorized reproductions eventually led to Fender's objections to Tokai's imports (the infamous *headstock sawing* rumour), and Norlin/Gibson taking Hoshino/Ibanez/Elger into court for patent infringement.

When Ibanez began having success basically reproducing Gibson guitars and selling them at a lower price on the market, Norlin (Gibson's owner at the time) sent off a cease-and-desist warning. Norlin's lawyers decided that the best way to proceed was to defend the decorative (the headstock) versus the functional (body design), and on June 28th, 1977 the case of Gibson vs. Elger Co. opened in Philadelphia Federal District Court. In early 1978, a resolution was agreed upon: Ibanez would stop reproducing Gibsons if Norlin would stop suing Ibanez. The case was officially closed on February 2, 1978.

The infringement lawsuit ironically might have been the kick in the pants that propelled Ibanez and other Japanese builders to get back into original designs. Ibanez stopped building Gibson exact reproductions, and moved on to other designs. By the early 1980s, certain guitar styles began appealing to other areas of the guitar market (notably the Hard Rock/Heavy Metal genre), and Ibanez's use of famous endorsers probably fueled the appeal. Ibanez's continuing program of original designs and artist involvement continued to work in the mid to late 1980s, and continues to support their position in the market today.

(Source: Michael Wright, Guitar Stories Volume One)

Model Dating Identification

In addition to the Ibanez company's model history, a serialization chart is provided in the back of the **Blue Book of Guitars** to further aid the dating of older Ibanez guitars (not all potentiometer builders use the EIA source code, so overseas-built potentiometer codes on Japanese guitars may not help in the way of clues).

1959-1967: Elger Acoustics are built in Ardmore, Pennsylvania; and are distributed by Medley Music, Grossman Music (Cleveland), Targ and Dinner (Chicago), and the Roger Balmer Company on the west coast. Elger imported from Japan the Tama acoustics, Ibanez acoustics, and some Elger electrics.

1971-1977: The copy era begins for Ibanez (*Faithful Reproductions*) as solid body electrics based on Gibson, Fender, and Rickenbacker models (both bolt-ons and set-necks) arrive. These are followed by copies of Martin, Guild, Gibson, and Fender acoustics. Ibanez opens an office and warehouse outside of Philadelphia, Pennsylvania to maintain quality control on imported guitars in 1972.

1973: Ibanez's **Artist** series acoustics and electrics are debuted. In 1974, the Artist-style neck joint; later in 1976 an Artist 'Les Paul' arrives. This sets the stage for the LP variant double cutaway Artist model in 1978.

1975: Ibanez began to use a meaningful numbering system as part of their warranty program. In general, the letter stands for the month (January = A, February = B, etc) and the following two digits are the year.

1981-1987: In 1984, the **Lonestar** acoustics are introduced, and Ibanez responds to the MIDI challenge of Roland by unveiling the **IMG-2010** MIDI guitar system.

1992-1993: The **ATL** acoustic/electric design is unveiled, and **RT** Series guitars debut in 1993.

(This overview, while brief, will hopefully identify years, trends, and series. For further information and deeper clarification, please refer to Michael Wright's Guitar Stories Volume One).

Grading	100%	EXCELLENT	AVERAGE

ACOUSTIC

Artwood Dreadnought Series

AW Series models specifications: Body Length 20", Body Width 15 3/4", Body Depth 4 3/4".

AW70 — dreadnought style body, solid Sitka spruce top, round soundhole, tortoiseshell pickguard, bound body, mahogany back/sides/neck, 14/20 fret rosewood fingerboard with pearl dot inlay, rosewood bridge with white black dot pins, Ibanez/'AW' logo on peghead, chrome hardware, 3 per side die-cast tuners. Available in Natural low gloss finish. Mfr. 1997 to date.

Mfr.'s Sug. Retail	$399	$299	$195	$125

AW100 — dreadnought style body, solid Sitka spruce top, round soundhole, tortoiseshell pickguard, bound body, mahogany back/sides/neck, 14/20 fret rosewood fingerboard with pearl dot inlay, rosewood bridge with white black dot pins, Ibanez/'A' logo on peghead, chrome hardware, 3 per side die-cast tuners. Available in Natural gloss finish. Current mfr.

Mfr.'s Sug. Retail	$449	$350	$225	$150

AW112 NT — similar to AW100, except features 12-string configuration, 6 per side tuners. Available in Natural gloss finish. Mfr. 1997 to date.

Mfr.'s Sug. Retail	$599	$425	$295	$195

AW300 — similar to the AW100, except features rosewood back/sides, abalone dot inlay, gold Grover tuners. Available in Natural gloss finish. Current mfr.

Mfr.'s Sug. Retail	$599	$475	$295	$175

AW500 — similar to the AW100, except features solid Engelmann spruce top, rosewood back/sides, herringbone rosette/body binding, abalone snowflake inlay, gold Grover tuners. Available in Natural gloss finish. Current mfr.

Mfr.'s Sug. Retail	$699	$550	$350	$225

AW600 — similar to the AW100, except features solid Engelmann spruce top, rosewood back/sides, Mexican abalone rosette/body binding, abalone snowflake inlay, gold Grover tuners. Available in Natural gloss finish. Disc. 1998.

		$425	$250

Last Mfr.'s Sug. Retail was $749.

AW900 AN — similar to the AW100, except features solid Engelmann spruce top, rosewood back/sides, Mexican abalone rosette/body binding, abalone snowflake inlay, gold Grover tuners. Available in Antique Stained gloss finish. Current mfr.

Mfr.'s Sug. Retail	$1,099	$895	$550	$375

Artwood Grand Auditorium Series

AG Series models specifications: Body Length 19", Body Width 14 3/4", Body Depth 4".

AG200 — tight waist/rounded lower bout body with single rounded cutaway, solid Engelmann spruce top, round soundhole, tortoiseshell pickguard, bound body, mahogany back/sides/neck, 14/20 fret rosewood fingerboard with pearl diamond inlay, rosewood bridge with snowflake inlay, white black dot pins, Ibanez/'AW' logo on peghead, chrome hardware, 3 per side Grover tuners. Available in Natural low gloss finish. Disc. 1998.

		$395	$225

Last Mfr.'s Sug. Retail was $669.

Artwood Grand Concert Series

AC Series models specifications: Body Length 18 1/2", Body Width 14 3/4", Body Depth 4 1/2".

AC50 LG — OM-style body, solid Sitka spruce top, round soundhole, tortoiseshell pickguard, maple back/sides/neck, 14/20 fret rosewood fingerboard with pearl dot inlay, rosewood bridge with white black dot pins, Ibanez/'AW' logo on peghead, chrome hardware, 3 per side die-cast tuners. Available in Natural low gloss finish. Mfr. 1998 to date.

Mfr.'s Sug. Retail	$339	$250	$160	$115

AC70 LG — similar to the AC50 LG, except features mahogany back/sides. Available in Natural low gloss finish. Mfr. 1997 to date.

Mfr.'s Sug. Retail	$399	$275	$195	$125

AC100 — OM-style body, solid Sitka spruce top, round soundhole, tortoiseshell pickguard, bound body, mahogany back/sides/neck, 14/20 fret rosewood fingerboard with pearl dot inlay, rosewood bridge with white black dot pins, Ibanez/'AW' logo on peghead, chrome hardware, 3 per side die-cast tuners. Available in Natural low gloss finish. Disc. 1998.

		$250	$150

Last Mfr.'s Sug. Retail was $449.

AC300 — similar to the AC100, except features rosewood back/sides, bound fingerboard/peghead, abalone dot fingerboard inlay, Grover tuners. Available in Natural gloss finish. Current mfr.

Mfr.'s Sug. Retail	$599	$475	$295	$200

Grading	100%	EXCELLENT	AVERAGE

AC900 — similar to the AC100, except features solid Engelmann spruce top, rosewood back/sides, bound fingerboard/peghead, abalone snowflake fingerboard inlay, gold hardware, Grover tuners. Available in Antique Stained gloss finish. Current mfr.

Mfr.'s Sug. Retail	$1,099	$875	$550	$375

Charleston Series

CR80 — auditorium style, spruce top, bound f-holes, 3-layer black pickguard, nato back/sides, mahogany neck, 14/22 fret bound rosewood fingerboard with pearl dot inlay, rosewood bridge with white black dot pins, blackface peghead with screened logo, 3 per side chrome tuners. Available in Brown Sunburst and Cherry Sunburst finishes. Mfd. 1994 to 1996.

	$225	$150

Last Mfr.'s Sug. Retail was $500.

CR100E — similar to CR80, except has thinner body, piezo bridge pickup, 4 band EQ. Disc. 1996.

	$325	$200

Last Mfr.'s Sug. Retail was $700.

Classic (GA) Series

GA5 — classical style, spruce top, round soundhole, wood inlay rosette, mahogany back/sides, mahogany neck, 12/19 fret rosewood fingerboard, rosewood tied bridge, 3 per side chrome tuners. Available in Natural gloss finish. Mfr. 1998 to date.

Mfr.'s Sug. Retail	$239	$175	$110	$75

GA7 — similar to the GA5, except features rosewood back/sides, gold tuners. Available in Natural gloss finish. Mfr. 1998 to date.

Mfr.'s Sug. Retail	$279	$195	$135	$95

GA10 — classical style, spruce top, round soundhole, bound body, wood inlay rosette, nato back/sides, mahogany neck, 12/19 fret rosewood fingerboard, rosewood tied bridge, rosewood peghead veneer, 3 per side chrome tuners with pearloid buttons. Available in Natural gloss finish. Mfr. 1994 to 1996, 1998 to date.

Mfr.'s Sug. Retail	$259	$195	$120	$90

Add $40 for Natural gloss finish **(Model GA30)**.

GA30 — similar to the GA10, except features mahogany back/sides, gold tuners. Available in Natural gloss finish. Mfr. 1998 to date.

Mfr.'s Sug. Retail	$299	$205	$135	$95

Day Tripper Series

DT 10 — spruce top, mahogany back/sides, rosewood fingerboard with pearl dot inlay, rosewood bridge, chrome die cast tuners. Available in Natural gloss finish. Mfr. 1998 to date.

Mfr.'s Sug. Retail	$249	$175	$115	$85

DT 10 CA — similar to the DT 10. Available in Natural gloss finish. Mfr. 1998 to date.

Mfr.'s Sug. Retail	$329	$225	$150	$100

Performance Series Mini Jumbo Models

Mini Jumbo models specifications: Body Length 19", Body Width 14 1/2", Body Depth 3 3/4".

PC5 NT — miniature jumbo style, spruce top, round soundhole, black body binding, 5 stripe rosette, nato back/sides/neck, 14/20 fret rosewood fingerboard with pearl dot inlay, rosewood bridge with white black dot pins, 3 per side chrome covered tuners. Available in Natural low gloss finish. Mfr. 1998 to date.

Mfr.'s Sug. Retail	$259	$195	$115	$85

Add $20 for limited edition Black gloss finish **(Model PC5 BK)**.
Add $20 for limited edition Tobacco Sunburst gloss finish **(Model PC5 TS)**.

Performance Series

The different Ibanez **Jam Pack** combinations include a PF guitar, gig bag, instructional video, electronic tuner, extra strings, strap, chord chart, picks, and a free subscription to **Plugged In** (the official Ibanez newsletter).

PF GUITAR JAM PACK (IJP1) PACKAGE — dreadnought style, spruce top, round soundhole, black pickguard, 3 stripe rosette, nato back/sides, mahogany neck, 14/20 fret rosewood fingerboard with pearl dot inlay, rosewood bridge with black pins, 3 per side covered tuners. Available in Natural low gloss finish. Current mfr.

Mfr.'s Sug. Retail	$329

PF GUITAR Jam Pack (IJP1 BK) Package — similar to the IJP1 Jam Pack. Available in Black finish. Mfr. 1997 to date.

Mfr.'s Sug. Retail	$349

PF GUITAR Jam Pack (IJP1 SM) Package — similar to the IJP1 Jam Pack, except features Grand Concert size acoustic. Available in Natural finish. Mfr. 1998 to date.

Mfr.'s Sug. Retail	$329

PF GUITAR Jam Pack (IJP1 CL) Package — similar to the IJP1 Jam Pack, except features Classical acoustic. Available in Natural finish. Mfr. 1998 to date.

Mfr.'s Sug. Retail	$319

PF3 — dreadnought style, spruce top, round soundhole, black pickguard, bound body, 3 stripe rosette, nato back/sides, mahogany neck, 14/20 fret rosewood fingerboard with pearl dot inlay, rosewood bridge with black white dot pins, 3 per side chrome tuners. Available in Natural finish. Mfd. 1994 to 1997.

	$100	$70

Last Mfr.'s Sug. Retail was $220.

Grading	100%	EXCELLENT	AVERAGE

PF5 NT — dreadnought style, spruce top, round soundhole, bound body, 5 stripe rosette, mahogany back/sides/neck, 14/20 fret rosewood fingerboard with pearl dot inlay, rosewood bridge with white black dot pins, 3 per side chrome covered tuners. Available in Natural gloss finish. Mfr. 1992 to date.

Mfr.'s Sug. Retail	$259	$195	$115	$85

    Add $20 for Black gloss finish **(Model PF5 BK)**.

    Add $40 for left-handed configuration **(Model PF5 L NT)**.

    In 1994, black pickguard was introduced.

PF5 S — similar to PF5, except features solid spruce top, pearl snowflake fingerboard inlay. Mfd. 1994 to 1996.

        $175 $115

        Last Mfr.'s Sug. Retail was $390.

PF5 12 — similar to PF5, except in 12-string configuration, 6 per side tuners, black pickguard. Available in Natural low gloss finish. Mfr. 1994 to date.

Mfr.'s Sug. Retail	$299	$210	$135	$95

PF10 — dreadnought style, spruce top, round soundhole, bound body, 5 stripe rosette, mahogany back/sides/neck, 14/20 fret rosewood fingerboard with pearl dot inlay, rosewood bridge with black white dot pins, 3 per side chrome die-cast tuners. Available in Natural gloss finish. Mfr. 1991 to date.

Mfr.'s Sug. Retail	$319	$225	$150	$100

    Add $20 for left-handed configuration **(Model PF10 L)**.

    Add $60 for Black gloss finish **(Model PF10 BK)**. When this option was discontinued in 1998, the list price for a PF10 BK was $399.

    In 1994, black pickguard was introduced.

PF10 12 — similar to PF10, except in 12-string configuration, 6 per side tuners. Available in Natural gloss finish. Current mfr.

Mfr.'s Sug. Retail	$369	$275	$175	$125

PF18 S — similar to the PF10, except features solid spruce top. Available in Natural gloss finish. Mfd. 1992 to date.

        $195 $120

        Last Mfr.'s Sug. Retail was $440.

PF20 — similar to PF10, except features flame maple top, 3 per side chrome enclosed tuners. Available in Traditional Violin finish. Mfd. 1991 to 1996.

        $175 $110

        Last Mfr.'s Sug. Retail was $370.

    In 1994, black pickguard was introduced.

PF25 — similar to PF10, except features herringbone body binding, oak back/sides, 14/20 fret rosewood fingerboard with pearl snowflake inlay. Available in Natural finish. Mfr. 1994 to 1996.

        $175 $110

        Last Mfr.'s Sug. Retail was $360.

PF30 — similar to PF10, except features cedar top, 3 per side chrome enclosed tuners. Available in Natural finish. Mfd. 1991 to 1992.

        $130 $85

        Last Mfr.'s Sug. Retail was $290.

PF40 — similar to PF10, except features flame maple top, 3 per side chrome diecast tuners. Available in Natural finish. Mfd. 1991 to 1996.

        $195 $125

        Last Mfr.'s Sug. Retail was $430.

    In 1994, black pickguard was introduced, spruce top, flame maple back/sides replaced original items.

PF40 FM — similar to PF40, except has flame maple top. Available in Natural and Transparent Blue finishes. Mfr. 1994 to 1996.

        $225 $150

        Last Mfr.'s Sug. Retail was $500.

PF50 — dreadnought style, spruce top, round soundhole, herringbone bound body and rosette, rosewood back/sides, mahogany neck, 14/20 fret bound rosewood fingerboard with abalone dot inlay, rosewood bridge with black abalone dot pins, bound peghead, 3 per side chrome diecast tuners. Available in Natural finish. Mfd. 1991 to 1994.

        $195 $125

        Last Mfr.'s Sug. Retail was $430.

PF50 S — similar to PF50, except has solid spruce top. Disc. 1994.

        $250 $175

        Last Mfr.'s Sug. Retail was $550.

PF50 12 — similar to PF50, except has 12-string configuration, 6 per side tuners. Disc. 1994.

        $225 $150

        Last Mfr.'s Sug. Retail was $480.

PF75 M — similar to PF50, except features flame maple back/sides, maple neck, 14/20 fret bound maple fingerboard with black dot inlays, rosewood bridge with white abalone dot pins, bound peghead with abalone Ibanez logo inlay. Available in Natural finish. Mfd. 1992 to 1996.

        $250 $175

        Last Mfr.'s Sug. Retail was $550.

Grading	100%	EXCELLENT	AVERAGE

PF80 V — similar to PF50, except features ovankol top, ovankol back/sides. Available in Natural finish. Mfr. 1994 to date.

	$160	**$100**
		Last Mfr.'s Sug. Retail was $320.

Ragtime Series

R001 — parlor style, solid spruce top, round soundhole, wooden inlay binding and rosette, rosewood back/sides/neck, 14/20 fret rosewood fingerboard, rosewood bridge with white black dot pins, gold hardware, 3 per side die-cast tuners. Available in Natural finish. Mfd. 1992 to 1994.

	$275	**$195**
		Last Mfr.'s Sug. Retail was $600.

R300 — similar to th R001, except features cedar top, mahogany back/sides/neck, chrome hardware. Available in Natural finish. Mfd. 1992 to 1994.

	$195	**$120**
		Last Mfr.'s Sug. Retail was $400.

R302 — similar to R001, except features 12-string configuration, 6 per side tuners, cedar top, mahogany back/sides/neck, chrome hardware. Available in Natural finish. Disc. 1994.

	$200	**$125**
		Last Mfr.'s Sug. Retail was $450.

R350 — similar to R001, except features cedar top, ovankol back/sides, mahogany neck, chrome hardware. Available in Natural finish. Disc. 1994.

	$200	**$125**
		Last Mfr.'s Sug. Retail was $450.

Tulsa Series

TU5 — grand concert style, round soundhole, bound body, 3 stripe rosette, nato back/sides, mahogany neck, 14/20 fret rosewood fingerboard with pearl dot inlay, rosewood bridge with black white dot pins, black pickguard, 3 per side chrome tuners. Available in Natural finish. Mfr. 1994 to 1996.

	$115	**$75**
		Last Mfr.'s Sug. Retail was $250.

Vintage (V) Series

Ibanez' Vintage models feature tempered mahogany necks (thinner and flatter profile) and synthetic Ivorex nuts and saddles.

V100 NT — dreadnought style, spruce top, round soundhole, body binding, mahogany back/sides, tempered mahogany neck, 14/20 fret rosewood fingerboard with pearl dot inlay, rosewood bridge with white bridgepins, 3 per side chrome die-cast tuners, tortoise pickguard. Available in Natural gloss finish. Mfr. 1998 to date.

Mfr.'s Sug. Retail	$339	$250	$150	$100

Add $30 for Black gloss finish (**Model V100 BK**).

ACOUSTIC ELECTRIC

PF GUITAR JAM PACK (IJP1 DE AMP) PACKAGE — dreadnought style, spruce top, round soundhole, black pickguard, 3 stripe rosette, nato back/sides, mahogany neck, 14/20 fret rosewood fingerboard with pearl dot inlay, rosewood bridge with black pins, 3 per side covered tuners. Available in Natural low gloss finish. Current mfr.

Mfr.'s Sug. Retail	$549

The Jam Pack includes an acoustic/electric model PF guitar, 10 watt acoustic amp, gig bag, instructional video, electronic tuner, extra strings, strap, chord chart, picks, and a free subscription to Plugged In (the official Ibanez newsletter).

ATL10 — single cutaway hollow style, spruce top, oval soundhole, bound body, 3 stripe rosette, maple back/sides/neck, 22 fret rosewood fingerboard with pearl dot inlays, rosewood bridge with white pearl dot pins, 6 per side black diecast tuners, piezo pickup, volume/3 band EQ controls. Available in Black and Blue Night finishes. Mfd. 1992 to 1996.

	$250	**$175**
		Last Mfr.'s Sug. Retail was $550.

AE (Acoustic/Electric) Series

AE Series models specifications: Body Length 20", Body Width 15 3/4", Body Depth 3".

AE10 — single rounded cutaway dreadnought style, spruce top, bound body, 3 stripe rosette, mahogany back/sides, mahogany neck, 14/21 fret rosewood fingerboard with pearl dot inlay, rosewood bridge with white black dot pins, wood peghead with screened plant/logo, 3 per side chrome die-cast tuners, piezo bridge pickup, AEQ-20 volume/tone/4 band EQ slider controls. Available in Natural low gloss finish. Current mfr.

Mfr.'s Sug. Retail	$449	$325	$215	$150

AE20 — similar to the AE10, except featured nato back/sides, 22 fret rosewood fingerboard with pearl dot inlay. Available in Natural gloss finish. Mfr. 1994 to 1996.

	$325	**$215**
		Last Mfr.'s Sug. Retail was $700.

AE20 N — similar to AE20, except has classic style body/peghead, no fingerboard inlay, rosewood tied bridge, 3 per side tuners with pearloid buttons. Disc. 1996.

	$315	**$215**
		Last Mfr.'s Sug. Retail was $700.

AE18 — similar to the AE10 (with the Ibanez AEQ system). Available in Natural gloss finish. Disc. 1998.

	$300	**$200**
		Last Mfr.'s Sug. Retail was $599.

ATL 10 BK
courtesy Ibanez USA

Grading	100%	EXCELLENT	AVERAGE

AE18 BK — similar to the AE18. Available in Black gloss finish. Current mfr.

Mfr.'s Sug. Retail	$599	$425	$295	$200

AE18 TBU — similar to the AE18. Available in Transparent Blue gloss finish. Mfr. 1998 to date.

Mfr.'s Sug. Retail	$599	$425	$295	$200

AE25 (TB, TS) — single rounded cutaway dreadnought style, flame maple top, bound body, 3 stripe rosette, bound body, maple back/sides, mahogany neck, 21 fret bound rosewood fingerboard with abalone dot inlay, rosewood bridge with white black dot pins, black peghead with screened plant/logo, 3 per side gold die-cast tuners, piezo bridge pickup, volume/tone/3 band EQ slider controls. Available in Transparent Blue (TB) and Tobacco Sunburst (TS) finishes. Current mfr.

Mfr.'s Sug. Retail	$699	$550	$350	$225

In 1998, Transparent Blue finish was discontinued.

AE40 — single rounded cutaway dreadnought style, figured maple top, bound body, 3 stripe rosette, nato back/sides, mahogany neck, 22 fret bound rosewood fingerboard with abalone/pearl block inlay, rosewood bridge with white black dot pins, bound peghead with screened plant/logo, 3 per side gold die-cast tuners with pearloid buttons, piezo bridge pickup, volume/tone/4 band EQ controls. Available in Honey Sunburst, Red Sunburst, and Transparent Blue finishes. Mfr. 1994 to 1996.

		$400	$275

Last Mfr.'s Sug. Retail was $900.

AE60S — similar to the AE40, except features solid spruce top, ovankol back/sides, bound blackface peghead with screened plant/logo. Available in Natural finish. Mfr. 1994 to 1996.

		$450	$300

Last Mfr.'s Sug. Retail was $1,000.

Artwood Dreadnought Series Acoustic/Electric

AW70 LG — dreadnought style, solid Sitka spruce top, round soundhole, tortoiseshell pickguard, bound body, mahogany back/sides/neck, 14/20 fret rosewood fingerboard with pearl dot inlay, rosewood bridge with white black dot pins, Ibanez/'AW' logo on peghead, chrome hardware, 3 per side die-cast tuners, Slim Jim pickup, volume/3 band EQ controls. Available in Natural low gloss finish. Mfr. 1998 to date.

Mfr.'s Sug. Retail	$399	$275	$195	$125

AW70 CE LG Limited Edition — similar to the AW70 LG, except features a single rounded cutaway body. Available in Natural low gloss finish. Mfr. 1998 to date.

Mfr.'s Sug. Retail	$599	$425	$295	$195

AW100 CE — dreadnought style body with single rounded cutaway, solid Sitka spruce top, round soundhole, tortoiseshell pickguard, bound body, mahogany back/sides/neck, 14/20 fret rosewood fingerboard with pearl dot inlay, rosewood bridge with white black dot pins, Ibanez/'AW' logo on peghead, chrome hardware, 3 per side die-cast tuners, Slim Jim pickup, volume/3 band EQ controls. Available in Natural gloss finish. Current mfr.

Mfr.'s Sug. Retail	$699	$550	$325	$225

Add $50 for Black gloss finish **(Model AW100 CE BK)**.

AW300CE — similar to the AW100, except features rosewood back/sides, abalone dot inlay, gold Grover tuners, Fishman pickup, volume/3 band EQ controls. Available in Natural gloss finish. Current mfr.

Mfr.'s Sug. Retail	$849	$695	$425	$295

Artwood Grand Auditorium Series Acoustic/Electric

AG200E — tight waist/rounded lower bout body with single rounded cutaway, solid Engelmann spruce top, round soundhole, tortoiseshell pickguard, bound body, rosewood back/sides/neck, 14/20 fret rosewood fingerboard with abalone snowflake inlay, rosewood bridge with white black dot pins, Ibanez/'AW' logo on peghead, gold hardware, 3 per side Grover tuners, Slim Jim pickup, volume/3 band EQ controls. Available in Natural gloss finish. Current mfr.

Mfr.'s Sug. Retail	$829	$675	$400	$275

Grading	100%	EXCELLENT	AVERAGE

AG600E — similar to the AG200 E, except features Mexican abalone rosette/binding, bound fingerboard/peghead, snowflake inlay on bridge, Fishman pickup, volume/3 band EQ controls. Available in Natural gloss finish. Current mfr.

Mfr.'s Sug. Retail	$999	$799	$495	$325

Classical Series Acoustic/Electric

GA6 CE — classical style body with single rounded cutaway, spruce top, round soundhole, wood inlay rosette, mahogany back/sides, mahogany neck, 12/19 fret rosewood fingerboard, rosewood tied bridge, 3 per side gold tuners, piezo pickup, volume/4 band EQ. Available in Natural gloss finish. Mfr. 1998 to date.

Mfr.'s Sug. Retail	$399	$275	$195	$125

Jumbo Series Acoustic/Electric

AJ307 CE 7-STRING — 7-string configuration, tight waist/rounded lower bout body with single rounded cutaway, solid Sitka spruce top, round soundhole, tortoiseshell pickguard, bound body, rosewood back/sides/neck, 14/20 fret rosewood fingerboard with abalone dot inlay, rosewood bridge with white bridgepins, Ibanez 'AW' logo on peghead, gold hardware, 4/3 per side Grover tuners, Fishman transducer, volume/3 band EQ controls. Available in Natural gloss finish. Current mfr.

Mfr.'s Sug. Retail	$1,099

Nomad Series Acoustic/Electric

N600 — single cutaway classical style, cedar top, round soundhole, 5 stripe bound body, wooden inlay rosette, mahogany back/sides/neck, 21 fret rosewood fingerboard with pearl dot inlays, rosewood bridge with white black dot pins, 3 per side chrome die-cast tuners, piezo pickup, volume/3 band EQ controls. Available in Natural finish. Mfd. 1992 to 1994.

		$275	$175

Last Mfr.'s Sug. Retail was $600.

N601 N — similar to the N600, except features slotted peghead, gold hardware, 3 per side open classic tuners. Available in Natural finish. Mfd. 1992 to 1994.

		$300	$200

Last Mfr.'s Sug. Retail was $680.

N700 D — single rounded cutaway dreadnought style, spruce top, round soundhole, 5 stripe bound body, wooden inlay rosette, ovankol back/sides, mahogany neck, 21 fret rosewood fingerboard with snowflake inlays, rosewood bridge with white black dot pins, 3 per side gold die-cast tuners, piezo pickup, volume/3 band EQ controls. Available in Natural finish. Mfd. 1992 to 1994.

		$325	$200

Last Mfr.'s Sug. Retail was $700.

N800 — single cutaway jumbo style, flame maple top, round soundhole, abalone bound body and rosette, flame maple back/sides, mahogany neck, 21 fret bound rosewood fingerboard with abalone block inlays, rosewood bridge with black white dot pins, bound peghead, 3 per side chrome die-cast tuners, piezo pickup, Matrix 4 band EQ. Available in Transparent Blue and Transparent Violin finishes. Mfd. 1992 to 1994.

		$375	$250

Last Mfr.'s Sug. Retail was $850.

N900 S — similar to N800, except has solid spruce top, gold diecast tuners. Disc. 1994.

		$500	$325

Last Mfr.'s Sug. Retail was $1,100.

Performer Series Acoustic/Electric

PF5 CE NT — single rounded cutaway dreadnought style, spruce top, round soundhole, bound body, 5 stripe rosette, mahogany back/sides/neck, 14/20 fret rosewood fingerboard with pearl dot inlay, rosewood bridge with white black dot pins, 3 per side chrome covered tuners, piezo bridge pickup, volume/3 band EQ. Available in Natural gloss finish. Mfr. 1994 to date.

Mfr.'s Sug. Retail	$399	$275	$195	$125

PF5 DE NT — similar to the PF5 CE NT, except has dreadnought body (no cutaway), passive volume/tone controls. Available in Natural gloss finish. Mfr. 1998 to date.

Mfr.'s Sug. Retail	$349	$250	$150	$100

Add $20 for Black gloss finish **(Model PF5 DE BK)**.

PF10 CE — similar to the PF5 CE, except features 3 per side chrome die-cast tuners. Available in Natural gloss finish. Mfd. 1992 to 1998.

		$300	$175

Last Mfr.'s Sug. Retail was $549.

PF18 S CE — similar to the PF5 CE, except features solid spruce top, 3 per side chrome diecast tuners. Available in Natural gloss finish. Mfd. 1994 to 1996.

		$300	$175

Last Mfr.'s Sug. Retail was $600.

Vintage Series Acoustic/Electric

V100 CE NT — dreadnought style body with single rounded cutaway, spruce top, round soundhole, body binding, mahogany back/sides, tempered mahogany neck, 14/20 fret rosewood fingerboard with pearl dot inlay, rosewood bridge with white bridgepins, 3 per side chrome die-cast tuners, tortoise pickguard. Available in Natural gloss finish, piezo bridge pickup, EQ30 volume/3 band EQ. Mfr. 1998 to date.

Mfr.'s Sug. Retail	$499	$350	$225	$150

ITHACA GUITAR WORKS

Instruments currently built in Ithaca, New York.

The Ithaca Guitar Works consists of both a retail music store and a custom guitar shop. Ithaca Guitar Works' shop offers repairs on stringed instruments as well as a nylon string acoustic guitar model.

ITHACA STRINGED INSTRUMENTS

Instruments currently built in Trumansburg, New York.

After a long association with Ithaca Guitar Works, luthiers Eric Aceto and Dan Hoffman established their own company in 1997. The company is now building the **Oneida** acoustic/electric guitar, scrolled acoustic instruments, *N.S. by Ithaca* electric violin, and the **Aceto/Violect** pickup system. The company also offers several other stringed instruments.

The **Oneida** acoustic/electric ($3,500) is constructed with a spruce or cedar top, mahogany or walnut back and sides, and an ebony fingerboard and bridge. For further information, please contact Ithaca Stringed Instruments via the Index of Current manufacturers located in the back of the book.

Ithaca acoustic
courtesy Ithaca Stringed Instruments

Ithaca acoustic
courtesy Ithaca Stringed Instruments

J

DOUGLAS R. JACKSON

Instruments currently built in Destin, Florida. Distributed through the Douglas R. Jackson Guitar Shop of Destin, Florida.

Luthier Douglas R. Jackson handcrafts his own acoustic and electric guitars, which are built on commission. On occasion, Jackson may build a model on speculation, but that is not the norm. All models are marketed through his guitar shop.

Jackson attended a guitar building school in the Spring of 1977. While enrolled, he was hired by the school to teach and perform repairs. Jackson taught two classes in the 1977 school year, and helped build over 150 instruments (plus his own personal guitars and repairs). Jackson then went to work for a vintage guitar dealer on and off for three years, while he studied just about anything he could get his hands on. During this research phase, Jackson continued to build three or four guitars a year (in addition to his shop repairs).

In 1986, Jackson moved from Arizona to his present location in Destin, Florida (the Pensacola/Fort Walton Beach area). Jackson currently owns and operates a 1,500 square foot building that houses his guitar shop and manufacturing equipment.

(Biography courtesy Douglas R. Jackson)

Jackson estimates that he has built close to 100 instruments consisting of acoustic and electric 6- and 12-string guitars, electric basses and mandolins, resonator guitars, along with a couple of dulcimers (both hammered and Appalachian).

ACOUSTIC

The majority of Jackson's acoustic guitars have been the dreadnought style, with his own scalloped bracing pattern. These dreadnought models feature herringbone trim on the front, back, back center strip, and soundhole; ebony fingerboards, bridges, and peghead laminates; curly maple binding, mother of pearl inlay; and spruce tops. The backs and sides are constructed out of either mahogany, Indian rosewood, curly koa, curly claro walnut, or curly maple (although other woods have been used through the years). Jackson now regularly makes a body size the same as a resonator or "classical in a steel-string".

Acoustic prices start at $2,000 for a plain mahogany body and go up according to the woods and appointments used. A used one in good condition may sell for $1,000 to $2,000, depending on how fancy a model it is.

Jackson Dreadnought
courtesy Doug Jackson

JAIME JULIA

Distributed by Manufacturas Alhambra S.L. of Muro del Alcoy, Spain.

Jaime Julia brand acoustic guitars are distributed by Manufacturas Alhambra S.L. of Muro del Alcoy, Spain. For information regarding model specifications and pricing, please contact Jaime Julia via the Index of Current Manufacturers located in the back of this edition.

JAMBOREE

Instruments produced in Japan.

The Jamboree trademark was a brandname used by U.S. importers Elger/Hoshino of Ardmore, Pennsylvania. Jamboree, along with others like Goldentone, King's Stone, and Elger were all used on Japanese guitars imported to the U.S. Elger/Hoshino evolved into Hoshino USA, the distributor of Ibanez guitars.

(Source: Michael Wright, Guitar Stories Volume One)

JAMMER

Instruments produced in Asia. Distributed by VMI Industries (Vega Musical Instruments) of Brea, California.

Jammer instruments are designed with the entry level and student guitarist in mind.

JASMINE

Instruments currently produced in Asia. Distributed by Kaman Music Corporation of Bloomfield, Connecticut.

The Jasmine trademark is a division of Takamine. Jasmine guitars can be viewed as an *entry-level* step into the Takamine product line. Jasmine guitars may not be as ornate, and may feature different construction methods than Takamine models.

J

Grading	100%	EXCELLENT	AVERAGE

ACOUSTIC

C Series Classicals

C-22 — classical style, agathis top, round soundhole, hardwood back/sides, nato neck, 12/19 fret rosewood fingerboard, rosewood tied bridge, 3 per side chrome tuners with pearloid buttons. Available in Natural finish. Current mfr.

Mfr.'s Sug. Retail	$249	$175	$115	$85

C-23 — classic style, spruce top, round soundhole, bound body, wood inlay rosette, mahogany back/sides, nato neck, 12/19 fret rosewood fingerboard, rosewood tied bridge, 3 per side chrome tuners with pearloid buttons. Available in Natural finish. Mfr. 1994 to date.

Mfr.'s Sug. Retail	$289	$200	$135	$95

Jackson Acoustic (Sunburst)
courtesy Doug Jackson

C-36 S
courtesy Kaman Music Corp.

J

Grading	100%	EXCELLENT	AVERAGE

C-26 — classic style, spruce top, round soundhole, 3 stripe bound body, wood inlay rosette, mahogany back/sides, nato neck, 12/19 fret rosewood fingerboard/bridge, 3 per side gold tuners with pearloid buttons. Available in Natural finish. Disc. 1994.

$150 $90
Last Mfr.'s Sug. Retail was $280.

C-27 — classic style, cedar top, round soundhole, bound body, wood inlay rosette, mahogany back/sides, nato neck, 12/19 fret rosewood fingerboard, rosewood tied bridge, 3 per side chrome tuners with pearloid buttons. Available in Natural finish. Mfd. 1994 to 1998.

$100 $65
Last Mfr.'s Sug. Retail was $200.

C-28 — classic style, spruce top, round soundhole, 3 stripe bound body, wood inlay rosette, rosewood back/sides, nato neck, 12/19 fret rosewood fingerboard, tied rosewood bridge, 3 per side gold tuners with pearloid buttons. Available in Natural finish. Disc. 1992.

$175 $115
Last Mfr.'s Sug. Retail was $350.

C-36 S — classic style, solid spruce top, round soundhole, 3 stripe bound body, wood inlay rosette, rosewood back/sides, nato neck, 12/19 fret rosewood fingerboard, tied rosewood bridge with marquetry inlay, 3 per side gold tuners with pearloid buttons. Available in Natural finish. Mfd. 1994 to 1998.

$225 $135
Last Mfr.'s Sug. Retail was $520.

C-48 M — single round cutaway classic style, figured maple top, round soundhole, 3 stripe bound body, wood inlay rosette, figured maple back/sides, nato neck, 12/19 fret rosewood fingerboard, tied rosewood bridge, figured maple veneered peghead, 3 per side gold tuners with pearloid buttons. Available in Natural finish. Mfd. 1994 to 1998.

$225 $135
Last Mfr.'s Sug. Retail was $500.

RQ-28 — requinto style, spruce top, round soundhole, bound body, wood inlay rosette, rosewood back/sides, nato neck, 12/19 fret extended rosewood fingerboard, tied rosewood bridge with marquetry inlay, 3 per side gold tuners with pearloid buttons. Available in Natural finish. Mfd. 1994 to 1998.

$195 $125
Last Mfr.'s Sug. Retail was $420.

S Series Dreadnoughts

S-31 — dreadnought style, spruce top, round soundhole, black pickguard, 3 stripe bound body/rosette, nato back/sides/neck, 14/20 fret rosewood fingerboard with pearl dot inlay, rosewood bridge with white pins, 3 per side chrome tuners. Available in Black finish. Mfr. 1994 to date.

Mfr.'s Sug. Retail	$389	$275	$125	$95

S-32 — dreadnought style, spruce top, round soundhole, black pickguard, 3 stripe bound body/rosette, nato back/sides/neck, 14/20 fret rosewood fingerboard with pearl dot inlay, rosewood bridge with white pins, 3 per side chrome diecast tuners. Available in Natural gloss finish. Current mfr.

Mfr.'s Sug. Retail	$269	$195	$125	$90

S-312 12-String — similar to the S-32, except features a 12-string configuration, 6 per side tuners, 5 stripe bound body/rosette. Available in Natural gloss finish. Current mfr.

Mfr.'s Sug. Retail	$319	$225	$150	$100

S-33 — dreadnought style, spruce top, round soundhole, black pickguard, stripe bound body/rosette, mahogany back/sides, nato neck, 14/20 fret rosewood fingerboard with pearl dot inlay, rosewood bridge with white black dot pins, 3 per side chrome diecast tuners. Available in Natural finish. Disc. 1998.

$200 $95
Last Mfr.'s Sug. Retail was $380.

S-37 — dreadnought style, spruce top, round soundhole, black pickguard, bound body, 3 stripe rosette, nato back/sides/neck, 14/20 fret rosewood fingerboard with pearl dot inlay, rosewood bridge with white pins, 3 per side diecast tuners. Available in Natural finish. Mfr. 1994 to 1998.

$125 $80
Last Mfr.'s Sug. Retail was $250.

S-38 — dreadnought style, solid spruce top, round soundhole, black pickguard, 3 stripe bound body/rosette, mahogany back/sides, nato neck, 14/20 fret bound rosewood fingerboard with pearl dot inlay, rosewood bridge with white pins, 3 per side chrome diecast tuners. Available in Natural finish. Current mfr.

Mfr.'s Sug. Retail	$319	$225	$150	$95

S-38 S — similar to the S-38, except features solid spruce top. Available in Natural finish. Current mfr.

Mfr.'s Sug. Retail	$389	$275	$175	$125

S-40 — dreadnought style, round soundhole, black pickguard, 3 stripe bound body/rosette, nato neck, 14/20 fret bound rosewood fingerboard with pearl dot inlay, rosewood bridge with white black dot pins, bound peghead, 3 per side chrome diecast tuners. Available in Natural finish. Disc. 1992.

$175 $115
Last Mfr.'s Sug. Retail was $350.

S-41 — dreadnought style, spruce top, round soundhole, black pickguard with white outline, 3 stripe bound body/rosette, daowood back/sides, nato neck, 14/20 fret bound rosewood fingerboard with pearl dot inlay, rosewood bridge with white black dot pins, 3 per side chrome diecast tuners. Available in Black finish. Disc. 1994.

$175 $115
Last Mfr.'s Sug. Retail was $360.

Grading	100%	EXCELLENT	AVERAGE

S-46 — dreadnought style, spruce top, round soundhole, black pickguard with white outline, 3 stripe bound body/rosette, daowood back/sides, nato neck, 14/20 fret bound rosewood fingerboard with pearl dot inlay, rosewood bridge with white black dot pins, 3 per side chrome diecast tuners. Available in White finish. Disc. 1992.

$195 $125
Last Mfr.'s Sug. Retail was $360.

S-49 — dreadnought style, mahogany top, round soundhole, black pickguard, 3 stripe bound body/rosette, mahogany back/sides, nato neck, 14/20 fret bound rosewood fingerboard with pearl dot inlay, rosewood bridge with white black dot pins, bound peghead, 3 per side chrome diecast tuners. Available in Natural finish. Disc. 1992.

$175 $115
Last Mfr.'s Sug. Retail was $360.

S-60 — dreadnought style, spruce top, round soundhole, black pickguard, 3 stripe bound body/rosette, rosewood back/sides, nato neck, 14/20 fret fingerboard with pearl dot inlay, rosewood bridge with white black dot pins, 3 per side chrome diecast tuners. Available in Natural finish. Disc. 1992.

$195 $125
Last Mfr.'s Sug. Retail was $390.

S-70 — dreadnought style, spruce top, round soundhole, black pickguard, 3 stripe bound body/rosette, Hawaiian koa back/sides, nato neck, 14/20 fret rosewood fingerboard with pearl dot inlay, rosewood bridge with white black dot pins, 3 per side chrome diecast tuners. Available in Natural finish. Disc. 1994.

$200 $125
Last Mfr.'s Sug. Retail was $400.

S-80 S — dreadnought style, solid spruce top, round soundhole, black pickguard, 3 stripe bound body/rosette, jacaranda back/sides, nato neck, 14/20 fret bound rosewood fingerboard with pearl dot inlay, rosewood bridge with white black dot pins, bound peghead, 3 per side gold diecast tuners. Available in Natural finish. Disc. 1998.

$300 $175
Last Mfr.'s Sug. Retail was $630.

Studio Series

Studio models are correctly proportioned sized classical models, and are available in 1/4 size, 1/2 size, 3/4 size, and full sized scale lengths. Studio Series models come equipped with a quality gig bag and shoulder strap.

STUDIO — classical style, spruce top, round soundhole, mahogany back/sides, nato neck, 12/19 fret rosewood fingerboard, rosewood tied bridge, slotted peghead, 3 per side chrome tuners. Available in Natural finish. Current mfr.

JS141 1/4 size, 22 1/2" scale.
Mfr.'s Sug. Retail $159

JS241 1/2 size, 23 5/16" scale.
Mfr.'s Sug. Retail $159

JS341 3/4 size, 24 3/4" scale.
Mfr.'s Sug. Retail $169

JS441 Full size, 25 11/16" scale.
Mfr.'s Sug. Retail $179

ACOUSTIC ELECTRIC

All models in this series have the following features: single round cutaway folk style, round soundhole, 3 stripe bound body/rosette, 21 fret bound rosewood fingerboard with pearl dot inlay, rosewood bridge with white black dot pins, body matching bound peghead, 3 per side chrome die cast tuners, crystal bridge pickups, 3 band EQ, unless otherwise listed.

ES Series

ES-31 C — single rounded cutaway dreadnought style body, spruce top, round soundhole, black pickguard, 3 stripe bound body/rosette, nato back/sides/neck, 14/20 fret rosewood fingerboard with pearl dot inlay, rosewood bridge with white pins, 3 per side chrome tuners. piezo bridge pickup, DJ-2 2 band EQ. Available in Black finish. Mfr. 1994 to date.

Mfr.'s Sug. Retail $419 $295 $195 $125

ES-32 C — single rounded cutaway dreadnought style, spruce top, round soundhole, black pickguard, 5 stripe bound body/rosette, mahogany back/sides, nato neck, 14/20 fret rosewood fingerboard with pearl dot inlay, rosewood bridge with white black dot pins, 3 per side chrome tuners, piezo bridge pickup, DJ-2 2 band EQ. Available in Natural finish. Mfr. 1994 to date.

Mfr.'s Sug. Retail $369 $275 $175 $125

ES-312 12-String — similar to the ES-32 C, except features non-cutaway body, nato back and sides, 12 string dreadnought style, 6 per side tuners. Available in Natural finish. Mfr. 1994 to date.

Mfr.'s Sug. Retail $369 $275 $175 $125

ES-33 C — single round cutaway dreadnought style, spruce top, round soundhole, black pickguard, stripe bound body/rosette, mahogany back/sides, nato neck, 14/20 fret rosewood fingerboard with pearl dot inlay, rosewood bridge with white black dot pins, 3 per side chrome diecast tuners, piezo bridge pickup, 3 band EQ control. Available in Natural finish. Disc. 1998.

$195 $125
Last Mfr.'s Sug. Retail was $480.

ES-33 C-TOB — similar to ES-33 C, except has single round cutaway, 6 crystal bridge pickups, 2 band EQ control. Available in Transparent Orangeburst finish. Disc. 1998.

$225 $125
Last Mfr.'s Sug. Retail was $490.

ES-33 C TOB
courtesy Kaman Music Corp.

TS-52 CR
courtesy Kaman Music Corp.

TS-26 C
courtesy Kaman Music Corp.

Grading	100%	EXCELLENT	AVERAGE

ES-40 C — single round cutaway dreadnought style, round soundhole, black pickguard, 3 stripe bound body/rosette, nato neck, 14/20 fret bound rosewood fingerboard with pearl dot inlay, rosewood bridge with white black dot pins, bound peghead, 3 per side chrome diecast tuners, piezo bridge pickup, 2 band EQ control. Available in Natural finish. Disc. 1994.

		$195	$125

Last Mfr.'s Sug. Retail was $390.

TC Series

TC-28 C — single round cutaway classic style, spruce top, round soundhole, 3 stripe bound body, wood inlay rosette, rosewood back/sides, nato neck, 12/19 fret rosewood fingerboard, tied rosewood bridge, 3 per side gold tuners with pearloid buttons, piezo bridge pickup, 4 band EQ. Available in Natural finish. Current mfr.

Mfr.'s Sug. Retail	$629	$450	$225	$175

TC-30 C — similar to the TC-28 C, except features walnut back/sides. Available in Amber finish. Current mfr.

Mfr.'s Sug. Retail	$629	$450	$225	$175

TC-48 MC — single round cutaway classic style, figured maple top, round soundhole, 3 stripe bound body, wood inlay rosette, figured maple back/sides, nato neck, 12/19 fret rosewood fingerboard, tied rosewood bridge, figured maple veneered peghead, 3 per side gold tuners with pearloid buttons, piezo bridge pickup, 4 band EQ. Available in Natural finish. Mfd. 1994 to 1998.

		$295	$175

Last Mfr.'s Sug. Retail was $650.

TS Series

TS-26 C — mahogany top/back/sides, abalone body purfling, nato neck, pearl diamond fingerboard inlay, black white dot bridge pins, gold diecast tuners. Available in White/Black finish. Mfd. 1994 to 1998.

		$325	$200

Last Mfr.'s Sug. Retail was $650.

TS-33 C — single rounded cutaway body, spruce top, mahogany back/sides, nato neck, rosewood fingerboard, rosewood bridge with black bridgepins, gold diecast tuners. Available in Natural finish. Current mfr.

Mfr.'s Sug. Retail	$569	$400	$275	$195

TS-38 C — single rounded cutaway dreadnought body, spruce top, round soundhole, rosewood back/sides, nato neck, 14/20 fret rosewood fingerboard with pearl dot inlay, rosewood bridge with white bridgepins, chrome diecast tuners. Available in Natural finish. Current mfr.

Mfr.'s Sug. Retail	$559	$395	$275	$195

TS-41 C — single round cutaway dreadnought style, spruce top, round soundhole, black pickguard with white outline, 3 stripe bound body/rosette, daowood back/sides, nato neck, 14/20 fret bound rosewood fingerboard with pearl dot inlay, rosewood bridge with white black dot pins, 3 per side chrome diecast tuners, bridge pickup, 4 band EQ control. Available in Black finish. Disc 1994.

		$225	$125

Last Mfr.'s Sug. Retail was $450.

TS-46 C — single round cutaway dreadnought style, spruce top, round soundhole, black pickguard with white outline, 3 stripe bound body/rosette, daowood back/sides, nato neck, 14/20 fret bound rosewood fingerboard with pearl dot inlay, rosewood bridge with white black dot pins, 3 per side chrome diecast tuners, bridge pickup, 4 band EQ control. Available in White finish. Disc. 1992.

		$225	$125

Last Mfr.'s Sug. Retail was $450.

TS-49 C — single round cutaway dreadnought style, mahogany top, round soundhole, black pickguard, 3 stripe bound body/rosette, mahogany back/sides, nato neck, 14/20 fret bound rosewood fingerboard with pearl dot inlay, rosewood bridge with white black dot pins, bound peghead, 3 per side chrome diecast tuners, bridge pickup, 4 band EQ control. Available in Natural finish. Disc. 1992.

		$225	$125

Last Mfr.'s Sug. Retail was $450.

TS-50 C — rounded cutaway dreadnought style, spruce top, round soundhole, black pickguard, 3 stripe bound body/rosette, flame maple back/sides, maple neck, 20 fret bound rosewood fingerboard with pearl dot inlay, rosewood bridge with white black dot pins, body matching peghead, 3 per side chrome diecast tuners, bridge pickup, 4 band volume/EQ control. Available in Blue Stain, Ebony Stain and Red Stain finishes. Disc. 1994.

		$300	$175

Last Mfr.'s Sug. Retail was $600.

TS-52 C MR — single round cutaway dreadnought style, ash top, round soundhole, black trilamated pickguard, ash back/sides, nato neck, 20 fret bound rosewood fingerboard with pearl dot inlay, rosewood bridge with white black dot pins, body matching bound peghead with screened logo, 3 per side chrome die cast tuners, piezo bridge pickup, 4 band EQ. Available in a Red Stain finishes. Mfd. 1994 to 1998.

		$300	$200

Last Mfr.'s Sug. Retail was $700.

TS-52 C ME — similar to the TS-52 CMR, except in an Ebony Stain finish. Mfd. 1994 to 1998.

		$300	$200

Last Mfr.'s Sug. Retail was $700.

TS-58 — jumbo style, cedar top, round soundhole, tortoise pickguard, 3 stripe bound body, wood inlay rosette, daowood back/sides, nato neck, 14/20 fret bound rosewood fingerboard with pearl diamond dot inlay, rosewood bridge with white black dot pins, bound peghead, 3 per side gold diecast tuners, piezo bridge pickup, 4 band EQ control. Available in Natural finish. Disc. 1998.

		$325	$200

Last Mfr.'s Sug. Retail was $650.

Grading		100%	EXCELLENT	AVERAGE

TS-60 — dreadnought style, spruce top, round soundhole, black pickguard, 3 stripe bound body/rosette, rosewood back/sides, nato neck, 14/20 fret fingerboard with pearl dot inlay, rosewood bridge with white black dot pins, 3 per side chrome diecast tuners, piezo bridge pickup, 4 band EQ. Available in Natural finish. Disc. 1994.

$250 $150
Last Mfr.'s Sug. Retail was $500.

TS-60 C — similar to TS-60, except has single round cutaway, piezo bridge pickup, 4 band EQ. Disc. 1994.

$275 $175
Last Mfr.'s Sug. Retail was $550.

TS-612 — dreadnought style, spruce top, round soundhole, black pickguard, 3 stripe bound body/rosette, rosewood back/sides, nato neck, 14/20 fret bound rosewood fingerboard with pearl dot inlay, rosewood bridge with white black dot pins, 6 per side chrome diecast tuners, piezo bridge pickup, 4 band EQ. Available in Natural finish. Disc. 1994.

$275 $175
Last Mfr.'s Sug. Retail was $560.

TS-612 C — similar to 612-TS, except has single round cutaway. Mfd. 1994 to 1998.

$350 $200
Last Mfr.'s Sug. Retail was $720.

TS-74 C — single round cutaway dreadnought style, cedar top, round soundhole, tortoise pickguard, 5 stripe bound body, wood inlay rosette, daowood back/sides, nato neck, 20 fret bound rosewood fingerboard with pearl diamond inlay, rosewood bridge with white black dot pins, bound blackface peghead with screened logo, 3 per side gold diecast tuners, piezo bridge pickup, 4 band EQ. Available in Natural finish. Mfd. 1994 to 1998.

$395 $200
Last Mfr.'s Sug. Retail was $700.

TS-91 C — similar to TS-74 C, except features daowood top/back/sides, nato neck. Available in Black finish. Current mfr.

Mfr.'s Sug. Retail	$629	$450	$275	$195

TS-92 C — similar to the TS-91 C, except features flame maple top/back/sides, maple neck. Available in Red Stain finish. Disc. 1994.

$250 $150
Last Mfr.'s Sug. Retail was $520.

TS-95 C — similar to the TS-91 C, except features flame maple top/back/sides, maple neck. Available in Ebony Stain finish. Disc. 1994.

$275 $175
Last Mfr.'s Sug. Retail was $520.

TS-96 C — similar to the TS-91 C, except features daowood top/back/sides, nato neck, black white dot bridge pins. Available in White finish. Disc. 1994.

$250 $150
Last Mfr.'s Sug. Retail was $480.

TS-97 C — similar to the TS-91 C, except features cedar top, daowood back/sides, nato neck, pearl diamond fingerboard inlay, gold diecast tuners. Available in Natural finish. Disc. 1998.

$300 $195
Last Mfr.'s Sug. Retail was $600.

TS-99 C — similar to the TS-91 C, except features daowood top/back/sides, nato neck. Available in Walnut Sunburst finish. Disc. 1994.

$250 $150
Last Mfr.'s Sug. Retail was $480.

TS-90C LW
courtesy Kaman Music Corp.

Artist Series

Artist series models feature the design of a slim body and a single cutaway.

TC-29 C — single round cutaway classic style, cedar top, round soundhole, 3 stripe bound body, wood inlay rosette, rosewood back/sides, nato neck, 19 fret rosewood fingerboard, tied rosewood bridge with wood marquetry inlay, 3 per side gold tuners with pearloid tuners, piezo bridge pickup, 3 band EQ. Available in Natural finish. Mfd. 1994 to 1998.

$375 $195
Last Mfr.'s Sug. Retail was $650.

TS-90 C-DW (DARK WALNUT) — burled mahogany top/back/sides, nato neck. Available in a Dark Walnut Stain finish. Mfr. 1994 to date.

Mfr.'s Sug. Retail	$699	$475	$250	$200

TS-90 C-LW — similar to the TS-90 C-DW (Dark Walnut), except finished in a Light Walnut Stain. Mfd. 1994 to 1998.

$325 $225
Last Mfr.'s Sug. Retail was $740.

TS-93 C-A — similar to TS-90 C-DW, except features silky oak top/back/sides, maple neck. Available in Amber finish. Mfd. 1994 to 1998.

$300 $195
Last Mfr.'s Sug. Retail was $680.

TS-98 C-FM — similar to TS-93 C-A, except features flame maple top/back/sides, maple neck. Available in Cherry Sunburst or Blue Stain finishes. Mfd. 1994 to 1998.

$300 $195
Last Mfr.'s Sug. Retail was $680.

TS-93 C
courtesy Kaman Music Corp.

J

Grading	100%	EXCELLENT	AVERAGE

ACOUSTIC ELECTRIC BASS

ES-100 C — single rounded cutaway body, round soundhole, black pickguard, nato neck, 14/20 fret bound rosewood fingerboard with dot inlay, rosewood bridge with white black dot pins, bound peghead, 2 per side chrome diecast tuners, piezo bridge pickup, 2 band EQ control. Available in Maple (ES-100 C-M), Natural (ES-100 C-4), and Sunburst (ES-100 C-1) finishes. Mfr. 1994 to date.

Mfr.'s Sug. Retail	$739	$550	$325	$250

JAX

Instruments produced in Taiwan during the early 1980s.

These solid body guitars consist of entry level designs based on classic American models.

(Source: Tony Bacon and Paul Day, The Guru's Guitar Guide)

JAY G

See chapter on House Brands.

This trademark has been identified as a *sub-brand* from the budget line of CHRIS guitars by the Jackson-Guldan company of Columbus, Ohio.

(Source: Willie G. Moseley, Stellas & Stratocasters)

J.B. PLAYER

Instruments currently produced in Asia; specific model Classical guitars are built in Spain. Distributed by MBT International of Charleston, South Carolina.

MBT International, owner of J.B. Player, is the parent company to the Hondo Guitar Company, Musicorp, Engl USA, and MBT Lighting and Sound.

J.B. Player offers a wide range of entry to student level instruments in acoustic or electric solid body guitars and basses. Many higher quality models that are currently offered may appeal to working musicians, and feature such parts as Schaller hardware, Wilkinson bridges, and APC pickups. The current catalog illustrates the four different levels offered: the **JBP Artist**, **Standard**, **Professional**, and **Sledgehammer** series.

ACOUSTIC

Artista Series Classical

J.B. Player offers four models of classical guitars, built in Spain. The **Granada** (list $299) has an Oregon pine top, and mahogany body. The **Morena** (list $385) has an Oregon pine top and rosewood body, while the **Flamenco** (list $399) has a sycamore body. The **Segovia** (list $579) features a solid cedar top and rosewood body.

Artist Series

JBA-1010 — grand auditorium style, flame maple top, round soundhole, multiple-ply body binding, mahogany back/sides, nato neck, 14/20 fret rosewood fingerboard with dot inlay, rosewood bridge with white dot pins, 3 per side diecast tuners. Available in Sunburst finish. Mfr. 1998 to date.

Mfr.'s Sug. Retail	$399	$275	$195	$135

JBA-1150 — auditorium style, solid cedar top, round soundhole, multiple-ply body binding, rosewood back/sides, mahogany neck, 14/20 fret rosewood fingerboard with dot inlay, rosewood bridge with white dot pins, blackface peghead, 3 per side diecast tuners. Available in Natural finish. Mfr. 1998 to date.

Mfr.'s Sug. Retail	$525	$375	$250	$175

JBA-1200 — dreadnought style, solid cedar top, black pickguard, round soundhole, mahogany back/sides/neck, 14/20 fret rosewood fingerboard with dot inlay, rosewood bridge with white dot pins, 3 per side diecast tuners. Available in Natural finish. Current mfr.

Mfr.'s Sug. Retail	$430	$325	$225	$150

Add $110 for 2 piece mahogany back and sides (Model JBA-1250).

Add $290 for 2 piece ovankol back and sides (Model JBA-1275).

JBA-1200-12 — similar to the JBA-1200, except features a 12-string configuration, 6 per side tuners. Available in Natural finish. Disc. 1998.

		$250	$125

Last Mfr.'s Sug. Retail was $475.

JBA-2000 — dreadnought style, solid spruce top, tortoise pickguard, round soundhole, 4 stripe bound body, abalone rosette, rosewood back/sides, mahogany neck, 14/20 fret bound rosewood fingerboard with abalone block inlay, rosewood bridge with white black dot pins, 3 per side gold tuners. Available in Natural finish. Mfr. 1994 to 1996.

		$275	$175

Last Mfr.'s Sug. Retail was $540.

JBA-1500 — similar to the JBA-2000, except features mahogany back and sides, no abalone rosette, black pickguard. Disc. 1998.

		$200	$125

Last Mfr.'s Sug. Retail was $395.

JBA-1520 — similar to the JBA-2000, except features mahogany back and sides, abalone-style rosette, black pickguard. Mfr. 1998 to date

Mfr.'s Sug. Retail	$299	$225	$150	$100

JBA-460
courtesy J.B. Player

Grading		100%	EXCELLENT	AVERAGE

JBA-2200 — similar to the JBA-2000, except features back and sides, herringbone rosette/body binding, bound fingerboard with pearl palm tree inlay. Current mfr.

Mfr.'s Sug. Retail	$620	$500	$325	$225

Standard Series

JB-95 COUNTRY JUMBO — jumbo style, maple top, round soundhole, 3 stripe bound body/rosette, mahogany back/sides, mahogany neck, 14/20 fret rosewood fingerboard with pearl dot inlay, rosewood bridge with black bridgepins, 3 per side chrome tuners. Available in Natural satin finish. Mfr. 1998 to date.

Mfr.'s Sug. Retail	$290	$200	$135	$95

JB-402 — dreadnought style, spruce top, round soundhole, black pickguard, bound body, 5 stripe rosette, nato back/sides/neck, 14/20 fret bound rosewood fingerboard with pearl dot inlay, rosewood bridge with white black dot pins, 3 per side chrome diecast tuners. Available in Natural finish. Current mfr.

Mfr.'s Sug. Retail	$275	$200	$135	$95

JB-403 — similar to JB-402, except has multiple-ply body binding. Available in Natural finish. Mfr. 1991 to 1994, 1998 to date.

Mfr.'s Sug. Retail	$299	$210	$150	$100

JB-405-12 12-STRING — dreadnought style, 12 string configuration, spruce top, round soundhole, black pickguard, stripe bound body/rosette, ash back/sides, bound mahogany neck, 14/20 fret bound rosewood fingerboard with pearl dot inlay, rosewood bridge with white black dot pins, 6 per side chrome diecast tuners. Available in Natural finish. Current mfr.

Mfr.'s Sug. Retail	$335	$235	$150	$100

JB-407 — dreadnought style, ash top, round soundhole, black pickguard, bound body, 5 stripe rosette, ash back/sides, nato mahogany neck, 14/20 fret bound fingerboard with pearl dot inlay, rosewood bridge with white black dot pins, 3 per side chrome diecast tuners. Available in Tobacco Sunburst finish. Current mfr.

Mfr.'s Sug. Retail	$280	$200	$125	$85

This model was optionally available with an acoustic pickup, active volume/3 band EQ (JB-407 E). This option discontinued in 1998.

JB-408 — similar to the JB-407, except features mahogany neck. Available in Transparent Blonde finish. Mfr. 1998 to date.

Mfr.'s Sug. Retail	$325	$225	$150	$100

JB-409 — dreadnought style, spruce top, round soundhole, black pickguard, bound body, 5 stripe rosette, mahogany back/sides/neck, 14/20 fret bound fingerboard with pearl dot inlay, rosewood bridge with white black dot pins, 3 per side chrome diecast tuners. Available in Black, Natural, and Tobacco Sunburst finish. Mfr. 1998 to date.

Mfr.'s Sug. Retail	$315	$210	$150	$100

JBL-409 — similar to the JB-409, except features a left-handed configuration. Available in Black, Natural, and Tobacco Sunburst finish. Mfr. 1998 to date.

Mfr.'s Sug. Retail	$330	$225	$150	$100

JB-450 — dreadnought style, spruce top, round soundhole, black pickguard, imitation abalone bound body/rosette, ash back/sides, mahogany neck, 14/20 fret bound rosewood fingerboard with hexagon imitation abalone inlay, rosewood bridge with white black dot pins, 3 per side chrome diecast tuners. Available in Natural finish. Current mfr.

Mfr.'s Sug. Retail	$315	$215	$150	$100

JB-502 — dreadnought style, spruce top, round soundhole, black pickguard, bound body, 5 ring rosette, mahogany finishes nato back/sides, nato neck, 14/20 fret rosewood fingerboard with pearl dot inlay, rosewood bridge with black bridgepins, 3 per side chrome diecast tuners. Available in Natural finish. Mfr. 1998 to date.

Mfr.'s Sug. Retail	$360	$250	$175	$115

JB-502-12 — similar to JB-502 except features a 12-string configuration, 6 per side tuners. Available in Natural finish. Mfr. 1998 to date.

Mfr.'s Sug. Retail	$395	$275	$175	$125

JB-506 — similar to JB-502 except features a blackface peghead. Available in Violin (shaded Brown Sunburst) finish. Mfr. 1998 to date.

Mfr.'s Sug. Retail	$375	$275	$175	$125

JB-505 — classical style, spruce top, round soundhole, herringbone bound body, wooden inlay rosette, ash back/sides, mahogany neck, 12/18 fret rosewood fingerboard, rosewood bridge, 3 per side chrome tuners with nylon buttons. Available in Natural finish. Disc. 1994.

			$130	$85

Last Mfr.'s Sug. Retail was $260.

JB-1000 — dreadnought style, spruce top, oval soundhole, black pickguard, 3 stripe bound body/rosette, mahogany back/sides/neck, 14/20 fret bound rosewood fingerboard with pearl dot inlay, rosewood bridge with white black dot pins, 3 per side chrome tuners. Available in Black and White (White finish model has black chrome tuners) finishes. Disc. 1996.

			$175	$115

Last Mfr.'s Sug. Retail was $325.

Add $70 for flame maple top and jacaranda back/sides (available in Natural finish).

JB-8000 — similar to the JB-1000, except features round soundhole, bound body, 5 stripe rosette, rosewood back/sides. Available in Natural finish. Disc. 1994.

			$200	$125

Last Mfr.'s Sug. Retail was $425.

JBA-2200
courtesy J.B. Player

J

Grading	100%	EXCELLENT	AVERAGE

JB-9000 — similar to the JB-1000, except features round soundhole, bound body, 5 stripe rosette. Available in Tobacco Sunburst finish. Disc. 1996.

	$195	**$125**

Last Mfr.'s Sug. Retail was $395.

JB-9000-12 — similar to JB-9000, except has 12 strings, black white dot pins, 6 per side tuners. Available in Natural finish.

	$200	**$135**

Last Mfr.'s Sug. Retail was $410.

JB-5000 — classical style, spruce top, round soundhole, bound body, wooden inlay rosette, mahogany back/sides/neck, 12/18 fret rosewood fingerboard, rosewood bridge, 3 per side gold tuners with pearloid buttons. Available in Natural finish. Disc. 1994.

	$175	**$100**

Last Mfr.'s Sug. Retail was $350.

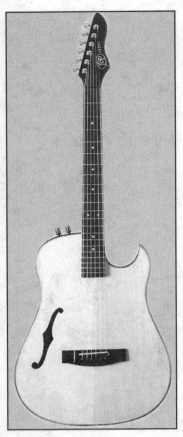

JBA-260
courtesy J.B. Player

Ridgeville by J.B. Player Series

J.B. Player's **Ridgeville** series offers three different model acoustic guitars. The **JBR-20** dreadnought (list $229) has a spruce top, mahogany back and sides, and diecast tuners. The **JBR-30** dreadnought (list $259) has a spruce top and Ovankol back and sides. The **JBR-10 C** classical (list $199) has an agathis top, mahogany back and sides, and plank-style tuners. All models are available in a Natural finish.

ACOUSTIC ELECTRIC

Artist Series Acoustic Electric

JB-300 E — single round cutaway dreadnought style, maple top, black pickguard, round soundhole, 3 stripe bound body/rosette, ash back/sides, mahogany neck, 20 fret bound rosewood fingerboard with pearl dot inlay, rosewood bridge with white black dot pins, bound blackface peghead with screened logo, 3 per side chrome tuners, acoustic pickup, volume/presence/3 band EQ control. Available in Brownburst, Cherryburst, Natural and White finishes. Mfr. 1994 to date.

Mfr.'s Sug. Retail	$440	$325	$175	$125

JBA-50 CEQ NYLON STRING — single rounded cutaway body, flame maple top, round soundhole, maple back/sides, mahogany neck, 12/19 fret rosewood fingerboard, rosewood tied bridge, slotted headstock, 3 per side gold tuners with white buttons, piezo pickup, active electronics. Available in Sunburst finish. Mfr. 1998 to date.

Mfr.'s Sug. Retail	$525	$375	$250	$175

JBA-65 CEQ — single rounded cutaway folk-style body, flame maple top, round soundhole, ash back/sides, mahogany neck, 14/20 fret rosewood fingerboard with white diamond inlay, rosewood bridge with white bridgepins, 3 per side gold tuners, piezo pickup, 3 band EQ, presence control, active electronics, pop-out battery compartment. Available in Natural (JBA-65 NCEQ) and Tobacco Sunburst (JBA-65 CEQ) finishes. Mfr. 1998 to date.

Mfr.'s Sug. Retail	$599	$375	$250	$175

JBA-97 CEQ — single rounded cutaway jumbo-style body, spruce top, round soundhole, mahogany back/sides/neck, 14/20 fret rosewood fingerboard with white dot inlay, rosewood bridge with white bridgepins, 3 per side gold tuners, piezo pickup, 3 band EQ, presence control, active electronics, pop-out battery compartment. Available in Natural satin finishes. Mfr. 1998 to date.

Mfr.'s Sug. Retail	$495	$350	$225	$150

JBA-260 — single cutaway alder body with carved tone chambers, spruce top, f-hole, mahogany neck, 21 fret rosewood fingerboard with dot inlay, rosewood bridge with black pins, 6 on a side diecast tuners, piezo pickup, volume/tone controls. Available in Natural finish. Disc. 1998.

	$400	**$250**

Last Mfr.'s Sug. Retail was $740.

JBA-910 — single round cutaway body, solid cedar top, round soundhole, body binding, 3 ring rosette, mahogany back/sides/neck, 14/20 fret bound rosewood fingerboard with pearl dot inlay, rosewood bridge with black bridgepins, 3 per side gold Schaller tuners with white pearloid buttons, piezo pickup, 3 band EQ, active electronics, 1/4" and XLR outputs. Available in Natural finishes. Current mfr.

Mfr.'s Sug. Retail	$775	$550	$375	$250

KJ-330-PU — single rounded cutaway body, tiger maple top, oval soundhole, abalone bound body/rosette, tiger maple back/sides, mahogany neck, 20 fret bound rosewood fingerboard with pearl split block inlay, rosewood bridge with white black dot pins, 3 per side gold tuners with amber buttons, acoustic pickup, 4 band EQ, active electronics. Available in Brownburst and Natural finishes. Mfr. 1994 to date.

Mfr.'s Sug. Retail	$675	$500	$325	$225

KJ-609-WPU — single round cutaway body, spruce top, round soundhole, 3 stripe bound body, abalone rosette, maple back/sides, mahogany neck, 14/20 fret rosewood fingerboard with pearl dot inlay, 12th fret pearl horns inlay, rosewood bridge with white black dot pins, 3 per side chrome tuners, acoustic pickup, active 4 band EQ, active electronics. Available in Natural finish. Mfr. 1994 to date.

Mfr.'s Sug. Retail	$660	$495	$325	$225

KJ-705-WPU — similar to the KJ-609-WPU, except features mahogany back/sides/neck. Available in Tobacco Sunburst finish. Disc. 1998.

	$425	**$250**

Last Mfr.'s Sug. Retail was $720.

JBA-910
courtesy J.B. Player

Grading	100%	EXCELLENT	AVERAGE

ACOUSTIC ELECTRIC BASS

JBA-3000 EAB — single round cutaway folk style, select spruce top, round soundhole, 3 stripe bound body/rosette, mahogany back/sides/neck, 22 fret bound rosewood fingerboard with pearl dot inlay, rosewood strings thru bridge, 2 per side chrome tuners, acoustic pickup, active 3 band EQ. Available in Natural finish. Mfr. 1994 to date.

Mfr.'s Sug. Retail	$720	$500	$325	$225

JBA-3000 EAB
courtesy J.B. Player

J D S

Instruments currently built in Asia. Exclusively distributed by Wolf Imports of St. Louis, Missouri.

J D S Limited Edition instruments are medium quality acoustic and solid body electric guitars that feature designs based on popular American classics.

JOHN PEARSE

Instruments built in Center Valley, Pennsylvania from 1996 to 1998. Distributed by Breezy Ridge Instruments, Inc. of Center Valley, Pennsylvania.

Starting with Herman Weissenborn's unusual styling, Breezy Ridge Instruments modified the design specifications and created a unique new generation of slide guitars. The John Pearse Vintage Acoustic Steel Guitars were available in 4 different models for the time span of about two years.

ACOUSTIC

All models are 37 7/8" in length, 2 7/8" deep, 10 1/4" wide at treble bout, and 15 3/8" wide at bass bout.

The **#100 ACJ** (retail list $1,695) has a solid acajoux top/back/sides/fingerboard, rosewood bridge, orange wood binding, and a vintage satin finish. The **#200 APM** (list $1,795) has an Engelmann spruce top, maple back and sides, rosewood fingerboard/bridge/binding, and vintage satinized Gold varnish; while the **#300 BW** has figured manzoniza walnut back/sides/fingerboard, rosewood and orange wood rope binding (list $1,995). Pearse's **#400 BAF** has highly figured afromosia top/back/sides/fingerboard, rosewood bridge, rosewood and orange wood rope binding, and a vintage satin finish for a retail price of $1,995. If the company name seems familiar, it's because Breezy Ridge is connected with John Pearse Strings - and John Pearse Strings has been producing some pretty fine guitar strings for quite some time.

JOHNSON

Instruments currently produced in Asia. Distributed by the Music Link of Brisbane, California.

The Music Link's Johnson guitars are offered in a wide range of acoustic and electric guitars, with prices aimed at the entry level and student guitarists.

There are also 8 different practice amps in the Johnson line, as well as numerous accessories like cases, Quartz tuners, and tuning machines. For further information regarding the Johnson products, contact the Music Link through the Index of Current Manufacturers located in the back of this edition.

ACOUSTIC

Johnson dreadnought models have laminated bodies and nato wood necks. Retail prices range from $89 up to $179. The Jumbo Cutaway model **JG-740** has a laminated flame maple top veneer, and is available in Blue, Green, Red, and Sunburst (list $199). Some models are also available with a piezo bridge pickup and on-board preamps.

Metal Body Series

Resonator models feature chrome-plated bell brass bodies, mahogany necks, 14/19 fret rosewood fingerboards, and 3 per side Gotoh tuners. The **JM-998-C Style 0-Cutaway** has a single rounded cutaway body (retail $1,650). Other Sterling Style O models include the full body **JM-998-D Style 0** is the same as the cutaway model (list $895); the **JM-998-R Style 0** full body model has a different pattern on the resonator plate (list $895).

Tricone Resonator Series

Johnson Tricone resonator guitars are modeled after the original, pre-World War II guitars. Models include chrome-plated bell brass bodies, mahogany necks, 12/19 fret rosewood fingerboards, and 3 per side Gotoh tuners. The **JM-991 Style I** plain body (no design) model lists at $1,650. The **JM-992 Style II** (list $2,200) has the Wild Rose engraved design; the **JM-993 Style III** (list $2,900) has the engraved Lily of the Valley design; and the **JM-993 Style IV** (list $3,500) has the engraved Chrysanthemum design.

JOHNSON GUITARS

Instruments currently built in Talkkeetna, Alaska.

Luthier Johnson started building guitars in 1981. Originally working out of a gutted R.V. trailer, Johnson now operates a one-man shop located in his home in rural Alaska which is located at the base of Mt. McKinley (North America's tallest mountain). Johnson has narrowed down his line of guitar models to a few select models; and as the single builder can give close attention to each commissioned guitar during construction. Johnson offers such custom options as a custom size or design, Englemann spruce or cedar tops, flame walnut back and sides, and on-board electronics. A standard hard shell case is included in the retail prices.

ACOUSTIC

Johnson offers 5 acoustic models and one archtop model. All models feature a Sitka spruce top, East Indian rosewood back and sides, 25.5" scale ebony fingerboard. The **Size A** Concert lists at $2,000, and is also available in a Classical version at $2,500. The **Size C** Grand Auditorium lists at $2,000, as well as the **Size D** Dreadnought and the **Size E** Jumbo.

The single cutaway **American Archtop** model has a hand-carved Sitka or Engelmann spruce top, flame maple back, sides, and neck, 2 f-holes, and an ebony fingerboard, tailpiece, and bridge (list $4,000).

J H S

Instruments built in Japan during the late 1970s.

The J H S trademark was the initials of the UK importer **John Hornby Skewes**, who founded his import company in 1965 (See ENCORE). The generally good quality instruments featured both original designs and those based on classic American designs. The line focused primarily on solid body guitars, much like the Encore line today.

(Source: Tony Bacon and Paul Day, The Guru's Guitar Guide)

JISHENG

Instruments currently produced in China. Distributed by Jisheng Musical Instruments Manufacturing Ltd. of Guangzhou, China.

Jisheng Musical Instruments Manufacturing Ltd. is currently offering a wide range of classical and dreadnought acoustic guitar models, as well as some acoustic/electric dreadnought models (some with single cutaway bodies). The company also produces violin models, and numerous gig bag/carrying bags for guitars, drums, and other musical instruments. For further information regarding company contacts, model pricing and specifications, contact Jisheng Musical Instruments Manufacturing Ltd. through the Index of Current Manufacturers located in the back of this edition.

J T G OF NASHVILLE

Instruments built in Japan. Distributed by JTG of Nashville located in Nashville, Tennessee.

The JTG of Nashville company is currently importing quality Japanese and Mexican acoustic guitars. For further information regarding JTG of Nashville's acoustic models, please contact JTG via the Index of Current Manufacturers located in the back of this edition.

JUDD GUITARS

Instruments currently built in Cranbrook (British Columbia), Canada.

Judd custom instruments are produced in Cranbrook, British Columbia. For information regarding model specifications and pricing, please contact Judd Guitars via the Index of Current Manufacturers located in the back of this edition.

JUNIOR

See chapter on House Brands.

This trademark has been identified as a Gibson built budget line available from 1919 through 1926. The pegheads carry no logo, and essentially are 'no-frills' versions of low end Gibsons. They will have a label different from the standard Gibson label of the time, but still credit Gibson as the manufacturer. As a Gibson-built budget line instrument these guitars do not possess an adjustable truss rod in the neck.

(Source: Walter Carter, Gibson Guitars: 100 Years of an American Icon)

J

K & S

Instruments currently built in Mexico. Distributed by K & S Guitars of Berkeley, California.

George Katechis and Marc Silber (K & S), two noted guitar experts, have re-introduced the Acoustic Hawaiian Slide Guitar. Born in the 1920s, this guitar design enjoyed moderate success before being overtaken by the louder resonator-driven National-style guitars of the early 1930s. The new instruments are modeled after designs by Weissenborn, Hilo, and Knutsen.

Prices start at $700 for these solid wood Acoustic Hawaiian Slide Guitars. Wood options include Canadian Cedar top and Spanish Cedar body; Sitka Spruce top and Spanish Cedar, Honduras Mahogany, Maple, or California Koa (Acacia) body, or all California Koa. Instruments are bound and feature Van Gent tuners.

STEPHEN KAKOS

Instruments built in Mound, Minnesota since 1975.

Luthier Stephen Kakos began building classical guitars in 1972, and turned to full time building in 1975. Kakos concentrates specifically on classical acoustics, although he has built a few flamenco guitars on request. In addition to guitar building, Kakos also performs some repairs. For further information on models and pricing, please contact luthier Kakos via the Index of Current Manufacturers located in the back of this book.

KALAMAZOO

See chapter on House Brands.

In the late 1930s, the Gibson guitar company decided to offer their own entry level guitars. While similar to models built for other distributors (Cromwell, Fascinator, or Capital) in construction, the Kalamazoo line was originally only offered for about five years. Models included flattop and archtop acoustics, lap steels (and amps), and mandolins.

Pre-War Kalamazoo instruments, like other Gibson budget instruments, do not have an adjustable truss rod (a key difference), different construction techniques, and no identifying Gibson logo.

In the mid 1960s, Gibson again released an entry level series of guitars under the Kalamazoo trademark, except all models were electric solid body guitars (except a flattop acoustic) that had a double offset cutaway body, bolt-on necks, six on a side headstock, and 1 or 2 pickups. The body profile of late 1960s models then switched to even dual cutaways. The second run of Kalamazoo models came to an end in the early 1970s. These Post-War models do feature an adjustable truss rod.

Kalamazoo serial numbers are impressed into the back of the headstock, and feature six digits like the regular Gibson line. However, the Kalamazoo numbers do not match or correspond with the Gibson serialization (in the back of this book). Further information regarding Kalamazoo serialization will appear in future editions of the Blue Book of Guitars.

(Source: Walter Carter, Gibson Guitars: 100 Years of an American Icon)

KALIL

Instruments currently built in McComb, Mississippi.

Luthier Edward E. Kalil builds instruments to custom order. Kalil currently offers acoustic steel and nylon models, as well as solid body electrics. Costs will vary due to complexity of the design and appointments.

Kalil began building guitars after attending a class at Guitar Research and Design (GRD) run by Charles Fox in South Strafford, Vermont. Kalil's class instructor was George Morris. Kalil has been a member of the Guild of American Luthiers (G.A.L.) since 1981, and a member of A.S.I.A. (Association of Stringed Instrument Artisans) since 1988.

Kalil instruments can be easily identified by the 'Kalil' headstock logo. Kalil also offers the Lick En Stik travel guitar, a full scale instrument with a compact body and built in amp (with variable distortion). For further information, contact luthier Edward E. Kalil via the Index of Current Manufacturers located in the back of this edition.

KAMICO

See chapter on House Brands.

This trademark has been identified as the "House Brand" of the Kay Guitar company. As one of the leading suppliers of "House Brand" guitars, Kay also supplied an entry-level budget line of guitars to various musical instrument distributors.

(Source: Willie G. Moseley, Stellas & Stratocasters)

KANSAS

Instruments built near Lawrence, Kansas.

The Kansas guitar company, located outside of Lawrence, Kansas built acoustic guitars from circa 1910 to World War II. During the war, the company switched over to producing gun stocks. After the war (circa 1946 to 1948) the company was sold to the employees, then went out of business.

A Kansas trademark later showed up on guitars featured by the Sears, Roebuck catalog until the catalog folded in 1991. It is unknown whether or not the two Kansas trademarks were related. Further information will be updated in future editions of the **Blue Book of Guitars.**

KAY

See chapter on House Brands.

Between the 1930s and the late 1960s, Kay stringed instruments were manufactured and distributed by the Kay Musical Instrument Company of Chicago, Illinois. Kay, along with Harmony, were the two larger suppliers of "House Brand" instruments for distributors and retailers.

The Kay trademark returned in the 1970s. Currently the instruments are produced in Asia, and are distributed by A.R. Musical Enterprises, Inc. of Fishers, Indiana.

Kay Deluxe Dobro
courtesy Hyatt W. Finley

The roots of the Kay Musical Instruments company begin back in 1890, when the Groeschel Company of Chicago, Illinois first began building bowl-back (or *potato bug*) mandolins. In 1918 Groeschel was changed to the Stromberg-Voisenet Company, and incorporated in 1921. Vice-president C. G. Stromberg directed production of guitars and banjos under the **Mayflower** trademark (See MAYFLOWER). This Stromberg is not to be confused with luthier Charles Stromberg (and son Elmer) of Boston, Massachusetts. Stromberg-Voisenet introduced the process of laminating wood tops and backs in 1924, and also began arching instruments tops and backs. Henry Kay Kuhrmeyer, who later became company president, offered use of his middle name on the more popular *Kay-Kraft* series of Stromberg-Voisenet's guitars, mandolins and banjos.

The Kay era began when Henry Kay Kuhrmeyer bought the Stromberg-Voisenet company in 1928. Kuhrmeyer renamed the company Kay Musical Instruments in 1931, and began mass-producing stringed instruments in large volume. Kay, like Washburn at the turn of the century, claimed production of almost 100,000 instruments a year by the mid 1930s. Kay instruments were both marketed by the company themselves, or produced for *jobbers* (distributors) and retail houses under various names. Rather than produce a list here, the **Blue Book of Guitars** has attempted to identify Kay-produced *House Brands* throughout the alphabetical listing in this text. Many of these instruments were entry level or students instruments then, and should be considered entry level even now. But as Jay Scott (author of **50's Cool: Kay Guitars**) points out, "True, the vast majority of Kay's student-grade and intermediate guitars were awful. But the top of each line - banjo, guitar and mandolin (especially the acoustic and electric jazz guitars and flattop acoustics) - were meritorious pieces of postwar musical art".

Kay introduced upright basses in 1937, and marketed them under both the Kay trademark and K. Meyer (a clever abbreviation of Kuhrmeyer?). After Leo Fender debuted his Precision electric bass at the 1951 NAMM trade show, Kay was the first company to join Fender in the electric bass market as they introduced their K-162 model in 1952. Kay also went on to produce some of the coolest mixtures of classic archtop design and '50s 'modern' acrylic headstocks on the "Gold K" line that debuted in 1957.

The Kay Musical Instrument company was sold to an investment group headed by Sydney Katz in 1955. Katz, a former manager of Harmony's service department, was more aggressive and competitive in the guitar market. Kay's production facilities expanded to try to meet the demand of the guitar market in the late 1950s and early 1960s. A large number of guitars were produced for Sears under their **Silvertone** trademark. At the peak of the guitar boom in 1964, Kay moved into a new million dollar facility located near Chicago's O'Hare Airport.

Unfortunately, by 1965 the guitar market was oversaturated as retail demand fell off. While Kay was still financially sound, Katz sold the company to Seeburg. Seeburg, a large jukebox manufacturer based in Chicago, owned Kay for a period of two years. At this time, the whole guitar industry was feeling the pinch of economics. Seeburg wanted to maintain their niche in the industry by acquiring Valco Guitars, Inc. (See NATIONAL or DOBRO) and producing their own amplifiers to go with the electric Kay guitars. Bob Keyworth, the executive vice-president in charge of Kay, suggested the opposite: Seeburg should sell Kay to Valco.

Robert Engelhardt, who succeeded Louis Dopyera in Valco's ownership in 1962, bought Kay from Seeburg in June 1967. Valco moved into the Kay facilities, but Engelhardt's company was underfinanced from the beginning. Engelhardt did make some deal with an investment group or financial company, but after two years the bills couldn't be paid. The investment group just showed up one day, and changed the plant locks. By 1969 or 1970, both Valco Guitars Inc., and the Kay trademark were out of business.

The rights to the Kay name were acquired by Sol Weindling and Barry Hornstein, who were importing Teisco Del Rey (Kawai) guitars to the U.S. market with their W.M.I. importing company. W.M.I. begins putting the Kay name on the Teisco products beginning in 1973, and continued on through the 1970s.

In 1980, Tony Blair of A.R. Enterprises purchased the Kay trademark. The Kay trademark is now on entry level/beginner guitars built in Asia.

(1950s/1960s company history courtesy Jay Scott, 50's Cool: Kay Guitars; contemporary history courtesy Michael Wright, Vintage Guitar Magazine)

KAY KRAFT

Sometimes hyphenated as KAY-KRAFT.

See KAY.

Instruments produced in Chicago, Illinois from the mid 1920s to the mid 1950s.

Henry Kay Kuhrmeyer, who worked his was up from company secretary, treasurer, and later president of Stromberg-Voisenet, lent his middle name to a popular selling line of guitars, mandolins, and banjos. When Kuhrmeyer gained control of Stromberg-Voisenet and changed the name to Kay Musical Instruments, he continued to use the Kay Kraft trademark. Instruments using this trademark could thus be either Stromberg-Voisenet or Kay (depending on the label) but was still produced by the *sameD company in the same* facilities.

KEL KROYDEN

See chapter on House Brands.

Faced with the severe American Depression of the 1930s, Gibson general manager Guy Hart converted most of company production to toy manufacturing as a means to keep his workforce employed. Kalamazoo Playthings produced wood blocks and wooden pull-toys from 1931 to 1933, while the Kel Kroyden offshoot built toy sailboats. Wood bodies, strings...and masts!

Kel Kroyden brand guitars seem to appear at the same time period that Kel Kroyden Toys were introduced. The "Kel" lettering is horizontal on the headstock, while "Kroyden" is lettered vertically.

(Source: Walter Carter, Gibson Guitars: 100 Years of an American Icon)

T. R. KELLISON

Instruments built in Billings, Montana since 1978.

Luthier T.R. Kellison has been handcrafting custom instruments since 1978.

KENT

Instruments were produced in Korea and Japan circa 1960s. Distributed in the U.S. by Buegeleisen & Jacobson of New York, New York; Maxwell Meyers in Texas; Southland Musical Merchandise Corporation in North Carolina; and Harris Fandel Corporation in Massachusetts.

The Kent trademark was used on a full line of acoustic and solid body electric guitars, banjos, and mandolins imported into the U.S. market during the 1960s. Some of the earlier Kent guitars were built in Japan by either the Teisco company or Guyatone, but the quality level at this time is down at the entry or student level. The majority of the models were built in Korea.

(Source: Walter Murray, Frankenstein Fretworks; and Michael Wright, Guitar Stories Volume One)

The address for Kent Guitars (as distributed by Buegeleisen & Jacobson) during the 1960s was 5 Union Square, New York (New York 10003).

ACOUSTIC

Many of the Kent models were patterned after Gibson models. For example, the Kent **KF-340** is roughly a Gibson Dove knock-off, as it includes the dove motif pickguard, double parallelogram pearl fingerboard inlay, and "moustache" bridge assembly with pearl dove inlay. Notable design differences include the **KF-340**'s zero fret (which the Dove does not), chrome tuners instead of gold, and an obvious quality level. The **KF-340** was available in Natural and Black finishes.

A Kent **KF-340** in average condition averages around $100 in value.

KEYSTONE STATE

See WEYMANN & SONS.

KIMAXE

Instruments produced in Korea and China. Distributed by Kenny & Michael's Co., Inc. of Los Angeles, California.

Kimaxe guitars are manufactured by Sang Jin Industrial Company, Ltd., which has a head office in Seoul, Korea and manufacturing facilities in four different places (Inchon, Bupyong, and Kongju, Korea; Tien Jin, China). Sang Jin Industrial Company, Ltd. is better known as a main supplier of guitars to world famous companies such as Fender, Hohner, and other buyers' own brand names for the past ten years. Sang Jin builds almost 10,000 guitars for these accounts each month. In 1994, Sang Jin established its own subsidary (Kenny and Michael's Company) in Los Angeles in order to distribute their own lines of **Kimaxe** electric guitars and **Corina** acoustic guitars.

KIMBARA

Instruments produced in Japan from the late 1960s to 1990.

Trademark re-introduced to British marketplace in 1995. Instruments currently produced in China. Distributed in the U.K. by FCN Music.

The Kimbara trademark was a brandname used by a UK importer on these Japanese-produced budget level instruments. Kimbara acoustics were first introduced in England in the late 1960s. During the 1970s, the Kimbara trademark was also applied to a number of solid body guitars based on classic American designs as well. Kimbara instruments are generally mid to good quality budget models, and a mainstay in the British market through 1990.

In 1995, FCN Music began importing Chinese-built classical and dreadnought acoustic guitars into England. Retail price-wise, the reborn line is back in its traditional niche.

(Source: Jerry Uwins, Guitar the Magazine [UK])

KIMBERLY

Instruments currently produced in Seoul, Korea. Distributed by the Kimex Trading Co., Ltd. of Seoul, Korea.

Instruments produced in Japan, circa 1960s to early 1970s. Distributed by Lafayette Company catalog sales.

According to initial research by Michael Wright in his book **Guitar Stories Volume One**, Kimberly-branded guitars produced in Japan were sold through the Lafayette company catalog. The U.S. importer during this time period has yet to be pinpointed. Recent evidence that arose indicates that the Teisco company was one of the production companies for this trademark. Photographic evidence of a Kimberly-branded **May Queen** (yes, that infamous Teisco model!) recently arrived at the offices of the **Blue Book of Guitars**. Fellow book enthusiasts are invited to send in photographs and information regarding their Kimberly guitars as well.

Current production of guitars under the Kimberly trademark is the Kimex Trading Co., Ltd. of Seoul, Korea. Kimex produces a number of guitar and bass models that favor classic American designs, and are designed with the entry level guitarist and student in mind.

KINGSTON

Instruments were produced in Japan from 1958 to 1967, and distributed in the U.S. by Westheimer Importing Corporation of Chicago, Illinois.

The Kingston brandname was used by U.S. importer Westheimer Importing Corporation of Chicago, Illinois. Jack Westheimer, who was one of the original guitar importers and distributors, is currently president of Cort Musical Instruments of Northbrook, Illinois. The Kingston trademark was used on a product line of acoustic and solid body electric guitars, electric bass guitars, banjos, and mandolins imported into the U.S. market during the 1960s. It has been estimated that 150,000 guitars were sold in the U.S. during the 1960s. Some of the earlier Kingston guitars were built in Japan by either the Teisco company or Guyatone.

(Source: Michael Wright, Guitar Stories Volume One)

KING'S STONE

Instruments produced in Japan.

The King's Stone trademark was a brandname used by U.S. importers Elger/Hoshino of Ardmore, Pennsylvania. King's Stone, along with others like Goldentone, Jamboree, and Elger were all used on Japanese guitars imported to the U.S. Elger/Hoshino evolved into Hoshino USA, distributor of Ibanez guitars.

(Source: Michael Wright, Guitar Stories Volume One)

KINSCHERFF

Instruments currently built in Austin, Texas.

Luthier Jamie Kinscherff has been hand crafting fine acoustic guitars for over the past 19 years. While Kinscherff has performed some repair work in the past (and accepts some currently), his main focus has been on building guitars. For further information regarding his acoustic guitars, please contact luthier Kinscherff through the Index of Current Manufacturers located in the rear of this book.

STEVE KLEIN

Klein Acoustic
courtesy Steve Klein

Instruments produced in Sonoma, California since 1976.

Steve Klein first began building electric guitars in Berkeley, California in 1967. A year later, Klein's grandmother introduced him to Dr. Michael Kasha at the University of California in Berkeley. Klein built his first acoustic after that meeting. He briefly attended the California College of Arts and Crafts in 1969, but left to continue building guitars.

In 1970, Klein built his second acoustic guitar. He moved to Colorado in the winter of 1970-1971, but later that summer accepted a job at *The American Dream* guitar shop back in San Diego (this shop was later bought by Bob Taylor and Kurt Listug, and grew into Taylor Guitars).

The third guitar Steve Klein built also had Kasha-inspired designs. Klein travelled to Detroit via Colorado, and met Richard Schneider. Schneider was building Kasha-style classical guitars at the time, and Klein thought that he was going to stay and apprentice with Schneider. Schneider looked at Klein's current guitar and said *Congratulations, You're a guitar builder*, and sent Klein back home.

In the fall of 1972 Klein received his business license. He designed the current acoustic body shape and flying brace, and started work on the Electric Bird guitar. Later the next summer, Klein had finished the first L-457 acoustic; and by 1974 had finished three more acoustics, his first 12 string guitar, and the first small (39.6) body. Klein made a deal with Clayton Johnson (staff member of 'Bill Gramm Presents') to be able to get into concerts to show guitars to professional musicians. Klein got to meet such notables as Stills, Crosby, Young, David Lindly, Doc Watson, Roy Buchanan, John Sebastion (Loving Spoonful), and others. In the summer of 1975, Klein went to Los Angeles with guitars to meet J.D. Souther; he received a commission from Joni Mitchell, and set up shop in Oakland.

In 1976, Klein finally settled into his current shop space in Sonoma. He continued building and designing guitars while doing some repair work. Two years later he finished Joni Mitchell's guitar, and the Electric Bird as well. In 1979, Klein met Steve Kauffman at a G.A.L. convention in Boston. That same year, Klein and Carl Margolis began developing a small electric model that was nicknamed *Lumpy* by David Lindly. Klein also did a side project of antique repair, furniture, and chairs for George Lucas at the Skywalker Ranch. On a more personal note, Klein married Lin Marie DeVincent in the spring of 1985, and Michael Hedges played at their wedding.

The MK Electric model was designed in conjunction with Ronnie Montrose in 1986. By 1988 the small Klein electric design was finished, and was debuted at a trade show in 1989. Klein Electric Division was later started that same year, and Steve Klein began designing an acoustic Harp guitar for Michael Hedges. A year later the acoustic Harp project was dropped in favor of an electrical Harp design instead (Hedges and guitar appeared on the cover of the October 1990 issue of **Guitar Player** magazine).

In the early 1990s, Klein began designing an acoustic bass guitar *for and with* Bob Taylor of Taylor Guitars. The first prototypes were assembled by Steve Kauffman in 1993. A large acoustic guitar order came in from Japan a year later, and the shipment was sent in 1995. In order to concentrate on the acoustic guitar production, Klein sold his Electric Division to Lorenzo German that same year, and the Electric Division still operates out of the original Klein Sonoma facilities. The Taylor/Klein acoustic bass went into production in 1996, and currently there is a waiting period on acoustic models.

In 1997, Klein went into business with Ed Dufault and opened Klein's Sonoma Music. Located on Broadway in Sonoma, California, the music shop services the local community as well as offering acoustic guitars built by Klein and other high grade builders like Michael Lewis.

ACOUSTIC

Klein currently focuses his attention on acoustic guitar building. His **Basic Klein Acoustic Guitar** features walnut back and sides, a spruce top, rosewood neck, ebony bridge and fretboard, and gold plated tuners with Ebony buttons. The model **S-39.6** carries a list price of $10,850; and the **L-45.7** is $11,150. Klein offers a fairly fancy ornamentaion package including mother-of-pearl snowflake inlays on the guitars. Optional custom features included a 12-string configuration, Florentine cutaway with hidden heel, and use of Brazilian Rosewood.

KNIGHT

Klein Acoustic
courtesy Steve Klein

Instruments made in England during the 1970s and 1980s. Instruments currently built in Surrey, England.

Luthier Dick Knight (1907-1996) was a well respected British guitar maker, and examples of his work were collected world-wide. Knight (born Stanley Charles Knight) specialized in archtop guitar construction, notably the *Imperial* model. While Knight began building his first guitars in the 1930s, he became more prominent in the 1970s (and 1980s), and featured such clients as Dave Gilmour, Paul McCartney, Pete Townshend, and Mike Rutherford (among others).

During Knight's formative years in the 1930s he worked for Lagonda, the motor vehicle manufacturer. After work, Knight would construct wood items at home, and lost the tips of his fingers in an accident. As this accident prevented him from playing guitar, he turned to making instruments as a hobby.

At the outbreak of World War II Knight met Ben and Lew Davis (the owners of Selmers music shop in London), as well as Joe Van Straten (Selmers' shop manager). In addition to instrument repair, Van Straten suggested the two work on producing a quality English archtop. When finances would not permit the business to carry on, Selmers asked Knight to produce some guitars.

Later, when Knight's wife became ill, he left his work at Selmers and professional guitar making for seventeen years. During this time period, he did produce a number of instruments under the 'KNIGHT' logo. Some of his earliest models do not have a name on the headstock. In addition to his archtop models, Knight produced flattop acoustic, solid body and *335*-style guitars. All Knight's instruments were produced with the same high degree of quality.

Recently, Knight's son-in-law Gordon Wells has been continuing to produce guitars and keep the Knight name alive in the guitar-building world.

(Source: Keith Smart, The Zemaitis Guitar Owners Club)

KNUTSON LUTHIERY

Instruments currently built in Forrestville, California.

Luthier John Knutson has been building and repairing stringed instruments in and around the San Francisco Bay area since 1978. As a custom builder of acoustic, archtop, and electric instruments, Knutson has produced hundreds of guitars, mandolins, dulcimers, and basses (including custom double- and triple-neck combinations). Knutson is currently producing the **Messenger** Upright Electric Bass (retail list $2,550), the **Songbird** Archtop guitar (list $3,750), and the **Songbird** Archtop mandolin (list $3,250). John Knutson holds the exclusive rights to the *Songbird* and *Messenger* trademarks. For further information contact luthier John Knutson through the Index of Current Manufacturers located in the back of this book.

KOHNO

Instruments built in Japan since the mid 1960s.

Luthier Masaru Kohno was noted as being the leading Japanese classical-style guitarmaker in author Tony Bacon's **Ultimate Guitar Book** (1991). Kohno studied under luthier Arcangel Fernandez in his Madrid workshop, and later opened his own operation in Tokyo during the late 1960s.

Knight Logo
courtesy Keith Smart

KOONTZ

See also STANDEL and HARPTONE.

Instruments built in Linden, New Jersey.

Luthier Stan Koontz designed several different models of acoustic and electric guitars and basses for Bob Crooks' Standel company. The instruments were built in Harptone's New Jersey facilities, and have the 'Standel' logo on the peghead. Koontz also built his own custom guitars that featured striking innovations as side-mounted electronics and a hinged internal f-hole cover.

(Source: Tom Wheeler, American Guitars)

K

KRAMER

Kramer (the original BKL company) was located in Neptune, New Jersey since its inception in 1975 to the late 1980s. Production of Kramer (KMI) instruments was at facilities in Eatontown, New Jersey.

The Kramer trademark is currently held by the Gibson Guitar Corporation of Nashville, Tennessee.

Gary Kramer and Dennis Berardi founded the firm in October of 1975 to produce guitars. Kramer, one of the ex-partners of Travis Bean, brought in his guitar building know-how to Berardi's previous retail experience. In the following April, Peter J. LaPlaca joined the two. LaPlaca had worked his way up through Norlin to vice presidency before joining Kramer and Berardi. The original company is named after their three initials: B, K, L.

Kramer (BKL) opened the Neptune factory on July 1, 1976. The first Kramer guitar was co-designed by luthier Phil Petillo, Berardi, and Kramer. Once the prototypes were completed and the factory tooled up, the first production run was completed on November 15, 1976. The first solid body guitars featured an original body design, and a bolt-on aluminum neck with rear wood inlays.

One month after the first production run was finished, Gary Kramer left the BKL company. Guitar production under the Kramer trademark continued. By the early 1980s, the company line consisted of 14 different guitar and bass designs with a price range of $649 to $1,418. Kramer's high profile continued to rise, thanks to an exclusive endorsement deal with Edward Van Halen. In the mid 1980s, the company flourished as they had the sole license to market the Floyd Rose tremolo system.

In 1985, Berardi bought the Spector company; production and distribution of Spector basses then originated from Kramer's facilities in New Jersey. Throughout the late 1980s, Kramer was one of the guitar companies favored by the hard rock/heavy metal bands (along with Charvel/Jackson). However, the company went into bankruptcy in 1989, attempted refinancing several times, and was purchased at auction by a group that incorporated the holdings under the company name of Kramer Musical Instruments in 1995. The newly-reformed Kramer (KMI) company had also acquired the rights to the Spector trademark and Spector instruments designs. Kramer (KMI) was located in Eatontown, New Jersey.

Kramer (KMI) re-introduced several new models at industry trade shows in 1995, again sporting an aluminum neck design. However, the company never did directly bring any large amount of products to the musical instrument market.

In 1997, the Gibson corporation acquired the Kramer trademark. By 1998, Gibson was displaying Kramer trademarked models at the Summer NAMM industry show (prices $TBA); ads in the print media followed a month later. It has been indicated by some Gibson company officals that the new Kramer 'SuperStrat' style models will be produced in Korea (like current Epiphone models). Expect further developments in the Kramer story in the next 6 to 9 months from Gibson.

Early 1950s Knight Archtop
courtesy Keith Smart

Grading	100%	EXCELLENT	AVERAGE

ACOUSTIC ELECTRIC

In 1988, Kramer offered several models designed by luthier Danny Ferrington. The Kramer Ferringtons were thinline, hollow body acoustics with bridge mounted piezo pickup systems, volume and tone controls. The six on a side headstocks and slimmer profile necks felt more like an electric guitar, and the instruments could be used in performances with minimal feedback problems.

FERRINGTON II KFS2 — offset double cutaway acoustic body, round soundhole, six on a side pointy headstock, chrome tuners, rosewood bridge, volume/2 tone knobs. Available in Black, Red, and White finishes. Mfd. 1986 to 1991.

$250 $150

Last Mfr.'s Sug. Retail was $550.

FERRINGTON II KFT2 — single cutaway acoustic body, round soundhole, six on a side pointy headstock, chrome tuners, rosewood bridge, volume/2 tone knobs. Available in Black, Red, and White finishes. Mfd. 1986 to 1991.

$250 $150

Last Mfr.'s Sug. Retail was $550.

DOUG KYLE

Instruments currently built in Hampstead (Devon), England.

Doug Kyle is currently offering handcrafted guitars. For additional information regarding models, pricing, and specifications, please contact luthier Kyle through the Index of Current Manufacturers located in the rear of this edition.

La CADIE

Instruments currently built in Saint John (New Brunswick), Canada.

Luthier Rod Hannah hand builds both dreadnought and 000 12-Fret acoustic guitars in "short lot" sizes (approximately 4 instruments at a time). Hannah feels that his "target audience" is recording and performing professional musicians. Retail list prices start at $3,000 (and up).

LA JOLLA LUTHIERS

Instruments built in San Diego, California (circa recent).

Luthier Wayne Harris and his shop produced both steel-string and classical guitar models. Both models feature the unusual "Bi Level" design (developed by Roger Pyltewski), in which the guitar's top is bent into two levels; the levels connect in a 10 degree "ramp" where the bridge is located. The purpose of this design (as addressed in their advertising) was "to increase the instrument's high overtones and overall perceived brilliancy and volume". Readers of the **Blue Book of Guitars** are encouraged to locate one of these guitars for testing purposes and send said results and photos to upcoming editions.

It is estimated that Harris built about 100 instruments a year. The **Collector's Series Bi Level** steel string model is a dreadnought-sized guitar with a Sitka spruce top, Brazilian rosewood body, fan bracing, adjustable truss rod, and mahogany neck (retail list was $2,167).

La Jolla Luthiers' last given address was P.O. Box 23366, San Diego, California 92123. The Blue Book of Guitars will continue to update this section in future editions.

La MANCHA

Instruments currently built in Paracho (Michoacan) Mexico. Distributed by La Mancha Guitars of Nashville, Tennessee.

Jerry Roberts has been providing fine classical guitars for over a quarter century. In 1996, Roberts debuted the La Mancha line, which offers handcrafted guitars inspired by Fleta, Friederick, Gilbert, Hauser, Ramierez, Romanillos, Ruck, and other legendary makers. La Mancha guitars are handmade by a team of highly skilled Mexican luthiers who are supervised by California luthiers Kenny Hill and Gil Carnal. The current **Nashville** model (list $2,500), is fashioned after a cutaway flamenco design in the style of Kenny Hill. For further information on models and availablility, please contact Jerry Roberts via the Index of Current Manufacturers located in the back of this book.

La PATRIE

Instruments built in La Patrie, Quebec, Canada since 1982. Distributed by La Si Do, Inc. of St. Laurent, Quebec.

The village of La Patrie, Quebec has long been associated with Robert Godin as far back as the introduction of the Norman Guitar Company in 1972. Other Godin trademark instruments have been built there for years, so it was fitting that the line of classical guitars introduced in 1982 should bear the name of the La Patrie village.

For full overall company history, see GODIN.

Grading	100%	EXCELLENT	AVERAGE

ACOUSTIC

La Patrie Series

All instruments in this series have the following features, unless otherwise listed: classic style, round soundhole, bound body, wood marquetry rosette, Honduras mahogany neck, 12/19 fret rosewood fingerboard, slotted peghead, 3 per side gold tuners with pearloid buttons. Available in a Natural finish of special alcohol lacquer (Mfd. 1982 to date). All models may be optionally equipped in a hardshell case.

COLLECTION (Model 0463) — solid spruce top, solid rosewood back/sides, ebony tied bridge, high gloss lacquer finish.

Mfr.'s Sug. Retail	$625	$500	$350	$225

Add $135 for EPM electronics **(Model 0470)**.

CONCERT (Model 0425) — solid cedar top, mahogany back/sides, rosewood tied bridge, high gloss lacquer finish.

Mfr.'s Sug. Retail	$392	$325	$200	$125

Add $40 for a left-handed configuration **(Model 0449)**.

Add $135 for EPM electronics **(Model 0432)**.

Add $175 for a left-handed configuration with EPM electronics **(Model 0456)**.

ETUDE (Model 0340) — solid cedar top, mahogany back/sides, rosewood tied bridge, lacquer satin finish.

Mfr.'s Sug. Retail	$325	$250	$150	$100

Add $35 for a left-handed configuration **(Model 0364)**.

Add $135 for EPM electronics **(Model 0357)**.

Add $170 for a left-handed configuration with EPM electronics **(Model 0371)**.

***Motif* (Model 8841)** — similar to the Etude, except features a more compact body. Available in semi gloss lacquer finish. Mfr. 1998 to date.

Mfr.'s Sug. Retail	$309	$225	$150	$100

Add $135 for EPM electronics **(Model 8858)**.

Grading	100%	EXCELLENT	AVERAGE

PRESENTATION (Model 0388) — solid spruce top, rosewood back/sides, rosewood tied bridge, semi-gloss lacquer finish.

Mfr.'s Sug. Retail	$475	$375	$250	$175

Add $135 for EPM electronics (**Model 0395**).

LaCOTE

Instruments built in Paris, France during the early to mid 1800s.

Luthier Rene Lacote was hand building acoustic guitars during the first half of the nineteenth century. According to author Tony Bacon, Lacote is sometimes credited with the invention of the scalloped fingerboard. Many of Lacote's guitars featured relatively small bodies braced with "transverse" strutting inside the top.

During the late 18th century, the European guitar was moving away from earlier designs containing 5 or 6 "courses" (a "course" was a pair of strings) to the simple six single string design. This design is closer to what the modern "classical" guitar looks like today. Lacote's designs in the 1830s followed the six string models.

(Source: Tony Bacon, The Ultimate Guitar Book)

MARK LACEY

Instruments currently built in Nashville, Tennessee.

Luthier Mark Lacey studied formal training in musical instrument technology at the London School of Design. Lacey has been repairing and building fine instruments since 1974. During that time, he spent two years affiliated at Gruhn Guitars in Nashville, Tennesee where he gained insight from noted vintage guitar expert George Gruhn.

LADY LUCK

Instruments produced in Korea since 1986. Distributed in the U.S., Europe, and South America by Lady Luck Industries, Inc. of Cary, Illinois.

President Terresa Miller has been offering a wide range of imported, affordable guitars that are designed for beginning students up to working professionals. Lady Luck guitar models are designed in the U.S. (specifications and colors). Lady Luck also offers several models of electric bass guitars along with the line of acoustic and electric guitars.

In addition to the Lady Luck and Nouveau brands, Lady Luck Industries also distributes Adder Plus pickups and EV Star Cables.

ACOUSTIC

Lady Luck acoustics feature dreadnought style models with bound tops, mahogany back and sides, rosewood fingerboards and bridges, and 3 on a side diecast tuners. The **LLAC1** has a Honeyburst satin finish; the **LLAC2** features a high gloss Tobacco Sunburst finish. The acoustic/electric **LLACE** model has a single rounded cutaway, and bound spruce top. Acoustic electrics have retail list prices that range from $310 to $378.

LAFAYETTE (Korea Mfr.)

Instruments built in Korea. Distributed by the More Company of Pooler, Georgia.

The More Company, distributors of Synsonic instruments, is also offering a wide range of acoustic and acoustic/electric guitars; and solid body electric guitars and basses. Acoustic models like the **SW 690** have a retail list price of $460; acoustic/electrics start at $500. Solid body electric models range from $350 up to $625, and basses run from $575 to $650. For additional information regarding models, specifications, and pricing, please contact Lafayette (a More Company) through the Index of Current Manufacturers located in the back of this edition.

LAGARDE

See COSI.

LAKEWOOD

Instruments built in Germany since 1985. Distributed in the U.S. by Dana B. Goods of Santa Barbara, California.

Luthier Martin Seeliger founded Lakewood Guitars in 1985. Seeliger apprenticed for three years with luthier Manfred Pletz, and then worked as a repairman for local music shops. His experience restoring and repairing different types and brands of acoustic guitars was utilized when he began designing his own style of acoustic steel string instruments.

Model Style Appointments

Style 14 to 18: All solid woods, wood binding, rosewood fingerboard, mother of pearl Lakewood peghead logo, bone nut, angled bridge saddle, and Schaller machine heads.

Style 22 to 32: All solid woods, wood binding, ebony fingerboard, mother of pearl Lakewood peghead logo, bone nut, angled bridge saddle, and Schaller machine heads.

Style 46 to 50: All solid woods, wood binding, ebony fingerboard, abalone Lakewood peghead logo on Brazilian rosewood veneer, bone nut, angled bridge saddle, and gold Schaller machine heads.

Style 54: All solid woods, wood binding, abalone top purfling, ebony fingerboard, abalone Lakewood peghead logo on Brazilian rosewood veneer, bone nut, angled bridge saddle, and gold Schaller machine heads with ebony buttons.

ACOUSTIC

All prices include a deluxe hardshell case. Lakewood offers two different neck widths (the Ragtime and the Medium), and a number of inlay options as well. **Deluxe** models have ebony fingerboards, custom abalone and wood soundhole rosettes, and peghead binding. The following price options are quoted at their suggested retail prices.

Add $130 for a left-handed cutaway body style.

Add $200 for Fishman Powerjack.

Lacey Virtuoso
courtesy Scott Chinery

L

Add $300 for L.R. Baggs ribbon transducer and remote control.
Add $490 for a cutaway body style.

Auditorium Series

Auditorium series guitars feature small bodies coupled with wider necks joined at the body at the twelfth fret.

A-14 DELUXE — solid spruce top, round soundhole, bound body, inlaid rosette, mahogany back/sides/neck, 12/19 fret rosewood fingerboard with pearl dot inlay, rosewood bridge with black white dot pins, chrome tuning pegs, mother of pearl Lakewood logo headstock inlay, 3 per side slotted headstock. Available in Natural gloss finish. Current mfr.
   Mfr.'s Sug. Retail $2,799

A-32 DELUXE — solid Sitka spruce top, round soundhole, bound body, inlaid rosette, East Indian rosewood back and sides, mahogany neck, 12/19 fret ebony fingerboard with pearl dot inlay, rosewood bridge with black white dot pins, chrome tuning pegs, abalone pearl Lakewood logo headstock inlay, 3 per side slotted headstock. Available in Natural gloss finish. Current mfr.
   Mfr.'s Sug. Retail $3,199

A-50 DELUXE — solid Sitka spruce top, round soundhole, bound body, inlaid rosette, flamed maple back and sides, mahogany neck, 12/19 fret ebony fingerboard with pearl dot inlay, rosewood bridge with black white dot pins, chrome tuning pegs, abalone pearl Lakewood logo headstock inlay, 3 per side slotted headstock. Available in Natural gloss finish. Current mfr.
   Mfr.'s Sug. Retail $4,399

A-54 DELUXE — solid European spruce top, round soundhole, abalone pearl bound body, abalone pearl rosette, Brazilian rosewood back and sides, mahogany neck, 12/19 fret ebony fingerboard with pearl dot inlay, rosewood bridge with black white dot pins, gold tuning machines with ebony buttons, abalone pearl Lakewood logo headstock inlay, 3 per side slotted headstock. Available in Natural gloss finish. Current mfr.
   Mfr.'s Sug. Retail $5,399

Dreadnought Series

Lakewood's Dreadnought series guitars feature arched tops and backs for improved dynamic response.
   Add $300 for a 12-string configuration.

D-14 — solid spruce top, round soundhole, wood binding, inlaid rosette, mahogany back/sides/neck, 14/20 fret rosewood fingerboard with pearl dot inlay, rosewood bridge with black white dot pins, 3 per side chrome tuners, white mother of pearl Lakewood logo headstock inlay. Available in Natural satin finish. Current mfr.
   Mfr.'s Sug. Retail $1,999

D-14 Deluxe — similar to the D-14, except features an ebony fingerboard. Available in Natural gloss finish. Current mfr.
   Mfr.'s Sug. Retail $2,299

D-18 — Sitka spruce top, round soundhole, wood binding, inlaid rosette, ovankol back and sides, mahogany neck, 14/20 fret rosewood fingerboard with pearl dot inlay, rosewood bridge with black white dot pins, 3 per side chrome tuners, white mother of pearl Lakewood logo headstock inlay. Available in Natural satin finish. Current mfr.
   Mfr.'s Sug. Retail $2,099

D-18 Deluxe — similar to the D-18, except features an ebony fingerboard. Available in Natural gloss finish. Current mfr.
   Mfr.'s Sug. Retail $2,399

D-22 — Sitka spruce top, round soundhole, wood binding, inlaid rosette, solid walnut back and sides, mahogany neck, 14/20 fret rosewood fingerboard with pearl dot inlay, rosewood bridge with black white dot pins, 3 per side chrome tuners, white mother of pearl Lakewood logo headstock inlay. Available in Natural satin finish. Current mfr.
   Mfr.'s Sug. Retail $2,199

D-22 Deluxe — similar to the D-22, except features an ebony fingerboard. Available in Natural gloss finish. Current mfr.
   Mfr.'s Sug. Retail $2,599

D-32 — Sitka spruce top, round soundhole, wood binding, inlaid rosette, solid East Indian rosewood back and sides, mahogany neck, 14/20 fret ebony fingerboard with pearl dot inlay, rosewood bridge with black white dot pins, 3 per side chrome tuners, abalone pearl Lakewood logo headstock inlay. Available in Natural satin finish. Current mfr.
   Mfr.'s Sug. Retail $2,399

D-32 Deluxe — similar to the D-32. Available in Natural gloss finish. Current mfr.
   Mfr.'s Sug. Retail $2,799

D-46 DELUXE — European spruce top, round soundhole, wood binding, abalone pearl inlaid rosette, solid East Indian rosewood back and sides, mahogany neck, 14/20 fret ebony fingerboard with pearl dot inlay, bound peghead, rosewood bridge with black white dot pins, 3 per side gold-plated tuners, abalone pearl Lakewood logo headstock inlay. Available in Natural gloss finish. Current mfr.
   Mfr.'s Sug. Retail $3,699

D-50 DELUXE — European spruce top, round soundhole, wood binding, abalone pearl inlaid rosette, solid flame maple back and sides, mahogany neck, 14/20 fret ebony fingerboard with pearl dot inlay, bound peghead, rosewood bridge with black white dot pins, 3 per side gold-plated tuners, abalone pearl Lakewood logo headstock inlay. Available in Natural gloss finish. Current mfr.
   Mfr.'s Sug. Retail $3,999

D-54 DELUXE — European spruce top, round soundhole, abalone pearl top binding, abalone pearl inlaid rosette, solid Brazilian rosewood back and sides, mahogany neck, 14/20 fret ebony fingerboard with pearl dot inlay, rosewood bridge with black white dot pins, 3 per side gold-plated tuners with ebony buttons, abalone pearl Lakewood logo headstock inlay. Available in Natural gloss finish. Current mfr.
    Mfr.'s Sug. Retail $4,999

Grand Concert Series

Grand Concert series guitars are slightly smaller and have a narrower waist than their counterpart Dreadnought series models.
Add $300 for 12-string configuration.

M-14 — grand concert style body, solid spruce top, round soundhole, wood binding, inlaid rosette, solid mahogany back and sides, mahogany neck, 14/20 fret rosewood fingerboard with pearl dot inlay, rosewood bridge with black white dot pins, 3 per side chrome tuners, white mother of pearl Lakewood logo headstock inlay. Available in Natural satin finish. Current mfr.
    Mfr.'s Sug. Retail $1,999

M-14 Deluxe — similar to the M-14, except features an ebony fingerboard. Available in Natural gloss finish. Current mfr.
    Mfr.'s Sug. Retail $2,299

M-18 — grand concert style body, Sitka spruce top, round soundhole, wood binding, inlaid rosette, solid ovankol back and sides, mahogany neck, 14/20 fret rosewood fingerboard with pearl dot inlay, rosewood bridge with black white dot pins, 3 per side chrome tuners, white mother of pearl Lakewood logo headstock inlay. Available in Natural satin finish. Current mfr.
    Mfr.'s Sug. Retail $2,099

M-18 Deluxe — similar to the M-18, except features an ebony fingerboard. Available in Natural gloss finish. Current mfr.
    Mfr.'s Sug. Retail $2,399

M-22 — grand concert style body, Sitka spruce top, round soundhole, wood binding, inlaid rosette, solid walnut back and sides, mahogany neck, 14/20 fret rosewood fingerboard with pearl dot inlay, rosewood bridge with black white dot pins, 3 per side chrome tuners, white mother of pearl Lakewood logo headstock inlay. Available in Natural satin finish. Current mfr.
    Mfr.'s Sug. Retail $2,199

M-22 Deluxe — similar to the M-22, except features an ebony fingerboard. Available in Natural gloss finish. Current mfr.
    Mfr.'s Sug. Retail $2,599

M-32 — grand concert style body, Sitka spruce top, round soundhole, wood binding, inlaid rosette, solid East Indian rosewood back and sides, mahogany neck, 14/20 fret ebony fingerboard with pearl dot inlay, rosewood bridge with black white dot pins, 3 per side chrome tuners, abalone pearl Lakewood logo headstock inlay. Available in Natural satin finish. Current mfr.
    Mfr.'s Sug. Retail $2,399

M-32 Deluxe — similar to the M-32, except features an ebony fingerboard. Available in Natural gloss finish. Current mfr.
    Mfr.'s Sug. Retail $2,799

M-46 DELUXE — grand concert style body, European spruce top, round soundhole, wood binding, custom abalone rosette, solid East Indian rosewood back and sides, mahogany neck, 14/20 fret ebony fingerboard with pearl dot inlay, bound peghead, rosewood bridge with black white dot pins, 3 per side gold-plated tuners, abalone pearl Lakewood logo headstock inlay. Available in Natural gloss finish. Current mfr.
    Mfr.'s Sug. Retail $3,699

M-50 DELUXE — grand concert style body, European spruce top, round soundhole, wood binding, custom abalone rosette, solid flamed maple back and sides, mahogany neck, 14/20 fret ebony fingerboard with pearl dot inlay, bound peghead, rosewood bridge with black white dot pins, 3 per side gold-plated tuners, abalone pearl Lakewood logo headstock inlay. Available in Natural gloss finish. Current mfr.
    Mfr.'s Sug. Retail $3,999

M-54 DELUXE — grand concert style body, European spruce top, round soundhole, abalone pearl top binding, abalone pearl rosette, solid Brazilian rosewood back and sides, mahogany neck, 14/20 fret ebony fingerboard with pearl dot inlay, rosewood bridge with black white dot pins, 3 per side gold-plated tuners with ebony buttons, abalone pearl Lakewood logo headstock inlay. Available in Natural gloss finish. Current mfr.
    Mfr.'s Sug. Retail $4,999

Jumbo Series

J-14 DELUXE — jumbo style body, solid spruce top, round soundhole, wood binding, inlaid rosette, solid mahogany back and sides, mahogany neck, 14/20 fret ebony fingerboard with pearl dot inlay, rosewood bridge with black white dot pins, 3 per side chrome tuners, white mother of pearl Lakewood logo headstock inlay. Available in Natural gloss finish. Current mfr.
    Mfr.'s Sug. Retail $2,799

J-46 DELUXE — jumbo style body, European spruce top, round soundhole, wood binding, custom abalone rosette, solid Indian rosewood back and sides, mahogany neck, 14/20 fret ebony fingerboard with pearl dot inlay, bound peghead, rosewood bridge with black white dot pins, 3 per side gold-plated tuners, abalone pearl Lakewood logo headstock inlay. Available in Natural gloss finish. Current mfr.
    Mfr.'s Sug. Retail $4,099

Leaf and Flower Headstock Inlay
courtesy Larrivee Guitars

L

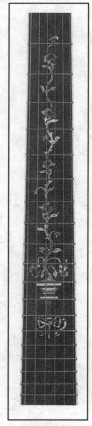

Vase and Vine Fingerboard Inlay
courtesy Larrivee Guitars

LANDOLA

Instruments currently built in Pietarsaari, Finland.

Landola has a tradition of guitar building that stretches back to 1942. In the late 1980s, Landola entered into a contract with Peavey to produce acoustic guitars for the U.S. company. Unfortunately, the company was not geared up for the production numbers that Peavey had projected, and this particular agreement had near disastrous results for the company.

However, Landola bounced back, and is currently offering a number of good quality acoustic guitar models. For further information regarding specific models and pricing, contact Landola Guitars (Audiosal OY AB) through the Index of Current Manufacturers located in the back of this edition.

ACOUSTIC

Landola offers several models of quality acoustic guitars. Models are constructed with spruce or cedar tops, mahogany or rosewood back/sides, artic birch or mahogany necks. Landola offers classical models like the **C-75 GL**, 7/8th size **C-21**, and cutaway body **CCE-110**; the **LR** series is a small bodied steel string **L**andola **R**agtime model. Both the **J** Series and the **JCE** Series models feature jumbo style bodies (the JCE models have a cutaway body). Landola **D** Series dreadnought features a solid spruce top, birch (or maple or mahogany) back and sides, and a mahogany neck.

LANGE

See PARAMOUNT.

See also ORPHEUM.

In the late 1890s, William L. Lange was a partner in Rettberg & Lange, a major East coast banjo producer and distributor. Lange expanded the company into the William L. Lange Company in the early 1920s, and supplied the C. Bruno & Son distributor with both **Paramount** and **Orpheum** banjo lines. In 1934, Lange debuted the Paramount guitar series - and some of the models were built by the C.F. Martin guitar company. Lange was quick to add Orpheum-branded guitars, and some of those models were built by Chicago's Kay company.

Lange's company went out of business in the early 1940s, but New York distributor Maurice Lipsky resumed distribution of Orpheum guitars in 1944. By the late 1940s, the Paramount guitar line was distributed by Gretsch & Brenner. Future model designations/indentifications will appear in updated editons of the **Blue Book of Guitars**.

(Source: Tom Wheeler, American Guitars)

LARK IN THE MORNING

Distributed by Lark In The Morning of Mendocino, California.

Lark In The Morning specializes in unusual instruments. Their production includes harp guitars, Cuban tres, Puerto Rican quatro, travel guitars, citterns, bajo sexto, vihuela, guitarrone, octave mandolins, steel guitars, and many others. For more information on their numerous stringed instruments and pricing, please contact the Lark In The Morning via the Index of Current Manufacturers located in the back of this edition.

GRIT LASKIN

Instruments currently built in Toronto, Canada.

Luthier Grit Laskin has been building high quality acoustic guitars for a number of years, and is well known for his inlay work. Laskin's workload keeps him slightly backlogged (a custom order from Laskin may require several years wait) but is well worth waiting for in terms of playability, construction, and any custom inlay work specified. For information regarding models and pricing, please contact Grit Laskin through the Index of Current Manufacturers located in the back of this edition.

LARRIVEE

Instruments currently produced in Vancouver, British Columbia (Canada). Distributed by Larrivee Guitars, Ltd. of Vancouver (British Columbia), Canada; also by Jean Larrivee Guitars Ltd. of Scottsdale, Arizona.

In 1967, luthier Jean Larrivee met and began studying under Edgar Munch. Larrivee guitars was founded in 1968, and guitar building was centered on classical models. The first steel string was introduced in 1971. Larrivee's attention to detail not only in guitar building but special inlay work soon made a Larrivee acoustic the sought after guitar to find.

Numerical Suffixes

Numerical suffixes listed below indicate individualized features per model suffix.

05 Mahogany Standard (mahogany back/sides).

09 Standard (pearl logo peghead inlay).

10 Deluxe (abalone purfling on top, abalone/pearl fingerboard inlay, peghead bordered by inlaid silver, hand-engraved Eagle, Gryphon, Pelican or Seahorse on headstock).

19 Special (abalone/pearl fingerboard inlay, hand-engraved Eagle, Gryphon, Pelican or Seahorse on headstock).

50 Standard (ebony fingerboard [pearl dot inlay available on request], pearl logo peghead inlay).

60 Special (Eagle [with feather fingerboard inlay], Stallion and Tiger peghead inlay).

70 DeLuxe (abalone purfled body/rosette, Eagle [with feather fingerboard inlay], Stallion and Tiger peghead inlay).

72 Presentation (abalone purfling on all bound edges, abalone rosette, abalone/pearl fingerboard inlay, peghead bordered by inlaid silver, hand-engraved Dancing Ladies, Genies, Jester, Mermaid on Seahorse or Tamborine Lady inlay on headstock, bridge wing inlays).

Female Genie Headstock Inlay
courtesy Larrivee Guitars

C-72 Presentation
courtesy Larrivee Guitars

Grading	100%	EXCELLENT	AVERAGE

Model Options

All instruments are available in left-handed versions at no additional charge. All instruments are also available with following options:

A 12 string variation is available in the following models for an additional $190: Cutaway, Cutaway Jumbo, Dreadnought, Jumbo, Larrivee and Larrivee Jumbo Series.

Add $140 for Fishman Matrix pickup.

Add $280 for Fishman pickup with preamp.

Add $1,000 for Brazilian rosewood (when available).

ACOUSTIC

Unless otherwise noted, all Larrivee models are constructed with the same standard materials: spruce top, round soundhole, wood body binding, wooden inlay rosette, transparent pickguard, rosewood or figured maple back/sides, mahogany neck, bound ebony fingerboard, ebony bridge with black pearl dot pins, and 3 per side chrome tuners.

Classic Series

Specifications: 66 mm Scale, 15" Lower Bout.

L-30 STANDARD — classic style, unbound fingerboard, tied bridge, 3 per side gold tuners with pearl buttons. Current mfr.

Mfr.'s Sug. Retail	$2,395	$1,800	$1,175	$795

C-30 Cutaway — similar to the L-30, except features single Florentine cutaway body. Current mfr.

Mfr.'s Sug. Retail	$2,695	$2,000	$1,350	$1,000

Cutaway Series

The instruments in this series have the Larrivee body style with a single sharp cutaway. Current mfr.

Specifications: 25 1/2" Scale, 20 1/4" Length, 16" Lower Bout, 4" Max Depth.

C-03 RE — ROSEWOOD STANDARD

Mfr.'s Sug. Retail	$1,495	$1,125	$725	$495

This model features a Fishman Prefix+ pickup

C-05 — MAHOGANY STANDARD

Mfr.'s Sug. Retail	$1,895	$1,425	$925	$625

C-09 — ROSEWOOD STANDARD

Mfr.'s Sug. Retail	$2,295	$1,725	$1,130	$750

C-10 — ROSEWOOD DELUXE

Mfr.'s Sug. Retail	$2,795	$2,100	$1,375	$925

Cutaway Jumbo Series

All the instruments in this series have jumbo Larrivee body styles with a single sharp cutaway. Current mfr.

LCJ-05 — MAHOGANY STANDARD

Mfr.'s Sug. Retail	$1,995	$1,500	$975	$660

LCJ-09 — ROSEWOOD STANDARD

Mfr.'s Sug. Retail	$2,495	$1,875	$1,225	$830

LCJ-10 — ROSEWOOD DELUXE

Mfr.'s Sug. Retail	$2,995	$2,250	$1,500	$1,000

LCJ-72 — PRESENTATION

Mfr.'s Sug. Retail	$5,995	$4,500	$3,000	$2,000

Cutaway Small Body Series

Fashioned after the Larrivee small body style, these instruments have a single sharp cutaway. Current mfr.

CS-05 — MAHOGANY STANDARD

Mfr.'s Sug. Retail	$1,895	$1,425	$925	$625

CS-09 — ROSEWOOD STANDARD

Mfr.'s Sug. Retail	$2,295	$1,725	$1,130	$750

CS-10 — ROSEWOOD DELUXE

Mfr.'s Sug. Retail	$2,795	$2,100	$1,375	$925

CS-72 — PRESENTATION

Mfr.'s Sug. Retail	$5,995	$4,500	$3,000	$2,000

D-Lite Series

All instruments in this series have slightly smaller dreadnought style bodies, and are optionally available with a gig bag.

Specifications: 24 1/2" Scale, 19" Length, 15" Lower Bout, 4 1/2" Max Depth.

D-LITE — dreadnought style, solid spruce top, wood fiber body binding, round soundhole, mahogany back/sides, mahogany neck, 14/20 fret ebony fingerboard, 3 per side chrome tuners, ebony bridge with white bridgepins, (satin) pickguard. Available in Natural satin finish. Mfr. 1997 to date.

Mfr.'s Sug. Retail	$749	$550	$350	$225

C-09 Standard
courtesy Larrivee Guitars

CS-19 Special
courtesy Larrivee Guitars

Grading	100%	EXCELLENT	AVERAGE

L-Lite — similar to the D-Lite, except features Larrivee body (Larrivee Series) design. Available in Natural satin finish. Mfr. 1997 to date.

Mfr.'s Sug. Retail	$749	$550	$350	$225

Dreadnought Series

All instruments in this series have dreadnought style bodies. Current mfr.

Specifications: 25 1/2" Scale, 19 3/4" Length, 16" Lower Bout, 4 1/2" Max Depth.

D-03 — MAHOGANY STANDARD

Mfr.'s Sug. Retail	$779	$595	$375	$250

D-03E Mahogany Standard — similar to the D-03, except features a Fishman Prefix+ pickup. Current mfr.

Mfr.'s Sug. Retail	$979	$725	$475	$325

D-03R Rosewood Standard — similar to the D-03, except features rosewood back/sides. Current mfr.

Mfr.'s Sug. Retail	$999	$750	$495	$325

D-03W Walnut Standard — similar to the D-03, except features walnut back/sides. Current mfr.

Mfr.'s Sug. Retail	$899	$675	$450	$300

D-05 — MAHOGANY STANDARD

Mfr.'s Sug. Retail	$1,595	$1,200	$775	$525

D-09 — ROSEWOOD STANDARD

Mfr.'s Sug. Retail	$1,995	$1,500	$975	$660

D-10 — ROSEWOOD DELUXE

Mfr.'s Sug. Retail	$2,495	$1,875	$1,225	$830

D-72 — PRESENTATION

Mfr.'s Sug. Retail	$5,495	$4,125	$2,695	$1,800

Koa Series

All instruments in this series have single sharp cutaway style bodies, koa top/back/sides, seashell fingerboard/bridge wing inlay, dolphin peghead inlay. Disc. 1994.

C-20 — Larrivee style body.

	$1,050	$695

Last Mfr.'s Sug. Retail was $2,110.

CJ-20 — Larrivee jumbo style body.

	$1,100	$725

Last Mfr.'s Sug. Retail was $2,210.

CS-20 — Larrivee small style body.

	$1,050	$695

Last Mfr.'s Sug. Retail was $2,110.

Larrivee Series

All instruments in this series have Larrivee style bodies. Current mfr.

Specifications: 25 1/2" Scale, 20 1/4" Length, 16" Lower Bout, 4" Max Depth.

L-03 — MAHOGANY STANDARD

Mfr.'s Sug. Retail	$779	$595	$375	$250

L-03E Mahogany Standard — similar to the L-03, except features a Fishman Prefix+ pickup. Current mfr.

Mfr.'s Sug. Retail	$979	$725	$475	$325

L-03R Rosewood Standard — similar to the L-03, except features rosewood back/sides. Current mfr.

Mfr.'s Sug. Retail	$999	$750	$495	$325

L-03W Walnut Standard — similar to the L-03, except features walnut back/sides. Current mfr.

Mfr.'s Sug. Retail	$899	$675	$450	$300

L-05 — MAHOGANY STANDARD

Mfr.'s Sug. Retail	$1,595	$1,200	$775	$525

L-09 — ROSEWOOD STANDARD

Mfr.'s Sug. Retail	$1,995	$1,500	$975	$660

L-10 — ROSEWOOD DELUXE

Mfr.'s Sug. Retail	$2,495	$1,875	$1,225	$830

L-72 — PRESENTATION

Mfr.'s Sug. Retail	$5,495	$4,125	$2,695	$1,800

Larrivee Jumbo Series

All instruments in this series have Larrivee Jumbo style bodies. Current mfr.

LJ-05 — MAHOGANY STANDARD

Mfr.'s Sug. Retail	$1,695	$1,275	$825	$550

LJ-09 — ROSEWOOD STANDARD

Mfr.'s Sug. Retail	$2,095	$1,575	$1,025	$695

The Jester Headstock Inlay
courtesy Larrivee Guitars

Leaf and Flower Headstock Inlay
courtesy Larrivee Guitars

L

Grading	100%	EXCELLENT	AVERAGE
LJ-10 — ROSEWOOD DELUXE			
Mfr.'s Sug. Retail $2,695	$2,000	$1,300	$895
LJ-72 — PRESENTATION			
Mfr.'s Sug. Retail $5,695	$4,275	$2,795	$1,875

Larrivee OM Series

All instruments in this series have Larrivee OM style bodies. Current mfr.

Specifications: 25 1/2" Scale, 20 1/4" Length, 16" Lower Bout, 4" Max Depth.

Grading	100%	EXCELLENT	AVERAGE
OM-03 — MAHOGANY STANDARD			
Mfr.'s Sug. Retail $779	$595	$375	$250
OM-03E Mahogany Standard — similar to the OM-03, except features a Fishman Prefix+ pickup. Current mfr.			
Mfr.'s Sug. Retail $979	$725	$475	$325
OM-03R Rosewood Standard — similar to the OM-03, except features rosewood back/sides. Current mfr.			
Mfr.'s Sug. Retail $999	$750	$495	$325
OM-03W Walnut Standard — similar to the OM-03, except features walnut back/sides. Current mfr.			
Mfr.'s Sug. Retail $899	$675	$450	$300
OM-05 — MAHOGANY STANDARD			
Mfr.'s Sug. Retail $1,595	$1,200	$775	$525
OM-09 — ROSEWOOD STANDARD			
Mfr.'s Sug. Retail $1,995	$1,500	$975	$660
OM-10 — ROSEWOOD DELUXE			
Mfr.'s Sug. Retail $2,495	$1,875	$1,225	$830
OM-72 — PRESENTATION			
Mfr.'s Sug. Retail $5,495	$4,125	$2,695	$1,800

Larrivee Small Series

All instruments in this series have Larrivee Small style bodies. Current mfr.

Grading	100%	EXCELLENT	AVERAGE
LS-05 — MAHOGANY STANDARD			
Mfr.'s Sug. Retail $1,595	$1,200	$775	$525
LS-09 — ROSEWOOD STANDARD			
Mfr.'s Sug. Retail $1,995	$1,500	$975	$660
LS-10 — ROSEWOOD DELUXE			
Mfr.'s Sug. Retail $2,495	$1,875	$1,225	$830
LS-72 — PRESENTATION			
Mfr.'s Sug. Retail $5,495	$4,125	$2,695	$1,800

Larrivee 00 Series

All instruments in this series have Larrivee 00 style bodies. Curr. mfr.

Grading	100%	EXCELLENT	AVERAGE
00-05 — MAHOGANY STANDARD			
Mfr.'s Sug. Retail $1,595	$1,200	$775	$525
00-09 — ROSEWOOD STANDARD			
Mfr.'s Sug. Retail $1,995	$1,500	$975	$660
00-10 — ROSEWOOD DELUXE			
Mfr.'s Sug. Retail $2,495	$1,875	$1,225	$830
00-72 — PRESENTATION			
Mfr.'s Sug. Retail $5,495	$4,125	$2,695	$1,800

Traditional Jumbo Series

All instruments in this series have Jumbo style bodies. Current mfr.

Specifications: 25 1/2" Scale, 20 5/8" Length, 17" Lower Bout, 4 3/4" Max Depth.

Grading	100%	EXCELLENT	AVERAGE
J-05 — MAHOGANY STANDARD			
Mfr.'s Sug. Retail $1,695	$1,275	$825	$550
J-09 — ROSEWOOD STANDARD			
Mfr.'s Sug. Retail $2,095	$1,575	$1,025	$695
J-10 — ROSEWOOD DELUXE			
Mfr.'s Sug. Retail $2,695	$2,000	$1,300	$895
J-72 — PRESENTATION			
Mfr.'s Sug. Retail $5,695	$4,275	$2,795	$1,875

OM-10 Deluxe
courtesy Larrivee Guitars

J-05-12
courtesy Larrivee Guitars

LARSON BROTHERS

Larson Brothers of Maurer & Co. (1900-1944).

Carl Larson immigrated from Sweden during the 1880s and began working in the musical instrument trade in the Chicago area. He soon sent for younger brother August who also had a great aptitude for woodworking. In 1900 August and other investors bought out Robert Maurer's Chicago-based business of manufacturing guitars and mandolins. August and Carl ran the business and maintained the Maurer & Co. name throughout their careers which ended with the death of August in 1944. During that period they produced a vast array of stringed instruments including guitars, harp guitars, mandolin orchestra pieces and harp mandolin orchestra pieces, and a few ukes, taro-patches, tiples, and mandolinettos. Through the years the styles changed and also the basic sizes of guitars and mandolins. They were built larger starting in the mid-1930s to accommodate the demand from players for more volume.

The Larson brothers "house" brand was the Maurer up to the transition period of the larger body instruments when the Euphonon brand was initiated for guitars and mandolins. The Maurer brand was used on guitars and mandolin orchestra pieces of many designs during that approximate 35-year period. The guitars ranged from oak body small guitars to pearl and abalone trimmed guitars and mandolins having tree-of-life inlays on the fingerboards. These are beautifully made instruments of the highest quality, but even the less fancy models are well made in the tradition of the Larson brothers' craftsmanship. The guitars with the 12-fret-to-the-body neck sizes came in widths of 12¾", 13½", 14" and 15".

The Larson brothers also built guitars, harp guitars, and mandolin orchestra pieces for Wm. C. Stahl of Milwaukee and W.J. Dyer of St. Paul, as well as other assorted suppliers who put their own name on the Larsons' products. Stahl and Dyer claimed to be the makers - a common practice during those "progressive years."

The Prairie State brand was added in the mid-1920s for guitars only. These followed the styles of the better and best grade Maurer models but incorporated one of three main systems of steel rods running the length of the guitar body. August was awarded three patents for these ideas which included side items such as adjustable bridges, fingerboards and necks.

The Prairie State guitars and the better and best grade Maurers and Stahls had a system of laminated top braces. August patented this idea in 1904 making the Larsons pioneers in designing the first guitars made for steel strings which are the only kind they ever made. The laminated braces were continued in the larger Prairie States and the better and best grade models of the Euphonon brand. An occasional Maurer brand instrument may be found in the larger size bodies which I attribute to those sold by Wack Sales Co. of Milwaukee during this later period. This outlet was not offered the Euphonon brand, so they sold them under the Maurer name.

The Larson brothers sold their wares to many prominent players from the radio stations in Chicago, mainly WLS and WJJD. These stations put on country music shows with live performances and became very popular. The Larsons also built three guitars for Les Paul, one of which was a step in developing the solid body guitar. A Larson fingerboard can be seen on what Les called "The Log" which he submitted to Gibson to sell his solid body idea. Gene Autry and Patsy Montana bought Euphonon guitars from the Larsons' shop in 1937.

The main brands produced by the Larsons were Maurer, Prairie State, Euphonon, W.J. Dyer, and Wm. C. Stahl, J.F. Stetson was Dyer's brand for their regular flat-top guitar, while the Dyer label was used for the "Symphony" series of harp-guitars and harp-mandolin family instruments.

The Larson brands were burned into the center inside back strip below the soundhole. Typically, if an instrument was altered from standard, it was not branded. This led to many not having any markings. All of the instruments built by the Larsons were handmade. Their degree of craftsmanship made them wonderful instruments to play and ensured that they would become highly collectible. Many people believe that the Larsons' products are as good as Martins and Gibsons, and some believe that they are better. The Larson-built guitars are considered the best harp guitars ever made!

More information regarding the individual brands can be found under their brand names: Maurer, Prairie State, Euphonon, Wm. C. Stahl and W.J. Dyer.

For more information regarding Maurer & Co. and the Larson Brothers, a Maurer/Prairie State catalog, Wm. C. Stahl catalog, the Larson patents, and a CD by Muriel Anderson which demonstrates the different sounds built into many styles of Larson-made guitars, see The Larsons' Creations, Guitars and Mandolins, by Robert Carl Hartman, Centerstream Publishing, P.O. Box 17878, Anaheim Hills CA 92807, phone/fax (714) 779-9390.

1917 photograph

August Larson
courtesy Robert Carl Hartman

LAUNHARDT & KOBS

Instruments currently produced in Wetslar, Germany.

Launhardt & Kobs specialize in high quality acoustic guitar models. Their classical series feature models like the **Prelude**, **Sarabande**, **Bourree**, and **Romantika** with slotted headstocks and traditional Spanish-style bodies. The jumbo-style models include the 6-string **Jack D.** and the 12-string **William D.** guitars.

Launhardt & Kobs also produces five Jazz Guitar (archtop) models, all with a 650 mm scale and choice of Attila Zoller or EMG pickups. In addition to the archtop models, Launhardt & Kobs also offers a Strat-style solid body **Model 1** and Tele-ish **Model 2** models under the L U K trademark.

The **Averell D.** akustik (acoustic bass) model has a single rounded cutaway body, and a 865 mm scale length. Both the **Model 3** and **Model 4** solid body electric basses have Jazz bass-stylings.

LEVIN

Instruments built in Sweden from 1900 to 1977. In the early 1970s, Levin was purchased by the Martin Guitar Company of Nazareth, Pennsylvania.

The Levin company of Sweden was founded by luthier Herman Karlsson Levin in 1900, and the first guitar and mandolin factory was set up in Gothenburg, Sweden. Prior to establishing his factory, luthier Levin had a shop in Manhattan.

Levin was purchased in the early 1970s by the Martin Guitar company. While early Levin models had some "Martin-esque" qualities prior to the sale, they definitely showed Martin influence afterwards. Production focused on flat-tops after the company changed hands. The last Levin guitars were built in 1977.

(Source: Aad Overseem, The Netherlands)

1939 photograph

Carl Larson
courtesy Robert Carl Hartman

ACOUSTIC

Levin built very good quality single cutaway one (or two) pickup archtops between the 1930s to the 1960s, as well as flat-top guitars, banjos, mandolins, lutes, and other stringed instruments. It is estimated that the company built more than 560,000 total instruments while in business.

LEVITCH

LEVITCH GUITAR WORKS.

Instruments currently built in Scotch Plains, New Jersey.

Luthier Richard Levitch has been offering custom handmade acoustic and electric guitars for the past 12 years. Levitch apprenticed to luthier Sam Koontz in Linden, New Jersey for five years.

In addition to his acoustic guitar models, Levitch offers electric guitars with a retail price starting at $950 (call for options).

ACOUSTIC

The Basic **Artisan** model (list $950) features a dreadnought or 15 1/2" round body, Sitka spruce top, mahogany (or maple or Indian rosewood) back and sides, maple or mahogany neck, ebony or rosewood fingerboard and bridge, black headpiece with mother of pearl or abalone inlay, gold or nickel plated tuners, plastic or wood binding, and an oval or round soundhole. The Artisan is finished with gloss or satin lacquer, and the price includes a hardshell case.

Options include an Engelmann spruce top (add $125), rounded or sharp cutaway (add $150), Fishman bridge pickup (add $200), and others.

Levitch optionally offers the following tonewoods for the back and sides of his Artisan model: figured bubinga, quilted and flame maple, Eucalyptus, Australian figured lacewood, figured paduak, figured walnut, and figured myrtle (add $150), flamed koa (add $200), Brazilian rosewood and quilted mahogany (call for prices). For further information regarding model and pricing information, contact luthier Richard Levitch at Levitch Guitar Works through the Index of Current Manufacturers located in the back of this edition.

MICHAEL A. LEWIS

Instruments currently built in Grass Valley, California.

Luthier Michael A. Lewis has been offering handcrafted banjos and mandolins since 1981, and recently began building flat top and archtop guitars. Lewis, a stringed instrument repairman since the early 1980s, began building the archtop and flat top models in 1993.

Lewis offers steel string flat top guitars inspired by those famous pre-war *herringbone* models. Soundboards are fashioned from either Sitka or Englemann spruce, Western red cedar, or coastal redwood (sequoia sempervirens).

Lewis' archtop models include the **Standard** and less ornate **Studio** models. Both models feature a rounded single cutaway body, raised pickguard, 2 original style f-holes, and bridge/trapeze tailpiece. Prices start at $6,700, but are determined by selection of materials, intricacy of inlay, and other appointments. The overall design is strongly influenced by D'Angelico's work, but has other concepts and considerations factored in. Built as acoustic instruments, the models are offered with the option of a floating Bartolini hum canceling jazz pickup (controls mounted on the pickguard).

LIIKANEN

Instruments currently built in Helsinki, Finland.

Liikanen Musical Instruments is a company formed by three experienced luthiers to construct high class concert acoustic guitars. The company was founded by Kauko Liikanen, who has been building guitars for more than 20 years. Keijo Liikanen joined the company in 1990, and in addition to his guitar building also manages the raw material supplies as well as the administrative duties. The company's youngest artisan, Kirsi Vaisanen, graduated from the Lutherie Department of Ikaalinen Institute of Arts and Crafts.

Liikanen guitars are crafted in their workshop in downtown Helsinki. Most models are built after commissioning, and delivery time is usually 6 months. Liikanen Musical Instruments offers both classical and flamenco guitar models, as well as other stringed instruments. For further information regarding specifications and pricing, contact Liikanen Musical Instruments via the Index of Current Manufacturers located in the back of this book.

LINCOLN

Instruments produced in Japan between the late 1970s and the early 1980s.

Lincoln instruments featured both original designs and designs based on classic American favorites; most guitars considered good quality.

(Source: Tony Bacon and Paul Day, The Guru's Guitar Guide)

LINDELL

Instruments produced in Japan during the mid 1960s.

Research continues into the Lindell trademark, as the producing company in Japan and the American distributor have yet to be identified. Further information will be reported in future editions of the **Blue Book of Guitars**.

WALTER LIPTON

Instruments currently built in Orford, New Hampshire.

Luthier Walter Lipton builds an estimated 10 hand crafted acoustic guitars each year. Lipton's retail list prices start around $2,250, and he offers both steel-string and classical style guitars. Lipton specializes in aged woods (10 to 20 years) and engraved mother-of-pearl inlays.

Lipton also operates the Euphanon Co., a parts supply house that offers woods, luthier tools, strings, and fretted instrument parts. For information regarding his products, specifications, and pricing, please contact Walter Lipton at the Euphanon Co. through the Index of Current Manufacturers located in the back of this edition.

LONE STAR

Instruments currently made in Paracho, Mexico. Distributed by LPD Music International.

Lone Star guitars are produced in the mountain village of Paracho, Mexico, which has a 200 year heritage of guitar building. Lone Star guitars are available with laminate, solid cedar, or solid spruce tops and are designed for the beginner to intermediate student. Retail list prices run from $165 up to $625; most instruments are priced around $250 to $439. For further information contact LPD Music International through the Index of Current Manufacturers located in the back of this book.

LoPRINZI

Instruments built in Rosemont, Hopeville, and Plainsboro, New Jersey from 1972 to 1980.

Thomas R. LoPrinzi, along with his brother Augustino, originally founded LoPrinzi guitars in New Jersey in early 1972. The business grew from a two- and three-man operation into a staff of 18 employees. Modern production techniques enabled the LoPrinzi brothers to pare the number of employees back to 7 while still producing 60 to 80 guitars a month in the late 1970s. Augustino LoPrinzi, tired of overseeing production, sold the business to Maark Corporation (a subsidiary of AMF). His brother Thomas was then named president of LoPrinzi Guitars. The AMF-owned company continued producing guitars for a number of years, and finally closed the doors in 1980. Years later, Augustino called AMF to request his old trademark back. Working with vice president Dick Hargraves, Augustino officially had the trademark transferred back, and has combined it to form the current "Augustino LoPrinzi" line of classical guitars.

(Source: Hal Hammer)

LoPrinzi guitars were available in three styles: Standard, Folk, and 12-String. Early designs featured German silver Spruce tops and Brazilian Rosewood; later models had tops built out of Canadian and Alaskan Spruce, and bodies constructed with Indian Rosewood, Flamed Maple, and Honduran Mahogany. All models have an adjustable truss rod, Ebony fingerboard, pearl or abalone inlays, and a Rosewood bridge.

LORD

Instruments built in Japan.

Guitars with the Lord trademark originated in Japan, and were distributed in the U.S. by the Halifax company.

(Source: Michael Wright, Guitar Stories Volume One)

LOTUS

Instruments produced in Korea, China, and India. Distributed by Midco International of Effingham, Illinois.

Lotus guitars are designed for the student or entry level guitarist. Lotus offers a wide range of acoustic and electric guitar models (a little something for everyone!).

In addition to the Electric guitar models, Lotus also offers 4 dreadnought acoustics, 2 banjo models, and 4 mandolins. Lotus Electric Basses are offered in a Precision-style L760, as well as a Jazz-style model L750JSB and two modern design basses (L770 4-string and L780 5-string).

LOWDEN

Instruments built by hand in Ireland since 1973. Distributed by Lowden Guitar Company, Ltd. of Newtownards, Northern Ireland.

In 1973, luthier George Lowden began designing and manufacturing hand built guitars in Ireland. Demand outgrew the one-person effort and the production of some models were farmed out to luthiers in Japan in 1981. However, full production was returned to Ireland in 1985.

ACOUSTIC

O Series (Standard Range)

0-10 — jumbo style, cedar top, round soundhole, wood bound body, wood inlay rosette, mahogany back/sides, 5-piece mahogany/roswood neck, 14/20 fret ebony fingerboard, rosewood bridge, rosewood veneered peghead with pearl logo inlay, 3 per side custom gold tuners with amber buttons. Available in Natural finish. Current mfr.

Mfr.'s Sug. Retail	$2,390	$1,800	$1,100	$770

0-12 — similar to O-10, except has spruce top. Current mfr.

Mfr.'s Sug. Retail	$2,390	$1,800	$1,100	$770

O12-12 — similar to O-10, except has spruce top, 12-string configuration, 6 per side tuners. Current mfr.

Mfr.'s Sug. Retail	$2,800	$2,100	$1,290	$900

0-22 — jumbo style, cedar top, round soundhole, wood bound body, wood inlay rosette, mahogany back/sides, mahogany/sycamore 5 piece neck, 14/20 fret ebony fingerboard, rosewood bridge, rosewood veneered peghead with pearl logo inlay, 3 per side gold tuners with amber buttons. Available in Natural finish. Disc. 1994.

			$990	$660

Last Mfr.'s Sug. Retail was $2,145.

0-22/12 — similar to O-22, except has 12-strings configuration, 6 per side tuners.

			$1,100	$735

Last Mfr.'s Sug. Retail was $2,445.

0-23 — jumbo style, cedar top, round soundhole, wood bound body, abalone/wood inlay rosette, walnut back/sides, mahogany/sycamore 5 piece neck, 14/20 fret ebony fingerboard, rosewood bridge, rosewood veneered peghead with pearl logo inlay, 3 per side gold tuners with amber buttons. Available in Natural finish. Current mfr.

Mfr.'s Sug. Retail	$2,390	$1,800	$1,100	$770

0-23
courtesy Lowden Guitars

Grading	100%	EXCELLENT	AVERAGE

O-25 — jumbo style, cedar top, round soundhole, wood bound body, wood inlay rosette, Indian rosewood back/sides, mahogany/rosewood 5 piece neck, 14/20 fret ebony fingerboard, rosewood bridge, pearl logo inlay and rosewood veneer on peghead, 3 per side gold tuners with amber buttons. Available in Natural finish. Current mfr.

Mfr.'s Sug. Retail	$2,800	$2,100	$1,290	$900

O25-12 — similar to O-25, except has 12-string configuration, 6 per side tuners. Disc. 1994.

		$1,240	$825

Last Mfr.'s Sug. Retail was $2,750.

O-32 — similar to O-25, except has spruce top, pearl tuner buttons.

Mfr.'s Sug. Retail	$2,800	$2,100	$1,290	$900

O32-12 — similar to O-32, except has 12-string configuration, 6 per side tuners with pearl buttons. Mfr. 1993 to date.

Mfr.'s Sug. Retail	$3,250	$2,450	$1,500	$1,050

D Series (Standard Range)

D Series guitars maintain the classic dreadnought design with a narrow neck for ease of playing.

D-10 — classic dreanought style guitar. Same Specifications as the O-10. Current mfr.

Mfr.'s Sug. Retail	$2,390	$1,800	$1,100	$770

D-12 — classic dreadnought style guitar. Same Specifications as the O-12. Current mfr.

Mfr.'s Sug. Retail	$2,390	$1,800	$1,100	$770

D12-12 — similar to the D-12, except has 12-string configuration, 6 per side tuners. Current mfr.

Mfr.'s Sug. Retail	$2,800	$2,100	$1,290	$900

D-22 — dreadnought style, cedar top, round soundhole, wood bound body, abalone rosette, mahogany back/sides, mahogany/sycamore 5 piece neck, 14/20 fret ebony fingerboard with pearl dot inlay, rosewood bridge, rosewood veneered peghead with pearl logo inlay, 3 per side gold tuners with amber buttons. Available in Natural finish. Mfd. 1993 to 1995.

		$1,075	$720

Last Mfr.'s Sug. Retail was $2,390.

D-23 — classic dreadnought style guitar. Same Specifications as the O-23. Current mfr.

Mfr.'s Sug. Retail	$2,390	$1,800	$1,100	$770

D-25 — classic dreadnought style guitar. Same Specifications as the O-25. Current mfr.

Mfr.'s Sug. Retail	$2,800	$2,100	$1,290	$900

D-32 — classic dreadnought style guitar. Same Specifications as the O-32. Current mfr.

Mfr.'s Sug. Retail	$2,800	$2,100	$1,290	$900

D32-12 — similar to the D-32, except has 12-string configuration, 6 per side tuners. Current mfr.

Mfr.'s Sug. Retail	$3,250	$2,450	$1,500	$1,050

F Series (Standard Range)

The F Series guitars are a mini-jumbo folk style with the standard Lowden neck.

F-10 — mini-jumbo folk guitar. Same Specifications as the O-10. Current mfr.

Mfr.'s Sug. Retail	$2,390	$1,800	$1,100	$770

F-12 — mini-jumbo folk guitar. Same Specifications as the O-12. Current mfr.

Mfr.'s Sug. Retail	$2,390	$1,800	$1,100	$770

F12-12 — similar to the F-12, except has 12-string configuration, 6 per side tuners. Current mfr.

Mfr.'s Sug. Retail	$2,800	$2,100	$1,290	$900

F-22 — folk style, cedar top, round soundhole, wood bound body, wood inlay rosette, mahogany back/sides, mahogany/rosewood 5 piece neck, 14/20 fret ebony fingerboard with pearl dot inlay, rosewood bridge, pearl logo inlay and rosewood veneer on peghead, 3 per side gold tuners with pearl buttons. Available in Natural finish. Disc. 1994.

		$990	$660

Last Mfr.'s Sug. Retail was $2,145.

F-24 — similar to F-22, except has spruce top, maple back/sides. Mfr. 1994 to 1995.

		$1,260	$840

Last Mfr.'s Sug. Retail was $2,790.

F-34 — similar to F-22, except has spruce top, koa back/sides. Mfr. 1994 to 1995.

		$1,440	$960

Last Mfr.'s Sug. Retail was $3,190.

F-23 — mini-jumbo folk guitar. Same Specifications as the O-23. Current mfr.

Mfr.'s Sug. Retail	$2,390	$1,800	$1,100	$770

F-25 — mini-jumbo folk guitar. Same Specifications as the O-25. Current mfr.

Mfr.'s Sug. Retail	$2,800	$2,100	$1,290	$900

F-32 — mini-jumbo folk guitar. Same Specifications as the O-32. Current mfr.

Mfr.'s Sug. Retail	$2,800	$2,100	$1,290	$900

D-10
courtesy Lowden Guitars

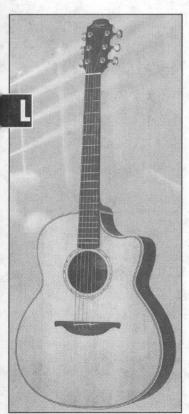

F-32 C
courtesy Lowden Guitars

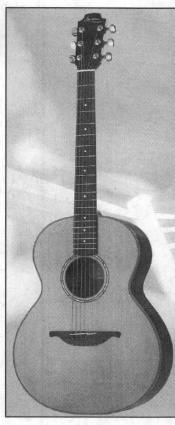

S-25
courtesy Lowden Guitars

Grading	100%	EXCELLENT	AVERAGE

F32-12 — similar to the F-32, except has 12-string configuration, 6 per side tuners. Current mfr.

Mfr.'s Sug. Retail	$3,250	$2,450	$1,500	$1,050

S Series (Standard Range)

S Series models feature a small compact body with a standard Lowden neck.

S-10 — small bodied folk guitar. Same Specifications as the O-10. Current mfr.

Mfr.'s Sug. Retail	$2,390	$1,800	$1,100	$770

S-12 — small bodied folk guitar. Same Specifications as the O-12. Current mfr.

Mfr.'s Sug. Retail	$2,390	$1,800	$1,100	$770

S12-12 — similar to the S-12, except has 12-string configuration, 6 per side tuners. Current mfr.

Mfr.'s Sug. Retail	$2,800	$2,100	$1,290	$900

S-23 — small bodied folk guitar. Same Specifications as the O-23. Current mfr.

Mfr.'s Sug. Retail	$2,390	$1,800	$1,100	$770

S-23S — folk style, German spruce top, round soundhole, wood bound body, abalone/wood inlay rosette, walnut back/sides, mahogany/sycamore 5 piece neck, 14/20 fret ebony fingerboard, rosewood bridge, rosewood veneered peghead with pearl logo inlay, 3 per side gold tuners with ebony buttons. Available in Natural finish. Mfd. 1994 to 1995.

		$1,075	$720
		Last Mfr.'s Sug. Retail was $2,390.	

S-25 — small bodied folk guitar. Same Specifications as the O-25. Current mfr.

Mfr.'s Sug. Retail	$2,800	$2,100	$1,290	$900

S-32 — small bodied folk guitar. Same Specifications as the O-32. Current mfr.

Mfr.'s Sug. Retail	$2,800	$2,100	$1,290	$900

S32-12 — similar to the S-32, except has 12-string configuration, 6 per side tuners. Current mfr.

Mfr.'s Sug. Retail	$3,250	$2,450	$1,500	$1,050

35 Series (Premier Range)

All Premier Guitars are available in the four distinctive Lowden body configurations (O, F, D, S). The 35 Series model features a choice of cedar or spruce top, wood bindings/purfling, round soundhole, abalone rosette, maple or mahogany neck, 14/20 fret ebony fingerboard, rosewood bridge, matching veneered peghead with pearl logo inlay, 3 per side custom gold tuners with amber buttons. Available in a Natural finish since 1996.

The 35 Series model is available in Indian rosewood, Claro walnut, or flamed maple at a suggested retail price of $3,550; and koa, Australian blackwood, quilted maple, or myrtle at $3,750. A Brazilian rosewood model has the suggested list price of $6,200.

38 Series (Premier Range)

The 38 Series is the top of the range Brazilian Rosewood Lowden Guitar. This model features black cedar top, abalone rosette, abalone/wood bound soundboard inlay, mahogany/rosewood 5-piece neck, 14/20 fret ebony fingerboard with leaf inlay, Brazilian rosewood bridge, Brazilian rosewood veneered peghead with pearl logo inlay, and 3 per side custom gold tuners with amber buttons. Available in a Natural finish. The suggested retail price is $6,200.

ACOUSTIC ELECTRIC

Stage Series (Standard Range)

LSE-I — venetian cutaway folk style, spruce top, round soundhole, wood bound body, wood inlay rosette, mahogany 2 piece neck, 20 fret ebony fingerboard, rosewood bridge, pearl logo inlay and rosewood veneer on peghead, 3 per side gold tuners with pearl buttons, transducer bridge pickup. Available in Natural finish. Current mfr.

Mfr.'s Sug. Retail	$3,200	$2,400	$1,475	$1,025

LSE-II — similar to LSE-I, except has Indian rosewood back/sides.

Mfr.'s Sug. Retail	$3,200	$2,400	$1,475	$1,025

S25 JAZZ — nylon string configuration, small body with cutaway. Same Specifications as the O-25, except features slotted peghead, 3 per side tuners with pearloid buttons, transducer bridge pickup, preamp. Mfr. 1993 to date.

Mfr.'s Sug. Retail	$3,200	$2,400	$1,475	$1,025

LUCENA

Distributed by Music Imports of San Diego, California.

Music Imports offers a number of quality Lucena guitar models. For further information regarding model specifications and pricing, please contact Music Imports through the Index of Current Manufacturers located in the rear of this edition.

LUCIDA

See JOHNSON.

Instruments currently produced in Asia. Distributed by the Music Link of Brisbane, California.

The Music Link offers 4 different models of Lucida classical acoustic guitars with prices aimed at the entry level and student guitarists (prices range from $79.95 to $189). For further information regarding the Lucida models, contact the Music Link through the Index of Current Manufacturers located in the back of this edition.

LUTHIER

Instruments currently built in Spain. Distributed by Luthier Music Corporation of New York, New York.

The Luthier Music Corporation is importing classical and flamenco guitars from Spain to the U.S. market. Models range from Student and Advanced Student up to Concert level acoustics. Luthier Music Corporation also distributes the 'Luthier' brand nylon strings. For further information regarding models and pricing, contact the Luthier Music Corporation via the Index of Current Manufacturers located in the back of this book.

LYLE

Instruments were built in Japan from 1969 to 1980. Distributed by the L.D. Heater company of Portland, Oregon.

The Lyle product line consisted of acoustic and acoustic/electric archtop guitars, as well as solid body electric guitars and basses. These entry level to intermediate quality guitars featured designs based on popular American models. These instruments were manufactured by the Matsumoku company, who supplied models for both the Arai (Aria, Aria Pro II) company and the early 1970s Epiphone models.

(Source: Michael Wright, Vintage Guitar Magazine)

G.W. LYON

Instruments built in Korea since the early 1990s. Distributed in the U.S. by Washburn International of Vernon Hills, Illinois.

G.W. Lyon offers a range of instruments designed for the student or beginner guitarist at affordable prices and decent entry level quality.

LYS

Instruments built in Canda circa late 1970s.

The **Blue Book of Guitars** recieved some information through the Internet this year that offered a connection between Lys acoustic guitars and the La Si Do company, makers of **Godin** and other fine acoustics and electrics. Further research continues into this trademark listing.

L

RIC McCURDY

Instruments currently built in New York City, New York.

Luthier Ric McCurdy has been producing custom guitars since 1983. Originally based in Santa Barbara, California, he moved to New York City in 1991 where he studied archtop guitar building with Bob Benedetto. Since then, he has been concentrating on building archtops and one-off custom guitars.

Currently using McCurdy guitars are ECM recording artist John Abercrombie and studio ace Joe Beck. All archtops feature the Kent Armstrong adjustable polepiece pickup which can be used with steel or bronze strings.

ACOUSTIC

The **Moderna** (list price $5,000) is a single cutaway archtop guitar, 16" wide at lower bout. This model features flame maple back and sides with a Sitka spruce top, multi-fine line binding on body head and pickguard, graphite reinforced maple neck with 25.5" scale, and abalone or pearl block inlays on a 22 fret ebony fingerboard. The finish is nitrocellulose lacquer.

The vintage styled **Kenmare** archtop is 17" across the lower bout, and has AAAA flame maple back and sides, and a Sitka spruce top. Other aspects of this model include bound f-holes, multi-ply fine line binding, 25.5" scale, graphite reinforced maple neck, split block inlay on 22 fret ebony fingerboard, vintage peghead inlay, and Cremona Amber nitrocellulose finish (list price $7,500).

McKERRIHAN

Instruments currently built in Phoenix, Arizona.

Luthier Glen E. McKerrihan handcrafts four different archtop guitar models that feature classic styling and single rounded cutaway bodies. All four models are available in 16" or 17" body widths. Models include the **Anastasia** (list $3,250), the **Finger Style** (list $3,750), the **Keenan** (list $3,000), and **Monk's Model** ($3,000). All models have hand carved aged solid tone woods, 25" scale length, ebony fingerboards, and 5-ply body binding.

MACCAFERRI

Instruments produced in Italy circa 1923. Instruments designed for the Selmer company in France date between 1931 to 1932.

Maccaferri instruments produced in America began circa the early 1950s and continued on as he stayed active in luthiery.

Italian-born luthier Mario Maccaferri (1900-1993) was a former classical guitarist turned guitar designer and builder. Born in Bologna, Italy in 1900, Maccaferri began his apprenticeship to luthier/guitarist Luigi Mozzani in 1911. At age 16 Maccaferri began classical guitar studies at the Academy in Siena, and graduated with highest possible honors in 1926.

Between 1931 and 1932, Maccaferri designed and built a series of instruments for the French Selmer company. Although they were used by such notables as Django Reinhardt, a dispute between the company and Maccaferri led to a short production run. In the two years (1931-1932) that Maccaferri was with Selmer, he estimated that perhaps 200 guitars were built.

In 1936 Maccaferri moved to New York. He founded Mastro Industries, which became a leading producer of plastic products such as clothespins (which he invented during World War II), acoustical tiles, and eventually Arthur Godfrey ukuleles.

In 1953, Maccaferri introduced another innovative guitar made out of plastic. This archtop guitar featured a through-neck design, 3 tuners per side headstock, and two f-holes. Despite the material involved, Maccaferri did not consider them to be a toy. Along with the archtop model Maccaferri produced a flattop version. But the 1953 market was not quite prepared for this new design, and Maccaferri took the product off the market and stored them until around 1980 (then released them again).

In the mid 1950s, Maccaferri was on friendly terms with Nat Daniels of Danelectro fame. As contemporaries, they would gather to discuss amplification in regards to guitar design, but nothing came of their talks. Maccaferri stayed busy with his plastics company and was approached by Ibanez in the early 1980s to endorse a guitar model. As part of the endorsement, Maccaferri was personally signing all the labels for the production run.

The Maccaferri-designed instruments were produced by the atelier of Henri Selmer and Co. of Paris, France between 1931 to 1932 as the Selmer modele Concert. However, due to the dispute between the company and Maccaferri, experts estimate that less than 300 were made (note Maccaferri's estimate, above).

(Source: George Gruhn and Dan Forte, Guitar Player magazine, February 1986; and Paul Hostetter, Guitares Maurice Dupont)

S.B. MACDONALD

Instruments currently built in Huntington (Long Island), New York.

Luthier S.B. MacDonald has been building and restoring stringed instruments for 20 years. His instruments are built by special order and designed around the needs of each customer. MacDonald offers acoustic, electric, and resophonic instruments. He is also a columnist for "20th Century Guitar" and "Acoustic Musician" magazines.

One of MacDonald's custom instruments is the Resonator Electric, a vintage-style semi-hollow body guitar with a resonator cone. The Resonator Electric features a maple neck, 21 fret ebony fingerboard, 6 on a side Grover tuners, Tele-style neck pickup/Fishman transducer in resonator cone, volume and tone controls, and cool retro colors. For further information on this model and others, contact luthier S.B. MacDonald through the Index of Current manufacturers located in the back of this edition.

McCurdy Archtop
courtesy Ric McCurdy

Cedar Top Acoustic
courtesy S.B. MacDonald

MAC YASUDA GUITARS

Also MASTERBILT GUITARS.

Instruments built in Old Hickory, Tennessee; final production (inlays) is set in California. Distributed by Mac Yasuda Enterprises of Irvine, California.

Mac Yasuda is internationally recognized as a vintage guitar authority and collector, and has been writing on the topic of vintage instruments for well over two decades. Many may not realize that Yasuda is also a first-rate musician who has appeared onstage at the WSM Grand Ole Opry. Yasuda began performing country music on a local radio show in Kobe, Japan at the age of 17, and joined the "Rodeo Rangers" as a singer a year later. This group gained popularity on radio and in nightclubs in western Japan.

In 1970, Yasuda arrived in the U.S. to study at Michigan Technological University. He traveled to Nashville, and later purchased his first vintage guitar from a Denver pawnshop. Since then, virtually thousands of vintage instruments have passed through his hands.

In the late 1980s, Yasuda met Greg Rich. Rich was then acquiring a reputation for his custom musical instruments created for a major guitar producer (located in Nashville). These specialized custom instruments had immediate appeal in the collectibles market. In 1992, Rich collaborated with Mark Taylor (see TUT TAYLOR, CRAFTERS OF TENNESSEE) to create a company to produce his latest custom designs. Mac Yasuda currently contracts Rich and Taylor to produce his namesake high quality, custom guitars. In 1997, Rich left the Masterbilt company.

ACOUSTIC

S.B. MacDonald acoustic
courtesy S.B. MacDonald

To show his appreciation for country music and the Grand Ole Opry, Yasuda decided to present custom guitars to several of the legendary Opry artists. Yasuda then contacted Rich and Taylor to produce the first of the Mac Yasuda guitars. In early 1995, these custom guitars were presented to Porter Wagoner, Billy Walker, and Jack Greene. Later presentations were made to Hank Snow, Del Reeves, and Jimmy C. Newman. As the gifts were presented, many other Grand Ole Opry stars became interested in the Mac Yasuda guitars.

In 1996, Yasuda and Rich decided to produce a line of guitars. The company was based in California, and debuted at the winter NAMM show in 1997 under the **Masterbilt** trademark. The company currently offers three models, as well as numerous custom options (finishes, custom inlay, hand engraving, binding, etc). Contact Mac Yasuda for current prices.

The **MYD-42** is a dreadnought sized model with either rosewood or maple back and sides. It features 42-style abalone on the top, tortoise style pickguard, ebony fingerboard with an intricate Tree of Life inlay, nickel Grover Imperial tuners, and a nitrocellulose finish.

The **MYD-45** (Mac Yasuda D-45) is also dreadnought sized, and has a selected spruce top with rosewood back and sides. This model features 45-style abalone trim on the top, back, and sides. Other features include a custom pearl inlaid pickguard, bridge, fingerboard, and peghead; ebony overlay on the front and back of the peghead; gold Grover Imperial tuners, and a nitrocellulose finish.

The jumbo size **MYJ-1000** model has rosewood or curly maple back and sides. The select spruce top has 42-style abalone on the top, combined with multi-layered binding on the back and sides. The pickguard, fingerboard, and peghead are inlaid with custom pearl. The tuning keys are gold Grover Imperial tuners, and is finished in either Natural or Sunburst nitrocellulose finish.

The **Art Deco Catalina** model has Sitka spruce top, selected curly maple back and sides, ebony fingerboard, and one-piece mahogany neck. This model features mother of pearl and abalone inlays depicting palm trees, moons, pyramids in an Art Deco motif; available in Antique Natural, Opaque Black, Pearl White, Translucent Blue, Translucent Green, and Translucent Red finishes.

M A D

M A D ARCHTOP GUITARS.

Instruments currently built in Geneva, Switzerland.

Luthier David Marioni is hand crafting **Virtuoso** model archtop guitars. This classic archtop design features a hand carved Swiss spruce top, flamed maple back and sides, laminated flame maple neck, and ebony fingerboard. The **Virtuoso** is available in a 16", 17", and 18" body widths. For further information, contact luthier David Marioni at M A D Archtop Guitars through the Index of Current Manufacturers located in the back of this book.

MADEIRA

See GUILD.

Instruments were built in Japan during the early 1970s to late 1980s.

The Madeira line was imported in to augment Guild sales in the U.S. between 1973 and 1974. The first run of solid body electrics consisted of entry level reproductions of classic Fender, Gibson, and even Guild designs (such as the S-100). The electric models were phased out in a year (1973 to 1974), but the acoustics were continued.

The solid body electrics were reintroduced briefly in the early 1980s, and then introduced again in 1990. The line consisted of three guitar models (ME-200, ME-300, ME-500) and one bass model (MBE-100). All shared similar design acoutrements such as bolt-on necks and various pickup configurations.

(Source: Michael Wright, Vintage Guitar Magazine)

MANEA CUSTOM GUITARS

Instruments currently built in Goodlettsville, Tennessee.

Luthier Dumitru Manea's goal is to make high quality affordable guitars for the beginner as well as professional recording artists. Manea has thirty years experience in woodworking and manufacturing techniques.

ACOUSTIC

Mahogany Resonator
courtesy S.B. MacDonald

Manea's new **Scodie** model is a 4-in-1 acoustic with a patented method to change from a 12 string configuration to 6-string, 9-string, or *Nashville* tuning in a matter of seconds.

Both the steel string model **M-2000** and classical model **AV-1** feature hand-carved spruce or cedar tops, mahogany or cedar necks and Indian rosewood back and sides. Both models feature ebony fingerboards and bridges, and a number of additionally priced design options. In addition to the AV-1, Manea also offers a Kid's Classical model (**CJ-11**) and two student models (**MP-14 Steel String** and **ME-14 Classical**).

MANSON

A.B. MANSON & COMPANY.

Instruments built in Devon, England from the late 1970s to date. Distributed in the U.S. by S.A. Music of Santa Barbara, California.

Stringed instruments bearing the Manson name come from two separate operations. Acoustic guitars, mandolins, bouzoukis (and even triplenecks!) are built by Andrew Manson at A.B. Manson & Company. Electric guitars and electric basses are built by Hugh Manson at Manson Handmade Instruments. Andrew and Hugh Manson have been plying their luthier skills for over twenty five years. Both Mansons draw on a wealth of luthier knowledge as they tailor the instrument directly to the player commissioning the work.

Hand sizing (for neck dimensions), custom wiring, or custom choice of wood - it's all done in house. Both facilities are located in Devon, and both Mansons build high quality instruments respective of their particular genre. U.S. retail prices range around $3,275 for various models like the **Dove**, **Heron**, and **Sandpiper**. For further information regarding model specifications, pricing, and availablility, please contact either Andrew or Hugh Manson via the Index of Current Manufacturers located in the back of this book.

According to authors Tony Bacon and Paul Day (The Guru's Guitar Guide), Manson instruments can be dated by the first two digits of the respective instrument's serial number.

MANZANITA GUITARS

Instruments currently built in Rosdorf, Germany.

Manzanita Guitars was founded in 1994 by Moritz Sattler and Manfred Pietrzok. During their first year of cooperation, they concentrated on building acoustic steel string guitars, blending traditional shapes with design and construction ideas that soon became accepted as typical for Manzanita.

In 1995 Moitz Sattler was commissioned to copy a 1929 Martin 000 and a 1932 Martin OM. Both resulting instruments were a success. Presently more than two thirds of his orders are reproductions of instruments of the same time period.

Manfred Pietrzok, on the other hand, was "forced" (by demand) to devote a large share of his work to building resophonic guitars. In cooperation with Martin Huch and Jorg Driesner, Pietrzok designed and constructed a solid body resophonic lapsteel guitar (**Crossbreed**) and a hollow neck resophonic guitar (**Hiro**).

In 1997 Jorg Driesner was asked to join Manzanita Guitars. Driesner has taken over the production of solid body resophonics and lapsteels. Shortly after joining, he added a roundneck solid body resophonic and a Tele-style thinline electric guitar to the Manzanita program. Manzanita Guitars feature 3 guitarmakers, 3 workshops, and more than 30 years of full time guitarmaking experience. For further information, please contact Manzanita Guitars through the Index of Current Manufacturers located in the back of this book.

MANZER

Instruments built in Toronto, Canada since 1978.

Luthier Linda Manzer was first inspired to build stringed instruments after seeing Joni Mitchell perform on a dulcimer in 1969. Manzer began building full time in 1974, and apprenticed under Jean Claude Larrivee until 1978. In 1983, Manzer spent several months with James D'Aquisto while learning the art of archtop guitar building. Manzer gained some industry attention after she completed Pat Metheny's "Pikasso" multi-necked guitar (the model has four necks sharing one common body and 42 strings). In 1990, Manzer was commissioned by the Canadian Museum of Civilization to create a guitar for one of their displays. In addition to building the high quality guitar that she is known for, Manzer included inlay designs in the shape of one of Canada's endangered species on the neck. The extra ornamentation served as a reminder for enviromental concerns. Noted players using Manzer guitars include Pat Metheny, Bruce Cockburn, and Heather Bishop.

ACOUSTIC

Archtop Series

All Manzer Archtops use only highest grade aged spruce tops and curly maple back, sides, and neck. Other features include an ebony fingerboard, bridge, and floating pickguard, as well as a gold plated height adjustment for the ebony tailpiece, and Schaller machine heads. Body depth is 3" at the side and 5" at the middle, a scale length of 25 1/4" (64 cm), and an overall length of 41" (104.5 cm) - except the Absynthe, which is 43" long (109 cm).

The **Studio** (list $8,000) is offered in either 16 1/2" or 17" lower bout width, and has ivoroid binding, dot inlay on fingerboard, Manzer signature inlay, and is available in a Blonde finish. The **Au Naturel** is 17" wide across the lower bout, and features all wood binding, highest grade woods, Orchid inlay and signature on the peghead, plain fingerboard, and art deco f-holes. This model is available in a Blonde finish, and has a retail list of $10,000.

The **Blue Note** model has a 5 ply maple/mahogany top and back, with curly maple sides and a body width of 16". Other features include an "In body" custom made PAF pickup that delivers rich warm tone with on-board volume and tone controls. Finished in a Light Tangerine Honey Burst, with all ebony appointments (list $5,500). The **JazzCAT** (list $11,000) is a 17" all wood model with contemporary A soundholes, bevelled veneered peghead, and Manzer signature inlay. This model is equipped with a Manzer JazzCAT pickup with adjustable polepieces, and is finished in Honey Tangerine. The 18" **Absynthe** has deluxe binding, highest grade woods, ebony bound fingerboard with split block inlay, and Orchid with engraved mother of pearl scroll inlay of peghead. This model is available in Blonde or custom colors, and has a list price of $14,000.

Flattop Series

There are several Manzer flattop models, each with their own "personality". Again, construction features aged spruce or Western cedar, Indian rosewood, and ebony. Manzer's most popular model, the **Manzer Steel String** ($5,000) has a 25½" scale, Rosewood back and sides, and an Ebony fingerboard. The **Baritone** ($5,500) was designed in conjunction with Craig Snyder, and features a longer 29" scale. The longer scale supports the lower tuning (either low B to B, or low A to A) thus giving guitars access to a fuller voice. Back and sides are contructed of Curly Koa, and the fingerboard and bridge are Ebony. The **Cowpoke** ($5,000) shares construction similarities with the standard Manzer, but features a larger and deeper body. Original inspiration was derived from a *tall guy who wanted a Manzer, only bigger!* The **Classical** ($6,000) offers a design that accomodates both traditional classical playing and modern jazz styles. A **12 String** configuration flat top is also offered ($5,500). All flattop models, with the exception of the **Little Manzer Steel** ($3,000) and the **Little Manzer Classical** ($3,400), are available in a single cutaway design for an additional $300.

Manzer Archtop
courtesy Linda Manzer

M

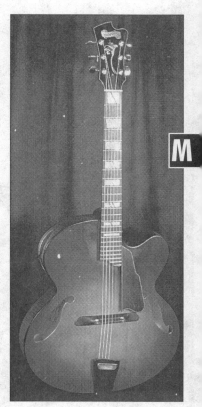

Manzer Blue Absynthe
courtesy Scott Chinery

JAMES L. MAPSON

Instruments currently built in Santa Ana, California.

Luthier James L. Mapson is currently offering a number of different archtop guitars built in small batches to control quality to the highest standards. Various aged tonewoods are available (AA, AAA, and Master grade maple and spruce from both domestic and European sources). Mapson originally studied aerospace and mechanical engineering, and built up a very successful engineering business. His experience with computer aided design (CAD) and aerospace product construction provided the basis for Mapson's archtop designs and construction - no sloppy tolerances here! As appointments vary from customer to customer, Mapson creates a CAD design to provide a rendering for customer approval prior to production.

Prices vary with each design, with base models starting at $3,000. Models include the Solo, Lusso, and the limited edition (only two built per year!) Avante. Contact luthier/designed James L. Mapson or visit Mapson's website for further information via the Index of Current Manufacturers located in the back of this book.

17" Nylon String Archtop
courtesy Stephanie Green

MARATHON

See chapter on House Brands.

This trademark had been identified as a *House Brand* previously used by Abercrombie & Fitch during the 1960s by author/researcher Willie G. Moseley. However, a number of newer guitars sporting the same trademark have been recently spotted. These guitars are built in Korea by the Samick company, and serve as an entry level instrument for the novice guitarist.

MARCHIONE

Instruments currently handcrafted in New York (Manhattan), New York.

Stephen Marchione builds recording quality archtop and special commission guitars. Marchione's clientele primarily consists of New York's top studio and stage players, and he has received commissions from the likes of Mark Whitfield, John Abercrombie, Vernon Reed, and Mark Knofler. Other notables playing Marchione's guitars are Georg Wadenius (Steely Dan's *Alive in America* CD), Mark Stewart (Bang on a Can's *Music for Airports* CD), and Kenny Brescia and Ira Seigel (soundtrack for the Broadway smash *Rent)*.

Marchione approaches his craft from many different angles. He understands players' sound and comfort needs as a guitar player himself. Marchione also seriously studies the great guitar and violin instruments in order to build archtop guitars that function as pinnacle pieces. When a player brings in a D'Aquisto or D'Angelico to Marchione's Manhattan shop, Marchione scrutinizes the instrument's construction, draws blueprints, and then quizzes the player about the instrument's best qualities. These important elements are then incorporated into his own designs.

The violin tradition has also figured prominently in Marchione's building. A hands-on understanding of cello arching is crucial to Marchione's ability to recreate the arching subtleties that imbue his archtop guitars with full acoustic volume and tambour. Marchione's friendship with violin maker Guy Rabut has impressed upon Marchione the importance of incorporating centuries of stringed instrument knowledge. Their friendship has also given Marchione the opportunity to measure and draw plans from Guarnieri cellows as well as Rabut's renowned instruments.

Personal musicianship, an exacting approach to guitar making, and the experience of hand building almost three hundred acoustic archtops, neck-throughs, and electric guitars are the groundwork for each and every Marchione guitar.

(Company information courtesy Stephanie Green)

ACOUSTIC

Archtop Models

There are several construction features that make Marchione's acoustic Archtops unique. Marchione chalk fits the neck dovetail joint to get a full contact suction fit - this provides the guitar with its long ringing sustain. Final top tuning is performed with the guitar strung up to pitch; thus, he can fine tune the tambour and volume of the guitar while it is being played (no guessing allowed!). Marchione also hand carves the soundboard recurve all the way around the perimeter of the soundboard, including the cutaway, making the whole instrument acoustically useful. In order to maximize the instrument's sound, Marchione suspends the pickguard, the entire fingerboard extension, the tailpiece, and the pickup over the top. Marchione has noticed from studying cellos and other acoustic guitars that as soon as anything touches the top, the instrument's sound is decreased by up to one-third.

Archtop guitars are available as Steel String or Nylon String models. All instruments feature loft-dried cello grade tonewoods including High Alpine Engelmann spruce (tops) and highly figured maple (back, sides, and necks). Other features include an ebony fingerboard, pickguard, tailpiece, and bridge. Instruments are constructed with all wood binding and purfling, and have mother of pearl inlay. The **Acoustic Archtop** model is featured in 16", 17", and 18" body widths, and are available with or without electronics. The retail list price is $16,500.

MARCO POLO

Instruments built in Japan circa early 1960s. Distributed by the Marco Polo Company of Santa Ana, California.

The Marco Polo product line offered acoustic flattops, thinline hollowbody acoustic/electric guitars, and solid body electric guitars and basses. These inexpensive Japanese-built instruments were the first to be advertised by its U.S. distributors, Harry Stewart and the Marco Polo company. While the manufacturers are currently unknown, it is estimated that some of the acoustics were built by Suzuki, and some electric models were produced by Guyatone.

(Source: Michael Wright, Vintage Guitar Magazine)

MARK WESCOTT GUITARS

Instruments currently built in Somers Point, New Jersey.

Mark Wescott's approach to guitar building is one of innovative design that is based on the importance of sound and the interaction between the guitar and the player. Wescott is one of the growing number of modern builders who are systematically re-examining the mechanics of how a guitar produces sound.

Wescott's backround in music began early as he grew up in a musical family where violins, violas, and cellos were always present. While Wescott first trained as an apprentice in cabinet making and furniture restoration, his musical backround led him back to creating high quality acoustic guitars.

Marchione custom Acoustic/Electric
courtesy Marchione Guitars

M

In 1980, Wescott built his first guitar under the guidance of George Morris, while attending the Charles Fox Guitar Research and Design School (GRD). Several years later, Wescott attended Richard Schneider's Kasha Design Seminar. Wescott continued on as resident luthier for three years at Schneider's Lost Mountain Center for the Guitar; it was there that he acquired a solid backround in the Kasha method of radial soundboard bracing. This method was first invented by Dr. Michael Kasha, and pioneered by Master Luthier Richard Schneider.

ACOUSTIC

Wescott designs his guitars (including the most recent **Intrepid** model) using the Kasha system of soundboard design. Asymetrical radial soundboard bracing in conjunction with the impedance matching bridge enables Wescott to tailor the tonal response of the instrument. The **Intrepid** model is available in 6- and 7-string configurations, and features a Sitka spruce top, East Indian rosewood back and sides, Honduran mahogany neck, 24 fret ebony fingerboard, Kasha-type bridge, 3 per side Schaller mini tuners, graphite soundboard braces, Wechter-style access panel (trap door) tail block. Commissioned retail price is $8,000, and comes complete with deluxe hardshell case.

MARLING

Instruments produced in Japan during the mid 1970s.

As the Italian-based EKO guitar company was winding down, they were marketing an EKO guitar copies built in Japan (although they may have been built by EKO). EKO offered a number of Marling acoustic models, as well as electric guitars. These guitar models were poor quality compared to the 1960s Italian EKOs.

(Source: Michael Wright, Guitar Stories Volume One)

MARONI

Instruments produced in Italy in the mid 1960s.

Reader Gene Van Alstyne of Cushing, Oklahoma called in this classical-styled guitar, built by *luthier Farfisa*. The guitar has a zero fret, a split saddle, 38mm tuning pegs, and a *Made in Italy* label in the soundhole. When the Farfisa name was uttered, the immediate talk turned to those 1960's organs. A connection, perhaps? Further research is underway.

MARTELLE

See chapter on House Brands.

The distributor of this Gibson-built budget line of guitars has not yet been identified. Built to the same standards as other Gibson guitars, they lack the one true *Gibson* touch: an adjustable truss rod. **House Brand** Gibsons were available to musical instrument distributors in the late 1930s and early 1940s.

(Source: Walter Carter, Gibson Guitars: 100 Years of an American Icon)

MARTIN

Instruments produced in Nazareth, Pennsylvania since 1839. C.F. Martin & Company was originally founded in New York in 1833.

The Martin Guitar company has the unique position of being the only company that has always been helmed by a Martin family member. Christian Frederick Martin, Sr. (1796-1873) came from a woodworking (cabinet making) family background. He learned guitar building as an employee for Johann Stauffer, and worked his way up to Stauffer's foreman in Vienna (Austria). Martin left Stauffer in 1825, and returned to his birthplace in Markneukirchen (Germany). Martin got caught up in an on-going dispute between the violin makers guild and the cabinet makers guild. Martin and his family emigrated to America in the fall of 1833, and by the end of the year set up a full line music store. The Martin store dealt in all types of musical instruments, sheet music, and repairs - as well as Martin's Stauffer-style guitars.

After six years, the Martin family moved to Nazareth, Pennsylvania. C.A. Zoebich & Sons, their New York sales agency, continued to hold "exclusive" rights to sell Martin guitars; so the Martin guitars retained their *New York* labels until a business falling-out occurred in 1898. The Martin family settled outside of town, and continued producing guitars that began to reflect less of a European design in favor of a more straightforward design. Christian Martin favored a deeper lower bout, Brazilian rosewood for the back and sides, cedar for necks, and a squared-off slotted peghead (with 3 tuners per side). Martin's scalloped X-bracing was developed and used begining in 1850 instead of the traditional "fan" bracing favored by Spanish luthiers (fan bracing is favored on classical guitars today).

In 1852, Martin standardized his body sizes, with "1" the largest and "3" the smallest (size 2 and 2 1/2 were also included). Two years later, a larger "0" and smaller "5" sizes were added as well. Martin also standardized his style (or design) distinctions in the mid 1850s, with the introduction of Style 17 in 1856 and Styles 18 and 27 a year later. **Thus, every Martin guitar has a two-part name: size number and style number.** Martin moved into town in 1857 (a few blocks north of town square), and built his guitar building factory right next door within two years.

C.F. Martin & Company was announced in 1867, and in three years a wide range of Styles were available. A larger body size, the **00** debuted in 1877. Under the direction of C.F. Martin, Jr. (1825-1888), the company decided to begin producing mandolins - which caused the business split with their New York sales agency. Martin bowl-back mandolins were offered beginning in 1895, three years before the snowflake inlay **Style 42** became available. Also as important, **Martin began serializing their guitars in 1898**. The company estimated that 8,000 guitars had been built between 1833 to 1898, and so started the serialization with number 8,000. This serialization line is still intact today (!), and functions as a useful tool in dating the vintage models. The 15" wide body **Size 000**, as well as more pearl inlay on Martin guitars were introduced in 1902, which led to the fancier **Style 45** two years later.

A major materials change occured in 1916, as mahogany replaced cedar as the chosen wood for neck building. White celluloid (ivoroid) became the new binding material in 1918. **The Martin company also took a big technological leap in 1922, as they adapted the Model 2 - 17 for steel strings instead of gut strings** (all models would switch to steel string configuration by 1929). To help stabilize the new amount of stress in the necks, an ebony bar was embedded in the neck (the ebony bar was replaced by a steel T-Bar in 1934). Martin briefly built banjos in the early to mid 1920s, and also built a fair share of good quality ukeleles and tiples.

In 1929, Martin was contacted by Perry Bechtel who was looking for a flat top guitar with 14 frets clear of the body (Martin's models all joined at the 12th fret). The company responded by building a 000 model with a slimmed down 14/20 fret neck

D-35
courtesy The Martin Guitar Company

- announced in the 1930 catalog as the **OM (Orchestra Model)** (the 14/20 fret neck was adopted by almost all models in the production line by 1934). Martin also began stamping the model name into the neck block of every guitar in 1931.

While the Jazz Age was raising a hubaloo, Martin was building arch top guitars. The three **C** models were introduced in 1931, and the **R-18** two years later. Martin arch top production lasted until 1942. The arch tops of 1931 have since been overshadowed by another model that debuted that year - Martin's 16" wide **Dreadnought** size. Guitar players were asking for more volume, but instead of making a bigger "0000" body, Martin chose to design a new type of acoustic guitar. Martin was already building a similar type of guitar originally as a model for the Oliver Ditson company in 1916; they just waited for the market to catch up to them!

The dreadnought acoustic (so named after large World War I battleships) with X-bracing is probably the most widely copied acoustic guitar design in the world today. A look at today's music market could confirm a large number of companies building a similar design, and the name "Dreadnought" has become an industry standard. Back in the 1930s, a singing cowboy of some repute decided to order a dreadnought size guitar in the Style 45. Gene Autry became the first owner of Martin's D-45.

Due to the use of heavy gauge steel strings, the Martin company stopped the practice of "scalloping" (shaving a concave surface) the braces on their guitar tops. 1947 saw the end of herringbone trim on the guitar tops, due to a lack of consistent sources (either German or American). The first two dozen (or so) 1947 D-28 models did have heringbone trim. Some thirty years later, Martin's HD-28 model debuted with the "restored" scalloped bracing and herringbone trim (this model is still in production today).

The folk boom of the late 1950s increased the demand for Martin guitars. The original factory produced around 6,000 guitars a year, but that wasn't enough. Martin began construction on a new facility in 1964, and when the new plant opened a year later, production began to go over 10,000 guitars a year. While expansion of the market is generally a good thing, the limited supply of raw materials is detrimental (to say the least!). In 1969, Brazil put an embargo on rosewood logs exported from their country. To solve this problem, Martin switched to Indian rosewood in 1969. Brazilian rosewood from legal sources does show up on certain limited edition models from time to time.

The 1970s was a period of fluctuation for the Martin company. Many aggressive foreign companies began importing products into the U.S. market, and were rarely challenged by complacent U.S. manufacturers. To combat the loss of sales in the entry level market, Martin started the **Sigma** line of overseas-produced guitars for dealers. Martin also bought **Levin**, the Swedish guitar company in 1973. The **Size M**, developed in part by Mark Silber, Matt Umanov, and Dave Bromberg, debuted in 1977. E Series electric guitars were briefly offered beginning in 1979 (up until 1983). A failed attempt at union organization at the Martin plant also occured in the late 1970s. Martin's Custom Shop was formally opened in 1979, and set the tone for other manufacturers' custom shop concepts.

The 1980s saw some innovations at the Martin company. Current CEO and Chairman of the Board Chris F. Martin IV assumed his duties at the youthful age of 28 in 1986. The Martin Guitar of the Month program, a limited production/custom guitar offering was introduced in 1984 (and continued through 1994, prior to the adoption of the Limited Edition series) as well as the new Jumbo **J** Series. The most mind-boggling event occured the next year: The Martin Company adopted the adjustable truss rod in 1985! Martin always maintained the point of view that a properly built guitar wouldn't need one. The Korean-built **Stinger** line of solid body electrics was offered the same year as the **Shenandoah** line of Japanese-produced parts/U.S. assembly.

The Martin company continues producing guitars in Pennsylvania. The new **Road** Series models, with their CNC-carved necks and laminated back and sides are being built in the same facilities that produce the solid wood body models and custom shop facilities. Martin has brought all model production (figuratively and literally) under one roof. Martin still experiments with other tone woods, and is concerned with dwindling supplies of traditional guitar building woods long used in their company history.

(Source: Mike Longworth, Martin Guitars: A History; Walter Carter, The Martin Book: A Complete History of Martin Guitars; and Tom Wheeler, American Guitars)

D12-28
courtesy The Martin Guitar Company

Visual Identification Features

Martin has been in the same location for 160 years and serialization has remained intact and consistent since their first instrument. When trying to determine the year of an instrument's construction, some quick notes about features can be helpful. The few notes contained herein are for readily identifying the instrument upon sight and are by no means meant to be used for truly accurate dating of an instrument. **All items discussed are for flat-top steel string guitars and involve instruments that are standard production models**.

The earliest dreadnoughts, and indeed just about all instruments produced with a neck that joins the body at the 12th fret, have bodies that are bell shaped on the top, as opposed to the more square shouldered styles of most dreadnoughts. Between 1929 to 1934, Martin began placing 14 fret necks on most of their instruments and this brought about the square shouldered body style. A few models maintained 12 fret necks into the late 1940s and several had a 12 fret neck until the late 1980s.

Turn of the century instruments have square slotted pegheads with the higher end models (models **42** and **45**) displaying an intricate pearl fern inlay that runs vertically up the peghead. This was replaced by a vertical inlay known as the *flowerpot* or the *torch* inlay, in approximately 1905. In 1932, the *C.F. Martin & Co. Est. 1833* scroll logo began appearing on certain models' pegheads. By approximately 1934, a solid peghead with a vertical pearl *C.F. Martin* inlay had replaced the former peghead design.

Bridges from the 1900s are rectangular with *pyramid* wings. In approximately 1929, the *belly* bridge replaced the rectangle bridge. This bridge has a straight slot cut across the entire length of the center section of the bridge. In 1965, the straight cut saddle slot was changed to a routed slot. It was in approximately 1936, that Martin began using the *tied* bridge on their classical instruments.

Pickguards were not standard features on instruments until 1931 (1930 on some OM models) when tortoise pickguards were introduced. In 1967, black pickguards became standard. In 1969, Martin stopped using Brazilian rosewood for its regular production instruments, ending with serial number **254498**. As a result, premiums are being asked for instruments manufactured from this exotic wood. After 1969, Martin began to use East Indian rosewood backs and sides on standard production instruments in Style 21 or higher (D-21, D-28, etc.); and mahogany backs and sides on Style 20 or lower (D-18, D-1220, etc.) production models.

Martin Instruments built for other Trademarks (Brandnames)

Martin did build guitars for other retailers, teachers, and musical instrument distributors; unlike Harmony's or Kay's house brands, though, "retitled" Martins were the exception and **not the rule**. If any of these trademarks are spotted, here's a partial hint to origin:

Bacon Banjo Company: Around 1924, Martin supplied a number of guitars without Martin stamps or labels. However, most of the Bacon-trademarked guitars were built by Regal (Chicago, Illinois).

Belltone: Only a few Style 3K guitars, mandolins, and ukeleles were built for the Perlburg and Halpin company of New York City, New York.

Martin Headstock
courtesy Martin Guitar Company

Bitting Special: Both guitars and mandolins were built for this well known music teacher in Bethlehem, Pennsylvania between 1916 to 1919.

Briggs Special: 65 specially trimmed mandolin models were built for the Briggs Music shop in Utica, New York circa 1914 to 1919.

C. Bruno: Long before they were acquired by Kaman Music, C. Bruno was associated with C.F. Martin in 1838. Guitars carry a paper label that says C.F. Martin & Bruno. Later C. Bruno & Sons guitars were not built by Martin.

Oliver Ditson & Co.: Ditson had stores in Boston, New York, and Philadelphia. Martin built guitars, bowl-back and flat mandolins, ukeleles, tiples, and taro patch stringed instruments for their stores. Martin built a dreadnought-style guitar for them in 1916, long before Martin offered it under their own trademark in 1931. Another Ditson branch in Chicago went on to fame producing and marketing Washburn guitars in the 1900s.

Carl Fischer: The Carl Fisher firm of New York City, New York ordered a number of special O-18T (tenor) guitars in 1929.

William Foden: Concert guitarist and teacher William Foden had his own series of Foden Specials built by Martin. These models were primarily sold to his students between 1900 to 1920. Foden's insistence on a twenty fret fingerboard is now a standard feature on Martin guitars.

J.A. Handley: J.A. Handley was an instructor in Lowell, Massachusetts. He is credited with the developement of the Style 6A mandolin.

Jenkins: This dealer in Kansas City, Missouri sold Martin ukeleles, renumbered #35 (Style 1) and #40 (Style 2).

Montgomery Ward: Martin had a short term deal with the Montgomery Ward company circa 1932. Martin supplied mahogany guitars, flat mandolins, and ukeleles.

Vahdah Olcott-Bickford: Vahdah Olcott-Bickford was a well-known concert artist and teacher. Guitars built to her specifications were called a Style 44, or Soloist.

Paramount: Paramount ordered about 30 special resonator models under the Paramount logo. Paramount was well known for their banjo models, which were not Martin instruments.

Rolando: The Rolando trademark shows up on a series of Martin-built koa Hawaiian-style guitars ordered by the Southern California Music Company (circa 1917-1920). Records also show a direct sale to J.J. Milligan Music.

Rudick's: The Rudick's firm of Akron, Ohio ordered a number of OO-17 guitars with the number O-55 stamped inside (circa 1935).

William J. Smith: The William J. Smith firm of New York City, New York had Martin-built ukeleles, taro patches and tiples in stock circa 1917.

Stetson: W.J. Dyer & Bro., known for their association with Larson Brothers acoustics, also specified 3 guitars for their Stetson trademark circa 1922.

S.S. Stewart: Distributors Buegeleisen and Jacobson of New York City, New York ordered ukeleles and other stringed instruments with their S.S. Stewart label circa 1923 to 1925.

John Wanamaker: The Wanamaker department store in Philadelphia, Pennsylvania ordered special models circa 1909.

H.A. Weymann & Son: The Weymann firm of Philadelphia, Pennsylvania was known for their banjos; Martin built a number of ukeleles and taro patches models around 1925.

Wolverine: The Wolverine trademark was applied to Martin-built guitars and mandolins for the Grinnell Brothers of Detroit, Michigan. Wolverine instruments carry the regular Martin serial numbers.

Rudolph Wurlitzer: The Wurlitzer music store chain ordered special model guitars between 1922 to 1924.

(Information on "Retitled" Martin instruments courtesy: Mike Longworth, *Martin Guitars: A History*; Walter Carter, *The Martin Book: A Complete History of Martin Guitars*; and Tom Wheeler, *American Guitars*)

Current Production Model Designation

The Martin model series listing follows the model nomenclature. Additional information within the following parentheses lists the Martin company's current **Series** designation. **To avoid any potential confusion, current models are listed just as their model name is stamped on their neck block** (Martin began stamping model designations on the neck block in 1930).

For example, Martin's new Road Series models feature common contruction design (models have solid spruce tops, and laminated back/sides). However, the models in the Road Series include both dreadnought size and 000 Auditorium size models (The DM, DR, and 000M).

Guitars of the Month/Martin Custom Shop Models

Martin's **Guitars of the Month** (started in 1984) and **Custom SHop** (since 1979) guitars are fancier or slightly different takes on established models. They are usually identified with a suffix (some have unusual prefixes, just to make things difficult: For example, a **1990 D-18MB** is a D-18 with maple binding). The D-18MB would probably trade at the high end of D-18 prices for that year, or maybe a little higher. It is not our intention to list every variation but the reader should be aware that these instruments do exist. Custom Shop guitars are stamped "Custom" on the neck block. Custom Shop instruments can only be valued on an individual basis.

Martin Guitars Made Before 1898

Any Martin guitar made before 1898 almost has to be dealt with on an individual basis - nearly all of them were rosewood construction; they featured different amounts of trim. From **Style 17** at the low end (at the time a rosewood and spruce guitar with relatively plain trim) to **Style 42** at the high end, the largest of these instruments would be considered small by today's standards. Martin guitars from before the turn of the century seem to start at about $1,500 for something in average condition (and not fancy), and go up in excess of $35,000 for the fanciest guitars.

In 1898 Martin started serially numbering their guitars. They estimated that they'd made about 8,000 guitars up to that time; that's when they started their numbering system. Some models with low production totals (10 or less, usually) may be ignored here.

"A" Mandolin
courtesy Martin Guitar Company

M

1834 Stauffer-style Martin
courtesy Buddy Summer

Grading	100%	Excellent	Average

1998 Martin D-18 VM
courtesy Buddy Summer

Common Martin Abbreviations

A - Ash (back and sides)

B - Brazilian (back and sides)

BK - Black

C - Cedar, Classical, or Cutaway

DB - Deep Body

E - Electric flat-top or Employees

FMG - Figured Mahogany

G - Gut (later nylon) String

GOM - Guitar of the Month

H - Hawaiian

K - Koa (back and sides)

LE - Limited Edition

LSH - Large Soundhole

M - Mahogany (back and sides)

MB - Maple binding

MP - Morado rosewood (back and sides)

P - Plectrum or Low Profile

R - Rosewood (back and sides)

S - Special or Special Order (pre 1995)

SE - Signature Edition

SP - Special (post 1995)

T - Tenor

V - Vintage (suffix for models after 1983)

W - Walnut (back and sides)

ACOUSTIC

A Sunburst finished Martin guitar generally commands a higher premium over a similar model in Natural finish. Depending on the model, this premium may be 20% to 30% higher.

Martin currently offers a wide variety of Acoustic Sound Reinforcement options that are installed at the factory, as well as other finishes. Retail list price includes a hardshell case.

Add $229 for Fishman Prefix.

Add $269 for Fishman Prefix Plus.

Add $299 for Fishman Prefix Onboard Blender.

Add $190 for Martin/Fishman Pro EQ (outboard preamp only).

Add $270 for Martin/Fishman SLI Matrix EQ.

Add $219 for L.R. Baggs RT System.

Add $335 for L.R. Baggs Dual SOurce System.

Add $100 for Martin Second Generation Thinline 332.

Add $179 for Martin Thinline 332 Plus with Active Jack.

Add $189 for Martin Thinline Gold Plus.

Add $220 for Sunburst, "Vintage" toner, or "Aging" toner finishes.

Add $250 for High Gloss finish.

D (Dreadnought) Series

Size D (Dreadnought) guitars feature a Lower Bout Width of 15 5/8 inches.

DM (Road Series)— solid spruce top, round soundhole, black body binding, laminated mahogany back/sides, mahogany neck, 14/20 fret rosewood fingerboard with white dot inlay, single band herringbone rosette, tortoise pickguard, 3 per side chrome tuners. Available in Natural satin finish. Mfr. 1996 to date.

Mfr.'s Sug. Retail	$899	$725	$595	$375

DCM (Road Series)— similar to DM, except features rounded Venetian cutaway. Mfr. 1996 to date.

Mfr.'s Sug. Retail	$1,150	$925	$750	$475

DM-12 (Road Series)— similar to DM, except has 12-string configuration, 6 per side tuners. Mfr. 1996 to date.

Mfr.'s Sug. Retail	$1,150	$925	$750	$475

DR (Road Series)— similar to DM, except features laminated rosewood back/sides. Available in Natural satin finish. Mfr. 1996 to date.

Mfr.'s Sug. Retail	$1,099	$875	$725	$450

DR
courtesy The Martin Guitar Company

M

Grading	100%	Excellent	Average

D-1 (1 Series) — solid Sitka spruce top, round soundhole, tortoise bound body, 3 stripe rosette, solid mahogany back, laminated mahogany sides, mahogany neck, 14/20 fret rosewood fingerboard with dot inlay, rosewood bridge with white black dot pins, tortoise pickguard, 3 per side chrome tuners. Available in Natural satin finish. Mfr. 1993 to date.

Mfr.'s Sug. Retail	$1,099	$875	$725	$450

D-1R (1 Series) — similar to D-1, except has rosewood back/sides. Mfr. 1994 to date.

Mfr.'s Sug. Retail	$1,300	$1,050	$850	$525

DC-1 (1 Series) — similar to D-1, except features a rounded Venetian cutaway. Mfr. 1996 to date.

Mfr.'s Sug. Retail	$1,300	$1,050	$850	$525

DC-1R (1 Series) — similar to D-1, except features a rounded Venetian cutaway, rosewood back/sides. Mfr. 1998 to date.

Mfr.'s Sug. Retail	$1,499

DC-1E (1 Series) — similar to D-1, except features a rounded Venetian cutaway, Martin Gold+Plus bridge pickup, Martin/Fishman Prefix preamp/EQ system. Current mfr.

Mfr.'s Sug. Retail	$1,499	$1,200	$975	$625

D12-1 (1 Series) — similar to D-1, except has a 12-string configuration, 6 per side headstock. Mfr. 1996 to date.

Mfr.'s Sug. Retail	$1,300	$1,050	$850	$535

D-2R (1 Series) — solid spruce top, round soundhole, ivoroid bound body, 3 stripe rosette, laminated East Indian rosewood back/sides, mahogany neck, 14/20 fret rosewood fingerboard with dot inlay, rosewood bridge with white black dot pins, black pickguard, 3 per side chrome tuners. Available in Natural satin finish. Mfr. 1996 to date.

Mfr.'s Sug. Retail	$1,349	$1,075	$875	$550

This model features appointments that pay tribute to the appearance of the D-28 model.

D-3R (1 Series) — similar to D-2R, except features bound fingerboard, 3-piece back of laminated East Indian rosewood. Available in Natural satin finish. Mfr. 1996 to date.

Mfr.'s Sug. Retail	$1,425	$1,150	$925	$595

This model features appointments that pay tribute to the appearance of the D-35 model.

D-15 (15 Series) — solid mahogany top, round soundhole, single band gold herringbone decal rosette, solid mahogany back/sides, mahogany neck, no body binding, 14/20 fret rosewood fingerboard with white dot inlay, rosewood bridge with white pins, tortoise pickguard, 3 per side chrome tuners. Current mfr.

Mfr.'s Sug. Retail	$849	$675	$550	$350

DC-15E (15 Series) — similar to D-15, except features a single rounded cutaway body, bridge pickup, on-board electronics. Available in Natural satin finish. Mfr. 1998 to date.

Mfr.'s Sug. Retail	$1,425

D-16T (16 Series) — spruce top, round soundhole, black pickguard, tortoise bound body, herringbone rosette, solid mahogany back/sides, mahogany neck, 14/20 fret rosewood fingerboard with pearl dot inlay, rosewood bridge with black pins, tortoise pickguard, 3 per side chrome tuners. Available in Natural satin finish. Mfr. 1986 to date.

1986-1997			$1,000	$750
Mfr.'s Sug. Retail	$1,650	$1,325	$1,075	$675

D-16 A — similar to the D-16, except features ash back/sides. Mfd. 1987-1988, 1990.

			$1,000	$750

D-16 K — similar to the D-16, except features Koa back/sides. Mfd. 1986.

			$1,200	$850

D-16 W — similar to the D-16, except features walnut back/sides. Mfd. 1987, 1990.

			$1,200	$850

D-16TR (16 Series) — similar to the D-16T, except has solid rosewood back/sides. Available in Natural satin finish. Mfr. 1996 to date.

Mfr.'s Sug. Retail	$1,850	$1,500	$1,200	$750

D-18 — solid spruce top, round soundhole, tortoise bound body, 3 stripe purfling/rosette, mahogany back/sides/neck, 12/19 fret ebony fingerboard with pearl dot inlay, ebony bridge with black white dot pins, 3 per side chrome tuners. Available in Natural finish. Mfd. 1932 to date.

1932-1933			$15,000 (and Up)	

In 1934, 14/20 fret fingerboard replaced the 12/19 fret fingerboard.

1934-1939			$14,000	$8,000
1940-1946			$8,000	$4,000
1947-1956			$3,800	$2,500
1957-1969			$2,500	$1,200
1970-1995			$1,200	$900

D-18 (Standard Series)

Mfr.'s Sug. Retail	$2,030	$1,625	$1,325	$395

Some early D-18 models have sold as high as $30,000.

In 1932, pickguard was optionally available.

By 1944, rosewood fingerboard/bridges replaced original items.

D-18 S — similar to D-18, except has prewar dreadnought style body, 12/20 fret fingerboard. Mfd. 1967 to 1993.

1967-1969			$2,000	$1,200
1970-1993			$1,800	$1,000

Last Mfr.'s Sug. Retail was $2,330.

D-18
courtesy Martin Guitar Company

Grading	100%	Excellent	Average

1941 Martin D-28
courtesy Buddy Summer

D12-18 — similar to D-18, except has 12 strings, 6 per side tuners. Mfd. 1973 to 1996.

		$1,200	$850

Last Mfr.'s Sug. Retail was $2,350.

D-18VM (Vintage Series) — solid spruce top, round soundhole, tortoise bound body, special design striped rosette, solid mahogany back/sides, mahogany neck, 14/20 fret ebony fingerboard with abalone dot inlay, ebony bridge with white black dot pins, beveled tortoise pickguard, (old style) squared off headstock, 3 per side open gear chrome tuners with "butterbean" knobs. Available in "Aging Toner" lacquer finish. Mfr. 1996 to date.

Mfr.'s Sug. Retail	$2,650	$2,125	$1,725	$1,100

D-18VMS (Vintage Series)— similar to the D-18VM, except features a 12/19 fret fingerboard, slotted headstock. Mfr. 1996 to date.

Mfr.'s Sug. Retail	$3,060	$2,500	$2,000	$1,250

D-19 — spruce top, round soundhole, black pickguard, 3 stripe bound body/rosette, mahogany back/sides/neck, 14/20 fret rosewood fingerboard with pearl dot inlay, rosewood bridge with white black dot pins, rosewood peghead veneer with logo decal, 3 per side chrome tuners. Available in Dark Brown finish. Mfd. 1976 to 1988.

		$1,200	$850

D12-20 — solid spruce top, round soundhole, black pickguard, 3 stripe bound body/rosette, mahogany back/sides/neck, 12/20 fret rosewood fingerboard with pearl dot inlay, rosewood bridge with black white dot pins, 6 per side chrome tuners. Available in Natural finish. Mfd. 1964 to 1991.

		$850	$750

Last Mfr.'s Sug. Retail was $2,480.

D-21 — spruce top, round soundhole, tortoise bound body, herringbone rosette, Brazilian rosewood back/sides, mahogany neck, 14/20 fret Brazilian rosewood fingerboard with pearl dot inlay, Brazilian rosewood bridge with black white dot bridgepins, 3 per side chrome tuners. Mfd. 1955 to 1969.

1955-1960		$4,000	$3,000
1961-1969		$3,200	$2,500

D-25K — spruce top, round soundhole, black pickguard, bound body, 4 stripe purfling, 5 stripe rosette, koa back/sides, mahogany neck, 14/20 fret rosewood fingerboard with pearl dot inlay, rosewood bridge with black white pins, rosewood veneered peghead with screened logo, 3 per side chrome tuners. Available in Natural finish. Mfd. 1980 to 1989.

		$1,200	$750

Last Mfr.'s Sug. Retail was $1,610.

D-25K2 — similar to D-25 K, except has koa top. Available in Natural finish. Mfd. 1980 to 1989.

		$1,200	$750

Last Mfr.'s Sug. Retail was $1,735.

D-28 — solid spruce top, round soundhole, black pickguard, bound body, herringbone purfling, 5 stripe rosette, rosewood 2 piece back/sides, 14/20 fret ebony fingerboard with pearl diamond inlay, ebony bridge with white black dot pins, 3 per side chrome tuners. finish. Mfd. 1931 to date.

Martin produced a number of D-28 Herringbone guitars between 1931 to 1933. A really clean, excellent plus D-28 from these three years may be worth over $35,000. The Blue Book of Guitars highly recommends that several professional appraisals be secured before buying/selling/trading any 1931-1933 D-28 guitars with herringbone trim.

1931-1939		$35,000	$20,000
1940-1946		$25,000	$20,000

1946 was the last year that the herringbone trim around the top was offered (although the last batch was in early 1947).

1947-1956		$6,500	$3,500
1957-1969		$4,000	$2,500
1970-1996		$1,800	$900

D-28 (Standard Series)

Mfr.'s Sug. Retail	$2,330	$1,865	$1,525	$975

By 1935, Shaded top finish was optionally available.

1936 was the last year for the 12 fret model. These models may command a higher premium.

In 1944, scalloped bracing was discontinued, and pearl dot fingerboard inlay replaced the split diamond inlays.

In 1969, Indian rosewood replaced Brazilian rosewood.

D-28 E — dreadnought style, spruce top, round soundhole, black pickguard, 3 stripe bound body/rosette, rosewood back/sides, 14/20 fret ebony fingerboard with pearl dot inlay, ebony bridge with white black dot pins, 3 per side tuners, gold hardware, 2 single coil exposed DeArmond pickups, 2 volume/2 tone controls, 3 position switch. Available in Natural finish. Mfd. 1959 to 1965.

		$1,275	$750

D-28S — similar to D-28, except has a bell shape dreadnought style body, 12/20 fret fingerboard, slotted headstock. Mfd. 1954 to 1993.

1954-1960		$6,500	$4,000
1961-1969		$4,200	$3,200
1970-1993		$1,800	$1,200

Last Mfr.'s Sug. Retail was $2,620.

D12-28 (Standard Series) — similar to D-28, except has 12 strings. Mfd. 1970 to date.

1970-1996		$1,400	$1,000
Mfr.'s Sug. Retail	$2,530	$2,025	$1,650	$1,050

D-28 S
courtesy Martin Guitar Company

M

Grading	100%	Excellent	Average

D-28V (Vintage Series) — similar to D-28, fashioned after the original dreadnought design, herringbone bound body, square headstock. Available in Antique Top finish. Mfd. 1983 to 1985.

		$4,500	$3,000

Last Mfr.'s Sug. Retail was $2,600.

DC-28 — similar to D-28, except has single round cutaway, 14/22 fret fingerboard. Mfd. 1981 to 1996.

1981-1989		$1,800	$1,200
1990-1996		$1,400	$925

Last Mfr.'s Sug. Retail was $2,810.

HD-28 (Standard Series) — solid spruce top, round soundhole, black pickguard, herringbone bound body/rosette, rosewood 2 piece back/sides, 14/20 fret ebony fingerboard with pearl dot inlay, ebony bridge with white black dot pins, 3 per side chrome tuners. Available in Natural finish. Mfd. 1976 to date.

1976-1997		$1,950	$1,200
Mfr.'s Sug. Retail $2,770	$2,200	$1,800	$1,150

This model is also available with solid red cedar top (CHD-28) or a larch top (LHD-28). The larch top was discontinued in 1994.

HD-28 2R — similar to HD-28, except has larger soundhole, 2 rows of herringbone purfling.

		$1,450	$925

Last Mfr.'s Sug. Retail was $2,900.

HD-28LSV LARGE SOUNDHOLE (Vintage Series) — Adirondack spruce top, oversized round soundhole, ivoroid body binding, 5 stripe rosette, rosewood back/sides, mahogany neck, 14/20 fret ivoroid bound rosewood fingerboard with pearl diamonds and squares inlay/side dot position markers, ebony bridge with white black dot pins, beveled tortoise pickguard, (old style) squared headstock, 3 per side Waverly tuners with ivoroid buttons. Available in Natural gloss finish. Mfr. 1998 to date.

Mfr.'s Sug. Retail $3,670	$2,950	$2,400	$1,525

This model is based on a 1934 D-28 once owned by Clarence White (Kentucky Colonels).

HD-28VR (Vintage Series) — solid spruce top, round soundhole, grained ivoroid body binding, 5 stripe rosette, solid rosewood back/sides, mahogany neck, 14/20 fret ebony fingerboard with pearl diamonds and squares inlay, ebony bridge with white black dot pins, beveled tortoise pickguard, (old style) squared headstock, 3 per side chrome tuners with "butterbean" buttons. Available in Natural gloss finish. Current mfr.

Mfr.'s Sug. Retail $3,260	$2,600	$2,125	$1,350

HD-28VS (Vintage Series) — similar to the HD-28VR, except features 12/19 fret fingerboard, slotted headstock. Available in Natural gloss and "Aging Toner" finishes. Current mfr.

Mfr.'s Sug. Retail $3,670	$2,950	$2,400	$1,525

CUSTOM 15 — similar to HD-28, except features tortoise pickguard, unbound ebony fingerboard, slotted-diamond inlay, chrome tuners. Available in Natural finish. Mfd. 1980 to 1995.

		$1,535	$1,025

Last Mfr.'s Sug. Retail was $3,070.

The Custom 15 was named after the 15th custom-ordered guitar of 1980. This model is similar to the HD-28, with added features.

D-35 — solid spruce top, round soundhole, tortoise pickguard, 5 stripe bound body/rosette, rosewood 3 piece back/sides, mahogany neck, 14/20 fret bound ebony fingerboard with pearl dot inlay, ebony bridge with white black dot pins, 3 per side chrome tuners. Available in Natural finish. Mfd. 1965 to date.

1965-1969		$3,200	$2,500
1970-1997		$1,800	$1,200

In 1967, black pickguard replaced original item.

D-35 (Standard Series)

Mfr.'s Sug. Retail $2,430	$1,950	$1,575	$1,000

D-35S — similar to D-35, except has a bell shape dreadnought style body, 12/20 fret fingerboard, slotted headstock. Mfd. 1966 to 1993.

1966-1969		$3,100	$2,500
1970-1993		$1,800	$1,200

Last Mfr.'s Sug. Retail was $2,760.

D12-35 — similar to D-35 S, except has 12 string configuration. Mfd. 1965 to 1993.

1965-1969		$1,900	$1,500
1970-1993		$1,000	$850

Last Mfr.'s Sug. Retail was $2,760.

HD-35 (Standard Series) — solid spruce top, round soundhole, black pickguard, herringbone bound body/rosette, rosewood 3 piece back/sides, 14/20 fret bound ebony fingerboard with pearl dot inlay, ebony bridge with white black dot pins, 3 per side chrome tuners. Available in Natural finish. Mfd. 1978 to date.

1978-1997		$1,950	$1,200
Mfr.'s Sug. Retail $3,140	$2,500	$2,050	$1,300

Also available with solid red cedar top (CHD-35).

D-37K — spruce top, round soundhole, tortoise pickguard, 5 stripe bound body, abalone rosette, figured koa 2 piece back/sides, mahogany neck, 14/20 fret ebony fingerboard with pearl inlay, ebony bridge with white black dot pins, koa peghead veneer with logo decal, 3 per side chrome tuners. Available in Amber Stain finish. Mfd. 1980 to 1995.

		$1,800	$1,300

Last Mfr.'s Sug. Retail was $2,740.

HD-28
courtesy Martin Guitar Company

1968 Martin D-35 12-String
courtesy Kenneth Little

Grading	100%	Excellent	Average

D-42
courtesy The Martin Guitar Company

M

1969 Martin D-45
courtesy Buddy Summer

D-37K2 — similar to D-37K, except has figured koa top, black pickguard.

		$1,800	$1,300

Last Mfr.'s Sug. Retail was $2,920.

D-40 (Standard Series) — solid spruce top, round soundhole, solid rosewood back/sides, abalone rosette, mahogany neck, 14/20 fret bound ebony fingerboard with abalone hexagon postion markers, bound headstock with (style 45) abalone pearl logo, 3 per side gold enclosed tuning machines. Available in Natural gloss finish. Current mfr.

Mfr.'s Sug. Retail	$3,250	$2,600	$2,100	$1,335

D-41 — solid spruce top, round soundhole, black pickguard, bound body, abalone purfling/rosette, rosewood back/sides, mahogany neck, 14/20 fret bound ebony fingerboard with abalone hexagon inlay, ebony bridge with white abalone dot pins, rosewood veneer on bound peghead with white pearl vertical logo inlay, 3 per side gold tuners. Available in Natural finish. Mfd. 1969 to date.

1969		$4,000	$3,200
1970-1997		$2,100	$1,750

D-41 (Standard Series)

Mfr.'s Sug. Retail	$3,960	$3,200	$2,575	$1,630

In 1987, tortoise pickguard, smaller abalone hexagon fingerboard inlay, abalone logo peghead inlay replaced original items.

D12-41 — similar to D-41, except has 12 strings, 12/20 fret fingerboard, 6 per side tuners. Mfd. 1988 to 1994.

		$1,850	$1,500

Last Mfr.'s Sug. Retail was $3,860.

D-41S — similar to D-41, except has a prewar dreadnought style body, 12/20 fret fingerboard, slotted headstock. Mfd. 1970 to 1993.

		$2,300	$2,000

Last Mfr.'s Sug. Retail was $3,720.

D-42 (Standard Series) — solid spruce top, round soundhole, abalone/grained ivoroid body binding, abalone rosette, solid rosewood back/sides, mahogany neck, 14/20 fret bound ebony fingerboard with pearl snowflake inlay, ebony bridge with white black dot pins, tortoise pickguard, 3 per side gold tuners. Available in Natural gloss finish. Mfr. 1996 to date.

Mfr.'s Sug. Retail	$4,850	$3,900	$3,150	$2,000

D-45 (PREWAR) — solid spruce top, round soundhole, bound body, abalone purfling back/top, abalone rosette, rosewood back/sides, mahogany neck, 14/20 fret bound ebony fingerboard with snowflake inlay, ebony bridge with white abalone dot pins, rosewood veneer on bound peghead with abalone vertical logo inlay, 3 per side chrome tuners. Available in Natural finish. Mfd. 1933 to 1942.

The prices of Prewar D-45s are constantly increasing. According to Martin production records, only 91 instruments were produced between 1933 and 1942. Currently, the market has only accounted for 72 of the 91. Furthermore, 25 of the 72 have been refinished or oversprayed. Depending on the condition, a Prewar D-45 may be worth $125,000 (or more). The Blue Book of Guitars highly recommends that several professional appraisals be secured before buying/selling/trading any Prewar Martin D-45.

D-45 — production resumed in 1968, and continues to date.

1968-1969		$15,000	$12,500
1970-1996		$6,000	$4,000

1968 and 1969 were the last full production models to be constructed with Brazilian Rosewood back and sides. The 1968 models command a slightly higher premium over the 1969 models.

D-45 (Standard Series)

Mfr.'s Sug. Retail	$7,480	$6,000	$4,900	$3,100

D-45S — similar to D-45, except has a prewar dreadnought style body, 12/20 fret fingerboard, slotted headstock. Mfd. 1969 to 1993.

		$6,000	$4,000

Last Mfr.'s Sug. Retail was $6,860.

The few Brazilian rosewood examples command a higher premium.

D-45VR (Vintage Series) — similar to D-45, except features highly colored abalone border around top/fingerboard perimeter/rosette, grained ivoroid binding, diamond and snowflake fingerboard inlay, gold Gotoh tuners. Current mfr.

Mfr.'s Sug. Retail	$8,600	$6,900	$5,600	$3,530

D12-45 — similar to D-45S, except has 12 strings, 6 per side tuners with pearl buttons. Mfd. 1969 to 1994.

		$4,500	$3,000

Last Mfr.'s Sug. Retail was $7,020.

The few Brazilian rosewood examples command a higher premium.

D-60 — solid spruce top, round soundhole, tortoise pickguard, 3 stripe bound body/rosette, birdseye maple back/sides, maple neck, 14/20 fret ebony fingerboard with pearl snowflake inlay, ebony bridge with white red dot pins, birdseye maple veneer on ebony bound peghead, 3 per side gold tuners with ebony buttons. Available in Natural finish. Mfd. 1989 to 1995.

		$1,250	$1,000

Last Mfr.'s Sug. Retail was $3,060.

D-62 — similar to D-60, except has figured maple back/sides, mahogany neck, figured maple peghead veneer, gold tuners with pearl buttons. Mfd. 1987 to 1995.

		$1,250	$1,000

Last Mfr.'s Sug. Retail was $2,420.

Grading	100%	Excellent	Average

D-76 (BICENTENNIAL LIMITED EDITION) — solid spruce top, round soundhole, black pickguard, herringbone bound body/rosette, rosewood 3 piece back/sides, mahogany neck, 14/20 fret ebony fingerboard with 13 pearl star inlays, ebony bridge with white black dot pins, rosewood peghead veneer with pearl eagle/logo inlay, 3 per side gold tuners. Available in Natural finish. Mfd. 1975 to 1976.

$3,500 $2,800

There were 1,976 models constructed, with an additional 98 (D-45 E) built exclusively for employees.

J (Jumbo) Series

Size J (Jumbo) guitars feature a Lower Bout Width of 16 inches, and a Body Depth of 4 7/8 inches. J Series models had the "M" suffix as part of the model designation until 1990. All J Series models have scalloped braces.

JM (Road Series) — solid spruce top, round soundhole, black body binding, laminated mahogany back/sides, mahogany neck, 14/20 rosewood fingerboard with white dot inlay, single band herringbone rosette, tortoise pickguard, 3 per side chrome tuners. Available in Natural satin finish. Mfr. 1998 to date.
Mfr.'s Sug. Retail $899

J-1 (1 Series) — solid Sitka spruce top, round soundhole, tortoise bound body, 3 stripe rosette, solid mahogany back, laminated mahogany sides, mahogany neck, 14/20 fret rosewood fingerboard with dot inlay, rosewood bridge with white black dot pins, tortoise pickguard, 3 per side chrome tuners. Available in Natural satin finish.
Mfr.'s Sug. Retail $1,099 $880 $725 $450

J-18 (Formerly J-18 M) — solid spruce top, round soundhole, tortoise pickguard, 5 stripe bound body/rosette, mahogany back/sides/neck, 14/20 fret rosewood fingerboard with pearl dot inlay, rosewood bridge with black white dot pins, rosewood peghead veneer, 3 per side chrome tuners with ebony buttons. Available in Natural finish. Mfd. 1987 to 1996.
$1,250 $700
Last Mfr.'s Sug. Retail was $2,300.

J-40
courtesy Martin Guitar Company

J-21 (Formerly J-21 M) — spruce top, round soundhole, tortoise pickguard, 5 stripe bound body/rosette, rosewood back/sides, mahogany neck, 14/20 fret rosewood fingerboard with pearl dot inlay, rosewood bridge with black white dot pins, rosewood veneer peghead, 3 per side chrome tuners. Available in Natural finish. Mfd. 1985 to 1996.
$1,400 $1,150
Last Mfr.'s Sug. Retail was $2,520.

J-21 MC — similar to J-21 M, except has single round cutaway, oval soundhole, 5 stripe rosette, ebony buttoned tuners. Mfd. 1987 only.
$1,050 $625
Last Mfr.'s Sug. Retail was $1,750.

J-40 (Formerly J-40 M) (Standard Series) — solid spruce top, round soundhole, black pickguard, 5 stripe bound body/rosette, rosewood back/sides, mahogany neck, 14/20 fret bound ebony fingerboard with abalone hexagon inlay, ebony bridge with white abalone dot pins, rosewood peghead veneer, 3 per side chrome tuners. Available in Natural finish. Mfd. 1985 to date.

1985-1997		$1,800	$1,250
Mfr.'s Sug. Retail	$3,250	$2,600 $2,125	$1,345

J-40 BK (Formerly J-40 MBK) — similar to J-40, except has Black Finish. Disc. 1996.
$1,725 $950
Last Mfr.'s Sug. Retail was $3,470.

JC-40 (Formerly J-40 MC) — similar to J-40, except has single round cutaway. Mfd. 1987 to 1996.
$1,900 $1,500
Last Mfr.'s Sug. Retail was $3,390.

J12-40 (Formerly J12-40 M) — similar to J-40, except has 12 strings, 6 per side gold tuners with ebony buttons. Mfd. 1987 to 1996.
$1,400 $1,150
Last Mfr.'s Sug. Retail was $3,350.

J-65 (Formerly J-65 M) — solid spruce top, round soundhole, tortoise pickguard, tortoise bound body, 3 stripe rosette, figured maple back/sides, maple neck, 14/20 fret bound ebony fingerboard with pearl dot inlay, ebony bridge with white red dot pins, rosewood peghead veneer with logo decal, 3 per side gold tuners with pearl buttons. Available in Natural finish. Mfd. 1985 to 1995.
$1,500 $975
Last Mfr.'s Sug. Retail was $2,520.

J12-65 (Formerly J12-65 M) — similar to J-65, except has 12 strings, 6 per side tuners. Mfd. 1985 to 1994.
$1,450 $1,150
Last Mfr.'s Sug. Retail was $2,610.

Custom J-65 (Also CMJ-65) — solid spruce top, round soundhole, tortoise pickguard, white body binding, herringbone purfling, 3 stripe rosette, figured maple back/sides, maple neck, 14/20 fret bound ebony fingerboard with pearl dot inlay, ebony bridge with white red dot pins, rosewood peghead veneer with logo decal, 3 per side gold tuners with pearl buttons. Available in Natural finish. Mfr. 1993 to 1996.
$1,750 $1,050
Last Mfr.'s Sug. Retail was $2,900.

Custom J-65 Electric — similar to Custom J-65, except has MEQ-932 acoustic amplification system. Mfd. 1993 to 1996.
$1,850 $1,100
Last Mfr.'s Sug. Retail was $3,070.

J-65
courtesy Martin Guitar Company

M

Grading	100%	Excellent	Average

HJ-28 (Standard Series) — solid spruce top, round soundhole, grained ivoroid body binding, 5 stripe rosette, solid rosewood back/sides, mahogany neck, 14/20 fret ebony fingerboard with pearl diamonds and squares inlay, ebony bridge with white black dot pins, beveled tortoise pickguard, (old style) squared headstock, 3 per side chrome tuners with "butterbean" knobs. Available in Natural gloss finish. Mfr. 1996 to date.

Mfr.'s Sug. Retail	$2,770	$2,200	$1,800	$1,150

M Series

Size M guitars feature a Lower Bout Width of 16 inches, and a Body Depth of 4 1/8 inches.

CM-0089 — spruce top, round soundhole, tortoise pickguard, bound body, herringbone purfling, pearl rosette, rosewood back/sides, mahogany neck, 14/20 fret ebony fingerboard with pearl dot inlay, rosewood bridge with white black dot pins, 3 per side chrome tuners. Available in Natural finish. Mfd. 1979 only.

There has not been sufficient quanity traded to quote prices.

Only 25 of these instruments were produced.

M-18 — spruce top, round soundhole, black pickguard, bound body, 3 stripe purfling/rosette, mahogany back/sides/neck, 14/20 fret rosewood fingerboard with pearl dot inlay, rosewood bridge with black white dot pins, 3 per side chrome tuners. Available in Natural finish. Mfd. 1984 to 1988.

$1,450 $1,000
Last Mfr.'s Sug. Retail was $1,550.

The first instruments of this line had ebony fingerboards/bridges. Three have a Blue/Red/White finish.

M-36 (FORMERLY M-35) — solid spruce top, round soundhole, tortoise pickguard, 5 stripe bound body/rosette, rosewood back/sides, mahogany neck, 14/20 fret bound ebony fingerboard with pearl dot inlay, rosewood bridge with white black dot pins, rosewood veneer on bound peghead, 3 per side chrome tuners. Available in Natural finish. Mfd. 1978 to 1996.

$1,600 $1,300
Last Mfr.'s Sug. Retail was $2,540.

Early production models came with an unbound peghead.

This instrument began production as the M-35. After 26 were manufactured, the model was renamed the M-36.

M-64 — similar to M-36, except has figured maple back/sides/neck, unbound fingerboard/peghead. Mfd. 1985 to 1995.

$1,600 $1,250
Last Mfr.'s Sug. Retail was $2,520.

MC-28 — single round cutaway body, solid spruce top, oval soundhole, black pickguard, 3 stripe bound body/rosette, rosewood back/sides, mahogany neck, 22 fret ebony fingerboard with pearl dot inlay, ebony bridge with white black dot pins, rosewood peghead veneer, 3 per side chrome tuners. Available in Natural finish. Mfd. 1981 to 1996.

$1,800 $1,500
Last Mfr.'s Sug. Retail was $2,810.

MC-37 K — single round cutaway body, spruce top, oval soundhole, tortoise pickguard, bound body, pearl rosette, figured koa back/sides, mahogany neck, 22 fret ebony fingerboard with abalone flake inlay, ebony bridge with white black dot pins, 3 per side chrome tuners. Available in Amber Stain finish. Mfd. 1981 to 1982, and 1988.

$2,000 $1,600
Last Mfr.'s Sug. Retail was $2,000.

18 of these instruments were produced.

MC-68 — single round cutaway body, solid spruce top, oval soundhole, tortoise pickguard, 5 stripe bound body/rosette, figured maple back/sides, maple neck, 22 fret bound ebony fingerboard with abalone dot inlay, ebony bridge with white abalone dot pins, rosewood veneer on bound peghead with abalone inlay, 3 per side gold tuners. Available in Natural and Sunburst finishes. Mfd. 1985 to 1995.

$2,000 $1,600
Last Mfr.'s Sug. Retail was $2,930.

OM (Orchestra Model) Series

Size OM (Orchestra Model) guitars feature a Lower Bout Width of 15 inches.

OM-18 — spruce top, tortoise pickguard, round soundhole, wooden bound body, rope pattern rosette, mahogany back/sides/neck, 14/20 fret ebony fingerboard with pearl dot inlay, ebony bridge with black pearl dot pins, 3 per side tuners with ivoroid buttons. Available in Natural finish. Mfd. 1930 to 1933.

$8,000 $6,000

This model had banjo style tuners from 1929 to 1931, then standard tuners from then on.

From 1929 to 1930, this model had no pickguard.

From 1930 to 1931, this model had a small pickguard.

From mid 1931 on, this model had a standard pickguard.

OM-21 (Standard Series) — solid spruce top, round soundhole, tortoise pickguard, bound body, herringbone rosette, rosewood back/sides, mahogany neck, 14/20 fret rosewood fingerboard with pearl dot inlay, rosewood bridge with black dot pins, 3 per side chrome tuners. Available in Natural finish. Mfd. 1992 to date.

1992-1997		$1,200	$1,000
Mfr.'s Sug. Retail	$2,110	$1,690	$1,375	$875

OM-28 — spruce top, round soundhole, black pickguard, 5 stripe bound body/rosette, rosewood back/sides, mahogany neck, 14/20 fret ebony fingerboard with pearl dot inlay, ebony bridge with white black dot pins, rosewood peghead veneer, 3 per side chrome tuners. Available in Natural finish. Mfd. 1929 to 1933.

$19,000 $10,000

A really clean, excellent plus OM-28 from these four years may be worth over $19,000.

J-1
courtesy The Martin Guitar Company

OM-21
courtesy The Martin Guitar Company

Grading	100%	Excellent	Average

OM-28VR (Vintage Series) — solid spruce top, round soundhole, 5 stripe rosette, grained ivoroid binding/herringbone purfling, rosewood back/sides, mahogany neck, 14/20 fret ebony fingerboard with pearl snowflake inlay, ebony bridge with white black dot pins, rosewood peghead veneer, squared off headstock, tortoise pickguard, 3 per side chrome tuners. Available in Natural gloss finish. Mfd. 1990 to date.

1990-1997		$1,750	$1,350
Mfr.'s Sug. Retail $3,620	$2,600	$2,150	$1,350

OM-45 (1930 to 1932 Mfr.) — solid spruce top, round soundhole, black pickguard, abalone bound body/rosette, rosewood back/sides, mahogany neck, 14/20 fret bound ebony fingerboard with abalone snowflake inlay, ebony bridge with white abalone dot pins, bound rosewood veneered peghead with abalone logo inlay, 3 per side gold banjo style tuners with ivoroid buttons. Available in Natural finish. Mfd. 1930 to 1932.

1930-1932	$35,000 (and Up)

OM-45 (1977 to 1994 Mfr.) — similar to OM-45, except has abalone hexagon fingerboard inlay, gold enclosed tuners. Mfd. 1977 to 1994.

1977-1994	$5,000	$4,000
		Last Mfr.'s Sug. Retail was $6,530.

OM-45 Deluxe — similar to OM-45, except has abalone vine pickguard inlay, abalone snowflake bridge wings inlay. Mfd. 1930.

$75,000 (and Up)

Only 14 instruments were built.

X Series

Martin debuted the X Series in 1998. The top, back, and sides of this model are constructed of a wood fiber derivative material that is laminated under high pressure. The resulting material is a pre-finished laminate that is shaped into the construction parts for the guitar building.

DXM (X Series) — laminated top, round soundhole, black body binding, laminated mahogany back/sides, solid mahogany neck, 14/20 morado fingerboard with white dot inlay, mahogany grained peghead veneer with gold silkscreen logo, applied gold/blackherringbone decal rosette, morado bridge with white bridgepins, tortoise pickguard, 3 per side chrome tuners. Available in Natural semi-gloss finish. Mfr. 1998 to date.

Mfr.'s Sug. Retail $599

DXME (X Series) — similar to the DXM, except features bridge pickuo, onboard electronics. Available in Natural semi-gloss finish. Mfr. 1998 to date.

Mfr.'s Sug. Retail $749

0000 (Grand Auditorium) Series

Size 0000 (Grand Auditorium) guitars feature a Lower Bout Width of 16 inches.

0000-1 (1 Series) — solid spruce top, round soundhole, tortoise body binding, solid mahogany back, laminated mahogany sides, mahogany neck, 3 stripe rosette, 14/20 fret rosewood fingerboard with dot inlay, rosewood bridge, chrome hardware, 3 per side tuners. Current mfr.

Mfr.'s Sug. Retail $1,099	$875	$725	$450

0000-28H (Standard Series) — solid spruce top, round soundhole, ivoroid body binding, solid rosewood back/sides, mahogany neck, 5 stripe rosette, 14/20 fret rosewood fingerboard with pearl dot inlay, rosewood bridge with white black dot pins, chrome hardware, 3 per side tuners. Current mfr.

Mfr.'s Sug. Retail $2,770	$2,225	$1,800	$1,150

0000-38 (Standard Series) (Formerly M-38) — solid spruce top, round soundhole, 5 stripe bound body, abalone rosette, solid rosewood back/sides, mahogany neck, 14/20 fret bound ebony fingerboard with pearl dot inlay, rosewood bridge with white black dot pins, rosewood veneer on bound peghead, tortoise pickguard, 3 per side chrome tuners. Available in Natural finish. Mfr. 1977 to date.

1977-1997		$1,750	$1,400
Mfr.'s Sug. Retail $3,150	$2,525	$2,100	$1,300

In 1996, the M-38 model was redesignated the 0000-38.

000 (Auditorium) Series

Size 000 (Auditorium) guitars feature a Lower Bout Width of 15 inches.

000-M (Road Series) — solid spruce top, round soundhole, black body binding, laminated mahogany back/sides, mahogany neck, 14/20 rosewood fingerboard with white dot inlay, single band herringbone rosette, tortoise pickguard, 3 per side chrome tuners. Available in Natural satin finish. Current mfr.

Mfr.'s Sug. Retail $899	$725	$595	$395

OOO-R (Road Series) — similar to the OOO-M, except features laminated rosewood back sides. Available in Natural satin finish. Mfr. 1998 to date.

Mfr.'s Sug. Retail $1,099

000-1 (1 Series) — solid Sitka spruce top, round soundhole, mahogany neck, solid mahogany back, 3-ply mahogany sides, 25.4" scale, 14/20 rosewood fingerboard with dot inlay, rosewood bridge, tortoise pickguard, 3 per side tuners, chrome hardware. Available in Natural satin finish. Mfr. 1996 to date.

Mfr.'s Sug. Retail $1,099	$875	$725	$450

000-1R (1 Series) — similar to the 000-1, except features 3-ply laminated Indian rosewood back and sides. Mfr. 1996 to date.

Mfr.'s Sug. Retail $1,300	$1,050	$850	$550

000C-1 (1 Series) — similar to the 000-1, except features a rounded Venetian cutaway. Current mfr.

Mfr.'s Sug. Retail $1,300	$1,050	$850	$550

OM-45
courtesy Martin Guitar Company

M-38
courtesy Martin Guitar Company

M

Grading	100%	Excellent	Average

000C-1E (1 Series) — similar to the 000-1, except features a rounded Venetian cutaway, Martin Gold+Plus bridge mounted pickup, Martin/Fishman Prefix preamp/EQ system. Current mfr.

Mfr.'s Sug. Retail	$1,499	$1,200	$975	$650

000-15 (15 Series) — solid mahogany top, round soundhole, single band gold herringbone decal rosette, solid mahogany back/sides, mahogany neck, no body binding, 14/20 fret rosewood fingerboard with white dot inlay, rosewood bridge with white pins, tortoise pickguard, 3 per side chrome tuners. Mfr. 1998 to date.

Mfr.'s Sug. Retail $849

000-16T (16 Series) — solid spruce top, round soundhole, tortoise bound body, herringbone rosette, solid mahogany back/sides, mahogany neck, 14/20 fret rosewood fingerboard with abalone diamonds/squares inlay, rosewood bridge with black white dot pins, tortoise pickguard, 3 per side chrome tuners. Available in Natural "Aging Toner" top/satin body finish. Mfd. 1989 to date.

1989-1997			$900	$750
Mfr.'s Sug. Retail	$1,650	$1,325	$1,075	$695

000-16TR — similar to the 000-16T, except features solid rosewood back and sides. Mfr. 1996 to date.

Mfr.'s Sug. Retail	$1,850	$1,500	$1,200	$850

000C-16T (16 Series) — similar to OOO-16, except has single rounded Ventian cutaway. Current mfr.

Mfr.'s Sug. Retail	$1,850	$1,500	$1,200	$900

000C-16 — similar to the OOO-16, except features an oval soundhole and single rounded Venetian cutaway. Mfd. 1990 to 1995.

	$1,100	$800

000C-16T — similar to the OOO-16, except features a single rounded Venetian cutaway. Mfd. 1990 to 1995.

	$900	$750

The OOOC-16T is similar to the OOOC-16, except has a round soundhole.

000-17 — mahogany top/back/sides, round soundhole, 3 stipe rosette, rosewood fingerboard with dot inlay, tortoise pickguard. Available in Natural finish. Mfd. 1952.

Only 25 instruments were produced. Although not a fancy model, the scarcity and lack of trading indicate that the seller can ask for what the market will bear.

000-18 — solid spruce top, round soundhole, black pickguard, wood bound body, rope rosette, rosewood back/sides, cedar neck, 12/19 fret ebony fingerboard, ebony pyramid bridge with black pearl dot pins, 3 per side brass tuners with ivory buttons. Available in Natural finish. Mfd. 1911 to 1931, 1931 to 1933, 1934 to date.

1911-1931		$5,500	$4,000
1931-1933		$7,000	$5,000
1934-1946		$5,000	$3,500
1947-1959		$2,250	$1,500
1960-1969		$1,500	$1,000
1970-1997		$1,000	$650

000-18 (Standard Series)

Mfr.'s Sug. Retail	$2,130	$1,700	$1,395	$995

In 1917, mahogany back/sides/neck replaced original items.

In 1920, 12/20 fret fingerboard became standard.

In 1929, straight bridge replaced original item.

In 1930, belly bridge replaced respective item.

In 1932, pickguard became optionally available.

In 1934, black body binding, all metal tuners replaced original items.

In 1934, 14/20 fret fingerboard replaced the 12/19 fret fingerboard (the first half production in 1934 featured an OM scale).

In 1935 and 1936, most OOO-18 models had rosewood fingerboard and bridge.

In 1937, ebony fingerboard and bridge replaced rosewood fingerboard and bridge.

In 1944, rosewood fingerboard and bridge replaced ebony fingerboard and bridge.

000-21 — solid spruce top, round soundhole, wood bound body, herringbone rosette, rosewood back/sides, cedar neck, 12/19 fret ebony fingerboard with pearl dot inlay, ebony pyramid bridge with black pearl dot pins, 3 per side brass tuners with ivory buttons. Available in Natural finish. Mfd. 1902 to 1959.

1902-1937		$7,500	$6,500
1938-1946		$6,000	$4,500
1947-1959		$3,500	$1,000

In 1923, mahogany neck, 12/20 fret fingerboard replaced original items.

In 1930, belly bridge replaced original item.

In 1932, pickguard became optionally available.

In 1939, 14/20 fret fingerboard replaced respective item.

In 1947, rosewood fingerboard/bridge replaced original item.

000C-16
courtesy Martin Guitar Company

1942 Martin 000-28
courtesy Buddy Summer

M

Grading	100%	Excellent	Average

000-28 — solid spruce top, round soundhole, ivory bound body, herringbone purfling, 5 stripe rosette, rosewood back/sides, cedar neck, 12/19 fret ebony fingerboard, ebony pyramid bridge with black pearl dot pins, 3 per side brass tuners with ivory buttons. Available in Natural finish. Mfd. 1902 to date.

1902-1933		$18,000	$9,000
1934-1946		$16,000	$8,000
1947-1959		$5,000	$3,500
1960-1969		$3,000	$2,200
1970-1997		$1,300	$800

000-28 (Standard Series)

Mfr.'s Sug. Retail	$2,430	$1,950	$1,575	$1,000

In 1901, pearl diamond fingerboard inlay was introduced.

In 1917, 12/20 fret fingerboard replaced original item, mahogany neck replaced original item.

In 1929, belly bridge replaced original item.

In 1932, pickguard became optionally available.

In 1934, pickguard became standard item, 14/20 fret fingerboard replaced respective item.

In 1944, pearl dot fingerboard inlay replaced original item.

In 1947, 5 stripe purfling replaced original item.

000-28 C — similar to OOO-28, except has classical style body. Mfd. 1962 to 1969.

		$1,700	$1,300

000-28 G — similar to the 000-28, except designed for gut (now nylon) string configuration. Mfd. 1937 to 1955.

1937-1946		$2,500	$2,000
1947-1955		$1,900	$1,500

ERIC CLAPTON SIGNATURE 000-28EC (Vintage Series) — solid Sitka spruce top, round soundhole, ivoroid body binding/herringbone purfling, herringbone rosette, solid East Indian rosewood back/sides, mahogany neck, 14/20 fret ebony fingerboard with abalone (pre-war style 28) snowflake inlay/mother of pearl Eric Clapton signature at 20th fret, rosewood bridge with white black dot pins, chrome hardware, 3 per side tuners. Available in Natural gloss finish. Mfr. 1996 to date.

Mfr.'s Sug. Retail	$3,500	$2,800	$2,275	$1,500

000-42 — solid spruce top, round soundhole, ivory bound body, pearl purfling/rosette, rosewood back/sides, cedar neck, 12/19 fret ivory bound ebony fingerboard with pearl diamond/snowflakes inlay, ivory bridge with black pearl dot pins, 3 per side silver tuners with pearl buttons. Available in Natural finish. Mfd. 1918 to 1942.

		$24,000	$19,000

The OOO-42 is the rarest OOO model.

In 1919, plastic body binding, ebony bridge replaced original items.

In 1923, mahogany neck, 12/20 fret fingerboard, nickel tuners replaced original items.

In 1929, belly bridge replaced original item.

In 1932, pickguard became optionally available.

In 1938, 14/20 fret fingerboard replaced respective item.

000-45 — solid spruce top, round soundhole, ivory bound body, pearl purfling top/back/sides, pearl rosette, rosewood back/sides, cedar neck, 12/19 fret ivory bound ebony fingerboard with pearl diamond/snowflakes inlay, ivory bridge with black pearl dot pins, pearl bound slotted peghead with pearl torch inlay, 3 per side silver tuners with pearl buttons. Available in Natural finish. Mfd. 1907 to 1942, 1970 to 1985.

1907-1942		$35,000	$28,000
1970-1985		$5,000	$4,000

Last Mfr.'s Sug. Retail was $6,530.

In 1917, 12/20 fret fingerboard replaced original item.

In 1919, ebony bridge replaced original item.

In 1923, plastic binding replaced original item.

In 1929, belly bridge replaced original item.

In 1932, pickguard became optionally available.

In 1934, pearl peghead logo inlay was introduced, 14/20 fret fingerboard replaced respective item.

In 1936, chrome tuners replaced original item.

In 1939, gold tuners replaced respective item.

00 (Grand Concert) Series

Size 00 (Grand Concert) guitars feature a Lower Bout Width of 14 1/8 inches.

00-1 (1 Series) — solid Sitka spruce top, round soundhole, mahogany neck, solid mahogany back, 3-ply mahogany sides, 14/20 rosewood fingerboard with dot inlay, rosewood bridge, tortoise pickguard, 3 per side tuners, chrome hardware. Available in Natural satin finish. Mfr. 1996 to date.

Mfr.'s Sug. Retail	$1,250	$1,000	$825	$525

000-28 EC
courtesy The Martin Guitar Company

1930 Martin 000-45
courtesy Buddy Summer

Grading	100%	Excellent	Average

00-1 R (1 Series)— similar to the 00-1, except features 3-ply laminated Indian rosewood back/sides. Mfr. 1996 to date.

Mfr.'s Sug. Retail $1,450	$1,150	$950	$600

00C-ME (Road Series)— similar to the 00-1, except features single rounded cutaway body, laminated mahogany back/sides, bridge pickup, on-board electronics. Mfr. 1998 to date.

Mfr.'s Sug. Retail $1,399

00-15 (15 Series) — solid mahogany top, round soundhole, single band gold herringbone decal rosette, solid mahogany back/sides, mahogany neck, no body binding, 14/20 fret rosewood fingerboard with white dot inlay, rosewood bridge with white pins, tortoise pickguard, 3 per side chrome tuners. Mfr. 1998 to date.

Mfr.'s Sug. Retail $849

00C-16 DB (16 Series) — single rounded cutaway body, spruce top, round soundhole, black pickguard, tortoise bound body, abalone pearl rosette,, solid mahogany back/sides, mahogany neck, 14/20 fret rosewood fingerboard with abalone fingerboard inlays, rosewood bridge with abalone snowflake inlay and black pins, tortoise pickguard, 3 per side chrome tuners. Available in Black gloss finish. Mfr. 1998 to date.

Mfr.'s Sug. Retail $2,300

00-16 C — solid spruce top, round soundhole, bound body, 3 stripe rosette, mahogany back/sides/neck, 12/19 fret rosewood fingerboard, tied rosewood bridge, slotted peghead, 3 per side tuners with pearl buttons. Available in Natural finish. Mfd. 1962 to 1994.

1962-1982		$700	$550
1983-1994		$1,625	$995

Last Mfr.'s Sug. Retail was $2,330.

The 00-16 C is a classical model (nylon string).

00-17 (1908 to 1917 Mfr.) — spruce top, round soundhole, 3 stripe bound body/rosette, mahogany back/sides/neck, 14/20 fret rosewood fingerboard, rosewood bridge with black pins, 3 per side tuners. Available in Dark Natural finish. Mfd. 1908 to 1917.

1908-1917		$3,000	$2,200

00-17 (1930 to 1960 Mfr.) — mahogany top, no body binding, rosewood fingerboard. Mfd. 1930 to 1960.

1930-1945		$1,500	$1,200
1946-1960		$1,200	$850

00-18 — 3 stripe rosette, mahogany back/sides, rosewood fingerboard/bridge. Mfd. 1898 to 1994.

1898-1931		$3,000	$2,500
1932-1946		$2,300	$2,000
1947-1959		$1,600	$1,200
1960-1969		$1,100	$600
1970-1994		$1,000	$750

Last Mfr.'s Sug. Retail was $2,480.

00-18 C — similar to the OO-18. Mfd. 1962 to 1992.

		$700	$500

The 00-18 C was a classical model (nylon string).

00-18 G — mahogany back/sides, ebony fingerboard/bridge. Available in polished lacquer finish. Mfd. 1936 to 1962.

1936-1946		$1,050	$800
1947-1962		$850	$600

The 00-18 G was a classical model (nylon string). The first models produced had pin bridges.

After the 1940s, these models came with a rosewood fingerboard/bridge.

00-18 H — similar to the 00-18, except features Hawaiian configuration (raised nut, flat fingerboard, flush frets, non-slanted saddle). Mfd. 1935 to 1941.

		$4,000	$3,000

Most of the OO-18 H models were in a Sunburst finish.

00-18 K — similar to the 00-18, except features koa top/back/sides. Mfd. 1918 to 1934.

		$3,000	$1,800

00-21 — spruce top, round soundhole, black pickguard, multibound body, 3 stripe rosette, rosewood back/sides, mahogany neck, 12/19 fret rosewood fingerboard with pearl dot inlay, rosewood bridge with black white dot pins, rosewood veneered solid peghead with screened logo, 3 per side chrome tuners. Available in Natural finish. Mfd. 1898 to 1995.

1898-1929		$5,000	$3,500
1930-1946		$5,500	$4,000
1947-1959		$3,500	$2,500
1960-1969		$2,000	$1,500
1970-1995		$1,000	$800

Last Mfr.'s Sug. Retail was $2,730.

00-21 NY — similar to the 00-21, except features no pickguard. Available in Natural finish. Mfd. 1961 to 1965.

		$2,500	$2,000

00-28 — herringbone bound body, 3 stripe rosette, rosewood back/sides ebony fingerboard/bridge. Mfd. 1898 to 1941.

		$16,000	$9,000

00-1
courtesy The Martin Guitar Company

00-1 R
courtesy The Martin Guitar Company

M

Grading	100%	Excellent	Average

00-28 C — 3 stripe rosette, rosewood back/sides, ebony fingerboard/bridge. Mfd. 1966 to 1994.

1966-1969		$1,500	$1,200
1970-1994		$1,000	$750

Last Mfr.'s Sug. Retail was $2,760.

The 00-28 C was a classical model (nylon string).

00-28 G — rosewood back/sides, 12/20 fret ebony fingerboard. Mfd. 1936 to 1962.

1936-1946		$2,200	$1,700
1947-1962		$1,600	$1,300

The 00-28 G was a classical model (nylon string).

00-28 K — similar to the 00-28, except features koa back/sides, raised nut, non-slanted saddle. Mfd. 1919 to 1933.

	$6,000	$4,000

00-30 — rosewood back/sides/fingerboard/bridge. Mfd. 1899 to 1921.

	$5,000	$3,000

00-42 — pearl bound body/rosette, rosewood back/sides/fingerboard/bridge. Mfd. 1898 to 1942.

	$12,000	$7,000

00-45 — pearl bound body/rosette/fingerboard/peghead, rosewood back/sides/fingerboard/bridge. Mfd. 1904 to 1938.

$20,000 (and Up)

0 (Concert) Series

Size 0 (Concert) guitars feature a Lower Bout Width of 13 1/2 inches.

0-15 — mahogany top, round soundhole, 2 stripe rosette, tortoise pickguard, mahogany back/sides/neck, 14/20 fret rosewood fingerboard with white dot inlay, rosewood bridge with white pins, black face peghead with logo decal, 3 per side nickel tuners with plastic buttons. Available in Natural finish. Mfd. 1935 and 1940 to 1961.

1935	$1,200	$800	
1940-1945		$1,000	$800
1946-1961		$850	$600

0-15T — similar to the 0-15, except has tenor neck. Mfd. 1960 to 1963.

	$600	$400

0-16NY — spruce top, round soundhole, 3 stripe bound body/rosette, mahogany back/sides/neck, 12/19 fret rosewood fingerboard, rosewood bridge with black white dot pins, slotted peghead 3 per side tuners with plastic buttons. Available in Natural finish. Mfd. 1961 to 1995.

1961-1980		$800	$650
1981-1995		$1,200	$795

0-16 — similar to the 0-16NY, except has tortoise pickguard. Available in Natural satin finish. Mfd. 1961.

	$800	$650

0-17 (1906 to 1917 Mfr.) — spruce top, round soundhole, mahogany back/sides, cedar neck, 12/20 fret ebony fingerboard with pearl dot inlay, ebony bridge with black pins, slotted peghead, 3 per side nickel tuners with plastic buttons. Available in Natural finish. Mfd. 1906 to 1917.

	$2,500	$2,000

In 1914, rosewood bound body, 3 stripe rosette was introduced.

0-17 (1929 to 1948, 1966 to 1968 Mfr.) — mahogany top/back/sides, round soundhole, cedar neck, 12/20 fret rosewood fingerboard with pearl dot inlay, rosewood bridge with black pins, slotted peghead, 3 per side nickel tuners with plastic buttons. Available in Natural finish. Mfd. 1929 to 1948, 1966 to 1968.

1929-1948		$1,400	$1,100
1966-1968		$850	$750

In 1929, rosewood bound body was discontinued.

In 1931, pickguard became optionally available.

In 1934, solid peghead and 14/20 fret fingerboard replaced original item.

0-17H — similar to the 0-17, except features flat fingerboard/flush frets, high nut, and non-slanted saddle. Mfd. 1930 to 1939.

	$1,800	$1,000

0-17T — similar to the 0-17, except has tenor neck. Mfd. 1932 to 1963.

1932-1945		$1,000	$750
1946-1960		$800	$600

0-18 — solid spruce top, round soundhole, wood bound body, rope rosette, rosewood back/sides, cedar neck, 12/19 fret ebony fingerboard, pyramid ebony bridge with black pearl dot pins, 3 per side brass tuners with ivory buttons. Available in Natural finish. Mfd. 1898 to 1995.

1898-1931		$2,600	$2,200
1932-1946		$2,100	$1,800
1947-1959		$1,400	$1,250
1960-1969		$1,100	$900
1970-1995		$800	$700

In 1909, pearl dot fingerboard inlay was introduced.

In 1917, mahogany back/sides/neck replaced original items.

1927 Martin 00-45
courtesy Buddy Summer

000C-1E
courtesy The Martin Guitar Company

Grading	100%	Excellent	Average

In 1919, rosewood bound body was introduced.

In 1920, 12/20 fret fingerboard became standard.

In 1921, straight bridge replaced original item.

In 1923, belly bridge replaced respective item.

In 1932, pickguard became optionally available.

In 1934, black body binding replaced original item.

By 1935, 14/20 fret fingerboard became standard item.

By 1945, rosewood fingerboard/bridge replaced original item.

0-18K — similar to the 0-18, except has koa top/back/sides. Mfd. 1918 to 1935.

		$2,200	$1,500

0-18T — similar to the 0-18, except has tenor neck. Mfd. 1929 to 1994.

1929-1945		$900	$800
1946-1994		$700	$650

0-21 — solid spruce top, round soundhole, wood bound body, herringbone rosette, rosewood back/sides, cedar neck, 12/19 fret ebony fingerboard with pearl dot inlay, pyramid ebony bridge with ebony pearl dot pins, 3 per side brass tuners with ivory buttons. Available in Natural finish. Mfd. 1898 to 1948.

1898-1931		$3,500	$3,000
1932-1948		$2,000	$1,800

In 1917, mahogany neck replaced original item.

In 1923, 12/20 fret fingerboard became standard item.

In 1927, belly bridge replaced original item.

In 1932, pickguard became optionally available.

0-21H — similar to the 0-21, except features flat fingerboard/flush frets, high nut, and non-slanted saddle. Mfd. 1918 only.

The O-21H model is very rare. Too few of these exist for accurate statistical representation.

0-21K — similar to the 0-21, except has koa top/back/sides. Mfd. 1919 to 1929.

		$3,200	$2,200

0-28 — solid spruce top, round soundhole, ivory bound body, herringbone rosette, rosewood back/sides, cedar neck, 12/19 fret ebony fingerboard, pyramid ebony bridge with ebony pearl dot pins, 3 per side brass tuners with ivory buttons. Available in Natural finish. Mfd. 1898 to 1931, 1937.

1898-1930		$5,500	$3,500
1931-1937		$5,500	$3,500

In 1901, pearl dot fingerboard inlay was introduced.

In 1917, 12/20 fret fingerboard replaced original item, mahogany neck replaced original item.

In 1929, belly bridge replaced original item.

In 1937, pickguard became standard item, 14/20 fret fingerboard replaced respective item.

0-28K — similar to the 0-28, except has koa top/back/sides. Mfd. 1917 to 1935.

		$4,000	$3,000

0-28T (1930 to 1931 Mfr.) — similar to the 0-28, except has tenor neck. Mfd. 1930 to 1931.

		$1,800	$1,500

0-30 — solid spruce top, round soundhole, ivory bound body/colored purfling, pearl rosette, Brazilian rosewood back/sides, cedar neck, 12/19 fret ivory bound ebony fingerboard with pearl dot inlay, pyramid ebony bridge with ebony pearl dot pins, 3 per side silver brass tuners. Available in Natural finish. Mfd. 1899 to 1921.

		$3,500	$3,000

Between 1917 to 1923, mahogany neck replaced the cedar neck.

0-34 — solid spruce top, round soundhole, ivory bound body/colored purfling, pearl rosette, Brazilian rosewood back/sides, cedar neck, 12/19 fret ivory bound ebony fingerboard with pearl slotted diamond inlay, pyramid ivory bridge with ebony pearl dot pins, 3 per side silver brass tuners. Available in Natural finish. Mfd. 1898 to 1899, 1907.

		$4,500	$3,500

0-40 — solid spruce top, round soundhole, ivory bound body, pearl rosette, Brazilian rosewood back/sides, cedar neck, 12/19 fret ebony fingerboard with pearl snowflake inlay, pyramid ivory bridge with ebony pearl dot pins, 3 per side silver brass tuners. Available in Natural finish. Mfd. 1912 to 1913.

The O-40 model is very rare. Too few of these exist for accurate statistical representation.

0-42 — solid spruce top, round soundhole, ivory bound body, pearl purfling/rosette, rosewood back/sides, cedar neck, 12/19 fret ivory bound ebony fingerboard with pearl diamond/snowflake inlay, pyramid ivory bridge with ebony pearl dot pins, 3 per side silver tuners with pearl buttons. Available in Natural finish. Mfd. 1898 to 1942.

		$9,000	$6,000

000-1 R
courtesy The Martin Guitar Company

M

000-18
courtesy The Martin Guitar Company

Grading	100%	Excellent	Average

In 1914, ivory peghead pegs were optionally available.

In 1919, plastic binding, ebony bridge replaced original items.

In 1923, mahogany neck, 12/20 fret fingerboard, nickel tuners replaced original items.

In 1929, belly bridge replaced original item.

0-45 — solid spruce top, round soundhole, ivory bound body, pearl purfling/rosette, Brazilian rosewood back/sides, cedar neck, 12/19 fret ivory bound ebony fingerboard with pearl snowflake/diamond inlay, pyramid ivory bridge with ebony pearl dot pins, ivory/pearl bound peghead with pearl torch inlay, 3 per side brass tuners with ivory buttons. Available in Natural finish. Mfd. 1904 to 1939.

| | **$16,000** | **$10,000** | |

In 1917, mahogany neck replaced the cedar neck, 12/20 fret fingerboard replaced the 12/19 fret fingerboard.

In 1919, plastic binding, ebony bridge replaced original items.

In 1929, belly bridge replaced original item.

Other Size Martin Models: Size 1, 2, 2 1/2, and 3

Between 1898 and 1938, Martin made guitars in these other small bodied sizes. The **Size 1** had a lower bout width of 12 3/4", the **Size 2** body width was 12", the **Size 2 1/2** body width was 11 5/8", and the **Size 3** had a body width of 11 1/4". Models can be cross-referenced in regards to styles by hyphenated description (for example, a 2-**17** or a 1-**45**).

Small Body Martin models tend to trade for close to the values of their single 0 stylistic counterparts (for example, a 1-18K would sell for a little less than an 0-18K).

5 Series

Size 5 guitars feature a Lower Bout Width of 11 1/4 inches.

5-16 — spruce top, round soundhole, 3 stripe bound body/rosette, mahogany back/sides/neck, 12/19 fret rosewood fingerboard, rosewood bridge with black white dot pins, 3 per side chrome tuners. Available in Natural finish. Mfd. 1962 to 1963.

| | **$800** | **$650** | |

5-17 (1912 to 1916 Mfr.) — spruce top, round soundhole, 3 black soundhole rings, mahogany back/sides/neck, 12/19 fret unbound ebony fingerboard, rosewood bridge with black pins, 3 per side die cast tuners with nickel buttons. Available in Dark finish. Mfd. 1912 to 1916.

The 5-17 model is very rare. Too few of these exist for accurate statistical representation.

5-17 (1927 to 1943 Mfr.) — similar to the 5-17 (1912 to 1916 Mfr.), except features mahogany top, rosewood fingerboard with dot inlay, 3 stripe top binding/rosette. Mfd. 1927 to 1943.

| | **$1,100** | **$900** | |

5-17T — similar to the 5-17 (1927 to 1943 Mfr.), except has tenor neck, 22" scale. Mfd. 1927 to 1949.

| | **$850** | **$600** | |

5-18 — rosewood back and sides, 5 stripe body binding, colored wood "rope" pattern soundhole, rectangular bridge, unbound ebony fingerboard, 3 per side tuners. Mfd. 1898 to 1989.

1898-1931	$2,100	$1,800
1932-1946	$1,800	$1,500
1947-1959	$1,200	$1,100
1960-1969	$1,000	$800
1970-1989	$800	$700

5-21 — rosewood back and sides, herringbone soundhole ring, 5 stripe body binding, unbound ebony fingerboard with slotted diamond inlay, 3 per side tuners. Mfd. 1902 to 1927.

| | **$2,800** | **$2,400** | |

5-28 — Brazilian rosewood back and sides, ivory bound top, herringbone top purfling, unbound ebony fingerboard with slotted diamond inlay, 3 per side tuners. Mfd. 1901 to 1939, 1968 to 1981.

1901-1939	$5,000	$3,500
1968-1969	$2,200	$2,000
1970-1981	$1,100	$800

7 Series

Size 7 guitars are designed to be a 7/8ths size dreadnought (scaled down body size).

7-28 — Indian rosewood back and sides, round soundhole, bound body, black pickguard, unbound eboy fingerbord, 3 per side tuners. Mfd. 1980 to 1987.

| | **$1,600** | **$1,100** | |

7-37K — similar to the 7-28, except features koa back and sides, pearl soundhole ring, tortoise pickguard, slotted diamond fingerboard inlay. Mfd. 1980 to 1987.

| | **$1,700** | **$1,200** | |

Archtop Series

Tailpiece variations were common on all arch and carved top instruments. Size C guitars feature a Lower Bout Width of 15 inches, while Size F guitars feature a Lower Bout Width of 16 inches.

Archtop series models with round soundholes tend to command a slightly higher premium.

000-28
courtesy The Martin Guitar Company

1968 Martin 5-18
courtesy Buddy Summer

M

Grading	100%	Excellent	Average

C-1 — carved spruce top, round soundhole, raised black pickguard, bound top/rosette, mahogany back/sides/neck, 14/20 fret rosewood fingerboard with white dot inlay, rosewood bridge/trapeze tailpiece, vertical pearl logo inlay on headstock, 3 per side nickel tuners. Available in Sunburst finish. Mfd. 1931 to 1942.

	$1,200	**$800**

In 1934, f-holes replaced original item.

C-2 — similar to C-1, except has stripe bound body/rosette, rosewood back/sides, ebony fingerboard with pearl snowflake inlay, ebony bridge. Available in Dark Lacquer finish. Mfd. 1931 to 1942.

	$1,800	**$1,200**

In 1934, f-holes replaced original item. Golden Brown top finish became standard.

In 1935, bound fingerboard, pickguard were introduced.

In 1939, hexagon fingerboard inlay was introduced.

C-3 — similar to C-1, except has 2 stripe bound body/rosette, pearl bound pickguard, rosewood back/sides, bound ebony fingerboard with pearl snowflake inlay, ebony bridge, gold tailpiece, bound peghead, gold single unit tuners. Available in Lacquer finish. Mfd. 1932 to 1935.

	$3,000	**$2,000**

In 1934, Stained top finish was introduced, bound pickguard, f-holes replaced original items.

F-1 — carved spruce top, f-holes, raised black pickguard, stripe bound top, mahogany back/sides/neck, 14/20 fret ebony fingerboard with white dot inlay, adjustable ebony bridge/trapeze tailpiece, logo decal on headstock, 3 per side nickel tuners. Available in Sunburst finish. Mfd. 1940 to 1942.

	$1,500	**$900**

F-2 — similar to F-1, except has rosewood back/sides.

	$3,000	**$2,000**

F-5 — similar to F-1, except features maple back/sides/neck. Mfd. 1940 only.

Only 2 instruments were produced. While pricing is an irrelevant issue with this model, it is significant more for what it is (a maple bodied archtop) than for how much it is. It is interesting that Martin saw a market for such a guitar, yet decided not to pursue it.

F-7 — similar to F-1, except has bound pickguard, rosewood back/sides, bound fingerboard with ivoroid hexagon inlay, bound peghead with pearl vertical logo inlay, chrome hardware. Available in Sunburst finish. Mfd. 1935 to 1942.

	$3,500	**$2,500**

In 1937, pearloid fingerboard inlay replaced original item.

F-9 — similar to F-1, except has stripe bound pickguard, rosewood back/sides, bound fingerboard with pearl hexagon inlay, bound peghead with pearl vertical logo inlay, gold hardware. Available in Golden Brown Sunburst finish. Mfd. 1935 to 1942.

	$4,000	**$3,500**

R-17 — arched mahogany top, f-holes, raised black (or tortoiseshell) pickguard, black)or tortoise) body binding, mahogany back/sides/neck, 14/20 fret rosewood fingerboard, rosewood bridge/trapeze tailpiece, logo decal on peghead, 3 per side nickel single unit tuners. Available in Sunburst finish. Mfd. 1934 to 1942.

	$750	**$550**

Body binding and pickguard color always match on the R-17 and R-18 acoustic archtop models (black binding with black pickguard, tortoise binding with tortoise pickguard).

R-18 — similar to R-17, except has arched spruce top, 3 stripe bound body/rosette, white dot fingerboard inlay. Mfd. 1932 to 1941.

	$900	**$600**

In 1933, f-holes replaced original item.

Backpacker Series

The Backpacker Travel Guitar was developed by luthier/designer Bob McNally in 1994. Backpackers have shown up in the most unusual of places, from the Space Shuttle to the Himalayas! Models are currently produced in Martin's Mexican facilities.

Add $125 for factory installed Martin 332 Thinline bridge pickup.

BACKPACKER — travel style "paddle"-shaped body, solid spruce top, round soundhole, one-piece mahogany body/neck with hollowed out sound cavity, 15 fret hardwood fingerboard with white dot inlay, hardwood bridge with white black dot pins, 3 per side chrome mini tuners. Available in Natural finish. Mfd. 1994 to date.

Mfr.'s Sug. Retail	$254	$168	$115	$85

Backpacker Classical — similar to Backpacker, except is designed for nylon strings. Current mfr.

Mfr.'s Sug. Retail	$254	$260	$175	$115

Backpacker Ukelele — similar to Backpacker, except in a ukelele configuration. Current mfr.

Mfr.'s Sug. Retail	$209	$165	$135	$75

This model is available in acoustic format only.

Classical Series

Size N (Classical) guitars feature a Lower Bout Width of 14 7/16 inches. Other models may differ.

N-10 — wooden inlay rosette, mahogany back/sides, rosewood fingerboard/bridge. Mfd. 1968 to 1993, 1995.

	$1,100	**$850**

Last Mfr.'s Sug. Retail was $2,620.

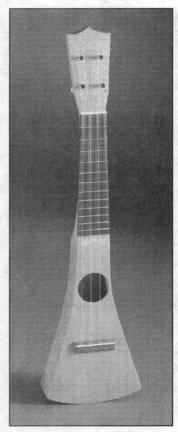

Backpacker Ukulele
courtesy The Martin Guitar Company

M

Martin Backpackers
courtesy The Martin Guitar Company

Grading	100%	Excellent	Average

N-20 — wooden inlay rosette, rosewood back/sides, ebony fingerboard/bridge. Mfd. 1968 to 1995.

1968-1969		$2,200	$1,850
1970-1995		$1,350	$1,000

Last Mfr.'s Sug. Retail was $3,190.

MARTIN/HUMPHREY C-TSH CLASSICAL (Standard Series) — solid Engleman spruce top, round soundhole, rose-patterned mosaic rosette, solid East Indian 2-piece back with (style 45) mosaic inlay strip, solid East Indian rosewood sides, rosewood/black/white body binding, mahogany neck, 12/19 "elevated" ebony fingerboard, slotted headstock, 3 per side gold tuners with white buttons. Available in Natural gloss finish. Mfr. 1996 to date.

Mfr.'s Sug. Retail	$3,750	$3,000	$2,450	$1,850

In 1996, luthier Thomas Humphrey contracted a standardized design of his Millennium design to the C.F. Martin Guitar company (see THOMAS HUMPHREY).

Martin/Humphrey C-1 R Classical (1 Series) — similar to the C-TSH Classical, except features a solid western red cedar top, laminated rosewood back/sides, black body binding, rosewood fingerboard and bridge. Available in Natural satin finish. Mfr. 1996 to date.

Mfr.'s Sug. Retail	$1,500	$1,200	$975	$650

C-TSH
courtesy The Martin Guitar Company

Custom Shop Models and Limited Editions

Martin formally opened their Custom Shop in 1979. As production for the first five years focused on one-of-a-kind custom creations, a catalog for pricing and listed options wasn't even printed! Many production runs that feature specialty woods are simply stamped "Custom" on the neck block.

Between 1983 to 1987, some of Martin's rosewood models were built using Brazilian rosewood. These guitars were initially stamped with a **V** (Vintage) after the model code; after 1985 the guitars were stamped with a **B** (Brazilian). Some "B" models do not have vintage features; some "V" models do not have Brazilian rosewood, but have vintage features.

(The source material for Martin's Custom Shop and Limited Edition models can be found in either Jim Washburn and Richard Johnson's "Martin Guitars: An Illustrated Celebration of America's Premier Guitarmaker", Rodale Books, 1997)

D-18LE (1986-1987) — D-18V style, quilted maple back/sides, herringbone backstrip, tortoiseshell pickguard. Available in Natural finish. Mfd. 1986 to 1987.

Model has not traded sufficiently to quote pricing.

It is estimated that about 30 instruments were produced.

D-16 Series Special (SP) Limited Editions

The D-16 Series Special (SP) edition models feature scalloped "X"-bracing, a (style 45) multi-colored back inlay strip, and compensated saddle. These models were introduced in 1996. While originally designated with a T (for example: SP D-16T), the T designation was dropped in 1998.

SP D-16 (Previously SP D-16T) — spruce top, round soundhole, black pickguard, tortoise bound body, abalone pearl rosette,, solid mahogany back/sides, mahogany neck, 14/20 fret rosewood fingerboard with abalone fingerboard inlays,, rosewood bridge with abalone snowflake inlay and black pins, tortoise pickguard, 3 per side chrome tuners. Available in Natural gloss finish. Mfr. 1996 to date.

Mfr.'s Sug. Retail	$1,800	$1,350	$1,175	$750

SP D-16B (16 Series) — similar to the SP D-16. Available in Black gloss finish. Mfr. 1998 to date.

Mfr.'s Sug. Retail	$2,200

SP D-16M (16 Series) — similar to the SP D-16, except features solid maple back/sides. Mfr. 1998 to date.

Mfr.'s Sug. Retail	$1,900

SP D-16R (Previously SP D-16TR) — similar to the SP D-16, except features solid East Indian rosewood back/sides. Mfr. 1996 to date.

Mfr.'s Sug. Retail	$2,000	$1,600	$1,300	$850

SP D-16W (16 Series) — similar to the SP D-16, except features solid walnut back/sides. Mfr. 1998 to date.

Mfr.'s Sug. Retail	$1,900

SP DC-16R (Previously SP DC-16TR) — similar to the SP D-16R, except features rounded Venetian cutaway. Mfr. 1996 to date.

Mfr.'s Sug. Retail	$2,300	$1,725	$1,450	$950

SP 000-16 (Previously SP 000-16T) — similar to SP D-16, except in 000 body size. Available in in Natural gloss finish. Mfr. 1997 to date.

Mfr.'s Sug. Retail	$1,800

SP 000-16R (Previously SP 000-16TR) — similar to SP 000-16, except features solid East Indian rosewood back and sides. Mfr. 1997 to date.

Mfr.'s Sug. Retail	$2,000

SP 000C-16R (Previously SP 000C-16TR) — similar to the SP 000-16R, except features a rounded Venetian cutaway. Mfr. 1997 to date.

Mfr.'s Sug. Retail	$2,300

Women and Music Series

In 1997, the Martin Guitar company specifically designed a guitar model for women. Martin's own Women and Music Program was responsible for initiating the first limited edition model.

M

C-1 R
courtesy The Martin Guitar Company

SP 000-16 T
courtesy The Martin Guitar Company

00-16 DB — 00 style body with extra deep mahogany sides, spruce top, black binding, round soundhole, classical-style wood mosiac rosette, OM-style black pickguard, mahogany back, 14/19 fret ebony fretboard with diamonds and squares inlay, slotted peghead, 3 per side tuners. Available in Natural finish. Mfd. 1997 only.

Model has not traded sufficiently to quote pricing.

Last Mfr.'s Sug. Retail was $2,100.

Only 97 instruments were sold.

00-16 BR — spruce top, black binding, round soundhole, mosaic soundhole rosette, solid rosewood sides, 25 1/2" scale, ebony fingerboard with pearl diamonds and squares inlay, slotted peghead, 3 per side Waverly tuners. Available in Natural finish. Mfd. 1998 only.

Mfr.'s Sug. Retail $2,400

Guitar of the Month Limited Editions

As customer demand opened up for specified, limited edition models, Martin announced the **Guitar of the Month** program in October, 1984. This ambitious plan to offer an announced custom built limited edition model every month was scaled back to four or five models per year. This program continued through 1994, then Martin switched to yearly offerings of limited edition models. Between 1984 to 1985, Guitar of the Month models have special paper labels signed by C.F. Martin III and C.F. Martin IV; models after 1986 are signed by C.F. Martin IV (unless otherwise listed below).

Some Guitar of the Month models are built in a "fixed", predetermined production amount; while others may be "open-ended" and are limited to the number sold (or ordered) through the calender year.

Prior to 1995, these Limited Edition models were labelled separately for Domestic (US) and Foreign markets: a model may be #1 of 100 in the US, while the next model may be numbered #1 of 12 (Overseas). Thus, the **total production** may be 112 for this model (and not the number given on the US label). Separate Foreign label editions are marked with a "*". In 1995, Martin began to issue one label worldwide.

A Special Note from Martin: "As a general rule, Martin has produced two prototypes of each limited edition, in order to develop model specifications and costing data. Generally these prototypes are NOT FOR SALE; however, due to space constrictions, many prototypes have already or eventually may be sold". The **Blue Book of Guitars** always recommends receiving as much paperwork with any guitar prototype to establish providence, as well as documenting legal ownership. Some prototypes may reach the collector's market through unauthorized channels, and unofficially be sold wherein the seller may not have full rights to make the sale.

Guitar of the Month models are usually identified with a suffix (some have unusual prefixes, just to make things difficult: For example, a HD-28 BLE (1990) is an HD-28 with Brazilian rosewood back and sides. Due to the limited production amounts (and fierce loyalty of Martin guitar owners), these specialty guitars rarely trade in the vintage market. Most models encountered are in the 95% to 98% (i.e. well cared for). As most of these models are based on stock Martins of the same year, it is assumed that these guitars would sell for the upper end of the "Excellent" price range, or perhaps the upper end plus an addtional 10% to 20%. Going back to our example of the HD-28 BLE, would probably trade at the high end of HD-28 prices for that year, or maybe a little higher (given that this model has Brazilian rosewood back and sides, a slightly higher adjustment is in order!)

For readers new to Martin products, please note: "Aging Toner" finish, or a " Toned Top" model refers to the golden-toned lacquer that is shot on the top (soundboard) of the guitar. The following models are listed as to the features that differ from similarly designated stock models (for that year).

(The source material for Martin's Guitar of the Month series courtesy Dick Boak, Martin Guitar Company. Additional detailed information can be found in either Jim Washburn and Richard Johnson's "Martin Guitars: An Illustrated Celebration of America's Premier Guitarmaker", Rodale Books, 1997; or Walter Carter's "The Martin Book: A Complete History of Martin Guitars", GPI Books, 1995)

OO-18V (October, 1984) — Prewar OO-18 style, 25.4" scale, tortoise binding, ebony fingerboard, gold tuners, tortoiseshell pickguard, ebony bridge. Available in "Aging Toner" finish.

Model has not traded sufficiently to quote pricing.

Last Mfr.'s Sug. Retail was $1,520.

Only 9 instruments were sold.

D-28 CUSTOM (November, 1984) — D-28 style, ebony fingerboard with snowflake inlay, unbound peghead with torch inlay, scalloped braces, stamped logo on back of peghead.

Model has not traded sufficiently to quote pricing.

Last Mfr.'s Sug. Retail was $2,000.

Only 43 instruments were sold.

M-21 CUSTOM (December, 1984) — Indian rosewood back/sides, tortoise binding, (Style 28) rosette, unbound rosewood fingerboard with slotted diamond inlay, tortoiseshell pickguard, black bridgepins with white dots. Available in "Aging Toner" finish.

Model has not traded sufficiently to quote pricing.

Last Mfr.'s Sug. Retail was $1,600.

Only 16 instruments were sold.

D-18V (September 1985) — Prewar D-18 style, tortoise binding, ebony fingerboard, tortoiseshell pickguard, ebony bridge.

Model has not traded sufficiently to quote pricing.

Last Mfr.'s Sug. Retail was $1,640.

Only 56 instruments were sold.

OM-28LE (October 1985) — OM-28 style, ivoroid binding, diamonds and squares fingerboard inlay, tortoiseshell pickguard under finish. Available in "Aging Toner" finish.

Model has not traded sufficiently to quote pricing.

Last Mfr.'s Sug. Retail was $2,180.

Only 41 instruments were sold (39 Domestic, 2 Foreign).

SP 000C-16 TR
courtesy The Martin Guitar Company

M

D-21LE (November 1985) — D-21 style, Indian rosewood back/sides, rosewood fingerboard, herringbone rosette, rosewood bridge, tortoise binding, tortoiseshell pickguard under finish.

Model has not traded sufficiently to quote pricing.

Last Mfr.'s Sug. Retail was $1,550.

Only 75 instruments were sold.

HD-28LE (December, 1985) — HD-28 style, scalloped bracing, herringbone top purfling/ivoroid binding, diamonds and squares fingerboard inlay, square peghead, tortoiseshell pickguard under finish, white bridgepins with red dots. Available in "Aging Toner" finish.

Model has not traded sufficiently to quote pricing.

Last Mfr.'s Sug. Retail was $2,100.

Only 87 instruments were sold.

J-21MC (1986) — J-21 style, cutaway body design, black binding, 9-ply rosette, tortoiseshell pickguard, chrome tuners with ebony buttons.

Model has not traded sufficiently to quote pricing.

Last Mfr.'s Sug. Retail was $1,750.

Only 56 instruments were sold (55 Domestic, 1 Foreign).

This model was the first J-style with a cutaway body shape.

HD-28SE (September, 1986) — HD-28 style, herringbone top purfling/ivoroid binding, diamonds and squares fingerboard inlay, tortoiseshell pickguard under finish, ebony tuner buttons. Available in "Toned Top" finish.

Model has not traded sufficiently to quote pricing.

Last Mfr.'s Sug. Retail was $2,300.

Only 138 instruments were sold (130 Domestic, 8 Foreign).

The underside of these tops are signed by C.F. Martin III, C.F. Martin IV, and company foremen.

D-62LE (October, 1986) — D-62 style, flamed maple back/sides, tortoise binding, snowflake fingerboard inlay, tortoiseshell pickguard, white bridgepins with tortoiseshell dots.

Model has not traded sufficiently to quote pricing.

Last Mfr.'s Sug. Retail was $2,100.

Only 48 instruments were sold (46 Domestic, 2 Foreign).

CUSTOM J-45M DELUXE (December, 1986) — J-45 style, Englemann or European spruce top, Indian rosewood back/sides, pearl rosette, pearl bordering/tortoise binding, pearl bound ebony fingerboard with hexagonal inlay, pearl bound tortoise pickguard, pearl hexagon outline inlay on bridge tips, gold tuners with small ebony buttons, black bridgepins with pearl dots.

Model has not traded sufficiently to quote pricing.

Last Mfr.'s Sug. Retail was $6,900.

Only 17 instruments were sold (16 Domestic, 1 Foreign).

D-45LE (September, 1987) — D-45 style, Brazilian rosewood back/sides, pearl bound fingerboard, hexagon outline fingerboard inlays, hexagon outline at bridge ends, pearl bound headstock, tortoiseshell pickguard, gold tuners with ebony buttons.

Model has not traded sufficiently to quote pricing.

Last Mfr.'s Sug. Retail was $7,500.

Only 50 instruments were sold (44 Domestic, 6 Foreign).

OO-21LE (September, 1987) — OO-21 style, 24.9" scale, scalloped braces, herringbone rosette, tortoise binding, slotted peghead, 14 fret ebony fingerboard, tortoiseshell pickguard, rectangular ebony bridge, black bridgepins with white dots, 3 per side tuners with pearloid buttons. Available in "Aging Toner" finish.

Model has not traded sufficiently to quote pricing.

Last Mfr.'s Sug. Retail was $2,350.

Only 19 instruments were sold (18 Domestic, 1 Foreign).

This model was optionally available without the tortoise pickguard.

HD-18LE (October, 1987) — D-18V style, scalloped braces, herringbone top trim/tortoise binding, tortoise pickguard, diamonds and squares inlay, ebony tuner buttons, black bridgepins with white dots. Available in "Aging Toner" finish.

Model has not traded sufficiently to quote pricing.

Last Mfr.'s Sug. Retail was $2,250.

Only 51 instruments were sold (50 Domestic, 1 Foreign).

J-40M BLE (November, 1987) — J-40 style, Brazilian rosewood back/sides, tortoise pickguard, snowflake fingerboard inlay, gold tuners with large pearloid buttons. Available in "Aging Toner" finish.

Model has not traded sufficiently to quote pricing.

Last Mfr.'s Sug. Retail was $3,000.

Only 17 instruments were sold (16 Domestic, 1 Foreign).

HD-28 BSE (1987) — D-28 style, Brazilian rosewood back/sides, ivoroid binding, tortoise pickguard, (Style 42) fingerboard inlay, gold tuners with ebony buttons. Available in "Aging Toner" finish.

Model has not traded sufficiently to quote pricing.

Last Mfr.'s Sug. Retail was $3,300.

Only 93 instruments were sold (88 Domestic, 5 Foreign).

The underside of these tops are signed by C.F. Martin IV and company supervisors.

HD-28
courtesy The Martin Guitar Company

HD-28 VS
courtesy The Martin Guitar Company

D-18 VMS
courtesy The Martin Guitar Company

D-42LE (1988) — D-42 style, scalloped braces, low profile neck, white binding, small hexagonal fingerboard inlay, gold tuners with large ebony buttons, tortoise pickguard.

Model has not traded sufficiently to quote pricing.

Last Mfr.'s Sug. Retail was $3,300.

Only 75 instruments were sold (69 Domestic, 6 Foreign).

The underside of the top is signed by the C.F. Martin IV and company foremen.

HD-28M (1988) — HD-28 style, mahogany back/sides, scalloped braces, herringbone top purfling, diamonds and squares inlay, gold tuners with large pearloid buttons, tortoise pickguard, white bridgepins with tortoise dots. Available in "Aging Toner" finish.

Model has not traded sufficiently to quote pricing.

Last Mfr.'s Sug. Retail was $2,170.

Only 81 instruments were sold (77 Domestic, 4 Foreign).

HD-28 PSE (1988) — HD-28 style, scalloped braces, low profile (P) neck, squared off peghead, herringbone top purfling/ivoroid binding, snowflake fingerboard inlay, 3 per side chrome tuners with ebony tuner buttons, tortoise pickguard, white bridgepins with tortoise dots. Available in "Aging Toner" finish.

Model has not traded sufficiently to quote pricing.

Last Mfr.'s Sug. Retail was $2,750.

Only 96 instruments were sold (93 Domestic, 3 Foreign).

The underside of the top is signed by the C.F. Martin IV and company supervisors.

M2C-28 (1988) — MC-28 style, double cutaway design, pearl single ring rosette, gold self-locking tuners with small ebony buttons, white bridgepins with pearl dots.

Model has not traded sufficiently to quote pricing.

Last Mfr.'s Sug. Retail was $2,700.

Only 22 instruments were sold (20 Domestic, 2 Foreign).

This model was optionally available with a pickguard, or Thinline pickup.

D-18 SPECIAL (Also D-18 GOM)(1989) — D-18 style, scalloped braces, low profile neck, rosewood binding, diamonds and squares fingerboard inlay, tortoise pickguard, black bridgepins with pearl dots, 3 per side Grover tuners.

Model has not traded sufficiently to quote pricing.

Last Mfr.'s Sug. Retail was $1,950.

Only 28 instruments were sold (15 Domestic, 13 Foreign).

D-41 BLE (1989) — D-41 style, Engelmann spruce top, Brazilian rosewood back/sides, scalloped braces, low profile neck, pearl bound headstock, pearl bound fingerboard with hexagon inlays, gold tuners with large ebony buttons, tortoise pickguard. Available in "Aging Toner" finish.

Model has not traded sufficiently to quote pricing.

Last Mfr.'s Sug. Retail was $4,800.

Only 39 instruments were sold (31 Domestic, 8 Foreign).

The underside of the top is signed by the C.F. Martin IV and company foremen.

HD-28GM GRAND MARQUIS (1989) — HD-28 style, scalloped braces, herringbone top purfling/tortoise binding, herringbone rosette, snowflake fingerboard inlay, snowflake inlay on bridge ends, "Grand Marquis" decal on back of peghead, gold tuners with embossed "M" on buttons, tortoiseshell pickguard, black bridgepins with abalone dots.

Model has not traded sufficiently to quote pricing.

Last Mfr.'s Sug. Retail was $3,198.

Only 120 instruments were sold (112 Domestic, 8 Foreign).

HOM-35 (1989) — OM-35 style, Brazilian rosewood sides/3-piece back, herringbone trim/top purfling, ivoroid binding top/back, ivoroid-bound ebony fingerboard with diamonds and squares inlay, gold tuners, tortoiseshell OM-style pickguard, white bridgepins with red dots, Martin stamp on back of peghead. Available in "Aging Toner" finish.

Model has not traded sufficiently to quote pricing.

Last Mfr.'s Sug. Retail was $4,000.

Only 60 instruments were sold (53 Domestic, 7 Foreign).

D-18MB (1990) — D-18 style, Engelmann spruce top, "X"-bracing, flamed maple binding/backstrip/peghead veneer, white bridgepins with red dots, ebony tuner buttons. Available in "Aging Toner" finish.

Model has not traded sufficiently to quote pricing.

Last Mfr.'s Sug. Retail was $2,300.

Only 99 instruments were sold (96 Domestic, 3 Foreign).

The underside of the top is signed by the company foremen.

D-40 BLE (1990) — D-40 style, Engelmann spruce top, Brazilian rosewood back/sides, bound top/back, pearl rosette, bound ebony fingerboard with snowflake inlay, 2 6-point snowflake inlay on bridge, bound peghead, engraved gold tuners with "M" buttons, tortoise pickguard, white bridgepins with pearl dots.

Model has not traded sufficiently to quote pricing.

Last Mfr.'s Sug. Retail was $5,598.

Only 58 instruments were sold (50 Domestic, 8 Foreign).

This model has a special label signed by C.F. Martin IV and Mike Longworth. Models came with a Mark Leaf hardshell case.

D-40
courtesy The Martin Guitar Company

M

HD-28 BLE (1990) — HD-28 style, Brazilian rosewood back/sides, low profile neck, herringbone top trim/ivoroid binding, herringbone rosette, ivoroid bound headstock, diamonds and squares fingerboard inlay, 3 per side chrome tuners, tortoise pickguard, white bridgepins with red dots. Available in "Aging Toner" finish.

> Model has not traded sufficiently to quote pricing.

Last Mfr.'s Sug. Retail was $3,900.

> Only 108 instruments were sold (100 Domestic, 8 Foreign).

OMC-28 (1990) — OM-28 style, rounded cutaway design, scalloped bracing, oval soundhole, low profile neck, "C.F. Martin in mother of pearl headstock inlay, gold tuners with small pearloid buttons, tortoise pickguard, white bridgepins with red dots.

> Model has not traded sufficiently to quote pricing.

Last Mfr.'s Sug. Retail was $3,148.

> Only 76 instruments were sold (74 Domestic, 2 Foreign).

D3-18 (1991) — Vintage D-18 style, 3-piece back, white purfling, tortoise-bound ebony fingerboard with mother of pearl diamonds and squares inlay, diamond inlays on bridge ends, tortoise pickguard, chrome tuners with embossed "M" on buttons, black bridgepins with white dots. Available in "Aging Toner" finish.

> Model has not traded sufficiently to quote pricing.

Last Mfr.'s Sug. Retail was $2,398.

> Only 80 instruments were sold (72 Domestic, 8 Foreign).

D-28 LSH (1991) — D-28 style, large soundhole (LSH) with 2 pearl soundhole rings, ivoroid binding, herringbone top trim, 22 fret fingerboard with snowflake inlay, snowflake inlay on bridge ends, tortoise pickguard, gold tuners, ebony tuner buttons with snowflake inlay. Available in "Aging Toner" finish.

> Model has not traded sufficiently to quote pricing.

Last Mfr.'s Sug. Retail was $4,398.

> Only 211 instruments were sold (200 Domestic, 11 Foreign).

> The underside of the top is signed by C.F. Martin IV and company employees. The label is signed by Les Wagner, who retired in 1991 after 47 years service with Martin guitar company.

D-45 KLE (1991) — D-45 style, Engelmann spruce top, flamed koa back/sides, ivoroid binding, pearl bound Brazilian rosewood peghead veneer, snowflake fingerboard inlay, tortoise pickguard, snowflake bridge inlays, gold tuners with embossed "M" on buttons. Available in "Aging Toner" finish.

> Model has not traded sufficiently to quote pricing.

Last Mfr.'s Sug. Retail was $7,800.

> Only 54 instruments were sold (50 Domestic, 4 Foreign).

> The underside of the top is signed by company employees.

> This model came with a Mark Leaf hardshell case.

D-18 VM
courtesy The Martin Guitar Company

OM-21 SPECIAL (1991) — OM-21 style, tortoise binding, striped Macassar ebony fingboard with mother of pearl diamonds and squares inlay, striped ebony bridge, herringbone rosette, tortoise-bound peghead with mother of pearl Martin logo inlay, gold tuners with pearloid buttons, OM-style tortoise pickguard, white bridgepins with red dots. Available in "Aging Toner" finish.

> Model has not traded sufficiently to quote pricing.

Last Mfr.'s Sug. Retail was $3,998.

> Only 36 instruments were sold (32 Domestic, 4 Foreign).

D-18 VINTAGE (1992) — D-18 style, scalloped braces, tortoise binding, ebony fingerboard, ebony bridge with saddle slot, tortoiseshell pickguard, 3 per side Grover tuners black bridgepins with white dots. Available in "Aging Toner" finish.

> Model has not traded sufficiently to quote pricing.

Last Mfr.'s Sug. Retail was $1,998.

> Only 218 instruments were sold (215 Domestic, 3 Foreign).

D-45S DELUXE (1992) — D-45 style, scalloped braces, ivoroid binding, neck joins at 12th fret, solid peghead with pearl borders, snowflake fingerboard inlay, snowflake inlay at bridge ends, pearl border on fingerboard, gold tuners with ebony buttons and pearl "M" inlay, tortoise pickguard. Available in "Aging Toner" finish.

> Model has not traded sufficiently to quote pricing.

Last Mfr.'s Sug. Retail was $9,760.

> Only 60 instruments were sold (50 Domestic, 10 Foreign).

> This modified version was based on a 1937 D-45S (12 fret version with solid peghead).

HD-28 C.T.B. (CUSTOM TORTOISE BOUND) (1992) — HD-28 style, tortoise binding, slotted peghead with torch pattern inlay, mother of pearl diamonds and squares fingerboard inlay with CFM script at 12th fret, gold tuners with embossed "M" on buttons, tortoiseshell pickguard, white bridgepins with red dots. Available in "Aging Toner" finish.

> Model has not traded sufficiently to quote pricing.

Last Mfr.'s Sug. Retail was $3,800.

> Only 97 instruments were sold (89 Domestic, 8 Foreign).

HJ-28 (1992) — HJ-28 style, rosewood back/sides, herringbone top purfling, ivoroid binding, unbound ebony fingerboard with diamonds and squares inlay, chrome tuners with embossed "M" on buttons, tortoiseshell pickguard, white bridgepins with red dots. Available in "Aging Toner" finish.

> Model has not traded sufficiently to quote pricing.

Last Mfr.'s Sug. Retail was $3,050.

> Only 69 instruments were sold (56 Domestic, 13 Foreign).

HJ-28
courtesy The Martin Guitar Company

D-45 VR
courtesy The Martin Guitar Company

HD-35
courtesy The Martin Guitar Company

D-28 1935 SPECIAL (1993) — D-28 style (more similar to the current HD-28 VR), Indian rosewood back/sides, scalloped bracing, ivoroid binding, square tapered peghead with Brazilian rosewood veneer, tortoiseshell pickguard.

Model has not traded sufficiently to quote pricing.

Last Mfr.'s Sug. Retail was $3,800.

Only 237 instruments were sold (217 Domestic, 20 Foreign).

This model is based on the D-28 with features available back in 1935.

This model was optionally available with a dark sunburst finish.

D-45 DELUXE (1993) — D-45 style, "bear claw" figured spruce top, Brazilian rosewood back/sides, ivoroid binding, bridge/pickguard inlay, highly figured pearl "Tree of Life" fingerboard inlay, peghead/fingerboard pearl borders, gold tuners with large gold buttons embossed with "M", fossilized ivory bridgepins with pearl dots, black pickguard. Available in "Aging Toner" finish.

Model has not traded sufficiently to quote pricing.

Last Mfr.'s Sug. Retail was $18,200.

Only 60 instruments were sold (50 Domestic, 10 Foreign).

D-93 (1993) — dreadnought style, mahogany back/sides, white binding, herringbone rosette, bound Brazilian rosewood veneer peghead, bound ebony fingerboard with diamonds and squares inlay/"CFM" script inlay at 3rd fret, diamond inlay at bridge ends, gold tuners with ebony buttons, tortoiseshell pickguard, white bridgepins with red dots. Available in "Aging Toner" finish.

Model has not traded sufficiently to quote pricing.

Last Mfr.'s Sug. Retail was $3,000.

Only 165 instruments were sold (148 Domestic, 17 Foreign).

This model commemorates Martin's 160 years of guitar building (1833 to 1993).

HD-28C LSH (1993) — HD-28 style, cutaway design, scalloped braces, herringbone top purfling, large soundhole, rosewood peghead veneer, tortoiseshell pickguard, white bridgepins with red dots, built-in pickup. Available in Sunburst finish.

Production amount unknown.

OM-28 PERRY BECHTEL (1993) — OM-28 (VR) style, herringbone top trim, ivoroid binding, wood purfling in rosette, diamonds and squares fingerboard inlay, Brazilian rosewood headstock veneer, pyramid bridge, chrome tuners with embossed "M" on buttons, tortoiseshell pickguard. Available in "Aging Toner" finish.

Model has not traded sufficiently to quote pricing.

Last Mfr.'s Sug. Retail was $4,000.

Only 94 instruments were sold (77 Domestic, 17 Foreign).

This model features a special label signed by Mrs. Ina Bechtel (Perry Bechtel's widow).

D-45 GENE AUTRY (1994) — D-45 style, scalloped braces, neck joins at 12th fret, "Gene Autry" pearl script fingerboard inlay, torch inlay on peghead, 3 per side Waverly tuners.

Model has not traded sufficiently to quote pricing.

Last Mfr.'s Sug. Retail was $22,000.

Only 66 instruments were sold (50 Domestic, 16 Foreign).

This model was also available with snowflake inlay and "Gene Autry" at 19th fret. The interior label is signed by Gene Autry.

HD-28GM LSH GRAND MARQUIS (1994) — HD-28 style, herringbone top purfling, tortoise binding, large soundhole with 2 herringbone soundhole rings, unbound ebony fingerboard with snowflake inlay and "Grand Marquis" in pearl script at 12th fret, "CF Martin" pearl logo inlay on peghead, snowflake inlay on bridge, tortoise pickguard, gold tuners with embossed "M" on buttons. Available in "Aging Toner" or Shaded top finishes.

Model has not traded sufficiently to quote pricing.

Last Mfr.'s Sug. Retail was $4,500 (Natural finish).
Last Mfr.'s Sug. Retail was $4,830 (Sunburst finish).

Only 151 instruments were sold (115 in Natural finish; 36 in Sunburst finish).

Of the 115 in Natural finish, 106 Domestic, 9 Foreign.

Of the 36 in Sunburst finish, 30 Domestic, 6 Foreign.

HJ-28M (1994) — jumbo style, mahogany back/sides, herringbone top purfling, ivoroid binding, striped Madagascar ebony fingerboard/bridge, chrome tuners with large ebony buttons and pearl "M" inlay, tortoiseshell pickguard, white bridgepins with tortoise dots. Available in "Aging Toner" finish.

Model has not traded sufficiently to quote pricing.

Last Mfr.'s Sug. Retail was $3,900.

Only 72 instruments were sold (60 Domestic, 12 Foreign).

This model has HD-28 (Vintage Series) features on a jumbo-style body.

OM-40LE (1994) — OM-40 style, Indian rosewood back/sides, herringbone top purfling, pearl rosette, pearl border on top, unbound ebony fingerboard with snowflake inlay, "CF Martin" pearl logo on unbound peghead, gold tuners with large ebony buttons and pearl 4-point snowflake inlays, white bridgepins with pearl dots. Available in Natural and Shaded Top finishes.

Model has not traded sufficiently to quote pricing.

Last Mfr.'s Sug. Retail was $7,100 (Natural finish).
Last Mfr.'s Sug. Retail was $7,430 (Sunburst finish).

Only 86 instruments were sold (57 in Natural finish; 29 in Sunburst finish).

Of the 57 in Natural finish, 45 Domestic, 12 Foreign.

Of the 29 in Sunburst finish, 20 Domestic, 9 Foreign.

This model has similar features that are found on current OM (Vintage Series) models.

1995 Limited Edition

ERIC CLAPTON SIGNATURE 000-42 EC — solid Sitka spruce top, 24.9" scale length, ivoroid body binding/herringbone purfling, herringbone rosette, solid East Indian rosewood back/sides, mahogany neck, 14/20 fret ebony fingerboard with special abalone inlay/mother of pearl Eric Clapton signature inlay, snowflake inlay on bridge, 3 per side tuners with "butterbean" buttons. Available in Natural gloss and Shaded Top finishes.

Model has not traded sufficiently to quote pricing.

Last Mfr.'s Sug. Retail was $8,100 (Natural finish).
Last Mfr.'s Sug. Retail was $8,320 (Sunburst finish).

Only 461 instruments were sold (433 in Natural finish; 28 in Sunburst finish).

D-18 GOLDEN ERA — D-18 style, abalone dot pattern on neck, Brazilian rosewood peghead veneer, old style logo. Available in Natural and Shaded Top finishes.

Model has not traded sufficiently to quote pricing.

Last Mfr.'s Sug. Retail was $3,100 (Natural finish).
Last Mfr.'s Sug. Retail was $8,320 (Sunburst finish).

Only 320 instruments were sold (272 in Natural finish; 48 in Sunburst finish).

This model was based on a 1937 D-18, and in addition to late 1930s styling also has similar features that are found on the current D-18VM (Vintage Series) models.

D-35 30TH ANNIVERSARY — D-35 style, Brazilian rosewood center wedge (3 pc. back)/peghead veneer, ivoroid binding, mitered fingerboard binding, "1965-1995" logo inlaid at 20th fret, tortoise pickguard, 3 per side gold tuners with "M" buttons. Available in Natural finish.

Model has not traded sufficiently to quote pricing.

Last Mfr.'s Sug. Retail was $4,000.

Only 207 instruments were sold.

HD-28 SO — HD-28 style, ivoroid binding, 12/19 fret fingerboard with mother of pearl *Sing Out!* logo inlay, slotted peghead. Available in Natural finish.

Model has not traded sufficiently to quote pricing.

Last Mfr.'s Sug. Retail was $4,500.

Only 45 instruments were sold.

This model celebrates the 45th Anniversary of Sing Out! magazine. The inside label is signed by Pete Seeger. The HD-28 SO has similar features that are found on current HD-28VS (Vintage Series) models.

00-40
courtesy The Martin Guitar Company

1996 Limited Editions

000-28 12 FRET GOLDEN ERA — bookmatched Sitka spruce top, round soundhole, wood rosette, 2-piece East Indian rosewood back, East Indian rosewood sides, herringbone marquetry/ivoroid body binding, 12/19 fret ebony fingerboard with abalone diamonds and squares inlay, ebony pyramid bridge, 3 per side Waverly-Sloane tuners. Available in "Aging Toner" lacquer finish.

Model has not traded sufficiently to quote pricing.

Last Mfr.'s Sug. Retail was $4,000.

Only 367 instruments were sold.

The edition run was limited to those guitars ordered in 1996. The pickguard was optional on this edition.

C.F. MARTIN SR. DELUXE D-45 — Sitka spruce top, Brazilian rosewood back/sides/headstock veneer, abalone/grained ivoroid body binding, abalone rosette, bound ebony fingerboard with abalone (style 45) snowflake inlay, abalone snowflake bridge inlay, 3 per side gold open geared tuners with "butterbean" knobs.

Model has not traded sufficiently to quote pricing.

Last Mfr.'s Sug. Retail was $19,500.

Only 91 instruments were sold.

C.F. Martin Sr. Commemorative D-45 — similar to the C.F. Martin Sr. Deluxe, except features East Indian rosewood back and sides, and standard Style 45 abalone body decoration.

Model has not traded sufficiently to quote pricing.

Last Mfr.'s Sug. Retail was $11,000.

Only 114 instruments were sold.

This model commemorates the 200 years since the birth of company founded C.F. Martin, Sr. (1796).

MARTY STUART HD-40MS — solid Sitka spruce top, round soundhole, pearl rosette, East Indian rosewood back/sides, grained ivoroid body/fingerboard/headstock binding, 103 piece pearl/abalone/recomposite stone fingerboard inlay (steer horns, horseshoes, dice, hearts, and flowers), 3 per side gold open geared tuners with "butterbean" knobs.

Model has not traded sufficiently to quote pricing.

Last Mfr.'s Sug. Retail was $5,400.

Only 250 instruments scheduled.

00-45
courtesy The Martin Guitar Company

M

1997 Martin 000-45 JR Jimmie Rogers
courtesy Buddy Summer

MTV-1 "MTV UNPLUGGED" DREADNOUGHT — solid Sitka spruce top, round soundhole, pearl rosette, East Indian rosewood bass (or top) side of guitar, mahogany treble (or lower) side of body, mahogany neck, 14/20 fret ebony fingerboard with paua shell "Unplugged" inlay, "MTV" pearl headstock inlay, ebony bridge. Available in Natural Gloss or Natural Satin finishes.

Model has not traded sufficiently to quote pricing.

Last Mfr.'s Sug. Retail was $2,200 (Satin finish).
Last Mfr.'s Sug. Retail was $2,450 (Gloss finish).

Only 697 instruments were sold.

1997 Limited Editions

00-45 ST STAUFFER LIMITED EDITION — Brazilian rosewood top/back/sides, abalone rosette/body binding, "ice cream cone" shaped neck heel, grained ivoroid bindings, Stauffer-style curved headstock, belly bridge with pyramid wings, black ebonized neck finish, Martin mother of pearl headstock inlay.

Model has not traded sufficiently to quote pricing.

Last Mfr.'s Sug. Retail was $20,000.

Only 25 instruments were sold.

00-40 ST Stauffer Limited Edition — similar to the 00-45, except features East Indian rosewood back and sides.

Model has not traded sufficiently to quote pricing.

Last Mfr.'s Sug. Retail was $7,900.

Only 75 instruments are scheduled. To date, 35 have been sold.

JIMMIE RODGERS 000-45 JR "BLUE YODEL" — bookmatched Adirondack spruce top, round soundhole, Brazilian rosewood back/sides, (style 45) pearl body inlay/ivoroid body binding, 12/19 fret bound ebony fingerboard with pearl "Jimmy Rodgers" inlay, pearl "Blue Yodel" peghead inlay, slotted headstock, snowflake inlay on bridge tips.

Model has not traded sufficiently to quote pricing.

Last Mfr.'s Sug. Retail was $25,000.

Only 100 instruments are scheduled. To date, 52 have been sold.

This model is the replica of Jimmie Rodgers' 1928 000-45. The limited editions are available with the optional "THANKS" printing on back.

ARLO GUTHRIE 0000-28H AG — M-38 style, Sitka spruce top, round soundhole, 3-piece abalone pearl rosette, East Indian rosewood back/sides, mahogany neck, herringbone body trim/ivoroid bindin, ebony fingerboard with circles and arrows/"Alice's Restaurant 30th"/Arlo Guthrie signature inlay, Martin raised gold logo/engraved pearl representation of Alice's restaurant peghead inlay.

Model has not traded sufficiently to quote pricing.

Last Mfr.'s Sug. Retail was $4,750.

Only 30 instruments were sold.

This model comes with a denim covered hardshell case.

Arlo Guthrie 000012-28H AG — similar to the Arlo Guthrie 0000-28H, except in a 12-string configuration, 6 per side tuners. Available in Natural finish.

Model has not traded sufficiently to quote pricing.

Last Mfr.'s Sug. Retail was $4,950.

Only 30 instruments were sold.

This model comes with a denim covered hardshell case.

PAUL SIMON OM-42 PS — solid Sitka spruce top, round soundhole, tortoise body binding, East Indian rosewood back/sides, 25.4" scale, 14/20 fret tortoise bound ebony fingerboard with (style 42) abalone pearl snowflake inlay/mother of pearl Paul Simon signature inlay, OM-style pickguard, snowflake inlay on bridge, nickel Waverly open geared tuners with ivoroid buttons.

Model has not traded sufficiently to quote pricing.

Last Mfr.'s Sug. Retail was $8,000.

Only 500 instruments are scheduled. To date only 223 have been sold.

The interior label of the instruments is signed by both Paul Simon and C.F. Martin IV.

CEO'S CHOICE LIMITED EDITION (CEO-1) — SP D-16T style, spruce top, round soundhole, abalone rosette, herringbone top trim, solid mahogany back/sides, ebony fingerboard with "hexagon outline"/mother of peral C.F. Martin IV signature inlays, hexagon outline on bridge, tortoise pickguard, 3 per side gold tuners with ebony buttons.

Model has not traded sufficiently to quote pricing.

Last Mfr.'s Sug. Retail was $2,600.

Only 128 instruments were sold.

Model design and appointments were chosen by CEO and Chairman of the Board, C.F. Martin IV. This model comes with an interior label signed by C.F. Martin IV, and a vintage "tweed" case.

CEO-1 R Limited Edition — similar to the CEO's Choice, except features solid East Indian rosewood back/sides.

Model has not traded sufficiently to quote pricing.

Last Mfr.'s Sug. Retail was $2,800.

Only 191 instruments were sold.

OM-42 PS
courtesy The Martin Guitar Company

JOHNNY CASH SIGNATURE D-42 JC — D-42 style, spruce top, round soundhole, pearl border/ivoroid body binding, 3-piece East Indian rosewood back, East Indian rosewood sides, 14/20 fret bound ebony fingerboard with abalone star inlay/Johnny Cash signature pearl inlay, abalone rosette, 3 per side vintage-style tuners. Available in Gloss Black lacquer finish.

Model has not traded sufficiently to quote pricing.

Last Mfr.'s Sug. Retail was $8,200.

Only 200 instruments are scheduled.

This model is the first limited edition model to be finished in Black.

KINGSTON TRIO SET: D-28, 0-18T, VEGA BANJO — All three models feature special mother of pearl "The Kingston Trio"/1957-1997 fingerboard inlay. The special D-28 model features a solid spruce top, East Indian back and sides, ebony fingerboard and bridge, and a Brazilian rosewood peghead veneer. The 0-18T tenor features a similar solid spruce top, ebony fingerboard and bridge, and mahogany back and sides.

This set has not traded sufficiently to quote pricing.

Last Mfr.'s Sug. Retail was $12,500.

There are 40 limited edition sets scheduled for production. To date, 34 sets have been sold.

In 1997, Martin noted that "Additional Kingston Trio D-28 models (D-28KT) will be offered after the limited edition sets are ordered". However, these models were not issued, nor were any additional prototypes constructed.

CEO-1
courtesy The Martin Guitar Company

1998 Limited Editions

JOAN BAEZ SIGNATURE 0-45 JB — 0-45 style, Sitka spruce top, abalone pearl rosette, abalone pearl/grained ivoroid binding, East Indian rosewood back/sides, 2-piece back, ebony fingerboard with style 45 abalone snowflake inlay.

Model has not traded sufficiently to quote pricing.

Last Mfr.'s Sug. Retail was $9,850.

Only 59 instruments are scheduled.

This model is the first "Woman & Music" program Artist's Signature edition.

00-21 GE GOLDEN ERA — 00-21 style, 12/19 fret fingerboard, slotted peghead.

Model has not traded sufficiently to quote pricing.

Last Mfr.'s Sug. Retail was $3,950.

This instrument has an open schedule for 1998.

OM-45 GE GOLDEN ERA — OM-45 style, Adirondack spruce top, tortoise teardrop-shaped pickguard with abalone inlay, 3 per side banjo tuners with mother of pearl buttons.

Model has not traded sufficiently to quote pricing.

Last Mfr.'s Sug. Retail was $27,500.

Only 14 instruments are scheduled. This model is a reproduction of the 1930 OM-45 (only 14 were originally made).

HANK WILLIAMS SR. COMMEMORATIVE D-28 HW — D-28 style, bookmatched spruce top, grained ivoroid binding, mahogany neck, 2 piece Brazilian rosewood back, ebony fingerboard with diamonds and squares inlay. Available in Natural finish.

Model has not traded sufficiently to quote pricing.

Last Mfr.'s Sug. Retail was $9,000.

Only 150 instruments are scheduled.

LESTER FLATT D-28 LF

— D-28 style, grained ivoroid body binding, Brazilian rosewood back/sides, ebony fingerboard with special Mike Longworth custom inlay reproduction, ebony bridge, enlarged tortoise pickguard.

Model has not traded sufficiently to quote pricing.

Last Mfr.'s Sug. Retail was $8,500.

Only 50 instruments are scheduled. Interior label in signed by C.F. Martin IV. Model includes a Geib Vintage Style deluxe hardshell case.

DON MCLEAN D-40 DM

— D-40 style, Engelmann spruce top, abalone pearl rosette, East Indian rosewood back/sides, mahogany neck, ebony fingerboard with custom hexagon inlay, bound ebony headplate, white body binding, tortoise pickguard. Available in Aging Toner finish.

Model has not traded sufficiently to quote pricing.

Last Mfr.'s Sug. Retail was $5,750.

Only 71 instruments are scheduled. The interior label is signed by Don McLean and C.F. Martin IV, and features McLean's handcolored Thumb's Up logo.

STEPHEN STILLS D-45 SS

— D-45 style, European Alpine spruce top, abalone pearl top/rosette/back/sides/endpiece/neck joint binding, pre-CITES Brazilian rosewood back and sides, tortoise pickguard with abalone 'Southern Cross' 5 star inlay.

Model has not traded sufficiently to quote pricing.

Last Mfr.'s Sug. Retail was $19,000.

Only 91 instruments are scheduled. The interior label is signed by Stephen Stills and C.F. Martin IV.

JIMMY BUFFET SIGNATURE HD-18 JB — vintage D-28 appointments, bookmatched spruce top, grained ivoroid binding, abalone rosette, selected mahogany back/sides, Palm Tree headstock inlay, tortoise pickguard.

Model has not traded sufficiently to quote pricing.

Last Mfr.'s Sug. Retail was $3,650.

Only 424 instruments are scheduled. The interior label is signed by both Jimmy Buffet and C.F. Martin IV.

CEO-1 R
courtesy The Martin Guitar Company

M

Grading	100%	Excellent	Average

WILLIE NELSON N-20 WN — N-20 style, Sitka spruce top, 25.4" scale, ebony fingerboard, square (non-tapered) slotted headstock, 3 per side Walverly Sloane tuners, Fishman transducer. Available in Aging Toner finish.

Model has not traded sufficiently to quote pricing.

Last Mfr.'s Sug. Retail was $5,500.

Only 100 total instruments are scheduled, between the N-20 WN and N-20 WN B. This model is a reproduction of Nelson's guitar, nicknamed "Trigger". The interior label is signed by Willie Nelson and C.F. Martin IV. This model is equipped with a Geib Deluxe hardshell case.

Willie Nelson N-20 WN B — similar to the Willie Nelson N-20 WN, except features Brazilian rosewood back/sides.

Model has not traded sufficiently to quote pricing.

Last Mfr.'s Sug. Retail was $9,800.

Only 30 of the 100 total instruments are scheduled to be produced with Brazilian rosewood back and sides.

STING CLASSICAL SIGNATURE CMSH — Martin/Humphrey classical style, Western red cedar top, solid quilted mahogany back/sides, tortoise body binding, mahogany neck, ebony fingerboard with inset abalone pearl bordering, Martin/Fishman Thinline Goldplus system. Available in Aging Toner finish.

Model has not traded sufficiently to quote pricing.

Last Mfr.'s Sug. Retail was $4,450.

Only 250 instruments are scheduled.

CEO'S CHOICE CEO-2 — abalone pearl rosette, black body binding, laminated Macassar striped ebony back/sides, ebony fingerboard fingerboard, with hollow hexagon inlay, ebony bridge with hollow hexagon inlay, 3 per side gold enclosed tuners with ebony buttons, tortoise pickguard.

Model has not traded sufficiently to quote pricing.

Last Mfr.'s Sug. Retail was $2,900.

This instrument has an open schedule for 1998. The interior label is signed by C.F. Martin IV.

EMPLOYEE MODEL EMP-1 — 000 style, single rounded cutaway body, wooden rosette, solid ovangkol 3 piece back with rosewood center wedge, solid ovangkol sides, abalone pearl peghead logo. Available in Natural finish.

Model has not traded sufficiently to quote pricing.

Last Mfr.'s Sug. Retail was $2,450.

Only 262 instruments are scheduled.

CONCEPT J CUTAWAY — solid spruce top, solid maple back/sides, abalone rosette, unbound body edges, ebony fingerboard with hollow hexagon inlay, ebony bridge with hollow hexagon inlay, active electronics. Available in "Holographic" finish (made with suspended metallic particles).

Model has not traded sufficiently to quote pricing.

Last Mfr.'s Sug. Retail was $4,100.

This instrument has an open schedule for 1998.

CERTIFIED WOOD MODEL SWD — cherry back/sides/neck (and interior blocks), katalox fingerboard and bridge, basswood interior lining. Available in Natural finish.

Model has not traded sufficiently to quote pricing.

Last Mfr.'s Sug. Retail was $1,399.

This instrument has an open schedule for 1998. This model features construction of woods certified by the Rainforest Alliance's "SmartWood" program.

ACOUSTIC BASS

Unless otherwise listed, all models have jumbo style bodies, and are available with fretless fingerboard at no additional charge.
Add $325 to all models for acoustic bridge pickup with active preamp, volume/tone control.

BM (Road Series) — solid spruce top, round soundhole, black body binding, laminated mahogany back/sides, mahogany neck, 14/20 rosewood fingerboard with white dot inlay, single band herringbone rosette, tortoise pickguard, 2 per side chrome tuners. Available in Natural satin finish. Mfr. 1998 to date.
Mfr.'s Sug. Retail $1,249

B-1 (1 Series) — solid Sitka spruce top, round soundhole, mahogany neck, solid mahogany back, 3-ply mahogany sides, 34" scale, 17/23 rosewood fingerboard with dot inlay, rosewood bridge, tortoise pickguard, 2 per side tuners, chrome hardware. Available in Natural satin finish. Current mfr.

Mfr.'s Sug. Retail $1,449	**$1,150**	**$950**	**$600**

B-40 — jumbo style, solid spruce top, round soundhole, black pickguard, 5 stripe bound body/rosette, rosewood back/sides, mahogany neck, 17/23 fret ebony fingerboard, ebony bridge with white black dot pins, rosewood peghead veneer, 2 per side chrome tuners. Available in Natural finish. Mfd. 1988 to 1996.

	$1,450	**$950**

Last Mfr.'s Sug. Retail was $2,900.

BC-40 — similar to B-40, except has single round cutaway, oval soundhole. Mfd. 1990 to 1996.

	$1,550	**$995**

Last Mfr.'s Sug. Retail was $3,120.

B-540 — similar to B-40, except has 5 strings, striped ebony fingerboard/bridge, 5/2 per side tuners. Mfd. 1992 to 1995.

	$1,600	**$950**

Last Mfr.'s Sug. Retail was $2,790.

B-65 — similar to B-40, except has tortoise pickguard, figured maple back/sides. Mfd. 1987 to 1995.

	$1,500	**$995**

Last Mfr.'s Sug. Retail was $2,610.

B-1 Acoustic Bass
courtesy The Martin Guitar Company

B-40
courtesy The Martin Guitar Company

MASTER

Instruments currently built in Los Angeles, California.

Luthier George Gorodnitski has been building fine handcrafted acoustic and semi-hollowbody electric guitars for a number of years. For further information, please contact luthier Gorodnitski through the Index of Current Manufacturers located in the back of this book.

MASTERBILT

See MAC YASUDA GUITARS.

MASTERTONE

See chapter on House Brands.

While the Mastertone designation was applied to high end Gibson banjos in the 1920s, the MASTERTONE trademark was used on a Gibson-produced budget line of electric guitars beginning in 1941. Some acoustic "Hawaiian" guitars from the 1930s by Gibson also carried the Mastertone label. While built to the same standards as other Gibson guitars, they lack the one "true" Gibson touch: an adjustable truss rod. "House Brand" Gibsons were available to musical instrument distributors in the late 1930s and early 1940s.

(Source: Walter Carter, Gibson Guitars: 100 Years of an American Icon)

TOM MATES

Instruments built in England.

Luthier Tom Mates produces handcrafted acoustic guitars. One notable player using a rather ornately inlaid version is Dave Pegg (of Jethro Tull).

(Source: Tony Bacon, The Ultimate Guitar Book)

MATON

Instruments produced in Australia since 1946.

Maton is Australia's longest established guitar manufacturer. The Maton trademark was established in 1946 by British emigre Bill May, a former woodworking teacher. His trademark name was a combination of his last name, and *tone* - just what every luthier seeks.

In the 1940s, it was a commonly held belief among Australian guitarists and musical instrument retailers that American guitars were the best in the world. While Bill May may have subscribed to that general idea, it didn't stop him from questioning why Australians shouldn't build their own guitars. As May related in a 1985 interview, "I wanted to make better guitars, beyond what people thought you had the ability to do. People asked 'How do you think you can do it..you've never been to see how it's done and what do you know about it? And it's Australia. You don't know anything here. If you want good instruments, you have to wait and get them from America'. But I didn't believe that".

May was raised with craftsman skills and a positive attitude, both for his own self esteem and for his country. Bill May originally completed his apprenticeship in cabinet making, and later an honors course in art and graphic design before he spent ten years as a woodwork teacher. When May couldn't find a decent sounding guitar in a reasonable price range, he began building guitars in the garage of his Thornbury home. While there was no wealth of guitar building information back in the 1940s, May learned from the various guitars that passed through his hands. Production tools for the time period were the same sort used by furniture craftsmen, like chisels, planes, or the occasional belt-sander or bench saw. Rather than knock out copies of American models, May produced designs that were distinctive in appearance and sound - and featured Australian woods and distinctly Australian names. After the humble beginnings in his garage, a factory was established outside of Melbourne in 1951. Maton guitars began to be offered through local stores; by the mid 1960s Maton instruments had established a solid reputation thoughout Australia.

May passed away on his 75th birthday in 1993, but the company continues to produce quality acoustic guitars. The modern factory located in Bayswater is certainly different from Maton's original site in Canterbury, but the traditional use of hand craftsmanship still co-exists with the new CNC router at the plant. While the focus of current production has been on acoustic guitars, the company also promises that there will be a return of production electrics later on.

(Company history courtesy John Stephenson, The Maton Book (1997); additional model descriptions courtesy Linda Kitchen (Bill May's daughter) and Haidin Demaj, Maton Guitars)

Maton estimates that 80,000 guitars were sold in the past forty years. The current company builds over 400 acoustics per month.

ACOUSTIC

Maton has been focused on producing quality acoustic guitar for the past several years. Current models feature Canadian Sitka spruce tops, Queensland maple and walnut as well as Tasmanian and Victorian blackwood in the back and sides. Other timbers include Brazilian and Indian rosewood, and rock maple. Most models feature solid wood back and sides. the acoustic/electric models feature an installed AP5 pickup and on-board preamp built by Australian piezo manufacturer GEC-Marconi.

R. MATSUOKA

Instruments produced in Japan circa late 1970s. Distributed by Unicord of Westbury, New York.

Luthier R. Matsuoka offered these good quality classical guitars that featured ebony fingerboards, select hardwoods, and a hand-rubbed finish. Suggested list prices are unknown at this time.

MAURER & CO.

See LARSON BROTHERS (1900-1944).

The Maurer brand was used by Robert Maurer prior to 1900 and by the Larson brothers, Carl and August, starting in 1900. The Larsons produced guitars, ukes, and mandolin family instruments under this brand until the mid-1930s when they, and

B-65
courtesy The Martin Guitar Company

14 1/2" Maurer
courtesy Robert Carl Hartman

Megas Custom
courtesy Scott Chinery

the rest of the industry, changed designs from the small body guitars with slot pegheads and 12-frets-to-the-body necks to larger bodies with necks becoming narrower but extending the fingerboard to now have 14 frets-to-the-body.

The most commonly found Maurer instrument is the flat-top guitar having either X-bracing or straight, ladder-type bracing. Some of the X-braced instruments have the laminated X-braces which were patented by August in 1904. The Maurers were offered in student grade, intermediate grade and best grade. The Maurer brand was also used on the harp guitar, uke, taro-patch, mandolinetto, mandola, octave mandolin, mando-cello, and mando-bass.

The style of the Maurers was carried through in the instruments sold to Wm. C. Stahl and the Prairie State brand. They ranged from the very plain to the pearl and abalone trimmed with the fanciest having a beautiful tree-of-life fingerboard. The Maurers are high quality instruments and are more commonly found than the other Larson brands.

For more detailed information regarding all the Larson brands, the Larson patents, and a Maurer/Prairie State catalog reprint, see The Larsons' Creations, Guitars and Mandolins, by Robert Carl Hartman, Centerstream Publishing, P.O. Box 17878, Anaheim Hills CA 92807, phone/fax (714) 779-9390.

MAXTONE

Instruments produced in Taiwan, and distributed by the Ta Feng Long Enterprises Company, Ltd. of Tai Chung, Taiwan.

Maxtone instruments are designed with the entry level to student quality guitars. For further information, contact Maxtone via the Index of Current Manufacturers located in the back of this book.

MAYFAIR

Instruments produced in Japan, circa 1960s.

Research continues on the Mayfair trademark.

MAYFLOWER

Instruments built in Chicago, Illinois from 1918 to 1928.

The Groeschel Company of Chicago, Illinois first began building bowl-back (or "potato bug") mandolins in 1890. In 1918 Groeschel was changed to the Stromberg-Voisenet Company, who produced guitars and banjos under the Mayflower trademark. This Stromberg company is not to be confused with luthier Charles Stromberg (and son Elmer) of Boston, Massachusetts.

Henry Kay Kuhrmeyer bought the Stromberg-Voisenet company in 1928, and renamed it Kay Musical Instruments in 1931 (See KAY).

TED MEGAS

Instruments built in San Francisco, California since 1989.

Luthier Ted Megas has been building guitars since 1975, and in 1989 began building arch top guitars, which represented the best combination of his musical interests and his knowledge and skills as a woodworker. For more information, please contact luthier Megas through the Index of Current Manufacturers, located in the back of this book.

Megas Archtop
courtesy Ted Megas

ACOUSTIC

Megas currently builds three arch top models. All his guitars have hand-carved Spruce tops, hand-carved, highly figured maple backs with matching matching sides, solid ebony fingerboard, bridge, pickguard, and peg overlay, figured hard maple neck and adjustable truss rod, high gloss nitro-celluose lacquer finish, and come with a 5-ply hardshell case. All models are made in 16", 17", and 18" bodies.

Add $250 for a floating Kent Armstrong pickup.

Add $300 for custom shading or Sunburst finish.

Add $500 for a 7-string configuration.

The **Athena** is classically styled with multi-lined plastic bindings throughout; split block MOP inlays on fingerboard; abalone dot side position markers; x-bracing; MOP nut; precision machined brass tailpiece construction with ebony overlay; and Schaller tuning machines with ebony buttons. List prices range from the 16" body width ($5,400), 17" width ($5,800), and the 18" width ($6,400).

The **Apollo** features wood bindings; abalone, dot side position makers; x-bracing; cello style f-holes; MOP nut; precision machined brass tailpiece construction with ebony overlay; and Schaller tuning machines with ebony buttons. List prices range from the 16" body width ($5,200), 17" width ($5,500), and the 18" width ($6,000).

The **Spartan** has a single bound body, neck, and peg head; parallel bracing; bone nut; ebony tailpiece with brass anchor; gold Gotoh tuning machines. List prices range from the 16" body width ($3,900), 17" width ($4,200), and the 18" width ($4,600).

JOHN F. MELLO

Instruments currently built in Kensington, California.

Since 1973, John Mello has been building classical and small-bodied steel- string guitars, with an emphasis on clarity, projection, and providing the player with a wide dynamic range and broad palette of colors to interpret his/her music. His building is informed by extensive experience in restoring master instruments by both historic and contemporary makers, and his guitars have been exhibited at the Renwick Gallery of the Smithsonian Institution, played on recordings by Douglas Woodful Harris and Alex Degrassi, and gained him mention as one of America's 17 best classical guitar makers by *Musician Magazine*.

MELPHONIC

Instruments built by Valco of Chicago, Illinois circa mid 1960s.

Melphonic resonator guitars were built by Valco (see VALCO or DOBRO).

(Source: Michael Wright, Vintage Guitar Magazine)

MENKEVICH GUITAR

Instruments currently built in Philadelphia, Pennsylvania.

Luthier Michael Menkevich has been handcrafting quality guitars for a number of years. For more information concerning model specifications and pricing, please contact luthier Menkevich through the Index of Current Manufacturers located in the back of this edition.

MERRILL

Instruments produced in New York, New York circa late 1880s.

Company president Neil Merrill began experimenting with aluminum in the mid-1880s. He debuted his aluminum bodied guitars in 1894 and offered a wide range of stringed instruments based on this design.

(Source: Tom Wheeler, American Guitars)

MERMER

Instruments currently built in Sebastian, Florida.

Luthier Richard Mermer, Jr. is producing concert quality, handcrafted instruments designed and built for the individual. Steel string, nylon string, electric-acoustic instruments, and acoustic Hawaiian steel guitars are offered.

All Mermer guitars feature: solid wood construction, choice of select tone woods, decorative wood binding, custom wood and stone inlay, custom scale lengths, fully compensated saddles and precision intonation, adjustable truss rod, choice of hardware and accessories, and optional pickup and microphone installation. For a list of options and additional information, visit Mermer Guitars on the internet; or for color brochure and information write to Mermer Guitars through the Index of Current Manufacturers located in the back of this book.

MESROBIAN

Instruments currently built in Salem, Massachusetts.

Luthier Carl Mesrobian offers a high quality, 17 inch archtop model that features a hand-graduated Sitka or European spruce top and figured maple back and sides. For additional information concerning specifications and pricing, please contact luthier Mesrobian through the Index of Current Manufacturers located in the back of this edition.

MICHAEL DOLAN

Instruments built in Sonoma County, California since 1977.

Luthier Michael Dolan has been handcrafting quality guitars for over twenty years. After Dolan graduated from Sonoma State University with a Bachelor of Arts degree in Fine Arts, he went to work for a prestigous bass and guitar manufacturer.

Dolan's full service shop offers custom built guitars and basses (solid body, arch-top, acoustic, neck-through, bolt-on, set-neck, and headless) as well as repairs and custom painting. He and his staff work in domestic and exotic woods, and use hardware and electronics from all well-known manufacturers. Finishes include their standard acrylic top coat/polester base, nitrocellulose, and hand rubbed oil.

As luthier Dolan likes to point out, a "Custom Guitar is a unique expression of the vision of a particular individual. Because there are so many options and variables, offering a price list has proven to be impractical." However, Dolan's prices generally start at $1,200 - and the average cost may run between $1,500 to $2,000. Prices are determined by the nature of the project, and the costs of components and building materials.

Working with their custom guitar order form, Michael Dolan can provide a firm up-front price quote. All custom guitars are guaranteed for tone, playability, and overall quality.

MIRAGE

Instruments produced in Taiwan during the late 1980s.

Entry level to intermediate quality guitars based on classic American designs.

(Source: Tony Bacon and Paul Day, The Guru's Guitar Guide)

BIL MITCHELL GUITARS

Instruments currently built in Wall, New Jersey.

Bil Mitchell has been building and designing guitars since 1979. After attending the Timberline school of Lutherie, Mitchell began focusing on acoustic guitars; in 1985 he began to pursue crafting guitars full time. Mitchell offers both one-of-a-kind and production guitars in a variety of models. For further information, contact Bil Mitchell via the Index of Current Manufacturers located in the back of the book.

The retail prices on Mitchell guitars run from $1,399 (MJ-10) up to $2,499 (MS-Manitou). Mitchell offers different body styles in his production series. 10 Series models feature solid Sitka spruce top, mahogany back/sides/neck, rosewood fingerboard and bridge; while the 15 Series (retail list $1,599) models have flame maple back and sides, and a maple neck. The 20 Series (retail list $1,799) features rosewood back and sides, and a mahogany neck. Mitchell's MS- Manitou Series has a singel cutaway body, flame maple neck/back/sides, ebony fingerboard and bridge, and a Fishman Matrix pickup.All models are offered with a wide range of options in wood choices, bindings, and inlays.

MOLL CUSTOM GUITARS

Instruments currently built in Springfield, Missouri.

Luthier W.E. Moll III is currently offering custom crafted archtop guitars and solid body bass models which feature premium materials, as well as restoration services for all stringed instruments. At Moll Custom Instruments, much of the training has been in applied acoustical physics, so instruments are built to perform acoustically before electronics are applied.

Mesrobian Archtop
courtesy Carl Mesrobian

M

Monteleone Rocket Convertible
courtesy Scott Chinery

Moll Custom Instruments offer three archtop models in either a 17" or 18" body width (a 19" body width is optionally available for an additional $500). The Classic (list $2,850) has a solid carved X-braced spruce top, solid carved maple back/sides/neck, ebony fingerboard, solid brass tailpiece, and Gotoh tuners. The Express (list $5,000) is a modern design archtop with teardrop-shaped soundholes and no extraneous binding. The D'Angelico-derived New Yorker has the fancy inlays and 'stairstep' bridge and pickguard that most jazz players lust after (list $6,500).

Moll custom basses feature laminated figured maple and American walnut in their through-body neck designs, and use active Seymour Duncan Basslines 'soapbar' pickups. Prices run from $2,800 (4-string), to $3,000 (5-string), and up to $$3,250 (6-string) base list prices.

MONTALVO

Instruments currently built Mexico. Distributed by K & S Guitars of Berkeley, California.

Montalvo guitars are the result of a collaboration between George Katechis-Montalvo (a highly skilled craftsman) and Marc Silber (a noted guitar historian, restorer and designer). Montalvo had already been importing guitars from Mexico since 1987. Silber joined him in 1990 to found the K & S Guitar Company. K & S introduced higher quality woods, glues, finishes and American builders' knowledge to the Mexican luthiers for actual production in Mexico. The resulting K & S guitars are set up and inspected at their Berkeley, California shop.

ACOUSTIC

Montalvo classical and flamenco acoustic guitars are constructed of Engelmann spruce or Canadian red cedar tops, mahogany or Spanish cedar necks, and rosewood or ebony fingerboards. Retail prices range from $900 up to $1,850.

MONTANA

Instruments are produced in Korea and distributed by the Kaman Music Corporation of Bloomfield, Connecticut.

Montana produces a range of acoustic and acoustic/electric guitars priced for the novice and intermediate players.

MONTCLAIR

See chapter on House brands.

This trademark has been identified as a *House Brand* of Montgomery Wards.

(Source: Willie G. Moseley, Stellas & Stratocasters)

JOHN MONTELEONE

Instruments currently built in Islip, New York.

Luthier John Monteleone has been building guitars and mandolins for almost three decades. A contemporary of James D'Aquisto, Monteleone performed repair and restoration work for a number of years while formulating his own archtop designs. Monteleone's archtop guitars feature such unique ideas as a flush-set truss rod cover, recessed tuning machine retainers, and a convex radiused headstock. For further information, please contact luthier John Monteleone via the Index of Current Manufacturers located in the back of this book.

MOON GUITARS LTD.

Instruments currently built in Glascow, Scotland.

Established by Jimmy Moon in 1979, the **Moon Guitars** name has become synonymous with custom built instruments of very high quality as they are producing modern instruments with strong traditional roots. Originally, Moon Guitars produced acoustic guitars, mandolins, mandolas, and dulcimers. Moon moved into the electric market during the eighties, producing for an impressive client list of famous names. A shift in the market pre-empted a return to building acoustics and mandolins (while continuing with custom built electrics, basses, and eletric mandolins).

Moon Guitars' latest successful development is the Moon *electro acoustic* mandolin, which comes in various body shapes with a piezo-based pickup system. For further information, please contact Moon Guitars Ltd. through the Index of Current Manufacturers located in the back of the book.

MOONSTONE

Instruments currently built in Eureka, California (Guitar production has been in different locations in California since 1972). Distributed directly by Moonstone Guitars of Eureka, California.

In 1972, self-taught luthier Steve Helgeson began building acoustic instruments in an old shingle mill located in Moonstone Heights, California. By 1974, Helgeson moved to Arcata, California, and began producing electric **Earth Axe** guitars. By 1976, Helgeson had moved to a larger shop and increased his model line and production. Helgeson hit boom sales in the early 1980s, but tapered off production after the market shifted in 1985. Rather than shift with the trends, Helgeson prefered to maintain his own designs. In 1988, a major disaster in the form of a deliberately set fire damaged some of his machinery. Steve's highly figured wood supply survived only a minor scorching. Helgeson moved and reopened his workshop in 1990 at the current location in Eureka, California, where he now offers a wide range of acoustic and eletric guitars and basses. In addition to the standard models, Moonstone also offers custom guitars designed in accordance with the customer's request. All current prices include a hardshell case.

All Moonstone instruments are constructed from highly figured woods. Where burl wood was not used in the construction, the wood used is highly figured. Almost all necks are reinforced with veneers, or stringers. Bass necks are reinforced with through body graphite stringers. Moonstone has always utilized exotic woods such as African purpleheart, paduak, wenge, koa, mahogany, Sitka and Engelman spruce, Myrtlewood, and black burl walnut.

Some older models can also be found with necks entirely made of graphite composite with phenolic fingerboards. Helgeson commissioned Modulus Graphite to produce these necks, and used them on models like the Eclipse Standard, Deluxe Basses, Vulcan Standard and Deluxe guitars, the M-80, D-81 Eagle 6- and 12-string models, as well as the D-81 Standard and the Moondolin (mandolin). In 1981, most wood necks were reinforced with a Graphite Aluminum Honeycomb Composite (G.A.H.C.) beam with stainless steel adjustment rod.

Monteleone Archtop
courtesy John Monteleone

Moonstone J-90 Eagle (Maple)
courtesy Steve Helgeson

Grading	100%	EXCELLENT	AVERAGE

ACOUSTIC

All necks currently are reinforced with 3/8" by 1/2" *U* channel graphite beam with a 3/16" adjustment rod.

D-81 EAGLE 6 — spruce top, round soundhole, black pickguard, bound body, wood inlay rosette, quilted maple back/sides, graphite neck, 14/20 fret bound phenolic fingerboard with abalone vine inlay, eagle shape ebony bridge with black pins, walnut burl peghead veneer with abalone halfmoon/logo inlay, 3 per side gold tuners. Available in Natural finish. Mfd. 1981 to 1984.

$1,025 $675

Last Mfr.'s Sug. Retail was $2,075.

D-81 Eagle 12 — similar to D-81 Eagle 6, except has 12 strings, 6 per side tuners.

$1,125 $745

Last Mfr.'s Sug. Retail was $2,255.

J-90 — Sitka spruce top, round soundhole, bound body, rifling twist rosette, wenge back/sides/neck, 14/20 fret bound ebony fingerboard with abalone/pearl flower/vine inlay, ebony bridge with pearl flower wing inlay, black pearl dot bridge pins, ebony peghead veneer with abalone halfmoon/logo inlay, 3 per side gold tuners. Available in Natural finish. Mfr. 1992 to date.

Mfr.'s Sug. Retail $3,450

Add $650 for J-90 Eagle Macassar Ebony with top rim inlay and full vine inlay.

J-90 Eagle — similar to the J-90, except features carved eagle bridge, bird fingerboard inlays. Current mfr.

Mfr.'s Sug. Retail $3,000

This model is optionally available with quilted Pacific or Canadian flame maple, rosewood, curly koa, or paduak back and sides (Call for prices); cutaway body design, abalone top purfling, Engelman spruce top.

ACOUSTIC BASS

B-95 — Engleman spruce top, round soundhole, 35" scale, 5-string configuration, wenge (or rosewood or curly koa or paduak or burl maple) back/sides/neck, ebony fingerboard with abalone filled mother of pearl inlays, 3/2 per side tuners. Available in Natural finish. Current mfr.

Mfr.'s Sug. Retail $3,500

Moonstone J-90 Eagle
courtesy Steve Helgeson

MORGAN

Instruments currently built in North Vancouver (British Columbia), Canada.

Morgan acoustic guitars are hand crafted by luthier David Iannone, and feature premier woods and construction techniques. Iannone began building guitars in 1981. His apprenticeship carried on a guitar lineage that dates back to the very birth of the modern classic guitar. Morgan Guitars, named after his first son, is Welsh for "working by the sea" (which he does).

ACOUSTIC

Morgan guitars all share the following features: high grade spruce or cedar top, rosewood (or mahogany or maple) back and sides, one piece mahogany neck, bound ebony fingerboard, wood binding and purfling, wood marquetry or abalone rosette, transparent or tortoiseshell pickguard, and Morgan engraved machine heads.

Morgan Rosewood model guitars are offered in configurations like the **Concert**, **OM**, **Dreadnought**, and **OO** models (list $2,095 each); **Concert Cutaway** ($2,410); **Classic** (list $2,510); and **Traditional Jumbo** ($2,200).

Morgan Mahogany model guitars are offered in configurations like the **Concert**, **OM**, **Dreadnought**, and **OO** models (list $1,695 each); **Concert Cutaway** ($2,010); and **Traditional Jumbo** ($1,800).

Options include a 12-string configuration ($230), figured maple back and sides, koa back and sides, Brazilian rosewood back and sides (call for quote), and other custom options.

MORIDAIRA

See also MORRIS.

Instruments produced in Japan.

The Moridaira company is an OEM manufacturer of guitars for other companies, under different trademark names. The company has produced a wide range of entry level to very good quality guitars through the years, depending on the outside company's specifications. Further research continues for upcoming editions of the **Blue Book of Guitars**.

MORRELL

Instruments built in Tennessee. Distributed by the Joe Morrell Music Distributing Company of Bristol, Tennessee.

The Joe Morrell Music Distributing company sells products wholesale to music dealers, instrument repair personnel, and instrument builders. Their current catalog offers a wide range of Morrell stringed instruments all built in the U.S., such as resonator guitars, lap steel guitars, dulcimers, and flaptop mandolins. In addition, the Morrell company also lists music songbooks, instructional videos, guitar cases, name brand guitar strings and accessories, guitar/banjo/violin parts, drum heads and drum parts, and other music store accessories. Besides their own U.S. built Morrell instruments, the Morrell company offers low cost, quality acoustic and electric instruments from overseas manufacturers.

Additional Morrell stringed instruments include their Tennessee Mountain dulcimer (list $119.95), Tennessee Flattop Mandolin (list $299.95), and Lap Steel guitars. A two octave student model in natural finish has a retail price of $219.95 (black or red sparkle finish is $50 extra), and the three octave Professional model Joe Morrell Pro 6 or Little Roy Wiggins 8 string have a retail price of $399.95 each.

Moonstone B-95
courtesy Steve Helgeson

Morse Archtop
courtesy John David Morse

ACOUSTIC

Morrell is currently offering the **FlintHill** series of resonator guitars, available in roundneck and squareneck models. These resonator models feature a maple top, walnut back and sides, walnut neck, ebony fingerboard, and 3 per side closed tuners. Models are available in Natural (**Model MDR-1/MDS-1**) and Tobacco Sunburst (**Model MDR-2/MDS-2**) finishes. All resonator models have a retail list price of $799. Morrell also stocks replacement parts for performing repairs on other resonator models.

MORRIS

Instruments produced in Korea. Distributed by the Moridaira company of Tokyo, Japan.

The Moridaira company offers a wide range of acoustic and solid body electric guitars designed for the beginning student up to the intermediate player under the Morris trademark. Moridaira has also built guitars (OEM) under other trademarks for a number of other guitar companies.

JOHN DAVID MORSE

Instruments built in Santa Cruz, California since 1978. Luthier Morse is currently concentrating on violin making.

Luthier John David Morse combined his artistic backgrounds in music, sculpture, and woodcarving with the practical scientific knowledge of stress points and construction techniques to produce a superior modern archtop guitar. Morse, a descendant of Samuel Morse (the telegraph and Morse code), studied under fine violin makers Henry Lannini and Arthur Conner to learn the wood carving craft. Morse still combines scientific processes in his building, and has identified means to recreate his hand graduated tops.

Morse is currently making high quality violins. A number of his violins are currently in use with the San Francisco Symphony, and he is building models for concertmaster Ramond Kobler and conductor Herbert Blomstedt. Any potential commissions for archtop guitar models should be discussed directly with luthier Morse.

GARY MORTORO

Instruments built in Miami, Florida since 1991.

Luthier Gary Mortoro combines his own guitar playing background with the time he spent studying archtop guitar building with Master Luthier Robert Benedetto. Mortoro has been building fine handcrafted instruments since 1991. Some of the high profile guitarists playing a Mortoro archtop include New York session artist Joe Cinderella, and Jimmy Vivino (Max Weinberg 7).

Mortoro currently offers four different archtop models that are available in both solid carved top and back as well as a laminated top and back version. For further information, please contact Gary Mortoro via the Index of Current Manufacturers located in the back of this book.

ACOUSTIC

Carved Solid Top/Back models have a carved select aged spruce top, flamed maple back and matching sides, flamed maple neck, and ebony tuner buttons.

Laminate models feature laminated tops and backs, with necks and sides of flamed maple.

All models feature a single rounded cutaway 17" body width and 3" body depth (custom body depth and neck dimensions are available at no extra charge). Mortoro features ebony construction on the fingerboard, pickguard, bridge, tailpiece, and truss rod cover; and also features a pearl headstock inlay, gold or black Schaller tuners, and a Benedetto floating pickup. Models are available with a choice of finishes. Add $30 for ebony tuner buttons (laminate body models only)

Add $100 for bound pickguard.

Add $350 for split block fingerboard inlay.

Add $700 for 7-string configuration.

Add $800 for 8-string configuration.

FREE FLIGHT (Volo Libero) — no body (or neck) binding, narrow or traditional pickguard. Current mfr.

    Carved Solid Top/Back

    Mfr.'s Sug. Retail   **$5,000**

    Laminate Body

    Mfr.'s Sug. Retail   **$3,000**

SONGBIRD (L'uccello Cantante) ò black/white body binding, narrow or traditional pickguard with inlay, inlaid tailpiece. Current mfr.

    Carved Solid Top/Back

    Mfr.'s Sug. Retail   **$5,700**

    Laminate Body (white body binding)

    Mfr.'s Sug. Retail   **$3,700**

    Add $250 for fingerboard block inlay.

STARLING (Il Storno) — multiple "bird" soundholes in upper and lower bout, "bird" cutout on side of upper bout, no body/neck binding, 12th fret pearl inlay, narrow pickguard. Current mfr.

    Carved Solid Top/Back

    Mfr.'s Sug. Retail   **$6,000**

    Laminate Body

    Mfr.'s Sug. Retail   **$4,000**

Mortoro's non-traditional "bird" soundholes in place of f-holes sets the Starling (Il Storno) into a new area where form and function cross into a nicely voiced, pleasant to the eye archtop design.

Mortoro 8 String Custom Archtop
courtesy Gary Mortoro

Free Bird (Uccello Libero) — 2 "bird" soundholes (instead of 2 f-holes), "bird" cutout on side of upper bout, no body/neck binding, 12th fret pearl inlay, narrow pickguard. Current mfr.

> Carved Solid Top/Back
> **Mfr.'s Sug. Retail**   **$5,000**
> Laminate Body
> **Mfr.'s Sug. Retail**   **$3,000**

MOSRITE

Instruments produced in Bakersfield, California during the 1960s; earlier models built in Los Angeles, California during the mid to late 1950s. Distribution in the 1990s was handled by Unified Sound Association, Inc. Production of Mosrite guitars ceased in 1994.

There were other factory sites around the U.S. during the 1970s and 1980s: other notable locations include Carson City, Nevada; Jonas Ridge, North Carolina; and Booneville, Arkansas (previous home of Baldwin-operated Gretsch production during the 1970s).

Luthier/designer Semie Moseley (1935-1992) was born in Durant, Oklahoma. The family moved to Bakersfield, California when Moseley was 9 years old, and Semie left school in the seventh grade to travel with an evangelistic group playing guitar.

Moseley, 18, was hired by Paul Barth to work at Rickenbacker in 1953. While at Rickenbacker, Moseley worked with Roger Rossmeisl. Rossmeisl's "German carve" technique was later featured on Moseley's guitar models as well. Moseley was later fired from Rickenbacker in 1955 for building his own guitar at their facilities. In the later years, Moseley always credited Barth and Rossmeisl (and the Rickenbacker company) for his beginning knowledge in guitar building.

With the help of Reverend Ray Boatright, who cosigned for guitar building tools at Sears, Moseley began building his original designs. The Mosrite trademark is named after **Mose**ley and Boat**right** ("-rite"). After leaving Rickenbacker, Moseley built custom instruments for various people around southern California, most notably Joe Maphis (of "Town Hall Party" fame). Moseley freelanced some work with Paul Barth's "Barth" guitars, as well as some neck work for Paul Bigsby.

After traveling for several months with another gospel group, Moseley returned to Bakersfield and again set up shop. Moseley built around 20 guitars for Bob Crooks (STANDEL). When Crooks asked for a Fender-styled guitar model, Moseley flipped a Stratocaster over, traced the rough outline, and built the forerunner to the "Ventures" model!

After Nokie Edwards (Ventures) borrowed a guitar for a recording session, Stan Wagner (Ventures Manager) called Moseley to propose a business collaboration. Mosrite would produce the instruments, and use the Venture's organization as the main distributor. The heyday of the Mosrite company was the years between 1963 and 1969. When the demand set in, the company went from producing 35 guitars a month to 50 and later 300. The Mosrite facility had 105 employees at one point, and offered several different models in addition to the Ventures model (such as the semi-hollowbody Celebrity series, the Combo, and the Joe Maphis series).

In 1963, investors sold the Dobro trademark to Moseley, who built the first 100 or 150 out of parts left over from the Dobro plant in Gardenia. Later Bakersfield Dobros can be identified by the serial number imprinted on the end of the fingerboard. The Mosrite company did not build the amplifiers which bear the Mosrite trademark; another facility built the Mosrite amplifiers and fuzz pedals, and paid for the rights to use the Mosrite name.

The amplifier line proved to be the undoing of Mosrite. While some of the larger amplifers are fine, one entry level model featured a poor design and a high failure rate. While covering for returns, the Ventures organization used up their line of credit at their bank, and the bank shut down the organization. In doing so, the Mosrite distribution was shut down as well. Moseley tried a deal with Vox (Thomas Organ) but the company was shut down in 1969. Moseley returned to the Gospel music circuit, and transfered the Dobro name to OMI in a series of negotiations.

Between the mid 1970s and the late 1980s, Moseley continued to find backers and sporadically build guitars. In 1972, Guitar Player magazine reported that "Semie Moseley is now working with Reinhold Plastics, Inc. to produce Mosrite of California guitars." Later that year, Moseley set up a tentative deal with Bud Ross at Kustom (Kustom Amplifiers) in Chanute, Kansas. Moseley was going to build a projected 200 guitars a month at his 1424 P Street location, and Ross' Kustom Electronics was going to be the distributor. This deal fell through, leaving Moseley free to strike up another deal in April of 1974 with Pacific Music Supply Company of Los Angeles, California. Pacific Music Supply Company had recently lost their Guild account, and was looking for another guitar line to distribute. One primary model in 1974 was the solid body Model 350 Stereo. The **Brass Rail** model was developed around 1976/1977. While shopping around his new model with "massive sustain", Moseley met a dealer in Hollywood Music in Los Angeles. This dealer had connections in Japan, and requested that Moseley begin recreating the original-style Ventures models. Moseley set out to build 35 to 50 of these reproductions per month for a number of months. Several years after Moseley recovered from an illness in 1983, he began rebuilding his dealer network with a number of models like the **V-88**, **M-88**, and **Ventures 1960's Reissues**. These models were built at his Jonas Ridge location.

Moseley's final guitar production was located in Booneville, Arkansas. The Unified Sound Association was located in a converted Walmart building, and an estimated 90% to 95% of production was earmarked for the Japanese market.

Moseley passed away in 1992. His two biggest loves were Gospel music, and building quality guitars. Throughout his nearly forty year career, he continued to persevere in his guitar building. Unified Sound Association stayed open through 1994 under the direction of Loretta Moseley, and then later closed its doors as well.

(Information courtesy of Andy Moseley and Hal Hammer [1996]; additional information courtesy Willie G. Moseley, Stellas and Stratocasters, and Tom Wheeler, American Guitars)

(Mosrite catalogs and file information courtesy John Kinnemeyer, JK Lutherie; model dating estimations courtesy Carlos Juan, Collectables & Vintage '95, Stuttgart, Germany)

> Mosrite guitars are easily identifiable by the "M" notch in the top of the headstock. Mosrite models produced in the 1960s have a "M" inital in a edged circle, and "Mosrite" (in block letters) "of California" (in smaller script) logo.
>
> Contrary to vintage guitar show information in the current "Age of Fendermania", Mosrite instruments were <u>not</u> available in those (rare) Fender finishes like "Candy Apple Red" and "Lake Placid Blue". Catalog colors were identified as Blue or Red. Mosrite did offer option colored finishes like Metallic Blue and Metallic Red.

M

Grading	100%	EXCELLENT	AVERAGE

Vibrato Identification

Semie's designs offered numerous innovations, most notable being the Vibra-Mute vibrato. This item was designed for the Ventures models and can be used to help identify early Mosrite instruments. The early vibratos (pre-1977) have Vibra-Mute and Mosrite on them, while later vibratos have Mosrite alone on them. More distinction can be made among the earliest instruments with Vibra-Mutes by observing the casting technique used. While the early vibratos were sandcast, later units were diecast (once funding was available).

Model Designation Description

During the heyday of Mosrite production in Bakersfield, model designations in the catalog would list a **Mark I** to designate a 6-string model, **Mark XII** to indicate the 12-string version, and **Mark X** to designate the bass model within a series. These Mark designations are a forerunner to - but not the same usage as - the later **1967-1969 Mark** "No Logo" series.

Mosrite Production Dates

Mosrite models in this edition of the **Blue Book of Guitars** feature estimated dates of production for each model. Just as it is easy to take for granted a sunny day in the Summer until it rains, most dealers and collectors take a Mosrite model as "Just a Mosrite" without really double checking the true nature of **which** model it really is. Of course, the corollary of this way of thinking is to assume that the Mosrite in question is going to end up in the Far East with the rest of them! Is Johnny Ramone the only current American guitar player to use these guitars? Are there no mega-Mosrite collectors? Ventures fans unite!

The **Blue Book of Guitars** is actively seeking additional input on Mosrite models, specifications, date of production, and any serialization information. This year's section is the official "Line Drawn in the Sand" for Mosrite fans - assume that this is Ground Zero, or the foundation to build upon. Any extra information gathered on Mosrite will be updated in future editions of the **Blue Book of Guitars**. For the time being, assume that **all Production Dates are either CIRCA and/or ESTIMATED**.

For further information regarding Mosrite electric models, please refer to the **5th Edition Blue Book of Electric Guitars**.

ACOUSTIC

The **D-8 Memhis** 5-string banjo was built between 1966 to 1969, and featured a maple top/back/sides, single body binding, 26" scale, East Indian rosewood fingerboard, Type C resonator and cover plate, 12 round mini-soundholes arranged around the resonator, bridge/metal tailpiece. The D-8 Memphis was available in a Blonde finish, and had a new retail list price of $229.00 (in 1966).

BALLADERE I (Model 401) — dreadnought style, 3 1/4" body depth, bound spruce top, round soundhole, mahogany back/sides, 24 1/2" scale, 14/20 fret Indian rosewood fingerboard, rosewood bridge with white bridgepins, 3 per side chrome enclosed tuners. Available Natural and Transparent Sunburst finishes. Mfd. 1966 to 1969.

$475	$275

Last Mfr.'s Sug. Retail was $198.00.

Balladere II (Model 402) — similar to the Balladere I, except features rosewood back/sides, 2 color laminated line purfling (top and back), bound fingerboard. Available Natural and Transparent Sunburst finishes. Mfd. 1968 to 1969.

Length ", Body Width ", Body Thickness 5".

$550	$350

Last Mfr.'s Sug. Retail was $398.00.

SERENADE — dreadnought style, spruce top, round soundhole, mahogany back/sides, mahogany neck, celluloid double binding on body, 14/20 fret rosewood fingerboard with dot inlay, rosewood bridge with white bridgepins, black celluloid "batwing" pickguard, 3 per side Kluson tuners. Available in Natural Spruce Top/Shaded Burgundy high gloss finish. Mfd. 1965 to 1969.

$450	$275

Last Mfr.'s Sug. Retail was $198.00.

A similar model, the Seranade I (Model 401) featured maple back and sides, and was available in Natural Spruce Top, Transparent Cherry Red and Transparent Sunburst finishes.

Dobro/Mosrite Resonator Models

In addition to the acoustic and electric guitars and basses, Semie Moseley and Mosrite produced **Dobro by Mosrite** between 1965 to 1969. "Dobro Goes Mod!!", proclaimed the catalogs, "The 'In' Sound". Many of these models (C-3, D-12, D-50, D-100 Californian kept the Dobro logo on the headstock, but added creme colored single coil pickups and a different soundhole mesh design.

C-3 MONTEREY (3/4 Size) — Dobro/Resonator style, 3 5/16" body depth, maple top, mahogany back/sides, 23 1/4" scale, 20 fret fingerboard, Type C resonator, bridge/metal tailpiece, solid peghead, 3 per side tuners. Available in Cherryburst, Deep Black, Metallic Blue, Metallic Red, Pearl White, and Sunburst finishes. Mfd. 1966 to 1969.

$400	$175

Last Mfr.'s Sug. Retail was $239.00.

C-3 E Monterey — similar to the C-3 Monterey, except features one single coil pickup. Available in Natural finish. Mfd. 1966 to 1969.

$450	$175

Last Mfr.'s Sug. Retail was $264.00.

D-12 COLUMBIA 12-STRING — Dobro/resonator style, 3 5/16" body depth, mahogany or maple body, 24 5/8" scale, 14/20 fret fingerboard, Type D resonator, bridge/metal tailpiece, 6 per side tuners. Available in Cherryburst, Deep Black, Metallic Blue, Metallic Red, Pearl White, and Sunburst finishes. Mfd. 1966 to 1969.

$600	$350

Last Mfr.'s Sug. Retail was $349.00.

D-12 E Columbia 12-String — similar to the D-12 Columbia, except features one single coil pickup. Available in Natural finish. Mfd. 1966 to 1969.

$625	$350

Last Mfr.'s Sug. Retail was $379.00.

Grading	100%	EXCELLENT	AVERAGE

D-50 RICHMOND — Dobro/resonator style, 3 5/8" body depth, mahogany or maple body, 2 small mesh-covered soundholes in upper bouts, Type D resonator, 24 5/8" scale, 14/20 fret rosewood fingerboard with dot inlay, bridge/metal taipiece, solid peghead, 3 per side tuners. Available in Cherryburst, Deep Black, Metallic Blue, Metallic Red, Pearl White, and Sunburst finishes. Mfd. 1966 to 1969.

$575 $350
Last Mfr.'s Sug. Retail was $298.00.

D-50 E RICHMOND — similar to the D-50 Richmond, except features one single coil pickup. Available in Natural finish. Mfd. 1966 to 1969.

$575 $350
Last Mfr.'s Sug. Retail was $349.00.

D-50 S UNCLE JOSH — Dobro/resonator style, 3 5/16" body depth, mahogany or maple body, 2 small mesh-covered soundholes in upper bouts, Type D resonator, 24 5/8" scale, 14/20 fret rosewood fingerboard with dot inlay, bridge/metal taipiece, slotted peghead, 3 per side tuners. Available in Cherryburst, Deep Black, Metallic Blue, Metallic Red, Pearl White, and Sunburst finishes. Mfd. 1966 to 1969.

$575 $350
Last Mfr.'s Sug. Retail was $298.00.

D-50 SE Uncle Josh — similar to the D-50 S Uncle Josh, except features one single coil pickup. Available in Natural finish. Mfd. 1966 to 1969.

$575 $350
Last Mfr.'s Sug. Retail was $349.00.

Mobro Series

The "Mobro" name is derived from "Mosrite Dobro"; in other words, Dobro models built by the Mosrite company.

MOBRO STANDARD — Resonator style, hollow wood body, 2 mesh covered mini-soundholes in upper bouts, 14/20 fret fingerboard, chrome resonator, bridge/metal tailpiece, Mosrite-style headstock, "Mosrite/Mobro" headstock logos, 3 per side chrome tuners. Available in Natural finish. Mfd. 1972 to 1973.

$550 $300
Last Mfr.'s Sug. Retail was $349.

Mobro Standard E — similar to the Mobro Standard, except features one single coil pickup. Available in Natural finish. Mfd. 1972 to 1973.

$575 $325
Last Mfr.'s Sug. Retail was $429.

MOBRO STEEL — similar to Mobro Standard, except features a metal body. Available in chrome finish. Mfd. 1972 to 1973.

$550 $300
Last Mfr.'s Sug. Retail was $349.

Mobro Steel E — similar to the Mobro Steel, except features one single coil pickup. Available in chrome finish. Mfd. 1972 to 1973.

$575 $325
Last Mfr.'s Sug. Retail was $429.

ACOUSTIC ELECTRIC

D-100 CALIFORNIAN (MARK I) — slim line semi-hollow dual cutaway bound body, maple neck, Type D resonator, 24 5/8" scale, 22 fret rosewood fingerboard with dot inlay, adjustable bridge/metal tailpiece, chrome hardware, 3 per side tuners, 2 exposed polepiece single coil pickups, volume/tone controls, 3 way selector toggle switch (controls plus a 1/4" jack mounted to celluloid controls plate). Available in Cherry and Cherry Sunburst finishes. Mfd. 1966 to 1969.

Length 41 1/2", Body Width 16 1/8", Body Thickness 3 1/2".

$700 $425
Last Mfr.'s Sug. Retail was $359.00.

In 1968, Deep Black, Metallic Blue, Metallic Red, Pearl White, and Transparent Sunburst finishes were introduced.

D-100 Californian 12-String (MARK XII) — similar to the D-100 Californian, except features 12-string configuration, 6 per side tuners. Mfd. 1966 to 1969.

Length 41 1/2", Body Width 16 1/8", Body Thickness 3 1/2".

$700 $425
Last Mfr.'s Sug. Retail was $398.00.

ACOUSTIC ELECTRIC BASS

D-100 CALIFORNIAN BASS (MARK X) — slim line semi-hollow dual cutaway bound body, maple neck, Type D resonator, 30 1/4" scale, 20 fret rosewood fingerboard with dot inlay, adjustable bridge/metal tailpiece, chrome hardware, 2 per side tuners, 2 exposed polepiece pickups, volume/tone controls, 3 way selector toggle switch (controls plus a 1/4" jack mounted to celluloid controls plate). Available in Cherry, Cherry Sunburst, and Natural finishes. Mfd. 1966 to 1969.

$700 $425
Last Mfr.'s Sug. Retail was $349.00.

MOSSMAN

Instruments built in Winfield, Kansas from 1969 to 1977. Some models were available from Mossman's private shop after 1977.

Current production of Mossman guitars has been centered in Sulphur Springs, Texas since 1989.

Luthier Stuart Mossman originally built acoustic guitars in his garage in 1969. Mossman then founded the S. L. Mossman Company, and set up a factory to produce guitars. Mossman inspected each finished guitar before shipping; the scale of the

Grading	100%	EXCELLENT	AVERAGE

Mossman factory was to build eight to ten guitars a day (at the most). Actually, when discussing acoustic guitars, it is prebably proper to say complete eight to ten guitars a day, as the actual construction would take longer to complete (gluing the bodies, neck/body joint assembly and set up, etc). It is estimated that around 1,400 guitars had been built between 1970 and 1975, when a fire struck the factory in February. With the support of local businessmen, Mossman returned to production. However, due to a disagreement with his distributors, the Mossman company closed shop in August of 1977. Stuart Mossman then opened a private shop, and offered a number of instruments privately.

In 1989, John Kinsey of Dallas, Texas resurrected the Mossman trademark. In mid 1990 Bob Casey joined the company as a part owner. The company operated in a suburb of Dallas until August of 1991 when it was moved to an old dairy barn in Sulpher Springs, Texas. The company has operated in Sulphur Springs since then. The Mossman line of acoustic guitars is still regarded as one of the finest handmade instruments in the country.

(Company history courtesy John Kinsey, Mossman Guitars)

Mossman Guitars manufactures basicaly the same models as Stuart Mossman manufactured in Winfield, Kansas. Some of the lower line models have been discontinued, but the mainstream line (Texas Plains, Winter Wheat, South Wind, and Golden Era) continue to be produced. Several improvements have been made to the standard models, such as scalloped bracing being made a standard feature. Mossman Guitars, Inc. has also developed the "next step in the evolution of x-bracing" that they refer to it as Suspension Bracing. This modification helps projection as well as producing a clear, clean punch on the lower end. For further information on Texas-made or Kansas-made Mossman instruments, please contact Mossman Guitars, Inc. through the Index of Current Manufacturers located in the back of this edition.

ACOUSTIC

In 1975, a fire started in the finishing area at Mossman Guitars. While no employees were hurt and the machinery suffered minor losses, the company's supply of Brazilian rosewood was depleted. Models that featured Brazilian Rosewood before the fire were converted to Indian rosewood after the fire (a minor instrument dating tip).

FLINT HILLS — dreadnought style, 25 3/4" scale, sitka spruce top, round soundhole, East Indian rosewood back/sides, 20 fret ebony fingerboard, ebony pin bridge, 3 per side Grover (or Schaller) tuners. Available in Natural finish. Mfd. 1969 to 1977.

$525　　　　$350
Last Mfr.'s Sug. Retail was $350.00.

This model was optionally available with abalone top and soundhole inlay as the Flint Hills Custom (retail list $525).

GOLDEN ERA — dreadnought style, 25 3/4" scale, German spruce top with abalone inlay, round soundhole, abalone trim, Brazilian rosewood back/sides, 20 fret ebony fingerboard, black pickguard, adjustable ebony bridge with white pins, 3 per side gold Grover (or Schaller) tuners. Available in Natural finish. Mfd. 1969 to 1977.

$1,100　　　　$725
Last Mfr.'s Sug. Retail was $750.00.

This model was optionally available with abalone 'tree of life' floral inlay as the Golden Era Custom (retail list price $900).

GREAT PLAINS — dreadnought style, 25 3/4" scale, German spruce top, round soundhole, herringbone inlay, Brazilian rosewood back/sides, 20 fret ebony fingerboard, ebony pin bridge, 3 per side Grover (or Schaller) tuners. Available in Natural finish. Mfd. 1969 to 1977.

$900　　　　$650
Last Mfr.'s Sug. Retail was $425.00.

TENNESSEE FLAT TOP — dreadnought style, 25 3/4" scale, sitka spruce top, round soundhole, black plastic body binding, Honduran mahogany back/sides, 20 fret rosewood fingerboard, adjustable bridge, 3 per side Grover (or Schaller) tuners. Available in Natural finish. Mfd. 1969 to 1977

$450　　　　$275
Last Mfr.'s Sug. Retail was $350.00.

MTD

Instruments built in Kingston, New York since 1994.

Luthier Michael Tobias has been handcrafting guitars and basses since 1977. The forerunner of MTD, Tobias Guitars was started in Orlando, Florida in April 1977. Tobias' first shop name was the Guitar Shop, and he sold that business in 1980 and moved to San Francisco to be partners in a short lived manufacturing business called Sierra Guitars. The business made about 50 instruments and then Tobias left San Francisco in May of 1981 to start a repair shop in Costa Mesa, California.

Several months later, Tobias left Costa Mesa and moved to Hollywood. Tobias Guitars continued to repair instruments and build custom basses for the next several years with the help of Bob Lee, and Kevin Almieda (Kevin went on to work for Music Man). The company moved into 1623 Cahuenga Boulevard in Hollywood and after a year quit the repair business. Tobias Guitars added Bob McDonald, lost Kevin to Music Man, and then got Makoto Onishi. The business grew in leaps and bounds. In June of 1988 the company had so many back orders, it did not accept any new orders until the January NAMM show in 1990.

After several attempts to move the business to larger, better equipped facilities, Michael Tobias sold Tobias Guitars to Gibson on 1/1/90. Late in 1992, it was decided that in the best corporate interests, Tobias Guitars would move to Nashville. Michael Tobias left the company in December 1992, and was a consultant for Gibson as they set up operations in Nashville.

By contractual agreement, after Tobias' consulting agreement with Gibson was up, he had a 1 year non competition term. That ended in December 1993. During that time, Tobias moved to The Catskills in upstate New York and set up a small custom shop. Tobias started designing new instruments and building prototypes in preparation for his new venture. The first instruments were named Eclipse. There are 50 of them and most all of them are 35" bolt ons. There are three neck-throughs. Tobias finally settled on MTD as the company name and trademark. As of this writing (10/1/97) he has delivered 250 MTD instruments delivered, including bolt-on basses, guitars, neck-through basses, and acoustic bass guitars.

Michael Tobias is currently building nearly 100 instuments per year, with the help of Chris Hofschneider (who works two days per week). Chris has at least 15 years experience, having worked for Sam Koontz, Spector Guitars, Kramer, and being on the road with bands like Bon Jovi and other New Jersey-based bands. Michael Tobias is also doing design and development work for other companies, such as Alvarez, Brian Moore Guitars, Modulus Guitars, Lakland, American Showster (with Chris Hofschneider) and the new Czech-built **Grendel** basses.

(Source: Michael Tobias, MTD fine hand made guitars and basses)

MTD Bass Specifications

All MTD instruments are delivered with a wenge neck/wenge fingerboard, or maple neck/wenge fingerboard; 21 frets plus a "Zero" fret, 35" scale length. Prices include plush hard shell cases.

The standard finish for body and neck is a tung oil base with a urethane top coat. Wood choices for bodies: swamp ash, poplar, and alder. Other woods, upon request, may require up charges. Exotic tops are subject to availability.

Add $100 for a lined fretless neck.

Add $150 for a hand rubbed oil stain.

Add $200 for satin epoxy coating on lined or unlined fretless fingerboard.

Add $200 for epoxy/oil urethane finished maple fingerboard.

Add $200 for a 24 fret fingerboard.

Add $350 for lacquer finish: sunburst (amber or brown), c-throughs (transparency) of red, coal blue, or honey gold.

Add $300 for a korina, Affican satinwood (Avadore), or lacewood body.

Add $350 for a left handed model.

Add $500 for a *10 Top* of burl, flamed, or quilted maple, myrtle, or mahogany.

ACOUSTIC BASS

Acoutic Basses are only available as a direct purchase from MTD. Models can be ordered in 34" or 35" scale.

Add $150 for Highlander system.

Add $175 for Fishman Transducer.

ABG 4 — 4 string Acoustic bass, flamed myrtle back and sides, spruce top. Mfr. 1994 to date.
  Mfr.'s Sug. Retail $2,500

ABG 5 — 5 string Acoustic bass, flamed myrtle back and sides, spruce top. Mfr. 1994 to date.
  Mfr.'s Sug. Retail $2,700

M

M

ARTHUR NAPOLITANO

Instruments currently built in Allentown, New Jersey.

Luthier Arthur Napolitano began building electric guitars in 1967, and offered repair services on instruments in 1978 in Watchung, New Jersey. Napolitano moved to Allentown in 1992, and began building archtop guitars in 1993.

Napolitano currently offers several different archtop models like the **Primavera**, **Acoustic**, **Philadelphian**, **Jazz Box**, and a **Seven-String** model. Prices range from $1,795 to $5,100.

NASH

Instruments built in Markneukirchen, Germany since 1996. Distributed in the U.S. by Musima North America of Tampa, Florida.

Nash acoustics guitars debuted in the United States, Canada, and South American markets in 1996. The guitars are built by Musima, Germany's largest acoustic guitar manufacturer (the company headquarters in Markneukirchen, Germany are near the Czech border). In 1991, Musima was purchased by industry veteran Helmet Stumpf. The Musima facilities currently employs 130 workers, and continue to produce Musima stringed instruments as well as the Nash acoustic guitars.

NASHVILLE GUITAR COMPANY

Instruments currently built in Nashville, Tennessee.

Luthier/musician Marty Lanham began working on stringed instruments in San Francisco during the late 1960s, and moved to Nashville in 1972. He accepted a job at Gruhn Guitar's repair shop, and spent eight years gaining knowledge and lutherie insight. In 1985, Lanham went into business custom building his own acoustic guitars.

Nashville Guitar's custom steel string acoustic models ($2,800 to $5,000) feature German or sitka spruce tops; mahogany, koa, Indian or Brazilian rosewood, Tasmanian blackwood, and Malagasy kingwood back and sides; mahogany neck, and an ebony or rosewood fingerboard.

NATIONAL

Instruments produced in Los Angeles, California during the mid 1920s to the mid 1930s.

Instruments produced in Chicago, Illinois from mid 1930s to 1969. After National moved production to Chicago in mid the 1930s, they formally changed the company name to VALCO (but still produced 'National' brand guitars).

Instruments produced in Japan circa 1970s. Distributed by Strum'n Drum of Chicago, Illinois. When Valco went out of business in 1969, the National trademark was acquired by Strum'n Drum, who then used the trademark on a series of Japanese built guitars.

The Dopyera family emigrated from the Austro-Hungary area to Southern Califonia in 1908. In the early 1920s, John and Rudy Dopyera began producing banjos in Southern California. They were approached by guitarist George Beauchamp to help solve his "volume" (or lack thereof) problem with other instruments in the vaudeville orchestra. In the course of their conversation, the idea of placing aluminum resonators in a guitar body for amplification purposes was developed. John Dopyera and his four brothers (plus some associates like George Beauchamp) formed National in 1925.

The initial partnership between Dopyera and Beauchamp lasted for about two years, and then John Dopyera left National to form the Dobro company. National's corporate officers in 1929 consisted of Ted E. Kleinmeyer (pres.), George Beauchamp (sec./gen. mngr.), Adolph Rickenbacker (engineer), and Paul Barth (vice pres.). In late 1929, Beauchamp left National, and joined up with Adolph Rickenbacker to form Ro-Pat-In (later Electro String/Rickenbacker).

At the onset of the American Depression, National was having financial difficulties. Louis Dopyera bought out the National company; and as he owned more than 50% of the stock in Dobro, "merged" the two companies back together (as National Dobro). In 1936, the decision was made to move the company to Chicago, Illinois. Chicago was a veritable hotbed of mass produced musical instruments during the early to pre-World War II 1900s. Manufacturers like Washburn and Regal had facilities, and major wholesalers and retailers like the Tonk Bros. and Lyon & Healy were based there. Victor Smith, Al Frost, and Louis Dopyera moved their operation to Chicago, and in 1943 formally announced the change to VALCO (The initials of their three first names: Victor-Al-Louis Company). Valco worked on war materials during World War II, and returned to instrument production afterwards. Valco produced the National/Supro/Airline fiberglass body guitars in the 1950s and 1960s, as well as wood-bodied models.

In 1969 or 1970, Valco Guitars, Inc. went out of business. The assets of Valco/Kay were auctioned off, and the rights to the National trademark were bought by the Chicago, Illinois-based importers Strum'n Drum. Strum'n Drum, which had been importing Japanese guitars under the **Norma** trademark, were quick to introduce National on a line of Japanese produced guitars that were distributed in the U.S. market. Author/researcher Michael Wright points out that the National "Big Daddy170 bolt-neck black LP copy was one of the first models that launched the Japanese "Copy Era" of the 1970s.

(Early company history courtesy Bob Brozman, The History and Artistry of National Resonator Instruments; model descriptions compiled by Dave Hull)

("Copy Era" National information courtesy Michael Wright)

National Resonator
courtesy Thoroughbred Music

Grading	100%	Excellent	Average

ACOUSTIC

Single Cone Models

STYLE O — nickel plated bell brass body, 2 f-holes, maple neck, 12/19 fret ebonized maple fingerboard with pearl dot inlay, 3 per side tuners. Available with Sandblasted Hawaiian Scene on body. Mfd. 1930 to 1941.

	100%	Average
Spanish 12 fret	$3,200	$2,500
Spanish 14 fret	$2,800	$2,200
Hawaiian	$2,300	$2,000

The 12 fret guitars with rolled in f-holes command a premium (produced for about one year).

The first few hundred Style O models featured steel bodies.

The Hawaiian Style O has a wooden neck.

Some 14 fret models may have parallelogram fingerboard inlays.

Until 1933, the f-holes were flat cut. After 1933, the f-holes were rolled in (these are the rarest and most expensive Style 0 models).

In late 1934, 14 fret fingerboard replaced 12 fret fingerboard.

STYLE N — German silver body, 12/19 fret fingerboard, square headstock with pearloid overlay (no sandblasting or etching design). Mfd. 1930 to 1934.

	100%	Average
Spanish 12 fret	$4,000	$3,500

THE DON #1 — German silver body, 14/20 fret fingerboard with dot inlay. Available with plain body with engraved edged borders.

	100%	Average
Spanish 14 fret	$3,000	$2,500

The Don guitar models are fairly rare and are rarely traded in the vintage market.

The Don #2 — similar to The Don #1, except features pearloid headstock overlay, pearl square fingerboard inlay. Available with geometric engraving.

	100%	Average
Spanish 14 fret	$3,300	$2,800

The Don #3 — similar to The Don #1, except features pearloid headstock overlay, pearl square fingerboard inlay. Available with Floral Pattern engraving.

	100%	Average
Spanish 14 fret	$3,500	$3,000

DUOLIAN — thinner gauge steel body, 2 flat cut f-holes, mahogany or maple neck, 12/19 fret dyed maple fingerboard with pearl or ivoroid dot inlay. Mfd. 1931 to 1934.

	100%	Average
Spanish 12 fret	$2,000	$1,500

14/20 fret fingerboard, basswood neck. Mfd. 1935 to 1940.

	100%	Average
Spanish 14 fret	$1,500	$1,200

After 1933, rolled in f-holes replaced flat cut f-holes.

Before 1938, Duolian models featured a crystalline paint finish.

TRIOLIAN — wooden body, 2 flat cut f-holes, 12/19 fret fingerboard. Available in Light Green finish with a light overspray of several colors; neck, fingerboard, and peghead featured matching finish. Decals were then placed on the body; early models feature a bouquet design, later models feature a hula girl design. Mfd. 1928 to 1941.

1928 (Tricone)

Only 12 of the 1928 Tricone Triolian models exist, making this an extremely rare model.

This version of the model has not traded sufficiently to quote pricing.

		100%	Average
1928-1929	wood body	$2,000	$1,500

In 1929, steel body replaced wooden bodies.

In 1933, rolled in f-holes replaced flat cut f-holes.

	100%	Average
1929-1934	$2,400	$1,800

In 1935, 14/20 fret fingerboard replaced 12/19 fret fingerboards.

	100%	Average
1935-1941	$1,800	$1,500

The first Triolians were an attempt to make a budget tricone. National then almost immediately switched to a single resonator cone on the wooden body; a steel body was later adopted.

Tricone Models

The Tricone Nationals came in two configurations: round neck **(Spanish)** and square neck **(Hawaiian)**. The round neck was basically a "German Silver" body with an attached wooden neck, while the square neck was a hollow extension of the body (all the way up to the attached wooden headstock). The tenor and plectrum instruments were built on a smaller triangular shaped body and only came in the Spanish style.

Generally speaking, the plectrum instruments will command a premium over the tenors. All of these instruments feature minor (and sometimes not so minor) changes through the years; a good place to research those would be Bob Brozman's fine work: "National Resonator Instruments" (published by Centerstream Publications).

STYLE 1 — German silver body, mahogany neck, ebony fingerboard with pearl dot inlay, National logo decal on headstock. Available in Plain (no engraving) body. Mfd. 1928 to 1941.

	100%	Average
Spanish	$4,000	$3,500
Hawaiian	$2,500	$1,500

Tenor and plectrum models feature maple necks.

	100%	Average
	$1,500	$1,000

Style 1 models below serial number 380 have a rosewood fingerboard instead of ebony.

National Duolian
courtesy Bluesland Amplifiers

N

Grading	100%	Excellent	Average

STYLE 2 — German silver body, mahogany neck, ebony fingerboard with pearl dot inlay, National logo decal on headstock. Available in a Wild Rose engraving pattern. Mfd. 1927 to 1939.

Spanish		$6,000	$5,000
Hawaiian		$3,000	$2,500

Tenor and plectrum models feature maple necks.

		$2,000	$1,500

Style 2 models below serial number 400 have a rosewood fingerboard instead of ebony.

STYLE 3 — German silver body, mahogany neck, ebony fingerboard with pearl square inlay, engraved National logo inlay on ebony peghead overlay (some models feature a pearloid engraved overlay). Available in a Lily of the Valley engraving pattern. Mfd. 1928 to 1941.

Spanish		$12,000	$8,000
Hawaiian		$5,000	$4,000

Tenor and plectrum models feature maple necks.

		$2,500	$1,800

STYLE 4 — German silver body, mahogany neck, ebony fingerboard with pearl square inlay, engraved National logo inlay on pearloid peghead overlay. Available in a Chrysanthemum engraving pattern. Mfd. 1928 to 1941.

Spanish		$15,000	$12,000
Hawaiian		$3,500	$2,500

STYLE 35 — nickel plated brass body, mahogany neck (Spanish) or integral neck (Hawaiian), ebony fingerboard with pearl dot inlay, black and white celluloid peghead overlay. Available in a Sandblasted Scene of a minstrel, colored with airbrushed enamel. Mfd. 1936 to 1940.

Spanish		$7,000	$6,000
Hawaiian		$2,200	$1,600

The Style 35 is extremely rare.

The Hawaiian featured an ebonoid fingerboard.

STYLE 97 — nickel plated brass body, mahogany neck (maple neck on Hawaiian), ebony fingerboard with pearl dot inlay, black and white celluloid peghead overlay. Available in a Sandblasted Scene of a female surfer, colored with airbrushed enamel. Mfd. 1936 to 1940.

Spanish		$6,000	$5,000
Hawaiian		$5,000	$4,000

Tenor and plectrum models feature maple necks, single resonator cone.

		$1,500	$1,000

The Style 97 is extremely rare.

The Hawaiian featured an ebonoid fingerboard.

The Hawaiian models tend to price closer to their Spanish sisters, because they are convertible.

Wooden Body Models

Wooden body Nationals have a single resonator cone.

ARAGON — 18" body width, spruce top, maple back and sides, 14 fret fingerboard with parallelogram inlays. Mfd. circa 1938 to 1941.

		$5,000	$4,000

Bodies for the Aragon model were produced by Harmony or Kay.

Havana — spruce top, 14 fret fingerboard. Mfd. circa 1938 to 1941.

		$1,500	$1,000

Not much is known about this guitar. The Havana was apparently introduced around the same time as the Aragon, and featured a Kay-built body.

EL TROVADOR — laminated mahogany body, mahogany neck, 12 fret fingerboard with pearl dot inlay, slotted peghead. Mfd. 1932 to 1933.

		$1,600	$1,200

The El Trovador model featured a Kay-built body.

ESTRALIA, ROSITA, TROJAN — wooden body. Mfd. circa 1930s to 1940s.

		$900	$600

Most of the wooden body Nationals (Estralia, Rosita, and Trojan) seen today are one of these models. These guitars feature Harmony bodies, usually of birch or basswood. In the words of National expert Bob Brozman, they produce a "mushy sound".

NATIONAL RESO-PHONIC GUITARS

Instruments built in San Luis Obispo, California since 1988.

Founders Don Young and McGregor Gaines met in 1981. Young had been employed on and off at OMI (building Dobro-style guitars) since the early 1970s. After their first meeting, Young got Gaines a job at OMI, where he was exposed to guitar production techniques. In the mid to late 1980s, both Young and Gaines had disagreements with the management at OMI over production and quality, and the two soon left to form the **National Reso-Phonic Guitars** company in 1988.

The company has been producing several models of resonator acoustic guitars in the last ten years. The most recent model the company has devised is the single cutaway resonator **Bendaway Radio Tone** model. For additional information concerning specifications and availability, contact National Reso-Phonic through the Index of Current Manufacturers located in the rear of this book.

(Early company history courtesy Bob Brozman, The History and Artistry of National Resonator Instruments)

National Reso-Phonic offers additional nickel-finished brass body models, such as the mirror finish Style "1" (retail list $2,750), hand-engraved Style "2" Wild Rose (list $3,600), and hand-engraved Style "4" Chrysanthamum (list $6,000). These three models are available in either single cone or tri-cone configurations.

In addition to their guitar models, National Reso-Phonic also offers the Style "N" Ukulele and Steel Ukulele models.

ACOUSTIC

BENDAWAY RADIO TONE — single rounded cutaway body, maple top/back/sides, slotted upper bout ports, maple neck, single cone resonator, 12/19 fret rosewood fingerboard with pearl dot inlay, biscuit bridge/trapeze tailpiece, chrome hardware, blackface peghead with logo/art deco design, 3 per side tuners. Available in Light Amber finish. Current mfr.

Mfr.'s Sug. Retail $1,500

DELPHI — hollow steel body, 2 f-holes, mahogany neck, 12/19 fret ivoroid bound rosewood fingerboard with pearl dot inlay, single cone resonator, spider bridge/chrome trapeze tailpiece, slotted headstock with logo, 3 per side chrome tuners. Available in Baked Wrinkle finish in a variety of colors. Current mfr.

Mfr.'s Sug. Retail $1,680

This model is available in a squareneck configuration.

ESTRALITA — hollow body, maple top/back/sides, 2 f-holes, maple neck, single cone resonator, 12/19 fret ivoroid bound rosewood fingerboard with pearl dot inlay, biscuit bridge/trapeze tailpiece, chrome hardware, ivoroid peghead overlay with logo, slotted peghead, 3 per side tuners. Available in Dark Walnut Burst finish. Current mfr.

Mfr.'s Sug. Retail $1,500

This model is available in a squareneck configuration.

POLYCHROME TRICONE — hollow steel body, "louver" upper bout soundports, maple neck, 12/19 fret bound rosewood fingerboard with pearl dot inlay, tri-cone resonator, bridge/chrome trapeze tailpiece, blackface headstock with logo/art deco design, 3 per side chrome tuners. Available in Baked Wrinkle finish in a variety of colors. Current mfr.

Mfr.'s Sug. Retail $2,000

RESOLECTRIC — single rounded cutaway solid maple body, maple neck, single cone resonator, 14/21 fret rosewood fingerboard with pearl dot inlay, biscuit bridge/trapeze tailpiece, chrome hardware, natural peghead with logo, 3 per side tuners, creme colored pickguard, creme colored Seymour Duncan P-90 single coil pickup, Highlander pickup, magnetic volume/Highlander volume/tone "chickenhead" knob controls, 3 way selector toggle switch. Available in Amber and Dark Walnut finishes. Current mfr.

Mfr.'s Sug. Retail $1,900

Earlier models may have a "lipstick tube" single coil pickup instead of the creme colored P-90 single coil pickup.

STYLE "O" — hollow nickel-plated brass body, 2 f-holes, maple neck, 12/19 fret bound ebony fingerboard with mother-of-pearl dot inlay, single cone resonator, spider bridge/chrome trapeze tailpiece, slotted peghead, blackface headstock with logo, 3 per side chrome tuners. Available in engraved Hawaiian finish (front and back). Current mfr.

Mfr.'s Sug. Retail $2,200

This model is available without etching for a plain mirror finish (Style "N").

STYLE "3" TRICONE — hollow nickel-plated brass body, "louver" upper bout soundports, mahogany neck, 12/19 fret bound ebony fingerboard with mother-of-pearl dot inlay, tri-cone resonator, bridge/chrome trapeze tailpiece, slotted peghead, ivoroid headstock overlay with logo, 3 per side chrome tuners. Available in hand-engraved Lily of the Valley finish. Current mfr.

Mfr.'s Sug. Retail $5,400

Style "3" Single Resonator — similar to the Style "3" Tricone, except has a single cone resonator, 2 f-holes. Current mfr.

Mfr.'s Sug. Retail $5,200

NEW WORLD GUITAR COMPANY

Instruments currently built in Ben Lomond, California.

New World Guitar Company was established in 1995 by American luthier Kenny Hill, in association with Swiss luthier Gil Carnal and guitar dealer Jerry Roberts. They specialize in the manufacture of high quality nylon string guitars directed at the wholesale market. They currently produce several models based on classical and flamenco guitars of recognized masters in the history of guitar building, such as Hauser, Fleta, Ramirez, Santos, and Panormo. The instruments are all handmade of the highest quality materials. They are concert quality instruments at very reasonable prices.

New World Guitar products are currently being marketed under the names La Mancha by Jerry Roberts (800-775-0650) and Hill/Carnal. Retail list prices are from $1,750 to $3,500 and dealer inquiries are encouraged.

NICKERSON

Instruments built in Northampton, Massachusetts since the early 1980s.

Luthier Brad Nickerson, born and raised on Cape Cod, Massachusetts, has been building archtop guitars since 1982. Nickerson attended the Berklee College of Music, and worked in the graphic arts field for a number of years. While continuing his interest in music, Nickerson received valuable advice from New York luthier Carlo Greco, as well as Cape Cod violin builder Donald MacKenzie. Nickerson also gained experience doing repair work for Bay State Vintage Guitars (Boston), and The Fretted Instrument Workshop (Amherst, Massachusetts).

With his partner Lyn Hardy, Nickerson builds archtop, flattop, and electric guitars on a custom order basis. Nickerson is also available for restorations and repair work. For further information regarding specifications and availability, please contact Nickerson Guitars via the Index of Current Manufacturers located in the back of this book.

Nickerson Corona
courtesy Brad Nickerson

Nickerson Equinox
courtesy Brad Nickerson

ACOUSTIC

Nickerson's instruments are constructed out of Sitka or European spruce tops, European cello or figured maple back and sides, and ebony tailpiece, bridge, and compound radius fingerboard.

Add $300 for left-handed configuration.

Add $500 for 7-string configuration.

CORONA — Sitka or European spruce top, figured maple back/sides, multiple-ply body binding, bound fingerboard/peghead/finger rest, macassar ebony tailpiece/finger rest/peghead, gold Schaller M6 tuners with ebony buttons. Available in Blonde, Cherry Sunburst, Brown Sunburst, or custom color nitrocellulose finishes. Current mfr.

Body Width 17", Body Depth 3" (or 3 1/8").

Mfr.'s Sug. Retail $5,700

EQUINOX — European spruce top, European cello maple back/sides, all wood binding, macassar ebony tailpiece/finger rest/peghead veneer, gold Schaller M6 tuners with ebony buttons or Waverly gold tuners. Available in Blonde finish. Current mfr.

Body Width 18".

Mfr.'s Sug. Retail $8,000

F C 3 — flattop model, single rounded cutaway, Sitka or European spruce top, wood purfling, cherry binding, Indian rosewood back/sides, laminated walnut neck, 25 1/4" scale, 20 fret fingerboard with pearl diamond inlays, macassar ebony peghead veneer, Schaller M6 mini tuners. Available in Natural finish. Current mfr.

Body Width 16", Body Depth 3 3/8" (or 4 3/8").

Mfr.'s Sug. Retail $2,300

This model is also offered in a non-cutaway boydy version as the Model F 3.

F C 3 S — similar to the F C 3. Available in Natural finish. Current mfr.

Body Width 15", Body Depth 3 3/8" (or 4 3/8").

Mfr.'s Sug. Retail $5,700

This model is also offered in a non-cutaway boydy version as the Model F 3 S.

SOLSTICE (Formerly L'ANIMA) — Sitka spruce top, maple back/sides, rock maple neck, body binding, macassar ebony tailpiece/finger rest, macassar ebony or figured maple or burl peghead veneer, Schaller M tuners. Available in Shaded Brown, Reddish Brown, and Burnt Tangerine nitrocellulose finishes. Current mfr.

Body Width 15 1/2", Body Depth 3" (or 2 7/8").

Mfr.'s Sug. Retail $3,300

Nickerson F C 3 S
courtesy Brad Nickerson

SKYLARK — semi-hollow mahogany body, carved spruce top, ivoroid body binding, macassar ebony tailpiece/finger rest/peghead veneer, Schaller M6 mini tuners. Available in custom color nitrocellulose finish. Current mfr.

Body Width 14 3/8", Body Depth 1 3/4".

Mfr.'s Sug. Retail $2,300

VIRTUOSO — European spruce top, European maple back/sides, all wood binding, macassar ebony tailpiece/finger rest, macassar ebony or figured maple or burl peghead veneer, gold Schaller M6 tuners with ebony buttons. Available in Shaded Brown, Reddish Brown, and Burnt Tangerine nitrocellulose finishes. Current mfr.

Body Width 17", Body Depth 3" (or 3 1/8").

Mfr.'s Sug. Retail $4,600

NOBLE

Instruments produced in Italy circa 1950s to 1964. Production models were then built in Japan circa 1965 to 1969. Distributed by Don Noble and Company of Chicago, Illinois.

Don E. Noble, accordionist and owner of Don Noble and Company (importers), began business importing Italian accordians. By 1950, Noble was also importing and distributing guitars (manufacturer unknown). In 1962 the company began distributing EKO and Oliviero Pigini guitars, and added Wandre instruments the following year.

In the mid 1960s, the Noble trademark was owned by importer/distributor Strum'N Drum of Chicago. The Noble brand was then used on Japanese-built solid body electrics (made by Tombo) through the late 1960s.

When the Valco/Kay holdings were auctioned off in 1969, Strum'N Drum bought the rights to the National trademark. Strum'N Drum began importing Japanese-built versions of popular American designs under the National logo, and discontinued the Noble trademark during the same time period.

(Source: Michael Wright, Vintage Guitar Magazine)

ROY NOBLE

Instruments currently built in California. Distributed by the Stringed Instument Division of Missoula, Montana.

Luthier Roy Noble has been handcrafting acoustic guitars for over 37 years. Noble has been plying his guitar building skills since the 1950s, when he first began building classical instruments after studying the construction of Jose Ramirez' Concert models. Noble later moved to a dreadnought steel string acoustic design in the late 1950s and early 1960s as he practiced his craft repairing vintage instruments, and has produced anywhere from two to twenty guitars a year since then. Noble constantly experimented with the traditional uses of tonewoods, and his designs reflect the innovative use of coco bolo in bridges, and western red cedar for tops.

In 1964/1965, Noble replaced the top and neck on Clarence White's pre-war Martin D-28 when it came in for repairs (this instrument is currently owned by Tony Rice). White so enjoyed the sound that he later recorded with two Noble acoustics in many of his studio recordings.

Nickerson Skylark
courtesy Brad Nickerson

Grading	100%	EXCELLENT	AVERAGE

(Source: Michael R. Stanger and Greg Boyd, Stringed Instrument Division)

Noble currently offers two models: an orchestra-sized acoustic or a dreadnought-sized acoustic. Models are built in one of three configurations. The Standard features mahogany and Indian rosewood construction, while the Deluxe features mahogany, Indian rosewood, koa, pau ferro, or coco bolo. The Custom offers construction with koa, pau ferro, coco bolo or CITES certified Brazilian rosewood. For further information regarding models, specifications, and pricing please contact the Stringed Instrument Division through the Index of Current Manufacturers located in the back of this book.

NORMA

Instruments were built in Japan between 1965 to 1970 by the Tombo company. Distributed by Strum'N Drum, Inc., of Chicago, Illinois.

These Japanese built guitars were distributed in the U.S. market by Strum'N Drum, Inc. of Chicago, Illinois. Strum'N Drum also distributed the Japanese-built Noble guitars of the mid to late 1960s, and National solid body guitars in the early 1970s.

(Source: Michael Wright, Guitar Stories Volume One)

NORMAN

Instruments built in La Patrie, Quebec, Canada since 1972. Norman Guitars are distributed by La Si Do, Inc., of St. Laurent, Canada.

In 1968, Robert Godin set up a custom guitar shop in Montreal called Harmonilab. Harmonilab quickly became known for its excellent work and musicians were coming from as far away as Quebec City to have their guitars adjusted. Harmonilab was the first guitar shop in Quebec to use professional strobe tuners for intonating guitars.

Although Harmonilab's business was flourishing, Robert was full of ideas for the design and construction of acoustic guitars. So, in 1972 the **Norman Guitar Company** was born. From the beginning the Norman guitars showed signs of the innovations that Godin would eventually bring to the guitar market. By 1978 Norman guitars had become quite successful in Canada and France, and continued expansion into the U.S. market. Today, Norman guitars and other members of the La Si Do guitar family are available all over the world.

For full company history, see GODIN.

Early models may be optionally equipped with L.R. Baggs electronics.

ACOUSTIC

B Series

B-15 (Model 0579) — dreadnought style, wild cherry top, round soundhole, black pickguard, bound body, black ring rosette, wild cherry back/sides, mahogany neck, 14/21 fret rosewood fingerboard with pearl dot inlay, rosewood bridge with white black dot pins, 3 per side chrome tuners. Available in Natural semi-gloss finish. Current model.

Mfr.'s Sug. Retail	$350	$275	$150	$115

Add $154 for Fishman Basic EQ electronics **(Model 7981)**.

Add $35 for a left-handed configuration **(Model 0715)**.

Add $189 for a left-handed configuration and Fishman Basic EQ electronics **(Model 8025)**.

B-15 Colored (Model 0586) — similar to B-15. Available in Burgundy (0586), Brown (0593), and TobaccoBurst (0609) semi-gloss finishes. Current mfr.

Mfr.'s Sug. Retail	$369	$295	$175	$115

Add $154 for Fishman Basic EQ electronics.

B-15 (12) (Model 0685) — similar to B-15, except has 12 strings, 6 per side tuners.

Mfr.'s Sug. Retail	$436	$350	$195	$150

Add $153 for Fishman Basic EQ electronics **(Model 8081)**.

Add $44 for a left-handed configuration **(Model 0807)**.

Add $198 for a left-handed configuration and Fishman Basic EQ electronics **(Model 8032)**.

B-20 (Model 0890) — dreadnought style, solid spruce top, round soundhole, black pickguard, bound body, one ring rosette, cherry back/sides, mahogany neck, 14/21 fret rosewood fingerboard with pearl dot inlay, rosewood bridge with white black dot pins, 3 per side chrome tuners. Available in Natural semi-gloss finish. Current model.

Mfr.'s Sug. Retail	$399	$325	$175	$125

Add $154 for Fishman Basic EQ electronics **(Model 8087)**.

Add $265 for Fishman Prefix EQ electronics **(Model 8094)**.

Add $41 for a left-handed configuration **(Model 0951)**.

Add $195 for a left-handed configuration and Fishman Basic EQ electronics **(Model 8124)**.

Add $306 for a left-handed configuration and Fishman Prefix EQ electronics **(Model 8131)**.

B-20 HG (Model 1019) — similar to B-20. Available in Natural high gloss lacquer finish. Current mfr.

Mfr.'s Sug. Retail	$477	$375	$250	$150

Add $376 for Fishman Blender EQ electronics **(Model 8179)**.

Add $265 for Fishman Prefix EQ electronics **(Model 8162)**.

Add $49 for a left-handed configuration **(Model 1040)**.

Add $425 for a left-handed configuration and Fishman Blender EQ electronics **(Model 8193)**.

Add $314 for a left-handed configuration and Fishman Prefix EQ electronics **(Model 8186)**.

Grading	100%	EXCELLENT	AVERAGE

B-20 (12) (Model 0920) — similar to B-20, except has 12 string configuration, 6 per side tuners. Available in Natural semi-gloss finish. Current mfr.

Mfr.'s Sug. Retail	$515	$395	$195	$150

Add $375 for Fishman Blender EQ electronics **(Model 8117)**.

Add $265 for Fishman Prefix EQ electronics **(Model 8100)**.

Add $50 for a left-handed configuration **(Model 0982)**.

Add $425 for a left-handed configuration and Fishman Blender EQ electronics**(Model 8155)**.

Add $315 for a left-handed configuration and Fishman Prefix EQ electronics**(Model 8148)**.

B-20 CW (Model 0517) — similar to B-20, except has single rounded cutaway body. Available in Natural semi-gloss finish. Current mfr.

Mfr.'s Sug. Retail	$525	$395	$200	$150

Add $375 for Fishman Blender EQ electronics **(Model 7943)**.

Add $265 for Fishman Prefix EQ electronics **(Model 7936)**.

B-20 CW HG (Model 0548) — similar to B-20, except has single rounded cutaway body. Available in Natural high gloss finish. Current mfr.

Mfr.'s Sug. Retail	$592	$475	$295	$195

Add $376 for Fishman Blender EQ electronics **(Model 7967)**.

Add $265 for Fishman Prefix EQ electronics **(Model 7950)**.

B-20 Folk (Model 0838) — similar to B-20, except has folk style body. Available in Natural semi-gloss finish. Current model.

Mfr.'s Sug. Retail	$399	$325	$175	$125

Add $154 for Fishman Basic EQ electronics **(Model 8049)**.

Add $265 for Fishman Prefix EQ electronics **(Model 8056)**.

Add $41 for a left-handed configuration **(Model 0869)**.

Add $195 for a left-handed configuration and Fishman Basic EQ electronics**(Model 8063)**.

Add $306 for a left-handed configuration and Fishman Prefix EQ electronics**(Model 8070)**.

B-50 (Model 1132) — dreadnought style, solid spruce top, round soundhole, black pickguard, bound body, 3 ring wooden inlay rosette, maple back/sides, mahogany neck, 14/21 fret rosewood fingerboard with pearl dot inlay, rosewood bridge with white black dot pins, 3 per side chrome tuners. Available in Natural high gloss finish. Current mfr.

Mfr.'s Sug. Retail	$745	$595	$300	$225

Add $375 for Fishman Blender EQ electronics **(Model 8230)**.

Add $265 for Fishman Prefix EQ electronics **(Model 8223)**.

B-50 (12) (Model 1163) — similar to B-50, except has 12 strings, 6 per side tuners. Available in Natural high gloss finish. Current mfr.

Mfr.'s Sug. Retail	$850	$695	$350	$275

Add $375 for Fishman Blender EQ electronics **(Model 8254)**.

Add $265 for Fishman Prefix EQ electronics **(Model 8247)**.

ST Series

ST-40 (Model 1071) — dreadnought style, solid cedar top, round soundhole, black pickguard, bound body, 3 stripe rosette, mahogany back/sides/neck, 14/21 fret rosewood fingerboard with pearl dot inlay, rosewood bridge with white black dot pins, 3 per side chrome tuners. Available in Natural semi-gloss finish. Current mfr.

Mfr.'s Sug. Retail	$450	$350	$195	$150

Add $375 for Fishman Blender EQ electronics **(Model 8216)**.

Add $265 for Fishman Prefix EQ electronics **(Model 8209)**.

ST-68 (Model 1255) — dreadnought style, solid spruce top, round soundhole, black pickguard, bound body, 3 ring wooden inlay rosette, solid rosewood back, rosewood sides, mahogany neck, 14/21 fret ebony fingerboard with pearl dot inlay, ebony bridge with white black dot pins, 3 per side chrome tuners. Available in Natural high gloss finish. Current mfr.

Mfr.'s Sug. Retail	$1,000	$825	$450	$350

Add $375 for Fishman Blender EQ electronics **(Model 8292)**.

Add $265 for Fishman Prefix EQ electronics **(Model 8285)**.

Add $100 for a left-handed configuration **(Model 1286)**.

Add $475 for a left-handed configuration and Fishman Blender EQ electronics**(Model 8315)**.

Add $365 for a left-handed configuration and Fishman Prefix EQ electronics**(Model 8308)**.

ST-68 CW (Model 8346) — similar to ST-68, except has a single rounded cutaway body. Available in Natural high gloss finish. Mfr. 1998 to date.

Mfr.'s Sug. Retail	$1,227

Add $376 for Fishman Blender EQ electronics **(Model 8339)**.

Add $265 for Fishman Prefix EQ electronics **(Model 8322)**.

NORTHWOOD GUITARS

Instruments currently built in Langley (British Columbia), Canada.

Northwood Guitars currently offers 4 models of acoustic guitars that feature solid tonewood tops, flamed or quilted maple and Indian rosewood back and sides, ebony fingerboards, and other wood appointments. Retail prices run from $1,999 up to $2,499.

N

NORTHWORTHY

Instruments built in England since 1987.

Northworthy currently offers hand crafted acoustic guitars, and well as custom and left-handed models. Previous original design solid body guitars are generally of very good quality, and feature such model designations as the **Dovedale**, **Edale**, and **Milldale**. Models include classical and dreadnought styles (also a few others), as well as a range of manddolins, mandolas, octave mandolins, bozoukis, and electric instruments. Interested persons are urged to contact Alan Marshall at Northworthy through the Index of Current Manufacturers located in the back of this book.

OAHU

Instrument production unknown. Distributed by the Oahu Publishing Company of Cleveland, Ohio.

The Oahu Publishing Company offered Hawaiian and Spanish style acoustic guitars, lap steels, sheet music, and a wide range of accessories during the Hawaiian music craze of pre-War America. Catalogs stress the fact that the company is a major music distributor (thus the question of who built the guitars is still unanswered).

OAKLAND

Instruments produced in Japan from the late 1970s through the early 1980s.

These good quality solid body guitars featured both original designs and designs based on classic American favorites.

(Source: Tony Bacon and Paul Day, The Guru's Guitar Guide)

ODELL

Instrument production unknown (possibly produced by the Vega Guitar Company of Boston, Massachusetts). Distributed through the Vega Guitar catalog circa early 1930s to the early 1950s.

Odell acoustic guitars with slotted headstocks were offered through early Vega Guitar catalogs in the early 1930s. In the 1932 catalog, the four Odell models were priced above Harmony guitars, but were not as pricey as the Vega models.

Other Odell *mystery guitars* appear at guitar shows from time to time. David Pavlick is the current owner of an interesting arch top model. The 3 tuners per side headstock features a decal which reads "Odell - Vega Co., - Boston", and features a 16 1/2" archtop body, one Duo-Tron pickup, 20 fret neck, volume/tone controls mounted on the trapeze tailpiece. Inside one f-hole there is "828H1325" stamped into the back wood. Any readers with further information are invited to write to the **Blue Book of Guitars**.

(Source: David J. Pavlick, Woodbury, Connecticut)

ACOUSTIC

The four Odell acoustic models featured in the 1932 catalog have a round soundhole, 3 per side brass or nickel-plated tuners, slotted headstock, pearl position dots, and are described as *full standard size* or *concert size*. The **Model A** had a white spruce top, mahogany body/neck, black and white purfling, blackwood fingerboard/bridge, and a 1930s list price of $15! The **Model B** featured a mahogany top/body/neck, and rosewood fingerboard/bridge (new list $20). The professional **Model C** had a black and white pyralin bound white spruce top, mahogany body, and a new price of $25. The quartet was rounded out by a 4-string **Tenor Guitar** ($15) with mahogany top/body/neck, with the neck joining the body at the 15th fret.

OLD KRAFTSMAN

See chapter on House Brands.

This trademark has been identified as a "House Brand" of Speigel, and was sold through the Speigel catalogs. The Old Kraftsman brand was used on a full line of acoustic, thinline acoustic/electric, and solid body guitars from circa 1930s to the 1960s. Old Kraftsman instruments were probably built by various companies in Chicago, including Kay and some models by Gibson.

(Source: Michael Wright, Vintage Guitar Magazine)

OLSEN AUDIO

Instruments currently built in Saskatoon (Saskatchewan), Canada.

Luthier Bryan Olsen has been building guitars and performing repairs for a number of years. His new project features a metal bodied tricone-style resonator guitar with a single cutaway. The body shape has been designed from the ground up, and has an innovative stacked cone tray assembly.

JAMES A. OLSON

Instruments currently built in Circle Pines, Minnesota.

Luthier James A. Olson began building acoustic guitars full time in 1977. Olson had previous backgrounds in woodworking and guitar playing, and combined his past favorites into his current occupation. Olson's creations have been used by James Taylor (since 1989), Phil Keaggy, Sting, Leo Kottke, Justin Hayward (Moody Blues), and Kathy Matthea.

Olson handcrafts 60 guitars a year, and currently has a waiting list. All models are custom made with a wide variety of options to choose from. Olson builds in either the **SJ** (Small Jumbo) or **Dreadnought** configuration, and features East Indian rosewood Back and sides, a Sitka spruce or western red cedar top, and a five piece laminated neck (rosewood center, maple, and mahogany outer sections). Either configuration also offers an Ebony fingerboard, bridge, and peghead overlay, tortoiseshell bound body, bound headstock and side purfling, Herringbone top purfling, mother-of-pearl fingerboard position dots, a carved volute on back of the headstock, chrome Schaller tuners, and gloss nitro-cellulose lacquer finish. Either the SJ or the Dreadnought configuration carries a retail list price of $3,595. For a complete listing of available options, or for further information please contact luthier Olson.

OLYMPIA

Instruments produced in Korea. Distributed by Tacoma Guitars USA of Tacoma, Washington.

Olympia instruments are engineered and set up in the U.S., and feature a number of "dreadnought" and "jumbo" body style models with designs based on the U.S.-produced Tacoma acoustic guitars. New retail prices run from $179 (**Model OD3**) up to $529 (acoustic/electric **Model EA15B**).

OMEGA INSTRUMENTS

Instruments currently built in Saylorsburg, Pennsylvania. Distributed by Kevin Gallagher Guitars, Inc. of Saylorsburg, Pennsylvania.

Luthier Kevin Gallagher is currently offering a range of quality, hand crafted acoustic guitars from his shop in Saylorsburg. Gallagher's Omega Instruments are offered in dreadnought, jumbo (and mini-jumbo), grand concert, and "000" style guitar models. In addition to a well built, good sounding instrument, Gallagher also offers high quality inlay work that ranges from simple dots to a full fingerboard vine inlay. Current retail prices range from $1,850 to $2,200; 000 models run $2,400 to $2,700. For further information, please contact Kevin Gallagher via the Index of Current Manufacturers located in the back of this book.

OPUS

Instruments produced in Japan.

The Opus trademark is a brandname of U.S. importers Ampeg/Selmer.

(Source: Michael Wright, Guitar Stories Volume One)

ORBIT

See TEISCO DEL REY.

Instruments built in Japan during the mid to late 1960s.

The Orbit trademark is the brandname of a UK importer. Orbit guitars were produced by the same folks who built Teisco guitars in Japan; so while there is the relative coolness of the original Teisco design, the entry level quality is the drawback.

(Source: Tony Bacon and Paul Day, The Guru's Guitar Guide)

ORIGINAL MUSIC INSTRUMENT COMPANY, INC.

Instruments currently produced in Nashville, Tennessee (previous production was located in Long Beach, California through December, 1996). Distributed by Gibson Guitar Corporation of Nashville, Tennessee.

In 1960, Emil Dopyera and brothers Rudy and John founded the Original Music Instrument company to build resonator guitars. They soon resumed production on models based on their wood-body Dobros. In the late 1960s, OMI also began production of metal-bodied resonators roughly similar to their old National designs. Ron Lazar, a Dopyera nephew, took over the business in the early 1970s. In 1993, OMI was sold to the Gibson Guitar Corporation, although production is still centered in California. For further information on OMI/Dobro, see current model listings under DOBRO.

(Early company history courtesy Bob Brozman, The History and Artistry of National Resonator Instruments)

ORPHEUM

See also LANGE.

Instruments manufactured in Chicago, Illinois circa 1930s to 1940s. Distributed by William L. Lange Company of New York, New York, and by C. Bruno & Son.

Instruments later manufactured in Japan circa 1960s. Distributed by Maurice Lipsky Music Company, Inc., of New York, New York.

Orpheum guitars were first introduced by distributor William L. Lange Company of New York in the mid 1930s. The Orpheum brand instruments were also distributed by C. Bruno & Son during this early period. It is estimated that some of the Orpheum models were built in Chicago, Illinois by the Kay company.

Lange's company went out of business in the early 1940s, but New York distributor Maurice Lipsky resumed distribution of Orpheum guitars circa 1944. The Maurice Lipsky Music Company continued distributing Orpheum guitars, through to the 1960s (See also DOMINO).

(Source: Tom Wheeler, American Guitars; Orpheum Manufacturing Company catalog courtesy John Kinnemeyer, JK Lutherie)

> Until more research is done in the Orpheum area, prices will continue to fluctuate. Be very cautious in the distinction between the American models and the later overseas models produced in Japan. "What the market will bear" remains the watchword for Orpheums.

OSCAR SCHMIDT

Instruments currently built in Korea, and distributed by Oscar Schmidt International of Vernon Hills, Illinois.

The original Oscar Schmidt company was based in Jersey City, New Jersey, and was established in the late 1800s by Oscar Schmidt and his son, Walter. The Oscar Schmidt company produced a wide range of stringed instruments and some of the tradenames utilized were Stella, Sovereign, and LaScala among others. The company later changed its name to Oscar Schmidt International, and in 1935 or 1936 followed with the Fretted Instrument Manufacturers. After the company went bankrupt, the Harmony Company of Chicago, Illinois purchased rights to use Oscar Schmidt's trademarks in 1939.

In the late 1900s, the Oscar Schmidt trademark was revived by the Washburn International Company of Illinois. Oscar Schmidt currently offers both acoustic guitars and other stringed instruments for the beginning student up to the intermediate player.

(Source: Tom Wheeler, American Guitars)

MM68-CCB Mandolin
courtesy Ovation

O

OUTBOUND

Instruments currently built in Boulder, Colorado.

Outbound is currently producing a scaled down travel guitar that maintains the look of a regular acoustic. For further information, please contact Outbound via the Index of Current Manufacturers located in the rear of this book.

OVATION

Instruments built in New Hartford, Connecticut since 1967. Distribution is handled by the Kaman Music Corporation of Bloomfield, Connecticut.

The Ovation guitar company, and the nature of the Ovation guitar's synthetic back are directly attributed to founder Charles H. Kaman's experiments in helicopter aviation. Kaman, who began playing guitar back in high school, trained in the field of aeronautics and graduated from the Catholic University in Washington, D.C. His first job in 1940 was with a division of United Aircraft, home of aircraft inventor Igor Sikorsky. In 1945, Kaman formed the Kaman Aircraft Corporation to pursue his helicopter-related inventions.

As the company began to grow, the decision was made around 1957 to diversify into manufacturing products in different fields. Kaman initially made overtures to the Martin company, as well as exploring both Harmony and Ludwig drums. Finally, the decision was made to start fresh. Due to research in vibrations and resonances in the materials used to build helicopter blades, guitar development began in 1964 with employees John Ringso and Jim Rickard. In fact, it was Rickard's pre-war Martin D-45 that was used as the "test standard". In 1967, the Ovation company name was chosen, incorporated, and settled into its "new facilities" in New Hartford, Connecticut. The first model named that year was the Balladeer.

Ovation guitars were debuted at the 1967 NAMM show. Early players and endorsers included Josh White, Charlie Byrd, and Glen Campbell. Piezo pickup equipped models were introduced in 1972, as well as other models. During the early 1970s, Kaman Music (Ovation's parent company) acquired the well-known music distributors Coast, and also part of the Takamine guitar company. By 1975, Ovation decided to release an entry level instrument, and the original Applause/Medallion/Matrix designs were first built in the U.S. before production moved into Korea.

In 1986, Kaman's oldest son became president of Kaman Music. Charles William *Bill* Kaman II had begun working in the Ovation factory at age 14. After graduating college in 1974, Bill was made Director of Development at the Moosup, Connecticut plant. A noted Travis Bean guitar collector (see Kaman's Travis Bean history later in this book), Bill Kaman remained active in the research and development aspect of model design. Kaman helped design the Viper III, and the UK II solidbodies.

Bill Kaman gathered all branches of the company *under one roof* as the Kaman Music Corporation (KMC) in 1986. As the Ovation branch was now concentrating on acoustic and acoustic/electric models, the corporation bought the independent Hamer company in 1988 as the means to re-enter the solid body guitar market. Furthermore, KMC began distributing Trace-Elliot amplifiers the same year, and bought the company in 1992. The Kaman Music Corporation acts as the parent company, and has expanded to cover just about all areas of the music business. As a result, the Ovation branch now concentrates specifically on producing the best acoustic guitars, with the same attention to detail that the company was founded on.

(Source: Walter Carter, The History of the Ovation Guitar)

Ovation Headstock
courtesy Ovation

FOUR DIGIT MODEL CODES

Ovation instruments are identified by a four digit model code. The individual numbers within the code will indicate production information about that model.

The **first** digit is (generally) always 1.

The **second** digit describes the type of guitar:

1	**Acoustic Roundbacks or Semi-hollow electrics**
2	**Solid Body or Semi-hollow body electrics**
3	**Ultra acoustics**
4	**Solid body**
5	**Acoustic/Electric cutaway Adamas and II/Elite/Ultra electric**
6	**Acoustic/Electric Roundbacks**
7	**Deep**
8	**Shallow**

The **third** digit indicates the depth of the guitar's bowl:

1	**Standard (5 1/2 13/16" deep)**
2	**Artist (5 1/2 1/8" deep)**
3	**Elite/Matrix electric deep bowl**
4	**Matrix shallow bowl**
5	**Custom Balladeer/Legend/Legend 12/Custom Legend 12/Anniversary**
6	**Cutaway electric, deep bowl**
7	**Cutaway electric, shallow bowl**
8	**Adamas (6 1/2 1/16" deep)**

The **fourth** digit indicates the model (for the first 8 acoustics):

1	**Balladeer**
2	**Deluxe Balladeer**
3	**Classic**
4	**Josh White**
5	**12 String**
6	**Contemporary Folk Classic**
7	**Glen Campbell Artist Balladeer**
8	**Glen Campbell 12 String**

Model 1767-4
courtesy Ovation

The color code follows the hyphen after the four digit model number. Colors available on Ovation guitars are Sunburst (1), Red (2), Natural (4), Black (5), White (6), LTD Nutmeg/Anniversary Brown/Beige/Tan (7), Blue (8), Brown (9), *Barnwood* [a grey to black sunburst] (B), and Honeyburst (H). Other specialty colors may have a 2- or 3-letter abbreviation.

(Information collected in Mr. Carter's Ovation Appendices was researched and compiled by Paul Bechtoldt)

ACOUSTIC

Ovation is currently offering a 8-string Mandolin **(Model MM68)** and 8-string Mandocello **(Model MC868)**. Both models feature a solid Sitka spruce top, 21 fret ebony fingerboard, gold hardware, and on-board preamp. The Mandolin has a list price of $1,499, and the Mandocello is $2,199.

Select Ovation acoustic/electric models can be ordered with a factory installed **Roland GK-2** synthesizer interface as an option. This option includes a magnetic hex pickup, synth/guitar mix controls, and a controller output jack.

All Ovation acoustic and acoustic/electric instruments have a synthetic rounded back/sides construction. The model number in parenthesis following the name is the current assigned **Model Number**.

Adamas Series

All Adamas models have a composite top consisting of 2 carbon-graphite layers around a birch core, and carved fiberglass body binding. There are also 11 various sized soundholes with leaf pattern maple veneer around them, situated around the upper bouts on both sides of the fingerboard. All models have 6 piezo bridge pickups, volume/3 band EQ controls, and an active OP-24 preamp. The Adamas model was introduced in 1976.

ADAMAS 6 (Model 1687) — composite top, mahogany neck, 14/24 fret walnut extended fingerboard with maple/ebony inlay, walnut bridge with carved flower designs, carved flower design on peghead, 3 per side gold tuners. Available in Blue finish. Disc. 1998.

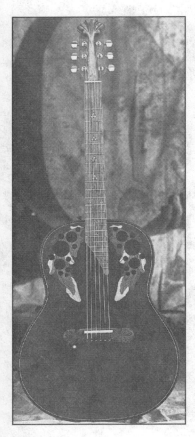

Model 1687-2
courtesy Ovation

$1,750 $1,050
Last Mfr.'s Sug. Retail was $3,099.

Earlier models may have Beige, Black, Brown, or Red finishes.

Adamas Cutaway (Model 1587) — similar to Adamas 6, except has venetian cutaway, no soundholes on cutaway side. Available in Black finish. Disc. 1998.

$1,825 $1,050
Last Mfr.'s Sug. Retail was $3,199.

Adamas 12 (Model 1688) — similar to Adamas 6, except has 12 strings. Available in Black finish. Disc. 1998.

$1,900 $1,100
Last Mfr.'s Sug. Retail was $3,299.

ADAMAS (Model 6581) — deep lyrachord bowl, carbon graphite/birch composite top, mahogany neck, 14/24 fret ebony extended fingerboard, ebony bridge, natural peghead with Adamas logo, 3 per side gold tuners, Optima pickup system. Available in High Gloss Black and Opaque Burgundy finishes. Mfr. 1998 to date.

Mfr.'s Sug. Retail $2,499

ADAMAS SMT (Model 1597) — mid depth Lyrachord bowl, carbon graphite/birch composite top, mahogany neck, 14/24 fret ebony extended fingerboard, ebony bridge, blackface peghead with Adamas logo, 3 per side gold tuners, CP-100 pickup, Optima pickup system. Available in Natural Graphite finish. Mfr. 1998 to date.

Mfr.'s Sug. Retail $1,799

ADAMAS Q (Model Q181) — deep carbon graphite bowl, carbon graphite top, through body graphite neck, 14/24 fret ebony extended fingerboard, ebony bridge, blackface peghead with Adamas logo, 3 per side gold tuners. Available in Natural Graphite finish. Mfr. 1998 to date.

Mfr.'s Sug. Retail $5,999

Adamas II Series

Similar to the original Adamas series, the Adamas II featured the standard Ovation headstock and bridge instead of the carved Walnut, and a five piece mahogany and maple laminate neck instead of the solid walnut neck. The Adamas II model was introduced in early 1982; the series was discontinued in 1998.

ADAMAS II (Model 1681) — composite top, mahogany/maple 5 piece neck, 14/24 fret walnut extended fingerboard with maple/ebony triangle inlay, walnut bridge, walnut veneer on peghead, 3 per side gold tuners. Available in Black, Blue, and Blue Green finishes. Disc. 1998.

$1,375 $795
Last Mfr.'s Sug. Retail was $2,399.

Adamas II Cutaway (Model 1581) — similar to Adamas II, except has venetian cutaway, no soundholes on cutaway side. Available in Blue finish. Disc. 1998.

$1,400 $850
Last Mfr.'s Sug. Retail was $2,499.

In 1994, soundholes on cutaway side were introduced.

Adamas II 12 (Model 1685) — similar to Adamas II, except has 12 strings, 6 per side tuners. Available in Black finish. Disc. 1998.

$1,475 $850
Last Mfr.'s Sug. Retail was $2,599.

Adamas II Cutaway Shallow (Model 1881) — similar to Adamas II, except has shallow bowl body, venetian cutaway. Available in Black and Blue Green finishes. Mfd. 1994 to 1998.

$1,400 $850
Last Mfr.'s Sug. Retail was $2,499.

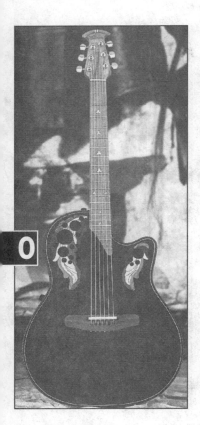

Model 1581-5
courtesy Ovation

O

Grading	100%	EXCELLENT	AVERAGE

Adamas II 12 Shallow (Model 1885) — similar to Adamas II, except has shallow bowl body, 12 strings, 6 per side tuners. Available in Black finish. Mfd. 1994 to 1998.

	$1,250	**$825**

Last Mfr.'s Sug. Retail was $2,699.

Balladeer Series

The Balladeer was the first model introduced by the Ovation company in 1967.

CUSTOM BALLADEER (Model 1712) — spruce top, round soundhole, 5 stripe bound body, leaf pattern rosette, 5 piece mahogany/maple neck, 14/20 fret ebony fingerboard, 12th fret pearl diamond/dot inlay, walnut strings through bridge with pearl dot inlay, 3 per side nickel tuners, 6 piezo bridge pickups, volume control, 3 band EQ, FET preamp. Available in Black, Natural, Sunburst and White finishes. Disc. 1996.

	$475	**$350**

Last Mfr.'s Sug. Retail was $995.

This model has cedar top optionally available. In 1994, the pearl dot bridge inlay was discontinued.

Custom Balladeer Cutaway (Model 1860) — similar to Custom Balladeer, except has single round cutaway, shallow bowl body. Disc. 1996.

	$575	**$375**

Last Mfr.'s Sug. Retail was $1,095.

Custom Balladeer 12 — similar to Custom Balladeer, except has 12 strings, 6 per side chrome tuners with pearloid buttons. Disc. 1994.

	$625	**$425**

Last Mfr.'s Sug. Retail was $1,250.

STANDARD BALLADEER (Model 1111) — folk style, spruce top, round soundhole, 5 stripe bound body, leaf pattern rosette, cedro neck, 14/20 fret rosewood fingerboard with pearl dot inlay, rosewood strings through bridge with pearl dot inlay, 3 per side chrome tuners. Available in Natural finish. Mfr. 1993 to date.

Mfr.'s Sug. Retail	$799	$650	$395	$275

Add $100 for 12-string configuration **(Model 1151)**.

Standard Balladeer Electric (Model 1711) — similar to Standard Balladeer, except has piezo bridge pickups, 4 band EQ. Available in Natural, Cadillac Green, and Cherry Cherryburst finishes. Current mfr.

Mfr.'s Sug. Retail	$949	$750	$475	$325

Add $100 for 12-string configuration **(Model 1751)**.

Standard Balladeer Cutaway (Model 1761) — similar to Standard Balladeer, except has single round cutaway, deep bowl, piezo bridge pickups, 4 band EQ. Available in Black, Natural, Cadillac Green, and Cherry Cherryburst finishes. Current mfr.

Mfr.'s Sug. Retail	$1,049	$850	$525	$350

Standard Balladeer Cutaway (Model 1861) — similar to Standard Balladeer, except has single round cutaway, super shallow bowl, piezo bridge pickups, 4 band EQ. Available in Black, Natural, Cadillac Green, and Cherry Cherryburst finishes. Current mfr.

Mfr.'s Sug. Retail	$1,049	$850	$525	$350

1711-CG Standard Balladeer
courtesy Ovation

Celebrity Series

The Celebrity series is Ovation's entry level introduction to the product line.

CELEBRITY (Model CC-01) — deep bowl, spruce top, round soundhole, bound body, leaf pattern rosette, 2-piece mahogany neck, 14/20 fret bound rosewood fingerboard with dot inlay, walnut bridge with pearloid dot inlays, rosewood veneer on peghead, 3 per side chrome tuners, piezo bridge pickup, DJ-4 preamp/electronics. Available in Natural and Mahogany finishes. Current mfr.

Mfr.'s Sug. Retail	$399	$325	$195	$125

Celebrity Shallow (Model CC-057) — similar to Celebrity, except features a super shallow cutaway bowl. Available in Natural, Black, Mahogany, and Ruby Red finishes. Current mfr.

Mfr.'s Sug. Retail	$599	$475	$295	$175

Add $50 for Honey burst finish.
Add $100 for mid depth cutaway bowl **(Model CC-047)**.

CELEBRITY (Model CC-11) — spruce top, round soundhole, 5 stripe bound body, leaf pattern rosette, mahogany neck, 14/20 fret bound rosewood fingerboard with pearl dot inlay, walnut bridge with pearloid dot inlays, rosewood veneer on peghead, 3 per side chrome tuners. Available in Barnboard, Brownburst, Natural, and Sunburst finishes. Disc. 1996.

	$195	**$125**

Last Mfr.'s Sug. Retail was $400.

Add $100 for 12-string configuration **(Model CC-15)**.
Add $200 for 12-string configuration, piezo bridge pickups, 4 band EQ **(Model CC-65)**. Available in Natural finish.

CELEBRITY TREKKER (Model CC-012) — compact mini body, spruce top, round soundhole, bound body, leaf pattern rosette, 2-piece mahogany neck, short scale 14/20 fret bound rosewood fingerboard with dot inlay, walnut bridge with pearloid dot inlays, rosewood veneer on peghead, 3 per side chrome tuners, piezo bridge pickup. Available in Black and Natural finishes. Mfr. 1998 to date.

Mfr.'s Sug. Retail	$399

Celebrity Electric (CC-67) — similar to Celebrity, except has piezo bridge pickups, 4 band EQ. Available in Barnboard, Brownburst and Natural finishes. Mfd. 1994 to 1996.

	$250	**$150**

Last Mfr.'s Sug. Retail was $500.

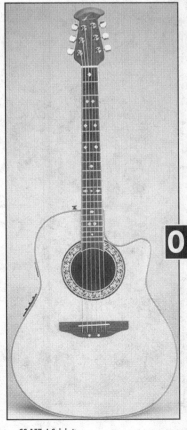

CC-157-4 Celebrity
courtesy Ovation

Grading	100%	EXCELLENT	AVERAGE

CELEBRITY CLASSIC (Model 1113) — classical style, spruce top, round soundhole, 5 stripe bound body, leaf pattern rosette, mahogany neck, 12/19 fret bound rosewood fingerboard, walnut bridge, 3 per side gold tuners with pearloid buttons. Available in Natural finish. Disc. 1996.

$195 $125
Last Mfr.'s Sug. Retail was $400.

Add $100 for piezo bridge pickups, 4 band EQ **(Model 1613)**. Available in Natural finish (Mfd. 1994 to 1996).
Add $200 for venetian cutaway, piezo bridge pickups, volume/tone control **(Model 1663)**.

CELEBRITY CUTAWAY — single round cutaway, spruce top, round soundhole, 5 stripe bound body, leaf pattern rosette, mahogany neck, 20 fret bound rosewood fingerboard with pearloid diamond/dot inlay, walnut bridge with pearloid dot inlay, walnut veneer on peghead, 3 per side chrome tuners, 6 piezo bridge pickups, volume/tone control. Available in Barnboard, Brownburst, Natural, and Sunburst finishes. Mfd. 1991 to 1996.

$250 $150
Last Mfr.'s Sug. Retail was $550.

Add $50 for shallow bowl body **(Celebrity Cutaway Shallow)**.

Celebrity Deluxe Series

The Celebrity Deluxe series features the same multiple soundholes of the Adamas and Elite designs on a laminated spruce or cedar top.

CELEBRITY DELUXE (Model CC-247) — mid depth Lyrachord bowl, solid spruce top, multi-sized soundholes with leaf pattern maple veneer, 5 stripe bound body, 2-piece nato neck, 14/23 fret bound rosewood extended fingerboard with pearl diamond/dot inlay, rosewood strings through bridge, rosewood veneered peghead with logo decal, 3 per side gold tuners, piezo bridge pickups, OP-24+ system. Available in Natural finish. Mfr. 1998 to date.

Mfr.'s Sug. Retail	$849	$650	$325	$275

Add $50 for 12-string configuration **(Model CS-245)**.

CELEBRITY DELUXE (Model CC-267) — cedar top, multi-sized soundholes with leaf pattern maple veneer, 5 stripe bound body, mahogany neck, 14/23 fret bound rosewood extended fingerboard with pearl diamond/dot inlay, rosewood strings through bridge, rosewood veneered peghead with logo decal, 3 per side gold tuners, piezo bridge pickups, 4 band EQ. Available in Antique Sunburst and Natural finishes. Disc. 1996.

$325 $200
Last Mfr.'s Retail was $650.

This model has spruce and sycamore tops optionally available.

Celebrity Deluxe Cutaway (Model CC-268) — similar to Celebrity Deluxe, except has single round cutaway. Available in Black, Natural and Wineburst finishes. Disc. 1996.

$350 $225
Last Mfr.'s Sug. Retail was $700.

Celebrity Deluxe Cutaway Shallow (Model CS-257) — similar to Celebrity Deluxe, except has spruce top, single round cutaway, shallow bowl body, OP-24 Plus preamp. Available in Black, Natural, and Ruby Redburst finishes. Current mfr.

Mfr.'s Sug. Retail	$749	$600	$300	$250

Add $50 for Autumnburst and Wineburst finishes.

Classic Series

CLASSIC — classical style, cedar top, round soundhole, 5 stripe bound body, leaf pattern rosette, 5 piece mahogany/maple neck, 12/19 fret extended ebony fingerboard, walnut bridge, walnut veneer on peghead, 3 per side gold tuners, piezo bridge pickup, volume/3 band EQ control, active preamp. Available in Natural finish. Disc. 1994.

$725 $450
Last Mfr.'s Sug. Retail was $1,420.

Classic Cutaway — similar to Classic, except has venetian cutaway. Available in Natural and White finishes. Disc. 1994.

$795 $500
Last Mfr.'s Sug. Retail was $1,520.

This model had shallow bowl optionally available.

Collector's Series

The Collector's Series offers limited edition guitars. Beginning in 1982, a different model is featured each year, and production of that model is limited to that year only. The following descriptions list the number of instruments built per model, and also the listed retail price.

(Information compiled by Paul Bechtoldt, and featured in Walter Carter's The History of the Ovation Guitar book.)

1982 COLLECTOR'S (Model 1982-8) — Bowl back acoustic guitar, round soundhole. Mfd. 1982 only.

$495 $300
Last Mfr.'s Sug. retail was $995.

A total of 1,908 guitars were produced.

1983 COLLECTOR'S (Model 1983-B) — Super shallow bowl, single cutaway, round soundhole. Available in Barnboard (exaggerated grain) finish. Mfd. 1983 only.

$495 $300
Last Mfr.'s Sug. retail was $995.

A total of 2,754 guitars were produced.

CC-257-1 Celebrity Deluxe
courtesy Ovation

CC-257-5 Celebrity Deluxe
courtesy Ovation

Grading	100%	EXCELLENT	AVERAGE

1984 COLLECTOR'S (Model 1984-5) — Elite model design, Super shallow bowl, single cutaway. Available in Ebony stain finish. Mfd. 1984 only.

$495 $300

Last Mfr.'s Sug. retail was $995.

A total of 2,637 guitars were produced.

1985 COLLECTOR'S (Model 1985-1) — Elite model design, Super shallow bowl, single cutaway. Available in Autumnburst finish. Mfd. 1985 only.

$540 $350

Last Mfr.'s Sug. retail was $1,095.

A total of 2,198 guitars were produced.

1985 Collector's (Model 2985-1) — similar to the 1985 Collector's model, except offered in limited quanities as a 12 string model. Available in Autumnburst finish. Mfd. 1985 only.

$595 $395

Last Mfr.'s Sug. retail was $1,195.

A total of 715 guitars were produced.

1986 COLLECTOR'S (Model 1986-6) — Super shallow bowl, single cutaway, round soundhole. Available in Pearl White finish. Mfd. 1986 only.

$540 $350

Last Mfr.'s Sug. retail was $1,095.

A total of 1,858 guitars were produced.

1986 Collector's (Model 2986-6) — similar to the 1986 Collector's model, except offered in limited quantities as a 12 string model. Available in Pearl White finish. Mfd. 1986 only.

$595 $395

Last Mfr.'s Sug. retail was $1,195.

A total of 392 guitars were produced.

1987 COLLECTOR'S (Model 1987-7) — Elite model design, deep bowl, single cutaway. Available in Nutmeg stain finish. Mfd. 1987 only.

$895 $560

Last Mfr.'s Sug. retail was $1,800.

A total of 820 guitars were produced.

1987 Collector's (Model 1987-5) — similar to the 1987 Collector's model, except offered in limited quantities in a Black finish. Mfd. 1987 only.

$895 $560

Last Mfr.'s Sug. retail was $1,800.

A total of 108 guitars were produced.

1988 COLLECTOR'S (Model 1988-P) — Elite model design, Super shallow bowl, single cutaway. Available in a Pewter finish. Mfd. 1988 only.

$595 $395

Last Mfr.'s Sug. retail was $1,195.

A total of 1,177 guitars were produced.

1989 COLLECTOR'S (Model 1989-8) — Super shallow bowl, single cutaway, round soundhole. Available in Blue Pearl finish. Mfd. 1989 only.

$645 $400

Last Mfr.'s Sug. retail was $1,299.

A total of 981 guitars were produced.

1990 COLLECTOR'S (Model 1990-7) — Elite model design, bird's eye maple top, deep bowl, single cutaway. Available in Nutmeg finish. Mfd. 1990 only.

$775 $495

Last Mfr.'s Sug. retail was $1,599.

A total of 500 guitars were produced.

1990 Collector's (Model 1990-1) — similar to the 1990 Collector's model (1990-7), except offered in extremely limited quantities in a Sunburst finish. Mfd. 1990 only.

$775 $495

Last Mfr.'s Sug. retail was $1,599.

A total of 50 guitars were produced.

1990 Collector's (Model 199S-7) — similar to the 1990 Collector's model (1990-7), except offered in limited quantities with a Super shallow bowl and Nutmeg finish. Mfd. 1990 only.

$775 $495

Last Mfr.'s Sug. retail was $1,599.

A total of 750 guitars were produced.

1990 Collector's (Model 199S-1) — similar to the 1990 Collector's model (1990-7), except offered in limited quantities with a Super shallow bowl and a Sunburst finish. Mfd. 1990 only.

$775 $495

Last Mfr.'s Sug. retail was $1,599.

A total of 100 guitars were produced.

1995 Collectors Edition
courtesy Ovation

1996 Collectors Edition
courtesy Ovation

Grading	100%	EXCELLENT	AVERAGE

1991 COLLECTOR'S (Model 1991-4) — Deep bowl, single cutaway, round soundhole. Available in Natural finish. Mfd. 1991 only.

$560 $350
Last Mfr.'s Sug. retail was $1,159.

A total of 1,464 guitars were produced.

1991 Collector's (Model 1991-5) — Deep bowl, single cutaway, round soundhole. Available in Black Metallic finish. Mfd. 1991 only.

$560 $350
Last Mfr.'s Sug. retail was $1,159.

A total of 292 guitars were produced.

1992 COLLECTOR'S (Model 1992-H) — Elite model design, quilted ash top, Super shallow bowl, single cutaway. Available in Honeyburst finish. Mfd. 1992 only.

$830 $520
Last Mfr.'s Sug. retail was $1,699.

A total of 1,995 guitars were produced.

1993 COLLECTOR'S (Model 1993-4) — single round cutaway folk style, solid spruce top, multi upper bout soundholes, 5 stripe bound body, multiple woods veneer around soundholes, medium bowl body, mahogany/padauk/ebony 5 piece neck, 22 fret ebony fingerboard with 12th fret banner inlay, strings through walnut bridge, maple logo inlay on peghead, 3 per side gold Schaller tuners with ebony buttons, piezo bridge pickup, volume/3 band EQ control, active preamp. Available in Natural finish. Mfd. 1993 only.

$735 $465
Last Mfr.'s Sug. retail was $1,499.

A total of 1,537 guitars were produced.

1994 COLLECTOR'S (Model 1994-7) — single round cutaway folk style, solid spruce top, round soundhole, bound body, multi wood purfling, ash/ebony/pearl rosette, medium bowl body, mahogany/ebony/purpleheart 5 piece neck, 21 fret ebony extended fingerboard with 12th fret banner inlay, strings through ebony bridge, ebony veneered peghead with screened logo, 3 per side gold tuners with ebony buttons, piezo bridge pickup, Optima EQ system. Available in Nutmeg finish. Mfd. 1994 only.

$830 $520
Last Mfr.'s Sug. retail was $1,695.

A total of 1,763 guitars were produced.

1995 COLLECTOR'S (Model 1995-7) — New mid-depth bowl, single cutaway, round soundhole. Available in Nutmeg finish. Mfd. 1995 only.

$935 $595
Last Mfr.'s Sug. retail was $1,899.

A total of 1,502 guitars were produced.

1996 COLLECTOR'S (Model 1996-TPB) — Solid Sitka Spruce top, Mid-depth bowl, single cutaway, five piece Mahogany/maple/ebony neck, bound ebony fingerboard with mother of pearl inlay, Stereo HexFX piezo pickup system, 3+3 headstock, round soundhole. Available in a Transparent Burgundy finish. Mfd. 1996 only.

$1,175 $700
Last Mfr.'s Sug. retail was $2,199.

A total of 1,280 guitars were produced.

1997 COLLECTOR'S (Model 1997-7N) — narrow waist ("salon style") walnut-bound body, solid Sitka spruce top, round soundhole, maple leaf rosette, unbound 14/20 fret fingerboard, CP 100 piezo pickup system, 3 per side slotted headstock with walnut veneer, onboard Stealth TS preamp. Available in Nutmeg Stain finish. Mfd. 1997 only.

Mfr.'s Sug. Retail $1,799

This model is also available with a wider neck as Model 1997-7W.

Every 1997 Collector's Series instrument is accompanied by a copy of Walter Carter's "The History of the Ovation Guitar" book.

Although this is the 1997 Collector's model, it is assumed that there may be a few still available among Ovation dealers (thus the retail list price is still listed).

1998 COLLECTOR'S (Model 1998) — single round cutaway style, figured maple top, laser cut leaf epaulets shaped with a cluster of 15 smaller soundholes, bound body, mid depth bowl body, 5-piece maple/mahogany neck, 22 fret rosewood fingerboard with 12th fret inlay, strings through rosewood bridge, 3 per side tuners, piezo bridge pickup, OP-24E system. Available in New England Burst finish. Mfd. 1998 only.

Mfr.'s Sug. Retail $1,649

Elite Series

The Elite Series design is similar to the Adamas models, but substitutes a solid Spruce or solid Cedar top in place of the composite materials. Standard models feature 22 soundholes of varying sizes, while the cutaway models only have 15 soundholes.

ELITE (Model 1718) — spruce top, 5 stripe bound body, 5 piece mahogany/maple neck, 14/22 fret extended rosewood fingerboard with maple triangle inlay, walnut bridge, 3 per side gold tuners, 6 piezo bridge pickups, volume control, 3 band EQ, active OP-24 preamp. Available in Black, Natural, Natural Cedar, Sunburst and White finishes. Disc. 1997.

$625 $450
Last Mfr.'s Sug. Retail was $1,395.

Model 1718-1
courtesy Ovation

O

Grading		100%	EXCELLENT	AVERAGE

Elite Cutaway (Model 1768) — similar to Elite, except has single cutaway body. Available in Sunburst finish. Current mfr.

Mfr.'s Sug. Retail	$1,699	$1,350	$825	$550

This model is optionally available with a cedar top, or shallow bowl body.

Elite Shallow (Model 1868) — similar to Elite, except has super shallow bowl body, single rounded cutaway. Available in Black, Black Cherryburst, Natural, and Sunburst finishes. Current mfr.

Mfr.'s Sug. Retail	$1,699	$1,350	$825	$550

Elite Shallow 12 (Model 1858) — similar to Elite Shallow, except has 12-string configuration. Available in Black Cherryburst and Sunburst finishes. Mfr. 1994 to date.

Mfr.'s Sug. Retail	$1,899	$1,500	$925	$625

CUSTOM ELITE (Model CE-768) — spruce top, single cutaway body, deep bowl, 5 piece mahogany/maple neck, 22 fret extended rosewood fingerboard with maple triangle inlay, walnut bridge, 3 per side gold tuners, piezo bridge pickup, volume control, 3 band EQ, active OP-X preamp. Available in Black Cherryburst finish. Current mfr.

Mfr.'s Sug. Retail	$1,999	$1,600	$965	$650

Custom Elite Shallow (Model CE-868) — similar to Elite, except has super shallow bowl body. Available in Black Cherryburst finish. Current mfr.

Mfr.'s Sug. Retail	$1,999	$1,600	$975	$650

ELITE STANDARD (Model 6718) — spruce top, 5 stripe bound body, mahogany neck, 14/22 fret extended rosewood fingerboard, strings through rosewood bridge with pearl dot inlay, rosewood veneered peghead with ebony/maple logo inlay, 3 per side chrome tuners, piezo bridge pickups, volume control, 3 band EQ, active preamp. Available in Cherry Sunburst, Root Beer and Vintage finishes. Mfd. 1993 to 1996.

			$575	$350

Last Mfr.'s Sug. Retail was $1,095.

Elite Standard Cutaway (Model 6778) — similar to Elite Standard, except has single round cutaway. Available in Black, Black Cherryburst, Cadillac Greenburst, and Natural finishes. Current mfr.

Mfr.'s Sug. Retail	$1,349	$1,100	$650	$450

Elite Standard Cutaway Shallow (Model 6868) — similar to Elite Standard Cutaway, except has a super shallow bowl body. Available in Black, Black Cherry, and Natural finishes.

Mfr.'s Sug. Retail	$1,349	$1,100	$650	$450

In 1998, Aspen Blue finish was introduced.

Model 6868-V
courtesy Ovation

Folklore Series

The Folklore series was introduced in 1979. Current listings feature the new updated versions that have been re-introduced to the Ovation line.

FOLKLORE (Model 6774) — single cutaway solid Sitka spruce top, round soundhole, mid-depth bowl back, inlaid rosette, 5 piece mahogany/maple neck, 21 fret ebony fingerboard, walnut bridge, 3 per side slotted headstock, OP-X preamp. Available in a Natural finish. Current mfr.

Mfr.'s Sug. Retail	$1,649	$1,325	$825	$550

Country Artist (Model 6773) — similar to Folklore model, except is designed for nylon string use. Available in Natural finish.

Mfr.'s Sug. Retail	$1,649	$1,325	$825	$550

PARLOR (Model 5741) — narrow waist ("salon style") body, mid-depth bowl back, solid Sitka spruce top, round soundhole, inlaid rosette, 5 piece mahogany/maple neck, unbound 14/21 fret ebony fingerboard, 3 per side headstock with walnut veneer, walnut bridge, CP 100 piezo pickup system, OP-X preamp. Available in Brown Sunburst finish. Mfr. 1998 to date.

Mfr.'s Sug. Retail	$1,499

Legend Series

The Legend series shares similar design patterns with the Custom Legend models, except a less ornate rosette and a standard Ovation bridge instead of the custom carved Walnut version. Outside of the all acoustic Model 1117, Legend series models feature the active OP-24 preamp electronics.

LEGEND (Model 1117) — spruce top, round soundhole, 5 stripe bound body, leaf pattern rosette, 5 piece mahogany/maple neck, 14/20 fret bound rosewood fingerboard with pearl diamond/dot inlay, walnut bridge, walnut veneer on peghead, 3 per side gold tuners. Available in Black, Natural, Sunburst and White finishes. Current mfr.

Mfr.'s Sug. Retail	$999	$795	$495	$325

In 1994, Cherry Cherryburst and Tobacco Sunburst finishes were introduced, bound ebony fingerboard replaced original item, Sunburst and White finishes were discontinued.

Legend Electric (Model 1717) — similar to Legend, except has piezo bridge pickup, volume control, 3 band EQ, OP-X active preamp. Available in Cherry Cherryburst and Natural finishes. Mfd. 1994 to 1998.

			$750	$450

Last Mfr.'s Sug. Retail was $1,349.

Legend 12 Electric — similar to Legend, except has 12-string configuration, 6 per side tuners, volume/3 band EQ controls, active preamp. Disc. 1994.

			$725	$475

Last Mfr.'s Sug. retail was $1,450.

Legend Cutaway Electric (Model 1777) — similar to Legend, except has single round cutaway, mid-depth bowl, volume control, 3 band EQ, OP-X active preamp. Available in Black, Cherry Cherryburst, Natural, and Red Stain finishes. Current mfr.

Mfr.'s Sug. Retail	$1,449	$1,150	$595	$450

Add $100 for Recording Model Telex mic/OptiMax preamp system **(Model 1777-4RM)**.

6773 Country Artist
courtesy Ovation

Grading	100%	EXCELLENT	AVERAGE

Legend Cutaway Electric Shallow (Model 1867) — similar to Legend Cutaway Electric, except has a super shallow bowl back. Available in Black, Cherry Cherryburst, Natural, and Red Stain finishes. Current mfr.

Mfr.'s Sug. Retail	$1,449	$1,150	$595	$450

Legend 12 Cutaway Electric (Model 1866) — similar to Legend Cutaway electric, except has 12-string configuration. Available in Black, Cherry Cherryburst and Natural finishes. Current mfr.

Mfr.'s Sug. Retail	$1,549	$1,235	$750	$525

NYLON STRING LEGEND (Model 1763) (Formerly NYLON STRING CLASSIC BALLADEER) — single round cutaway, AAA cedar top, round soundhole, 5 stripe bound body, leaf pattern rosette, 5 piece mahogany/maple neck, 19 fret ebony fingerboard, rosewood bridge, 3 per side gold tuners with pearloid buttons, piezo bridge pickup, volume/3 band EQ control, OP-X preamp. Available in Natural finish. Mfr. 1994 to date.

Mfr.'s Sug. Retail	$1,649	$1,325	$800	$550

    Add $100 for Recording Model with OptiMax preamp **(Model 1763-4RM)**.

    This model is available with a super shallow bowl body (Model 1863).

Custom Legend Series

    Custom Legend models have an AAA grade Solid Sitka Spruce top, spruce struts, custom bracing, and the active OP-24 piezo electronics package.

CUSTOM LEGEND (Model 1719) — spruce top, round soundhole, abalone bound body, abalone leaf pattern rosette, 5 piece mahogany/maple neck, 14/20 fret bound ebony fingerboard with abalone diamond/dot inlay, strings through walnut bridge with carved flower design/pearl dot inlay, walnut veneered peghead with abalone logo inlay, 3 per side gold tuners with pearloid buttons, piezo bridge pickups, volume control, 3 band EQ, active preamp. Available in Black, Natural, Sunburst and White finishes. Disc. 1996.

		$900	$525

    Last Mfr.'s Sug. Retail was $1,595.

Custom Legend Cutaway (Model 1769) — similar to Custom Legend, except has single rounded cutaway. Available in Cherry Cherryburst, Cadillac Greenburst, and Sunburst finishes. Current mfr.

Mfr.'s Sug. Retail	$1,999	$1,600	$975	$650

Custom Legend Shallow Cutaway (Model 1869) — similar to Custom Legend, except has single round cutaway body, super shallow bowl. Available in Black, Cherry Cherryburst, Natural, and Sunburst finishes. Current mfr.

Mfr.'s Sug. Retail	$1,999	$1,600	$975	$650

    Add $500 for factory installed Roland GR Series guitar synth pickup.

Custom Legend 12 (Model 1759) — similar to Custom Legend, except has 12-string configuration, 6 per side tuners. Available in Black and Natural finishes. Current mfr.

Mfr.'s Sug. Retail	$2,099	$1,675	$1,050	$695

CUSTOM LEGEND WITH ROLAND GR SYNTH (Model R 869) — similar to the Custom Legend, except has a factory installed Roland GR Series synthesizer interface. Available in Natural finish. Mfr. 1998 to date.

Mfr.'s Sug. Retail	$2,499

Longneck Series

LONGNECK (Model DS 768) — similar to the Elite model six string, except has a scale length of 28.35" and is tuned one full step lower than a standard guitar. Five piece maple and mahogany neck, gold-plated hardware, and OP-X preamp. Available in Natural and Cherry Cherryburst finishes. Mfr. 1995 to date.

Mfr.'s Sug. Retail	$1,899	$1,525	$925	$625

Matrix (Formerly Medallion) Series

    In 1976/1977, Ovation debuted the Medallion series guitars - which was later renamed the Matrix series. These models were produced in the U.S., and featured a wood top, synthetic bowl back, and plastic headstock overlay. The original list price was $249.

Pinnacle Series

PINNACLE — folk style, spruce top, 5 stripe bound body, leaf pattern rosette, mahogany neck, 14/20 fret rosewood fingerboard with white dot inlay, rosewood bridge with white dot inlay, rosewood veneer on peghead, 3 per side chrome tuners, 6 piezo bridge pickups, volume control, 3 band EQ, FET preamp. Available in Barnboard, Black, Ebony Stain, Natural, Opaque Blue, Sunburst, Transparent Blue Stain and White finishes. Mfd. 1991 to 1992.

		$450	$300

    Last Mfr.'s Sug. Retail was $900.

Pinnacle Shallow Cutaway — similar to Pinnacle, except has single round cutaway, shallow bowl body. Mfd. 1991 to 1994.

		$500	$330

    Last Mfr.'s Sug. Retail was $1,000.

Ultra Deluxe Series

    The Ultra Deluxe models feature a solid spruce top, two piece mahogany neck, on-board OP-24Plus electronics, and a 20 fret bound rosewood fingerboard.

ULTRA DELUXE (Model 1312-D) — spruce top, round soundhole, 5 stripe bound body, leaf pattern rosette, 14/20 fret bound rosewood fingerboard with abalone diamond/dot inlay, walnut bridge with white dot inlay, rosewood veneer on peghead, 3 per side gold tuners. Available in Barnboard, Black, Brownburst, Natural and Sunburst finishes. Disc. 1996.

		$225	$150

    Last Mfr.'s Sug. Retail was $500.

This model has flame maple top with Brownburst finish optionally available.

Model 1869-CCB
courtesy Ovation

Model 1759-4
courtesy Ovation

Grading	100%	EXCELLENT	AVERAGE

Ultra Deluxe Electric (Model 1517-D) — similar to Ultra Deluxe, except has piezo bridge pickup, 4 band EQ, FET preamp. Available in Black and Natural finishes. Mfd. 1994 to 1996.

$300 $195
Last Mfr.'s Sug. Retail was $600.

This model has flame maple top with Brownburst finish optionally available.

Ultra Deluxe 12 (Model 1515-D) — similar to Ultra Deluxe, except has 12 strings, 6 per side tuners. Disc. 1994.

$275 $175
Last Mfr.'s Sug. Retail was $530.

Ultra Deluxe 12 Electric — similar to Ultra Deluxe, except has 12 strings, 6 per side tuners, piezo bridge pickups, 4 band EQ, preamp. Available in Black and Natural finishes. Mfd. 1994 to 1996.

$350 $225
Last Mfr.'s Sug. Retail was $700.

Ultra Deluxe Cutaway (Model 1528-D) — similar to Ultra Deluxe, except has single round cutaway, piezo bridge pickup, volume/tone control, FET preamp. Available in Barnboard, Brownburst and Sunburst finishes. Disc. 1994.

$375 $225
Last Mfr.'s Sug. Retail was $730.

Ultra Deluxe Shallow Cutaway — similar to Ultra Deluxe, except has single round cutaway, shallow bowl body, piezo bridge pickups, volume/tone control, FET preamp. Available in Barnboard, Black, Brownburst, Natural, Redburst, Sunburst and White finishes. Disc. 1994.

$395 $250
Last Mfr.'s Sug. Retail was $700.

This model has flame maple top with Brownburst finish optionally available.

ACOUSTIC ELECTRIC

Viper Series

The Viper name is back! Originally a solid body guitar from the mid 1970s to the early 1980s, the Viper name has now been affixed to a new, 1990s acoustic/electric slim body design. The Viper model has a solid Spruce top, and a mahogany body with acoustic chambers. An on-board active electronics package (volume and three band EQ) allows control over feedback.

EA-68 Viper
courtesy Ovation

VIPER (Model EA 68) — single cutaway mahogany body with routed sound chamber, bound spruce top, 14 multi-size soundholes with various leaf wood overlay, 5 piece mahogany/maple neck, 24 fret bound ebony fingerboard, strings through rosewood bridge, rosewood veneered peghead with screened logo, 3 per side gold tuners, 6 piezo bridge pickups, volume/3 band EQ controls. Available in Black and Natural finishes. Mfr. 1994 to date.
Mfr.'s Sug. Retail $1,999 $1,600 $975 $650

VIPER 12 (Model EA 58) — similar to the Viper, except in 12 string variation. Available in Black and Natural finishes.
Mfr.'s Sug. Retail $2,099 $1,675 $1,075 $825

VIPER NYLON (Model EA 63) — similar to the Viper, except in 6 string nylon variation. Available in Black finish only.
Mfr.'s Sug. Retail $1,999 $1,600 $975 $650

ACOUSTIC ELECTRIC BASS

CELEBRITY (Model CC-074) — single round cutaway, spruce top, round soundhole, 5 stripe bound body, leaf pattern rosette, mahogany neck, 20 fret bound rosewood fingerboard with pearloid diamond/dot inlay, walnut bridge with pearloid dot inlay, walnut veneer on peghead, 2 per side chrome tuners, piezo bridge pickups, volume/tone control, FET preamp. Available in Ebony Stain, Natural, and Sunburst finishes. Mfd. 1993 to 1996, 1998 to date.
Mfr.'s Sug. Retail $799 $600 $395 $275

CELEBRITY DELUXE (Model CC-274) — similar to the Celebrity, except features cedar top, multi-sized soundholes with leaf pattern maple veneers, 22 fret rosewood extended fingerboard with pearl dot inlay, rosewood strings through bridge, rosewood veneered peghead with logo decal, 2 per side gold tuner, piezo bridge pickup, 4 band EQ. Available in Antique Sunburst, Black, Natural and Sunburst finishes. Mfd. 1994 to 1996.

$400 $275
Last Mfr.'s Sug. Retail was $800.

This model has spruce and sycamore tops optionally available.

Celebrity Deluxe 5 (Model CC-275) — similar to Celebrity Deluxe, except has 5 strings, 19 fret fingerboard, 3/2 per side chrome tuners. Available in Black finish. Mfd. 1994 to date.

$425 $275
Last Mfr.'s Sug. Retail was $850.

ELITE (Model B-768) — single round cutaway, spruce top, 5 stripe bound body, multiple soundholes around the top bouts with leaf pattern veneer, 5 piece mahogany/maple neck, 22 fret extended rosewood fingerboard with maple triangle inlay, walnut bridge, 2 per side gold tuners, piezo bridge pickup, volume/3 band EQ control, active preamp. Available in Black, Natural and Sunburst finishes. Mfd. 1992 to date.
Mfr.'s Sug. Retail $2,199 $1,750 $1,075 $725

In 1994, bound fingerboard was introduced, Sunburst finish was discontinued.

ELITE 5 (Model B-5768) — similar to the Elite bass, except has five strings and a 2/3 headstock design. Available in Black and Natural finishes. Mfd. 1995 to 1998.

$1,375 $795
Last Mfr.'s Sug. Retail was $2,399.

Model B768-4
courtesy Ovation

O

EAB 68-CCB
courtesy Ovation

VIPER BASS (Model EAB 68) — single cutaway mahogany body with routed sound chamber, bound spruce top, 14 multi-size soundholes with various leaf wood overlay, 5 piece mahogany/maple neck, 24 fret bound ebony fingerboard, strings through rosewood bridge, rosewood veneered peghead with screened logo, 2 per side gold tuners, 4 piezo bridge pickups, volume/3 band EQ controls. Available in Black, Cherry Cherryburst, and Natural finishes. Mfr. 1994 to date.

Mfr.'s Sug. Retail	$2,399	$1,900	$1,175	$795

PACE

Instruments produced in Korea, circa early 1970s.

Pace brand guitars were moderate quality acoustics imported to the U.S. market.

The Pace model **F-200** featured a spruce top, round soundhole, mahogany back and sides, black pickguard, 14/20 fret rosewood fingerboard, rosewood bridge with black bridge pins, 3 per side closed chrome tuners.

Pace acoustic guitars in average condition range in price between $100 to $150.

(Source: Walter Murray, Frankenstein Fretworks)

PALMER

Instruments produced in Asia from the late 1980s to date. Distributed by Chesbro Music Company of Idaho Falls, Idaho, and Tropical Music Corporation of Miami, Florida.

Both the Chesbro Music Company and Tropical Music Corporation are distributing Palmer brand acoustic and classical models. These models are geared towards the entry level or student guitarist.

During the late 1980s, Palmer offered instruments were entry level solid body guitars that feature designs based on traditional American designs. Solid body models were marketed under the trademark (or model designation) of **Biscayne**, **Growler**, **Baby**, and **Six**. The Biscayne trademark is still distributed by Tropical Music Corporation.

Palmer acoustic guitars are usually priced in the used market between $79 up to $299.

PANORMO

Instruments built in London, England during the early nineteenth century.

During the early 1800s, luthier Louis Panormo ran a productive workshop in London. Panormo, the son of an Italian violin-maker, was one of the few outside of Spain that braced the tops of his acoustics with "fan-strutting", and advertised himself as the "only maker of guitars in the Spanish style".

(Source: Tony Bacon, The Ultimate Guitar Book)

PARAMOUNT

See LANGE.

Instruments produced in America during the 1930s and 1940s.

In 1934, the William L. Lange Company (New York) debuted the Paramount guitar series - and some of the models were built by the C.F. Martin guitar company. However, Lange's company went out of business in the early 1940s. In the late 1940s, the Paramount guitar line was re-introduced and distributed by Gretsch & Brenner.

(Source: Tom Wheeler, American Guitars)

PAUL REED SMITH

Instruments currently produced in Stevensville, Maryland.

PRS Guitars was originally located in Annapolis, Maryland from 1985 to 1996. In 1996, PRS Guitars completed the move to newer and larger facilities in Stevensville, Maryland.

Combining the best aspects of vintage design traditions in modern instruments, luthier Paul Reed Smith devised a guitar that became very influential during the late 1980s. With meticulous attention to detail, design, and production combined with the concept of "graded" figured wood tops, PRS guitars became touchstone to today's high end guitar market. The concept of a *ten top* (denoting the flame in the maple figuring) began at PRS Guitars, and to hear the slang phrase "It's a ten top with birds" is magic at guitar shows nowadays.

Paul Reed Smith built his first guitar for a college music class. Drawing on his high school shop classes and his musical experiences, his first attempt gained him an *A*. Working out of his home attic in the mid 1970s, Smith began designing and revising his guitar models while involved with the guitar repair trade. He continued to work out of a small repair shop for the better part of eight years, and was selling a number of hand crafted guitars between 1976 through 1984 without major advertising. By 1982 he had finished designing and building a guitar that combined his original ideas with traditional ones.

In 1985, Smith received some major financial backing and was able to start limited handmade production of the PRS Custom model. Part of the new finances guaranteed his high quality products would finally see advertising in the major magazines (a corollary to this is the interesting phenomonon that most magazines generally don't review products unless the manufacturer advertises in the magazine - ever see a **Blue Book of Guitars** review in *Guitar Player* magazine?). One major difference between PRS and other guitar companies of the 1980s is Smith made - or had exclusively made - all of his own components for his own guitars. Of course, choosing highly figured woods for construction wasn't a bad choice either! Through the years, Paul Reed Smith has continued to experiment with pickup design, body and neck variations, and even amplification and speaker systems.

(Source: Ed Roman, Ed Roman Guitars)

Grading	100%	EXCELLENT	AVERAGE

ACOUSTIC

This series of instruments was designed and built by Dana Bourgeois and Paul Reed Smith.

CUSTOM CUTAWAY — single flat cutaway dreadnought style, spruce top, round soundhole, abalone bound body and rosette, figured maple back/sides, mahogany neck, 20 fret Brazilian rosewood fingerboard with abalone bird inlay, Brazilian rosewood bridge with ebony pearl dot pins, 3 per side chrome locking PRS tuners, volume/tone control, preamp system. Available in Amber Sunburst, Antique Natural, Black Cherry, Grayblack and Walnut Sunburst finishes. Disc. 1992.

$1,295   **$N/A**
Last Mfr.'s Sug. Retail was $2,590.

MAHOGANY CUTAWAY — single flat cutaway dreadnought style, spruce top, round soundhole, wood bound body and rosette, mahogany back/sides/neck, 20 fret rosewood fingerboard, rosewood bridge with ebony pearl dot pins, rosewood veneer on peghead, 3 per side chrome locking PRS tuners, volume/tone control, preamp system. Available in Antique Natural, Black and Natural finishes. Disc. 1992.

$1,475   **$N/A**
Last Mfr.'s Sug. Retail was $1,970.

ROSEWOOD SIGNATURE — dreadnought style, spruce top, round soundhole, abalone bound body and rosette, rosewood back/sides, mahogany neck, 20 fret Brazilian rosewood fingerboard with abalone bird inlay, Brazilian rosewood bridge with ebony pearl dot pins, 3 per side gold locking PRS tuners, gold endpin, volume/tone control, preamp system. Available in Antique Natural and Rosewood Sunburst finishes. Disc. 1992.

$3,195   **$N/A**
Last Mfr.'s Sug. Retail was $3,190.

PEAVEY

Instruments built in Meridian and Leaksville, Mississippi. Distributed by Peavey Electronics Corporation of Meridian, Mississippi since 1965.

Peavey also has a factory and distribution center in Corby, England to help serve and service the overseas market.

Peavey Electronics is one of the very few major American musical instrument manufacturers still run by the original founding member and owner. Hartley Peavey grew up in Meridian, Mississippi and spent some time working in his father's music store repairing record players. He gained some recognition locally for the guitar amplifiers he built by hand while he was still in school, and decided months prior to college graduation to go into business for himself. In 1965 Peavey Electronics was started out of the basement of Peavey's parents home. Due to the saturated guitar amp market of the late 1960s, Peavey switched to building P.A. systems and components. By 1968 the product demand was great enough to warrant building a small cement block factory on rented land and hire another staff member.

The demand for Peavey products continued to grow, and by the early 1970s the company's roster had expanded to 150 employees. Emphasis was still placed on P.A. construction, although both guitar and bass amps were doing well. The Peavey company continued to diversify and produce all the components needed to build the finished product. After twelve years of manufacturing, the first series of Peavey guitars was begun in 1977, and introduced at the 1978 NAMM show. An advertising circular used by Peavey in the late '70s compared the price of an American built T-60 (plus case) for $350 versus the Fender Stratocaster's list price of $790 or a Gibson Les Paul for $998.50 (list). In light of those list prices, it's also easy to see where the Japanese guitarmakers had plenty of manuevering room during their "copy" era.

The "T-Series" guitars were introduced in 1978, and the line expanded from three models up to a total of seven in five years. In 1983, the product line changed, and introduced both the mildly wacky Mystic and Razer original designs (the Mantis was added in 1984) and the more conservative Patriot, Horizon, and Milestone guitars. The Fury and Foundation basses were also added at this time. After five years of stop tailpieces, the first Peavey "Octave Plus" vibratos were offered (later superceded by the Power bend model). Pickup designs also shifted from the humbuckers to single or double "blade" pickups.

Models that debuted in 1985 included the vaguely stratish Predator, and the first doubleneck (!), the Hydra. In response to the guitar industry shifting to "superstrat" models, the Impact was introduced in 1986. Guitars also had the option of a Kahler locking tremolo, and two offsprings of the '84 Mantis were released: The Vortex I or Vortex II. The Nitro series of guitars were available in 1987, as well as the Falcon, Unity, and Dyna-Bass. Finally, to answer companies like Kramer or Charvel, the Tracer series and the Vandenberg model(s) debuted in 1988.

As the U.S. guitar market grew more conservative, models like the Generation S-1 and Destiny guitars showed up in guitar shops. Peavey basses continued to evolve into sleeker and more solid instruments like the Palaedium, TL series or B Ninety. 1994 saw the release of the MIDIBASE (later the Cyberbass) that combined magnetic pickups with a MIDI-controller section.

One of Peavey's biggest breakthroughs in recent years was the development of the Peavey EVH amplifier, developed in conjunction with Edward Van Halen. Due to the success and acceptance of the EVH 5150 amplifier, Van Halen withdrew his connection with his signature Ernie Ball model (which is still in production as the Axis model), and designed a "new" **Wolfgang** model with Peavey. This new model had a one year "waiting period" from when it was announced at the NAMM industry trade show to actual production. Many Peavey dealers who did receive early models generally sold them at new retail (no discount) for a number of months due to slow supply and re-supply.

Rather than stay stuck in a design "holding pattern", Peavey continues to change and revise guitar and bass designs, and they continue the almost twenty year tradition of American built electric guitars and basses.

(Model History, nomenclature, and description courtesy Grant Brown, Peavey Repair section)

Information on virtually any Peavey product, or a product's schematic is available through Peavey Repair. Grant Brown, the head of the Repair section, has been with Peavey Electronics for over eighteen years.

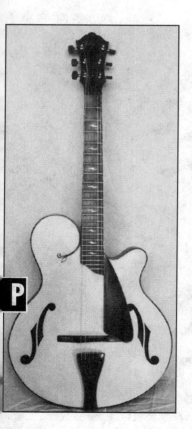

Pederson Archtop
courtesy Craig Pederson

Grading	100%	EXCELLENT	AVERAGE

ACOUSTIC

In 1994, a series of Peavey acoustic guitars was announced. Although some models were shipped in quantity, the acoustic line was not as wide spread as other guitar models that were introduced. Peavey acoustics have a solid Alpine Spruce top, and either laminated or solid rosewood sides, and a mahogany neck. So, if some Peavey acoustics are encountered, the following list will at least indicate the range envisioned.

Compact Cutaway Series

Two models comprise the Compact body design that featured a single cutaway: the **CC-37PE** ($1,099) had a five piece mahogany/rosewood neck, piezo pickup system, and Schaller hardware; the **CC-3712PE** ($1,149) was the accompanying 12 string model.

Dreadnought Series

The **SD-9P** ($499) was the only model to feature a solid cedar top in the dreadnought design. The **SD-11P** ($599) featured the same body design with a Spruce top and laminated mahogany sides and back, and the **DD-21P** ($699) substitutes laminated rosewood in place of the mahogany. The **SD-11PCE** ($759) featured a single cutaway and piezo under-the-bridge pickup system with 3 band EQ and volume control.

Jumbo Series

The **CJ-33PE** ($1,049) featured the Jumbo body design and a piezo system; the **CJ-3312PE** ($1,099) was the accompanying 12 string model.

ACOUSTIC ELECTRIC

ECOUSTIC — single rounded cutaway dreadnought style, cedar top, oval soundhole, bound body, 5 stripe rosette, mahogany back/sides, maple neck, 22 fret rosewood fingerboard with white dot inlay, rosewood bridge with white pins, 3 per side gold tuners, piezo bridge pickup, 3 band EQ. Available in Black, Natural, and Transparent Red finishes. Current mfr.

Mfr.'s Sug. Retail	$959	$780	$475	$320

ECOUSTIC ATS — single rounded cutaway dreadnought style, Maple top, oval soundhole, bound body, 5 stripe rosette, Poplar back/sides, Rock Maple neck, 22 fret rosewood fingerboard with white dot inlay, rosewood ATS Tremolo bridge with white pins, 3 per side chrome tuners, piezo bridge pickup, 3 band EQ. Available in Black, Natural and Transparent Red finishes. Mfr. 1995 to date.

Mfr.'s Sug. Retail	$999	$799	$490	$330

Pederson Resonator
courtesy Craig Pederson

CRAIG PEDERSON

Instruments currently built in Brooklyn, New York. Distributed by Rudy's Music Shop of New York City, New York.

Luthier Craig Pederson has been building guitars for the past 27 years. While currently based in New York (on the fourth floor of the Gretsch building!), Pederson has had workshops in Minneapolis, Minnesota as well as Albuquerque, New Mexico. Throughout his luthier career, Pederson has produced various acoustic guitar models, semi-hollow body guitars, and archtop guitars.

In addition to his various guitar models, Pederson also produces mandolins, mandolas, and mandocellos. Flat top models start at $1,300 (add $200 for wood binding), and caved top models start at $3,200 (add $300 for wood binding). Call for a price quote for custom options on any Pederson stringed instrument.

ACOUSTIC

All prices include a Harptone hardshell case. Pederson's **Archtop** guitars have a list price begining at $4,000.
Add $500 for wood binding on all guitar models (the following model prices quoted are for plastic body binding).

PEDERSON NYLON STRING — rounded body with venetian cutaway, round soundhole, set-in neck, rosette, 20 fret fingerboard, 3 per side tuners. Current mfr.

Cypress Flamenco
Mfr.'s Sug. Retail $2,370

Rosewood Classic
Mfr.'s Sug. Retail $2,370

PEDERSON RESONATOR — rounded body with florentine cutaway, set-in neck, 20 fret fingerboard, 3 per side tuners, resonator, round covered soundhole on bass bout. Current mfr.

Curly Maple
Mfr.'s Sug. Retail $2,670

Mahogany
Mfr.'s Sug. Retail $2,470

Rosewood
Mfr.'s Sug. Retail $2,670

PEDERSON STEEL STRING — rounded body with florentine cutaway, round soundhole, set-in neck, rosette, 20 fret fingerboard, 3 per side tuners. Current mfr.

Curly Maple
Mfr.'s Sug. Retail $2,370

Mahogany
Mfr.'s Sug. Retail $2,170

Rosewood
Mfr.'s Sug. Retail $2,370

P

Pederson Acoustic
courtesy Craig Pederson

PENNCO

Instruments produced in Japan circa 1970s. DIstributed by the Philadelphia Music Company of Philadelphia, Pennsylvania.

This trademark has been identified as a *House Brand* of the Philadelphia Music Company of Philadelphia, Pennsylvania, the U.S. distributor of these Japanese-built instruments. The Pennco (sometimes misspelled *Penco)* brandname was applied to a full range of acoustic and solid body electric guitars, many entry level to intermediate quality versions of popular American designs.

(Source: Michael Wright, Vintage Guitar Magazine)

PENNCREST

See chapter on House Brands.

This trademark has been identified as a *House Brand* of J. C. Penneys.

(Source: Willie G. Moseley, Stellas & Stratocasters)

PETE BACK

Instruments built in Richmond (North Yorkshire), England since 1975.

Luthier Pete Back is noted for his custom handcrafted guitars of the highest quality. His electric, folk and classical guitar construction uses the finest woods available. Pete has his own original designs, but will make whatever the guitarist requires. He also offers repairs (refretting, set-ups, and resprays). Back's prices start at 650 (English pounds), depending on parts and materials.

PHILLIP J. PETILLO

Petillo Masterpiece Guitars and Accessories was founded in 1968. Custom handcrafted instruments are currently built in Ocean, New Jersey.

Luthier Phillip J. Petillo has been creating, repairing, and restoring guitars and other instruments for over thirty years. Petillo was one of the original co-designers of the Kramer aluminum neck guitar in 1976, and built the four prototypes for Kramer (BKL). Later, he severed his connections with the company.

Currently, Petillo makes acoustic carved top and back guitars, flat top acoustics, semi-hollow body guitars, and solid body guitars and basses. Petillo also makes and repairs the bowed instruments. Petillo, a holder of a BS, MS, and PHD in Engineering, also offers his talents in Engineering for product development, research and development, engineering, and prototype building for the musical instruments industry.

Phillip and Lucille Petillo are the founders and officers of a research corporation that developes devices and technology for the medical industry. While seeming unrelated to the music industry, the Phil-Lu Incorporated company illustrates Petillo's problem-solving skills applied in different fields of study.

Petillo estimates that he hand builds between 8 to 20 guitars a year on his current schedule. Prices begin at $1,200 and are priced by nature of design and materials utilized. Custom Marquetry Inlay and other ornamental work is priced by the square inch. Petillo offers 170 different choices of lumbers, veneers, and mother-of-pearl.

Restoration, alteration and repair work are price quoted upon inspection of the instrument. In addition, he markets his patented products such as Petillo Frets, the Acoustic Tonal Sensor, Petillo Strings and Polish, and a fret micro-polishing system.

Some of his clients include: Tal Farlow, Chuck Wayne, Jim Croce, Elvis Presley, James Taylor, Tom Petty, Howie Epstein, Dave Mason, The Blues Brothers, Bruce Springsteen, Gary Talent, Steve Van Zant, Southside Johnny, and many others.

PETROS

Instruments built in Holland, Wisconsin since 1972.

Luthier Bruce Petros has been handcrafting guitars for over twenty five years. Petros currently offers handmade acoustic dreadnought and fingerstyle guitars (retail list price starts at $3,600), as well as a classical model and a 4-string solid body electric bass. In addition to his guitars, Petros is a complete repair shop and authorized repair center for Martin and other companies.

Petros is also the manufacturer/distributor of High Cliff Acoustic guitar strings and guitar care products that include: Professional Fingerboard Oil, Miracle Finish Restorer, and Professional Guitar Polish.

ACOUSTIC

All Petros guitars feature an arched Sitka spruce top, spruce/ebony bridgeplate, ebony fingerboard/bridge, wood binding and purfling, Grover tuners, and a enviro-friendly gloss finish.

The **D** body size is a dreadnought style guitar with a tighter "waist", and the **FS** body style has a smaller body/wider neck more suited for fingerstyle playing.

The **Apple Creek** model features black walnut back/sides, abalone dot fingerboard markers, and abalone rosette. The **Holland Rose** is a walnut guitar with a Rose fingerboard inlay from the 12th to 17th fret; while the **Jordan** features a Dove fingerboard inlay. The **High Cliff** model features a unique fingerboard/rosette inlay, curly maple binding, bound fingerboard, and a set of gold Grover tuners. Petros' limited edition **The Rite of Spring** has a unique *Tulip Headstock*, curly maple binding, abalone purfling, gold Grover tuners, and *Tulip* rosette/fingerboard inlays.

PHIL

Instruments currently produced in Korea.

The Myung Sung Music Ind. Co., Ltd. is currently offering a wide range of well constructed solid body electric guitar models. The **Phil Pro Series** offers models with offset double cutaway bodies, bolt-on necks, and double locking tremolo systems. Even more intriguing is the **Tulip Series**, which features a body with a rounded lower bout and rounded horns that resembles a profile of a tulip (it's a pretty clever design). For further information, please contact the Myung Sung Music Co., Ltd. through the Index of Current Manufacturers located in the back of this book.

PIMENTEL & SONS

Instruments built in Albuquerque, New Mexico since 1951.

Luthier Lorenzo Pimentel builds high quality classical and steel string acoustic guitars and requintos. Pimentel, originally born in Durango, Mexico, learned guitar making from his older brothers. Though trained as a baker, Pimentel moved to El Paso, Texas, in 1948 to work for master violin maker Nagoles. A few years later, Pimentel moved to Albuquerque, and began building guitars as his livelihood.

Today, Lorenzo Pimentel and his sons handcraft perhaps 40 to 80 guitars a month, and the entire family is involved in some aspect of the business.

ACOUSTIC

List prices may run from $700 up to $3,000, depending on the model and woods used in the contruction. Only Lorenzo Pimentel builds the top-of-the-line **Grand Concert** model, while his sons professionally build other models in the line.

RONALD PINKHAM

Instruments currently built in Glen Cove, Maine. Distributed by Woodsound Studio of Glen Cove, Maine.

Luthier Ronald Pinkham currently offers high quality concert-grade classic and steel-string acoustic guitars, as well as cellos. Pinkham also has one of the largest orchestral and fretted instrument repair facilities in New England. For further information, please contact luthier Pinkham through the Index of Current Manufacturers located in the rear of this book.

PMC GUITARS

Instruments currently built in Asia. Distributed by Sound Trek Distributors of Tampa, Florida.

PMC guitars are good quality acoustics designed for the entry or student level up to the medium grade player. For further information regarding model specifications and pricing, contact Sound Trek Distributors via the Index of Current Manufacturers located in the rear of this edition.

PRAIRIE STATE

See LARSON BROTHERS (1900-1944).

The Larson brothers added the Prairie State brand to Maurer & Co. in the mid-1920s. This brand was used exclusively for guitars. The main difference between the Maurer and the Prairie State was the use of a support rod and an adjustable rod running the length of the guitar body from end block to neck block. These 12-fret-to-the-body guitars have the double rod system, which may vary according to the period it was made because August Larson was awarded three patents for these ideas. The rod closest to the sound-hole is larger than the lower one, and, in some cases, is capable of making adjustments to the fingerboard height. The function of the lower rod is to change the angle of the neck. Most all Prairie States have laminated top braces and laminated necks. They were built in the lower bout widths of 13½", 14" and 15" for the standard models, but special order guitars were built up to 21" wide. In the Mid-1930s, the Prairie State guitars were built in the larger 14-fret-to-the-body sizes, all now sporting the large rod only. The common body widths of these are 15", 16", 17", 19" and a rare 21". The single cutaway style was used on one known 19" f-hole and one 21" guitar. The Prairie State guitar is rarer than the other Larson brands. They are of very high quality and are sought by players and collectors. The rigid body produces great sustain and a somewhat different sound from the Maurers and Euphonon guitars. Almost all the Prairie State guitars were made with beautiful rosewood back and sides except the f-hole models which were commonly made with maple bodies, all having select spruce tops.

For more information regarding other Larson-made brands, see MAURER, EUPHONON, WM. C. STAHL, W.J. DYER, and THE LARSON BROTHERS.

For more detailed information regarding all the Larson brands and a Maurer/Prairie State catalog reprint, see **The Larsons' Creations, Guitars and Mandolins,** *by Robert Carl Hartman, Centerstream Publishing, P.O. Box 17878, Anaheim Hills CA 92807, phone/fax (714) 779-9390.*

PRAIRIE VOICE

See chapter on House Brands.

This trademark has been identified as a Harmony-built "Roy Rodgers" style guitar built specifically for the yearly Canadian "Calgary Stampede". The **Blue Book of Guitars** is interested in more information on either the guitars produced for this celebration, or the celebration itself!

(Source: Willie G. Moseley, Stellas & Stratocasters)

PREMIER

Instruments currently produced in Korea. Distributed in the U.S. market by Entertainment Music Marketing Corporation (EMMC) of Deer Park, New York.

Instruments produced in New York during the 1950s and 1960s. Later models manufactured in Japan.

Premier was the brandname of the Peter Sorkin Music Company. Premier-branded solid body guitars were built at the Multivox company of New York, and distribution of those and the later Japanese built Premiers was handled by the Sorkin company of New York City, New York. Other guitars built and distributed (possibly as rebrands) were **ROYCE, STRAD-O-LIN, BELLTONE,** and **MARVEL.**

Current Premier models are built in Korea, and feature a slimmed (or sleek) strat-style guitar body and P-style bass body. New list prices range from $229 to $289.

Premier solid body guitars featured a double offset cutaway body, and the upper bout had a "carved scroll"design, bolt-on necks, a bound rosewood fingerboard, 3+3 headstocks (initially; later models featured 6-on-a-side), and single coil pickups. Later models of the mid to late 1960s featured wood bodies covered in sparkly plastic.

Towards the end of the U.S. production in the mid 1960s, the **Custom** line of guitars featured numerous body/neck/electronics/hardware parts from overseas manufacturers like Italy and Japan. The guitars were then assembled in the U.S., and available through the early 1970s.

P

Some models, like the acoustic line, were completely made in Japan during the early 1970s. Some Japanese-built versions of popular American designs were introduced in 1974, but were discontinued two years later. By the mid-1970s, both the Sorkin company and Premier guitars had ceased. Multivox continued importing and distributing Hofner instruments as well as Multivox amplifiers through the early 1980s. Hofners are currently distributed by the Entertainment Music Marketing Corporation of New York, as well as the current line of Premier solid body electric guitars and basses.

(Source: Michael Wright, Guitar Stories Volume One)

RICHARD PRENKERT

Instruments currently built in the U.S. Distributed by Kirkpatrick Guitar Studios of Baltimore, Maryland.

Luthier Richard Prenkert is currently building high quality classical guitars.

PRUDENCIO SAEZ

Instruments currently produced in Spain. Distributed by Saga Musical Instruments of San Francisco, California.

Prudencio Saez classical acoustics are designed for the beginning to advancing player. Handmade in Spain, these guitars feature a solid cedar top, mahogany neck, rosewood fingerboard and bridge, an inlaid marquetry rosette, clear high gloss finish, and a slotted 3 per side headstock. Some models feature mahogany back and sides (like the **PS-4A** and **PS-6A**) while others have walnut backs and sides (**PS-8A**).

PURE-TONE

See chapter on House Brands.

This trademark has been identified as a *House Brand* of Selmer (UK).

(Source: Willie G. Moseley, Stellas & Stratocasters)

P

RAIMUNDO

Distributed by Luthier Music Corporation of New York, New York, and Music Imports of San Diego, California.

Raimundo offers a wide range of classical and flamenco-style acoustic guitars.

RAINSONG

Instruments currently produced in Maui, Hawaii since 1994. Distributed by Kuau Technology, Ltd. since 1985. Previous instrument production was a joint effort between facilities in Hawaii and Albuquerque, New Mexico.

Kuau Technology, Ltd. was initally founded in 1982 by Dr. John A. Decker, Jr. to research and provide development on optical instrumentation and marine navigation. Decker, a physicist with degrees in engineering, also enjoys playing classical guitar. Since 1985, the company began concentrating on developing and manufacturing graphite/epoxy Classical and Steel String guitars. Members of the design team included Dr. Decker, as well as noted luthier Lorenzo Pimentel and composite materials expert George M. Clayton. In the company's beginning, the R & D facility was in Maui, Hawaii; and manufacturing was split between Escondido, California and Pimentel and Sons guitar makers of Albuquerque, New Mexico. The California facility handled the work on the composite materials, and the Pimentels in New Mexico supplied the lutherie and finishing work (Pimentel and Sons themselves build quality wooden guitars). The Rainsong All-Graphite acoustic guitar has been commerically available since 1992.

In December 1994, full production facilities were opened in Maui, Hawaii. George Clayton of Bi-Mar Productions assisted in development of the factory and manufacturing processes, then returned to the mainland to continue his own work. The product line has expanded to include classical models, steel string acoustic guitars and basses, acoustic/electric models, and hollowbody electric guitars and basses. Kuau Technologies, Ltd. currently employs ten people on their production staff.

Rainsong guitars and basses feature Rainsong's proprietary graphite/epoxy technology, Schaller tuning machines, optional Fishman transducers, and EMG pickups (on applicable models). Models also available with a single cutaway, in left-handed configurations, a choice of three peghead inlay designs, side-dot fret markers, and wood marquetry rosette. Instruments shipped in a hardshell case.

ACOUSTIC

The Rainsong **Limited Edition** model features a Fishman Prefix Pro pickup system, and an abalone inlay on the 12th fret. They are available in Burgundy, Platinum, and Sapphire finishes. Only 300 models are scheduled in the Edition (list $1,995).

The **Russ Freeman Signature Jazz** model is available in 6-string (list $2,995) and 12-string ($3,295) configurations.

RainSong guitars are optionally available with peghead inlay like the **Maui Girl**, **Modest Maui Girl**, and a **Whale** design. Prices range from $100 to $150 for peghead inlay.

CLASSICAL — black unidirectional-graphite soundboard, 650 mm scale, 2" width at nut, slotted (open) peghead with 3 per side tuners, gold Schaller tuners with ebony buttons, and abalone rosette. Current mfr.

Mfr.'s Sug. Retail $2,195

The Classical model is patterned after Pimentel & Sons "Grand Concert" model.

FLAMENCO — similar to the Classical, except has solid headstock. Current mfr.

Mfr.'s Sug. Retail $2,195

6-STRING DREADNOUGHT — dreadnought size body, choice of 14/20 or 12/20 fret fingerboard, solid peghead, Schaller black tuning pegs, shark inlay design on the twelfth fret, side dot markers, Fishman Prefix transducer, volume/tone controls. Current mfr.

Mfr.'s Sug. Retail $2,195

12-String Dreadnought — similar to the 6-String Dreadnought, except features 12-string configuration, 6 per side tuners. Mfr. 1997 to date.

Mfr.'s Sug. Retail $2,195

12-FRET WINDSONG — jumbo size single cutaway body, 12/20 fret fingerboard, solid peghead, Fishman Prefix transducer, Schaller black tuning pegs, shark inlay design on the twelfth fret, and side dot markers. Current mfr.

Mfr.'s Sug. Retail $2,195

14-Fret WindSong — similar to the 12-Fret WindSong, except the neck joins the body at the 14th freth, 14/20 fingerboard. Current mfr.

Mfr.'s Sug. Retail $2,195

12-String WindSong — similar to the 14-Fret WindSong, except has 12-string configuration, 6 per side tuners. Mfr. 1997 to date.

Mfr.'s Sug. Retail $2,195

ACOUSTIC BASS

ACOUSTIC BASS — body patterned similar to the Windsong guitar, 844 mm scale, 4-string configuration, 2 per side tuners, solid headstock, abalone rosette, side dot fret markers, Fishman Prefix transducer/preamp, volume/tone controls. Current mfr.

Mfr.'s Sug. Retail $2,195

Add $250 for fretless fingerboard (**Model Fretless Bass**).

R

ACOUSTIC ELECTRIC

6-STRING JAZZ GUITAR — single cutaway body, f-holes, 648 mm scale, 3+3 headstock, black Schaller tuning machines, graphite tailpiece, EMG 91 Custom pickup, Mike Christian tune-o-matic acoustic piezo bridge, volume/tone controls, 3-way pickup selector. Current mfr.
   Mfr.'s Sug. Retail $2,495

12-String Jazz Guitar (Formerly StormSong) — similar to the 6-String Jazz Guitar, except features a 12-string configuration, 6 per side tuners, EMG 89R humbucking pickups, 5-way pickup selector. Mfr. 1997 to date.
   Mfr.'s Sug. Retail $2,495

WINDSONG ACOUSTIC/ELECTRIC — similar to the Windsong acoustic model, except has thinner body, oval soundhole, Fishman Axis-M transducer/preamp, and oval abalone rosette. Current mfr.
   Mfr.'s Sug. Retail $4,000

STAGESONG — similar to the Windsong Acoustic/Electric model, except has no soundhole in the top soundboard. Current mfr.
   Mfr.'s Sug. Retail $2,195

12-String StageSong — similar to the StageSong, except features 12-string configuration, 6 per side tuners. Mfr. 1997 to date.
   Mfr.'s Sug. Retail $2,195

STAGESONG CLASSICAL — similar to the Stagesong, except has classical stylings. Current mfr.
   Mfr.'s Sug. Retail $2,195

ACOUSTIC ELECTRIC BASS

STAGESONG BASS — similar to the Acoustic Bass, except has no soundhole in the top soundboard. Current mfr.
   Mfr.'s Sug. Retail $2,195

RALEIGH

Instruments built in Chicago, Illinois. Distributed by the Aloha Publishing and Musical Instrument Company of Chicago, Illinois.

The Aloha company was founded in 1935 by J. M. Raleigh. True to the nature of a "House Brand" distributor, Raleigh's company distributed both Aloha instruments and amplifiers and Raleigh brand instruments through his Chicago office. Acoustic guitars were supplied by Harmony, and initial amplifiers and guitars for the Aloha trademark were supplied by the Alamo company of San Antonio, Texas. By the mid 1950s, Aloha was producing their own amps, but continued using Alamo products.

   (Source: Michael Wright, Vintage Guitar Magazine)

JOSE RAMIREZ

Instruments built in Madrid, Spain for four generations. Distributed in the U.S. exclusively by Guitar Salon International of Santa Monica, California.

Jose' Ramirez (1858-1923), originally apprenticed with luthier Francisco Gonzalez, began the family business in 1882. Many well known players, such as Segovia, Tarrega, Sabicas, Llobet, Yepes, and others had used Ramirez guitars during the course of their careers. The Madrid-based family business then passed to Jose' II (1885-1957), and then to Jose' III (born 1922-1994).

The acoustic guitars today are built in the workshop that is supervised by Jose' Ramirez IV. Ramirez IV, born in 1953, apprenticed in the family workshop when he was eighteen years old. By 1976, he had approached journeyman status, and within three years was working in maestro status. His sister, Amalia Ramirez, oversees the business side of the company.

In the early 1980s, the family workshop employed 17 workers and was producing 1,000 guitars a year. In the mid 1990s, the Ramirez workshop cut back production numbers to the amount the workshop could build without sub-contracting to outside builders. This level of supervision aids in maintaining the high quality of the guitars that carry the Ramirez name.

ACOUSTIC

The Madrid workshop continues to produce a full line of classical and flamenco guitars, lauds, bandurrias, and even cutaway guitar models with installed pickups. Ramirez continues to offer the two top of the line models, the **Tradicional** and the **Especial**.

RANGE RIDER

See chapter on House Brands.

This trademark has been identified as a "House Brand" of the Monroe Catalog House.

   (Source: Willie G. Moseley, Stellas & Stratocasters)

RECORDING KING

See chapter on House Brands.

The Recording King trademark was the House Brand of Montgomery Wards, and was used on a full range of acoustic flattops, electric lap steels, acoustic and electric archtop guitars, mandolins, and banjos. Instruments were built by a number of American manufacturers such as Gibson, Gretsch, and Kay between the 1930s through the early 1940s.

The high end models of the Recording King line were built by Gibson, but the low end models were built by other Chicago-based manufacturers. Recording King models built by Gibson will not have an adjustable truss rod (like other budget brands Gibson produced). Chances are that the low end, Chicago-built models do not either. Recording King had a number of endorsers, such as singing cowboy movie star Ray Whitley, country singer/songwriter Carson Robison, and multi-instrumental virtuoso Roy Smeck.

   (Source: Walter Carter, Gibson Guitars: 100 Years of an American Icon)

R

J. K. REDGATE

Instruments currently built in Adelaide, Australia. Distributed exclusively in the U.S by Classic Guitars International of Westlake Village, California.

Luthier Jim Redgate was born in London, England in 1963. His family emigrated to Australia in 1966. Redgate left school at age 15 to pursue a trade in plumbing. After his apprenticeship, Redgate began pursuing a career in music. Disappointed in a music shop's lackluster repair of his guitar, Redgate decided to fix the guitar himself (a neck reset performed on the kitchen table!).

Redgate has been building guitars since 1984. An accomplished player himself, Redgate holds a Bachelor of Music Performance in Classical Guitar from the Elder Conservatorium. Although not formally trained in guitar building, his backround in guitar playing comes to bear in his guitar design.

In 1992, Redgate became a full time luthier - and began marketing worldwide by 1995. Redgate is well known for his classical concert guitars with carbon fibre reinforced lattice bracing and arched backs. His high grade construction materials include Brazilian rosewood, W.R. cedar, German spruce, black ebony, and Honduras mahogany.

Redgate builds about fifteen or so guitars a year, with minimal use of power tools. This limited number of instruments are available from Jim Redgate direct, and custom requirements can be catered for. Retail list price in the U.S. is $5,400. For further information, please contact Jim Redgate via the Index of Current Manufacturers located in the back of this book.

REDONDO

See chapter on House Brands.

This trademark has been identified as a *House Brand* of the Tosca Company.

(Source: Willie G. Moseley, Stellas & Stratocasters)

REEDMAN

Instruments built in Korea. Distributed by Reedman America of Whittier, California.

The Reedman Musical Instrument company is currently offering a wide range of good quality acoustic, acoustic/electric, and solid body electric guitars. For further information, please contact Reedman America through the Index of Current Manufacturers located in the back of this book.

REGAL

Instruments currently produced in Korea. Distributed by Saga Musical Instruments of San Francisco, California.

Original Regal instruments produced beginning 1896 in Indianapolis, Indiana. Regal reappeared in Chicago, Illinois in 1908, possibly tied to Lyon and Healy (WASHBURN). U.S. production was centered in Chicago from 1908 through the late 1960s.

Models from the mid 1950s to the late 1960s produced in Chicago, Illinois by the Harmony company. Some Regal models licensed to Fender, and some appear with Fender logo during the late 1950s to mid 1960s (prior to Fender's own flat-top and Coronado series).

Emil Wulschner was a retailer and wholesaler in Indianapolis, Indiana during the 1880s. In the early 1890s he added his stepson to the company, and changed the name to "Wulschner and Son". They opened a factory around 1896 to build guitars and mandolins under three different trademarks: Regal, University, and 20th Century. Though Wulschner passed away in 1900, the factory continued on through 1902 or 1903 under control of a larger corporation. The business end of the company let it go when the economy faltered during those final years. This is the end of the original Regal trademarked instruments.

In 1904 Lyon & Healy (WASHBURN) purchased the rights to the Regal trademark, thousands of completed and works in progress instruments, and the company stockpile of raw materials. A new Regal company debuted in Chicago, Illinois in 1908 (it is not certain what happened during those four years) and it is supposed that they were tied to Lyon & Healy. The new company marketed ukeleles and tenor guitars, but not six string guitars. However, experts have agreed that Regal built guitar models for other labels (Bruno, Weyman, Stahl, and Lyon & Healy) during the 1910-1920 era. Regal eventually announced that their six string models would be distributed through a number of wholesalers.

In 1930, the Tonk Bros. Company acquired the rights to the Washburn trademark when the then-current holder (J. R. Stewart Co.) went bankrupt. Regal bought the rights to the **Stewart** and **LeDomino** names from Tonk Bros., and was making fretted instruments for all three trademarks. Also in the early 1930s, Regal had licensed the use of Dobro resonators in a series of guitars. In 1934 they acquired the rights to manufacture Dobro brand instruments when National-Dobro moved to Chicago from California. Regal then announced that they would be joining the name brand guitar producers that sold direct to dealers in 1938. Regal was, in effect, another producer of "house brand" guitars prior to World War II.

It has been estimated by one source that Regal-built Dobros stopped in 1940, and were not built from then on. During World War II, guitar production lines were converted to the war effort. After the war, the Regal Musical Instrument company's production was not as great as the pre-war production amounts. In 1954 the trademark and company fixtures were sold to Harmony. Harmony and Kay, were the other major producers of *House Brand* instruments. Regal guitars were licensed to Fender in the late 1950s, and some of the Harmony built "Regals" were rebranded with the Fender logo. This agreement continued up until the mid 1960s, when Fender introduced their own flat-top guitars.

In 1987, Saga Musical Instruments reintroduced the Regal trademark to the U.S. market. Regal now offers a traditional resonator guitar in both a roundneck and squareneck versions. Saga, located in San Francisco, also offers the **Blueridge** line of acoustic instruments, as well as mandolins, and stringed instrument parts and replacement pieces.

(Early Regal history courtesy John Teagle, Washburn: Over One Hundred Years of Fine Stringed Instruments. This noteworthy book brilliantly unravels core histories of Washburn, Regal, and Lyon & Healy and is a recommended must read to guitar collectors.)

(Harmony) Regal H6382 Deluxe Grand Concert
1973 Harmony Catalog

R

ACOUSTIC

All of the new Regal RD-45 resonator guitar models feature a mahogany body and neck, multi-ply white body binding, a bound rosewood fingerboard with mother of pearl position dots, chrome hardware, and a 10 1/2" spun aluminum cone with the traditional *spider* bridge.

The **RD-45** roundneck resonator has a spruce top, solid 3+3 peghead, a 21 fret neck that joins at the 14th fret, and an adjustable truss rod. Available in Black, Cherryburst, Natural, and Sunburst. The all-mahogany version **(RD-45 M)** has a gloss finish.

The **RD-45S** squareneck resonator model also has a spruce top, and a more traditional slotted 3+3 peghead, as well as the 14/21 fret neck. The RD-45 S models are also available in Black, Cherryburst, Natural, and Sunburst. The all-mahogany version **(RD-45S M)** has a gloss finish.

Regal briefly offered the **RD-65** resonator guitar. This roundneck model features all maple body construction, a mahogany neck, bound 14/21 fret rosewood fingerboard with mother of pearl position dots, solid 3+3 peghead, and a 7-ply white/black/white body binding. The **RD-65S** squareneck model is similar in construction, except has a slotted 3+3 headstock, 12th fret neck joint, and all white body binding. Both models have a Sunburst finish. Regal's **RD-65M** has a body constructed out of mahogany with the same specifications as the RD-65. The RD-65M has a dark-stained high gloss finish. All three of the **RD-65** series resonators are now discontinued.

ACOUSTIC BASS

Regal has recently introduced the **RD-05** resonator bass guitar. Similar to the RD-45 resonator guitar models, the RD-05 has 23 fret neck that joins the body at the 17th fret, a 2+2 solid headstock, and a spruce top. The RD-05 is currently available in a Sunburst finish only.

REX

See chapter on House Brands.

In the early 1900s, the Rex models were Kay-built student quality guitars distributed by the Fred Gretsch Manufacturing Company. By 1920 the Fred Gretsch Mfg. Co. had settled into its new ten story building in Brooklyn, New York, and was offering music dealers a very large line of instruments that included banjos, mandolins, guitars, violins, drums, and other band instruments. Gretsch distributed both the **20th Century** and **Rex** trademarks prior to introduction of the **Gretsch** trademark in 1933.

Another Rex trademark has also been identified as a House Brand of the Great West Music Wholesalers of Canada by author/researcher Willie G. Moseley.

TOM RIBBECKE

Instruments built in the San Francisco bay area in California since 1973.

Luthier Tom Ribbecke has been building and repairing guitars and basses for over twenty three years in the San Francsico bay area. Ribbecke's first lutherie business opened in 1975 in San Francisco's Mission District, and remained open and busy for ten years. In 1985 Ribbecke closed down the storefront in order to focus directly on client commissions.

Ribbecke guitars are entirely hand built by the luthier himself, while working directly with the customer. Beyond his signature and serial number of the piece, Ribbecke also offers a history of the origin of all materials involved in construction.

All prices quoted are the base price new, and does not reflect additions to the comissioned piece. For further information, please contact luthier Tom Ribbecke through the Index of Current Manufacturers located in the back of this book.

ACOUSTIC

Ribbecke 17" Archtop courtesy Tom Ribbecke

16" (OR 17") ARCH TOP STANDARD — Construction material as quoted in the base price is good Quality Domestic Figured Maple back and sides, Sitka Spruce top, Ebony fingerboard, Ebony pickguard, gold hardware, and solid Ebony tailpiece. Available in 25.4", 25", or 24.75" scale length. Current mfr.
> Mfr.'s Sug. Retail $8,000
>> Add $300 for mother of pearl block inlay.
>> Add $300 for pickup and volume control.
>> Add $400 for Sunburst finish.
>> Add $800 for wood body binding.
>> Add $1,000 for 18" body width (Call for specifics).
>> Add $1,000 for 7-string configuration.
>> Add $1,000 for 8-string configuration (Call for specifics).

> Earlier models were designated either a Monterey or Homage model; the Monterey features a cascade type peghead design, while the Homage features a peghead design reminiscent of a D'Angelico.

ACOUSTIC STEEL STRING — First Quality Spruce top, Indian Rosewood back and sides, Ebony fingerboard, Ebony Bridge, and dot inlays. Current mfr.
> Mfr.'s Sug. Retail $4,000
>> Add $300 for wood body binding.

SOUND BUBBLE STEEL STRING — Solid carved top, First Quality Indian Rosewood back and sides, Ebony fingerboard, Ebony bridge, and dot inlays. Current mfr.
> Mfr.'s Sug. Retail $4,500
>> Add $300 for wood body binding.

> The Sound Bubble, a slightly domed area on the bass side of the lower bout, increases the guitar's ability to translate the energy of the strings into sound. Patented in 1981 by artisan Charles Kelly and luthier Tom Ribbecke.

ACOUSTIC BASS

CARVED TOP ACOUSTIC BASS — Solid carved Spruce top with elliptical soundhole, Maple back and sides, Ebony fingerboard, 34" scale, chrome hardware, and dot inlays. Available in Natural finish only. Current mfr.
> Mfr.'s Sug. Retail $5,000

Grading	100%	EXCELLENT	AVERAGE

RICHTER

See chapter on House Brands.

This trademark has been identified as a *House Brand* of Montgomery Wards. Judging from the impressed stamp on the back of the headstock, instruments built by the Richter Manufacturing Company were produced in Chicago, Illinois. The production date is still unknown, but the instruments seem to have a pre-World War II aura about them - 1930s to 1940s, perhaps? Research on this brand is still underway.

(Information courtesy Bob Smith, Cassville, Wisconsin)

RICKENBACKER

Instruments produced in Santa Ana, California. Distributed by Rickenbacker International Corporation of Santa Ana, California. Rickenbacker instruments have been produced in California since 1931.

In 1925, John Dopyera (and brothers) joined up with George Beauchamp and Adolph Rickenbacker and formed National to build resonator guitars. Beauchamp's attitudes over spending money caused John Dopyera to leave National and start the Dobro company. While at National, Beauchamp, Rickenbacker and Dopyera's nephew, Paul Barth, designed the *Frying Pan* electric lap steel. In 1929 or 1930, Beauchamp was either forced out or fired from National - and so allied himself with Adolph Rickenbacker (National's tool and die man) and Barth to form **Ro-Pat-In**.

In the summer of 1931, Ro-Pat-In started building aluminum versions of the *Frying Pan* prototype. Early models have *Electro* on the headstock. Two years later, *Rickenbacker* (or sometimes *Rickenbacher)* was added to the headstock, and Ro-Pat-In was formally changed to the Electro String Instrument Corporation. Beauchamp left Electro sometime in 1940, and Barth left in 1956 to form his own company.

In December of 1953, F.C. Hall bought out the interests of Rickenbacker and his two partners. The agreement stated that the purchase was complete, and Electro could "continue indefinitely to use the trade name Rickenbacker." Hall, founder of Radio-Tel and the exclusive Fender distributor, had his Fender distributorship bought out by Leo Fender and Don Randall. The Rickenbacker company was formed in 1965 as an organizational change (Electro is still the manufacturer, and Rickenbacker is the sales company). Rickenbacker instruments gained popularity as the Beatles relied on a number of their guitars in the 1960s. One slight area of confusion: the model names and numbers differ from the U.S. market to models imported in to the U.K. market during the short period in the 1960s when Rose Morris represented Rickenbacker in the U.K (at all other times, the model numbers worldwide have been identical to the U.S. market).

In 1984 John Hall (F.C. Hall's son) officially took control by purchasing his father's interests in both the Rickenbacker, Inc. and Electro String companies. Hall formed the Rickenbacker International Corporation (RIC) to combine both interests.

(Source: John C. Hall, Chief Executive Officer, Rickenbacker International Corporation; and Tom Wheeler, American Guitar)

Rickenbacker currently offers the 5002V58 Mandolin, a vintage-style solid body electric mandolin based on a similar model issued in 1958. The current reproduction has a maple and walnut laminated body, 8 string configuration, and single coil pickups. Available in Fireglo or Mapleglo finishes (retail list is $1,489).

For further information regarding Rickenbacker electric models, please refer to the **5th Edition Blue Book of Electric Guitars**.

Ribbecke Archtop
courtesy Scott Chinery

ACOUSTIC ARCHTOP

760J JAZZ-BO — single rounded cutaway hollow body, bound carved spruce top, set-in neck, solid maple sides, carved maple back, 2 bound catseye f-holes, 14/21 fret rosewood fingerboard with pearl triangle inlay, adjustable rosewood bridge/metal trapeze tailpiece, 3 per side tuners, gold hardware. Available in Natural and Sunburst finishes. Current mfr.

Mfr.'s Sug. Retail	$4,649	$3,725	$2,275	$1,550

ACOUSTIC

385 — dreadnought style, maple top, round soundhole, pickguard, checkered body/rosette, maple back/sides/neck, 21 fret rosewood fingerboard with pearl triangle inlay, rosewood bridge with white pins. Available in Burst finishes. Mfd. 1958 to 1972.

1958-1965	$1,795	$1,175
1966-1972	$1,075	$850

This model was also available in a classic style body (Model 385-S).

385-J — similar to 385, except has jumbo style body.

	$1,850	$1,295

390 — while a few prototypes were made (circa 1957), this model was never put into production.

700 Series

700 COMSTOCK (Model 700C) — jumbo style, bound spruce top, round soundhole, solid maple back/sides, 14/21 fret rosewood fingerboard with pearl triangle inlay, rosewood bridge, 3 per side tuners, chrome hardware. Available in Natural finish. Current mfr.

Mfr.'s Sug. Retail	$2,189	$1,750	$1,075	$725

700 Comstock 12 String (Model 700C/12) — similar to the 700 Comstock, except has a 12-string configuration, 6 per side tuners. Current mfr.

Mfr.'s Sug. Retail	$2,289	$1,825	$1,125	$750

700 SHASTA (Model 700S) — similar to the 700 Comstock, except features solid rosewood back/sides. Current mfr.

Mfr.'s Sug. Retail	$2,289	$1,825	$1,150	$750

R

Grading	100%	EXCELLENT	AVERAGE

700 Shasta 12 String (Model 700S/12) — similar to the 700 Shasta, except has a 12-string configuration, 6 per side tuners. Current mfr.

Mfr.'s Sug. Retail	$2,389	$1,900	$1,175	$795

730 LARAMIE (Model 730L) — dreadnought style, bound spruce top, round soundhole, solid maple back/sides, 14/21 fret rosewood fingerboard with pearl triangle inlay, rosewood bridge, 3 per side tuners, chrome hardware. Available in Natural finish. Current mfr.

Mfr.'s Sug. Retail	$1,949	$1,550	$975	$650

730 Laramie 12 String (Model 730L/12) — similar to the 730 Laramie, except has a 12-string configuration, 6 per side tuners. Current mfr.

Mfr.'s Sug. Retail	$2,049	$1,650	$1,000	$695

730 SHILOH (Model 730S) — similar to the 730 Laramie, except features solid rosewood back/sides. Current mfr.

Mfr.'s Sug. Retail	$2,049	$1,650	$1,000	$695

730 Shiloh 12 (Model 730S/12) — similar to the 730 Shiloh, except has a 12-string configuration, 6 per side tuners. Current mfr.

Mfr.'s Sug. Retail	$2,149	$1,725	$1,050	$725

RICKMANN

Instruments built in Japan during the late 1970s.

The Rickmann trademark is a brandname used by a UK importer. Instruments are generally intermediate quality copies of classic American designs.

(Source: Tony Bacon and Paul Day, The Guru's Guitar Guide)

RICO

See B. C. RICH

RIEGER-KLOSS

See B D DEY.

STEVE RIPLEY

Instruments built in Tulsa, Oklahoma.

Luthier Steve Ripley had established a reputation as both a guitarist and recording engineer prior to debuting his Stereo Guitar models at the 1983 NAMM show. Ripley's designs were later licensed by Kramer (BKL). In 1986, Ripley moved to Tulsa, Oklahoma and two years later severed his relationship with Kramer. Any other updates will be featured in future editions of the **Blue Book of Guitars**.

(Source: Tom Wheeler, American Guitars)

MIKHAIL ROBERT

Instruments currently built in Canada. Distributed by Kirkpatrick Guitar Studio of Baltimore, Marlyland.

Luthier Mikhail Robert has been consistently producing high quality classical guitars.

RODIER

Instruments built in Kansas City, Kansas circa 1900s.

While not much information is known about the Rodier instruments, Mr. Jim Reynolds of Independence, Missouri is currently researching materials for an upcoming book. Interested persons can contact Mr. Reynolds through the **Blue Book of Guitars**.

RODRIQUEZ GUITARS

Instruments currently built in Madrid, Spain. Distributed in the U.S. market by Fender Musical Instruments Corporation of Scottsdale, Arizona.

Luthier Manuel Rodriguez, grandson of noted flamenco guitarist Manuel Rodriguez Marequi, has been building classical style guitars for a number of years. He began learning guitar construction at the age of 13 in Madrid and apprenticed in several shops before opening his own. Rodriguez emigrated to Los Angeles in 1959 and professionally built guitars for nearly 15 years. In 1973, Rodriguez returned to Spain and currently builds high quality instruments.

ACOUSTIC

A (Model 094-9100) — classical style, solid Canadian red cedar top, round soundhole, Indian rosewood back/sides, sapele neck, rosewood fingerboard, 3 per side goldplated standard tuners. Available in Natural Gloss finish. Current mfr.

Mfr.'s Sug. Retail	$675	$510	$335	$225

B (Model 094-9140) — classical style, solid Canadian red cedar top, round soundhole, Indian rosewood back/sides, sapele neck, ebony fingerboard, 3 per side goldplated standard tuners. Available in Natural Gloss finish. Current mfr.

Mfr.'s Sug. Retail	$785	$590	$390	$265

C (Model 094-9180) — classical style, solid Canadian red cedar top, round soundhole, Indian rosewood back/sides, cedar neck with ebony reinforcement, ebony fingerboard, 3 per side goldplated standard tuners. Available in Natural Gloss finish. Current mfr.

Mfr.'s Sug. Retail	$930	$700	$465	$315

R

Grading	100%	EXCELLENT	AVERAGE

C-1 (Model 094-9030) — classical style, solid Canadian red cedar top, round soundhole, Indian rosewood back/sides, sapele neck, rosewood fingerboard, 3 per side nickelplated tuners. Available in Natural Gloss finish. Current mfr.

Mfr.'s Sug. Retail	$485	$365	$240	$170

C-1 M (Model 094-9015) — similar to the C-1, except features Natural Satin finish. Current mfr.

Mfr.'s Sug. Retail	$435	$325	$220	$150

C-3 (Model 094-9080) — classical style, solid Canadian red cedar top, round soundhole, Indian rosewood back/sides, sapele neck, rosewood fingerboard, 3 per side nickelplated tuners. Available in Natural Gloss finish. Current mfr.

Mfr.'s Sug. Retail	$555	$420	$275	$190

C-3 F (Model 094-9082) — flamenco style, solid German spruce top, round soundhole, sycamore back/sides, sapele neck, rosewood fingerboard, 3 per side nickelplated tuners. Available in Natural Gloss finish. Current mfr.

Mfr.'s Sug. Retail	$565	$425	$285	$195

D (Model 094-9240) — classical style, solid Canadian red cedar top, round soundhole, Indian rosewood back/sides, Honduran cedar neck with ebony reinforcement, ebony fingerboard, 3 per side goldplated standard tuners. Available in Natural Gloss finish. Current mfr.

Mfr.'s Sug. Retail	$1,225	$920	$610	$415

E (Model 094-9300) — classical style, solid Canadian red cedar top, round soundhole, solid Indian rosewood back/sides, Honduran cedar neck with ebony reinforcement, ebony fingerboard, 3 per side goldplated standard tuners. Available in Natural Gloss finish. Current mfr.

Mfr.'s Sug. Retail	$1,800	$1,350	$890	$600

FC (Model 094-9360) — classical style, solid Canadian red cedar top, round soundhole, solid Indian rosewood back/sides, Honduran cedar neck with ebony reinforcement, ebony fingerboard, 3 per side goldplated standard tuners. Available in Natural Gloss finish. Current mfr.

Mfr.'s Sug. Retail	$2,200	$1,650	$1,090	$750

FF (Model 094-9280) — flamenco style, solid German cedar top, round soundhole, solid cypress back/sides, Honduran cedar neck with ebony reinforcement, ebony fingerboard, 3 per side goldplated standard tuners. Available in Natural Gloss finish. Current mfr.

Mfr.'s Sug. Retail	$1,250	$940	$620	$420

FG (Model 094-9400) — classical style, solid Canadian red cedar top, round soundhole, solid Indian rosewood back/sides, Honduran cedar neck with ebony reinforcement, ebony fingerboard, 3 per side goldplated deluxe tuners. Available in Natural Gloss finish. Current mfr.

Mfr.'s Sug. Retail	$2,790	$2,100	$1,380	$945

Rodriguez Signature Series

The following four models are completely hand made. The Brazilian rosewood used in Rodriguez guitars has been aged for over twenty five years. CITES Treaty documentation is available upon request. List prices include a hardshell case.

NORMAN RODRIGUEZ (Model 094-9420) — classical style, solid Canadian red cedar top, round soundhole, solid Brazilian rosewood back/sides, Honduran cedar neck with ebony reinforcement, ebony fingerboard, 3 per side goldplated deluxe tuners. Available in Natural Gloss finish. Current mfr.

Mfr.'s Sug. Retail	$4,500	$3,600	$2,340	$1,530

MANUEL RODRIGUEZ JR. (Model 094-9440) — classical style, solid Canadian red cedar top, round soundhole, solid Indian rosewood back/sides, Honduran cedar neck with ebony reinforcement, ebony fingerboard, 3 per side goldplated deluxe tuners. Available in Natural Gloss finish. Current mfr.

Mfr.'s Sug. Retail	$5,500	$4,400	$2,860	$1,870

MANUEL RODRIGUEZ JR. (Model 094-9480) — classical style, solid Canadian red cedar top, round soundhole, solid Brazilian rosewood back/sides, Honduran cedar neck with ebony reinforcement, ebony fingerboard, 3 per side goldplated deluxe tuners. Available in Natural Gloss finish. Current mfr.

Mfr.'s Sug. Retail	$7,500	$6,000	$3,900	$2,550

MANUEL RODRIGUEZ SR. (Model 094-9451) — classical style, solid Canadian red cedar top, round soundhole, solid Brazilian rosewood back/sides, Honduran cedar neck with ebony reinforcement, ebony fingerboard, 3 per side goldplated deluxe tuners. Available in Natural Gloss finish. Current mfr.

Mfr.'s Sug. Retail	$19,000	$15,200	$N/A	$N/A

ACOUSTIC ELECTRIC

Rodriguez Nylon String Acoustic Electrics feature a cutaway design and built-in electronics.

BC (Model 094-9150) — classical style with cutaway design, solid Canadian red cedar top, round soundhole, Indian rosewood back/sides, sapele neck, ebony fingerboard, 3 per side goldplated standard tuners, L.R. Baggs pickup, on-board preamp, volume/3 band EQ/mid-sweep contols. Available in Natural Gloss finish. Current mfr.

Mfr.'s Sug. Retail	$1,295	$970	$635	$430

CC (Model 094-9190) — classical style with cutaway design, solid Canadian red cedar top, round soundhole, Indian rosewood back/sides, cedar neck with ebony reinforcement, ebony fingerboard, 3 per side goldplated standard tuners, L.R. Baggs pickup, on-board preamp, volume/3 band EQ/mid-sweep contols. Available in Natural Gloss finish. Current mfr.

Mfr.'s Sug. Retail	$1,495	$1,120	$740	$500

R

ROGER

Instruments built in West Germany from the late 1950s to mid 1960s.

Luthier Wenzel Rossmeisl built very good to high quality archtop guitars as well as a semi-solid body guitar called "Model 54". Rossmeisl derived the trademark name in honor of his son, Roger Rossmeisl.

Roger Rossmeisl (1927-1979) was raised in Germany and learned luthier skills from his father, Wenzel. One particular feature was the "German Carve", a feature used by Wenzel to carve an indented plane around the body outline on the guitar's top. Roger Rossmeisl then travelled to America, where he briefly worked for Gibson in Kalamazoo, Michigan (in a climate not unlike his native Germany). Shortly thereafter he moved to California, and was employed at the Rickenbacker company. During his tenure at Rickenbacker, Rossmeisl was responsible for the design of the Capri and Combo guitars, and custom designs. His apprentice was a young Semie Moseley, who later introduced the "German Carve" on his own Mosrite brand guitars. Rossmeisl left Rickenbacker in 1962 to help Fender develop their own line of acoustic guitars (Fender had been licensing Harmony-made Regals up till then), and later introduced the Montego and LTD archtop electrics.

ROGERS

See chapter on House Brands.

This trademark has been identified as a "House Brand" of Selmer (UK).

(Source: Willie G. Moseley, Stellas & Stratocasters)

ROGUE

Instruments produced in Korea. Distributed by Musician's Friend of Medford, Oregon.

Musician's Friend distributes a line of good quality student and entry level instruments through their mail order catalog. Musician's Friend now offers a wide range of good quality guitars at an affordable price. For further information, contact Musician's Friend through the Index of Current Manufacturers located in the back of this book.

ROK AXE

Instruments currently produced in Korea. Distributed by Muse of Inchon, Korea.

The Muse company is currently offering a wide range of electric guitar and bass models, as well as a number of acoustic guitar models. Rok Axe models are generally fine entry level to student quality instruments. For further information, contact Rok Axe via the Index of Current Manufacturers located in the back of this edition.

JONATHAN W. ROSE

Instruments currently built in Strasburg, Virginia.

Luthier Jonathan W. Rose creates one-of-a-kind guitars, specializing in archtops. His aim is to push current design and tonal parameters. Rose's goal is to work closely with each client, giving them exactly what they want - a very personal instrument. For further information, contact Jonathan W. Rose via the Index of Current Manufacturers located in the back of this book.

ROYALIST

See chapter on House Brands.

This trademark has been identified as a "House Brand" of the RCA Victor Records Store.

(Source: Willie G. Moseley, Stellas & Stratocasters)

RUBIO

Instruments built in Spain, America, and England throughout this luthier's career.

English Master Luthier David Rubio apprenticed in Madrid, Spain at the workshop of Domingo Esteso (which was maintained by Esteso's nephews). In 1961 Rubio built guitars in New York City, New York. Returning to England in 1967, he set up a workshop and continued his guitar building. One of Rubio's apprentices was Paul Fischer, who has gone on to gain respect for his own creations.

ROBERT RUCK

Instruments built in Washington since 1966.

Luthier Robert Ruck has been building high quality classical guitars since 1966. Ruck hand-crafts between 25-30 guitars a year, and estimates that he has produced around 600 instruments altogether. Ruck's guitars are sought after by classical guitarists, and do not surface too often on the collectible market. For further information as to models, specifications, and availablility, please contact luthier Ruck via the Index of Current Manufacturers located in the back of this book.

R

S

SAEHAN

Instruments currently built in Korea. Distributed by the Saehan International Co., Ltd. of Seoul, Korea.

The Saehan International company offers a wide range of acoustic guitars from standard to cutaway model dreadnoughts, jumbo style body designs, and acoustic/electric models. For further information, please contact the Saehan International company via the Index of Current Manufacturers located in the back of this book.

T. SAKASHTA GUITARS

Instruments built in Van Nuys, California. Distribution is directly handled by T. Sakashta Guitars of Van Nuys, California.

Luthier Taku Sakashta builds high quality acoustic Archtop and steel string guitars. All are offered with custom options per model.

ACOUSTIC

Because the following archtop models are available with numerous custom body wood choices, hardware wood choices, and finishes, The **Blue Book of Guitars** recommends contacting luthier Sakashta in regards to exact pricing. The following information is offered as a guideline to the available models produced by luthier Sakashta.

Archtop Series

The **Avalon** features a 17" single cutaway body constructed of AAA quarter-sawn Sitka spruce top and AA Eastern rock maple sides and matching back. The neck is one piece Honduran mahogany neck with an East Indian rosewood fingerboard and pearl inlays. The Avalon also has either an ebony or rosewood tailpiece, and a rosewood bridge, pickguard, and peghead overlay.

The **Karizma** also features 17" single cutaway body. The top is built of AAA quarter-sawn Engleman spruce, and has sides and matching back of AA Eastern rock maple. The neck again is one piece Honduran mahogany, with East Indian rosewood fingerboard with pearl inlays. The Karizma has either an ebony or rosewood tailpiece, rosewood bridge, pickguard, and peghead overlay.

Steel String Acoustic Guitars

The following steel string models are available with numerous custom wood options for tops, backs and sides. Addition of custom choices will add to the base price quoted. All Steel String Acoustic guitar models are equipped with a deluxe hardshell case as part of the asking price.

The **Auditorium** model features a top of Sitka or Engleman spruce, or Western red cedar. The back and matching sides are constructed of East Indian rosewood; and the bound Honduras mahogany one piece neck has a Gaboon ebony fingerboard and peghead with diamond or dot position markers. The Auditorium also has a Brazilian rosewood bridge, Abalone soundhole ring decoration, three on a side Schaller tuning machines, and a nitrocellulose natural lacquer finish. The **S O** model is similar to the Auditorium model, except the design is slightly modified.

The **Dreadnought** model features the same construction materials, but designed along the lines of a dreadnought style guitar. Though similar, the **S D** model is a modified version of the Dreadnought.

The **Jumbo** model features the same construction materials as well, and is a full sized acoustic guitar design. The modified version **S J** model is similar in base design to the Jumbo.

SAMICK

Instruments produced in Korea since 1965. Current production of instruments is in Korea and City of Industry, California. Distributed in the U.S. market by Samick Music Corporation of City of Industry, California.

For a number of years, the Samick corporation was the "phantom builder" of instruments for a number of other trademarks. In fact, when the Samick trademark was finally introduced to the U.S. guitar market, a number of consumers thought that the company was brand new! However, Samick has been producing both upright and grand pianos, as well as stringed instruments for nearly forty years.

The **Samick Piano Co.** was established in Korea in 1958. By January of 1960 they had started to produce upright pianos, and within four years became the first Korean piano exporter. One year later in 1965, the company began maufacturing guitars, and by the early 1970s expanded to produce grand pianos and harmonicas as well. In 1973 the company incorporated as the **Samick Musical Instruments Mfg. Co., Ltd.** to reflect the diversity it encompassed. Samick continued to expand into guitar production. They opened a branch office in Los Angeles in 1978, a brand new guitar factory in 1979, and a branch office in West Germany one month before 1981.

Throughout the 1980s Samick continued to grow, prosper, and win awards for quality products and company productivity. The **Samick Products Co.** was established in 1986 as an affiliate producer of other products, and the company was listed on the Korean Stock Exchange in September of 1988. With their size of production facilities (the company claims to be *cranking out over a million guitars a year*, according to a recent brochure), Samick could be referred to as modern day producer of *House Brand* guitars as well as their own brand. In the past couple of years Samick acquired Valley Arts, a guitar company known for its one-of-a-kind instruments and custom guitars. This merger stabilized Valley Arts as the custom shop *wing* of Samick, as well as supplying Samick with quality American designed guitars.

Samick continues to expand their line of guitar models through the use of innovative designs, partnerships with high exposure endorsees (like Blues Saraceno and Ray Benson), and new projects such as the Robert Johnson Commemorative and the D'Leco Charlie Christian Commemorative guitars.

(Samick Company History courtesy Rick Clapper; Model Specifications courtesy Dee Hoyt)

In addition to their acoustic and electric guitars and basses, Samick offers a wide range of other stringed instruments such as autoharps, banjos, mandolins, and violins.

SM 50 S Mandolin
courtesy Samick

Grading	100%	EXCELLENT	AVERAGE

ACOUSTIC

American Classic Classical Series

SC-430 S N (Formerly LE GRANDE) — classical style, solid spruce top, round soundhole, bound body, wooden inlay rosette, rosewood back/sides, nato neck, 12/19 fret rosewood fingerboard, rosewood bridge, 3 per side gold tuners. Available in Natural finish. Current mfr.

Mfr.'s Sug. Retail	$450	$340	$225	$150

SC-433 — similar to the SC-430 S N, except features solid cedar top, laser-cut soundhole mosaic. Mfr. 1997 to date.

Mfr.'s Sug. Retail	$450	$340	$225	$150

American Classic Concert Folk Series

SR-100 — folk (wide shoulder/narrow waist) style, solid spruce top, round soundhole, bound body, multistripe purfling/rosette, sapele back/sides, 14/20 fret rosewood fingerboard with dot inlay, rosewood bridge with black white dot pins, slotted headstock, 3 per side chrome die-cast tuners. Available in Natural finish. Current mfr.

Mfr.'s Sug. Retail	$470	$355	$235	$160

SR-200 — similar to the SR-100, except features jacaranda back/sides, snowflake fingerboard inlay. Available in Natural finish. Current mfr.

Mfr.'s Sug. Retail	$790	$600	$390	$265

American Classic Dreadnought Series

SW-790 S — dreadnought style, solid spruce top, round soundhole, bound body, multistripe purfling/rosette, solid jacaranda back/sides, 14/20 fret ebony fingerboard with ornate abalone inlay, rosewood bridge with black white dot pins, tortoiseshell pickguard, 3 per side chrome tuners. Available in Natural finish. Current mfr.

Mfr.'s Sug. Retail	$850	$640	$420	$285

American Classic Super Jumbo Series

SJ-210 (Formerly MAGNOLIA) — jumbo style, sycamore top, round soundhole, black pickguard, 5 stripe bound body/rosette, nato back/sides/neck, 14/20 fret bound rosewood fingerboard with pearl dot inlay, rosewood bridge with white black dot pins, 3 per side black chrome tuners. Available in Black and White finishes. Disc. 1994.

		$150	$100
			Last Mfr.'s Sug. Retail was $330.

SJD-210 — jumbo style body, spruce top, metal resonator/2 screened soundholes, bound body, mahogany back/sides/neck, 14/20 fret bound rosewood fingerboard with pearl dot inlay, covered bridge/metal trapeze tailpiece, 3 per side chrome die-cast tuners. Available in Natural finish. Current mfr.

Mfr.'s Sug. Retail	$550	$415	$275	$185

Artist Series Elmore James Estate Dreadnought

EJ-1 — dreadnought style, spruce top, round soundhole, mahogany back/sides, 9-string configuration, rosewood bridge with black pins, chrome tuners, built-in guitar slide holder. Available in Natural finish. New 1997.

Mfr.'s Sug. Retail	$398

Artist Classical Series

Instruments in this series have a classical style body, round soundhole, bound body, wooden inlay rosette, 12/19 fret fingerboard, slotted peghead, tied bridge, 3 per side chrome tuners as following features (unless otherwise listed).

SC-310 (Formerly SEVILLE) — select spruce top, mahogany back/sides/neck, rosewood fingerboard/bridge. Available in Pumpkin finish. Current mfr.

Mfr.'s Sug. Retail	$250	$190	$125	$85

SC-330 (Formerly DEL REY) — select spruce top, rosewood back/sides, mahogany neck, rosewood fingerboard/bridge. Available in Pumpkin finish. Current mfr.

Mfr.'s Sug. Retail	$370	$280	$185	$125

SC-410 S — solid cedar top, sapele back/sides, mahogany neck, rosewood fingerboard/bridge. Available in Pumpkin finish. Mfr. 1997 to date.

Mfr.'s Sug. Retail	$350	$265	$175	$120

SC-450 (Formerly LA TOUR) — select spruce top, sapele back/sides, nato neck, rosewood fingerboard/bridge. Available in Pumpkin finish. Current mfr.

Mfr.'s Sug. Retail	$280	$210	$140	$95

SC-450 S (Formerly SC-430) — similar to the SC-450, except features solid spruce top. Available in Pumpkin finish. Current mfr.

Mfr.'s Sug. Retail	$350	$265	$175	$120

Artist Concert Folk Series

Instruments in this series have a wide shoulder/narrow waist *folk*-style body, round soundhole, bound body, multistripe purfling/rosette, 14/20 fret rosewood fingerboard with dot inlay, rosewood bridge with black white dot pins, 3 per side chrome tuners as following features (unless otherwise listed).

SF-115 — select natural spruce top, mahogany back/sides/neck, chrome tuners. Available in Natural finish. Current mfr.

Mfr.'s Sug. Retail	$250	$190	$125	$85

SC-450
courtesy Samick

Grading	100%	EXCELLENT	AVERAGE

SF-210 (Formerly SF-210 M SWEETWATER) — select natural spruce top, mahogany back/sides/neck, die-cast chrome tuners. Available in Natural finish. Current mfr.

Mfr.'s Sug. Retail	$280	$210	$140	$95

SF-291 (Formerly CHEYENNE) — solid spruce top, solid rosewood back/sides, nato neck, rosewood veneer on peghead, gold plated die-cast tuners. Available in Natural finish. Current mfr.

Mfr.'s Sug. Retail	$440	$330	$220	$145

Artist Dreadnought Series

SW-21 NM — dreadnought style, select natural spruce top, round soundhole, black pickguard, ivory body binding, multistripe rosette, nato back/sides/neck, 14/20 fret rosewood fingerboard with white dot inlay, rosewood bridge with black pins, 3 per side die-cast tuners. Available in Natural finishes. New 1997.

Mfr.'s Sug. Retail	$238	$144	$70	$60

SW-015 D (Formerly SANTA FE) — dreadnought style, mahogany top, round soundhole, black pickguard, bound body, multistripe rosette, mahogany back/sides/neck, 14/20 fret rosewood fingerboard with white dot inlay, rosewood bridge with white black dot pins, 3 per side die-cast tuners. Available in Black, Natural, and White gloss finishes. Mfr. 1994 to date.

Mfr.'s Sug. Retail	$260	$195	$130	$85

Add $10 for Black (BK) and White (WH) finishes.

SW-115-12 — dreadnought style, 12-string configuration, select natural spruce top, round soundhole, black pickguard, bound body, multistripe rosette, mahogany back/sides/neck, 14/20 fret rosewood fingerboard with white dot inlay, rosewood bridge with white black dot pins, 6 per side standard tuners. Available in Natural finish. Current mfr.

Mfr.'s Sug. Retail	$270	$200	$135	$90

SW-210 (Formerly GREENBRIAR) — dreadnought style, select natural spruce top, round soundhole, black pickguard, bound body, multistripe rosette, mahogany back/sides/neck, 14/20 fret rosewood fingerboard with white dot inlay, rosewood bridge black pins, 3 per side die-cast tuners. Available in Natural finish. Current mfr.

Mfr.'s Sug. Retail	$300	$225	$150	$100

SW-210 LH (Formerly Beaumont) — similar to the SW-210, except in a left-handed configuration. Current mfr.

Mfr.'s Sug. Retail	$310	$235	$155	$105

SW-210 BB 1 — similar to the SW-210, except features select natural bamboo top/back/sides. Available in Natural finish. Mfr. 1997 to date.

Mfr.'s Sug. Retail	$470	$355	$235	$160

SW-210 S (Formerly Bluebird) — similar to the SW-210, except features a solid spruce top. Current mfr.

Mfr.'s Sug. Retail	$400	$300	$200	$135

SW-210-12 (Formerly Savannah) — similar to the SW-210, except in a 12-String configuration, 6 per side tuners. Current mfr.

Mfr.'s Sug. Retail	$350	$265	$175	$120

SW-230-12 HS (Formerly VICKSBURG) — dreadnought style, 12-String configuration, solid spruce top, round soundhole, black pickguard, bound body, herringbone purfling/rosette, rosewood back/sides, mahogany neck, 14/20 fret rosewood fingerboard with pearl dot inlay, rosewood bridge with black white dot pins, 6 per side tuners gold die cast tuners. Available in Natural finish. Current mfr.

Mfr.'s Sug. Retail	$520	$390	$260	$175

SW-250 (Formerly ASPEN) — dreadnought style, spruce top, round soundhole, black pickguard, 3 stripe bound body/rosette, sapele back/sides, nato neck, 14/20 fret rosewood fingerboard, rosewood bridge with white black dot pins, rosewood veneer on peghead, 3 per side chrome tuners. Available in Natural finish. Disc. 1994.

	$115	$75

Last Mfr.'s Sug. Retail was $250.

SW-260-12 B (Formerly NIGHTINGALE 12) — dreadnought style, 12-string configuration, maple top, round soundhole, black pickguard, bound body, multistripe purfling/rosette, mahogany back/sides/neck, 14/20 fret rosewood fingerboard with pearl dot inlay, rosewood bridge with black pins, 6 per side chrome die-cast tuners. Available in Black gloss finish. Current mfr.

Mfr.'s Sug. Retail	$380	$285	$190	$130

SW-270 HS NM (Formerly JASMINE) — dreadnought style, cedar top, round soundhole, black pickguard, bound body, herringbone purfling/rosette, walnut back/sides, mahogany neck, 14/20 fret bound rosewood fingerboard with pearl block inlay, bound peghead with pearl logo inlay, rosewood bridge with white black dot pins, 3 per side chrome die-cast tuners. Available in Natural finish. Current mfr.

Mfr.'s Sug. Retail	$400	$300	$200	$135

SW-292 S (Formerly NIGHTINGALE) — dreadnought style, solid spruce top, round soundhole, black pickguard, 3 stripe bound body/rosette, mock birdseye maple back/sides, nato neck, 14/20 fret bound rosewood fingerboard with pearl dot inlay, rosewood bridge with white black dot pins, bound headstock, 3 per side chrome tuners. Available in Transparent Black finish. Disc. 1994.

	$160	$105

Last Mfr.'s Sug. Retail was $350.

SW-630 HS (Previously LAUREL) — dreadnought style, solid spruce top, round soundhole, black pickguard, bound body, herringbone purfling/rosette, rosewood back/sides, mahogany neck, 14/20 fret bound rosewood fingerboard with pearl tree-of-life inlay, rosewood bridge with white black dot pins, bound peghead with pearl logo inlay, 3 per side gold die-cast tuners. Available in Natural finish. Current mfr.

Mfr.'s Sug. Retail	$500	$375	$245	$165

SW-210 LH
courtesy Samick

SW-630 HS
courtesy Samick

Grading	100%	EXCELLENT	AVERAGE

SD-50
courtesy Samick

SW-730 SP — dreadnought style, solid spruce top, round soundhole, black pickguard, bound body, multistripe purfling/rosette, rosewood back/sides, mahogany neck, 14/20 fret ebony fingerboard with abalone dot inlay, ebony bridge with black white dot pins, bound peghead with abalone logo inlay, 3 per side chrome tuners. Available in Natural finish. Mfr. 1994 to 1996.

$380 $250
Last Mfr.'s Sug. Retail was $840.

SW-790 SP — similar to the SW-730 SP, except features jacaranda back/sides, bound fingerboard. Available in Natural finish. Mfr. 1994 to 1996.

$325 $220
Last Mfr.'s Sug. Retail was $720.

Exotic Wood Series

SD-50 — dreadnought style, spruce top, round soundhole, black pickguard, bound body, multistripe purfling/rosette, maple back/sides, mahogany neck, 14/20 fret rosewood fingerboard with pearl diamond/dot inlay, maple veneered peghead with pearl split diamond/logo inlay, rosewood bridge with white black dot pins, 3 per side chrome tuners. Available in Natural finish. Mfr. 1994 to 1995.

$150 $100
Last Mfr.'s Sug. Retail was $300.

SD-60 S — dreadnought style, solid spruce top, round soundhole, black pickguard, bound body, multistripe purfling/rosette, bubinga back/sides, mahogany neck, 14/20 fret rosewood fingerboard with abalone diamond/dot inlay, rosewood bridge with white black dot pins, bubinga veneered peghead with abalone split diamond/logo inlay, 3 per side chrome tuners. Available in Natural finish. Mfr. 1994 to 1995.

$225 $150
Last Mfr.'s Sug. Retail was $450.

SD-80 CS — dreadnought style, figured maple top, round soundhole, black pickguard, bound body, multistripe purfling/rosette, maple back/sides, mahogany neck, 14/20 fret bound rosewood fingerboard with abalone pearl diamond/dot inlay, bound peghead with abalone split diamond/logo inlay, rosewood bridge with white black dot pins, 3 per side chrome tuners. Available in Sunburst finish. Mfr. 1994 to 1995.

$175 $115
Last Mfr.'s Sug. Retail was $350.

Pro Series

All instruments in this series are handmade. This series was also known as the **Handcrafted Series**.

S-7 — concert style, spruce top, round soundhole, rosewood pickguard, bound body, multistripe wood purfling/rosette, rosewood back/sides, mahogany neck, 14/20 fret bound ebony fingerboard with pearl dot inlay, ebony bridge with black white dot pins, pearl peghead logo inlay, 3 per side chrome tuners. Available in Natural finish. Mfr. 1994 to 1995.

$350 $230
Last Mfr.'s Sug. Retail was $700.

SK-5 (Formerly MARSEILLES) — folk style, solid spruce top, round soundhole, tortoise shell pickguard, wooden bound body, wooden inlay rosette, ovankol back/sides, nato neck, 14/20 fret bound rosewood fingerboard with pearl dot inlay, ebony bridge with white black dot pins, ovankol veneer on peghead with pearl logo inlay, 3 per side chrome tuners. Available in Natural finish. Disc. 1994.

$230 $150
Last Mfr.'s Sug. Retail was $460.

SK-7 (Formerly VERSAILLES) — similar to Marseilles, except has solid cedar top, rosewood back/sides, brown white dot bridge pins. Disc. 1994.

$350 $230
Last Mfr.'s Sug. Retail was $700.

Standard Acoustic Series

C-41 — dreadnought style, mahogany top, round soundhole, black pickguard, bound body, multistripe rosette, mahogany back/sides/neck, 14/20 fret rosewood fingerboard with dot inlay, rosewood bridge with black pins, 3 per side chrome tuners. Available in Black satin, Natural, and White satin finishes. Disc. 1995.

$70 $50
Last Mfr.'s Sug. Retail was $160.

LF-006 — smaller scale (36" length) folk style, Nato top/back/sides/neck, bound body, round soundhole, rosewood fingerboard with dot inlay, rosewood bridge with black pins, 3 per side chrome tuners. Available in Natural satin finish. Current mfr.
Mfr.'s Sug. Retail $124 $95 $60 $40

LF-009 — smaller scale (39" length) folk style, Nato top/back/sides/neck, bound body, round soundhole, rosewood fingerboard with dot inlay, rosewood bridge with black pins, 3 per side chrome tuners. Available in Natural satin finish. Current mfr.
Mfr.'s Sug. Retail $128 $100 $65 $45

LF-015 — (full scale) folk style, Nato top/back/sides/neck, bound body, round soundhole, rosewood fingerboard with dot inlay, rosewood bridge with black pins, 3 per side chrome tuners. Available in Natural satin finish. Current mfr.
Mfr.'s Sug. Retail $156 $120 $75 $55

LW-015 — dreadnought style, Nato top, round soundhole, black pickguard, bound body, multistripe rosette, nato back/sides/neck, 14/20 fret rosewood fingerboard with dot inlay, rosewood bridge with black pins, 3 per side chrome tuners. Available in Natural satin finish. Mfr. 1994 to date.
Mfr.'s Sug. Retail $156 $120 $75 $55

LW-015 LH — similar to the LW-015, except in a left-handed configuration. Available in Natural satin finish. Current mfr.
Mfr.'s Sug. Retail $170 $130 $85 $60

Grading	100%	EXCELLENT	AVERAGE

LW-015 G — similar to the LW-015. Available in Black, Sunburst, and White gloss finishes. Current mfr.

Mfr.'s Sug. Retail	$210	$160	$105	$75

LW-020 G — similar to the LW-015, except features solid natural Agathis top, 3 per side enclosed tuners. Available in Blonde (top only) finish. Current mfr.

Mfr.'s Sug. Retail	$174	$130	$90	$60

LW-025 G — dreadnought style, spruce top, round soundhole, black pickguard, bound body, multistripe rosette, nato back/sides, mahogany neck, 14/20 fret rosewood fingerboard with dot inlay, rosewood bridge with white black dot pins, 3 per side chrome die-cast tuners. Available in Natural gloss finish. Mfr. 1994 to date.

Mfr.'s Sug. Retail	$210	$160	$110	$75

LW-027 G — similar to the LW-025 G, except features ovankol back/sides. Available in Natural gloss finish. Current mfr.

Mfr.'s Sug. Retail	$250	$190	$125	$85

LW-028 A new — similar to the LW-025 G, except features ivory body binding, 3 per side Grover tuners. Available in Natural satin finish. Mfr. 1997 to date.

Mfr.'s Sug. Retail	$200	$150	$100	$70

Standard Classical Series

Instruments in this series have a classical style body, round soundhole, bound body, marquetry rosette, 12/19 fret fingerboard, slotted peghead, tied bridge, 3 per side tuners as following features (unless otherwise listed).

LC-006 — smaller scale (36" length) classical style, Nato top/back/sides/neck, rosewood fingerboard/bridge, chrome tuners. Available in Natural satin finish. Mfr. 1997 to date.

Mfr.'s Sug. Retail	$120	$90	$60	$40

LC-009 — smaller scale (39" length) classical style, Nato top/back/sides/neck, rosewood fingerboard/bridge, chrome tuners. Available in Natural satin finish. Mfr. 1997 to date.

Mfr.'s Sug. Retail	$124	$95	$60	$40

LC-015 G — Nato mahogany top/back/sides/neck, rosewood fingerboard/bridge, chrome tuners. Available in Natural gloss finish. Mfr. 1994 to date.

Mfr.'s Sug. Retail	$140	$105	$70	$45

LC-025 G — natural spruce top, mahogany back/sides/neck, rosewood fingerboard/bridge, chrome tuners. Available in Natural finish. Mfr. 1994 to date.

Mfr.'s Sug. Retail	$184	$140	$90	$60

LC-034 G new — solid spruce top, ovangol back/sides, mahogany neck, rosewood fingerboard/bridge, gold plated tuners. Available in Natural finish. Mfr. 1997 to date.

Mfr.'s Sug. Retail	$210	$160	$110	$75

ACOUSTIC ELECTRIC

American Classic Acoustic/Electric Classical Series

SC-438 ES FS — classical style, solid cedar top, round soundhole, bound body, laser-cut sunflower mosaic, rosewood back/sides, nato neck, 12/19 fret rosewood fingerboard, rosewood bridge, 3 per side gold tuners, piezo pickup, volume/3 band EQ slider controls. Available in Natural finish. Current mfr.

Mfr.'s Sug. Retail	$650	$490	$320	$215

American Classic Super Jumbo Acoustic/Electric Series

SJ-218 CE — jumbo style body with single rounded cutaway, spruce top, round soundhole, black pickguard, bound body, abalone rosette, nato back/sides/neck, 14/20 fret rosewood fingerboard with abalone dot inlay, rosewood bridge with white black dot pins, 3 per side Gotoh tuners, piezo pickup, volume/3 band EQ slider controls. Available in Natural finish. Current mfr.

Mfr.'s Sug. Retail	$600	$450	$295	$200

American Classic Acoustic/Electric Dreadnought Series

AMCT-CE — thin line depth dreadnought body with single florentine cutaway, solid spruce top, bound body, rosewood back/sides, mahogany neck, 14/20 fret bound extended rosewood fingerboard with abalone diamond inlay, ebony bridge and pins, 6 on a side chrome die-cast tuners, piezo bridge pickup, volume/3 band EQ slider controls. Available in Natural (N), Transparent Purple (TP), and Vintage Sunburst (VSB). Current mfr.

Mfr.'s Sug. Retail	$570	$425	$280	$190

LC-015 G
courtesy Samick

EAG-89 N
courtesy Samick

Grading	100%	EXCELLENT	AVERAGE

SW-218 CE TT — dreadnought style with single rounded cutaway, spruce top, laser cut round soundhole design, bound body, mahogany back/sides/neck, 14/20 fret rosewood fingerboard with white dot inlay, rosewood bridge with black white dot pins, 3 per side die-cast tuners. piezo bridge pickup, volume/3 band EQ slider controls, XLR jack. Available in Natural finish. Current mfr.

Mfr.'s Sug. Retail	$550	$415	$275	$185

American Classic Thin Line Dreadnought Series:

EAG-88 (Formerly BLUE RIDGE) — single round cutaway flat-top body, spruce top, oval soundhole, bound body, wood purfling, abalone rosette, maple back/sides, mahogany neck, 24 fret bound extended rosewood fingerboard with pearl dot inlay, rosewood bridge, bound peghead with screened logo, 6 on a side black chrome tuners, piezo bridge pickup, volume/tone controls. Available in Natural finish. Disc. 1995.

		$225	$150

Last Mfr.'s Sug. Retail was $500.

Earlier models had a figured maple top, 22 fret bound rosewood fingerboard, and were available in Blue Burst, Natural, and Tobacco Sunburst finishes.

EAG-89 — similar to the EAG-88, except features a figured maple top, rosewood back/sides, gold tuners. Available in Natural, Red Stain, and Sunburst finishes. Disc. 1995.

		$270	$180

Last Mfr.'s Sug. Retail was $600.

EAG-93 — thin line depth dreadnought body with single rounded cutaway, solid spruce top, oval soundhole, bound body, abalone purfling/rosette, rosewood back/sides, mahogany neck, 24 fret bound extended ebony fingerboard with pearl eagle inlay, rosewood bridge, abalone bound peghead with screened logo, 6 on side tuners, black hardware, piezo bridge pickup, volume/3 band EQ slider controls. Available in Natural finish. Mfr. 1994 to date.

Mfr.'s Sug. Retail	$1,400	$1,050	$685	$465

Artist Series Acoustic/Electric Classical Series

SCT-450 CE (Formerly GRANADA) — single round cutaway classical style, select spruce top, round soundhole, bound body, wooden inlay rosette, rosewood back/sides, nato neck, 12/19 fret rosewood fingerboard, rosewood bridge, rosewood peghead veneer, 3 per side chrome tuners, active piezo pickup, volume/tone slider controls. Available in Natural finish. Current mfr.

Mfr.'s Sug. Retail	$440	$330	$220	$150

Artist Series Electric/Acoustic Steel String Dreadnought Series

SW-115 DE — dreadnought style, select natural spruce top, round soundhole, black pickguard, bound body, multistripe rosette, mahogany back/sides/neck, 14/20 fret rosewood fingerboard with white dot inlay, rosewood bridge with white black dot pins, 3 per side die-cast tuners, neck pickup, volume/tone controls. Available in Black, Natural, and White gloss finishes. Mfr. 1994 to date.

Mfr.'s Sug. Retail	$290	$220	$145	$100

Add $10 for Black (BK) and White (WH) finishes.

SW-210 CE (Formerly LAREDO) — dreadnought style with single rounded cutaway, select natural spruce top, round soundhole, black pickguard, bound body, multistripe rosette, mahogany back/sides/neck, 14/20 fret rosewood fingerboard with white dot inlay, rosewood bridge with white black dot pins, 3 per side die-cast tuners. piezo bridge pickup, volume/3 band EQ slider controls. Available in Natural finish. Current mfr.

Mfr.'s Sug. Retail	$420	$315	$210	$145

SW-220 HS CE (Formerly AUSTIN) — dreadnought style with single rounded cutaway, solid cedar top, oval soundhole, 5 stripe bound body/rosette, cedar back/sides, maple neck, 14/20 fret bound rosewood fingerboard with pearl dot inlay, stylized pearl inlay at 12th fret, rosewood bridge with white black dot pins, cedar veneer on bound peghead, 3 per side gold tuners, piezo pickup, volume/tone slider control. Available in Natural finish. Disc. 1994.

		$205	$135

Last Mfr.'s Sug. Retail was $450.

SW-260 CE N (Formerly GALLOWAY) — single rounded cutaway dreadnought style, maple top, round soundhole, tortoise pickguard, bound body, multistripe purfling/rosette, maple back/sides/neck, 14/20 fret bound rosewood fingerboard with pearl diamond/dot inlay, rosewood bridge with white black dot pins, bound peghead with pearl logo inlay, 3 per side die-cast chrome tuners, piezo bridge pickup, volume/3 band EQ slider controls. Available in Natural finish. Current mfr.

Mfr.'s Sug. Retail	$480	$360	$240	$160

Artist Series Thin Line Electric Dreadnought Series

SDT-110 CE OSM — thin line depth dreadnought style with single rounded cutaway, kusu top/back/sides/headstock, round soundhole, tortoise pickguard, bound body, multistripe purfling/rosette, 14/20 fret bound rosewood fingerboard with pearl diamond/dot inlay, rosewood bridge with white black dot pins, bound peghead with pearl logo inlay, 3 per side die-cast chrome tuners, piezo bridge pickup, volume/3 band EQ slider controls. Available in Cherry Sunburst finish. Current mfr.

Mfr.'s Sug. Retail	$570	$430	$280	$190

SWT-210 CE — thin line depth dreadnought style with single rounded cutaway, spruce top, round soundhole, mahogany back/sides/neck, 14/20 fret rosewood fingerboard, rosewood bridge with white black dot pins, 3 per side chrome tuners, piezo bridge pickup, volume/tone controls. Available in Natural finish. Current mfr.

Mfr.'s Sug. Retail	$470	$350	$230	$160

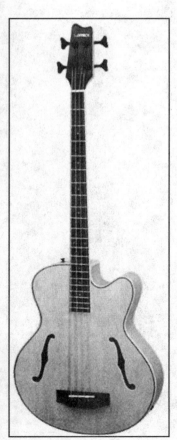

HFB-590 N
courtesy Samick

Grading	100%	EXCELLENT	AVERAGE

SWT-217 CE ASHTR — thin line depth dreadnought style with single rounded cutaway, ash top, round soundhole, mahogany back/sides/neck, 14/20 fret bound rosewood fingerboard with pearl diamond inlay, rosewood bridge with white black dot pins, 3 per side die-cast chrome tuners, piezo bridge pickup, volume/3 band EQ slider controls. Available in Transparent Red finish. Current mfr.

Mfr.'s Sug. Retail	$550	$415	$275	$185

Pro Series Acoustic/Electric

All instruments in this series are handmade. This series was also known as the **Handcrafted Series**.

S-7 EC (Formerly CHAMBRAY) — single round cutaway folk style, solid cedar top, round soundhole, rosewood pickguard, wooden bound body, wooden inlay rosette, rosewood back/sides, nato neck, 14/20 fret ebony fingerboard with pearl dot inlay, ebony bridge with black white dot pins, rosewood veneer on peghead with pearl logo inlay, 3 per side Schaller gold tuners with pearl buttons, acoustic pickup, volume/tone control, preamp. Available in Natural finish. Disc. 1995.

		$550	$365

Last Mfr.'s Sug. Retail was $1,100.

SDT-10 CE — single round cutaway dreadnought style, ash top, round soundhole, tortoise pickguard, bound body, multistripe purfling/rosette, ash back/sides, maple neck, 14/20 fret bound rosewood fingerboard with pearl diamond/dot inlay, rosewood bridge with white black dot pins, bound peghead with pearl logo inlay, 3 per side chrome tuners, piezo bridge pickup, 4 band EQ. Available in Natural finish. Mfr. 1994 to 1995.

		$225	$150

Last Mfr.'s Sug. Retail was $450.

Standard Acoustic/Electric Series

LW-015 E — dreadnought style, Nato top, round soundhole, black pickguard, bound body, multistripe rosette, nato back/sides/neck, 14/20 fret rosewood fingerboard with dot inlay, rosewood bridge with black pins, 3 per side chrome tuners, piezo bridge pickup, volume/tone controls. Available in Natural satin finish. Current mfr.

Mfr.'s Sug. Retail	$196	$150	$100	$70

LWO-15 E LH — similar to the LW-015, except in a left-handed configuration. Available in Natural satin finish. Current mfr.

Mfr.'s Sug. Retail	$210	$160	$110	$75

LW-025 G CEQ — dreadnought style with single rounded cutaway, spruce top, round soundhole, black pickguard, bound body, multistripe rosette, nato back/sides, mahogany neck, 14/20 fret rosewood fingerboard with dot inlay, rosewood bridge with white black dot pins, 3 per side chrome die-cast tuners, piezo pickup, volume/EQ slider controls. Available in Natural gloss finish. Mfr. 1997 to date.

Mfr.'s Sug. Retail	$190	$145	$95	$65

LW-044 G CEQ new — similar to the LW-025 G CEQ, except features ovankol back/sides, ABS body binding. Available in Natural gloss finish. Mfr. 1997 to date.

Mfr.'s Sug. Retail	$300	$225	$150	$100

ACOUSTIC ELECTRIC BASS

American Classic Acoustic/Electric Bass Series

HFB-590 N (Formerly KINGSTON) — single round cutaway flat-top body, maple top, bound body, bound f-holes, maple back/sides/neck, 21 fret bound rosewood fingerboard with pearl dot inlay, strings through rosewood bridge, blackface peghead with pearl logo inlay, 2 per side black chrome tuners, piezo bridge pickup, 4 band EQ. Available in Natural finish. Current mfr.

Mfr.'s Sug. Retail	$850	$640	$420	$285

Earlier models were also available in Black, Pearl White, and Tobacco Sunburst finishes.

HFB-690 RB TBK — similar to HF590, except has 5 strings, arched quilted maple top, 3/2 per side tuners. Available in Transparent Black finish. Mfr. 1994 to 1995.

		$475	$315

Last Mfr.'s Sug. Retail was $950.

This model was optionally available with a birdseye maple fretless fingerboard and Natural finish (Model HFB5-690 RB FL N).

HFB5-690 RB FL N
courtesy Samick

KIRK SAND

Instruments currently built in Laguna Beach, California.

Luthier Kirk Sand began playing guitar at six years old and played professionally and taught until the age of nineteen when he moved from his hometown of Springfield, Illinois to Southern California to study classical guitar.

His love of the instrument led him to co-establish the Guitar Shoppe in 1972 with Jim Matthews in Laguna Beach, California, which produces some of the finest custom instruments built today as well as being one of the premier repair facilities on the West Coast. The head of the repair section is Mark Angus (see ANGUS GUITARS) who works full-time as well as building his custom acoustics throughout the year.

By 1979, Kirk's twenty years of dedicated experience with guitars, guitar repair and restoration inspired him to begin building guitars of his own design. Sand guitars feature Sitka or Engleman Spruce tops, Brazilian or Indian rosewood backs and sides, ebony fingerboards, and custom designed active electronics. For further information, contact Sand Guitars through the Index of Current Manufacturers located in the back of this book.

Sand Guitar
courtesy Kirk Sand

Grading		100%	EXCELLENT	AVERAGE

Archtop Model
courtesy Santa Cruz Guitar Co.

SANDNER

Instruments produced between 1948 to 1959.

The Sandner trademark can be found on a series of acoustic archtops. These models may have **Alosa** or **Standard** on the headstock (or tailpiece). Reseasrch continues into the Sandner (or Alosa) trademark.

SANOX

Instruments produced in Japan from the late 1970s through the mid 1980s.

Intermediate to good quality guitars featuring some original designs and some designs based on American classics.

(Source: Tony Bacon and Paul Day, The Guru's Guitar Guide)

SANTA CRUZ

Instruments built in Santa Cruz, California since 1976. Distributed by the Santa Cruz Guitar Company (SCGC) located in Santa Cruz, California.

The Santa Cruz Guitar company has been creating high quality acoustic guitars since 1976. Founded by Richard Hoover, who first became interested in guitar building around 1969, and moved to Santa Cruz in 1972 where he studied once a week under a classical guitar builder. Hoover continued honing his skills through daily on-the-job training and talking with other builders. While he was learning the guitar building trade, Hoover was still playing guitar professionally. Hoover ran his own shop for a number of years, producing guitars under the *Rodeo* trademark.

The Santa Cruz Guitar Company was formed by Richard Hoover and two partners in 1976. Their objective was to build acoustic guitars with consistent quality. By drawing on building traditions of the classical guitar and violin builders, Hoover based the new company's building concept on wood choice, voicing the tops, and tuning the guitar bodies. The company's production of individually-built guitars has expanded by working with a group of established luthiers. Santa Cruz now offers fifteen different guitar models with a wide variety of custom options. It is estimated that over half of the guitars are made to order to customer's specifications.

ACOUSTIC ARCHTOP

ARCHTOP — single rounded cutaway, bound carved Engelman or Sitka spruce top, raised bound ebony pickguard, bound f-holes, multi-wood purfling, German maple back/sides/neck, 21 fret bound ebony fingerboard with abalone fan inlay, adjustable ebony bridge/fingers tailpiece, ebony veneered bound peghead with abalone logo inlay, 3 per side tuners, gold hardware. Available in Natural finish. Current mfr.

This instrument comes in three different body dimensions (measured across the lower bout). listed below:

16 Inch Body				
Mfr.'s Sug. Retail	$10,500	$8,500	$5,500	$3,600
17 Inch Body				
Mfr.'s Sug. Retail	$10,950	$8,800	$5,725	$3,775
18 Inch Body				
Mfr.'s Sug. Retail	$14,000	$11,200	$7,400	$4,800

ACOUSTIC

Santa Cruz offers a wide range of custom options on their guitar models. These options include different wood for tops, back/sides, tinted and Sunburst finishes, abalone, wood, or herringbone binding, and 12-string configurations. For current option pricing, availability, or further information, please contact the Santa Cruz Guitar Company via the Index of Current Manufacturers located in the rear of this book.

All models have round soundholes with wood inlay rosettes, ivoroid body binding with wood purfling, and Natural finish (unless otherwise listed).

MODEL D — dreadnought style, Sitka spruce top, Indian rosewood back/sides, mahogany neck, 14/20 fret bound ebony fingerboard, ebony bridge with black pearl dot pins, ebony veneer on bound peghead with pearl logo inlay, 3 per side chrome Scaller tuners. Current mfr.

Mfr.'s Sug. Retail	$2,500	$1,950	$1,275	$850

12 Fret D Model — Sitka spruce top, herringbone purfling/rosette, tortoise pickguard, mahogany back/sides, 12/20 fret ebony fingerboard with pearl diamond inlay, ebony bridge with pearl dot pins, ebony veneer on slotted peghead with pearl logo inlay, 3 per side Waverly tuners. Current mfr.

Mfr.'s Sug. Retail	$3,250	$2,900	$1,850	$1,225

MODEL F — Sitka spruce top, Indian rosewood back/sides, mahogany neck, 14/21 fret bound ebony fingerboard with abalone fan inlay, ebony bridge with black pearl dot pins, ebony veneer on bound peghead with pearl logo inlay, 3 per side chrome Schaller tuners. Current mfr.

Mfr.'s Sug. Retail	$3,150	$2,500	$1,325	$950

MODEL FS — single rounded cutaway, Red cedar top, Indian rosewood back/sides, mahogany neck, 21 fret ebony fingerboard, Brazilian rosewood binding, ebony bridge with black pearl dot pins, 3 per side gold Schaller tuners with ebony buttons. Current mfr.

Mfr.'s Sug. Retail	$3,800	$3,300	$2,175	$1,425

MODEL H — Sitka spruce top, Indian rosewood back/sides, mahogany neck, 14/20 fret bound ebony fingerboard, ebony bridge with black pearl pins, ebony veneer on bound peghead, 3 per side chrome Schaller tuners with ebony buttons. Current mfr.

Mfr.'s Sug. Retail	$2,800	$2,250	$1,450	$950

Model F
courtesy Santa Cruz Guitar Co.

Grading	100%	EXCELLENT	AVERAGE

Model H A/E — spruce top, mahogany back/sides/neck, abalone top border and rosette, 21 fret ebony fingerboard with pearl/gold ring inlay, ebony bridge with black pearl dot pins, 3 per side gold Schaller tuners with ebony buttons, bridge pickup with micro drive preamp. Current mfr.

Mfr.'s Sug. Retail	$3,850	$3,100	$2,000	$1,325

MODEL PJ — parlour-size, Sitka spruce top, Indian rosewood back/sides, mahogany neck, herringbone border, 14/20 fret bound ebony fingerboard with diamond and squares inlay, ebony bridge with pearl dot bridgepins, 3 per side chrome Waverly tuners with ebony buttons. Current mfr.

Mfr.'s Sug. Retail	$3,000	$2,300	$1,500	$975

MODEL OO — similar to the Model PJ, except features a slotted peghead. Current mfr.

Mfr.'s Sug. Retail	$3,400	$2,900	$1,850	$1,225

MODEL OOO-12 — Sitka spruce top, tortoise pickguard, Indian rosewood back/sides, mahogany neck, 25.375" scale, 12/19 fret bound ebony fingerboard with pearl diamond and squares inlay, slotted headstock, ebony bridge with ebony mother of pearl dot pins, ebony peghead veneer, 3 per side Waverly W-16 tuners. Mfr. 1995 to date.

Mfr.'s Sug. Retail	$3,600	$2,900	$1,850	$1,220

MODEL OM — Sitka spruce top, tortoise pickguard, Indian rosewood back/sides, mahogany neck, 14/20 fret bound ebony fingerboard with pearl dot inlay, ebony bridge with black pearl dot pins, ebony peghead veneer, 3 per side chrome Waverly tuners. Current mfr.

Mfr.'s Sug. Retail	$3,150	$2,450	$1,600	$1,050

JANIS IAN MODEL — parlour-size with single rounded cutaway, Sitka spruce top, abalone rosette, Indian rosewood back/sides, mahogany neck, 14/20 fret bound ebony fingerboard with gold ring inlay/rude girl logo, ebony bridge with pearl dot bridgepins, 3 per side black Schaller tuners, L.R. Baggs pickup system. Available in all Black finish. Current mfr.

Mfr.'s Sug. Retail	$3,675	$2,595	$1,000	$775

TONY RICE MODEL — dreadnought style, Sitka spruce top, tortoise pickguard, herringbone bound body/rosette, Indian rosewood back/sides, mahogany neck, 14/20 fret bound ebony fingerboard with pearl logo inlay at 12th fret, Tony Rice signature on label, ebony bridge with black pearl dot pins, ebony peghead veneer, 3 per side chrome Waverly tuners. Current mfr.

Mfr.'s Sug. Retail	$3,300	$2,550	$1,675	$1,100

This model was designed in conjunction with guitarist Tony Rice.

VINTAGE ARTIST — dreadnought style, Sitka spruce top, tortoise pickguard, herringbone body trim, mahogany back/sides/neck, 14/21 fret bound ebony fingerboard with pearl dot inlay, ebony bridge with black pearl dot pins, Brazilian rosewood veneer on bound peghead with pearl logo inlay, 3 per side Waverly tuners. Current mfr.

Mfr.'s Sug. Retail	$3,100	$2,450	$1,600	$1,050

OM Model
courtesy Santa Cruz Guitar Co.

SANTA ROSA

Instruments built in Asia. Distributed by A R Musical Enterprises of Fishers, Indiana.

Santa Rosa acoustic guitars are geared more towards the entry level or student guitarist.

ED SCHAEFER

Instruments currently built in Fort Worth, Texas.

Luthier Ed Schaefer studied classical guitar in college while working as a guitar tech at R.B.I. The Rhythm Band Instrument Company was a sister company of I.M.C. (International Music Corporation - See HONDO or CHARVEL/JACKSON). Schaefer's main job was fret re-surfacing and set-ups on imported guitars that sat out on ships for too long! Schaefer's first lutherie attempt was building a classical guitar (with the guidance of Irving Sloan's guitar construction book).

In April, 1997, Schaefer attended Tom Ribbecke's Archtop "Boot Camp" to learn acoustic archtop construction. In addition to his twenty-five year career as a professional painter, Schaefer is currently building archtop guitars on a custom commissioned basis.

ACOUSTIC

Schaefer's archtop models feature AAA Sitka or Englemann spruce tops, American sycamore backs and sides, and 3-piece sycamore necks. Schaefer's professional painting backround has led him to the opinion that "Nitrocellulose lacquer - the only way" to finish guitars. Schaefer is currently constructing his archtop guitars on a custom order, commission basis. For further information regarding specifications and pricing, please contact Ed Schaefer through the Index of Current Manufacturers located in the back of this edition.

THEO SCHARPACH

Instruments built in the Netherlands since 1979.

Luthier Theo Scharpach was born in Vienna, Austria, and was originally trained in the restoration of high quality antique furniture. Scharpach currently resides in Bergeyk, the Netherlands, and has been plying his lutherie skills for over seventeen years. His current models range from classical designed nylon string guitars to more experimental 7- and 8-stringed models. Scharpach should be contacted in regard to pricing on commissioned guitar works.

All commissioned guitars are tailored to the individual player. Scharpach maintains a number of core designs such as the **SKD**, and **SKW** which feature conventional soundholes and an open-strung headstocks. The **Arch** model is a semi-acoustic designed for nylon strings, and has an onboard piezo system and microphone (as well as a High Tech class I preamp and an outboard Applied Acoustics blend box). The **Dolphin** model features a four octave fretboard, while the **Classical Guitar** has two soundholes for very good sound projection.

A true copy of the original Slemer guitar is also available. This guitar has a carved top and uses original material for sides, back, and neck. This model is played by the famous French gypsy player Raphael Fays. Also available are Baritone and Twelve string guitars. The Twelve string has a special headstock construction and double top and second bridge built inside to reduce string tension while adding bass to the guitar. New this year is the nylon string jazz guitar, the **TearDrop**. This model has a flat top and great curly maple carved back.

Schaefer Archtop
courtesy Edward Schaefer

Scharpach Blue Vienna
courtesy Scott Chinery

As the only European guitarmaker invited to deliver a contribution to the famous "Blue Guitar" collection of Scott Chinery, Scharpach's **Blue Vienna** was noted for its massive silver carved coverplate and beautiful handmade titanium tuning machines.

All guitars are made by hand by the master himself. This leads to a small production each year, but the attention to detail results in unique, beautiful instruments. For further information (and nice pictures), take a look at the Patrick van Gerwen site on the internet (www.iaehv.nl/users/pvg1/ts.html).

TIM SCHEERHORN

Instruments built in Kentwood, Michigan since 1989. Instruments are available through Scheerhorn or Elderly Instruments of Lansing, Michigan.

Luthier Tim Scheerhorn has background training as a tool and die maker, a tool engineer, and is a specialist in process automation for manufacturing. In the past, his hobbies generally involved rebuilding something - either boats or classic cars. But in 1986, Scheerhorn picked up a resonator guitar and later found himself immersed in the world of custom guitar building.

Although Scheerhorn did have prior experience setting up banjos and resonator guitars for other players, he had never built a musical instrument from scratch. He did possess a new OMI Dobro, and a Regal from the 1930s. In February of 1989, Scheerhorn began building guitars based on the Regal model and his own innovations. In the summer of 1989 the guitar was tested by Mike Auldridge (Seldom Scene) at the Winterhawk festival in New York. Encouraged by Auldridge's enthusiasm, Scheerhorn returned to his workshop and continued building.

Scheerhorn limits production to 3 or 4 instruments a month. All guitars are handbuilt by Scheerhorn.

ACOUSTIC

Both Scheerhorn models share the same revised resonator design. The resonators are built of bright chrome plated brass, Spun Quarterman cone, and a spider bridge of aluminum. The bridge insert is made of hard maple with ebony tops. Both models also feature chrome Schaller M-6 tuning machines.

The **Curly Maple Regal Body** model ($2,450) has a bookmatched solid curly Maple top, with matching sides and back. The three piece neck consists of Curly Maple and Walnut, and has a 19 fret ebony fingerboard. The body and neck are bound in either an ivoroid or dark tortoise (natural blond finish), and finished in hand-rubbed lacquer. The **Curly Maple Large Body** model has similar specifications, but with a larger body size (longer, deeper, wider) for additional volume and projection (list $2,650).

The **Mahogany/Spruce Regal Body** model ($2,450) has a book-matched quartersawn Sitka Spruce top, solid mahogany back and sides, and a two piece mahogany neck. The **Mahogany/Spruce Large Body** model has similar specifications, but with a larger body size for additional volume and projection (list $2,650).

Scheerhorn also builds a Weissenborn Style Reissue dubbed the **"Scheerhorn Hawaiian"** ($2,500). The body is constructed out of solid Figured Koa (top, back, and sides), and the peghead has a Curly Maple overlay. The bridge is cocobolo with a bone saddle, and the cocobolo fingerboard has Curly Maple binding and abalone inlays. This model also features Kluson style tuners, a built in McIntyre pickup, and a hand-rubbed lacquer finish.

Scheerhorn's newest model in the **Acoustic/Electric** (list $1,875), which features solid curly maple top/back/sides and neck, ebony fingerboard with flush frets, a 9" Quarterman cone and National-style coverplate, a Seymour Duncan mini-humbucker/McIntyre transducer pickups (with volume and tone for each system) and a 3-way selector switch. This model is wired for stero.

RICHARD SCHNEIDER

Instruments formerly built in Washington State, and other locations. Distributed by the Lost Mountain Center for the Guitar of Carlsborg, Washington.

In 1996, when luthier/designer Richard Schneider was asked what he considered his occupation, he simply replied, "I don't make guitars, I make guitar makers". While known for his Kasha-inspired acoustic guitar designs, Schneider also trained and encouraged younger builders to continue crafting guitars. At last count, some 21 full term apprentices had been taught in the craft of classical guitar design. Schneider is best known for his over 25 year collaboration with Dr. Michael Kasha, in their advanced design for the classical guitar. Kasha, the Director of Institue of Molecular Biophysics at Florida State University, worked with Schneider to pioneer an entirely new and scientific way of designing and constructing classical guitars. This advanced design has been the topic of controversy for a number of years in the classical guitar community.

Schneider first apprenticed with Juan Pimentel in Mexico City, Mexico from 1963 to 1965. Schneider served as proprietor of **Estudio be las Guitarra** from 1965 to 1972, which housed a guitar making workshop, retail store and music instruction studio. It was during this time period that Schneider began his collaboration with Dr. Kasha. In 1973, Schneider became the director and owner of the Studio of Richard Schneider in Kalamazoo, Michigan. This studio was devoted solely to classical guitar design and fine construction using the Kasha/Schneider design. Schneider was a consultant to the Gibson Guitar company between 1973 to 1978. His duties included design, engineering, and production procedures for the **Mark** series guitars, which was based on the Kasha/Schneider design. He also designed the **The Les Paul** electric guitar model. In 1983, Schneider also engineered and built five **Taxi** prototypes for Silver Street, Inc. of Elkhart, Indiana.

In 1984, Schneider moved his family and workshop to Sequim, Washington. The Lost Mountain Center for the Guitar was founded in 1986 as a non-profit organization whose purposes include research, development, and information disseminating about improvements in guitar design. Schneider continued to make improvements to his Kasha/Schneider design, which made significant improvements to the tonal functions and playability. Luthier Richard Schneider passed away in January, 1997.

(Biography courtesy Bob Fischer, Lost Mountain Center)

Schneider estimated that he constructed over 200 guitars by 1996. Approximately 60 were handcrafted traditional concert guitars, while 50 models were the advanced Schneider/Kasha design. Rather than assign a serial number to his guitars, Schneider used to name them instead.

In addition to his own guitar designs, Schneider assumed that he had built over 100 prototypes for the Gibson Guitar company, and Baldwin-era Gretsches.

Schneider met with Maestro Andres Segovia on 18 separate occasions, and auditioned new instruments with Segovia on 6 of these visits for purposes of critique and analysis. After Segovia passed away, Schneider then consulted with guitarist Kurt Rodarmer, whose new CD The Goldberg Variations features two of Schneider's guitars.

ERIC SCHOENBERG

Instruments built in Nazareth, Pennsylvania from 1985 to 1996. Shoenberg Guitars set up a new, separate production facility in Massachusetts in 1997.

Eric Schoenberg is regarded as one of the finest ragtime and fingerstyle guitarists of the last twenty years. While operating out of the Music Emporium in Massachusetts, Schoenberg released a number of high quality acoustic guitars that were built in conjunction with the C.F. Martin company of Nazareth, Pennsylvania, and individually finished by either Schoenberg or luthier Dana Bourgeois. The Martin facilities assembled the bodies, then final touches were controlled by Schoenberg and Bourgeois. Luthier Bourgeois was involved in the project from 1986 to mid 1990. Luthier T.J. Thompson worked with Schoenberg from the mid 1990s until 1995. In 1997, Shoenberg Guitars began setting up a production facility in Massachusetts run by Julius Borges.

ACOUSTIC

Schoenberg debuted the **Soloist** model in the late 1980s. The Soloist was a modern version of a Martin OM-style acoustic, and featured top grade woods originally overseen by Bourgeois. The Soloist model featured a European spruce top, Brazilian back and sides, a one piece mahogany neck, 20 fret ebony fingerboard with diamond shaped pearl inlays, and Kluson-styled Grover tuning machines. Retail list price back in the late 1980s was $2,850 (which seems more than reasonable now!).

SHELDON SCHWARTZ

Instruments currently built in Toronto (Ontario), Canada.

Luthier Sheldon Schwartz currently offers high quality handcrafted acoustic guitars that are immaculately constructed. Schwartz began working on guitars at fifteen, and has had lutherie associations with such builders as Grit Laskin and Linda Manzer. In 1992, Schwartz began building full time, and attended vintage guitar shows to display his work.

ACOUSTIC

Schwartz prefers working with the top quality, master grade woods that generally don't show up in the large production factories, and matches back, sides, tops, and necks for both appearance and tonal qualities. Depending on the commission, Schwartz also works in other woods such as Engelmann spruce, Bearclaw Sitka spruce, and Brazilian Rosewood; and will negotiate rates on custom inlay work.

Add $250 for Curly Maple back and sides.

Add $350 for Venetian (rounded) cutaway.

Add $550 for Curly Koa back and sides.

Schwartz Custom Acoustic
courtesy Sheldon Schwartz

BASIC MODEL SIX STRING — dreadnought style, Sitka spruce top, dovetail mahogany neck, 25 1/2" scale, bound ebony fingerboard with two abalone dots at 12th fret, East Indian back and sides, abalone rosette, rosewood binding/heelcap/headstock veneer, mitered top/back purfling, ebony bridge, solid Spanish cedar lining, bone nut and saddle, brass dot side postition markers, 3 per side Schaller M6 tuning machines. With Natural high gloss nitrocellulose finish. Current mfr.

Mfr.'s Sug. Retail $2,500

Price includes hardshell case.

This model has a 16 1/8" lower bout. A clear Mylar pickguard is available on request.

Basic Model Plus — similar to the Basic Model Six String, except features hand picked, color matched abalone top purfling. Current mfr.

Mfr.'s Sug. Retail $3,150

Limited Edition Model — similar to the Basic Model Six string, except has 130 year old birdseye maple back and sides, *reclaimed* salmon trap soundboard, brazilian rosewood fingerboard, bridge, binding, and front and back headstock veneers, gold tuners, gold mother of pearl 12 fret position marker, and color matched abalone top purfling. Current mfr.

Mfr.'s Sug. Retail $4,300

Price includes Carlton fiberglass case.

SEAGULL GUITARS

Instruments built in La Patrie, Quebec, Canada since 1980. Seagull Acoustic Guitars are distributed by La Si Do, Inc., of St. Laurent, Canada.

In 1968 Robert Godin set up a custom guitar shop in Montreal called Harmonilab. Harmonilab quickly became known for its excellent work and musicians were coming from as far away as Quebec City to have their guitars adjusted.

Although Harmonilab's business was flourishing, Robert was full of ideas for the design and construction of acoustic guitars. So in 1972 the **Norman Guitar Company** was born. From the beginning the Norman guitars showed signs of the innovations that Godin would eventually bring to the guitar market. By 1978 Norman guitars had become quite successful in Canada and France.

In 1980 Godin introduced the Seagull guitar. With many innovations like a bolt-on neck (for consistent neck pitch), pointed headstock (straight string pull) and a handmade solid top, the Seagull was designed for an ease of play for the entry level to intermediate guitar player. Most striking was the satin lacquer finish. Godin borrowed the finishing idea that was used on fine violins, and applied it to the acoustic guitar. When the final version of the Seagull guitar went into production, Godin went about the business of finding a sales force to help introduce the Seagull into the U.S. market. Several independent U.S. sales agents jumped at the chance to get involved with this new guitar, and armed with samples, off they went into the market. A couple of months passed, and not one guitar was sold. Rather than retreat back to Harmonilab, Godin decided that he would have to get out there himself and explain the Seagull guitar concept. So he bought himself an old Ford Econoline van and stuffed it full of about 85 guitars, and started driving through New England visiting guitar shops and introducing the Seagull guitar. Acceptance of this new guitar spread, and by 1985 La Si Do was incorporated and the factory in La Patrie expanded to meet the growing demand.

For full company history, see GODIN.

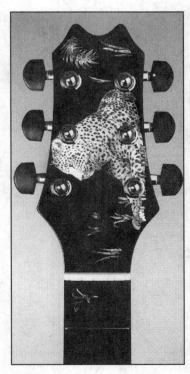

Headstock Detail
courtesy Sheldon Schwartz

Grading	100%	EXCELLENT	AVERAGE

ACOUSTIC

GRAND ARTIST (Model 10561) — solid spruce top, black pickguard, round soundhole, multi-stripe rosette, solid rosewood back, laminated rosewood sides, Honduran mahogany neck, 25 11/32" scale, 14/21 fret rosewood fingerboard with pearl dot inlay, bound headstock, rosewood bridge with white bridgepins, 3 per side chrome tuners. Available in Natural high gloss lacquer finish. Mfd. 1993 to date.

Mfr.'s Sug. Retail	$995	$795	$525	$350

This model is designed to be a modern version of a "turn of the century" parlor guitar.

S 6 (Model 10257) — dreadnought style bound body, solid cedar top, black pickguard, round soundhole, multistripe rosette, wild cherry back/sides, mahogany neck, 14/21 fret rosewood fingerboard with pearl dot inlay, rosewood bridge with white black dot pins, blackface peghead with screened logo, 3 per side chrome tuners. Available in Natural finish. Mfd. 1993 to date.

Mfr.'s Sug. Retail	$395	$296	$155	$125

This model has single round cutaway (Model 2214), or left-handed version (Model 10288).

S 12 — similar to S 6, except has 12 strings, 6 per side tuners. Disc. 1998.

		$225	$125

Last Mfr.'s Sug. Retail was $450.

S 6 DELUXE — dreadnought style bound body, solid spruce top, black pickguard, round soundhole, multistripe rosette, wild cherry back/sides, mahogany neck, 14/21 fret rosewood fingerboard with pearl dot inlay, rosewood bridge with white black dot pins, blackface peghead with screened logo, 3 per side chrome tuners. Available in Honeyburst and Natural finishes. Disc. 1998.

		$225	$125

Last Mfr.'s Sug. Retail was $435.

This model has single round cutaway or left-hand version optionally available.

S 12 Deluxe — similar to S 6 Deluxe, except has 12 strings, 6 per side tuners. Disc. 1998.

		$225	$150

Last Mfr.'s Sug. Retail was $495.

S 6 MAHOGANY (Model 1767) — dreadnought style bound body, solid cedar top, black pickguard, round soundhole, multistripe rosette, mahogany back/sides/neck, 14/21 fret rosewood fingerboard with pearl dot inlay, rosewood bridge with white black dot pins, blackface peghead with screened logo, 3 per side chrome tuners. Available in Natural finish. Current mfr.

Mfr.'s Sug. Retail	$450	$350	$175	$125

This model has left-handed version optionally available (Model 1804).

Performance Series

S 6 FLAME MAPLE CUTAWAY (Model 2375) — round cutaway dreadnought style bound body, solid spruce top, round-soundhole, herringbone rosette, maple back/sides, mahogany neck, 21 fret ebony fingerboard with offset dot inlay, ebony bridge with white black dot pins, bound flame maple veneered peghead with screened logo, 3 per side gold tuners. Available in Blackburst and Natural finishes. Current mfr.

Mfr.'s Sug. Retail	$895	$695	$375	$275

S 6 Flame Maple Micro EQ (Model 2399) — similar to S 6 Flame Maple, except features piezo bridge pickup, onboard EQ. Current mfr.

Mfr.'s Sug. Retail	$1,084	$795	$550	$425

SM 6 (Model 1927) — round cutaway dreadnought style bound body, solid spruce top, black pickguard, round soundhole, multistripe rosette, mahogany back/sides/neck, 14/21 fret rosewood fingerboard with pearl dot inlay, rosewood bridge with white black dot pins, blackface peghead with screened logo, 3 per side chrome tuners. Available in Natural finish. Current mfr.

Mfr.'s Sug. Retail	$537	$425	$250	$175

SM 12 (Model 1972) — similar to SM 6, 12 strings, 6 per side tuners. Current mfr.

Mfr.'s Sug. Retail	$620	$495	$250	$200

SEBRING

Instruments currently built in Korea. Distributed by V.M.I. Industries of Brea, California.

Sebring instruments are designed towards the intermediate level guitar student. For further information, contact V.M.I. Industries through the Index of Current Manufacturers located in the rear of this book.

SEDONA

Instruments currently built in Asia. Distributed by V M I Industries of Brea, California.

Sedona offers a range of instruments that appeal to the beginning guitarist and entry level player. For further information, contact V M I Industries through the Index of Current Manufacturers located in the back of this book.

SEGOVIA

Instruments produced in Asia. Distributed by the L.A. Guitar Works of Reseda, California.

Segovia acoustic dreadnought guitars are offered with solid headstocks, spruce tops, and 3 per side chrome tuning machines. Available in Natural Spruce or Spruce Sunburst finishes. List price is $225.

SEKOVA

Instruments produced in Japan.

Sekova brand instruments were distributed in the U.S. market by the U.S. Musical Merchandise Corporation of New York, New York.

(Source: Michael Wright, Guitar Stories Volume One)

HENRI SELMER & CO.

Instruments built in Paris, France between 1931 to 1952.

Between 1931 and 1932, Mario Maccaferri designed and built a series of instruments for the French Selmer company. They were originally referred to as the "modele Concert", and featured a "D" shaped soundhole. Although they were used by such notables as Django Reinhardt, a dispute between the company and Maccaferri led to a short production run. In the two years (1931-1932) that Maccaferri was with Selmer, he estimated that perhaps 200 guitars were built. After Macaferri left the business arrangement, the Selmer company continued to produce acoustic guitar models that featured an oval soundhole and a longer scale. All in all, an estimated 950 guitars were built.

(Source: Paul Hostetter, Guitares Maurice Dupont)

SEXAUER

Instruments hand-built in Vancouver (British Columbia), Canada from 1967 through 1977, and in Sausalito, California since 1979.

Luthier Bruce Sexauer has been handcrafting contemporary flat-top acoustic guitars since 1967. For the last several years, Sexauer has become increasingly interested in Archtop guitars, and in addition to his quality carved tops has become well known for his highly innovative **Coo'stik Dominator** (a successful interpretation of the Selmer/Macaferri concept).

While Sexauer continues to build true custom guitars, he also offers several standard models. The noted prices represent the simplest trim level, and most customers choose to indulge themselves somewhat more. The FT-15 ($1,950) is a concert sized flat-top model, while the FT-16 ($2,175) is full sized. Sexauer offers a jazz-style hand carved archtop model in both a 16" body width (JZ-16) at $4,200, and 17" body width (JZ-17) for $4,650. His Coo'stik Dominator has a list price of $3,500.

SHANTI

Instruments currently built in Avery, California.

Luthier Michael Hornick has been handcrafting acoustic guitars under the **Shanti** trademark for the past several years. All guitars are designed with input from the commissioning player, so specifications on woods and inlay work will vary. Contact Michael Hornick for further details.

Hornick produces about 9 or 10 guitars a year. In addition, Hornick hosts a mandolin-building course each year at the RockyGrass Festival in Lyons, Colorado; and has been affiliated with the Troubadour singer/songwriter competition in Telluride, Colorado for a good number of years.

SHENANDOAH

Instruments assembled from imported Japanese components in Nazareth, Pennsylvania between 1983 to 1996. Distributed by the C. F. Martin Guitar Company of Nazarath, Pennsylvania.

Shenandoah production began in 1983. Initially viewed as a way to offer *entry-level* models for Martin dealers, Shenandoah models featured Japanese-built unfinished body and neck kits imported to the Martin plant for final assembly and finishing. However, Shenandoah guitars are not as ornate, and may feature different construction methods than the Martin models.

While this may have been cost effective to some degree, the labor intensive work of assembly and finishing at the Martin plant led Martin to considering producing the whole guitar in Nazareth - which led to the introduction of Martin's U.S.-built **Road** and **1** Series.

Instruments were produced in Japan and assembled in the U.S. between 1983 to 1993; full Japanese production was featured between 1994 to 1996. Shenandoah model codes add a -32 suffix after a Martin-style model designation. Thus, a D-1832 is Shenandoah's version of a D-18. Models carrying a CS prefix designation indicate a custom model, usually fancier than the standard version (custom models were built in limited runs of 25 instruments).

ACOUSTIC

Some models have a factory installed thinline bridge pickup. Most models feature a tortoiseshell pickguard, and laminated back/sides.

C-20 — classic style, solid spruce top, round soundhole, wooden bound body, wooden inlay rosette, rosewood back/sides, nato neck, 12/19 fret ebonized rosewood fingerboard, ebonized rosewood tied bridge, rosewood peghead veneer, 3 per side gold tuners with pearl buttons. Available in Natural and Yellow Stained Top finishes.

$535 $370
Last Mfr.'s Sug. Retail was $1,280.

This model had no factory installed pickup.

D-1832 — dreadnought style, solid spruce top, round soundhole, tortoise pickguard, 3 stripe bound body/rosette, mahogany back/sides, nato neck, 14/20 fret rosewood fingerboard with pearl dot inlay, rosewood bridge with black pins, rosewood peghead veneer, 3 per side chrome tuners. Available in Natural finish.

$450 $250
Last Mfr.'s Sug. Retail was $1,075.

Shenandoah C-20
courtesy The Martin Guitar Company

Grading	100%	EXCELLENT	AVERAGE

Shenandoah SE-2832
courtesy The Martin Guitar Company

D-1932 — similar to D-1832, except has quilted mahogany veneer back/sides.

	$620	**$425**

Add $20 for twelve string version (D12-1932).

Last Mfr.'s Sug. Retail was $1,320.

D-2832 — dreadnought style, solid spruce top, round soundhole, tortoise pickguard, 3 stripe bound body/rosette, rosewood back/sides, nato neck, 14/20 fret ebonized rosewood fingerboard with pearl dot inlay, ebonized rosewood bridge with white black dot pins, rosewood peghead veneer, 3 per side chrome tuners. Available in Natural finish.

	$550	**$350**

Add $75 for 12 string version of this model (D12-2832).

Last Mfr.'s Sug. Retail was $1,125.

HD-2832 — similar to D-2832, except has herringbone purfling.

	$600	**$400**

D-3532 — similar to D-2832, except has bound fingerboard.

	$550	**$400**

Last Mfr.'s Sug. Retail was $1,175.

D-4132 — similar to D-2832, except has abalone bound body/rosette, bound fingerboard with abalone hexagon inlay, white abalone dot bridge pins, bound peghead, gold tuners.

	$780	**$575**

Last Mfr.'s Sug. Retail was $1,750.

D-6032 — similar to D-2832, tortoise binding, except has birdseye maple back/sides.

	$525	**$365**

Last Mfr.'s Sug. Retail was $1,320.

D-6732 — dreadnought style body, solid spruce top, round soundhole, tortoise pickguard, tortoise binding, 3 stripe rosette, quilted ash back/sides, nato neck, 14/20 fret bound ebonized rosewood neck with pearl dot inlay, pearl vine/diamond inlay at 12th fret, ebonized rosewood bridge with white black dot pins, bound peghead with quilted ash veneer, 3 per side gold tuners with ebony buttons. Available in Natural finish.

	$625	**$480**

Last Mfr.'s Sug. Retail was $1,490.

SE-2832 — single round cutaway folk style, solid spruce top, round soundhole, 3 stripe bound body/rosette, rosewood back/sides, nato neck, 14/21 fret bound ebonized rosewood fingerboard with pearl diamond inlay, ebonized rosewood bridge with white black dot pins, rosewood veneer peghead, 3 per side chrome tuners, active EQ with volume/treble/mid/bass slider control. Available in Natural and Sunburst Top finishes.

	$600	**$460**

Last Mfr.'s Sug. Retail was $1,470.

SE-6032 — similar to SE-2832, except has tortoise binding, birdseye maple back/sides/peghead veneer, pearl tuner buttons. Available in Burgundy Burst, Dark Sunburst and Natural finishes.

	$660	**$520**

Last Mfr.'s Sug. Retail was $1,540.

000-2832 — folk style, solid spruce top, round soundhole, tortoise shell pickguard, 3 stripe bound body/rosette, rosewood back/sides, nato neck, 14/20 fret ebonized rosewood fingerboard with pearl dot inlay, ebonized rosewood bridge with white black dot pins, rosewood peghead veneer with abalone torch inlay, 3 per side chrome tuners. Available in Natural finish.

	$550	**$350**

Last Mfr.'s Sug. Retail was $1,210.

SHERWOOD

See chapter on House Brands.

This trademark has been identified as a *House Brand* of Montgomery Wards.

(Source: Willie G. Moseley, Stellas & Stratocasters)

SHO-BUD

Also SHO-BRO.

Instruments built in the U.S. during circa early 1970s. Distributed through the Gretsch Guitar company catalog between 1972 to 1975; possibly as late as 1979.

While this company is best known for their pedal steel guitars, the company did produce a number of acoustic guitars. Sho-Bud and Sho-Bro guitars were designed by Shot Jackson (known for his Sho-Bud pedal steel guitars). Two models appear in the Gretsch catalogs of the early 1970s: The **Sho Bro**, a resonator with a single cutaway body and dot fingerboard inlays; and the **Sho Bud**, a non-cutaway model with inlays similar to the Sho-Bud lap steels (the four suits of the card deck).

(Information courtesy John Brinkmann, Waco Vintage Instruments; and John Sheridan)

ACOUSTIC

Sho-Bro resonator guitars in the early 1970s featured a 17" body (4 5/8" body depth) with maple back and sides, bound rosewood fingerboard, 3 per side polished plated geared tuners, metal resonator, 2 grill covered soundholes. The **Model 6031 Hawaiian** model has a squared neck, and playing card suites fingerboard inlays; the **Model 6030 Spanish** model has a rounded neck and "thumbprint" fingerboard inlays.

Later Sho-Bud acoustics have spruce tops and mahogany necks. The **Club (Model 7720)** features mahogany sides, and a 2-piece back; the **Diamond (Model 7722)** features rosewood sides and the 2-piece back. The **Heart (Model 7724)** has rosewood back and sides, mother-of-pearl inlays, and abalone purfling; the **Spade (Model 7726)** features a rosewood fingerboard, ebony bridge, and abalone bridge pins. The aptly named **Grand Slam (Model 7728)** has jacaranda back and sides, and an inlaid heel plate.

Grading	100%	EXCELLENT	AVERAGE

Sho-Bud and Sho-Bro acoustic guitars turn up infrequently at guitar shows. Average prices run from $800 to $1,200; buyers in the market have more control in the buy/sell arena by choking up on their wallets similar to big league baseball players choking up on their bats during a big ball game!

SHUTT

Instruments built in Topeka, Kansas circa 1900s.

While not much information is known about the Shutt instruments, Mr. Jim Reynolds of Independence, Missouri is currently researching materials for an upcoming book. Interested persons can contact Mr. Reynolds through the **Blue Book of Guitars**.

SIGMA

Instruments initially assembled in Asia, with final finishing/inspection in Nazareth, Pennsylvania. Distributed by the C. F. Martin Guitar Company of Nazareth, Pennsylvania.

In 1970, the Martin Guitar Company expanded its product line by introducing the Sigma line. The instruments begin their assembly in Japan, and then are shipped in to Pennsylvania where the Martin company can oversee the final finishing and setup. Sigma guitars are great introductory models to the classic Martin design.

(Source: Michael Wright, Guitar Stories Volume One)

ACOUSTIC

2 Series

CS-2 — classic style, spruce top, round soundhole, bound body, wooden inlay rosette, mahogany back/sides/neck, 20/19 fret ebonized fingerboard/tied bridge, 3 per side chrome tuners. Available in Natural finish. Disc. 1994.

$115 $80
Last Mfr.'s Sug. Retail was $295.

DM-2 — dreadnought style, spruce top, round soundhole, tortoise shell pickguard, 3 stripe bound body/rosette, mahogany back/sides/neck, 14/20 fret rosewood fingerboard with pearl dot inlay, rosewood bridge with black white dot pins, 3 per side chrome tuners. Available in Natural finish. Disc. 1994.

$140 $100

     Add $45 for 12 string version **(DM12-2)**.

Last Mfr.'s Sug. Retail was $375.

DM-2E/WH — similar to DM-2, except has ebonized fingerboard/bridge, acoustic pickup, 3 band EQ with volume control. Available in White finish. Disc. 1994.

$260 $175

     Add $25 for single round cutaway, white black dot bridge pins. Available in Black finish (DM-2CEB).

Last Mfr.'s Sug. Retail was $630.

DR-2 — similar to DM-2, except has rosewood back/sides, ebonized fingerboard/bridge. Disc. 1994.

$190 $150
Last Mfr.'s Sug. Retail was $510.

GCS-2 — similar to DM-2, except has grand concert style body. Disc. 1994.

$175 $100
Last Mfr.'s Sug. Retail was $420.

Marquis Series

This series was introduced in 1987.

CS-1 — classic style, spruce top, round soundhole, bound body, wooden inlay rosette, mahogany back/sides/neck, 20/19 fret ebonized fingerboard/tied bridge, 3 per side chrome tuners. Available in Antique Stain finish. Disc. 1996.

$75 $50
Last Mfr.'s Sug. Retail was $210.

DM-1 — dreadnought style, spruce top, round soundhole, black pickguard, bound body, 3 stripe rosette, mahogany back/sides/neck, 14/20 fret ebonized fingerboard with pearl dot inlay, ebonized bridge with black pins, 3 per side chrome tuners. Available in Natural finish. Disc. 1996.

$100 $65
Last Mfr.'s Sug. Retail was $260.

     Add $25 for 12 string version **(DM12-1)**.

FDM-1 — similar to DM-1, except has folk style body. Mfr. 1994 to 1996.

$100 $60
Last Mfr.'s Sug. Retail was $255.

GCS-1 — similar to DM-1, except has grand concert style body. Disc. 1996.

$100 $65
Last Mfr.'s Sug. Retail was $260.

CS-4 — classic style, spruce top, round soundhole, bound body, wooden inlay rosette, mahogany back/sides/neck, 12/19 fret rosewood fingerboard, rosewood tied bridge, rosewood peghead veneer, 3 per side chrome tuners with pearl buttons. Available in Antique finish. Disc. 1996.

$140 $85
Last Mfr.'s Sug. Retail was $340.

Sigma DR-41
courtesy The Martin Guitar Company

Sigma DM12-1
courtesy The Martin Guitar Company

Sigma DT-4N
courtesy The Martin Guitar Company

Grading	100%	EXCELLENT	AVERAGE

DM-4 — dreadnought style, spruce top, round soundhole, black pickguard, 3 stripe bound body/rosette, mahogany back/sides/neck, 14/20 fret ebonized fingerboard with pearl dot inlay, pearl horizontal teardrop inlay at 12th fret, ebonized bridge with black white dot pins, rosewood peghead veneer, 3 per side chrome tuners. Available in Black and Natural finishes. Disc. 1996.

		$170	$115
			Last Mfr.'s Sug. Retail was $430.

Add $30 for Black finish.
Add $40 for 12 string version (**DM12-4**).
Add $40 for left handed version (**DM-4L**).
Subtract $20 for stained mahogany top (**DM-4M**).
Add $45 for herringbone bound body/rosette (**DM-4H**).
Add $45 for Antique and Tobacco Sunburst finishes (**DM-4Y** and **DM-4S**).

In 1994, Antique finish (DM-4Y) was discontinued.

DM-4C — similar to DM-4, except has single round cutaway. Mfr. 1994 to 1996.

		$200	$140
			Last Mfr.'s Sug. Retail was $505.

Add $45 for Black finish.

DM-4CV — similar to DM-4, except has venetian cutaway. Available in Violin finish.

		$185	$120
			Last Mfr.'s Sug. Retail was $560.

DM-4C/3B — similar to DM-4, except has single round cutaway, acoustic pickup, 3 band EQ with volume control. Available in Natural finish. Disc. 1994.

		$300	$235
			Last Mfr.'s Sug. Retail was $715.

DM12-4 — similar to DM-4, except has 12 strings, 6 per side tuners. Mfr. 1994 to 1996.

		$185	$120
			Last Mfr.'s Sug. Retail was $470.

DR-4H — similar to DM-4, except has tortoise pickguard, herringbone bound body/rosette, rosewood back/sides. Available in Natural finish.

		$200	$145
			Last Mfr.'s Sug. Retail was $510.

DT-4N — similar to DM-4, except has chestnut back/sides/peghead veneer. Available in Violin finish.

		$200	$140
			Last Mfr.'s Sug. Retail was $495.

Add $35 for Violin finish (**DT-4**).
Add $75 for 12 string version (**DT12-4**).

DV-4 — similar to DM-4, except has ovankol back/sides. Available in Antique finish. Disc. 1994.

		$195	$145
			Last Mfr.'s Sug. Retail was $595.

GCS-4 — grand concert style, spruce top, round soundhole, black pickguard, 5 stripe bound body/rosette, mahogany back/sides/neck, 14/20 fret ebonized fingerboard with pearl dot inlay, horizontal teardrop inlay at 12th fret, ebonized bridge with black white dot pins, rosewood peghead veneer, 3 per side chrome tuners. Available in Natural finish. Disc. 1996.

		$160	$100
			Last Mfr.'s Sug. Retail was $395.

GCS-4C — similar to GCS-4, except has single round cutaway. Disc. 1994.

		$200	$140
			Last Mfr.'s Sug. Retail was $550.

GCS-4C/3B — similar to GCS-4, except has single round cutaway, acoustic pickup, 3 band EQ with volume control. Disc. 1994.

		$300	$235
			Last Mfr.'s Sug. Retail was $715.

Studio Series (formerly the Generation III Series)

CS-1 ST — classic style, solid spruce top, round soundhole, bound body, wood inlay rosette, mahogany back/sides/neck, 14/19 fret ebonized fingerboard, ebonized tied bridge, 3 per side chrome tuners with nylon buttons. Available in Natural finish. Mfd. 1994 to 1996.

		$135	$85
			Last Mfr.'s Sug. Retail was $335.

CR-8 — classic style, solid spruce top, round soundhole, bound body, wooden inlay rosette, rosewood back/sides, mahogany neck, 12/19 fret ebonized fingerboard/tied bridge, 3 per side gold tuners with pearl buttons. Available in Natural finish. Disc. 1996.

		$215	$145
			Last Mfr.'s Sug. Retail was $570.

DM-1 ST — dreadnought style, solid spruce top, round soundhole, tortoise pickguard, 3 stripe bound body/rosette, mahogany back/sides/neck, 14/20 fret ebonized fingerboard with pearl dot inlay, ebonized bridge with black white dot pins, abalone logo peghead inlay, 3 per side chrome tuners. Available in Natural finish. Mfd. 1994 to 1996.

		$145	$85
			Last Mfr.'s Sug. Retail was $345.

Sigma CS-1 ST
courtesy The Martin Guitar Company

Grading	100%	EXCELLENT	AVERAGE

DR-1 ST — similar to DM-1 ST, except has rosewood back/sides. Mfd. 1994 to 1996.

$140 $85
Last Mfr.'s Sug. Retail was $375.

DM12-1 ST — similar to DM-1 ST, except has 12 strings, 6 per side tuners. Mfd. 1994 to 1996.

$185 $135
Last Mfr.'s Sug. Retail was $410.

DM-18 — dreadnought style, solid spruce top, round soundhole, tortoise pickguard, 3 stripe bound body/rosette, mahogany back/sides/neck, 14/20 fret ebonized fingerboard with pearl dot inlay, ebonized bridge with black white dot pins, abalone logo peghead inlay, 3 per side chrome tuners. Available in Natural finish. Disc. 1996.

$225 $150
Last Mfr.'s Sug. Retail was $525.

DR-28 — dreadnought style, solid spruce top, round soundhole, tortoise shell pickguard, 3 stripe bound body/rosette, rosewood back/sides, mahogany neck, 14/20 fret ebonized fingerboard with pearl dot inlay, ebonized bridge with white abalone dot pins, rosewood veneered peghead with abalone logo inlay, 3 per side chrome tuners. Available in Natural finish. Disc. 1996.

$275 $200
Last Mfr.'s Sug. Retail was $620.

DR-28H — similar to DR-28, except has herringbone bound body, pearl diamond fingerboard inlay.

$300 $215
Last Mfr.'s Sug. Retail was $670.

Add $35 for 12 string version (**DR12-28H**). Mfd. 1993 to 1996.

DR-35 — dreadnought style, solid spruce top, round soundhole, tortoise shell pickguard, 5 stripe bound body/rosette, rosewood back/sides, mahogany neck, 14/20 fret bound ebonized fingerboard with pearl dot inlay, ebonized bridge with white abalone dot pins, bound rosewood veneered peghead with abalone logo inlay, 3 per side chrome tuners. Available in Natural finish. Disc. 1996.

$300 $215
Last Mfr.'s Sug. Retail was $655.

DR-41 — dreadnought style, solid spruce top, round soundhole, tortoise shell pickguard, abalone bound body/rosette, rosewood back/sides, mahogany neck, 14/20 fret bound ebonized fingerboard with abalone hexagon inlay, ebonized bridge with white abalone dot pins, bound rosewood veneered peghead with abalone logo inlay, 3 per side chrome tuners. Available in Natural finish. Disc. 1996.

$315 $225
Last Mfr.'s Sug. Retail was $725.

DR-45 — dreadnought style, solid spruce top, round soundhole, tortoise shell pickguard, abalone bound body/rosette, rosewood back/sides, mahogany neck, 14/20 fret abalone bound rosewood fingerboard with abalone hexagon inlay, rosewood bridge with white abalone dot pins, abalone bound rosewood veneered peghead with abalone logo inlay, 3 per side gold tuners. Available in Natural finish. Mfd. 1994 to 1996.

$760 $600
Last Mfr.'s Sug. Retail was $1,745.

Sigma DR-28 H
courtesy The Martin Guitar Company

FD-16M — folk style, spruce top, round soundhole, black pickguard, bound body, 3 stripe rosette, mahogany back/sides/neck, 14/20 fret ebonized fingerboard with pearl dot inlay, ebonized bridge with black pins, 3 per side chrome tuners. Available in Natural finish. Mfd. 1994 to 1996.

$180 $115
Last Mfr.'s Sug. Retail was $460.

000-18M — auditorium style, solid spruce top, round soundhole, tortoise pickguard, 3 stripe bound body, 5 stripe rosette, mahogany back/sides/neck, 14/20 fret ebonized fingerboard with pearl dot inlay, ebonized bridge with black white dot pins, rosewood peghead veneer with abalone logo inlay, 3 per side chrome tuners. Available in Antique finish. Mfd. 1993 to 1996.

$215 $135
Last Mfr.'s Sug. Retail was $525.

000-18MC/3B — similar to 000-18M, except has venetian cutaway, acoustic pickup, 3 band EQ with volume control. Disc. 1994.

$320 $240
Last Mfr.'s Sug. Retail was $940.

ACOUSTIC BASS

STB-M/E — jumbo style, spruce top, round soundhole, tortoise pickguard, 5 stripe bound body/rosette, maple back/sides/neck, 15/21 fret ebonized fingerboard with pearl dot inlay, ebonized strings through bridge with pearl dot inlay, maple peghead veneer, 2 per side chrome tuners, acoustic pickup, 3 band EQ with volume control. Available in Natural finish. Mfd. 1993 to 1996.

$510 $400
Last Mfr.'s Sug. Retail was $1,145.

STB-R/E — similar to STB-M, except has black pickguard, rosewood back/sides.

$565 $370
Last Mfr.'s Sug. Retail was $1,160.

STB-M — similar to STB-M/E, except has no acoustic pickup, 3 band EQ with volume control. Mfd. 1994 to 1996.

$345 $260
Last Mfr.'s Sug. Retail was $785.

Add $15 for black pickguard, rosewood back/sides.

Sigma 000-18MC/3B
courtesy Martin Guitar Company

Grading	100%	EXCELLENT	AVERAGE

Sigma SE-18/3B
courtesy Martin Guitar Company

ACOUSTIC ELECTRIC

SE Series

SE-1 — single round cutaway folk style, spruce top, round soundhole, 3 stripe bound body/rosette, mahogany back/sides/neck, 22 fret bound ebonized fingerboard with pearl dot inlay, ebonized bridge with white black dot pins, rosewood peghead veneer with abalone logo inlay, 3 per side chrome tuners, acoustic pickup, volume/2 band EQ control. Available in Black and Natural finishes. Mfd. 1994 to 1996.

	$245	$185	

Last Mfr.'s Sug. Retail was $565.

SE-18/2BC — single round cutaway folk style, spruce top, round soundhole, 3 stripe bound body/rosette, mahogany back/sides/neck, 22 fret bound ebonized fingerboard with pearl dot inlay, ebonized bridge with white black dot pins, rosewood peghead veneer with abalone logo inlay, 3 per side chrome tuners, acoustic pickup, 2 band EQ with chorus effect, volume control. Available in Black, Natural, Red and Tobacco Sunburst finishes. Mfd. 1993 to 1994.

	$300	$200	

Last Mfr.'s Sug. Retail was $905.

SE-18/3B — similar to SE-18/2BC, except has 3 band EQ with volume control. Available in Natural and Tobacco Sunburst finishes. Mfd. 1993 to 1994.

	$275	$200	

Last Mfr.'s Sug. Retail was $860.

SIGNET

Instruments produced in Japan circa early 1970s.

The Signet trademark was a brandname used by U.S. importers Ampeg/Selmer.

(Source: Michael Wright, Guitar Stories Volume One)

SILVERTONE

See chapter on House Brands.

This trademark has been identified as a "House Brand" owned and used by Sears and Roebuck between 1941 to 1970. There was no company or factory; Sears owned the name and applied it to various products from such manufacturers as HARMONY, VALCO, DANELECTRO, and KAY. Sears and Roebuck acquired Harmony in 1916 to control its respectable ukulele production. Harmony generally sold around 40 percent of its guitar production to Sears. The following is a word of caution: Just because it says **Silvertone**, do not automatically assume it is a Danelectro! In fact, study the guitar to determine possible origin (Harmony, Valco and Kay were originally built in Illinois, Danelectro in New Jersey; so all were U.S. However, mid 1960s models were built in Japan by Teisco, as well!). Best of all, play it! If it looks good, and sounds okay - it was meant to be played. As most Silvertones were sold either through the catalog or in a store, they will generally be entry level quality instruments.

Certain Silvertone models have garnered some notoriety, such as the Danelectro-produced combination of guitar and amp-in-case. Sears also marketed the Teisco company's TRG-1 (or TRE-100) electric guitar with amp built in! This guitar has a six-on-a-side "Silvertone" headstock, and a single cutaway *pregnant Telecaster* body design (the small built-in speaker is in the *tummy*). Harmony produced a number of electric hollowbody guitars (like the Sovereign) for the Silvertone label; Kay also offered a version of their *Thin Twin* model as well as arch top models.

> Silvertone pricing depends primarily on Kay and Harmony versus Danelectro for company of origin. Currently, the market is favoring the Danelectro Silvertones, although certain Harmony hollow body electrics do possess eye-catching appeal. Prices may range from $199 up to $600.

SIMON & PATRICK

Instruments built in La Patrie, Quebec, Canada since 1985. Simon & Patrick Acoustic Guitars are distributed by La Si Do, Inc., of St. Laurent, Canada.

Robert Godin set up a custom guitar shop in Montreal called Harmonilab in 1968. Harmonilab quickly became known for its excellent work and musicians were coming from as far away as Quebec City to have their guitars adjusted.

Although Harmonilab's business was flourishing, Robert was full of ideas for the design and construction of acoustic guitars. So in 1972 the **Norman Guitar Company** was born. From the beginning the Norman guitars showed signs of the innovations that Godin would eventually bring to the guitar market.

By 1978 Norman guitars had become quite successful in Canada and France. In 1980 Godin introduced the Seagull guitar. With many innovations like a bolt-on neck, pointed headstock and a handmade solid top, the Seagull was designed for an ease of play for the entry level to intermediate guitar player. Godin borrowed the finishing idea that was used on fine violins (a satin-finish lacquer), and applied it to the acoustic guitar.

Acceptance of this new guitar spread, and by 1985 La Si Do was incorporated and the factory in La Patrie expanded to meet the growing demand. In 1985 Godin introduced the Simon & Patrick line (named after his two sons) for people interested in a more traditional instrument. Simon & Patrick guitars still maintained a number of Seagull innovations.

For full company history, see GODIN.

ACOUSTIC GUITAR

Sigma DR-1 ST CE
courtesy The Martin Guitar Company

S & P 6 (Model 2719) — solid cedar top, wild cherry back and sides, rosewood fingerboard and bridge, 3 per side headstock, lacquer finish. Current mfr.

Mfr.'s Sug. Retail	$395	$325	$225	$175

Guitar is available with a solid spruce top **(Model 2795)**.
Guitar is available in a left-handed version **(Model 2757)**.

Grading	100%	EXCELLENT	AVERAGE

Guitar may be optionally equipped with EPM electronics **(Model 2726)**.

S & P 12 (Model 2733) — similar to S & P 6, except as a 12 string model with 6 on a side tuners. Current mfr.

Mfr.'s Sug. Retail	$462	$400	$300	$250

S & P CUTAWAY (Model 2559) — similar to S & P 6, except model is a steel-string cutaway. Current mfr.

Mfr.'s Sug. Retail	$520	$500	$400	$325

Guitar is only available in a right-handed configuration.

S & P 6 MAHOGANY (Model 2870) — similar to the S & P 6, only has mahogany back and sides instead of wild-cherry, and has a satin lacqer finish. Current mfr.

Mfr.'s Sug. Retail	$450	$395	$300	$225

Guitar is available with a solid spruce top **(Model 2917)**.

Guitar is available in a left-handed version **(Model 2894)**.

Guitar may be optionally equipped with EPM electronics **(Model 2887)**.

Simon & Patrick Pro Series

S & P 6 PRO MAHOGANY (Model 2955) — similar to the S & P 6, except has a solid spruce top, mahogany back and sides, mahogany neck, and high gloss lacquer finish. Current mfr.

Mfr.'s Sug. Retail	$760	$700	$575	$450

Guitar is available in a left-handed version **(Model 3006)**.

Guitar may be optionally equipped with L.R. Baggs electronics **(Model 8353)**.

S & P 6 PRO FLAME MAPLE (Model 3051) — similar to the S & P Pro Mahogany, except has flame maple sides and solid back. Current mfr.

Mfr.'s Sug. Retail	$850	$795	$675	$540

Guitar is available in a left-handed version **(Model 3105)**.

Guitar may be optionally equipped with L.R. Baggs electronics **(Model 8377)**.

S & P 6 PRO Flame Maple Cutaway (Model 2665) — similar to S & P 6 Pro Flame Maple, but body is in the cutaway configuration. Current mfr.

Mfr.'s Sug. Retail	$995	$925	$800	$675

S & P 6 PRO ROSEWOOD (Model 3150) — similar to the S & P Pro Mahogany, except has Indian rosewood back and sides. Current mfr.

Mfr.'s Sug. Retail	$1,005	$925	$825	$695

Guitar is available in a left-handed version **(Model 3204)**.

Guitar may be optionally equipped with L.R. Baggs electronics **(Model 8391)**.

S & P 6 PRO Rosewood Cutaway (Model 2603) — similar to S & P 6 Pro Rosewood, except features cutaway configuration. Current mfr.

Mfr.'s Sug. Retail	$1,160	$1,075	$800	$700

S & P 6 PRO QUILTED MAPLE (Model 3259) — similar to the S & P Pro Mahogany, except the back and sides are solid quilted maple. Current mfr.

Mfr.'s Sug. Retail	$1,290	$1,100	$825	$725

Guitar is available in a left-handed version **(Model 3303)**.

Guitar may be optionally equipped with L.R. Baggs electronics **(Model 8414)**.

DANIEL SLAMAN

Instruments built in Den Haag, Netherlands since 1978. Distributed through Luthier Slaman's workshop; Casa Benelly in Den Haag; and La Guitarra Buena in Amsterdam.

Luthier Daniel Slaman began building classical guitars in 1978. Slaman participated in a guitar making Masterclass hosted by Jose L. Romanillos in 1988, and professes a strong design influence by Romanillos. In 1997, Slaman and Robert Benedetto presented guitar making workshops at the Instrument Museum in Berlin during the *History of the Guitar in Rock and Jazz* exhibition.

Slaman introduced a number of new acoustic models in 1996 as well. By slightly offsetting the body contour, Slaman produced a cutaway on his classical model (which allows access to all 20 frets); this model has been named the **Classic Access** (list price $3,000). A variation named the **Flamenco Access** (list $2,500) is in the works. Another model is a European jazz guitar inspired by the Selmer models built in France from 1932 to 1952. Slaman's **Modele Jazz** is offered as brand new, or with antique parts and distressing as the **Modele Jazz Patina** (prices start at $2,500). List prices include a Hiscox case.

The majority of Slaman's instruments were built after 1992. Slaman currently produces between ten and fifteen handcrafted instruments a year, although archtop building is more time consuming and thus tends to slow down the building schedule.

ACOUSTIC

Luthier Slaman uses European Spruce for his classical guitar tops, and either Brazilian or Indian Rosewood, Cocobolo or Maple for the back and sides. When building **flamenco instruments**, Slaman offers soundboards of either European Spruce or Western red Cedar, and bodies of Spanish Cypress or Rosewood. Prices on classical models start at $3,000; and flamenco models begin at $2,500.

NORTH SEA STANDARD 17" — carved Sitka spruce top, two piece flamed maple back with matching sides/neck, ebony fingerboard with mother of pearl/Mexican green abalone inlays, ebony tailpiece/pickguard, Brazilian rosewood bridge/headplate, 3 per side Schaller gold tuning machines. Available in hand-applied nitrocellulose finish. Current mfr.

Mfr.'s Sug. Retail	$4,500

Add $250 for 18" or 18 1/2" wide body.

List price includes a Calton DeLuxe fibreglass case.

Slaman Classic Access
courtesy Daniel Slaman

This model is available with an optional Benedetto S-6 suspended pickup.

This model is available with select aged European Cello grade flamed maple back and sides as the North Sea Cello 17".

This model is available with special Thuya wood headplate/pickguard/bridge wings/tailpiece as the North Sea Special 17".

North Sea Natural 17" — similar to the North Sea Standard, except features all wood binding (no plastic), no pearl inlay.
Mfr.'s Sug. Retail $4,500

North Sea 7-String Swing — similar to the North Sea, except in a 7-string configuration, 4/3 per side headstock. Current mfr.
Mfr.'s Sug. Retail $4,500

North Sea Orchestra — similar to the North Sea, except has non-cutaway body style, 18" width (across lower bout), European spruce top, European flamed maple back/sides/neck. Current mfr.
Mfr.'s Sug. Retail $4,750

SLINGERLAND

Instruments built in Chicago, Illinois from the mid 1930s to circa mid 1940s.

Slingerland is perhaps better known for the drums the company produced. The Slingerland Banjo and Drum Company was established in 1916 in Chicago. In terms of construction, a banjo and drum do have several similarites (the soundhead stretched over a circular frame and held by a retaining ring). The company introduced the **Marvel** line of carved top guitars in 1936. A catalog of the time shows that Slingerland guitars were also sold under various brandnames such as **Songster**, **College Pal**, and **May-Bell**, as well as the Slingerland trademark.

(Source: Tom Wheeler, American Guitars)

SMALLMAN GUITARS

Instruments built in New South Wales, Australia from the early 1980s on.

Luthier Greg Smallman continues to push the mechanical limits on the classical guitar form. Though the instruments look conventional, Smallman utilizes a flexible criss-cross lattice-like internal strutting composed of balsawood reinforced by carbon fiber under a thin top to increase the volume of the guitar. Backs and sides are constructed from laminated rosewood, which reduces the amount of energy that they might absorb from the top, which also enhances the guitar's projection. Smallman favors cedar for his guitar tops.

(Source: Tony Bacon, The Ultimate Guitar Book)

Luthier Smallman makes a small number of guitars each year, has a moderately high asking price, and has a long waiting list. 'Used' Smallman guitars rarely turn up on the secondary market.

STEFAN SOBELL

Instruments currently built in England.

Luthier Stefan Sobell was a pioneer in the developement of the "cittern" (similar to a long necked mandolin) in the early 1970s (the cittern proved popular in the British Celtic music revival). Sobell then changed to building acoustic guitars in the early 1980s. Currently he produces about 35 guitars a year, "bent" or carved top "flat tops" (the top and back feature a cylindrical arch). Sobell also builds citterns, mandolins, and Irish bouzoukis.

SONNET

Instruments produced in Japan.

Sonnet guitars were distributed in the U.S. by the Daimaru New York Corporation of New York, New York.

(Source: Michael Wright, Guitar Stories Volume One)

SORRENTINO

Instruments built by Epiphone in New York, New York circa mid 1930s. Distributed by C.M.I. (Chicago Musical Instruments)
.

Sorrentino guitar
courtesy Tam Milano

In the new book, **Epiphone: The House of Stathopoulo**, authors Jim Fisch and L.B. Fred indicate that Sorrentino instruments were built by Epaminondas Stathopoulos' Epiphone company during the mid 1930s. Unlike other 1930s *budget* lines, the Sorrentinos are similar in quality and prices to Epiphones during this time period. Of the six models (Luxor, Premier, Artist, Avon, Lido, and Arcadia), two models were even higher priced than their Epiphone counterpart!

Sorrentinos share construction designs and serialization similar to same-period Epiphones, and headstock designs similar to the Epiphone-built Howard brand models. Sorrentinos, like budget line Gibsons, do not have a truss rod in the neck. Labels inside the body read: Sorrentino Mfg. Co., USA.

(Source: Jim Fisch and L.B. Fred, Epiphone: The House of Stathopoulo)

S.S. STEWART

Instruments also produced as STEWART & BAUER.

Instruments produced in Philadelphia, Pennsylvania, during the late 1800s.

S.S. Stewart was a major banjo producer of the late 1800s, and was one of the first to apply mass production techniques to instrument building with good consequences. Stewart became partners with well-known guitar builder George Bauer, and issued guitars under the **Stewart & Bauer** trademark from Philadelphia.

After the company was dissolved, Stewart's family put out guitars under the **S.S. Stewart's Sons** trademark. The **Stewart** name also appears on a series of entry level to medium grade guitars built by Harmony (circa 1950s); and others for Weymann. These later models are not at the same level of quality as the Philadelphia-era models.

(Source: Tom Wheeler, American Guitars)

WM. C. STAHL

See LARSON BROTHERS (1900-1944).

William C. Stahl was a prominent music publisher and teacher of guitar, mandolin, and banjo in Milwaukee from the turn of the century to the early 1940s. He sold instruments to his students but also advertised heavily in the trade papers. The Larson brothers of Maurer & Co. in Chicago supplied most of his guitar and mandolin family instruments, the remainder being made by Washburn, Regal, or others.

The Larson-made Stahl guitars followed the designs of the Maurer and Prairie State brands also built by the Larsons. The difference in the Stahl labeled guitars is that maple is used for bracing rather than spruce. Some of the top-of-the-line Stahl guitars have the Prairie State system of steel rods which strengthen the body and add sustain as well as help to produce a somewhat different sound from other Larson brands. The Larson-made Stahl instruments have a Stahl logo burned or stamped on the inside center strip. Author Robert Hartman believes that Stahl's paper label was also used on some Larsons, as well as the ones made by other builders. Stahl offered guitars and mandolins ranging in quality from student grade to the highest degree of presentation grade instruments.

For more information regarding other Larson-made brands, see MAURER, PRAIRIE STATE, EUPHONON, W.J. DYER, and THE LARSON BROTHERS.

For more detailed information regarding all the Larson brands and a Stahl catalog reprint, see The Larsons' Creations, Guitars and Mandolins, by Robert Carl Hartman, Centerstream Publishing, P.O. Box 17878, Anaheim Hills CA 92807, phone/fax (714) 779-9390.

STELLA

See HARMONY.

See OSCAR SCHMIDT.

STEVENS CUSTOM GUITARS

Instruments currently built in Munchen (Munich), Germany.

Werner Kozlik, Stefan Zirnbauer, and the other guitar builders at Stevens Custom Guitars are crafting high quality acoustic models. For additional information regarding models and specifications, please contact Stevens Custom Guitars through the Index of Current Manufacturers located in the back of this book.

GILBERT L. STILES

Instruments built in Independence, West Virginia and Hialeah, Florida between 1960 to 1994.

Luthier/designer Gilbert L. Stiles (1914-1994) had a background of working with wood, be it millwork, logging or housebuilding. In 1960, he set his mind to building a solid body guitar, and continued building instruments for over the next thirty years. In 1963, Stiles moved to Hialeah, Florida. Later on in his career, Stiles also taught for the Augusta Heritage Program at the Davis and Elkins College in Elkins, West Virginia.

Stiles built solid body electrics, arch tops, flattop guitars, mandolins, and other stringed instruments. It has been estimated that Stiles had produced over 1,000 solid body electric guitars and 500 acoustics during his career. His arch top and mandolins are still held in high esteem, as well as his banjos.

Stiles guitars generally have Stiles or G L Stiles on the headstock, or Lee Stiles engraved on a plate at the neck/body joint of a bolt-on designed solid body. Dating a Stiles instrument is difficult, given that only the electric solids were given serial numbers consecutively, and would only indicate which number guitar it was, not when built.

(Source: Michael Wright, Guitar Stories Volume One)

STOLL

Instruments built in Taunusstein, Germany since 1983. Distributed in the U.S. by Salwender International of Trabuco Canyon, California.

Christian Stoll began his lutherie career in the mid 1970s as an apprentice at Hopf guitars, then left to study under Dragan Musulin. Stoll finished his period of apprenticeship with Andreas Wahl, and founded the Stoll Guitar Company in 1983.

Between 1983 to 1985, Stoll produced custom orders for classical and steel string models (and some electric guitars and basses), and began to work on developing an acoustic bass guitar. In 1988, Stoll began adding other luthiers to his workshop, and currently has three on staff.

Stoll also offers the McLoud acoustic pickup system on a number of his acoustic models. This internal system features a piezo pickup, endpin jack, and a battery clip for 9 volt batteries.

ACOUSTIC

Stoll offers hand crafted steel string acoustic guitar and acoustic bass models. The models are built from quality wood, and inlays and trim are used sparingly as the emphasis is on tone and craftsmanship. Guitars are then finished in nitrocellulose lacquer or Shellac (French polish method).

Classical models feature solid cedar or spruce tops, rosewood or ovankol sides and backs, 20 fret ebony fingerboards, and Schaller tuners. The Steel String acoustics have solid spruce tops, maple or rosewood backs and sides, cedro necks, 21 fret rosewood or ebony fingerboards and chrome or gold Schaller tuners. All models are available with options like cutaways, left-handed configurations, and more.

SPEXX acoustic basses feature a wider cutaway body design, solid spruce top, maple back and sides, a 21 fret ebony fingerboard, and gold Schaller tuners. Basses are available in fretless, left-handed, 5- and 6-string configurations.

15" Euphonon with a Stahl label
courtesy Robert Carl Hartman

(Harmony) Stella H6134
1973 Harmony Catalog

STRADIVARI

Instruments built in Italy during the late 1600s.

While this reknowned builder is revered for his violins, luthier Antonio Stradivari (1644-1737) did build a few guitars; a handful survive today. The overall design and appearance is reminiscent of the elegant yet simple violins that command such interest today.

(Source: Tony Bacon, The Ultimate Guitar Book)

STRAD-O-LIN

Instruments produced in New York during the 1950s and 1960s. Later models manufactured in Japan.

Strad-O-Lin was a brandname of the Peter Sorkin Music Company. A number of solid body guitars were built at the Multivox company of New York, and distribution of those and the later Japanese built models were handled by the Sorkin company of New York City, New York. Other guitars built and distributed (possibly as rebrands) were ROYCE, PREMIER, BELLTONE, and MARVEL.

STROMBERG

Instruments built in Boston, Massachusetts between 1906 and the mid-1950s.

The Stromberg business was started in Boston, Massachusetts in 1906 by Charles Stromberg (born in Sweden 1866) who immigrated to Boston in April 1886. Charles Stromberg was a master luthier. He specialized in banjo, drum, mandolin, and guitars after working for several years at Thompson and Odell (est. 1874), a Boston based firm that manufactured brass instruments, percussion instruments, fretted instruments, music publications, stringed instruments, and accessories. Thompson & Odell sold the manufacturing of the fretted instrument business to the Vega Company in Boston in 1905. Stromberg was one of the country's leading repairers of harps with his masterful ability in carving headstocks, replacing sound boards, and making new machine mechanisms. His reputation among Boston's early engravers, violin, drum, banjo, and piano makers was very high. Charles, in addition, repaired violins, cellos, and basses. Repairs were a steady source of income for the Stromberg business. His oldest son, Harry (born in Chelsea, Massachusetts 1890), worked with Charles from 1907 on and his youngest son, Elmer (born in Chelsea in 1895), apprenticed at the shop with older brother Harry from July 1910 until March 1917, when Elmer left the business to serve in World War I. He returned to the business in March 1919 after serving his country for two years in France.

At that time, the shop was located at 40 Sudbury Street and later moved to 19 Washington Street in early 1920s. Shop locations were in an area based in the heart of Boston's famous Scollay Square with burlesque and theater establishments. The Strombergs produced drums, mandolins, guitars, and banjos during the early 1920s from the 19 Washington Street location.

Throughout the 1920s (the Jazz Age of banjo music), the Strombergs produced custom tenor banjos. They competed with other banjo manufacturers, and were part of the eastern corridor in banjo manufacturing. The Stromberg reputation was very strong in Boston and the New England area. Banjoists who often desired a custom made instrument chose the Stromberg banjo as it was highly decorative and the sound would carry for the player in large dance halls. In October of 1926, Elmer Stromberg applied for a patent for a series of tubes around the tone chamber of the banjo just under the head. This created a new sustaining sound and more volume and was called the "Cupperphone". The Stromberg Cupperphone banjo consisted of 41 hollow, perforated metal tubes $^{13}/_{16}$ inches high and $^{13}/_{16}$ inches in diameter fitted to the wooden rim to produce a louder and clearer tone. This was an option for the banjos, and this Cupperphone feature made the Stromberg banjo one of the loudest and heaviest built in the country. The two models offered at this time were the **Deluxe**, and **Marimba** models. The patent was granted in June of 1928.

Harry Stromberg left the business in 1927. By the late 1920s, banjo players were beginning to switch from banjo to guitar to create deeper sounding rhythm sections in orchestras. As the style of music changed, the guitar needed to be heard better. While musicians' needs focused towards the guitar, the banjo's popularity declined and Elmer began producing archtop guitars for Boston musicians.

In June of 1927, the shop relocated to 40 Hanover Street where they began producing archtop guitars. By the early 1930s, banjo players began ordering guitars. As early as 1927, Elmer began taking guitar orders, and offered several types based on a 16 inch body, called the **G** series. The models **G1**, **G2**, and **Deluxe** models were offered featuring a small headstock, with laminated body and segmented f-holes.

During the American Depression of the 1930s, Elmer wanted as many musicians as possible to enjoy his instruments and kept the cost of the instrument affordable. After the Depression, the guitars began to change in looks and construction. By the mid 1930s (1935-37), musicians requested fancier models with larger bodies that could produce more volume. The Stromberg guitar went through at least two major headstock dimension sizes and designs and body specifications between 1936 and 1940. Elmer's response to players' needs (and the competition) was to widen the body on the G series guitars to $17^3/_8$ inches, and add two more models: the 19 inch **Master 400** model was introduced around 1937/38, and the **Master 300** was introduced in the same time period. The larger body dimensions of the Master 300 and 400 made them the largest guitars offered from any maker.

Elmer's top-of-the-line model was the Master 400. This guitar would set the Stromberg guitar apart from other rhythm acoustic archtop guitars, especially during the swing era: Elmer added decorative pearl inlay to the headstock, additional binding, and a fine graduated top carving that would carry its sound volume across the brass sections of a large orchestra. By 1940, a new, longer headstock style and the single diagonal brace were added to Master series guitars, switching from a traditional parallel bracing to a single brace for yet more carrying power. The graduation of the tops also changed during this period. By 1940 to '41, a single tension rod adjustment was added to the Master series (and was later added to the Deluxe and G series). By 1941, the G1 and G3 series body dimensions increased to $17^3/_8$ inches, and featured a new tailpiece design that was "Y" shaped in design. The f-holes became non-segmented and followed the graceful design of the Deluxe model.

Elmer Stromberg built all of the guitars and the majority of banjos. His name never appeared on an instrument, with the exception of a Deluxe Cutaway (serial number 634, a short scale made for guitarist Hank Garland). Every label read **Charles A. Stromberg and Son** with a lifetime guarantee to the original purchaser. Elmer is described by many players who knew him as a gentle man with a heart of gold. He wanted to please his family of guitarists with the best instrument he could make.

(Stromberg history and model specifications courtesy Jim Speros. Speros is currently compiling a Stromberg text, portions of which were supplied to this edition of the Blue Book of Guitars. Interested parties can contact Speros through Stromberg Research, P.O. Box 51, Lincoln, Massachusetts 01773.)

The apparent rarity of the individual guitars (it is estimated that only 640 guitars were produced), like D'Angelicos, combined with condition and demand, makes it difficult to set a selling price in the vintage market. The Blue Book of Guitars recommends at least two or three professional appraisals or estimates before buying/selling/trading any Stromberg guitar (or any other Stromberg instrument, especially the banjos).

STROMBERG GUITAR IDENTIFICATION

Early **G** series (G1, G2, G3, Deluxe) from 1927-1930 has a 16 inch body and a label reading "40 Hanover Street, Tel Bowdoin 1228R-1728-M" (Stromberg's current business card). Narrow banjo-style headstock, Stromberg logo, Victorian-style, hand-painted with floral accents. Fingerboard (G1, G2, G3) mother-of-pearl inlays, diamond shape, oval at 14th fret. The Deluxe model featured solid pearl blocks position markers on an ebony fingerboard. The headstock was Victorian-style, engraved, hand-painted. Pressed back Indian Rosewood or maple, carved spruce top, segmented f-holes. Trapeze-style tailpiece brass with chrome plating on models G1, G2, and G3 (gold plated on the Deluxe model). All shared rosewood bridge with adjustments for bridge height, top location thumb adjustments. Bracing: two parallel braces, 3 ladder type braces.

Mid- to late 1930s (1935-37), the **G-100, G1, G3, Deluxe, Ultra Deluxe**, 17$^3/_8$ inch body. Blond finish guitars began appearing during the late 1930s. Construction featured a pressed back, carved spruce top, Grover tailpiece (chrome plated). Blue shipping labels inside guitar body read "Charles A. Stromberg & Son" in the late 1930s was typewritten or handwritten. The headstock shape changed to a larger bout and from the early 1930s had a laminated, embossed, plastic engraved Stromberg logo characterizing the new style. Bracing: dual parallel bracing top. The Master 400 had a "stubby" style headstock, parallel braced top, inlaid mother-of-pearl or Victorian laminated style.

1940s Style Guitars

Master 400: body size 19 inches wide x 21$^3/_4$ inch length. Top: carved and graduated spruce $^7/_8$ inch thickness. F-holes bound white/black, neck was a 5-piece rock maple with Ivoroid binding (black and white) on fingerboard. The bridge was adjustable compensating rosewood and pickguard was imitation tortoise shell that was inlaid with white and black Ivoroid borders. Available in Natural or Sunburst finishes. Ebony fingerboard, position markers were three segmented pearl blocks. Bracing: single diagonal brace from upper bout to lower bout (began about 1940). Tailpiece: 5 Cutout "Y" shaped with Stromberg engraving (gold plated).

Master 300: body size 19 inches wide x 21$^3/_4$ inch length. Top: carved and graduated spruce $^7/_8$ inch thickness. F-holes bound white. Neck: rock maple with ebony fingerboard, position markers solid pearl block. Ivoroid binding on fingerboard (black and white). Bridge: adjustable compensating rosewood. The pickguard was imitation tortoise shell inlaid with white and black Ivoroid borders. Available in Natural or Sunburst finishes. Bracing: single diagonal brace from upper bout to lower bout (began about 1940). Tailpiece: 5 Cutout "Y" shaped with Stromberg engraving (gold plated).

Deluxe: body size 17$^3/_8$ inches wide x 20$^3/_4$ inch length. Top: graduated and carved spruce $^7/_8$ inch thickness. F-holes Ivoroid bound (white/black). Bridge: adjustable compensating rosewood. The pickguard was imitation tortoise shell inlaid with white and black Ivoroid borders. Available in Natural or Sunburst finishes. The ebony fingerboard had position markers solid pearl blocks. Bracing: single diagonal brace from upper bout to lower bout (1940-41). Tailpiece: 5 Cutout "Y" shaped (gold plated).

G-3: body size 17$^3/_8$ inches wide x 20$^3/_4$ inch length. Top: graduated and carved spruce $^7/_8$ inch thickness. F-holes not bound. Bridge: adjustable compensating rosewood. The pickguard was imitation tortoise shell inlaid with white and black Ivoroid borders. Available in Natural or Sunburst finishes. The rosewood fingerboard had position markers of two segmented pearl blocks. Bracing: single diagonal brace from upper bout to lower bout (mid- to late 1940s). Tailpiece: 3 Cutout "Y" shaped (gold plated).

G-1: body size 17$^3/_8$ inches wide 20$^3/_4$ inch length. Top: graduated and carved spruce $^7/_8$ inch thickness. F-hole not bound. Bridge: adjustable compensating rosewood. The pickguard was imitation tortoise shell inlaid with white and black Ivoroid borders. Available in Natural or Sunburst finishes. The rosewood fingerboard had position markers of diamond shaped pearl with four indented circle cutouts in inner corners. Bracing: single diagonal brace from upper bout to lower bout (mid to late '40s). Tailpiece: 3 Cutout "Y" shaped (chrome plated).

CUTAWAYS

Introduced in 1949.

Master 400: body size 18$^3/_8$ inches wide x 21$^3/_4$ inch length. Top: carved and graduated spruce $^7/_8$ inch thickness. F-holes bound white/black. Neck: 5 piece rock maple. Ivoroid binding on fingerboard (black and white). Bridge: adjustable compensating rosewood. The pickguard was imitation tortoise shell inlaid with white and black Ivoroid borders. Available in Natural or Sunburst finishes. Ebony fingerboard had position markers of three segmented pearl blocks or solid pearl blocks. Bracing: single diagonal brace from upper bout to lower bout. Tailpiece: 5 Cutout "Y" shaped with the new Stromberg Logo engraved and gold plated.

Deluxe Cutaway: body size 17$^3/_8$ inches wide x 20$^3/_4$ inch length. Top: graduated and carved spruce $^7/_8$ inch thickness. F-holes Ivoroid bound white/black. Bridge: adjustable compensating rosewood. The pickguard was imitation tortoise shell inlaid with white and black Ivoroid borders. Available in Natural or Sunburst finishes. Position markers were solid pearl blocks. Bracing: single diagonal brace from upper bout to lower bout. Tailpiece: 5 Cutout "Y" shaped with Stromberg engraving (gold plated).

G-5 Cutaway (introduced 1950): body size 17$^3/_8$ inches wide x 20$^3/_4$ inch length. Top: graduated and carved spruce $^7/_8$ thickness. F-holes Ivoroid bound white. Bridge: adjustable compensating rosewood. Pickguard was imitation tortoise shell inlaid with white and black Ivoroid borders. Available in Natural or Sunburst finishes. Ebony fingerboard had position markers of solid pearl blocks. Bracing: single diagonal brace from upper bout to lower bout. Tailpiece: 3 Cutout "Y" shaped with Stromberg engraving (gold plated).

G-3 Cutaway: body size 17$^3/_8$ inches wide x 20$^3/_4$ inch length. Top: graduated and carved spruce $^7/_8$ thickness. F-hole unbound. Bridge: adjustable compensating rosewood. The pickguard was imitation tortoise shell inlaid with white and black Ivoroid borders. Available in Natural or Sunburst finishes. Rosewood fingerboard had position markers of split pearl blocks. Bracing: single diagonal brace from upper bout to lower bout. Tailpiece: 3 Cutout "Y" shaped (gold plated).

STUDIO KING

See chapter on House Brands.

While this trademark has been identified as a *House Brand*, the distributor is currently unknown at this time. As information is uncovered, future listings in the **Blue Book of Guitars** will be updated.

(Source: Willie G. Moseley, Stellas & Stratocasters)

SUPERIOR

See chapter on House Brands.

While this trademark has been identified as a "House Brand", the distributor is currently unknown. As information is uncovered, future editions of the **Blue Book of Guitars** will be updated.

(Source: Willie G. Moseley, Stellas & Stratocasters)

SUPERTONE

See chapter on House Brands.

This trademark has been identified as a *House Brand* of Sears, Roebuck and Company between 1914 to 1941. Instruments produced by various (probably) Chicago-based manufacturers, especially Harmony (then a Sears subsidiary). Sears used the Supertone trademark on a full range of guitars, lap steels, banjos, mandolins, ukuleles, and amplifiers.

In 1940, then-company president Jay Krause bought Harmony from Sears by acquiring the controlling stock, and continued to expand the company's production. By 1941, Sears had retired the Supertone trademark in favor of the new *Silvertone* name. Harmony, though a separate business entity, still sold guitars to Sears for sale under this new brandname.

(Source: Michael Wright, Vintage Guitar Magazine)

SUPRO

See chapter on House Brands.

The Supro trademark was the budget brand of the National Dobro company (See NATIONAL or VALCO), who also supplied Montgomery Wards with Supro models under the **Airline** trademark. National offered budget versions of their designs under the Supro brandname beginning in 1935.

When National moved to Chicago in 1936, the Supro name was on wood-bodied lap steels, amplifiers, and electric Spanish arch top guitars. The first solid body Supro electrics were introduced in 1952, and the fiberglass models began in 1962 (there's almost thirty years of conventionally built guitars in the Supro history).

In 1962, Valco Manufacturing Company name was changed to Valco Guitars, Inc. (the same year that fiberglass models debuted). Kay purchased Valco in 1967, so there are some Kay-built guitars under the Supro brandname. Kay went bankrupt in 1968, and both the Supro and National trademarks were acquired by Chicago's own Strum 'N Drum company. The National name was used on a number of Japanese-built imports, but not the Supro name.

Archer's Music of Fresno, California bought the rights to the Supro name in the early 1980s. They marketed a number of Supro guitars constructed from new old stock (N.O.S.) parts for a limited period of time.

(Source: Michael Wright, Vintage Guitar Magazine)

SUZUKI

Instruments built in Korea. Previously distributed in the U.S. market by Suzuki Guitars of San Diego, California.

Suzuki, noted for their quality pianos, offered a range of acoustic and electric guitars designed for the beginning student to intermediate player. In 1996, the company discontinued the guitar line completely. Suzuki guitars are similar to other trademarked models from Korea at comparable prices.

20TH CENTURY

Instruments were produced by REGAL (original company of Wulschner & Son) in the late 1890s through the mid 1900s.

Indianapolis retailer/wholesaler Emil Wulschner introduced the Regal line in the 1880s, and in 1896 opened a factory to build guitars and mandolins under the following three trademarks: REGAL, 20th CENTURY, and UNIVERSITY. In the early 1900s the 20th Century trademark was a *sub-brand* distributed by the Fred Gretsch Manufacturing Company. By 1920 the Fred Gretsch Mfg. Co. had settled into its new ten story building in Brooklyn, New York, and was offering music dealers a very large line of instruments that included banjos, mandolins, guitars, violins, drums, and other band instruments. Gretsch used both the 20th Century and Rex trademarks prior to introduction of the GRETSCH trademark in 1933.

TACOMA

Instruments produced in Tacoma, Washington since 1995. Distributed by Tacoma Guitars direct sales force.

Tacoma Guitars is the newest USA-produced acoustic guitar line. The company estimates that 55 to 70 guitars are produced a day, and all models feature a unique bracing pattern that is called the *Voice Support Bracing*.

ACOUSTIC

PAPOOSE (Model P1) — travel sized solid mahogany body and sides, cedar top, mahogany neck, 15/21 fret rosewood fingerboard with white dot inlay, *quotation mark* soundhole in bass bout, *pinless* bridge, 3 per side headstock, chrome hardware. Available in Natural satin finish. Mfr. 1995 to date.

Mfr.'s Sug. Retail	$479

Add $100 for piezo pickup and endpin jack **(Model Papoose P1E)**.

This model is voiced as a tenor-style guitar (up a fourth) from a standard acoustic guitar.

CHIEF (Model C1C) — similar to the Papoose, except has full sized body/neck, single rounded cutaway. Mfr. 1997 to date.

Mfr.'s Sug. Retail	$839

Add $250 for Fishman Prefix piezo pickup system **(Model Chief C1CE)**.

DM10 — dreadnought style, solid Sitka spruce top, round soundhole with abalone trim, mahogany back/sides, tortoise body binding, mahogany neck, 14/20 fret rosewood fingerboard with white dot inlay, rosewood bridge, 3 per side headstock, chrome hardware. Available in Natural satin finish. Mfr. 1997 to date.

Mfr.'s Sug. Retail	$799

Add $250 for Fishman piezo pickup and active EQ **(Model DM10E)**.

DR20 — similar to the DM10, except features rosewood back/sides, herringbone pufling/ivoroid body binding. Available in Natural gloss finish. Mfr. 1997 to date.

Mfr.'s Sug. Retail	$1,099

Add $150 for Fishman Basic piezo pickup and active EQ **(Model DR20E)**.

PM20 — rounded lower bout/slim waist style, solid Sitka spruce top, round soundhole with abalone trim, mahogany back/sides, herringbone purfling/ivoroid body binding, 25.5" scale, mahogany neck, 14/20 fret bound rosewood fingerboard with white dot inlay, rosewood bridge, 3 per side headstock, chrome hardware. Available in Natural gloss finish. Mfr. 1997 to date.

Mfr.'s Sug. Retail	$999

Add $250 for Fishman Prefix piezo pickup and active EQ **(Model PM20E)**.

PK30 — similar to the DM10, except features koa back/sides, bound flamed koa peghead with maple logo inlay, abalone position markers. Available in Natural gloss finish. Mfr. 1997 to date.

Mfr.'s Sug. Retail	$1,299

Add $250 for Fishman Prefix piezo pickup and active EQ **(Model PK30E)**.

ACOUSTIC ELECTRIC

JK50CE — rounded lower bout/slim waist style with single rounded cutaway, solid Sitka spruce top, round soundhole with abalone trim, koa back/sides, herringbone purfling/ivoroid body binding, mahogany neck, 14/20 fret bound rosewood fingerboard with abalone inlay, bound flamed koa peghead with maple logo inlay, rosewood bridge, 3 per side headstock, chrome hardware, Fishman Prefix system. Available in Natural satin finish. Mfr. 1997 to date.

Mfr.'s Sug. Retail	$1,599

TAKAMINE

Instruments manufactured in Japan. Distributed by the Kaman Music Corporation of Bloomfield, Connecticut.

The Takamine brand was originally set up to be Martin's Sigma series with the help of Coast distributors. However, when the Kaman Music Corporation (Ovation) bought Coast, Martin had to contract Sigma production elsewhere. Ovation encouraged Takamine to enter the market under their own trademark, and have since distributed the guitars in the U.S. market.

(Source: Michael Wright, Guitar Stories Volume One)

During the 1980s, Takamine offered an acoustic model with a V-shaped body. Originally dubbed the "Acoustic Flying V", the name was later changed to the "Flying A". This model was available in Natural, Metallic Red, and Metallic Blue finishes.

Takamine uses certain designation to indicate aspects of the model: The E prefix indicates an acoustic/electric model, the C prefix indicates a cutaway body, and the -12 indicates as 12-string configuration.

3 Band EQ Closeup
courtesy Takamine

Takamine EA-360 "Flying A"
courtesy Thoroughbred Music

Grading	100%	EXCELLENT	AVERAGE

ACOUSTIC

G-334
courtesy Takamine

G-10 — dreadnought style, cedar top, round soundhole, bound body, multi stripe purfling/rosette, mahogany back/sides/neck, 14/20 fret rosewood fingerboard, rosewood bridge with white black dot pins, 3 per side gold tuners. Available in Natural finish. Mfr. 1994 to date.

Mfr.'s Sug. Retail	$499	$360	$180	$150

EG-10C — similar to G-10, except has single round cutaway, crystal bridge pickups, 4 band EQ. Available in Natural finish. Mfr. 1994 to date.

Mfr.'s Sug. Retail	$749	$560	$280	$230

G-124 — classical style, spruce top, round soundhole, bound body, wood marquetry rosette, nato back/sides, mahogany neck, 12/19 fret rosewood fingerboard, tied rosewood bridge, 3 per side chrome tuners with plastic buttons. Available in Natural finish. Mfr. 1994 to date.

Mfr.'s Sug. Retail	$399	$275	$135	$115

Add $40 for solid spruce top (G-124S).

EG-124C — similar to G-124, except has single round cutaway, crystal bridge pickups, 4 band EQ. Available in Natural finish. Mfr. 1994 to date.

Mfr.'s Sug. Retail	$699	$525	$310	$225

300 Series

G-330 — dreadnought style, spruce top, round soundhole, black pickguard, 3 stripe bound body and rosette, mahogany back/sides/neck, 14/20 fret rosewood fingerboard with white dot inlay, rosewood bridge with white pins, 3 per side chrome tuners. Available in Natural finish. Current mfr.

Mfr.'s Sug. Retail	$399	$280	$140	$115

In 1993, Red Stain finish was introduced (discontinued 1994).

EG-330C — similar to G-330, except has single round cutaway, crystal bridge pickups, 4 band EQ. Available in Natural finish. Mfr. 1994 to date.

Mfr.'s Sug. Retail	$669	$450	$220	$180

G-332 — dreadnought style, solid spruce top, round soundhole, black pickguard, 3 stripe bound body and rosette, mahogany back/sides/neck, 14/20 fret rosewood fingerboard with white dot inlay, rosewood bridge with white pins, 3 per side chrome tuners. Available in Natural finish. Current mfr.

Mfr.'s Sug. Retail	$499	$375	$160	$130

EG-332C — similar to G-332, except has single round cutaway, crystal bridge pickups, 4 band EQ. Available in Natural finish. Mfr. 1994 to date.

Mfr.'s Sug. Retail	$699	$495	$240	$195

G-334 — dreadnought style, spruce top, round soundhole, black pickguard, wood bound body and rosette, rosewood back/sides, mahogany neck, 14/20 fret bound rosewood fingerboard with pearl dot inlay, rosewood bridge with white black dot pins, 3 per side gold tuners. Available in Natural and Black finishes. Disc. 1994.

		$250	$165

Last Mfr.'s Sug. Retail was $500.

EG-334C — similar to G-334, except has single rounded cutaway, crystal bridge pickups, 4 band EQ. Available in Natural finish. Mfr. 1994 to date.

Mfr.'s Sug. Retail	$799	$560	$280	$230

EG-334BC (Also EG-334RC) — similar to G-334, except has single rounded cutaway, crystal bridge pickups, 4 band EQ. Available in Black (B) Stain and Red (R) Stain finishes. Mfr. 1994 to date.

Mfr.'s Sug. Retail	$849	$640	$300	$245

G-335 — dreadnought style, spruce top, round soundhole, black pickguard, 3 stripe bound body and rosette, mahogany back/sides/neck, 14/20 fret rosewood fingerboard with white dot inlay, rosewood bridge with white pins, 6 per side chrome tuners. Available in Natural finish. Current mfr.

Mfr.'s Sug. Retail	$599	$460	$200	$165

F-340 — dreadnought style, spruce top, round soundhole, black pickguard, 3 stripe bound body and rosette, mahogany back/sides/neck, 14/20 fret rosewood fingerboard with pearl dot inlay, rosewood bridge with black white dot pins, 3 per side chrome tuners. Available in Natural finish. Current mfr.

Mfr.'s Sug. Retail	$769	$580	$260	$215

F-340S — similar to F-340, except has solid spruce top. Current mfr.

Mfr.'s Sug. Retail	$899	$645	$315	$260

F-341 — dreadnought style, spruce top, round soundhole, black pickguard, 5 stripe bound body and rosette, campnosparma back/sides, mahogany neck, 14/20 fret bound rosewood fingerboard with pearl dot inlay, rosewood bridge with white black dot pins, bound peghead, 3 per side chrome tuners. Available in Black finish. Disc. 1996.

		$390	$260

Last Mfr.'s Sug. Retail was $780.

EF-341 — similar to F-341, except has crystal bridge pickups, 3 band EQ. Current mfr.

Mfr.'s Sug. Retail	$1,129	$835	$490	$325

EF-341C — similar to F-341, except has single rounded cutaway, crystal bridge pickups, 3 band EQ. Current mfr.

Mfr.'s Sug. Retail	$1,219	$956	$530	$355

FP-400 S
courtesy Takamine

Grading	100%	EXCELLENT	AVERAGE

EF-381C — dreadnought style, single rounded cutaway, 12-string configuration, spruce top, round soundhole, black pickguard, 5 stripe bound body/rosette, campnosparma back/sides, mahogany neck, 14/20 fret rosewood fingerboard with pearl diamond/dot inlay, rosewood bridge with white black dot pins, 6 per side chrome tuners, crystal bridge pickups, 3 band EQ. Available in Black finish. Current mfr.

Mfr.'s Sug. Retail	$1,309	$995	$575	$390

F-385 — dreadnought style, spruce top, round soundhole, black pickguard, 5 stripe bound body/rosette, mahogany back/sides/neck, 14/20 fret rosewood fingerboard with pearl dot inlay, rosewood bridge with black white dot pins, 6 per side chrome tuners. Available in Natural finish. Current mfr.

Mfr.'s Sug. Retail	$859	$700	$400	$245

EF-385 — similar to F-385, except has crystal bridge pickup, 3 band EQ.

Mfr.'s Sug. Retail	$1,059	$960	$680	$415

360 Series

F-60S — dreadnought style, solid spruce top, round soundhole, black pickguard, 5 stripe bound body/rosette, rosewood back/sides, 14/20 fret bound rosewood fingerboard with pearl dot inlay, rosewood bridge with white black dot pins, 3 per side chrome tuners. Available in Natural finish. Current mfr.

Mfr.'s Sug. Retail	$1,089	$955	$675	$410

Add $130 for left handed version of this model (F-360SLH).

Classic Series

C-128 — classical style, spruce top, round soundhole, 5 stripe bound body, wooden rosette, rosewood back/sides, mahogany neck, 12/19 fret rosewood fingerboard, rosewood bridge, 3 per side gold tuners with nylon buttons. Available in Natural finish. Current mfr.

Mfr.'s Sug. Retail	$629	$440	$220	$180

EC-128 — similar to C-128, except has mahogany back/sides, crystal bridge pickups, 3 band EQ.

Mfr.'s Sug. Retail	$869	$700	$480	$245

C-132S — classical style, solid cedar top, round soundhole, 5 stripe bound body, wooden rosette, rosewood back/sides, mahogany neck, 12/19 fret rosewood fingerboard, rosewood bridge, 3 per side gold tuners with nylon buttons. Available in Natural finish. Current mfr.

Mfr.'s Sug. Retail	$829	$650	$335	$245

EC-132C — similar to C-132S, except has single rounded cutaway, spruce top, crystal bridge pickups, 3 band EQ.

Mfr.'s Sug. Retail	$1,049	$840	$560	$300

CP-132SC — similar to C-132S, except single rounded cutaway, crystal bridge pickup, parametric EQ.

Mfr.'s Sug. Retail	$1,249	$985	$560	$380

Hirade Series

This series was designed by Mass Hirade, Takamine founder.

H-5 — classical style, solid cedar top, round soundhole, 5 stripe wood bound body, wooden rosette, rosewood back/sides, mahogany neck, 12/19 fret ebony fingerboard, ebony bridge, 3 per side gold tuners with pearl buttons. Available in Natural finish. Current mfr.

Mfr.'s Sug. Retail	$1,599	$1,125	$520	$430

H-8 — similar to H-5, except features a solid spruce top.

Mfr.'s Sug. Retail	$2,199	$1,500	$720	$595

H-15 — classical style, solid spruce top, round soundhole, wood bound body, wooden rosette, rosewood back/sides, mahogany neck, 12/19 fret ebony fingerboard, ebony bridge with rosette matching inlay, 3 per side gold tuners with pearl buttons. Available in Natural finish. Current mfr.

Mfr.'s Sug. Retail	$3,899	$2,760	$1,350	$1,115

HP-7 — classical style, solid cedar top, round soundhole, 5 stripe wood bound body, wooden rosette, rosewood back/sides, mahogany neck, 12/19 fret ebony fingerboard, ebony bridge, 3 per side gold tuners with pearl buttons, crystal bridge pickups, parametric EQ. Available in Natural finish. Current mfr.

Mfr.'s Sug. Retail	$2,349	$1,675	$780	$645

Natural Series

N-10 — dreadnought style, solid cedar top, round soundhole, 3 stripe bound body, 5 stripe rosette, mahogany back/sides/neck, 14/20 fret rosewood fingerboard, rosewood strings through bridge, 3 per side gold tuners with amber buttons. Available in Natural finish. Current mfr.

Mfr.'s Sug. Retail	$949	$660	$325	$270

EN-10 — similar to N-10, except has crystal bridge pickup, 3 band EQ.

Mfr.'s Sug. Retail	$1,239	$980	$500	$370

EN-10C — similar to N-10, except has single rounded cutaway, crystal bridge pickup, 3 band EQ.

Mfr.'s Sug. Retail	$1,329	$1,000	$525	$400

N-15 — dreadnought style, solid cedar top, round soundhole, 3 stripe bound body, 5 stripe rosette, rosewood back/sides, mahogany neck, 14/20 fret rosewood fingerboard, rosewood strings through bridge, 3 per side gold tuners with amber buttons. Available in Natural finish. Current mfr.

Mfr.'s Sug. Retail	$1,139	$965	$470	$350

NP-15C — similar to N-15, except has single round cutaway, crystal bridge pickups, parametric EQ.

Mfr.'s Sug. Retail	$1,579	$1,175	$730	$535

EF-381 C
courtesy Takamine

CP-132 SC
courtesy Takamine

Grading	100%	EXCELLENT	AVERAGE

NP-18C — dreadnought style, single rounded cutaway, solid spruce top, round soundhole, abalone bound body/rosette, rosewood back/sides, mahogany neck, 14/20 fret ebony fingerboard, ebony strings through bridge, abalone logo peghead inlay, 3 per side gold tuners with amber buttons, crystal bridge pickup, parametric EQ. Available in Natural finish. Current mfr.

Mfr.'s Sug. Retail	$2,199	$1,650	$875	$555

N-20 — jumbo style, solid cedar top, round soundhole, 3 stripe bound body, 5 stripe rosette, mahogany back/sides/neck, 14/20 fret rosewood fingerboard, rosewood strings through bridge, 3 per side gold tuners with amber buttons. Available in Natural finish. Disc. 1996.

	100%	EXCELLENT	AVERAGE
		$470	$310

Last Mfr.'s Sug. Retail was $940.

EN-20 — similar to N-20, except has crystal bridge pickup, 3 band EQ.

Mfr.'s Sug. Retail	$1,389	$1,080	$740	$465

NP-25C — jumbo style, single rounded cutaway, solid cedar top, round soundhole, 3 stripe bound body, 5 stripe rosette, mahogany back/sides/neck, 14/20 fret rosewood fingerboard, rosewood strings through bridge, 3 per side gold tuners, crystal bridge pickups, parametric EQ. Available in Natural finish. Mfr. 1994 to date.

Mfr.'s Sug. Retail	$1,679	$1,200	$850	$550

N-40 — dreadnought style, solid red cedar top, round soundhole, 3 stripe bound body, 5 stripe rosette, mahogany back/sides/neck, 14/20 fret rosewood fingerboard, rosewood strings through bridge, 3 per side gold tuners. Available in Natural finish. Mfr. 1994 to date.

Mfr.'s Sug. Retail	$949	$755	$325	$270

EN-40C — similar to N-40, except has single round cutaway, crystal bridge pickups, 3 band EQ. Mfr. 1994 to date.

Mfr.'s Sug. Retail	$1,239	$995	$530	$355

NP-45C — dreadnought style, single rounded cutaway, red cedar top, round soundhole, 3 stripe bound body, 5 stripe rosette, rosewood back/sides, mahogany neck, 14/20 fret rosewood fingerboard, rosewood strings through bridge, 3 per side gold tuners, crystal bridge pickups, parametric EQ. Available in Natural finish. Mfr. 1994 to date.

Mfr.'s Sug. Retail	$1,489	$1,075	$635	$440

NP-65C — "country classic" body style, single rounded cutaway, solid cedar top, round soundhole, 3 stripe bound body, wooden rosette, rosewood back/sides, mahogany neck, 20 fret ebony fingerboard, classic style ebony bridge, classic style peghead, 3 per side gold tuners with amber buttons, crystal bridge pickups, parametric EQ. Available in Natural finish. Current mfr.

Mfr.'s Sug. Retail	$1,499	$1,050	$615	$425

Santa Fe Series

Santa Fe series instruments feature turquoise or abalone inlays and rosette designs with a Southwestern flavor.

ESF-93 — folk style, single rounded cutaway, solid cedar top, round soundhole, multi bound, wood inlay rosette, silky oak back/sides, mahogany neck, 21 fret ebony fingerboard with turquoise eagle inlay, ebony bridge with white black dot pins, silky oak peghead veneer with turquoise dot/abalone logo inlay, 3 per side gold tuners with amber buttons, piezo bridge pickups, parametric EQ, active electronics. Available in Natural finish. Mfd. 1993 only.

		$750	$495

Last Mfr.'s Sug. Retail was $1,500.

PSF-15C — dreadnought style, single rounded cutaway, solid cedar top, round soundhole, 3 stripe bound body/black crow rosette, rosewood sides, bookmatched rosewood back, mahogany neck, 21 fret rosewood fingerboard with turquoise dot inlay, turquoise eagle inlay at 12th fret, black headstock, rosewood bridge, 3 per side gold tuners, bridge pickup, preamp and parametric EQ. Available in Natural finish. Mfr. 1993 to date.

Mfr.'s Sug. Retail	$1,699	$900	$540	$450

PSF-35C — folk style, single rounded cutaway, solid cedar top, round soundhole, 3 stripe bound body/black crow rosette, rosewood back/sides, mahogany neck, 21 fret rosewood fingerboard with turquoise dot inlay, turquoise eagle inlay at 12th fret, open classical-style headstock, rosewood bridge, 3 per side gold tuners with amber buttons, bridge pickup, preamp and parametric EQ. Available in Natural finish. Mfd. 1993 to 1995.

		$750	$495

Last Mfr.'s Sug. Retail was $1,699.50.

PSF-48C — folk style, single rounded cutaway, solid spruce top, round soundhole, multi-bound body, wood inlay rosette, rosewood back/sides, mahogany neck, 21 fret ebony fingerboard with green abalone eagle inlay, strings through ebony bridge, rosewood peghead veneer with abalone dot/logo inlay, 3 per side gold tuners with amber buttons, piezo bridge pickups, parametric EQ, active electronics. Available in Natural finish. Mfr. 1993 to date.

Mfr.'s Sug. Retail	$1,999	$1,440	$720	$595

PSF-65C — folk style, single rounded cutaway, solid cedar top, round soundhole, 3 stripe bound body/black crow rosette, rosewood back/sides, mahogany neck, 21 fret rosewood fingerboard with turquoise dot inlay, turquoise eagle inlay at 12th fret, open classical-style headstock, rosewood bridge, 3 per side gold tuners, bridge pickup, preamp and parametric EQ. Available in Natural finish. Mfr. 1993 to date.

Mfr.'s Sug. Retail	$1,699	$1,200	$600	$495

The PSF-65C was designed for nylon string use.

H-5
courtesy Takamine

NP-18 C
courtesy Takamine

Grading		100%	EXCELLENT	AVERAGE

PSF-94 — folk style, single rounded cutaway, solid cedar top, round soundhole, multi-layer binding, wood inlay rosette, koa back/sides, mahogany neck, 20 fret rosewood fingerboard with abalone eagle inlay, rosewood strings through bridge, koa peghead veneer with abalone logo inlay, 3 per side gold tuners with brown pearl buttons, piezo bridge pickups, parametric EQ. Available in Natural finish. Mfd. 1994 only.

$925 $610
Last Mfr.'s Sug. Retail was $1,850.

Specials Series

EF-325SRC — dreadnought style, single rounded cutaway, solid spruce top, round soundhole, black pickguard, 5 stripe bound body/rosette, bubinga back/sides, mahogany neck, 14/20 fret bound rosewood fingerboard with pearl dot inlay, rosewood bridge with white black dot pins, 3 per side chrome tuners, crystal bridge pickups, 3 band EQ. Available in Clear Red finish. Current mfr.

Mfr.'s Sug. Retail	$1,295	$975	$560	$380

EF-350 MC
courtesy Takamine

TAMA

Instruments produced in Japan from 1975 through 1979 by Ibanez. Distributed in the U.S. by the Chesbro Music Company of Idaho Falls, Idaho.

The Tama trademark is better known on the Hoshino-produced quality drum sets. Never the less, the Tama trademark was used on 2 series of acoustic guitars offered during the mid to late 1970s. The first series introduced was entry level to good quality D-45 shaped acoustics that featured a laminated top. However, the quality level jumped on the second series. The second series featured a solid top, mahogany neck, and East Indian and Brazilian rosewoods, as well as a light oil finish.

One way to determine a solid top acoustic from a ply or laminated top is to check the cross section of the wood on the edge of the soundhole. If the wood seems continuous, it's probably a solid top. If you can see layers, or if the inside of the edge is painted (check the wood inside the top - if it is different in appearance from the outside it's probably laminated), then the top is plywood. No, it's not the sheets that you build houses with! A ply wood top is several layers of wood glued and pressed together. However, a solid top guitar will resonate better (because it's one piece of wood) and the tone will get better as the wood ages.

(Tama Guitars overview courtesy Michael R. Stanger, Stringed Instrument Division of Missoula, Montana)

TANARA

Instruments built in Korea and Indonesia. Distributed by the Chesbro Music Company of Idaho Falls, Idaho.

Tanara offers a range of acoustic and electric guitars designed for the entry level to student guitarist.

ACOUSTIC

Acoustic Series

All Tanara guitar models feature a round soundhole, 3 per side headstock, chrome hardware, and a Natural finish (unless otherwise specified).

SC26 — concert size steel string, pacific spruce top, mahogany back/sides. Current mfr.

Mfr.'s Sug. Retail	$219	$165	$110	$75

SD24 — dreadnought size, pacific spruce top, mahogany back/sides. Available in Natural gloss finish. Current mfr.

Mfr.'s Sug. Retail	$219	$165	$110	$75

SD26 — dreadnought size, natural spruce top, mahogany back/sides, adjustable neck, 3 per side machine heads. Available in Black, Brown Sunburst, and Natural gloss finish. Current mfr.

Mfr.'s Sug. Retail	$239	$180	$120	$80

SD30 — dreadnought size, spruce top, mahogany back/sides, rosewood fingerboard/bridge, scalloped 'X-bracing', 3 per side die-cast tuners. Available in Natural satin finish. Current mfr.

Mfr.'s Sug. Retail	$339	$255	$170	$115

SD32 — similar to the SD30, except in a 12-string configuration, 6 per side tuners, covered tuning gears. Current mfr.

Mfr.'s Sug. Retail	$379	$285	$185	$125

Classical Series

TC26 — concert size, spruce top, mahogany back/sides, adjustable neck, 3 per side butterfly knobs. Available in Pumpkin Amber finish. Current mfr.

Mfr.'s Sug. Retail	$189	$140	$90	$65

TC46 — similar to the TC26, except features ovankol back/sides, multiple binding. Available in Pumpkin Amber finish. Current mfr.

Mfr.'s Sug. Retail	$259	$195	$130	$90

ACOUSTIC ELECTRIC

TSF1 — grand concert size with single cutaway, spruce top, mahogany back/sides, bound body/headstock, bound rosewood fingerboard with offset pearl position markers, rosewood bridge, 3 per side chrome tuners, piezo pickup, volume/3 band EQ controls. Current mfr.

Mfr.'s Sug. Retail	$569	$425	$280	$190

TSJ5 — solid spruce top, mahogany back/sides/neck, rosewood fingerboard, 3 per side gold tuners, Fishman pickup, volume/EQ controls. Current mfr.

Mfr.'s Sug. Retail	$669	$500	$330	$225

Tama 3557-12
courtesy Dan Holden

Grading	100%	EXCELLENT	AVERAGE

ACOUSTIC ELECTRIC BASS

TR720BF — select maple top, maple back/sides/neck, die-cast tuners. Available in Natural finish. Current mfr.

Mfr.'s Sug. Retail	$779	$585	$385	$260

TANGLEWOOD

Instruments currently produced in Korea and Indonesia. Distributed by the European Music Company, Ltd. of Kent, England.

The European Music Company, Ltd. is currently offering a wide range of acoustic and electric guitar models under the **Tanglewood** trademark. These solidly built instruments offer the beginning and intermediate player a quality guitar for the price. For further information regarding model specification and pricing, contact the European Music Company, Ltd. through the Index of Current Manufacturers located in the back of this edition.

TAYLOR

Instruments currently built in El Cajon, California. Distributed by Taylor Guitars of El Cajon, California.

Previous production was based in Lemon Grove, California from 1974 through 1987.

Founding partners Bob Taylor, Steve Schemmer, and Kurt Listug were all working at the American Dream guitar repair shop in Lemon Grove, California, in the early 1970s. In 1974, the trio bought the shop and converted it into a guitar building factory. The company went through early *growing pains* throughout the late 1970s, but slowly and surely the guitars began catching on. In 1983, Listug and Taylor bought out Schemmer's share of the company, and re-incorporated. Fueled by sales of models such as the **Grand Concert** in 1984, the company expanded into new facilities in Santee, California (near El Cajon) three years later. Taylor and Listug continue to experiment with guitar construction and models - A good example would be the **Baby Taylor** model (list $299) which is a 3/4 size guitar with a solid top and laminated back and sides.

Bob Taylor
courtesy Taylor Guitars

Taylor Model Designations

Each Taylor model number also describes the particular guitar in relationship to the overa ll product line. The first of three numbers denotes the series (Taylor series comprise a specific combination of woods, bindings, inlays, etc).

The second number indicates whether it is a six string **(1)**, or a 12 string **(5)**. The exception to this rule is the 400 series, which include models 420 and 422.

Finally, the third number indicates the body size: Dreadnought **(0)**, Grand Concert **(2)**, and Jumbo **(5)**. The Grand Auditorium size models carry a prefix of **GA**.

Any upper case letters that follow the three digit designation may indicate a cutaway **(C)** or a left-handed model **(L)**.

Taylor Body Dimensions

Dreadnought: Body Width 16", Body Length 20", Body Depth 4 5/8".

Grand Auditorium: Body Width 16", Body Length 20", Body Depth 4 5/8".

Grand Concert: Body Width 15", Body Length 19 1/2", Body Depth 4 1/8".

Jumbo: Body Width 17", Body Length 21", Body Depth 4 5/8".

ACOUSTIC

Taylor Retail list prices do not include a case. Cases carry an additional cost. TC Series h ardshell cases retail at $299, and SC Series SKB/Taylor cases retail at $199.

Taylor acoustics are available with a wide range of custom options, including Engelmann spru ce tops or Fishman transducer systems. . There is not charge for a left-handed configuration (not available on all models).
Add $240 for Sunburst finish.

BABY TAYLOR — 3/4 size, dreadnought body, solid Sitka spruce top, round soundhole, laser-etched rosette, mahogany veneer back/sides, mahogany neck, 14/19 fret ebony fingerboard with pearloid dot inlay, ebony bridge, Lexan peghead veneer, 3 per side chrome diecast tuners. Available in Natural satin finish. Mfr. 1997 to date.

Mfr.'s Sug. Retail	$299	$250	$150	$100

Baby Taylor M — similar to the Baby Taylor, except features a mahogany top. Available in Natural satin finish. Current Mfr.

Mfr.'s Sug. Retail	$299	$250	$150	$100

300 Series

The 300 series models each feature a solid Sitka spruce top, sapele mahogany back and sides, 3- ply black plastic body binding, plastic ring inlay rosette, mahogany neck, 25 1/2" scale, 20 fret ebony fingerboard with pearl dot inlay, India n rosewood peghead veneer, ebony bridge, Tusq nut and saddle.

310 — dreadnought body, tortoise shell pickguard, 6-string configuration, 3 per side chrome Grover tuners. Available in Natural satin finish with gloss top. Mfr. 1998 to date.

Mfr.'s Sug. Retail	$999	$795	$525	$375

310 CE — similar to the 310, except features a single Venetian cutaway dreadnought body, Fishman Prefix electronics. Available in Natural satin finish with gloss top. Mfr. 1998 to date.

Mfr.'s Sug. Retail	$1,359	$1,100	$700	$475

312 CE — grand concert body with single Venetian cutaway, tortoise shell pickguard, 6-string configuration, 3 per side chrome Grover tuners, Fishman Prefix electronics. Available in Natural satin finish with gloss top. Mfr. 1998 to date.

Mfr.'s Sug. Retail	$1,419	$1,150	$750	$475

Grading	100%	EXCELLENT	AVERAGE

314 — grand auditorium body, tortoise shell pickguard, 6-string configuration, 3 per side chrome Grover tuners. Available in Natural satin finish with gloss top. Mfr. 1998 to date.

Mfr.'s Sug. Retail	$1,119	$895	$575	$375

314 CE — similar to the 314, except features a single Venetian cutaway dreadnought body, Fishman Prefix electronics. Available in Natural satin finish with gloss top. Mfr. 1998 to date.

Mfr.'s Sug. Retail	$1,479	$1,185	$775	$500

355 — jumbo body, tortoise shell pickguard, 12-string configuration, 6 per side chrome Grover tuners. Available in Natural satin finish with gloss top. Mfr. 1998 to date.

Mfr.'s Sug. Retail	$1,359	$1,100	$700	$475

400 Series

In 1998, Taylor changed the 400 series' mahogany or maple back and sides in favor of solid Ova ngkol (also spelled Ovankol). All 6-string models feature scalloped bracing. Earlier acoustic/electric models may be equipped with an optiona l Acoustic Matrix pickup system.

410 — dreadnought body, solid (Sitka) spruce top, round soundhole, tortoise shell pickguard, white plastic body binding, 3-ply body, 3 ring inlay rosette, solid mahogany back/sides, mahogany neck, 14/20 fret rosewood fingerboard with pearl dot inlay, rosewood bridge, rosewood veneer on peghead, 3 per side chrome Grover tuners. Available in Natural satin finish with gloss top. Current mfr.

Mfr.'s Sug. Retail	$1,239	$995	$650	$425

In 1994, pearl peghead logo inlay was introduced.

In 1998, Ovankol back/sides replaced mahogany back/sides; ebony fingerboard replaced the rosewood fingerboard; ebony bridge replaced the rosewood bridge.

410 CE — similar to 410, except has an single Venetian cutaway body, Fishman Prefix system. Available in Natural satin finish with gloss top. Current mfr.

Mfr.'s Sug. Retail	$1,599	$1,275	$825	$550

420 — similar to 410, except has maple back and sides. Available in natural finish. Disc, 1997.

	$750	$425

Last Mfr.'s Sug. Retail was $1,198.

420 PF Limited Edition — similar to 410, except has solid pau ferro back and sides. Disc. 1997.

	$650	$425

Last Mfr.'s Sug. Retail was $1,400.

450 — similar to 410, except has 12-string configuration, 6 per side tuners. Disc. 1997.

	$795	$475

Last Mfr.'s Sug. Retail was $1,298.

412 — grand concert body, solid spruce top, round soundhole, tortoise shell pickguard, white plastic body binding, 3-ply body, 3 ring inlay rosette, solid mahogany back/sides, mahogany neck, 14/20 fret rosewood fingerboard with pearl dot inlay, rosewood bridge, rosewood veneer on peghead, 3 per side chrome Grover tuners. Available in Natural satin finish with gloss top. Disc. 1998.

	$625	$375

Last Mfr.'s Sug. Retail was $998.

412 CE — similar to the 412, except features single Venetian cutaway body, Ovangkol back/sides, ebony fingerboard, ebony bridge, Fishman Prefix electronics. Available in Natural satin finish with gloss top. Mfr. 1998 to date.

Mfr.'s Sug. Retail	$1,659	$1,350	$850	$575

422 — similar to 412, except has maple back and sides. Disc. 1998.

	$750	$425

Last Mfr.'s Sug. Retail was $1,198.

414 — grand auditorium body, solid Sitka spruce top, round soundhole, tortoise shell pickguard, white plastic body binding, 3-ply body, 3 ring inlay rosette, solid Ovangkol back/sides, mahogany neck, 14/20 fret ebony fingerboard with pearl dot inlay, ebony bridge, rosewood veneer on peghead, 3 per side chrome Grover tuners. Available in Natural satin finish with gloss top. Mfr. 1998 to date.

Mfr.'s Sug. Retail	$1,359	$1,100	$700	$475

414 CE — similar to 414, except has a single Venetian cutaway body, Fishman Prefix system. Available in Natural satin finish with gloss top. Current mfr.

Mfr.'s Sug. Retail	$1,719	$1,375	$895	$595

415 — jumbo body, solid Sitka spruce top, round soundhole, tortoise shell pickguard, white plastic body binding, 3-ply body, 3 ring inlay rosette, solid Ovangkol back/sides, mahogany neck, 14/20 fret ebony fingerboard with pearl dot inlay, ebony bridge, rosewood veneer on peghead, 3 per side chrome Grover tuners. Available in Natural satin finish with gloss top. Mfr. 1998 to date.

Mfr.'s Sug. Retail	$1,359	$1,100	$700	$475

500 Series

The 500 series models feature solid mahogany backs and sides; current fancy appointments inc lude abalone inlay on the soundhole rosettes and pearl diamond inlays on the fingerboard.

410 Model
courtesy Taylor Guitars

Grading	100%	EXCELLENT	AVERAGE

510 — dreadnought body, solid Engelmann spruce top, round soundhole, tortoise shell pickguard, 3 stripe bound body/rosette, solid mahogany back/sides/neck, 14/20 fret ebony fingerboard with pearl dot inlay, ebony bridge with black pins, rosewood veneer on peghead, 3 per side gold tuners. Available in Natural gloss finish. Current mfr.

Mfr.'s Sug. Retail	$1,739	$1,400	$900	$600

In 1994, pearl peghead logo inlay, abalone rosette, abalone 'slotted' diamond fingerboard inlay, black abalone dot bridgepins replaced original items.

In 1998, chrome Grover tuners replaced the gold-plated tuners.

510 CE — similar to 510, except has a single Venetian cutaway body, Fishman Onboard Blender system. Available in Natural gloss finish. Mfr. 1998 to date.

Mfr.'s Sug. Retail	$2,099	$1,675	$1,100	$700

512 — grand concert body, solid Engelmann spruce top, round soundhole, tortoise shell pickguard, 3 stripe bound body/rosette, solid mahogany back/sides/neck, 14/20 fret ebony fingerboard with pearl dot inlay, ebony bridge with black pins, rosewood veneer on peghead, 3 per side gold tuners. Available in Natural gloss finish. Current mfr.

Mfr.'s Sug. Retail	$1,859	$1,495	$975	$650

In 1994, pearl peghead logo inlay, abalone rosette, abalone 'slotted' diamond fingerboard inlay, black abalone dot bridgepins replaced original items.

In 1998, chrome Grover tuners replaced the gold-plated tuners.

514 C — grand auditorium body with single Venetian cutaway, solid Western red cedar top, round soundhole, tortoise shell pickguard, 3 stripe bound body/rosette, solid mahogany back/sides/neck, 14/20 fret ebony fingerboard with pearl dot inlay, ebony bridge with black pins, rosewood veneer on peghead, 3 per side gold tuners. Available in Natural gloss finish. Disc. 1998.

		$1,350	$795

Last Mfr.'s Sug. Retail was $2,198.

In 1994, pearl peghead logo inlay, abalone rosette, abalone 'slotted' diamond fingerboard inlay, black abalone dot bridgepins replaced original items.

In 1998, chrome Grover tuners replaced the gold-plated tuners.

514 CE — similar to 514 C, except has a Fishman Onboard Blender system. Available in Natural gloss finish. Mfr. 1998.

Mfr.'s Sug. Retail	$2,459	$1,950	$1,295	$850

555 — jumbo body, 12-string configuration, solid Sitka spruce top, round soundhole, tortoise shell pickguard, 3 stripe bound body/rosette, solid mahogany back/sides/neck, 14/20 fret ebony fingerboard with pearl dot inlay, ebony bridge with black pins, rosewood veneer on peghead, 6 per side gold tuners. Available in Natural gloss finish. Current mfr.

Mfr.'s Sug. Retail	$2,219	$1,775	$1,150	$750

In 1994, pearl peghead logo inlay, abalone rosette, abalone 'slotted' diamond fingerboard inlay, black abalone dot bridgepins replaced original items.

In 1998, chrome Grover tuners replaced the gold-plated tuners.

600 Series

The 600 series features curly maple back and side, scalloped bracing (on the 6-string models), an abalone soundhole rosette, and pearl "Leaf Pattern" inlays.

The models originally featured Amber-stained back and sides and gloss finish. In 1998, when 5 acoustic/electric models debuted, the stain colors expanded to Amber, Black, Blue, Green, Natural, and Red (and gloss finish).

610 — dreadnought body, solid spruce top, round soundhole, tortoise shell pickguard, white plasic body binding, ring design rosette, solid maple back/sides, mahogany neck, 14/20 fret bound rosewood fingerboard with pearl dot inlay, rosewood bridge with black pins, rosewood veneer on peghead, 3 per side gold Grover tuners. Available in Amber Stain finish. Current mfr.

		$1,150	$675

Last Mfr.'s Sug. Retail was $1,898.

In 1994, the abalone rosette, bound ebony fingerboard with pearl leaf inlay, ebony bridge with black abalone dot bridge pins, ebony peghead veneer with pearl logo inlay replaced original items.

610 CE — similar to 610, except has an single Venetian cutaway body, Sitka spruce top, Big leaf maple back/sides, Fishman Onboard Blender system. Available in Amber, Black, Blue, Green, Natural, and Red gloss finishes. Mfr. 1998 to date.

Mfr.'s Sug. Retail	$2,459

612 — grand concert body, solid spruce top, round soundhole, tortoise shell pickguard, 3 stripe bound body/rosette, solid maple back/sides, mahogany neck, 14/20 fret bound rosewood fingerboard with pearl dot inlay, rosewood bridge with black pins, rosewood veneer on peghead, 3 per side gold tuners. Available in Natural finish. Disc. 1992.

		$775	$600

Last Mfr.'s Sug. Retail was $1,840.

612 C — similar to 612, except has single Venetian cutaway body. Mfd. 1993 to 1998.

		$1,350	$775

Last Mfr.'s Sug. Retail was $2,198.

In 1994, single round cutaway, abalone rosette, bound ebony fingerboard with pearl leaf inlay, ebony bridge with black abalone dot bridge pins, ebony peghead veneer with pearl logo inlay replaced original items.

510 Model
courtesy Taylor Guitars

615 Model
courtesy Taylor Guitars

Grading	100%	EXCELLENT	AVERAGE

612 CE — similar to 612, except has an single Venetian cutaway body, Sitka spruce top, Big leaf maple back/sides, Fishman Onboard Blender system. Available in Amber, Black, Blue, Green, Natural, and Red gloss finishes. Mfr. 1998 to date.
Mfr.'s Sug. Retail $2,579

614 C — grand auditorium body, with single Venetian cutaway, solid spruce top, round soundhole, tortoise shell pickguard, 3 stripe bound body/rosette, solid maple back/sides, mahogany neck, 14/20 fret bound rosewood fingerboard with pearl dot inlay, rosewood bridge with black pins, rosewood veneer on peghead, 3 per side gold tuners. Available in Natural finish. Disc. 1998.

	$1,400	$895	

Last Mfr.'s Sug. Retail was $2,298.

614 CE — similar to 614, except has an single Venetian cutaway body, Sitka spruce top, Big leaf maple back/sides, Fishman Onboard Blender system. Available in Amber, Black, Blue, Green, Natural, and Red gloss finishes. Mfr. 1998 to date.
Mfr.'s Sug. Retail $2,699

615 — jumbo body, solid spruce top, round soundhole, tortoise pickguard, 3 stripe bound body/rosette, solid maple back/sides, mahogany neck, 14/20 fret bound rosewood fingerboard with pearl dot inlay, rosewood bridge with black pins, rosewood veneer on peghead, 3 per side gold tuners. Available in Natural finish. Disc. 1998.

	$1,350	$775	

Last Mfr.'s Sug. Retail was $2,198.

In 1994, abalone rosette, bound ebony fingerboard with pearl leaf inlay, ebony bridge with black abalone dot bridge pins, ebony peghead veneer with pearl logo inlay replaced original items.

615 CE — similar to 615, except has an single Venetian cutaway body, Sitka spruce top, Big leaf maple back/sides, Fishman Onboard Blender system. Available in Amber, Black, Blue, Green, Natural, and Red gloss finishes. Mfr. 1998 to date.
Mfr.'s Sug. Retail $2,699

655 — jumbo body, 12-string configuration, solid spruce top, round soundhole, tortoise pickguard, 3 stripe bound body/rosette, solid maple back/sides, mahogany neck, 14/20 fret bound rosewood fingerboard with pearl dot inlay, rosewood bridge with black pins, rosewood veneer on peghead, 6 per side gold tuners. Available in Natural finish. Disc. 1998.

	$1,475	$850	

Last Mfr.'s Sug. Retail was $2,398.

655 CE — similar to 655, except has an single Venetian cutaway body, Sitka spruce top, Big leaf maple back/sides, Fishman Onboard Blender system. Available in Amber, Black, Blue, Green, Natural, and Red gloss finishes. Mfr. 1998 to date.
Mfr.'s Sug. Retail $2,939

700 Series

The 700 Series models feature Indian rosewood back and sides, abalone soundhole rosette and neck dot inlays. Models prior to 1998 have solid spruce tops; models after 1998 now feature Western red cedar tops.

710 — dreadnought body, solid spruce top, round soundhole, tortoise shell pickguard, 3 stripe bound body/rosette, rosewood back/sides, mahogany neck, 14/20 fret ebony fingerboard with pearl dot inlay, ebony bridge with black pins, rosewood veneer on peghead, 3 per side gold tuners. Available in Natural finish. Current mfr.

Mfr.'s Sug. Retail $1,979	$1,575	$1,000	$675

In 1994, abalone rosette, abalone dot fingerboard inlay, black abalone dot bridge pins, pearl logo peghead inlay replaced original items.

In 1998, a Western Red cedar top replaced spruce top.

710 CE — similar to 710, except has a single Venetian cutaway body, Fishman Onboard Blender system. Available in Natural gloss finish. Mfr. 1998 to date.

Mfr.'s Sug. Retail $2,339	$1,875	$1,225	$800

750 — similar to 710, except has 12-string configuration, 6 per side tuners. Disc. 1998.

	$1,150	$675	

Last Mfr.'s Sug. Retail was $1,898.

712 — grand concert body, solid spruce top, round soundhole, tortoise shell pickguard, 3 stripe bound body and rosette, rosewood back/sides, mahogany neck, 14/20 fret ebony fingerboard with pearl dot inlay, ebony bridge with black pins, rosewood veneer on peghead, 3 per side gold tuners. Available in Natural finish. Current mfr.

Mfr.'s Sug. Retail $2,099	$1,675	$1,100	$725

In 1994, abalone rosette, abalone dot fingerboard inlay, black abalone dot bridge pins, pearl logo peghead inlay replaced original items.

In 1998, a Western Red cedar top replaced spruce top.

714 — grand auditorium body, solid spruce top, round soundhole, tortoise shell pickguard, 3 stripe bound body and rosette, rosewood back/sides, mahogany neck, 14/20 fret ebony fingerboard with pearl dot inlay, ebony bridge with black pins, rosewood veneer on peghead, 3 per side gold tuners. Available in Natural finish. Current mfr.

Mfr.'s Sug. Retail $2,219	$1,775	$1,150	$750

In 1998, a Western Red cedar top replaced spruce top.

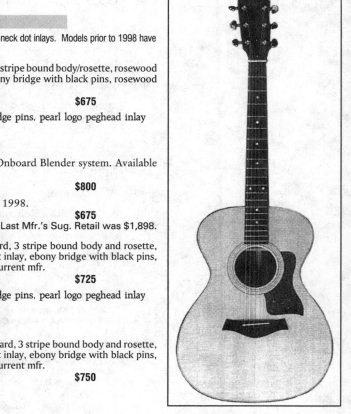

712 Model
courtesy Taylor Guitars

Grading	100%	EXCELLENT	AVERAGE

714 CE — similar to 714, except has a single Venetian cutaway body, Fishman Onboard Blender system. Available in Natural gloss finish. Mfr. 1998 to date.

Mfr.'s Sug. Retail	$2,579	$2,100	$1,350	$895

800 Series

The Taylor 800 series are referred to as "the decendants of Bob Taylor's original design". These deluxe models feature Indian rosewood back and sides, scalloped bracing (on 6-string models), abalone soundhole rosette, and pearl "Progressive Diamond" fretboard inlay.

810 — dreadnought body, solid (Sitka) spruce top, round soundhole, tortoise shell pickguard, 3 stripe bound body, abalone rosette, Indian rosewood back/sides, mahogany neck, 14/20 fret bound rosewood fingerboard with pearl snowflake inlay, rosewood bridge with black abalone dot pins, rosewood veneer on bound peghead with pearl logo inlay, 3 per side gold tuners. Available in Natural finish. Current mfr.

Mfr.'s Sug. Retail	$2,219	$1,775	$1,150	$750

In 1994, pearl progressive diamond fingerboard inlay replaced the snowflake inlay.

In 1998, ebony fingerboard replaced rosewood fingerboard; ebony bridge replaced the rosewood bridge.

810 CE — similar to 810, except has a single Florentine or Venetian cutaway body, Fishman Onboard Blender system. Available in Natural gloss finish. Mfr. 1998 to date.

Mfr.'s Sug. Retail	$2,579	$2,100	$1,350	$895

812 — grand concert body, solid (Sitka) spruce top, round soundhole, tortoise shell pickguard, 3 stripe bound body, abalone rosette, rosewood back/sides, mahogany neck, 14/20 fret bound rosewood fingerboard with pearl snowflake inlay, rosewood bridge with black abalone dot pins, rosewood veneer on bound peghead with pearl logo inlay, 3 per side gold tuners. Available in Natural finish. Disc. 1992.

		$995	$650

Last Mfr.'s Sug. Retail was $1,960.

812 C — similar to 812, except has single sharp cutaway. Mfd. 1993 to 1998.

		$1,350	$800

Last Mfr.'s Sug. Retail was $2,298.

In 1994, single round cutaway, pearl progressive diamond fingerboard inlay replaced original items.

812 CE — similar to 812, except has a single Florentine or Venetian cutaway body, Fishman Onboard Blender system. Available in Natural gloss finish. Mfr. 1998 to date.

Mfr.'s Sug. Retail	$2,699	$2,150	$1,400	$925

814 C — grand auditorium body with single rounded cutaway, solid (Sitka) spruce top, round soundhole, tortoise pickguard, 3 stripe bound body, abalone rosette, rosewood back/sides, mahogany neck, 14/20 fret bound rosewood fingerboard with pearl snowflake inlay, rosewood bridge with black abalone dot pins, rosewood veneer on bound peghead with pearl logo inlay, 3 per side gold tuners. Disc. 1998.

		$1,450	$825

Last Mfr.'s Sug. Retail was $2,398.

814 CE — similar to 814 C, except has a Fishman Onboard Blender system. Available in Natural gloss finish. Mfr. 1998 to date.

Mfr.'s Sug. Retail	$2,819	$2,250	$1,475	$950

815 C — jumbo body with single sharp cutaway, solid (Sitka) spruce top, round soundhole, tortoise pickguard, 3 stripe bound body, abalone rosette, rosewood back/sides, mahogany neck, 14/20 fret bound rosewood fingerboard with pearl snowflake inlay, rosewood bridge with black abalone dot pins, rosewood veneer on bound peghead with pearl logo inlay, 3 per side gold tuners. Mfr. 1993 to date.

		$1,450	$825

Last Mfr.'s Sug. Retail was $2,398.

In 1994, pearl progressive diamond fingerboard inlay replaced original item.

815 CE — similar to 815 C, except has a Fishman Onboard Blender system. Available in Natural gloss finish. Mfr. 1998 to date.

Mfr.'s Sug. Retail	$2,819	$2,250	$1,475	$950

855 — jumbo body, 12-string configuration, solid (Sitka) spruce top, round soundhole, tortoise shell pickguard, 3 stripe bound body, abalone rosette, rosewood back/sides, mahogany neck, 14/20 fret bound rosewood fingerboard with pearl snowflake inlay, rosewood bridge with black abalone dot pins, rosewood veneer on bound peghead with pearl logo inlay, 6 per side gold tuners. Available in Natural finish. Current mfr.

Mfr.'s Sug. Retail	$2,699	$2,150	$1,400	$925

In 1994, pearl progressive diamond fingerboard inlay replaced original item.

900 Series

The deluxe 900 series models feature Engelmann spruce tops, Indian rosewood back and sides, scalloped bracing (on the 6-string models), abalone top edging combined with rosewood binding, distinct abalone soundhole rosette, and the abalone and pearl "Cindy" design fingerboard inlays.

910 — dreadnought body, solid (Engelmann) spruce top, round soundhole, tortoise shell pickguard, abalone edge inlay/rosewood body binding, abalone rosette, maple back/sides/neck, 14/20 fret ebony fingerboard with abalone stylized inlay, ebony bridge with black abalone dot pins, rosewood peghead veneer with abalone stylized T/logo inlay, 3 per side gold tuners. Available in Natural finish. Current mfr.

Mfr.'s Sug. Retail	$3,779	$3,200	$2,275	$N/A

In 1993, rosewood back/sides, mahogany neck were optionally available.

In 1994, abalone purfling, abalone flower fingerboard inlay replaced original items, abalone stylized T peghead inlay was discontinued.

Grading	100%	EXCELLENT	AVERAGE

912 — grand concert body, solid (Engelmann) spruce top, round soundhole, tortoise shell pickguard, wood bound body, abalone rosette, maple back/sides/neck, 14/20 fret ebony fingerboard with abalone stylized inlay, ebony bridge with black abalone dot pins, rosewood veneer with abalone stylized T/logo inlay on peghead, 3 per side gold tuners. Available in Natural finish. Disc. 1992.

	$1,325	$N/A	
		Last Mfr.'s Sug. Retail was $2,715.	

912 C — similar to 912, except has single Florentine or Venetian cutaway body. Mfr. 1993 to date.

Mfr.'s Sug. Retail	$4,139	$3,500	$2,500	$N/A

In 1994, abalone purfling, abalone flower fingerboard inlay replaced original items, abalone stylized T peghead inlay was discontinued.

914 C — similar to the 921, except features a grand auditorium body with a single Florentine or Venetian cutaway. Current mfr.

Mfr.'s Sug. Retail	$4,259	$3,625	$2,550	$N/A

915 — jumbo body, solid spruce top, round soundhole, tortoise pickguard, wood bound body, abalone rosette, maple back/sides/neck, 14/20 fret ebony fingerboard with abalone stylized inlay, ebony bridge with black abalone dot pins, rosewood veneer with abalone stylized T/logo inlay on peghead, 3 per side gold tuners. Available in Natural finish. Disc. 1992.

	$1,400	$N/A	
		Last Mfr.'s Sug. Retail was $2,815.	

915 C — similar to 915, except has single Florentine or Venetian cutaway body. Mfr. 1998 to date.

Mfr.'s Sug. Retail	$4,259	$3,625	$2,550	$N/A

955 — jumbo body, 12-string configuration, solid spruce top, round soundhole, tortoise shell pickguard, wood bound body, abalone rosette, maple back/sides/neck, 14/20 fret ebony fingerboard with abalone stylized inlay, ebony bridge with black abalone dot pins, rosewood veneer with abalone stylized T/logo inlay on peghead, 6 per side gold tuners. Available in Natural finish. Current mfr.

Mfr.'s Sug. Retail	$4,139	$3,500	$2,500	$N/A

Koa Series

Different Koa Series models feature Engelmann spruce, Western Red cedar, or Hawaiian koa tops. Each model features Hawaiian koa back and sides, tortoiseshell body binding, abalone rosette, mahogany neck, 20 fret ebony fingerboard with a special 1995 Limited Edition pattern, ebony bridge with black bridgepins, ebony peghead veneer, gold plated Grover tuners.

K 10 — dreadnought body, Engelmann spruce top, 6-string configuration, 3 per side tuners. Available in Natural gloss finish. Mfr. 1998 to date.

Mfr.'s Sug. Retail	$2,699

K 14 C — grand auditorium body with single Venetian cutaway, Western Red cedar top, 6-string configuration, 3 per side tuners. Available in Natural gloss finish. Mfr. 1998 to date.

Mfr.'s Sug. Retail	$3,179

K 20 — dreadnought body, koa top/back/sides/neck, round soundhole, tortoise pickguard, 3 stripe bound body, abalone rosette, 14/20 fret rosewood fingerboard with pearl diamond inlay, rosewood bridge with black abalone dot pins, ebony veneer with abalone logo inlay on peghead, 3 per side gold tuners. Available in Natural finish. Disc. 1992.

	$1,050	$695
	Last Mfr.'s Sug. Retail was $2,115.	

This model had solid spruce top optionally available.

K 20 C — similar to the K 20, except features single Venetian cutaway body, Hawaiian koa top, mahogany neck, ebony fingerboard with 1995 Limited Edition pattern inlay, ebony bridge, tortoise body binding. Available in Natural gloss finish. Mfr. 1998 to date.

Mfr.'s Sug. Retail	$3,179

K 22 (Version I) — grand concert body, koa top/back/sides/neck, round soundhole, tortoise pickguard, 3 stripe bound body, abalone rosette, 14/20 fret rosewood fingerboard with pearl diamond inlay, rosewood bridge with black abalone dot pins, ebony veneer with abalone logo inlay on peghead, 3 per side gold tuners. Available in Natural finish. Disc. 1992.

	$1,000	$700
	Last Mfr.'s Sug. Retail was $2,190.	

K 22 (Version II) — similar to the K 22 (Version I), except features a Hawaiian koa top, mahogany neck, tortoise body binding, 14/20 fret ebony fingerboard with the 1995 Limited Edition pattern inlay, ebony bridge. Mfr. 1998 to date.

Mfr.'s Sug. Retail	$3,059

K 65 — jumbo body, Hawaiian koa top, 12-string configuration, 6 per side tuners. Available in Natural gloss finish. Mfr. 1998 to date.

Mfr.'s Sug. Retail	$3,419

Presentation Series

The Taylor **Presentation Series** guitar models each feature a solid Engelmann spruce top, scalloped 'X' bracing (tapered on the PS 55), ivoroid body binding with abalone edging, solid Hawaiian Koa back and sides, abalone soundhole rosette, mahogany neck, 25 1/2" scale, 20 fret ebony fingerboard with "Byzantine" fretboard inlays, ebony bridge, ebony peghead veneer, Tusq nut and saddle, and gold Schaller tuners with ebony buttons.

PS 10 — dreadnought body, 6-string configuration, 3 per side tuners. Available in Natural gloss finish. Current mfr.

Mfr.'s Sug. Retail	$9,059	$7,700	$6,000	$N/A

K-20 Model
courtesy Taylor Guitars

Grading	100%	EXCELLENT	AVERAGE

PS 12 C — grand concert body with single Venetian cutaway, 6-string configuration, 3 per side tuners. Available in Natural gloss finish. Current mfr.

Mfr.'s Sug. Retail	$9,419	$8,000	$6,150	$N/A

PS 14 C — grand auditorium body with single Venetian cutaway, 6-string configuration, 3 per side tuners. Available in Natural gloss finish. Current mfr.

Mfr.'s Sug. Retail	$9,539	$8,100	$6,200	$N/A

PS 15 — jumbo body, 6-string configuration, 3 per side tuners. Available in Natural gloss finish. Current mfr.

Mfr.'s Sug. Retail	$9,299	$7,900	$6,000	$N/A

PS 55 — jumbo body, 12-string configuration, 6 per side tuners. Available in Natural gloss finish. Current mfr.

Mfr.'s Sug. Retail	$9,419	$8,000	$6,200	$N/A

Signature Series

DCSM DAN CRARY SIGNATURE — single rounded cutaway dreadnought body, Sitka spruce top, round soundhole, tortoise pickguard, 5 stripe white plastic body binding, abalone rosette, Indian rosewood back/sides, mahogany neck, 25 1/2" scale, 14/20 fret bound ebony fingerboard with pearl diamond inlay, ebony bridge with black abalone dot pins, bound rosewood peghead veneer with pearl logo inlay, 3 per side gold tuners. Available in Natural gloss finish. Current mfr.

Body Width 16", Body Length 20", Body Depth 4 5/8".

Mfr.'s Sug. Retail	$2,459	$1,975	$1,475	$N/A

This model was designed in conjunction with guitarist Dan Crary.

LKSM LEO KOTTKE SIGNATURE — 12 string configuration, jumbo body, spruce top, round soundhole, rosewood body binding, rosette, American mahogany back/sides, mahogany neck, 14/20 fret ebony fingerboard, ebony bridge with black pins, rosewood peghead veneer with pearl logo inlay, 6 per side gold tuners. Available in Natural finish. Current mfr.

Body Width 17", Body Length 21", Body Depth 4 5/8".

Mfr.'s Sug. Retail	$2,819	$2,250	$1,695	$N/A

In 1994, 12th fret fingerboard inlay was discontinued.

This model was designed in conjunction with guitarist Leo Kottke.

LKSM-6 Leo Kottke Signature — similar to the LKSM, except in a 6-string configuration, 3 per side tuners. Available in Natural gloss finish. Mfr. 1997 to date.

Body Width 17", Body Length 21", Body Depth 4 5/8".

Mfr.'s Sug. Retail	$2,699	$2,150	$1,625	$N/A

Walnut Series

Different Walnut Series models feature Sitka Spruce, Western Red cedar, or Claro Walnut tops. Each Walnut Series guitar models feature scalloped 'X' bracing (tapered on the W 65), ivoroid body binding with abalone edging, solid Claro Walnut back and sides, abalone soundhole rosette, mahogany neck, 25 1/2" scale, 20 fret ebony fingerboard with Original 900 Series inlay pattern, ebony bridge, ebony peghead veneer, Tusq nut and saddle, and gold Grover tuners. Taylor's Walnut Series was introduced in 1998.

W 10 — dreadnought body, Sitka spruce top, 6-string configuration, 3 per side tuners. Available in Natural gloss finish. Mfr. 1998 to date.

Mfr.'s Sug. Retail	$3,179

W 12 C — grand concert body with single Venetian cutaway, Western Red cedar top, 6-string configuration, 3 per side tuners. Available in Natural gloss finish. Mfr. 1998 to date.

Mfr.'s Sug. Retail	$3,539

W 14 C — grand auditorium body with single Venetian cutaway, Western Red cedar top, 6-string configuration, 3 per side tuners. Available in Natural gloss finish. Mfr. 1998 to date.

Mfr.'s Sug. Retail	$3,659

W 15 — jumbo body, Sitka spruce top, 6-string configuration, 3 per side tuners. Available in Natural gloss finish. Mfr. 1998 to date.

Mfr.'s Sug. Retail	$3,419

W 65 — jumbo body, Claro walnut top, 12-string configuration, 6 per side tuners. Available in Natural gloss finish. Current mfr.

Mfr.'s Sug. Retail	$3,779

ACOUSTIC BASS

AB Series

Bob Taylor and Steve Klein collaborated on an acoustic bass design in a 34" scale with a Fishman pickup system. The rugged padded gig bag for the AB Series basses lists at $155.

AB 1 — single rounded cutaway body, Sitka spruce top, round soundhole ofset to the treble bout, tuned Imbuia ring rosette, Imbuia 'Brazilian Walnut' back/sides, mahogany neck/Imbuia peghead, 24 fret ebony fingerboard with pearl 'Steve Klein' signature inlay, ebony bridge, Imbuia peghead veneer, 2 per side chrome Grover tuners. Available in Natural satin finish. Current mfr.

Mfr.'s Sug. Retail	$2,595	$2,100	$1,350	$895

AB 2 — similar to the AB 1, except features Imbuia top. Available in Natural satin finish. Current mfr.

Mfr.'s Sug. Retail	$2,595	$2,100	$1,350	$895

Grading	100%	EXCELLENT	AVERAGE

AB 3 — similar to the AB 1, except features big leaf maple back/sides, tuned ebony ring rosette, maple neck, ebony peghead veneer, white plastic body binding. Available in Amber, Black, Blue, Green, Natural, and Red gloss finishes. Current mfr.

Mfr.'s Sug. Retail	$2,595	$2,100	$1,350	$895

TEISCO

See TEISCO DEL REY.

Instruments produced in Japan. Distributed in the U.S. by Westheimer Musical Instruments of Evanston, Illinois.

One of the original Teisco importers was George Rose of Los Angeles, California. Some instruments may bear the shortened "Teisco" logo, many others were shipped in unlabeled. Please: no jokes about Teisco "no-casters".

(Source: Michael Wright, Guitar Stories Volume One)

TEISCO DEL REY

Instruments produced in Japan from 1956 to 1973. Distributed in the U.S. by Westheimer Musical Instruments of Evanston, Illinois.

In 1946, Mr. Atswo Kaneko and Mr. Doryu Matsuda founded the Aoi Onpa Kenkyujo company, makers of the guitars bearing the Teisco and other trademarks (the company name roughly translates to the **Hollyhock Soundwave or Electricity Laboratories**). The Teisco name was chosen by Mr. Kaneko, and was used primarily in domestic markets. Early models include lap steel and electric-Spanish guitars. By the 1950s, the company was producing slab-bodied designs with bolt-on necks. In 1956, the company name was changed to the Nippon Onpa Kogyo Co., Ltd. - but the guitars still stayed Teisco!

As the demand for guitars in the U.S. market began to expand, Mr. Jack Westheimer of WMI Corporation of Evanston, Illinois started to import Japanese guitars in the late 1950s, perhaps circa 1958. WMI began importing the Teisco-built Kingston guitars in 1961, and also used the Teisco Del Rey trademark extensively beginning in 1964. Other Teisco-built guitars had different trademarks (a *rebranding* technique), and the different brandnames will generally indicate the U.S. importer/distributor. The Japanese company again changed names, this time to the Teisco Co. Ltd. The Teisco line included all manners of solid body and semi-hollowbody guitars, and their niche in the American guitar market (as entry level or beginner's guitars) assured steady sales.

In 1967, the Kawai Corporation purchased the Teisco company. Not one to ruin a good thing, Kawai continued exporting the Teisco line to the U.S. (although they did change some designs through the years) until 1973. Due to the recent popularity in the Teisco name, Kawai actually produced some limited edition Teisco Spectrum Five models lately in Japan, although they were not made available to the U.S. market.

(Source: Michael Wright, Vintage Guitar Magazine)

Threet Leaf Headstock Inlay
courtesy Judy Threet

One dating method for identifying Teisco guitars (serial numbers are non-existent, and some electronic parts may not conform to the U.S. EIA code) is the change in pickguards that occurred in 1965. Pre-1965 pickguards are plastic construction, while 1965 and post-1965 pickguards are striped metal.

Pricing on Teisco Del Rey models and other Teiscos remains a bit strange. Most models that hang on walls are tagged at $99 (and sometimes lower), but clean cool shaped models sometimes command the $200 to $300 range. However, due to the association of the Spectrum Five model with Eddie Van Halen (he posed with a Spectrum Five on the cover of some German music magazine, if the story is true), some Spectrum Fives are now priced (used) at $1,000!

TELE-STAR

Instruments produced in Japan circa late 1960s to 1983.

The Tele-Star trademark was distributed in the U.S. by the Tele-Star Musical Instrument Corporation of New York, New York. Tele-Star offered a full range of acoustic, thinline acoustic/electric hollow body, and solid body electric guitars and basses. Many built by Kawai of Japan, and some models feature sparkle finishes.

(Source: Michael Wright, Vintage Guitar Magazine)

TEXARKANA

Instruments currently built in Korea. Distributed by the V. J. Rendano Music Company, Inc. of Youngstown, Ohio.

Texarkana offers a number of acoustic guitar models designed for the entry level or beginning guitar student. Suggested new retail prices range from $129 (dreadnought style) up to $379 (cutaway dreadnought with piezo pickup system).

THOMAS

Instruments produced in Italy from the late 1960s through the early 1970s.

Thomas semi-hollowbodies are medium quality guitars that feature original designs.

(Source: Tony Bacon and Paul Day, The Guru's Guitar Guide)

Threet Mountain Headstock Inlay
courtesy Judy Threet

Threet Acoustic
courtesy Judy Threet

THOS SHA CZAR

Instruments built in Valley Stream, New York circa late 1970s through 1980s.

Luthier/designer Tom Leiberman of "The Woodshop" in Valley Stream, New York built a number of acoustic bowl-back basses for the past number of years. In addition to a custom bass built several years ago for Jack Cassidy (Hot Tuna), Leiberman also built the **Stanley Clarke Bass** back in the 1970s. Leiberman current focuses his talents on furniture, but may accept custom commissions.

(Preliminary information courtesy Jeff Meyer)

In the late 1970s, Leiberman's Thos Sha Czar bowl-backed basses had a list price of $4,000. Specifications will be available in future editions of the Blue Book of Guitars.

THREET GUITARS

Instruments built in Calgary (Alberta), Canada since 1990.

Always interested in music, luthier Judy Threet had been playing guitar both semi-professionally and for pleasure for many years. Initially pursuing an academic career, she earned her Ph.D in Philosophy at Stanford (Palo Alto, California) in 1986; she then taught for a few years at the University of Calgary (Alberta, Canada). While teaching in Calgary, Threet met luthier Michael Heiden (see HEIDEN STRINGED INSTRUMENTS) and learned the art of inlay ("as a diversion", she claims).

Living in Calgary at the time, Heiden was gaining a reputation as a highly gifted luthier - and as a result was becoming increasingly busy. Heiden needed some help at his shop (especially doing inlay work), and Threet's Fine Arts backround from her early university days served her well as she offered to help. Over the next year and a half, Threet spent time away from her teaching career working with Heiden on inlays, and in the process began to learn the rudiments of guitar building.

In 1990, Threet decided to switch careers and become a luthier. She asked Heiden to teach her how to build and repair guitars, and it was agreed that under his careful supervision she would build a guitar from start to finish. When Heiden subsequently moved to British Columbia, Threet opened her own shop in 1991. Initially concentrating on guitar repair, Threet's focus shifted to building acoustic guitars. She designed and completed eight guitars by the end of 1994.

In her current location (a warehouse loft in one of Calgary's oldest areas), Threet individually handcrafts acoustic guitars and often customizes them to her client's wishes. Custom inlays are a specialty and are highly encouraged.

Threet guitars are relatively small-bodied instruments, usually with Sitka spruce tops and mahogany backs and sides. Lightweight but strong, they are especially well-suited to fingerstyle playing. Threet estimates that she produces 10 to 12 instruments on a yearly basis.

ACOUSTIC

Threet individually handcrafts each guitar, and takes great care in choosing the tonewoods and in voicing the tops. Necks are entirely handcarved and are joined in the traditional dove-tail joint. Each instrument is monitored throughout the building process to optimize its tone. Many *Custom Options*, such as a left-handed configuration, or an Englemann spruce top, or Koa or Walnut back and sides are available; most at an additional cost.

All 4 Threet models are available in 2 set styles: **Standard** and **Deluxe**. Customers can also design their own guitar as a **Custom** model. The **Standard** configuration includes a Sitka spruce top, Honduran mahogany back and sides, tortoise-shell plastic body binding, cocobola fingerboard/bridge/faceplate, wood purfling rosette, a 14/20 fret fingerboard with pearl dot inlay, and a natural nitrocellulose lacquer finish. The **Deluxe** configuration differs with an ebony with holly purfling body/fingerboard/headstock binding, Indian rosewood fingerboard/bridge, ebony faceplate, abalone rosette, pearl snowflake position markers/small asymetrical "torch", and a rosewood/ebony/holly backstrip.

The four Threet acoustic models correspond roughly to the traditional sizes of *0, 00, 000,* and *Dreadnought*. Threet's **Model A** is practically a parlor sized guitar, with dimensions: Body Length - 18 3/8", Width - 13 3/4", and Depth - 3 1/2" tapering to 4 1/4".

The **Model B** is a slightly larger parlor sized guitar: Body Length - 18 7/8", Width - 14 1/8", and Depth - 3 1/2" tapering to 4 1/8".

The **Model C** is larger still, with dimensions: Body Length - 19 3/8", Width - 14 1/2", and Depth - 3 1/2" tapering to 4 1/8".

The **Model D** is a hybrid size best described as a cross between a *Model C* and a dreadnought: Body Length - 20", Width - 15 1/4", and Depth - 3 1/2" tapering to 4 1/2". Models A, B, and C have a 24 27/32" scale, while the Model D has a 25 11/32" scale. For further information regarding pricing, inlay work, and additional model specifiactions, please contact luthier Judy Threet via the Index of Current Manufacturers located in the back of this edition.

TILTON

Instruments manufactured in Boston, Massachusetts from 1865 to the early 1900s.

The Oliver Ditson Company, Inc. was formed in 1835 by music publisher Oliver Ditson (1811-1888). Ditson was a primary force in music merchandising, distribution, and retail sales on the East Coast. He also helped establish two musical instrument manufacturers: The John Church Company of Cincinnati, Ohio, and Lyon & Healy (Washburn) in Chicago, Illinois.

In 1865 Ditson established a manufacturing branch of his company under the supervision of John Haynes, called the John C. Haynes Company. This branch built guitars for a number of trademarks, such as **Bay State**, **Tilton**, and **Haynes Excelsior**.

(Source: Tom Wheeler, American Guitars)

TIMELESS INSTRUMENTS

Instruments currently built in Tugaske (Saskatchewan), Canada.

In addition to his custom built stringed instruments, luthier David Freeman also offers acoustic guitar lutherie training, as well as lutherie supplies. For further information, please contact luthier Freeman via the Index of Current Manufactuers located in the back of this book.

BILL TIPPIN

Instruments currently built in Marblehead, Massachusetts.

Luthier Bill Tippin started building guitars in 1978 on a part time basis for his friends. In 1992, the "part time" became full time when he founded his Tippin Guitar Company. Tippin and his craftsmen are now creating a range of acoustic guitar and acoustic bass models. For further information, contact Bill Tippin through the Index of Current Manufacturers located in the back of this book.

Threet Polar Bear Headstock Inlay
courtesy Judy Threet

T

TOMMYHAWK

Instruments currently built in New Jersey. Distributed by Tom Barth's Music Box of Dover, New Jersey.

Designer Tom Barth offers a 24" travel-style guitar that is a one-piece carved mahogany body (back, sides, neck, and bracing). The solid spruce top, bridge, and top bracing are then glued on - forming a solid, tone projecting little guitar! In 1997, the soundhole was redesigned into a more elliptical shape. Retail list price on the **Original** is $350. Barth's full size (25 1/2" scale) electric/acoustic has a double cutaway body, 'Tele'-style neck with a 21 fret rosewood or maple fingerboard, and a Seymour Duncan Duckbucker pickup (retail list $595).

TONEMASTER

See chapter on House Brands.

This trademark has been identified as a "House Brand" ascribed to several distributors such as Harris-Teller of Illinois, Schmidt of Minnesota, and Squire of Michigan. While one recognized source has claimed that instruments under this trademark were built by HARMONY, author/researcher Willie G. Moseley has also seen this brand on a VALCO-made lap steel.

(Source: Willie G. Moseley, Stellas & Stratocasters)

TORRES

Instruments built in Spain.

Noted luthier Don Antonio de Torres Jurado (1817-1892) has been identified as the leading craftsman of what scholars have termed the "third renaissance" of the guitar, and developed the guitar to its current *classical* configuration.

Before the early 1800s, the European guitar featured five *courses*, which could be a single string or a pair of strings. Torres' new design focused on the five individual strings, and also added the low 'E' string for a total of six individual strings. Torres developed a larger bodied guitar design, and fan-bracing to support a thinner, more resonant top. The new design offered a larger tonal range (especially in the bass response), and was widely adopted both in Spain and throughout Europe.

Torres had two workshops during his career. He produced guitars both in Seville (1852-1869), and his place of birth, Almeria (1875-1892). It has been estimated that Torres built about 320 guitars during his two workshop period. Only 66 instruments have been identified as his work.

(Source: Tony Bacon, The Ultimate Guitar Book)

TOYOTA

Instruments produced in Japan circa early 1970s.

Toyota guitars were distributed in the U.S. by the Hershman company of New York, New York. The Toyota trademark was applied to a full range of acoustic, thinline acoustic/electric hollow body, and solid body electric guitars and basses.

(Source: Michael Wright, Guitar Stories Volume One)

JEFF TRAUGOTT

Instruments built in Santa Cruz, California since 1991.

Luthier Jeff Traugott builds a line of high-end acoustic steel string guitars. He focuses on high-level craftsmanship, as well as a clean, sophisticated sense of design. Traugott Guitars has a reputation for excellent projection and clear, bell-like tones up and down the neck.

Jeff Traugott apprenticed to David Morse in 1982, then worked with a partner for five years beforeworking as the foreman for the Santa Cruz Guitar Company for 4 1/2 years. He began his own company in 1991 and currently builds 15-20 guitars per year.

For more information on model speifiaction, pricing, and availablility, please contact Jeff Traugott via the Index of Current Manufacturers located in the back of this book.

JAMES W. TRIGGS

Instruments currently built in Nashville, Tennessee.

Luthier Jim Triggs began building mandolins during high school and progressed to selling his instruments at bluegrass festivals. Triggs was hired by Gibson a year before the guitar company acquired the Flatiron Works in Boseman, Montana, and then taught the Montana crafsmen how to build in the Gibson style. Triggs then worked in (and later managed) the Gibson Custom shop. In 1992, Triggs left Gibson to begin building D'Angelico replica archtops for a distributor. Other builders and players recognized that Triggs was building the D'Angelico II archtops, and so convinced him to build archtop guitars under his own name.

Jim Triggs is currently offering several archtop, flattop, and semi-hollowbody guitar models. Triggs incorporates features of older pre-WWII archtop guitars into his designs, and has a number of inlay and fancy hardware options to further beautify his already elaborate guitars.

Tommyhawk
courtesy Tom Barth

Triggs New Yorker
courtesy Scott Chinery

T

U

DALE UNGER

Instruments built in Stroudsburg, Pennsylvania since 1996.

Dale Unger was an apprentice to Bob Benedetto for four years, and has since opened up his own shop. For further information, see AMERICAN ARCHTOP.

UNICORD

See UNIVOX.

Instruments produced in Japan.

The Merson Musical Supply Company of Westbury, New York was the primary importer of Univox guitars. Merson evolved into Unicord, and also became a distributor for Westbury brand guitars.

(Source: Michael Wright, Guitar Stories Volume One)

UNITY

Instruments built by the Unity Guitar Company of Vicksburg and Kalamazoo, Michigan since 1994.

The Unity Guitar Company was founded by Aaron Cowles and Kevin Moats in 1994. Cowles, a former Gibson employee (from 1961 to 1983) opened his own music and repair shop after the Kalamazoo plant was closed down. Moats, son of Heritage Guitar's J.P. Moats, comes from a family background of musical instrument building.

In 1994, Unity offered a limited edition of the **100th Anniversary Model** arch top guitar, which celebrates the 100 years of musical instrument building in Kalamazoo, Michigan. The inlay work was done by Maudie Moore (Moore's Engraving), who has over thirty years experience. Unity was scheduled to begin offering their Custom Carved series of Arch top guitars in 1995.

6-String Archtop
courtesy Dale Unger

UNIVERSITY

Instruments were produced by REGAL (original company of Wulschner & Son) in the late 1890s.

Indianapolis retailer/wholesaler Emil Wulschner introduced the Regal line in the 1880s, and in 1896 opened a factory to build guitars and mandolins under the following three trademarks: REGAL, 20th CENTURY, and UNIVERSITY. After Wulschner's death in 1900, the factory became part of a larger corporation.

(Source: John Teagle, Washburn: Over One Hundred Years of Fine Stringed Instruments)

UNIVOX

Instruments built in Japan circa 1969 to 1978, and imported into the U.S. by the Merson Musical Supply Company of Westbury, New York.

Merson Musical Supply later evolved into the Unicord company. The Univox trademark was offered on a full range of acoustic, thinline acoustic/electric hollow body, and solid body electric guitars and basses. The majority of the Univox guitars produced were built by Arai of Japan (See Aria), and are entry level to intermediate quality for players.

(Source: Michael Wright, Guitar Stories Volume One)

7-String Archtop
courtesy Dale Unger

U

VAGABOND

Instruments currently built in Albany, New York.

Luthier Kevin Smith's Vagabond Travel Guitar has been "defining the acoustic travel guitar since 1981". Smith says that his design is the perfect balance of playability, portability, and sound in an attractive shape.

The Vagabond Travel Guitar has a solid spruce top, mahogany integral neck, adjustable truss rod, 24.5" scale with 21 full frets. The **Standard** model (list $399) has laminated maple back and sides, black and white binding, Gotoh open tuners, and a deluxe travel bag. The **Deluxe** (list $499) is similar, but has purpleheart and herringbone custom bindings, a tortoiseshell pickguard, and Schaller mini tuners. Both models are available with a Fishman transducer or Fishman Matrix active system.

VALCO

See NATIONAL.

Louis Dopyera bought out the National company, and as he owned more than 50% of the stock in Dobro, "merged" the two companies back together (as National Dobro). In 1936, the decision was made to move the company to Chicago, Illinois. Chicago was a veritable hotbed of mass produced musical instruments during the early to pre-World War II 1900s. Manufacturers like Washburn and Regal had facilities, and major wholesalers and retailers like the Tonk Bros. and Lyon & Healy were based there. Victor Smith, Al Frost, and Louis Dopyera moved their operation to Chicago, and in 1943 formally announced the change to VALCO (the initials of their three first names: V-A-L company). Valco worked on war materials during World War II, and returned to instrument production afterwards. Valco produced the National/Supro/Airline fiberglass body guitars in the 1950s and 1960s, as well as wood-bodied models. In the late 1960s, Valco was absorbed by the Kay company (See KAY). In 1968, Kay/Valco Guitars, Inc. went out of business. Both the National and the Supro trademarks were purchased at the 1969 liquidation auction by Chicago's Strum 'N Drum Music Company.

(Source: Tom Wheeler, American Guitars)

VALLEY ARTS

Instruments produced in City of Industry, California since 1993. Previous production was based in North Hollywood, California from 1979 to 1993. Distributed by the Samick Music Corporation of City of Industry, California.

Valley Arts originally began as a North Hollywood teaching studio in 1963. The facilities relocated to Studio City, California and through the years became known as a respected retail store that specialized in professional quality music gear. Production moved back to North Hollywood and into larger facilities in 1989, and luthier/co-owner Michael McGuire directed a staff of 15 employees.

In 1992, the Samick corporation became involved in a joint venture with Valley Arts, and by June of 1993 had acquired full ownership of the company. Samick operates Valley Arts as the custom shop *wing* for the company, as well as utilizing Valley Arts designs for their Samick production guitars built overseas.

Grading	100%	EXCELLENT	AVERAGE

ACOUSTIC

VALLEY ARTS GRAND (Model VAGD-1) — dreadnought style, solid AAA spruce top, herringbone binding, round soundhole, mahogany neck, 25 1/2" scale, ebony fingerboard/bridge, rosewood back/sides, tortoise pickguard, 3 per side tuners, gold hardware. Available in Natural finish. Current mfr.

Mfr.'s Sug. Retail	$1,580	$1,185	$775	$525

VALLEY ARTS GRAND CONCERT (Model VAGC-1) — 'OOO' style, solid AAA spruce top, herringbone binding, round soundhole, mahogany neck, 25" scale, ebony fingerboard/bridge, rosewood back/sides, tortoise pickguard, 3 per side tuners, gold hardware. Available in Natural finish. Current mfr.

Mfr.'s Sug. Retail	$1,580	$1,185	$775	$525

ACOUSTIC ELECTRIC

VALLEY ARTS GRAND ELECTRIC (Model VAGD-1E) — dreadnought style, solid AAA spruce top, herringbone binding, round soundhole, mahogany neck, 25 1/2" scale, ebony fingerboard/bridge, rosewood back/sides, tortoise pickguard, 3 per side tuners, gold hardware, piezo bridge pickup, volume/3 band active EQ. Available in Natural finish. Current mfr.

Mfr.'s Sug. Retail	$1,720	$1,290	$845	$570

VALLEY ARTS GRAND CONCERT ELECTRIC (Model VAGD-1E) — 'OOO' style, solid AAA spruce top, herringbone binding, round soundhole, mahogany neck, 25" scale, ebony fingerboard/bridge, rosewood back/sides, tortoise pickguard, 3 per side tuners, gold hardware, piezo bridge pickup, volume/3 band active EQ. Available in Natural finish. Current mfr.

Mfr.'s Sug. Retail	$1,720	$1,290	$845	$570

Robert Johnson Estate Commemorative Series

RJ 1935 N — jumbo style body, solid spruce top, round soundhole, maple back/sides, 12/19 fret rosewood fingerboard with pearl dot inlay, rosewood bridge, 3 per side deluxe Kluson tuners, engraved plate on headstock. Available in Natural (N) and Vintage Black Burst (B) finishes. Mfr. 1994 to 1996.

Model has not traded sufficiently to quote pricing.

Grading	100%	EXCELLENT	AVERAGE

VANTAGE

Instruments currently produced in Korea. Original production was based in Japan from 1977 to 1990. Distributed by Music Industries Corporation of Floral Park, New York, since 1987.

This trademark was established in Matsumoto, Japan, around 1977. Instruments have been manufactured in Korea since 1990. Vantage offers a wide range of guitars designed for the beginning student to the intermediate player.

ACOUSTIC

Classic Series

VCT-20 CE
courtesy Vantage

VC-10 — classical style, spruce top, round soundhole, bound body, wooden inlay rosette, nato back/sides/neck, 12/19 fret rosewood fingerboard/tied bridge, rosewood peghead veneer, 3 per side chrome tuners with plastic buttons. Available in Light Pumpkin finish. Current mfr.

		$100	$65
		Last Mfr.'s Sug. Retail was $200.	

VC-20 — classic style, cedar top, round soundhole, bound body, wooden inlay rosette, ovankol back/sides, nato neck, 12/19 fret rosewood fingerboard/tied bridge, ovankol peghead veneer, 3 per side gold tuners with plastic buttons. Available in Natural finish. Current mfr.

Mfr.'s Sug. Retail	$339	$255	$165	$115

VC-20CE — similar to VSC-20, except has single round cutaway, piezo bridge pickup, 3 band EQ with volume slide control.

Mfr.'s Sug. Retail	$439	$325	$215	$145

VSC-30 — similar to VSC-20, except has rosewood back/sides. Available in Light Pumpkin finish.

Mfr.'s Sug. Retail	$429	$320	$200	$135

Dreadnought Series

VS-5 — dreadnought style, spruce top, round soundhole, black pickguard, bound body, 3 stripe rosette, nato back/sides/neck, 14/20 fret nato fingerboard with white dot inlay, ebonized maple bridge with white black dot pins, 3 per side chrome tuners. Available in Natural finish. Current mfr.

Mfr.'s Sug. Retail	$319	$240	$150	$100
Add $10 for left-handed version (**Model VS-5/LH**).				

VS-10 — similar to VS-5, except has 3 stripe bound body.

Mfr.'s Sug. Retail	$329	$235	$140	$90

VS-12 — similar to VS-10, except has 12 strings, 6 per side tuners.

Mfr.'s Sug. Retail	$329	$235	$140	$90
Add $10 for Black finish (**Model VS-12B**).				

VS-15 — dreadnought style, spruce top, round soundhole, black pickguard, 3 stripe bound body/rosette, nato back/sides/neck, 14/20 fret rosewood fingerboard with white dot inlay, rosewood bridge with black white dot pins, 3 per side chrome tuners. Available in Natural finish. Current mfr.

Mfr.'s Sug. Retail	$309	$225	$120	$80

VS-20 — dreadnought style, nato top, round soundhole, black pickguard, 3 stripe bound body/rosette, nato back/sides/neck, 14/20 fret bound rosewood fingerboard with white dot inlay, rosewood bridge with white black dot pins, bound peghead, 3 per side chrome tuners. Available in Black, Natural and Tobacco Sunburst finishes. Curr. mfr.

Mfr.'s Sug. Retail	$369	$275	$185	$125

VS-25 — dreadnought style, cedar top, round soundhole, black pickguard, herringbone bound body/rosette, ovankol back/sides, mahogany neck, 14/20 fret rosewood fingerboard with white dot inlay, rosewood bridge with white black dot pins, 3 per side tuners. Available in Natural finish. Current mfr.

Mfr.'s Sug. Retail	$379	$255	$165	$115
Add $50 for solid cedar top (**Model VS-25S**).				
Add $60 for left-handed version with solid cedar top (**Model VS-25S/LH**).				

VS-25SCE — similar to VS-25, except has single sharp cutaway, solid cedar top, piezo bridge pickup, 3 band EQ with volume slide control.

Mfr.'s Sug. Retail	$459	$345	$225	$150

VS-25SCE-12 — similar to VS-25SCE, except has 12 strings, 6 per side tuners.

Mfr.'s Sug. Retail	$629	$475	$300	$215

VS-30 — dreadnought style, maple top, round soundhole, black pickguard, 3 stripe bound body/rosette, maple back/sides/neck, 14/20 fret bound rosewood fingerboard with white dot inlay, rosewood bridge with white black dot pins, bound peghead, 3 per side chrome tuners. Available in Natural finish. Current mfr.

Mfr.'s Sug. Retail	$379	$285	$190	$125

VS-33 — dreadnought style, spruce top, round soundhole, black pickguard, 5 stripe bound body/rosette, oak back/sides, mahogany neck, 14/20 fret bound rosewood fingerboard, rosewood bridge with white black dot pins, bound peghead, 3 per side chrome tuners. Available in Transparent Black, Transparent Blue and Transparent Red finishes. Current mfr.

Mfr.'s Sug. Retail	$399	$295	$200	$125

Grading	100%	EXCELLENT	AVERAGE

VS-35CE — single sharp cutaway dreadnought style, nato top, oval soundhole, 3 stripe bound body/rosette, nato back/sides/neck, 20 fret bound rosewood fingerboard with white dot inlay, rosewood bridge with white black dot pins, bound peghead, 3 per side chrome tuners, piezo bridge pickup, 3 band EQ with volume slide control. Available in Black and Tobacco Sunburst finishes. Disc. 1997.

$215 $140
Last Mfr.'s Sug. Retail was $430.

Add $10 for left-handed version of this model (**Model VS-35CE/LH**).

VS-50S — dreadnought style, solid spruce top, round soundhole, black pickguard, herringbone bound body/rosette, nato back/sides/neck, 14/20 fret rosewood fingerboard with white dot inlay, rosewood bridge with white black dot pins, bound peghead, 3 per side gold tuners. Available in Natural finish. Current mfr.

| Mfr.'s Sug. Retail | $449 | $335 | $220 | $150 |

Add $10 for left-handed version of this model (**Model VS-50S/LH**).

ACOUSTIC ELECTRIC

VS-40CE — single sharp cutaway dreadnought style, nato top, oval soundhole, 3 stripe bound body/rosette, nato back/sides/neck, 20 fret bound rosewood fingerboard with white dot inlay, rosewood bridge with white black dot pins, bound peghead, 3 per side chrome tuners, piezo bridge pickup, 3 band EQ with volume slide control. Available in Black and White finishes. Current mfr.

| Mfr.'s Sug. Retail | $499 | $375 | $245 | $165 |

VS-40CE/M — similar to VS-40CE, except has maple back/sides.

| Mfr.'s Sug. Retail | $519 | $390 | $250 | $170 |

Add $10 for left-handed version of this model (**Model VS-40CE/MLH**).

Add $10 for 12 string version of this model (**VS-40CEM-12**).

VST-40SCE — single sharp cutaway dreadnought style, solid spruce top, round soundhole, 3 stripe bound body, herringbone rosette, nato back/sides/neck, 20 fret rosewood fingerboard with white dot inlay, rosewood bridge with white black dot pins, bound peghead, 3 per side gold tuners, piezo bridge pickup, 3 band EQ with volume slide control. Available in Natural finish. Curr. mfr.

$250 $165
Last Mfr.'s Sug. Retail was $500.

VST-33 CE/TBL
courtesy Vantage

VANTEK

Instruments produced in Korea, and distributed by Music Industries Corporation of Floral Park, New York.

These instruments are built with the entry level player or beginning student in mind by Vantage in Korea.

VARSITY

See WEYMANN & SONS.

VEGA

Instruments are currently built in Korea, and distributed by ANTARES.

Historically, Vega guitars were produced in Boston, Massachusetts.

The predessor company to Vega was founded in 1881 by Swedish immigrant Julius Nelson, C. F. Sunderberg, Mr. Swenson, and several other men. Nelson was the foreman of a 20-odd man workforce (which later rose to 130 employees during the 1920s banjo boom). Nelson, and his brother Carl, gradually bought out the other partners, and incorporated in 1903 as Vega (which means 'star'). In 1904, Vega acquired banjo maker A. C. Fairbanks & Company after Fairbanks suffered a fire, and Fairbank's David L. Day became Vega's general manager.

Vega built banjos under the Bacon trademark, named after popular banjo artist Frederick J. Bacon. Bacon set up his own production facility in Connecticut in 1921, and a year later wooed Day away from Vega to become the vice president in the newly reformed **Bacon & Day** company. While this company marketed several models of guitars, they had no facility for building them. It is speculated that the Bacon & Day guitars were built by the Regal company of Chicago, Illinois.

In the mid 1920s Vega began marketing a guitar called the **Vegaphone**. By the early 1930s, Vega started concentrating more on guitar production, and less on banjo making. Vega debuted its Electrovox electric guitar and amplifier in 1936, and a electric volume control footpedal in 1937. Vega is reported to have built over 40,000 guitars during the 1930s.

In the 1940s, Vega continued to introduce models such as the Duo-Tron and the Supertron; and by 1949 had become both a guitar producer and a guitar wholesaler as it bought bodies built by Harmony. In 1970 Vega was acquired by the C. F. Martin company for its banjo operations. Martin soon folded Vega's guitar production, and applied the trademark to a line of imported guitars. Ten years later, Martin sold the Vega trademark rights to a Korean guitar production company.

(Source: Tom Wheeler, American Guitars)

VENSON

Instruments currently produced in Seoul, Korea. Distributed by Sungbo Industrial Co., Ltd.

Sungbo Industrial Co., Ltd. is currently offering a wide range of acoustic guitars and acoustic basses under the **Venson** trademark. The acoustic guitar line contains a number of dreadnought, jumbo, and classical models. For further information, please contact Sungbo Industrial Co., Ltd. through the Index of Current Manufacturers located in the back of this edition.

V

VENTURA

Instruments produced in Japan circa 1970s.

Ventura guitars were distributed in the U.S. market by C. Bruno & Company of New York, New York. Ventura models were both full body and thinline hollow body electric archtop guitars, and generally medium to good quality versions of popular American models.

(Source: Michael Wright, Guitar Stories Volume One; and Sam Maggio)

During the 1970s, a "Barney Kessel Custom"-style copy (the model is a V-1400, by the way) had a suggested retail price of $199.50. If one of these guitars gets sold at a big guitar show for $200 to $250, does this mean that the guitar "has appreciated in value" or the retail price of today's Korean semi-hollow body guitars has risen over the past twenty five years? Traditionally, there is a ceiling to how high a price can raise on imported laminate wood semi-hollow body guitars - but who can put a price tag on that intangible "funkiness" factor?

VERSOUL

Instruments built in Helsinki, Finland since 1994.

Versoul Ltd. was founded in 1994 by Kari Nieminen, who has over 20 years background in guitar making and design. Nieminen combines concern for the acoustic tone of his instruments with his innovative designs to produce a masterful instrument. Nieminen's production is on a limited basis (he estimates about one guitar a week) in his humidity controlled workshop.

Both the handcrafted **Zoel** and **Touco** acoustic models reflect his commitment to excellence. Models are available in Silver label (mahogany body), Gold label (Indian rosewood body), and Platinum label (Honduran rosewood body) configurations. The Zoel model has a squared-shoulder design, with spruce top and reverse headstock. Nieminen is also offering an **Acoustic Sitar Guitar**, which provides instant exotic sitar sound with adjustable bridge piece for each string (and 13 sympathetic strings). The fingerboard is scalloped, and the guitar has an extra long scale length for twanging sound.

Nieminen's newest model is the electric solid body **Raya**. This model is constructed out of Finnish alder, with a set-in mahogany neck, and 22 fret ebony fingerboard. The Raya features 2 Versoul single coil pickups, and a reverse headstock. For further information, please contact luthier Nieminen via the Index of Current Manufacturers located in the back of this book.

VESTAX

Instruments currently built in Japan. Distributed by the Vestax Corporation of Fairfield, California.

Vestax offers high quality guitars including one model that echos the classic designs of the 1940s and 1950s, as well as a semi-hollow electric model. The D'Angelico-Vestax **Phil Upchurch** model is a single cutaway *New Yorker*-style acoustic with bound body, 2 bound f-holes, bound headstock, 3 per side gold tuners, 22 fret bound ebony fingerboard with pearl block inlay, raised rosewood pickguard, adjustable rosewood bridge/'stairstep' rosewood tailpiece, floating humbucker pickup. Vestax's **Superior Limited Series** semi-hollow **GV-98** looks like a double cutaway 'Strat' or 'PRS' design, but features hollowed out tone chambers under the flamed maple top. The **GV-98** has a Wilkinson VSVG (GG) tremolo bridge, 2 single coil/humbucker pickups, and 22 fret fingerboard. For further information, please contact Vestax via the Index of Current Manufacturers located in the back of this book. All Vestax models may not be available in the U.S. market.

VICTOR

See chapter on House Brands.

This trademark has been identified as a "House Brand" of the RCA Victor Record Stores.

(Source: Willie G. Moseley, Stellas & Stratocasters)

VINTAGE

Instruments are currently produced in Asia. Distributed by John Hornby Skewes & Co., Ltd. of Garforth (Leeds), England.

The **Vintage** trademark is the brand name of UK importer John Hornby Skewes & Co., Ltd.

ACOUSTIC

EY 200 DREADNOUGHT — dreadnought style, tighter waist, round soundhole, spruce top, mahogany back/sides, Nato neck, 14/20 fret rosewood fingerboard with white dot inlay, rosewood bridge, chrome hardware, 3 per side headstock, black pickguard with flower decorations. Available in Natural finish. Current mfr.
Mfr.'s Sug. Retail   **$TBA**

F 300 FOLK — rounded folk style, tighter waist, round soundhole, laminated spruce top, Nato back/sides/neck, 14/20 fret rosewood fingerboard with white dot inlay, rosewood bridge, chrome hardware, 3 per side headstock, black pickguard. Available in Natural finish. Current mfr.
Mfr.'s Sug. Retail   **$TBA**

ACOUSTIC ELECTRIC

EY 60 ELECTRO — dreadnought style, single rounded cutaway, 2 f-holes, birds eye maple top, mahogany back/sides, Nato neck, 14/20 fret rosewood fingerboard with white dot inlay, rosewood bridge/gold-plated trapeze tailpiece, 3 per side headstock, chrome tuners, piezo pickup, 4 band EQ, XLR D.I. output. Available in Vintage Sunburst finish. Current mfr.
Mfr.'s Sug. Retail   **$TBA**

EM 132 Electro — dreadnought style, single rounded cutaway, round soundhole, flamed maple top, ash back/sides, Nato neck, 14/20 fret rosewood fingerboard with white dot inlay, rosewood bridge, 3 per side headstock, chrome hardware, piezo pickup, 4 band EQ. Available in Gold Flame finish. Current mfr.
Mfr.'s Sug. Retail   **$TBA**

VIVI-TONE

Instruments built in Kalamazoo, Michigan circa early 1930s.

After pioneering such high quality instruments for Gibson in the 1920s (such as the F-5 Mandolin), Designer/engineer/builder Lloyd Loar founded the Vivi-Tone company to continue exploring designs too radical for Gibson. It is rumored that Loar designed a form of stand-up bass that was amplified while at Gibson, but this prototype was never developed into a production model.

Loar, along with partners Lewis A. Williams and Walter Moon started Vivi-Tone in 1933. Loar continued building his pioneering designs, such as an acoustic guitar with sound holes in the rear, but failed to find commercial success. However, it is because of his early successes at Gibson that researchers approach the Vivi-tone designs with some wonderment instead of discounting the radical ideas altogether.

(Source: Tom Wheeler, American Guitars)

VOX

Vox Jumbo
'60s Vox Catalog (Reprint)

Instruments originally built in England from 1961 to 1964; production was then moved to Italy for the mid 1960s up to the early 1970s.

After Italian production ceased, some solid body models were built in Japan during the 1980s.

The Vox company, perhaps better known for its amplifier design, also built fashionable and functional guitars and basses during the 1960s. While the early guitar models produced tended to be entry level instruments based on popular Fender designs, later models expressed an originality that fit in well with the 1960s British "Pop" music explosion.

Thomas Walter Jennings was born in London, England on February 28, 1917. During World War II he saw action with the English Royal Engineers, and received a medical discharge in 1941. By 1944 Jennings had a part-time business dealing in secondhand accordians and other musical instruments, and by 1946 had set up shop. Along with fellow musical acquaintance Derek Underdown, Jennings produced the Univox organ in 1951 and formed the Jennings Organ Company not long after. Based on the success of his organs for several years, Jennings teamed up with engineer Dick Denney to build amplifiers under the Vox trademark. In mid 1958, Jennings reincorporated the company as Jennings Musical Instruments (JMI). When rock 'n roll hit Britain, Vox amps were there.

The first Vox guitars were introduced in 1961. Early models like the **Stroller** or **Clubman** were entry level instruments based on Fender designs. Quality improved a great deal when Vox brought in necks built by EKO in Recanati, Italy. Tom Jennings then assembled a three engineer design team of Bob Pearson (quality and materials control), Mike Bennett (prototypes), and Ken Wilson (styling design) to develop a more original-looking instrument. The resulting 5-sided **Phantom** in late 1962 featured a Strat-ish three single coil pickup selection and a Bigsby-derived tremolo. Further Phantom models were developed in 1963, as well as the **Mark VI** series ("teardrop" body shapes). When production moved to Italy in 1964, Vox guitars were built by EKO. Vox also offered a 12-string **Mandoguitar**, and a double cutaway 12-string called the **Bouzouki**. A number of hollowbody models such as the **Lynx**, **Bobcat**, and **Cougar** were made by Crucianelli in Italy during the mid 1960s.

In order to generate funds for the company, Jennings sold a substantial amount of shares to the Royston group in 1964, and later that same year the entire shareholding was acquired. JMI was officially renamed Vox Sound Ltd. Thomas Organs was already supplying JMI for organs in the British market, and was looking for a reciprocal agreement to import Vox amps to the U.S. market. However, Joe Benaron (president of Thomas Organs) was really into transistors, and began *supplementing* the British tube models with solid-state amps developed at Thomas laboratories at Sepulveda, California. To clearly illustrate this sorry state of affairs, compare a U.S. **Super Beatle** amp against a British **AC-100**.

The Vox line began the slump that befell other corporate-run music instrument producers during the late 1960s and 1970s. Soon Japanese-built models appeared on the market with Vox on their headstock, including a Les Paul-derived issued in 1970. Later, the Vox name appeared on a series of original design solid body guitars (**24 series**, **25 series**, **White Shadows**) during the early to mid 1980s. Distribution in the U.S. during this time period was through the Pennino Music Company of Westminster, California; and Allstate Music Supply Corporation of Greensboro, North Carolina.

The Vox trademark was later purchased by the Korg company (Korg USA in the American Market). Korg USA distributes Korg synthesizers, Marshall Amplifiers, Parker guitars, and the new line of Vox amplifiers in the U.S. market. In 1998, Korg/Vox debuted 5 "new" electric guitar models which feature designs based on previous Vox models.

Vox's new models include the Mark III model VM3B with Bigsby tremolo (list $1,400), the Mark III model VM3F with fixed tailpiece (list $1,200), the Mark III model VM3CFWD with fixed tailpiece, chrome pickguard, and matching finish headstock (list $1,300), the Mark VI model VM6V with Bigsby tremolo (list $1,400), and the Mark XII model VMXII 12-string guitar (list $1,400).

Model Name Identification

Identification of Vox instruments is fairly easy, as the model names generally appear on the pickguards. However, there are models and configurations that do need to be doublechecked! Collectible Vox guitars seem to be the models built between 1962 and 1969, and solid body models are favored over the hollowbody ones.

ACOUSTIC

In the mid to late 1960s, Thomas Organ distributed a number of Vox acoustic guitars. Steel-string models such as the **Country Western**, **Folk XII**, and **Fold Twelve Electro** had a simple horizontal *Vox* logo on the peghead. The **Rio Grande**, **Shenandoah** (12-string), and **Silver Sage** (12-string) had more ornate inlay decorations around the logo, and the horizontal Vox lettering was thicker.

V

W & S

See WEYMANN & SONS.

WABASH

See chapter on House Brands.

This trademark has been identified as a "House Brand" of Wexler.

(Source: Willie G. Moseley, Stellas & Stratocasters)

WALKER GUITARS

Instruments built in North Stonington, Connecticut since 1984.

Luthier Kim Walker was involved in the musical instrument making business since 1973, and began building F-5 style mandolins in 1982. Walker worked for a number of years at George Gruhn's repair and restoration workshop, were hew was able to work in close association with other fine instrument builders such as Mark Lacey, Paul McGill, and Steven Gilchrist. Walker later served as both a prototype builder and R&D/Custom shop supervisor at Guild beginning in 1986.

Walker currently offers three different archtop models, and his combination of premier woods and over twenty years experience make for a truly solid, high quality guitar. Models like the **Black Tie**, **Excel**, and **Classic** are traditional style archtops with different appointments and body binding styles, while the top-of-the-line **Empress** is a limited edition custom model. Walker as builds flat top acoustic guitars that feature pre-war style scalloped bracing, and are finished in a gloss varnish. For further information on model specifications, pricing, and availability please contact luthier Walker via the Index of Current Manufacturers located in the back of this book.

WARWICK

Instruments produced in Markneukirchen, Germany by Warwick Gmbh & Co., Musicequipment KG since 1982. Distributed exclusively in the U.S. by Dana B. Goods of Santa Barbara, California.

Hans Peter Wilfer, son of Framus' Frederick Wilfer, established the Warwick trademark in 1982 in Erlangen (Bavaria). Wilfer literally grew up in the Framus factories of his father, and learned all aspects of construction and production 'right at the source'. The high quality of Warwick basses quickly gained notice with bass players worldwide.

In 1995, Warwick moved to Markneukirchen (in the Saxon Vogtland) to take advantage of the centuries of instrument-making traditions. Construction of the new plant provided the opportunity to install new state-of-the-art machinery to go with the skilled craftsmen. The Warwick company continues to focus on producing high quality bass guitars; and since 1993, Warwick also offers a full range of bass amplification systems and speaker cabinets.

Grading	100%	EXCELLENT	AVERAGE

ACOUSTIC BASS

ALIEN — single sharp cutaway concert style, spruce top, asymmetrical soundhole located in upper bout, rosewood thumb rest, wood bound body, ovankol soundhole cap, ovankol back/sides, 2 piece mahogany neck with wenge center strip, 24 fret wenge fingerboard, wenge/metal bridge, ebony peghead veneer with pearl W inlay, 2 per side chrome tuners, piezo pickup, 4 band EQ, active electronics. Available in Natural finish. Disc. 1994.

$1,575 $995

Last Mfr.'s Sug. Retail was $3,300.

WASHBURN

Instruments currently produced both in Chicago, Illinois and Korea. Distributed by Washburn International, located in Vernon Hills, Illinois.

Historically, Washburn instruments were produced in the Chicago, Illinois area from numerous sources from the late 1800s to 1940s. When the trademark was revived in the 1960s, instruments were produced first in Japan, and then later in Korea.

The Washburn trademark was originated by the Lyon & Healy company of Chicago, Illinois. George Washburn Lyon and Patrick Joseph Healy were chosen by Oliver Ditson, who had formed the Oliver Ditson Company, Inc. in 1835 as a musical publisher. Ditson was a primary force in music merchandising, distribution, and retail sales on the East Coast. In 1864 the Lyon & Healy music store opened for business. The late 1800s found the company ever expanding from retail, to producer, and finally distributor. The Washburn trademark was formally filed for in 1887, and the name applied to quality stringed instruments produced by a manufacturing department of Lyon & Healy.

Lyon & Healy were part of the Chicago musical instrument production conglomerate that produced musical instruments throughout the early and mid 1900s. As in business, if there is demand, a successful business will supply. Due to their early pioneering of mass production, the Washburn facility averaged up to one hundred instruments a day! Lyon & Healy/Washburn were eventually overtaken by the Tonk Bros. company, and the Washburn trademark was eventually discarded.

When the trademark was revived in 1964, the inital production of acoustic guitars came from Japan. Washburn electric guitars were re-introduced to the American market in 1979, and featured U.S. designs on Japanese-built instruments. Production of the entry level models was switched to Korea during the mid to late 1980s. As the company gained a larger foothold in the

Walker Archtop
courtesy Kim Walker

Warwick Alien Acoustic Bass
courtesy Warwick

Grading	100%	EXCELLENT	AVERAGE

guitar market, American production was reintroduced in the late 1980s as well. Grover Jackson (ex-Jackson/Chavel) was instrumental in introducing new designs for Washburn for the Chicago series in 1993.

In 1998, Washburn adopted the Buzz Feiten *Tuning System* on the American-produced models. The Buzz Feiten Tuning System is a new 'tempered' tuning sytem that produces a more "in-tune" guitar.

(Early company history courtesy of John Teagle in his book Washburn: Over One Hundred Years of Fine Stringed Instruments. **The actual history is a lot more involved and convoluted than the above outline suggests, and Teagle's book does a fine job of unravelling the narrative)**

ACOUSTIC

Classic Guitar Series

C20 — classic style, spruce top, round soundhole, 3 stripe bound body, wooden inlay rosette, mahogany back/sides/neck, 12/19 fret rosewood fingerboard, tied rosewood bridge, 3 per side nylon head chrome tuners. Available in Natural finish. Mfr. 1994 to 1996.

	$90	$60

Last Mfr.'s Sug. Retail was $180.

C40 — classic style, spruce top, round soundhole, 3 stripe bound body, wooden inlay rosette, ovankol back/sides, mahogany neck, 12/19 fret rosewood fingerboard, tied rosewood bridge, 3 per side nylon head chrome tuners. Available in Natural finish. Current mfr.

Mfr.'s Sug. Retail	$299	$225	$150	$100

C60 ZARAZOGA — classic style, spruce top, round soundhole, 3 stripe bound body, wooden inlay rosette, rosewood back/sides, mahogany neck, 12/19 fret rosewood fingerboard, tied rosewood bridge, rosewood peghead veneer, 3 per side nylon head gold tuners. Available in Natural finish. Disc. 1994.

	$175	$120

Last Mfr.'s Sug. Retail was $370.

C80 S — classic style, solid cedar top, round soundhole, 3 stripe bound body, wooden inlay rosette, rosewood back/sides, mahogany neck, 12/19 fret rosewood fingerboard, tied rosewood bridge, rosewood peghead veneer, 3 per side nylon head gold tuners. Available in Natural finish. Current mfr.

Mfr.'s Sug. Retail	$649	$525	$350	$225

C100 S W VALENCIA — classic style, solid cedar top, round soundhole, 3 stripe bound body, wood marquetry rosette, rosewood back/sides, mahogany neck, 12/19 fret ebony fingerboard, jacaranda bridge with bone saddle, rosewood peghead veneer, 3 per side pearl head gold tuners. Available in Natural finish. Disc. 1991.

	$650	$475

Last Mfr.'s Sug. Retail was $1,500.

C200 S W Sevilla — similar to C100 S W, except has ebony reinforcement in the neck. Disc. 1991.

	$650	$475

Last Mfr.'s Sug. Retail was $1,900.

Dreadnought Series

D8 — dreadnought style, spruce top, round soundhole, black pickguard, bound body, 3 stripe purfling/rosette, mahogany back/sides/neck, 14/20 fret rosewood fingerboard with pearl dot inlay, rosewood bridge with black white dot pins, rosewood peghead veneer with screened logo, 3 per side chrome tuners. Available in Natural finish. Mfd. 1994 to 1996.

	$100	$65

Last Mfr.'s Sug. Retail was $200.

D8 M — similar to D8, except has mahogany top. Mfd. 1994 to 1996.

	$95	$65

Last Mfr.'s Sug. Retail was $190.

D10 — dreadnought style, select spruce top, round soundhole, black pickguard, 3 stripe bound body and rosette, mahogany back/sides/neck, 14/20 fret rosewood fingerboard with pearl dot inlay, rosewood bridge with pearl dot black pins, 3 per side chrome Grover tuners. Available in Black, Natural and Sunburst finishes. Current mfr.

Mfr.'s Sug. Retail	$329	$250	$150	$100

D10 M — similar to D10, except has mahogany top. Available in Caribbean Blue, Mahogany, and Transparent Wine Red finishes. Current mfr.

Mfr.'s Sug. Retail	$299	$225	$150	$100

D10 Q — similar to D10, except has a quilted maple top. Available in Sunburst finish. Current mfr.

Mfr.'s Sug. Retail	$399	$295	$195	$125

D11 — similar to D10, except has a mountain ash top, mountain ash back/sides. Available in Antique Natural, Brown, Transparent Red, and Transparent Blue finishes. Current mfr.

Mfr.'s Sug. Retail	$369	$275	$175	$125

D12 — dreadnought style, spruce top, round soundhole, black pickguard, 3 stripe bound body and rosette, mahogany back/sides/neck, 14/20 fret rosewood fingerboard with pearl dot inlay, rosewood bridge with pearl dot black pins, 3 per side chrome diecast tuners. Available in Black, Brown, Natural and White finishes. Disc. 1994.

	$175	$100

Last Mfr.'s Sug. Retail was $350.

D12 LH — similar to D12, except in left-handed configuration. Available in Natural finish. Disc. 1996.

	$195	$100

Last Mfr.'s Sug. Retail was $380.

D51 SW Apache
courtesy Washburn

Grading	100%	EXCELLENT	AVERAGE

D1212 — similar to D12, except features 12-string configuration, 6 per side chrome diecast tuners. Available in Black, Brown, Natural, Tobacco Sunburst, and White finishes. Disc. 1996.

		$195	$125

Last Mfr.'s Sug. Retail was $400.

D12 S — similar to D12, except has solid spruce top. Available in Black and Natural finishes. Mfr. 1994 to date.

Mfr.'s Sug. Retail	$449	$325	$225	$150

D12 S LH — similar to D12 S, except in left-handed configuration. Available in Natural finish. Current mfr.

Mfr.'s Sug. Retail	$499	$350	$225	$150

D12 S 12 — similar to D12 S, except features 12-string configuration, 6 per side chrome diecast tuners. Available in Natural finish. Current mfr.

Mfr.'s Sug. Retail	$499	$350	$225	$150

D13 — dreadnought style, spruce top, round soundhole, black pickguard, 3 stripe bound body and rosette, ovankol back/sides, mahogany neck, 14/20 fret rosewood fingerboard with pearl dot inlay, rosewood bridge with white black dot pins, 3 per side chrome diecast tuners. Available in Natural finish. Disc. 1994.

		$195	$125

Last Mfr.'s Sug. Retail was $390.

D1312 12-String — similar to D13, except has 12-string configuration, 6 per side tuners. Disc. 1994.

		$225	$125

Last Mfr.'s Sug. Retail was $450.

D13 S — similar to D13, except has solid spruce top. Available in Natural finish. Mfr. 1994 to 1996, 1998 to date.

Mfr.'s Sug. Retail	$499	$350	$225	$150

D1312 S 12-String — similar to D13, except has 12-string configuration, solid spruce top, 6 per side tuners. Mfd. 1994 to 1996.

		$250	$150

Last Mfr.'s Sug. Retail was $500.

D14 — dreadnought style, spruce top, round soundhole, tortoise pickguard, 3 stripe bound body and rosette, rosewood back/sides, mahogany neck, 14/20 fret rosewood fingerboard with pearl dot inlay, rosewood bridge with pearl dot white pins, 3 per side chrome diecast tuners. Available in Natural and Tobacco finishes. Disc. 1992.

		$175	$100

Last Mfr.'s Sug. Retail was $350.

D20 — dreadnought style, Hawaiian koa top, round soundhole, 3 stripe bound body/rosette, Hawaiian koa back/sides, mahogany neck, 14/20 fret rosewood fingerboard with pearl dot inlay, rosewood bridge with white bridgepins, 3 per side gold diecast tuners. Available in Natural finish. Current mfr.

Mfr.'s Sug. Retail	$799	$595	$375	$250

D20 S — dreadnought style, solid spruce top, round soundhole, tortoise shell pickguard, 3 stripe bound body and rosette, flame maple back/sides, mahogany neck, 14/20 fret rosewood fingerboard with pearl diamond/12th fret W inlay, rosewood bridge with pearl dot white pins, rosewood veneer on peghead, 3 per side chrome diecast tuners. Available in Natural finish. Disc. 1994.

		$275	$175

Last Mfr.'s Sug. Retail was $530.

D21 S — dreadnought style, solid spruce top, round soundhole, tortoise shell pickguard, 3 stripe bound body/rosette, rosewood back/sides, mahogany neck, 14/20 fret rosewood fingerboard with pearl diamond/12th fret W inlay, rosewood bridge with pearl dot white pins, rosewood peghead veneer, 3 per side gold diecast tuners. Available in Natural and Tobacco Sunburst finishes. Current mfr.

Mfr.'s Sug. Retail	$699	$525	$325	$225

In 1994, Tobacco Sunburst finish was discontinued.

D21 S LH — similar to D21S, except is left handed. Available in Natural finish. Disc. 1992.

		$250	$150

Last Mfr.'s Sug. Retail was $510.

D28 S — dreadnought style, solid spruce top, round soundhole, black pickguard, 3 stripe bound body and rosette, 3 piece rosewood back/sides, mahogany neck, 14/20 fret bound rosewood fingerboard with snowflake inlay, rosewood bridge with pearl dot white pins, bound peghead, 3 per side gold diecast tuners. Available in Natural finish. Disc. 1996.

		$300	$195

Last Mfr.'s Sug. Retail was $600.

D28 S LH — similar to D28 S, except has left-handed configuration. Disc. 1992.

		$295	$175

Last Mfr.'s Sug. Retail was $580.

D28 S 12 — similar to D28 S, except has 12-string configuration, 6 per side tuners. Disc. 1994.

		$325	$200

Last Mfr.'s Sug. Retail was $650.

D28 12 LH — similar to D28 S, except is select spruce top, left-handed configuration, 12-string configuration, 6 per side tuners. Disc. 1992.

		$325	$200

Last Mfr.'s Sug. Retail was $620.

W

D55 SW Cherokee
courtesy Washburn

D96 SW Paramount
courtesy Washburn

Grading	100%	EXCELLENT	AVERAGE

D48 S Comanche
courtesy Washburn

D29 S (ORIGINAL VERSION) — dreadnought style, solid cedar top, round soundhole, tortoise shell pickguard, 3 stripe bound body and rosette, rosewood back/sides, 5 piece mahogany/rosewood neck, 14/20 fret rosewood fingerboard with diamond/12th fret W inlay, rosewood bridge with pearl dot white pins, 3 per side gold diecast tuners. Available in Natural finish. Disc. 1994.

	$275	$175	

Last Mfr.'s Sug. Retail was $550.

D29 S (2nd Version) — similar to the D29 S (Original Version), except features a solid spruce top, jacaranda back/sides. Available in Natural finish. Current mfr.

Mfr.'s Sug. Retail	$899	$675	$425	$295

D31 S — dreadnought style, solid spruce top, round soundhole, tortoise shell pickguard, 3 stripe bound body/rosette, flamed maple back/sides, mahogany neck, 14/20 fret rosewood fingerboard with pearl dot inlay, rosewood bridge with white bridgepins, 3 per side gold diecast tuners. Available in Natural finish. Mfr. 1998 to date.

Mfr.'s Sug. Retail	$999	$750	$450	$325

D33 S — similar to the D31 S, except features rosewood back/sides. Available in Natural finish. Mfr. 1998 to date.

Mfr.'s Sug. Retail	$1,099	$825	$525	$350

D61 S W PRAIRIE SONG — dreadnought style, solid spruce top, round soundhole, rosewood pickguard, 3 stripe bound body, 5 stripe rosette, rosewood back/sides, mahogany neck, 14/20 fret rosewood fingerboard with pearl dot inlay, rosewood bridge with pearl dot black pins, rosewood veneer on peghead, 3 per side chrome diecast tuners. Available in Natural finish. Disc. 1994.

	$600	$375	

Last Mfr.'s Sug. Retail was $1,200.

In 1993, ovankol back/sides replaced original item.

D61 S W 12 — similar to D61 S W, except has 12-string configuration, 6 per side tuners. Disc. 1992.

	$475	$300	

Last Mfr.'s Sug. Retail was $940.

D68 S W HARVEST — dreadnought style, solid spruce top, round soundhole, rosewood pickguard, maple/rosewood binding and rosette, rosewood back/sides, 5 piece mahogany/rosewood neck, 14/20 fret rosewood fingerboard with pearl dot inlay, ebony bridge with pearl dot black pins, rosewood veneered maple bound peghead with abalone Washburn inlay, 3 per side chrome diecast tuners with pearloid buttons. Available in Natural finish. Disc. 1994.

	$750	$495	

Last Mfr.'s Sug. Retail was $1,500.

D70 S W HARVEST DELUXE — dreadnought style, solid spruce top, round soundhole, rosewood pickguard, maple/rosewood bound body, abalone inlay rosette, 3 piece rosewood back/sides, 5 piece mahogany/rosewood neck, 14/20 fret ebony fingerboard with abalone eye inlay, ebony bridge with abalone box inlay and Washburn inlay, 3 per side chrome diecast tuners with pearloid buttons. Available in Natural finish. Mfd. 1990 to 1994.

	$950	$650	

Last Mfr.'s Sug. Retail was $2,000.

D90 S W Golden Harvest — similar to D70 S W, except has abalone bound body, tree of life abalone inlay on fingerboard, unbound peghead and pearloid head gold diecast tuners. Disc. 1994.

	$1,800	$1,100	

Last Mfr.'s Sug. Retail was $4,000.

D200 S K — dreadnought style, solid spruce top, round soundhole, tortoise shell pickguard, bound body, 3 stripe rosette, flamed maple back/sides, mahogany neck, 14/20 fret bound rosewood fingerboard with pearl dot inlay, rosewood bridge with white bridgepins, 3 per side gold diecast tuners. Available in Natural finish. Mfr. 1998 to date.

Mfr.'s Sug. Retail	$1,549	$1,150	$700	$495

This model features the Buzz Feiten Tuning System.

D250 S K — similar to the D200 S K, except features rosewood back/sides. Available in Natural finish. Mfr. 1998 to date.

Mfr.'s Sug. Retail	$1,599	$1,200	$750	$525

This model features the Buzz Feiten Tuning System.

Folk Series

F1 S JOEY — smaller travel guitar, solid spruce top, round soundhole, ovankol back/sides, mahogany neck, rosewood fingerboard with pearl dot inlay, rosewood bridge with white bridgepins, 3 per side chrome Grover tuners. Available in Natural finish. Mfr. 1998 to date.

Mfr.'s Sug. Retail	$299			

F11 — folk style, mountain ash top, round soundhole, bound body, 3 stripe purfling/rosette, mountain ash back/sides, mahogany neck, 14/20 fret bound rosewood fingerboard with pearl dot inlay, rosewood bridge with black bridgepins, 3 per side chrome Grover tuners. Available in Antique Natural, Brown, and Natural finishes. Current mfr.

Mfr.'s Sug. Retail	$359	$275	$175	$125

Jumbo Series

F-21 S
courtesy Washburn

D24 S 12 12-String — jumbo style, solid spruce top, round soundhole, tortoise pickguard, bound body, 3 stripe purfling/rosette, mahogany back/sides/neck, 14/20 fret rosewood fingerboard with pearl dot inlay, rosewood bridge with white black dot pins, 6 per side chrome Grover tuners. Available in Natural finish. Mfr. 1994 to date.

Mfr.'s Sug. Retail	$799	$575	$375	$250

Grading	100%	EXCELLENT	AVERAGE

D25 S — jumbo style, solid spruce top, round soundhole, tortoise pickguard, bound body 3 stripe purfling/rosette, mahogany back/sides/neck, 14/20 fret rosewood fingerboard with pearl diamond/12th fret 'W' inlay, rosewood bridge with pearl dot white pins, 3 per side gold diecast tuners. Available in Natural and Tobacco Sunburst finishes. Mfr. 1993 to date.

Mfr.'s Sug. Retail	$699	$525	$325	$200

In 1994, bound fingerboard/peghead, Tobacco Sunburst finish were introduced; 12th fret inlay was discontinued.

D25 S 12 — similar to D25 S, except has 12-string configuration, 6 per side tuners. Disc. 1994.

$250 $150

Last Mfr.'s Sug. Retail was $500.

D30 S — jumbo style, solid cedar top, round soundhole, tortoise pickguard, bound body, 3 stripe purfling, 5 stripe rosette, birdseye maple back/sides, mahogany neck, 14/20 fret rosewood fingerboard with pearl dot inlay, rosewood bridge with pearl dot white pins and bone saddle, birdseye maple peghead veneer, 3 per side chrome diecast tuners. Available in Natural finish. Disc. 1994.

$375 $250

Last Mfr.'s Sug. Retail was $750.

D32 S — similar to D30S, except has Makassar back/sides, bound fingerboard/peghead, Makassar veneer on peghead. Disc. 1994.

$400 $275

Last Mfr.'s Sug. Retail was $800.

D32 S 12 12-String — similar to D32S, except has 12-string configuration, 6 per side tuners. Disc. 1992.

$400 $275

Last Mfr.'s Sug. Retail was $780.

D34 S — jumbo style, solid spruce top, round soundhole, bound body 3 stripe purfling/rosette, mahogany back/sides, mahogany neck, 14/20 fret rosewood fingerboard with pearl dot inlay, rosewood bridge with white bridgepins, 3 per side gold diecast tuners. Available in Natural finish. Current mfr.

Mfr.'s Sug. Retail	$729	$550	$350	$225

R312 Presentation
courtesy Washburn

R Series (Also 1896 Reissue Series)

R301 — concert style, solid spruce top, round soundhole, bound body, 3 stripe purfling/rosette, mahogany back/sides/neck, 12/18 fret rosewood fingerboard with pearl dot inlay, rosewood bridge with black white dot pins, rosewood veneered slotted peghead, 3 per side diecast chrome tuners. Available in Natural finish. Mfd. 1994 to 1996.

$300 $195

Last Mfr.'s Sug. Retail was $600.

This instrument is a reissue of a model available in 1896.

R306 — similar to R301, except features solid cedar top, rosewood back/sides, mahogany neck, 12/18 fret rosewood fingerboard with pearl multi symbol inlay, rosewood bridge with carved fans/pearl dot inlay, white abalone dot bridge pins, rosewood veneered slotted peghead with pearl fan/diamond inlay, 3 per side diecast chrome tuners with pearl buttons. Available in Natural finish. Mfd. 1993 to 1996.

$400 $265

Last Mfr.'s Sug. Retail was $800.

This instrument is a reissue of a model available in 1896.

R310 — parlor (concert) style, solid spruce top, round soundhole, bound body, 3 stripe purfling/rosette, rosewood back/sides, mahogany neck, 12/18 fret rosewood fingerboard with pearl dot inlay, rosewood bridge with black bridgepins, rosewood veneered slotted peghead, 3 per side diecast chrome tuners. Available in Natural finish. Disc. 1998.

$725 $475

Last Mfr.'s Sug. Retail was $1,499.

WD Series

WD20 S — dreadnought style, solid spruce top, round soundhole, black pickguard, bound body, 3 stripe rosette, mahogany back/sides/neck, 14/20 fret rosewood fingerboard with pearl dot inlay, rosewood bridge with black white dot pins, rosewood peghead veneer with screened logo, 3 per side chrome tuners. Available in Natural finish. Mfd. 1993 to date.

Mfr.'s Sug. Retail	$629	$475	$300	$200

WD40 S — similar to WD20 S, except features a solid cedar top, rosewood back/sides, mahogany neck. Available in Natural finish. Mfd. 1993 to 1996.

$265 $175

Last Mfr.'s Sug. Retail was $530.

Stephen's Extended Cutaway Series

This series has a patented neck to body joint called the Stephen's Extended Cutaway (designed by Stephen Davies) that allows full access to all 24 frets.

DC60 LEXINGTON — single round cutaway dreadnought style, solid spruce top, oval soundhole, bound body, 3 stripe purfling/rosette, ovankol back/sides, mahogany neck, 24 fret bound rosewood fingerboard with pearl dot inlay, rosewood bridge with black dot pins, 3 per side pearloid chrome diecast tuners. Available in Natural finish. Disc. 1992.

$425 $275

Last Mfr.'s Sug. Retail was $830.

DC80 Charleston — similar to DC60 Lexington, except features a solid cedar top, rosewood back/sides, mahogany neck, 24 fret bound rosewood fingerboard with diamond inlay, rosewood bridge with pearl dot white pins, rosewood veneer on bound peghead, 3 per side pearloid head gold diecast tuners. Available in Natural finish. Disc. 1992.

$450 $300

Last Mfr.'s Sug. Retail was $900.

WD20 S
courtesy Washburn

W

Grading	100%	EXCELLENT	AVERAGE

C64 CE
courtesy Washburn

J20 S — jumbo style, solid cedar top, oval soundhole, bound body, 5 stripe rosette, walnut back/sides, mahogany neck, 21 fret rosewood fingerboard with pearl snowflake inlay at 12th fret, rosewood bridge with pearl dot white pins and bone saddle, walnut veneer on peghead, 3 per side chrome diecast tuners. Available in Natural finish. Disc. 1994.

$450 $300
Last Mfr.'s Sug. Retail was $900.

J50 S — similar to J20 S, except features a solid spruce top, birdseye maple back/sides, 21 fret bound rosewood fingerboard with pearl snowflake inlay at the 12th fret, birds eye maple veneer on bound peghead, 3 per side pearl button gold diecast tuners. Available in Natural finish. Disc. 1994.

$575 $375
Last Mfr.'s Sug. Retail was $1,150.

ACOUSTIC ELECTRIC

Classic Acoustic Electric

C64 CE — single rounded cutaway classical body, spruce top, round soundhole, bound body, wood marquetry rosette, ovankol back/sides, mahogany neck, 19 fret rosewood fingerboard, tied rosewood bridge, 3 per side gold tuners with nylon buttons, acoustic bridge pickup, volume/tone controls, EQUIS Standard preamp. Available in Natural finish. Mfr. 1994 to date.

Mfr.'s Sug. Retail	$769	$575	$350	$250

C84 CE — single rounded cutaway body, solid spruce top, round soundhole, 3 stripe bound body, wood marquetry rosette, rosewood back/sides, mahogany neck, 12/19 fret rosewood fingerboard, tied rosewood bridge, rosewood peghead veneer, 3 per side nylon head gold tuners, acoustic bridge pickup, 4 band EQ. Available in Natural finish. Disc. 1996.

$350 $225
Last Mfr.'s Sug. Retail was $650.

In 1994, solid cedar top replaced original item.

C94 S CE — similar to the C84CE, except features solid cedar top, wooden inlay rosette, jacaranda back/sides, 19 fret rosewood fingerboard, volume/tone control, 3 band EQ. Available in Natural finish. Mfd. 1994 to 1996.

$450 $275
Last Mfr.'s Sug. Retail was $900.

C104 S CE — single rounded cutaway classical body, solid cedar top, round soundhole, bound body, wood marquetry rosette, rosewood back/sides, mahogany neck, 19 fret rosewood fingerboard, tied rosewood bridge, 3 per side gold tuners with nylon buttons, acoustic bridge pickup, volume/tone controls, EQUIS Silver preamp. Available in Natural finish. Mfr. 1997 to date.

Mfr.'s Sug. Retail	$1,099	$825	$525	$350

EC41 TANGLEWOOD — classical style, spruce top, oval soundhole, 5 stripe bound body/rosette, ovankol back/sides, mahogany neck, 21 fret bound rosewood fingerboard with pearl dot inlay, rosewood bridge, ovankol veneer on bound peghead, 3 per side pearl button gold tuners, EQUIS II preamp system. Available in Natural finish. Disc 1992.

$350 $225
Last Mfr.'s Sug. Retail was $700.

Dreadnought Acoustic Electric Series

D10 E — dreadnought style, select spruce top, round soundhole, black pickguard, 3 stripe bound body/rosette, mahogany back/sides/neck, 14/20 fret rosewood fingerboard with pearl dot inlay, rosewood bridge with pearl dot black pins, 3 per side chrome Grover tuners, piezo bridge pickup, volume/tone controls, passive preamp. Available in Black and Natural finishes. Current mfr.

Mfr.'s Sug. Retail	$399	$300	$195	$125

D10 CE — single rounded cutaway dreadnought style, select spruce top, round soundhole, black pickguard, 3 stripe bound body and rosette, mahogany back/sides/neck, 14/20 fret rosewood fingerboard with pearl dot inlay, rosewood bridge with pearl dot black pins, 3 per side chrome Grover tuners, piezo bridge pickup, volume/tone controls, 3 band EQ, EQUIS Standard preamp. Available in Black and Natural finishes. Mfr. 1993 to date.

Mfr.'s Sug. Retail	$549	$425	$255	$195

D10 DE LH — similar to the D12 CE, except features a left-handed configuration. Available in Natural finish. Current mfr.

Mfr.'s Sug. Retail	$599	$450	$295	$195

D10 CE M — similar to the D10 CE, except features a mahogany top (and mahogany back/sides). Available in Transparent Wine Red and Caribbean Blue finishes. Current mfr.

Mfr.'s Sug. Retail	$499	$375	$225	$150

D10 CE Q — similar to the D10 CE, except features a quilted maple top. Available in Sunburst finish. Current mfr.

Mfr.'s Sug. Retail	$599	$450	$295	$195

D12 CE — single rounded cutaway dreadnought style, spruce top, round soundhole, black pickguard, 3 stripe bound body and rosette, mahogany back/sides/neck, 14/20 fret rosewood fingerboard with pearl dot inlay/pearl W inlay at 12th fret, rosewood bridge with pearl dot black pins, 3 per side chrome diecast tuners, piezo bridge pickup, volume/tone control, 3 band EQ, EQUIS Standard preamp. Available in Black, Natural, Tobacco Sunburst, White, and Woodstone Brown finishes. Mfd. 1993 to 1994.

$295 $200
Last Mfr.'s Sug. Retail was $600.

D12 S CE — similar to the D12 CE, except features a solid spruce top. Available in Black and Natural finishes. Mfr. 1994 to date.

Mfr.'s Sug. Retail	$599	$450	$295	$195

C104 SCE
courtesy Washburn

Grading	100%	EXCELLENT	AVERAGE

D1212 CE — similar to D12 CE, except has 12-string configuration, 6 per side tuners. Available in Natural and Tobacco Sunburst finishes. Disc. 1994.

$350 $225
Last Mfr.'s Sug. Retail was $680.

D1212 E — similar to D12 CE, except has non-cutaway body, 12-string configuration, 6 per side tuners. Available in Natural finish. Mfd. 1994 to 1996.

$275 $175
Last Mfr.'s Sug. Retail was $530.

D17 S CE — single rounded cutaway dreadnought style, solid spruce top, round soundhole, black pickguard, 3 stripe bound body/rosette, mahogany back/sides/neck, 20 fret bound rosewood fingerboard with pearl diamond inlay, stylized W inlay at 12th fret, rosewood bridge with black white dot pins, pearl diamond inlay on bridge wings, bound peghead, 3 per side gold tuners with pearl buttons, acoustic bridge pickup, volume/tone control, 3 band EQ, 1/4/XLR output jack. Available in Black and Natural finishes. Disc. 1996.

$395 $250
Last Mfr.'s Sug. Retail was $800.

Add $50 for 12-string configuration of this model (**D17 S CE 12**). Available in Natural finish only.

D17 CE — similar to D17 S CE, except has flamed sycamore top/back/sides. Available in Brown and Wine Red finishes. Disc. 1998.

$575 $325
Last Mfr.'s Sug. Retail was $999.

D17 CE 12 12-String — similar to D17 S CE, except has 12-string configuration, 6 per side tuners, flamed sycamore top/back/sides. Disc. 1994.

$450 $295
Last Mfr.'s Sug. Retail was $880.

D21 SE — dreadnought style, solid spruce top, round soundhole, tortoise shell pickguard, 3 stripe bound body and rosette, flame maple back/sides, mahogany neck, 14/20 fret rosewood fingerboard with pearl diamond/12th fret W inlay, rosewood bridge with pearl dot white pins, rosewood veneer on peghead, 3 per side chrome diecast tuners, acoustic bridge pickup, volume/tone control, 3 band EQ. Available in Natural finish. Disc. 1992.

$275 $175
Last Mfr.'s Sug. Retail was $570.

D61 S CE — single round cutaway dreadnought style, solid spruce top, round soundhole, wood bound body, 3 stripe wood purfling, 5 stripe rosette, ovankol back/sides, mahogany neck, 14/20 fret rosewood fingerboard with pearl dot inlay, rosewood bridge with pearl dot black pins, rosewood peghead veneer, 3 per side chrome diecast tuners. Available in Natural finish. Mfd. 1993 to 1996.

$650 $495
Last Mfr.'s Sug. Retail was $1,500.

D68 S CE — single rounded cutaway dreadnought style, solid spruce top, round soundhole, wood body binding, 5 stripe wood purfling/rosette, rosewood back/sides, 5 piece mahogany/rosewood neck, 14/20 fret rosewood fingerboard with pearl dot inlay, rosewood bridge with black pearl dot pins, rosewood veneered maple bound peghead with abalone Washburn inlay, 3 per side pearloid head chrome diecast tuners, rosewood pickguard, acoustic bridge pickup, 4 band EQ. Available in Natural finish. Mfd. 1993 to 1996.

$850 $575
Last Mfr.'s Sug. Retail was $1,800.

WD20 S CE — single rounded cutaway dreadnought style, solid spruce top, round soundhole, black pickguard, bound body, 3 stripe rosette, mahogany back/sides/neck, 14/20 fret rosewood fingerboard with pearl dot inlay, rosewood bridge with black white dot pins, rosewood peghead veneer with screened logo, 3 per side chrome tuners, acoustic bridge pickup, volume/tone control, 3 band EQ. Available in Natural finish. Mfd. 1994 to 1996.

$350 $225
Last Mfr.'s Sug. Retail was $700.

D17 CE WR
courtesy Washburn

Festival Series

Washburn's Festival Series models are equipped with EQUIS preamp systems and Fishman USA pick ups.

EA10 — deep single sharp cutaway jumbo body, spruce top, oval soundhole, bound body, 3 stripe purfling/rosette, mahogany back/sides/neck, 21 fret bound rosewood fingerboard with pearl dot inlay, rosewood bridge with white black dot pins, bound peghead with screened logo, 3 per side chrome Grover tuners, acoustic bridge pickup, Equis Standard preamp. Available in Black and Natural finishes. Mfr. 1994 to date.

Mfr.'s Sug. Retail	$769	$575	$375	$250

EA18 — similar to the EA10, except features a thin single sharp cutaway folk body, ash top, ash back/sides. Available in Transparent Red and Tobacco Sunburst finishes. Mfr. 1997 to date.

Mfr.'s Sug. Retail	$849	$625	$375	$250

EA20 NEWPORT — thin single sharp cutaway jumbo body, select spruce or mahogany top, oval soundhole, bound body, 3 stripe rosette, mahogany back/sides/neck, 21 fret rosewood fingerboard with pearl dot inlay, rosewood bridge with pearl dot white pins, 3 per side Grover diecast tuners, acoustic bridge pickup, Equis Gold preamp. Available in Black and Tobacco Sunburst finishes. Mfd. 1979 to date.

Mfr.'s Sug. Retail	$999	$775	$495	$325

In 1994, Natural finish was introduced.

EA2012 — similar to EA20, except has 12 strings, 6 per side tuners. Available in Black and Natural finishes. Disc. 1994.

$450 $300
Last Mfr.'s Sug. Retail was $900.

EA20 TS
courtesy Washburn

Grading	100%	EXCELLENT	AVERAGE

EA20 X Melissa — similar to EA20, except has special 'Melissa' fingerboard inlay. Available in Black finish. Mfd. 1995 only.

		$575	$N/A

Last Mfr.'s Sug. Retail was $949.

This model was designed in conjunction with Greg Allman (Allman Brothers). It is estimated that only 500 instruments were built

EA22 NUNO BETTENCOURT LIMITED EDITION — single sharp cutaway folk style, spruce top, oval soundhole, bound body, 5 stripe purfling, 9 stripe rosette, mahogany back/sides/neck, 21 fret bound rosewood fingerboard with pearl wings inlay, rosewood bridge with white black dot pins, bound blackface peghead with screened signature/logo, 3 per side chrome Grover tuners, acoustic bridge pickup, volume/tone control, 3 band EQ, numbered commemorative metal plate inside body. Available in Black finish. Mfd. 1994 to 1996.

		$500	$350

Last Mfr.'s Sug. Retail was $1,000.

EA26 Craig Chacquico
courtesy Washburn

EA26 CRAIG CHACQUICO SIGNATURE — thin single sharp cutaway jumbo body, select spruce top, oval soundhole, bound body, abalone rosette, mahogany back/sides/neck, 21 fret rosewood fingerboard with special abalone position markers, rosewood bridge with pearl dot white pins, 3 per side Grover diecast tuners, gold hardware, acoustic bridge pickup, volume/tone controls, Equis Gold preamp. Available in Black, Natural, and White finishes. Current mfr.

Mfr.'s Sug. Retail	$1,299	$1,000	$600	$425

EA27 K — similar to the EA26, except features chrome hardware, EQUIS Silver preamp. Available in Natural finish. Mfr. 1997 to date.

Mfr.'s Sug. Retail	$1,449	$1,100	$675	$475

EA30 MONTEREY — single sharp cutaway dreadnought style, spruce top, oval soundhole, bound body, 3 stripe purfling, 5 stripe rosette, flame maple back/sides, mahogany neck, 21 fret rosewood fingerboard, rosewood bridge with white pearl dot pins, 3 per side chrome diecast tuners, acoustic bridge pickup, volume/tone control, 3 band EQ. Available in Natural, Transparent Red, Transparent Blue and Transparent Black finishes. Disc. 1992.

		$375	$225

Last Mfr.'s Sug. Retail was $730.

Add $40 for 12-string configuration of this model **(Model EA3012)**. Available in Natural finish.

Add $100 for left-handed configuration of this model **(Model EA30 LH)**.

EA33 S K — deep single sharp cutaway jumbo body, solid spruce top, oval soundhole, bound body, 3 stripe rosette, flamed maple back/sides, mahogany neck, 21 fret rosewood fingerboard with pearl dot inlay, rosewood bridge with pearl dot white pins, 3 per side Grover diecast tuners, gold hardware, acoustic bridge pickup, volume/tone controls, Equis Gold preamp. Available in Natural finish. Current mfr.

Mfr.'s Sug. Retail	$1,799	$1,350	$850	$595

This model features the Buzz Feiten Tuning System.

EA36 MARQUEE (Formerly EA46) — single cutaway dreadnought style, figured maple top, 3 stripe bound body, diagonal sound channels, figured maple back/sides, mahogany neck, 23 fret rosewood bound fingerboard with pearl diamond inlay, rosewood bridge with pearl dot black pins, flame maple veneer on bound peghead, 3 per side pearl button gold diecast tuners, acoustic bridge pickup, Equis Gold preamp. Available in Natural and Tobacco Sunburst finishes. Disc. 1998.

		$625	$400

Last Mfr.'s Sug. Retail was $1,199.

EA3612 — similar to EA36, except has 12 strings, 6 per side tuners. Disc. 1994.

		$525	$350

Last Mfr.'s Sug. Retail was $1,050.

EA40 WOODSTOCK — single sharp cutaway dreadnought style, arched spruce top, oval soundhole, bound body, abalone purfling/rosette, mahogany back/sides/neck, 21 fret bound rosewood fingerboard, rosewood bridge with pearl dot black pins, 3 per side chrome diecast tuners, EQUIS II preamp system. Available in Black and White finishes. Disc. 1992.

		$550	$350

Last Mfr.'s Sug. Retail was $1,100.

Add $40 for string version of this model **(Model EA4012)**. Disc. 1992.

This model had birdseye maple back/sides with Natural finish optionally available.

EA44 — single sharp cutaway dreadnought style, solid cedar top, oval soundhole, bound body, 3 stripe purfling/rosette, rosewood back/sides, mahogany neck, 20 fret bound rosewood fingerboard with pearl diamond inlay, rosewood bridge with white black pins, bound peghead with rosewood veneer, 3 per side chrome tuners with pearl buttons, acoustic bridge pickup, volume/tone control, 3 band EQ. Available in Black, Natural and Tobacco Sunburst finishes. Disc. 1994.

		$550	$350

Last Mfr.'s Sug. Retail was $1,100.

EA45 — similar to EA44. Available in Natural and Tobacco Sunburst finishes. Disc. 1996

		$575	$375

Last Mfr.'s Sug. Retail was $1,150.

Grading	100%	EXCELLENT	AVERAGE

EA220 DOUBLENECK — deep single sharp cutaway jumbo body, select spruce top, oval soundhole, bound body, 3 stripe rosette, mahogany back/sides/neck, 21 fret rosewood fingerboard with pearl dot inlay, rosewood bridge with pearl dot white pins, 12-string configuration neck (6 per side Grover diecast tuners), 6-string configuration neck (3 per side Grover diecast tuners), chrome hardware, acoustic bridge pickups, volume/tone controls, neck selector toggle switch, Equis Gold preamp. Available in Black and Natural finishes. Current mfr.

Mfr.'s Sug. Retail	$2,499	$1,900	$1,150	$800

Jumbo Acoustic Electric Series

J21 CE — single rounded cutaway jumbo body, spruce top, oval soundhole, bound body, 3 stripe purfling, 5 stripe rosette, mahogany back/sides/neck, 21 fret bound rosewood fingerboard, pearl diamond inlay at 12th fret, rosewood bridge with white black dot pins, bound rosewood veneered peghead with screened logo, 3 per side chrome tuners, acoustic bridge pickup, 4 band EQ. Available in Black, Natural, and Tobacco Sunburst finishes. Mfd. 1994 to 1996.

		$325	$225

Last Mfr.'s Sug. Retail was $650.

J28 S CE — single rounded cutaway jumbo body, solid spruce top, round soundhole, bound body, inlaid rosette, mahogany back/sides/neck, 14/20 fret bound rosewood fingerboard with pearl 'crown' inlay, rosewood bridge with white bridgepins, 3 per side chrome Grover tuners, piezo bridge pickup, volume/3 band EQ controls, EQUIS Gold preamp. Available in Tobaco Sunburst finish. Current mfr.

Mfr.'s Sug. Retail	$1,299	$1,000	$625	$425

J30 S CE — similar to J28 S CE. Available in Black, Transparent Wine Red, and Natural finishes. Mfr. 1998 to date.

Mfr.'s Sug. Retail	$1,799	$1,350	$850	$575

This model features the Buzz Feiten Tuning System.

J61 S CE K — similar to J28 S CE, except features flamed maple back/sides. Available in Natural and Tobacco Sunburst finishes. Current mfr.

Mfr.'s Sug. Retail	$1,999	$1,500	$925	$650

Red Rocker (RR) Series

These models were designed in conjunction with guitarist Sammy Hagar.

RR150 — single Florentine cutaway semi-hollow alder body, bound quilted maple top, mahogany neck, 22 fret rosewood fingerboard with pearl dot inlay, blackface peghead, rosewood bridge, 3 per side Grover tuners, chrome hardware, 2 exposed coil humbucker pickups/acoustic piezo pickup, 2 volume/tone controls, 3 position toggle switch. Available in Black and Transparent Red finishes. Mfd. 1997 to date.

Mfr.'s Sug. Retail	$1,199	$900	$550	$395

RR300 (U.S. Mfr.) — similar to the MR250, except features a mahogany body, bound spruce top, P-90-style single coil pickup/Fishman bridge transducer. Available in Transparent Red and Vintage Sunburst finishes. Mfr. 1997 to date.

Mfr.'s Sug. Retail	$1,999	$1,495	$925	$650

This model features the Buzz Feiten Tuning System.

Solid Body Series

SBC20 — single rounded cutaway classic style, spruce top, round soundhole, bound body, wooden inlay rosette, routed out mahogany body, mahogany neck, 22 fret rosewood fingerboard with pearl dot inlay, rosewood bridge, 3 per side chrome diecast tuners, Sensor pickups, volume/tone control. Available in Natural finish. Disc. 1992.

		$275	$175

Last Mfr.'s Sug. Retail was $550.

SBC70 — single cutaway classic style routed out mahogany body, multi-bound spruce top, mahogany neck, 22 fret bound rosewood fingerboard, tied rosewood bridge, rosewood veneered slotted peghead, 3 per side chrome tuners with pearloid buttons, acoustic bridge pickup, volume/tone controls. Available in Natural finish. Mfd. 1994 to 1996.

		$350	$225

Last Mfr.'s Sug. Retail was $700.

SBF24 — single round cutaway dreadnought style, spruce top, round soundhole, bound body, wooden inlay rosette, routed out mahogany body, mahogany neck, 22 fret rosewood fingerboard with pearl dot inlay, rosewood bridge with white pearl dot pins, 3 per side chrome diecast tuners, Sensor pickups, volume/tone control, active electronics. Available in Natural, Pearl White and Black finishes. Disc. 1992.

		$275	$175

Last Mfr.'s Sug. Retail was $570.

SBF80 — single cutaway dreadnought style routed out mahogany body, multi-bound figured maple top, mahogany neck, 22 fret bound rosewood fingerboard with pearl slotted diamond inlay, rosewood bridge with white abalone dot pins, bound figured maple peghead with screened logo, 3 per side chrome Grover tuners with pearloid buttons, acoustic bridge pickup, volume/treble/bass controls, active electronics. Available in Cherry Sunburst finish. Mfd. 1993 to 1996.

		$375	$250

Last Mfr.'s Sug. Retail was $750.

Stephen's Extended Cutaway Series Acoustic Electric

DC60 E — single round cutaway dreadnought style, solid spruce top, oval soundhole, bound body, 3 stripe purfling/rosette, ovankol back/sides, mahogany neck, 24 fret bound rosewood fingerboard with pearl dot inlay, rosewood bridge with black dot pins, 3 per side pearloid chrome diecast tuners, acoustic bridge pickup, 4 band EQ. Disc. 1994.

		$700	$450

Last Mfr.'s Sug. Retail was $1,400.

EA220
courtesy Washburn

W

Grading	100%	EXCELLENT	AVERAGE

AB30
courtesy Washburn

DC80 E — similar to DC60 E, except features a solid cedar top, rosewood back/sides, mahogany neck, 24 fret bound rosewood fingerboard with diamond inlay, rosewood bridge with pearl dot white pins, rosewood veneer on bound peghead, 3 per side pearloid head gold diecast tuners, acoustic bridge pickup, 4 band EQ. Disc. 1994.

		$750	$495

Last Mfr.'s Sug. Retail was $1,500.

ACOUSTIC ELECTRIC BASS

AB Series

AB10 — single sharp cutaway thin jumbo body, select spruce top, diagonal slotted sound channels (soundhole), bound body, mahogany back/sides, maple neck, 23 fret rosewood fingerboard with pearl dot inlay, rosewood bridge with brass insert, 2 per side tuners, chrome hardware, EQUIS Silver bass preamp system. Available in Black and Natural finishes. Mfr. 1997 to date.

Mfr.'s Sug. Retail	$999	$750	$450	$325

AB20 — single sharp cutaway thin jumbo body, mahogany top, diagonal sound channels, bound body, mahogany back/sides, maple neck, 23 fret rosewood fingerboard with pearl dot inlay, rosewood bridge with brass insert, 2 per side tuners, chrome hardware, EQUIS Gold bass preamp system. Available in Black, Natural, and Tobacco Sunburst finishes. Current mfr.

Mfr.'s Sug. Retail	$1,199	$900	$550	$395

This model was available with a fretless fingerboard (this option discontinued in 1996).

In 1997, Natural finish was discontinued.

AB25 — similar to AB20, except has 5 strings. Available in Black and Tobacco Sunburst finishes. Disc. 1996.

		$500	$325

Last Mfr.'s Sug. Retail was $1,049.

AB32 — similar to AB20, except has single rounded cutaway deep dreadnought body, select spruce top, oval soundhole, EQUIS Silver bass preamp system. Available in Natural and Tobacco Sunburst finishes.

Mfr.'s Sug. Retail	$1,099	$825	$525	$350

AB40 — single round cutaway jumbo style, arched spruce top, diagonal sound channels, bound body, quilted ash back/sides, multi layer maple neck, 24 fret bound ebony fingerboard with pearl dot inlay, ebonized rosewood bridge with brass insert, bound peghead with pearl Washburn logo and stylized inlay, 2 per side tuners, gold hardware, active electronics, volume/2 tone controls, EQUIS II bass preamp system. Available in Natural and Tobacco Sunburst finishes. Disc. 1996.

		$1,100	$750

Last Mfr.'s Sug. Retail was $2,250.

Subtract $150 for fretless fingerboard (**Model AB40 FL**).

AB42 — similar to AB40, except has humbucker pickup. Available in Tobacco Sunburst finish. Disc. 1996.

		$1,150	$825

Last Mfr.'s Sug. Retail was $2,500.

AB45 — similar to AB40, except has 5-string configuration, 3/2 per side tuners. Available in Tobacco Sunburst finish. Disc. 1991.

		$1,150	$825

Last Mfr.'s Sug. Retail was $2,300.

DAVID WEBBER

Instruments currently built in North Vancouver, Canada.

Luthier David Webber and his "small factory" build high quality acoustic guitars. For further information regarding model pricing and specification, please contact David Webber via the Index of Current Manufacturers located in the rear of this edition.

ABRAHAM WECHTER

Instruments built in Paw Paw, Michigan. Distributed by Wechter Guitars of Paw Paw, Michigan. Distributed in Japan by Okada International, Inc. of Tokyo, Japan.

Luthier Abraham Wechter began his guitar building career in the early 1970s by making dulcimers and repairing guitars in Seattle, Washington. Shortly thereafter he started looking for a mentor to apprentice with. In December of 1974, he moved to Detroit to begin an apprenticeship with Richard Schneider. He was captivated by Schneider's art, along with the scientific work Schneider was doing with Dr. Kasha.

Wechter worked with Schneider developing prototypes for what later became the "Mark" project at Gibson Guitars. Schneider was working regularly for Gibson developing prototypes, and as a result Wechter started working for Gibson as a model (prototype) builder. Schneider and Wechter moved to Kalamazoo in December 1976. After a few years, Wechter was given the opportunity to work as an independent consultant to Gibson. He continued on until June of 1984, performing prototype work on many of the guitars Gibson produced during that time period.

While at Gibson, Wechter continued his apprenticeship with Schneider, building handmade, world-class guitars. He actually rented space from Schneider during this time and started building his own models. In 1984, when Gibson moved to Nashville, Wechter decided to remain in Michigan. Wechter moved to Paw Paw, Michigan, a rural town about 20 miles west of Kalamazoo, where he set up shop and started designing and building his own guitars.

Wechter built handmade classical, jazz-nylon, bass, and steel-string acoustic guitars. He did a tremendous amount of research into how and why guitars perform. As a result, he became sought after by many high profile people in the industry. Between 1985 and 1995, Wechter designed and hand built guitars for artists like John McLaughlin, Steve Howe, Al DiMeola, Giovanni, John Denver, Earl Klugh, and Jonas Hellborg. During this time period he developed a reputation as one of the world's finest craftsman and guitar designers.

In November of 1994, Wechter built a prototype of an innovative new design, and realized that it would have applications far beyond the high price range he was working in. This was the birth of the Pathmaker guitar. The Pathmaker model is a revolutionary acoustic guitar. The double cutaway construction (patent pending) provides a full 19 frets clear of the body in a design that is both inherently stable and visually striking.

Wechter is currently laying the groundwork for mass production and distribution of the Pathmaker - the first production models were scheduled for January, 1997. A limited number of handmade premier models are being built, along with a small number of classical and jazz-nylon guitars. For more information on availability and pricing, contact Wechter Guitars via the Index of Current Manufacturers located in the back of this book.

(Biography courtesy Abraham Wechter and Michael Davidson, August 2, 1996)

ACOUSTIC

In November of 1994, Wechter built a prototype of an innovative new design that led to the i ntroduction of the **Pathmaker**. The unique double cutaway body design features a neck with 19 frets clear of the body.

Earlier model may be equipped with either a Fishman Axis system or Axis+ or Axis-M. The Pathmak er "Recessed Tailblock" has a Fishman Matrix transducer mounted on the tailblock of the instrument.

Add $50 for a Fishman Onboard Blender.

Add $150 for an Engelmann spruce top.

PATHMAKER STANDARD — dual cutaway acoustic body, solid Sitka spruce top, solid mahogany or rosewood back/sides, round soundhole, abalone rosette, wood binding, mahogany neck, 19/22 fret rosewood fingerboard with offset abalone dot inlay, 3 per side tuners, rosewood peghead veneer with mother of pearl logo inlay, rosewood bridge with white bridgepins, tortoise pickguard, Fishman Prefix + system. Available in Natural gloss finish. Current mfr.

Mahogany back and sides.
Mfr.'s Sug. Retail $1,899

Rosewood back and sides.
Mfr.'s Sug. Retail $1,999
Add $60 for cedar top.

Add $75 for Autumn Brown top toner finish.

This model is also available in a Satin gloss finish. List price includes a hardshell case.

Pathmaker Elite Nylon String — similar to the Pathmaker Standard, except features a nylon string configuration. Available in Natural gloss finish. Current mfr.

Mahogany back and sides.
Mfr.'s Sug. Retail $2,049

Rosewood back and sides.
Mfr.'s Sug. Retail $2,149
Add $60 for cedar top.

Add $75 for Autumn Brown top toner finish.

This model is also available in a Satin gloss finish. List price includes a hardshell case.

Pathmaker Starburst — similar to the Pathmaker Standard, except features white ABS body binding. Available in Tobacco Brown Starburst finish. Current mfr.

Mahogany back and sides.
Mfr.'s Sug. Retail $2,099

Rosewood back and sides.
Mfr.'s Sug. Retail $2,199

WEISSENBORN

H. WEISSENBORN

Instruments built in California during the 1920s and early 1930s.

H. Weissenborn instruments were favorites of slide guitar players in Hawaii and the West Coast in the early 1900s. All four models featured koa construction, and different binding packages per model. Further model specifications and information updates will be contained in future editions of the **Blue Book of Guitars**.

WEYMANN & SON

Instruments built in Philadelphia, Pennsylvania from 1864 to the early part of the 1900s. Some models under the Weymann & Son trademark were built by Regal (Chicago, Illinois), and Vega (Boston, Massachusetts).

H.A. Weymann & Son, Incorporated was established in 1864 in Philadelphia. Later, it incorporated as the Weymann Company in 1904, and distributed numerous guitar models that ranged from entry level student up to fine quality. Other trademarks may include **Weymann**, **Keystone State**, **W & S**, and **Varsity**. Some of the guitars were actually produced by Vega or Regal, and share similarities to the company of origin's production instruments.

MARK WHITEBROOK

Instruments built in California during the 1970s.

Mark Whitebrook was an apprentice to luthier Roy Noble for a number of years. Whitebrook built high quality acoustic guitars, and was luthier to James Taylor for a number of years. Further information will be updated in future editions of the **Blue Book of Guitars**.

Weissenborn Model 1
courtesy Gary Sullivan

WINDSOR

See chapter on House Brands.

The Windsor trademark was a *House Brand* for Montgomery Wards around the turn of the century (circa 1890s to mid 1910s). These beginner's grade acoustic flattop guitars and mandolins were built by various American manufacturers such as Lyon & Healy (and possibly Harmony).

(Source: Michael Wright, Vintage Guitar Magazine)

KATHY WINGERT

KATHY WINGERT GUITARS

Instruments currently produced in California.

Luthier Kathy Wingert is currently offering a number of hand crafted acoustic guitars. For more information regarding model specifications and pricing, contact Kathy Wingert through the Index of Current Manufacturers located in the back of this edition.

WINSTON

Instruments produced in Japan circa early 1960s to late 1960s. Distributed in the U.S. by Buegeleisen & Jacobson of New York, New York.

The Winston trademark was a brandname used by U.S. importers Buegeleisen & Jacobson of New York, New York. The Winston brand appeared on a full range of acoustic guitars, thinline acoustic/electric archtops, and solid body electric guitars and basses. Winston instruments are generally the shorter scale beginner's guitar. Although the manufacturers are unknown, some models appear to be built by Guyatone.

(Source: Michael Wright, Vintage Guitar Magazine)

RANDY WOOD

Instruments built in Savannah, Georgia, since 1978. Distributed exclusively by Joe Pichkur's Guitar Center of Floral Park, New York.

Luthier Randy Wood was one of three partners who formed GTR, Inc. in Nashville in 1970. Wood left GTR to form the Old Time Picking Parlor in 1972, a combination custom instrument shop and nightclub that featured Bluegrass music. In 1978, he sold the Parlor and moved to Savannah, Georgia to concentrate on instruments building. Since then, he has produced over 1,500 stringed instruments from guitars to mandolins, dobros, violins, and banjos.

YAMAHA

Instruments currently produced in U.S., Taiwan, and Indonesia. Distributed in the U.S. by the Yamaha Corporation of America, located in Buena Park, California.

Instruments previously produced in Japan. Yamaha company headquarters is located in Hamamatsu, Japan.

Yamaha has a tradition of building musical instruments for over 100 years. The first Yamaha solid body electric guitars were introduced to the American market in 1966. While the first series relied on designs based on classic American favorites, the second series developed more original designs. In the mid 1970s, Yamaha was recognized as the first Oriental brand to emerge as a prominent force equal to the big-name US builders.

Production shifted to Taiwan in the early 1980s as Yamaha built its own facility to maintain quality. In 1990, the Yamaha Corporation of America (located in Buena Park, California) opened the Yamaha Guitar Development (YGD) center in North Hollywood, California. The Yamaha Guitar Development center focuses on design, prototyping, and customizing both current and new models. The YGD also custom builds and maintains many of the Yamaha artist's instruments. The center's address on Weddington Street probably was the namesake of the Weddington series instruments of the early 1990s.

The Yamaha company is active in producing a full range of musical instruments, including band instruments, stringed instruments, amplifiers, and P.A. equipment.

Grading	100%	EXCELLENT	AVERAGE

ACOUSTIC

Classical Series

C40 — classical style, spruce top, round soundhole, jetulong back/sides, nato neck, 14/20 fret sonokeling fingerboard, tied sonokeling bridge, 3 per side chrome tuners. Available in Natural finish. Current mfr.

Mfr.'s Sug. Retail	$199	$150	$100	$75

CG40 A — classical style, spruce top, round soundhole, bound body, wooden inlay rosette, jelutong back/sides, nato neck, 12/19 fret sonokeling fingerboard/bridge, 3 per side chrome tuners. Available in Natural finish. Disc. 1996.

		$95	$50

Last Mfr.'s Sug. Retail was $170.

G50 A — similar to the CG40 A, except has judaswood back/sides, bubinga fretboard, red/black rosette, pearl tuner buttons. Mfd. 1970 to 1973.

		$75	$35

This model was also available with a pine top.

CG90 M A — classical style, spruce top, round soundhole, bound body, wooden inlay rosette, nato back/sides/neck, 12/19 fret bubinga fingerboard, rosewood bridge, 3 per side chrome tuners. Available in Natural finish. Current mfr.

Mfr.'s Sug. Retail	$259	$195	$120	$85

CG100 A — classical style, spruce top, round soundhole, bound body, wooden inlay rosette, nato back/sides/neck, 12/19 fret bubinga fingerboard, nato bridge, 3 per side chrome tuners. Available in Natural finish. Current mfr.

Mfr.'s Sug. Retail	$279	$215	$135	$95

CS100 A — similar to CG100 A, except has 7/8 size body. Mfr. 1994 to 1996.

		$135	$90

Last Mfr.'s Sug. Retail was $310.

CG110 A — classical style, spruce top, round soundhole, bound body, wooden inlay rosette, nato back/sides/neck, 12/19 fret bubinga fingerboard, nato bridge, 3 per side chrome tuners. Available in Natural finish. Current mfr.

Mfr.'s Sug. Retail	$319	$225	$110	$90

CG110 S A — similar to CG110 A, except has solid spruce top. Mfr. 1994 to date.

Mfr.'s Sug. Retail	$379	$295	$175	$125

CG120 A — similar to CG110 A, except has different rosette, rosewood fingerboard and bridge.

Mfr.'s Sug. Retail	$359	$275	$175	$125

CG130 A — classical style, spruce top, round soundhole, bound body, wooden inlay rosette, rosewood back/sides, nato neck, 12/19 fret bubinga fingerboard, rosewood bridge, 3 per side gold tuners. Disc. 1996.

		$175	$100

Last Mfr.'s Sug. Retail was $390.

CG130 S A — similar to CG110 S A, except has solid spruce top, nato back/sides, Indian rosewood fingerboard. Available in Natural finish. Mfr. 1998 to date.

Mfr.'s Sug. Retail	$409			

Grading	100%	EXCELLENT	AVERAGE

CG150 S A — classical style, solid spruce top, round soundhole, bound body, wooden inlay rosette, ovankol back/sides, nato neck, 12/19 fret rosewood fingerboard, rosewood bridge, rosewood veneer on peghead, 3 per side gold tuners. Available in Natural finish. Current mfr.

	Mfr.'s Sug. Retail	$469	$350	$225	$150

> This model is optionally available with a solid cedar top (Model CG150 CA).

CG170 S A — classical style, solid spruce top, round soundhole, wooden inlay bound body and rosette, rosewood back/sides, nato neck, 12/19 fret rosewood fingerboard, rosewood bridge, rosewood veneer on peghead, 3 per side gold tuners. Available in Natural finish. Current mfr.

	Mfr.'s Sug. Retail	$609	$450	$295	$195

> This model is optionally available with a solid cedar top (Model CG170 CA).

CG180 S A — similar to 170 S A, except has different binding/rosette, ebony fingerboard.

	Mfr.'s Sug. Retail	$739	$550	$350	$250

CS100 A — 7/8th scale classical style, spruce top, round soundhole, nato back/sides/neck, 12/19 fret bubinga fingerboard, nato bridge, 3 per side tuners. Available in Natural finish. Current mfr.

	Mfr.'s Sug. Retail	$309	$225	$150	$100

DW Series

DW4 S — dreadnought style, solid spruce top, round soundhole, nato back/sides/neck, 14/20 fret rosewood fingerboard, rosewood bridge, 3 per side gold tuners. Available in Natural finish. Current mfr.

	Mfr.'s Sug. Retail	$599	$450	$295	$195

> Add $50 for 12-string configuration (**Model DW4 S-12**).

> This model is also available left-handed with electronics (Model SW4 S LE) and with a cutaway body/electronics (Model DW4 S C).

DW5 S — similar to the DW4 S. Available in Natural and Tobacco Sunburst finishes. Current mfr.

	Mfr.'s Sug. Retail	$649	$475	$295	$195

DW105 — dreadnought style, solid spruce top, round soundhole, nato back/sides/neck, 14/20 fret rosewood fingerboard, rosewood bridge, 3 per side chrome tuners. Available in Natural satin finish. Current mfr.

	Mfr.'s Sug. Retail	$599	$450	$295	$195

FG (Dreadnought) Series

JR1 (FG JUNIOR) — (travel guitar) 3/4 size dreadnought body, spruce top, round soundhole, teardrop-shaped tortoise pickguard, black body binding, 2 stripe rosette, meranti back/sides, nato neck, 14/20 fret rosewood fingerboard with pearl dot inlay, rosewood bridge with white bridgepins, 3 per side chrome tuners. Available in Natural finish. Mfr. 1998 to date.

	Mfr.'s Sug. Retail	$169

FG300 A — dreadnought style, spruce top, round soundhole, bound body, 3 stripe rosette, black pickguard, jetulong back/sides, nato neck, 14/20 fret sonokeling fingerboard with pearl dot inlay, sonokeling bridge with white pins, 3 per side chrome tuners with plastic buttons. Available in Natural finish. Disc. 1996.

		$100	$65
			Last Mfr.'s Sug. Retail was $230.

FG400 A — dreadnought style, spruce top, round soundhole, bound body, 3 stripe rosette, black pickguard, nato back/sides/neck, 14/20 fret bubinga fingerboard with pearl dot inlay, nato bridge with white pins, 3 per side chrome tuners with plastic buttons. Available in Natural finish. Disc. 1994.

		$125	$80
			Last Mfr.'s Sug. Retail was $260.

FG401 — similar to FG400A, except has jumbo style body. Available in Natural finish. Mfd. 1994 to 1997.

		$150	$85
			Last Mfr.'s Sug. Retail was $319.

FG402 — dreadnought style, spruce top, round soundhole, black pickguard, bound body, 5 stripe rosette, nato back/sides/neck, 14/20 fret rosewood fingerboard with pearl dot inlay, nato bridge with white bridgepins, 3 per side diecast chrome tuners. Available in Natural finish. Mfr. 1998 to date.

	Mfr.'s Sug. Retail	$319

FG410 A — dreadnought style, spruce top, round soundhole, bound body, 5 stripe rosette, black pickguard, nato back/sides/neck, 14/20 fret bubinga fingerboard with pearl dot inlay, nato bridge with white pearl dot pins, 3 per side chrome tuners with plastic buttons. Available in Natural finish. Disc. 1994.

		$175	$100
			Last Mfr.'s Sug. Retail was $330.

FG410-12 A — similar to FG410 A, except has 12 strings, 6 per side tuners. Disc. 1994.

		$200	$125
			Last Mfr.'s Sug. Retail was $360.

FG410 E A — similar to FG410 A, except has piezo pickups and volume/2 tone controls. Disc. 1994

		$225	$150
			Last Mfr.'s Sug. Retail was $520.

Grading	100%	EXCELLENT	AVERAGE

FG411 — dreadnought style, spruce top, round soundhole, black pickguard, bound body, 5 stripe rosette, nato back/sides/neck, 14/20 fret rosewood fingerboard with pearl dot inlay, nato bridge with white black dot pins, 3 per side diecast chrome tuners. Available in Natural and Violin Sunburst finishes. Mfd. 1994 to 1997.

$200 $125
Last Mfr.'s Sug. Retail was $399.

Add $50 for left-handed configuration (**Model FG411 L**).

This model had agathis back/sides/neck with Black finish optionally available.

FG411-12 — similar to FG411, except has 12 strings, bubinga fingerboard, 6 per side tuners. Mfd. 1994 to 1997.

$225 $150
Last Mfr.'s Sug. Retail was $449.

FG411 C — similar to FG411, except has single round cutaway body. Available in Natural finish. Mfd. 1994 to 1996.

$225 $150
Last Mfr.'s Sug. Retail was $600.

This model has agathis back/sides optionally available.

FG411 C-12 — similar to FG411, except has 12 strings, single round cutaway, 6 per side tuners, piezo bridge pickup, volume/treble/bass controls.

$300 $200
Last Mfr.'s Sug. Retail was $750.

This model has agathis back/sides with Black finish optionally available.

FG411 S — dreadnought style, solid spruce top, round soundhole, black pickguard, bound body, 5 stripe rosette, nato back/sides/neck, 14/20 fret rosewood fingerboard with pearl dot inlay, nato bridge with white black dot pins, 3 per side diecast tuners. Available in Violin Sunburst finish. Mfd. 1994 to 1998.

$225 $125
Last Mfr.'s Sug. Retail was $449.

Add $50 for left-handed configuration (**Model FG411 S L**).

FG411 S C — similar to FG411S, except has single round cutaway, solid spruce top, piezo bridge pickup, volume/treble/bass controls. Available in Natural and Violin Sunburst finishes. Mfd. 1994 to 1996.

$275 $200
Last Mfr.'s Sug. Retail was $660.

FG411 S-12 — similar to FG411S, except has 12 strings, 6 per side tuners. Disc. 1996.

$250 $175
Last Mfr.'s Sug. Retail was $490.

FG412 — dreadnought style, spruce top, round soundhole, black pickguard, bound body, 5 stripe rosette, nato back/sides/neck, 14/20 fret rosewood fingerboard with pearl dot inlay, nato bridge with white bridgepins, 3 per side chrome diecast tuners. Available in Black, Natural, and Violin Sunburst finishes. Mfr. 1998 to date.

Mfr.'s Sug. Retail $399

Add $20 for left-handed configuration (**Model FG412 L**). Available in Natural finish only.

FG412-12 — similar to FG412, except has 12-string configuration, 6 per side tuners. Available in Natural finish. Mfr. 1998 to date.

Mfr.'s Sug. Retail $449

FG412 S — similar to FG412, except has a solid spruce top. Available in Natural finish. Mfr. 1998 to date.

Mfr.'s Sug. Retail $449

FG420 A — dreadnought style, spruce top, round soundhole, black pickguard, 3 stripe bound body, abalone rosette, nato back/sides/neck, 14/20 fret bound bubinga fingerboard with pearl dot inlay, rosewood bridge with white pearl dot pins, 3 per side chrome tuners. Available in Natural finish. Disc. 1994.

$175 $100
Last Mfr.'s Sug. Retail was $380.

This model was also available in a left-handed version (Model FG420 L A).

FG420-12 A — similar to FG420A, except has 12 strings, 6 per side tuners. Disc. 1994

$200 $125
Last Mfr.'s Sug. Retail was $420.

FG420 E-12 A — similar to FG420A, except has 12 strings, piezo electric pickups and volume/treble/bass controls. Disc. 1998.

$225 $150
Last Mfr.'s Sug. Retail was $530.

FG421 — dreadnought style, spruce top, black pickguard, round soundhole, 5 stripe bound body/rosette, nato back/sides/neck, 14/20 fret bound rosewood fingerboard with pearl dot inlay, rosewood bridge with white black dot pins, 3 per side diecast chrome tuners. Available in Natural finish. Mfd. 1994 to 1996.

$225 $125
Last Mfr.'s Sug. Retail was $430.

FG422 — dreadnought style, spruce top, round soundhole, black pickguard, bound body, 5 stripe rosette, nato back/sides/neck, 14/20 fret bound rosewood fingerboard with pearl dot inlay, nato bridge with white bridgepins, 3 per side diecast chrome tuners. Available in Natural, Oriental BlueBurst, and Tobacco Sunburst finishes. Mfr. 1998 to date.

Mfr.'s Sug. Retail $449

Grading	100%	EXCELLENT	AVERAGE

FG430 A — dreadnought style, spruce top, round soundhole, black pickguard, 3 stripe bound body, abalone rosette, nato back/sides/neck, 14/20 fret bound rosewood fingerboard with pearl dot inlay, rosewood bridge with white pearl dot pins, bound peghead, 3 per side chrome tuners. Available in Natural finish. Disc. 1994.

| | $225 | $125 | |

Last Mfr.'s Sug. Retail was $430.

FG432 — dreadnought style, spruce top, round soundhole, black pickguard, bound body, 5 stripe rosette, nato back/sides/neck, 14/20 fret bound rosewood fingerboard with pearl dot inlay, bound headstock, nato bridge with white bridgepins, 3 per side diecast chrome tuners. Available in Natural finish. Mfr. 1998 to date.

Mfr.'s Sug. Retail $479

FG432 S — similar to FG432, except features a solid spruce top. Available in Natural finish. Mfr. 1998 to date.

Mfr.'s Sug. Retail $519

FG435 A — dreadnought style, spruce top, round soundhole, black pickguard, agathis back/sides, nato neck, 14/20 bound bubinga fingerboard with pearl snowflake inlay, rosewood bridge with white pearl dot pins, bound peghead, 3 per side chrome tuners. Available in Black, Marine Blue, Oriental Blue, Tinted and Tobacco Brown Sunburst finishes. Disc. 1994.

| | $200 | $125 | |

Last Mfr.'s Sug. Retail was $420.

FG441 — dreadnought style, spruce top, round soundhole, black pickguard, 3 stripe bound body, abalone rosette, ovankol back/sides, nato neck, 14/20 fret bound rosewood fingerboard with pearl dot inlay, rosewood bridge with black white dot pins, bound blackface peghead with pearl leaf/logo inlay, 3 per side chrome tuners. Available in Natural and Tobacco Brown Sunburst finishes. Mfd. 1994 to 1997.

| | $225 | $150 | |

Last Mfr.'s Sug. Retail was $460.

Add $70 for left-handed configuration (**Model FG441 L**).

This model had agathis back/sides with Black finish optionally available.

FG441 C — similar to FG441, except has single round cutaway, piezo bridge pickup, volume/treble/bass controls. Available in Natural and Tobacco Brown Sunburst finishes. Mfd. 1994 to 1996.

| | $375 | $250 | |

Last Mfr.'s Sug. Retail was $750.

This model had agathis back/sides with Black and Marine Blue finish optionally available.

FG441 S — similar to FG441, except has solid spruce top. Available in Natural finish. Mfd. 1994 to 1997.

| | $250 | $150 | |

Last Mfr.'s Sug. Retail was $529.

FG441 S-12 — similar to FG44 1, except has 12 strings, solid spruce top, 6 per side tuners. Available in Natural finish. Mfd. 1994 to 1996.

| | $295 | $175 | |

Last Mfr.'s Sug. Retail was $580.

FG450 S A — dreadnought style, solid spruce top, round soundhole, black pickguard, bound body, abalone rosette, ovankol back/sides, nato neck, 14/20 fret bound rosewood fingerboard with pearl snowflake inlay, rosewood bridge with black pearl dot pins, bound peghead with rosewood veneer, 3 per side chrome tuners. Available in Natural finish. Disc. 1994.

| | $225 | $150 | |

Last Mfr.'s Sug. Retail was $500.

This model had left-handed configuration (Model FG450 S L A) optionally available.

FG460 S A — similar to 450S A, except has rosewood back/sides, gold hardware. Disc 1994.

| | $295 | $175 | |

Last Mfr.'s Sug. Retail was $590.

FG460 S-12 A — similar to FG450SA, except has 12 strings, rosewood back/sides, 6 per side tuners, gold hardware. Disc 1994.

| | $300 | $200 | |

Last Mfr.'s Sug. Retail was $620.

FG461 S — dreadnought style, solid spruce top, round soundhole, black pickguard, bound body, abalone purfling/rosette, rosewood back/sides, nato neck, 14/20 fret bound rosewood fingerboard with pearl cross inlay, rosewood bridge with black pearl dot inlay, bound blackface peghead with pearl leaf/logo inlay, 3 per side diecast gold tuners. Available in Natural finish. Mfd. 1994 to 1997.

| | $325 | $200 | |

Last Mfr.'s Sug. Retail was $679.

FG470 S A — dreadnought style, solid spruce top, round soundhole, black pickguard, bound body, abalone rosette, rosewood back/sides, nato neck, 14/20 fret bound rosewood fingerboard with pearl snowflake inlay, rosewood bridge with black pearl dot pins, bound peghead with rosewood veneer, 3 per side gold tuners. Available in Natural finish. Disc 1994.

| | $350 | $225 | |

Last Mfr.'s Sug. Retail was $660.

Grading	100%	EXCELLENT	AVERAGE

FJ (Jumbo) Series

CJ12 — 'country' jumbo style, spruce top, round soundhole, bound body, 3 stripe rosette, black pickguard, rosewood back/sides, mahogany neck, 14/20 fret rosewood fingerboard with pearl dot inlay, rosewood bridge with white pins, 3 per side gold tuners with plastic buttons. Available in Natural finish. Current mfr.

Mfr.'s Sug. Retail	$699	$525	$325	$225

F310 — jumbo style, spruce top, round soundhole, bound body, 3 stripe rosette, black pickguard, jetulong back/sides, nato neck, 14/20 fret sonokeling fingerboard with pearl dot inlay, sonokeling bridge with white pins, 3 per side chrome tuners. Available in Natural finish. Current mfr.

Mfr.'s Sug. Retail	$249	$195	$125	$90

> This model is also available in the Yamaha Gig Maker package, along with a case, digital tuner, strings, string winder, polish and cloth, picks, a strap, and a video (retail list $309).

FJ645 A — jumbo style, spruce top, round soundhole, black pickguard, bound body, abalone rosette, agathis back/sides, nato neck, 14/20 fret bound rosewood fingerboard with pearl pyramid inlay, nato bridge with white pearl dot pins, bound peghead, 3 per side chrome tuners. Available in Black Burst finish. Disc. 1994.

		$275	$175	

Last Mfr.'s Sug. Retail was $550.

FJ651 — jumbo style, spruce top, round soundhole, black pickguard, 5 stripe bound body/rosette, agathis back/sides, mahogany neck, 14/20 fret bound rosewood fingerboard with pearl pentagon inlay, rosewood bridge with white black dot inlay, bound blackface peghead with pearl leaves/logo inlay, 3 per side diecast gold tuners. Available in Violin Sunburst finish. Mfd. 1994 to 1997.

		$275	$175	

Last Mfr.'s Sug. Retail was $560.

FS Series

FS310 A — parlor style, spruce top, round soundhole, black pickguard, bound body, 5 stripe rosette, nato back/sides/neck, 14/20 fret bubinga fingerboard with pearl dot inlay, nato bridge with white pins, 3 per side chrome tuners. Available in Natural finish. Disc. 1995.

		$150	$85	

Last Mfr.'s Sug. Retail was $330.

FS311 — 7/8th scale dreadnought body, spruce top, round soundhole, bound body, 3 stripe rosette, black pickguard, nato back/sides/neck, 14/20 fret rosewood fingerboard with pearl dot inlay, rosewood bridge with white pins, 3 per side chrome tuners. Available in Natural finish. Current mfr.

Mfr.'s Sug. Retail	$399	$225	$125	$90

Handcrafted Series Classicals

GC30 — classic style, solid white spruce top, round soundhole, bound body, wooden inlay rosette, rosewood back/sides, mahogany neck, 12/19 fret ebony fingerboard, jacaranda bridge, rosewood peghead veneer, 3 per side gold tuners. Available in Natural finish. Disc. 1998.

		$600	$425	

Last Mfr.'s Sug. Retail was $1,379.

> This model had solid cedar top (Model GC30C) optionally available.

GC40 — classic style, solid white spruce top, round soundhole, bound body, wooden inlay rosette, jacaranda back/sides, mahogany neck, 12/19 fret ebony fingerboard, jacaranda bridge, jacaranda peghead veneer, 3 per side gold tuners. Available in Natural finish. Disc. 1996.

		$950	$625	

Last Mfr.'s Sug. Retail was $2,000.

> This model had solid cedar top (Model GC40C) optionally available.

GC50 — classic style, solid spruce top, round soundhole, bound body, wooden inlay rosette, jacaranda back/sides, mahogany neck, 12/19 fret ebony fingerboard, jacaranda bridge, jacaranda peghead veneer with stylized Y groove, 3 per side gold tuners. Available in Lacquer finish. Disc. 1998.

		$1,550	$1,000	

Last Mfr.'s Sug. Retail was $3,799.

> This model had solid cedar top (Model GC50C) optionally available.

GC60 — classic style, solid spruce top, round soundhole, bound body, wooden inlay rosette, jacaranda back/sides, mahogany neck, 12/19 fret ebony fingerboard, jacaranda bridge, jacaranda peghead veneer with stylized Y groove, 3 per side gold tuners. Available in Lacquer finish. Disc. 1998.

		$2,850	$1,650	

Last Mfr.'s Sug. Retail was $4,999.

> This model had solid cedar top (Model GC60C) optionally available.

GC70 — classic style, solid spruce top, round soundhole, bound body, wooden inlay rosette, jacaranda back/sides, mahogany neck, 12/19 fret ebony fingerboard, jacaranda bridge, jacaranda peghead veneer with stylized Y groove, 3 per side gold tuners. Available in Shellac finish. Disc. 1998.

		$,3395	$1,925	

Last Mfr.'s Sug. Retail was $5,799.

> This model had solid cedar top (Model GC70C) optionally available.

> This model was available with no peghead groove (Model GC71).

Grading	100%	EXCELLENT	AVERAGE

GD10 — classic style, solid spruce top, round soundhole, wooden inlay rosette, rosewood back/sides, mahogany neck, 12/19 fret ebony fingerboard, rosewood bridge, rosewood peghead veneer, 3 per side gold tuners. Available in Natural finish. Disc. 1998.

	$350	$225
		Last Mfr.'s Sug. Retail was $799.

This model had solid cedar top (Model GD10C) optionally available.

GD20 — classic style, solid spruce top, round soundhole, wooden inlay rosette, rosewood back/sides, mahogany neck, 12/19 fret ebony fingerboard, rosewood bridge, rosewood peghead veneer, 3 per side gold tuners. Available in Natural finish. Disc. 1996.

	$450	$300
		Last Mfr.'s Sug. Retail was $950.

This model had solid cedar top (Model GD20C) optionally available.

L Series

LA8 — dreadnought style, solid spruce top, round soundhole, 3 stripe bound body, abalone rosette, rosewood back/sides, mahogany neck, 14/20 fret bound ebony fingerboard with pearl snowflake/cross inlay, ebony bridge with white black dot pins, bound rosewood veneered peghead with pearl logo inlay, 3 per side gold tuners. Available in Natural finish. Mfd. 1994 to 1998.

	$450	$300
		Last Mfr.'s Sug. Retail was $949.

LA18 — mid-size dreadnought style, solid spruce top, round soundhole, bound body, abalone rosette, mahogany back/sides, mahogany neck, 14/20 fret bound ebony fingerboard with pearl dot inlay, ebony bridge with white pearl dot pins, bound peghead with rosewood veneer and pearl/abalone double L inlay, 3 per side gold tuners. Available in Natural finish. Disc. 1996.

	$525	$350
		Last Mfr.'s Sug. Retail was $1,130.

LA28 — similar to LA18, except has rosewood back/sides and pearl diamond inlay. Disc. 1996.

	$700	$450
		Last Mfr.'s Sug. Retail was $1,600.

LD10 — dreadnought style, solid white spruce top, round soundhole, black pickguard, abalone bound body and rosette, rosewood back/sides, mahogany neck, 14/20 fret bound rosewood fingerboard with pearl dot inlay, rosewood bridge with black pearl dot pins, bound peghead with rosewood veneer, 3 per side gold tuners. Available in Natural finish. Disc. 1996.

	$350	$225
		Last Mfr.'s Sug. Retail was $760.

LD10E — similar to LD10, except has piezo electric pickups and pop up volume/2 tone and mix controls. Disc. 1996.

	$425	$275
		Last Mfr.'s Sug. Retail was $950.

LL15 — dreadnought style, solid spruce top, round soundhole, black pickguard, 5 stripe bound body and rosette, mahogany back/sides/neck, 14/20 fret ebony fingerboard with pearl dot inlay, ebony bridge with black pearl dot pins, rosewood veneer on peghead, 3 per side gold tuners. Available in Natural finish. Disc. 1996.

	$525	$350
		Last Mfr.'s Sug. Retail was $1,130.

LL35 — dreadnought style, solid white spruce top, round soundhole, black pickguard, 3 stripe bound body, abalone rosette, jacaranda back/sides, mahogany neck, 14/20 fret bound ebony fingerboard with pearl snowflake inlay, ebony bridge with black pearl dot pins, bound peghead with rosewood veneer and pearl/abalone double L inlay, 3 per side gold tuners. Available in Natural finish. Disc. 1996.

	$875	$575
		Last Mfr.'s Sug. Retail was $1,900.

LW15 — dreadnought style, solid spruce top, round soundhole, black pickguard, 5 stripe bound body/rosette, mahogany back/sides/neck, 14/20 fret bound rosewood fingerboard with pearl flower inlay, rosewood bridge with black white dot pins, bound rosewood veneered peghead with pearl logo inlay, 3 per side chrome tuners. Available in Natural finish. Mfr. 1994 to 1996.

	$350	$225
		Last Mfr.'s Sug. Retail was $700.

LW25 — dreadnought style, solid spruce top, round soundhole, black pickguard, 5 stripe bound body/rosette, rosewood back/sides, mahogany neck, 14/20 fret bound ebony fingerboard with pearl flower inlay, ebony bridge with black white dot pins, bound rosewood veneered peghead with pearl logo inlay, 3 per side gold tuners. Available in Natural finish. Mfr. 1994 to 1996.

	$400	$250
		Last Mfr.'s Sug. Retail was $800.

ACOUSTIC ELECTRIC

APX Series

APX T1 (TRAVEL SERIES) — single rounded cutaway body, spruce top, oval soundhole, bound body, 3 stripe rosette, agathis/alder back/sides, maple neck, 23 5/8" scale, 22 fret rosewood fingerboard with pearl dot inlay, string-through rosewood bridge, blackface peghead with screened flowers/logo, 3 per side chrome tuners, piezo bridge pickup, volume/tone controls. Available in BlueBurst and Violin Sunburst finishes. Mfr. 1998 to date.

Mfr.'s Sug. Retail	$449

This model is available in a nylon string configuration (Model APX T1 N).

Grading	100%	EXCELLENT	AVERAGE

APX 4 A — single round cutaway dreadnought style, spruce top, oval soundhole, 5 stripe bound body and rosette, nato back/sides, nato neck, 25 1/2" scale, 22 fret rosewood fingerboard with pearl dot inlay, rosewood bridge with white bridgepins, blackface peghead with screened flowers/logo, 3 per side chrome tuners, piezo bridge pickup, volume/treble/bass controls. Available in Black, Natural and Violin Sunburst finishes. Current mfr.

Mfr.'s Sug. Retail	$649	$495	$295	$195

APX 4 A Special — similar to APX 4 A, except has flamed sycamore top, volume/mute/3 band EQ controls. Available in Marine BlueBurst and Tobacco Brown Sunburst finishes. Mfr. 1998 to date.

Mfr.'s Sug. Retail	$749

APX 4-12 A — similar to APX4, except has 12 strings, 6 per side tuners. Mfr. 1994 to date.

Mfr.'s Sug. Retail	$679	$500	$300	$225

APX 6 — single round cutaway dreadnought style, spruce top, oval soundhole, 5 stripe bound body, wooden inlay rosette cap, nato back/sides, nato neck, 24 fret extended rosewood fingerboard with pearl dot inlay, rosewood bridge with white pearl dot pins, 3 per sides chrome tuners, bridge/body piezo pickups, pop up volume/treble/bass/mix controls. Available in Black, Cherry Sunburst and Cream White finishes. Disc. 1994.

		$375	$225

Last Mfr.'s Sug. Retail was $730.

APX 6 A — similar to APX 6, except has volume/tone controls, 3 band EQ. Mfr. 1994 to date.

Mfr.'s Sug. Retail	$819	$625	$375	$275

Add $180 for left-handed configuration (**Model APX 6 L A**).

APX 6 N A — classical style, spruce top, oval soundhole, 5 stripe bound body, wooden inlay rosette, ovankol back/sides, nato neck, 14/22 fret rosewood fingerboard, rosewood bridge, 3 per side gold tuners, bridge/body piezo pickups, volume/treble/bass/mix controls. Available in Natural finish. Current mfr.

Mfr.'s Sug. Retail	$799	$595	$375	$250

APX 7 — single round cutaway dreadnought style, spruce top, oval soundhole, 5 stripe bound body, wooden inlay rosette cap, agathis back/sides, mahogany neck, 24 fret extended bound rosewood fingerboard with pearl dot inlay, rosewood bridge with white pearl dot pins, bound peghead, 3 per side gold tuners, 2 bridge/body piezo pickups, volume/treble/bass/mix controls. Available in Black, Blue Burst and Light Brown Sunburst finishes. Disc. 1996.

		$425	$275

Last Mfr.'s Sug. Retail was $850

This model was optionally available with ovankol back/sides (Model APX 7 CT).

APX 7 CN — single round cutaway classic style, spruce top, oval soundhole, 5 stripe bound body, rosette decal, ovankol back/sides, nato neck, 24 fret extended rosewood fingerboard, rosewood tied bridge, rosewood veneered peghead, 3 per side gold tuners with pearloid buttons, piezo bridge pickup, volume/tone controls, 3 band EQ. Available in Natural finish. Mfd. 1994 to 1996.

		$450	$300

Last Mfr.'s Sug. Retail was $900

APX 8 A — similar to APX 7, except has bridge piezo pickup, mode switch. Available in Gray Burst and Light Brown Sunburst finishes.

Mfr.'s Sug. Retail	$1,099	$825	$525	$350

Add $100 for 12-string configuration (**Model APX 8-12 A**).

APX 8 C — single round cutaway folk style, spruce top, oval soundhole, 5 stripe bound body, wooden abalone inlay rosette cap, agathis back/sides, mahogany neck, 24 fret bound extended fingerboard with pearl dot inlay, rosewood bridge with white black dot pins, bound blackface peghead with screened leaves/logo, 3 per side gold tuners, piezo bridge pickups, volume/tone/mix controls, 3 band EQ. Available in Blackburst, Brownburst, and Translucent Blueburst finishes. Mfd. 1994 to 1996.

		$625	$375

Last Mfr.'s Sug. Retail was $1,100.

APX 8 C-12 — similar to APX 8 C, except has 12 strings, 6 per side tuners. Mfr. 1994 to 1996.

		$650	$375

Last Mfr.'s Sug. Retail was $1,190.

APX 8 D — similar to APX8C, except has solid spruce top. Mfd. 1994 to 1996.

		$650	$375

Last Mfr.'s Sug. Retail was $1,200

APX 9-12 — single round cutaway dreadnought style, spruce top, oval soundhole, 5 stripe bound body, wooden inlay rosette cap, agathis back/sides, mahogany neck, 24 fret extended bound rosewood fingerboard with pearl dot inlay, rosewood bridge with white pearl dot pins, bound peghead, 6 per side chrome tuners, 2 bridge/body piezo pickups, volume/treble/bass/mix controls, mode switch. Available in Black, Blue Burst, and Light Brown Sunburst finishes. Disc. 1994.

		$575	$350

Last Mfr.'s Sug. Retail was $1,150.

APX 10 A — single round cutaway dreadnought style, spruce top, oval soundhole, 5 stripe bound body, abalone rosette cap, ovangkol back/sides, mahogany neck, 24 fret extended bound ebony fingerboard with pearl diamond inlay, ebony bridge with white pearl dot pins, bound peghead, 3 per side gold tuners, bridge/body piezo pickups, volume/treble/bass/mix controls, mode switch. Available in Antique Stain Sunburst, Black Burst and Burgundy Red finishes. Mfr. 1993 to date.

Mfr.'s Sug. Retail	$1,499	$1,125	$695	$475

Add $60 for left-handed configuration (**Model APX 10 L A**).

In 1994, Antique Brown Sunburst finish was introduced. Burgundy Red finish was discontinued.

Grading	100%	EXCELLENT	AVERAGE

APX 10 N A — single round cutaway classic style, spruce top, oval soundhole, 5 stripe bound body, wooden inlay rosette, rosewood back/sides, mahogany neck, 24 fret ebony fingerboard, rosewood bridge, rosewood veneer on peghead, 3 per side gold tuners, bridge/body piezo pickups, volume/treble/bass/mix controls, mode switch. Available in Natural finish. Current mfr.

Mfr.'s Sug. Retail	$1,299	$975	$600	$425

APX 10 CT — similar to APX 10 C, except has rosewood back/sides. Available in Natural finish. Mfd. 1994 to 1996.

			$725	$495

Last Mfr.'s Sug. Retail was $1,500.

APX 20 C — single round cutaway dreadnought style, spruce top, oval soundhole, abalone bound body, abalone rosette cap, sycamore back/sides, mahogany neck, 24 fret extended bound ebony fingerboard with abalone/pearl pentagon inlay, ebony bridge with white pearl dot pins, bound peghead, 3 per side gold tuners, bridge/body piezo pickups, volume/treble/bass/mix controls, mode switch. Available in Cream White and Light Brown Sunburst finishes. Disc. 1996.

			$800	$530

Last Mfr.'s Sug. Retail was $1,600.

In 1994, volume/tone/mix controls, 3 band EQ replaced original item.

Classical Acoustic Electric Series

CG110 CE — single rounded cutaway classical body, spruce top, round soundhole, bound body, wooden inlay rosette, nato back/sides/neck, 12/19 fret rosewood fingerboard, rosewood bridge, 3 per side chrome tuners, piezo bridge pickup, volume/3 band EQ controls. Available in Natural finish. Current mfr.

Mfr.'s Sug. Retail	$629	$475	$295	$195

CG150 CCE — similar to the CG110 CE, except features a cedar top, ovankol back/sides, gold hardware. Available in Natural finish. Current mfr.

Mfr.'s Sug. Retail	$729	$550	$325	$250

Compass Series

Compass Series (CPX) models have bodies which are larger than the APX Series models.

CPX 7 — single rounded cutaway jumbo style, spruce top, round soundhole, bound body, inlaid rosette, mahogany back/sides, mahogany neck, 25 1/2" scale, 14/20 fret bound Indian rosewood fingerboard with offset pearl triangle inlay, Indian rosewood bridge with black pearl dot pins, 3 per side chrome tuners, piezo bridge pickups, volume/mid-shape/3 band EQ controls. Available in Natural finish. Mfr. 1998 to date.

Mfr.'s Sug. Retail	$1,099

CPX 10 — similar to the CPX 7, except features solid spruce top, rosewood back/sides, ebony fingerboard/bridge. Available in Natural finish. Mfr. 1998 to date.

Mfr.'s Sug. Retail	$1,399

FGX Series

FGX 412 — dreadnought style, spruce top, round soundhole, black pickguard, bound body, 5 stripe rosette, nato back/sides/neck, 14/20 fret rosewood fingerboard with pearl dot inlay, nato bridge with white bridgepins, 3 per side chrome diecast tuners, piezo bridge pickup, volume/mute.3 band EQ controls. Available in Natural finish. Mfr. 1998 to date.

Mfr.'s Sug. Retail	$519

FGX 412 C — similar to FGX 412, except has a single rounded cutaway body. Available in Natural, Marine BlueBurst, and Violin Sunburst finishes. Mfr. 1998 to date.

Mfr.'s Sug. Retail	$649

FGX 412 C-12 — similar to FGX 412, except has a single rounded cutaway body, 12-string configuration, 6 per side tuners. Available in Black, Natural, and Violin Sunburst finishes. Mfr. 1998 to date.

Mfr.'s Sug. Retail	$649

FGX 412 S C — similar to FGX 412, except has a solid spruce top. Available in Natural and Tobacco Sunburst finishes. Mfr. 1998 to date.

Mfr.'s Sug. Retail	$449

YAMAKI

See DAION.

Instruments produced in Japan during the late 1970s through the 1980s.

YAMATO

Instruments produced in Japan during the late 1970s to the early 1980s.

Yamato guitars are medium quality instruments that feature both original and designs based on classic American favorites.

(Source: Tony Bacon and Paul Day, The Guru's Guitar Guide)

YURIY

Instruments built in Wheeling, Illinois since 1990.

Luthier Yuriy Shishkov was born in 1964 in St. Petersburg. As with many other guitarmakers, Shishkov began his career from discovering a big personal attraction to music. After spending 10 years playing guitars that he found unsatisfactory, Yuriy attempted to build his own instrument in 1986. The results amazed everyone who played the instrument, including Yuriy himself! From this initial bit of success, Yuriy gained a reputation as a luthier as well as several orders for guitars.

In 1990, Yuriy moved to Chicago, Illinois. A year later, he secured a job at Washburn International, a major guitar company based in Chicago. His experience with personal guitar building lead him to a position of handling the difficult repairs, restorations, intricate inlay work, company prototypes, and the custom-built instruments for the artist endorsees.

Luthier Yuriy Shishkov is currently offering custom designed and construction of instruments from solid body guitars to his current passion of archtop acoustics and hollow body electrics. For additional information regarding pricing and availability, contact luthier Yuriy Shishkov through the Index of Current Manufacturers located in the back of this edition.

ACOUSTIC

Yuriy currently features a number of Jazz-style archtop guitars. Models include the 16" **Minuet** (list $3,700) or **Soprano** ($3,900), 17" **Capitol** ($4,300), **Sunset** ($4,600), and **Concerto** ($4,900), and 18" **Imperial** ($5,400) and **Triumph** ($5,900). Archtop models include features like hand-carved spruce tops, figured maple back and sides, rock maple necks, and rosewood fingerboard. Models are finished in nitrocellulose lacquer finishes.

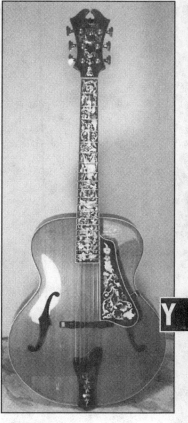

Yuriy Archtop
courtesy Yuriy Shishkov

Headstock Detail
courtesy Yuriy Shishkov

Y

Z

ZEIDLER

Instruments currently built in Philadelphia, Pennsylvania.

Luthier John R. Zeidler has been building quality custom instruments for over eighteen years. Zeidler's background encompasses woodworking, metalsmithing, tool making and music. Zeidler is currently producing high quality archtop and flattop guitars, as well as mandolins.

ACOUSTIC ARCHTOP

ARCH TOP— select Sitka spruce top, curly maple back and sides, 5-piece laminated mahogany/maple/rosewood neck, 2 f-holes, 22 fret bound ebony fingerboard, ebony head veneer/bridge, ebony/gold-plated brass hinged tailpiece, mother of pearl truss rod cover, black/white body binding, 3 per side gold-plated Schaller tuners. Available in high gloss nitrcellulose finish. Current mfr.

    Mfr.'s Sug. Retail   **$7,500**

JAZZ (16" or 17" BODY)— hand graduated Sitka spruce top, curly maple back and sides, 2-piece laminated curly maple neck, 2 f-holes, 22 fret bound ebony fingerboard with pearl diamond inlay, ebony head veneer/bridge, ebony/gold-plated brass hinged tailpiece, mother of pearl truss rod cover, black/white body binding, 3 per side gold-plated Schaller tuners. Available in high gloss nitrcellulose finish. Current mfr.

    Mfr.'s Sug. Retail   **$9,000**
        Add $1,000 for 18" body width **(Model Jazz 18")**.

JAZZ DELUXE (16" or 17" BODY)— hand split select Adirondack spruce top, highly figured curly maple back and sides, 2-piece laminated curly maple neck, 2 f-holes, 22 fret bound ebony fingerboard, ebony head veneer/bridge, ebony/gold-plated brass hinged tailpiece, mother of pearl truss rod cover, celluloid body binding, 3 per side gold-plated Schaller tuners. Available in high gloss spirit varnish finish. Current mfr.

    Mfr.'s Sug. Retail   **$11,000**
        Add $1,000 for 18" body width **(Model Jazz Deluxe 18")**.

ACOUSTIC

AUDITORIUM— tight waist/rounded lower bout design, hand split select Sitka spruce top, East Indian rosewood back and sides, 5-piece laminated mahogany/maple/rosewood neck, round soundhole, 20 fret ebony fingerboard, ebony head veneer/bridge, mother of pearl truss rod cover, tortoiseshell pickguard, black/white body binding, 3 per side gold-plated Schaller tuners. Available in high gloss nitrocellulose finish. Current mfr.

    Mfr.'s Sug. Retail   **$4,500**
        Add $500 for cutaway body design.

EXCALIBUR— sloped shoulder design, hand split select Sitka spruce top, East Indian rosewood back and sides, 5-piece laminated mahogany/maple/rosewood neck, round soundhole, 20 fret ebony fingerboard, ebony head veneer/bridge, mother of pearl truss rod cover, tortoiseshell pickguard, black/white body binding, 3 per side gold-plated Schaller tuners. Available in high gloss nitrocellulose finish. Current mfr.

    Mfr.'s Sug. Retail   **$4,500**
        Add $500 for cutaway body design.

*Zeidler Jazz Deluxe Special
courtesy Scott Chinery*

ZEMAITIS

Instruments handbuilt in England since 1957.

Tony Zemaitis was born Antanus (Anthony) Casimere (Charles) Zemaitis in 1935. While his grandparents were Lithuanian, both Tony and his parents were born in the UK. At age 16 he left college to be an apprentice at cabinet making. As part of a hobby, he refashioned an old damaged guitar found in the family attic. In 1955, the first turning point to luthiery: Zemaitis built his first *half decent* guitar, a classical, nylon string with peghead. In the mid to late 1950s, Zemaitis served for two years in Britian's National Service.

Upon his return to civilian life, Zemaitis continued his guitar building hobby, only now a number of the guitars began turning up onto the folk scene. By 1960 he was selling guitars for the price of the materials, and a number of the originals that Zemaitis calls **Oldies** still exist. Early users include Spencer Davis, Long John Baldry, and Jimi Hendrix.

In 1965, Zemaitis' *hobby* had acquired enough interest that he was able to become self employed. By the late 1960s, the orders were coming in from a number of top players such as Ron Wood, Eric Clapton, and George Harrison. The house and shop all moved lock, stock , and barrel to Kent in 1972. A **Student** model was introduced in 1980, but proved to be too popular and time consuming to produce the number of orders, so it was discontinued.

In 1995, Zemaitis celebrated the 40th Anniversary of the first classical guitar he built in 1955. Guitar production is limited to 10 guitars a year. Now over sixty, Zemaitis reports that he is *still fit, healthy and going strong*, and what started as a pleasant hobby has still remained pleasurable through the years.

    (Source: Tony Zemaitis, March 1996)

    (Information courtesy Keith Smart and Keith Rogers, The Z Gazette: magazine of the Zemaitis Guitar Owners Club based in England)

AUTHENTICITY

In the late 1980s, Zemaitis was surprised to see that his guitars were even more valuable in the secondhand market than originally priced. As his relative output is limited, an alarming trend of forgeries has emerged in England, Japan, and the U.S. Serial number identification and dating on guitars will continue to be unreported in this edition, due to the number of forgeries that keep turning up (and we're not going to add tips to the "help-yourself merchants" as Tony likes to call them). To clarify matters simply: **Tony Zemaitis has granted NO ONE permission to build reproductions and NO licensing deals have been made to any company.**

Points to Consider When Buying a Zemaitis

Prior to spending a large amount of money on what may very well turn out to be a copy of a Zemaitis, it is always best to ask for advice. Indeed, Mr. Zemaitis may have a refurbished model in stock at a more reasonable price. If you do telephone, please be brief and only call during office hours.

There are German, Japanese, and English copies. At first glance they may look a little like a Zemaitis, but they will not sound like one due to the use of second-rate materials. Because of the mass produced nature of these fakes, the intonation and general finish will be inferior to the genuine article. Even more alarming, what starts out as a cheap copy changes hands once or twice and eventually ends up being advertised as *the real thing* without proper research.

The more difficult *fakes* (?) to spot are the genuine Zemaitis guitars that started life as a cheaper version (Student or Test model), and has been unofficially upgraded. In other words, a plain front guitar suddenly becomes a Pearl Front guitar. While parts and pieces will be genuine, the newer finish and general appearance are nothing like the real thing.

Always ask for a receipt, even if you are not buying from a shop. Always check the spelling of *Zemaitis*. Look at the engraving, and make sure that it is engraved by hand (not photo etching - it is too clean and has not been worked on by hand).

(reprinted courtesy Keith Smart, The Z Gazette)

The Blue Book of Guitars strongly recommends two or three written estimates of any ZEMAITIS instrument from accredited sources. If possible, ask to see the original paperwork. Here are two more serious tips: Usually the person who commissioned the guitar has their initials on the truss rod cover. Also, review the printed label and logo (there's only one correct spelling for Mr. Zemaitis' name - and contrary to word of mouth, he does not intentionally misspell it on his guitars.

MODEL DESCRIPTIONS

Here is a brief overview of model histories and designations. During the late 1950s, a few basic acoustic models were built to learn about sizes, shapes, wood response, and soundholes. From 1960 to 1964, guitar building was still a hobby, so there was no particular standard; also, the paper labels inside are hand labeled.

In 1965, Zemaitis *turned pro* and introduced the **Standard, Superior,** and **Custom** models of acoustic guitars. These terms are relative, not definitive as there is some overlapping from piece to piece. While some soundholes are round, there are a number of acoustic guitars built with the *heart shaped* sound hole.

The electric solidbody guitar was discussed and inspired by Eric Clapton on a visit to Zemaitis' workshop in 1969. The handful of early models had aluminum plates on the faces, and later were followed by solid silver, then finally returned to aluminum as the British tax people proved difficult. Zemaitis' good friend and engraver Danny O'Brien handles the ornate engraving on the M/F (**Metal Front**) models. The first *test* guitar was sold off cheaply at the time, but the second was purchased by Tony McPhee (Groundhogs); the third guitar built was purchased by Ron Wood. The M/F guitar model has since moved worldwide. There is a variation model called the **Disc Front** which has a round faced metal plate around the pickups as opposed to the entire front. An ultimate version called the Pearl Front is just that: a pearl topped solid body guitar - and the written description hardly does justice to the actual piece.

The **Student** model was introduced in 1980. Designed as a basic guitar that could be later upgraded, the model proved so popular that it was quickly discontinued for fear that the production would overtake other work altogether! In the late 1980s, clients began asking for either more decorations or copies of older models. At this point Zemaitis upgraded his system to the **Custom, Deluxe,** and **Custom Deluxe** which are still in use to date. Again, these three models are relative, not definitive as some crossing back and forth does go on.

ZIMNICKI

Instruments currently built in Allen Park, Michigan.

Luthier Gary Zimnicki has been developing his guitar building skills since 1978, and is currently focusing on building quality archtop and flattop guitars. For further information, please call Gary Zimnicki via the Index of Current Manufacturers located in the back of this book.

ACOUSTIC

Zimnicki uses aged tonewoods for his carved graduated tops, and wood bindings. Due to the nature of these commissioned pieces, the customer determines the body size, neck scale, types of wood/fingerboard inlays/pickups, and finish.

Add $150 for European maple back on the archtop models.

Add $200 for sunburst finish.

ACOUSTIC ARCHTOP — single cutaway bound body, carved arched top, 2 f-holes, ebony tailpiece/full contact bridge/fingerboard, 3 per side Schaller gold tuners. Available in Natural and Translucent high gloss Nitrocellulose lacquer finishes. Current mfr.

| **Mfr.'s Sug. Retail** | **$4,750** |

Price includes hardshell case.

CLASSICAL — classical style, round soundhole with rosette, 14/20 fret unbound fingerboard, 3 per side headstock, classical style tied bridge. Current mfr.

| **Mfr.'s Sug. Retail** | **$2,500** |

Price includes hardshell case.

Zimnicki Archtop
courtesy Gary Zimnicki

Z

FLATTOP STEEL STRING — exaggerated waist dreadnought style, single rounded cutaway, round soundhole with rosette, 12/20 or 14/20 fret unbound fingerboard, 3 per side headstock, conventional style bridge. Current mfr.

Mfr.'s Sug. Retail   **$2,500**

Price includes hardshell case.

This model is available in a non-cutaway configuration.

ACOUSTIC ELECTRIC ARCHTOP

ELECTRIC ARCHTOP — similar in construction to the Acoustic Archtop, except has gold-plated *harp* tailpiece, footed ebony bridge, pickup and volume/tone controls mounted on soundboard. Current mfr.

Mfr.'s Sug. Retail   **$4,100**

Price includes hardshell case.

Z

Guitar Serialization

AMERICAN ARCHTOP SERIALIZATION

According to luthier Dale Unger, the digits after the dash in the serial number are the year the guitar was completed.

BENEDETTO SERIAL NUMBERS

As of August 1997, Robert Benedetto had completed a total of over 670 instruments. Over 400 are archtop guitars, with the remainder comprising of 48 violins, 5 violas, 1 classical guitar, 2 mandolins, 8 semi-hollow electrics, 209 electric solid body guitars and basses, and one cello.

Archtop guitars are numbered in their own series, comprising of a four or five digit number. The last two digits in the number indicate the year the guitar was made; the preceding digits indicate the instrument's number.

Example: Guitar # 29193 would be the 291st archtop, made in 1993.

Violins and violas have a separate numbering system apart from the archtops, as do the electric solidbody guitars and basses. Mandolins were not numbered. The 8 semi-hollow electrics and the one classical guitar made are within the archtop numbering system.

From Robert Benedetto's Serial Number Logbook

(Note: year listed on the right indicates date shipped, not made)

0168 (#1)	1968	12085 through 12885	1985
0270 (#2)	1970	12986 through 13586	1986
0372	1972	13686 through 13987-A	1987
0473	1973	14087 through 16488	1988
0575 through 0676	1976	16588 through 19189	1989
0777 through 1177	1977	19289 through 22490-A	1990
1277 through 2778	1978	22591 through 25091	1991
2879 through 4279	1979	25192 through 28092	1992
4380 through 5580	1980	28193 through 30293	1993
5681 through 7381	1981	30393 through 32994	1994
7482 through 9582	1982	33095 through 36595	1995
9682 through 10983	1983	36696 through 39496	1996
11084 through 11984	1984	39597 through 40497	1997 (to date)

(Benedetto did not adopt his current serial number system until his third guitar, serial #0372)

Seven guitar serial numbers are follwed by the letter "A". Example: archtop guitar #23891 and #23891-A are two separate instruments even though both are numbered the "238th".

Further information and a full serial number list can be found in Robert Benedetto's own book, **Making an Archtop Guitar** *(Center stream Publishing, 1994).*

BREEDLOVE SERIALIZATION

Breedlove serial numbers can be found on the guitar's label inside the guitar (look through the soundhole). The first two digits of the serial number are the year (last two digits of the year; i.e., "19XX") the guitar was built.

BUSCARINO SERIAL NUMBERS

Luthier John Buscarino had the priviledge of apprenticing with not one but two Master Builders, Augustino LoPrinzi and Robert Benedetto. Buscarino formed his first company, **Nova U.S.A.** in 1981; he changed the company to **Buscarino Guitars** in 1990.

The last two digits of the Buscarino serial number are the year the guitar was completed.

COLLINGS SERIALIZATION

Collings guitar serial numbers are expressed as the date, which is written on the label on the inside of the guitar. However, here is a more expanded view on Collings serialization:

Flattop Serialization

1975-1987: Guitars do not posses a serial number. Most are marked with a handwritten date on the underside of the top. Some guitars from 1987 may have a serial number.

1988 to date: Guitars began a consecutive numbering series that began with number 175. The serial number is stamped on the neck block.

Archtop Serialization

Before 1991: Archtops before 1991 had their own separate serialization.

1991 to date: Archtops are now numbered with a two part serial number. The first number indicates the archtop as part of the general company serialization; and the second number indicates the ranking in the archtop series list.

(Serialization information courtesy Collings Guitars, Inc.)

D'ANGELICO SERIAL NUMBERS

Master Luthier John D'Angelico (1905-1964) opened his own shop at age 27, and every guitar was hand built - many to the specifications or nuances of the customer commissioning the instrument. In the course of his brief lifetime, he created 1,164 numbered guitars, as well as unnumbered mandolins, novelty instruments, and the necks for the plywood semi-hollowbody electrics. The nature of this list is to help identify the numbered guitars as to the date produced.

D'Angelico kept a pair of ledger books and some loose sheets of paper as a log of the guitars created, models, date of completion (or possibly the date of shipping), the person or business to whom the guitar was sold, and the date. The following list is a rough approximation of the ledgers and records.

First *Loose Sheets*		**Ledger Book One**	
1002 through 1073	1932 to 1934	1169 through 1456	1936 to 1939
		1457 through 1831	1940 to 1949

1832 through 1849	1950	2123	1961

Ledger Book Two

Second *Loose Sheets*

1850 through 2098	1950 to 1959	2124 through 2164	Dates not recorded
2099 through 2122	1960		

Again, I must stress that the above system is a guide only. In 1991, author Paul William Schmidt published a book entitled *Acquired of the Angels: The lives and works of Master Guitar Makers John D'Angelico and James L. D'Aquisto* (The Scarecrow Press, Inc.; Metuchen, N.J. & London). In appendix 1 the entire ledger information is reprinted save information on persons or businesses to whom the guitar was sold. This book is fully recommended to anyone seeking information on luthiers John D'Angelico and James L. D'Aquisto.

D'AQUISTO SERIAL NUMBERS

Master Luthier James L. D'Aquisto (1935-1995) met John D'Angelico around 1953. At the early age of 17 D'Aquisto became D'Angelico's apprentice, and by 1959 was handling the decorative procedures and other lutherie jobs.

D'Aquisto, like his mentor before him, kept ledger books as a log of the guitars created, models, date of completion (or possibly the date of shipping), the person or business to whom the guitar was sold, and the date. The following list is a rough approximation of the ledger. As the original pages contain some idiosyncrasies, the following list will by nature be inaccurate as well - and should only be used as a guide for dating individual instruments. The nature of this list is only to help identify the numbered guitars as to the date produced.

The D'Aquisto Ledger

1001 through 1035	1965 to 1969	1085 through 1133	1975 to 1979
1036 through 1084	1970 to 1974	1134 through 1175	1980 to 1984
		1176 through 1228	1985 to 1990

Beginning in 1988, serial number was 1230.

Other guitars that D'Aquisto built had their own serial numbers. For example, solid body and semi-hollow body guitars from 1976 to 1987 had an *E* before the three digit number. D'Aquisto also built some classical models, some flat-top acoustics, and some hollow body electric models (hollowbody guitars run from #1 to #30, 1976 to 1980; and #101 to #118, 1982 to 1988).

In 1991, author Paul William Schmidt published a book entitled *Acquired of the Angels: The Lives and Works of Master Guitar Makers John D'Angelico and James L. D'Aquisto* (The Scarecrow Press, Inc.; Metuchen, N.J. & London). In appendix 2 the entire ledger information is reprinted up to the year 1988 except for information on persons or businesses to whom the guitar was sold. This book is fully recommended to anyone seeking information on luthiers John D'Angelico and James L. D'Aquisto.

DOBRO SERIAL NUMBERS

The convoluted history of the Dopyera brothers (Dobro, National Dobro, Valco, Original Music Instrument Company) has been discussed in a number of wonderful guitar texts. Serialization of Dobro instruments is far less tangled, but there are different forms of the numbers to contend with. Dobro serial numbers should always be used in conjunction with other identifying features for dating purposes.

Dobro was founded in Los Angeles in 1929, and production continued until the outbreak of World War II in 1942 (resonator guitar production ends). The numbers listed by year are the serialization ranges, not production amounts.

# 900 - 2999	1928-1930
# 3000 - 3999	1930-1931

Between 1931 to 1932, the *cyclops* models carried a serial number code of B XXX.

# 5000 - 5599	1932-1933
# 5700 - 7699	1934-1936
# 8000 - 9999	1937-1942

In the mid 1950s, Rudy and Ed Dopyera return to building wood bodied Dobros from pre-war parts under the trademark of **DB Original**. The serialization of these models is still unknown.

In 1961, Louis Dopyera of Valco transfers the **Dobro** trademark to Rudy and Ed. These models are distinguished by a serialization code of **D** plus three digits.

After Semie Moseley gained the rights to the Dobro trademark, the Original Music Instrument Company was founded in 1967 by Ed, Rudy, and Gabriela Lazar. OMI regained the Dobro name in 1970, and instituted a new coding on the instruments. The code had a prefix of **D** (Wood body) or **B** (Metal body), followed by three or four digits (production ranking) and a single digit to indicate the year, thus:

D XXXX Y	OMI Dobro coding 1970 - 1979

The code reversed itself in 1980. The single digit prefix indicated the year/decade, then three or four digits (production ranking), another single digit to indicate the year, then the body material designation (D or B), like:

8 XXXX YD	OMI Dobro coding 1980 - 1987

In 1988, the code became a little more specialized, and shared more information. The prefix consisted of a letter and number that indicated the model style, three or four digits for production ranking, another letter for neck style, 2 digits for year of production, and the body material designation (D or B):

AX XXXX NYYD	OMI Dobro coding 1988 - 1992

In 1993, Gibson bought OMI/Dobro. Production was maintained at the California location from 1993 to 1996, and the serialization stayed similar to the 1988 - 1992 style coding. In 1997, Gibson moved Dobro to Nashville, and is in the process of constructing facilities for the new production. It is unknown what serialization code will be used next year.

EPIPHONE SERIAL NUMBERS

In 1917, Epaminondas *Epi* Stathopoulos began using the **House of Stathopoulo** brand on the family's luthiery business. By 1923 the business was incorporated, and a year later the new trademark was unveiled on a line of banjos. Stathopoulos combined his nickname *Epi* with the Greek word for sound, *phone*. When the company was recapitalized in 1928, it became the **Epiphone Banjo Company**.

Guitars were introduced in 1930, and were built in New York City, New York through 1953. Company manufacturing was moved to Philadelphia due to union harrassment in New York, and Epiphone continued on through 1957. Serial numbers on original Epiphones can be found on the label.

Epiphone **Electar** electric instruments were numbered consecutively, using a die stamped number on the back of the headstock. The numbering began at 000 in 1935, terminating at about 9000 in 1944. Between about 1944 and 1950, the two number prefixes 15, 25, 26, 60, 75, or 85 were assigned to specific models. These were followed by three digits which were the actual "serial" number. In 1951, electric instruments were brought under the same numbering system as acoustics, and serial numbers were relocated to a paper label in the instrument's interior. Some transitional instruments bear both impressed numbers and a paper label with differing numbers. The latter are the more accurate for use in dating.

Number	Year		
1000 - 3000		11000	1937
[electrics only]	1937-1938	12000	1938
4000 - 5000		13000	1939-1940
[electrics only]	1939-1941	14000 - 15000	1941-1942
5000 [acoustics]	1932	16000 - 18000	1943
6000	1933	19000	1944
7000	1934	In 1944, a change was made in the numbering sequence.	
8000 - 9000	1935	Number	Year
10000	1930-1932, 1936	51000 - 52000	1944
		52000 - 54000	1945

ELECTRIC INSTRUMENTS (Numbers are approximate):

Number	Year		Year	Number
54000 - 55000	1946		1935	000 to 249
56000	1947		1936	250 to 749
57000	1948		1937	750 to 1499
58000	1949		1938	1500 to 2499
59000	1950		1939	2500 to 3499
60000 - 63000	1951		1940	3500 to 4999
64000	1952		1941	5000 to 6499
64000 - 66000	1953		1942	6500 to 7499
68000	1954		1943	7500 to 8299
69000	1955-1957		1944	8300 to 9000

In May of 1957, Epiphone was purchased by CMI and became a division of Gibson. Parts and materials were shipped to the new home in Kalamazoo, Michigan. Ex-Epiphone workers in New Berlin, New York "celebrated" by hosting a bonfire behind the plant with available lumber (finished and unfinished!).

Gibson built Epiphone guitars in Kalamazoo from 1958 to 1969. Hollow body guitars had the serial number on the label inside, and prefixed with a "A-" plus four digits for the first three years. Electric solid body guitars had the serial number inked on the back of the headstock, and the first number indicates the year: "8" (1958), "9" (1959), and "0" (1960).

In 1960, the numbering scheme changed as all models had the serial number pressed into the back on the headstock. There were numerous examples of duplication of serial numbers, so when dating a Epiphone from this time period consideration of parts/configuration and other details is equally important.

Number	Year		Number	Year
100 - 41199	1961		368640 - 369890	1966
41200 - 61180	1962		370000 - 370999	1967
61450 - 64222	1963		380000 - 380999	1966 to 1968*
64240 - 70501	1964		381000 - 385309	1966
71180 - 95846	1962* *(Numerical sequence may not coincide to year sequence)		390000 - 390998	1967
			400001 - 400999	1965 to 1968*
95849 - 99999	1963*		401000 - 408699	1966
000001 - 099999	1967*		408800 - 409250	1966 or 1967
100000 - 106099	1963 or 1967*		420000 - 438922	1966
106100 - 108999	1963		500000 - 500999	1965 to 1966, or 1968 to 1969*
109000 - 109999	1963 or 1967*		501009 - 501600	1965
110000 - 111549	1963		501601 - 501702	1968
111550 - 115799	1963 or 1967*		501703 - 502706	1965 or 1968*
115800 - 118299	1963		503010 - 503109	1968
Number	**Year**		**Number**	**Year**
118300 - 120999	1963 or 1967*		503405 - 520955	1965 or 1968*
121000 - 139999	1963		520956 - 530056	1968
140000 - 140100	1963 or 1967*		530061 - 530850	1966 or 1968 or 1969*
140101 - 144304	1963		530851 - 530993	1968 or 1969
144305 - 144380	1963 or 1964		530994 - 539999	1969
144381 - 145000	1963		540000 - 540795	1966 or 1969*
147001 - 149891	1963 or 1964		540796 - 545009	1969
149892 - 152989	1963		555000 - 556909	1966*
152990 - 174222	1964		558012 - 567400	1969
174223 - 179098	1964 or 1965		570099 - 570755	1966*
179099 - 199999	1964		580000 - 580999	1969
200000 - 250199	1964		600000 - 600999	1966 to 1969*
250540 - 290998	1965		601000 - 606090	1969
300000 - 305999	1965		700000 - 700799	1966 or 1967*
Number	**Year**		750000 - 750999	1968 or 1969
306000 - 306099	1965 or 1967*		800000 - 800999	1966 to 1969*
307000 - 307984	1965		801000 - 812838	1966 or 1969*
309653 - 310999	1965 or 1967*		812900 - 819999	1969
311000 - 320149	1965		820000 - 820087	1966 or 1969*
320150 - 320699	1967*		820088 - 823830	1966*
320700 - 325999	1967*		824000 - 824999	1969
325000 - 326999	1965 or 1966		828002 - 847488	1966 or 1969*
327000 - 329999	1965		847499 - 858999	1966 or 1969*
330000 - 330999	1965 or 1967 or 1968*		859001 - 895038	1967*
331000 - 346119	1965		895039 - 896999	1968*
346120 - 347099	1965 or 1966		897000 - 898999	1967 or 1969*
348000 - 349100	1966		899000 - 972864	1968*
349101 - 368639	1965			

In 1970, production of Epiphone instruments moved to Japan. Japanese Epiphones were manufactured between 1970 to 1983. According to author/researcher Walter Carter, the serial numbers on these are unreliable as a usable tool for dating models. Comparison to catalogs is one of the few means available. Earlier Kalamazoo labels were generally orange with black printing and said "Made in Kalamazoo", while the Japanese instruments featured blue labels which read "Epiphone of Kalamazoo, Michigan" (note that it doesn't say made in Kalamazoo, nor does it say Made in Japan). While not a solid rule of thumb, research of the model should be more thorough than just glancing at the label.

During the early 1980s, the Japanese production costs became pricey due to the changing ratio of the dollar/yen. Production moved to Korea, and again the serial numbers are not an exact science as a dating mechanism. In 1993, a structure was developed where the number (or pair of numbers) following the initial letter indicates the year of production (i.e. "3" indicates 1993, or a "93" would indicate the same).

Some top of the line Epiphones were produced in the U.S. at either Gibson's Nashville or Montana facilities in the 1990s. These instruments are the only ones that correspond to the standard post-1977 Gibson serialization. Like Gibson numbers, there are 8 digits in the complete number, and follows the code of YDDDYNNN. The YY (first and fifth) indicate the year built. DDD indicates the day of the year (so DDD can't be above 365), and the NNN indicates the instrument's production ranking for that day (NNN = 021 = 21st guitar built). The Nashville facility begins each day at number 501, and the Montana workshop begins at number 101. **However**, in 1994, the Nashville-produced Epiphones were configured as YYNNNNNN: YY = 94 (the year) and NNNNNN is the ranking for the entire year.

Information for this chart of Epiphone serial numbers can be found in Walter Carter's book Epiphone: The Complete History (Hal Leonard, 1995). Not only a fascinating story and chronology of the original Epiphone company and its continuation, but also an overview of product catalogs as well as serial numbers. Walter Carter serves as the Gibson Historian as well as being a noted songwriter and author. He also wrote The Martin Book, and co-authored several with expert George Gruhn including Gruhn's Guide to Vintage Guitars, Acoustic Guitars and Other Fretted Instruments, and Electric Guitars and Basses: A Photographic History (the later all available through GPI/Miller-Freeman books).

FENDER SERIALIZATION

Serial numbers, in general, are found on the bridgeplate, the neckplate, the backplate or the peghead. From 1950-1954, serial numbers are found on the bridgeplate or vibrato backplate. From 1954-1976, the serial numbers are found on the neckplate, both top or bottom of the plate. From 1976 to date, the serial number appears with the peghead decal. Vintage Reissues have their serial numbers on the neckplate and have been in use since 1982.

The Fender company also stamped (or handwrote) the production date on the heel of the neck, in the body routs, on the pickups, and near the wiring harness (the body, pickup, and wiring dating was only done sporadically, during certain time periods). However, the neck date (and body date) indicate when the neck (or body) part was completed! Fender produces necks and guitar bodies separately, and bolts the two together during final production. Therefore, the date on the neck will generally be weeks or months before the actual production date.

When trying to determine the manufacturing date of an instrument by serialization, it is best to keep in mind that there are no clear cut boundaries between where the numbers began and where they ended. There were constant overlapping of serial numbers between years and models. The following are approximate numbers and dates.

1950	0001-0750	1957	14900-025200
1951	0200-1900	1958	022700-38200
1952	0400-4900	1959	31400-60600
1953	2020-5030	1960	44200-58600
1954	2780-7340	1961	55500-81700
1955	6600-12800	1962	71600-99800
1956	7800-16000	1963	81600-99200

In 1962, as the serialization count neared 100000, for one reason or another, the transition did not occur. Instead, an L preceded a 5 digit sequence. It ran this way from 1962 to 1965.

1962	L00400-L13200	1964	L20600-L76200
1963	L00200-L40300	1965	L34980-L69900

In 1965, when CBS bought Fender Musical Instruments, Inc., the serialization has come to be known as the F Series, due to an "F" being stamped onto the neckplate. This series of numbers went from 1965 to 1973. The approximate numbers and years are as follows:

1965	100001-147400	1970	278910-305415
1966	112170-600200	1971	272500-380020
1967	162165-602550	1972	301395-412360
1968	211480-627740	1973	359415-418360
1969	238945-290835		

In early 1973, Fender stopped the practice of writing/stamping the production date on the heel of the neck (through 1982). The following are rough approximations for the years 1973 to 1976:

Early 1973 to Late 1976:	400000 series	Mid 1974 to Mid 1976:	600000 series
Late 1973 to Late 1976:	500000 series	Mid 1976 to Late 1976:	700000 series

In late 1976, Fender decided to move to a new numbering scheme for their serialization. The numbers appeared on the pegheads and for the remainder of 1976 they had a prefix of 76 or S6 preceding a 5 digit sequence. In 1977, the serialization went to a letter for the decade, followed by a single digit for the year and then 5 to 6 digits. Examples of the letter/digit code follow like this: S for the '70s, E for the '80s, N for the '90s, etc.

1970s	S	(example) S8 - 1978
1980s	E	(example) E1 - 1981
1990s	N	(example) N2 - 1992

While the idea was fine, the actuality was a different matter. Instrument production did not meet the levels for which decals had been produced, so there are several overlapping years. **Sometimes several prefixes found within a single year's production**. Here is the revised table of letter/digit year codes:

1976	S6 (also 76)	1989	E8 and E9
1977	S7 and S8	1990	E9, N9, and N0
1978	S7, S8, and S9	1991	N0 (plus 6 digits)
1979	S9 and E0	1992	N2
1980-1981	S9, E0, and E1	1993	N3
1982	E1, E2, and E3	1994	N4
1984-1985	E3 and E4	1995	N5
1985-1986	*No U.S. Production	1996	N6
1987	E4	1997	N7
1988	E4 and E8		

Serialization on Fender Japan models

Fender Japan was established in March, 1982, in a negotiation between CBS/Fender, Kanda Shokai, and Yamano Music. Instruments were built by Fuji Gen Gakki, initially for the European market. When the Vintage/Reissues models were offered in the early 1980s, a *V* in the serial number indicated U.S. production, while a *JV* stood for Fender Japan-built models. For the first two years of Japanese production, serial numbers consisted of a 2 letter prefix to indicate the year, followed by five digits. In late 1984, this code was changed to a single letter prefix and six digits. Note the overlapping year/multi-prefix letter codes:

1982-1984	JV	1989-1990	I and J
1983-1984	SQ	1990-1991	K
1984-1987	E (plus 6 digits)	1991-1992	L
1985-1986	A, B, and C	1992-1993	M
1986-1987	F	1993-1994	N
1987-1988+	G	1994-1995	O
1988-1989	H	1995-1996	P

Dating a Fender instrument by serialization alone can get you within an approximate range of years, but should not be used as a definitive means to determine the year of actual production.

(Fender Serialization overview courtesy A.R. Duchossoir; Later year production codes courtesy Michael Wright, Vintage Guitar Magazine)

FRAMUS SERIAL NUMBERS

Framus serial numbers were generally placed on the back of the peghead or on a label inside the body. The main body of the serial number is followed by an additional pair of digits and a letter. This additional pair of numbers indicate the production year.

For example:

51334 63L =	1963
65939 70L =	1970

(Serial number information courtesy Tony Bacon and Barry Moorehouse, The Bass Book, GPI Books, 1995)

GIBSON SERIALIZATION

Identifying Gibson instruments by serial number is tricky at best and downright impossible in some cases. The best methods of identifying them is by using a combination of the serial number, the factory order number and any features that are particular to a specific time that changes may have occurred in instrument design (i.e. logo design change, headstock volutes, etc). There have been 6 different serial number styles used to date on Gibson instruments.

The first serialization started in 1902 and ran until 1947. The serial numbers started with number 100 and go to 99999. All numbers are approximates. In most cases, only the upper end instruments were assigned identification numbers.

YEAR	LAST #	YEAR	LAST #
1903	1150	1925	82700
1904	1850	1926	83600
1905	2550	1927	85400
1906	3350	1928	87300
1907	4250	1929	89750
1908	5450	1930	90200
1909	6950	1931	90450
1910	8750	1932	90700
1911	10850	1933	91400
1912	13350	1934	92300
1913	16100	1935	92800
1914	20150	1936	94100
1915	25150	1937	95200
1916	32000	1938	95750
1917	39500	1939	96050
1918	47900	1940	96600
1919	53800	1941	97400
1920	62200	1942	97700
1921	69300	1943	97850
1922	71400	1944	98250
1923	74900	1945	98650
1924	80300	1946	99300
		1947	99999

White oval labels were used on instruments from 1902 to 1954, at which time the oval label was changed to an orange color. On instruments with round soundholes, this label is visible directly below it. On f-hole instruments, it is visible through the upper f-hole. The second type of serial numbers used started with an *A* prefix and ran from 1947 to 1961. The first number is A 100.

YEAR	LAST #	YEAR	LAST #
1947	A 1305	1955	A 21910
1948	A 2665	1956	A 24755
1949	A 4410	1957	A 26820
1950	A 6595	1958	A 28880
1951	A 9420	1959	A 32285
1952	A 12460	1960	A 35645
1953	A 17435	1961	A 36150
1954	A 18665		

When production of solid body guitars began, an entirely new serial number system was developed. Though not used on the earliest instruments produced (those done in 1952), a few of these instruments have 3 digits stamped on the headstock top. Some time in 1953, instruments were ink stamped on the headstock back with 5 or 6 digit numbers, the first indicating the year, the following numbers are production numbers. The production numbers run in a consecutive order and, aside from a few oddities in the change over years (1961-1962), it is fairly accurate to use them when identifying solid body instruments produced between 1953 and 1961. Examples of this system:

4 2205 = 1954	
614562 = 1956	

In 1961 Gibson started a new serial number system that covered all instrument lines. It consisted of numbers that are impressed into the wood. It is also generally known to be the most frustrating and hard to understand system that Gibson has employed. The numbers were used between the years 1961-1969. There are several instances where batches of numbers are switched in order, duplicated, not just once, but up to four times, and seem to be randomly assigned, throughout the decade. In general though, the numbers are approximately as follows:

YEAR	APPROXIMATE SERIAL RANGE	YEAR	APPROXIMATE SERIAL RANGE
1961	100-42440	1967	010000-042900
1962	42441-61180	1967	044000-044100
1963	61450-64220	1967	050000-054400
1964	64240-70500	1967	055000-063999
1962	71180-96600	1967	064000-066010
1963	96601-99999	1967	067000-070910
1967	000001-008010	1967	090000-099999

YEAR	APPROXIMATE SERIAL RANGE	YEAR	APPROXIMATE SERIAL RANGE
1963, 1967	100000-106099	1966	427000-429180
1963	106100-108900	1966	430005-438530
1963, 1967	109000-109999	1966	438800-438925
1963	110000-111549		
1963, 1967	111550-115799	YEAR	APPROXIMATE SERIAL RANGE
1963	115800-118299	1965, 1966, 1968, 1969	500000-500999
		1965	501010-501600
1963, 1967	118300-120999	1968	501601-501702
1963	121000-139999	1965, 1968	501703-502706
1963, 1967	140000-140100	1968	503010-503110
1963	140101-144304	1965, 1968	503405-520955
1964	144305-144380	1968	520956-530056
1963	144381-145000	1966, 1968, 1969	530061-530850
1963	147009-149864	1968, 1969	530851-530993
1964	149865-149891	1969	530994-539999
1963	149892-152989	1966, 1969	540000-540795
1964	152990-174222	1969	540796-545009
1964, 1965	174223-176643	1966	550000-556910
1964	176644-199999	1969	558012-567400
1964	200000-250335	1966	570099-570755
1965	250336-291000	1969	580000-580999
1965	301755-302100	1966, 1967, 1968, 1969	600000-600999
1965	302754-305983	1969	601000-601090
1965, 1967	306000-306100	1969	605901-606090
1965, 1967	307000-307985	1966, 1967	700000-700799
1965, 1967	309848-310999	1968, 1969	750000-750999
1965	311000-320149	1966, 1967, 1968, 1969	800000-800999
1967	320150-320699	1966, 1969	801000-812838
1965	320700-321100	1969	812900-814999
1965	322000-326600	1969	817000-819999
1965	328000-328500	1966, 1969	820000-820087
1965	328700-329179	1966	820088-823830
1965, 1967	329180-330199	1969	824000-824999
1965, 1967, 1968	330200-332240	1966, 1969	828002-847488
1965	332241-347090	1966	847499-858999
1965	348000-348092	1967	859001-880089
1966	348093-349100	1967	893401-895038
1965	349121-368638	1968	895039-896999
1966	368640-369890	1967	897000-898999
1967	370000-370999	1968	899000-899999
1966	380000-385309	1968	900000-902250
1967	390000-390998	1968	903000-920899
1965, 1966, 1967, 1968	400001-400999	1968	940000-941009
1966	401000-407985	1968	942001-943000
1966	408000-408690	1968	945000-945450
1966	408800-409250	1968	947415-956000
1966	420000-426090	1968	959000-960909
		1968	970000-972864

From 1970-1975 the method of serializing instruments at Gibson became even more randomized. All numbers were impressed into the wood and a six digit number assigned, though no particular order was given and some instruments had a letter prefix. The orange labels inside hollow bodied instruments were discontinued in 1970 and were replaced by white and orange rectangle labels on the acoustics, and small black, purple and white rectangle labels were placed on electric models.

In 1970, the words **MADE IN USA** was impressed into the back of instrument headstocks (although a few instruments from the 1950s also had *MADE IN USA* impressed into their headstocks as well).

Year(s)	Approximate Series Manufacture
1970, 1971, and 1972	100000s, 600000s, 700000s, 900000s
1973	000001s, 100000s, 200000s, 800000s and a few "A" + 6 digit numbers
1974 and 1975	100000s, 200000s, 300000s, 400000s, 500000s, 600000s, 800000s and a few *A-B-C-D-E-F* + 6 digit numbers

During the period from 1975-1977 Gibson used a transfer that had eight digit numbers, the first two indicate the year, 99=1975, 00=1976 and 06=1977, the following six digits are in the 100000 to 200000 range. *MADE IN USA* was also included on the transfer and some models had *LIMITED EDITION* also applied. A few bolt-on neck instruments had a date ink stamped on the heel area.

In 1977, Gibson first introduced the serialization method that is in practice today. This updated system utilizes an impressed eight digit numbering scheme that covers both serializing and dating functions. The pattern is as follows:

YDDDYPPP

YY is the production year

DDD is the day of the year

PPP is the plant designation and/or instrument rank.

The numbers 001-499 show Kalamazoo production, 500-999 show Nashville production. The Kalamazoo numbers were discontinued in 1984.

When acoustic production began at the plant built in Bozeman, Montana (in 1989), the series' numbers were reorganized. Bozeman instruments began using 001-299 designations and, in 1990, Nashville instruments began using 300-999 designations. It should also be noted that the Nashville plant has not reached the 900s since 1977, so these numbers have been reserved for prototypes. Examples:

70108276 means the instrument was produced on Jan.10, 1978, in Kalamazoo and was the 276th instrument stamped that day.

82765501 means the instrument was produced on Oct. 3, 1985, in Nashville and was the 1st instrument stamped that day.

However, it has come to light recently that the Kalamazoo plant did not directly switch over to the "new" 8 digit serialization method in 1977. When the Nashville Gibson plant was opened in 1974, it was decided that the bulk of the production of products would be run in the South; the Kalamazoo plant would produce the higher end (fancier) models in the North. Of course, many of the older guitar builders and craftsmen were still in Kalamazoo; and if they weren't ready to change how they built guitars, then they may not have been ready to change how they numbered them! Certain guitar models built in the late 1970s can be used to demonstrate the old-style 6 digit serial numbers. **It is estimated that Gibson's Kalamazoo plant continued to use the 6 digit serial numbers through 1978 and 1979.** So double check the serial numbers on those 1970s L-5s, Super 400s, and Super 5 BJBs!

Gibson's F O N System

In addition to the above serial number information, Gibson also used **Factory Order Numbers (F O N) to track batches of instruments being produced at the time. In the earlier years at Gibson, guitars were normally built in batches of 40 instruments. Gibson's Factory Order Numbers were** an internal coding that followed the group of instruments through the factory. Thus, the older Gibson guitars may have a serial number and a F O N. The F O N may indicate the year, batch number, and the ranking (order of production within the batch of 40).

This system is useful in helping to date and authenticate instruments. There are three separate groupings of numbers that have been identified and are used for their accuracy. The numbers are usually stamped or written on the instrument's back and seen through the lower F hole or round soundhole, or maybe impressed on the back of the headstock.

1908-1923 Approximate #s

YEAR	F O N
1908	259
1909	309
1910	545, 927
1911	1260, 1295
1912	1408, 1593
1913	1811, 1902
1914	1936, 2152
1915	2209, 3207

YEAR	F O N
1916	2667, 3508
1917	3246, 11010
1918	9839, 11159
1919	11146, 11212
1920	11329, 11367
1921	11375, 11527
1922	11565, 11729
1923	11973

F O Ns for the years 1935-1941 usually consisted of the batch number, a letter for the year and the instrument number. Examples are as follows:

722 A 23

465 D 58

863 E 02.

Code Letter and Year			
A	1935	D	1938
B	1936	E	1939
C	1937	F	1940
		G	1941

Code Letter F O Ns were discontinued after 1941, and any instruments made during or right after World War II do not bear an F O N codes. In 1949, a four digit F O N was used, but not in conjunction with any code letter indicating the year.

From 1952-1961, the F O N scheme followed the pattern of a letter, the batch number and an instrument ranking number (when the guitar was built in the run of 40). The F O N is the only identification number on Gibson's lower grade models (like the ES-125, ES-140, J-160E, etc.) which do not feature a paper label. Higher grade models (such as the Super 400, L-5, J-200, etc.) feature both a serial number **and** a F O N. When both numbers are present on a higher grade model, remember that the F O N was assigned at the beginning of the production run, while the serial number was recorded later (before shipping). The serial number would properly indicate the actual date of the guitar. F O N examples run thus:

Y 2230 21

V 4867 8

R 6785 15

Code Letter and Year			
Z	1952	U	1957
Y	1953	T	1958
X	1954	S	1959
W	1955	R	1960
V	1956	Q	1961

After 1961 the use of FONs was discontinued at Gibson.

There are still some variances that Gibson uses on some instruments produced today, but for the most part the above can be used for identifying instruments. For the most accurate identification you would need to contact the Gibson Guitar Corporation itself.

GRETSCH SERIALIZATION

Before World War II, serial numbers were penciled onto the inside backs of Gretsch's higher end instruments. By 1949, small labels bearing *Fred Gretsch Mfg. Co.*, serial and model number replaced the penciled numbers inside the instruments. This label was replaced by a different style label, an orange and grey one, sometime in 1957. A few variations of this scheme occurred throughout the company's history, the most common being the use of impressed numbers in the headstock of instruments, beginning about 1949. Serial numbers were also stamped into the headstock nameplate of a few models. The numbers remain consecutive throughout and the following chart gives approximations of the years they occurred.

APPROXIMATE SERIALIZATION RANGE	YEARS	APPROXIMATE SERIALIZATION RANGE	YEARS
001 - 1000	1939-1945	21001 - 26000	1957
1001 - 2000	1946-1949	26001 - 30000	1958
2001 - 3000	1950	30001 - 34000	1959
3001 - 5000	1951	34001 - 39000	1960
5001 - 6000	1952	39001 - 45000	1961
6001 - 8000	1953	45001 - 52000	1962
8001 - 12000	1954	52001 - 63000	1963
12001 - 16000	1955	63001 - 78000	1964
16001 - 21000	1956	78001 - 85000	1965

In the latter part of 1965, Gretsch decided to begin using a date coded system of serialization. It consists of the first digit (sometimes two) that identified the month; the second or third identifying the year, and the remaining digit (or digits) represented the number of the instrument in production for that month. Some examples of this system would be:

997   September, 1969 (7th instrument produced)

11255   November, 1972 (55th instrument produced)

On solid body instruments, impressed headstock numbers were used. In 1967, *Made in USA* was added. Hollow body instruments still made use of a label placed on the inside back of the instrument.

Around circa 1973, the label style changed once again, becoming a black and white rectangle with *Gretsch Guitars* and the date coded serialization on it. A hyphen was also added between the month and the year to help avoid confusion, thus:

12-4387   December, 1974 (387th instrument produced)

3-745   March, 1977 (45th instrument produced)

GUILD SERIALIZATION

Guild Serialization went through three distinct phases, and can be both a helpful guide as well as confusing when trying to determine the manufacturing date of a guitar. The primary idea to realize is that most Guild models use a **separate serial numbering system for each guitar model** - there is no "overall system" to plug a number into! While serial numbers are sometimes a helpful tool, other dating devices like potentiomter codes or dating by hardware may be more exact.

1952-1965: Between the inception of the Guild company in 1952 to 1965, the serialization was sequential for all models.

APPROXIMATE LAST NUMBER	YEAR		
		8348	1958
350	1952	12035	1959
840	1953	14713	1960
1526	1954	18419	1961
2468	1955	22722	1962
3830	1956	28943	1963
5712	1957	38636	1964
		46606	1965

1966-1969: While some models retained the serialization from the original series, many models were designated with a 2 letter prefix and an independent numbering series for each individual model between 1966 to 1969.

Continued Original Serialization Series APPROXIMATE LAST NUMBER	YEAR		
		46637	1967
		46656	1968
46608	1966	46695	1969

The models that were numbered with the new 2 letter prefix started each separate serial number series with 101.

1970-1979: The following chart details the serial numbers as produced through the 1970s. There are no corresponding model names or numbers for this time period.

APPROXIMATE LAST NUMBER	YEAR		
		112803	1974
		130304	1975
50978	1970	149625	1976
61463	1971	169867	1977
75602	1972	190567	1978
95496	1973	211877	1979

1979-1989: In 1979, Guild returned to the separate prefix/serial number system. Serial numbers after the 2 letter prefix in each separate system began with 100001 (thus, you would need a serialization table for each model/by year to date by serialization alone). In 1987, a third system was devised. In some cases, the **Model Designation** became the *prefix* for the serial number. For example:

D300041   D-30, #0041 (41st D-30 instrument produced)

With acoustic models, you can cross-reference the model name to the serial number to judge the rest of the serialization; the resulting serial number must still be checked in the serialization table.

1990-Date: Guild continued with the separate prefix/serialization system. In 1994, only the Model Prefix and last serial numbers for each model were recorded; better records continued in 1995.

Guild Custom Shop: The three Guild Custom Shop models (**45th Anniversary**, **Deco**, and **Finesse**) all use a completely different serial numbering system. Each instrument has a serial number on the back of the headstock that indicates the "which number out of the complete series". Inside the guitar there is a seven digit code: The first three numbers (starting with #500) indicate the production sequence, while the last four digits indicate the date of production (the 4th and 7th digit **in reverse** indicate the year, the 5th and 6th digits are the month).

Guild has a series of charts available on their website (www.guildguitars.com) to help date a guitar during different manufacturing periods. Through the years (and different owners of the company), some of the historical documentation has been lost or destroyed. However, these tables are some of the most comprehensive available to the public.

(Serialization reference source: Hans Moust, The Guild Guitar Book; and Jay Pilzer, Guild authority; additional company information courtesy Bill Acton, Guild Guitars)

IBANEZ SERIALIZATION

Author/researcher Michael Wright successfully discussed the Ibanez/Hoshino history in his book, *Guitar Stories Volume One* (Vintage Guitar Books, 1995). Early serial numbers and foreign-built potentiometer codes on Japanese guitars aren't much help in the way of clues, but Ibanez did institute a meaningful numbering system as part of their warranty program in 1975.

Before 1987: In general, Ibanez serial numbers between 1975 to 1987 had seven digits, arranged **XYYZZZZ**. The letter prefix ("X") stands for the month (January = A, February = B, etc. on to L); the next following two digits ("YY") are the year. The rest of the four digits are sequential production ranking numbers.

An outside source indicated that the month/letter code prefix was discontinued in 1988, and the previous dating code was discontinued in 1990. However (or whatever), in 1987 the **XYYZZZZ** still appeared the same, but the new listing shifted to **XYZZZZZ**.

1987 and After: The opening prefix ("X") now indicates production **location** instead of month: **F** (Fuji, Japan), or **C** (Cort, Korea). The first digit ("Y") indicates the year: As in 198**Y** - and as in 199**Y**. Bright-eyed serialization students will notice that there is some inherent problems with the post-1987 system! All following numbers again are the production ranking code (**ZZZZZ**).

(Source: Michael Wright, Guitar Stories Volume One)

MARTIN GUITAR SERIAL NUMBERS

YEAR	LAST #		
		1910	11203
1898	8348	1911	11413
1899	8716	1912	11565
1900	9128	1913	11821
1901	9310	1914	12047
1902	9528	1915	12209
1903	9810	1916	12390
1904	9988	1917	12988
1905	10120	**YEAR**	**LAST #**
1906	10329	1918	13450
1907	10727	1919	14512
1908	10883	1920	15848
1909	11018	1921	16758

YEAR	LAST #	YEAR	LAST #
1922	17839	1961	181297
1923	19891	1962	187384
1924	22008	1963	193327
1925	24116	1964	199626
1926	28689	1965	207030
1927	34435	**YEAR**	**LAST #**
1928	37568	1966	217215
1929	40843	1967	230095
1930	45317	1968	241925
1931	49589	1969	256003
1932	52590	1970	271633
1933	55084	1971	294270
1934	58679	1972	313302
1935	61947	1973	333873
1936	65176	1974	353387
1937	68865	1975	371828
YEAR	**LAST #**	1976	388800
1938	71866	1977	399625
1939	74061	1978	407800
1940	76734	1979	419900
1941	80013	1980	430300
1942	83107	1981	436474
1943	86724	1982	439627
1944	90149	1983	446101
1945	93623	1984	453300
1946	98158	1985	460575
1947	103468	1986	468175
1948	108269	1987	476216
1949	112961	1988	483952
1950	117961	1989	493279
1951	122799	1990	503309
1952	128436	1991	512487
1953	134501	1992	522655
1954	141345	1993	535223
1955	147328	1994	551696
1956	152775	1995	570434
1957	159061	1996	PENDING
1958	165576	1997	PENDING
1959	171047	1998	PENDING
1960	175689		

MOONSTONE SERIALIZATION

The most important factor in determining the year of manufacture for Moonstone instruments is that each model had its own set of serial numbers. There is no grouping of models by year of manufacture.

D-81 EAGLE

	L001-L004	1981
	L005-L011	1982

EAGLE (Electrics)

	52950-52952	1980
	52953-52954	1981
	52955-52959	1982
	52960	1983

EARTHAXE
(26 total instruments made)

	0001-0013	1975
	0014-0026	1976

ECLIPSE Guitar models
(81 total instruments made)

	79001-79003	1979
	8004-8036	1980
	8037-8040	1981
	1041-1052	1981
	1053-1075	1982
	1076-1081	1983

ECLIPSE Bass models
(124 total instruments made)

	3801-3821	1980
	3822-3828	1981
	3029-3062	1981
	3063-3109	1982
	3110-3118	1983
	3119-3123	1984

EXPLODER Guitar models
(65 total instruments made)

	7801-7806	1980
	7007-7020	1981
	7021-7052	1982
	7053-7065	1983

EXPLODER Bass models
(35 total instruments made)

	6801-6803	1980
	6004-6013	1981
	6014-6031	1982
	6032-6035	1983

FLYING V Guitar models
(52 total instruments made)

	5801-5812	1980
	5013-5028	1981
	5029-5045	1982
	5046-5048	1983
	5049-5052	1984

FLYING V Bass models
(6 total instruments made)

	9001-9006	1981

M-80
(64 total instruments made)

	4801-4808	1980
	4809-4816	1981
	4017-4031	1981
	4032-4052	1982
	4053-4064	1983

MOONDOLINS

T001-T002	1981
T003-T006	1983
T007	1984

VULCAN Guitar models
(162 total instruments made)

5027	1977
5028-5034	1978
107835-107838	1978
17939-179115	1979
179116-179120	1980
80121-80129	1980

80130-80134	1981
8135-8167	1981
8168-8185	1982
8186-8191	1983
7988-7991	1984

VULCAN Bass models
(19 total instruments made)

V001-V002	1982
V003-V016	1983
V017-V019	1984

OVATION SERIALIZATION

Three Digit numbers (no letter prefix)

006-319	1966
320-999	1967 (February - November)

Four Digit numbers (no letter prefix)

1000-	1967 (November) to 1968 (July)

Five Digit numbers (no letter prefix)

10000-	1970 (February) to 1972 (May)

Six Digit numbers (1971 to Present, except Adamas models)

000001-007000	1972 (May - December)
007001-020000	1973
020001-039000	1974
039001-067000	1975
067001-086000	1976
086001-103000	1977 (January - September)
103001-126000	1977 (September) to 1978 (April)
126001-157000	1978 (April - December)
157001-203000	1979
211011-214933	1980
214934-263633	1981
263634-291456	1982
291457-302669	1983
302670-303319	1984 [Elite models only]
315001-331879	1984 (May - December) [Balladeer models only]
303320-356000	1985 to 1986
357000-367999	1987
368000-382106	1988
382107-392900	1989
403760-420400	1990
421000-430680	1991
402700-406000	1992
446001-457810	1992

457811-470769	1993
470770-484400	1994
484401-501470	1995
501470-507000	1996
PENDING	1997
PENDING	1998

Adamas Models Serialization
Serialization for the Adamas models begins with number 0077 on September, 1977.

0077-0099	1977
0100-0608	1978
0609-1058	1979
1059-1670	1980
1671-2668	1981
2669-3242	1982
3243-3859	1983
3860-4109	1984
4110-4251	1985
4252-4283	1986
4284-4427	1987
4428-4696	1988
4697-4974	1989
4975-5541	1990
5542-6278	1991
6279-7088	1992
7089-8159	1993
8160-9778	1994
9779-11213	1995
11214-12000	1996
PENDING	1997
PENDING	1998

Letter Prefix plus digits

A + 3 digits	1968 (July - November)
B + 3 digits	1968 (November) to 1969 (February)
B + 5 digits	1974 to 1979 [Magnum solid body basses]
C + 3 digits	1969 (February - September)
D + 3 digits	1969 (September) to 1970 (February)
E + 4 digits	1973 (January) to 1975 (February) [solid bodies]
E + 5 digits	1975 (February) to 1980 [solid bodies]
E + 6 digits	1980 (late) to 1981 [UK II guitars]
F Prefix	1968 (July) to 1970 (February)
G Prefix	1968 (July) to 1970 (February)
H Prefix	1970 to 1973 [Electric Storm series]
I Prefix	1970 to 1973 [Electric Storm series]
J Prefix	1970 to 1973 [Electric Storm series]
L Prefix	1970 to 1973 [Electric Storm series]

(Source: Walter Carter, The History of the Ovation Guitar. Information collected in Mr. Carter's Ovation Appendices was researched and compiled by Paul Bechtoldt)

RICKENBACKER SERIAL NUMBERS

Rickenbacker offered a number of guitar models as well as lap steels prior to World War II, such as the **Ken Roberts Spanish** electric f-hole flattop (mid 1930s to 1940) and the **559** model archtop in the early 1940s. The company put production on hold during the war; in 1946, began producing an **Electric Spanish** archtop. Serialization on early Rickenbacker models from 1931 to 1953 is unreliable, but models may be dated by patent information. This method should be used in conjunction with comparisons of parts, and design changes.

In 1953, Rickenbacker/Electro was purchased by Francis C. Hall. The **Combo 600** and **Combo 800** models debuted in 1954. From 1954 on, the serial number appears on the bridge or jackplate of the instrument. The Rickenbacker serial numbers during the 1950s have four to seven digits. The letter within the code indicates the type of instrument (Combo/guitar, bass, mandolin, etc), and the number after the letter indicates the year of production:

Example: X(X)B7XX   (A bass from 1957)

1961 to 1986: In 1961, the serialization scheme changes. The new code has **two letter** prefixes, followed by digits. The first letter prefix indicates the year; the second digit indicates the month of production.

PREFIX	YEAR		PREFIX	YEAR
A	1961		T	1980
B	1962		U	1981
C	1963		V	1982
D	1964		W	1983
E	1965		X	1984
F	1966		Y	1985
G	1967		Z	1986
H	1968		PREFIX	MONTH
I	1969		A	January
J	1970		B	February
K	1971		C	March
L	1972		D	April
M	1973		E	May
N	1974		F	June
O	1975		G	July
P	1976		H	August
Q	1977		I	September
R	1978		J	October
S	1979		K	November
			L	December

In 1987, the serialization was revised, again. The updated serial number code has letter prefix (A to L) that still indicates month; the following digit that indicates the year:

DIGIT	YEAR			
0	1987		5	1992
1	1988		6	1993
2	1989		7	1994
3	1990		8	1995
4	1991		9	1996

The following digits after the month/year digits are production (for example, L2XXXX would be an instrument built in December, 1989).

Rickenbacker is currently not disclosing the current system of serialization. If a collector or dealer needs a recent instrument dated, Rickenbacker invites individuals to contact the company through the Customer Service department.

STROMBERG SERIALIZATION

This Boston-based instrument shop was founded by Charles Stromberg, a Swedish immigrant, in 1906. Stromberg generally concentrated on banjo and drum building, leaving the guitar lutherie to his son Elmer. Elmer joined the family business in 1910, and began building guitars in the late 1920s.

Total production of guitars reached about 640. The labels on the guitars were business cards, so the instruments can be dated (roughly) by the telephone number on the cards.

Bowdoin 1228R-1728-M	1920-1927		the Blue shipping labels inside
Bowdoin 1242 W	1927-1929		the guitar body were either
Bowdoin 1878 R	1929-1932		typewritten or handwritten)
CA 3174	1932-1945 (In the late 1930s,	CA 7-3174	1949-1955

(Source: Jim Speros, Stromberg research)

TAKAMINE SERIALIZATION

The eight digit serial number on Takamine instruments can be deciphered by breaking down the number into 4 groups of two digits, thus:

YYMMDDXX   = (YY)(MM)(DD)(XX)

The first two digits (YY) indicate the year; the next two digits (MM) indicate the month; the third group of digits (DD) indicates the day of production; and the remaining two digits indicates the ranking in the number of instruments produced that day. If a nine digit serial number is encountered, assume that the last three digits indicate the production ranking.

TAYLOR SERIAL NUMBERS

In 1974, Taylor Guitars began a serialization system that uses the first two digits in the instrument's serial number to indicate the year the instruments was manufactured (for example, the year of 1977 = **77**XXX).

THREET GUITARS SERIALIZATION

The serial number on Threet acoustic guitars consists of a letter followed by three (sometimes four) numbers. The letter indicates the model:

A	Parlor-size (similar to a traditional Model O)
B	A "large person's" Parlor-size (similar to a Model OO)
C	Larger, balanced sound Parlor-size (similar to a Model OOO)
D	Cross between a Model C and a Dreadnought

The first two numbers indicate the year the guitar was started (and, hopefully, completed). The third (and occasionally fourth) number indicate the guitar's "rank" in that year's production. For example:

C 964 =   Model C   built in 1996   4th Guitar Produced

Keep in mind, Threet guitars are offered in both a *Standard* and *Deluxe* versions. Review the appointments to determine the level of construction, and watch for *Custom* level inlays as well.

(Source: Judy Threet, Threet Guitars)

WASHBURN SERIALIZATION

The Washburn trademark was introduced by the Lyon & Healy company of Chicago, Illinois in 1864. While this trademark has changed hands a number of times, the historical records have not! Washburn suffered a fire in the 1920s that destoyed all records and paperwork that was on file; in the 1950s, another fire destroyed the accumulated files yet again.

When the trademark was revived yet again in 1964, the first production of Washburn acoustic guitars was in Japan. Washburn electric guitars debuted in 1979, and featured U.S. designs and Japanese production.

Production of Washburn guitars changed to Korea in the mid to late 1980s; a number of U.S.-produced **Chicago Series** models were introduced in the late 1980s as well. Serial numbers from 1988 on use the first two digits of the instrument's serial number to indicate the year the instrument was produced (19**88** = **88**XXX). This process works for most, but not all, of the instruments since then.

Washburn Limited Editions feature the year in the model name. For example, **D-95 LTD** is a Limited Edition introduced in 1995. No corresponding serialization information is available at this time.

(Washburn information courtesy Dr. Duck's AxWax)

YAMAHA SERIAL NUMBERS

Yamaha instruments were originally produced in Japan; production switched to Taiwan in the early 1980s. Instruments are currently produced in the U.S., Taiwan, and Indonesia. It is important to recognize that Yamaha uses two different serialization systems, based on the country of origin (in fact, decoding the serial number is the first clue to country of origin).

Japanese-produced Yamaha instruments have a letter/number code that indicates production date. The first two letters of the serial number indicate the year and month of production (the first letter indicates the year, the second letter indicates the month). Yamaha's coding system substitutes a letter for a number indicating year and month, thus:

CODE LETTER	MONTH or YEAR NUMBER		
H	1	N	7
I	2	O	8
J	3	P	9
K	4	X	10
L	5	Y	11
M	6	Z	12

For example, an "H" in the first of two letters would be a "1", indicating the last digit of the year (1981 or 1991). An "H" in the second of two letters would also be a "1", indicating the first month (January). Like Hamer, the digits will cycle around every 10 years.

After the two letter prefixes, 5 digits follow. The first two digits represent the day of the month, and the three digits indicate the production ranking for that day. For example:

NZ19218   December 19, 1987 (or 1997); #218.

The example's code should be properly broken down as N - Z - 27 - 428. The "N" in the first of the two letters would be a "7", indicating the last digit of the year (1987 or 1997). The "Z" in the second of the two letters would be a "12", indicating the 12th month (December). The two digit pair after the letters is the day of the month, the 19th. The final three digits indicate production ranking, therefore this imaginary guitar is the 218th instrument built that day.

Yamaha **APX**, **FG**, and **CG** instruments from Taiwan and Indonesia feature 8 digit serial numbers. In this coding scheme, the first digit represents the last digit of the year (for example, 1987 = 7); the second and third numbers indicate the month (numbers 01 through 12); the fourth and fifth numbers will indicate the day of the month, and the final three digits will indicate the production ranking of the instrument.

This system works for most (but not all) of Yamaha products. If a serial number doesn't fit the coding system, Yamaha offers internal research via their website - just email your request in.

House Brands

Identifying "House Brands" Musical Instruments, "All Cats are Grey in the Dark"

The phenomenon of large production companies producing "house brand" instruments dates back to the late 1800s and early 1900s. A "house brand" is defined as a trademark used by distributors/wholesalers/sellers to represent their respective company instead of the manufacturer. These brands are found (for the most part) on budget instruments, although some models are currently sought after by players and collectors on the basis of playability, tone, or relative degree of "coolness" they project.

In the 1800s, many guitar manufacturers were located in New York and Philadelphia; by the early 1900s large guitar factories were centered in Chicago. The "Big Three" that evolved out of the early 1930s were Harmony, Kay, and Valco. Valco, producer of **National** and **Supro** instruments, produced the **Airline** house brand as well as bodies and resonator parts that were sold to Harmony and Kay. However, the majority of house brand instruments found today probably originated at either Harmony or Kay. On the East Coast, Danelectro was a large builder/supplier to Sears & Roebuck under Sears' **Silvertone** label (sometimes up to 85 percent of Danelectro's output).

Prior to World War II, Harmony and Kay sold straight to wholesalers like catalogue houses and large distributors. In turn, these wholesalers would send their salesmen and "reps" out on the road to generate sales — no territories, no music store chains — just straight sales. Business was fierce, and companies used their own private labels to denote "their" product. House brands were typically used as a marketing tool for distributors, wholesalers, and/or retailers to try to eliminate consumer shopping for the best price on popular makes and models of the time. How could you shop a trademark that didn't exist anywhere else? Tom Wheeler, in his book **American Guitars**, quoted former Harmony president Charles A. Rubovits' recollection that the company built 57 private brands for the wholesalers — and sold over five million guitars.

An informative essay about house brands and their place in the vintage guitar spectrum can be found in **Stellas & Stratocasters** (Vintage Guitar Books) by Willie G. Moseley, feature writer/columnist for *Vintage Guitar Magazine*. Moseley's commentary includes a listing of thirty-eight brands and their retailers/distributors, brief ancedotes about the major American manufacturers of budget instruments (Harmony, Kay, etc.) and photos of twenty-five American made house brand instruments.

Since writing that article, Moseley has advised the **Blue Book of Guitars**: "I've come across a couple of other house brands in my travels; one example was a low-end, Stella-type variant with 'Superior' sloppily screen-printed on its headstock. It was one of those cheap, beginner's instruments that were and still are at the nadir of American-made guitars, but so far I haven't been able to determine anything about its brand name...not that it matters too much!"

"It's my opinion, and I dare say the opinion of most vintage guitar enthusiasts, that a good rule of thumb concerning the collectibility of house brands would be something along the lines of 'If it was a budget instrument **then**, it's **proportionally** a budget instrument **now**.' Regretably, as the interest in vintage guitars continues to grow, some individuals and/or businesses tend to assume that simply because an instrument is 'old' and/or 'discontinued' and/or 'American-made', that automatically makes it 'a collector's item' and/or 'valuable'. That's certainly not the case, **especially** with house brands. It's disheartening to walk into a pawn shop and see a Kay-made Silvertone archtop acoustic from the Sixties labeled as an 'antique' and priced at $499, when the instrument is worth no more than $100 in the vintage guitar market, and such incidents are apparently on the increase. And that's unfortunate for everybody."

The **Blue Book of Guitars** is continuing to collect data and evaluate the collectibility and pricing on these house brand instruments. Condition is a large factor in the pricing, as a thirty-to-forty year old guitar ordered from a catalog may have been used/abused by younger members of a household (to the detriment of the instrument). House brand guitars may be antiques, they may be somewhat collectible, and they may be "classic pieces of Americana" (as one antique shop's sign declared), but they should still be relatively inexpensive when compared to the rest of the vintage guitar market. I believe Mr. Moseley to be correct in his C-note assessment of this aspect of the vintage market (at 80% to 90% condition); other music markets that service players and students may find pricing at a slightly wider range of $75 to $150 depending on other factors (playability, possessing an adjustable truss rod, appearance/"coolness" factor, a solid wood top versus plywood, veneer sides, additional parts, etc.). This is the bottom line: this book should help identify the brand/original company, give a few hints as to the quality and desirability, and a price range. The rest is up to you! We will continue to survey the market for pricing trends and "hot" models — further information will be included in upcoming editions of the **Blue Book of Guitars**.

Steven Cherne, Author
Blue Book of Guitars™

Hall of Confusion

With apologies to the 1970 #1 hit song *Ball of Confusion (by the Temptations)* we here at **Blue Book** have opened up this Hall as an addendum to the guitar text. In the course of research, cross-referencing, and too much coffee, certain names of companies appear but can't be pinned down. We assume that instruments that appear in advertising and discussed in books were produced; we also assume (at the risk of making an **ass** of **u** and **me**) that somebody owns them, plays them, and has some information that they can share about them!

One great source of tracking down the "unsung heros" of independent lutherie has been the Internet, specifically the outstanding site maintained by luthier Anthony Huvard: Luthiers Around The World at **www.cybozone.com/fg/luthier.html** If you are an independent guitar builder, or small guitar producing company (or even part of the big MI scene), then you need to be listed here! Another great source in learning about the Classical guitar tradition was Guitar And Guitar Builder at **www.cyberg8t.com/gfa/guitar-builders.html**, which spotlighted a number of the Classical guitar builders and dealers.

Research for future editions of the **Blue Book of Guitars** is an on-going process. What we don't know, we ask; we also enjoy *putting the spotlight* on those sources of information that help us gather knowledge. Anyone interested in writing about any of the following companies or trademarks is invited to contact us at the following:

Blue Book of Guitars, 8009 34th Avenue South Suite #175, Minneapolis, Minnesota 55425
800.877.4867, (FAX) 612. 853.1486
http//:www.bluebookinc.com, email: guitars@bluebookinc.com

We'll be happy to hear from you. In the meantime, let's take a little stroll down the Hall and maybe a diligent player/reader/luthier can shed some light in the dark corners...

Alcivar
(set-neck Gibson copies - Korean?)
Alex Axe
(El Matador bass)
Alliance (France)
Anson Custom Guitars
Steve Beaney (UK luthier)
Marc Beneteau
Acoustic guitar models
Either Quebec or Ontario, Canada
(Sent in by Paul Ruta)
Bremer
Brunet
(The Metalmaster)
Burny (Fernandes line)
Centerstage
Columbia
(Spotted by Michael Wright)
Concorde
Damila Guitars
Steve Davis (luthier)
DD Guitar Design
Deathless Creations
Dega
(Europe, 1960s)
Del Vecchio
Dixon
Erickson
Firstman (Japan)
Fisher Communications
Gadden
Gajic Guitars
(UK luthier Lazar Gajic)
Gamma
(1964-1965, semi-hollowbody Les Paul Style)
(Sent in by John Gallagher of Haverstown, Pennsylvania)
Goldklang (acoustics)
Griffin
(The Bat)
Guitarlia
Halifax
(Hofner 'Beatle Bass'-style copies)
Halle
Richard Harris
(Indianapolis, Indiana)
Hasselberger
Hauke
Hawk (guitars and basses)
Karl Hawser
(Model 610)
Hendrick
(Catalyst model)

Herndon
Classical model made in the U.S.
(Spotted by Brian Mays)
Hernandis
Medium quality acoustic guitars
(Japan, early 1970s)
Nick Hoffman Guitars
(Brian Jones Model)
Holzappel & Beitel
(late 1800s)
Honey
(Japan, 1960s)
Hummingbird
(Japan, 1960s)
Idol
Doug Irwin (luthier)
Joaquim Duarte
(Spotted by Gary Whitehead of Ottawa, Ontario)
Joshia De Jonge
JK Bennett
(Widowmaker model)
Peter Kawa (independent luthier)
K-Muse Photon
Distributed by Phi Tech (late 1980s).
Kamouraska
(Etude model)
Distributed from Canada.
Kansas
(circa 1910 to 1984, Lawrence, Kansas)
Killer Guitars
Kraft
Kulick Custom Guitars and Basses
(Luthier/repairman Barry Kulick)
New York City, New York (circa 1978-1990)
La Primera
Distributed by Pennino of Westminister, California (late 1970s?).
Lang
Archtops built during the 1950s and 1960s.
McBride
(Side Arm model)
Marc Maingard (South Africa luthier)
Mains Custom Guitars
Manhattan (acoustics)
Mann (Japan)
Marsdan Guitar Mfg.
(The Sasquatch)
Mario Mazzella (luthier)
Maybell
M C I/Intertek

Melofonic (1930s ?)
Merrari
(935 Shark V, Explorer)
Miller
Built by E.L. Miller of Parkersburg, West Virginia.
Minister (Japan)
Mitre Guitars
MJH Guitars
(luthier Michael Jacobson-Hardy)
Mory
(Japan, 1960s)
Naruber
(Japan, 1960s)
Neily
Noble Guitars
(UK luthier David Noble)
North American Instruments
(The Custom Legend series)
Northern
LP copy guitar model
Distributed in Canada (circa early/mid 1970s)
(Sent in by Paul Ruta)
Oneida
Pagani (late 1800s)
Panaramic
(Europe, 1960s)
Panoramic
Mid-1950s Italian single cutaway thinline hollow body guitars
(Sent in by David Mignella of Rhode Island)
Distributed by Sam Ash Music Stores.
Shelley Park
Pedulla-Orsini
(Distributed by Wurlitzer circa 1970s)
Pekko Bass (Finland)
Phoenix (Phoenix, Arizona)
Pittilla
Pleasant
Quantum
R.A. Gresco
Rainier
(Bolt-on neck LP copy)
Paul Richardson
(UK guitar builder)
Roch
Santa Fe Guitars (Santa Fe, New Mexico)
Saunders
(DC-111 bass, Cougar guitar)
Ken Savage (UK luthier)
Roch Schneider
Schroeder

Scorpion Custom Guitars
Silver Mellowtone
(Japan, 1960s)
Silver Street
(Nightwing Series)
Company was based in Michigan (and/or Indiana) during the mid to late 1980s, and built other guitars such as the Taxi, Cobra, and Spitfire models.
Skylark
Distributed by J.C. Penney (early 1980s)
Skylark
Alembic-style neck through designs by Matsumoku
(Sent in by David Mignella of Rhode Island)
Ervin Somogyi (luthier)
St. Blues
(St. Louis, Missouri)
Strings 'n Things
(Memphis, Tennessee)
John Starrett
State of the Art
(bound body Strat-style guitars)
Splendor
(Japan, 1960s)
J. R. Stetson & Co.
D. W. Stevens
(Golden, Colorado)
Stevenson
J. R. Stewart
Stutz
Tilben Company
Time Guitars
(Luthier Alan Stack)
Toledo
(Japan, late 1960s/early 1970s)
Tombo
Tornese
Toucan Guitars
Vintage Guitar Company
(The Groovemaster model)
Voss
(circa late 1960s)
Walthari Mittenwald (acoustics)
Westminster
Distributed by Pennino of Westminister, California (late 1970s?)
David Wren (luthier)
Acoustic guitar models
Toronto, Canada
(Sent in by Paul Ruta)

Strings/Trademark Index

Another aspect of tone generation is Strings. How strings interact with the instrument and the player is another crucial portion of the overall "chain" of the sound produced.

The following is a brief review of String Companies.

ADAMAS
Distributed by Kaman Music (OVATION)
P.O. Box 507
Bloomfield CT 06002-0507
203.243.7941
www.kamanmusic.com

CHARLIE STRINGER SNARLING DOGS STRINGS
Dept. GW
P.O. Box 4241
Warren NJ 07059
908.469.2828
(FAX) 908.469.2882

CONCERTISTE
Picato Musician Strings
Unit 24, Treorchy Ind. Est.
Treorchy Mid Glamorgan
United Kingdom CF42 6EJ
44.144.343.7928
(FAX) 44.144.343.3624

J. D'ADDARIO
J. D'Addario & Co.
595 Smith Street
Farmingdale NY 11735
800.323.2746
516.391.5400
(FAX) 516.391.5410
strings@daddario.com
www.daddario.com

D'AQUISTO
20 E. Industry Court
P.O. Box 569
Deer Park NY 11729
516.586.4426

DEAN MARKLEY
3350 Scott Blvd. #45
Santa Clara CA 95054
408.988.2456
www.deanmarkley.com

DR STRINGS
7 Palisades Avenue
Emerson NJ 07630
201.599.0100
(FAX) 201.599.0404
email: DRStrings@aol.com

ELIXIR STRINGS
W. L. Gore & Associates
888.367.5533
email: mail@goremusic.com
www.goremusic.com

ERNIE BALL
P.O. Box 4117
San Luis Obispo CA 93401
805.544.7726

EVERLY
Everly Music Company
P.O. Box 7304-286
North Hollywood CA 91603
888.4EVERLY

FENDER
Fender Musical Instruments Corp.
7975 N Hayden Road
Scottsdale AZ 85258
602.596.9690
(FAX) 602.596.1385
www.fender.com

GHS
G.H.S. Corporation
P.O. Box 136
2813 Wilber Avenue
Battle Creek MI 49016
800.388.4447
616.968.3351
(FAX) 616.968.6913
rmcfee@tdsnet.com
www.ghsstrings.com

GIBSON
Gibson Strings & Accessories
A Manufacturing Division of Gibson Guitar Corp.
1725 Fleetwood Drive
Elgin IL 60123
800.544.2766
708.741.7315
(FAX) 708.741.4644
www.gibson.com

JOHN PEARSE STRINGS
P.O. Box 295
Center Valley PA 18034
610.691.3302

LABELLA
256 Broadway
Newburg NY 12550
914.562.4400

MARI
14 W. 71st Street
New York NY 10023-4209
212.799.6781
(FAX) 212.721.3932

MARTIN STRINGS
C.F.Martin & Co.
510 Sycamore Street
Nazareth PA 18064
800.633.2060
info@mguitar.com
www.mguitar.com

MAXIMA
57 Crooks Avenue
Clifton NJ 07011
201.722.3333
garpc@ix.netcom.com

SABINE
NitroStasis Strings
13301 Highway 441
Alachua FL 32615-8544
904.418.2000
(FAX) 904.418.2001
sabine@sabineinc.com
www.sabineinc.com

S.I.T. STRINGS
815 S. Broadway
Akron OH 44311
330.434.8010
email: sitstrings@aol.com

THOMASTIK-INFELD
P.O. Box 93
Northport NY 11768
800.644.5268
email: 100420.745@compuserve.com
http://kfs.oeaw.ac.at/thom/home.html

YAMAHA STRINGS
6600 Orangethorpe Avenue
Buena Park CA 90620
714.522.9011
(FAX) 714.739.2680

SUNRISE
Sunrise Pickup Systems
8101 Orion Ave. #19
Van Nuys CA 91406
818.785.3428
(FAX) 818.785.9972
JimSunrise@earthlink.net
www.Sunrisepickups.com

VAN ZANDT
Distributed and Produced by VAN ZANDT Pickups
205 Robinson Rd.
Combine TX 75159
214.476.8844
(FAX) 214.476.8844

ZETA
Zeta Music Systems
2230 Livingston St.
Oakland CA 94606
800.622.6434
510.261.1702
(FAX) 510.261.1708

Lutherie Organizations

Association of Stringed Instrument Artisans (ASIA)
c/o David Vinopal
P.O. Box 341
Paul Smiths NY 12970
518.891.5379
(GUITARMAKER is the quarterly newsletter/publication of ASIA)

Guild of American Luthiers (GAL)
8222 South Park Avenue
Tacoma WA 98408
206.472.7853
(AMERICAN LUTHERIE is the quarterly journal of GAL)

Fretted Instrument Guild of America
c/o Glen Lemmer, Editor
2344 S. Oakley Avenue
Chicago IL 60608
(FIGA, official publication)

Trademark Index

ABILENE
Distributed by Advantage Worldwide
800.MUS.ICAL
800.687.4225

ACADEMY
Distributed by Lark in the Morning
P.O. Box 1176
Mendocino CA 95460-1176
707.964.5569
(FAX) 707.964.1979
larkinam@larkinam.com
www.larkinam.com

A.C.E. GUITARS
30 Centre Road, #4
Somersworth NH 03878
603.692.5971
(FAX) 603.592.6015
allan@nh.ultranet.com

LAVEZZI ADALBERTO
Via Cav. di Vitt. Veneto 8
44011 Argenta (FE)
Italy
0532.805845

JOE ALESSI
Instrumental Music Service
221 High Street
Pottstown PA 19464
monjakwa@ptd.net

ALHAMBRA
Manufacturas Alhambra, S.L.
Duquesa de Almo-dovar, 17
Muro del Alcoy, Ali-cante E-03830
Spain
346.553.0011
(FAX) 346.651.6302

ALLEN GUITARS & MANDOLINS
Randy Allen
P.O. Box 1883
Colfax CA 95713
916.346.6590
allen@allenguitar.com
www.allenguitar.com

RICHARD C. ALLEN
R.C. Dick Allen
2801 New Deal Road
Almonte CA 91733
818.442.8806

GUITARRAS ALMANSA
Poligono Industrial El Mugron
C/.Aparadoras 8
(P.O. Box 397)
Almansa Albacete
Spain E-02640
34.67.345678
(FAX) 34.67.345787

ALVAREZ
A Division of St. Louis Music, Inc.
1400 Ferguson Avenue
St. Louis MO 63133
800.727.4512
314.727.4512
(FAX) 314.727.8929

ALVAREZ YAIRI
A Division of St. Louis Music, Inc.
1400 Ferguson Avenue
St. Louis MO 63133
800.727.4512
314.727.4512
(FAX) 314.727.8929

JUAN CARLOS MORAGA ALVAREZ
Rio Blanco 217
Chaiten Chile
jmoraga@entel.cl

AMADA
Distributed by Geneva International Corporation
29 E. Hintz Road
Wheeling IL 60090
800.533.2388
847.520.9970
(FAX) 847.520.9593
geneva-intl@msn.com
www.guitars~amada.com
www.music~instruments~lidl.com

AMALIO BURGUET
Distributed by Saga Musical Instruments
P.O. Box 2841
South San Francisco CA 94083
800.BUY.SAGA
415.742.6888
(FAX) 415.871.7590

AMERICAN ACOUSTECH
4405 Ridge Road W.
Rochester NY 14626-3549
716.352.3225
(FAX) 716.352.8614

AMERICAN ARCHTOP
Dale Unger, Luthier
RD #6, Box 6379-B
Stroudsburg PA 18360
717.992.4956

AMIGO
Distributed by Midco International
P.O. Box 748
908 W. Fayette Avenue
Effingham IL 62401
800.35.MIDCO
800.356.4326
(FAX) 800.700.7006

ANDERSEN STRINGED INSTRUMENTS
Steven Andersen
7811 Greenwood Avenue North
Seattle WA 98103
206.782.8630
(FAX) 206.782.9345
www.hacyon.com/ralevine/andersen

JOHN ANDERSON
Panasonic
Willoughby Road
Bracknell
England
john.anderson@b-e-grp.demon.co.uk

RICARDO FERREIRA
ANDRE
Lisboa Portugal
bizet90@hotmail.com

ANGELO
T. Angelo Industrial Co. Ltd.
4862 Soi Phomjit
Rama IV Road
Prakanong Klongtoey
Bangkok 10110
Thailand
662.392.1041
(FAX) 662.712.1153
aprasart@loxinfo.co.th

ANGUS GUITARS
P.O. Box 737
Laguna Beach CA 92652-0737
714.497.3198
714.497.2110

ANTARES
Distributed by VMI Industries
Vega Musical Instruments
P.O. Box 1357
2980-D Enterprise Street
Brea CA 92822-1357
800.237.4864
714.572.1492
(FAX) 714.572.9321

ANTONIO LORCA
Distributed by David Perry Guitar Imports
14519 Woodstar Court
Leesburg VA 22075-6055
800.593.1331
703.771.1331
(FAX) 703.771.8170

SCANDURRA ANTONIO
Via Palazzotto 50
Catania Italy
095.431901

NICK APOLLONIO
P.O. Box 791
Rockport ME 04856
207.236.6312

APPLAUSE
Distributed by the Kaman Music Corporation
P.O. Box 507
Bloomfield CT 06002-0507
800.647.2244
860.243.7105
(FAX) 860.243.7287
www.kamanmusic.com

ARBOR
Distributed by Midco International
P.O. Box 748
Effingham IL 62401
800.356.4326
217.342.9211
(FAX) 217.347.0316

ARIA
ARIA PRO II
Aria USA/NHF
9244 Commerce High-way
Pennsauken NJ 08110
800.524.0441
609.663.8900
(FAX) 609.663.0436
ariagtrs@aol.com
www.ariausa.com

ARIANA
Distributed by Aria USA/NHF
9244 Commerce High-way
Pennsauken NJ 08110
800.524.0441
609.663.8900
(Fax) 609.663.0436

GEORGE DAVID ARMSTRONG
G.D. Armstrong - Luthier
16783 NW Greenhoot
Yamhill OR 97148
goldmanarmstrong@msn.com

ART AND LUTHERIE
Distibuted by La Si Do, Inc.
4240 Sere'
St. Laurent Quebec
Canada H4T 1A6
514.343.5560
(FAX) 514.343.5098
sales@lasido.com
www.lasido.com

ARTESANO
Distributed by Juan Orozco Corporation
P.O. Box 812
Maunabo PR 00707
800.499.5042
809.861.1045
(FAX) 09.861.4122

MARIO ARTESE
Liutisti & Liutai
Via Cattaneo, 11/g
Cosenza
Italy 87100
maartese@tin.it

ARTISTA
Distributed by Musicorp/MBT
Hondo Guitar Company
P.O. Box 30819
Charleston SC 29417
800.845.1922
803.763.9083
(FAX) 803.763.9096

ASHLAND
Distributed by VMI Industries
Vega Musical Instruments
P.O. Box 1357
2980-D Enterprise Street
Brea CA 92822-1357
800.237.4864
714.572.1492
(FAX) 714.572.9321

ASPEN
Distributed by the International Music Corporation (IMC)
1316 E. Lancaster Ave-nue
Fort Worth TX 76102
800.433.5627
817.336.5114
(FAX) 817.870.1271

ASPRI CREATIVE ACOUSTICS
12145 de l'Acadie
Montreal PQ
Canada H3M 2V1
514.333.2853
(FAX) 514.333.3153

ASTURIAS
Distributed by J.T.G. of NASHVILLE
5350 Hillsboro Road
Nashville TN 37215
615.665.8384
(FAX) 615.665.9468

ASTRO GUITARS, INC.
Ken Harris
1256 Industrial Blvd.
Port St. Lucie FL 33452

ATELIER Z
Day's Corporation
MH-Building 4F 3-15-7
Nishi-Shinjuku
Shinjuku-Ku
Tokyo 160
Japan
81.3.3377.0157
(FAX) 81.3.3377.0183
f2615943@nv.aif.or.jp

AUGUSTINO LOPRINZI GUITARS
Augustino LoPrinzi
1929 Drew Street
Clearwater FL 34625
813.447.2276
loprinzi@gate.net
equitablebusiness.com/loprinzi_guitars

AUSTIN
A Division of St. Louis Music, Inc.
1400 Ferguson Avenue
St. Louis MO 63133
800.727.4512
314.727.4512
(FAX) 314.727.8929

ALAIN AVENTINI
Chez Scotto Musique
180, Rue de Rome
13006 Marseille
France
melodiccontrol@usa.net

AXELSON
Axelson Guitar
706 Lake Avenue South
Duluth MN 55802
218.720.6086

AXTECH
Saehan International Co., Ltd.
R# 1503 Leaders B/D
1599-11
Seocho-Dong, Seocho-Ku
Seoul Korea
82.2.523.6459
(FAX) 82.2.523.6455
(FAX) 82.2.523.6457

R. J. AYLWARD
The Loft, Unit 19
19 Bourne Road
Bexley, Kent
DA5 1LR England
01322.553393

BAARSLAG AND ESPINOZA
Rene Baarslag, Gerente
Lista de Correos
Lanjaron
Granada 18420
Spain

ROGER BACORN CUSTOM GUITARS
Nichols NY

BARANIK GUITAR
1739 E. Broadway
Road
Tempe AZ 85282
602.755.7155

BARDSONG RECYCLED STRING INSTRUMENTS
Shawn & Jenny Spencer
588 Highcrest Drive
Nashville TN 37211
bardsong@bellsouth.net
spaceformusic.com/bardsong

CARL BARNEY
P.O. Box 128
Southbury CT 06488
203.264.9207

GUITARRIA GERMAN PEREZ BARRANCO
*German Perez,
Barranco, Luthier*
Cuesta de Gomerez 10
Granada 18009
Spain
guitarras_german@hotmail.com
www.geocities.com/nashville/8901

B.C. RICH
B.C. Rich International, Inc.
17205 Eucalyptus
Suite B-5
Hesperia CA 92345
760.956.1599
(FAX) 760.956.1565
www.bcrichguitars.com
B.C. Rich Guitars USA
432 N. Arrowhead Ave.
San Bernadino CA
92401
909.888.6080
(FAX) 909.884.1767
*Distributed by Davitt & Hanser
Music
(NJ, Platinum, and
Bronze Series)*
4940 Delhi Pike
Cincinnati OH 45238
800.999.5558
513.451.5000
(FAX) 513.347.2298

B D DEY
*B D Dey Musical
Instruments*
Dlouha 4309
Zlin 760 01
Czech Republic
00420.67.36702
(FAX) 00420.67.36629
mmmusic@zl.unext.cz
www.inext.cz/bddey

BEAR CREEK GUITARS
556 Spencer Street
Monterey CA 93940
408.657.9399
(FAX) 408.375.4029
bcguitar@bcguitar.com
www.bcguitar.com

JUSTIN BELSHE
3606 59th Street
Lubbock TX 79413
jbelshe@aol.com

BELTONA
8 Knowle Road
Leeds LS4 2PJ
United Kingdom
44.113.275.3454
(FAX) 44.113.275.3454

THOMAS E. BELTRAN
137 North Larchmont
Blvd.
Suite 256
Los Angeles CA
90004
tbeltran@wavenet.com

ROBERT BENEDETTO
RR 1 - Box 1347
E. Stroudsburg PA
18301
717.223.0883
(FAX) 717.223.7711
www.benedetto-guitars.com

PETER BENGTSSON
*Peter Bengtsson
Instrumentateljen*
Backavagen 9
S-29475 Solvesborg
Sweden
peter.bengtsson@instat.se

MICHAEL AND MARJORIE BENNETT
Bennett's Music
16134 NE 87th
Redmond WA 98052

ROBERT A. BENNETT
3971 Saranac Drive
Sharpsville PA 16150
decase@aol.com

BENTLY
A Division of St. Louis Music, Inc.
1400 Ferguson Avenue
St. Louis MO 63133
800.727.4512
314.727.4512
(FAX) 314.727.8929

BERTRAM HEARTWOOD GUITARS
Jay Bertram
P.O. Box 474
Albany KY 42602-0474

BEYOND THE TREES
Fred Carlson
1987 Smith Grade
Santa Cruz CA 95060
408.423.9264
wildsols@BeyondTheTrees.com
www.BeyondTheTrees.com

BIGHEART
BigHeart Slide Company
937 Rashford Drive
Placentia CA 92870
714.993.1573
(FAX) 714.579.3019
bgheart1@aol.com
www.bigheartslide.com

BISCAYNE
*Distributed by Tropical Music
Corporation*
7091 N.W. 51st Street
Miami FL 33166-5629
305.594.3909
(FAX) 305.594.0786
www.tropicalmusic.com

HERMANN BISCHOFBERGER
1314 E. John
Seattle WA 98102

BLACK MOUNTAIN INSTRUMENTS
David Johnston
100 Foothill Blvd.
Calistoga CA 94515
david@blackmtninstruments.com
www.blackmtninstruments.com

TOM BLACKSHEAR
17303 Springhill Drive
San Antonio TX
78232-1552
210.494.1141
(FAX) 210.494.1141

BLAIR GUITARS LTD.
24 Haverhill Street
Andover MA 01810
978.749.0088
(FAX) 806.872.9942

BLANCHARD GUITARS
Mark Blanchard
P.O. Box 8030
Mammoth Lakes CA
93546
760.934.4386
(FAX) 760.934.2281
markath@qnet.com
www.qnet.com/~markathblanchard.guitars.htm

BILL BLAND
3367 N. Winstel Blvd.
Tucson AZ 85716
giapetto@msn.com

BLUERIDGE
*Distributed by Saga Musical
Instruments*
429 Littlefield Avenue
P.O. Box 2841
South San Francisco
CA 94080
800.BUY.SAGA
415.588.5558
(FAX) 415.871.7590

BLUESOUTH
BlueSouth Guitars
P.O. Box 3562
Florence AL 35630
205.764.7431
ronnie@hiwaay.net

BOAZ ELKAYAM GUITARS
11208 Huston Street
#2
North Hollywood CA
91601
818.766.4456

BOOM BASSES
*Distributed by Donnell
Enterprises*
24 Parkhurst Street
Chico CA 95628-6856
800.585.7659
(FAX) 916.893.4845
Donnellent@aol.com

ENRICO BOTTELLI
Via Cuzzi 16
20155 Milano
Italy
02.39214715

MARIO BOUCHARD
*Lutherie Mario Bouchard
Enr.*
295, Avenue Giguere
Suite 005
Vanier Quebec
Canada G1M 1X7
guitar@total.net
www.total.net/~guitar/

PHILIP AND PAM BOULDING
P.O Box 4086
Seattle WA 98104

DANA BOURGEOIS GUITARS
235 Goddard Road
Lewiston ME 04240
207.786.9320
(FAX) 207.786.4018
dana@danabourgeois.com
www.danabourgeois.com
*Distributed by Akai Musical
Instrument Corporation*
4710 Mercantile Drive
Fort Worth TX 76137
800.433.5627
817.831.9203
akaiUSA@ix.netcom.com
www.akai.com/akaipro

RALPH S. BOWN
The Old Coach House
1, Paver Lane
Walmgate York Y01
2TS
England
01904.621011

JAMES C. BOYCE
North Falmouth MA
508.563.9494
umboyce@capecod.net

BOZO PODUNAVAC
2340 Englewood Road
Englewood FL 34233-633
941.474.3288

AARON BRADFORD
Dixieland Guitars
9512 Downing Street
Richmond VA 23233
bradfor@erols.com

BRANDENBURG STRINGED INSTRUMENTS
Dietrich Knapp
7355 Eagle Creek Drive
Centerville OH 45459
pimmel90@aol.com

BREEDLOVE GUITAR CO.
19885 8th Street
Bend OR 97701
541.385.8339
(FAX) 541.385.8183
slhender@breedloveguitars.com
www.breedloveguitars.com

BRIDWELL WORKSHOP
426 W. Wilson Street
Palatine IL 60067-4920
847.934.0374
Bridwshp@aol.com

CLINT BRILEY
Briley Guitars
1926 Albany Drive
Clearwater FL 34623
813.669.0256
randyk@flanet.com

EDUARDO THIAGO AREAS BRITO
Shin QI-08 CONJ-09
Casa 16
Brasilia DF 71520-290
botafogo@mre.gov.br

JAMES BROWN
13174 S. 18th Street
Vicksburg MI 49097

BRUKO
*Distributed by Lark in the
Morning*
P.O Box 1176
Mendocino CA 95460-1176
707.964.5569
(FAX) 707.964.1979
larkinam@larkinam.com
www.larkinam.com

RICHARD E. BRUNE
800 Greenwood Street
Evanston IL 6021-4312

BRUZE CONTRABASS
6922 Kramer Street
San Diego CA 92111
619.541.2635

CYNDY BURTON
2812 SE 37th Avenue
Portland OR 97202

BUSCARINO GUITARS, INC.
John Buscarino
9075-B 130th Avenue
North
Largo FL 33773
813.586.4992
(FAX) 813.581.4535
www.netace.com/buscarino

CRAIG BUZZART
5235 Diane Way
Santa Rosa CA 95409-5118
Craig_Buzzart@lamg.com

KURT CADDY
11852 N. Ridgetop
Lane
Brighton MO 65617
kcaddy@sbuniv.edu

JOHN CALKIN
P.O. Box 421
Greenville VA 24440

CALVIN CRAMER
*Distributed by Musima North
America, Inc.*
13540 N. Florida Avenue
Suite 206 A
Tampa FL 33613
813.961.8357
(FAX) 813.961.8514

FRED W. CAMPBELL
F.W. Campbell & Sons
1709 Little Orchard
San Jose CA 95125
laquerboy@aol.com

M. CAMPELLONE GUITARS
Mark Campellone
(Box 125)
725 Branch Avenue
Providence RI 02904
401.351.4229
www.businesson.com/
guitars/index.htm

GUITARRES CAMPS, S.L.
Javier Camps Masos
Canigo, 25
Porqueres 17834
Spain
jcamps13@piue.xtec.es

LUCIO ANTONIO CARBONE
Via C. Goldoni 77
20129 Milano
Italy
02.70100028

STEVE CARLISLE
12510 Sagamore Forest Lane
Reistertown MD 23136

BOB CARMAN
Kathy & Bob's Planet
1702 E. Pepper Circle # 3
Mesa AZ 85203
bobcrmn@worldnet.att.net

CARMODY GUITARS LTD.
Jim Carmody
1060 Clearview Avenue
Burlington Ontario
Canada L7T 2J1
ginette.drovin@sympatico.ca

CARODYCE INSTRUMENTS
Tim Deacon
11 Castle Road
Weybridge
Surrey KT13 9QP
England
www.cybozone.com/fg/deacon.html

JAMES CARRETT
430 Stenner Street
Toowoomba Queensland
Australia 4350
carrettj@ozemail.com.au

CHRISTOPHER CARRINGTON
Open Ocean Music
8255 San Cristobal
Dallas TX 75128
neptune@isource.net
www.isource.net/~neptune

KEN CARTWRIGHT
Cartwright's Music Repair Shop
189 Liberty Street NE
Salem OR 97301

CARVIN
12340 World Trade Drive
San Diego CA 92128
800.854.2235
619.487.8700
(FAX) 619.487.8160
www.carvinguitars.com

CASELEY GUITAR COMPANY
Glen Caseley
105 - 272 E. 4th
Vancouver British Columbia
Canada V5T 4S2

IGNACIO CASTRILLON
Calle 73 #49-60
Medellin Columbia

DAVE CASSOTTA
SonFather Guitars
5000 Plumbago Place
Rocklin CA 95677
sfguitar@inreach.com
home.inreach.com/sfguitar/

CATALUNA
Distributed by Reliance International Corporation
3rd Fl., No. 175, Sec. 2
An-Ho Road
P.O. Box No. 96-140
Taipei 106
Taiwan R.O.C.
886.2.736.8151
(FAX) 886.2.738.6491
(FAX) 886.2.738.2614

CATCHINGS GUITARS
Tom Catchings
330 Jackson Avenue
McComb MS 39648
tomcat@telapex.com

C B ALYN GUITARWORKS
935 Galloway Street
Pacific Palisades CA 90272
310.454.8196
(FAX) 310.459.7517

CARLO CECCON
Via Alessi, 13
Milan 20123
Italy
39.2.389955409
ceccon@iol.it

CARLO CECCONI
Via Alpi Apuane 44
Roma 00141
Italy
06.8170176

CELEBRITY
Distributed by the Kaman Music Corporation
P.O. Box 507
Bloomfield CT 06002-0507
800.647.2244
860.243.7105
(FAX) 860.243.7287
www.kamanmusic.com

CFOX
Charles Fox Guitars
468 Moore Lane
Healdsburg CA 95448
707.433.8228
(FAX) 707.433.8180
cfox@wco.com
www.wco.com/~cfox
www.cfoxguitars.com

CHABOT GUITAR CO.
Paul Chabot
18033 East Gunnison Place
Aurora CO 80017
guitarmaker@milehigh.net
www.milehigh.net/guitarmaker

FERNANDEZ SETIAHADI CHANDRA
Perumahan Griya Pabean LI/F55
Sidoarjo Surabaya
East Java
Indonesia

CHAPEC
Chapec Companhia Industrial de Alimentos
Gustavo Antonio De Nadal
Rua Lauro Miller, 304-E, Centro
Chapec SC 89.800-000
55.(049)723.0295

CHAPIN GUITARS
1709-D Little Orchard
San Jose CA 95125
408.295.6252
shaydz@earthlink.net

WILLIAM CHAPMAN STRINGED INSTRUMENTS
Columbia SC

CHAPPELL GUITARS
2619 Columbia Avenue
Richmond CA 94804
510.528.2904
(FAX) 510.528.8310
guitarsrus@earthlink.net
www.home.earthlink.net/~guitarsrus

CHARVEL
Distributed by Akai Musical Instrument Corporation
4710 Mercantile Drive
Fort Worth TX 76137
800.433.5627
817.831.9203
akaiUSA@ix.netcom.com
www.akai.com/akaipro

CHATWORTH GUITARS
England
01423.536383

CHORDACOPIA GUITARS
Peter Roehling
31881 Florida Street
Redlands CA 92373
peter_roehling@eee.org

CHRIS LARKIN CUSTOM
Fine Handmade Guitars
Castlegregory
Co. Kerry
Ireland
353.66.39330
(FAX) 353.66.39330

CIGANA
Guitarras Cigana, Lda.
Av. Agostinho Ribeiro
Edificio Sta. Ovaia - BL 4
Felgueiras
Portugal
351.55.925785
(FAX) 351.55.925785

CIMARRON GUITARS
538 Sherman
P.O. Box 511
Ridgway CO 81432-0511
970.626.4464

CITRON
Harvey Citron Enterprises
282 Chestnut Hill Road #4

Woodstock NY 12498
914.679.7138
(FAX) 914.679.3221
harvey@citron-guitars.com
www.citron-guitars.com

EUGENE CLARK
P.O. Box 710
El Cerrito CA 94530

NEIL ALEXANDER CLARK
Fishguard
West Wales
United Kingdom

ED CLAXTON GUITARS
Ed CLaxton
2527-C Mission Street
Santa Cruz CA 95060
408.469.4563
(FAX) 408.426.9875

C L E GUITARS
Corey L. Eller
RD 4, Box 79A
Moundsville WV 26041

CLOUTIER GUITARS
Steve Cloutier
Tree Frog Instruments
521 Short Street
Faribault MN 55021
treefrog@ptel.net
www.means.net/~treefrog/cloutierguitars.html

JEFFREY C. COLE
Cole Studios
4862 Country Road 12
Andover NY 14806
colestu@vivanet.com

COLIN'S GUITAR WORKS
M. Colin Burch
1205-B Antioch Pike
Nashville TN 37211
cgw@vol.com
www.vol.com/~cgw

COLLINGS
Collings Guitars, Inc.
11025 Signal Hill Drive
Austin TX 78737-2834
512.288.7776
(FAX) 512.288.6045
www.collingsguitars.com

COLLOPY GUITARS
Richard Collopy
301 Balboa Street
San Francisco CA 94118
415.221.2990
(FAX) 415.221.6380
rcollopy@pacbell.net

BILL COMINS
P.O. Box 611
Willow Grove PA 19090
215.784.0314
(FAX) 215.784.0314

CONDE HERMANOS
Conde Hermanos - Sobrino de Esteso
C/Felipe V, 2
Madrid
Spain
condehermanos@mx2.redestb.es
www.condehermanos.com
Distributed by the Luthier Music Corporation
341 W. 44th Street
New York NY 10036
212.397.6038
(FAX) 212.397.6048
luthier@tiac.net
www.tiac/net/users/luthier

MIKE CONNER
Fretted Instrument Adjustment & Repair
7010 Longshore Avenue
Seneca SC 29672
j_m_conner@valenite.com

COOG INSTRUMENTS
Ronald Cook
218 Plateau Avenue
Santa Cruz CA 95060
coog@slip.net
www.coog.com

CORDOBA
Distributed by Guitar Salon International
3100 Donald Douglas Loop North
Santa Monica CA 90405
310.399.2181
310.396.9283
GSImail@guitarsalon.com
www.guitarsalon.com

HUMBERTO CORREA
Flores Condor de Columbia
Carrera 12A #77A-05
Bogata
Columbia

CORT MUSICAL INSTRUMENTS
3451 W. Commercial Avenue
Northbrook IL 60062
847.498.6491
(FAX) 847.498.5370
postmaster@cort.com
www.cort.com

COSI
Composite Stringed Instruments
Distributed by ATN International
Rue de l'Avenir
Z.I. des Playes
83140 Six-Fours-Les Plages
France
+33.494.879878
(FAX) +33.494.060915
cosi_atn_int@compuserve.com

PETER COURA
Guitar Center
SchumannStr. 15
60325 Frankfurt
Germany
011.49.6975.2744

AARON COWLES
Aaron's Music Service
113 S. Main
Vicksburg MI 49097

CRAFTER
Exclusively distributed in the U.S. by HSS
A Division of Hohner, Inc.
10223 Sycamore Drive
Ashland VA 23005
804.550.2700
(FAX) 801.550.2670

CRAFTERS OF TENNESSEE, LLC
Mark Taylor
14860 Lebanon Road
Old Hickory TN 37138
615.773.7200
(FAX) 615.773.7201
cmtaylor@usit.net

CUDNEY GUITARS
Russ Cudney
P.O. Box 998
Oakley CA 94561
axmaker@ix.netcom.com
www2.netcom.com/~
axmaker/guitars.html

CUMBUS
Distributed by Lark in the Morning
P.O Box 1176
Mendocino CA 95460-1176
707.964.5569
(FAX) 707.964.1979
larkinam@larkinam.com
www.larkinam.com

WILLIAM R. CUMPIANO
Stringfellow Guitars
237 B South Street
Northampton MA 01060
413.586.3730
(FAX) 413.585.1595
eljibaro@crocker.com

CURBOW
Curbow String Instruments, Inc.
24 Allen Lane
Morgantown GA 30560
706.374.2873
(FAX) 706.374.2530
curbow@copperhill.com

CUSTOM AX GUITARS
Edison NJ

THE CUSTOM JOB
Angwin CA

PAUL CYAMPAGNE
8660 Jeanne - Mance
Montreal Quebec
Canada H2P 2S6

DAVID DAILY
Distributed by Kirkpatrick Guitar Studio
4607 Maple Avenue
Baltimore MD 21227-4023
410.242.2744
(FAX) 410.242.0326
info@guitar1stop.com

DAKOTA
Dakota Guitars
Distributed by Sound Trek Distributors U.S.A.
2119 W. Hillsborough Avenue
Tampa FL 33603
888.466.TREK
www.sound-trek.com

TED DALACK
8940 Bay Drive
Gainesville GA 30506
770.889.1104

TITO DALMEDO
Preston
England
01772.718907
0973.163205

D'ANGELICO
Distributed by Vestax
Vestax Corporation
2-37-1 Kamiuma
Setagayaku
Tokyo 154-0011
03.3412.7011
(FAX) 03.3412.7013
vestax-corporation@msn.com

D'ANGELICO II
Archtop Enterprises, Inc.
1980 Broadcast Plaza
Merrick NY 11566
516.868.4877
516.223.3421

D'ANGELICO REPLICA
Working Musician
1760 Claridge Street
Arcadia CA 91006
818.255.5554

D'ARCY GUITARS
Paul Avenell
Belmont Road
Brisbane Queensland
Australia 4153
pavmuse@powerup.com.au

JAY DARMSTADTER
1724 Allied Street
Charlottesville VA 22901

DAVID L. DART
P.O. Box 322
520 Hwy 128
Navarro CA 95463
ddart@pacific.net
www.luthier.com

DAVE MAIZE ACOUSTIC BASS GUITARS
Dave Maize
999 Holton Road
Talent OR 97540
503.535.9052
(FAX) 503.535.9052
dmaize@wave.net
www.vertexgroup.com/maize

DAVIDSON STRINGED INSTRUMENTS
P.O. Box 150758
Lakewood CO 80215
303.984.1896
guitars@rmi.net

PETER DAVIES
23 Heathwood Road
Cardiff
Wales CF4 4JL
United Kingdom
petelorna@aol.com

J. THOMAS DAVIS
3135 N. High Street
Columbus OH 43202-1125
614.263.0264
(FAX) 614.447.0174
JTDGuitars@aol.com

K.D. DAVIS GUITARS
Kevin D. Davis
853 Second Street West
Sonoma CA 95476
inivekdboy@sprynet.com

KYLE DAVIS
Just Guitars
106 Forest Lane
Madisonville KY 42431
cbta@vci.net

RICK DAVIS
Running Dog
RD 2, Box 57
Richmond VT 05477

WILLIAM DAVIS
Handbuilt Guitars
57 Main Street
Boxford MA 01921
508.887.0282
(FAX) 508.887.7214

DE CAVA FRETTED INSTRUMENTS
James R. De Cava
P.O. Box 131
Stratford CT 06497
203.377.0096
888.661.0229
JRDeCava@aol.com

D. C. HILDER BUILDER
2 Yorkshire Street N.
Guelph Ontario
Canada N1H 5A5
519.821.6030

LOREN PAUL DECK
Wire & Wood Guitars
306 S. Oak Knoll Avenue
Pasadena CA 91101
wirewood@macconnect.co
www.macconnect.com/~wirewood

DE LORENE ACOUSTICS, INC.
7304 184th Street
Surrey British Columbia
Canada V4N 3G5
604.574.8041
(FAX) 604.574.4889

DEAN
Distributed by Armadillo Enterprises
15251 Roosevelt Blvd.
Suite 206
Clearwater FL 33760
800.793.5273
727.796.8868
(FAX) 727.797.9448
gtr&bass@armadilloent.co
www.armadilloent.com

DEAN USA
7091 N.W. 51st Street
Miami FL 33166
305.594.3909
(FAX) 305.594.0786

DEAR GUITARS
Distributed by L.A. Guitar Works
19320 Vanowen Street
Reseda CA 91335
818.758.8787
(FAX) 818.758.8788

DEERING BANJO COMPANY
7936 Lester Avenue
Lemon Grove CA 91945-1822
800.845.7791
619.464.8252
(FAX) 619.464.0833
Deeringban@aol.com
www.torranceweb.com/category/music/deering/deering.htm

DEIMEL GUITARWORKS
Frank Deimel
Bautzener Str. 14
10829 Berlin
Germany
deimelguitarwoks@berlin.snafu.de

R. J. DiCARLO
Classical Guitar Maker
141 Roosevelt Avenue
Massapequa Park NY 11762
516.795.3941

DILLON
Dillon Guitars
RR # 4 Box 115 A
Bloomsburg PA 17815-9124
717.784.7552
(FAX) 717.387.8135

ROB DINES
Robz Guitars
473 California Street
Santa Clara CA 95050
rdines@divi.com

MARTIN DIXON
England
01487.823182

DOBRO
Distributed by Gibson Musical Instruments
1818 Elm Hill Park
Nashville TN 37210-3781
800.283.7135
615.871.4500
(FAX) 615.889.5509
www.gibson.com

GARY DONEFER
Slugmeister Bass and Guitar
P.O. Box 1718
Mendocino CA 95460
gdonefer@mcn.org

MICHAEL DUNN
708 3rd Avenue
New Westminster British Columbia
Canada V3M 1N7
604.524.1943
www.portal.ca/~django/guitars.html

DUNWELL GUITARS
Magnolia Star Route
1891 CR 68-J
Nederland CO 80466
303.939.8870
dunwell@jnov.colorado.edu

GUITARES MAURICE DUPONT
Maurice Dupont, Luthier
20, Port-Boutiers
16100 Cognac France
Distributed by Paul Hostetter
2550 Smith Grade
Santa Cruz CA 95060
408.427.2241
(FAX) 408.427.0343
music@cruzio.com

DURANGO
Distributed by Saga Musical Instruments
429 Littlefield Avenue
South San Francisco CA 94080
800.BUY.SAGA
415.588.5558
415.871.7590

EAGLE
Eagle Country Instruments
Rieslingweg 12C
Murr Germany
49.714.424736
(FAX) 49.714.4209115

BRIAN EASTWOOD GUITARS
Brian Eastwood
408 Newchurch Road
Stacksteads
Bacup OL13 0LD
England
011.44.1706.874549

DILLON

CHRIS ECCLESHALL
Unit 2
Webber's Way
Darington, Totnes
Devon
England TQ9 6JY
01803.862364

E. C. POL GUITAR COMPANY
Jay Duncan
Vancouver British Columbia
Canada
www.personal.smartt.com/~amirault/duncan.html

EDWARDS GUITAR RESEARCH LTD.
Bill Edwards
8892 N. 56th Street
Temple Terrace FL 33617

MICK EDWARDS
48 Dukes Lane
Adelaide
South Australia 5000
micke@adelaide.on.net

EHLERS GUITARS
Rob Ehlers
408 4th Avenue
Oregon City OR 97045
503.655.7546

EICHELBAUM CUSTOM GUITARS
1735 Mountain Avenue
Santa Barbara CA 93101
805.563.6028
samusic@samusic.com
www.samusic.com

EISELE
Donn Eisele
923 Mokapu Blvd.
Kailua HI 96734
808.254.6679
Eiselegtr@aol.com

EKO MUSICAL INSTRUMENTS
Zona Ind. E. Fermi
62010 Montelupone
(MC)
Italy
0733.226271
(FAX) 0733.226546
info@eko.it
www.eko.it
www.ekoguitars.com

EL CID
Distributed by L.A. Guitar Works
19320 Vanowen Street
Reseda CA
818.758.8787
(FAX) 818.758.8788

JEFFREY ELLIOT
2812 SE 37th Avenue
Portland OR 97202
www.cybozone.com/fg/elliot.html

KLAS ELDH
Friman Vag
Froson Osterund
Sweden 83254
eldh@mail.bip.net
www.home6.swipnet.se/~w-62511/klas/klasbas.htm

ENCORE

Distributed by John Hornby Skewes & Co., Ltd.
Salem House
Parkinson Approach
Garforth Leeds
LS25 2HR England
0113.286.6411
(FAX) 0113.286.8518

EPI

Distributed by Gibson Musical Instruments
1050 Acorn Drive
Suite A
Nashville TN 37210
800.283.7135
615.871.4500
(FAX) 615.872.7768
www.gibson.com

EPIPHONE

Distributed by Gibson Musical Instruments
Epiphone Company
645 Massman Drive
Nashville TN 37210
800.283.7135
615.871.4500
(FAX) 615.872.7768
jazor@gibson.com
www.gibson.com

MATS ERIKSSON

Hansta 3
Vingaker
Sweden S-64391
mats.eriksson@vingaker.
mail.telia.com

ERRINGTON GUITARS

Cravengate
Richmond, North Yorks
England DL10 4RE
01748.824700

ESPANOLA

Distributed by V.J. Rendano Music Company, Inc.
7152 Market Street
Youngstown OH
44512
800.321.4048
330.758.0881
(FAX) 330.758.1096

La ESPANOLA

GUITARRAS ESPANOLA

Prol. 20 de Noviembre
1513
Paracho Michoacan
60250
Mexico
91.452.50152
(FAX) 91.452.50074

ESTEVE GUITARS

GUITARRAS FRANCISCO ESTEVE

Camino al Mar, 15
46120 Alboraya
Valencia Espana
346.18.55974
(FAX) 346.18.56077
Distributed by Fernandez Music
P.O. Box 5153
Irvine CA 92716
949.856.1537
949.856.1529
fernandezmusic@worldnet
.att.net

EUPHANON COMPANY

Walter Lipton
P.O. Box 100
Orford NH 03777
603.353.4882

EVANS GUITAR PRODUCTS

Robert Tilley
961 Dunford Avenue
Victoria British Colum-
bia
Canada V9B 2S4

EVD STRING INSTRUMENTS

Edward W. Dick
1869 S. Pearl Street
Denver CO 80210
evd303@aol.com
www.musicore.com/evd

EVERETT GUITARS

Kent Everett
2338 Johnson Ferry Rd.
Atlanta GA 30341
770.451.2485
everett@pop.mindspring.com

EVERGREEN MOUNTAIN INSTRUMENTS

Jerry Nolte
1608 Jasper
Cove OR 97824
www.eosc.osshe.edu/~
jkraft/jnhome.htm

NEIL L. FABRICANT

821 Westfield Avenue
Elizabeth NJ 07208
drfab@aol.com

MARTIN FAIR

Route 1, Box 174
Santa Fe NM 87501

FAIR LADY

Kwo Hsiao Company, Ltd.
3 FL. No. 297-4
Sec. 3
Roosevelt Road
Taipei
Taiwan
886.2.2362.7585
886.2.2362.0710
(FAX) 886.2.2363.8530
kwohsiao@ms19.hinet.net

FENDER

Fender Musical Instruments Corporation
7975 North Hayden
Road
Scottsdale AZ 85258-
3246
602.596.9690
(FAX) 602.596.1384
www.fender.com

FERNANDES

Fernandes Guitars U.S.A., Inc.
12600 Saticoy Street
South
North Hollywood CA
91605
800.318.8599
818.764.8383
(FAX) 818.764.0080
fernandes1@aol.com
www.fernandesguitars.com

MARIO ROSAZZA FERRARIS

Via P. Cossa 3
Roma
Italy
06.3230741

DANNY FERRINGTON

P.O. Box 923
Pacific Palisades CA
90272
310.454.0692

JOSE ANTONIO RUOTOLO FILHO

Rua dos Trilhos, 2096
Sao Paulo SP 03168-
010
ruotolo@mandic.com.br

FINOCCHIO GUITARS

Frank Finocchio
20 South Maple Street
Easton PA 18042
610.258.2268

FITZPATRICK JAZZ GUITARS

54 Enfield Avenue
Wickford RI 02852
401.294.4801

FLANDERS CUSTOM GUITARS

Distributed by Fretboard Korner
520 Hawkins Avenue
Lake Ronkonkoma NY
11779-2327
516.588.4167
Fretboard@CrysJen.com
www.CrysJen.com

FLEISHMAN INSTRUMENTS

Harry Fleishman, Luthier
4500 Whitney Place
Boulder CO 80303
303.499.1614

W. FLOHR

Jazzebel
Kerktoren 4
Middelburg Zld
Netherlands
flos1@pi.net

RUBEN FLORES

P.O. Box 2746
Seal Beach CA 90740
310.598.9800
(FAX) 310.598.9800

E.A. FOLEY GUITARS

Ed Foley
P.O. Box 646
Andover NJ 07821
973.786.6077
(FAX) 973.786.5627

ALAN FONTANILLA

P.O. Box 31423
San Francisco CA
94131
415.642.9375

FOSTER GUITAR MANUFACTURING

Jimmy Foster
76353 Eugene Wallace
Road
Covington LA 70435
504.892.9822
guitars@neosoft.com
www.fosterguitars.com

MAURIZIO FOTI

Via Alessi 13
Milan
Italy 20123
39.2.58101241
mf@iol.it

FRAMUS

Postfach 10010
D-08258 Mark-
neukirchen
Germany
3742.25550
(FAX) 3742.55599
wwpresse@aol.com

FREDDY'S FRETS

2520 Meritt Road
Welland Ontario
Canada L3B 5N5
905.384.0303
(FAX) 905.384.0014
freddy@cgocable.net
www.cgocable.net/~freddy/

FRISCO GUITAR WORKS

Frisco TX

FROGGY BOTTOM GUITARS

RR 1 Box 1505
Timson Hill Road
Newfane VT 05345
802.348.6665
(FAX) 802.348.6665
froggy@sover.net

FRUDUA GUITAR WORKS

Via Zappa Ceroni
18-40026 Imola (BO)
Italy
0542.45002
(FAX) 0542.43810
www.ispitalia.it/frudua.htm

GERGORY FURAN LUTHERIE

38 Stillbrook Court
West Hill
Ontario
Canada M1E 3W7
gfuran@ican.net

FYLDE GUITARS

Hartness Road
Gilwilly Industrial Estate
Penrith Cumbria
England PR4 2TZ
01768.891515
(FAX) 01768.868998

JOE GALLACHER

Gallacher Guitars
255 Kooba Street
Albury NSW
Australia 2640
stuart@dragnet.com.au

J. W. GALLAGHER & SON

Gallagher Guitar Company
(P.O. Box 128)
7 Main Street
Wartrace TN 37183
931.389.6455
(FAX) 931.389.6455
DonG@mail.cafes.net
www.dnj.com/gallagher/inde
x.html

GALLOUP GUITARS

Bryan Galloup
10495 Northland Drive
Big Rapids MI 49307
800.278.0089
616.796.5611
luthier@netonecom.net

STEVE GANZ GUITARS

Steve Ganz
3629 Illinois Lane
Bellingham WA 98226
sganz_guitars@geocities
.com
www.geocities.com/vienna/
2242/

GARDNER GUITARS

Michael Gardner
8976 Rosetta Circle
Sacramento CA 95826
drguitar@midtown.net

MARK GASSER

Distributed by GuitArts
P.O. Box 2015
Cottonwood AZ 86326
520.646.7233
sean@verdenet.com
www.dreamweavers.net/
guitarts

GAZELLE GUITARS

Bill Pfleging
Glasco Turnpike
Woodstock NY 12498
songcraftr@aol.com

GAZER GUITARS

Roanoke VA

GC GUITARS

Gill Chavez
5934 El Mio Drive
Los Angeles CA
90042
gcmqr@earthlink.com

GENEVA

Distributed by Geneva International Corporation.
29 E. Hintz Road
Wheeling IL 60090
800.533.2388
847.520.9970
(FAX) 847.520.9593
geneva-intl@msn.com
www.guitars~amada.com
www.music~instruments~
lidl.com

MICK GENTRY

Flinders Avenue
Molendinar Queens-
land
Australia 4214
mickgrep@fan.net.au

GHOST INSTRUMENT COMPANY

Tom Morici
P.O. Box 1368
Anaconda MT 59711
tm51mt@aol.com

CORTESI GIANCARLO

Via Don Carlo 65
Albana S. Alessandro
(BG)
Italy 24061
035.580369

GIANNINI

Distributed by Music Industries Corporation
99 Tulip Avenue
Suite 101
Floral Park NY 11001
800.431.6699
516.352.4110
(FAX) 516.352.0754
mic@musicindustries.com
www.musicindustries.com

GIBSON

Gibson Musical Instruments
1818 Elm Hill Pike
Nashville TN 37210-
3781
800.846.4376
615.871.4500
(FAX) 615.889.5509
jazor@gibson.com
www.gibson.com

BILL GIEBITZ
Strait Music Company
805 W. 5th Street
Austin TX 78703
giebitz@dfti.com

GIFFIN GUITARS
Alingsas Sweden

JOHN AND BILL GILBERT
1485 LaHonda Road
Woodside CA 94062
415.851.1239
(FAX) 415-851-3284

GILCHRIST MANDOLINS AND GUITARS
Stephen Gilchrist
c/o Carmel Music Company
P.O. Box 2296
Carmel CA 93921-2296
408.624.8078

GERARD GILET
Gilet Guitars & Guitarwoods
Factory 5/6 Booralee Street
Botany NSW
Australia 2019
www.spirit.com.au/~
gramac/gilet/giletintro.html

GILLHAM'S GUITAR WORKS
Stephen Gillham
116 S. Channel Drive
Wrightsville NC 28480

GIUSSANI GIOACHINO
Podere Aile
Anghiari (Ariezzo)
Italy 52031

GIRDIS
Robert Girdis
8745 Evanston Avenue North
Seattle WA 98103
www.cybozone.com/fg/girdis.html

GITARRENBAU
Susann Albrecht & Jens Kummer
GleimstraBe 56
10437 Berlin
Germany
030.442.0196

GODIN
Godin Guitars
Distributed by La Si Do, Inc.
4240 Sere Street
St. Laurent Quebec
Canada H4T 1A6
514.343.5560
(FAX) 514.343.5098
sales@lasido.com
www.lasido.com

THE GOLDEN WOOD
33700 S. Highway One
Gualala CA 95445
707.884.4213
dbucher@mcn.org

THE GOLDFINGER CO.
Glenn Richard Thommassen
Valervn. 67
Moss
Norway 1537
glennrichardthommassen
@broderdue.com

OZHAN GOLEBATMAZ
100 Yil AA-14
Balgat - Ankara
Turkey
c/o: kemal@tel-soft.com

ROBERT GOMES
914 A Mission Street
Santa Cruz CA 95060-3504
sequoia@cruzio.com

JAMES GOODALL GUITARS
James Goodall
P.O. Box 3542
Kailua-Kona HI 96745
808.329.8237
(FAX) 808.325.7842
goodall@aloha.net
www.goodallguitars.com

GOODMAN GUITARS
Brad Goodman
47 Juniper Circle
Brewster NY
914.278.8847

GOUGI FABRICE
L'Atelier de Lutherie Fabrice Gougi
Rue de la Gare
Penmarsh
France 29760
gougi@wanadoo.fr

GOYA
Distributed by the Martin Guitar Company
510 Sycamore Street
Nazareth PA 18064-9233
800.345.3103
610.759.2837
(FAX) 610.759.5757
info@mguitar.com
www.mguitar.com

OSKAR GRAF
P.O. Box 2502
Clarendon Ontario
Canada K0H 1J0
613.279.2610
grafco@frontenac.net
www.neteyes.com/graf/

JIM GRAINGER
Custom Fretted Instruments & Repair
400 Firetower Road
Sparta TN 38583
customfret@juno.com

GRANATA GUITARS
Peter Granata
Oak Ridge NJ

KEVIN GRAY
Kevin Gray Guitars
P.O. Box 12056
Dallas TX 75225
214.692.1064

GREEN MOUNTAIN GUITARS
Built by the Breedlove Guitar Company
19885 8th St.
Tumalo OR 97701
801.486.0222
(FAX) 541.385.8183

JAMES D. GREGORY
Jim Gregory Guitar/Repair
17133 West Munyon Road
Cane Hill AR 72717
jgregory@lincoln.mwsc.k12.ar.us

GREMLIN
Distributed by Midco International
P.O. Box 748
Effingham IL 62401
800.356.4326
217.342.9211
(FAX) 217.347.0316

GRETSCH
Fred Gretsch Enterprises, Ltd.
P.O. Box 2468
Savannah GA 31402
912.748.7070
(FAX) 912.748.6005
www.gretsch.com

JACK GRETZ
Distributed by Magdon Music
jackguitrs@aol.com

JOHN GREVEN
Greven Guitars
1108 E. First Street
Bloomington IN 47401
812.334.2853
(FAX) 812.334.2853
tortise@bluemarble.net

GRIFFITHS GUITAR WORKS
St. John's, Newfoundland
Canada

GRIMES GUITARS
Stephen Grimes
(P.O. Box 537)
755-G Kamehameiki
Kula HI 96790
808.878.2076
(FAX) 808.878.2076
grimer@maui.net
www.maui.net/~grimer/index.html

GROVES CUSTOM GUITARS
Gordon S. Groves
46 N. Westmoreland Avenue
Tucson AZ 85745
520.882.7953
ggroves100@earthlink.net

GUILD
60 Industrial Drive
Westerly RI 02891
401.596.0141
(FAX) 401.596.0436
Distributed by the Fender Musical Instrument Corp.
Fender Musical Instruments Corporation
7975 North Hayden Road
Scottsdale AZ 85258-3246
602.596.9690
(FAX) 602.596.1384
www.fender.com

GUITAR FACTORY
The Guitar Factory
2816 Edgewater Drive
Orlando FL 32804
800.541.1070
407.425.1070
(FAX) 407.425.7276
felsfam@magicnet.net
members.aol.com/gif89/index.html

THE GUITAR FARM
RR 1, Box 60
Sperryville VA 22740-9604
540.987.9744
(FAX) 640.987.9419

GUITARLAB
Kiyoshi Itoh
Funabashi, Chiba
Japan

WOLFGANG GUTSCHER
33-35 St. John's Square
Unit 51
Pennybank Chambers
London EC1 M4DS
England
wolfgang.gutscher@
easynet.co.uk

PAUL GUY GUITARS
Paul Guy
Katarina Bangata 65
Stockholm
Sweden 11642
paul@guyguitars.se
www.home3.swipnet.se/~
w-37192/

HAGENLOCHER GUITARRAS
Henner Hagenlocher
Calle Guadarrama 3 Bajo
Granada
Spain E-18009
henner@valnet.es

PER HALLGREN
Skraddarns Vag 14
Grabo
Sweden
per.hallgren@mbox301
.swipnet.se

HANNAH GUITARS
1216 Sand Cove Road
Saint John NB
Canada E2M 5V8
506.648.4827
rhannah@nbsympatico.ca
www.atsonline.com/info/hannah/rod.htm

HANIKA GITARREN
Armin Hanika
Egerstrasse 12A
Baiersdorf Bayern
D-91083 Germany
armin.hanika@t-online.de

RICHARD HARRIS
7610 Chris Anne Drive
Indianapolis IN 46237

HERMANN HAUSER
Clemens-Seidl-Str. 5-7
Reisbach/Vils
94419 Germany
49.8734.255
(FAX) 49.8734.7665

LES HAYNIE
Eureka Springs AR
501.253.8941

HEIDEN STRINGED INSTRUMENTS
Michael Heiden
7285 Hinkley Road
Chilliwac, British Columbia
Canada V2P 6H3
604.794.7261
mheiden@uniserve.com

PULFER HEIDI
Via Piccinino 3
Rimini
Italy 47037
0541.27997

HEINS GUITARS
Heins Gitaaratelier
Hoogend 26
8601 AE Sneek
Holland
+31.0515.423848
(FAX) +31.0515.423848

JOHN HEINZ
Prototech Engineering
5 Hunter Avenue
Joliet IL 60436
jwheinz@juno.com

WILLIAM HENDERSON
Distributed by Kirkpatrick Guitar Studio
4607 Maple Avenue
Baltimore MD 21227-4023
410.242.2744
(FAX) 410.242.0326
info@guitar1stop.com

HENRY
Henry Guitars
75 Bennett Street
Suite D-1
Atlanta GA 30309
404.351.9255

HERITAGE
Heritage Guitar, Inc.
225 Parsons Street
Kalamazoo MI 49007
616.385.5721
(FAX) 616.385.3519

JAVIER HERNANDEZ
Humlegardsgatan 13
Stockholm
Sweden 12244
x-herdz@swipnet.se

JIRI LEBEDA HFI
Jasminova 32
10600 Praha 10
Czech Republic
420.2.7553.472
420.602.255.120

H.G. LEACH GUITARS
P.O. Box 1315
Cedar Ridge CA 95924
916.477.2938

DENNIS HILL
Dennis Hill, Luthier
Leitz Music, Inc.
508 Harrison Avenue
Panama City FL 32401
850.769.0111
(FAX) 850.785.1779
(Studio) 850.769.3009

KENNY HILL GUITARS
501 Maple Avenue
Ben Lomond CA 95005
408.336.2436
(FAX) 408.336.2436
khill@cruzio.com

JAMES HILL
The Heron
England
012.47.469090

CHRIS HINTON
Hinton Custom Inlays
Ashland WI 54806
hiton@ncis.net

HIRADE
Also HIRADE CONCERT
Distributed by the Kaman Music Corporation
P.O. Box 507
Bloomfield CT 06002-0507
800.647.2244
860.243.7105
(FAX) 860.243.7287
www.kamanmusic.com

HOFFMAN GUITARS
Charles A. Hoffman
2219 East Franklin Avenue
Minneapolis MN 55404
612.338.1079
choffman@hoffmanguitars.com
www.hoffmanguitars.com

CRAIG HOFFMAN
Hoffman Stringed Instruments and Repairs
2660 South Yonkers Road
Raleigh NC 27604

HOFNER
Karl Hofner GmbH
EgerlandstraBe 38
91083 Baiersdorf-Hagenau
Germany
9131.7758.0
(FAX) 9131.7758.58
Distributed by Boosey & Hawkes
1925 Enterprise Court
Libertyville IL 60048
800.426.7068
847.816.2500
(FAX) 847.816.2514
booseyH@aol.com
www.boosey.com

HOHNER
Exclusively distributed in the U.S. by HSS
(A Division of Hohner, Inc.)
Lakeridge Park
10223 Sycamore Drive
Ashland VA 23005
800.446.6010
804.550.2700
(FAX) 804.550.2670
www.hohnerusa.com

HOLLENBECK GUITARS
160 Half Moon Street
Lincoln IL 62656
217.732.6933
HollenbGtr@aol.com
majazzg@dove-world.net

HOLLISTER GUITARS
138 Turner Street
Dedham MA 02026
617.251.6688

STEPHEN HOLST GUITARS
Stephen Holst
254 E. 30th Avenue
Eugene OR 97405
541.687.7845
(FAX) 541.687.7845
guitars@rio.com
www.tio.com/~guitars/

EDWARD D. HOOD
Yondern and Back
1315 1/2 W. 5th Street
Port Angeles WA 98363
ehood@olypen.com

HONDO
Hondo Guitar Company
Distributed by Musicorp/MBT
P.O. Box 30819
Charleston SC 29417
800.845.1922
803.763.9083
(FAX) 803.763.9096
www.hondo.com

DIETER HOPF
Distributed by the Luthier Music Corporation
341 W. 44th Street
New York NY 10036
212.397.6038
(FAX) 212.397.6048
luthier@tiac.net
www.tiac/net/users/luthier

HOYER
International Distribution by Musikwarengrosshandel Mario Pellarin
Toyota-Allee 19
D-50858 Koeln (Cologne)
Germany
49.2234.16011
(FAX) 49.2234.14042
106131.523@compuserve.com
www.pellarin.de

BENITO HUIPE
Distributed by Casa Talamantes
529 Adams NE
Albuquerque NM 87108-
505.265.2977
(FAX) 505.265.2977

THOMAS HUMPHREY
37 W. 26th Street
New York NY 10010
212.696.1693

ROBERT J. HUNTER
1400 West 3rd Street
Waterloo IA 50701

HUSS AND DALTON GUITAR COMPANY
102 Wayne Avenue
(P.O. Box 537)
Stuarts Draft VA 24477
540.337.3382
(FAX) 540.337.3382
hdguitar@cfw.com
www.dezines.com/hdguitar

ANTHONY J. HUVARD
P.O. Box 130
Sandston VA 23150
gitarmkr@cybozone.com
www.cybozone.com/luthier/index.html

HWANG-CARLOS GUITARS
Leo Hwang-Carlos
8 Easthampton Road
Northampton MA 01060
lhwangca@mtholyoke.edu

HYUNDAI
Hyundai Guitars
126 Route 303
West Nyack NY 10994
914.353.3520
(FAX) 914.353.3540

IBANEZ
Hoshino (USA), Inc.
1726 Winchester Road
Bensalem PA 19020-0886
800.669.4226
215.638.8670

(FAX) 215.245.8583
www.ibanez.com
Ibanez Canada
2165-46th Avenue
Lachine Quebec H8T 2P1
Ibanez Australia
88 Bourke Road
Alexandria Sydney NSW 2015
Ibanez New Zealand
5 Amokura Street
Henderson Auckland

ITHACA GUITAR WORKS
215 N. Cayuga
Ithaca NY 14850
607.272.2602
www.guitarworks.com

ITHACA STRINGED INSTRUMENTS
Eric Aceto
D. S. Hoffman
6115 Mount Road
Trumansburg NY 14886
607.387.3544
(FAX) 607.387.3544

JACKSON GUITARWORKS
Herndon VA

DOUGLAS R. JACKSON GUITARS
Douglas R. Jackson, Luthier
P.O. Box 5149
Destin FL 32540
Or,
175 Stahlman Avenue
Destin FL 32541
850.654.1048
(FAX) 850.654.1048

PAUL JACOBSON
www.cybozone.com/fg/jacobson.html

JAEN ARCHTOP GUITARS
Fernando Alonso Jaen
C/Solana de Opanel
14 Bis - 2
Madrid
Spain 28091
falonso@alcatel.es

JAIME JULIA
Distributed by Manufacturas Alhambra S.L.
Duquesa de Almodovar, 11
Muro del Alcoy 03830
Spain
34.655.30011
(FAX) 34.655.30190

JAMMER
Distributed by VMI Industries
Vega Musical Instruments
P.O. Box 1357
2980-D Enterprise Street
Brea CA 92822-1357
800.237.4864
714.572.1492
(FAX) 714.572.9321

STEVE JARMAN GUITARS
Steve Jarman, Luthier
Bexleyheath, Kent
England
jarman@btinternet.com
www.btinternet.com/~sjguitars/

JASMINE
Distributed by the Kaman Music Corporation
P.O. Box 507
Bloomfield CT 06002-0507
800.647.2244
860.243.7105
(FAX) 860.243.7287
www.kamanmusic.com

J.B. PLAYER
Distributed by J.B. Player International
PO Box 30819
Charleston SC 29417
800.845.1922
803.763.9083
(FAX) 803.763.9096
www.jbplayer.com

J D S
Distributed by Wolf Imports, Inc.
1933 Woodson Road
St. Louis MO 63114
800.844.9653
314.429.3439
(FAX) 314.429.3255

JEANNIE
Jeannie Pickguards and Guitar Accessories
292 Atherton Avenue
Pittsburg CA 94565
510.439.1447

CHRIS JENKINS
829 Kingston Drive
Mansfield TX 76063
cjenkins@arlington.net

PACO JIMENEZ
Avda. de Italia, 4-D
Granada
Spain
paco@100mbps.es
www.100mbps.es/paco/pacoweb.html

JISHENG
Jisheng Musical Instruments Manfacturing Ltd.
Rm. 111, Bldg. 41
Taoyuanst., Xihu Road
Guangzhou
P. R. China
0086.20.81840008
(FAX) 0086.20.81845765
gzjsheng@publicl.guangzhou.gd.cn

J L D RESEARCH AND DEVELOPMENT
James Oliver
2431 S. Lake Letta Drive #2
Avon Park FL 33825
jldrd@digital.net
www.digital.net/~jlddoc/

J M S CUSTOM GUITARS
J. Michael Sperzel
1308 Everett Avenue
No. Two
Louisville KY 40204

LEIF JORGEN JOHANSEN
Nordassloyfa 11A
Oslo
Norway 1250
226.22228

JENS JOHANSSON
Odenskogvagen 84
Ostersund
Sweden
vfhs@algonet.se

JOHNSON
Distributed by The Music Link
P.O. Box 162
Brisbane CA 94005
888.552.5465
650.615.8991
(FAX) 650.615.8997
thelink@@musiclinkcorp.com

JOHNSON GUITARS
P.O. Box 222
Talkeetna AK 99676
907.733.2005
(FAX) 907.733.2777
jguitars@alaska.net

JONES GUITARS
Steve Jones, Luthier
Brookfield Road
Brookfield Works
Leeds Yorkshire
England LS6 4EH
cwj27@aol.com

ARTHUR MILES JONES
Fretworks
4027 4th Street SE
Calgary Alberta
Canada T2G 2W4
fretwork@fretwork.com
www.fretwork.com

RICK OWEN JONES
Coconut Grove Music
418 Kuulei Road
Kailua HI 96734

SERGIE DE JONGE
Oshawa, Ontario
Canada
www.cybozone.com/fg/jonge.html

JOSHUA GUITARS
Distributed by L.A. Guitar Works
19320 Vanowen Street
Reseda CA 91335
818.758.8787
(FAX) 818.758.8788

J.T.G. OF NASHVILLE
5350 Hillsboro Road
Nashville TN 37215
615.665.8384
(FAX) 615.665.9468

BOB JUZEK
Metropolitan Music Company
P.O. Box 1415
Mountain Road
Stowe VT 05672-9598

J W L INSTRUMENT
Jokke Lagerqvist
Tallgatan 7
HOK
Sweden 56013
jokke@jwl.pp.se
www.flashback.net/~guitar

K & S GUITARS, INC.
2923 Adeline Street
Berkeley, CA 94703
510.843.2883
510.548.7538
(FAX) 510.644.1958
BMIEX@GLOBEL.CALIFORNIA.COM
www.california.com/~kands

STEPHEN KAKOS
6381 Maple Road
Mound MN 55364
612.472.4732
(FAX) 612.472.4732

KALIL
Edward E. Kalil
Kalil Fine Handcrafted Guitars
132 S. Front Street
McComb MS 39648
edekalil@aol.com
members.aol.com/edekalil/
kalil.html

VARINDER KAMBO
15 Scenic Drive
South Salem NY
10590
vkhalsa@bestweb.net

PETER KAWA
508.697.8485

KAY
*Distributed by A.R. Musical
Enterprises, Inc.*
9031 Technology Drive
Fishers IN 46038
800.428.4807
317.577.6999
(FAX) 317.577.7288

WILLIAM C. KELDAY
The Guitar Workshop
Unit 3
Aldessan House
The Clachan Campsie
Glen
Glasgow G65 7AB
Scotland
billguitmk@aol.com

KELLER CUSTOM GUITARS
P.O. Box 244
Mandan ND 58554
701.663.1153
(FAX) 701.667.2197

KELLER GUITARS
Alphonse J. Keller
Bayreutherstrasse 4-6
Erlangen Bavaria
91054 Germany

T. R. KELLISON
1739 Grand Avenue
Billings MT 59102
406.245.4212
www.imt.net/~evolve/
guitarshop/index.html

JEFF KEMP
P.O. Box 943
Armidale NSW
Australia 2350
www.ozemail.com.au/~jeff
kemp/classical/guitar.html

KERSENBROCK GUITARS
111 S. Third
Lindsborg KS 67456
785.227.2968

**KGB MUSICAL
INSTRUMENTS**
61 Derby Road
Birkenhead
Merseyside L42 7HA
England
0151.6473268

KIMAXE
*Distributed by Kenny &
Michael's Company, Inc.*
811 E. 14th Place
Los Angeles CA
90021
213.746.2848
213.747.1671
(FAX) 213.747.1161

KIMBARA
Distributed by FCN Music
Morley Road
Tonbridge
Kent TN9 1RA
01732.366.421

KIMBERLY
Kimex Trading Co., Ltd.
Room 1411, Han Suh
River Park
11-11, Yeo Eui Do-
Dong
Yeong Deung Po-Ku,
Seoul Korea
82.2.786.1014
82.2.783.0408
(FAX) 82.2.786.5578

KINKADE
18 Clevedon Terrace
Kingsdown
Bristol BS6 5TX
England
0117.9243279

JOHN KINNAIRD
100 Rolling Road
Social Circle GA
30025
jhkjr@bellsouth.net

KINSCHERFF
Jamie Kinscherff
102 West Annie
Austin TX 78704
512.447.1944

STEVE KLEIN
Klein Acoustic Guitars
2560 Knob Hill Road
Sonoma CA 95476
707.938.4639
(FAX) 707.938.4639
info@klein.micronet.org
www.kleinguitars.com

THOMAS KNATT
Luthiers Workshop
Waltham MA

JOHN KNAUFF
Neo CLassic Guitars
6839 Kerrywood Circle
Centreville VA 20121
jknauff@visa.com

KNIGHT GUITARS
Woodham Lane
New Haw, Weybridge
Surrey, England
01932.353131

KNUTSON LUTHIERY
*Custom Guitar and
Mandolin Works*
P.O. Box 945
Forrestville CA 95436
707.887.2709
mssngr@sonic.net
www.sonic.net/mssngr

MARTIN KOCH
Hartbergerstrasse 22
A-8200 Gleisdorf
Austria
koch@kwb.tv-graz.ac.at
www.cis.tv-graz.ac.at/iwb/
martin/welcome.html

MASARU KOHNO
www.cybozone.com/fg/kohn
o.html

KOLEKOLE GUITARS
Dave DeGomez
Norwood MA

BILL KOUCKY
Route #2
Box 424
East Jordan MI 49072

RANDALL KRAL
First Fret Acoustics
6793 Scott Road
Parker CO 80134

KRAMER
*Kramer Guitars
Distributed by Gibson Musical
Instruments*
1050 Acorn Drive
Suite A
Nashville TN 37210
800.283.7135
615.871.4500
(FAX) 615.872.7768
www.gibson.com

ERIK KRAUSE
Die Gitarrenwerkstatt
Haslacher Str. 10
79115 Freiburg
Germany
ekrause@ruf.uni-freiburg.de
www.gitarrenwerkstatt.de

**KAZIMIERZ M.
KRAWCZAK**
63 Marshall Avenue
Warwick RI 02886
401.739.3215

CRAIG KREIDER
Lee Harbor, Inc.
1708 Lincoln Avenue
Panama City FL 33972

MAX KRIMMEL
Salina Star Road
Boulder CO 80302

GREG KROCHMAN
The Classic Ax
1024 16th Avenue
South
Suite 203
Nashville TN 37212

JAMES KRUEGER
Broken String Music
133 Imperial Crescent
Bradford Ontario
Canada L3Z 2N3
krugdesn@pathcom.com

K S M GUITARS
Kevin S. Moore
349 North Main
Logan UT 84321

DOUG KYLE
Fursdon, Moreton
Hampstead, Devon
England TQ13 8QT
44.647.70394

La CADIE
Distributed by Hannah Guitars
1216 Sand Cove Road
Saint John NB
Canada E2M 5V8
506.648.4827
rhannah@nb.sympatico.ca
www.atsonline.com/info/
hannah/rod.htm

La MANCHA
Distributed by Hep Cat
2605-A Fessey Park
Road
Nashville TN 37204
800.775.0650
615.385.3676
www.lamancha.com

La PATRIE GUITARS
Distributed By La Si Do, Inc.
4240 Sere'
St. Laurent Quebec
Canada H4T 1A6
514.343.5560
(FAX) 514.343.5098

La ROCQUE GUITARS
Joerg Scherbaum
Furtwaengler Str. 9A
70195 Stuttgart
Germany
joerg.scherbaum@
metronet.de

MARK LACEY
Lacey Guitars
P.O. Box 24646
Nashville TN 37202
615.952.3045
laceygtr@ix.netcom.com

LADY LUCK
Lady Luck Industries, Inc.
P.O. Box 195
Cary IL 60013
708.639.8607
(FAX) 708.639.7010
www.ladyluck.com

LAFAYETTE
A More Company
200 Governor Treutlen
Road
P.O. Box 956
Pooler GA 31322
912.748.1101
(FAX) 912.748.1106
brown@synsonics.com
www.synsonics.com

LAKEWOOD GUITARS
Zum Bahnhopf 6a
35394 Giessen
Germany
0641.43088
(FAX) 0641.491398
www.lakewoodguitars.com
*Distributed in the U.S. by Dana
B. Goods*
5427 Hollister Avenue
Santa Barbara CA
3111-2345
800.765.8663
805.964.9610
(FAX) 805.964.9749
72431.416@compuserve
.com
www.danabgoods.com
Distributed in the U.K. by Picato
Unit 24
Treorchy Industrial Es-
tate
Treorchy, Mid Glamor-
gan
England CF42 6EJ
01443.437982
(FAX) 01443.433624
*Distributed in Japan by
Nakabayashi Boeki*
8-3, Nonowari, Kanie
Honmachi
Kanie, Aichi 497
Japan
05679.5.6310
(FAX) 05679.5.6309

LANDOLA
*Landola Guitars
Audiasal OY AB*
P.O. Box 39
Pietarsaari
Finland 68601
+358.6.723.0407
(FAX) +358.6.723.4564
landola@multi.fi
www.landola.fi

LARK IN THE MORNING
P.O Box 1176
Mendocino CA 95460-
1176
707.964.5569
(FAX) 707.964.1979
larkinam@larkinam.com
www.larkinam.com

KRISTOPHER LARSON
The Loft
315 N. 36th Street
Seattle WA 98103

GRIT LASKIN
Toronto, Canada
416.536.2135

LARRIVEE
Larrivee Guitars, Ltd.
1896 Victoria Diversion
Vancouver British Co-
lumbia
Canada V5N 2K4
604.879.8111
(FAX) 604.879.5440
answers@larrivee.com
www.larrivee.com
*Distributed by Jean Larrivee
Guitars Ltd.*
8860 East Pershing
Avenue
Scottsdale AZ 85260
602.860.1876
602.860.1895

LAUGHLIN GUITARS
Bob Laughlin, Luthier
1551 East 4th Avenue
#163
Vancouver British Co-
lumbia
Canada V5N 1J7
bob_laughlin@douglas.bc.c
www.douglas.bc.ca/~
laughlin

LAUNHARDT & KOBS
Garbenheimer StraBe
34
35578 Wetzlar
Germany
6441.905260
(FAX) 6441.905261

LAWRENCE FINE GUITARS
Larry Mills
6530 Baywood Lane
North College Hill OH
45224

LEVESQUE GUITARS
Alan Levesque
6204 Moray Avenue
New Port Richey FL
34653
levesque@gate.net

LEVITCH GUITAR WORKS
Richard Levitch
2292 Stocker Lane
Scotch Plains NJ
07076
levitch@bellatlantic.net
www.levitchguitar.com

**MICHAEL LEWIS
INSTRUMENTS**
*Fine Guitars and
Mandolins*
20807 E. Spring
Ranches Rd.
Grass Valley VA 95949
916.272.4124
malewis@nccn.net

JAMES D. LILLARD
Jay Dee's Guitar Repair
1869 Madison Avenue
Memphis TN 38104-
2621
jaydeegtr@aol.com
members.aol.com/jaydeegtr/
index.html

LIIKANEN
Liikanen Musical Instruments KY
Vaaksyntie 4
Helsinki
Finland 00510
+358.9.701.5335
(FAX) +358.9.701.5335

LINDSEY INSTRUMENTS
Kaono Lindsey
2806 Booth Road
Pauoa Valley HI 96813
ukuman@lava.net

JEFF LIVERMAN
1722 Elmsmere
Richmond VA 23227

THOMAS B. LIVESEY
T. B. Livesey Guitars
P.O. Box 215
Gin Gin Queensland
Australia 4671
couzens@mpx.com.au
www.mpx.com.au

LKS GUITARS and MANDOLINS
Lawrence K. Smith
8 Mt. Gilead Road
Thirroul NSW
Australia
lksguitars@ozemail.com.au
www.ozemail.com.au/~lksguit

THOMAS LLOYD GUITARS
Chris Wynne
15 Yarra Street
Yarra Glen
Melbourne Victoria
Australia 3775
matty@wire.net.au

HANS VAN LOBEN SELS
Teut 96
Amersfoort 3811 W2
Netherlands
loben@kpd.nl
www.domeinen.net/lobelsels

LONE STAR
Lone Star Guitar Company
Distributed by LPD Music International
2104-B Greenbriar
Southlake TX 76092
888.421.2207
817.421.2207
(FAX) 817.488.1507

ABEL GARCIA LOPEZ
Guerrero 383
C.P. 60250
Paracho Michoacan
Mexico
52.(452)50239
(FAX) 52.(452)50873

FRIGNANI LORENZO
Via F. Baracca 38
41031 Camposanto (MO)
Italy
0535.87056

LOTUS
Distributed by Midco International
P.O. Box 748
Effingham IL 62401
800.356.4326
217.342.9211
(FAX) 217.347.0316

LOWDEN
The Lowden Guitar Co., Ltd.

Andy Kidd
8 Glenford Way
Newtownards Co.
Northern Ireland B23 4BX
44.01247.820.542
(FAX) 44.01247.820.650
wilson@germanco.dnet.co.uk

LUCENA
Distributed by Music Imports
3322-C Glacier Avenue
San Diego CA 92120
800.748.5711
619.578.3443
(FAX) 619.280.7180

LOVADINA LUCIANO
Via Verdi 5
31030 Arcade (TV)
Italy
0422.720212
(FAX) 0422.720212

LUCIDA
Distributed by The Music Link
P.O. Box 162
Brisbane CA 94005
888.552.5465
650.615.8991
(FAX) 650.615.8997
thelink@musiclinkcorp.com

CHRISTOPHER LUCK
RR #2, Box 1590
SOuth China ME 04358
celuck@pivot.net

ARBAN LUIS
Via Darwin 17
52100 Arezzo
Italy
0575.381709

LUTHIER
Distributed by the Luthier Music Corporation
341 W. 44th Street
New York NY 10036
212.397.6038
(FAX) 212.397.6048
luthier@tiac.net
www.tiac/net/users/luthier

G.W. LYON
Distributed by Washburn International
255 Corporate Woods Parkway
Vernon Hills IL 60061-3109
800.US.SOUND
708.913.5511
(FAX) 708.913.7772
jhawk103@aol.com
www.washburn.com

GRAHAM McARTHUR
9 Eileen Street
Modbury South Australia
Australia 5092
grahammc@camtech.net.au

RIC McCURDY
19 Hudson Street
New York NY 10013-3822
212.274.8352
McCurdygtr@aol.com

McDERMOTT GUITARS
Dennis McDermott
Bizarre Guitars
1930 S. Greenwood
Wichita KS 67211

GRAHAM McDONALD
P.O. Box 365
Jamison ACT
Australia 2614
www.spirit.com.au/~gramac/instruments.html

MCGILL GUITARS
Paul McGill
808 Kendall Drive
Nashville TN 37209
conecaster@aol.com
www.backporchmusic.com

McHUGH GUITARS
P.O. Box 2216
Northbrook IL 60065-2216
847.498.3319

McLEOD HANDCRAFTED INSTRUMENTS
Dan McLeod
37539 97th Street East
Littlerock CA 93543
dgmcleod@qnet.com

McKERRIHAN
Glen E. McKerrihan
548 West Jackson Street
Phoenix AZ 85003
602.957.3671
602.253.0731
(FAX) 602.253.4072

S.B. MACDONALD CUSTOM INSTRUMENTS
Scott MacDonald
22 Fairmont Street
Huntington NY 11743
516.421.9056
guitardoc@earthlink.net
www.home.earthlink.net/~guitardoc/

M.A.C. SOUND
See PHILLIP MURRAY

MAC YASUDA GUITARS
Mac Yasuda
17971 Skypark Circle
Suite L
Irvine CA 92614
949.474.6020
(FAX) 949.474.7571
www.masterbiltguitar.com
Masterbilt Guitar Company
1027 N. Coast Highway
Suite A
Laguna Beach CA 92651
714.494.2285
(FAX) 714.494.9947

M A D CUSTOM GUITARS
David Marioni
#3, Rue John Grasset
CH-1205 Geneva
Switzerland
41.22.321.9935
(FAX) 41.22.321.9935
info@madguitars.ch
www.madguitars.ch/madguitars

MADDEN GUITARS
Paul K. Madden
202 Fifth Avenue North
Franklin TN 37064
strgwndr@aol.com
www.tndirectory.com/maddenguitars

BENOIT MAILLETTE
Custom Hand Made Guitars
79 16th Avenue
Roxboro Quebec
Canada H8Y 2Y2
masson@worldnet.att.net
www.home.att.net/~masson/bm.html

GEORGE MAJKOWSKI
13012 Pt. Richmond Drive NW
Gig Harbor WA 98332
jurek@wolfenet.com

GUITARRERIA MALDONADO & HIJOS
Luis Miguel Maldonado Ruiz
Avda Velazquez, 57
Malaga
Spain 29004
Pedro Maldonado Ruiz
Avda Isabel Manoja, 4
Torremolinos
Spain 29620

MANEA CUSTOM GUITARS
246 St. Rt. 994
Boaz KY 42027
502.658.3866
(FAX) 502.658.3866

MANSON
A.B. Manson & Co.
Easterbrook, Hittisliegh
Exeter EX6 6LR
England
0647.24139
(FAX) 0647.24140
Manson Guitars
Vellake, Sandford
Crediton, Devon EX17 4EH
United Kingdom
44.01363.775603
Distributed in the U.S. by Eichelbaum Guitars
1735 Mountain Avenue
Santa Barbara CA 93101
805.563.6028
samusic@samusic.com
www.samusic.com

MANZANITAS GUITARS
Sellenfried 3
D-37124 Rosdorf
Germany
49.551.782.417
(FAX) 49.551.782.417
jdriesner@aol.com
www.members.aol.com/manzguitar/index.htm

MANZER GUITARS
Linda Manzer, Luthier
65 Metcalfe Street
Toronto Ontario
Canada M4X 1R9
416.927.1539
(FAX) 416.927.8233
manzer@interlog.com
www.manzer.com

MAPSON INSTRUMENTS
James L. Mapson
3230 S. Susan Street
Santa Ana CA 92704
714.754.6566
(FAX) 714.751.9062
JLMapson@aol.com
www.archtops.com

MARCHIONE GUITARS
Stephen Marchione
20 West 20th Street
Suite 806
New York NY 10011
212.675.5215
(FAX) 212.675.6356
www.marchione.com/

EGGERT MAR MARINOSSON
Tonastoedin h/f
Skipholt 50 D
Reykjavik
Iceland 105

GRIMALDI MARIO
Via Lamarmora 2
Trisobbio (AL)
Italy 15070
0143.831947

NOVELLI MARIO
Via Nogariole 43
Giavera del Montello (TV)
Italy
0422.770216

MARK WESCOTT GUITARS
Mark Wescott
411 W. New York Avenue
Somers Point NJ 08244
609.927.2890
wescott3@ix.netcom.com

MARTELL GUITARS UNLIMITED
Kris Martell
2158 East 39th Avenue
Vancouver British Columbia
Canada V5P 1H7
amirault@smartt.com
www.personal.smartt.com/~amirault/

MARTHA'S VINEYARD GUITAR COMPANY

MARTIN
The C.F. Martin Guitar Company
510 Sycamore Street
Nazareth PA 18064-9233
800.345.3103
610.759.2837
(FAX) 610.759.5757
info@mguitar.com
www.mguitar.com

ELLIO MARTINA
Eefde
The Netherlands

MASTER

MATLIN GUITARS
David Matlin
Mendocino CA
www.mcn.org/MenComNet/Business/Retail/matlin/matlin1.html

MATON GUITARS
9-11 Kelvin Road
North Bayswater, Victoria
Australia 3153
03.9720.7529
(FAX) 03.9720.7273

MAUEL GUITARS
Hank Mauel
77 Sylvan Vista Drive
Auburn CA 95603
whmauel@neworld.net

MAUI MUSIC
Maui Music Guitars & Acoustic Bass
808.667.5711

MAXTONE
Maxtone Musical Instrument Mfg. Co., Ltd.
(Ta Feng Long Enterprises Co., Ltd.)
3F, #400 Taichung-Kang Road, Sec. 1
Tai Chung Taiwan ROC
886.90.493024
(FAX) 886.4.3212493
maxtone@ms7.hinet.net

M B GUITARS
Mike Beckert
Marion Music
4970 Stack Blvd. # b-3
Melbourne FL 32901
mbeckert@digital.net

MIKE MEARS
Windy Hill GuitarWorks
10160 Hampton Road
Fairfax Station VA 22039
mearsman2@aol.com

TED MEGAS
Arch Top Guitar Maker
1070 Van Dyke
San Francisco CA 94124
415.822.3100
(FAX) 415.822.1454
tmegas@infinex.com

JOHN F. MELLO
John F. Mello, Luthier
437 Colusa Avenue
Kensington CA 94707-1545
510.528.1080
johnfmello@bcg.net
www.johnfmello.com

MELOBAR
Melobar Guitars, Inc.
Distributed by Smith Family Music Products
9175 Butte Road
Sweet ID 83670
800.942.6509
208.584.3349
(FAX) 208.584.3312
Enhancr@micron.net

JOSE MENDEZ
Oncativo 2026
Lanus 1824
Buenos Aires
Argentina
cc951048@bed.buenayre.com.ar

MENKEVICH GUITARS
Michael Menkevich
1401 Church Street
Philadelphia PA 19124
215.288.8417
menkguitar@icdc.com
www.icdc.com/~menkevich

MERCHANT
Merchant Vertical Bass Co.
307 Seventh Avenue
New York NY 10001-6007
212.989.2517

STEVE MERKEL
Integrity Music
1000 Cody Road
Mobile AL 36695

MERMER GUITARS
Richard Mermer, Jr.
P.O. Box 782132
Sebastian FL 32958-4014
561.388.0317
mermer@gate.net
www.gate.net/~mermer

MERVI
Guitarras Mervi S.L.
Abellaroi, 3
San Antonio de Ben-ageber
Valencia 46814
Spain
346.1350336
(FAX) 346.1350220

MESROBIAN
Carl Mesrobian
P.O. Box 204
Salem MA 01970-0204
508.740.6986
cmguitar@gis.net
www.gis.net/~smguitar

MESSENGER
Messenger Upright Electric Bass
P.O. Box 945
Forrestville CA 95436
707.887.2709
mssngr@sonic.net
www.sonic.net/mssngr

MICHAEL DOLAN
3222 Airway Dr. #4
Santa Rosa CA 95403
707.575.0654

SERGE MICHAUD
See SERGE

DELLA GIUSTINA MICHELE
Via della Seta 35
Italy
0438.912378

MILBURN GUITARS
Orville and Robert Milburn
28093 Liberty Road
Sweet Home OR 97386
omilburn@dswebnet.com
www.weber.u.washington.edu/~patm

BIL MITCHELL GUITARS
906 17th St.
Wall NJ 07719-3103
908.681.3430

AARON J. MITCHNECK
Back Mountain Music Company
433 S. Memorial High-way
Trucksville PA 18708
ajnemasis@aol.com

MOJO GUITARS
David Amirault
6630 Sussex Avenue #301
Burnaby British Colum-bia
Canada V5H 3C6
amirault@smartt.com
www.personal.smartt.com/~amirault

MOLINI CUSTOM GUITARS
Mark Moye
441 Briarwood Road
Columbia SC 29206
molini@mailexcite.com

MOLL CUSTOM GUITARS
Bill Moll
720 E. Cherokee
Springfield MO 65807-2706
417.883.9946
mollinst@ix.netcom.com
www.mollinst.com

MONCLOA GUITARS
Daniel Moncloa
M. Prado Ugarteche 626
La Estancia, La Molina
Lima 12
Peru
511.368.0260
511.479.8456
(FAX) 511.479.0266
daniel@net.casopidata.com.pe
www.members.tripod.com/~moncloa

MONTALVO
Distributed by K & S Guitars
2923 Adeline St.
Berkeley CA 94703
510.843.2883
510.548.7538
(FAX) 510.644.1958
BMIEX@globel.california.co
www.california.com/~kands

MONTANA
Distributed by the Kaman Music Corporation
P.O. Box 507
Bloomfield CT 06002-0507
800.647.2244
860.243.7105
(FAX) 860.243.7287
www.kamanmusic.com

JOHN MONTELEONE
Custom Mandolin and Guitar Maker
(P.O. Box 52
Islip NY 11751)
41 Degnon Blvd.
Bay Shore NY 11706
516.277.3620
(FAX) 516.277.3639

MOON GUITARS LTD.
974 Pollokshaws Road
Glascow
Scotland G41 2HA
0044.141.632.9526
(FAX) 0044.141.632.9526

FERGUS MOONEY
4579 Chatterton Way
Victoria British Colum-bia
Canada A8X 4Y7
fmooney@direct.ca

MOONSTONE GUITARS
P.O. Box 757
Eureka CA 95502
707.445.9045
www.northcoast.com/~moongtar

MORENA
Distributed by Guitarras Espanola
Prol. 20 de Noviembre 1513
Paracho Michoacan 60250
Mexico
52.452.50152
(FAX) 52.452.50074

MORGAN GUITARS
3007 Plymouth Drive
North Vancouver Brit-ish Columbia
Canada V7H 1C6
604.929.6577

MORRELL
Distributed by the Joe Morrell Music Distributing Co.
2306 West State Street
Bristol TN 37620
800.545.5811

MORRIS
Moridaira Musical Instrument Company, Ltd.
2-7-4 Iwatioto-Cho
Chiyoda-Ku
Tokyo 101
Japan
81.3.3862.1641
(FAX) 81.3.3864.7454
mmi@kiwi.co.jp

MARCELLO MORRONE
Via Panebianco II
Strada 32
Cosenza
Italy 87100
mmorron@tin.it

JOHN DAVID MORSE
3235 Paper Mill Rd.
Soquel CA 95073
408.426.4745

MORTORO
Gary Mortoro
P.O. Box 161225
Miami FL 33116-1225
305.238.7947
(FAX) 305.259.8745

MOSSMAN
1813 Main Street
Sulphur Springs TX 75482
903.885.4992
(RES) 903.885.9749

MOUNTAIN
Distributed by Music Imports
3322-C Glacier Avenue
San Diego CA 92120
800.748.5711
619.578.3443
(FAX) 619.280.7180

MTD
Michael Tobias Design
760 Zena Highwoods Road
Kingston NY 12401
914.246.0670
(FAX) 914.246.1670
mike@mtobias.com
www.mtobias.com/mtd

C. D. MUNSON
Red Wing Tech Inc.
Hwy. 58 & Pioneer Road
Red Wing MN 55066

PHILLIP MURRAY
M.A.C. Sound
No. 17 Idrone Close
Knocklyon
Dublin 16
Ireland
phillip@clubi.ie

MUSICIAN SOUND DESIGN
Lindenstr. 32
50674 Koln (Cologne)
Germany
221.2409614
(FAX) 221.2409615

KNUT MYHRVOLD
Gitar Doktor'n
Haukedalsv. 66
3960 Stathelle
Norway
gitardoktorn@tm.telia.no

CHRISTOPHER MYLES
P.O. Box 675
Silverton CO 81433-0675
970.387.0185

MYTHIC GUITAR COMPANY
Wind O'Neal
Glen Burnie MD 21060
winds@sprynet.com
home.sprynet.com/sprynet/winds

ARTHUR NAPOLITANO
P.O. Box 0294
Allentown NJ 08501
609.259.8818

NASH
Distributed by Musima North America, Inc.
13540 N. Florida Ave-nue
Suite 206 A
Tampa FL
813.961.8357
(FAX) 813.961.8514

NASHVILLE GUITAR COMPANY
Marty Lanham
(P.O. Box 160412)
4309 Burrus Avenue
Nashville TN 37216
615.262.4891
(FAX) 615.262.4891
nashguitar@aol.com
www.members.aol.com/nashguitar

NATIONAL RESO-PHONIC
National Reso-Phonic Guitars, Inc.
871 Via Esteban #C
San Luis Obispo CA 93401
805.546.8442
(FAX) 805.546.8430
natres@nationalguitars.co
www.nationalguitars.com

N B CUSTOM GUITARS
1251 10th Street
Courtenay, British Co-lumbia
Canada V9N 1R8
250.338.6834
nbcustom@island.net
www.island.net/~nbcustom/

NEW WORLD GUITAR COMPANY
P.O. Box 986
Ben Lomond CA 95005
408.336.2436
(FAX) 408.336.2436
khill@cruzio.com

DAVID NEWTON
Beaumont TX
d.newton@worldnet.att.net

NICKERSON GUITARS
Brad Nickerson
8 Easthampton Rd.
Northampton MA 01060
413.586.8521

NIGHTINGALE
25 Denmark Street
London WC2H 8NJ
England
0171.379.3572

NIXON CUSTOM GUITARS
Stephen Nixon
47 A McCurtain Street
Cork
Ireland
arthive@indigo.ie

ROY NOBLE
Distributed by Stringed Instrument Division
123 W. Alder
Missoula MT 59802
406.549.1502
(FAX) 406.549.3380

NORMAN
Distributed by La Si Do, Inc.
4240 Sere Street
St. Laurent Quebec
Canada H4T 1A6
514.343.5560
(FAX) 514.343.5098
sales@lasido.com
www.lasido.com

SUSAN NORRIS
Vermont Musical Instrument Builders Cooperative
RD #1, Box 2250
Plainfield VT 05667

JAMES NORTH
810.227.7072
www.ismi.net/upnorth

NORTHWOOD GUITARS
#4 - 20701 Langley By-Pass
Langley BC
Canada V3A 5E8
604.533.5777
(FAX) 604.532.7815

NORTHWORTHY MUSICAL INSTRUMENTS
Main Road
Hulland Ward
ashbourne Derbyshire
England DE6 3EA
1335.370806
(FAX) 1335.370806
Northwrthy@aol.com

LAWRENCE NYBERG
Acoustic Guitars & Bouzoukis
6320 Bond Road
Hornby Island
Canada V0R 1Z0
nyberg@island.net
www.ice.el.utwente.nl/~han/bouzouki/nyberg.html

OLD WOODS GUITARS
Stacy Woods
3354 Bagdad Road
Bagdad KY 40003
gufb27a@prodigy.com

OLSEN AUDIO
117 Elm Street
Saskatoon SK
Canada S7J 0G6
306.244.4973
bolsen@sk.sympatico.ca

JAMES OLSON
Olson Guitars
11840 Sunset Avenue
Circle Pines MN 55014
612.780.5301
(FAX) 612.780.8513

OLYMPIA GUITARS
Distributed by Tacoma Guitars
4615 E. 192nd St.
Tacoma WA 98446
206.847.6508
(FAX) 206.847.8524
TacomaGtr@aol.com
www.TacomaGuitars.com

OMEGA INSTRUMENTS
Kevin Gallagher Guitars, Inc.
RR 3, Box 3384
Saylorsburg PA 18353
610.381.4041
(FAX) 717.992.9285

GEERT VAN OPSTAL
Berkenlaan 8
Leon op Zand
CH 5175
Netherlands
0130.416362690
luthier@worldonline.nl

TYLER OREHEK
162 West 54th Street
Suite 10 A
New York NY 10019
orehek@aol.com

JOSE ORIBE GUITARS
2141 Lakeview Road
Vista CA 92084-7713
619.727.2230
(FAX) 619.727.2238
oribeg@aol.com
members.aol.com/oribeg
www.cybozone.com/fg/oribe.html

OSCAR SCHMIDT
Oscar Schmidt International
Distributed by Washburn International
255 Corporate Woods Parkway
Vernon Hills IL 600061-3109
800.877.6863
847.913.5511
(FAX) 847.913.7772
washburn@washburn.com
www.washburn.com

VINCE OTTALAGANO
Vishnu Music
(P.O. Box 1248)
64 North Main Street
Gloversville NY 12078
vincent@superior.net

OUTBOUND
Outbound Instruments
1319 Spruce Street, Suite 205

Boulder CO 80302
800.487.1887
303.449.1887
(FAX) 303.447.1905
moorejt@indra.com

OVATION
Distributed by the Kaman Music Corporation
P.O. Box 507
Bloomfield CT 06002-0507
800.647.2244
860.509.8888
(FAX) 860.509.8891
info-kmc@kaman.com
www.kamanmusic.com

GREGORY OXRIEDER
Handmade Guitars
10617 NE 13th
Bellevue WA 98004

PALMER
Distributed by Chesbro Music Company
P.O. Box 2009
Idaho Falls ID 83403
800.CHE.SBRO
800.243.7276
(FAX) 208.522.8712
cmc@srv.net
Distributed by Tropical Music Corporation
7091 N.W. 51st Street
Miami FL 33166-5629
305.594.3909
(FAX) 305.594.0786
www.tropicalmusic.com

PALMWOOD GUITARS & STRINGED INSTRUMENTS
Michael J. Palm
92 Thomas Street
Wellington Pt. Queensland
Australia 4159
c/o:
  j.owens@qca.gu.edu.qu

CORIANI PAOLO
Via Barchetta 98
Moderna
Italy 41100
075.8041485

SHELLEY PARK
604.254.8210

PARROT PRODUCTIONS
Kevin Zaccheo
2390 Ocean Pines
Berlin MD 215811
kraccheo@dmv.com

LUIGI DE PASCALI
P.O. Box
Avuily - Geneva
Switzerland 1237
41.22.756.25.38

PAUL REED SMITH
Paul Reed Smith Guitars
107 Log Canoe Circle
Stevensville MD 21666
410.643.9970
(FAX) 410.643.9980
www.prsguitars.com

STEVEN OWSLEY SMITH
Taos NM

PAUL'S GUITARS
Paul Ritten
740 N. 10th Street
Spearfish SD 57783
ccr7861@mystic.bhsu.edu

GEORGE & NOAH PEACOCK
Peacock Music
2200 15th Street
San Francisco CA 94114
viotarla@pacbell.net

PEAVEY
Peavey Electronics Corporation
711 A Street
Meridian MS 39301
601.483.5365
(FAX) 601.486.1278
www.peavey.com

DARRYL J. PECK
D.J. Peck Guitar Builder
2 Indian Road
Dudley MA 01571
c-dpeck@ma.ultranet.com

PEDERSON GUITARS
Gretsch Building #4
60 Broadway
4th Floor West
Brooklyn NY 11211
718.599.6442
Distributed by Rudy's Music Shop
169 West 48th St.
New York NY 10036
212.391.1699
(FAX) 212.768.3782

PEGASUS
Pegasus Guitars and Ukuleles
Bob Gleason
45 Pohaku Street
Hilo HI 96720-4572
808.935.7301
(FAX) 808.935.7301

DARYL PERRY
The Guitar Suite
500-100 Arthur Street
Winnipeg Manitoba
Canada R3B 1H3

PHILLIP PETILLO
Petillo Masterpiece Guitars
1206 Herbert Avenue
Ocean NJ 07712
908.531.6338

PETROS GUITARS
Bruce Petros
345 Country Road CE
Holland WI 54130-8967
414.766.1295
petros@atw.earthreach.co
www.atw.earthreach.com/~petros

MARCO ANTONIO PETTA
Av. 1, Hoyada de Milla, No. 0-259
Merida
Venezuela 5201-A

PHIL
Myung Sung Music Ind. Co., Ltd.
#143 Deung Won Ri
Jori-Myon Paju-City
Kyungki-Do Korea
82.348.941.5477
(FAX) 82.348.941.7938

PHIL HARMONIC GUITARS
Phil Orlikowski
4388 County Road 7640

West Plains MO 65775
sparky@townsqr.com

PHOENIX
Phoenix Guitar Company
6030 E. Le Marche
Scottsdale AZ 85254
602.553.0005
(FAX) 602.553.0646

PICATO
Distributed by Saga Musical Instruments
429 Littlefield Avenue
South San Francisco CA 94080
800.BUY.SAGA
415.588.5558
415.871.7590

PIMENTEL & SONS GUITAR MAKERS
Lorenzo Pimentel
3316 LaFayette NE
Albuquerque NM 87107
505.884.1669
pimentel@rt66.com
www.rt66.com/~pimentel

RONALD PINKHAM
Distributed by Woodsound Studio
P.O. Box 149
Glen Cove ME 04846
207.596.7407

PLANET GUITARS
Augustin Henriques
1117 Semlin Drive
Vancouver British Columbia
Canada V5L 4K3
classical@musician.org
www.intergate.bc.ca/business/magi

PMC GUITARS
Distributed by Sound Trek Distributors U.S.A.
2119 W. Hillsborough Avenue
Tampa FL 33603
888.466.TREK
www.sound-trek.com

POSHEK
Joe Poshek
751 Rembrandt
Laguna Beach CA 92651
poshek@aol.com

PREMIER
Premier Guitars & Amps
Distributed by the Entertainment Music Marketing Corp.
770-12 Grand Blvd.
Deer park NY 117219
800.345.6013
516.243.0600
(FAX) 516.243.0605

RICHARD PRENKERT
Distributed by Kirkpatrick Guitar Studio
4607 Maple Avenue
Baltimore MD 21227-4023
410.242.2744
(FAX) 410.242.0326
info@guitar1stop.com

JOHN PRICE
*Distributed by the Luthier
Music Corporation*
341 W. 44th Street
New York NY 10036
212.397.6038
(FAX) 212.397.6048
luthier@tiac.net
www.tiac/net/users/luthier

PRICE ENTERPRISES
Gary H. Price
P.O. Box 1115
Jones OK 73049
ghprice@telepath.com

THOMAS PRISLOE
P.O. Box 99
Mesa CO 81643
prisloe@gj.net
www.gj.net/~prisloe

PRUDENCIO SAEZ
*Distributed by Saga Musical
Instruments*
429 Littlefield Avenue
P.O. Box 2841
South San Francisco
CA 94080
800.BUY.SAGA
415.742.6888
(FAX) 415.871.7590

FABIO RAGGHIANTI
Via Fornace 10
Caprigna (LU)
Italy 55045
0584.796050

RICHARD RAIMI
4028 Woodland Park
Avenue N.
Seattle WA

RAIMUNDO
Raimundo y Aparicio S.A.
C/. Islas Canarias, 3
Poligono Industrial
Fuente del Jarro
46988 Paterna (Valencia)
Spain
34.6.132.1404
(FAX) 34.6.132.0902
raimundo.guitar@chip10.es
*Distributed in the U.S. by
Luthier Music Corporation*
341 W. 44th Street
New York NY 10036-
0774
212.397.6038
(FAX) 212.397.6048
Distributed by Music Imports
3322-C Glacier Avenue
San Diego CA 92120
800.748.5711
619.578.3443
(FAX) 619.280.7180

RAINSONG
*Rainsong Graphite
Guitars*
300 Ohukai Road #C-
214
Kihei HI 96753
*Distributed by Kuau
Technology, Ltd.*
P.O. Box 1031
Puunene HI 96784
800.788.5828
808.879.0434
(FAX) 808.879.4261
rainsongki@aol.com
www.rainsong.com

RALSTON
P.O. Box 138
Grant Town WV
26574
304.278.5645

JOSE RAMIREZ
*Distributed by Guitar Salon
International*
3100 Donald Douglas
Loop N.
Santa Monica CA
90405
310.399.2181
(FAX) 310.399.9283
GSImail@guitarsalon.com
www.guitarsalon.com

**RAFAEL MONTES
RAMIREZ LUTHIERS,
S.L.**
Apartado 126
Cerdanyola Del Valles
Barcelona E-08290
Spain
luthiers@abaforum.es

CARLO RASPAGNI
Via Vitt. Veneto 7
Vignate (MI)
Italy
02.9566089

RAVEN
*c/o Bearingdale Guitars
& Basses*
01582.597651
(FAX) 01582.599994

RAYA AND RAYA
*Antonio Raya Ferrer,
Luthier*
Paseo del Salon 9
Granada
Spain 18009

RBC
Robert Bustos
995 W. 3rd Street
North Vancouver British Columbia
Canada V7P 1E4
amirault@smartt.com
www.personal.smartt.com/~
amirault/rbc.html

**READ CUSTOM
INSTRUMENTS**
Bolton MA

J. K. REDGATE GUITARS
46 Penno Parade North
Adelaide South Australia
Australia 5052
61.8.370.3198
(FAX) 61.8.370.3198
redgate@ozemail.com.au
www.ozemail.com.au/~
redgate/
*Distributed by Classic Guitars
International*
2899 Agoura Road,
Suite 701
Westlake Village CA
91361
805.495.0490
(FAX) 805.381.0329

JOHAN REBERGEN
Joh. Camphuysstraat
47
Utrecht 3534 ES
Holland

REEDMAN
*Distributed by Reedman
America*
13006 Philadelphia
Street, Suite 301
Whittier CA 90601
310.698.2645
(FAX) 310.698.1074

REGAL
*Distributed by Saga Musical
Instruments*
429 Littlefield Avenue
South San Francisco
CA 94080
800.BUY.SAGA
415.588.5558
415.871.7590

THOMAS REIN
*Thomas Rein Classical
Guitars*
334 Marion Avenue
St. Louis MO 63119

JON REYNOLDS
The Custom Job
P.O. Box 872
Angwin CA 94508
thecustomjob@angelfire.co
www.angelfire.com/biz/thecu
stomjob

RHINEHART GUITARS
Billy Rhinehart
14 Second Street
Athens OH 45701
www.eurekanet.com/~rhine
hart

RIBBECKE GUITARS
Tom Ribbecke
P.O. Box 1581
Santa Rosa CA 95402
707.433.3778

KEN RICE
701 Cypress Wood
Cove
Chesapeake VA 23323
krice@macs.net

RICKENBACKER
*Rickenbacker
International
Corporation*
3895 S. Main Street
Santa Ana CA 92707-
5710
714.545.5574
(FAX) 714.754.0135
info@rickenbacker.com
www.rickenbacker.com

GEORGE RIZSANYI
Hands On Music
50 King Street E.
Bowmanville Ontario
Canada L1N 1C2
fretboy@gsfmicro.com
www.gsfmicro.com

GARY RIZZOLO
The Guitar Company
113 York Street
Sandy Bay Hobart
Tasmania 7005
rizzolo@netspace.net.au

MIKHAIL ROBERT
*Distributed by Kirkpatrick Guitar
Studio*
4607 Maple Avenue
Baltimore MD 21227-
4023
410.242.2744
(FAX) 410.242.0326
info@guitar1stop.com

THAD ROBOSSON
Precision Guitar
4442 N. 7th Avenue
Suite 6
Phoenix AZ 85013
tmrob@primenet.com

RODRIGUEZ
*Distributed by the Fender
Musical Instrument Corp.*
7975 North Hayden
Road
Scottsdale AZ 85258-
3246
602.596.9690
(FAX) 602.596.1384
www.fender.com

**ALBERTO PAREDES
RODRIGUEZ**
Transversal 68D #79A-
15
Santafe de Bogot
Bogot
Columbia
albertoparedes@hotmail.com

RODRIGUEZ GUITARS
Tom Rodriguez
929 Meyers Street
Richmond VA 23230

ROGUE
*Distributed in the U.S by
Musician's Friend*
931 Chevy Way
Medford OR 97504
Also:
P.O. Box 4520
Medford OR 97501
800.776.5176
(FAX) 541.776.1370
support@musiciansfriend
.com
www.musiciansfriend.com

**ROMANTIC GUITAR &
MANDOLIN CO.**
Roman Tarnovetsky
25 Wood Street 2411
Toronto Ontario
Canada M4Y 2P9
romantic@aracnet.net

JEAN ROMPRE
Jean Rompre Luthier Enr.
460 Ste. - Catherine
West.
Montreal Quebec
Canada H3B 1A7
ad791876@er.uquam.ca

JONATHAN W. ROSE
*Specializing in Archtop
designs*
46 Calamus Lane
Strasburg VA 22657
540.465.4964

ROGER ROSE
620 B Blandy Drive
Colts Neck NJ 07722-
5034
rose@myhost.com

GERALD ROSENTHAL
69 Plympton Street
Waltham MA 02154

ROBERT RUCK
37676 Hood Canal
Drive NE
Hansville WA 98340
360.297.4024

STEVE RYDER
*Steve Ryder Stringed
Instruments*
93 Washington Avenue
Portland ME 04101
strydah@cybertours.com
sjryder.com

SAEHAN
*Saehan International
Co., Ltd.*
Bldg. 1599-11
Sedcho Dong #1503
15th Floor
Seoul Korea
82.2.523.6459
(FAX) 82.2.523.6455-7

ERIC SAHLIN
4324 E. 37th Avenue
Spokane WA 99223

T. SAKASHTA GUITARS
Taku Sakashta, Luthier
1905 Sperring Road
#21
Sonoma CA 95476
707.938.8604
(FAX) 707.938.5246

SAMICK
*Samick Music
Corporation*
18521 Railroad Street
City of Industry CA
91748
800.592.9393
818.964.4700
(FAX) 818.965.5224
samick_music@earthlink
.net

CAMILLO SAMPAOLO
Viale Isonzo 60
Milano
Italy 20135
sampa@planet.it
members.planet.it/freewww/
sampa/home.html

DR. BILL SAMSON
88 Grove Road
West Ferry
Dundee
Scotland DD5 7AB
wbs@sol.co.uk

SAND GUITARS
Kirk R. Sand
The Guitar Shoppe
1027 B. North Coast
Hwy.
Laguna Beach CA
92651
714.497.2110

**SANDEN ACOUSTIC
GUITARS**
Michael Sanden
Karl X Gustavs Gata 33
Helsingborg
Sweden 25439

SANTA CRUZ
*Santa Cruz Guitar
Company*
328 Ingalls Street
Santa Cruz CA 95060
408.425.0999
(FAX) 408.425.3604
scgc@cruzio.com
www.santacruzguitar.com

SANTA FE GUITARS
*Santa Fe Violin Guitar
Works*
1412 Llano St.
Santa Fe NM 87505
505.988.4240

SANTA ROSA
*Distributed by A.R. Musical
Enterprises, Inc.*
9031 Technology Drive
Fishers IN 46038
800.428.4807
317.577.6999
(FAX) 317.577.7288

SANTER GUITARS
Lewis Santer
2216 Calaveras Avenue
Davis CA 95616
lewis@davis.com

LOVERDE SANTO
Via del Ciclamino 42
Catania
Italy 95121
095.451046

STEPHEN NEAL SAQUI
The Blue Guitar
San Diego CA
saqui@anarchyx.com
www.ax.com/users/saqui/
steve

KAZVO SATO
Heiligenstrasse 27
66740 Saarlouis
Saar
Germany

SCHAEFER GUITARS
Ed Shaefer
5904 Sandra Drive
Fort Worth TX 76133
817.346.0855

THEO SCHARPACH
Acterste Aa 14
5571 VE Bergeyk
The Netherlands
31.497.541278
(FAX) 31.497.541278

SCHATTEN DESIGN
Les Schatten
124 Ottawa Street S.
Kitchener Ontario
Canada
ischattn@netcom.ca

SCHEERHORN
*Scheerhorn Custom
Resonator Guitars*
1454 52nd St.
Kentwood MI 49508
616.281.3927

BRUCE VANDER SCHEL
West Music Company
1212 5th Street
Coralville IA 52241
bruce@avalon.net
www.avalon.net/~bruce

IVON SCHMUKLER
*Artisan Fretted
Instruments*
8 Easthampton Road
Northampton MA
01060
leeds@crocker.com

RICHARD SCHNEIDER
*Richard Schneider Estate
Lost Mountain Center for
the Guitar*
P.O. Box 44
Carlsborg WA 98324
360.683.2778

**ERIC SCHOENBERG
GUITARS**
106 Main Street
Tiburon CA 94920
415.789.0846
www.wenet.net/~guitar

SCHRAMM GUITARS
David D. Schramm
926 West Princeton
Avenue
Fresno CA 93075

SCHWARTZ GUITARS
Sheldon Schwartz
371 Bradwick Drive
Unit 5
Concord Ontario
Canada L4K 2P4
905.738.0024

**FLIP VAN DOMBURG
SCIPIO**
Staten Island NY

ROGER SCRAFFORD
Seattle WA

SEAGULL
Seagull Guitars
Distributed by La Si Do, Inc.
4240 Sere Street
St. Laurent Quebec
Canada H4T 1A6
514.343.5560
(FAX) 514.343.5098
sales@lasido.com
www.lasido.com

SEBRING
Distributed by VMI Industries
*Vega Musical
Instruments*
P.O. Box 1357
2980-D Enterprise
Street
Brea CA 92822-1357
800.237.4864
714.572.1492
(FAX) 714.572.9321

SEDONA
Distributed by VMI Industries
*Vega Musical
Instruments*
P.O. Box 1357
2980-D Enterprise
Street
Brea CA 92822-1357
800.237.4864
714.572.1492
(FAX) 714.572.9321

SEGOVIA
Distributed by L.A. Guitar Works
19320 Vanowen Street
Reseda CA
818.758.8787
(FAX) 818.758.8788

SELMER
The Selmer Co. Inc.
P.O. Box 310
Elkhart IN 46515
800.348.7426
219.522.1675
www.selmer.com

**DOUGLAS SPRIGGS
SELSAM**
Selsam Innovations
8211 Michael Drive
Huntington Beach CA
92647

SERENA
Distributed by Saga Musical
Instruments
429 Littlefield Avenue
P.O. Box 2841
South San Francisco
CA 94080
800.BUY.SAGA
415.742.6888
(FAX) 415.871.7590

SERGE GUITARS
Serge Michaud
63 Rue Boisvert
St. Etienne Quebec
Canada G6J 1G3
smichaud@sympatico.ca

www3.sympatico.ca/
smichaud

SEXAUER
Bruce Sexauer, Luthier
265 B Gate 5 Road
Saulsalito CA 94965
800.735.0650
luthier@hooked.net
www.hooked.net~luthier

SHANTI GUITARS
Michael Hornick
P.O. Box 341
Avery CA 95224
209.795.5299

**SHELTON-FARRETTA
GUITARS**
John Shelton
5040 SE 115th
Portland OR 97266
jshelton@teleport.com
www.teleport.com/~
jshelton/

SHENANDOAH
Distributed by the Martin Guitar
Company
510 Sycamore Street
Nazareth PA 18064-
9233
800.345.3103
610.759.2837
(FAX) 610.759.5757
info@mguitar.com
www.mguitar.com

DAVID SHEPPARD
Sheppard Instruments & Repairs
1820 Spring Garden
Street
Greensboro NC 27403

CHARLES R. SHIFFLETT
H-R Guitars
124 7 Avenue SW
High River Alberta
Canada T1V 1A2
403.652.1526
105025.2644@compuserve
.com

SHO-BUD
P.O. Box 358
Ridgeland SC 29936

**SIERRA VISTA GUITAR
COMPANY**
Tombstone AZ

SIGMA
Distributed by the Martin Guitar
Company
510 Sycamore Street
Nazareth PA 18064-
9233
800.345.3103
610.759.2837
(FAX) 610.759.5757
info@mguitar.com
www.mguitar.com

SIGURDSON GUITARS
Jeff Sigurdson
2158 East 39th Avenue
Vancouver British Co-
lumbia
Canada V5P 1H7
amirault@smartt.com
www.personal.smartt.com/~
amirault/sigurdson.html

SILBER
Distributed by K & S
Guitars
2923 Adeline Street
Berkeley CA 94703
510.843.2883
510.548.7538

(FAX) 510.644.1958
BMIEX@GLOBEL.CALIFORN
IA.COM
www.california.com/~kands

DENNIS SILER
Jack's Music
3190 Highway 95
Hattieville AR 72063
siler@petit-jean.pjtc.tec
.ar.us

JOHN SILVER
#5 Chester Road
Parkwood
Johannesburg
South Africa

SIMON & PATRICK
Distributed by La Si Do, Inc.
4240 Sere Street
St. Laurent Quebec
Canada H4T 1A6
514.343.5560
(FAX) 514.343.5098
sales@lasido.com
www.lasido.com

MIKE SKORSKI
Mike's Guitars at Jones Music
161-B RObertsville
Road
Oak Ridge TN 37830
biz2biz@nxs.net

DANIEL SLAMAN
Westeinde 58
2512 H E
Den Haag The Nether-
lands
31.70.389.42.32
(FAX) 31.70.364.62.89

**A. LAWRENCE SMART,
LUTHIER**
John Kinnaird
501 E. Park
Social Circle GA
30025
jhkjr@mindspring.com

SOLID ROCK GUITARS
Mark Vinciguerra
1415 River Street
Palatka FL 32177
srg@gbso.net

SOMERVELL GUITARS
Douglas P. Somervell
2443 Green Cove Road
Brasstown NC 28902
somervell@grove.net
wyattweb.com/freepage/s/so
mervell@grove.net/home.s
html

LARRY STAMM
P.O. Box 561
McBride British Co-
lumbia
Canada V0J 2E0
larryst@vis.bc.ca

LES STANSELL
P.O. Box 6056
Pistol River OR 97444

JERRY STARR
411 61st Street
Albuquerque NM
87121

STAUFER GUITARS
Andre Waldenmaier
Theodor Engel-Str. 46
Escenbach
Germany 73107
07161.45480
(FAX) 07161.45480

JOEL A. STAUFFER
Front Porch Dreams Guitars
35786 165th Avenue
Goodhue MN 55027

BOB ST. CYR
14 Beverly Street
Waterloo Ontario
Canada N2L 2H6
bobstcy@golden.net
www.gsfmicro.com

STEELE GUITARS
John Steele
641 West D. Street
South
Dixon CA 95620
jwsteele@ucdavis.edu

STEELE GUITARS
K. Doug Steele
112-B Edwardia Drive
Greensboro NC 27409

STELLING
Stelling Banjo Works, Ltd.
7258 Banjo Lane
Afton VA 22920
800.5.STRING
804.295.1917
(FAX) 804.971.8309
stelling@stellingbanjo.com
www.stellingbanjo.com

THOM STEVENS
Hawknest Company
2472 Citation Court
Wexford PA 15090
hawknest@nauticom.net

**STEVENS CUSTOM
GUITARS**
Muhldorfstr. 8
Aufgang 5
Muchen
Germany D-81671
089.490.00785
(FAX) 089.49000785
www.guitars.de

DANIEL STICKEL
710 West 15th
Suite 21
North Vancouver Brit-
ish Columbia
Canada V3M 3K6

STOLL
Christian Stoll
Aarstr. 268
65232 Taunusstein
Germany
61.28.982864
(FAX) 61.28.86867
Distributed by Salwender
International
1140 N. Lemon Street
#M
Orange CA 92867
714.583.1285
(FAX) 714.583.9331
uwe@salwender.com
www.salwender.com

STONEMAN
Stoneman Guitars
20 Russell Blvd.
Bradford PA 16701
814.362.8820

STRINGFELLOW
Distributed by Bill Cumpiano
P.O. Box 329
Leeds MA 01053-
3730
413.586.3730
(FAX) 413.585.1595
eljibaro@crocker.com
www.crocker.com/~eljibaro

ROGER STROMBERG
Andgraend 28
Lulea
Sweden
roger.stromberg@usa.net

BILL STULTZ
Bill's Guitar Repair
1600 Robin Road
Martinsville IN 46151
bbstultz@tecwrite.co

SUPERIOR GUITAR WORKS
Tim and Cindy Huenke
4047 Cresson Street,
2nd Floor
Philadelphia PA 19127
superiorguitar@pipeline.com

TOM SYDOW
Tom S. Guitar Works
16105 Castile Drive
Whittier CA 90603

ANDREA TACCHI
Concert Guitar Maker
Via Monte Oliveto 20
Firenze
Italy 50124
tacchi@dada.it

TACOMA GUITARS
4615 E. 192nd St.
Tacoma WA 98446
800.743.8830
206.847.6508
(FAX) 206.847.8524
TacomaGtr@aol.com
www.TacomaGuitars.com

TAKAMINE
Distributed by the Kaman Music Corporation
P.O. Box 507
Bloomfield CT 06002-0507
800.647.2244
860.509.8888
(FAX) 860.509.8891
info-kmc@kaman.com
www.kamanmusic.com

TANARA
Distributed by the Chesbro Music Company
P.O. Box 2009
327 Broadway
Idaho Falls ID 83403-2009
800.CHE.SBRO
800.243.7276
(FAX) 208.522.8712
cmc@srv.net

TANGLEWOOD
Distributed by European Music Company, Ltd.
Unit 6
Concorde Business Centre
Main Road
Biggin Hill
Kent
England TN16 3YN
01959.571600
(FAX) 01959.572267

Z. Q. TATE
Fretted Instrument Engineering
37 Scout Avenue
Auckland
New Zealand
(FAX) 64.9.620.8790
croydon-mcrae@xtra.co.nz

CHARLES S. TAUBER
Hamilton, Ontario
Canada
www.cybozone.com/fg/
tauber.html

TAYLOR GUITARS
1940 Gillespie Way
El Cajon CA 92020
800.943.6782
619.258.1207
(Fax) 619.258.4052
srapp@taylorguitars.com

STEVE TAYLOR
13 Atkins Lane
Newport News VA
23602

TEXARKANA
Distributed by V.J. Rendano Music Company, Inc.
7152 Market Street
Youngstown OH
44512
800.321.4048
330.758.0881
(FAX) 330.758.1096

OTIS A. THOMAS
Baddeck, Cape Breton
Nova Scotia
Canada

THOMPSON GUITARS
Ted Thompson
9905 Coldstream
Creek Road
Vernon British
Columbia
Canada V1B 1C8
604.542.9410
(FAX) 604.542.9410

BILL THRASH
P.O. Box 1783
Las Cruces NM 87901
thrash@riolink.com

THREET GUITARS
Judy Threet
1215 13th Street SE
Suite 212
Calgary Alberta
Canada T2G 3J4

THUNDERHOUSE INSTRUMENTS
Yuri Amatnieks
2809 Bucklepost Cres.
Mississauga Ontario
Canada L5N 1X6
amatniek@inforamp.net

ROGER THURMAN
Thurman Guitar & Violin Repair, Inc.
900 Franklin Avenue
Kent OH 44240
rogluthier@aol.com
members.aol.com/rogluthier/
index/html

ROBERT TICE
HCR #1, Box 465
Sciota PA 18354
luthier@epix.net

TIMELESS INSTRUMENTS
David Freeman
P.O. Box 51
Tugaske SK
Canada S0H 4B0
888.884.2753
306.759.2042
(FAX) 306.759.2729
www3.sk.sympatico.ca/
timeless

JERRY TIMM
4512 47th Street S.E.
Auburn WA 98092
253.833.8667
(FAX) 253.833.1820

TIPPIN GUITAR COMPANY
Bill Tippin
3 Beacon Street
Marblehead MA
01945
617.631.5749
www.tiac.net/users/keri/
Tippin.htm

INGVARD TJELTA
Nadienne GWS
Nordahlgriegsgate 21
Moss
Norway 1524
(47) 69.25.45.84

OTIS A. TOMAS
RR 4, Baddeck
Cape Breton Nova
Scotia
Canada BO3 1B0

TOMMYHAWK
Tom Barth's Music Box
1910 Rt. 10
Succasunna NJ 07876
800.558.4295
201.366.6611
(FAX) 201.366.5243
NJLUCK@aol.com
www.gbase.com/tbmusic/

RICHARD P. TOPF
Topf Tech
2230 East Hamilton
Avenue
Orange CA 92867

TORTORICI GUITARS
Ben Tortorici
2111 Palo Verde Ave-
nue
Long Beach CA
90815-3323
tortorici@luthiers.com
www.tortorici-guitars.com

JEFF TRAUGOTT GUITARS
Jeff Traugott
2553 B Mission Street
Santa Cruz CA 95060
408.426.2313
(FAX) 408.426.2313

J. TRIGGS GUITARS
Fine Hand Made Guitars & Mandolins
James Triggs
P.O. Box 394
Stilwell KS 66085
913.681.9703
(FAX) 913.681.9703

TRINITY GUITARS
Jim Holler, Builder
2089 Camp Street
Jamestown NY
ajrb30a@prodigy.com

DALE UNGER
See AMERICAN ARCHTOP.

TREVOR USHER
Sounds in Scale
Trefaes Bella, Sarn
Pwllhei, Gynedd
United Kingdom LL53
8RL

VAGABOND
Vagabond Travel Guitar
String Smith Custom Guitars
(P.O. Box 845)
34 Learned Street
Albany NY 12201
800.801.1341
518.436.9942
vagabond@stringsmith.co
www.stringsmith.com

JAN VAISTO
Malvavagen 23
Akersbera
Sweden 18435
jan.vaisto@mailbox
.swipnet.se

ETINNE VALLEE
25 Jolicouer, Suite 3
Victoriaville Quebec
Canada G6P 2P8

VALLEY ARTS
Distributed by Samick Music Corporation
18521 Railroad Street
City of Industry CA
91748
800.592.9393
818.964.4700
(FAX) 818.965.5224
samick_music@earthlink
.net

VANTAGE
Distributed by Music Industries Corporation
99 Tulip Avenue
Suite 101
Floral Park NY 11001
800.431.6699
516.352.4110
(FAX) 516.352.0754
mic@musicindustries.com
www.musicindustries.com

VANTEK
Distributed by Music Industries Corporation
99 Tulip Avenue
Suite 101
Floral Park NY 11001
800.431.6699
516.352.4110
(FAX) 516.352.0754
mic@musicindustries.com
www.musicindustries.com

CHARLES VEGA
2101 Carterdale Road
Baltimore MD 21209-4523
410.664.6506

VENSON
Sungbo Industrial Co. Ltd.
C.P.O. Box 10580
Seoul
Korea
(FAX) 82.2.3473.5626

VERSOUL
Kutomotie 13
Fin-00380 Helsinki
Finland
358.0565.1876
(FAX) 358.0565.1876

VESTAX
Vestax Corporation
2-37-1 Kamiuma
Setagayaku
Tokyo 154-0011
03.3412.7011
(FAX) 03.3412.7013
vestax-corporation@msn
.com

Vestax Musical Electronics Corporation
2870 Cordelia Rd.,
Suite 100
Fairfield CA 94585
707.427.1920
(FAX) 707.427.2023

JOSE MA. VILAPLANA
Distributed by Manufacturas Alhambra, S.L.
Duquesa de Almo-
dovar, 11
Muro del Alcoy 03830
Spain
34.6.55.30011
(FAX) 34.6.55.30190

CIPRIANI VINCENZO
Via Cimabue 5
S. Madrid d. Angeli
Assisi (PG)
Italy 06088
075.8041485 BREAK =

VINTAGE
Distributed by John Hornby Skewes & Co., Ltd.
Salem House
Parkinson Approach
Garforth Leeds
LS25 2HR England
44.113.286.5381
(FAX) 44.113.286.8518

VINTAGE DESIGNS
Ray Whitaker
Route 7, Box 1538-X
Manning SC 29102-9242
803.473.3707
vin_designs@ftc-i.net
www.geocities.com/
nashville/2041

VIPUR GUITARS
Pretoria
South Africa

V.J. RENDANO
See ESPANOLA.
See KARERA.
See TEXARKANA.

VOLBRECHT GUITARS
Ron Volbrecht
130 North Artist Drive
Nashville IN 47448
ozbond@mon-
roe.lib.in.us

MATTHIAS WAGNER
Ruschstr. 5
Vogtsburg
Germany D-79235
matthias.wagner_lavten
@t-online.de

WALKER GUITARS
Kim Walker
314 Pendleton Hill Rd.
North Stonington CT
06359
203.599.8753

WARWICK
Warwick GmbH & Co.
Music Equipment KG
Postfach 10010
D-08258 Mark-
  neukirchen
Germany
3742.25550
(FAX) 3742.55599
Exclusively Distributed in the
U.S. by Dana B. Goods
5427 Hollister Avenue
Santa Barbara CA
  93111-2345
800.765.8663
805.964.9610
(FAX) 805.964.9749
72431.416@compuserve
.com
www.danabgoods.com

WASHBURN
Distributed by Washburn
International
255 Corporate Woods
  Parkway
Vernon Hills IL 60061-
  3109
800.US.SOUND
(800.877.6863)
847.913.5511
(FAX) 847.913.7772
washburn@washburn.com
www.washburn.com

WATTS GUITARS
Gary Watts
2457 NW Grant Avenue
Corvallis OR 97330

WEBBER GUITARS
David Webber
135 A Crown Street
North Vancouver Brit-
  ish Columbia
Canada V7J 1G4
604.980.0315
www.webberguitars.com

WECHTER GUITARS
Abraham Wechter
(P.O. Box 91)
200 S. Gremps
Paw Paw MI 49079
616.657.3479
(FAX) 616.657.3479
wechter@guitar.net
michaeld@net-link.net

www.guitar.net/wechterguit
ars/
Exclusive Sales and Marketing
Lasar Music Corporation
P.O. Box 2045
Brentwood TN 37027
615.337.4913
(FAX) 615.373.4986
lanez9@idt.net
Distributed in Japan by Okada
International, Inc.
Mr. Sei
2-15-8 Tamazusumi
Setagaya-ku
Tokyo
Japan 158
03.3703.3221
(AFX) 03.3703.1821

RON WEGELIN
1414 W. 14st
Scottsbluff NV 69361
rwegelin@panesu.esu14.k12
.ne.us

SYLVAN WELLS
618 N. Wild Olive
Daytona Beach FL
  33118
swells@america.com

WENTZELL GUITARS
Michael F. Wentzell
609 Longstreet Circle
Summerville SC
  29483
wguitars@cchat.com
www.cchat.com/wguitars

STEVE WESLEY
Taree, NSW
Australia

RICH WESTERMAN
6780 Warren
St. Anne IL 60964
musicadtk@keynet.net
www.execpe.com/~danb/m
andolin/westerman.html

WHEAT COMPANY
Arroyo Grande CA

J. WHITE
England
01252.520911

**WHITSETT GUITAR
WORKS**

William (Bill) D. Whitsett
2369 Browning Street
Sarasota FL 34237
ellisjazz@worldnet.att.net

JAMES WIESNER
Tyrson's Wood
Ojai CA 93023
tyrswood@pacbell.net
home.pacbell.net/tyrswood/
index.html

RENE WILHELMY
8415 Rue Foucher
Montreal Quebec
Canada H2P 2CZ
rwil@infobahnos.com
www.infobahnos.com/~
rwil/

**WILLIAMS GUITAR MFG.
LTD.**
Laurie Williams
  Spicer Road RD 3
  Kaitaia Northlands
  New Zealand 0500
laurie@williams-guitars
.co.nz

WILLIAMS GUITARS
Paul Williams
209 Rogers Avenue
Mt. Sterling KY 40353
prwilliams@kih.net

SCOTT A. WILLIAMS
312 Diamon Road
Jackson NJ 08527
tabla@mail.superlink.net

STAN WILLIAMS
9 Belmont Drive
Rome GA 30165

DAVE WILLIAMSON
Common Bond, Acoustic Music
Route 1
Troy MT 59935

**WIND MOUNTAIN
GUITARS**
William Myres
P.O. Box 477
Carson WA 98610
williammyres@linkport.com

WINDROSE
Distributed by VMI Industries

Vega Musical
Instruments
P.O. Box 1357
2980-D Enterprise
  Street
Brea CA 92822-1357
800.237.4864
714.572.1492
(FAX) 714.572.9321

**KATHY WINGERT
GUITARS**
Kathy Wingert
310.522.9596

RANDY WOOD
Distributed Exclusively
by Joe Pichkur's Guitar
Center
306 Jericho Turnpike
Floral Park NY 11001
516.488.5343

GARY WOODALL
229 N.W. 19th Street
Richmond IN 47374
mandolin@info-
com.com

WORLAND GUITARS
Jim Worland
810 N. First Street
Rockford IL 61107
815.961.8854
worland.james@mcleodusa
.net

WYZA GUITARS
Bill Wyza

YAMAHA
Yamaha Corporation of
America
6600 Orangethorpe
  Avenue
Buena Park CA 90620
800.322.4322
714.522.9011
(FAX) 714.522.9587
www.yamahaguitars.com

JOSEPH YANUZIELLO
Toronto Canada
Distributed by Elderly
Instruments
1100 N. Washington
Lansing MI 48906
517.372.7890

PETER MICHAEL YELDA
1127 Peach Street
San Luis Obispo CA
  93401

C. H. JEFFREY YONG
Guitar Institute Malaysia
55-2, Jalan 5/76 B
Desa Pandan
Kuala Lumpur 55100
tcmych@tm.net.my

GEORGE YONTZ GUITARS
George W. Yontz, Jr.
5563 Archer Road
Brethren MI 49619
yontz@manistee-isd
.k12.mi.us

YURIY
Yuriy Guitars
P.O. Box 4914
Buffalo Grove IL
  60089
847.670.1169
www.yuriyguitars.com

J. R. ZEIDLER GUITARS
John R. Zeidler
1441 S. Broad St.
Philadelphia PA 19147
215.271.6858
jrzeidler@aol.com
www.cyboard.com/ent/
zeidler.html

A.C. ZEMAITIS
Anthony (Tony) C.
Zemaitis, Luthier
108 Walderslade Road
Chatham Kent
England ME5 0LL
(MEDWAY) 01634.865086

ZIMNICKI
Zimnicki Guitars
15106 Garfield
Allen Park MI 48101
313.381.2817
gkbmtzim@aol.com

ZUNI
Zuni Instrument Woods
and Custom Guitars
702 S. Illinois Avenue,
  Ste. 101
Carbondale IL 62901
618.893.2988
(FAX) 618.893.4436

PHIL ZYCHOWSKI
Ranger, GA

Index

PAGES 437- 472

Music legends; Johnny Cash, Don McLean, and Elvis Presley.

The sound in your mind.

That's what you pay for when you buy a Gibson flattop or ...
your mind's ear—the best you can think of.
Nothing to try your patience, break your mood. Gibson ...
every detail. So you get low, fast effortless action ...
Beautiful woods, too. Mahogany, rosewood ...
and cherry sunburst finishes. Twelve ...
get the full story.

(Illustration: Gibson Hummingbird with cherry sunburst finish)

ACOUSTIC POWER!